SCHOOL OF GOVERNMENT
North Carolina Benchmarking Project

Final Report on City Services for Fiscal Year 2019–2020

PERFORMANCE AND COST DATA

AUGUST 2021

COSPONSORED BY:

THE CITIES OF APEX, CHAPEL HILL, CHARLOTTE, CONCORD, GOLDSBORO, GREENSBORO, HICKORY, RALEIGH, WILSON, AND WINSTON-SALEM

SCHOOL OF GOVERNMENT

NORTH CAROLINA LOCAL GOVERNMENT BUDGET ASSOCIATION

The School of Government at the University of North Carolina at Chapel Hill works to improve the lives of North Carolinians by engaging in practical scholarship that helps public officials and citizens understand and improve state and local government. Established in 1931 as the Institute of Government, the School provides educational, advisory, and research services for state and local governments. The School of Government is also home to a nationally ranked Master of Public Administration program, the North Carolina Judicial College, and specialized centers focused on community and economic development, information technology, and environmental finance.

As the largest university-based local government training, advisory, and research organization in the United States, the School of Government offers up to 200 courses, webinars, and specialized conferences for more than 12,000 public officials each year. In addition, faculty members annually publish approximately 50 books, manuals, reports, articles, bulletins, and other print and online content related to state and local government. The School also produces the *Daily Bulletin Online* each day the General Assembly is in session, reporting on activities for members of the legislature and others who need to follow the course of legislation.

Operating support for the School of Government's programs and activities comes from many sources, including state appropriations, local government membership dues, private contributions, publication sales, course fees, and service contracts.

Visit sog.unc.edu or call 919.966.5381 for more information on the School's courses, publications, programs, and services.

School of Government
CB# 3330 Knapp Building,
The University of North Carolina at Chapel Hill,
Chapel Hill, NC 27599-3330

Preparation and printing of this report were made possible
by funding from the participating cities.

Printed in the United States of America

25 24 23 22 21 1 2 3 4 5

ISBN 978-1-64238-036-1

CONTENTS

SCHOOL OF GOVERNMENT

North Carolina Benchmarking Project

PREFACE

North Carolina municipalities are continually looking for ways to improve the efficiency and effectiveness of service delivery. As part of this effort, a group of municipalities joined together with the School of Government at the University of North Carolina at Chapel Hill and the North Carolina Local Government Budget Association to create an ongoing project to compare performance and cost data for selected governmental services. This joint undertaking is known as the North Carolina Local Government Performance Measurement Project or, more commonly, the North Carolina Benchmarking Project. This report presents performance and cost data for the fiscal year ending June 30, 2020, for the ten North Carolina municipalities participating in the benchmarking project: Apex, Chapel Hill, Charlotte, Concord, Goldsboro, Greensboro, Hickory, Raleigh, Wilson, and Winston-Salem. Twenty-four previous reports regarding municipal services have been published.

The benchmarking project is a collaborative effort. Officials from the participating local governments, including budget and finance staff, program and service staff, and city and town managers, have made vital contributions to the success of the project. Special thanks are owed to the members of the steering committee, who provide the necessary leadership demanded by such a project: Amanda Grogan, Budget and Management Analyst of Apex; Matthew Brinkley, Budget Manager, Brian Murphy Budget and Management Analyst of Chapel Hill; Jordan Paschal, Budget Analyst of Charlotte; Lesley Reder, Budget and Performance Manager, Amanda Newton, Management Analyst, and Brandon Edwards, Management Analyst of Concord; Octavius Murphy, Assistant to the Manager of Goldsboro; Tracy Nash, Budget Analyst of Greensboro; Cameron McHargue, Budget Analyst of Hickory; Toy Beeninga, Budget Analyst and Greg Reger, Budget Analysis of Raleigh; Lanette Pridgen, Financial Analyst of Wilson; and Heather Curry, Budget and Evaluation Analyst of Winston-Salem.

The benchmarking project receives contributions from other individuals who strongly support benchmarking and performance measurement. William C. Rivenbark and David N. Ammons, faculty members of the School of Government, serve as project advisors. Special thanks go to Michael R. Smith, dean of the School of Government, and Aimee Wall, senior associate dean of the School of Government, for their leadership and support of the benchmarking project. The author wishes to acknowledge other School of Government staff who have contributed many hours to the benchmarking project, including Kevin Justice and Melissa Twomey in Strategic Communications.

Dale J. Roenigk
July 2021

UNC SCHOOL OF GOVERNMENT
North Carolina Benchmarking Project

Performance and Cost Data

INTRODUCTION

SCHOOL OF GOVERNMENT
North Carolina Benchmarking Project

INTRODUCTION

Can local governments measure their performance and cost in a meaningful way? Can performance measures in one local government be legitimately compared to the those of another? In the fall of 1995, fourteen large municipalities and counties in North Carolina agreed to participate in a collaborative project to answer these and other questions relating to benchmarking. Seven of the jurisdictions were municipalities, forming Phase I of what is now known as the North Carolina Local Government Performance Measurement Project or, more commonly, the North Carolina Benchmarking Project. The other seven jurisdictions were counties, constituting Phase II of the benchmarking project. A third phase of the benchmarking project began in January 1997, consisting of fourteen municipal and county, small- and medium-sized North Carolina jurisdictions. These phases represented the pilot stage of the benchmarking project.

Since the beginning, the benchmarking project has proceeded with an ongoing agreement to collect, clean, and report comparative performance and cost data from the participating municipalities. Listed below are the ten municipalities that are included in this report:

- Apex
- Chapel Hill
- Charlotte
- Concord
- Goldsboro
- Greensboro
- Hickory
- Raleigh
- Wilson
- Winston-Salem

This project was the result of a joint undertaking of the participating municipalities, the School of Government, and the North Carolina Local Government Budget Association. The North Carolina League of Municipalities and the Local Government Commission also contributed to the development of this project. The goals of the benchmarking project are:

1. to develop/expand the use of performance measurement in local government,
2. to produce reliable performance and cost data for comparison, and
3. to facilitate the use of performance and cost data for service improvement.

SERVICES

This report presents performance and cost data and accompanying explanatory information for the following service areas:

- Residential Refuse Collection
- Household Recycling
- Yard Waste/Leaf Collection
- Police Services
- Emergency Communications
- Asphalt Maintenance and Repair
- Fire Services
- Building Inspections
- Fleet Maintenance
- Central Human Resources
- Water Services
- Wastewater Services
- Core Parks and Recreation

The participating units did not agree to continue the benchmarking project to endure the challenges of data collection and "data cleaning" simply to produce a report. They continue with the belief that performance measurement and benchmarking are catalysts to service improvement. No jurisdiction can be the best in every service that it provides, highlighting the notion that even outstanding performers can learn from the practices of others. Performance measurement and benchmarking are about tracking performance and cost data and making changes based on both internal and external comparisons over time.

This report is the twenty-fifth publication representing municipal services. The previous twenty-four reports and their publication dates are listed below:

- *Performance and Cost Data: Phase I City Services* (October 1997)
- *Performance and Cost Data: Phase III City Services* (March 1999)
- *Final Report on City Services for Fiscal Year 1997–98* (March 1999)
- *Final Report on City Services for Fiscal Year 1998–99* (February 2000)
- *Final Report on City Services for Fiscal Year 1999–2000* (February 2001)
- *Final Report on City Services for Fiscal Year 2000–2001* (February 2002)
- *Final Report on City Services for Fiscal Year 2001–2002* (February 2003)
- *Final Report on City Services for Fiscal Year 2002–2003* (February 2004)
- *Final Report on City Services for Fiscal Year 2003–2004* (February 2005)
- *Final Report on City Services for Fiscal Year 2004–2005* (February 2006)
- *Final Report on City Services for Fiscal Year 2005–2006* (February 2007)
- *Final Report on City Services for Fiscal Year 2006–2007* (February 2008)
- *Final Report on City Services for Fiscal Year 2007–2008* (February 2009)
- *Final Report on City Services for Fiscal Year 2008–2009* (February 2010)
- *Final Report on City Services for Fiscal Year 2009–2010* (February 2011)
- *Final Report on City Services for Fiscal Year 2010–2011* (February 2012)
- *Final Report on City Services for Fiscal Year 2011–2012* (February 2013)
- *Final Report on City Services for Fiscal Year 2012–2013* (February 2014)

- *Final Report on City Services for Fiscal Year 2013–2014* (February 2015)
- *Final Report on City Services for Fiscal Year 2014–2015* (February 2016)
- *Final Report on City Services for Fiscal Year 2015–2016* (May 2017)
- *Final Report on City Services for Fiscal Year 2016–2017* (May 2018)
- *Final Report on City Services for Fiscal Year 2017–2018* (April 2019)
- *Final Report on City Services for Fiscal Year 2018–2019* (June 2020)

REPORTING FORMAT

This is primarily a data report. It incorporates graphs, summary tables, and explanatory information to present the performance and cost results for each service area under study. The results of each service area by municipality are displayed in a standard, two-page format. The following information is contained in this report:

1. **Explanatory Information.** This segment of the report describes how the service is provided and identifies the conditions or dimensions that affect the performance and cost data of service delivery.
2. **Municipal Profile.** This section includes a limited number of characteristics of each municipality, such as population density and median family income, which may affect service performance and cost. Some of the general characteristics, such as population, appear in the municipal profiles for all of the service areas. Others, such as weather and tax base served, appear only in selected profiles.
3. **Service Profile.** This area provides input and output data and identifies important dimensions of service delivery.
4. **Full Cost Profile.** A cost accounting model is used to calculate the full or total cost of providing each service area under study. Although the cost data were collected in detail, using a collection instrument with more than seventy specific line items, the reporting format aggregates the detailed cost data into three general categories for the purpose of presentation: personal services for the direct expenses of salaries, wages, and related fringe benefits; operating costs which include direct operating expenses and indirect cost allocations; and capital costs that represent depreciation of equipment and facilities.
5. **Resource Measures.** These measures gauge the amount of resources or inputs municipalities allocate for the provision of a given service.
6. **Performance Measures.** Three types of performance measures are used and reported: workload, efficiency, and effectiveness. A municipality's performance is compared to the performance average, noting that the average is based on services with numerous variations and should be viewed with caution. The measures used in this report do not assess total service performance. They gauge certain service dimensions and should be approached with an understanding of the service being provided.

SUMMARY OF OVERALL RESULTS

What the project has achieved

1. The project's methodology, consisting of service profiles, performance measures, cost accounting, and an explanation of results, works extremely well for data

consistency and comparability. The project's accounting model is especially effective in producing reliable and materially accurate cost data.

2. The performance data have been used in numerous jurisdictions for service improvement, especially in the areas of residential refuse collection, household recycling, police services, and fleet services.
3. The project's success directly correlates with consensus among numerous local government officials from the participating units regarding service definitions and measurement formulas.

What we have learned

1. Local governments can produce accurate, reliable, and comparable performance and cost data, which can then be used for service improvement.
2. Specific service definitions are vital to performance measurement, including explanatory information.
3. Data availability and quality are very important to performance measurement.
4. Performance measurement and cost accounting are time consuming. However, performance measures provide valuable feedback when the goal is to deliver quality services at a reasonable cost.

READING THE REPORT

This report presents the performance and cost data for the ten North Carolina municipalities participating in the benchmarking project for the fiscal year ending June 30, 2020. It also presents multiyear data for participants based on the number of fiscal years each municipality has participated in the benchmarking project. The following table lists the five fiscal years of performance measures contained within the present report and the corresponding municipalities by fiscal year of participation.

Final Report	Jurisdictions
Final Report on City Services for Fiscal Year 2015–2016	Apex, Asheville, Burlington, Cary, Chapel Hill, Charlotte, Concord, Greensboro, Greenville, Hickory, High Point, Raleigh, Salisbury, Wilson, and Winston-Salem
Final Report on City Services for Fiscal Year 2016–2017	Apex, Asheville, Chapel Hill, Charlotte, Concord, Goldsboro, Greensboro, Greenville, Hickory, High Point, Raleigh, Salisbury, Wilson, and Winston-Salem
Final Report on City Services for Fiscal Year 2017–2018	Apex, Asheville, Chapel Hill, Charlotte, Concord, Goldsboro, Greensboro, Greenville, Hickory, High Point, Mooresville, Raleigh, Wilson, and Winston-Salem
Final Report on City Services for Fiscal Year 2018–2019	Apex, Asheville, Chapel Hill, Charlotte, Concord, Goldsboro, Greensboro, Greenville, Hickory, Mooresville, Raleigh, Wilson, and Winston-Salem
Final Report on City Services for Fiscal Year 2019–2020	Apex, Chapel Hill, Charlotte, Concord, Goldsboro, Greensboro, Hickory, Raleigh, Wilson, and Winston-Salem

The municipal profile, full cost profile, service profile, and explanatory information for each municipality are based solely on performance and cost data for the fiscal year ending June 30, 2020. Readers should be extremely careful when interpreting the performance and cost data of municipalities with multi-year data. Municipal profiles, full cost profiles, service profiles, and explanatory information that support performance measures for the fiscal years ending June 30, 2016, through June 30, 2019, are located in prior year performance and cost data reports and can be obtained from the School of Government.

The benchmarking project considers new service areas and service changes on an annual basis under the guidance of the steering committee. Asphalt Maintenance and Repair represented a new service area for the fiscal year ending June 30, 2000. This service was previously reported as Street Pavement Maintenance. Police Services represented a new service area for the fiscal year ending June 30, 2001. This service was presented as Police Patrol and Police Investigations in prior reports. Fleet Maintenance represented a new service area for the fiscal year ending June 30, 2002. Central Human Resources represented a new service area for the fiscal year ending June 30, 2004. Water Services represented a new service area added in the fiscal year ending June 30, 2007. Wastewater Services was added in the fiscal year ending June 30, 2012. Finally, Core Parks and Recreation was added in the fiscal year ending June 30, 2013.

Municipalities do not participate in every service area for a variety of reasons. Certain ones do not participate in Emergency Communications and Building Inspections because those services are often county functions. In some cases, a municipality may not participate due to organizational structures or other issues. The following table provides the jurisdictions participating in each service area contained in this report.

Service Area	Jurisdictions
Residential Refuse Collection	Apex, Chapel Hill, Charlotte, Concord, Goldsboro, Greensboro, Hickory, Raleigh, Wilson, and Winston-Salem
Household Recycling	Apex, Charlotte, Concord, Goldsboro, Greensboro, Hickory, Raleigh, Wilson, and Winston-Salem
Yard Waste/Leaf Collection	Apex, Chapel Hill, Charlotte, Concord, Goldsboro, Greensboro, Hickory, Raleigh, Wilson, and Winston-Salem
Police Services	Apex, Chapel Hill, Concord, Goldsboro, Greensboro, Hickory, Raleigh, Wilson, and Winston-Salem
Emergency Communications	Apex, Concord, Greensboro, Hickory, Raleigh, and Winston-Salem
Asphalt Maintenance and Repair	Apex, Chapel Hill, Charlotte, Concord, Goldsboro, Greensboro, Hickory, Raleigh, Wilson, and Winston-Salem
Fire Services	Apex, Chapel Hill, Charlotte, Concord, Goldsboro, Greensboro, Hickory, Raleigh, Wilson, and Winston-Salem
Building Inspections	Apex, Chapel Hill, Goldsboro, Greensboro, Raleigh, Wilson, and Winston-Salem
Fleet Maintenance	Apex, Chapel Hill, Charlotte, Concord, Goldsboro, Greensboro, Hickory, Raleigh, Wilson, and Winston-Salem

Service Area	Jurisdictions
Central Human Resources	Apex, Chapel Hill, Charlotte, Concord, Goldsboro, Greensboro, Hickory, Raleigh, Wilson, and Winston-Salem
Water Services	Apex, Charlotte, Concord, Goldsboro, Greensboro, Hickory, Raleigh, Wilson, and Winston-Salem
Wastewater Services	Apex, Charlotte, Concord, Goldsboro, Greensboro, Hickory, Raleigh, Wilson, and Winston-Salem
Core Parks and Recreation	Apex, Chapel Hill, Concord, Goldsboro, Greensboro, Hickory, Raleigh, Wilson, and Winston-Salem

It also should be noted that not all municipalities submit performance and cost data for each performance measure contained within the respective service area. Therefore, data are missing for selected performance measures regardless of service participation.

Performance and Cost Data

RESIDENTIAL REFUSE COLLECTION

SCHOOL OF GOVERNMENT
North Carolina Benchmarking Project

PERFORMANCE MEASURES FOR RESIDENTIAL REFUSE COLLECTION

SERVICE DEFINITION

This is regularly scheduled collection of household refuse or "garbage" from residential premises and other locations, including small businesses, using containers small enough that residents and/or workers can move or lift them manually. The service excludes collection of waste from dumpsters; regular or special collection of yard waste and leaves; collection of recyclable materials, white goods, or other bulky items; and any special or nonroutine service provided to residences. Transportation of refuse to a landfill or a transfer station is included, but the disposal of refuse and tipping costs is excluded.

NOTES ON PERFORMANCE MEASURES

1. Tons of (Residential) Refuse Collected per 1,000 Population and per 1,000 (Residential) Collection Points

"Tons of refuse collected" is widely used as a measure of workload for this service. A collection point or pickup point is a single locale (active address) from which residential refuse is collected. It can be a single-family residence, a condominium, an apartment, or a small business that uses containers that residents or sanitation workers can move or lift. Pickup points directly generate collection work, so this measure provides a good assessment of workload. "Tons of refuse collected per 1,000 population" and "per 1,000 collection points" also serve as measures of need for this service. Because of citizen expectations and public health requirements, sanitation crews or contractors must pick up all, or virtually all, household refuse that residents put out for collection.

2. Cost per Ton of Residential Refuse Collected and Cost per Residential Collection Point

These are the project's principal measures of efficiency for this service. Because of differences in the number of people per household and the percentage of the municipal population served by curbside collection, comparisons for these two efficiency measures can vary.

3. Full-Time Equivalent (FTE) Positions

The number of full-time equivalent (FTE) positions for residential refuse collection is the number of employees directly involved in providing the service as approved in the annual operating budget during the fiscal year. This number includes both full-time and part-time workers and both permanent and temporary workers. One FTE equates to 2,080 hours of work per year. Any combination of employees providing 2,080 hours of work annually equals one FTE. Cost data reflect all such workers. The measure "tons collected per collection FTE," however, includes only those workers who actually collect refuse and not supervisory or support personnel.

4. Number of Complaints and Number of Valid Complaints

All of the participating units take calls about residential refuse collection, and nearly all maintain records of one kind or another about such calls. However, the municipalities follow very different procedures in processing and recording these calls and in determining which ones are complaints and which are not. For these reasons, the project is able to present limited comparative data about complaints or valid complaints for residential refuse collection or other solid waste services. Nonetheless, the project recommends that the participating municipalities devise common criteria for identifying complaints and procedures for processing and recording calls.

Residential Refuse Collection

Summary of Key Dimensions of Service

City or Town	Normal Collection Location	Collection Points	Tons Collected	Weekly Routes	Percentage Contracted Service	Crew Size (most commonly used)	City FTE Collection Positions	Main Equipment		Landfill/Transfer	
								Packers	Automated	Trips per Day	Distance
Apex	Curbside	19,679	16,384	20	100%	Contracted	Contracted	Contracted	Contracted	1.5	7 miles
Chapel Hill	Curbside	12,230	6,829	27	0%	1 & 3 person	12.71	7	0	1	18 miles
Charlotte	Curbside	223,131	211,114	330	0%	1 & 2 person	81	7	59	1.3	22 miles
Concord	Curbside	34,130	33,951	5	100%	Contracted	Contracted	Contractor - 2	Contractor - 6	1	8 miles
Goldsboro	Curbside	14,372	11,263	11,263	1%	1 & 3 person	6	1	3	6	11 miles
Greensboro	Curbside	91,075	67,455	68	0%	1 & 2 person	27	5	18	1.8	8 miles
Hickory	Curbside	12,116	10,158	15	0%	1 & 2 person	3.75	1	4	2	5 miles
Raleigh	Curbside	131,952	94,435	88	0%	1 & 3 person	73	10	22	1.5	15 miles
Wilson	Curbside	21,111	23,080	27	0%	1 & 3 person	11	2	5	2	10 miles
Winston-Salem	Curbside	81,589	65,319	96	0%	1 & 3 person	65	11	13	1	12 miles

NOTES

All of the municipalities currently collect residential refuse once per week.
All of the municipalities have special provisions for collecting from the back or side yards of individuals with disabilities or mobility restrictions.

EXPLANATORY FACTORS

These are factors that the project found affected residential refuse collection performance and cost in one or more of the municipalities:

Backyard or curbside collection
Routing
Climate
Topographic conditions
Population density
Size of crews
Type of equipment used (automated)
Privatization
Participation in recycling program
Economies of scale
Distance to landfill/transfer station
Fee policies (volume-based or other)

Apex — Residential Refuse Collection

Fiscal Year 2019-20

Explanatory Information

Service Level and Delivery

Apex contracts with Waste Industries for refuse collection, disposal, and recycling. Only the refuse collection is reflected on this page.

Residents pay $8.30 per month for collection. Refuse is collected once a week at curbside, although backyard collection is provided for disabled customers at no additional charge. Residents receiving service are provided with one ninety-six-gallon container. The service also includes a small number of businesses in the downtown area that use the standard carts but receive service twice a week.

The contractor collects five days a week from different routes. Trash is trucked to the landfill.

The contractor collected 16,384 tons of residential refuse during the fiscal year, at a cost of $76 per ton. The cost per ton does not include the disposal cost at the landfill.

Conditions Affecting Service, Performance, and Costs

Municipal Profile

Population (OSBM 2019)	61,319
Land Area (Square Miles)	23.61
Persons per Square Mile	2,597
Median Household Income U.S. Census 2016	$84,000

Service Profile

FTE Positions—Collection	Contractor
FTE Positions—Other	Contractor
Type of Equipment	Contractor
Size of Crews (most commonly used)	Contractor
Weekly Routes	20
Average Distance to Disposal Site	7 miles
Average Daily Trips to Disposal Site	1.5
Percentage of Service Contracted	100%
Collection Frequency	1 x week
General Collection Location	Curbside
Residential Customers (number represents collection points)	19,679
Tons Collected	16,384
Monthly Service Fee	$8.30

Full Cost Profile

Cost Breakdown by Percentage	
Personal Services	0.0%
Operating Costs	100.0%
Capital Costs	0.0%
TOTAL	100.0%

Cost Breakdown in Dollars	
Personal Services	$0
Operating Costs	$1,237,867
Capital Costs	$0
TOTAL	$1,237,867

Residential Refuse Collection

Key: Apex ▒ Benchmarking Average — Fiscal Years 2016 through 2020

Resource Measures

Residential Refuse Collection Costs per Capita

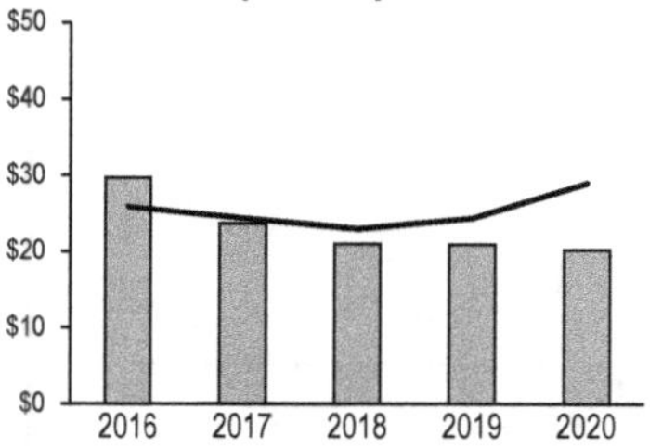

	2016	2017	2018	2019	2020
Apex	$29.73	$23.64	$21.00	$20.88	$20.19
Average	$25.84	$24.39	$22.93	$24.37	$29.01

Residential Refuse FTEs per 10,000 Population

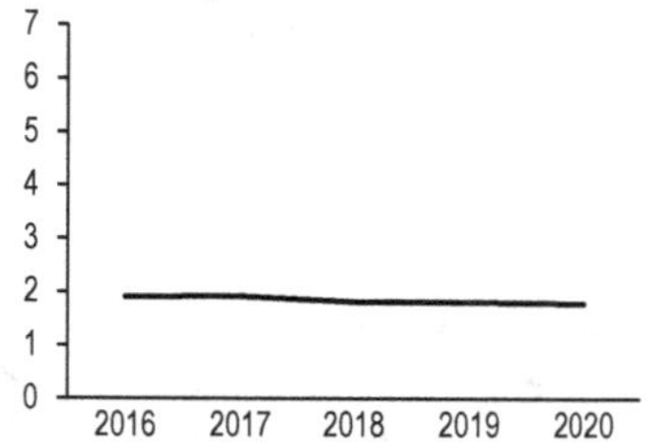

	2016	2017	2018	2019	2020
Apex					
Average	1.91	1.91	1.81	1.81	1.79

Workload Measures

Residential Refuse Tons per 1,000 Population

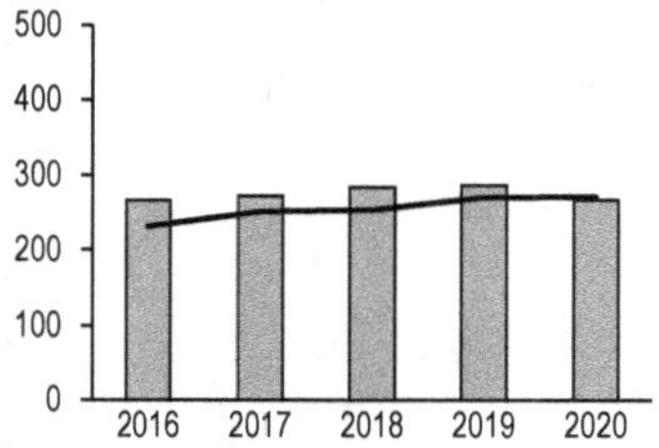

	2016	2017	2018	2019	2020
Apex	267	273	284	287	267
Average	232	251	254	271	271

Residential Refuse Tons per 1,000 Collection Points

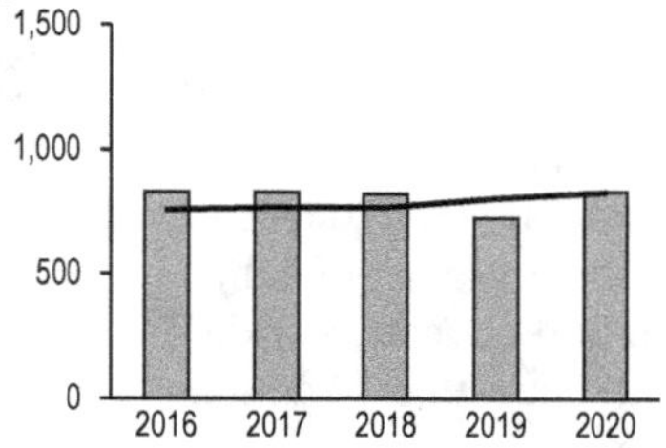

	2016	2017	2018	2019	2020
Apex	829	829	822	724	833
Average	759	767	769	806	830

Efficiency Measures

Residential Refuse Collection Cost per Ton Collected

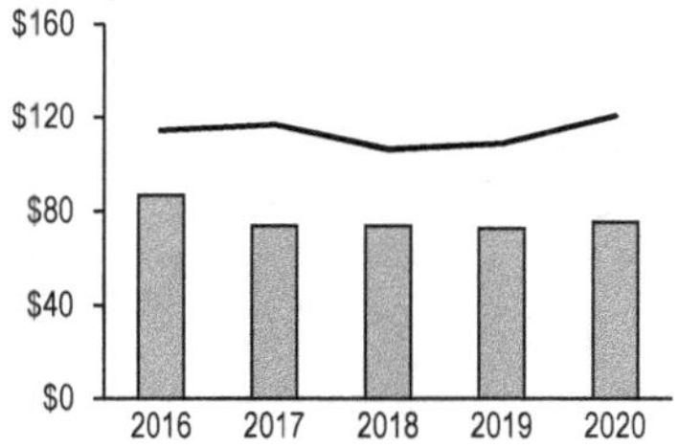

	2016	2017	2018	2019	2020
Apex	$87	$74	$74	$73	$76
Average	$114	$117	$106	$109	$121

Residential Refuse Collection Cost per Collection Point

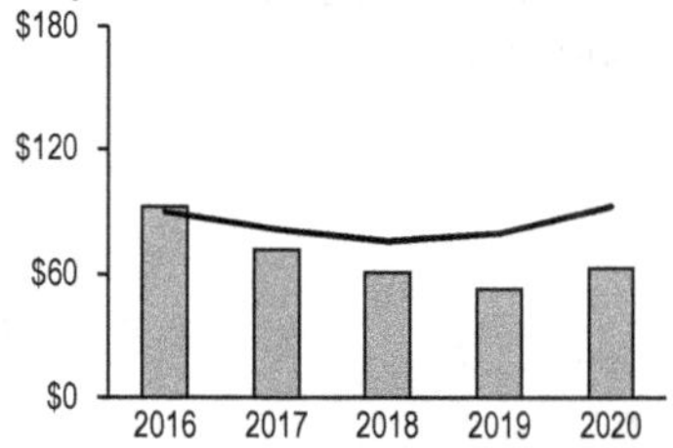

	2016	2017	2018	2019	2020
Apex	$92	$72	$61	$53	$63
Average	$90	$82	$76	$80	$93

Refuse Tons Collected per Municipal Collection FTE

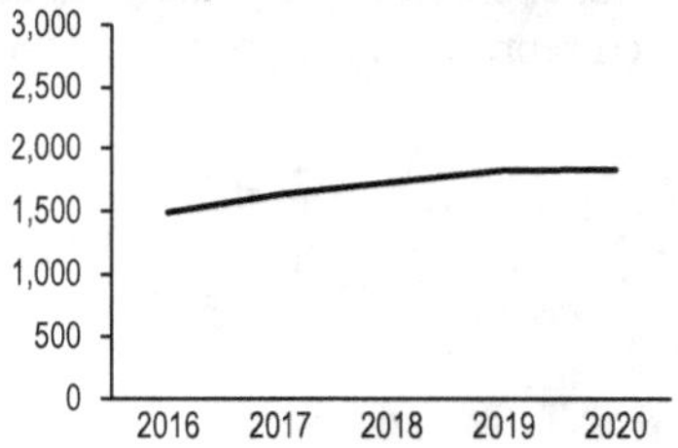

	2016	2017	2018	2019	2020
Apex					
Average	1,489	1,633	1,730	1,822	1,828

Effectiveness Measures

Complaints per 1,000 Collection Points

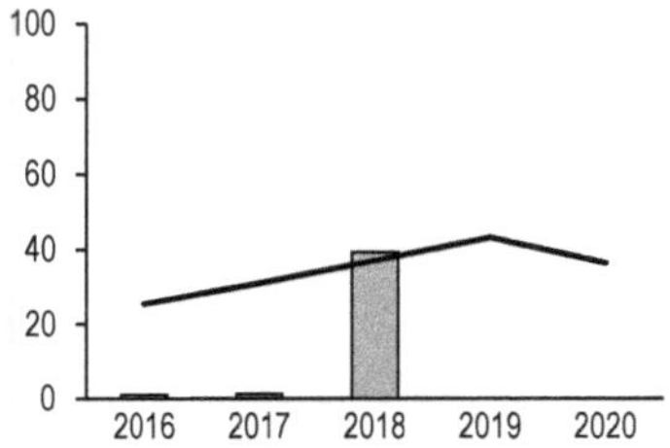

	2016	2017	2018	2019	2020
Apex	1.0	1.3	39.2		
Average	25.4	31 1	37.1	43.2	36.4

Valid Complaints per 1,000 Collection Points

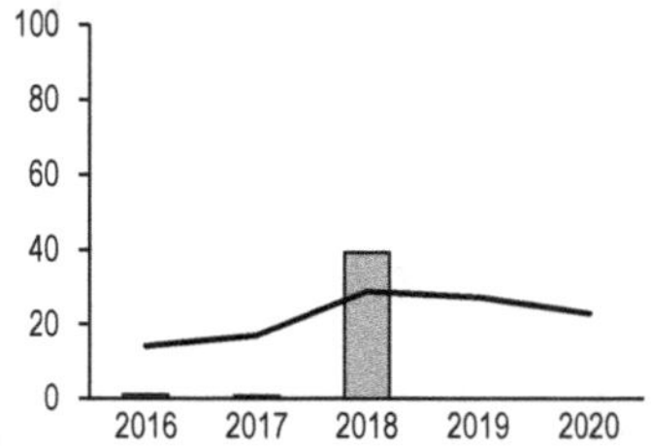

	2016	2017	2018	2019	2020
Apex	1.0	0.8	39.2		
Average	14.2	17.1	28.9	27.4	23.0

Fiscal Year 2019-20

Explanatory Information

Service Level and Delivery

Chapel Hill residential refuse collection is performed by the Solid Waste Services Division under the Public Works Department. The Town provides weekly household waste collection Mondays and Tuesdays with no fees charged.

Residential refuse is collected by seven 3-person crews using rear packers two days per week. The packer crews are staffed with three persons; one driver and two collectors. The trucks average one trip to the transfer station with the distance averaging 18 miles one way. A lift gate truck is also used to collect bulky items and electronics for a fee five days per week. Two pickup trucks are also used to collect medical exemptions, pedestrian trash cans, and streets not accessible to rear packers with one truck running seven days per week and the other running two days per week.

The town collected 6,829 tons of residential refuse during the fiscal year at a cost of $298 per ton or $166 per collection point. The cost does not include the disposal cost of $43.00 per ton at the transfer station for the tipping fee. Residents receive one roll-out cart at no charge but can purchase an additional cart for $60 per cart. Residents can also purchase their own trash cans, but these must be 32 gallons or smaller and weigh less than 60 pounds when full.

Conditions Affecting Service, Performance, and Costs

The out-of-town transfer station is the primary disposal location for Chapel Hill. Orange County had the highest waste reduction rate (64 percent) in North Carolina in FY 2014–15. The town provides special exemptions for backyard collections for 470 collection points, which represents 3.9 percent of the total collection points.

Municipal Profile

Population (OSBM 2019)	63,639
Land Area (Square Miles)	21.31
Persons per Square Mile	2,987
Median Household Income U.S. Census 2016	$60,802

Service Profile

FTE Positions—Collection	12.7
FTE Positions—Other	1.1
Type of Equipment	7 packers 1 Lift-Gate Truck and 2 Pickups
Size of Crews (most commonly used)	1 & 3 person
Weekly Routes	27
Average Distance to Disposal Site	18 miles
Average Daily Route Trips to Disposal Site	1
Percentage of Service Contracted	0%
Collection Frequency	1 x week
General Collection Location	Curbside
Residential Customers (number represents collection points)	12,230
Tons Collected	6,829
Monthly Service Fee	No

Full Cost Profile

Cost Breakdown by Percentage	
Personal Services	42.2%
Operating Costs	44.5%
Capital Costs	13.3%
TOTAL	100.0%
Cost Breakdown in Dollars	
Personal Services	$856,514
Operating Costs	$905,145
Capital Costs	$270,137
TOTAL	$2,031,796

Chapel Hill — Residential Refuse Collection

Key: Chapel Hill ■ Benchmarking Average — Fiscal Years 2016 through 2020

Resource Measures

Residential Refuse Collection Costs per Capita

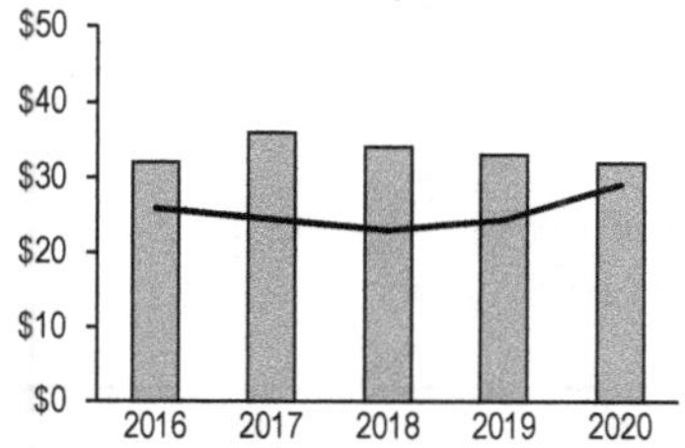

	2016	2017	2018	2019	2020
Chapel Hill	$32.09	$35.94	$34.06	$33.05	$31.93
Average	$25.84	$24.39	$22.93	$24.37	$29.01

Residential Refuse FTEs per 10,000 Population

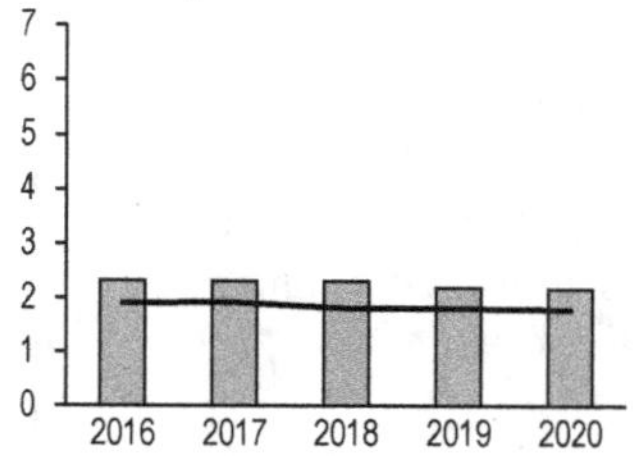

	2016	2017	2018	2019	2020
Chapel Hill	2.32	2.31	2.31	2.19	2.17
Average	1.91	1.91	1.81	1.81	1.79

Workload Measures

Residential Refuse Tons per 1,000 Population

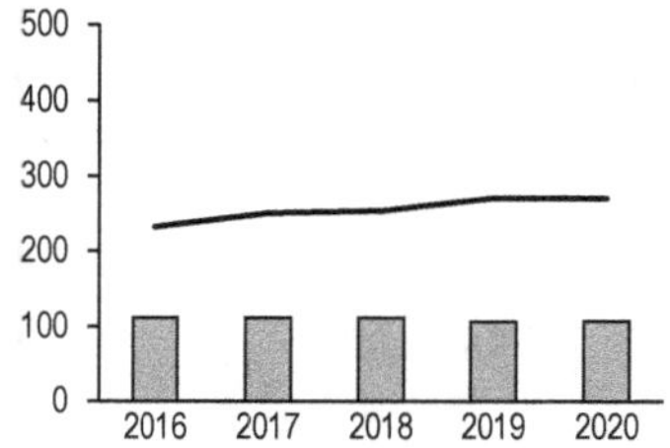

	2016	2017	2018	2019	2020
Chapel Hill	112	112	112	107	107
Average	232	251	254	271	271

Residential Refuse Tons per 1,000 Collection Points

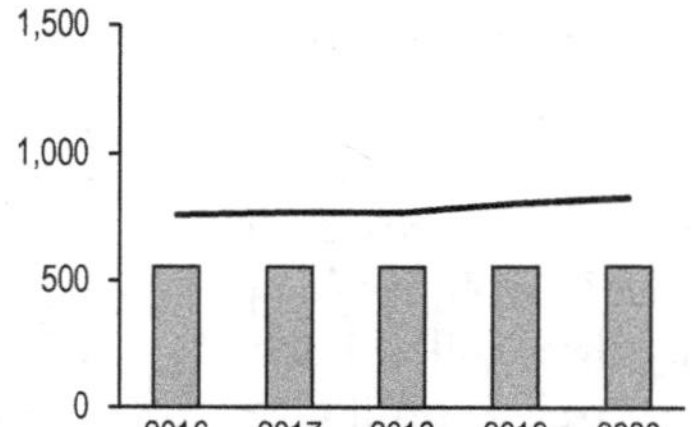

	2016	2017	2018	2019	2020
Chapel Hill	553	554	552	555	558
Average	759	767	769	806	830

Efficiency Measures

Residential Refuse Collection Cost per Ton Collected

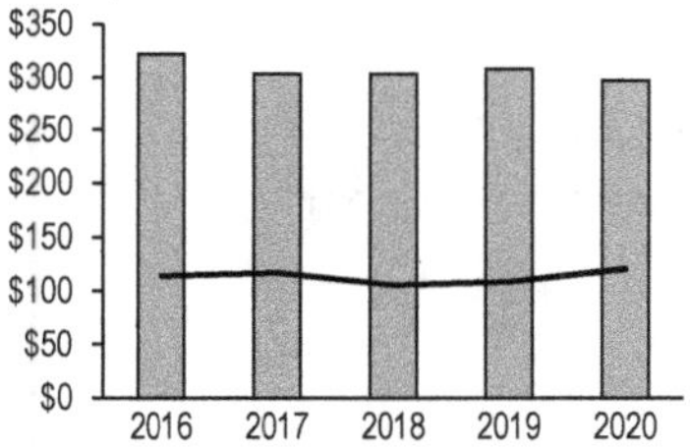

	2016	2017	2018	2019	2020
Chapel Hill	$322	$304	$304	$308	$298
Average	$114	$117	$106	$109	$121

Residential Refuse Collection Cost per Collection Point

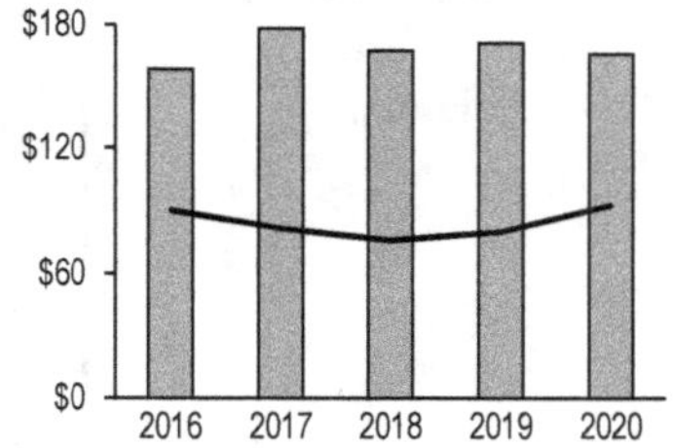

	2016	2017	2018	2019	2020
Chapel Hill	$159	$178	$168	$171	$166
Average	$90	$82	$76	$80	$93

Refuse Tons Collected per Municipal Collection FTE

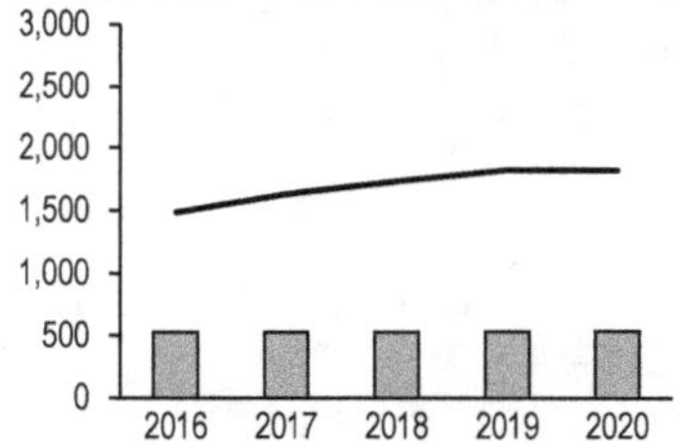

	2016	2017	2018	2019	2020
Chapel Hill	525	526	529	533	537
Average	1,489	1,633	1,730	1,822	1,828

Effectiveness Measures

Complaints per 1,000 Collection Points

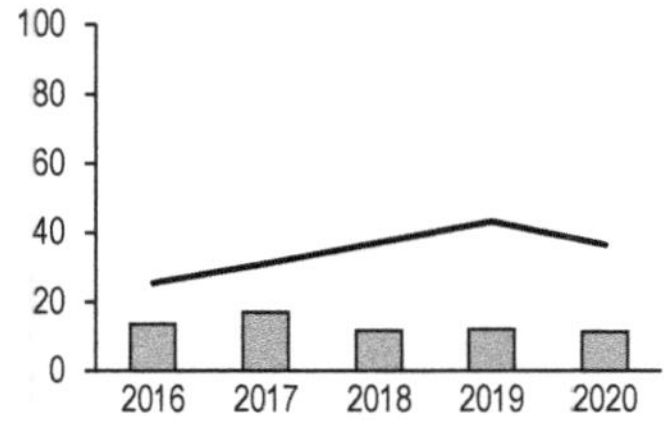

	2016	2017	2018	2019	2020
Chapel Hill	13.5	17.1	11.7	12.1	11.3
Average	25.4	31.1	37.1	43.2	36.4

Valid Complaints per 1,000 Collection Points

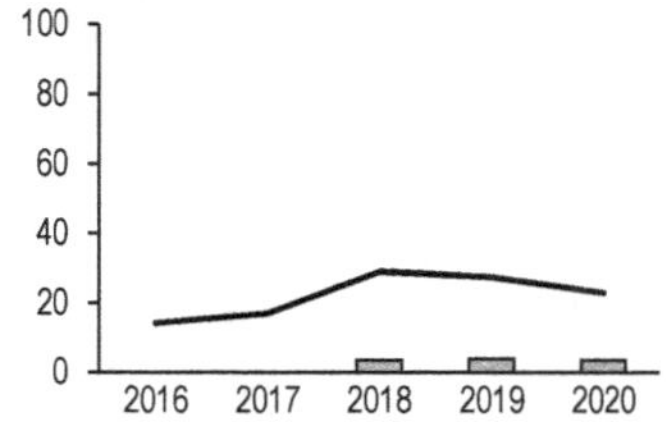

	2016	2017	2018	2019	2020
Chapel Hill			3.6	3.9	3.6
Average	14.2	17.1	28.9	27.4	23.0

Charlotte — Residential Refuse Collection

Fiscal Year 2019-20

Explanatory Information

Service Level and Delivery

Charlotte collects residential refuse once a week at curbside. Backyard service is available only to those persons with valid medical reasons and physician certification. The city charges an annual fee of $58 for refuse services, which is paid on the property tax bill; the fee applies to both collection and disposal costs and is meant to be just a portion of cost recovery for services.

City crews are composed primarily of one driver, each operating an automated packer. There were fifty-nine of these crews for FY 2019–20. In addition, three crews, each composed of one driver and one laborer, collected refuse using semi-automated packers. These crews are used primarily for backyard service for those citizens with disabilities and some multifamily complexes with less than thirty units. Small business garbage is collected by four crews, each composed of one driver and one laborer, using rear loaders. Costs include reserve crews that were used as needed throughout the year.

The city serviced 320 daily collection routes once each week during the fiscal year, with an average of 1.3 trips to the landfill per day per route at an average one-way distance of twenty-three miles. Each single-family residence is provided one ninety-six-gallon rollout container. An additional receptacle may be purchased for a nominal one-time fee. Charlotte collected 211,114 tons of residential refuse during the fiscal year, at a cost of $91 per ton. The cost per ton does not include the disposal cost of $34.50 representing the landfill tipping fee.

Conditions Affecting Service, Performance, and Costs

Charlotte is highly automated in the area of residential refuse collection. It considers all complaints to be valid complaints.

Municipal Profile

Population (OSBM 2019)	863,985
Land Area (Square Miles)	307.41
Persons per Square Mile	2,811
Median Household Income U.S. Census 2016	$46,975

Service Profile

FTE Positions—Collection	81.0
FTE Positions—Other	7.0
Type of Equipment	59 automated packers 7 packers
Size of Crews (most commonly used)	1 & 2 person
Weekly Routes	330
Average Distance to Disposal Site	23 miles
Average Daily Trips to Disposal Site	1.3
Percentage of Service Contracted	0%
Collection Frequency	1 x week
General Collection Location	Curbside
Residential Customers (number represents collection points)	223,131
Tons Collected	211,114
Annual Service Fee	$58.06

Full Cost Profile

Cost Breakdown by Percentage	
Personal Services	35.8%
Operating Costs	45.9%
Capital Costs	18.3%
TOTAL	100.0%

Cost Breakdown in Dollars	
Personal Services	$6,890,042
Operating Costs	$8,814,776
Capital Costs	$3,519,515
TOTAL	$19,224,333

Charlotte

Residential Refuse Collection

Key: Charlotte ▪ Benchmarking Average — Fiscal Years 2016 through 2020

Resource Measures

Residential Refuse Collection Costs per Capita

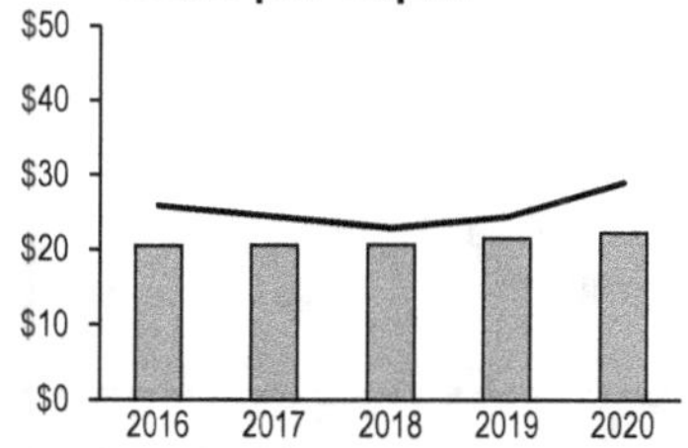

	2016	2017	2018	2019	2020
Charlotte	$20.50	$20.59	$20.64	$21.53	$22.25
Average	$25.84	$24.39	$22.93	$24.37	$29.01

Residential Refuse FTEs per 10,000 Population

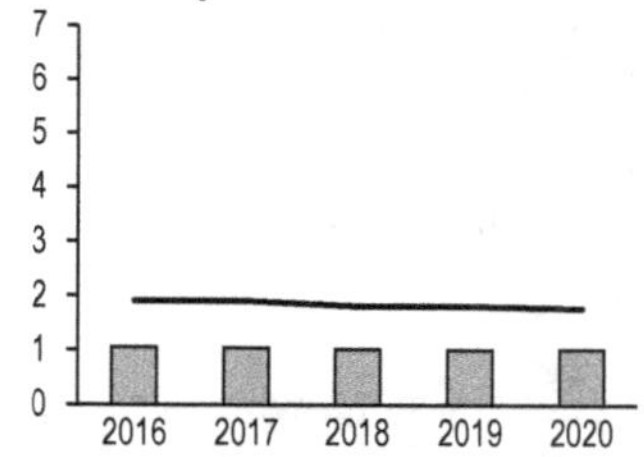

	2016	2017	2018	2019	2020
Charlotte	1.05	1.04	1.02	1.01	1.02
Average	1.91	1.91	1.81	1.81	1.79

Workload Measures

Residential Refuse Tons per 1,000 Population

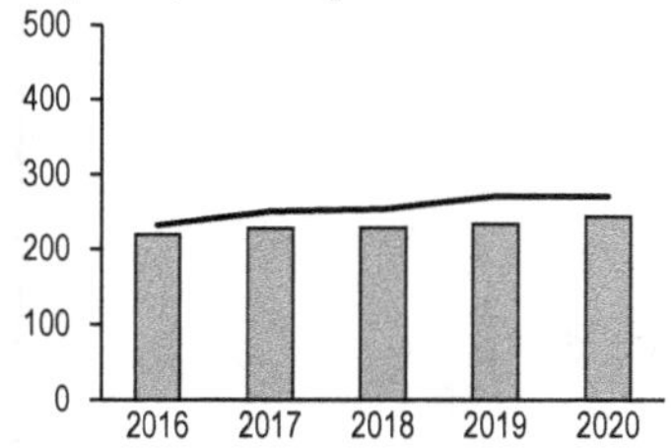

	2016	2017	2018	2019	2020
Charlotte	220	228	229	234	244
Average	232	251	254	271	271

Residential Refuse Tons per 1,000 Collection Points

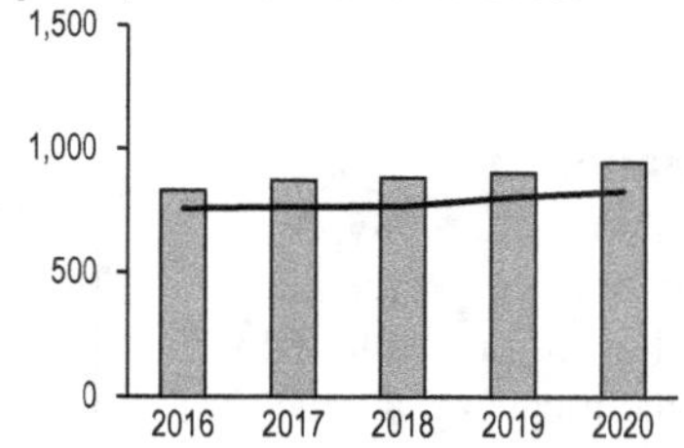

	2016	2017	2018	2019	2020
Charlotte	834	873	884	902	946
Average	759	767	769	806	830

Efficiency Measures

Residential Refuse Collection Cost per Ton Collected

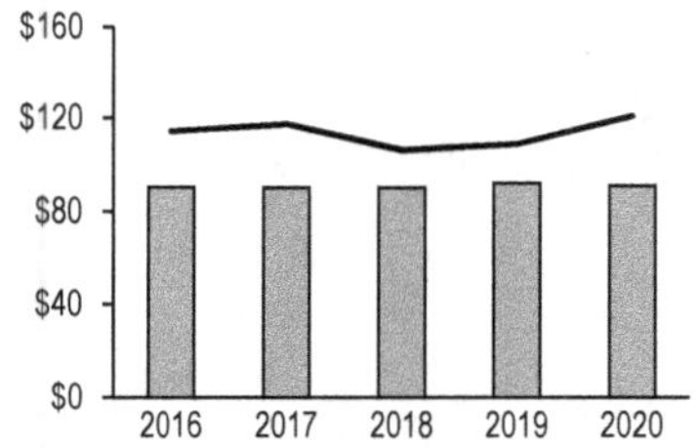

	2016	2017	2018	2019	2020
Charlotte	$90	$90	$90	$92	$91
Average	$114	$117	$106	$109	$121

Residential Refuse Collection Cost per Collection Point

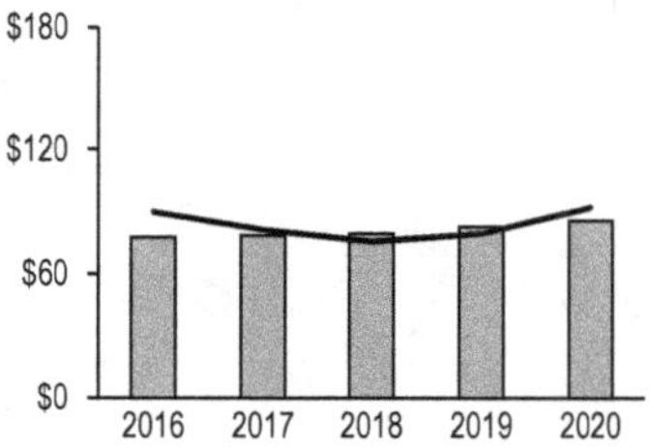

	2016	2017	2018	2019	2020
Charlotte	$78	$79	$80	$83	$86
Average	$90	$82	$76	$80	$93

Refuse Tons Collected per Municipal Collection FTE

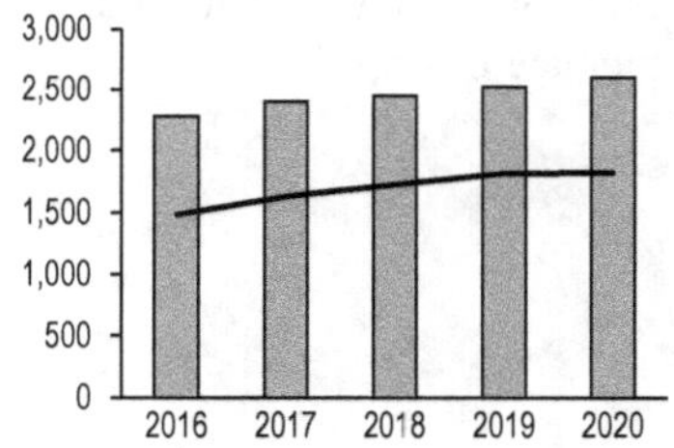

	2016	2017	2018	2019	2020
Charlotte	2,276	2,397	2,450	2,524	2,606
Average	1,489	1,633	1,730	1,822	1,828

Effectiveness Measures

Complaints per 1,000 Collection Points

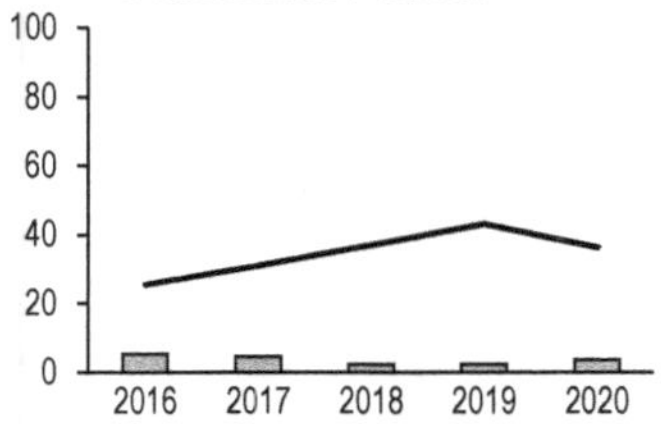

	2016	2017	2018	2019	2020
Charlotte	5.3	4.7	2.4	2.4	3.7
Average	25.4	31.1	37.1	43.2	36.4

Valid Complaints per 1,000 Collection Points

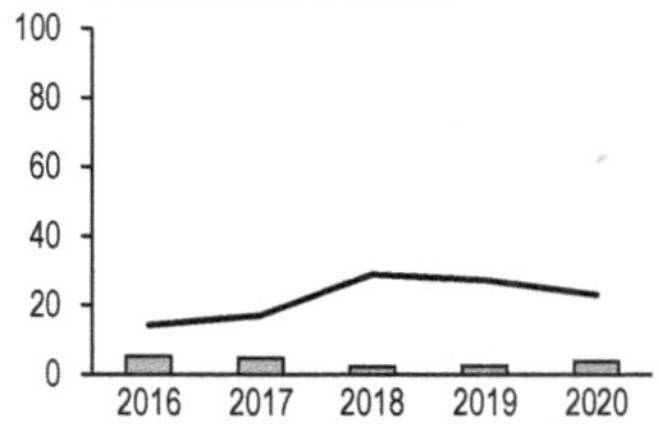

	2016	2017	2018	2019	2020
Charlotte	5.3	4.7	2.4	2.4	3.7
Average	14.2	17.1	28.9	27.4	23.0

Concord — Residential Refuse Collection

Fiscal Year 2019-20

Explanatory Information

Service Level and Delivery
Residential refuse collection service is provided once a week at curbside to Concord residents. Backyard service is available for the elderly and disabled. The city has provided residential refuse collection service under contract for many years. The cost of the contract for the year was approximately $2.4 million.

The contractor primarily used five automated packers, each with one person. Residents used one ninety-five-gallon cart, with extra carts available for larger families or unusual circumstances.

The contractor serviced twenty-five collection routes each week, with an average distance per route per day to the landfill of eight miles. The packers made an average of one trip to the landfill per day per route. The contractor collected 33,951 tons of residential refuse during the fiscal year, at a cost of $91 per ton.

Conditions Affecting Service, Performance, and Costs
Concord is one of only two jurisdictions participating in the benchmarking project that contracts 100 percent of its residential refuse collection service. Therefore, "tons collected per collection FTE" is not used for Concord as a performance measure, as this reflects only municipal workers.

Concord's "total tons collected" includes bulk trash, which is collected along with residential refuse and cannot be separated for reporting purposes.

Concord defines valid complaints to mean any missed collection or request for service as determined by the city to result from contractor negligence or omission.

Municipal Profile

Population (OSBM 2019)	95,453
Land Area (Square Miles)	63.65
Persons per Square Mile	1,500
Median Household Income U.S. Census 2016	$50,863

Service Profile

FTE Positions—Collection	0.6 City
FTE Positions—Other	2.09 City
Type of Equipment	6 automated packers 2 packers
Size of Crews (most commonly used)	Contractor
Weekly Routes	25
Average Distance to Disposal Site	8 miles
Average Daily Trips to Disposal Site	1
Percentage of Service Contracted	100%
Collection Frequency	1 x week
General Collection Location	Curbside
Residential Customers (number represents collection points)	34,130
Tons Collected	33,951
Monthly Service Fee	$2.24

Full Cost Profile

Cost Breakdown by Percentage	
Personal Services	5.5%
Operating Costs	93.9%
Capital Costs	0.6%
TOTAL	100.0%

Cost Breakdown in Dollars	
Personal Services	$167,569
Operating Costs	$2,886,610
Capital Costs	$19,175
TOTAL	$3,073,354

Concord

Residential Refuse Collection

Key: Concord ▩ Benchmarking Average — Fiscal Years 2016 through 2020

Resource Measures

Residential Refuse Collection Costs per Capita

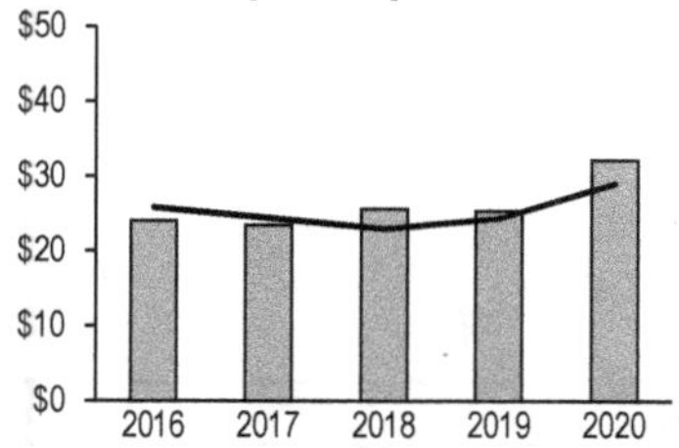

	2016	2017	2018	2019	2020
Concord	$24.04	$23.46	$25.65	$25.37	$32.20
Average	$25.84	$24.39	$22.93	$24.37	$29.01

Residential Refuse FTEs per 10,000 Population

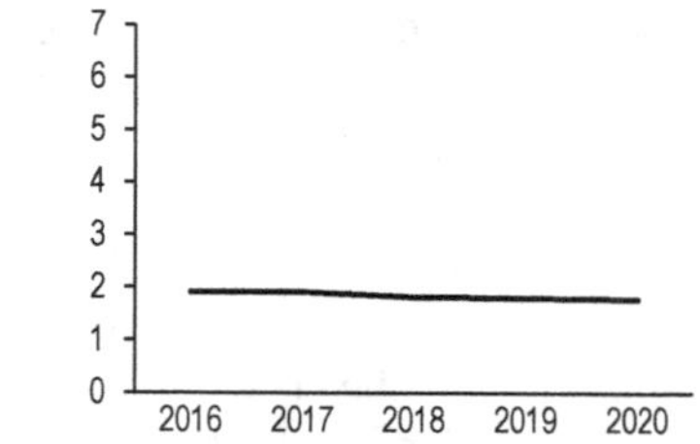

	2016	2017	2018	2019	2020
Concord					
Average	1.91	1.91	1.81	1.81	1.79

Workload Measures

Residential Refuse Tons per 1,000 Population

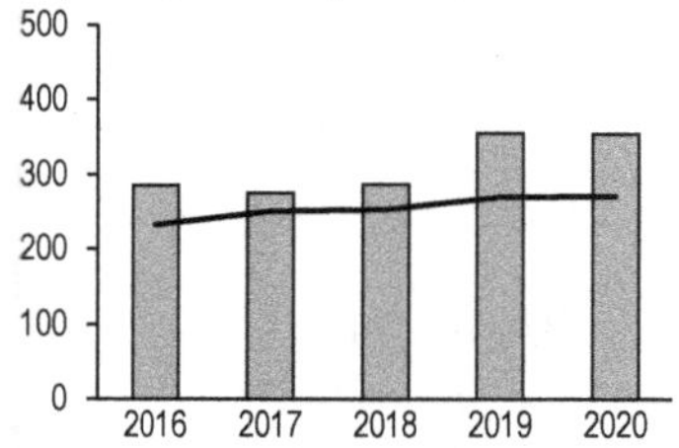

	2016	2017	2018	2019	2020
Concord	286	275	287	356	356
Average	232	251	254	271	271

Residential Refuse Tons per 1,000 Collection Points

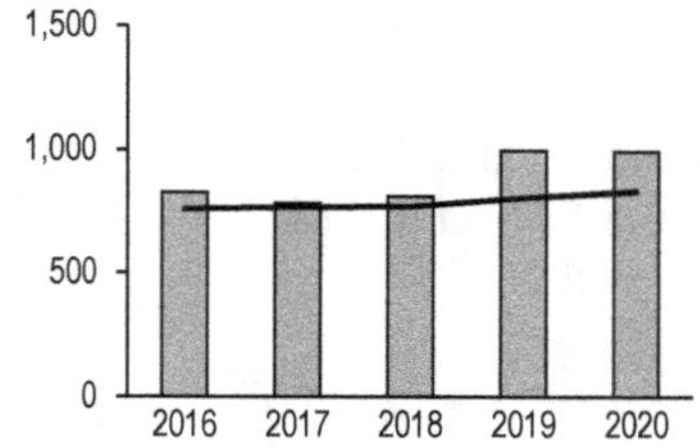

	2016	2017	2018	2019	2020
Concord	825	783	810	996	995
Average	759	767	769	806	830

Efficiency Measures

Residential Refuse Collection Cost per Ton Collected

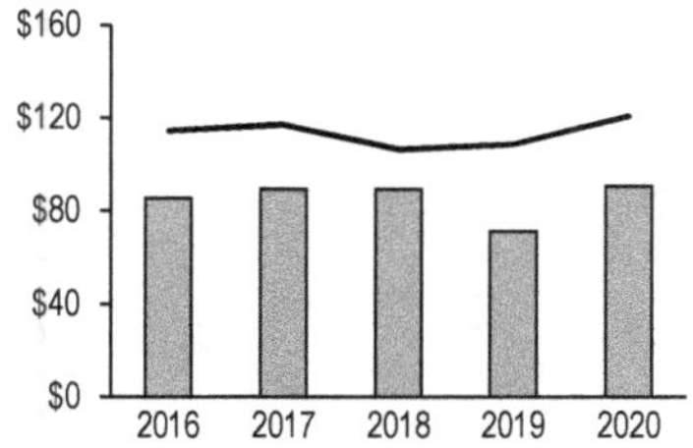

	2016	2017	2018	2019	2020
Concord	$85	$89	$89	$71	$91
Average	$114	$117	$106	$109	$121

Residential Refuse Collection Cost per Collection Point

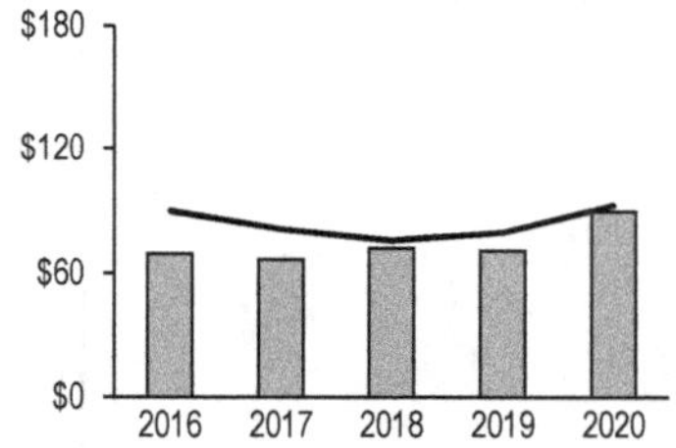

	2016	2017	2018	2019	2020
Concord	$69	$67	$72	$71	$90
Average	$90	$82	$76	$80	$93

Refuse Tons Collected per Municipal Collection FTE

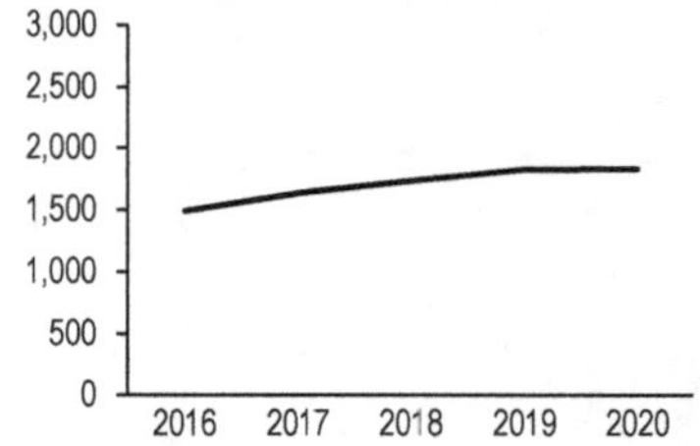

	2016	2017	2018	2019	2020
Concord					
Average	1,489	1,633	1,730	1,822	1,828

Effectiveness Measures

Complaints per 1,000 Collection Points

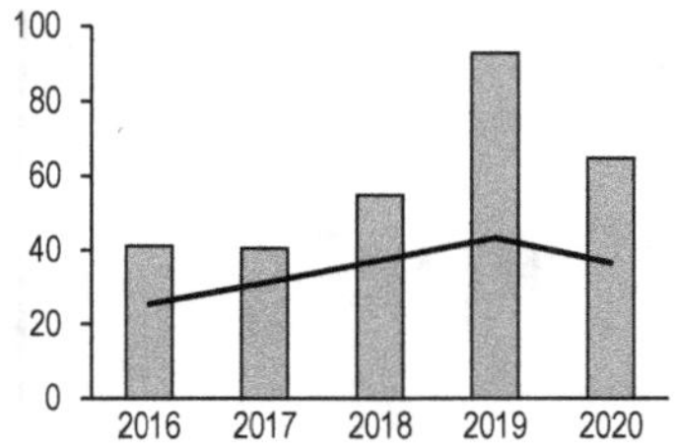

	2016	2017	2018	2019	2020
Concord	41.2	40.5	54.9	92.8	64.7
Average	25.4	31.1	37.1	43.2	36.4

Valid Complaints per 1,000 Collection Points

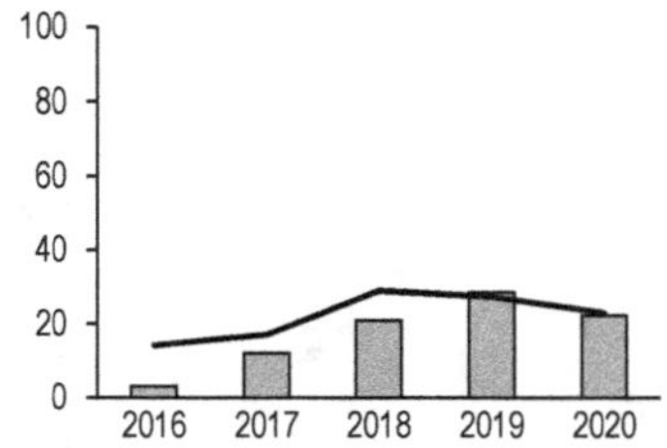

	2016	2017	2018	2019	2020
Concord	3.1	12.0	20.8	28.4	22.2
Average	14.2	17.1	28.9	27.4	23.0

Fiscal Year 2019-20

Explanatory Information

Service Level and Delivery

Goldsboro provides residential refuse collection once a week at curbside for residents. Collection is done by the Solid Waste Division of the Public Works Department. Backyard collection is available for the disabled. Currently the city charges a monthly fee of $22, which includes refuse, recycling, and leaf and limb pickup.

There are three automated trucks with a single driver and one crew with a driver and two collectors using a rear loader. Collection trucks run four days per week. Crews drive eleven miles to a transfer station.

The city collected 11,263 tons of residential refuse during the fiscal year from 14,372 collection points at a cost of $183 per ton. The collection costs do not include a disposal cost at the transfer station of $31.50 per ton.

Conditions Affecting Service, Performance, and Costs

The City of Goldsboro joined the Benchmarking Project in July 2017, with the first year of data showing for FY 2016–17.

Goldsboro contracts refuse collection for one small neighborhood where a hill and tight roads make it infeasible to use city trucks.

Municipal Profile

Population (OSBM 2019)	33,969
Land Area (Square Miles)	29.45
Persons per Square Mile	1,154
Median Household Income U.S. Census 2016	$32,148

Service Profile

FTE Positions—Collection	6.0
FTE Positions—Other	1.2
Type of Equipment	3 automated packers 1 packer
Size of Crews (most commonly used)	1 & 3 person
Weekly Routes	16
Average Distance to Disposal Site	11 miles
Average Daily Trips to Disposal Site	6
Percentage of Service Contracted	0.1%
Collection Frequency	1 x week
General Collection Location	Curbside
Residential Customers (number represents collection points)	14,372
Tons Collected	11,263
Monthly Service Fee	$22

Full Cost Profile

Cost Breakdown by Percentage	
Personal Services	52.9%
Operating Costs	34.2%
Capital Costs	13.0%
TOTAL	100.0%

Cost Breakdown in Dollars	
Personal Services	$1,088,815
Operating Costs	$703,665
Capital Costs	$267,637
TOTAL	$2,060,117

Goldsboro — Residential Refuse Collection

Key: Goldsboro ▒ Benchmarking Average — Fiscal Years 2016 through 2020

Resource Measures

Residential Refuse Collection Costs per Capita

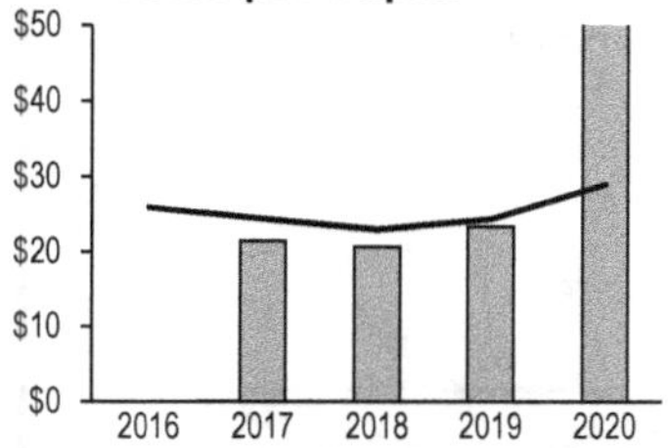

	2016	2017	2018	2019	2020
Goldsboro		$21.44	$20.66	$23.39	$60.65
Average	$25.84	$24.39	$22.93	$24.37	$29.01

Residential Refuse FTEs per 10,000 Population

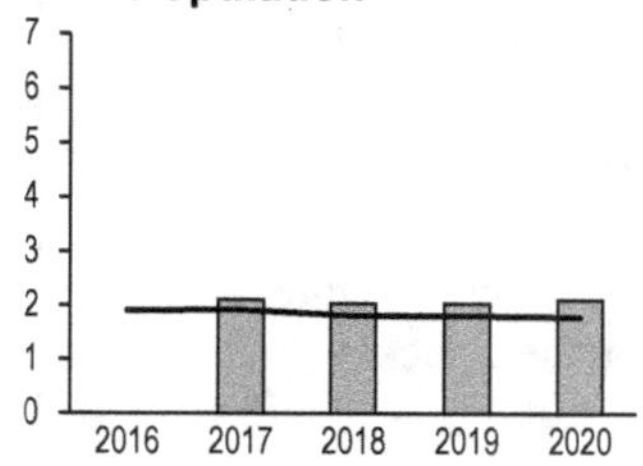

	2016	2017	2018	2019	2020
Goldsboro		2.11	2.03	2.03	2.11
Average	1.91	1.91	1.81	1.81	1.79

Workload Measures

Residential Refuse Tons per 1,000 Population

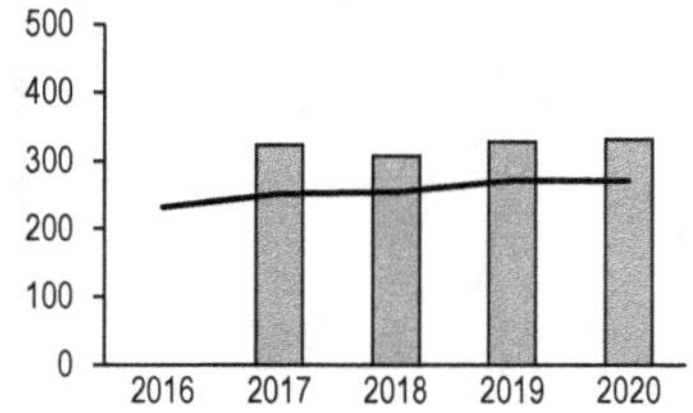

	2016	2017	2018	2019	2020
Goldsboro		323	307	328	332
Average	232	251	254	271	271

Residential Refuse Tons per 1,000 Collection Points

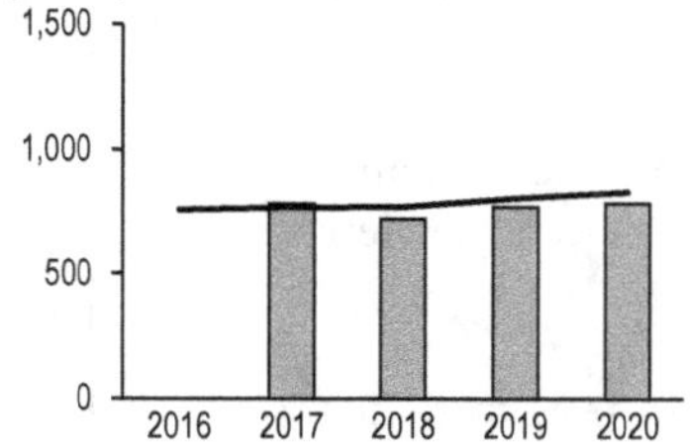

	2016	2017	2018	2019	2020
Goldsboro		783	720	768	784
Average	759	767	769	806	830

Efficiency Measures

Residential Refuse Collection Cost per Ton Collected

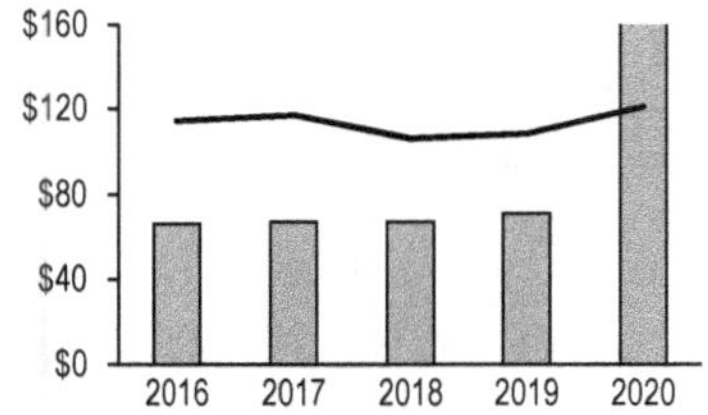

	2016	2017	2018	2019	2020
Goldsboro	$66	$67	$67	$71	$183
Average	$114	$117	$106	$109	$121

Residential Refuse Collection Cost per Collection Point

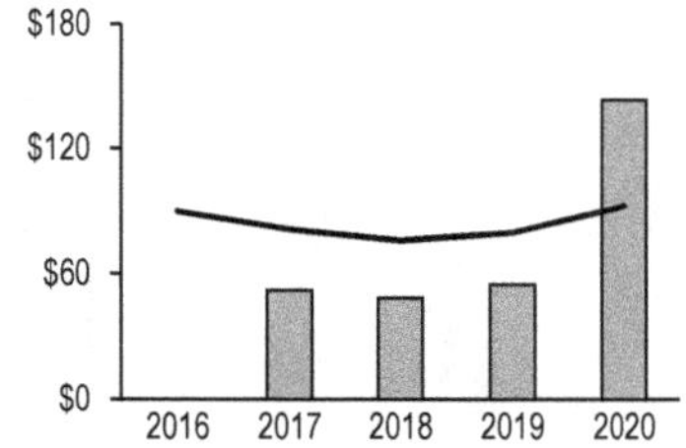

	2016	2017	2018	2019	2020
Goldsboro		$52	$48	$55	$143
Average	$90	$82	$76	$80	$93

Refuse Tons Collected per Municipal Collection FTE

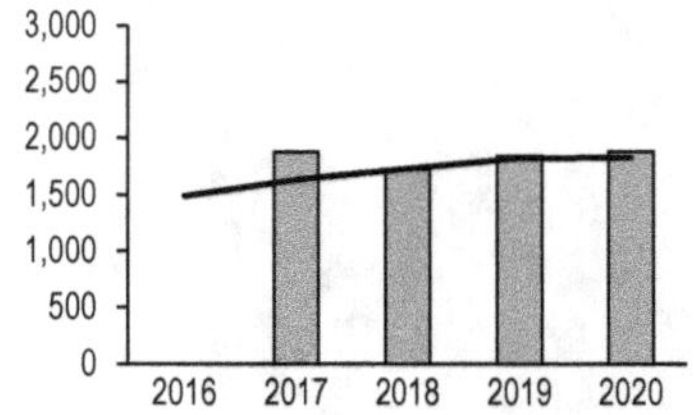

	2016	2017	2018	2019	2020
Goldsboro		1,874	1,724	1,841	1,877
Average	1,489	1,633	1,730	1,822	1,828

Effectiveness Measures

Complaints per 1,000 Collection Points

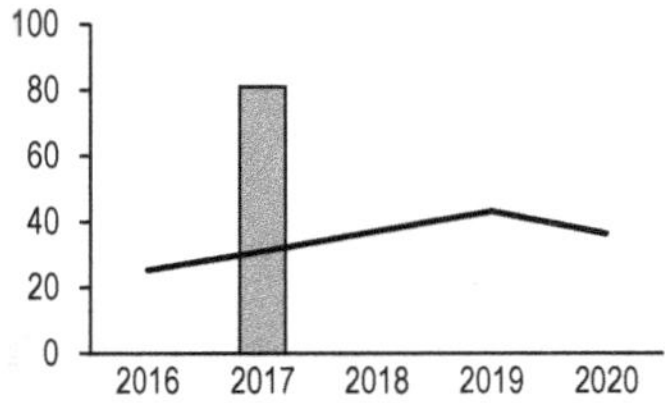

	2016	2017	2018	2019	2020
Goldsboro		81.0			
Average	25.4	31.1	37.1	43.2	36.4

Valid Complaints per 1,000 Collection Points

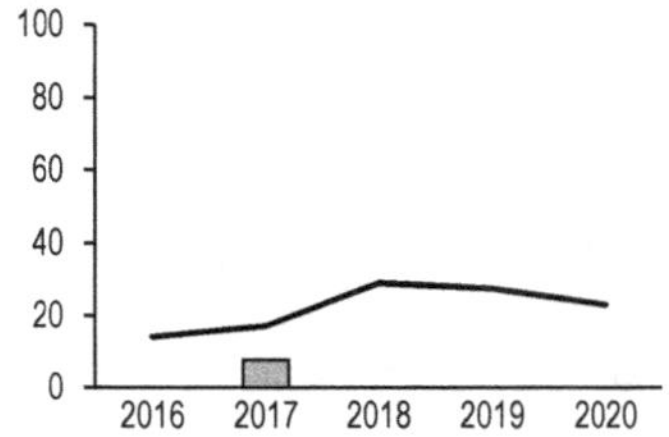

	2016	2017	2018	2019	2020
Goldsboro		7.7			
Average	14.2	17.1	28.9	27.4	23.0

Greensboro — Residential Refuse Collection

Fiscal Year 2019-20

Explanatory Information

Service Level and Delivery
Greensboro provides once-a-week collection of residential refuse at curbside. Each resident is provided up to two ninety-gallon carts. Currently there is no fee for residential collection of refuse.

There were twenty-three city crews for the fiscal year. Eighteen crews each have one driver operating an automated packer. Five crews use rear loaders.

The city used sixty-eight collection routes during the fiscal year, with each packer making an average of 1.8 trips per day to a municipal solid waste transfer station and the travel distance averaging eight miles.

The city collected 67,455 tons of residential refuse during the fiscal year at a cost of $105 per ton.

Greensboro defines automated packers as one-armed automated-loading packers that are operated by one person. Rear loaders are rear-loading packer trucks.

Conditions Affecting Service, Performance, and Costs
Greensboro is highly automated in the area of residential refuse collection.

Municipal Profile

Population (OSBM 2019)	293,730
Land Area (Square Miles)	129.62
Persons per Square Mile	2,266
Median Household Income U.S. Census 2016	$40,760

Service Profile

FTE Positions—Collection	27.0
FTE Positions—Other	4.0
Type of Equipment	18 automated packers 5 packers
Size of Crews (most commonly used)	1 & 2 person
Weekly Routes	68
Average Distance to Disposal Site	8.0
Average Daily Trips to Disposal Site	1.8
Percentage of Service Contracted	0.0%
Collection Frequency	1 x week
General Collection Location	Curbside
Residential Customers (number represents collection points)	91075
Tons Collected	67,455
Monthly Service Fee	$2.50

Full Cost Profile

Cost Breakdown by Percentage	
Personal Services	20.4%
Operating Costs	79.6%
Capital Costs	0.0%
TOTAL	100.0%

Cost Breakdown in Dollars	
Personal Services	$1,445,749
Operating Costs	$5,627,486
Capital Costs	$0
TOTAL	$7,073,235

Greensboro

Residential Refuse Collection

Key: Greensboro ▪ Benchmarking Average — Fiscal Years 2016 through 2020

Resource Measures

Residential Refuse Collection Costs per Capita

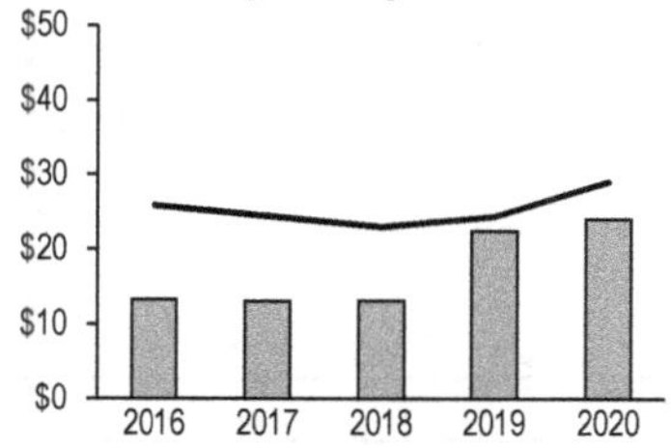

	2016	2017	2018	2019	2020
Greensboro	$13.27	$13.04	$13.16	$22.42	$24.08
Average	$25.84	$24.39	$22.93	$24.37	$29.01

Residential Refuse FTEs per 10,000 Population

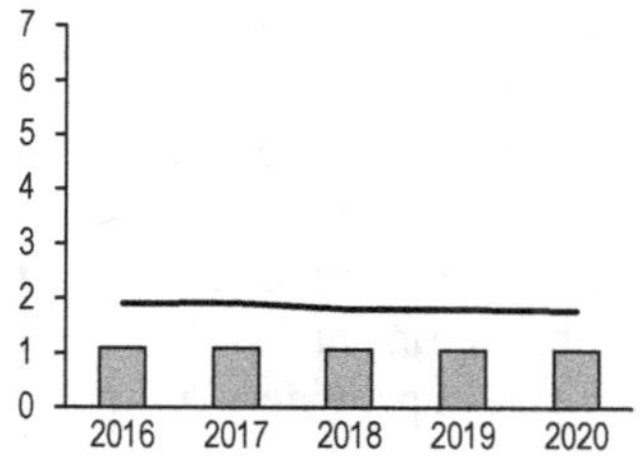

	2016	2017	2018	2019	2020
Greensboro	1.10	1.09	1.08	1.06	1.06
Average	1.91	1.91	1.81	1.81	1.79

Workload Measures

Residential Refuse Tons per 1,000 Population

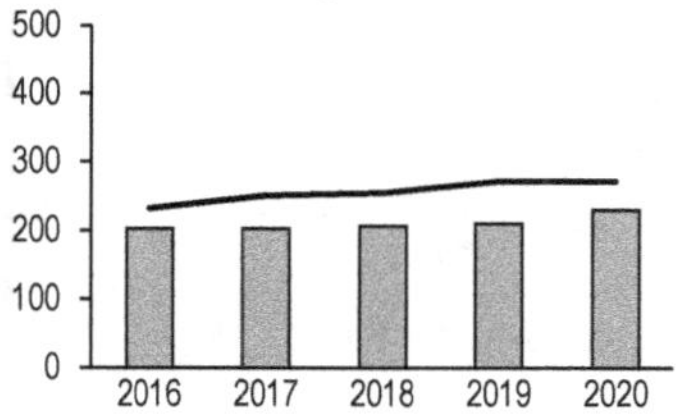

	2016	2017	2018	2019	2020
Greensboro	202	203	206	210	230
Average	232	251	254	271	271

Residential Refuse Tons per 1,000 Collection Points

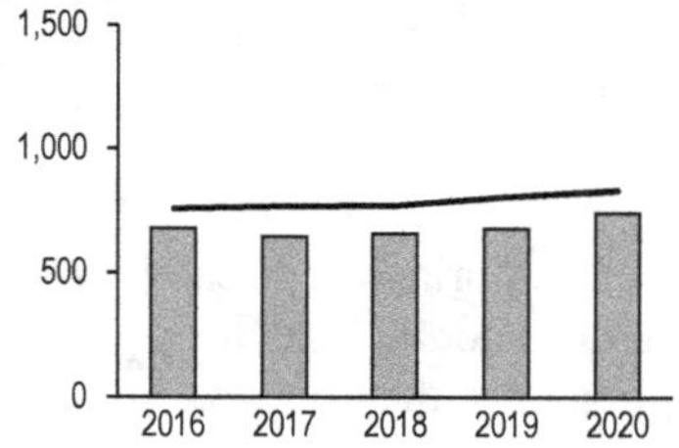

	2016	2017	2018	2019	2020
Greensboro	678	646	658	677	741
Average	759	767	769	806	830

Efficiency Measures

Residential Refuse Collection Cost per Ton Collected

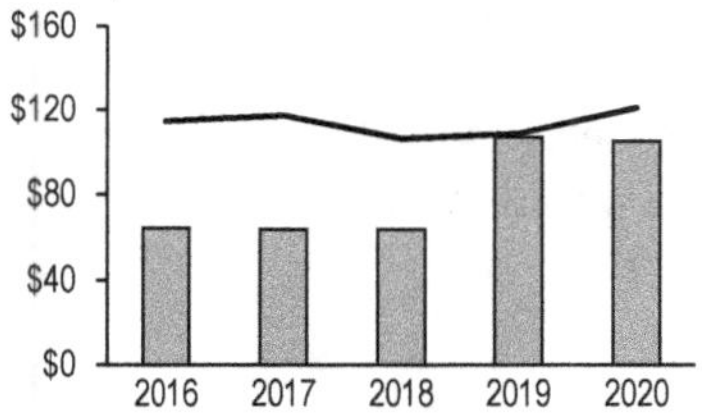

	2016	2017	2018	2019	2020
Greensboro	$64	$64	$64	$107	$105
Average	$114	$117	$106	$109	$121

Residential Refuse Collection Cost per Collection Point

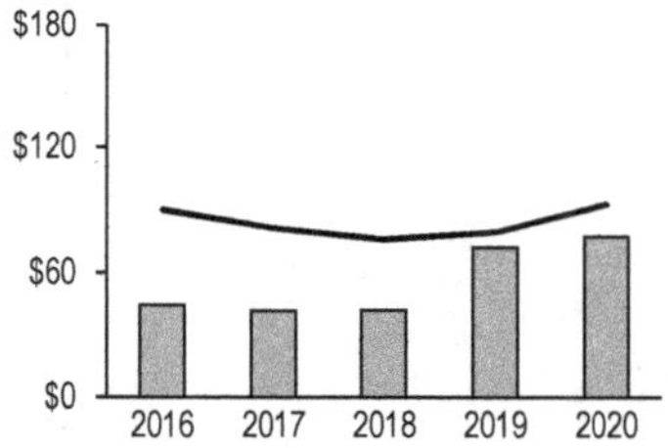

	2016	2017	2018	2019	2020
Greensboro	$45	$42	$42	$72	$78
Average	$90	$82	$76	$80	$93

Refuse Tons Collected per Municipal Collection FTE

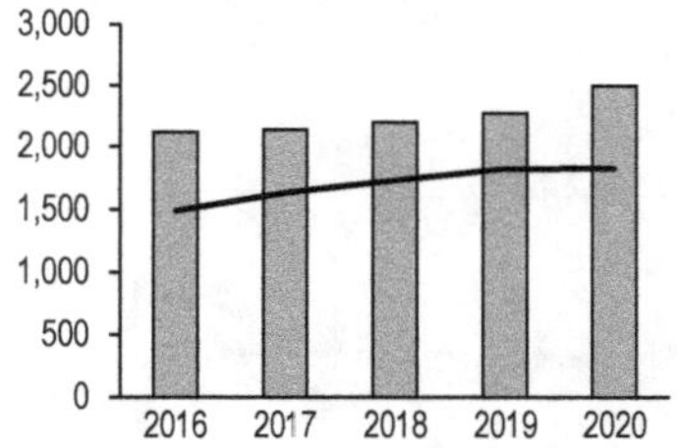

	2016	2017	2018	2019	2020
Greensboro	2,116	2,134	2,196	2,273	2,498
Average	1,489	1,633	1,730	1,822	1,828

Effectiveness Measures

Complaints per 1,000 Collection Points

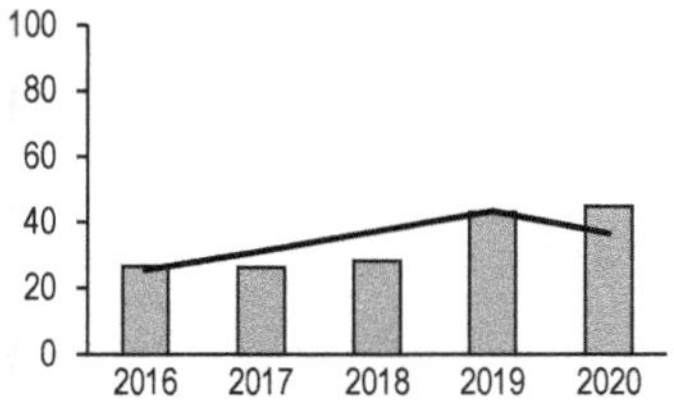

	2016	2017	2018	2019	2020
Greensboro	26.6	26.2	28.2	42.9	44.7
Average	25.4	31.1	37.1	43.2	36.4

Valid Complaints per 1,000 Collection Points

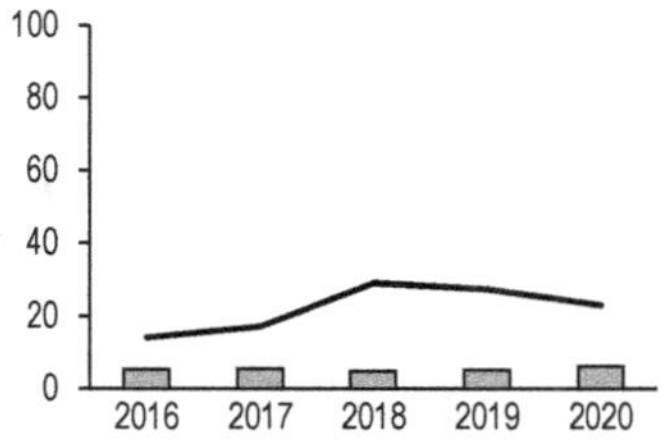

	2016	2017	2018	2019	2020
Greensboro	5.4	5.5	4.9	5.2	6.3
Average	14.2	17.1	28.9	27.4	23.0

Hickory

Residential Refuse Collection

Fiscal Year 2019-20

Explanatory Information

Service Level and Delivery

Hickory collects refuse from residential premises once a week at curbside, although backyard collection is provided for elderly and disabled citizens. A monthly solid waste fee of $22.50 per cart was charged for residential refuse collection service during FY 2019–20. Each residence uses a cart provided by the city for residential refuse collection. Each cart has a capacity of ninety-six gallons and is provided at no charge. Upon request, a second cart is provided to the customer for an additional solid-waste fee.

The city used four one-person crews operating automated packers, with three of these trucks running full-time and one one-fourth of the time. A regular packer truck with one driver and one crew member works about half-time collecting on one-way streets and dead ends.

Fifteen collection routes were used during the fiscal year, with an average of two trips to the transfer station per day per route. The average distance to the transfer station per route was five miles.

Hickory collected 10,158 tons of residential refuse during the fiscal year, at a cost of $40 per ton. The cost per ton does not include the disposal cost of $35.70, representing the tipping fee at the Catawba County landfill.

Hickory defines automated packers as trucks with mechanical arms.

Conditions Affecting Service, Performance, and Costs

Hickory is highly automated in the area of residential refuse collection.

Municipal Profile

Population (OSBM 2019)	41,409
Land Area (Square Miles)	30.50
Persons per Square Mile	1,358
Median Household Income U.S. Census 2016	$35,353

Service Profile

FTE Positions—Collection	3.75
FTE Positions—Other	0.82
Type of Equipment	4 automated packers 1 packer
Size of Crews (most commonly used)	1 & 2 person
Weekly Routes	15
Average Distance to Disposal Site	5 miles
Average Daily Trips to Disposal Site	2
Percentage of Service Contracted	0%
Collection Frequency	1 x week
General Collection Location	Curbside
Residential Customers (number represents collection points)	12,116
Tons Collected	10,158
Monthly Service Fee	$22.50

Full Cost Profile

Cost Breakdown by Percentage	
Personal Services	44.0%
Operating Costs	42.4%
Capital Costs	13.6%
TOTAL	100.0%

Cost Breakdown in Dollars	
Personal Services	$179,696
Operating Costs	$172,953
Capital Costs	$55,469
TOTAL	$408,118

Key: Hickory ▒ Benchmarking Average — Fiscal Years 2016 through 2020

Resource Measures

Residential Refuse Collection Costs per Capita

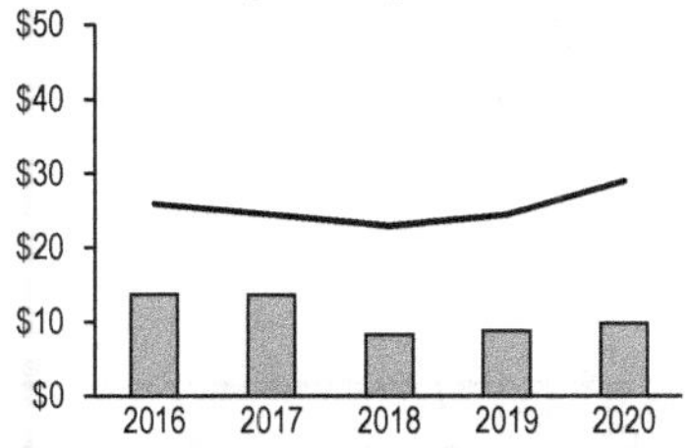

	2016	2017	2018	2019	2020
Hickory	$13.80	$13.68	$8.31	$8.84	$9.86
Average	$25.84	$24.39	$22.93	$24.37	$29.01

Residential Refuse FTEs per 10,000 Population

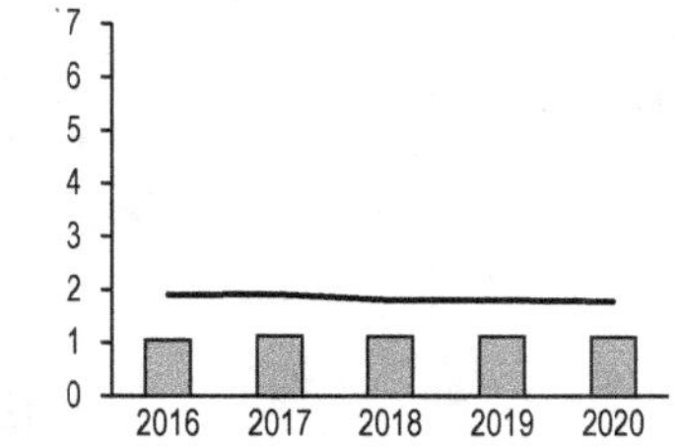

	2016	2017	2018	2019	2020
Hickory	1.05	1.13	1.12	1.12	1.10
Average	1.91	1.91	1.81	1.81	1.79

Workload Measures

Residential Refuse Tons per 1,000 Population

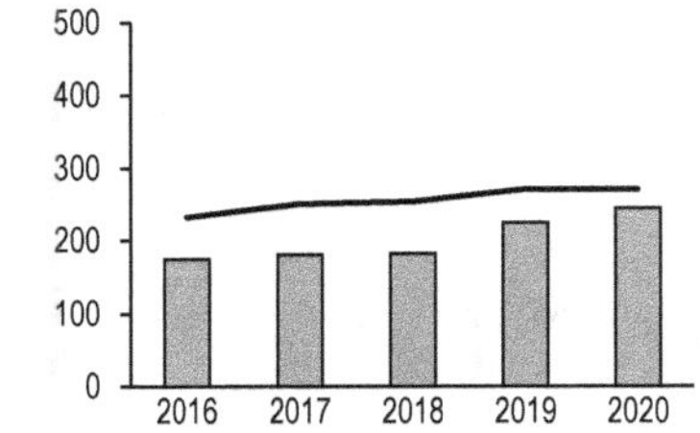

	2016	2017	2018	2019	2020
Hickory	175	180	182	225	245
Average	232	251	254	271	271

Residential Refuse Tons per 1,000 Collection Points

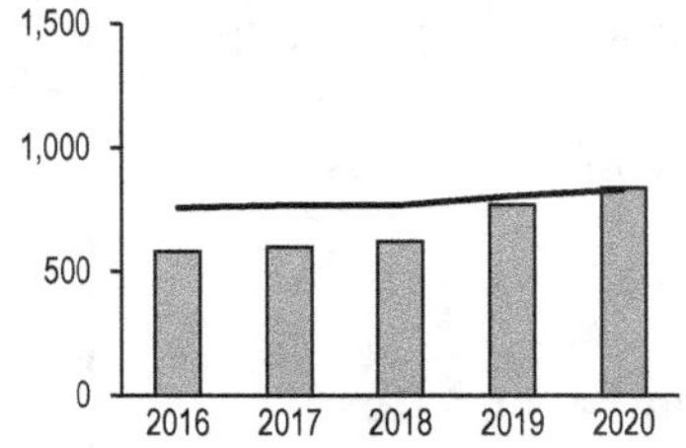

	2016	2017	2018	2019	2020
Hickory	579	598	620	771	838
Average	759	767	769	806	830

Efficiency Measures

Residential Refuse Collection Cost per Ton Collected

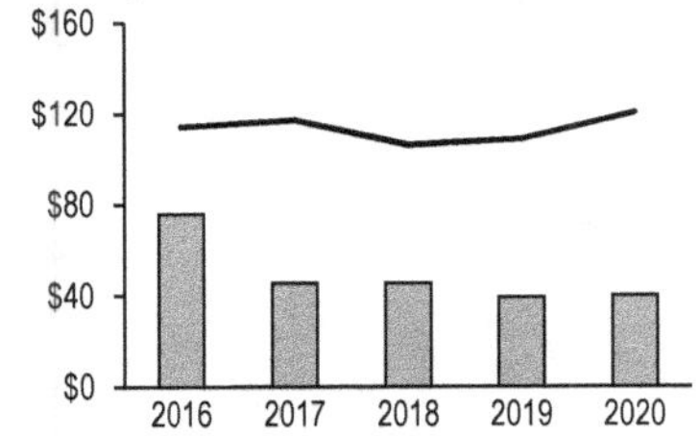

	2016	2017	2018	2019	2020
Hickory	$76	$46	$46	$39	$40
Average	$114	$117	$106	$109	$121

Residential Refuse Collection Cost per Collection Point

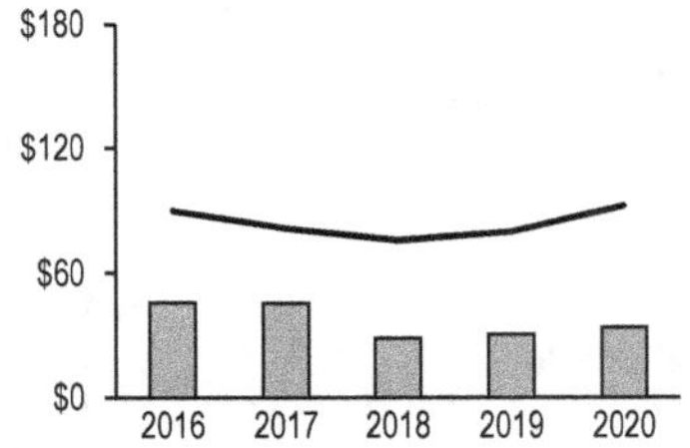

	2016	2017	2018	2019	2020
Hickory	$46	$45	$28	$30	$34
Average	$90	$82	$76	$80	$93

Refuse Tons Collected per Municipal Collection FTE

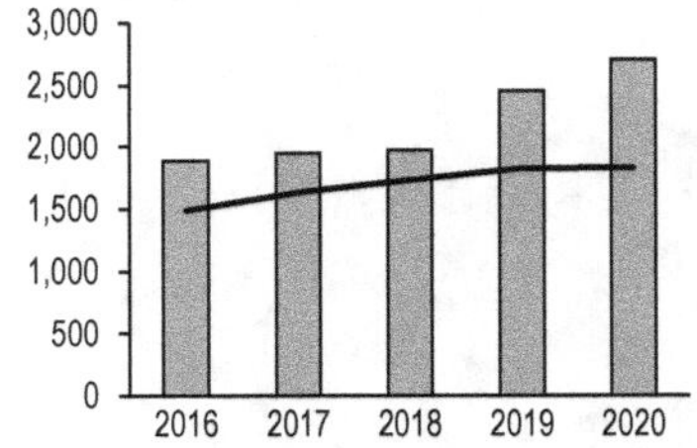

	2016	2017	2018	2019	2020
Hickory	1,883	1,945	1,973	2,456	2,709
Average	1,489	1,633	1,730	1,822	1,828

Effectiveness Measures

Complaints per 1,000 Collection Points

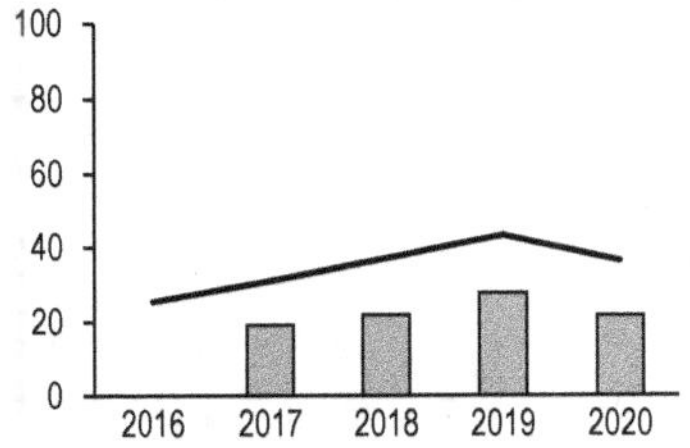

	2016	2017	2018	2019	2020
Hickory		19.2	21.9	27.8	21.7
Average	25.4	31.1	37.1	43.2	36.4

Valid Complaints per 1,000 Collection Points

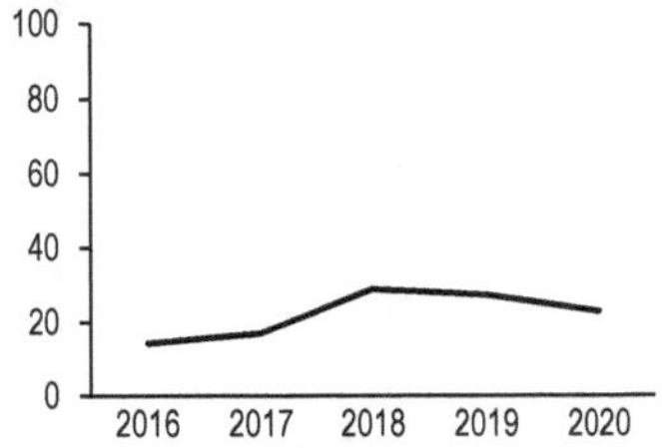

	2016	2017	2018	2019	2020
Hickory					0.0
Average	14.2	17.1	28.9	27.4	23.0

Fiscal Year 2019-20

Explanatory Information

Service Level and Delivery
Raleigh provides residential refuse collection service once per week at curbside. Backyard collection service is provided for customers who have been certified by a physician as being unable to move a cart to the curb and who have no able-bodied resident to provide assistance. The city charges a monthly fee of $14.45 for refuse collection.

The city employed twenty-two automated trucks with a single driver and ten crews of three on semi-automated trucks for primary collection. A total of 88 collection routes were used per week with a average truck making 1.5 trips per day to the disposal site, covering a distance of fifteen miles.

Each customer has up to two ninety-five-gallon roll-out carts provided and paid for by the city. The city collected 94,435 tons of residential refuse during the fiscal year, at a cost per ton of $151 or $108 per collection point. Not included in the cost per ton was a $30 landfill tipping fee.

Conditions Affecting Service, Performance, and Costs
Raleigh rejoined the Benchmarking Project in July 2016, with the first year of data showing for FY 2015–16.

Municipal Profile

Population (OSBM 2019)	475,580
Land Area (Square Miles)	146.47
Persons per Square Mile	3,247
Median Household Income U.S. Census 2016	$46,612

Service Profile

FTE Positions—Collection	73.0
FTE Positions—Other	4.0
Type of Equipment	22 automated packers 10 packers
Size of Crews (most commonly used)	1 & 3 person
Weekly Routes	88
Average Distance to Disposal Site	15 miles
Average Daily Trips to Disposal Site	1.5
Percentage of Service Contracted	0%
Collection Frequency	1 x week
General Collection Location	Curbside
Residential Customers (number represents collection points)	131,952
Tons Collected	94,435
Monthly Service Fee	$14.45

Full Cost Profile

Cost Breakdown by Percentage	
Personal Services	37.1%
Operating Costs	29.5%
Capital Costs	33.4%
TOTAL	100.0%

Cost Breakdown in Dollars	
Personal Services	$5,291,876
Operating Costs	$4,214,640
Capital Costs	$4,775,851
TOTAL	$14,282,367

Raleigh

Residential Refuse Collection

Key: Raleigh ■ Benchmarking Average — Fiscal Years 2016 through 2020

Resource Measures

Residential Refuse Collection Costs per Capita

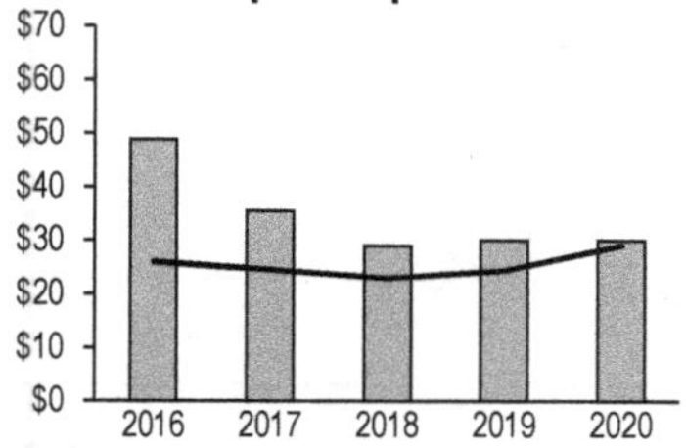

	2016	2017	2018	2019	2020
Raleigh	$48.80	$35.54	$28.89	$29.97	$30.03
Average	$25.84	$24.39	$22.93	$24.37	$29.01

Residential Refuse FTEs per 10,000 Population

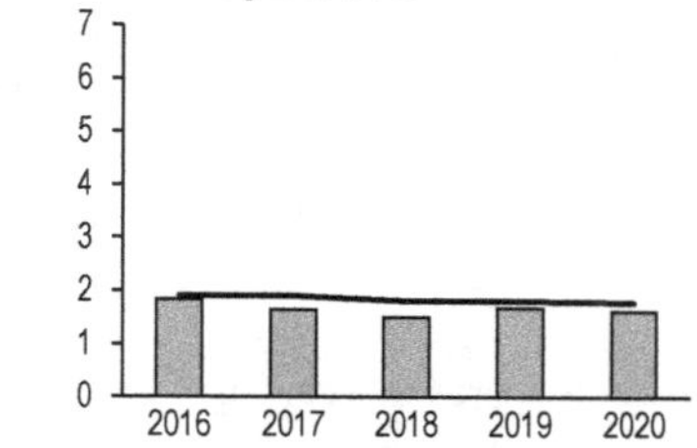

	2016	2017	2018	2019	2020
Raleigh	1.84	1.65	1.50	1.68	1.62
Average	1.91	1.91	1.81	1.81	1.79

Workload Measures

Residential Refuse Tons per 1,000 Population

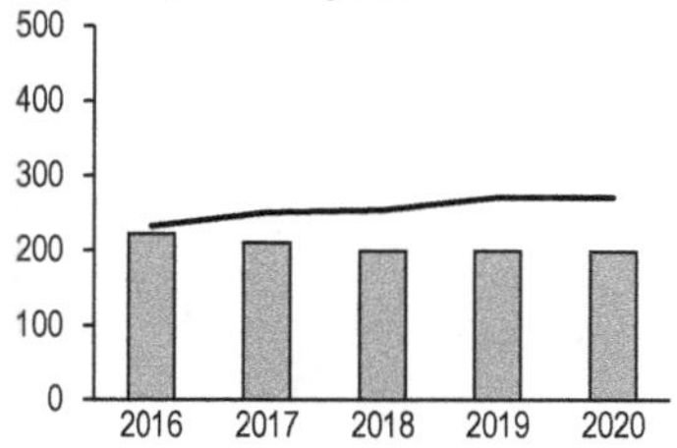

	2016	2017	2018	2019	2020
Raleigh	222	210	200	199	199
Average	232	251	254	271	271

Residential Refuse Tons per 1,000 Collection Points

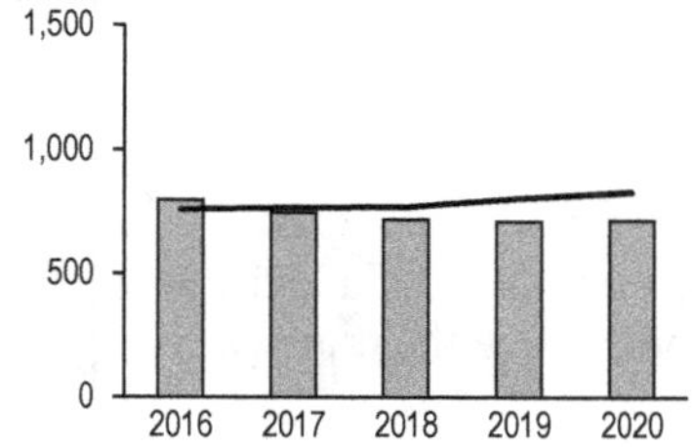

	2016	2017	2018	2019	2020
Raleigh	797	748	718	712	716
Average	759	767	769	806	830

Efficiency Measures

Residential Refuse Collection Cost per Ton Collected

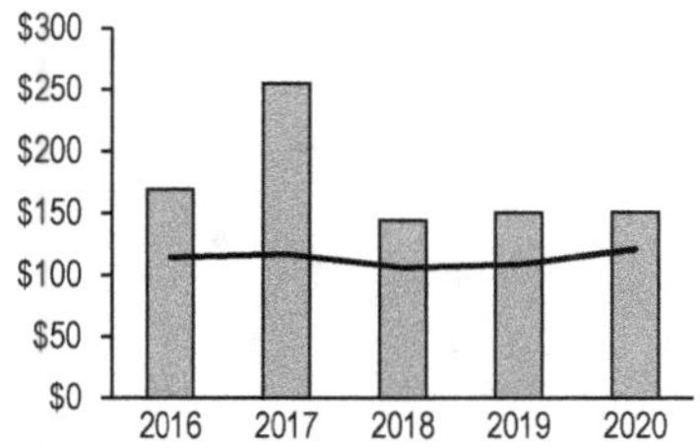

	2016	2017	2018	2019	2020
Raleigh	$169	$255	$145	$150	$151
Average	$114	$117	$106	$109	$121

Residential Refuse Collection Cost per Collection Point

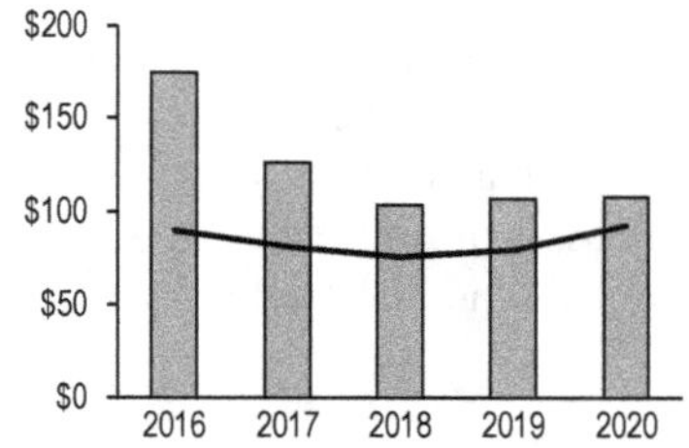

	2016	2017	2018	2019	2020
Raleigh	$175	$126	$104	$107	$108
Average	$90	$82	$76	$80	$93

Refuse Tons Collected per Municipal Collection FTE

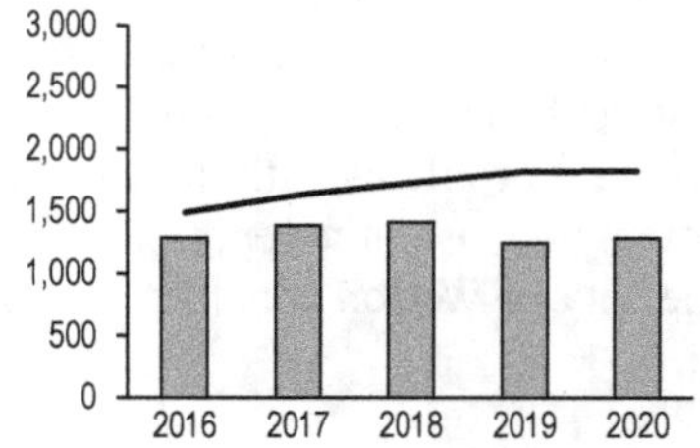

	2016	2017	2018	2019	2020
Raleigh	1,290	1,386	1,414	1,250	1,294
Average	1,489	1,633	1,730	1,822	1,828

Effectiveness Measures

Complaints per 1,000 Collection Points

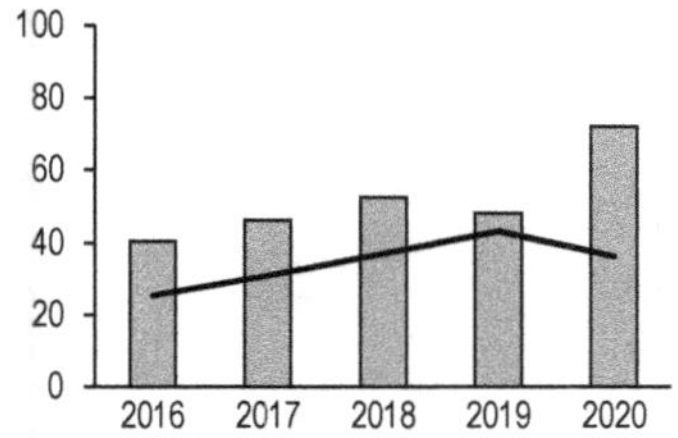

	2016	2017	2018	2019	2020
Raleigh	40.6	46.3	52.5	48.4	72.1
Average	25.4	31.1	37.1	43.2	36.4

Valid Complaints per 1,000 Collection Points

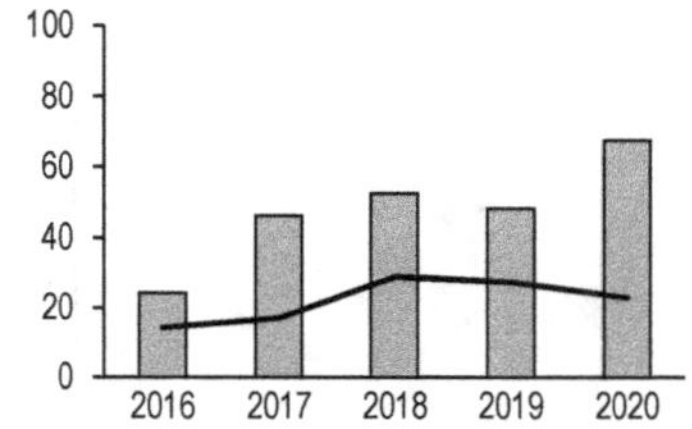

	2016	2017	2018	2019	2020
Raleigh	24.4	46.3	52.5	48.4	67.5
Average	14.2	17.1	28.9	27.4	23.0

Fiscal Year 2019-20

Explanatory Information

Service Level and Delivery

Residential refuse collection service is provided once a week at curbside to Wilson residents. Senior citizens and disabled persons may apply for and receive backyard pickup. There is currently a monthly $20.00 fee per household for the residential refuse collection service.

During the fiscal year, the city used five one-person crews working from automated packers. The city also used two three-person crews, each composed of one driver and two collectors working from semi-automated rear loaders. Residents are required to use ninety-six-gallon roll-out containers.

The city serviced twenty-four collection routes each week during the fiscal year. The packers made an average of two trips to the disposal facility per day per route, with the distance to the transfer station being ten miles.

Wilson collected 23,080 tons of residential refuse during the fiscal year, at a cost of $61 per ton. The cost per ton does not include the disposal cost of $42.30, representing the tipping fee at the transfer station.

Conditions Affecting Service, Performance, and Costs

During FY 2017–18, Wilson made sweeping route changes and added additional entry level positions and two new supervisors.

Wilson began using a new system for tracking all call-ins into "FixIt Wilson" during FY 2017–18. Complaints include missed trash; spilled trash; improper place of container; vehicle or other obstructions blocking pickup; and other issues. Not all of these represent problems with the collection staff. This change in the system increased the reported number of complaints or problems. The City of Wilson considers all complaints to be valid complaints.

Municipal Profile

Population (OSBM 2019)	49,384
Land Area (Square Miles)	31.02
Persons per Square Mile	1,592
Median Household Income U.S. Census 2016	$35,409

Service Profile

FTE Positions—Collection	11.0
FTE Positions—Other	1.0
Type of Equipment	5 automated packers 2 packers
Size of Crews (most commonly used)	1 & 3 person
Weekly Routes	27
Average Distance to Disposal Site	10 miles
Average Daily Trips to Disposal Site	2
Percentage of Service Contracted	0%
Collection Frequency	1 x week
General Collection Location	Curbside
Residential Customers (number represents collection points)	21,111
Tons Collected	23,080
Monthly Service Fee	$20.00

Full Cost Profile

Cost Breakdown by Percentage	
Personal Services	39.3%
Operating Costs	33.4%
Capital Costs	27.2%
TOTAL	100.0%

Cost Breakdown in Dollars	
Personal Services	$551,529
Operating Costs	$468,465
Capital Costs	$382,031
TOTAL	$1,402,025

Wilson

Residential Refuse Collection

Key: Wilson ■ Benchmarking Average — Fiscal Years 2016 through 2020

Resource Measures

Residential Refuse Collection Costs per Capita

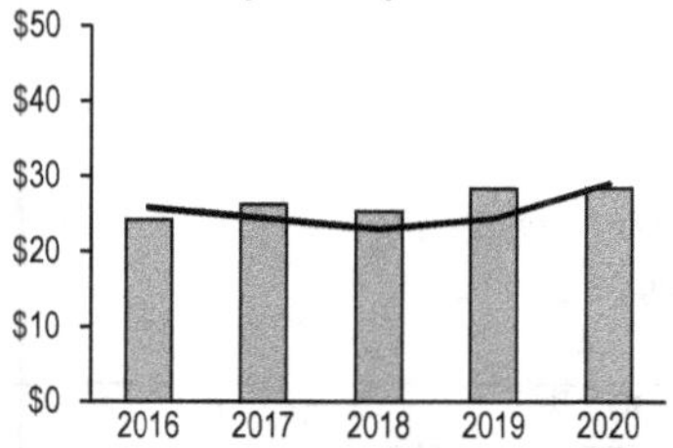

	2016	2017	2018	2019	2020
Wilson	$24.19	$26.23	$25.27	$28.36	$28.39
Average	$25.84	$24.39	$22.93	$24.37	$29.01

Residential Refuse FTEs per 10,000 Population

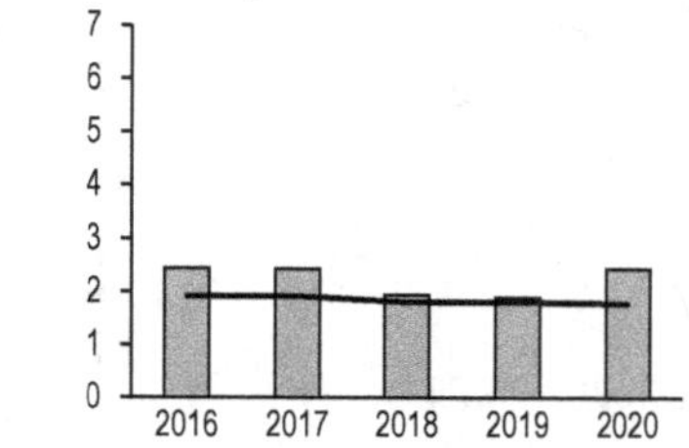

	2016	2017	2018	2019	2020
Wilson	2.43	2.43	1.93	1.89	2.43
Average	1.91	1.91	1.81	1.81	1.79

Workload Measures

Residential Refuse Tons per 1,000 Population

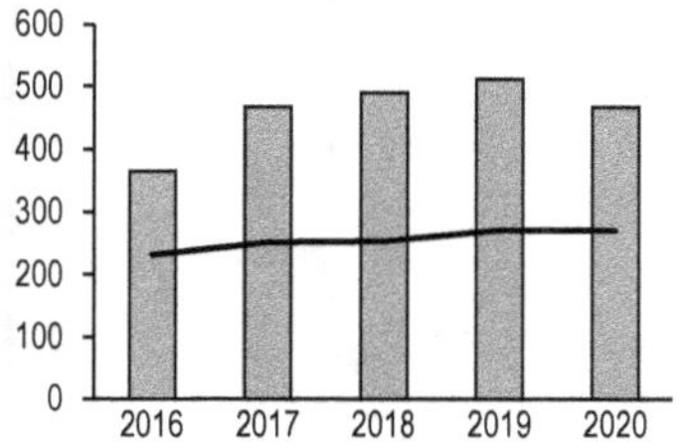

	2016	2017	2018	2019	2020
Wilson	365	467	491	512	467
Average	232	251	254	271	271

Residential Refuse Tons per 1,000 Collection Points

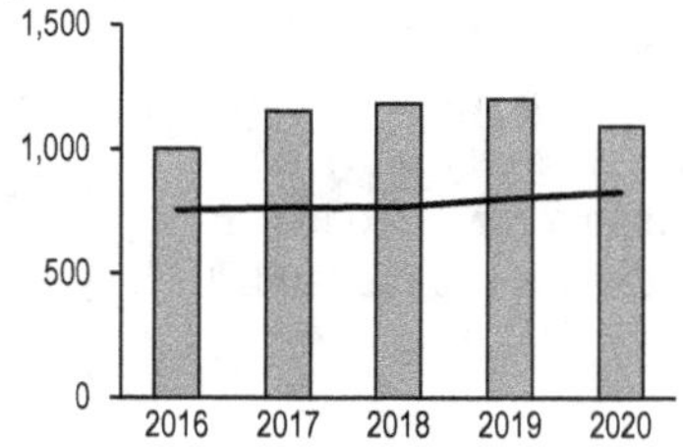

	2016	2017	2018	2019	2020
Wilson	1,001	1,153	1,183	1,201	1,093
Average	759	767	769	806	830

Efficiency Measures

Residential Refuse Collection Cost per Ton Collected

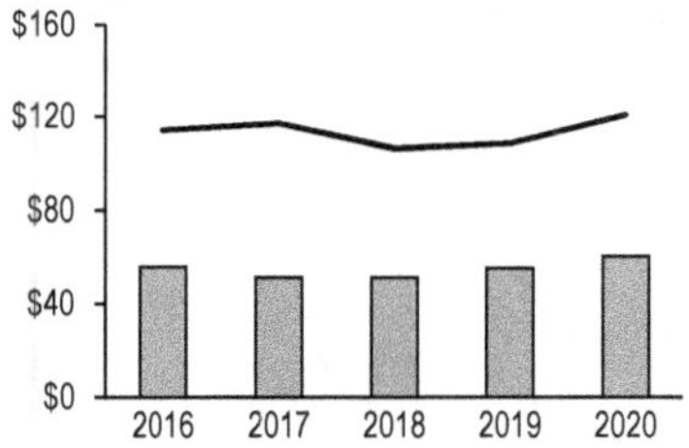

	2016	2017	2018	2019	2020
Wilson	$56	$51	$51	$55	$61
Average	$114	$117	$106	$109	$121

Residential Refuse Collection Cost per Collection Point

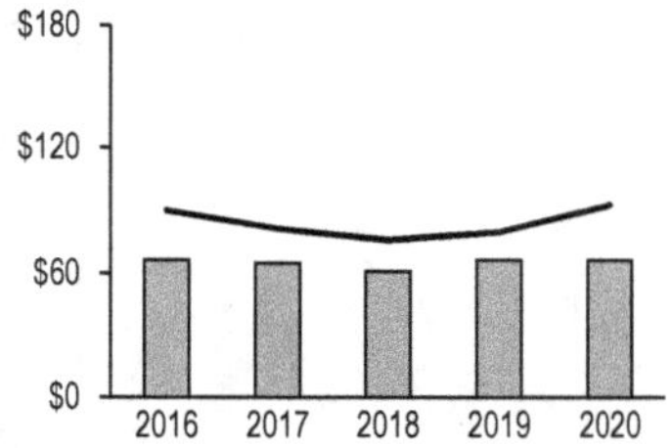

	2016	2017	2018	2019	2020
Wilson	$66	$65	$61	$67	$66
Average	$90	$82	$76	$80	$93

Refuse Tons Collected per Municipal Collection FTE

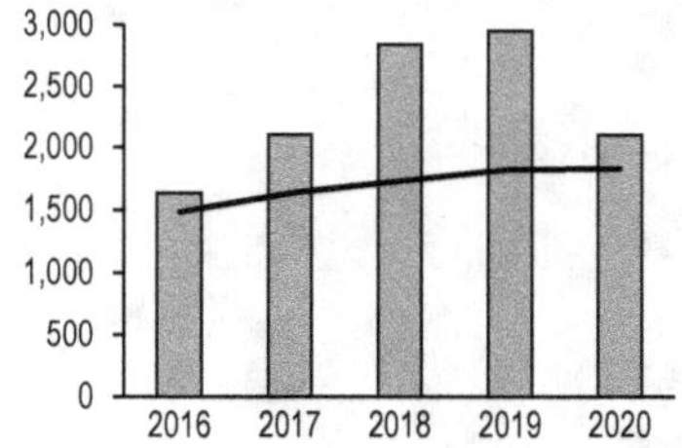

	2016	2017	2018	2019	2020
Wilson	1,636	2,098	2,838	2,953	2,098
Average	1,489	1,633	1,730	1,822	1,828

Effectiveness Measures

Complaints per 1,000 Collection Points

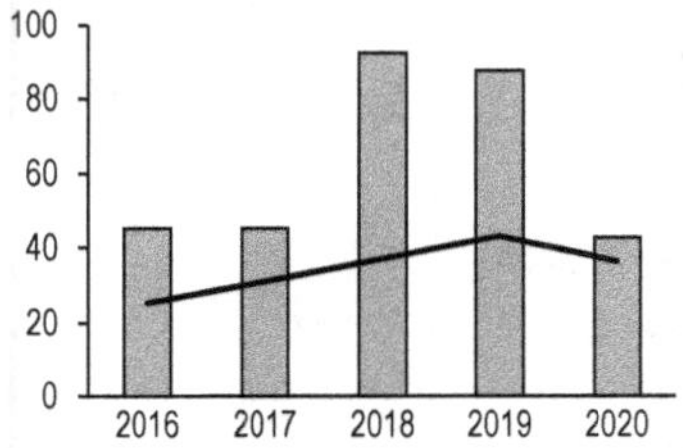

	2016	2017	2018	2019	2020
Wilson	45.1	45.1	92.5	87.8	42.7
Average	25.4	31.1	37.1	43.2	36.4

Valid Complaints per 1,000 Collection Points

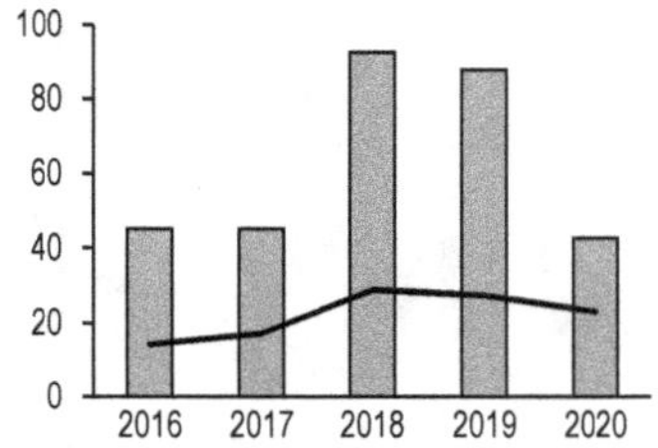

	2016	2017	2018	2019	2020
Wilson	45.1	45.1	92.5	87.8	42.7
Average	14.2	17.1	28.9	27.4	23.0

Winston-Salem Residential Refuse Collection

Fiscal Year 2019-20

Explanatory Information

Service Level and Delivery

Winston-Salem collects residential refuse once per week from curbside. The city implemented a voluntary curbside collection program in March 2005. In October 2010, the city began the transition to mandatory curbside collection. The transition to a curbside-only collection system was completed during FY 2011–12.

The city uses thirteen one-person crews to collect residential refuse plus eleven three-person crews, each composed of a driver and two collectors equipped with rear-loading packers.

Residents may use three thirty-two-gallon containers or one ninety-six-gallon roll-out cart. There was no fee for the residential refuse service during the fiscal year.

The city collected 65,319 tons of residential refuse during the fiscal year from 81,589 collection points. The cost per ton was $114, which does not include the tipping fee of $36 per ton. The city serviced 96 collection routes during the fiscal year, with an average of one trip per route per day to the landfill. The average distance to the landfill was twelve miles.

Conditions Affecting Service, Performance, and Costs

Municipal Profile

Population (OSBM 2019)	244,739
Land Area (Square Miles)	132.59
Persons per Square Mile	1,846
Median Household Income U.S. Census 2016	$40,584

Service Profile

FTE Positions—Collection	65.0
FTE Positions—Other	3.0
Type of Equipment	13 automated packers 11 packers
Size of Crews (most commonly used)	1 & 3 person
Weekly Routes	96
Average Distance to Disposal Site	12 miles
Average Daily Trips to Disposal Site	1
Percentage of Service Contracted	0%
Collection Frequency	1 x week
General Collection Location	Curbside
Residential Customers (number represents collection points)	81,589
Tons Collected	65,319
Monthly Service Fee	No

Full Cost Profile

Cost Breakdown by Percentage	
Personal Services	48.0%
Operating Costs	32.4%
Capital Costs	19.7%
TOTAL	100.0%

Cost Breakdown in Dollars	
Personal Services	$3,580,221
Operating Costs	$2,416,098
Capital Costs	$1,467,542
TOTAL	$7,463,861

Key: Winston-Salem ▒ Benchmarking Average — Fiscal Years 2016 through 2020

Resource Measures

Residential Refuse Collection Costs per Capita

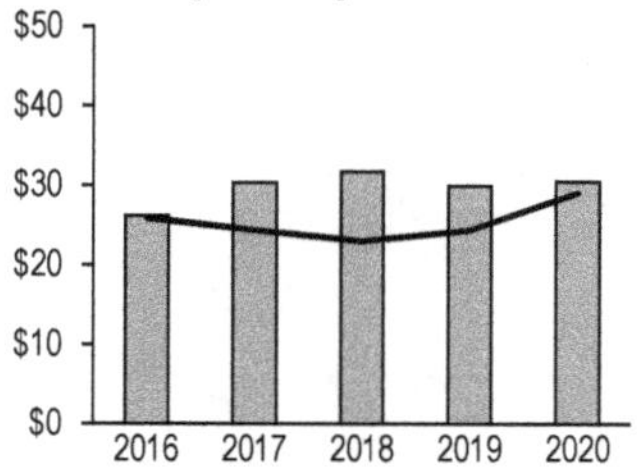

	2016	2017	2018	2019	2020
Winston-Salem	$26.13	$30.33	$31.66	$29.90	$30.50
Average	$25.84	$24.39	$22.93	$24.37	$29.01

Residential Refuse FTEs per 10,000 Population

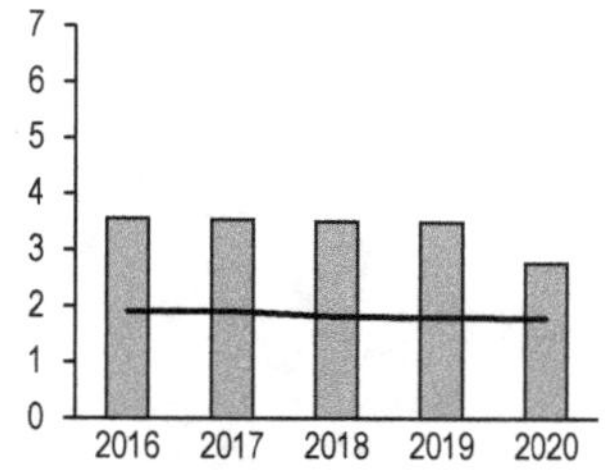

	2016	2017	2018	2019	2020
Winston-Salem	3.56	3.53	3.50	3.49	2.78
Average	1.91	1.91	1.81	1.81	1.79

Workload Measures

Residential Refuse Tons per 1,000 Population

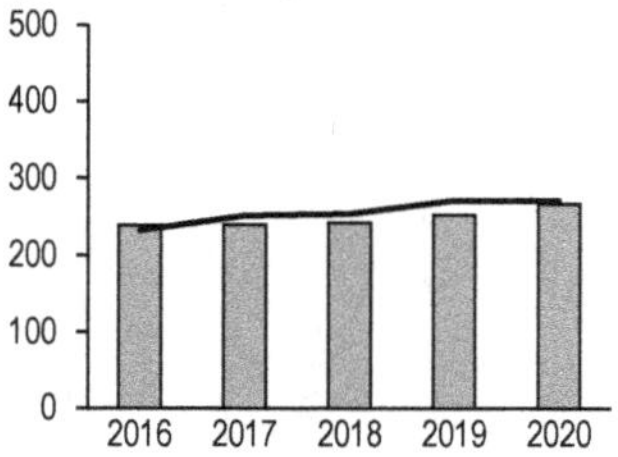

	2016	2017	2018	2019	2020
Winston-Salem	239	240	242	252	267
Average	232	251	254	271	271

Residential Refuse Tons per 1,000 Collection Points

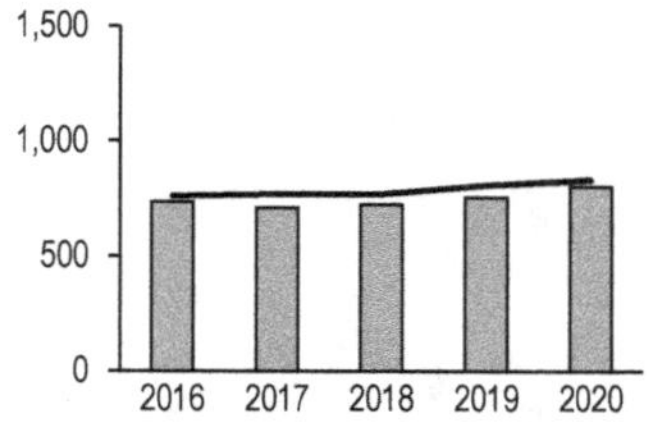

	2016	2017	2018	2019	2020
Winston-Salem	732	707	722	753	801
Average	759	767	769	806	830

Efficiency Measures

Residential Refuse Collection Cost per Ton Collected

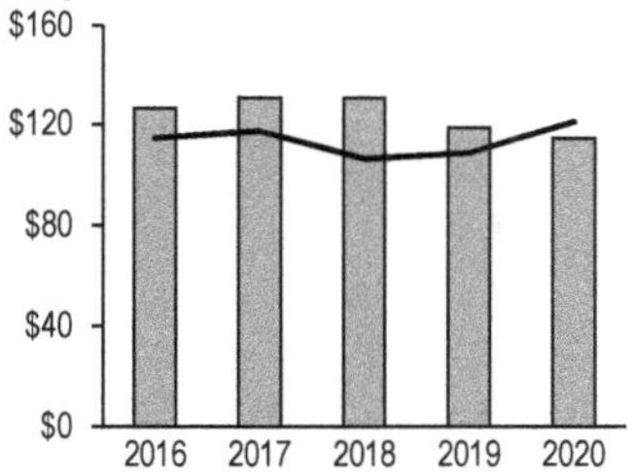

	2016	2017	2018	2019	2020
Winston-Salem	$126	$131	$131	$119	$114
Average	$114	$117	$106	$109	$121

Residential Refuse Collection Cost per Collection Point

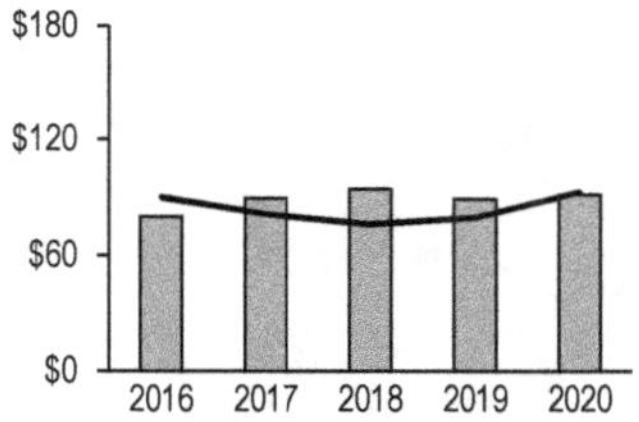

	2016	2017	2018	2019	2020
Winston-Salem	$80	$89	$94	$89	$91
Average	$90	$82	$76	$80	$93

Refuse Tons Collected per Municipal Collection FTE

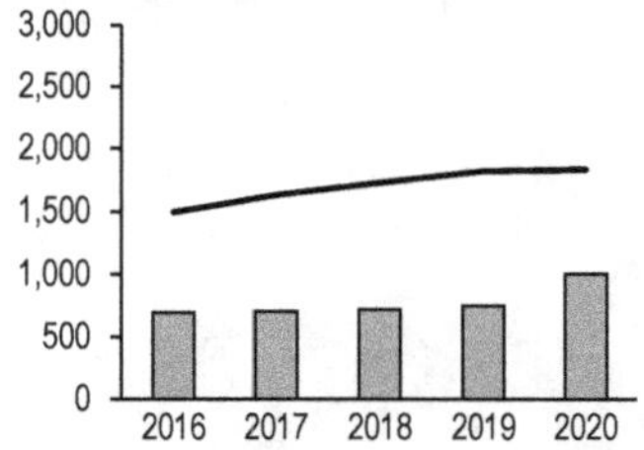

	2016	2017	2018	2019	2020
Winston-Salem	696	704	718	749	1,005
Average	1,489	1,633	1,730	1,822	1,828

Effectiveness Measures

Complaints per 1,000 Collection Points

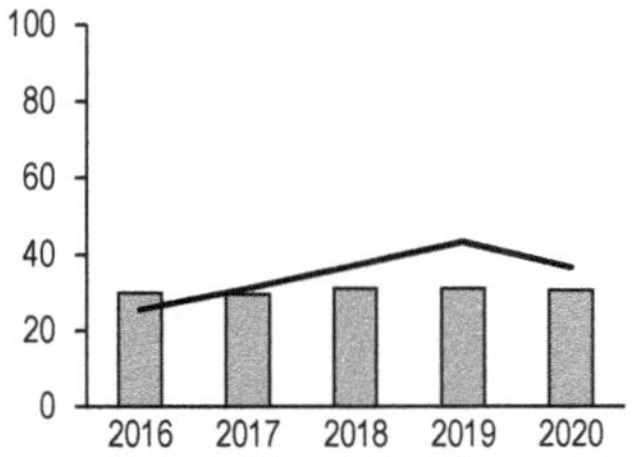

	2016	2017	2018	2019	2020
Winston-Salem	29.9	29.5	31.1	31.1	30.6
Average	25.4	31.1	37.1	43.2	36.4

Valid Complaints per 1,000 Collection Points

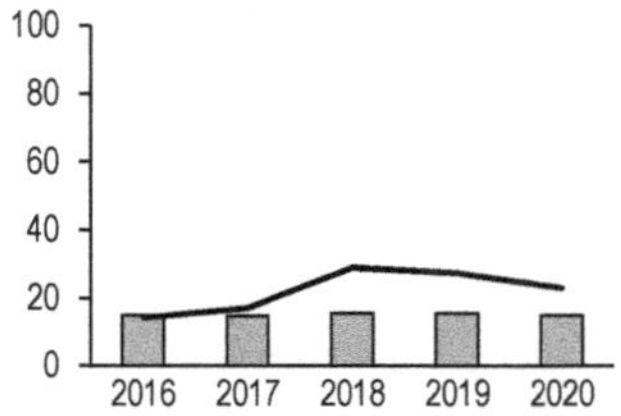

	2016	2017	2018	2019	2020
Winston-Salem	15.0	14.7	15.6	15.6	14.9
Average	14.2	17.1	28.9	27.4	23.0

SCHOOL OF GOVERNMENT
North Carolina Benchmarking Project

Performance and Cost Data

HOUSEHOLD RECYCLING

PERFORMANCE MEASURES FOR HOUSEHOLD RECYCLING

SERVICE DEFINITION

This includes both curbside collection and processing of household recyclable materials from residences and certain other locations and the drop-off of such materials by citizens at recycling stations or centers. The recyclable materials collected are mainly aluminum and steel cans, plastics, glass bottles, newspapers, magazines, and cardboard. The curbside portion of this service involves regularly scheduled collection that utilizes containers small enough that residents and/or workers can move or lift them. The service definition excludes collection of yard waste, leaves, and commercial recycling.

NOTES ON PERFORMANCE MEASURES

1. Workload and Efficiency Measures

The same sorts of workload and efficiency measures are used for household recycling as for residential refuse collection. The project's workload measures for household recycling are tons of recyclable materials collected per 1,000 population and per 1,000 collection points, and the efficiency measures for this service are cost per ton of recyclable materials collected, cost per collection point, and tons of household recyclable materials collected per full-time equivalent (FTE) position directly involved in household recycling. FTEs for recycling are calculated in the same way as they are for residential refuse collection. Only those FTE positions that actually collect recyclables are used for the measure "tons collected per FTE."

2. Tons of Solid Waste Landfilled per 1,000 Population

"Tons solid waste landfilled per 1,000 population" is used as a workload measure. Although not all residential refuse is recyclable, much more of it is likely to be recycled in the future as recycling technology improves and markets for recyclable materials grow. Thus, tons of solid waste landfilled per 1,000 population serves as a useful indicator of the need for household recycling.

3. Community Set-Out Rate in Household Recycling

The project uses this as a measure the effectiveness of household recycling. Residents in municipalities with curbside recycling choose whether to participate in the program and decide the extent of their participation. As the portion of households participating in household recycling grows, the more effective recycling is likely to be in reducing the volume of residential refuse. This measure combines the set-out rate for those participating and the participation rate to estimate the percentage of potential households that are actually recycling.

4. Tons of Household Recyclable Materials Collected as a Percentage of the Sum of Tons of Residential Refuse Collected Plus Tons of Household Recyclable Materials Collected

This measure assesses the magnitude of household recycling in relation to residential refuse collected for disposal. A household recycling program is effective to the extent it diverts residential refuse from the disposal stream.

Household Recycling

Summary of Key Dimensions of Service

City or Town	Drop-Off Sites		Collection Frequency	Collection Points	Community Set-Out Rate	Tons Collected	Percentage of Waste Stream Diverted from Landfill	Percentage Service Contracted	Municipal FTE Collection Positions
	City Owned	Other							
Apex	0	0	1 x week	19,910	NA	5,398	25%	100%	NA
Charlotte	0	9	1 x 2 weeks	221,992	29%	48,316	19%	100%	NA
Concord	0	1	1 x 2 weeks	34,130	70%	6,177	15%	100%	1.3
Goldsboro	0	0	1 x 2 weeks	14,372	NA	1,067	9%	0.1%	4.0
Greensboro	2	0	1 x 2 weeks	91,075	48%	13,539	17%	NA	15
Hickory	2	0	1 x 2 weeks	12,116	69%	2,680	21%	93%	0.5
Raleigh	2	1	1 x 2 weeks	190,585	NA	29,102	24%	NA	39
Wilson	0	0	1 x 2 weeks	21,111	53%	1,705	7%	NA	7
Winston-Salem	9	0	1 x 2 weeks	81,589	60%	16,254	20%	100%	NA

NOTES

Community Set-Out Rate is a combination of the participation rate and the participant's set-out rate.

EXPLANATORY FACTORS

These are factors that the project found affected household recycling collection performance and cost in one or more of the municipalities:

Types of items eligible for recycling
Landfill tipping fees for solid waste
Commitment of city officials to recycling
Number of drop-off centers
Community education
Market prices for recyclable materials
Demographic makeup of community

Fiscal Year 2019-20

Explanatory Information

Service Level and Delivery

Apex contracts with Waste Industries for refuse collection, disposal, and recycling. Only the recycling collection is reflected on this page. The town offers curbside recycling to all residents. Residents pay a $4.28 fee per container per month. Most residents have a sixty-four-gallon cart though some have eighteen-gallon containers.

The following materials are collected:

- plastics
- paperboard
- chipboard
- paper tubes
- corrugated cardboard
- aluminum
- tin and steel cans
- glass
- newspaper
- magazines and catalogs
- phone books

Residents living within Apex are encouraged to participate in the curbside recycling program. The program serves 19,910 residences.

Conditions Affecting Service, Performance, and Costs

Municipal Profile

Population (OSBM 2019)	61,319
Land Area (Square Miles)	23.61
Persons per Square Mile	2,597
Median Household Income U.S. Census 2016	$84,000

Service Profile

FTE Positions—Collection	Contractor
FTE Positions—Other	Contractor
Number of City Drop-Off Centers	0
Other Drop-Off Centers	0
Percentage of Service Contracted	100%
Collection Frequency	1 x week
General Collection Location	Curbside
Recyclables Sorted at Curb	No
Collection Points	19,910
Tons of Recyclables Collected	
Curbside	5,398
City Drop-Off Centers	0
Total Tons Collected	5,398
Monthly Service Fee	$4.28
Revenue from Sale of Recyclables	$0
Sale Revenue as Percentage of Cost	NA

Full Cost Profile

Cost Breakdown by Percentage	
Personal Services	0.0%
Operating Costs	100.0%
Capital Costs	0.0%
TOTAL	100.0%
Cost Breakdown in Dollars	
Personal Services	$0
Operating Costs	$1,037,366
Capital Costs	$0
TOTAL	$1,037,366

Apex

Household Recycling

Key: Apex ▒ Benchmarking Average — Fiscal Years 2016 through 2020

Resource Measures

Recycling Services Cost per Capita

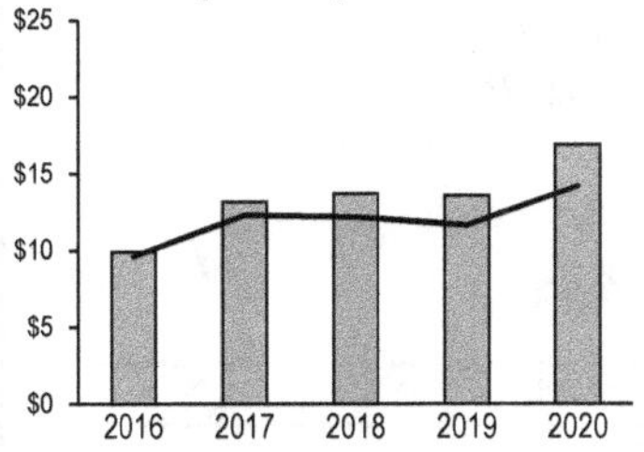

	2016	2017	2018	2019	2020
Apex	$9.92	$13.17	$13.73	$13.58	$16.92
Average	$9.60	$12.29	$12.17	$11.65	$14.17

Recycling Services FTEs per 10,000 Population

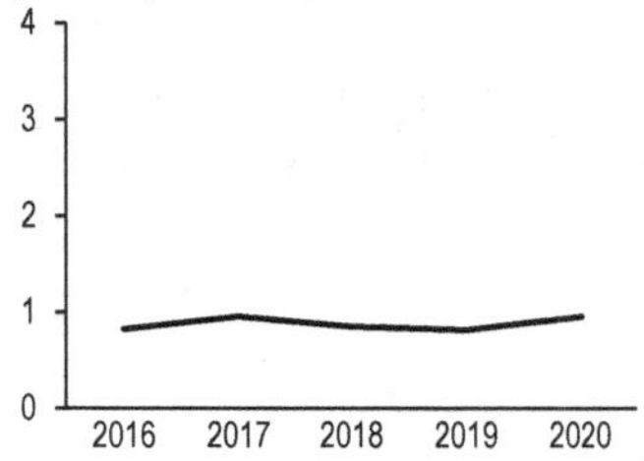

	2016	2017	2018	2019	2020
Apex					
Average	0.82	0.96	0.85	0.82	0.95

Workload Measures

Tons Recyclables Collected per 1,000 Population

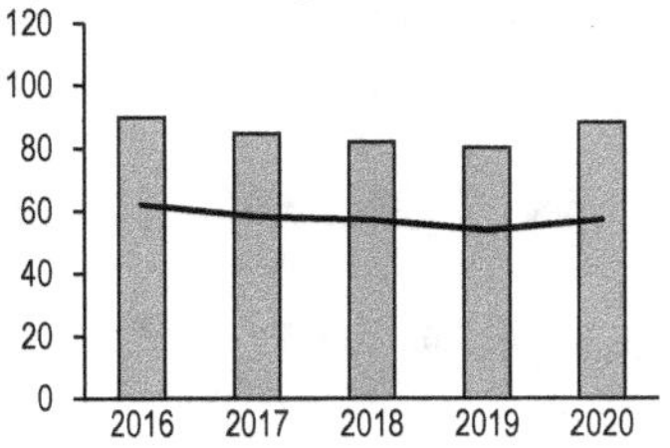

	2016	2017	2018	2019	2020
Apex	89.7	84.6	82.1	80.1	88.0
Average	62.1	58.2	57.1	53.7	57.0

Tons Recyclables Collected per 1,000 Collection Points

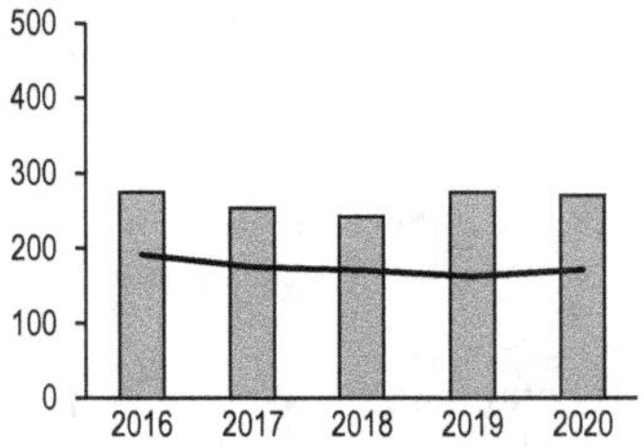

	2016	2017	2018	2019	2020
Apex	275	253	242	275	271
Average	192	175	171	163	172

Tons Solid Waste Landfilled per 1,000 Population

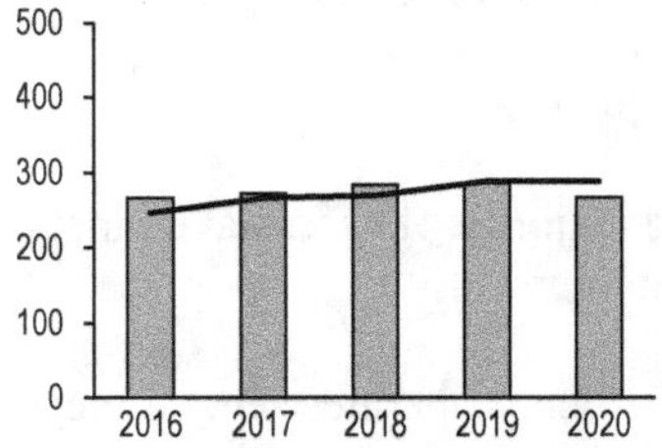

	2016	2017	2018	2019	2020
Apex	266.6	272.8	284.0	286.9	267.2
Average	246.9	266.6	269.8	289.2	289.6

Efficiency Measures

Recycling Services Cost per Ton Collected

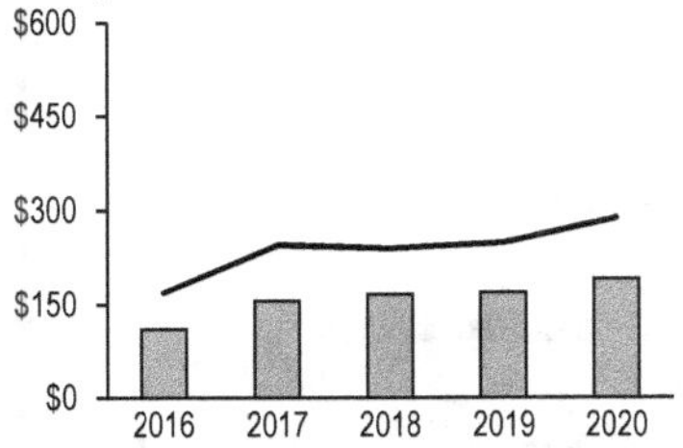

	2016	2017	2018	2019	2020
Apex	$111	$156	$167	$169	$192
Average	$169	$246	$240	$250	$288

Recycling Services Cost per Collection Point

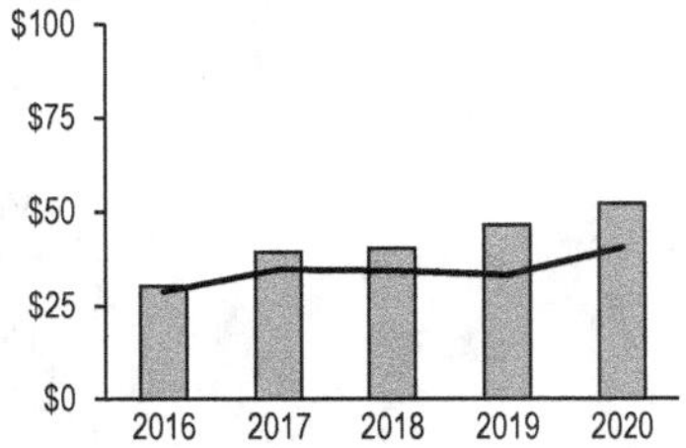

	2016	2017	2018	2019	2020
Apex	$30.38	$39.40	$40.43	$46.53	$52.10
Average	$28.82	$34.78	$34.40	$33.24	$40.46

Tons Collected Curbside per Municipal FTE

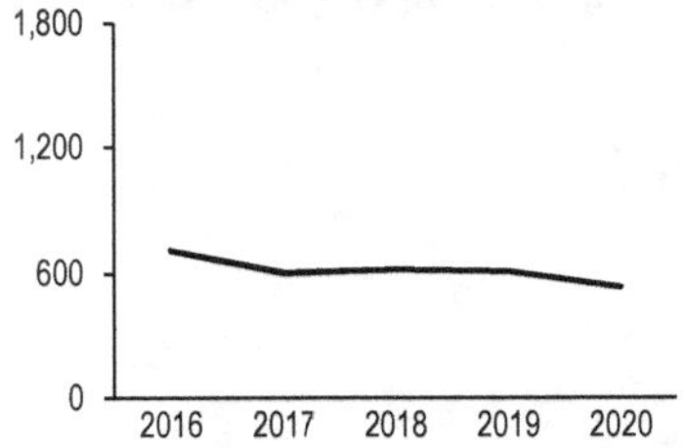

	2016	2017	2018	2019	2020
Apex					
Average	711	602	620	610	536

Effectiveness Measures

Community Set-Out Rate

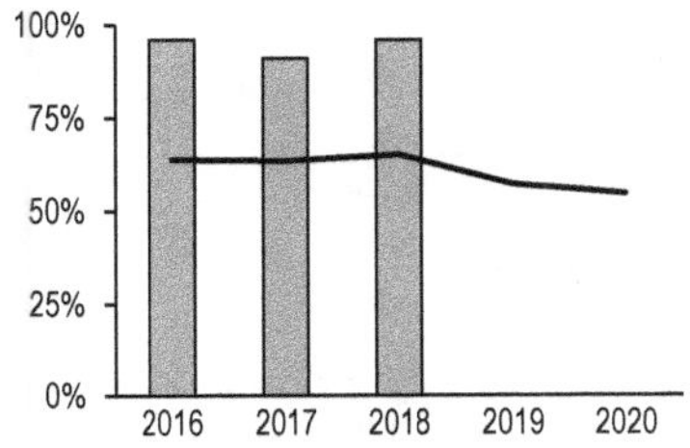

	2016	2017	2018	2019	2020
Apex	96.0%	91.0%	96.0%		
Average	63.9%	63.5%	65.1%	57.2%	54.8%

Tons Recycled as Percentage of Tons Refuse and Recyclables Collected

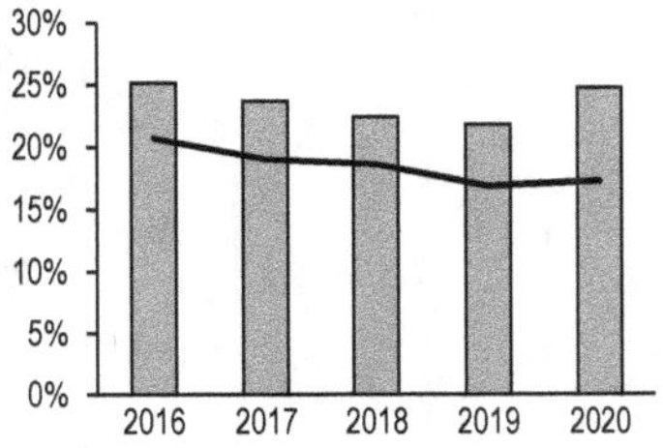

	2016	2017	2018	2019	2020
Apex	25.2%	23.7%	22.4%	21.8%	24.8%
Average	20.7%	19.1%	18.6%	16.9%	17.3%

Charlotte — Household Recycling

Fiscal Year 2019-20

Explanatory Information

Service Level and Delivery

Charlotte provides curbside recycling collection to single-family residential customers once every two weeks. Recycling collection is entirely provided by a contractor. Materials collected in the recycling program include the following:

- glass
- plastic
- aluminum
- newspaper
- magazines
- catalogs
- phone books
- cardboard
- milk cartons
- aerosol cans
- juice boxes

The majority of users have ninety-five or ninety-six-gallon roll-out containers.

The county operates several recycling drop-off centers that are available for use by citizens of Charlotte and Mecklenburg County. Tonnage from the drop-off centers is not included in this report.

Conditions Affecting Service, Performance, and Costs

The set-out rate is calculated daily, as the trucks are outfitted with Radio Frequency Identification (RFID) readers and the recycling carts have RFID chips installed.

Municipal Profile

Population (OSBM 2019)	863,985
Land Area (Square Miles)	307.41
Persons per Square Mile	2,811
Median Household Income U.S. Census 2016	$46,975

Service Profile

FTE Positions—Collection	Contractor
FTE Positions—Other	Contractor
Number of City Drop-Off Centers	0
Other Drop-Off Centers	9
Percentage of Service Contracted	100%
Collection Frequency	Every 2 weeks
General Collection Location	Curbside
Recyclables Sorted at Curb	No
Collection Points	221,992
Tons of Recyclables Collected	
Curbside	48,316
City Drop-Off Centers	0
Total Tons Collected	48,316
Monthly Service Fee	0
Revenue from Sale of Recyclables	$0
Sale Revenue as Percentage of Cost	NA

Full Cost Profile

Cost Breakdown by Percentage	
Personal Services	0.0%
Operating Costs	99.1%
Capital Costs	0.9%
TOTAL	100.0%
Cost Breakdown in Dollars	
Personal Services	$0
Operating Costs	$7,311,997
Capital Costs	$67,279
TOTAL	$7,379,276

Charlotte — Household Recycling

Key: Charlotte ▪ Benchmarking Average — Fiscal Years 2016 through 2020

Resource Measures

Recycling Services Cost per Capita

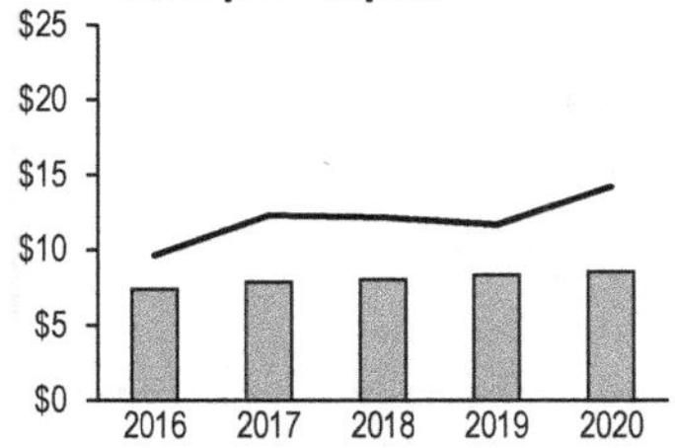

	2016	2017	2018	2019	2020
Charlotte	$7.39	$7.86	$8.05	$8.32	$8.54
Average	$9.60	$12.29	$12.17	$11.65	$14.17

Recycling Services FTEs per 10,000 Population

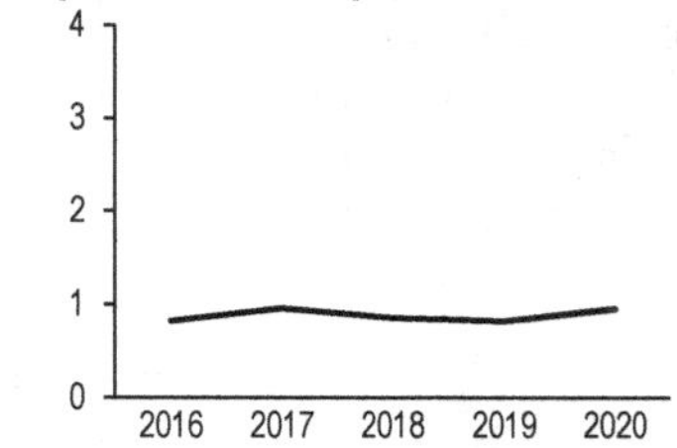

	2016	2017	2018	2019	2020
Charlotte					
Average	0.82	0.96	0.85	0.82	0.95

Workload Measures

Tons Recyclables Collected per 1,000 Population

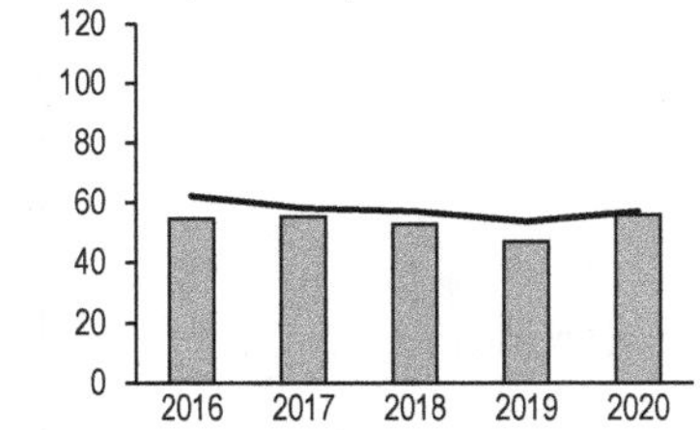

	2016	2017	2018	2019	2020
Charlotte	54.7	55.2	52.7	47.0	55.9
Average	62.1	58.2	57.1	53.7	57.0

Tons Recyclables Collected per 1,000 Collection Points

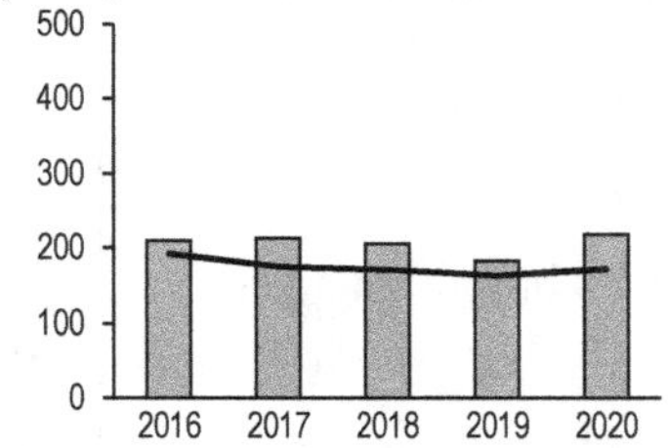

	2016	2017	2018	2019	2020
Charlotte	209	213	205	182	218
Average	192	175	171	163	172

Tons Solid Waste Landfilled per 1,000 Population

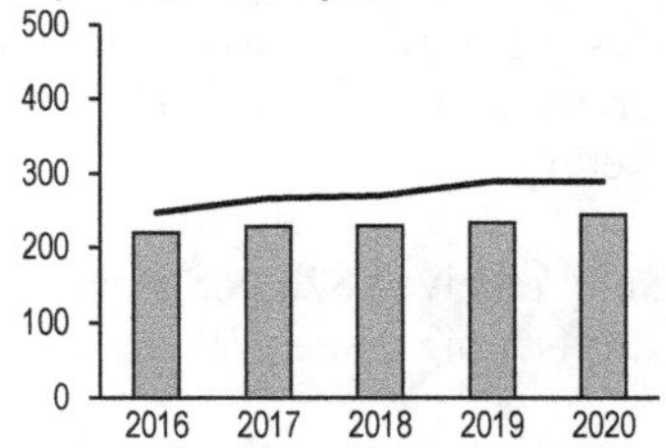

	2016	2017	2018	2019	2020
Charlotte	219.7	228.1	229.0	233.8	244.3
Average	246.9	266.6	269.8	289.2	289.6

Efficiency Measures

Recycling Services Cost per Ton Collected

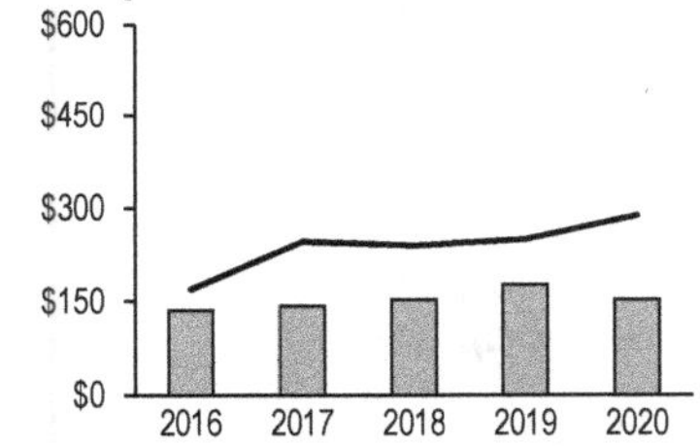

	2016	2017	2018	2019	2020
Charlotte	$135	$142	$153	$177	$153
Average	$169	$246	$240	$250	$288

Recycling Services Cost per Collection Point

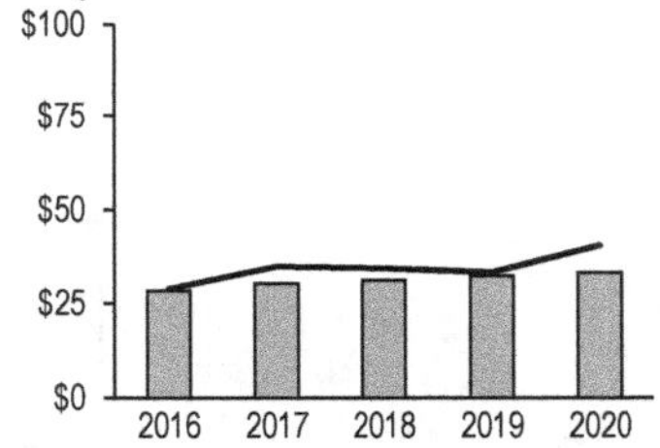

	2016	2017	2018	2019	2020
Charlotte	$28.29	$30.28	$31.24	$32.28	$33.24
Average	$28.82	$34.78	$34.40	$33.24	$40.46

Tons Collected Curbside per Municipal FTE

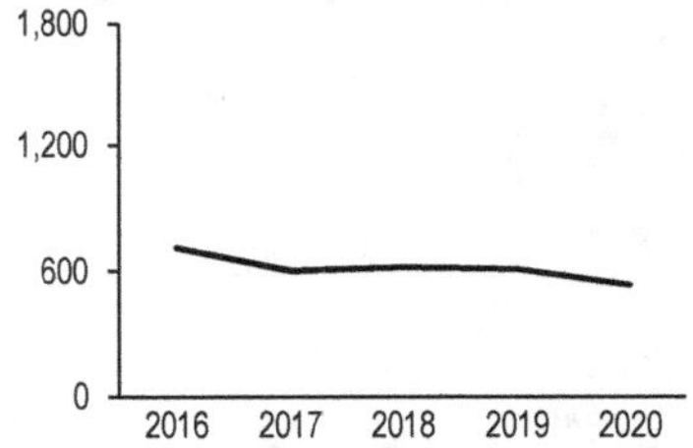

	2016	2017	2018	2019	2020
Charlotte					
Average	711	602	620	610	536

Effectiveness Measures

Community Set-Out Rate

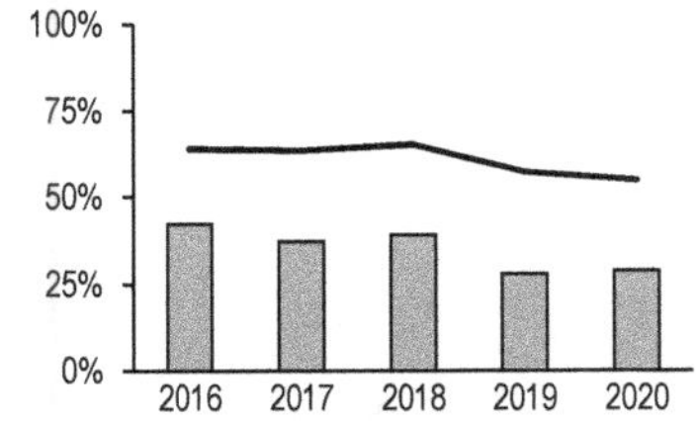

	2016	2017	2018	2019	2020
Charlotte	42.2%	37.2%	39.2%	28.0%	29.0%
Average	63.9%	63.5%	65.1%	57.2%	54.8%

Tons Recycled as Percentage of Tons Refuse and Recyclables Collected

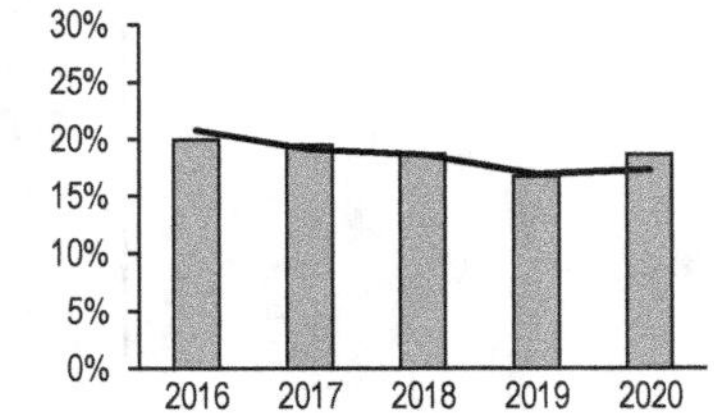

	2016	2017	2018	2019	2020
Charlotte	19.9%	19.5%	18.7%	16.7%	18.6%
Average	20.7%	19.1%	18.6%	16.9%	17.3%

Fiscal Year 2019-20

Explanatory Information

Service Level and Delivery
Concord provides biweekly curbside collection of recyclable materials from households. The city uses a contractor to provide recycling collection. Residents place materials into a ninety-five-gallon cart. The recyclable materials collected include:

- glass
- newspaper
- magazines
- mixed paper and mail
- No. 1 and No. 2 plastics
- metal and aluminum food and beverage containers

Concord uses a contract collector for regular residential curbside recycling. The materials are collected on a commingled basis biweekly from each participating resident and delivered to a materials recovery facility (MRF) in Charlotte for separation and marketing.

The city received $20,965 from the sale of recyclables during the year, offsetting some of the costs.

Conditions Affecting Service, Performance, and Costs

Municipal Profile

Population (OSBM 2019)	95,453
Land Area (Square Miles)	63.65
Persons per Square Mile	1,500
Median Household Income U.S. Census 2016	$50,863

Service Profile

FTE Positions—Collection	1.3
FTE Positions—Other	1.74
Number of City Drop-Off Centers	0
Other Drop-Off Centers	1
Percentage of Service Contracted	100%
Collection Frequency	Every 2 weeks
General Collection Location	Curbside
Recyclables Sorted at Curb	No
Collection Points	34,130
Tons of Recyclables Collected	
Curbside	6,177
City Drop-Off Centers	0
Total Tons Collected	6,177
Monthly Service Fee	2.24
Revenue from Sale of Recyclables	$20,965
Sale Revenue as Percentage of Cost	1.1%

Full Cost Profile

Cost Breakdown by Percentage	
Personal Services	9.6%
Operating Costs	88.9%
Capital Costs	1.6%
TOTAL	100.0%
Cost Breakdown in Dollars	
Personal Services	$189,331
Operating Costs	$1,753,667
Capital Costs	$30,729
TOTAL	$1,973,727

Concord

Household Recycling

Key: Concord ■ Benchmarking Average — Fiscal Years 2016 through 2020

Resource Measures

Recycling Services Cost per Capita

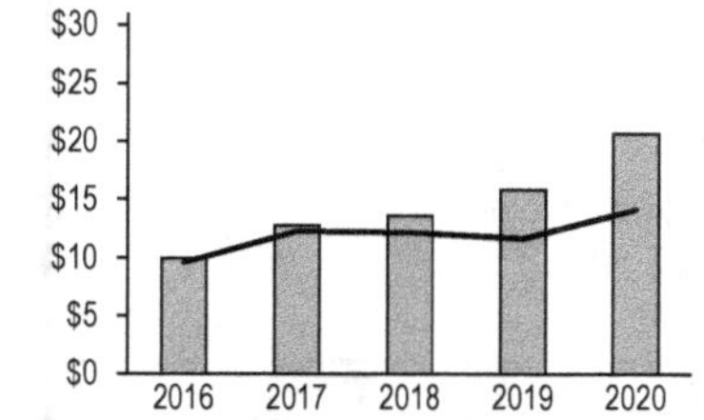

	2016	2017	2018	2019	2020
Concord	$9.96	$12.78	$13.62	$15.83	$20.68
Average	$9.60	$12.29	$12.17	$11.65	$14.17

Recycling Services FTEs per 10,000 Population

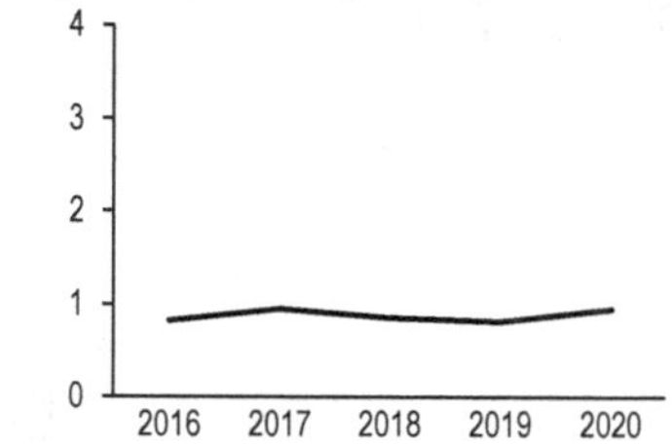

	2016	2017	2018	2019	2020
Concord					
Average	0.82	0.96	0.85	0.82	0.95

Workload Measures

Tons Recyclables Collected per 1,000 Population

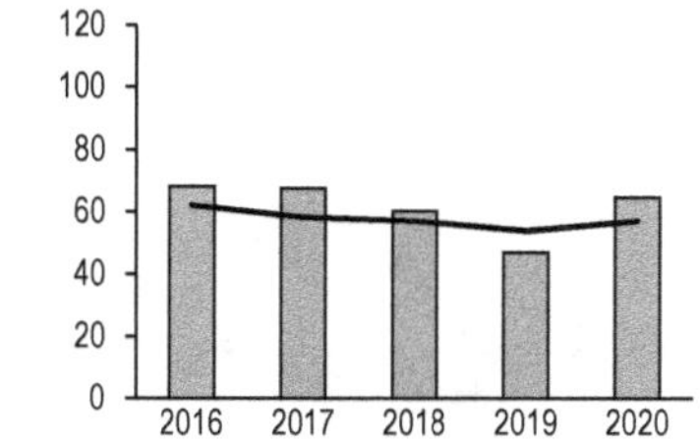

	2016	2017	2018	2019	2020
Concord	68.2	67.6	60.2	47.0	64.7
Average	62.1	58.2	57.1	53.7	57.0

Tons Recyclables Collected per 1,000 Collection Points

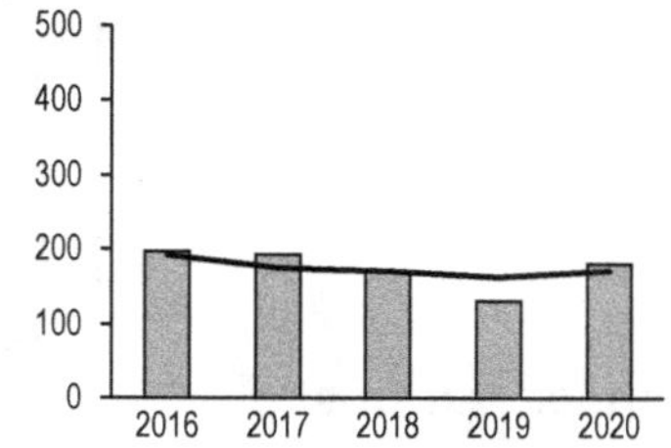

	2016	2017	2018	2019	2020
Concord	197	192	170	131	181
Average	192	175	171	163	172

Tons Solid Waste Landfilled per 1,000 Population

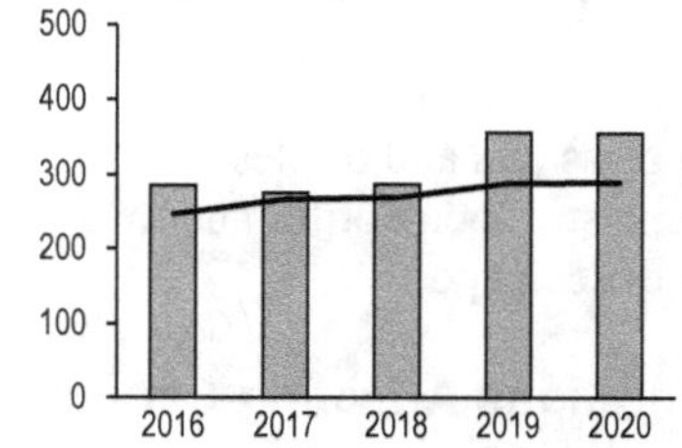

	2016	2017	2018	2019	2020
Concord	285.6	275.3	287.5	355.9	355.7
Average	246.9	266.6	269.8	289.2	289.6

Efficiency Measures

Recycling Services Cost per Ton Collected

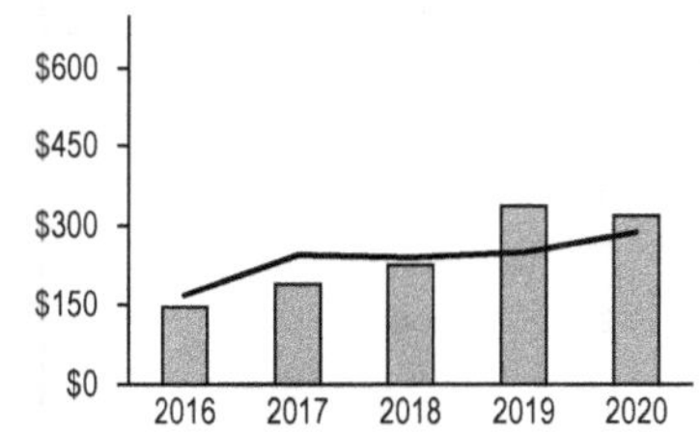

	2016	2017	2018	2019	2020
Concord	$146	$189	$226	$337	$320
Average	$169	$246	$240	$250	$288

Recycling Services Cost per Collection Point

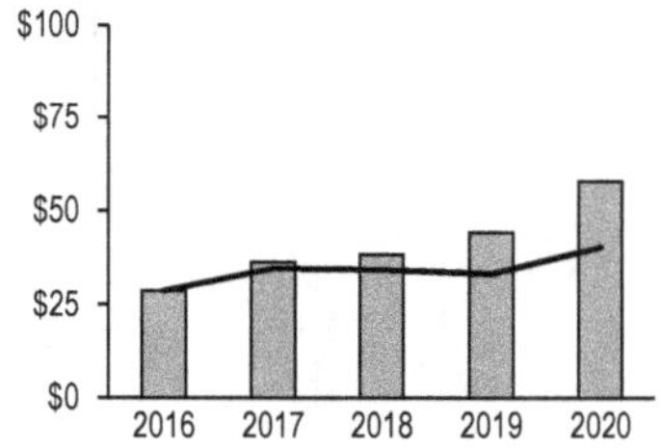

	2016	2017	2018	2019	2020
Concord	$28.77	$36.36	$38.36	$44.29	$57.83
Average	$28.82	$34.78	$34.40	$33.24	$40.46

Tons Collected Curbside per Municipal FTE

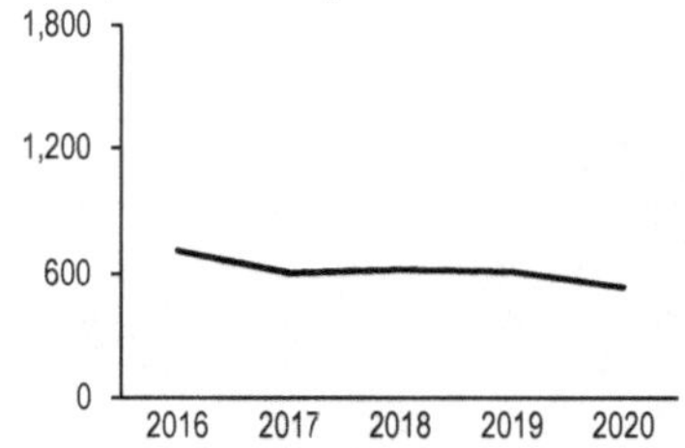

	2016	2017	2018	2019	2020
Concord					
Average	711	602	620	610	536

Effectiveness Measures

Community Set-Out Rate

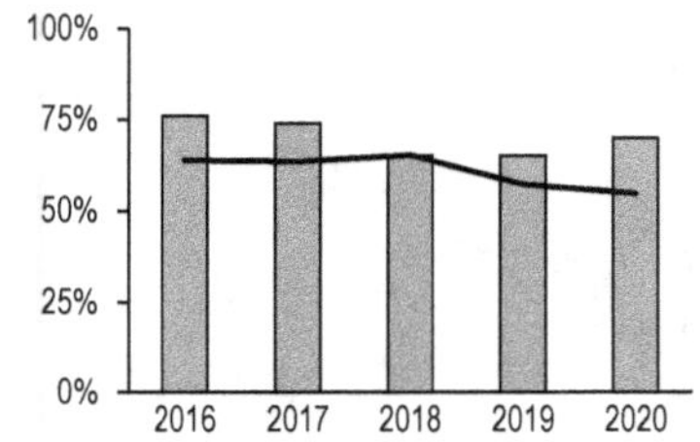

	2016	2017	2018	2019	2020
Concord	76.0%	74.0%	65.0%	65.0%	70.0%
Average	63.9%	63.5%	65.1%	57.2%	54.8%

Tons Recycled as Percentage of Tons Refuse and Recyclables Collected

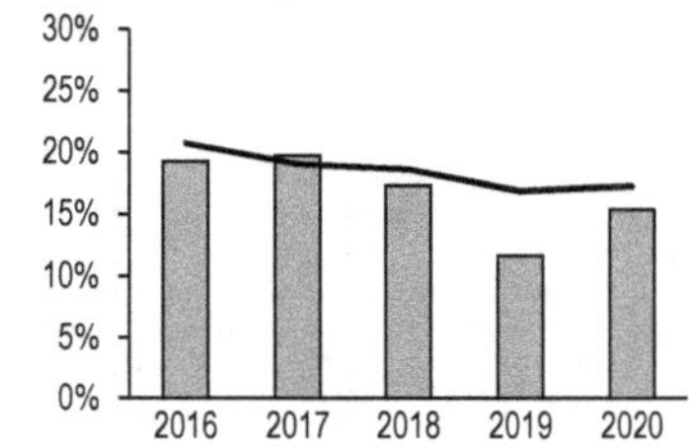

	2016	2017	2018	2019	2020
Concord	19.3%	19.7%	17.3%	11.7%	15.4%
Average	20.7%	19.1%	18.6%	16.9%	17.3%

Fiscal Year 2019-20

Explanatory Information

Service Level and Delivery

Goldsboro operates a recycling system with curbside collection for residents. Recycling is picked up by the Solid Waste Division of the Public Works Department. Collection is done every two weeks. Residents pay a fee that covers all solid waste services, including recycling. Residents use a ninety-five-gallon container provided by the city.

Goldsboro's recycling is not sorted curbside. Materials collected by the household recycling program include:

- No. 1 and No. 2 plastics
- newspaper
- magazines
- telephone books
- cardboard
- aluminum and steel cans
- glass jars and bottles
- plastic soda bottles and milk jugs
- office paper

Conditions Affecting Service, Performance, and Costs

The City of Goldsboro joined the Benchmarking Project in July 2017, with the first year of data showing for FY 2016–17.

Goldsboro contracts recycling collection for one small neighborhood where a hill and tight roads make it infeasible to use city trucks.

Municipal Profile

Population (OSBM 2019)	33,969
Land Area (Square Miles)	29.45
Persons per Square Mile	1,154
Median Household Income U.S. Census 2016	$32,148

Service Profile

FTE Positions—Collection	4.0
FTE Positions—Other	1.2
Number of City Drop-Off Centers	0
Other Drop-Off Centers	0
Percentage of Service Contracted	0.1%
Collection Frequency	Every 2 weeks
General Collection Location	Curbside
Recyclables Sorted at Curb	No
Collection Points	14,372
Tons of Recyclables Collected	
Curbside	1,067
City Drop-Off Centers	0
Total Tons Collected	1,067
Monthly Service Fee	0
Revenue from Sale of Recyclables	$0
Sale Revenue as Percentage of Cost	NA

Full Cost Profile

Cost Breakdown by Percentage	
Personal Services	52.9%
Operating Costs	34.2%
Capital Costs	13.0%
TOTAL	100.0%
Cost Breakdown in Dollars	
Personal Services	$450,544
Operating Costs	$291,172
Capital Costs	$110,746
TOTAL	$852,462

Goldsboro — Household Recycling

Key: Goldsboro ■ Benchmarking Average — Fiscal Years 2016 through 2020

Resource Measures

Recycling Services Cost per Capita

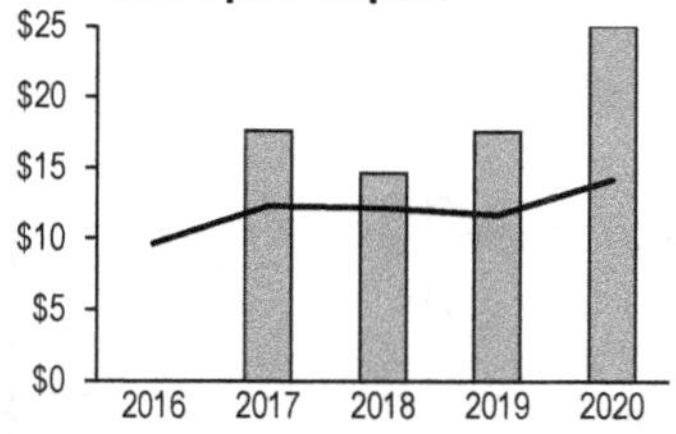

	2016	2017	2018	2019	2020
Goldsboro		$17.59	$14.61	$17.55	$25.10
Average	$9.60	$12.29	$12.17	$11.65	$14.17

Recycling Services FTEs per 10,000 Population

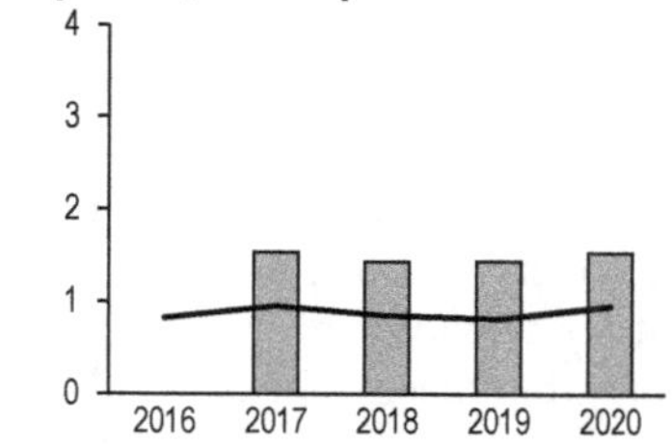

	2016	2017	2018	2019	2020
Goldsboro		1.53	1.43	1.44	1.53
Average	0.82	0.96	0.85	0.82	0.95

Workload Measures

Tons Recyclables Collected per 1,000 Population

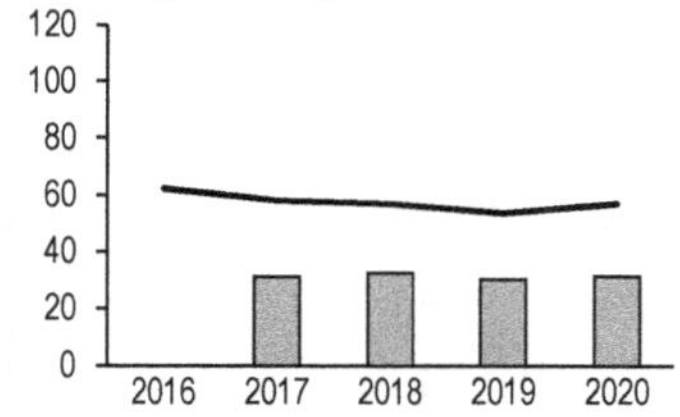

	2016	2017	2018	2019	2020
Goldsboro		31.2	32.6	30.3	31.4
Average	62.1	58.2	57.1	53.7	57.0

Tons Recyclables Collected per 1,000 Collection Points

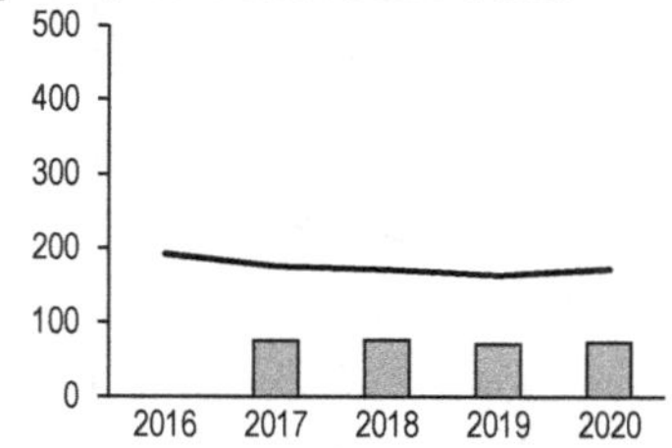

	2016	2017	2018	2019	2020
Goldsboro		75	76	71	74
Average	192	175	171	163	172

Tons Solid Waste Landfilled per 1,000 Population

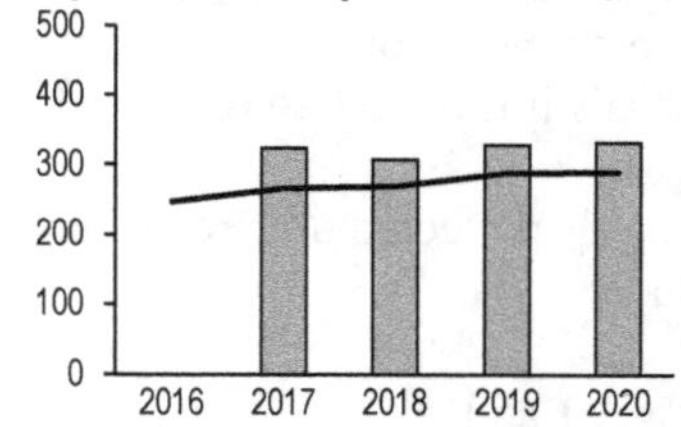

	2016	2017	2018	2019	2020
Goldsboro		323.4	307.1	328.4	331.6
Average	246.9	266.6	269.8	289.2	289.6

Efficiency Measures

Recycling Services Cost per Ton Collected

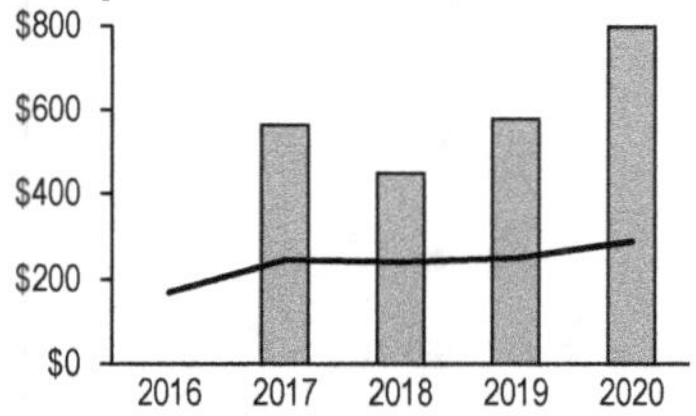

	2016	2017	2018	2019	2020
Goldsboro		$564	$448	$578	$799
Average	$169	$246	$240	$250	$288

Recycling Services Cost per Collection Point

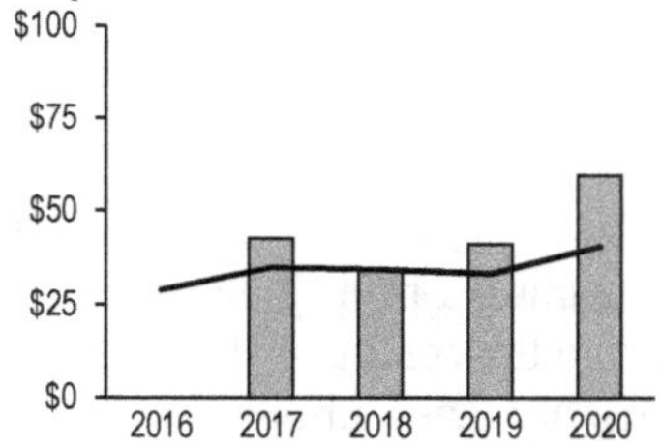

	2016	2017	2018	2019	2020
Goldsboro		$42.57	$34.24	$41.06	$59.31
Average	$28.82	$34.78	$34.40	$33.24	$40.46

Tons Collected Curbside per Municipal FTE

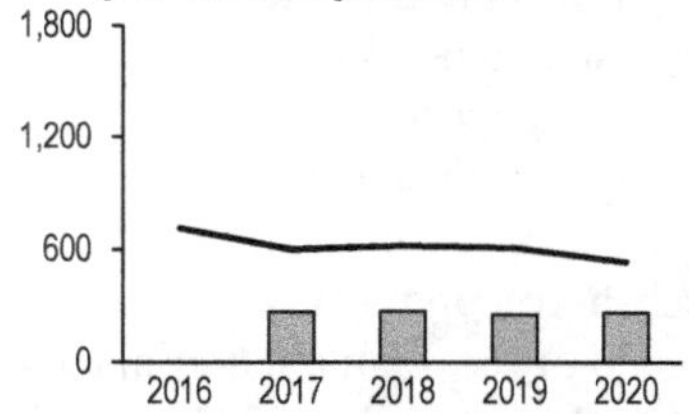

	2016	2017	2018	2019	2020
Goldsboro		271	275	255	266
Average	711	602	620	610	536

Effectiveness Measures

Community Set-Out Rate

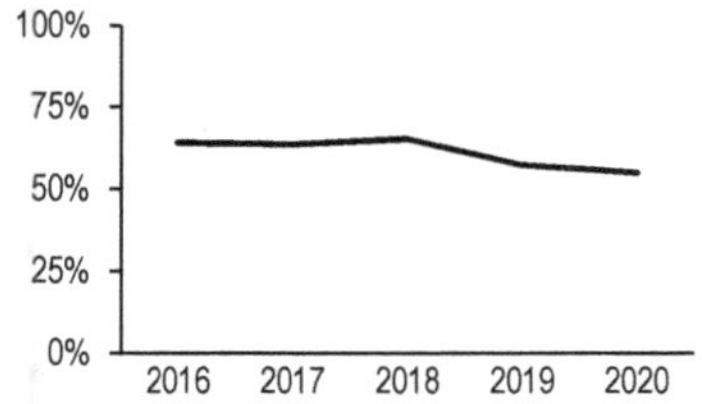

	2016	2017	2018	2019	2020
Goldsboro					
Average	63.9%	63.5%	65.1%	57.2%	54.8%

Tons Recycled as Percentage of Tons Refuse and Recyclables Collected

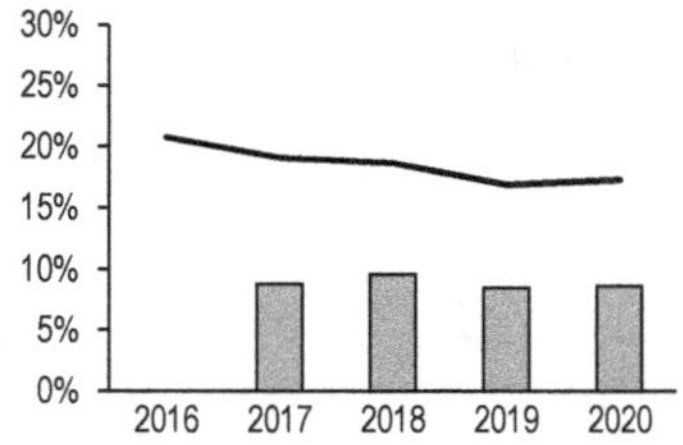

	2016	2017	2018	2019	2020
Goldsboro		8.8%	9.6%	8.5%	8.7%
Average	20.7%	19.1%	18.6%	16.9%	17.3%

Fiscal Year 2019-20

Explanatory Information

Service Level and Delivery

Greensboro operates a voluntary commingled collection process for its recycling customers. Recycling services are provided to the community by means of single ninety-six or sixty-four-gallon automated containers and by green translucent bags. Partnerships also are maintained with fire departments, the county school system, the extension office, and the parks department for providing drop-off sites. There are twenty city-owned drop-off sites, but these collected tons are not reported in Greensboro's data.

Recycling pickup is done every other week. Recycling materials are not sorted curbside. Instead, they are set out in one container, picked up by an automated-collection crew, and taken to an off-site contractor that sorts and recycles the materials. Greensboro provides the collection pickup and delivery to the contractor's location, while the contractor provides for recovery of materials and disposal of the residuals it is unable to recycle.

Materials collected by Greensboro's household recycling program include:

- No. 1 and No. 2 plastics
- newspaper
- magazines
- telephone books
- cardboard
- aluminum and steel cans
- chipboard (cereal boxes)
- glass jars and bottles
- plastic soda bottles and milk jugs
- office paper
- empty aerosol cans

Greensboro contracts with a private firm for separation, packaging, and sale of recyclable materials. City payments to the contractor for the fiscal year are included in total cost. Greensboro gets additional revenues from the sale of recyclables from nonresidential sources, but these are not counted here.

Conditions Affecting Service, Performance, and Costs

Greensboro is highly automated in gathering materials from its recycling program.

The set-out rate was based on a manual count done on a biweekly basis.

Municipal Profile

Population (OSBM 2019)	293,730
Land Area (Square Miles)	129.62
Persons per Square Mile	2,266
Median Household Income U.S. Census 2016	$40,760

Service Profile

FTE Positions—Collection	15.0
FTE Positions—Other	4.0
Number of City Drop-Off Centers	2
Other Drop-Off Centers	0
Percentage of Service Contracted	0%
Collection Frequency	Every 2 weeks
General Collection Location	Curbside
Recyclables Sorted at Curb	No
Collection Points	91,075
Tons of Recyclables Collected	
Curbside	13,539
City Drop-Off Centers	0
Total Tons Collected	13,539
Monthly Service Fee	2.5
Revenue from Sale of Recyclables	$0
Sale Revenue as Percentage of Cost	NA

Full Cost Profile

Cost Breakdown by Percentage	
Personal Services	28.0%
Operating Costs	72.0%
Capital Costs	0.0%
TOTAL	100.0%
Cost Breakdown in Dollars	
Personal Services	$977,248
Operating Costs	$2,511,970
Capital Costs	$0
TOTAL	$3,489,218

Greensboro — Household Recycling

Key: Greensboro ■ Benchmarking Average — Fiscal Years 2016 through 2020

Resource Measures

Recycling Services Cost per Capita

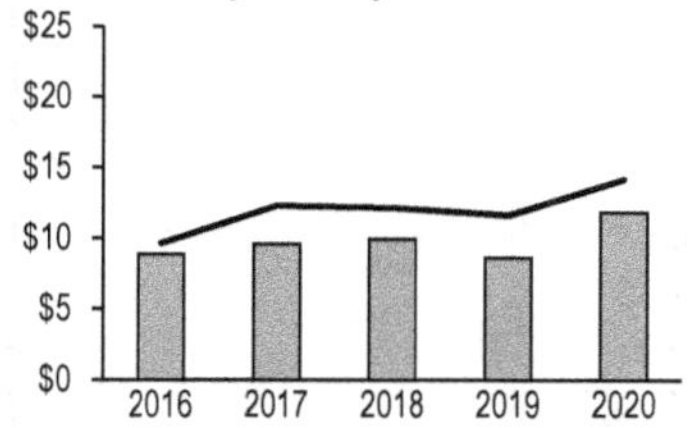

	2016	2017	2018	2019	2020
Greensboro	$8.86	$9.58	$9.96	$8.63	$11.88
Average	$9.60	$12.29	$12.17	$11.65	$14.17

Recycling Services FTEs per 10,000 Population

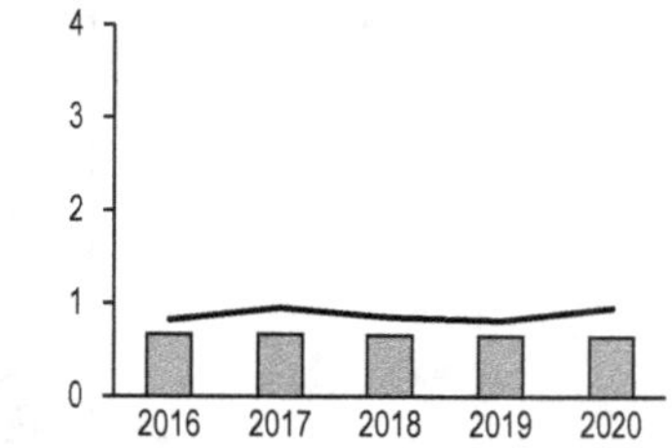

	2016	2017	2018	2019	2020
Greensboro	0.67	0.67	0.66	0.65	0.65
Average	0.82	0.96	0.85	0.82	0.95

Workload Measures

Tons Recyclables Collected per 1,000 Population

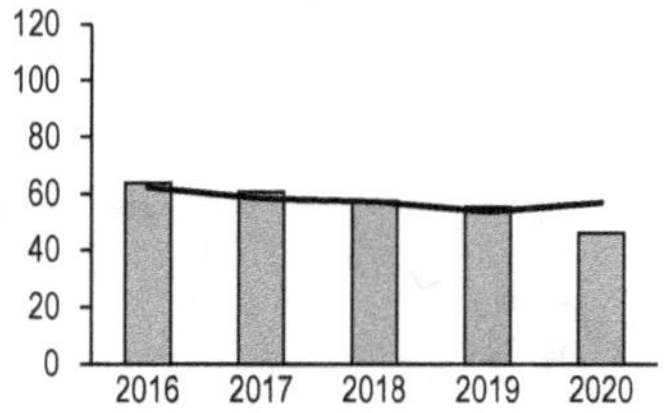

	2016	2017	2018	2019	2020
Greensboro	63.8	60.5	57.5	55.4	46.1
Average	62.1	58.2	57.1	53.7	57.0

Tons Recyclables Collected per 1,000 Collection Points

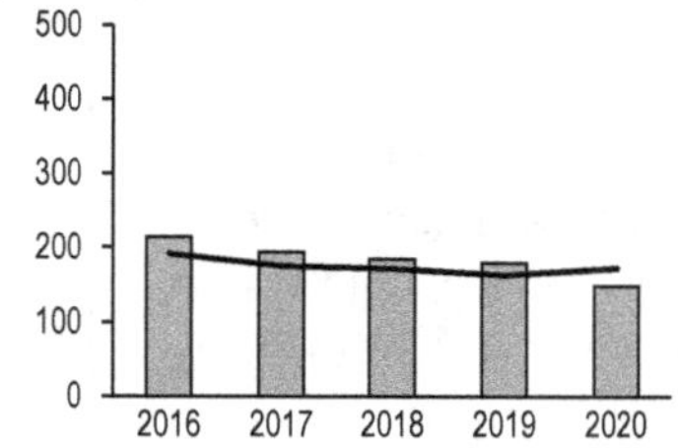

	2016	2017	2018	2019	2020
Greensboro	214	193	184	179	149
Average	192	175	171	163	172

Tons Solid Waste Landfilled per 1,000 Population

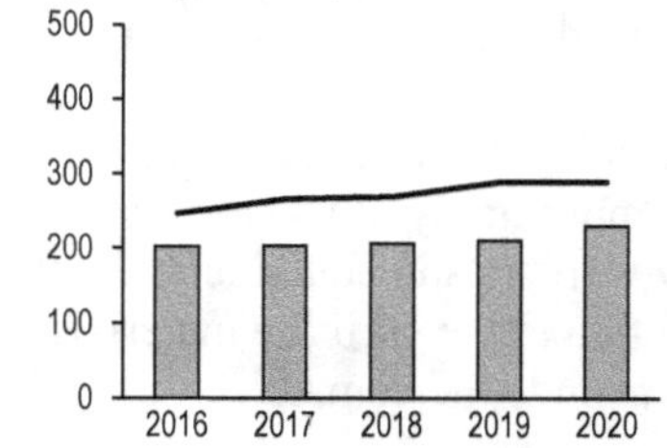

	2016	2017	2018	2019	2020
Greensboro	202.0	202.6	205.8	210.0	229.6
Average	246.9	266.6	269.8	289.2	289.6

Efficiency Measures

Recycling Services Cost per Ton Collected

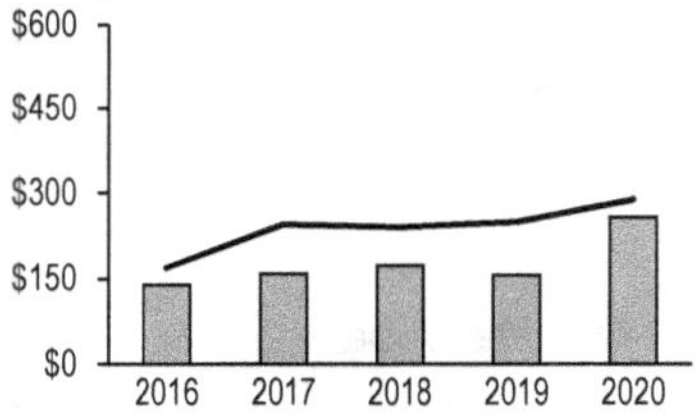

	2016	2017	2018	2019	2020
Greensboro	$139	$158	$173	$156	$258
Average	$169	$246	$240	$250	$288

Recycling Services Cost per Collection Point

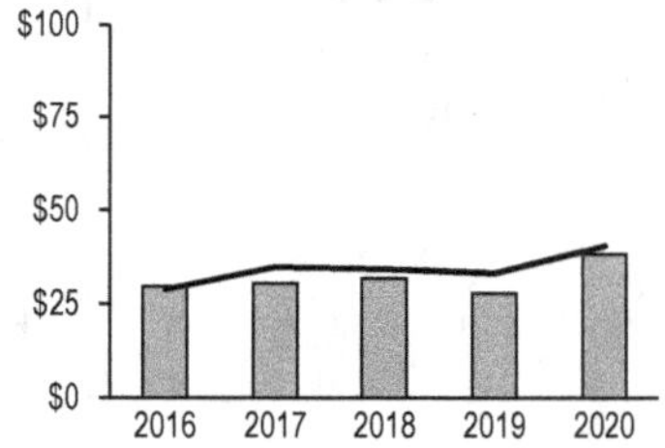

	2016	2017	2018	2019	2020
Greensboro	$29.74	$30.52	$31.86	$27.84	$38.31
Average	$28.82	$34.78	$34.40	$33.24	$40.46

Tons Collected Curbside per Municipal FTE

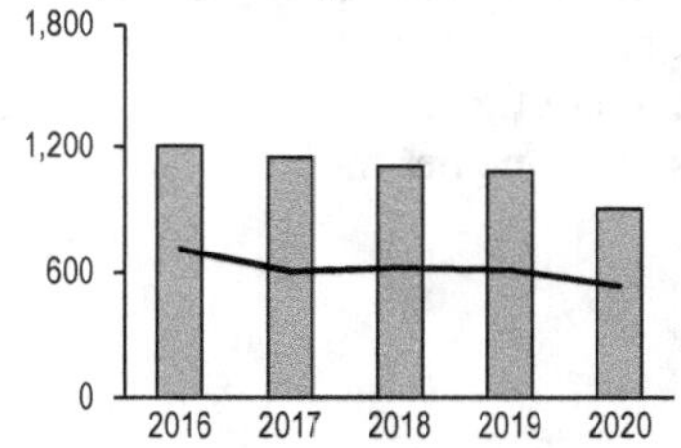

	2016	2017	2018	2019	2020
Greensboro	1,204	1,148	1,104	1,079	903
Average	711	602	620	610	536

Effectiveness Measures

Community Set-Out Rate

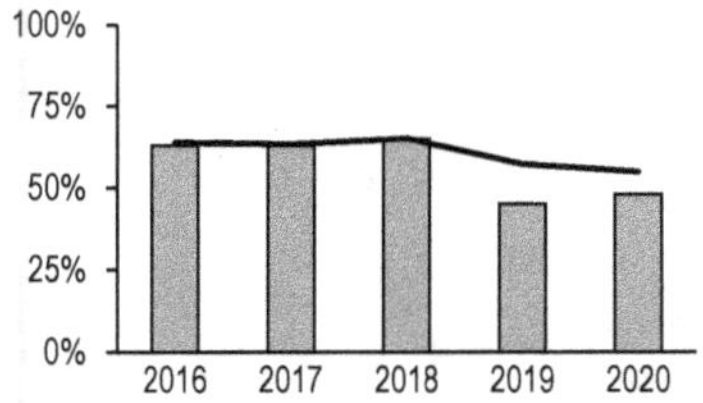

	2016	2017	2018	2019	2020
Greensboro	63.0%	63.0%	64.9%	45.0%	48.0%
Average	63.9%	63.5%	65.1%	57.2%	54.8%

Tons Recycled as Percentage of Tons Refuse and Recyclables Collected

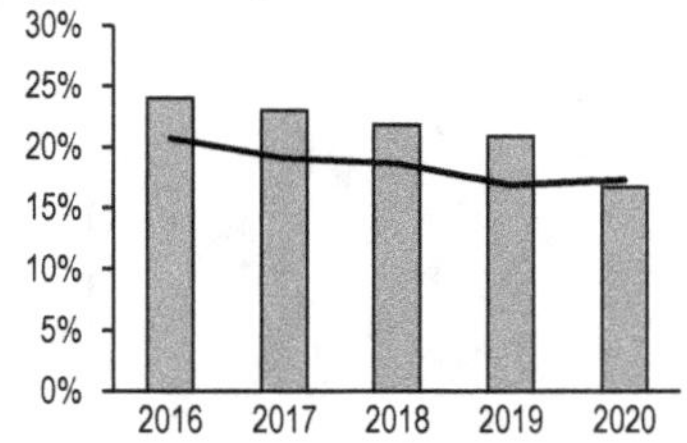

	2016	2017	2018	2019	2020
Greensboro	24.0%	23.0%	21.8%	20.9%	16.7%
Average	20.7%	19.1%	18.6%	16.9%	17.3%

Fiscal Year 2019-20

Explanatory Information

Service Level and Delivery
Hickory offers curbside collection of recyclable materials every other week to its residents through a contractual agreement. The recycling materials collected include:

- newspaper and magazines
- aluminum and steel cans
- No. 1 and No. 2 plastics
- glass—all colors
- phone books and junk mail

Hickory's household recycling program also uses two drop-off recycling centers. One is staffed, and the other is not. These centers collect antifreeze and oil in addition to the same household materials that are collected at the curb. Tonnage and costs for this service are included in the performance and cost data.

A separate commercial recycling program that services businesses and multifamily units is operated by the city. The program utilizes city workers and equipment to collect cardboard and paper in addition to the curbside materials. The performance and cost data do not include the commercial program.

The city charges residents a monthly fee for recycling, which is included in the monthly solid waste fee. In the fiscal year, the city collected $23,115 in revenue from the sale of recyclables, partially offsetting program costs.

Conditions Affecting Service, Performance, and Costs
The set-out rate is calculated on a monthly basis by the contractor. While not tracked, missed recycling pickups are minimal and average less than one per month.

Municipal Profile

Population (OSBM 2019)	41,409
Land Area (Square Miles)	30.50
Persons per Square Mile	1,358
Median Household Income U.S. Census 2016	$35,353

Service Profile

FTE Positions—Collection	0.5 City
FTE Positions—Other	0.27 City
Number of City Drop-Off Centers	2
Other Drop-Off Centers	0
Percentage of Service Contracted	93%
Collection Frequency	Every 2 weeks
General Collection Location	Curbside
Recyclables Sorted at Curb	No
Collection Points	12,116
Tons of Recyclables Collected	
Curbside	2,483
City Drop-Off Centers	197
Total Tons Collected	2,680
Monthly Service Fee	0
Revenue from Sale of Recyclables	$23,115
Sale Revenue as Percentage of Cost	4.7%

Full Cost Profile

Cost Breakdown by Percentage	
Personal Services	10.6%
Operating Costs	87.6%
Capital Costs	1.8%
TOTAL	100.0%
Cost Breakdown in Dollars	
Personal Services	$52,451
Operating Costs	$433,322
Capital Costs	$9,018
TOTAL	$494,791

Hickory

Household Recycling

Key: Hickory ▪ Benchmarking Average — Fiscal Years 2016 through 2020

Resource Measures

Recycling Services Cost per Capita

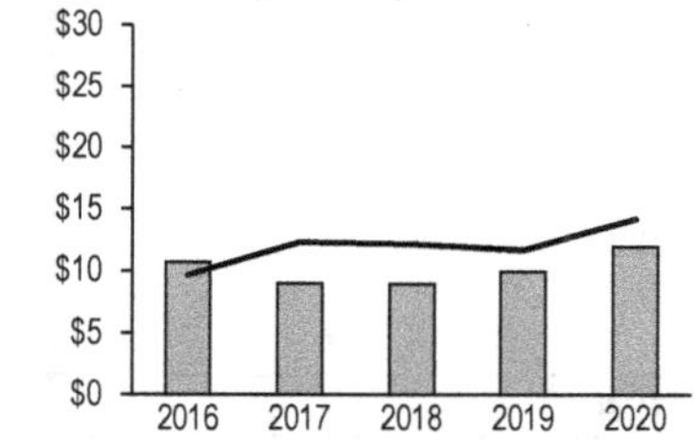

	2016	2017	2018	2019	2020
Hickory	$10.68	$8.96	$8.95	$9.94	$11.95
Average	$9.60	$12.29	$12.17	$11.65	$14.17

Recycling Services FTEs per 10,000 Population

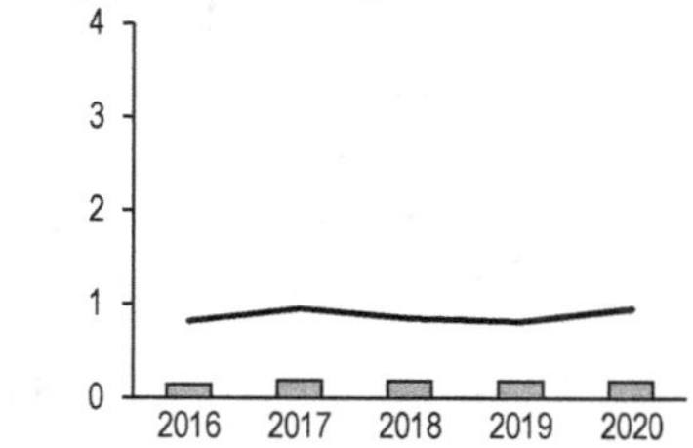

	2016	2017	2018	2019	2020
Hickory	0.15	0.19	0.19	0.19	0.19
Average	0.82	0.96	0.85	0.82	0.95

Workload Measures

Tons Recyclables Collected per 1,000 Population

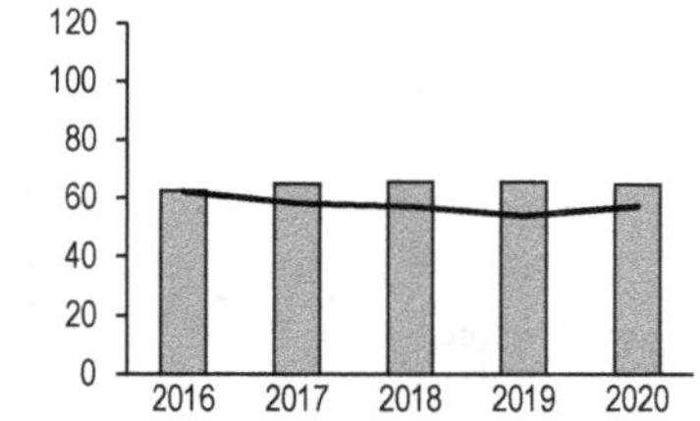

	2016	2017	2018	2019	2020
Hickory	62.5	64.8	65.6	65.5	64.7
Average	62.1	58.2	57.1	53.7	57.0

Tons Recyclables Collected per 1,000 Collection Points

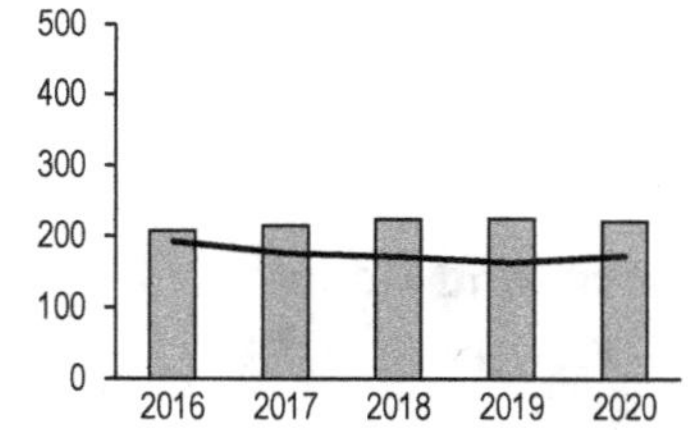

	2016	2017	2018	2019	2020
Hickory	207	215	223	225	221
Average	192	175	171	163	172

Tons Solid Waste Landfilled per 1,000 Population

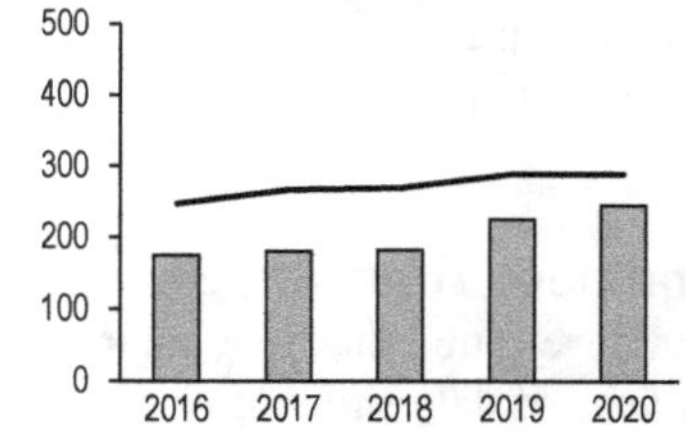

	2016	2017	2018	2019	2020
Hickory	175.0	180.3	182.0	225.0	245.3
Average	246.9	266.6	269.8	289.2	289.6

Efficiency Measures

Recycling Services Cost per Ton Collected

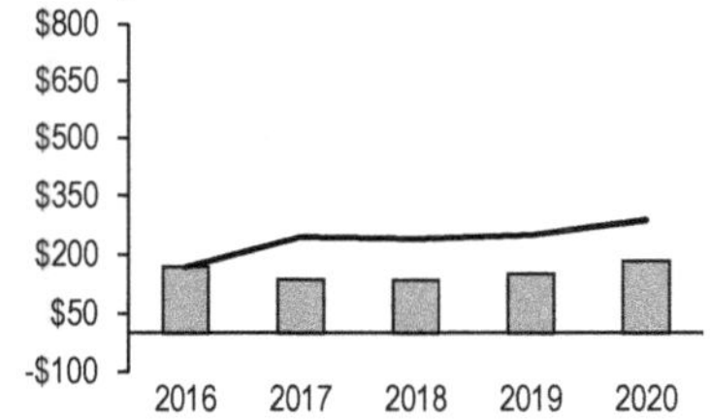

	2016	2017	2018	2019	2020
Hickory	$171	$138	$136	$152	$185
Average	$169	$246	$240	$250	$288

Recycling Services Cost per Collection Point

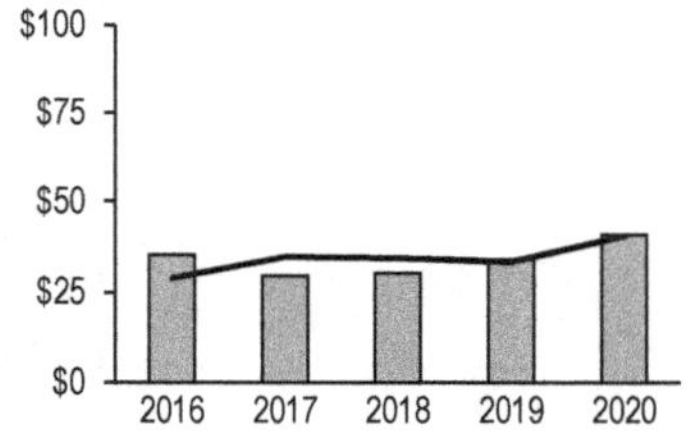

	2016	2017	2018	2019	2020
Hickory	$35.34	$29.70	$30.47	$34.07	$40.84
Average	$28.82	$34.78	$34.40	$33.24	$40.46

Tons Collected Curbside per Municipal FTE

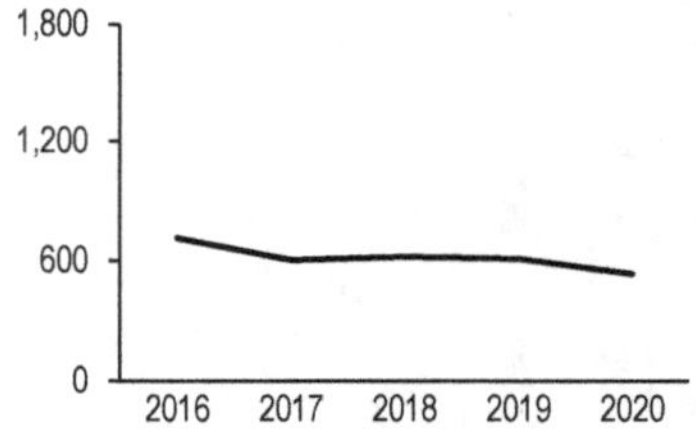

	2016	2017	2018	2019	2020
Hickory					
Average	711	602	620	610	536

Effectiveness Measures

Community Set-Out Rate

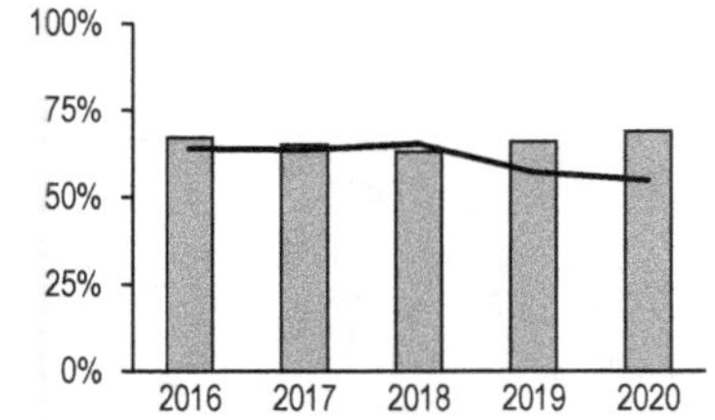

	2016	2017	2018	2019	2020
Hickory	67.0%	65.0%	63.0%	66.0%	68.9%
Average	63.9%	63.5%	65.1%	57.2%	54.8%

Tons Recycled as Percentage of Tons Refuse and Recyclables Collected

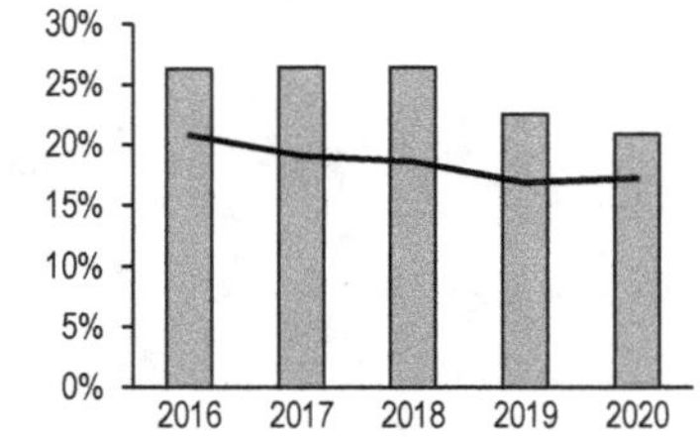

	2016	2017	2018	2019	2020
Hickory	26.3%	26.4%	26.5%	22.5%	20.9%
Average	20.7%	19.1%	18.6%	16.9%	17.3%

Raleigh

Household Recycling

Fiscal Year 2019-20

Explanatory Information

Service Level and Delivery

Raleigh provides curbside collection of recyclables every other week. Three drop-off centers for use by all residents and small businesses are also available. Customers are allowed two ninety-five-gallon carts. A few townhome locations use smaller eighteen-gallon bins due to the difficulty of moving carts to a pickup location.

Recyclables collected include:

- plastic
- glass
- metal and aluminum cans
- magazines
- newspaper
- phone books
- cardboard
- mixed paper

Conditions Affecting Service, Performance, and Costs

Raleigh rejoined the Benchmarking Project in July 2016, with the first year of data showing for FY 2015–16.

Municipal Profile

Population (OSBM 2019)	475,580
Land Area (Square Miles)	146.47
Persons per Square Mile	3,247
Median Household Income U.S. Census 2016	$46,612

Service Profile

FTE Positions—Collection	39.0
FTE Positions—Other	3.0
Number of City Drop-Off Centers	2
Other Drop-Off Centers	1
Percentage of Service Contracted	0%
Collection Frequency	Every 2 weeks
General Collection Location	Curbside
Recyclables Sorted at Curb	No
Collection Points	190,585
Tons of Recyclables Collected	
Curbside	28,445
City Drop-Off Centers	657
Total Tons Collected	29,102
Monthly Service Fee	$2.60
Revenue from Sale of Recyclables	$0
Sale Revenue as Percentage of Cost	NA

Full Cost Profile

Cost Breakdown by Percentage	
Personal Services	41.5%
Operating Costs	32.9%
Capital Costs	25.6%
TOTAL	100.0%
Cost Breakdown in Dollars	
Personal Services	$2,458,700
Operating Costs	$1,944,579
Capital Costs	$1,516,237
TOTAL	$5,919,516

Raleigh

Household Recycling

Key: Raleigh ▒ Benchmarking Average — Fiscal Years 2016 through 2020

Resource Measures

Recycling Services Cost per Capita

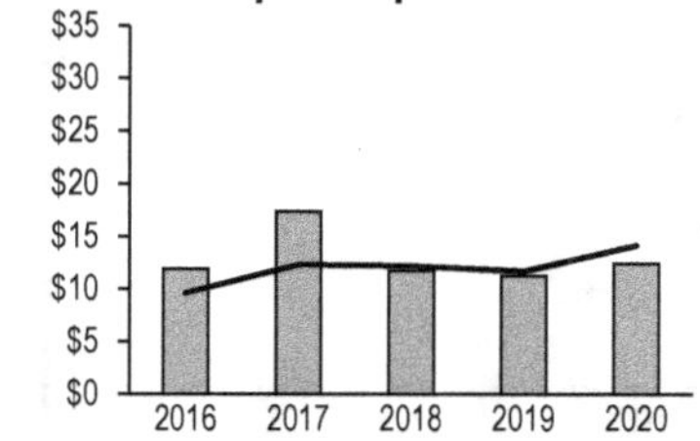

	2016	2017	2018	2019	2020
Raleigh	$11.90	$17.39	$11.74	$11.22	$12.45
Average	$9.60	$12.29	$12.17	$11.65	$14.17

Recycling Services FTEs per 10,000 Population

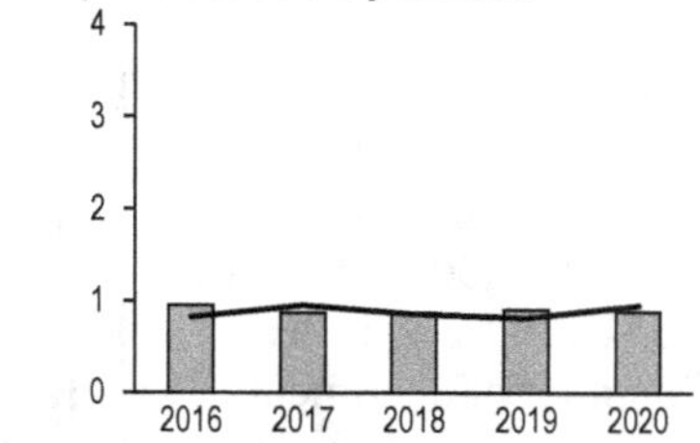

	2016	2017	2018	2019	2020
Raleigh	0.95	0.87	0.87	0.90	0.88
Average	0.82	0.96	0.85	0.82	0.95

Workload Measures

Tons Recyclables Collected per 1,000 Population

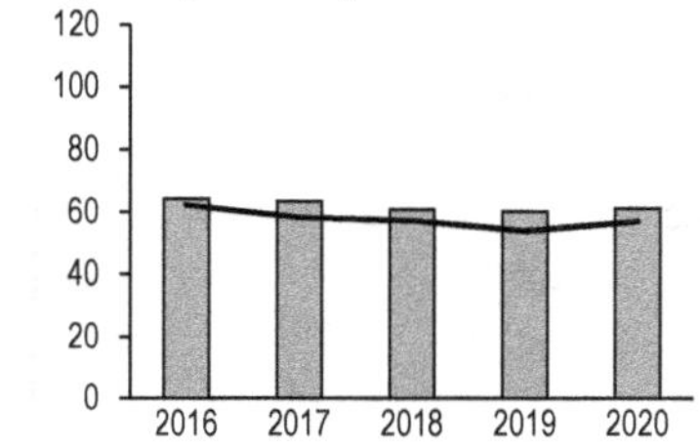

	2016	2017	2018	2019	2020
Raleigh	64.1	63.3	60.6	60.2	61.2
Average	62.1	58.2	57.1	53.7	57.0

Tons Recyclables Collected per 1,000 Collection Points

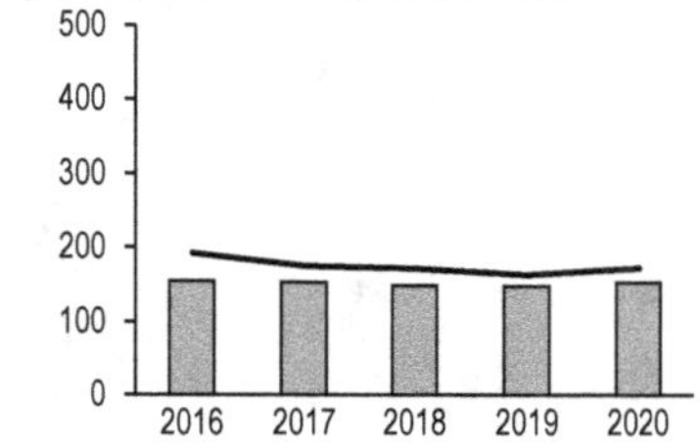

	2016	2017	2018	2019	2020
Raleigh	154	153	149	147	153
Average	192	175	171	163	172

Tons Solid Waste Landfilled per 1,000 Population

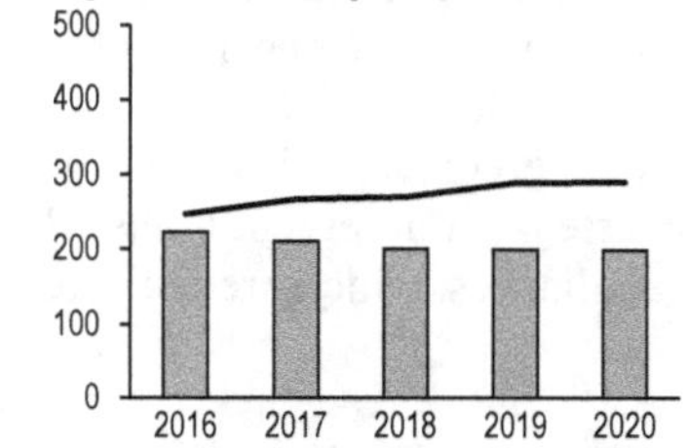

	2016	2017	2018	2019	2020
Raleigh	222.4	210.1	199.7	199.2	198.6
Average	246.9	266.6	269.8	289.2	289.6

Efficiency Measures

Recycling Services Cost per Ton Collected

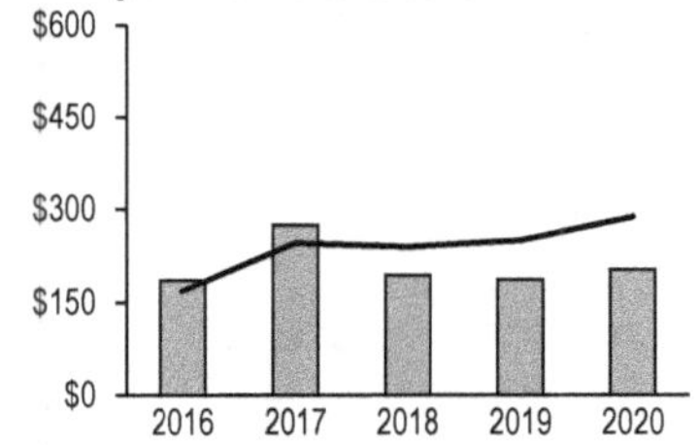

	2016	2017	2018	2019	2020
Raleigh	$186	$275	$194	$186	$203
Average	$169	$246	$240	$250	$288

Recycling Services Cost per Collection Point

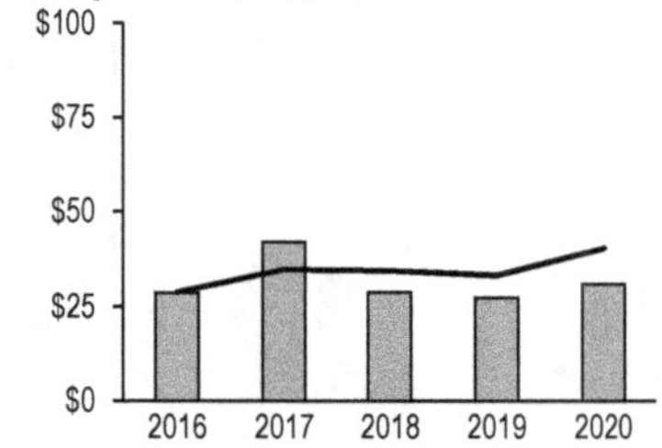

	2016	2017	2018	2019	2020
Raleigh	$28.65	$42.02	$28.79	$27.48	$31.06
Average	$28.82	$34.78	$34.40	$33.24	$40.46

Tons Collected Curbside per Municipal FTE

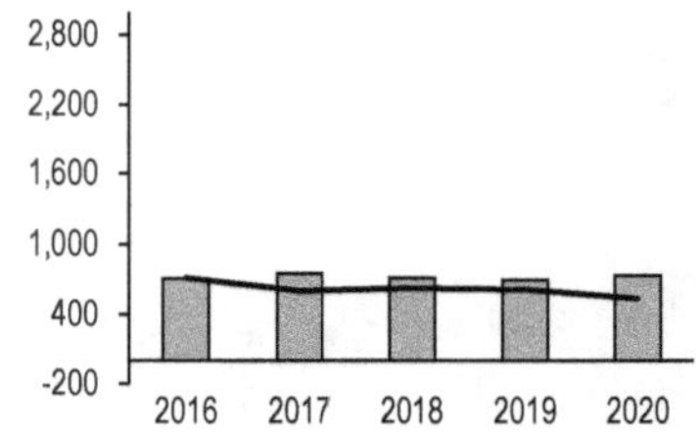

	2016	2017	2018	2019	2020
Raleigh	702	745	710	694	729
Average	711	602	620	610	536

Effectiveness Measures

Community Set-Out Rate

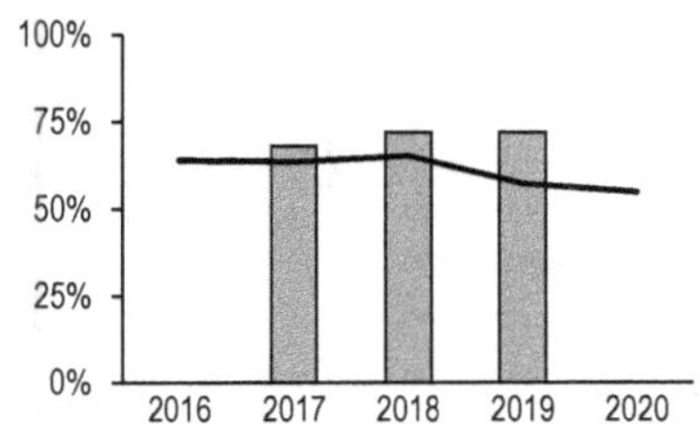

	2016	2017	2018	2019	2020
Raleigh		68.0%	72.0%	72.0%	
Average	63.9%	63.5%	65.1%	57.2%	54.8%

Tons Recycled as Percentage of Tons Refuse and Recyclables Collected

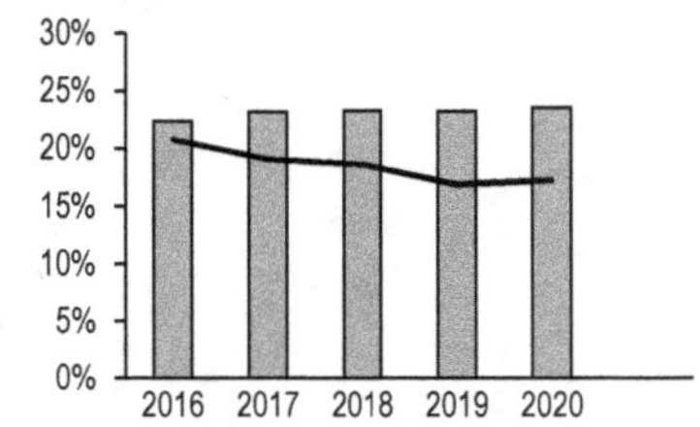

	2016	2017	2018	2019	2020
Raleigh	22.4%	23.2%	23.3%	23.2%	23.6%
Average	20.7%	19.1%	18.6%	16.9%	17.3%

Wilson — Household Recycling

Fiscal Year 2019-20

Explanatory Information

Service Level and Delivery

Wilson's household recycling program provides curbside pickup of materials once each week to residents on the same day as residential refuse collection but by different crews. Wilson began a pilot program in July 2015 that shifted to collection being done once every two weeks. This pilot phase initially covered about 2,800 homes, and each received a ninety-six-gallon roll-out cart. The transition was largely completed in 2018 except for a small number of apartments and town homes that could not be collected with automated trucks but instead required rear loaders. The recycling program is part of the Division of Environmental Services.

The following materials are collected:

- aluminum and steel cans
- No. 1 and No. 2 plastic containers
- newsprint
- clear, green, and brown glass
- waste oil, fluorescent bulbs, electronics, and small appliances, which are collected curbside on a call-in basis

Conditions Affecting Service, Performance, and Costs

The set-out rate was calculated on a monthly basis by drivers on the recycling trucks using counters.

The initial pilot phase for recycling begun in July 2015 helped lower overall costs notably.

Municipal Profile

Population (OSBM 2019)	49,384
Land Area (Square Miles)	31.02
Persons per Square Mile	1,592
Median Household Income U.S. Census 2016	$35,409

Service Profile

FTE Positions—Collection	7.0
FTE Positions—Other	0.5
Number of City Drop-Off Centers	0
Other Drop-Off Centers	0
Percentage of Service Contracted	0%
Collection Frequency	
for 96-gallon carts	Every 2 weeks
for 18-gallon cart	Every week
General Collection Location	Curbside
Recyclables Sorted at Curb	No
Collection Points	21,111
Tons of Recyclables Collected	
Curbside	1,705
City Drop-Off Centers	0
Total Tons Collected	1,705
Monthly Service Fee	$20.00
Revenue from Sale of Recyclables	NA

Full Cost Profile

Cost Breakdown by Percentage	
Personal Services	38.7%
Operating Costs	39.1%
Capital Costs	22.2%
TOTAL	100.0%
Cost Breakdown in Dollars	
Personal Services	$246,940
Operating Costs	$250,022
Capital Costs	$141,830
TOTAL	$638,792

Wilson

Household Recycling

Key: Wilson ▒ Benchmarking Average — Fiscal Years 2016 through 2020

Resource Measures

Recycling Services Cost per Capita

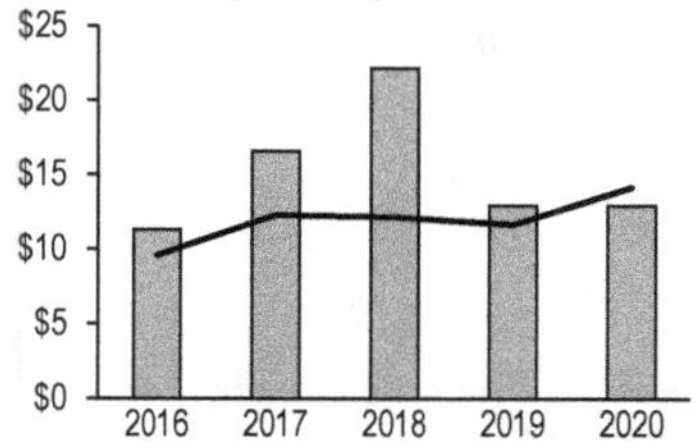

	2016	2017	2018	2019	2020
Wilson	$11.31	$16.56	$22.16	$12.95	$12.94
Average	$9.60	$12.29	$12.17	$11.65	$14.17

Recycling Services FTEs per 10,000 Population

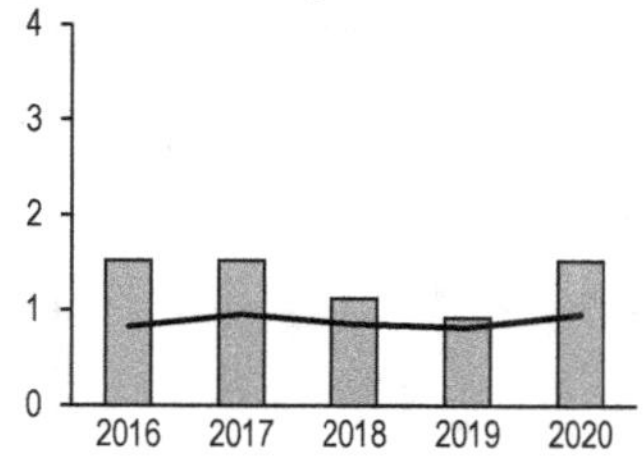

	2016	2017	2018	2019	2020
Wilson	1.52	1.52	1.12	0.92	1.52
Average	0.82	0.96	0.85	0.82	0.95

Workload Measures

Tons Recyclables Collected per 1,000 Population

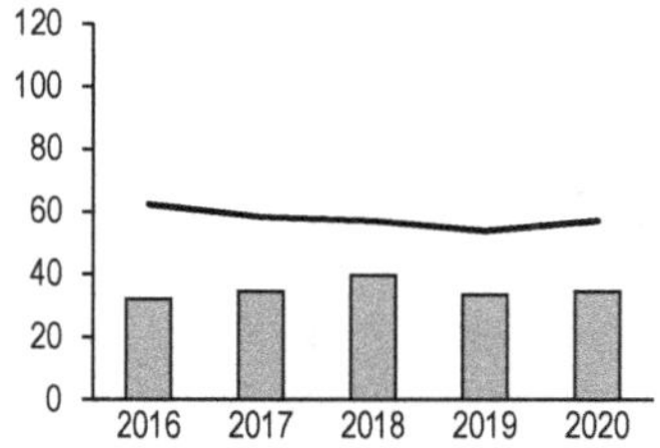

	2016	2017	2018	2019	2020
Wilson	32.1	34.5	39.7	33.5	34.5
Average	62.1	58.2	57.1	53.7	57.0

Tons Recyclables Collected per 1,000 Collection Points

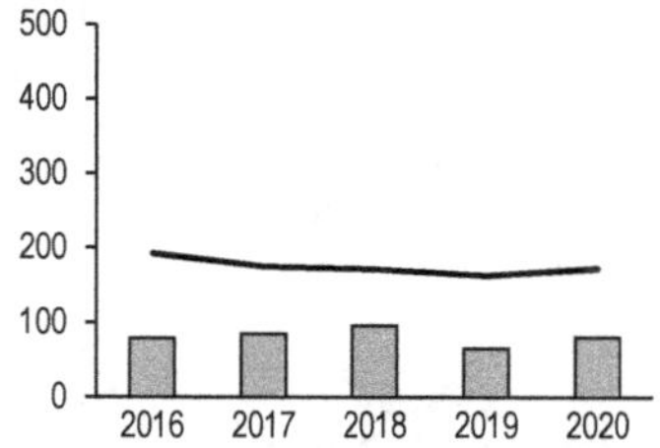

	2016	2017	2018	2019	2020
Wilson	79	85	96	66	81
Average	192	175	171	163	172

Tons Solid Waste Landfilled per 1,000 Population

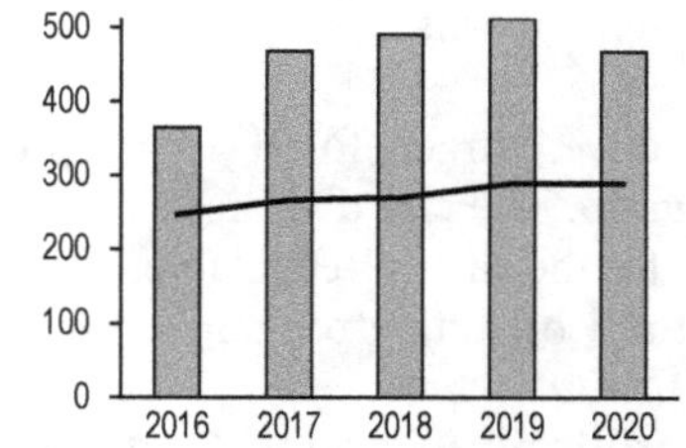

	2016	2017	2018	2019	2020
Wilson	364.7	467.1	490.7	511.7	467.4
Average	246.9	266.6	269.8	289.2	289.6

Efficiency Measures

Recycling Services Cost per Ton Collected

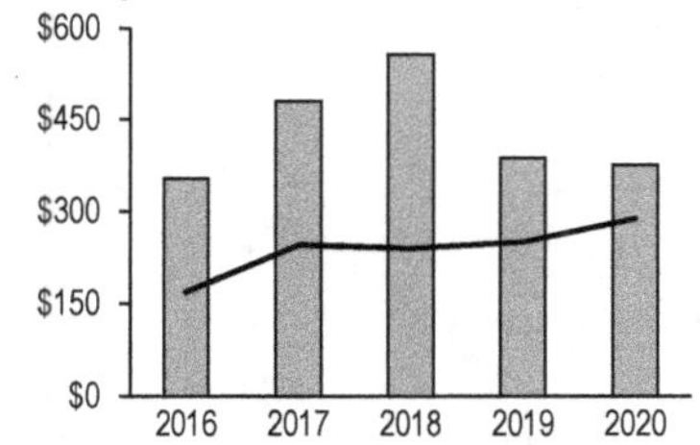

	2016	2017	2018	2019	2020
Wilson	$352	$480	$558	$386	$375
Average	$169	$246	$240	$250	$288

Recycling Services Cost per Collection Point

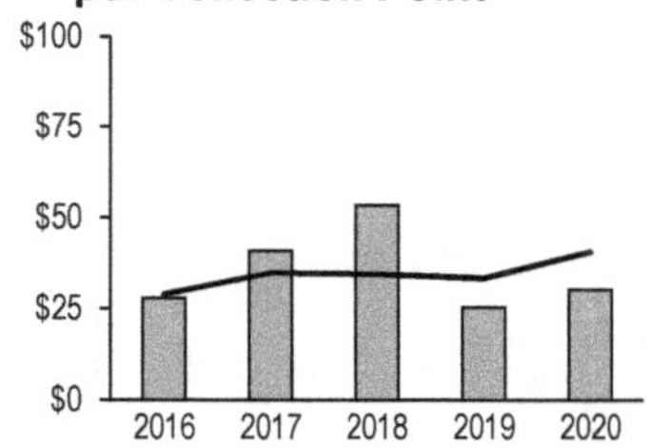

	2016	2017	2018	2019	2020
Wilson	$27.96	$40.87	$53.42	$25.31	$30.26
Average	$28.82	$34.78	$34.40	$33.24	$40.46

Tons Collected Curbside per Municipal FTE

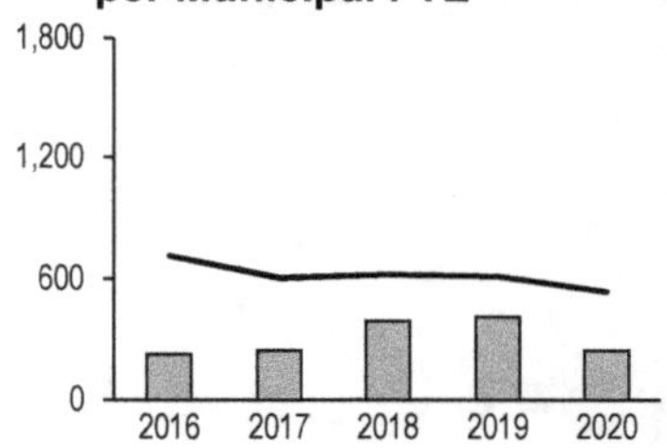

	2016	2017	2018	2019	2020
Wilson	227	244	390	411	244
Average	711	602	620	610	536

Effectiveness Measures

Community Set-Out Rate

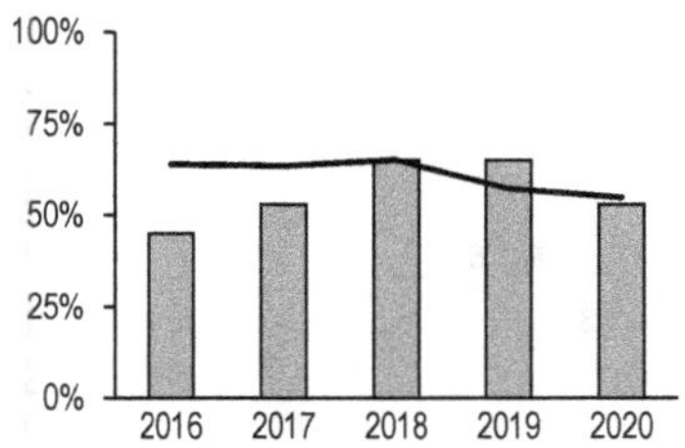

	2016	2017	2018	2019	2020
Wilson	45.0%	53.0%	65.0%	65.0%	53.0%
Average	63.9%	63.5%	65.1%	57.2%	54.8%

Tons Recycled as Percentage of Tons Refuse and Recyclables Collected

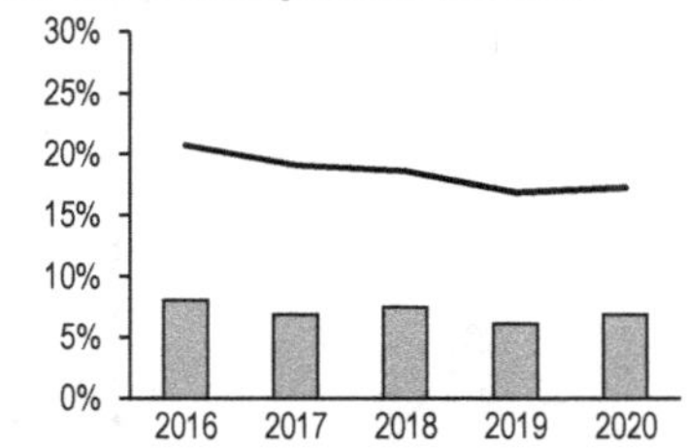

	2016	2017	2018	2019	2020
Wilson	8.1%	6.9%	7.5%	6.2%	6.9%
Average	20.7%	19.1%	18.6%	16.9%	17.3%

Winston-Salem — Household Recycling

Fiscal Year 2019-20

Explanatory Information

Service Level and Delivery

Winston-Salem provides biweekly curbside household recycling service to its single-family residences using ninety-six-gallon carts. The city provides nine drop-off sites for cardboard at its fire stations plus two full-service drop-off sites. Items collected in the city's curbside household recycling program include:

- aluminum and steel cans
- all plastic bottles
- green, amber, and clear glass
- newspaper
- magazines, telephone books, and junk mail
- chipboard
- corrugated cardboard (no bundling requirement)
- office paper
- aerosol cans

The city contracts for 100 percent of its curbside household recycling program. The city does not charge a recycling fee. Revenue to the city for the sale of recyclables was $127,639 during the year, partially offsetting program costs.

Conditions Affecting Service, Performance, and Costs

Complaints include calls reported to the city. The contractor has a separate customer service hotline.

Municipal Profile

Population (OSBM 2019)	244,739
Land Area (Square Miles)	132.59
Persons per Square Mile	1,846
Median Household Income U.S. Census 2016	$40,584

Service Profile

FTE Positions—Collection	Contractor
FTE Positions—Other	1.0
Number of City Drop-Off Centers	9
Other Drop-Off Centers	0
Percentage of Service Contracted	100%
Collection Frequency	Every 2 weeks
General Collection Location	Curbside
Recyclables Sorted at Curb	No
Collection Points	81,589
Tons of Recyclables Collected	
Curbside	15,154
City Drop-Off Centers	1,100
Total Tons Collected	16,254
Monthly Service Fee	0
Revenue from Sale of Recyclables	$127,639
Sale Revenue as Percentage of Cost	7.4%

Full Cost Profile

Cost Breakdown by Percentage	
Personal Services	5.1%
Operating Costs	94.9%
Capital Costs	0.0%
TOTAL	100.0%
Cost Breakdown in Dollars	
Personal Services	$88,750
Operating Costs	$1,642,635
Capital Costs	$0
TOTAL	$1,731,385

Winston-Salem — Household Recycling

Key: Winston-Salem ▩ Benchmarking Average — Fiscal Years 2016 through 2020

Resource Measures

Recycling Services Cost per Capita

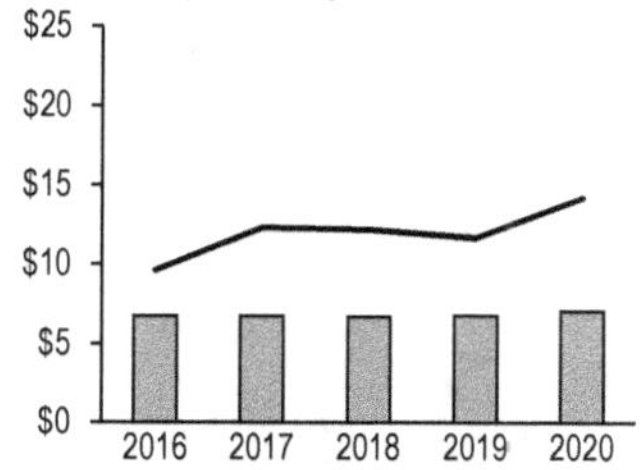

	2016	2017	2018	2019	2020
Winston-Salem	$6.73	$6.75	$6.69	$6.81	$7.07
Average	$9.60	$12.29	$12.17	$11.65	$14.17

Recycling Services FTEs per 10,000 Population

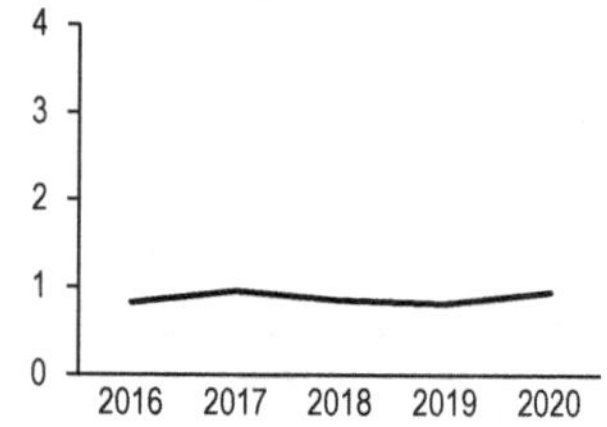

	2016	2017	2018	2019	2020
Winston-Salem					
Average	0.82	0.96	0.85	0.82	0.95

Workload Measures

Tons Recyclables Collected per 1,000 Population

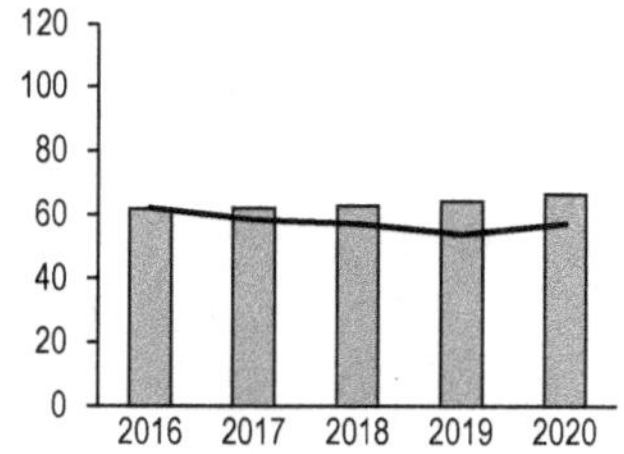

	2016	2017	2018	2019	2020
Winston-Salem	61.7	62.0	62.7	64.2	66.4
Average	62.1	58.2	57.1	53.7	57.0

Tons Recyclables Collected per 1,000 Collection Points

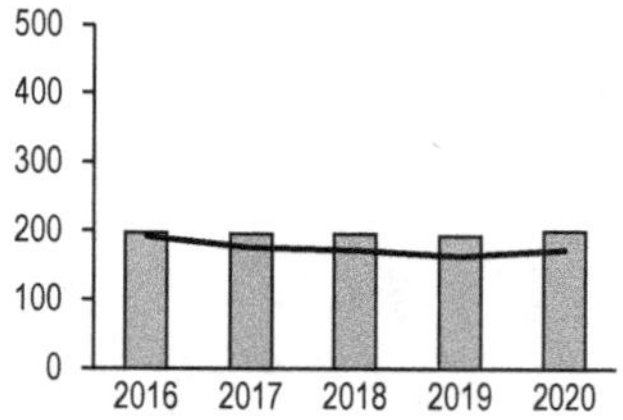

	2016	2017	2018	2019	2020
Winston-Salem	196	195	195	192	199
Average	192	175	171	163	172

Tons Solid Waste Landfilled per 1,000 Population

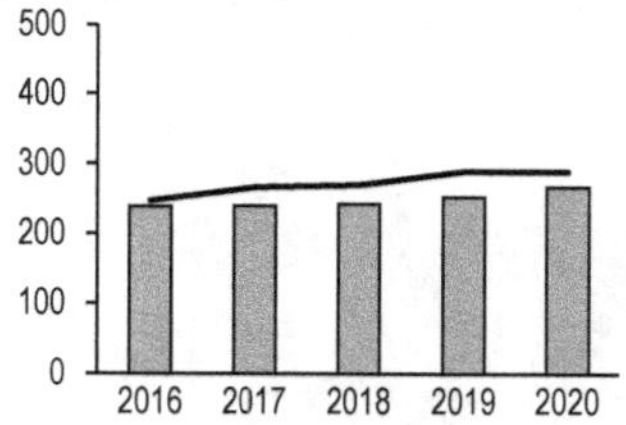

	2016	2017	2018	2019	2020
Winston-Salem	238.9	239.8	242.3	252.2	266.9
Average	246.9	266.6	269.8	289.2	289.6

Efficiency Measures

Recycling Services Cost per Ton Collected

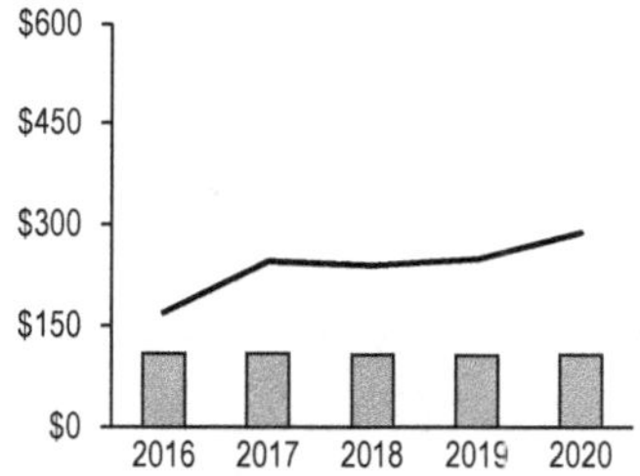

	2016	2017	2018	2019	2020
Winston-Salem	$109	$109	$107	$106	$107
Average	$169	$246	$240	$250	$288

Recycling Services Cost per Collection Point

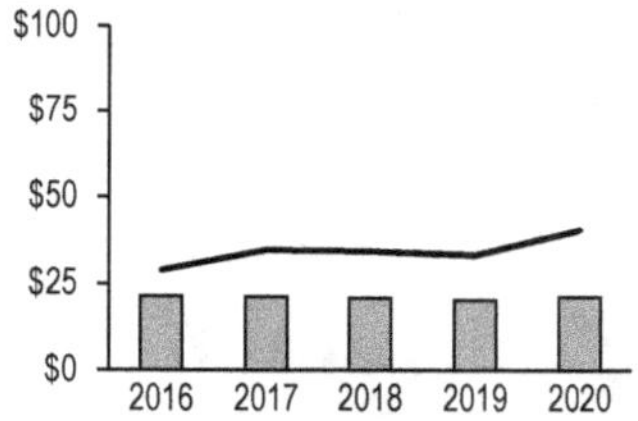

	2016	2017	2018	2019	2020
Winston-Salem	$21.44	$21.24	$20.82	$20.31	$21.22
Average	$28.82	$34.78	$34.40	$33.24	$40.46

Tons Collected Curbside per Municipal FTE

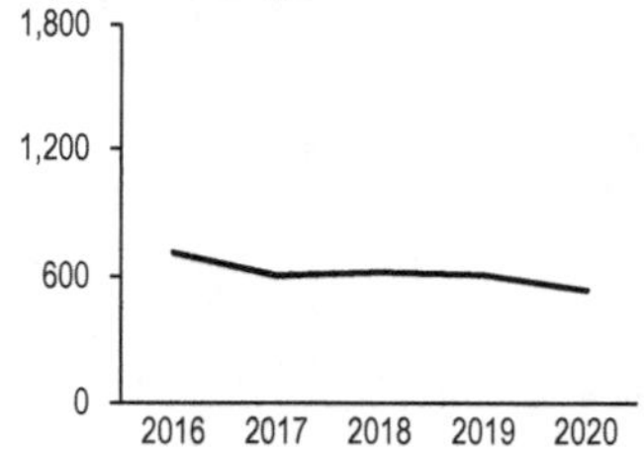

	2016	2017	2018	2019	2020
Winston-Salem					
Average	711	602	620	610	536

Effectiveness Measures

Community Set-Out Rate

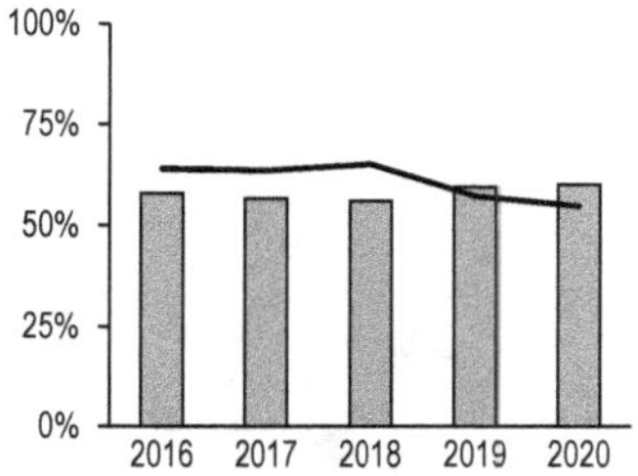

	2016	2017	2018	2019	2020
Winston-Salem	57.9%	56.7%	56.0%	59.5%	60.0%
Average	63.9%	63.5%	65.1%	57.2%	54.8%

Tons Recycled as Percentage of Tons Refuse and Recyclables Collected

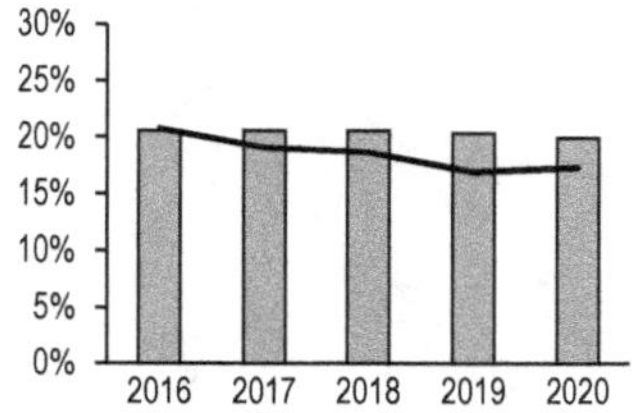

	2016	2017	2018	2019	2020
Winston-Salem	20.5%	20.5%	20.6%	20.3%	19.9%
Average	20.7%	19.1%	18.6%	16.9%	17.3%

SCHOOL OF GOVERNMENT
North Carolina Benchmarking Project

Performance and Cost Data

YARD WASTE / LEAF COLLECTION

PERFORMANCE MEASURES FOR YARD WASTE/LEAF COLLECTION

SERVICE DEFINITION

Yard waste and leaf collection includes regularly scheduled or special collection of these items. Such collection may occur from the curb, backyard, or another locale. Yard waste and leaves may be bagged, placed in containers, or loose. The service definition excludes the collection of white goods and other bulky items. Although some municipalities collect yard waste and leaves with household refuse or other trash, they separate the items at some point in the collection process because yard waste and leaves cannot be placed in landfills.

NOTES ON PERFORMANCE MEASURES

1. Tons Collected per 1,000 Population and per 1,000 Collection Points

These are the same performance measures that are used for residential refuse collection, except that tonnage is for yard waste, leaves, and miscellaneous trash rather than residential refuse. "Collection points" refers to the number of residential premises served by regularly scheduled collection of yard waste, leaves, and miscellaneous trash.

2. Cost per Ton Collected

Cost is measured using the project's full cost accounting model, calculating direct, indirect, and capital costs. Tons are as defined above.

3. Tons Collected per Collection FTE

The number of full-time equivalent (FTE) positions refers to the number of employees or laborers who were directly involved in collection of yard waste, leaves, and miscellaneous trash during the fiscal year. This number includes temporary, permanent, full-time, and part-time workers. Such workers can be sanitation, street, or other municipal employees. One FTE equals 2,080 hours of work per year. Any combination of employees providing 2,080 hours of work per year is one FTE.

4. Complaints (and Valid Complaints) per 10,000 Collection Points

Complaints are those tracked by each jurisdiction, using its own criteria and procedures. Collection points are as defined above. The municipalities follow very different procedures in processing and recording these calls and in determining which ones are complaints and which are not. For these reasons, the project is able to present only limited comparative data about complaints or valid complaints. Nonetheless, the project recommends that the participating municipalities devise common criteria for identifying complaints and procedures for processing and recording calls.

Yard Waste/Leaf Collection

Summary of Key Dimensions of Service

City or Town	Yard Waste Collection		Seasonal Loose Leaf Collection	Collection Points	Tons Collected		Collection FTE Positions
	Location	Frequency			Yard Waste	Seasonal Leaves	
Apex	Curbside	1 x week	NA	19,484	7,014	na	16.0
Chapel Hill	Curbside	1 x week	2-6 sweeps	12,230	3,313	4,260	14.6
Charlotte	Curbside	1 x week	NA	221,992	48,316	na	71.0
Concord	Curbside	1 x week	3 sweeps	34,130	8,352	1,932	21.5
Goldsboro	Curbside	1 x 2 weeks	1 x 2 weeks	14,372	6,280	3,384	14.0
Greensboro	Curbside	1 x week	2 sweeps	91,075	10,969	11,883	42.2
Hickory	Curbside	1 x week	2 sweeps	12,116	11,331	3,568	4.3
Raleigh	Curbside	1 x week	2 sweeps	130,646	14,427	13,950	96.0
Wilson	Curbside	1 x week	1 x 3 weeks	21,500	9,211	1,204	15.0
Winston-Salem	Curbside	Yard Waste Cart 1 x week Brush every 10 days	1 x 3 weeks	81,589 for Leaves and brush, 15,022 for Yard Waste	21,942	16,252	70.8

NOTES

Municipalities with no reported seasonal leaf collection collect leaves as part of their yard waste collection programs.

EXPLANATORY FACTORS

These are factors that the project found affected yard waste and leaf collection performance and cost in one or more of the municipalities:

- Whether or not a fee is charged for collection
- Residential/commercial/industrial nature of the community
- Policies regarding sizes and types of items collected
- Extent of seasonal leaf collection service
- Landfill policies and tipping fees

Fiscal Year 2019-20

Explanatory Information

Service Level and Delivery

The Town of Apex collects yard waste curbside once per week for all city residents. The town collects vegetative matter from residential landscaping. The town does not operate a seasonal leaf collection, but leaves are collected year-round as part of the weekly service. Land clearing debris is not collected. The town charges $8.51 per month for collection of yard waste.

There are three grass/vacuum trucks, two two-person limb-chipping crews, and one grapple-truck operator for larger items. These crews cover the town every week using a five-day-a-week schedule.

Conditions Affecting Service, Performance, and Costs

Municipal Profile

Population (OSBM 2019)	61,319
Land Area (Square Miles)	23.61
Persons per Square Mile	2,597
Median Household Income U.S. Census 2016	$84,000

Service Profile

FTE Positions—Collection	17.0
FTE Positions—Other	2.8
Collection Frequency	
Yard Waste	1 x week
Collection Points	19,484
Tons Collected	
Yard Waste	7,014
Seasonal Leaves	with yard waste
Total Tons Collected	7,014
Monthly Service Fee	$8.51

Full Cost Profile

Cost Breakdown by Percentage	
Personal Services	47.1%
Operating Costs	35.0%
Capital Costs	17.8%
TOTAL	100.0%
Cost Breakdown in Dollars	
Personal Services	$1,084,867
Operating Costs	$806,891
Capital Costs	$410,676
TOTAL	$2,302,434

Apex — Yard Waste/Leaf Collection

Key: Apex ■ Benchmarking Average — Fiscal Years 2016 through 2020

Resource Measures

Yard Waste and Leaf Collection Costs per Capita

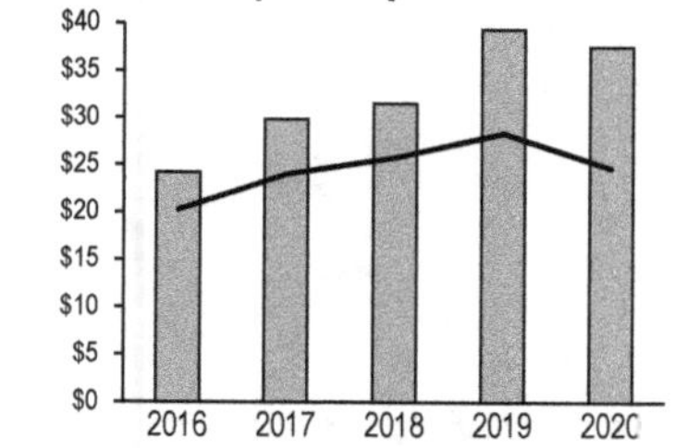

	2016	2017	2018	2019	2020
Apex	$24.19	$29.82	$31.53	$39.40	$37.55
Average	$20.26	$24.02	$25.75	$28.32	$24.62

Yard Waste and Leaf Collection FTEs per 10,000 Population

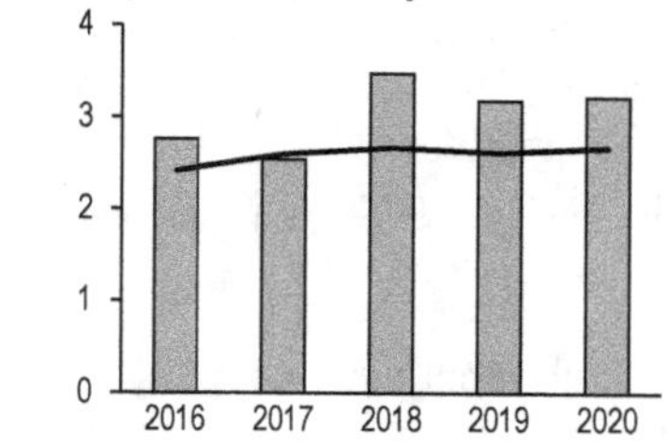

	2016	2017	2018	2019	2020
Apex	2.8	2.5	3.5	3.2	3.2
Average	2.4	2.6	2.7	2.6	2.7

Workload Measures

Yard Waste and Leaf Tons Collected per 1,000 Population

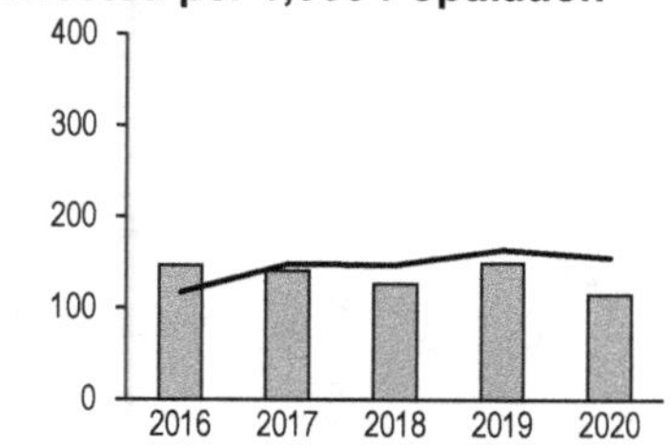

	2016	2017	2018	2019	2020
Apex	146	140	126	149	114
Average	117	147	147	164	155

Yard Waste and Leaf Tons Collected

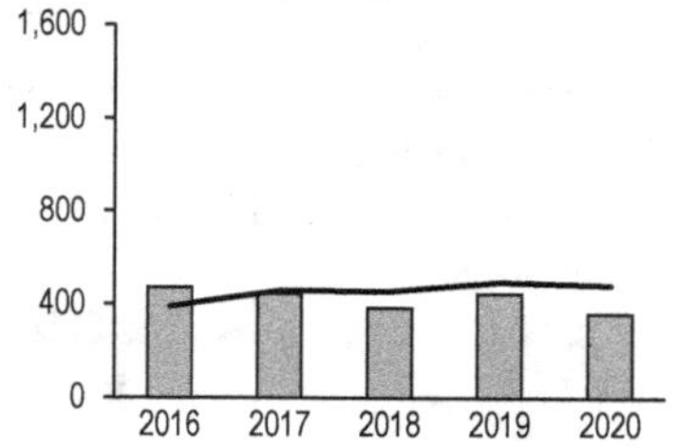

	2016	2017	2018	2019	2020
Apex	471	445	384	446	360
Average	391	459	454	495	482

Efficiency Measures

Yard Waste and Leaf Collection Cost per Collection Point

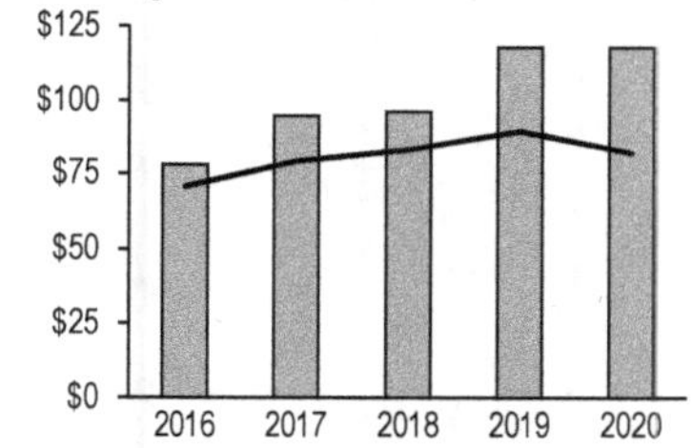

	2016	2017	2018	2019	2020
Apex	$78	$95	$96	$118	$118
Average	$71	$79	$83	$89	$82

Yard Waste and Leaf Collection Cost per Ton Collected

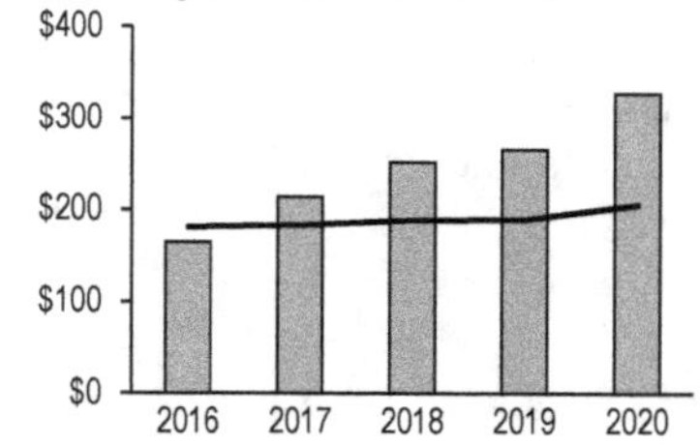

	2016	2017	2018	2019	2020
Apex	$165	$213	$251	$265	$328
Average	$181	$183	$189	$189	$205

Yard Waste and Leaf Tons Collected per Collection FTE

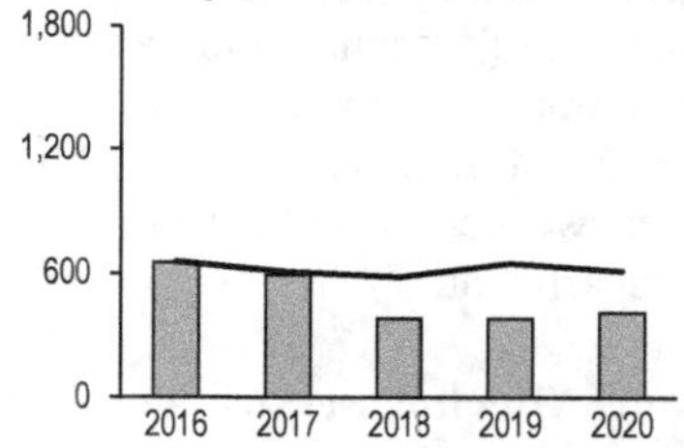

	2016	2017	2018	2019	2020
Apex	654	594	381	381	413
Average	655	607	582	651	613

Effectiveness Measures

Collection Complaints per 10,000 Collection Points

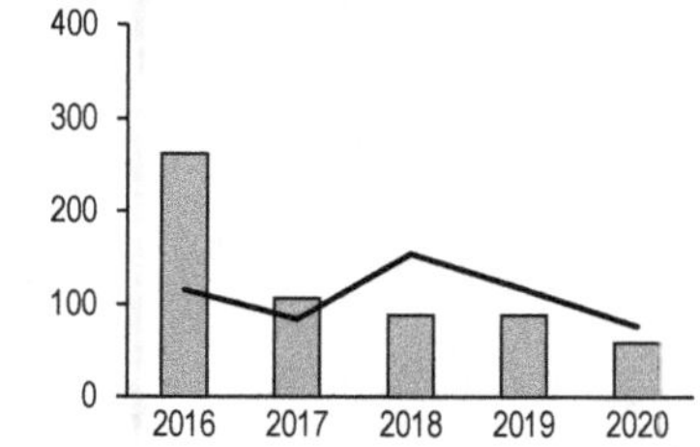

	2016	2017	2018	2019	2020
Apex	262	106	88	88	59
Average	115	84	154	117	76

Valid Complaints per 10,000 Collection Points

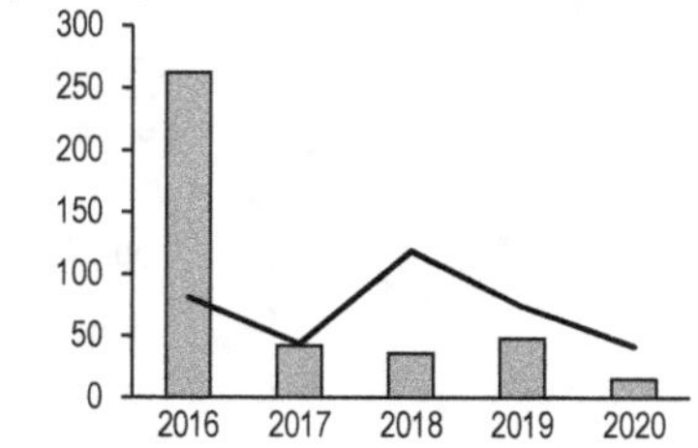

	2016	2017	2018	2019	2020
Apex	262	42	36	48	15
Average	81	44	119	74	42

Fiscal Year 2019-20

Explanatory Information

Service Level and Delivery
Yard waste collection is managed by the Solid Waste Services Division of the Public Works Department. Yard waste includes organic materials, such as leaves, stems, grass, limbs, and other residential organic matter. The town does not collect large logs or stumps, or debris from lot clearing.

Yard waste is collected once per week curbside with no monthly fee. Yard waste is collected by seven three-person crews using rear packers two days per week. The Town collects small yard waste materials placed in roll carts, other rigid containers, or paper yard waste bags. The Town collects large yard waste materials in loose piles. Yard waste piles larger than three cubic yards are collected for a fee. The Town does not collect yard waste in plastic bags.

Residents can rent a 10-cubic-yard roll-off container or schedule a paid knuckle boom collection for large projects. These larger loads are collected by a one-person crew using a knuckle boom truck and a hook-lift truck five days per week. Residents pay a fee of $35 per day or $60 per week to rent a roll-off container for collection. The fee for a knuckle boom collection is $125.

Seasonal leaf collection is managed by the Streets and Construction Services Division of the Public Works Department. Seasonal leaf collection is run with five or six cycles in a season from mid-October to early March. Only loose leaves and pine straw free of limbs or other debris are collected curbside. Leaf crews consist of a driver, a raker, and a machine operator. Crews may make use of seasonal labor, and three to six crews are used depending on the volume of leaves at the curb for collection. During peak leaf fall, crews also pull the curb line in conjunction with street sweepers from the Stormwater Program of the Public Works Department.

Conditions Affecting Service, Performance, and Costs

Municipal Profile

Population (OSBM 2019)	63,639
Land Area (Square Miles)	21.31
Persons per Square Mile	2,987
Median Household Income	$60,802
U.S. Census 2016	

Service Profile

FTE Positions—Collection	15.6
FTE Positions—Other	0.2
Collection Frequency	
Yard Waste	1 x week
Seasonal Leaf Collection	5-6 sweeps
Collection Points	12,230
Tons Collected	
Yard Waste	3,313
Seasonal Leaves	4,260
Total Tons Collected	7,573
Monthly Service Fee	Resdients may purchase cart for $50 but not required

Full Cost Profile

Cost Breakdown by Percentage	
Personal Services	45.1%
Operating Costs	36.1%
Capital Costs	18.9%
TOTAL	100.0%
Cost Breakdown in Dollars	
Personal Services	$1,026,766
Operating Costs	$821,771
Capital Costs	$429,984
TOTAL	$2,278,521

Chapel Hill — Yard Waste/Leaf Collection

Key: Chapel Hill ■ Benchmarking Average — Fiscal Years 2016 through 2020

Resource Measures

Yard Waste and Leaf Collection Costs per Capita

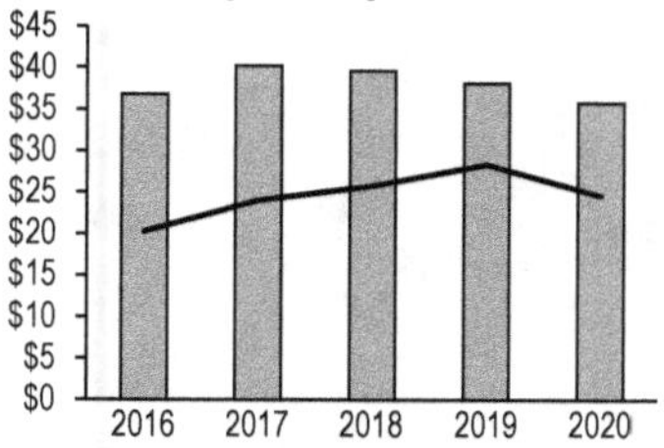

	2016	2017	2018	2019	2020
Chapel Hill	$36.77	$40.18	$39.55	$38.09	$35.80
Average	$20.26	$24.02	$25.75	$28.32	$24.62

Yard Waste and Leaf Collection FTEs per 10,000 Population

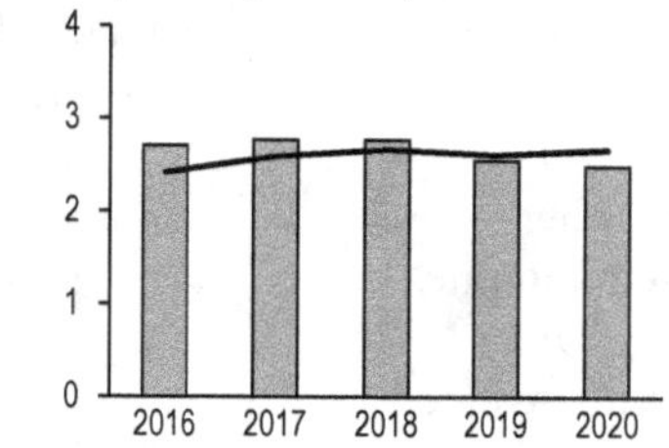

	2016	2017	2018	2019	2020
Chapel Hill	2.7	2.8	2.8	2.5	2.5
Average	2.4	2.6	2.7	2.6	2.7

Workload Measures

Yard Waste and Leaf Tons Collected per 1,000 Population

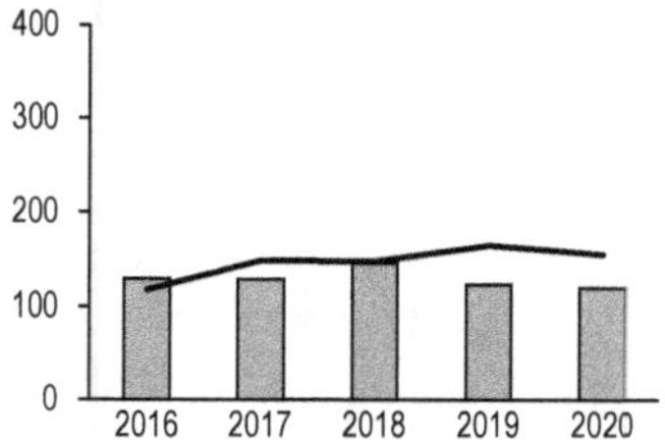

	2016	2017	2018	2019	2020
Chapel Hill	129	128	145	123	119
Average	117	147	147	164	155

Yard Waste and Leaf Tons Collected

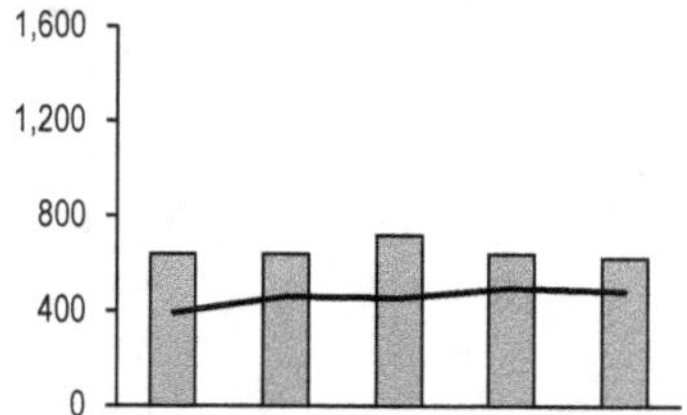

	2016	2017	2018	2019	2020
Chapel Hill	636	636	715	637	619
Average	391	459	454	495	482

Efficiency Measures

Yard Waste and Leaf Collection Cost per Collection Point

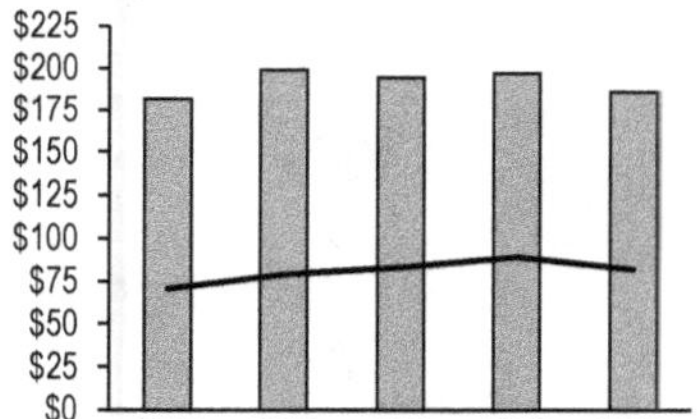

	2016	2017	2018	2019	2020
Chapel Hill	$182	$199	$195	$197	$186
Average	$71	$79	$83	$89	$82

Yard Waste and Leaf Collection Cost per Ton Collected

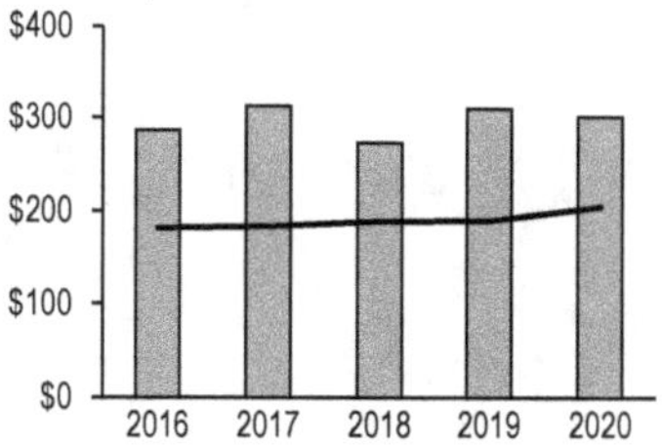

	2016	2017	2018	2019	2020
Chapel Hill	$286	$313	$272	$310	$301
Average	$181	$183	$189	$189	$205

Yard Waste and Leaf Tons Collected per Collection FTE

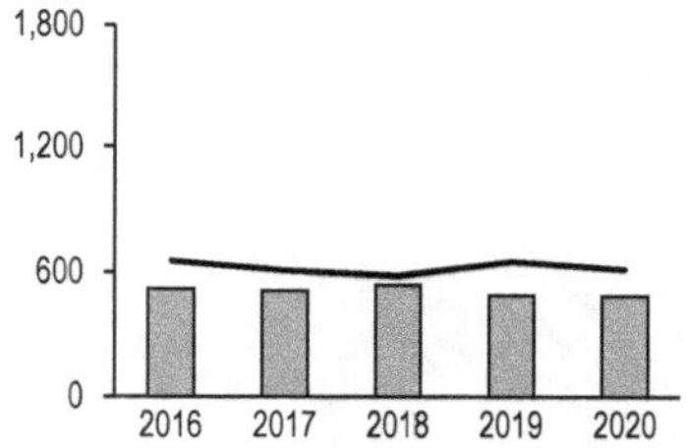

	2016	2017	2018	2019	2020
Chapel Hill	519	509	538	489	485
Average	655	607	582	651	613

Effectiveness Measures

Collection Complaints per 10,000 Collection Points

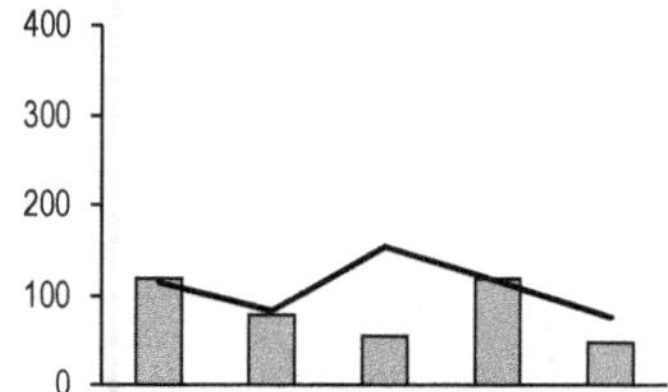

	2016	2017	2018	2019	2020
Chapel Hill	119	79	55	120	48
Average	115	84	154	117	76

Valid Complaints per 10,000 Collection Points

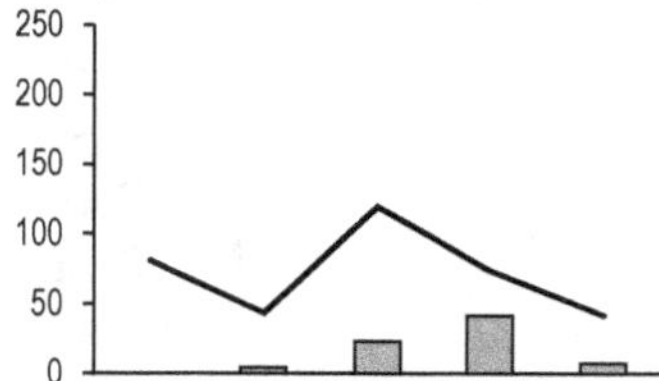

	2016	2017	2018	2019	2020
Chapel Hill		4	23	42	7
Average	81	44	119	74	42

Fiscal Year 2019-20

Explanatory Information

Service Level and Delivery
Charlotte collects yard waste once per week curbside. The city performs all yard waste collection.

Yard waste includes leaves, stems, grass, limbs, and other residential organic matter. Limbs should be separated into piles small enough for one individual to handle. Leaves and grass clippings must be placed in untied plastic bags or in uncovered trash cans. Yard waste placed at the curb by a commercial landscaping service will not be collected by the city. The city of Charlotte used thirty-four two-person crews working from rear loaders to service the entire city. Additional trucks and staff are allocated as a yard waste reserve.

Leaves are collected in bags and are debagged at the curb as part of the regular yard waste service. A special seasonal leaf collection is not done by the City of Charlotte.

Conditions Affecting Service, Performance, and Costs

Municipal Profile

Population (OSBM 2019)	863,985
Land Area (Square Miles)	307.41
Persons per Square Mile	2,811
Median Household Income U.S. Census 2016	$46,975

Service Profile

FTE Positions—Collection	74.00
FTE Positions—Other	0.00
Collection Frequency	
Yard Waste	1 x week
Collection Points	221,992
Tons Collected	
Yard Waste	48,316
Seasonal Leaves	with yard waste
Total Tons Collected	48,316
Monthly Service Fee	No

Full Cost Profile

Cost Breakdown by Percentage	
Personal Services	39.9%
Operating Costs	44.3%
Capital Costs	15.7%
TOTAL	100.0%
Cost Breakdown in Dollars	
Personal Services	$4,750,370
Operating Costs	$5,275,703
Capital Costs	$1,873,699
TOTAL	$11,899,772

Charlotte

Yard Waste/Leaf Collection

Key: Charlotte ▒ Benchmarking Average — Fiscal Years 2016 through 2020

Resource Measures

Yard Waste and Leaf Collection Costs per Capita

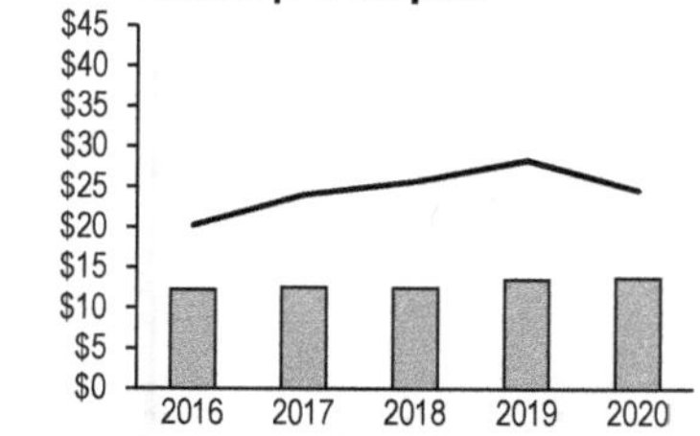

	2016	2017	2018	2019	2020
Charlotte	$12.25	$12.58	$12.51	$13.56	$13.77
Average	$20.26	$24.02	$25.75	$28.32	$24.62

Yard Waste and Leaf Collection FTEs per 10,000 Population

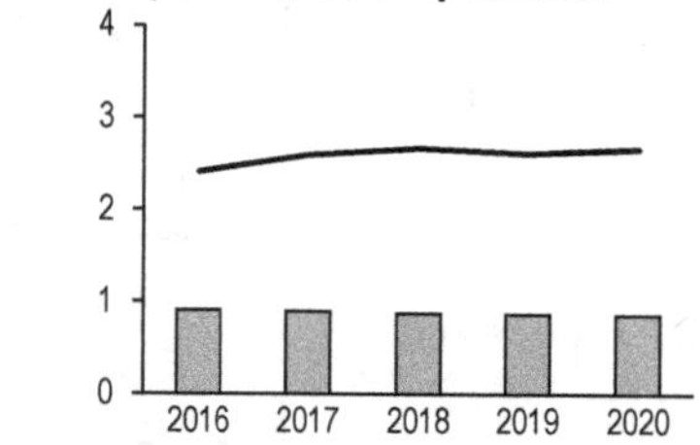

	2016	2017	2018	2019	2020
Charlotte	0.9	0.9	0.9	0.9	0.9
Average	2.4	2.6	2.7	2.6	2.7

Workload Measures

Yard Waste and Leaf Tons Collected per 1,000 Population

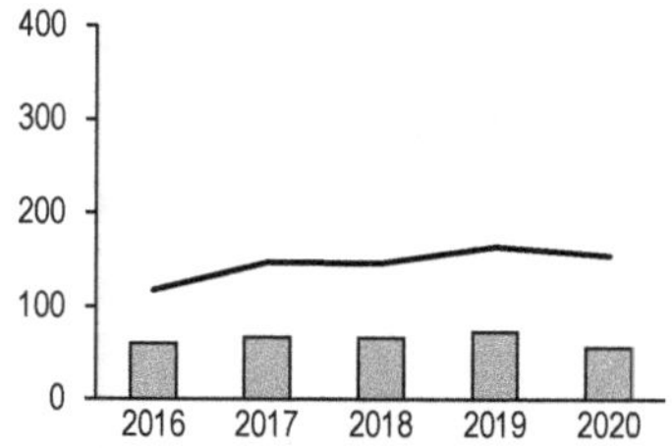

	2016	2017	2018	2019	2020
Charlotte	60	67	66	72	56
Average	117	147	147	164	155

Yard Waste and Leaf Tons Collected per 1,000 Collection Points

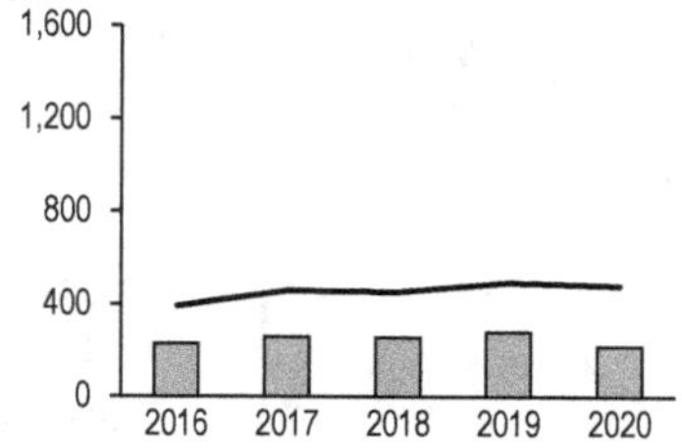

	2016	2017	2018	2019	2020
Charlotte	228	258	257	281	218
Average	391	459	454	495	482

Efficiency Measures

Yard Waste and Leaf Collection Cost per Collection Point

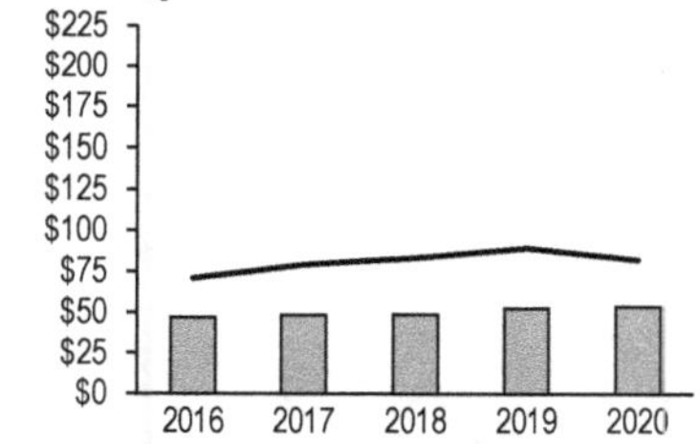

	2016	2017	2018	2019	2020
Charlotte	$47	$48	$49	$53	$54
Average	$71	$79	$83	$89	$82

Yard Waste and Leaf Collection Cost per Ton Collected

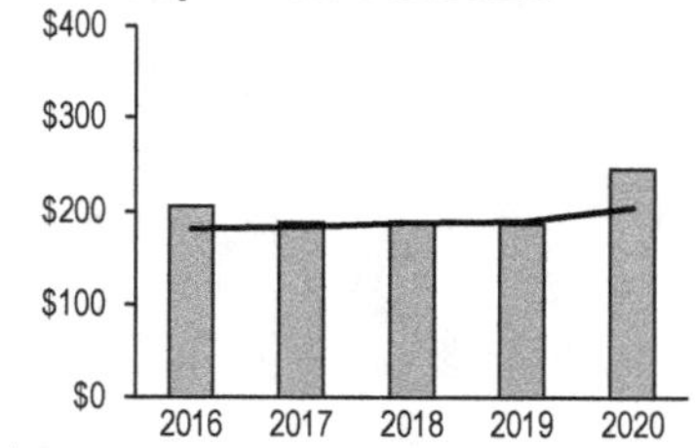

	2016	2017	2018	2019	2020
Charlotte	$206	$188	$189	$187	$246
Average	$181	$183	$189	$189	$205

Yard Waste and Leaf Tons Collected per Collection FTE

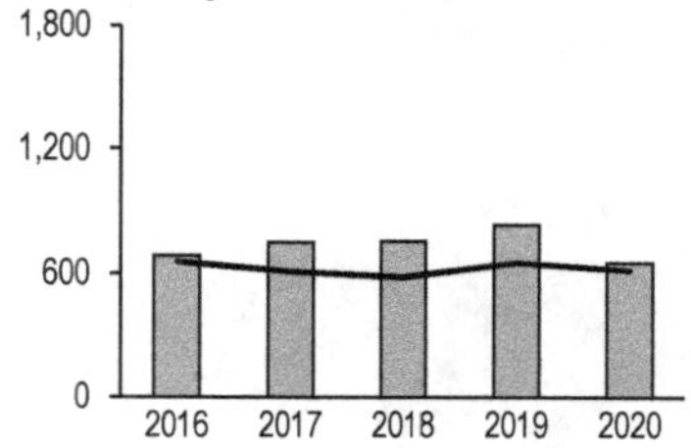

	2016	2017	2018	2019	2020
Charlotte	687	750	755	835	653
Average	655	607	582	651	613

Effectiveness Measures

Collection Complaints per 10,000 Collection Points

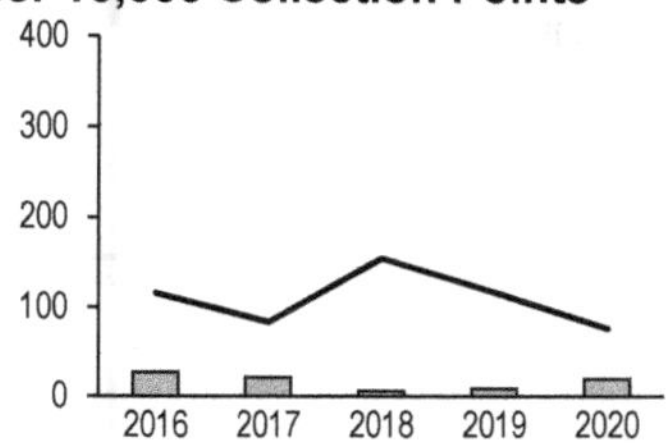

	2016	2017	2018	2019	2020
Charlotte	27	21	6	9	20
Average	115	84	154	117	76

Valid Complaints per 10,000 Collection Points

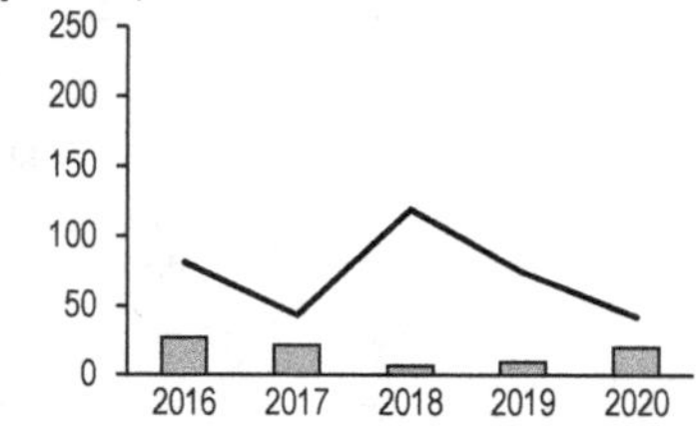

	2016	2017	2018	2019	2020
Charlotte	27	21	6	9	20
Average	81	44	119	74	42

Fiscal Year 2019-20

Explanatory Information

Service Level and Delivery
Concord collects all yard waste once per week. Yard waste includes limbs, logs, grass clippings, shrubbery clippings, and leaves.

Concord uses three two-person crews with rearloaders and six two-person crews with knuckleboom trucks to collect limbs and brush on a weekly basis.

Concord's seasonal loose leaf collection runs from November through mid-February. Each street is serviced following a publicized schedule a minimum of three times for loose leaf collection during this period. Residents who bag their leaves receive weekly collection along with the normal yard waste collection program.

Conditions Affecting Service, Performance, and Costs
Concord provides a high level of service in this area, which make the costs per collection point and per ton appear high.

Municipal Profile

Population (OSBM 2019)	95,453
Land Area (Square Miles)	63.65
Persons per Square Mile	1,500
Median Household Income U.S. Census 2016	$50,863

Service Profile

FTE Positions—Collection	23.45
FTE Positions—Other	2.32
Collection Frequency	
Yard Waste	1 x week
Seasonal Leaf Collection	3 sweeps
Collection Points	34,130
Tons Collected	
Yard Waste	8,352
Seasonal Leaves	1,932
Total Tons Collected	10,284
Monthly Service Fee	No

Full Cost Profile

Cost Breakdown by Percentage	
Personal Services	53.6%
Operating Costs	28.4%
Capital Costs	18.0%
TOTAL	100.0%
Cost Breakdown in Dollars	
Personal Services	$1,605,625
Operating Costs	$848,879
Capital Costs	$538,522
TOTAL	$2,993,026

Concord

Yard Waste/Leaf Collection

Key: Concord ▒ Benchmarking Average — Fiscal Years 2016 through 2020

Resource Measures

Yard Waste and Leaf Collection Costs per Capita

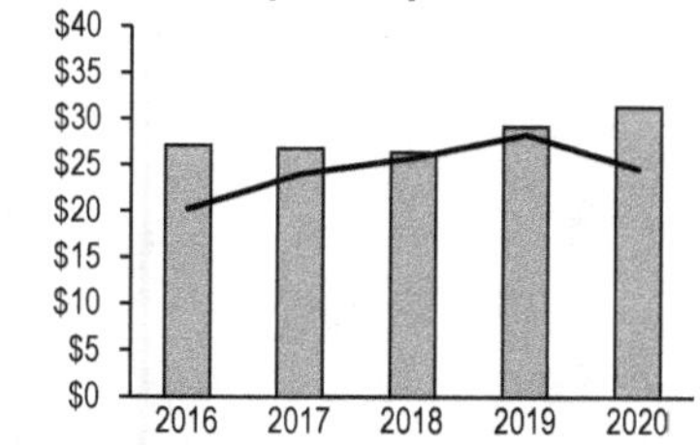

	2016	2017	2018	2019	2020
Concord	$27.10	$26.73	$26.36	$29.21	$31.36
Average	$20.26	$24.02	$25.75	$28.32	$24.62

Yard Waste and Leaf Collection FTEs per 10,000 Population

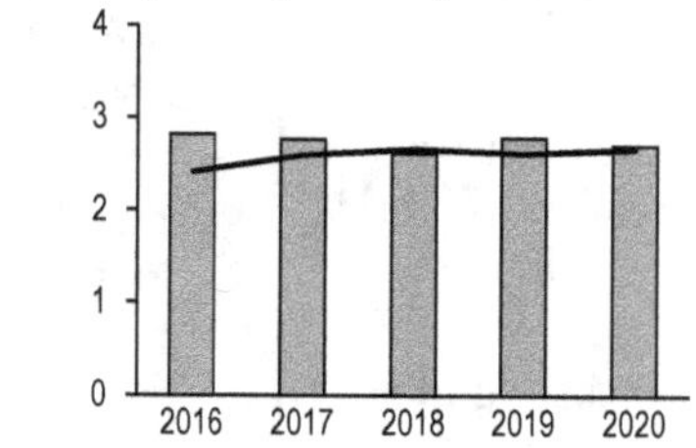

	2016	2017	2018	2019	2020
Concord	2.8	2.8	2.6	2.8	2.7
Average	2.4	2.6	2.7	2.6	2.7

Workload Measures

Yard Waste and Leaf Tons Collected per 1,000 Population

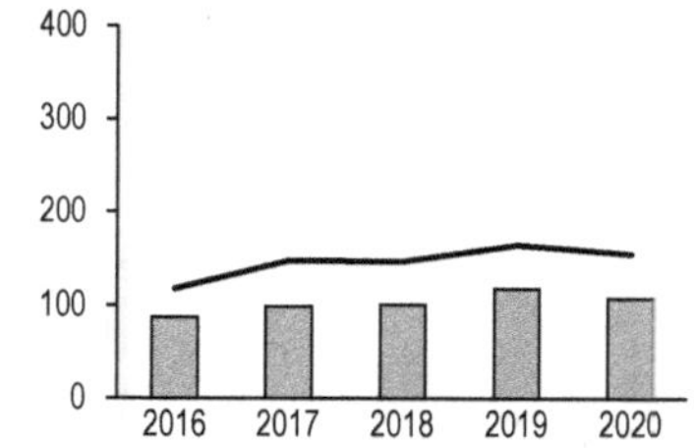

	2016	2017	2018	2019	2020
Concord	87	99	101	118	108
Average	117	147	147	164	155

Yard Waste and Leaf Tons Collected

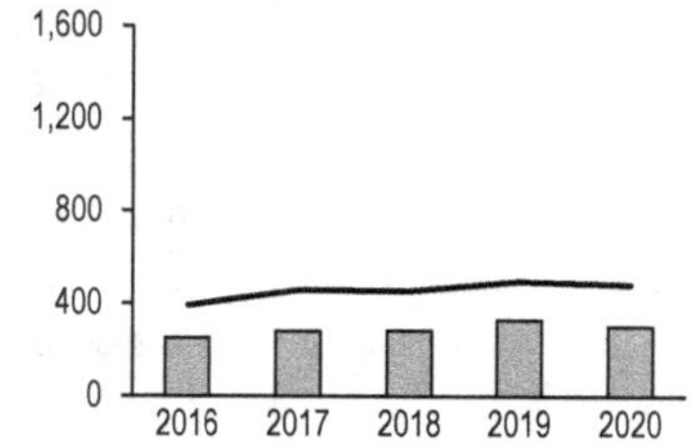

	2016	2017	2018	2019	2020
Concord	251	281	284	330	301
Average	391	459	454	495	482

Efficiency Measures

Yard Waste and Leaf Collection Cost per Collection Point

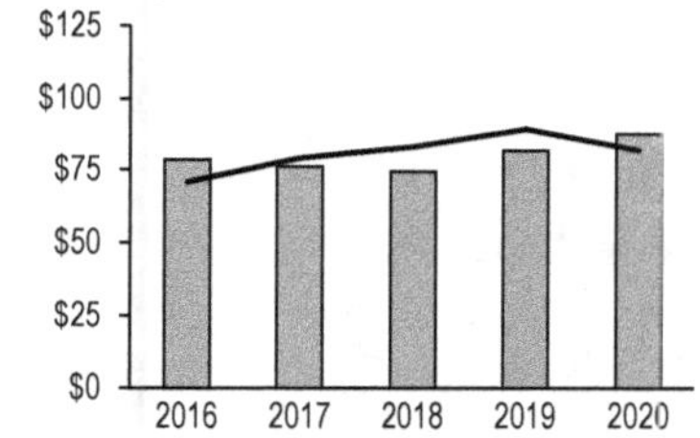

	2016	2017	2018	2019	2020
Concord	$78	$76	$74	$82	$88
Average	$71	$79	$83	$89	$82

Yard Waste and Leaf Collection Cost per Ton Collected

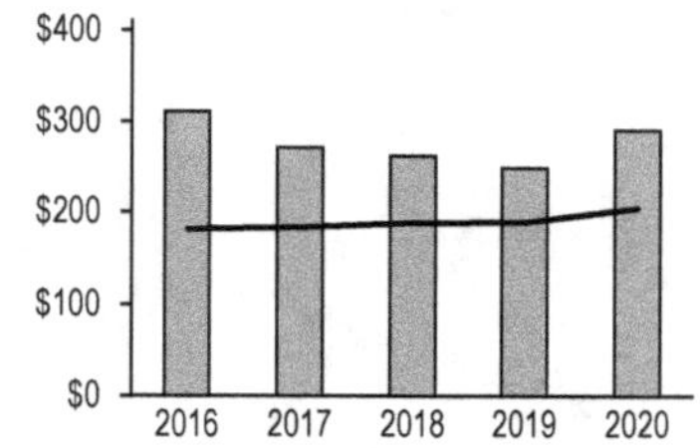

	2016	2017	2018	2019	2020
Concord	$311	$271	$261	$248	$291
Average	$181	$183	$189	$189	$205

Yard Waste and Leaf Tons Collected per Collection FTE

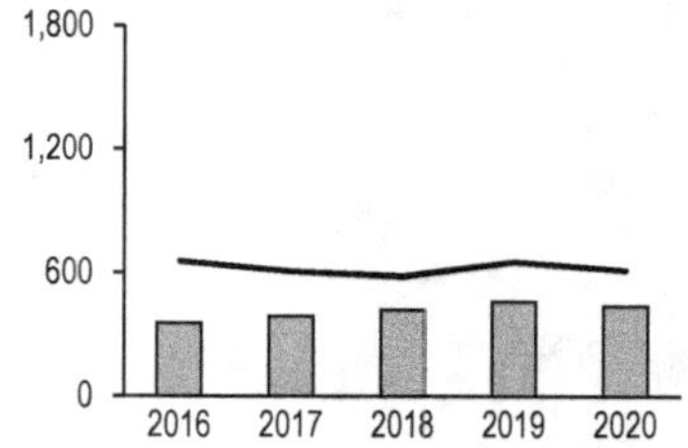

	2016	2017	2018	2019	2020
Concord	358	390	422	460	439
Average	655	607	582	651	613

Effectiveness Measures

Collection Complaints per 10,000 Collection Points

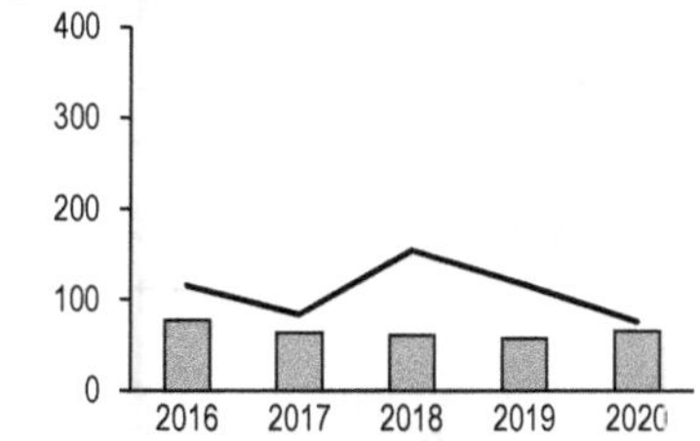

	2016	2017	2018	2019	2020
Concord	78	63	60	57	66
Average	115	84	154	117	76

Valid Complaints per 10,000 Collection Points

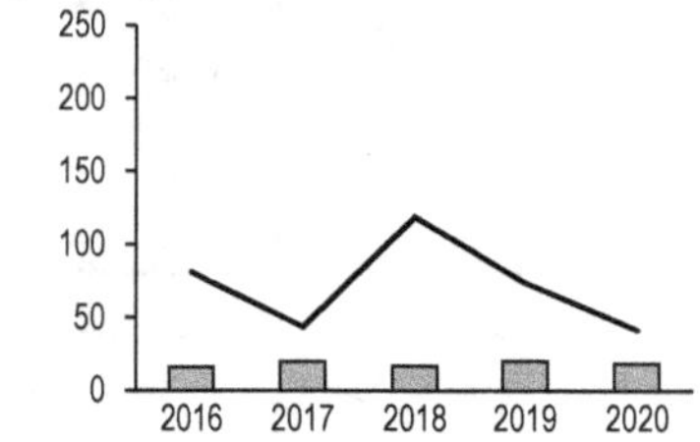

	2016	2017	2018	2019	2020
Concord	16	20	16	20	18
Average	81	44	119	74	42

Goldsboro — Yard Waste/Leaf Collection

Fiscal Year 2019-20

Explanatory Information

Service Level and Delivery

Goldsboro provides yard waste and seasonal leaf collection through the Solid Waste Division of the Public Works Department. Yard waste includes grass clippings, vines, garden and hedge trimmings, shrubbery, and other vegetative debris. Yard waste must be placed at the curbside in loose piles.

Yard waste is collected by four two-person crews consisting of one driver and one collector. Yard waste is collected every two weeks rotating through different sections of the city.

Seasonal leaf collection is done during the months of October through February. Collection is done every two weeks. Five crews are used for seasonal leaf collection consisting of one driver and two collectors per crew. One of the seasonal collectors is a temporary employee, while the driver and the other collector are permanent employees. Leaves must be placed loose or in a leaf cage at the curb.

Conditions Affecting Service, Performance, and Costs

The City of Goldsboro joined the Benchmarking Project in July 2017, with the first year of data showing for FY 2016–17.

Municipal Profile

Population (OSBM 2019)	33,969
Land Area (Square Miles)	29.45
Persons per Square Mile	1,154
Median Household Income U.S. Census 2016	$32,148

Service Profile

FTE Positions—Collection	15.00
FTE Positions—Other	1.33
Collection Frequency	
Yard Waste	1 x 2 weeks
Seasonal Leaf Collection	1 x 2 weeks
Collection Points	14,372
Tons Collected	
Yard Waste	6,280
Seasonal Leaves	3,384
Total Tons Collected	9,664
Monthly Service Fee	No

Full Cost Profile

Cost Breakdown by Percentage	
Personal Services	52.9%
Operating Costs	34.2%
Capital Costs	13.0%
TOTAL	100.0%
Cost Breakdown in Dollars	
Personal Services	$337,908
Operating Costs	$218,380
Capital Costs	$83,059
TOTAL	$639,347

Goldsboro

Yard Waste/Leaf Collection

Key: Goldsboro ▒ Benchmarking Average — Fiscal Years 2016 through 2020

Resource Measures

Yard Waste and Leaf Collection Costs per Capita

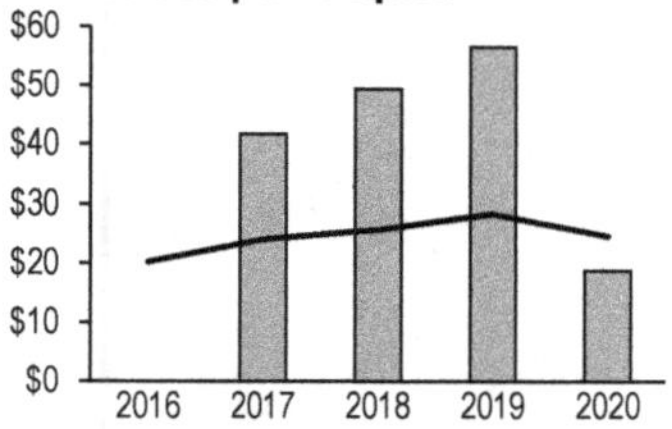

	2016	2017	2018	2019	2020
Goldsboro		$41.72	$49.39	$56.53	$18.82
Average	$20.26	$24.02	$25.75	$28.32	$24.62

Yard Waste and Leaf Collection FTEs per 10,000 Population

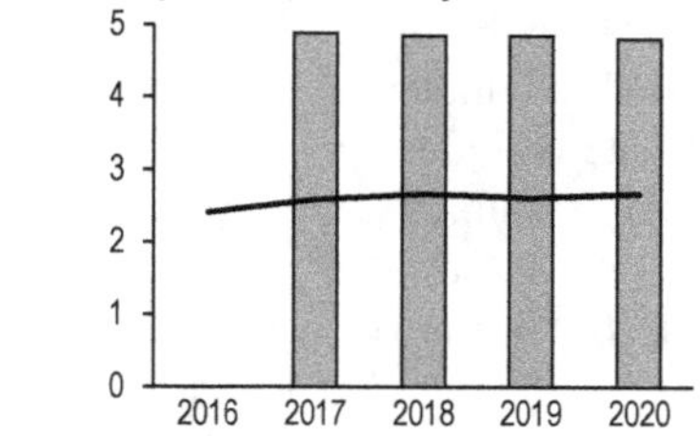

	2016	2017	2018	2019	2020
Goldsboro		4.9	4.8	4.9	4.8
Average	2.4	2.6	2.7	2.6	2.7

Workload Measures

Yard Waste and Leaf Tons Collected per 1,000 Population

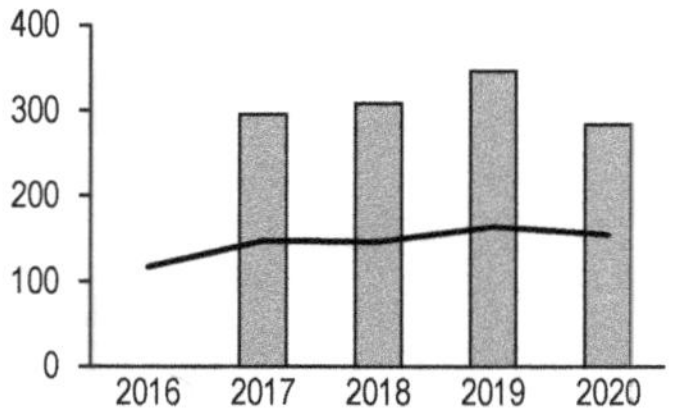

	2016	2017	2018	2019	2020
Goldsboro		296	309	346	284
Average	117	147	147	164	155

Yard Waste and Leaf Tons Collected per 1,000 Collection Points

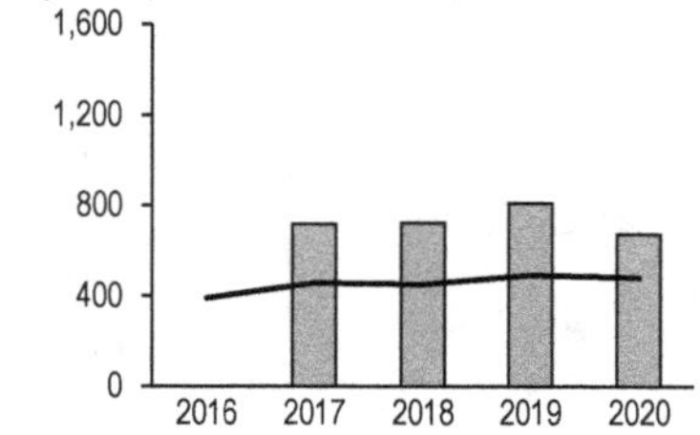

	2016	2017	2018	2019	2020
Goldsboro		716	724	811	672
Average	391	459	454	495	482

Efficiency Measures

Yard Waste and Leaf Collection Cost per Collection Point

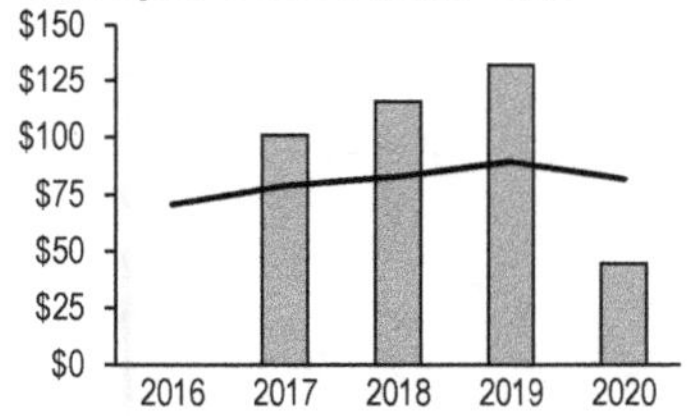

	2016	2017	2018	2019	2020
Goldsboro		$101	$116	$132	$44
Average	$71	$79	$83	$89	$82

Yard Waste and Leaf Collection Cost per Ton Collected

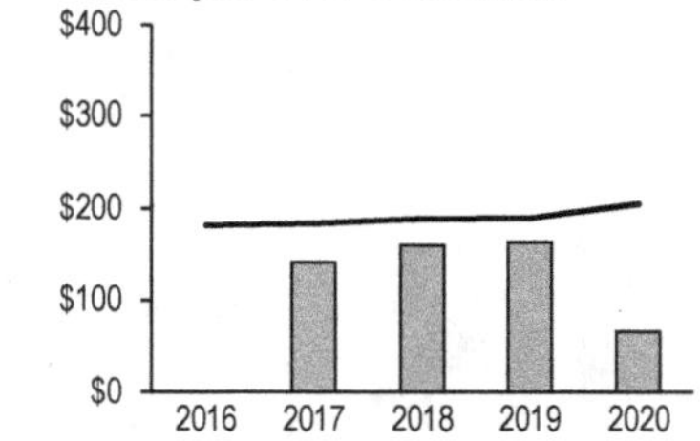

	2016	2017	2018	2019	2020
Goldsboro		$141	$160	$163	$66
Average	$181	$183	$189	$189	$205

Yard Waste and Leaf Tons Collected per Collection FTE

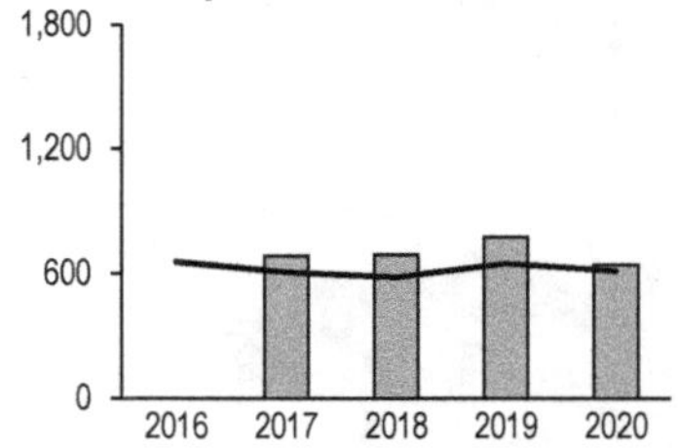

	2016	2017	2018	2019	2020
Goldsboro		686	693	777	644
Average	655	607	582	651	613

Effectiveness Measures

Collection Complaints per 10,000 Collection Points

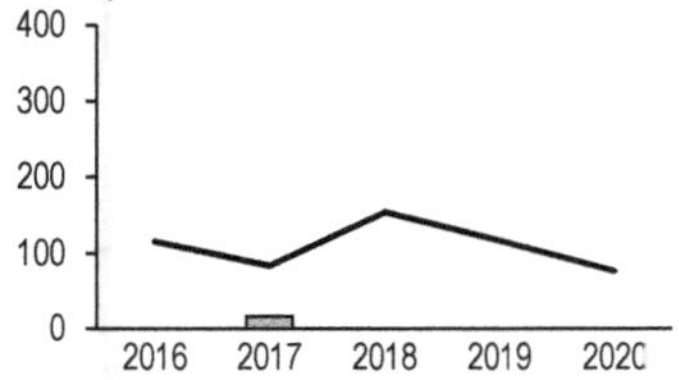

	2016	2017	2018	2019	2020
Goldsboro		17			
Average	115	84	154	117	76

Valid Complaints per 10,000 Collection Points

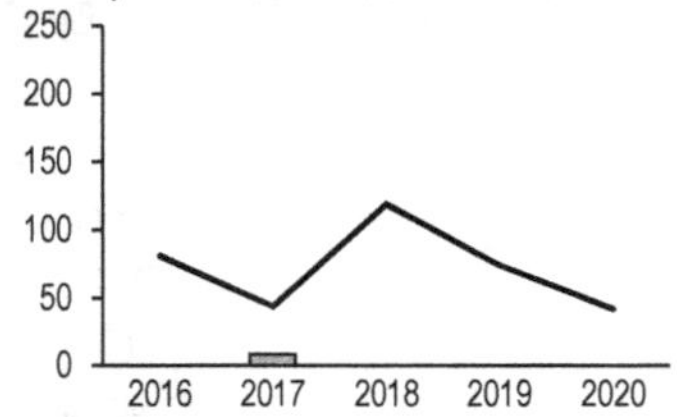

	2016	2017	2018	2019	2020
Goldsboro		8			
Average	81	44	119	74	42

Fiscal Year 2019-20

Explanatory Information

Service Level and Delivery

Greensboro collects yard waste once per week curbside, either in clear plastic bags, thirty-five-gallon containers, or tied in bundles not to exceed 50 pounds or 5 feet in length. Yard waste includes grass, weeds, leaves, tree trimmings, plants, shrubbery trimmings, and other materials generated in yard maintenance. Yard waste does include some bagged leaves during the fall, and this waste is not broken out separately into leaf collection.

The city provides yard waste service to all single-family residences inside the city limits. Yard waste crews include nine two-person crews that rotate between driver and collector. The crews work four days per week, ten hours per day.

Seasonal leaf collection (October through January) is provided by Greensboro's Field Operations Division. Leaves are picked up a minimum of two times from November until mid-January by vacuuming the leaves from the curb.

Conditions Affecting Service, Performance, and Costs

Municipal Profile

Population (OSBM 2019)	293,730
Land Area (Square Miles)	129.62
Persons per Square Mile	2,266
Median Household Income U.S. Census 2016	$40,760

Service Profile

FTE Positions—Collection	44.79
FTE Positions—Other	1.15
Collection Frequency	
Yard Waste	1 x week
Seasonal Leaf Collection	2 sweeps
Collection Points	91,075
Tons Collected	
Yard Waste	10,969
Seasonal Leaves	11,883
Total Tons Collected	22,852
Monthly Service Fee	No

Full Cost Profile

Cost Breakdown by Percentage	
Personal Services	34.8%
Operating Costs	65.2%
Capital Costs	0.0%
TOTAL	100.0%
Cost Breakdown in Dollars	
Personal Services	$1,227,118
Operating Costs	$2,299,054
Capital Costs	$0
TOTAL	$3,526,172

Greensboro

Yard Waste/Leaf Collection

Key: Greensboro ▒ Benchmarking Average — Fiscal Years 2016 through 2020

Resource Measures

Yard Waste and Leaf Collection Costs per Capita

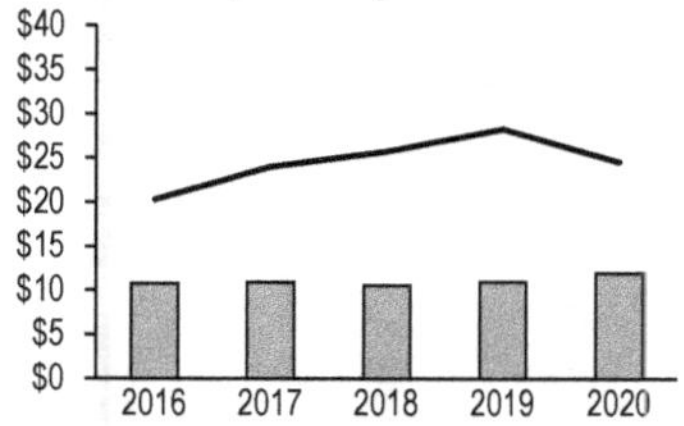

	2016	2017	2018	2019	2020
Greensboro	$10.74	$10.92	$10.50	$10.98	$12.00
Average	$20.26	$24.02	$25.75	$28.32	$24.62

Yard Waste and Leaf Collection FTEs per 10,000 Population

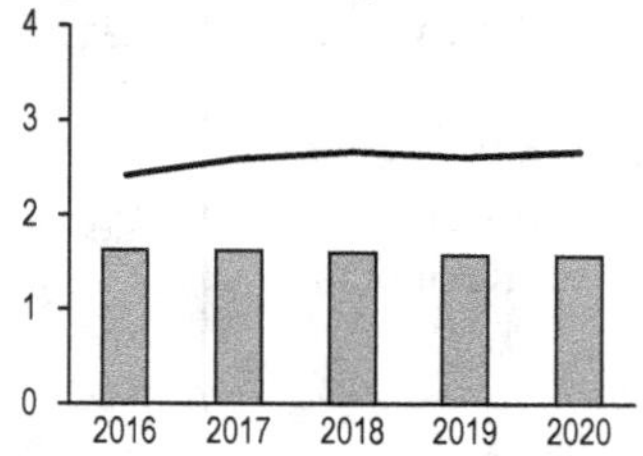

	2016	2017	2018	2019	2020
Greensboro	1.6	1.6	1.6	1.6	1.6
Average	2.4	2.6	2.7	2.6	2.7

Workload Measures

Yard Waste and Leaf Tons Collected per 1,000 Population

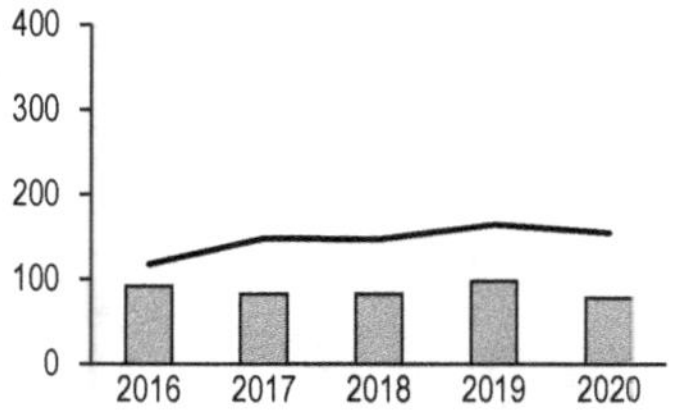

	2016	2017	2018	2019	2020
Greensboro	92	82	82	97	78
Average	117	147	147	164	155

Yard Waste and Leaf Tons Collected

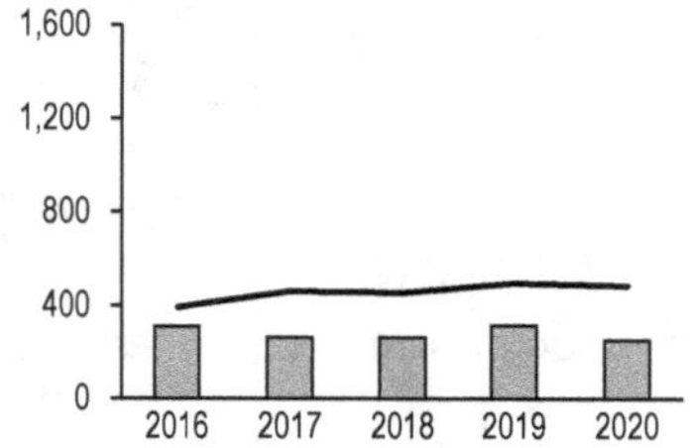

	2016	2017	2018	2019	2020
Greensboro	308	262	264	314	251
Average	391	459	454	495	482

Efficiency Measures

Yard Waste and Leaf Collection Cost per Collection Point

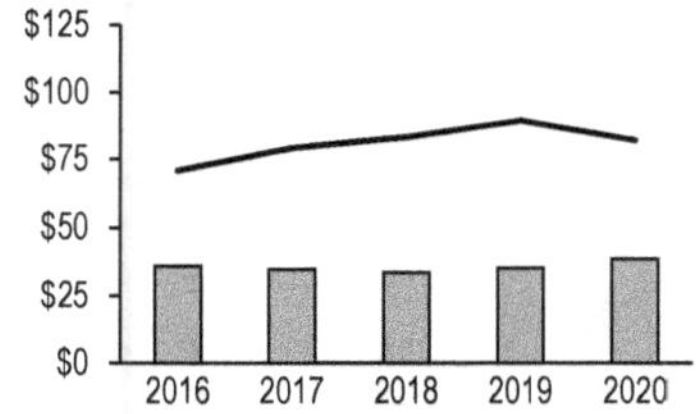

	2016	2017	2018	2019	2020
Greensboro	$36	$35	$34	$35	$39
Average	$71	$79	$83	$89	$82

Yard Waste and Leaf Collection Cost per Ton Collected

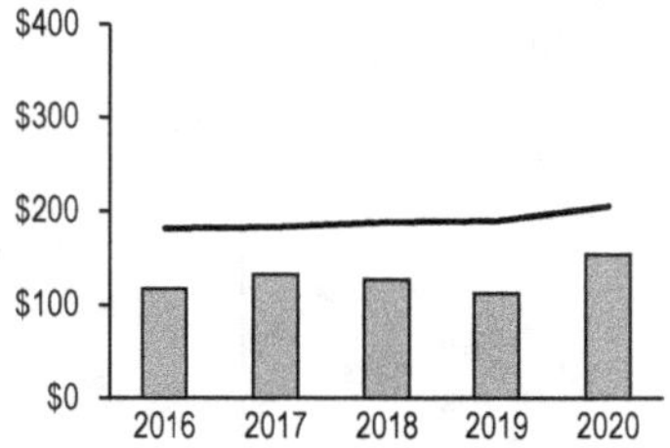

	2016	2017	2018	2019	2020
Greensboro	$117	$133	$127	$113	$154
Average	$181	$183	$189	$189	$205

Yard Waste and Leaf Tons Collected per Collection FTE

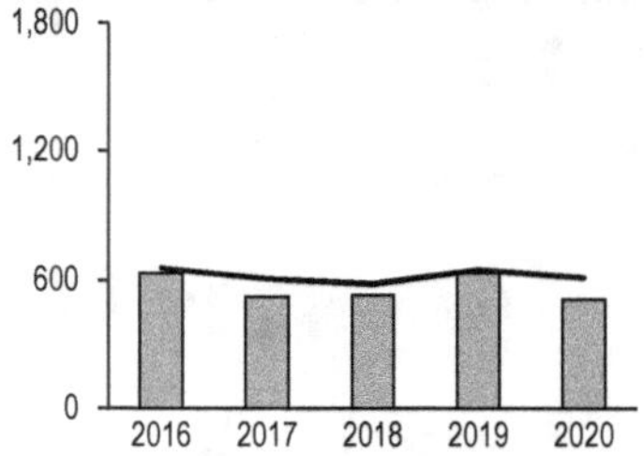

	2016	2017	2018	2019	2020
Greensboro	632	522	530	635	510
Average	655	607	582	651	613

Effectiveness Measures

Collection Complaints per 10,000 Collection Points

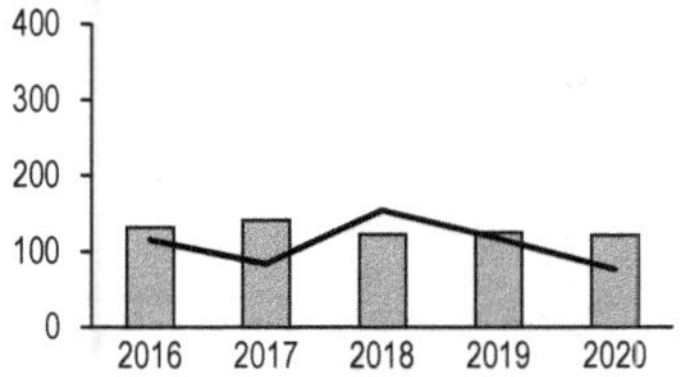

	2016	2017	2018	2019	2020
Greensboro	132	141	122	125	121
Average	115	84	154	117	76

Valid Complaints per 10,000 Collection Points

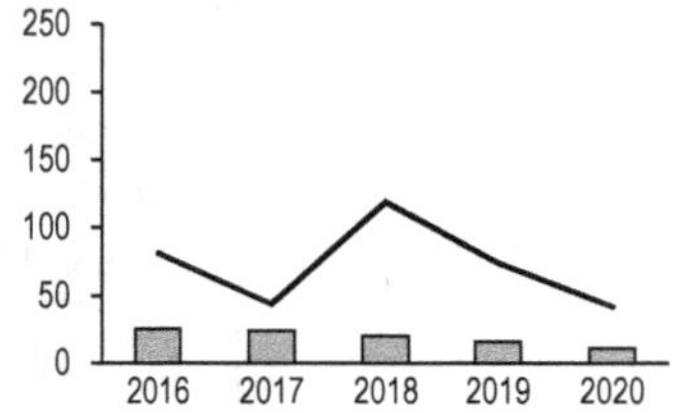

	2016	2017	2018	2019	2020
Greensboro	26	24	20	16	11
Average	81	44	119	74	42

Fiscal Year 2019-20

Explanatory Information

Service Level and Delivery

Hickory collects yard waste once per week curbside. Yard waste includes tree limbs less than 6 feet in length and 6 inches in diameter, shrubs, grass clippings, leaves, and other vegetative matter. The city does not charge a separate fee for yard waste, leaves, or bulky items. It is part of the solid waste fee. Residents use either clear plastic bags or open containers.

Hickory is divided into five sections for the yard waste program. Three routes are serviced each day within each section, using three rear loaders with crews comprised of one driver and one laborer each. Large piles are collected with a knuckle boom loader with one driver on a scheduled basis working about half-time.

All yard waste is collected and stockpiled at the city yard waste facility. Debris is ground into mulch or compost and sold back to citizens or used for city projects.

The city's seasonal leaf collection service runs from November to January. There are two sweeps down each city street during this time. City crews use leaf vacuums to collect leaves in box trucks. Hickory uses temporary contract workers to help with leaf collection. These seasonal employees are counted in the total employee count, but only for the one-fourth of the year they work.

Conditions Affecting Service, Performance, and Costs

Hickory's yard waste collection is set up to provide regular service but also takes requests for service when collection is needed. These calls for service cannot be separated out from actual complaints, so complaint data cannot be reported for this service area.

Municipal Profile

Population (OSBM 2019)	41,409
Land Area (Square Miles)	30.50
Persons per Square Mile	1,358
Median Household Income U.S. Census 2016	$35,353

Service Profile

FTE Positions—Collection	9.75
FTE Positions—Other	0.7
Collection Frequency	
Yard Waste	1 x week
Seasonal Leaf Collection	2 sweeps
Collection Points	12,116
Tons Collected	
Yard Waste	11,331
Seasonal Leaves	3,568
Total Tons Collected	14,899
Monthly Service Fee	No

Full Cost Profile

Cost Breakdown by Percentage	
Personal Services	44.2%
Operating Costs	42.2%
Capital Costs	13.6%
TOTAL	100.0%
Cost Breakdown in Dollars	
Personal Services	$409,720
Operating Costs	$391,311
Capital Costs	$126,474
TOTAL	$927,505

Key: Hickory ▪ Benchmarking Average — Fiscal Years 2016 through 2020

Resource Measures

Yard Waste and Leaf Collection Costs per Capita

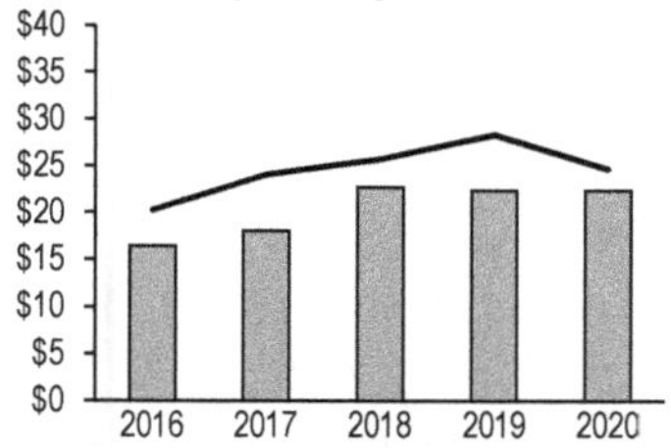

	2016	2017	2018	2019	2020
Hickory	$16.47	$18.07	$22.69	$22.36	$22.40
Average	$20.26	$24.02	$25.75	$28.32	$24.62

Yard Waste and Leaf Collection FTEs per 10,000 Population

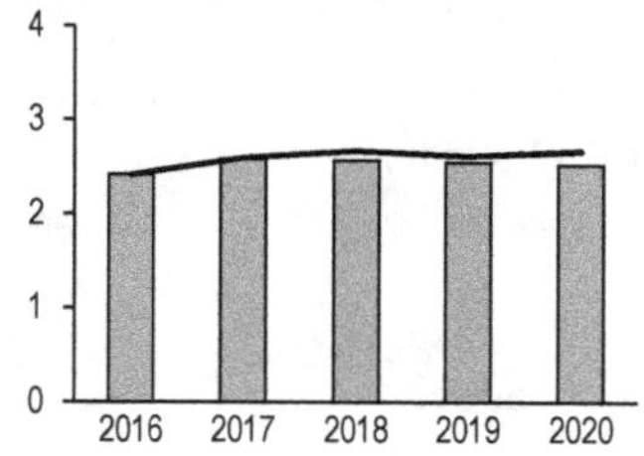

	2016	2017	2018	2019	2020
Hickory	2.4	2.6	2.6	2.5	2.5
Average	2.4	2.6	2.7	2.6	2.7

Workload Measures

Yard Waste and Leaf Tons Collected per 1,000 Population

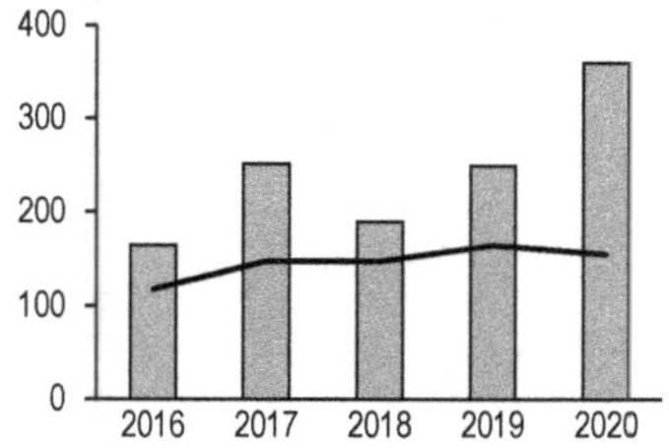

	2016	2017	2018	2019	2020
Hickory	164	251	189	250	360
Average	117	147	147	164	155

Yard Waste and Leaf Tons Collected

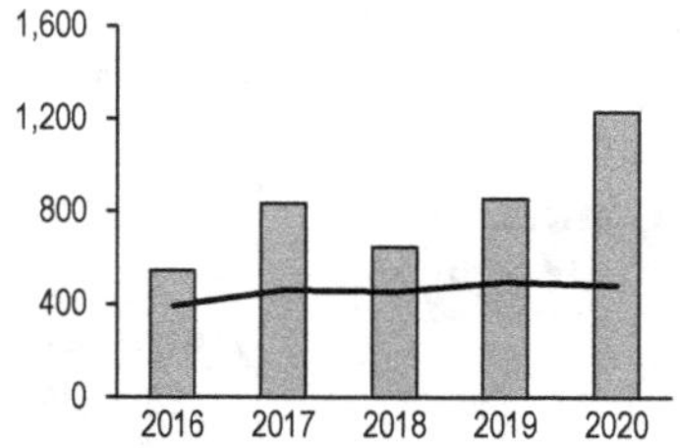

	2016	2017	2018	2019	2020
Hickory	543	834	645	855	1,230
Average	391	459	454	495	482

Efficiency Measures

Yard Waste and Leaf Collection Cost per Collection Point

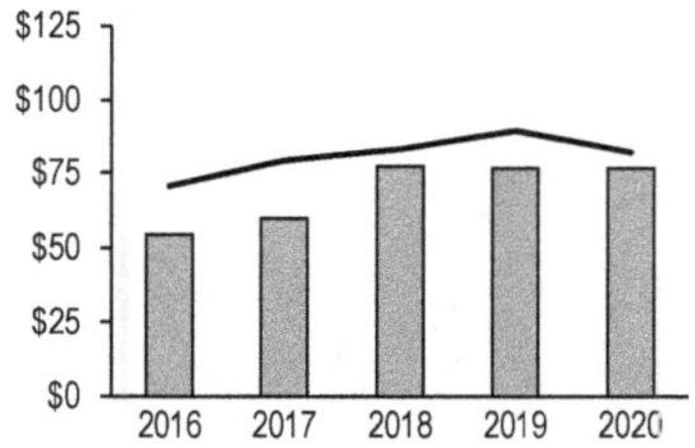

	2016	2017	2018	2019	2020
Hickory	$54	$60	$77	$77	$77
Average	$71	$79	$83	$89	$82

Yard Waste and Leaf Collection Cost per Ton Collected

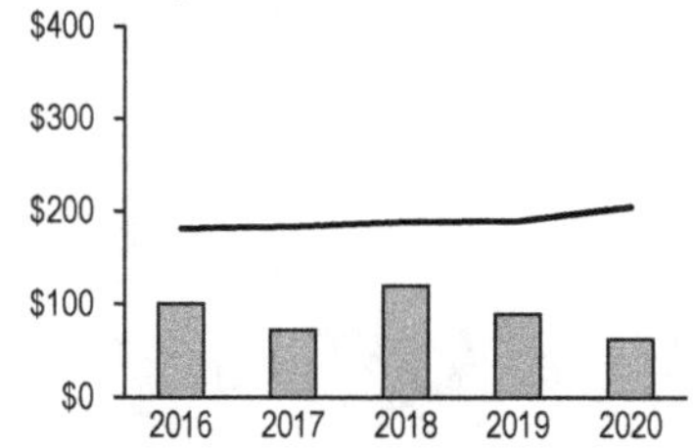

	2016	2017	2018	2019	2020
Hickory	$100	$72	$120	$90	$62
Average	$181	$183	$189	$189	$205

Yard Waste and Leaf Tons Collected per Collection FTE

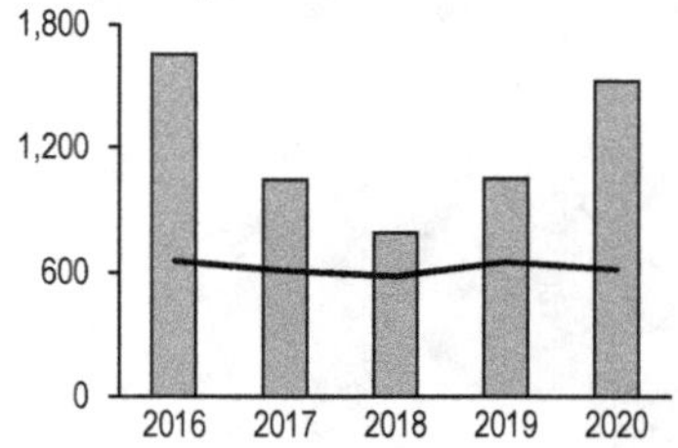

	2016	2017	2018	2019	2020
Hickory	1,657	1,043	790	1,048	1,528
Average	655	607	582	651	613

Effectiveness Measures

Collection Complaints per 10,000 Collection Points

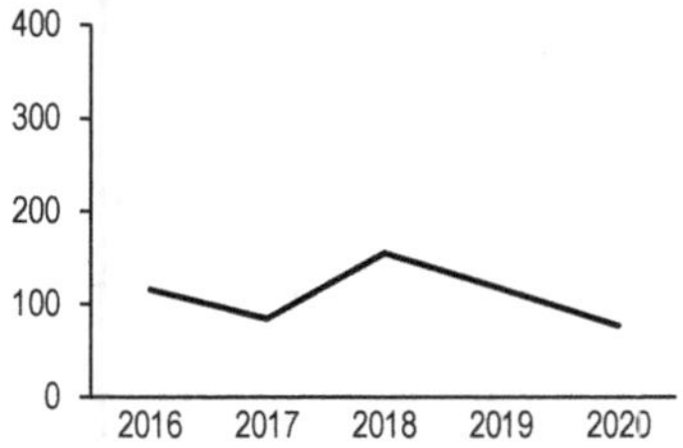

	2016	2017	2018	2019	2020
Hickory					
Average	115	84	154	117	76

Valid Complaints per 10,000 Collection Points

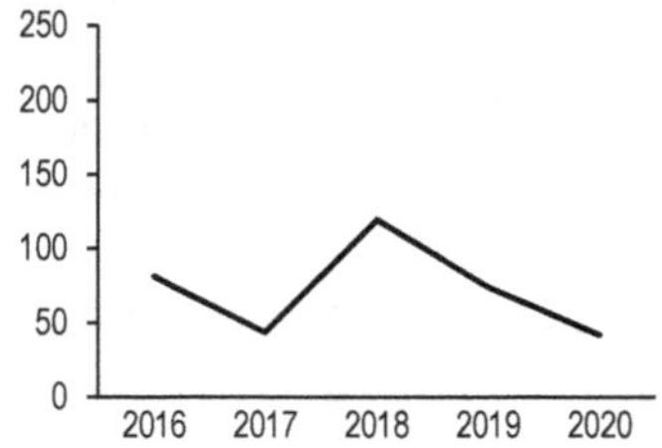

	2016	2017	2018	2019	2020
Hickory					
Average	81	44	119	74	42

Raleigh

Yard Waste/Leaf Collection

Fiscal Year 2019-20

Explanatory Information

Service Level and Delivery

Yard waste is picked up weekly at the curb in Raleigh by the Solid Waste Services Department. Yard waste must be bagged or containerized with a limit of fifteen bags. Bags must be clear or biodegradable.

The city uses twelve three-person crews to collect yard waste on the same day as trash collection. Temporary crews are added during leaf season as yard waste volume picks up.

Loose Leaf collection is done by the Transportation Field Services Division. Loose leaves are collected curbside during leaf season, which runs from November to February. Two sweeps of the city are completed during leaf season. The first sweep is usually completed by mid-January, and the second sweep is usually completed by the end of February. Loose leaves must be placed at the street and must be free of debris to be collected.

Conditions Affecting Service, Performance, and Costs

Raleigh rejoined the Benchmarking Project in July 2016, with the first year of data showing for FY 2015–16.

Municipal Profile

Population (OSBM 2019)	475,580
Land Area (Square Miles)	146.47
Persons per Square Mile	3,247
Median Household Income U.S. Census 2016	$46,612

Service Profile

FTE Positions—Collection	103.0
FTE Positions—Other	4.5
Collection Frequency	
Yard Waste	1 x week
Seasonal Leaf Collection	2 sweeps
Collection Points	130,646
Tons Collected	
Yard Waste	14,427
Seasonal Leaves	13,950
Total Tons Collected	28,377
Monthly Service Fee	
Yard Waste	Yes
Seasonal Leaf Collection	No

Full Cost Profile

Cost Breakdown by Percentage	
Personal Services	49.3%
Operating Costs	37.8%
Capital Costs	12.9%
TOTAL	100.0%
Cost Breakdown in Dollars	
Personal Services	$3,781,663
Operating Costs	$2,900,516
Capital Costs	$994,050
TOTAL	$7,676,229

Raleigh

Yard Waste/Leaf Collection

Key: Raleigh ▒ Benchmarking Average — Fiscal Years 2016 through 2020

Resource Measures

Yard Waste and Leaf Collection Costs per Capita

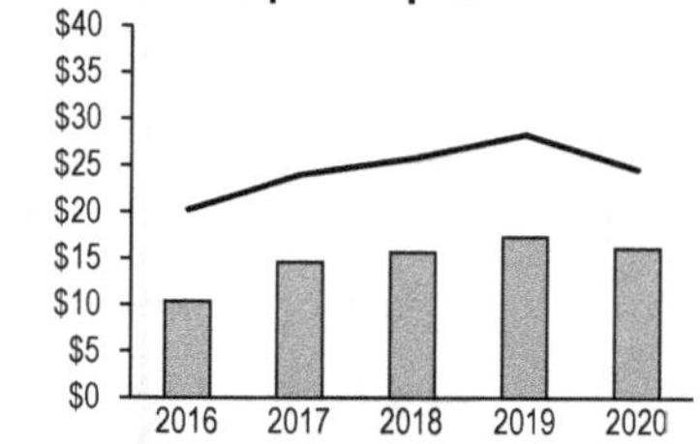

	2016	2017	2018	2019	2020
Raleigh	$10.31	$14.59	$15.66	$17.35	$16.14
Average	$20.26	$24.02	$25.75	$28.32	$24.62

Yard Waste and Leaf Collection FTEs per 10,000 Population

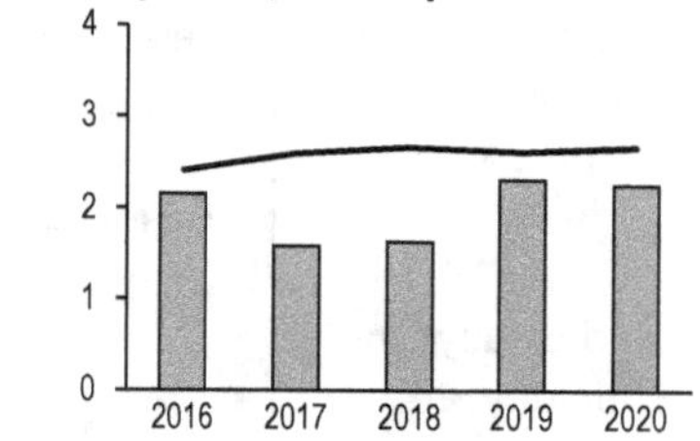

	2016	2017	2018	2019	2020
Raleigh	2.2	1.6	1.6	2.3	2.3
Average	2.4	2.6	2.7	2.6	2.7

Workload Measures

Yard Waste and Leaf Tons Collected per 1,000 Population

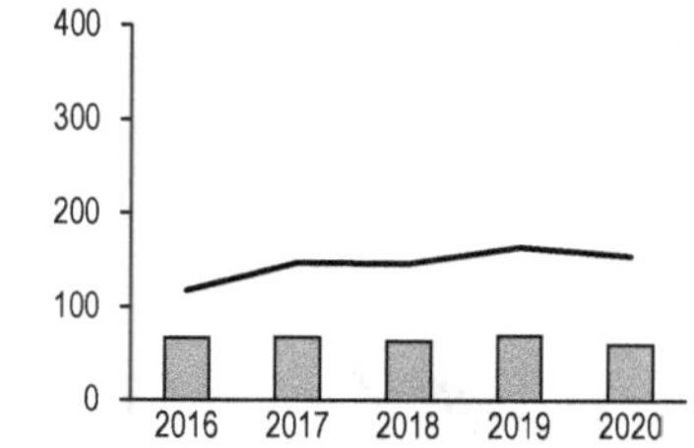

	2016	2017	2018	2019	2020
Raleigh	67	68	63	69	60
Average	117	147	147	164	155

Yard Waste and Leaf Tons Collected per 1,000 Collection Points

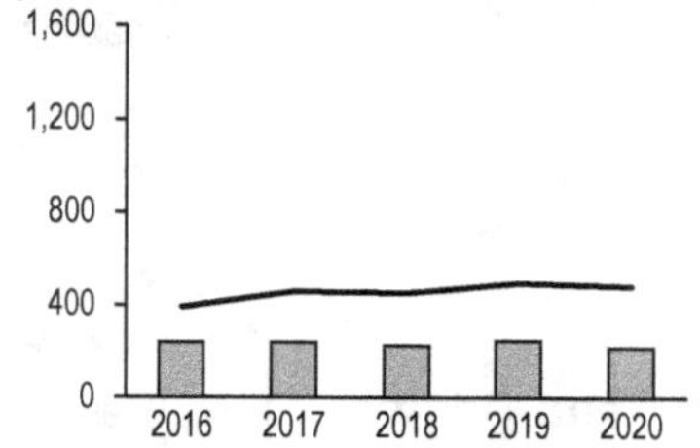

	2016	2017	2018	2019	2020
Raleigh	239	240	227	247	217
Average	391	459	454	495	482

Efficiency Measures

Yard Waste and Leaf Collection Cost per Collection Point

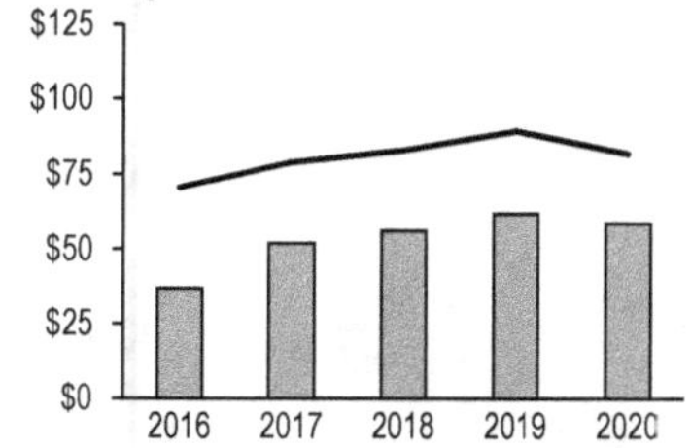

	2016	2017	2018	2019	2020
Raleigh	$37	$52	$56	$62	$59
Average	$71	$79	$83	$89	$82

Yard Waste and Leaf Collection Cost per Ton Collected

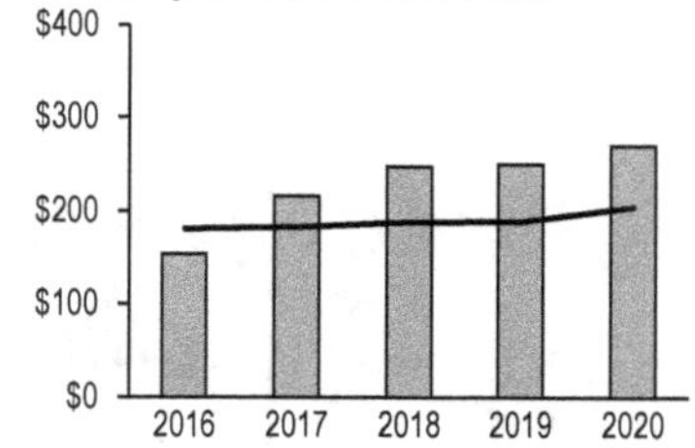

	2016	2017	2018	2019	2020
Raleigh	$154	$216	$248	$251	$271
Average	$181	$183	$189	$189	$205

Yard Waste and Leaf Tons Collected per Collection FTE

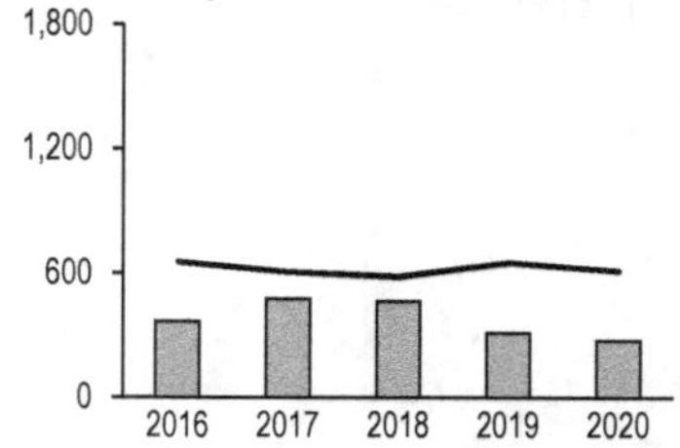

	2016	2017	2018	2019	2020
Raleigh	364	473	461	312	276
Average	655	607	582	651	613

Effectiveness Measures

Collection Complaints per 10,000 Collection Points

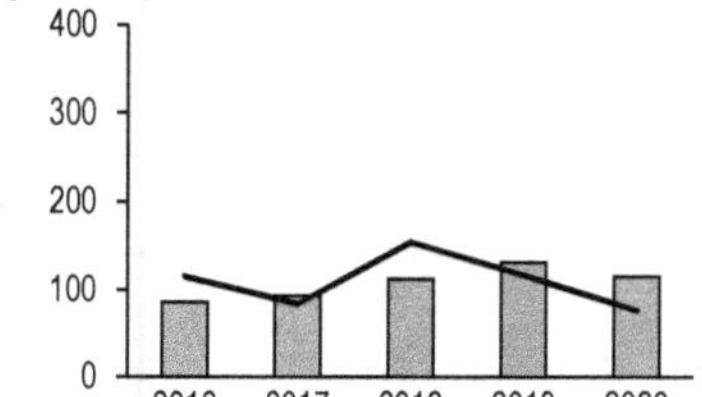

	2016	2017	2018	2019	2020
Raleigh	86	93	113	132	116
Average	115	84	154	117	76

Valid Complaints per 10,000 Collection Points

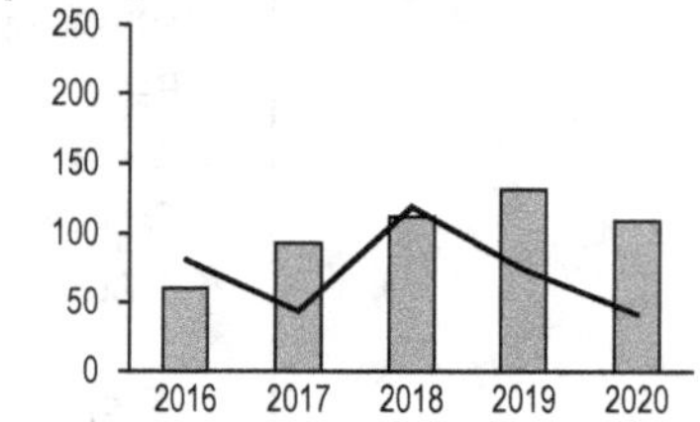

	2016	2017	2018	2019	2020
Raleigh	60	93	112	132	109
Average	81	44	119	74	42

Fiscal Year 2019-20

Explanatory Information

Service Level and Delivery

Yard waste is containerized in bags, sheets, roll-out containers, or other container types for collection by rear-loader packers. Yard waste is collected once per week by compost crews on the same day as residential refuse collection.

The city uses two three-person crews on Tuesdays and Fridays and three or four three-person crews on Mondays and Thursdays to collect yard waste. Each crew is composed of one driver and two workers. These crews rotate collection between residential refuse and yard waste. A one-person crew uses a knuckle boom truck to collect large limbs daily.

The city's leaf season is from mid-October to mid-January. Leaves are collected loose at the curb on a one-to-three-week cycle. The city uses leaf vacuum machines and compacting leaf trucks to collect loose leaves.

Six to eight three-person crews are used to collect loose leaves. The drivers are permanent employees. Collectors are seasonal employees.

Conditions Affecting Service, Performance, and Costs

Wilson began using a new automated system for tracking all call-ins into "Fix-It Wilson" during FY 2017–2018. The contacts for yard waste include all items related to limbs, leaves, and compost. Previously all complaints were received by telephone and documented by hand in a notebook. The jump in complaints is connected to the implementation of this new system rather than changes in service.

Municipal Profile

Population (OSBM 2019)	49,384
Land Area (Square Miles)	31.02
Persons per Square Mile	1,592
Median Household Income U.S. Census 2016	$35,409

Service Profile

FTE Positions—Collection	15.5
FTE Positions—Other	0.0
Collection Frequency	
Yard Waste	1 x week
Seasonal Leaf Collection	1 x 3 weeks
Collection Points	21,500
Tons Collected	
Yard Waste	9,211
Seasonal Leaves	1,204
Total Tons Collected	10,415
Monthly Service Fee	Included in solid waste fee

Full Cost Profile

Cost Breakdown by Percentage	
Personal Services	51.5%
Operating Costs	30.8%
Capital Costs	17.7%
TOTAL	100.0%
Cost Breakdown in Dollars	
Personal Services	$717,194
Operating Costs	$429,531
Capital Costs	$246,059
TOTAL	$1,392,784

Wilson

Yard Waste/Leaf Collection

Key: Wilson ■ Benchmarking Average — Fiscal Years 2016 through 2020

Resource Measures

Yard Waste and Leaf Collection Costs per Capita

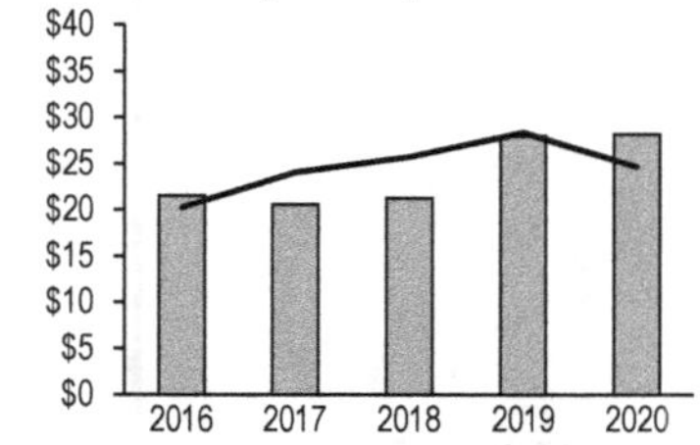

	2016	2017	2018	2019	2020
Wilson	$21.50	$20.57	$21.28	$27.98	$28.20
Average	$20.26	$24.02	$25.75	$28.32	$24.62

Yard Waste and Leaf Collection FTEs per 10,000 Population

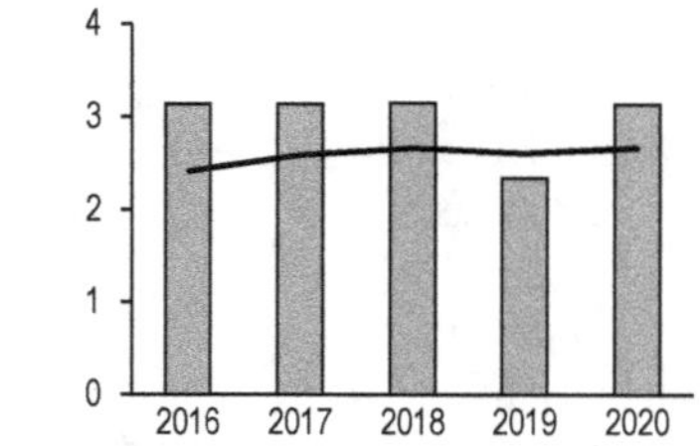

	2016	2017	2018	2019	2020
Wilson	3.1	3.1	3.2	2.3	3.1
Average	2.4	2.6	2.7	2.6	2.7

Workload Measures

Yard Waste and Leaf Tons Collected per 1,000 Population

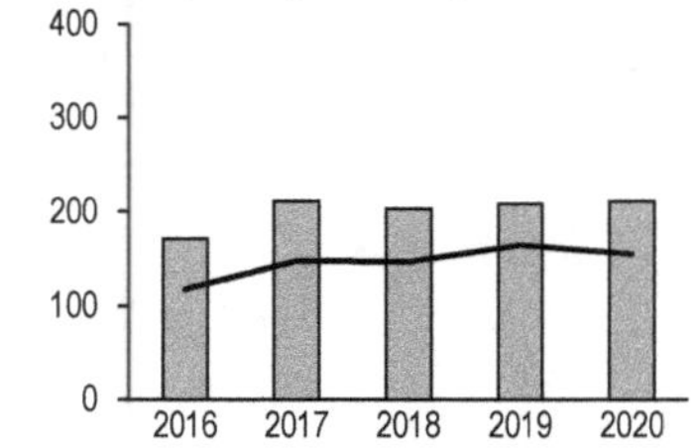

	2016	2017	2018	2019	2020
Wilson	171	211	203	208	211
Average	117	147	147	164	155

Yard Waste and Leaf Tons Collected

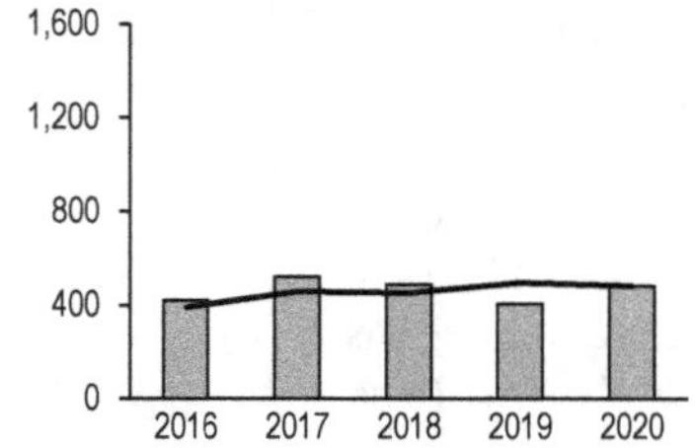

	2016	2017	2018	2019	2020
Wilson	422	520	489	407	484
Average	391	459	454	495	482

Efficiency Measures

Yard Waste and Leaf Collection Cost per Collection Point

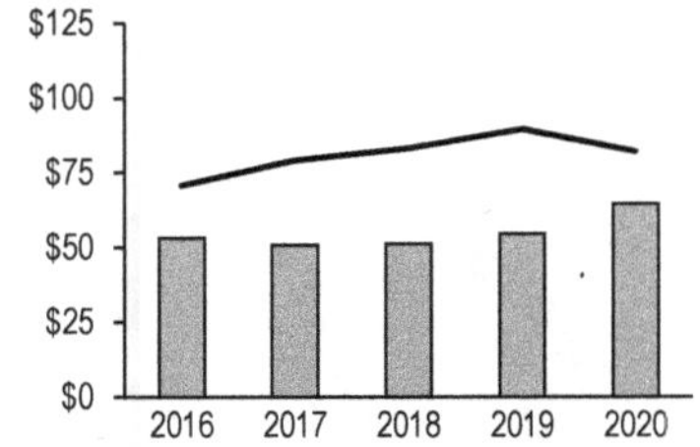

	2016	2017	2018	2019	2020
Wilson	$53	$51	$51	$55	$65
Average	$71	$79	$83	$89	$82

Yard Waste and Leaf Collection Cost per Ton Collected

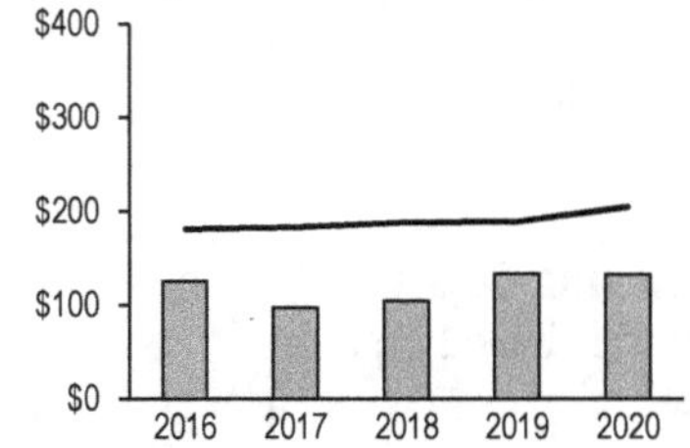

	2016	2017	2018	2019	2020
Wilson	$126	$98	$105	$134	$134
Average	$181	$183	$189	$189	$205

Yard Waste and Leaf Tons Collected per Collection FTE

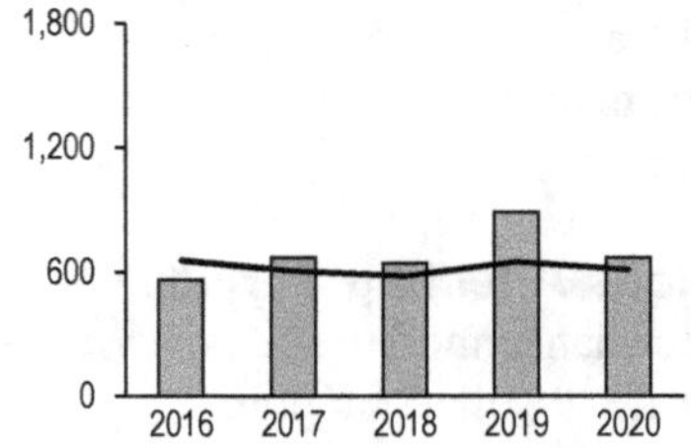

	2016	2017	2018	2019	2020
Wilson	562	672	643	889	672
Average	655	607	582	651	613

Effectiveness Measures

Collection Complaints per 10,000 Collection Points

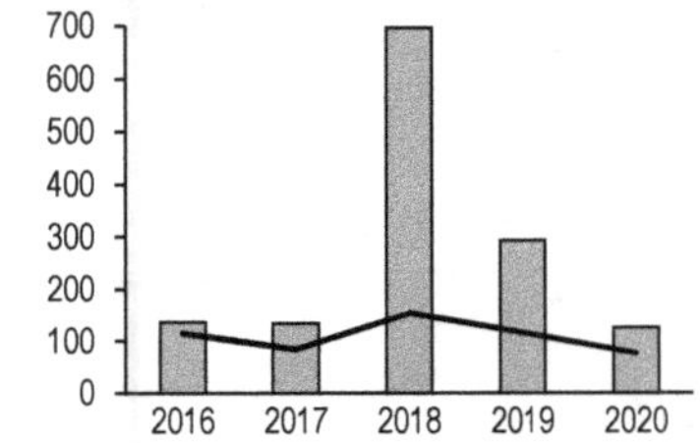

	2016	2017	2018	2019	2020
Wilson	137	135	697	293	126
Average	115	84	154	117	76

Valid Complaints per 10,000 Collection Points

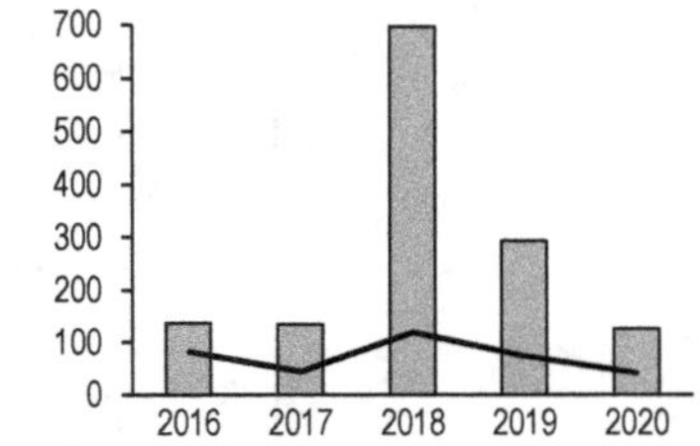

	2016	2017	2018	2019	2020
Wilson	137	135	697	293	126
Average	81	44	119	74	42

Fiscal Year 2019-20

Explanatory Information

Service Level and Delivery

The city operates a curbside collection program for brush, leaves, and bulky items. Brush is collected throughout the year, while leaves and bulky items are collected on a seasonal basis. Brush is defined as small tree limbs, branches, and shrubbery clippings. Tree and shrubbery limbs cannot be larger than 6 inches in diameter or 6 feet in length. A city ordinance requires that brush be collected once every ten working days except during leaf season. There are no separate fees for the curbside collection program. The brush collection program gathered 21,942 tons across the city.

The yard waste cart program provides weekly collection of containerized yard waste placed in ninety-six-gallon carts. The city uses six one-person crews using automated packers and one two-person crew using a rear-loading packer to service these carts. Collection is provided Monday through Thursday. Carts are delivered on Friday. Residents who participate in the yard waste cart program pay an annual $60 fee. Residents also pay for the ninety-six-gallon carts at a cost of $60 if the cart is picked up or $65 if the cart is delivered. A household can have up to three carts. The yard cart program serviced 13,828 customers in the fiscal year picking up 7,379 tons.

The city's seasonal leaf collection program picks up leaves that are deposited at the curb between November 1 and January 15. Loose leaves are vacuumed two to three times during this time period. Containerized leaves are collected throughout the year as part of the yard waste program. The city uses thirty-two crews for seasonal leaf collection, with a combination of equipment operators, maintenance workers, and both permanent and seasonal workers.

Conditions Affecting Service, Performance, and Costs

The performance measure "cost per collection point" is based on a total of 81,589 collection points.

Municipal Profile

Population (OSBM 2019)	244,739
Land Area (Square Miles)	132.59
Persons per Square Mile	1,846
Median Household Income U.S. Census 2016	$40,584

Service Profile

FTE Positions—Collection	74.5
FTE Positions—Other	1.4
Collection Frequency	
Yard Waste	1 x week
Seasonal Leaf Collection	1 x 3 weeks
Brush	1 x 10 days
Collection Points	81,589
Tons Collected	
Yard Waste	21,942
Seasonal Leaves	16,252
Total Tons Collected	38,193
Monthly Service Fee	$60 per year for cart

Full Cost Profile

Cost Breakdown by Percentage	
Personal Services	54.6%
Operating Costs	26.5%
Capital Costs	18.9%
TOTAL	100.0%
Cost Breakdown in Dollars	
Personal Services	$4,033,784
Operating Costs	$1,954,407
Capital Costs	$1,395,715
TOTAL	$7,383,906

Winston-Salem — Yard Waste/Leaf Collection

Key: Winston-Salem ■ Benchmarking Average — Fiscal Years 2016 through 2020

Resource Measures

Yard Waste and Leaf Collection Costs per Capita

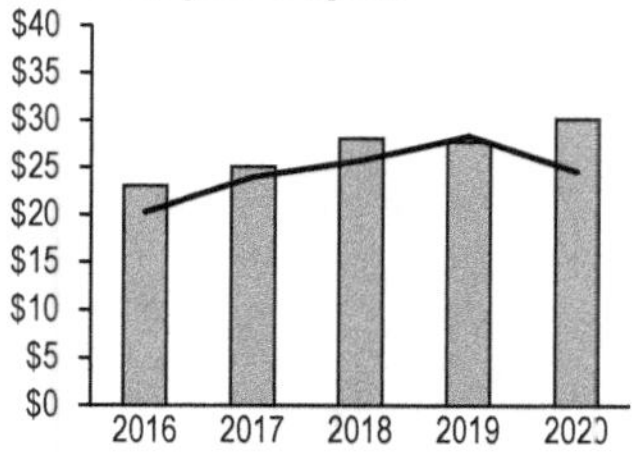

	2016	2017	2018	2019	2020
Winston-Salem	$23.03	$25.06	$28.05	$27.76	$30.17
Average	$20.26	$24.02	$25.75	$28.32	$24.62

Yard Waste and Leaf Collection FTEs per 10,000 Population

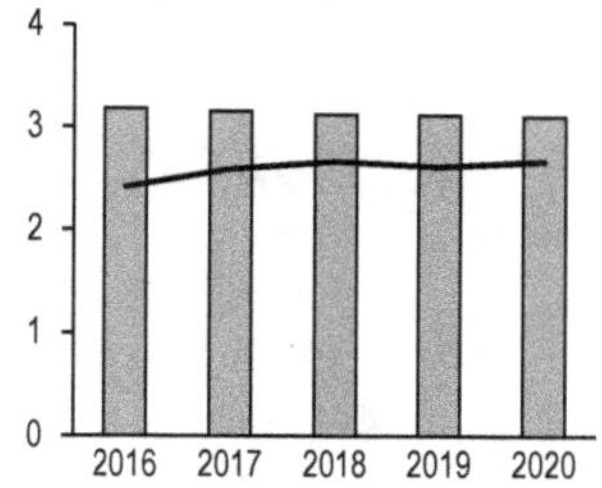

	2016	2017	2018	2019	2020
Winston-Salem	3.2	3.2	3.1	3.1	3.1
Average	2.4	2.6	2.7	2.6	2.7

Workload Measures

Yard Waste and Leaf Tons Collected per 1,000 Population

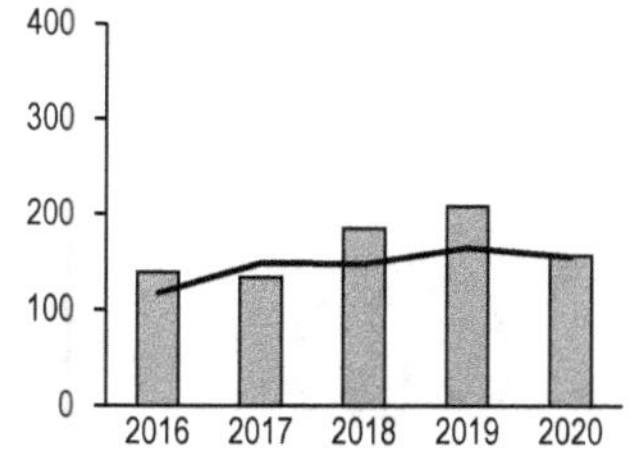

	2016	2017	2018	2019	2020
Winston-Salem	138	133	184	208	156
Average	117	147	147	164	155

Yard Waste and Leaf Tons Collected

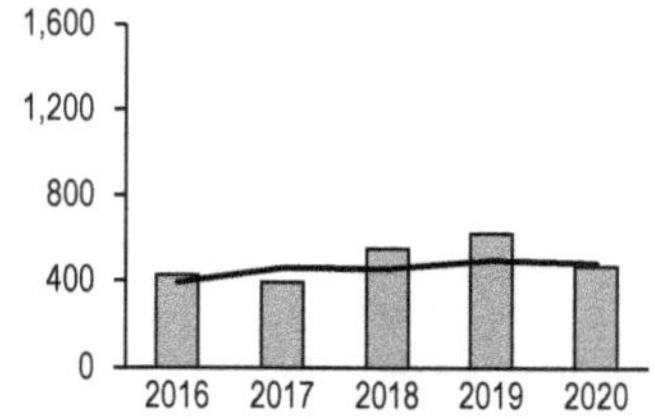

	2016	2017	2018	2019	2020
Winston-Salem	424	392	549	621	468
Average	391	459	454	495	482

Efficiency Measures

Yard Waste and Leaf Collection Cost per Collection Point

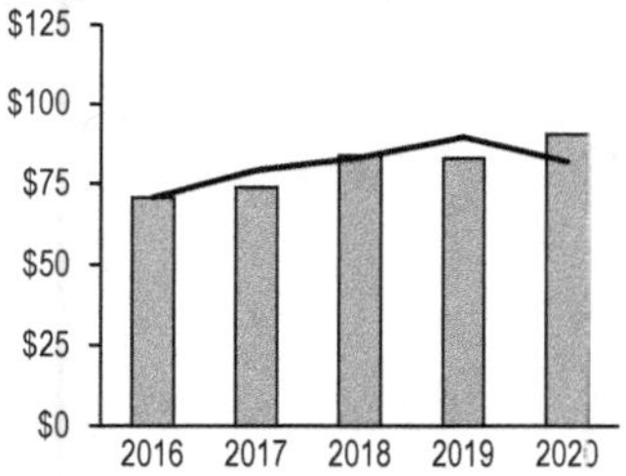

	2016	2017	2018	2019	2020
Winston-Salem	$71	$74	$84	$83	$91
Average	$71	$79	$83	$89	$82

Yard Waste and Leaf Collection Cost per Ton Collected

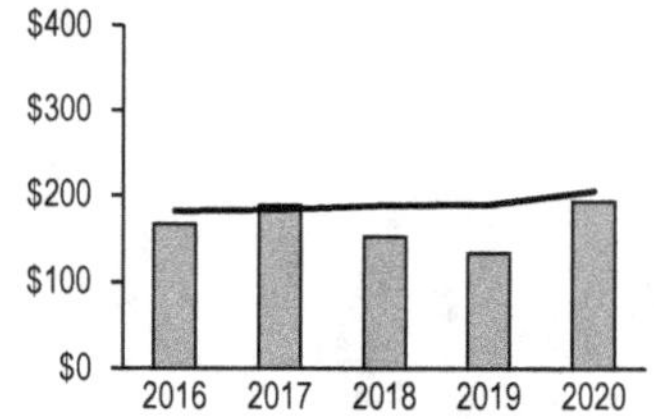

	2016	2017	2018	2019	2020
Winston-Salem	$167	$188	$152	$133	$193
Average	$181	$183	$189	$189	$205

Yard Waste and Leaf Tons Collected per Collection FTE

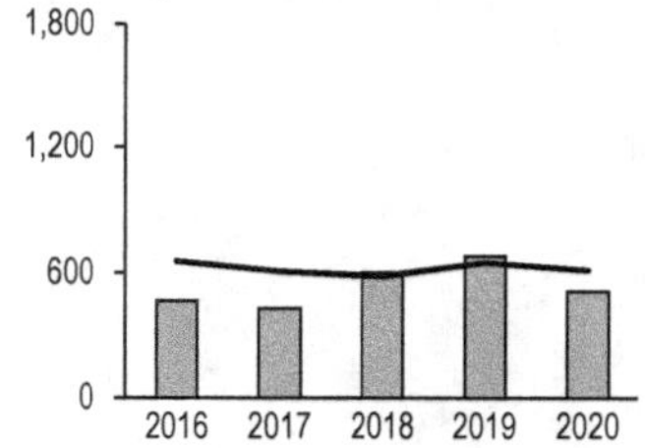

	2016	2017	2018	2019	2020
Winston-Salem	466	430	601	680	513
Average	655	607	582	651	613

Effectiveness Measures

Collection Complaints per 10,000 Collection Points

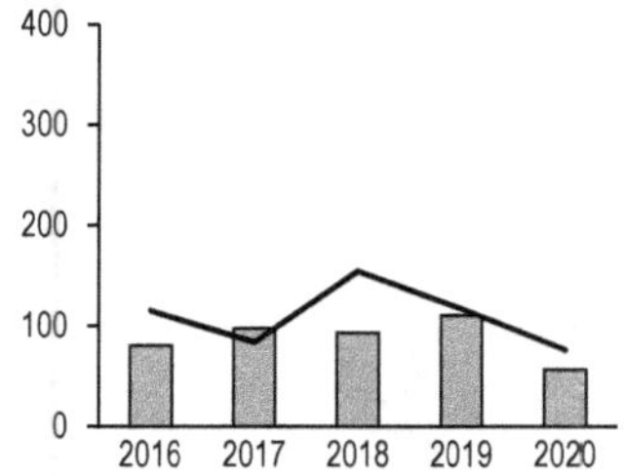

	2016	2017	2018	2019	2020
Winston-Salem	80	97	93	110	57
Average	115	84	154	117	76

Valid Complaints per 10,000 Collection Points

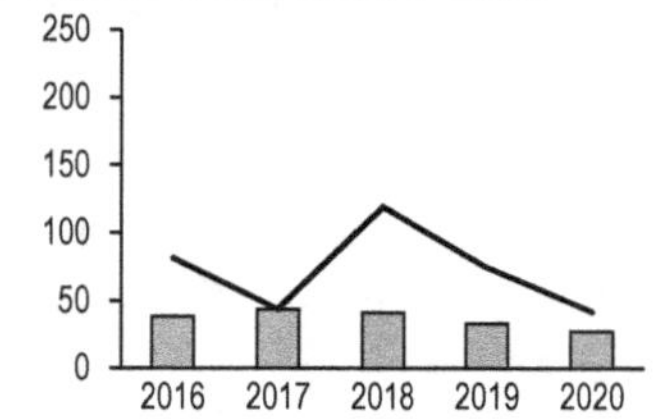

	2016	2017	2018	2019	2020
Winston-Salem	39	44	41	33	28
Average	81	44	119	74	42

SCHOOL OF GOVERNMENT
North Carolina Benchmarking Project

Performance and Cost Data

POLICE SERVICES

PERFORMANCE MEASURES FOR POLICE SERVICES

SERVICE DEFINITION

Police Services consist of all police activities performed by sworn and non-sworn personnel. This includes, but is not limited to, activities performed by patrol, traffic, investigations, special units, support staff, supervisors, and police administration. This definition captures all functions of the police department except for emergency communications.

NOTES ON PERFORMANCE MEASURES

1. Dispatched Calls

These are calls resulting in the dispatch of an officer. Most dispatches result from calls coming into the emergency communications center or the police department, but some are self-initiated by officers on duty. Multiple calls resulting in the dispatch of several officers are counted as one.

2. Uniform Crime Reporting (UCR) Part I Crimes

Uniform Crime Reporting (UCR) Part I crimes include crimes against persons (criminal homicide, forcible rape, robbery, and aggravated assault) and crimes against property (burglary, larceny, motor vehicle theft, and arson).

3. Incident-Based Reporting (IBR) Part I Crimes

Incident-Based Reporting (IBR) Part I crimes include crimes against persons (criminal homicide, forcible rape, robbery, and aggravated assault) and crimes against property (burglary, larceny, motor vehicle theft, and arson). The difference between the UCR method and the IBR method for reporting crimes is that IBR counts crime and arrest activities at the incident level, as opposed to counting only the most serious crime with multiple offenses.

4. Full-Time Equivalent (FTE) Positions: Sworn Officers

The number of full-time equivalent (FTE) positions is the number of budgeted positions for sworn officers during the fiscal year.

5. Response Time to High Priority Calls

Each police department defines high priority calls somewhat differently. The definitions generally refer to crimes in progress or situations where there are risks of injury or threats to life or property. Response time commences with the dispatch of an officer and ends with the arrival of the officer at the scene of the incident. The officer may be dispatched while on patrol or from the police station.

Police Services

Summary of Key Dimensions of Service

City or Town	Police Department Accredited?	Number of Sworn Officers	Average Length of Service for Sworn Officers (Years)	Number of Patrol Vehicles	Reporting Format	Part I Crimes			Part II Crimes	Dispatched Calls	Number of Traffic Accidents
						Against Persons	Against Property	Total			
Apex	Yes	96.0	13.1	112	IBR	33	612	645	1,697	60,834	1,023
Chapel Hill	No	117	12.8	77	IBR	80	910	990	2,633	27,679	974
Concord	No	187	6.2	226	IBR	98	1,514	1,612	2,276	124,351	3,506
Goldsboro	No	108	10.4	101	IBR	217	1,882	2,099	1,761	53,479	1,441
Greensboro	Yes	675	11.6	223	IBR	2,472	10,677	13,149	13,967	208,373	8,979
Hickory	No	116	8.2	144	IBR	150	1,803	1,953	4,324	98,159	2,321
Raleigh	Yes	796	12.5	820	NIBRS	1,587	10,660	12,247	NA	357,903	31,425
Wilson	Yes	125	10.7	128	IBR	230	1,432	1,662	2,686	104,481	2,563
Winston-Salem	Yes	558	11.5	418	NIBRS	2,861	12,342	15,203	32,151	213,719	9,969

EXPLANATORY FACTORS

These are factors that the project found affected police services performance and cost in one or more of the municipalities:

Demographic makeup of the community
Community policing policies
Population density and land area
Downtown area characteristics
Use of incident-based reporting
Presence of unique problems in particular areas, such as drugs or gangs
Emphasis on quick response to all calls
Vehicle take-home policy
Beat structure
Use of special units

Fiscal Year 2019-20

Explanatory Information

Service Level and Delivery

The Town of Apex Police Department provides an array of police services, including patrol, investigations, a special response unit, and school resource officers at the high school and middle schools located in the town.

The city had ninety-six sworn officer positions authorized for the year, with an average length of service of over thirteen years. Police services occupies a headquarters located in downtown Apex, newly built in 2010, which houses all divisions in the department. There is also an unmanned substation attached to one of the town fire stations.

Officers in Apex in the patrol division work twelve-hour modified DuPont schedules. Each patrol squad is also assigned a flex officer. The traffic unit works a modified DuPont schedule based on crash statistics. The investigations division works Monday through Friday from 8 a.m. to 5 p.m., with one investigator working from 2 p.m. to 11 p.m. The investigator working the late shift is also the on-call investigator, and this position rotates every week.

Patrol and investigation units are assigned individual vehicles. Command staff also have individually assigned vehicles, which are the only take-home vehicles in the fleet.

The police department was successful in clearing a total of 217 Part I cases during the fiscal year.

The definition of a high-priority call in Apex is any call which the immediate arrival and presence of the police may prevent death or injury or alleviate the threat of death or injury.

Conditions Affecting Service, Performance, and Costs

Municipal Profile

Population (OSBM 2019)	61,319
Land Area (Square Miles)	23.61
Persons per Square Mile	2,597
Median Household Income	$84,000
U.S. Census 2016	

Service Profile

FTE Positions—Sworn	96.0
FTE Positions—Other	9.0
Marked and Unmarked Patrol Vehicles	112
Part I Crimes Reported	
Homicide	0
Rape	7
Robbery	1
Assault	25
Burglary	108
Larceny	487
Auto Theft	17
Arson	0
TOTAL	645
Part II Crimes Reported	1,697
Part I Crimes Cleared	
Persons	19
Property	198
TOTAL	217
Reporting Format	IBR
Number of Calls Dispatched	60,834
Number of Traffic Accidents	1,023
Property Damage for Accidents	$4,796,077

Full Cost Profile

Cost Breakdown by Percentage	
Personal Services	65.2%
Operating Costs	22.3%
Capital Costs	12.5%
TOTAL	100.0%
Cost Breakdown in Dollars	
Personal Services	$9,088,808
Operating Costs	$3,110,832
Capital Costs	$1,737,941
TOTAL	$13,937,581

Key: Apex ▒ Benchmarking Average —

Fiscal Years 2016 through 2020

Resource Measures

Police Services Costs per Capita

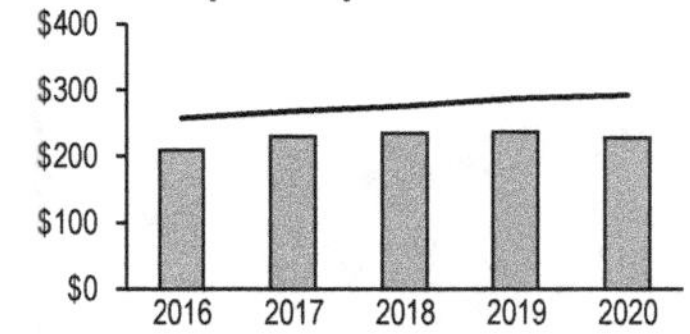

	2016	2017	2018	2019	2020
Apex	$209	$229	$234	$236	$227
Average	$257	$267	$275	$286	$291

Total Police Services Personnel per 10,000 Population

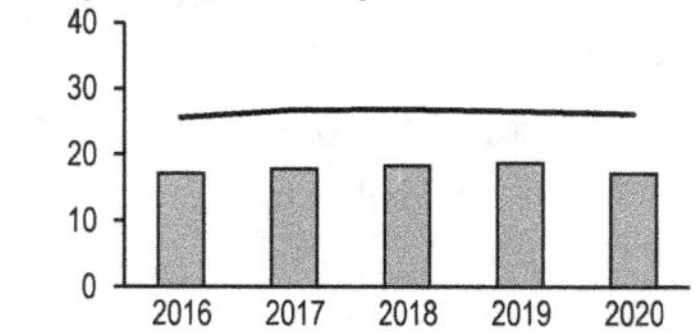

	2016	2017	2018	2019	2020
Apex	17.2	17.8	18.3	18.7	17.1
Average	25.6	26.6	26.7	26.5	26.1

Sworn Police Officers per 10,000 Population

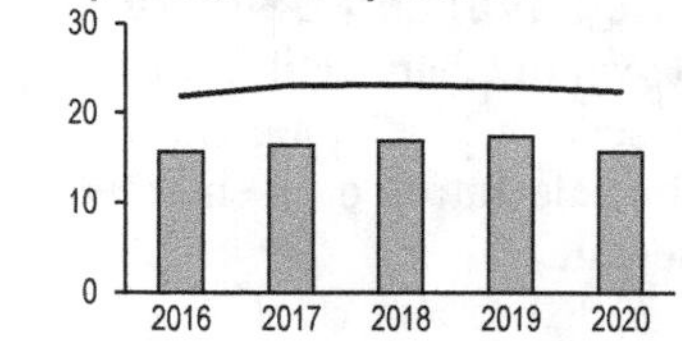

	2016	2017	2018	2019	2020
Apex	15.6	16.4	16.8	17.4	15.7
Average	21.8	23.0	23.1	22.9	22.4

Workload Measures

Calls Dispatched per 1,000 Population

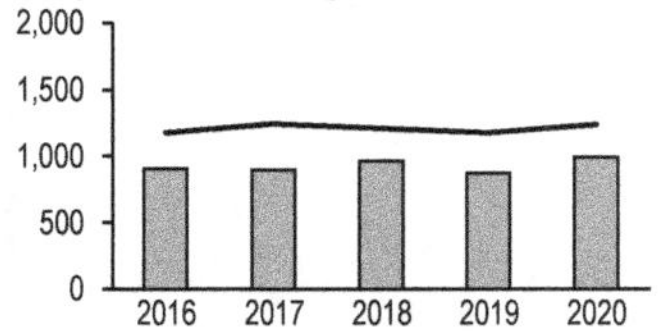

	2016	2017	2018	2019	2020
Apex	905	898	965	873	992
Average	1,176	1,246	1,211	1,178	1,236

Part I Crimes per 1,000 Population

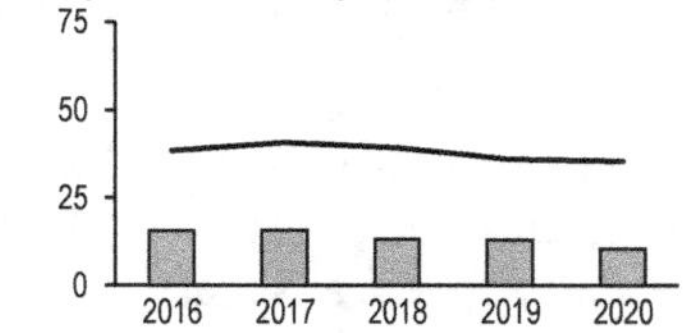

	2016	2017	2018	2019	2020
Apex	15.5	15.8	13.2	13.1	10.5
Average	38.3	40.8	39.3	35.9	35.4

Efficiency Measures

Police Services Cost per Call Dispatched

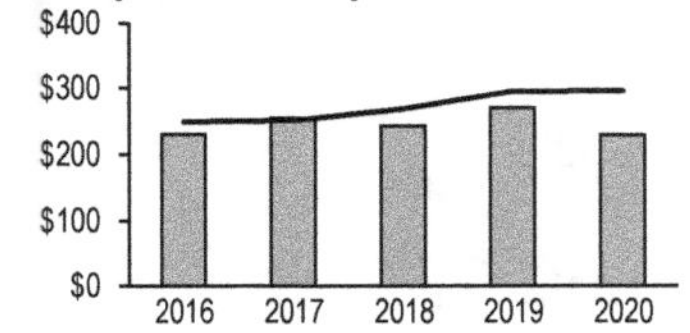

	2016	2017	2018	2019	2020
Apex	$230	$255	$243	$270	$229
Average	$248	$251	$268	$294	$296

Calls Dispatched per Sworn Officer

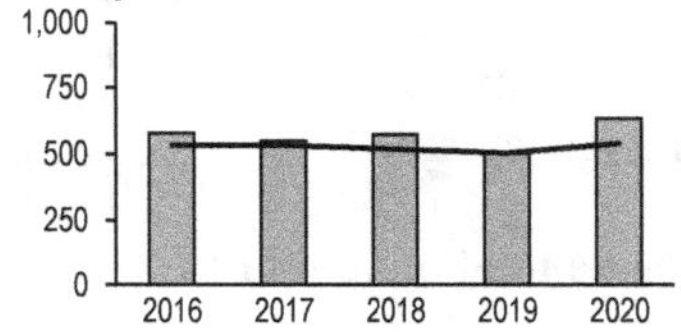

	2016	2017	2018	2019	2020
Apex	578	548	573	502	634
Average	531	532	518	501	539

Police Services Cost per Part I Case Cleared

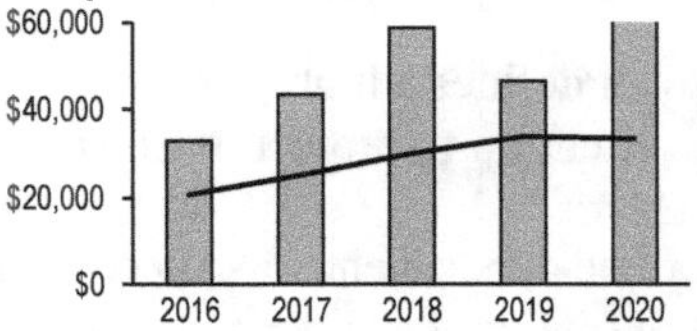

	2016	2017	2018	2019	2020
Apex	$32,860	$43,413	$58,864	$46,407	$64,228
Average	$20,634	$25,225	$30,061	$33,791	$33,378

Part I Cases Cleared per Sworn Officer

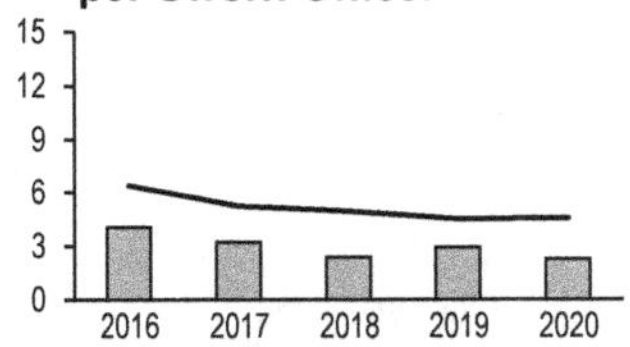

	2016	2017	2018	2019	2020
Apex	4.1	3.2	2.4	2.9	2.3
Average	6.4	5.2	4.9	4.5	4.5

Effectiveness Measures

Percentage of Part I Cases Cleared of Those Reported

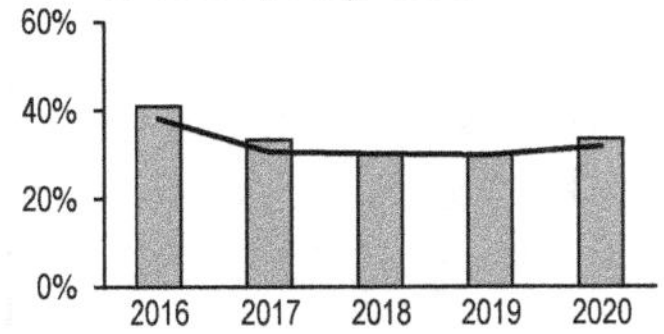

	2016	2017	2018	2019	2020
Apex	40.9%	33.4%	30.1%	30.1%	33.6%
Average	38.2%	30.7%	30.1%	30.0%	31.8%

Response Time to High Priority Calls in Minutes

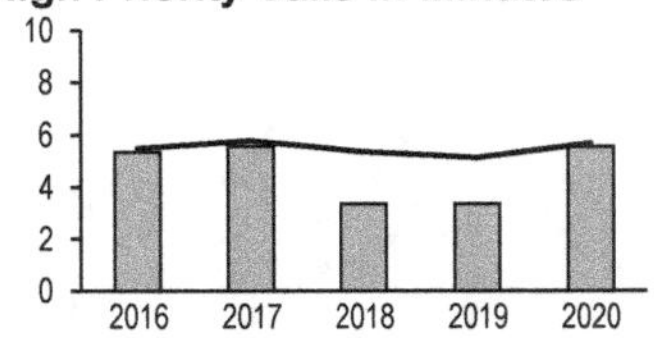

	2016	2017	2018	2019	2020
Apex	5.4	5.6	3.4	3.4	5.5
Average	5.5	5.8	5.3	5.1	5.7

Fiscal Year 2019-20

Explanatory Information

Service Level and Delivery

The Town of Chapel Hill Police Department provides an array of police services, including patrol, investigations, a special response unit, bicycle patrol, drug enforcement, limited laboratory work, and a canine unit.

The town had 117 sworn officer positions authorized for the fiscal year, with an average length of service of 12.8 years. Police headquarters is located in a separate building. The department also operates four substations. Three of the substations function as offices for community services, and the fourth is located downtown and functions as a space for report processing but is not regularly staffed.

In order to provide continuous service to the citizens of Chapel Hill, officers work twelve hour shifts and are assigned to either day (6 a.m. to 6 p.m.) or night (6 p.m. to 6 a.m.) shifts. Each shift selects a number of officers to report one to two hours early to cover calls that occur leading up to shift change.

Vehicles are allocated to divisions in the department and are assigned by unit level supervisors. Individual assignments are made for certain positions, but the only officers allowed to take home vehicles are K9 units, administrative officers, and on-call investigators.

The town defines a high-priority call as one that requires immediate police attention to protect persons or render emergency aid.

The police department was successful in clearing a total of 409 Part I cases during the fiscal year.

Conditions Affecting Service, Performance, and Costs

Reported cases cleared was up in FY 2015–16 by 68 percent for Part I crimes over the prior year. This was due to an improvement in data tracking.

The average response time to high-priority calls reflects the response time of the first arriving unit. Self-initiated calls with a response time of zero are included in the average response time to high-priority calls.

Municipal Profile

Population (OSBM 2019)	63,639
Land Area (Square Miles)	21.31
Persons per Square Mile	2,987
Median Household Income U.S. Census 2016	$60,802

Service Profile

FTE Positions—Sworn	117.0
FTE Positions—Other	16.0
Marked and Unmarked Patrol Vehicles	77
Part I Crimes Reported	
Homicide	0
Rape	10
Robbery	23
Assault	47
Burglary	177
Larceny	687
Auto Theft	43
Arson	3
TOTAL	990
Part II Crimes Reported	2,633
Part I Crimes Cleared	
Persons	36
Property	373
TOTAL	409
Reporting Format	IBR
Number of Calls Dispatched	27,679
Number of Traffic Accidents	974
Property Damage for Accidents	$4,919,225

Full Cost Profile

Cost Breakdown by Percentage	
Personal Services	63.7%
Operating Costs	29.4%
Capital Costs	7.0%
TOTAL	100.0%
Cost Breakdown in Dollars	
Personal Services	$10,536,593
Operating Costs	$4,862,715
Capital Costs	$1,152,707
TOTAL	$16,552,015

Key: Chapel Hill ■ Benchmarking Average — Fiscal Years 2016 through 2020

Resource Measures

Police Services Costs per Capita

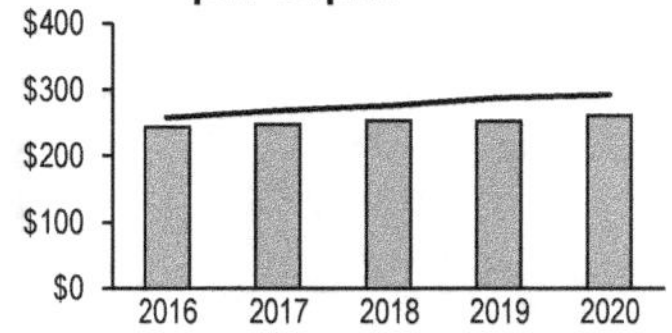

	2016	2017	2018	2019	2020
Chapel Hill	$243	$246	$253	$252	$260
Average	$257	$267	$275	$286	$291

Total Police Services Personnel per 10,000 Population

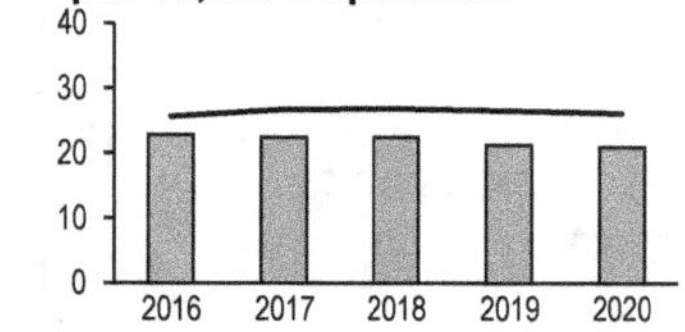

	2016	2017	2018	2019	2020
Chapel Hill	22.8	22.4	22.4	21.2	20.9
Average	25.6	26.6	26.7	26.5	26.1

Sworn Police Officers per 10,000 Population

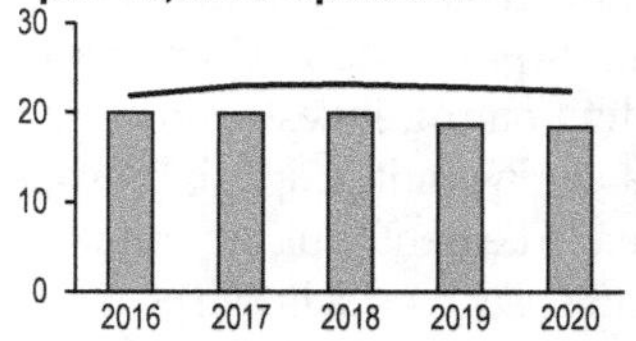

	2016	2017	2018	2019	2020
Chapel Hill	20.0	19.9	19.9	18.7	18.4
Average	21.8	23.0	23.1	22.9	22.4

Workload Measures

Calls Dispatched per 1,000 Population

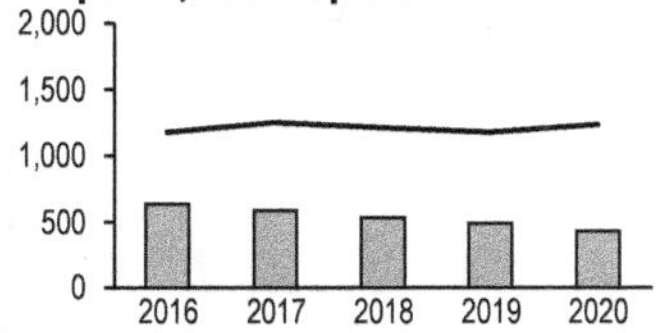

	2016	2017	2018	2019	2020
Chapel Hill	638	589	535	492	435
Average	1,176	1,246	1,211	1,178	1,236

Part I Crimes per 1,000 Population

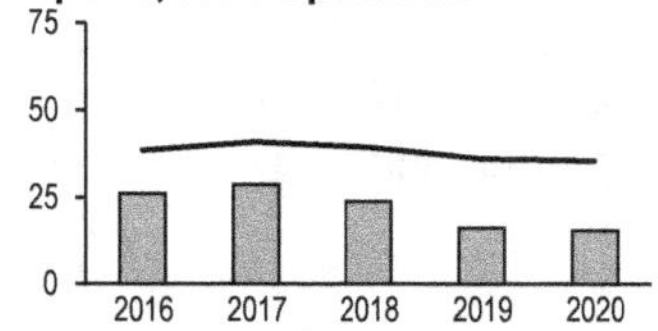

	2016	2017	2018	2019	2020
Chapel Hill	26.0	28.7	23.9	16.3	15.6
Average	38.3	40.8	39.3	35.9	35.4

Efficiency Measures

Police Services Cost per Call Dispatched

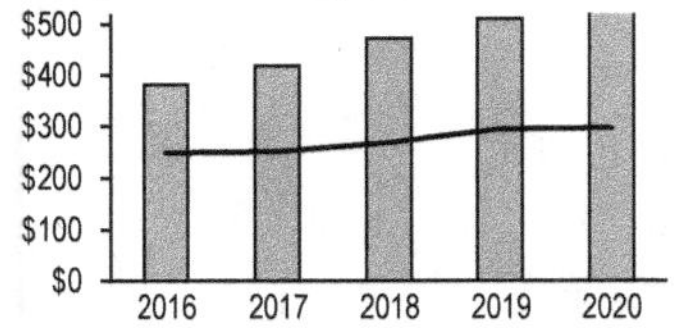

	2016	2017	2018	2019	2020
Chapel Hill	$381	$418	$473	$512	$598
Average	$248	$251	$268	$294	$296

Calls Dispatched per Sworn Officer

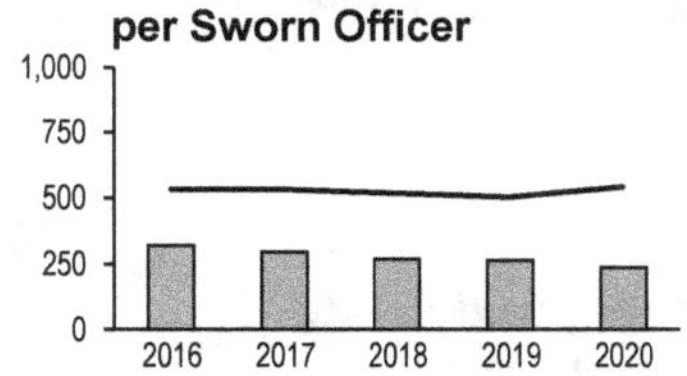

	2016	2017	2018	2019	2020
Chapel Hill	319	296	270	264	237
Average	531	532	518	501	539

Police Services Cost per Part I Case Cleared

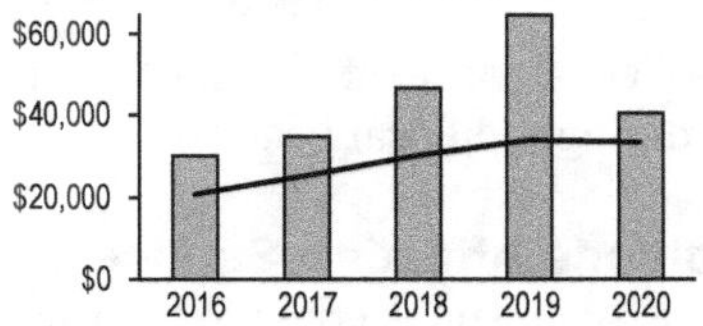

	2016	2017	2018	2019	2020
Chapel Hill	$30,063	$34,782	$46,509	$64,744	$40,469
Average	$20,634	$25,225	$30,061	$33,791	$33,378

Part I Cases Cleared per Sworn Officer

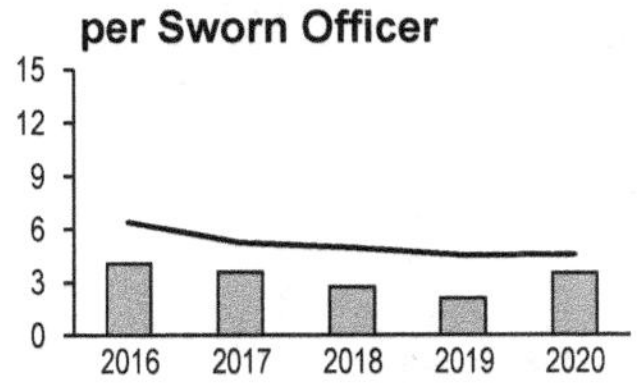

	2016	2017	2018	2019	2020
Chapel Hill	4.1	3.6	2.7	2.1	3.5
Average	6.4	5.2	4.9	4.5	4.5

Effectiveness Measures

Percentage of Part I Cases Cleared of Those Reported

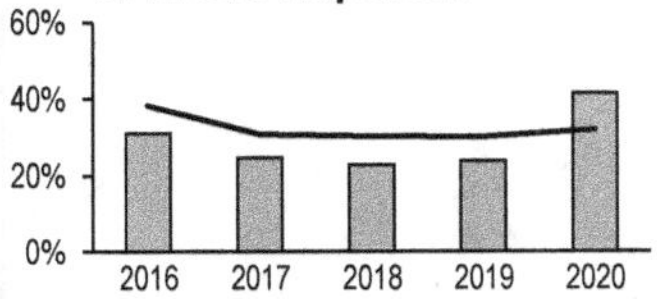

	2016	2017	2018	2019	2020
Chapel Hill	31.1%	24.7%	22.8%	23.9%	41.3%
Average	38.2%	30.7%	30.1%	30.0%	31.8%

Response Time to High Priority Calls in Minutes

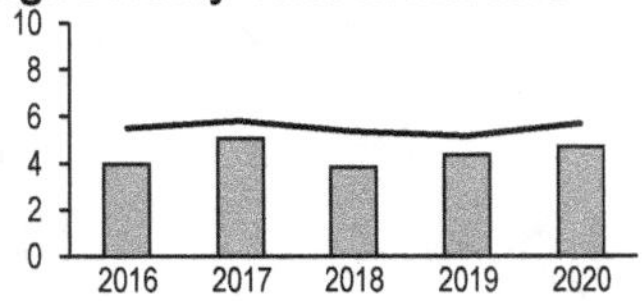

	2016	2017	2018	2019	2020
Chapel Hill	4.0	5.1	3.8	4.4	4.7
Average	5.5	5.8	5.3	5.1	5.7

Fiscal Year 2019-20

Explanatory Information

Service Level and Delivery

Concord's police department provides an array of police services, including patrol, investigations, a traffic unit, a telephone response unit, a canine unit, a special response unit, a bicycle patrol unit, a drug enforcement unit, a limited forensic laboratory, and other programs, such as school resource officers.

The city had 187 sworn officer positions authorized for the fiscal year, with an average length of service of 6.2 years. The police headquarters is in a new separate building located downtown. Four substations are used: two in fire stations and two in shopping malls.

Uniformed patrol officers work twelve-hour rotating shifts. Investigators work five eight-hour days on first and second shifts. District Commanders have the authority to change individual schedules to meet peak demands.

The city defines high-priority emergency calls as those involving an assault in progress, personal injury, breaking and entering, or robbery in progress.

Concord uses a one-on-one car plan. Officers may take their vehicles home if they live in the city or within one mile of the city limits.

The police department was successful in clearing a total of 599 Part I cases during the fiscal year.

Conditions Affecting Service, Performance, and Costs

The average response time to high-priority calls reflects the response time of the first arriving unit. Self-initiated calls are not included.

Concord's high clearance rate has been driven by a focus on clearing larceny cases by arrest or by exhausting leads as quickly as possible. Because larcenies are the largest category of Part I crimes, this effort has substantially improved the overall clearance rate. The lower clearance rates in the last few years is driven mostly by more accurate data reporting rather than a drop in results.

Municipal Profile

Population (OSBM 2019)	95,453
Land Area (Square Miles)	63.65
Persons per Square Mile	1,500
Median Household Income U.S. Census 2016	$50,863

Service Profile

FTE Positions—Sworn	187.00
FTE Positions—Other	21.0
Marked and Unmarked Patrol Vehicles	226
Part I Crimes Reported	
Homicide	5
Rape	10
Robbery	26
Assault	57
Burglary	111
Larceny	1,276
Auto Theft	122
Arson	5
TOTAL	1,612
Part II Crimes Reported	2,276
Part I Crimes Cleared	
Persons	64
Property	535
TOTAL	599
Reporting Format	IBR
Number of Calls Dispatched	124,351
Number of Traffic Accidents	3,506
Property Damage for Accidents	$12,941,870

Full Cost Profile

Cost Breakdown by Percentage	
Personal Services	67.4%
Operating Costs	23.7%
Capital Costs	8.9%
TOTAL	100.0%
Cost Breakdown in Dollars	
Personal Services	$17,069,870
Operating Costs	$5,997,753
Capital Costs	$2,251,430
TOTAL	$25,319,053

Concord

Police Services

Key: Concord ▒ Benchmarking Average — Fiscal Years 2016 through 2020

Resource Measures

Police Services Costs per Capita

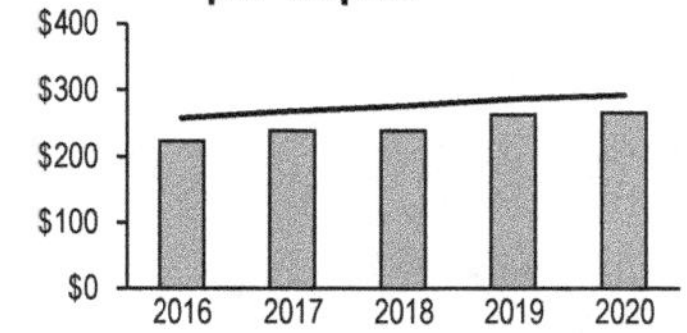

	2016	2017	2018	2019	2020
Concord	$223	$239	$238	$263	$265
Average	$257	$267	$275	$286	$291

Total Police Services Personnel per 10,000 Population

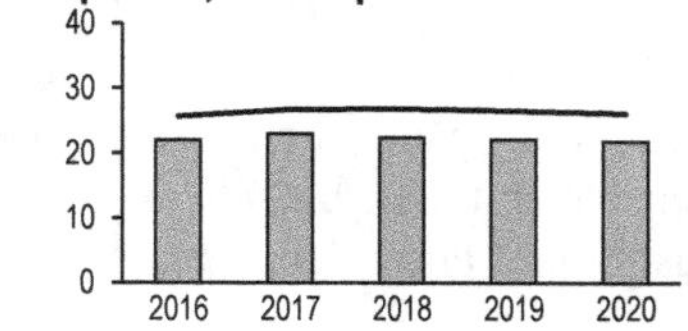

	2016	2017	2018	2019	2020
Concord	22.1	23.0	22.5	22.1	21.8
Average	25.6	26.6	26.7	26.5	26.1

Sworn Police Officers per 10,000 Population

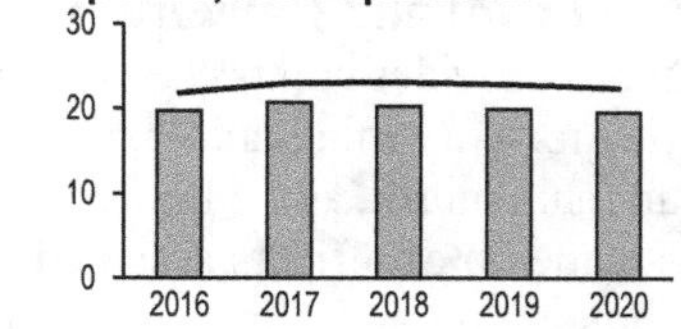

	2016	2017	2018	2019	2020
Concord	19.8	20.7	20.3	20.0	19.6
Average	21.8	23.0	23.1	22.9	22.4

Workload Measures

Calls Dispatched per 1,000 Population

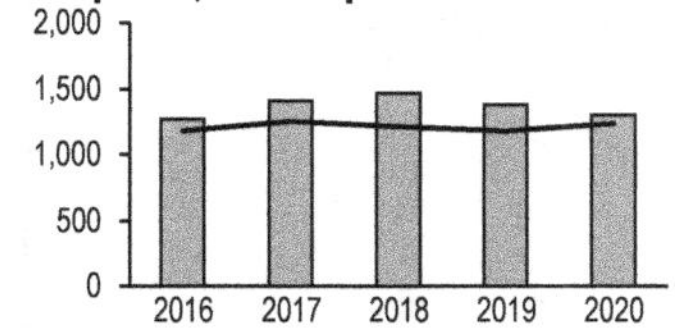

	2016	2017	2018	2019	2020
Concord	1,271	1,411	1,469	1,382	1,303
Average	1,176	1,246	1,211	1,178	1,236

Part I Crimes per 1,000 Population

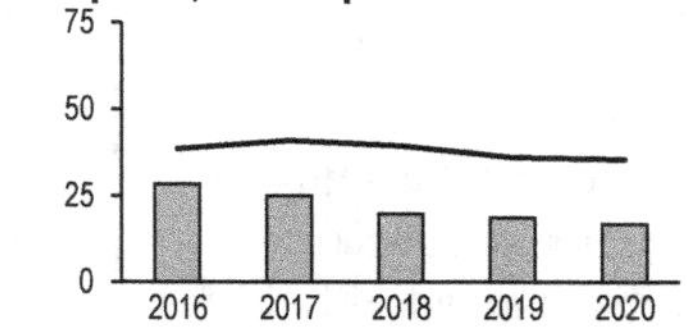

	2016	2017	2018	2019	2020
Concord	28.3	25.0	19.9	18.6	16.9
Average	38.3	40.8	39.3	35.9	35.4

Efficiency Measures

Police Services Cost per Call Dispatched

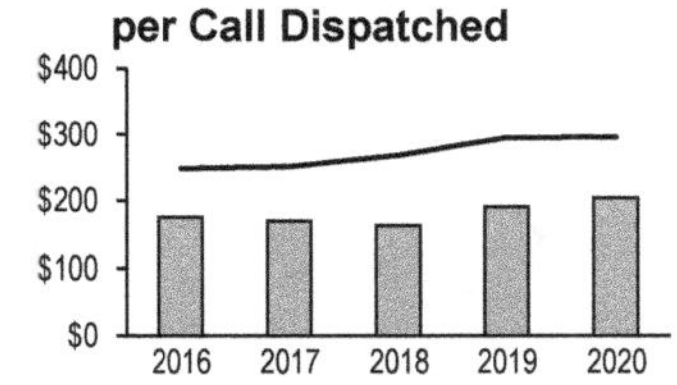

	2016	2017	2018	2019	2020
Concord	$175	$169	$162	$190	$204
Average	$248	$251	$268	$294	$296

Calls Dispatched per Sworn Officer

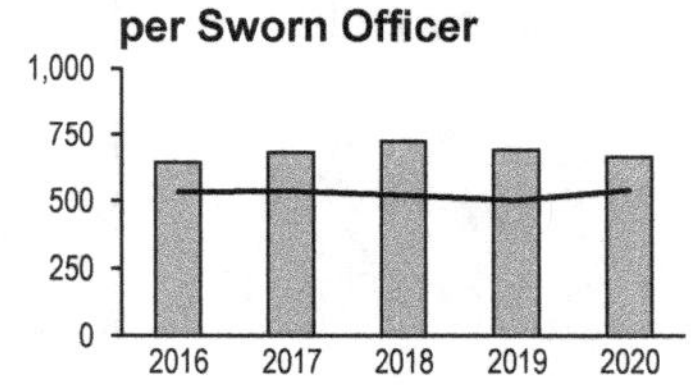

	2016	2017	2018	2019	2020
Concord	643	681	725	692	665
Average	531	532	518	501	539

Police Services Cost per Part I Case Cleared

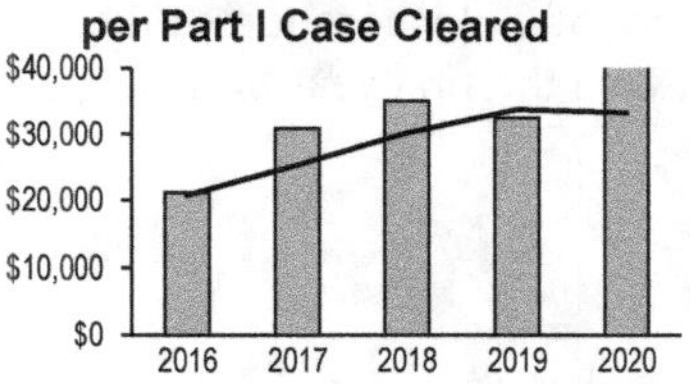

	2016	2017	2018	2019	2020
Concord	$21,121	$30,846	$35,154	$32,628	$42,269
Average	$20,634	$25,225	$30,061	$33,791	$33,378

Part I Cases Cleared per Sworn Officer

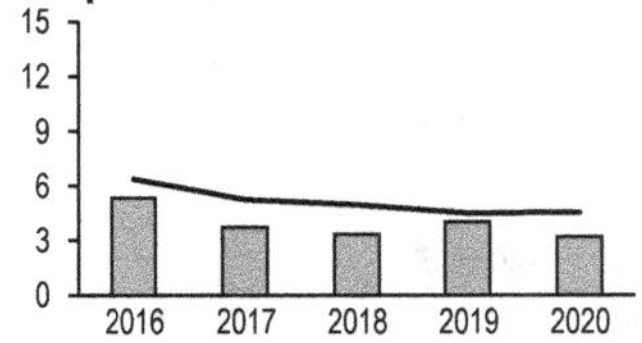

	2016	2017	2018	2019	2020
Concord	5.3	3.7	3.3	4.0	3.2
Average	6.4	5.2	4.9	4.5	4.5

Effectiveness Measures

Percentage of Part I Cases Cleared of Those Reported

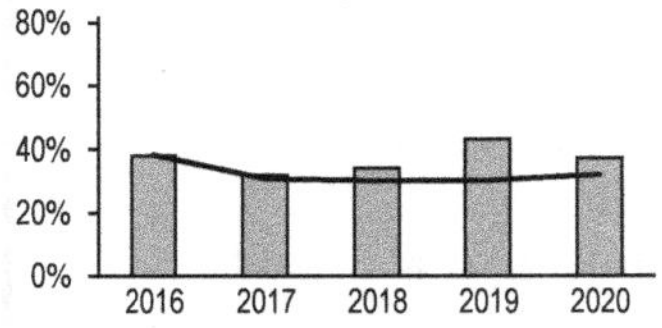

	2016	2017	2018	2019	2020
Concord	38.0%	32.0%	34.1%	43.2%	37.2%
Average	38.2%	30.7%	30.1%	30.0%	31.8%

Response Time to High Priority Calls in Minutes

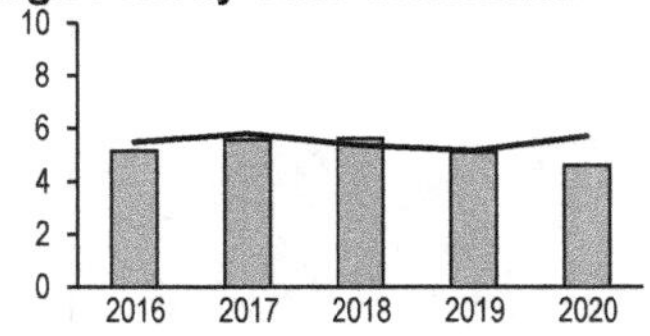

	2016	2017	2018	2019	2020
Concord	5.2	5.6	5.6	5.1	4.6
Average	5.5	5.8	5.3	5.1	5.7

Fiscal Year 2019-20

Explanatory Information

Service Level and Delivery

Goldsboro provides comprehensive police services, including patrol, investigations, a canine unit, a bicycle patrol unit, a drug enforcement unit, animal control, and a limited service forensics unit. The bicycle unit is made up of officers assigned to the housing unit and selective enforcement unit and is not a stand-alone unit.

The city had 108 sworn officers authorized for the fiscal year with an average length of service of 10.43 years. The police department is housed in a complex that is shared with the fire department, with each department having its own entrance but sharing a gym and locker rooms.

Uniformed officers work a total of 2,052 hours per year while investigators work a total of 2,080 hours. Schedules can be adjusted at any time according to call demand, special events, or special incidents. Officers are assigned a vehicle once they are out of field training. They can drive a vehicle home if they live within Wayne County.

Conditions Affecting Service, Performance, and Costs

The City of Goldsboro joined the Benchmarking Project in July 2017, with the first year of data showing for FY 2016–17.

Municipal Profile

Population (OSBM 2019)	33,969
Land Area (Square Miles)	29.45
Persons per Square Mile	1,154
Median Household Income U.S. Census 2016	$32,148

Service Profile

FTE Positions—Sworn	108.0
FTE Positions—Other	13.0
Marked and Unmarked Patrol Vehicles	101
Part I Crimes Reported	
Homicide	0
Rape	10
Robbery	51
Assault	156
Burglary	323
Larceny	1,461
Auto Theft	95
Arson	3
TOTAL	2,099
Part II Crimes Reported	1,761
Part I Crimes Cleared	
Persons	76
Property	418
TOTAL	494
Reporting Format	IBR
Number of Calls Dispatched	53,479
Number of Traffic Accidents	1,441
Property Damage for Accidents	$6,133,874

Full Cost Profile

Cost Breakdown by Percentage	
Personal Services	82.2%
Operating Costs	15.2%
Capital Costs	2.6%
TOTAL	100.0%
Cost Breakdown in Dollars	
Personal Services	$7,929,840
Operating Costs	$1,463,508
Capital Costs	$254,124
TOTAL	$9,647,472

Key: Goldsboro ■ Benchmarking Average — Fiscal Years 2016 through 2020

Resource Measures

Police Services Costs per Capita

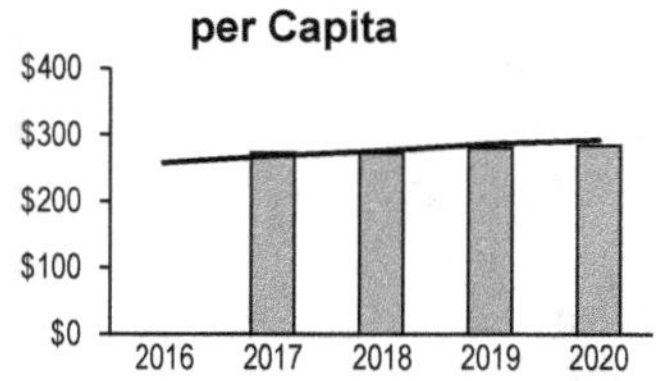

	2016	2017	2018	2019	2020
Goldsboro		$272	$273	$280	$284
Average	$257	$267	$275	$286	$291

Total Police Services Personnel per 10,000 Population

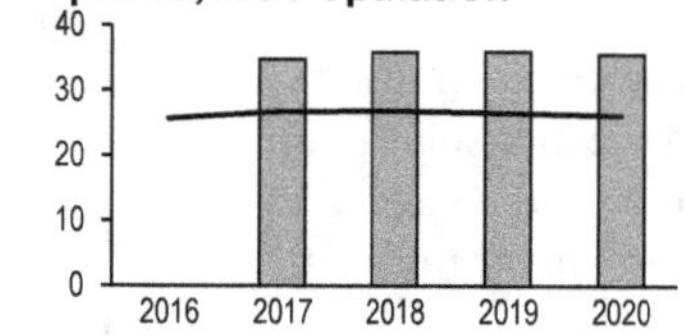

	2016	2017	2018	2019	2020
Goldsboro		34.8	35.9	36.0	35.6
Average	25.6	26.6	26.7	26.5	26.1

Sworn Police Officers per 10,000 Population

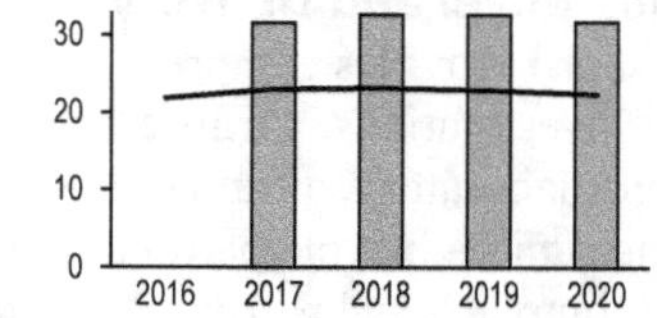

	2016	2017	2018	2019	2020
Goldsboro		31.6	32.7	32.7	31.8
Average	21.8	23.0	23.1	22.9	22.4

Workload Measures

Calls Dispatched per 1,000 Population

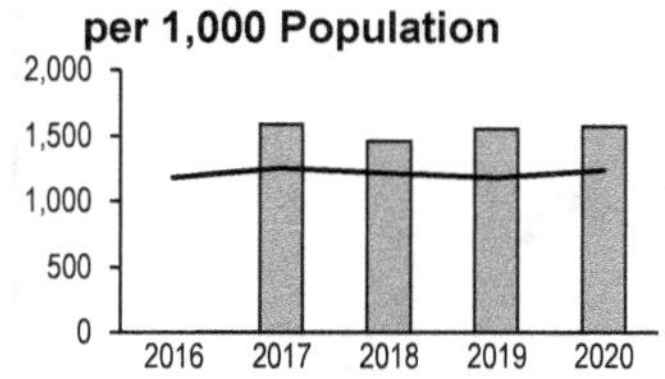

	2016	2017	2018	2019	2020
Goldsboro		1,588	1,458	1,555	1,574
Average	1,176	1,246	1,211	1,178	1,236

Part I Crimes per 1,000 Population

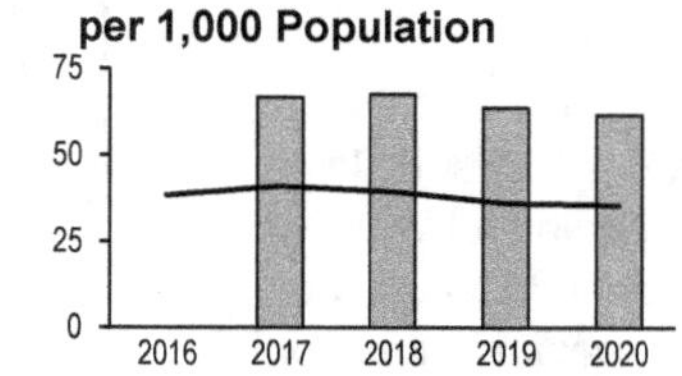

	2016	2017	2018	2019	2020
Goldsboro		66.7	67.6	63.8	61.8
Average	38.3	40.8	39.3	35.9	35.4

Efficiency Measures

Police Services Cost per Call Dispatched

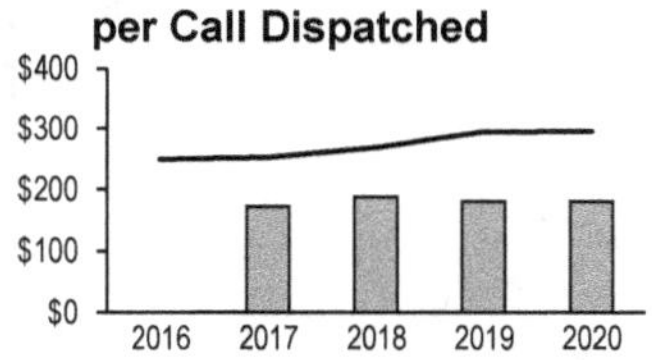

	2016	2017	2018	2019	2020
Goldsboro		$171	$187	$180	$180
Average	$248	$251	$268	$294	$296

Calls Dispatched per Sworn Officer

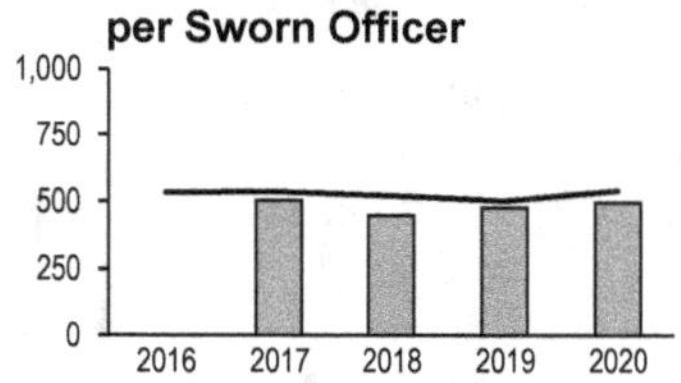

	2016	2017	2018	2019	2020
Goldsboro		502	447	476	495
Average	531	532	518	501	539

Police Services Cost per Part I Case Cleared

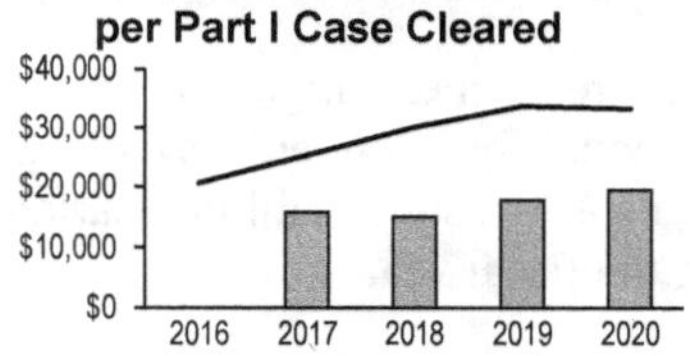

	2016	2017	2018	2019	2020
Goldsboro		$15,735	$15,039	$17,835	$19,529
Average	$20,634	$25,225	$30,061	$33,791	$33,378

Part I Cases Cleared per Sworn Officer

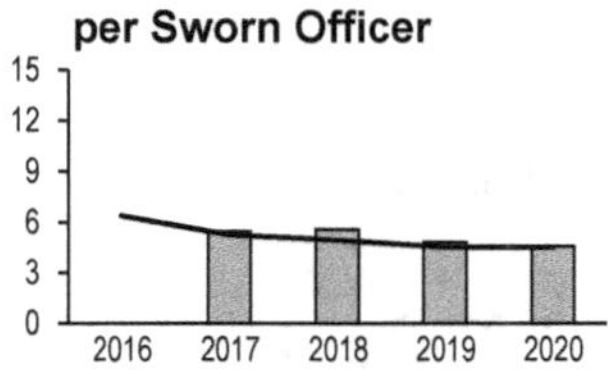

	2016	2017	2018	2019	2020
Goldsboro		5.5	5.6	4.8	4.6
Average	6.4	5.2	4.9	4.5	4.5

Effectiveness Measures

Percentage of Part I Cases Cleared of Those Reported

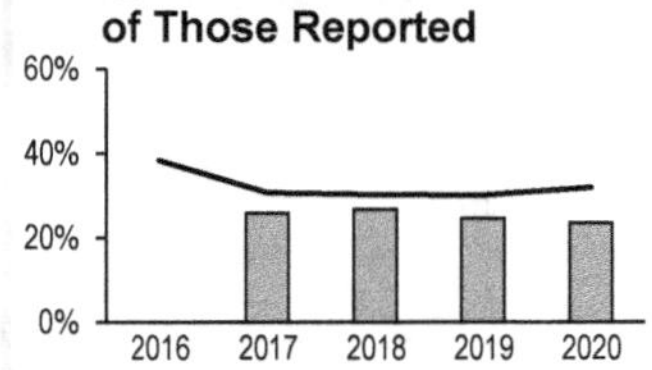

	2016	2017	2018	2019	2020
Goldsboro		25.9%	26.8%	24.6%	23.5%
Average	38.2%	30.7%	30.1%	30.0%	31.8%

Response Time to High Priority Calls in Minutes

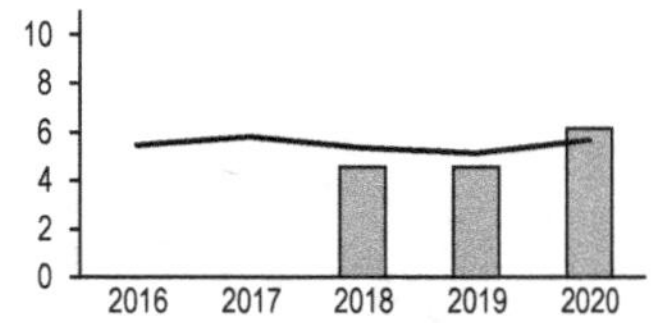

	2016	2017	2018	2019	2020
Goldsboro			4.6	4.6	6.2
Average	5.5	5.8	5.3	5.1	5.7

Fiscal Year 2019-20

Explanatory Information

Service Level and Delivery
Greensboro provides comprehensive police services, including patrol, investigations, a traffic unit, a telephone response unit, a forensics laboratory, a canine unit, a motorcycle unit, a special response unit, a bicycle patrol unit, a drug enforcement unit, and a student outreach and recruiting program.

The city had 675 sworn officer positions authorized for the fiscal year, with an average length of service of 11.6 years. The police department is housed in a stand-alone headquarters facility. The city also has three substations that serve as remote line-up facilities.

Patrol officers work a four-days-on and four-days-off fixed schedule. There are four shifts each day, with each patrol officer shift lasting eleven hours. Investigators and administrative personnel work Monday through Friday from 8 a.m. to 5 p.m. Schedules can be adjusted at any time according to call demand, special events, or special incidents.

Line patrol officers do take vehicles home during their tour of duty. Patrol supervisors, division commanders, and some investigators take vehicles home, depending on their assignments.

Greensboro defines a high-priority emergency call as one where there is a potential for imminent serious injury or death. The police department was successful in clearing a total of 2,916 Part I cases during the fiscal year.

Conditions Affecting Service, Performance, and Costs
The average response time to high-priority calls reflects the response time of the first arriving unit. Self-initiated calls with a response time of zero are included in the average response time to high-priority calls, with the exception of traffic stops and report-only calls.

Municipal Profile

Population (OSBM 2019)	293,730
Land Area (Square Miles)	129.62
Persons per Square Mile	2,266
Median Household Income U.S. Census 2016	$40,760

Service Profile

FTE Positions—Sworn	675.0
FTE Positions—Other	112.0
Marked and Unmarked Patrol Vehicles	223
Part I Crimes Reported	
Homicide	44
Rape	92
Robbery	621
Assault	1,715
Burglary	2,094
Larceny	7,451
Auto Theft	1,029
Arson	103
TOTAL	13,149
Part II Crimes Reported	13,967
Part I Crimes Cleared	
Persons	601
Property	2,315
TOTAL	2,916
Reporting Format	IBR
Number of Calls Dispatched	208,373
Number of Traffic Accidents	8,979
Property Damage for Accidents	$36,699,901

Full Cost Profile

Cost Breakdown by Percentage	
Personal Services	75.6%
Operating Costs	24.4%
Capital Costs	0.0%
TOTAL	100.0%
Cost Breakdown in Dollars	
Personal Services	$64,607,080
Operating Costs	$20,860,117
Capital Costs	$0
TOTAL	$85,467,197

Key: Greensboro ■ Benchmarking Average — Fiscal Years 2016 through 2020

Resource Measures

Police Services Costs per Capita

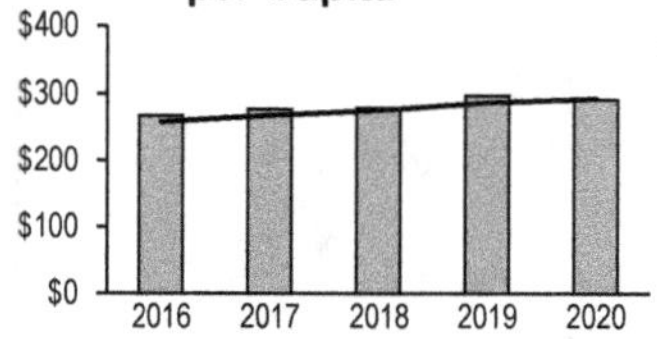

	2016	2017	2018	2019	2020
Greensboro	$266	$276	$278	$297	$291
Average	$257	$267	$275	$286	$291

Total Police Services Personnel per 10,000 Population

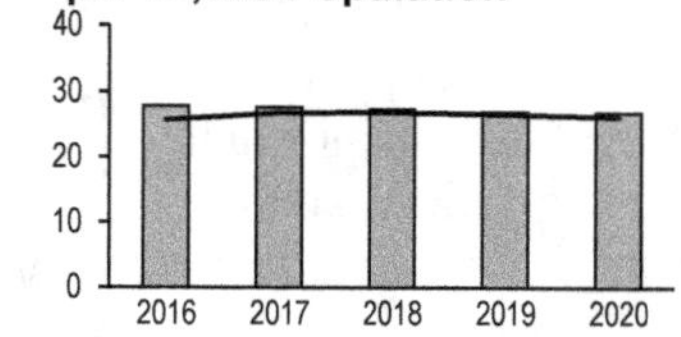

	2016	2017	2018	2019	2020
Greensboro	27.8	27.6	27.3	26.9	26.8
Average	25.6	26.6	26.7	26.5	26.1

Sworn Police Officers per 10,000 Population

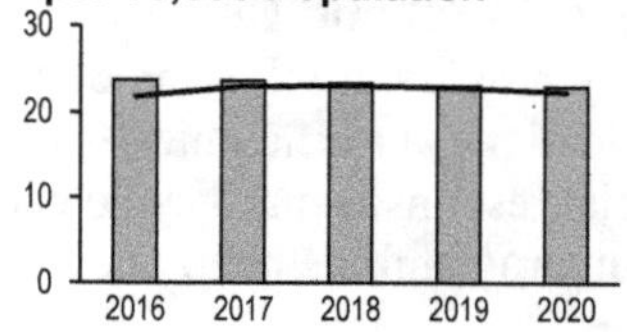

	2016	2017	2018	2019	2020
Greensboro	23.8	23.7	23.4	23.1	23.0
Average	21.8	23.0	23.1	22.9	22.4

Workload Measures

Calls Dispatched per 1,000 Population

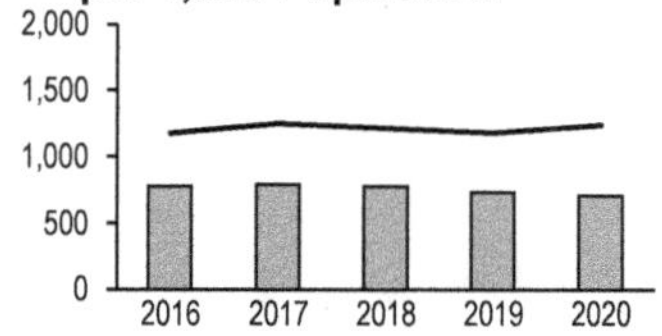

	2016	2017	2018	2019	2020
Greensboro	779	791	776	736	709
Average	1,176	1,246	1,211	1,178	1,236

Part I Crimes per 1,000 Population

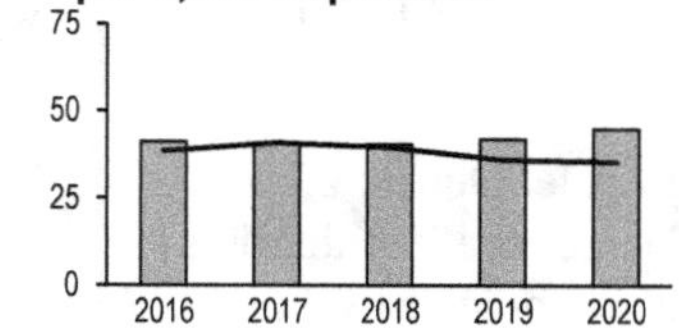

	2016	2017	2018	2019	2020
Greensboro	41.0	40.7	40.3	41.8	44.8
Average	38.3	40.8	39.3	35.9	35.4

Efficiency Measures

Police Services Cost per Call Dispatched

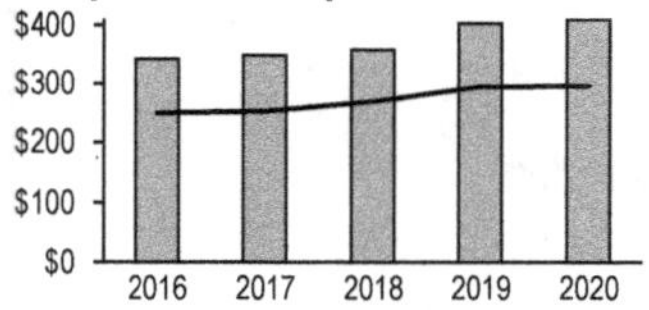

	2016	2017	2018	2019	2020
Greensboro	$342	$349	$359	$403	$410
Average	$248	$251	$268	$294	$296

Calls Dispatched per Sworn Officer

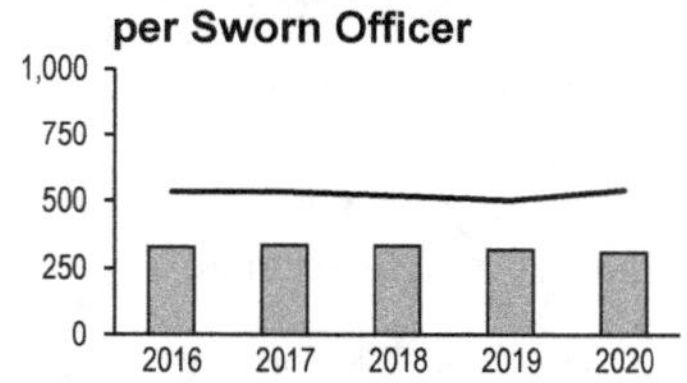

	2016	2017	2018	2019	2020
Greensboro	327	334	332	319	309
Average	531	532	518	501	539

Police Services Cost per Part I Case Cleared

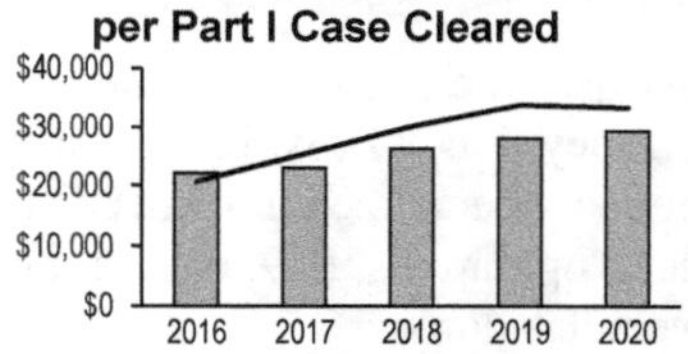

	2016	2017	2018	2019	2020
Greensboro	$22,107	$22,942	$26,279	$28,049	$29,310
Average	$20,634	$25,225	$30,061	$33,791	$33,378

Part I Cases Cleared per Sworn Officer

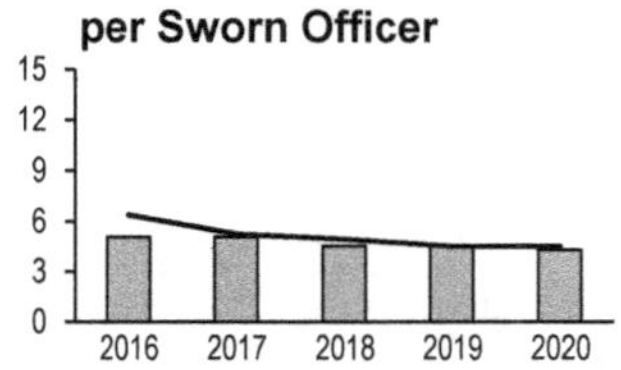

	2016	2017	2018	2019	2020
Greensboro	5.1	5.1	4.5	4.6	4.3
Average	6.4	5.2	4.9	4.5	4.5

Effectiveness Measures

Percentage of Part I Cases Cleared of Those Reported

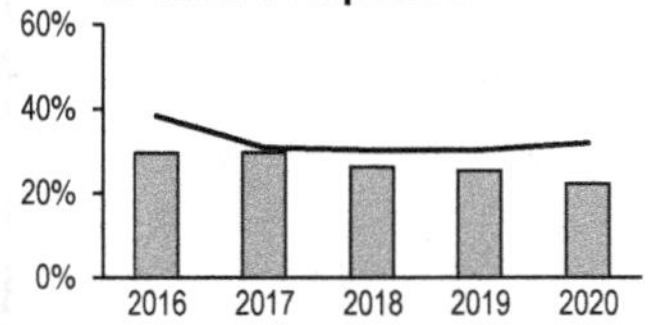

	2016	2017	2018	2019	2020
Greensboro	29.4%	29.6%	26.3%	25.3%	22.2%
Average	38.2%	30.7%	30.1%	30.0%	31.8%

Response Time to High Priority Calls in Minutes

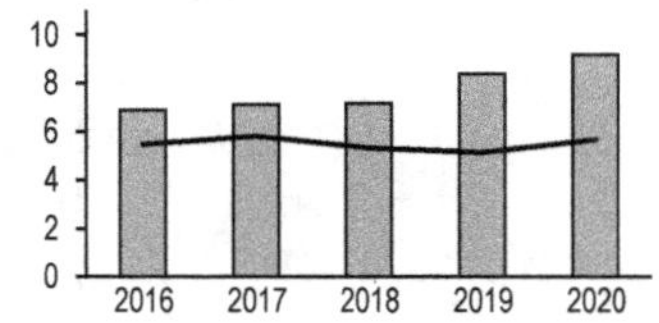

	2016	2017	2018	2019	2020
Greensboro	6.9	7.1	7.2	8.4	9.2
Average	5.5	5.8	5.3	5.1	5.7

Fiscal Year 2019-20

Explanatory Information

Service Level and Delivery

Hickory provides a full array of police services, including patrol, investigations, a traffic unit, a small laboratory facility, a canine unit, a special response unit, bicycle patrol, a jail/holding facility, animal control, drug enforcement, and a DARE program.

The city had 116 sworn officer positions authorized for the fiscal year, with an average length of service of 8.2 years. The police department occupies its own three-story facility, completed in January 1996. Each of the five community police areas has an office located in its respective community. These offices are not staffed. They are used for interviews, to obtain information, to store supplies, and to make phone calls.

Patrol officers work a fourteen-day, 80.5-hour cycle. During this period, officers work seven 11.5-hour days. Each of the five districts is commanded by a lieutenant who establishes schedules based on need.

Investigators work Monday through Friday, either from 8:30 a.m. to 5:00 p.m. or 3:30 p.m. to 12:00 a.m. for the second-shift on-call investigators.

Hickory uses the one-officer, one-car plan. Officers take vehicles home if they live in or within one mile of the city. Officers who are members of specialized units needed for emergency response, such as special operations, K-9, or criminial investigations, may also take their vehicles home.

Hickory defines high-priority emergency calls as those situations that present an in-progress threat to life or serious property loss. Officers are authorized to utilize blue lights and sirens during responses and may exceed posted speed limits by up to 20 miles per hour.

The police department was successful in clearing a total of 711 Part I cases during the fiscal year.

Conditions Affecting Service, Performance, and Costs

The average response time to high-priority calls reflects the response time of the first arriving unit. Self-initiated calls with a response time of zero are included in the average response time to high-priority calls.

Municipal Profile

Population (OSBM 2019)	41,409
Land Area (Square Miles)	30.50
Persons per Square Mile	1,358
Median Household Income	$35,353
U.S. Census 2016	

Service Profile

FTE Positions—Sworn	116.0
FTE Positions—Other	36.0
Marked and Unmarked Patrol Vehicles	144
Part I Crimes Reported	
Homicide	4
Rape	12
Robbery	35
Assault	99
Burglary	226
Larceny	1,433
Auto Theft	139
Arson	5
TOTAL	1,953
Part II Crimes Reported	4,324
Part I Crimes Cleared	
Persons	86
Property	625
TOTAL	711
Reporting Format	IBR
Number of Calls Dispatched	98,159
Number of Traffic Accidents	2,321
Property Damage for Accidents	$9,120,051

Full Cost Profile

Cost Breakdown by Percentage	
Personal Services	66.7%
Operating Costs	25.1%
Capital Costs	8.2%
TOTAL	100.0%
Cost Breakdown in Dollars	
Personal Services	$9,318,685
Operating Costs	$3,509,017
Capital Costs	$1,140,931
TOTAL	$13,968,633

Hickory

Police Services

Key: Hickory ▒ Benchmarking Average —

Fiscal Years 2016 through 2020

Resource Measures

Police Services Costs per Capita

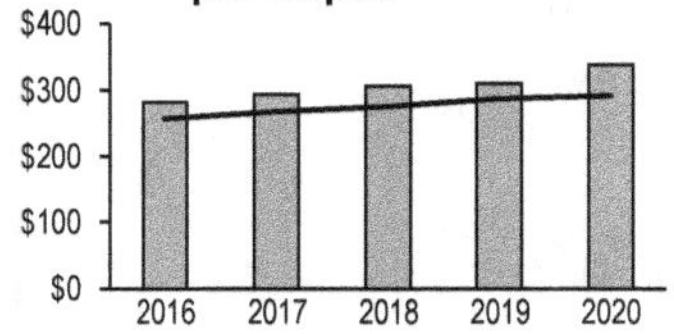

	2016	2017	2018	2019	2020
Hickory	$281	$293	$306	$310	$337
Average	$257	$267	$275	$286	$291

Total Police Services Personnel per 10,000 Population

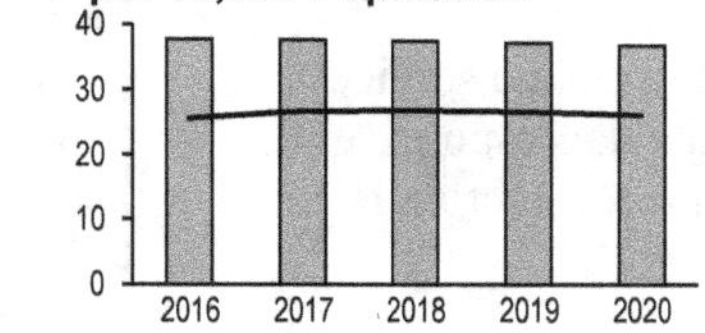

	2016	2017	2018	2019	2020
Hickory	37.7	37.6	37.4	37.1	36.7
Average	25.6	26.6	26.7	26.5	26.1

Sworn Police Officers per 10,000 Population

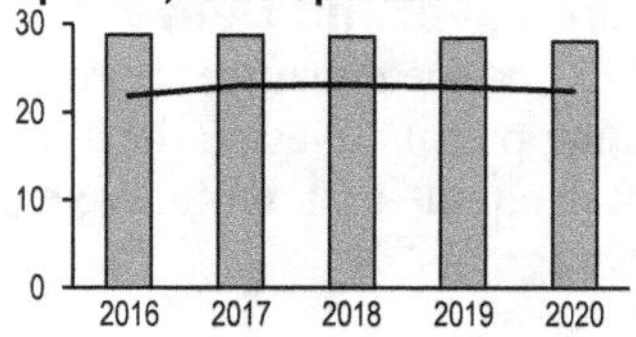

	2016	2017	2018	2019	2020
Hickory	28.7	28.7	28.5	28.3	28.0
Average	21.8	23.0	23.1	22.9	22.4

Workload Measures

Calls Dispatched per 1,000 Population

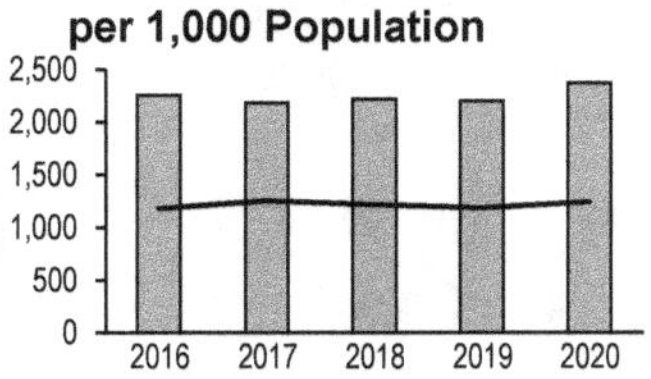

	2016	2017	2018	2019	2020
Hickory	2,253	2,179	2,215	2,199	2,370
Average	1,176	1,246	1,211	1,178	1,236

Part I Crimes per 1,000 Population

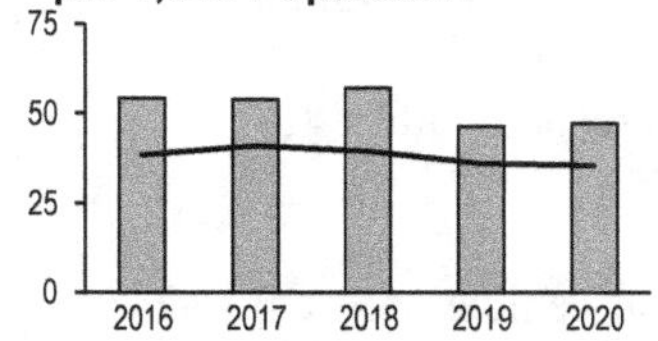

	2016	2017	2018	2019	2020
Hickory	54.2	53.8	57.0	46.4	47.2
Average	38.3	40.8	39.3	35.9	35.4

Efficiency Measures

Police Services Cost per Call Dispatched

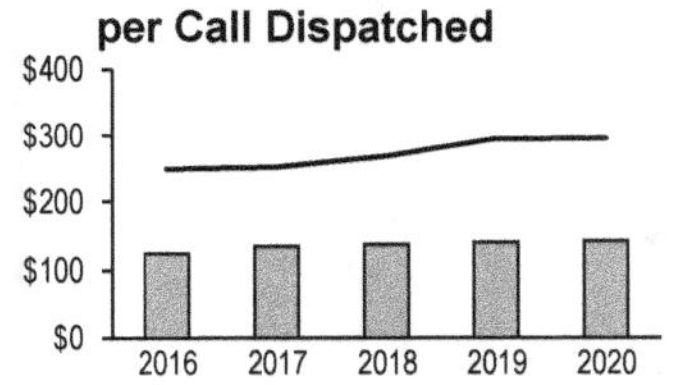

	2016	2017	2018	2019	2020
Hickory	$125	$135	$138	$141	$142
Average	$248	$251	$268	$294	$296

Calls Dispatched per Sworn Officer

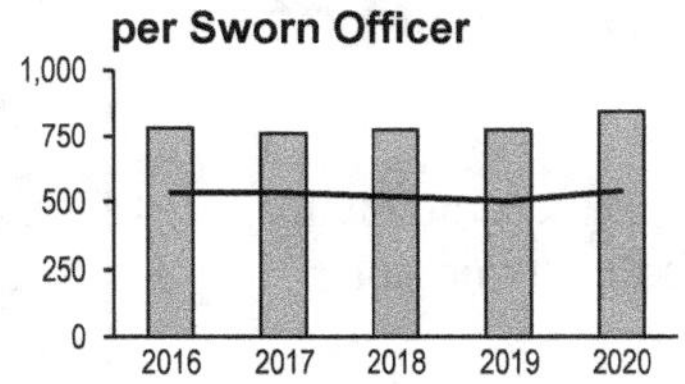

	2016	2017	2018	2019	2020
Hickory	784	760	776	776	846
Average	531	532	518	501	539

Police Services Cost per Part I Case Cleared

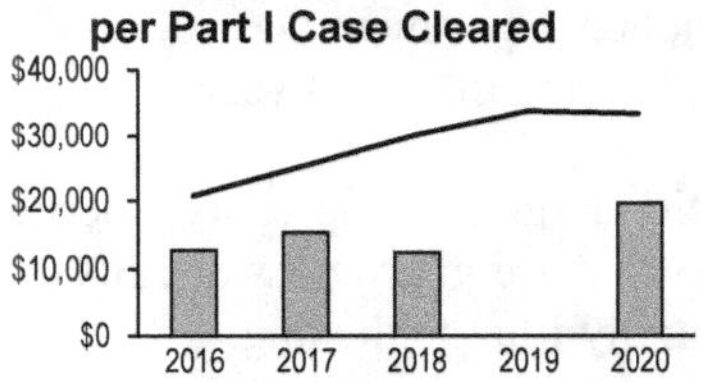

	2016	2017	2018	2019	2020
Hickory	$12,697	$15,338	$12,330		$19,646
Average	$20,634	$25,225	$30,061	$33,791	$33,378

Part I Cases Cleared per Sworn Officer

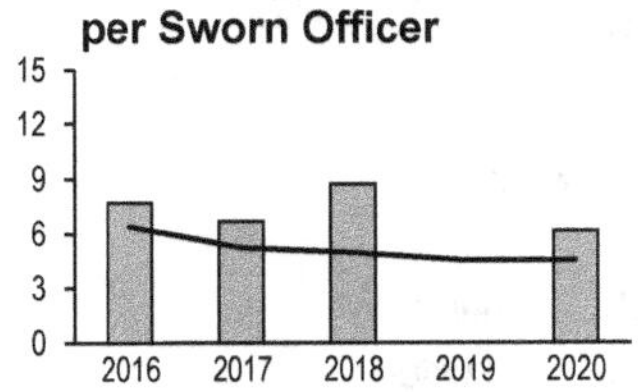

	2016	2017	2018	2019	2020
Hickory	7.7	6.7	8.7		6.1
Average	6.4	5.2	4.9	4.5	4.5

Effectiveness Measures

Percentage of Part I Cases Cleared of Those Reported

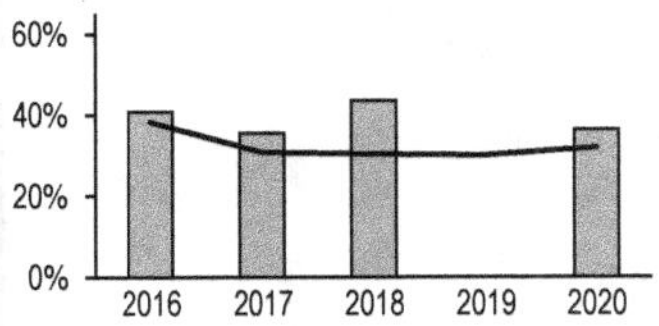

	2016	2017	2018	2019	2020
Hickory	40.9%	35.6%	43.5%		36.4%
Average	38.2%	30.7%	30.1%	30.0%	31.8%

Response Time to High Priority Calls in Minutes

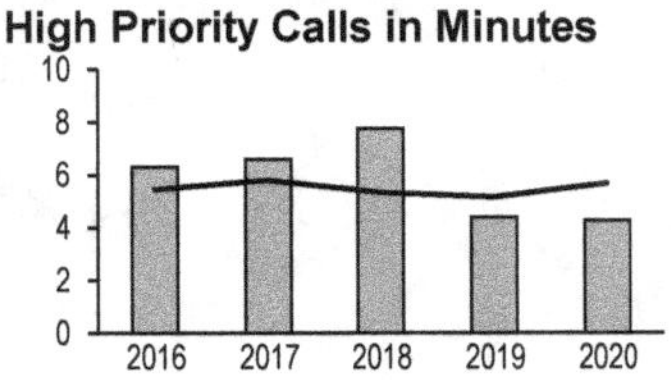

	2016	2017	2018	2019	2020
Hickory	6.3	6.6	7.8	4.4	4.3
Average	5.5	5.8	5.3	5.1	5.7

Fiscal Year 2019-20

Explanatory Information

Service Level and Delivery

Raleigh's police department provides an array of police services, including patrol, investigations, canine unit, special response unit, mounted equine unit, motorcycle unit, drug enforcement units, and other programs.

The city had 796 sworn officer positions authorized for the fiscal year, with an average length of service of 12.45 years. The police department has ten substations around the city.

Patrol officers work a twelve-hour schedule rotating between days and nights every twenty-eight days. Detectives work an 8.4 hour schedule each weekday rotating between a day shift and an evening shift. Most detectives are in a pool that shares responsibilities to cover weekend duty and midnight shifts.

The Field Operations Division has a take-home vehicle program for officers with two years of service and living inside the city limits with a safe driving record. Detectives and Special Operation Divisions have take-home vehicles for units on call or call-back status.

The police department was successful in clearing a total of 3,417 Part I cases during the fiscal year.

The city defines high-priority emergency calls as those involving crimes that are in progress or calls that are life-threatening or potentially life-threatening.

Conditions Affecting Service, Performance, and Costs

Raleigh rejoined the Benchmarking Project in July 2016, with the first year of data showing for FY 2015–16.

The average response time to high-priority calls reflects the response time of each arriving unit. Self-initiated calls are not included in the average response time to high-priority calls.

Municipal Profile

Population (OSBM 2019)	475,580
Land Area (Square Miles)	146.47
Persons per Square Mile	3,247
Median Household Income U.S. Census 2016	$46,612

Service Profile

FTE Positions—Sworn	796.0
FTE Positions—Other	105.0
Marked and Unmarked Patrol Vehicles	820
Part I Crimes Reported	
Homicide	26
Rape	178
Robbery	498
Assault	885
Burglary	1,391
Larceny	8,207
Auto Theft	1,006
Arson	56
TOTAL	12,247
Part II Crimes Reported	NA
Part I Crimes Cleared	
Persons	760
Property	2,657
TOTAL	3,417
Reporting Format	NIBRS
Number of Calls Dispatched	357,903
Number of Traffic Accidents	31,425
Property Damage for Accidents	$3,764,396

Full Cost Profile

Cost Breakdown by Percentage	
Personal Services	75.9%
Operating Costs	15.4%
Capital Costs	8.7%
TOTAL	100.0%
Cost Breakdown in Dollars	
Personal Services	$93,539,913
Operating Costs	$19,004,403
Capital Costs	$10,727,911
TOTAL	$123,272,227

Raleigh

Police Services

Key: Raleigh ■ Benchmarking Average — Fiscal Years 2016 through 2020

Resource Measures

Police Services Costs per Capita

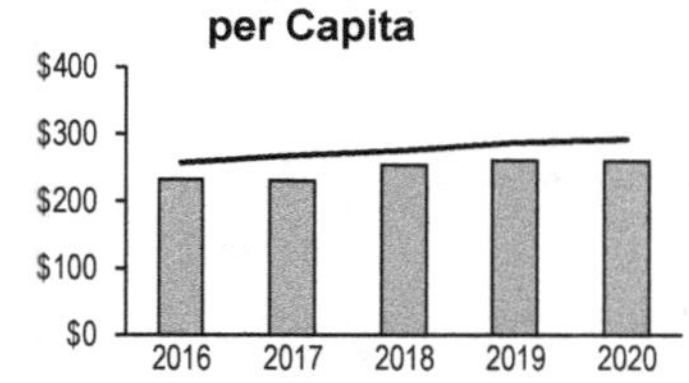

	2016	2017	2018	2019	2020
Raleigh	$232	$230	$253	$260	$259
Average	$257	$267	$275	$286	$291

Total Police Services Personnel per 10,000 Population

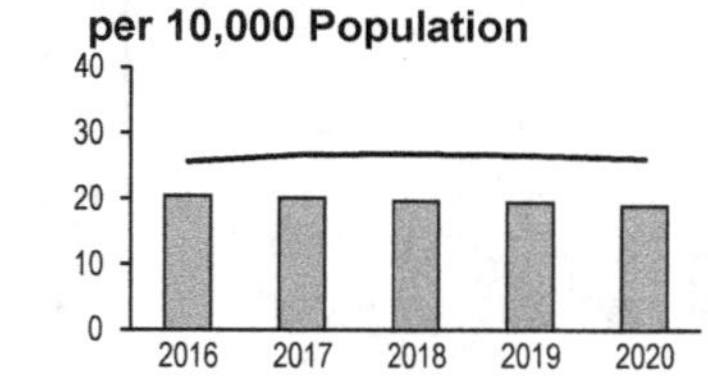

	2016	2017	2018	2019	2020
Raleigh	20.4	20.1	19.6	19.4	18.9
Average	25.6	26.6	26.7	26.5	26.1

Sworn Police Officers per 10,000 Population

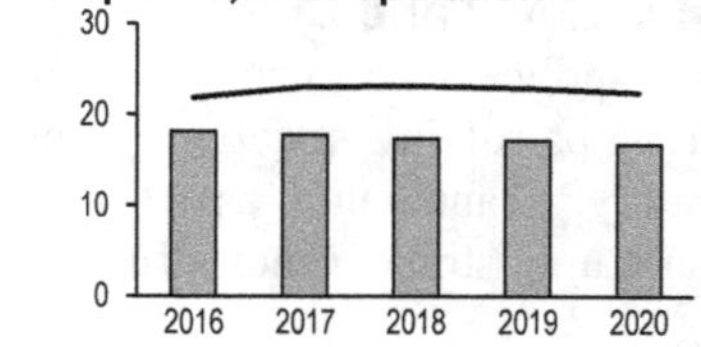

	2016	2017	2018	2019	2020
Raleigh	18.1	17.8	17.4	17.1	16.7
Average	21.8	23.0	23.1	22.9	22.4

Workload Measures

Calls Dispatched per 1,000 Population

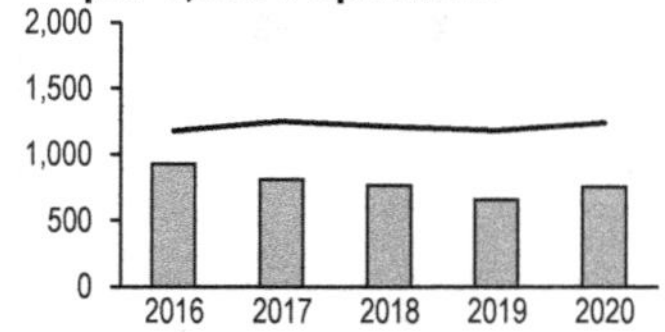

	2016	2017	2018	2019	2020
Raleigh	925	807	766	657	753
Average	1,176	1,246	1,211	1,178	1,236

Part I Crimes per 1,000 Population

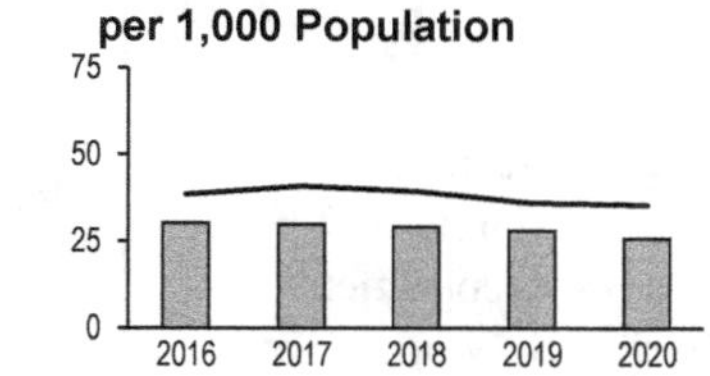

	2016	2017	2018	2019	2020
Raleigh	30.1	29.7	28.9	27.9	25.8
Average	38.3	40.8	39.3	35.9	35.4

Efficiency Measures

Police Services Cost per Call Dispatched

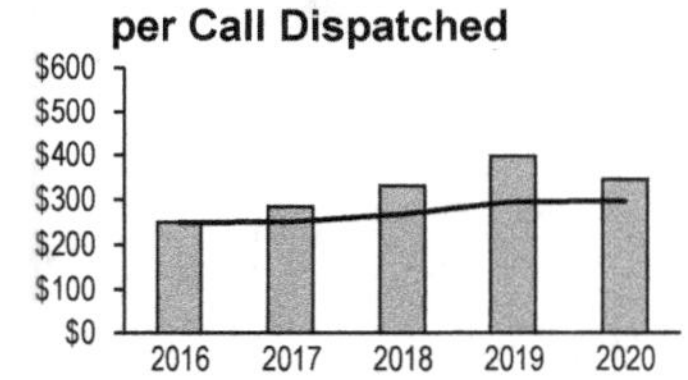

	2016	2017	2018	2019	2020
Raleigh	$251	$285	$330	$397	$344
Average	$248	$251	$268	$294	$296

Calls Dispatched per Sworn Officer

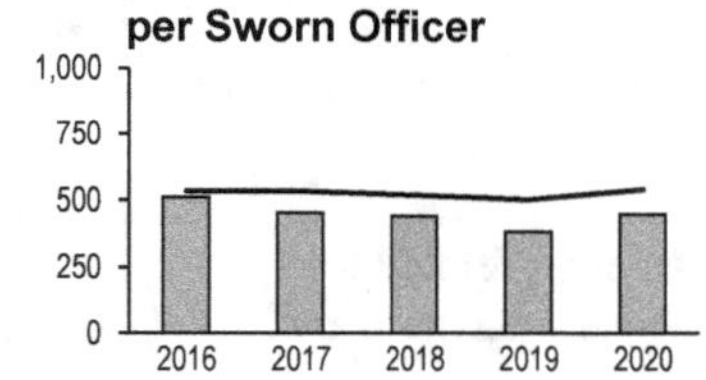

	2016	2017	2018	2019	2020
Raleigh	510	453	441	383	450
Average	531	532	518	501	539

Police Services Cost per Part I Case Cleared

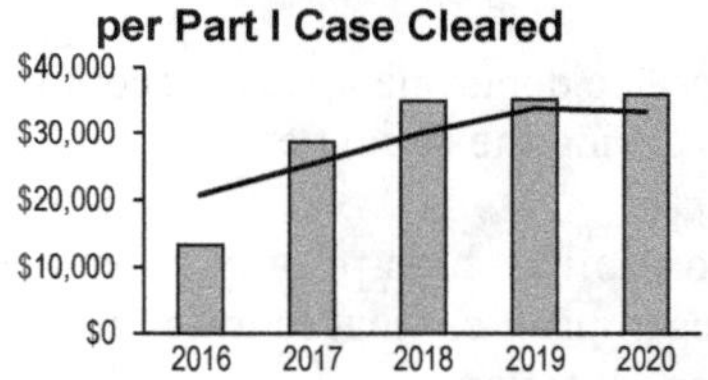

	2016	2017	2018	2019	2020
Raleigh	$13,291	$28,604	$35,008	$35,287	$36,076
Average	$20,634	$25,225	$30,061	$33,791	$33,378

Part I Cases Cleared per Sworn Officer

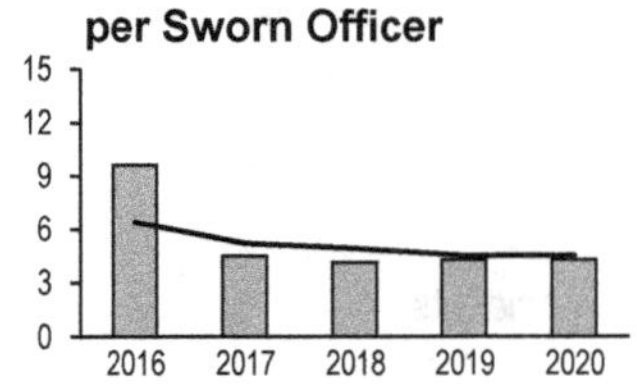

	2016	2017	2018	2019	2020
Raleigh	9.6	4.5	4.2	4.3	4.3
Average	6.4	5.2	4.9	4.5	4.5

Effectiveness Measures

Percentage of Part I Cases Cleared of Those Reported

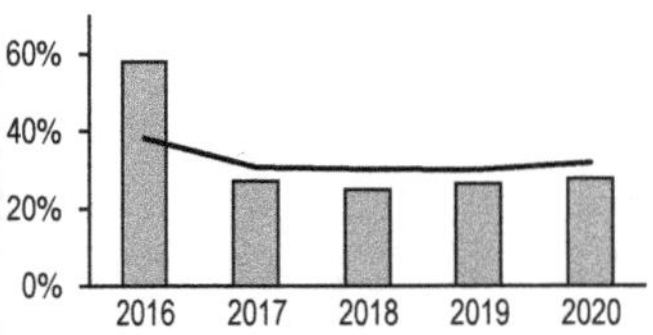

	2016	2017	2018	2019	2020
Raleigh	57.9%	27.1%	25.0%	26.5%	27.9%
Average	38.2%	30.7%	30.1%	30.0%	31.8%

Response Time to High Priority Calls in Minutes

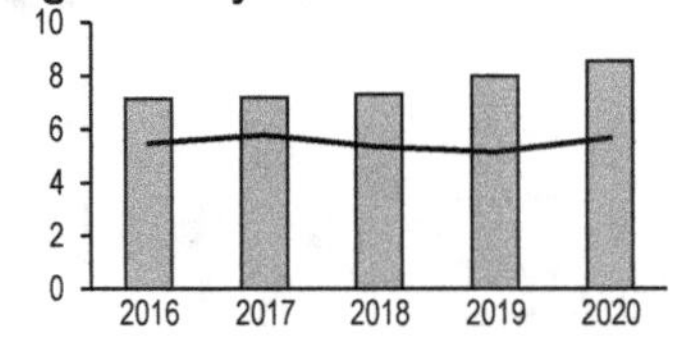

	2016	2017	2018	2019	2020
Raleigh	7.2	7.2	7.3	8.0	8.6
Average	5.5	5.8	5.3	5.1	5.7

Wilson — Police Services

Fiscal Year 2019-20

Explanatory Information

Service Level and Delivery

Wilson's police department provides an array of police services, including patrol, investigations, a telephone response unit, a forensics laboratory, a canine unit, a part-time mounted equine unit, a special response unit, street crimes, drug enforcement, and other services.

The city had 125 sworn officer positions authorized for the fiscal year, with an average length of service of 10.7 years. The main police department headquarters is located in downtown Wilson, housing administration, records, property, major case investigations, police information services, victim services, evidence, and recruitment and training. There are five substations.

Patrol officers work twelve-hour shifts, working fourteen days of a twenty-eight day cycle (168 hours). Shifts are either 7 a.m. to 7 p.m. or 7 p.m. to 7 a.m. and are rotated every two weeks. Department needs may cause shifts to vary. Investigators generally work eight-hour shifts five days per week. Shifts are 8 a.m. to 5 p.m.

Each patrol officer is assigned a vehicle and may take the vehicle home if he or she resides in the city. Officers living outside the city limits park their vehicles at businesses.

The police department was successful in clearing a total of 630 Part I cases during the fiscal year.

Wilson defines high-priority emergency calls as calls related to crimes in progress that require immediate response: murder, rape, robbery, burglary, arson/fire, and assaults.

Conditions Affecting Service, Performance, and Costs

The average response time to high-priority calls reflects the response time of the first unit to arrive. Self-initiated calls with a response time of zero are not included in the average response time to high-priority calls.

Municipal Profile

Population (OSBM 2019)	49,384
Land Area (Square Miles)	31.02
Persons per Square Mile	1,592
Median Household Income U.S. Census 2016	$35,409

Service Profile

FTE Positions—Sworn	125.0
FTE Positions—Other	17.0
Marked and Unmarked Patrol Vehicles	128
Part I Crimes Reported	
Homicide	6
Rape	15
Robbery	57
Assault	152
Burglary	310
Larceny	1,006
Auto Theft	103
Arson	13
TOTAL	1,662
Part II Crimes Reported	2,686
Part I Crimes Cleared	
Persons	144
Property	486
TOTAL	630
Reporting Format	IBR
Number of Calls Dispatched	104,481
Number of Traffic Accidents	2,563
Property Damage for Accidents	na

Full Cost Profile

Cost Breakdown by Percentage	
Personal Services	71.1%
Operating Costs	22.5%
Capital Costs	6.3%
TOTAL	100.0%
Cost Breakdown in Dollars	
Personal Services	$12,904,283
Operating Costs	$4,090,589
Capital Costs	$1,150,124
TOTAL	$18,144,996

Key: Wilson ▪ Benchmarking Average — Fiscal Years 2016 through 2020

Resource Measures

Police Services Costs per Capita

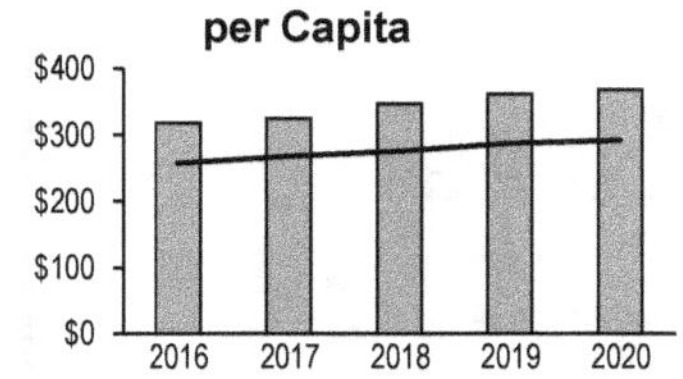

	2016	2017	2018	2019	2020
Wilson	$317	$324	$347	$361	$367
Average	$257	$267	$275	$286	$291

Total Police Services Personnel per 10,000 Population

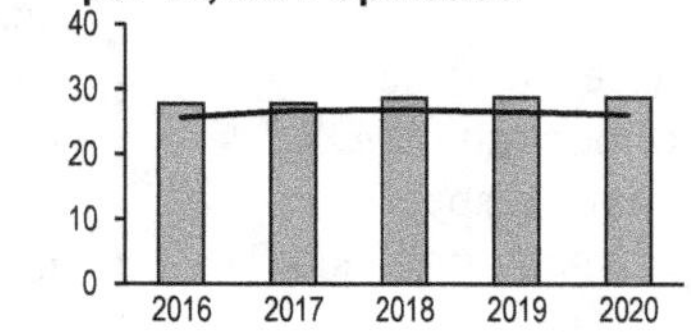

	2016	2017	2018	2019	2020
Wilson	27.8	27.7	28.7	28.7	28.8
Average	25.6	26.6	26.7	26.5	26.1

Sworn Police Officers per 10,000 Population

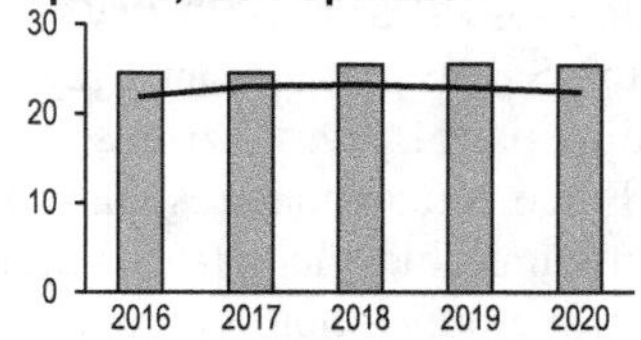

	2016	2017	2018	2019	2020
Wilson	24.5	24.5	25.4	25.5	25.3
Average	21.8	23.0	23.1	22.9	22.4

Workload Measures

Calls Dispatched per 1,000 Population

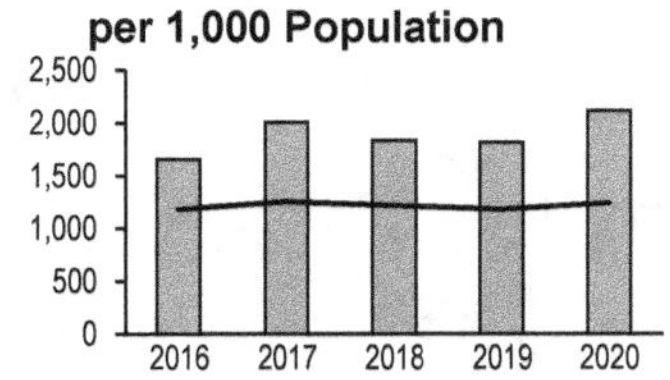

	2016	2017	2018	2019	2020
Wilson	1,659	2,008	1,835	1,820	2,116
Average	1,176	1,246	1,211	1,178	1,236

Part I Crimes per 1,000 Population

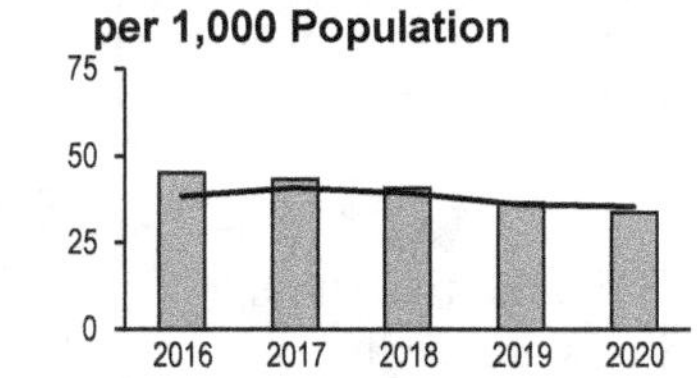

	2016	2017	2018	2019	2020
Wilson	45.3	43.3	40.8	36.4	33.7
Average	38.3	40.8	39.3	35.9	35.4

Efficiency Measures

Police Services Cost per Call Dispatched

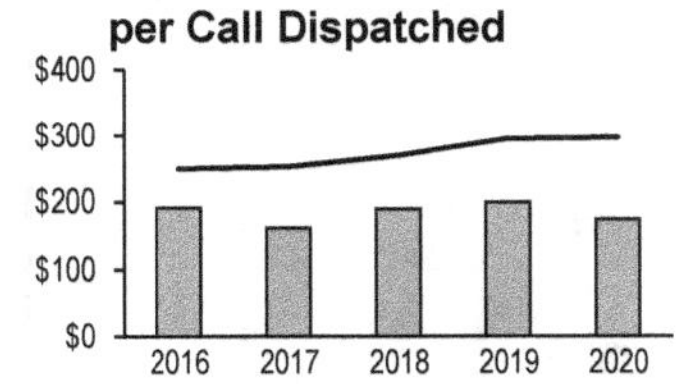

	2016	2017	2018	2019	2020
Wilson	$191	$161	$189	$198	$174
Average	$248	$251	$268	$294	$296

Calls Dispatched per Sworn Officer

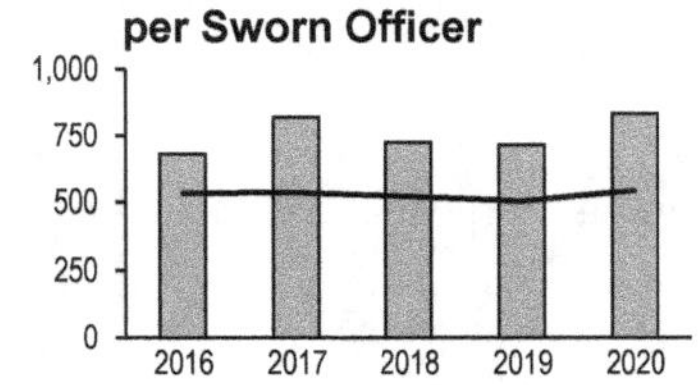

	2016	2017	2018	2019	2020
Wilson	677	820	722	714	836
Average	531	532	518	501	539

Police Services Cost per Part I Case Cleared

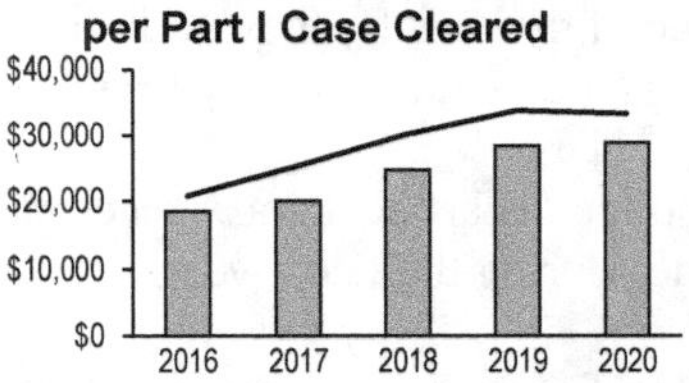

	2016	2017	2018	2019	2020
Wilson	$18,555	$20,033	$24,656	$28,401	$28,802
Average	$20,634	$25,225	$30,061	$33,791	$33,378

Part I Cases Cleared per Sworn Officer

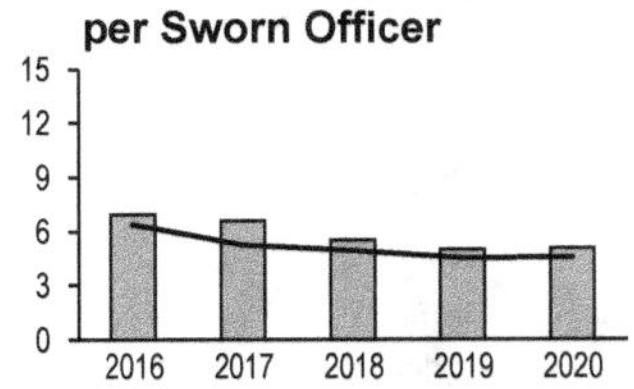

	2016	2017	2018	2019	2020
Wilson	7.0	6.6	5.5	5.0	5.0
Average	6.4	5.2	4.9	4.5	4.5

Effectiveness Measures

Percentage of Part I Cases Cleared of Those Reported

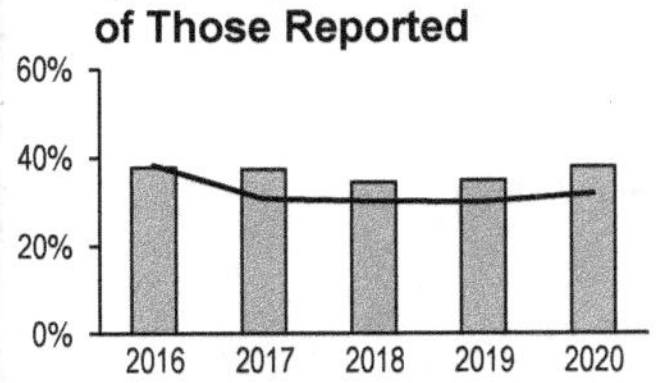

	2016	2017	2018	2019	2020
Wilson	37.8%	37.3%	34.5%	34.8%	37.9%
Average	38.2%	30.7%	30.1%	30.0%	31.8%

Response Time to High Priority Calls in Minutes

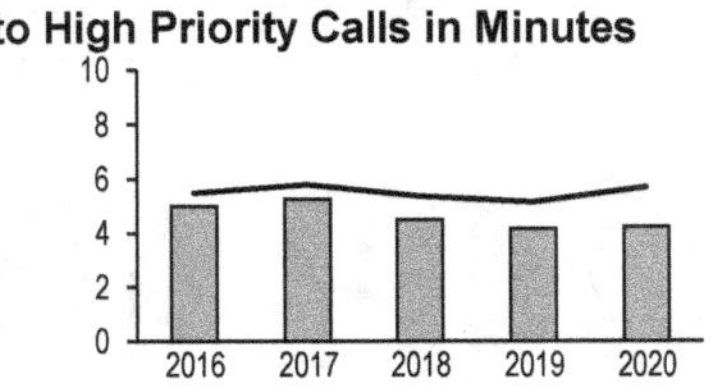

	2016	2017	2018	2019	2020
Wilson	5.0	5.3	4.5	4.2	4.2
Average	5.5	5.8	5.3	5.1	5.7

Fiscal Year 2019-20

Explanatory Information

Service Level and Delivery

Winston-Salem provides an array of police services to its citizens, including patrol, investigations, a traffic enforcement unit, a DWI Task Force, a telephone response unit, a canine unit, a special response unit, bicycle patrol, drug enforcement, a gang unit, and other crime prevention programs.

The city had 558 sworn officer positions authorized for the fiscal year, with an average length of service of 11.52 years. The police department occupies the public safety center. It houses the police department, emergency communications, and the fire department administration. The special investigations division occupies offices in leased space in another facility. A downtown bike patrol office is maintained in the central downtown area.

The department employs a forward-rotating schedule of five shifts. Officers work five days on and four days off. Shifts are ten hours in length. The majority of investigators work Monday through Friday from 8 a.m. to 5 p.m.

Patrol vehicles are assigned to individual officers. Officers residing within Forsyth County take their vehicles home. If officers reside outside of the county, they park their vehicles in a residential or business area within the city limits.

The police department was successful in clearing a total of 4,031 Part I crimes during the fiscal year.

Winston-Salem defines highest-priority emergency calls as those dealing with a significant threat of imminent injury to persons or with crimes against persons that are in progress or have just occurred and where the suspect is still there.

Conditions Affecting Service, Performance, and Costs

The average response time to high-priority calls reflects the response time of the first arriving unit. Self-initiated calls with a response time of zero are included in the average response time to high-priority calls.

The Winston-Salem Police Department does not investigate arsons, so arsons are not included in the crimes reported here. Arson investigations are handled by the Winston-Salem Fire Department.

Municipal Profile

Population (OSBM 2019)	244,739
Land Area (Square Miles)	132.59
Persons per Square Mile	1,846
Median Household Income U.S. Census 2016	$40,584

Service Profile

FTE Positions—Sworn	558.0
FTE Positions—Other	127.0
Marked and Unmarked Patrol Vehicles	418
Part I Crimes Reported	
Homicide	31
Rape	121
Robbery	340
Assault	2,369
Burglary	2,111
Larceny	9,213
Auto Theft	1,018
Arson	na
TOTAL	15,203
Part II Crimes Reported	32,151
Part I Crimes Cleared	
Persons	1,000
Property	3,031
TOTAL	4,031
Reporting Format	NIBRS
Number of Calls Dispatched	213,719
Number of Traffic Accidents	9,969
Property Damage for Accidents	$36,250,713

Full Cost Profile

Cost Breakdown by Percentage	
Personal Services	76.3%
Operating Costs	14.8%
Capital Costs	8.9%
TOTAL	100.0%
Cost Breakdown in Dollars	
Personal Services	$61,741,861
Operating Costs	$11,966,848
Capital Costs	$7,205,183
TOTAL	$80,913,892

Key: Winston-Salem ■ Benchmarking Average — Fiscal Years 2016 through 2020

Resource Measures

Police Services Costs per Capita

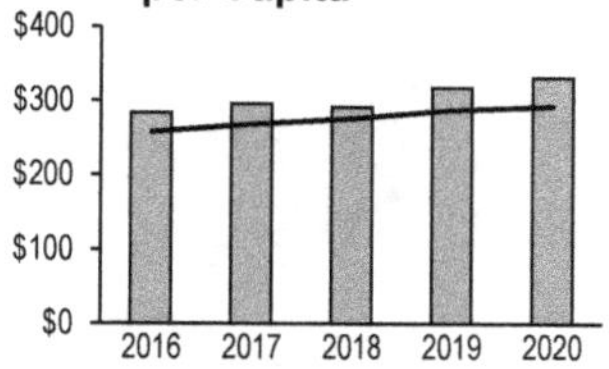

	2016	2017	2018	2019	2020
Winston-Salem	$283	$295	$291	$317	$331
Average	$257	$267	$275	$286	$291

Total Police Services Personnel per 10,000 Population

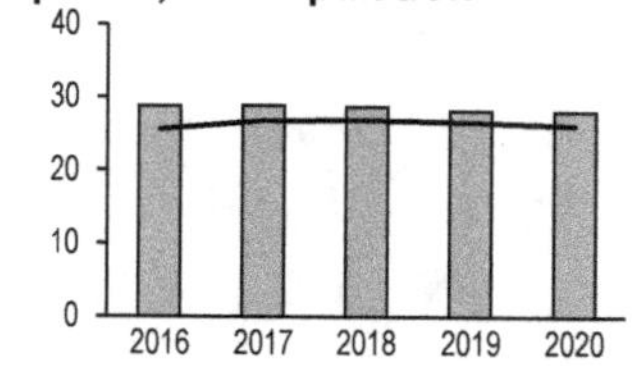

	2016	2017	2018	2019	2020
Winston-Salem	28.8	28.8	28.6	28.1	28.0
Average	25.6	26.6	26.7	26.5	26.1

Sworn Police Officers per 10,000 Population

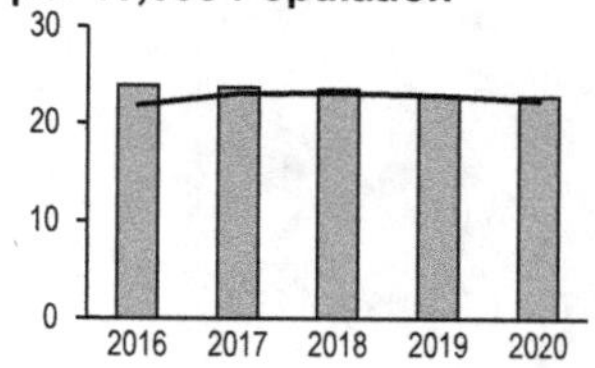

	2016	2017	2018	2019	2020
Winston-Salem	23.9	23.7	23.5	22.9	22.8
Average	21.8	23.0	23.1	22.9	22.4

Workload Measures

Calls Dispatched per 1,000 Population

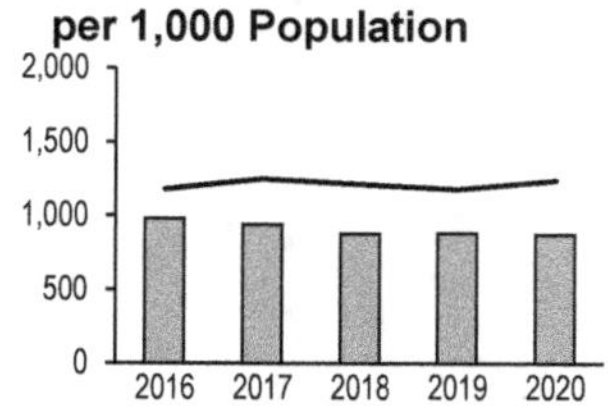

	2016	2017	2018	2019	2020
Winston-Salem	977	939	879	884	873
Average	1,176	1,246	1,211	1,178	1,236

Part I Crimes per 1,000 Population

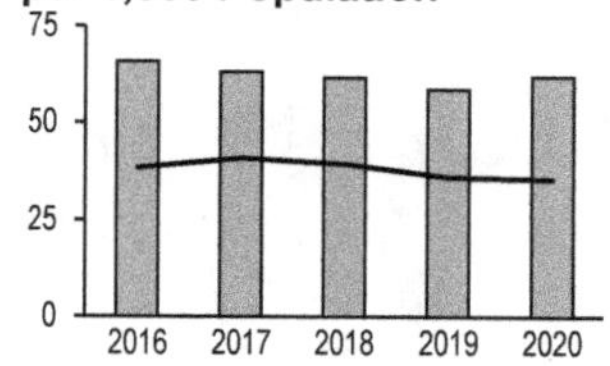

	2016	2017	2018	2019	2020
Winston-Salem	65.9	63.2	61.6	58.7	62.1
Average	38.3	40.8	39.3	35.9	35.4

Efficiency Measures

Police Services Cost per Call Dispatched

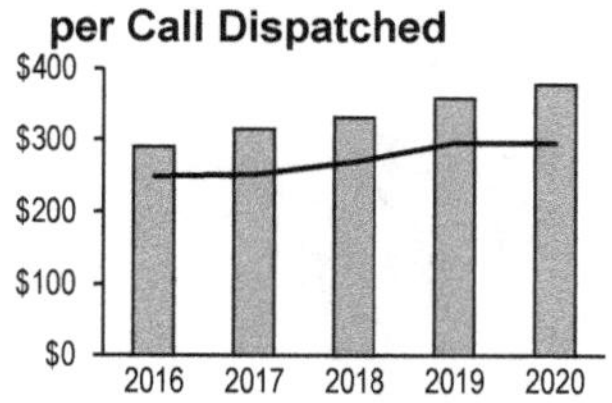

	2016	2017	2018	2019	2020
Winston-Salem	$290	$314	$331	$359	$379
Average	$248	$251	$268	$294	$296

Calls Dispatched per Sworn Officer

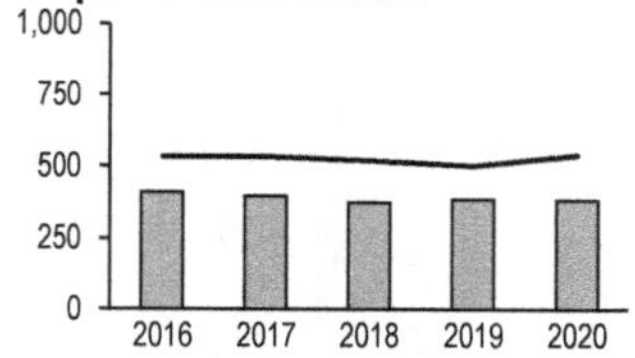

	2016	2017	2018	2019	2020
Winston-Salem	410	396	375	386	383
Average	531	532	518	501	539

Police Services Cost per Part I Case Cleared

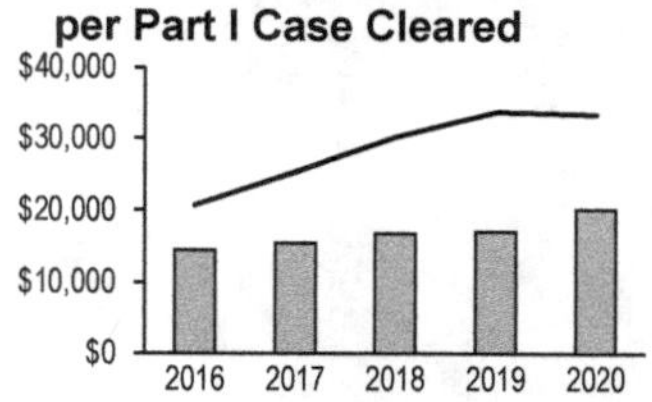

	2016	2017	2018	2019	2020
Winston-Salem	$14,381	$15,330	$16,711	$16,977	$20,073
Average	$20,634	$25,225	$30,061	$33,791	$33,378

Part I Cases Cleared per Sworn Officer

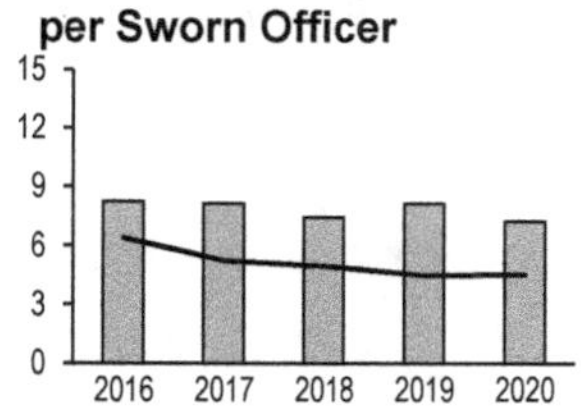

	2016	2017	2018	2019	2020
Winston-Salem	8.2	8.1	7.4	8.1	7.2
Average	6.4	5.2	4.9	4.5	4.5

Effectiveness Measures

Percentage of Part I Cases Cleared of Those Reported

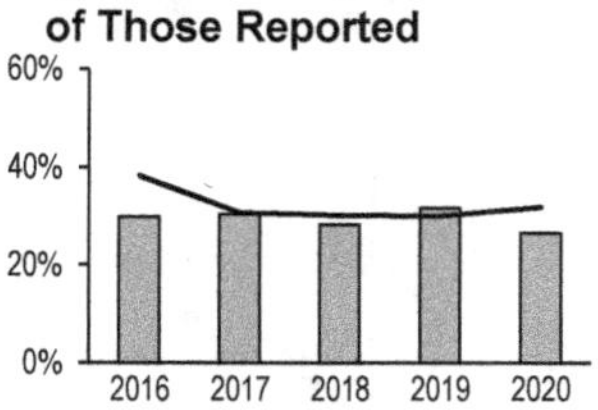

	2016	2017	2018	2019	2020
Winston-Salem	29.9%	30.4%	28.3%	31.8%	26.5%
Average	38.2%	30.7%	30.1%	30.0%	31.8%

Response Time to High Priority Calls in Minutes

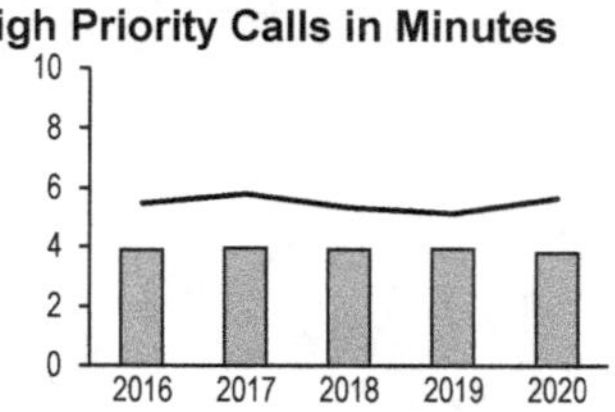

	2016	2017	2018	2019	2020
Winston-Salem	3.9	4.0	3.9	3.9	3.8
Average	5.5	5.8	5.3	5.1	5.7

UNC | SCHOOL OF GOVERNMENT
North Carolina Benchmarking Project

Performance and Cost Data

EMERGENCY COMMUNICATIONS

PERFORMANCE MEASURES FOR EMERGENCY COMMUNICATIONS

SERVICE DEFINITION

This service refers to the receipt and handling of 911 and other calls by an emergency communications center. Such a center must answer all calls, including those that come in over 911 lines and others that come in over regular phone lines. Some calls result in the dispatch of a police or other emergency response unit. Others do not.

NOTES ON PERFORMANCE MEASURES

1. Number of Calls Answered and Number of Calls Dispatched per 1,000 Population

These are used as measures of workload. All calls coming into a police emergency communications center must be answered; therefore, these measures assess service workload. Calls coming into a center also reflect the actual or existing, if not full potential, need for emergency communications services. Many calls coming into a center are dispatched. Others come in over regular telephone lines, and still others may be referred to the center by an external call-taker, such as a county emergency communications center.

2. Telecommunicators

Telecommunicators are the personnel who handle the calls in the communication centers. They may take calls, dispatch calls, or do both. Telecommunicators receive specialized training. They work on a shift schedule that generally allows twenty-four-hour-a-day, seven-day-a-week coverage.

3. Average Number of Seconds from Initial Ring to Answer and Percentage of Calls Answered within Twenty Seconds

These are effectiveness measures that assess how quickly telecommunicators answer calls.

4. Average Processing Time (Seconds)

This is an effectiveness measure representing the average time in seconds between when the telecommunicator answers the telephone and when computer-aided dispatch (CAD) entry begins. This measure is often referred to as "talk time."

5. For Calls Dispatched, Average Number of Seconds from CAD Entry to Dispatch—Highest Priority Calls

Some calls result in the dispatch of a police or other emergency response unit to a life-threatening or other similar emergency situation. Other calls result in a dispatch to a serious—but not emergency—situation. Other calls do not result in a dispatch. This measure assesses dispatch time for high priority, emergency situations.

Emergency Communications

Summary of Key Dimensions of Service

City or Town	Population Served	Number of FTEs	Average Length of Service for Call Takers (in Years)	Total Incoming Calls Handled	Total E-911 Calls Handled	Total Dispatches	Outgoing Calls Other than Dispatches
Apex	61,319	11.0	13.8	39,021	3,907	60,834	10,287
Concord	95,453	25.5	9.1	95,822	29,081	132,591	30,992
Greensboro	536,096	98.0	10.5	524,888	323,899	421,076	194,238
Hickory	41,409	14.0	4.5	114,966	15,042	98,159	27,561
Raleigh	1,085,297	129.0	5.5	835,150	553,997	487,264	288,455
Winston-Salem	244,739	47.0	9.5	446,177	209,526	237,578	70,822

NOTES

The population served by the municipal emergency communications center may go beyond municipal boundaries up to the entire county in cases where the service is a consolidated center.

EXPLANATORY FACTORS

These are factors that the project found affected emergency communication performance and cost in one or more of the municipalities:

Types of emergency response units dispatched, such as police, fire, and EMS
Number and proportion of nonemergency calls received by center
Types of assistance or advice, such as medical, that telecommunicators provide over the phone
Technology available to telecommunication centers
City's definition of what constitutes an "emergency" and "highest priority" call
Service to city only or to city and outlying areas
Training of telecommunicators
Demographic makeup of community
Organizational configuration and staffing for service

Fiscal Year 2019-20

Explanatory Information

Service Level and Delivery

The Apex Emergency Communications Center is a division within the Apex Police Department. This center is a secondary public safety answering point within Wake County, using Raleigh computer-aided dispatch (CAD) as a remote position. The communications center dispatches calls for police, fire, public works, and utilities.

The town owns a 150-foot radio tower that is tied into the Wake County radio system. The system is an 800 MHz system tied into the state VIPER system for radio operations.

Apex's emergency communications center handled a total of 39,021 incoming calls in the fiscal year and dispatched 60,834 calls. The city defines highest-priority emergency calls as those with immediate life or property risk or in-progress calls.

Conditions Affecting Service, Performance, and Costs

CAD entry for Apex does not begin immediately but is activated by operators.

Municipal Profile

Population (OSBM 2019)	61,319
Land Area (Square Miles)	21.55
Persons per Square Mile	2,846
Median Household Income U.S. Census 2016	$84,000
County	Wake

Service Profile

Primary or Secondary Answering Point	Secondary
Calls Dispatched	
Police	Yes
Fire	No
Other	Yes
FTE Positions	
Telecommunicators/Call-Takers	9.20
Other	1.80
Total Positions	11.00
Average Length of Service for Call-Takers	13.8 years
Total Incoming Calls	39,021
Total 911 Calls	3,907
Total Calls Dispatched	60,834
Outgoing Calls Other than Dispatch	10,287
Revenue from E-911 Fees	None

Full Cost Profile

Cost Breakdown by Percentage	
Personal Services	62.4%
Operating Costs	29.8%
Capital Costs	7.8%
TOTAL	100.0%
Cost Breakdown in Dollars	
Personal Services	$871,029
Operating Costs	$416,403
Capital Costs	$108,937
TOTAL	$1,396,369

Key: Apex ■ Benchmarking Average — Fiscal Years 2016 through 2020

Resource Measures

Emergency Communications Services Costs per Capita

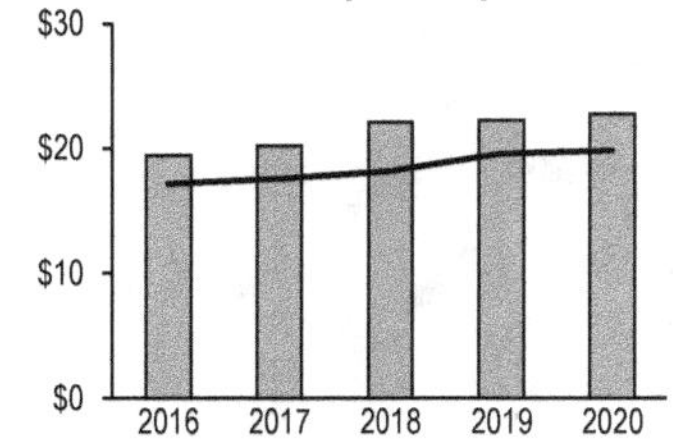

	2016	2017	2018	2019	2020
Apex	$19.43	$20.19	$22.13	$22.25	$22.77
Average	$17.16	$17.58	$18.22	$19.32	$19.83

Emergency Communications FTEs per 10,000 Population

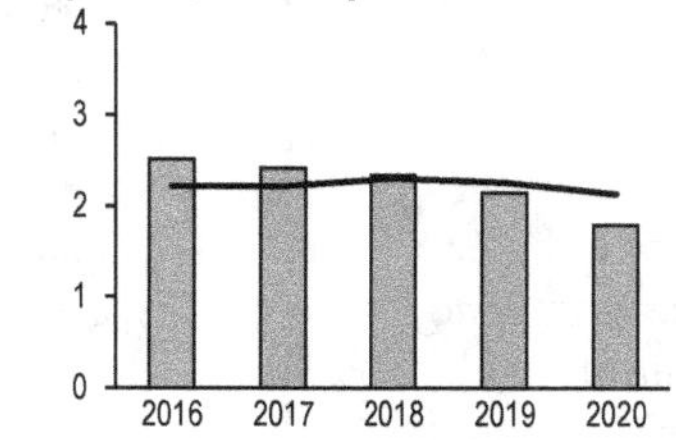

	2016	2017	2018	2019	2020
Apex	2.51	2.41	2.34	2.14	1.79
Average	2.22	2.21	2.30	2.26	2.13

Workload Measures

Total Calls Answered per 1,000 Population

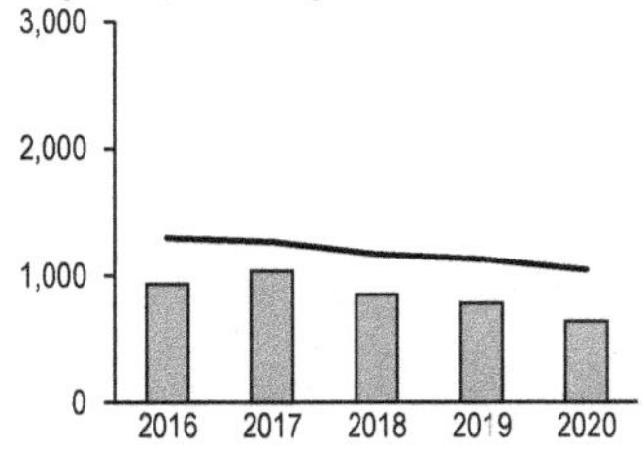

	2016	2017	2018	2019	2020
Apex	933	1,033	847	782	636
Average	1,296	1,264	1,166	1,130	1,042

Calls Dispatched per 1,000 Population

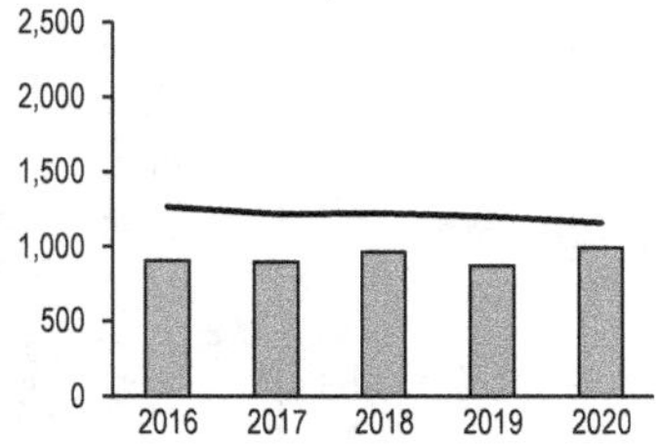

	2016	2017	2018	2019	2020
Apex	905	898	965	873	992
Average	1,267	1,222	1,225	1,204	1,159

E-911 Calls as a Percentage of All Incoming Calls

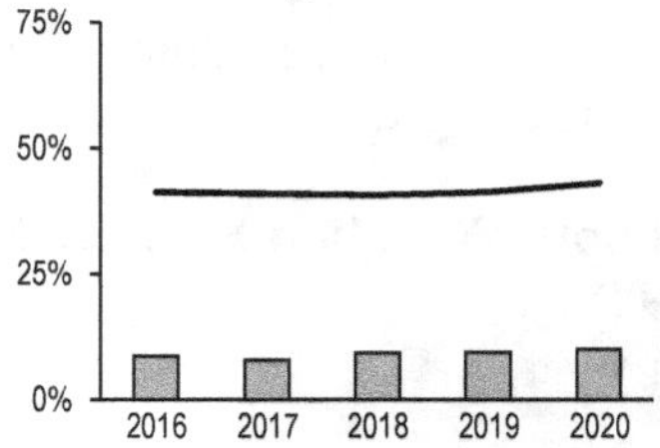

	2016	2017	2018	2019	2020
Apex	8.6%	7.8%	9.1%	9.3%	10.0%
Average	41.3%	41.0%	40.8%	41.4%	43.1%

Efficiency Measures

Calls Answered per Telecommunicator

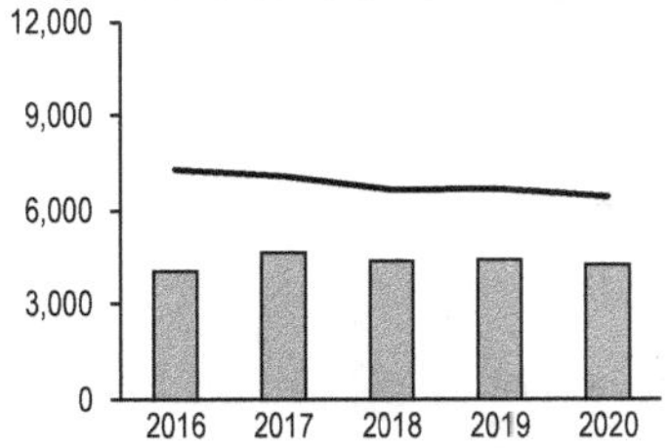

	2016	2017	2018	2019	2020
Apex	4,014	4,638	4,369	4,399	4,241
Average	7,274	7,068	6,655	6,675	6,425

Calls Dispatched per Telecommunicator

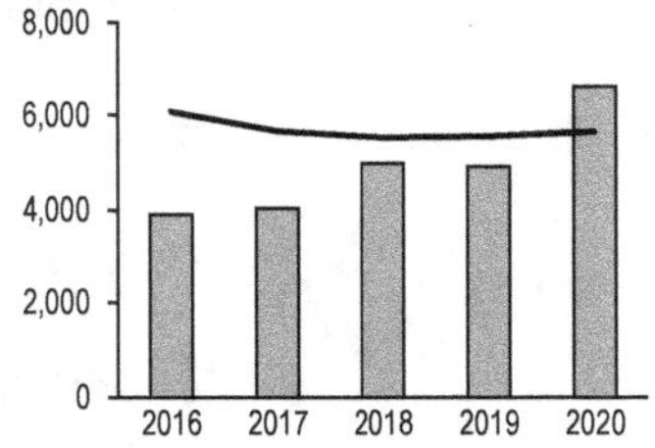

	2016	2017	2018	2019	2020
Apex	3,894	4,030	4,977	4,912	6,612
Average	6,069	5,660	5,529	5,556	5,650

Emergency Communications Cost per Call Dispatched

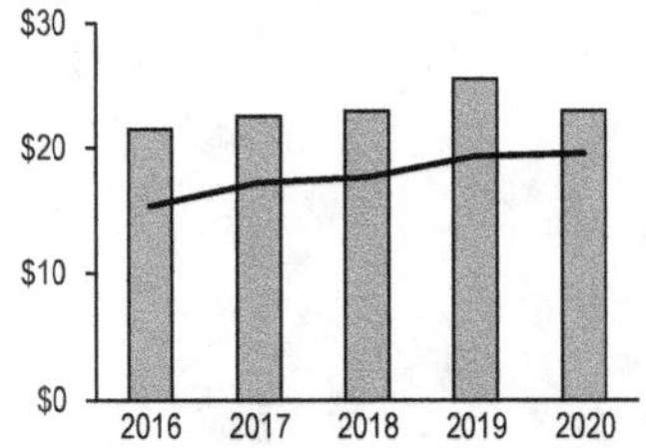

	2016	2017	2018	2019	2020
Apex	$21.47	$22.49	$22.93	$25.50	$22.95
Average	$15.44	$17.28	$17.65	$19.34	$19.57

Effectiveness Measures

Number of Seconds from Initial Ring to Answer

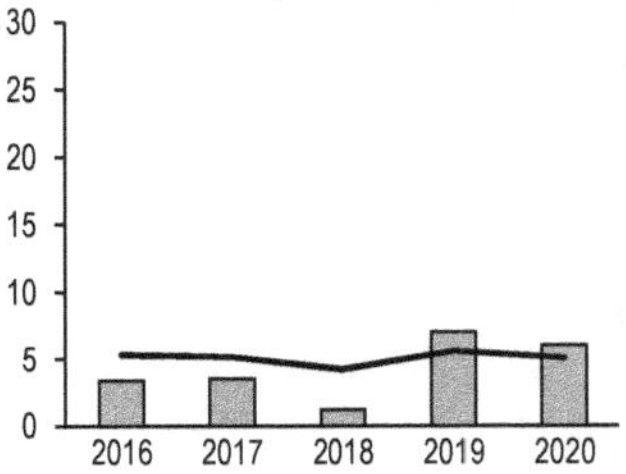

	2016	2017	2018	2019	2020
Apex	3	4	1	7	6
Average	5	5	4	6	5

Percent of E-911 Calls Answered within Twenty Seconds

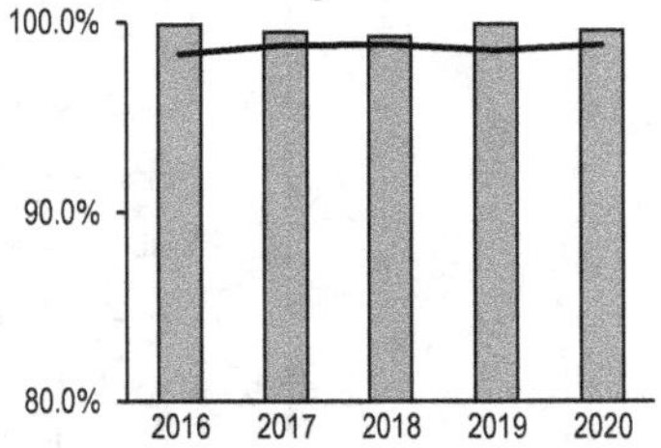

	2016	2017	2018	2019	2020
Apex	99.9%	99.4%	99.2%	99.9%	99.5%
Average	98.3%	98.8%	98.8%	98.5%	98.8%

Average Time in Seconds from CAD Entry to Dispatch for Priority One Calls

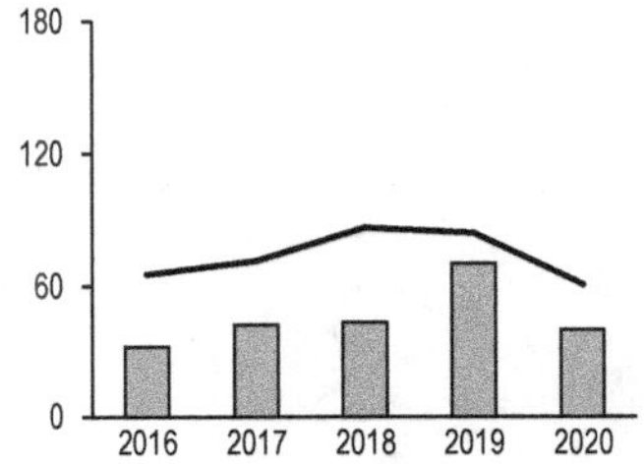

	2016	2017	2018	2019	2020
Apex	32	42	43	70	40
Average	65	71	86	84	61

Fiscal Year 2019-20

Explanatory Information

Service Level and Delivery

Concord's emergency communications center handles E-911 and non-emergency calls for the city. The emergency communications function of the city is separate from the police and fire functions and does not answer or transfer administrative calls for those departments. The emergency communications center does answer calls for utility and other city departments after hours, which is reflected in the number of incoming calls.

The city uses an 800 MHz system, which is a twelve-channel, five-site system shared with Cabarrus County and the City of Kannapolis.

Concord's center handled a total of 95,822 calls in the fiscal year, dispatching 132,591 calls.

Conditions Affecting Service, Performance, and Costs

Municipal Profile

Population (OSBM 2019)	95,453
Land Area (Square Miles)	63.65
Persons per Square Mile	1,500
Median Household Income U.S. Census 2016	$50,863
County	Cabarrus

Service Profile

Primary or Secondary Answering Point	Primary
Calls Dispatched	
Police	Yes
Fire	Yes
Other	Yes
FTE Positions	
Telecommunicators/Call-Takers	23.5
Other	2.0
Total Positions	25.5
Average Length of Service for Call-Takers	9.1 years
Total Incoming Calls	95,822
Total 911 Calls	29,081
Total Calls Dispatched	132,591
Outgoing Calls Other than Dispatch	30,992
Revenue from E-911 Fees	None

Full Cost Profile

Cost Breakdown by Percentage	
Personal Services	80.0%
Operating Costs	18.0%
Capital Costs	2.0%
TOTAL	100.0%
Cost Breakdown in Dollars	
Personal Services	$1,552,189
Operating Costs	$350,153
Capital Costs	$37,955
TOTAL	$1,940,297

Concord — Emergency Communications

Key: Concord ▪ Benchmarking Average — Fiscal Years 2016 through 2020

Resource Measures

Emergency Communications Services Costs per Capita

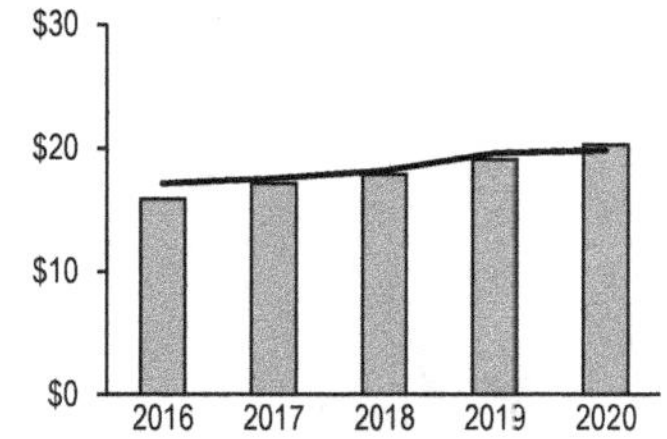

	2016	2017	2018	2019	2020
Concord	$15.91	$17.16	$17.91	$19.08	$20.33
Average	$17.16	$17.58	$18.22	$19.62	$19.83

Emergency Communications FTEs per 10,000 Population

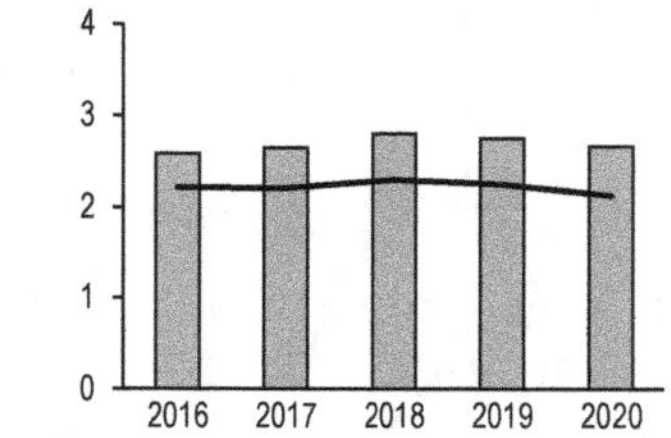

	2016	2017	2018	2019	2020
Concord	2.58	2.65	2.81	2.75	2.67
Average	2.22	2.21	2.30	2.26	2.13

Workload Measures

Total Calls Answered per 1,000 Population

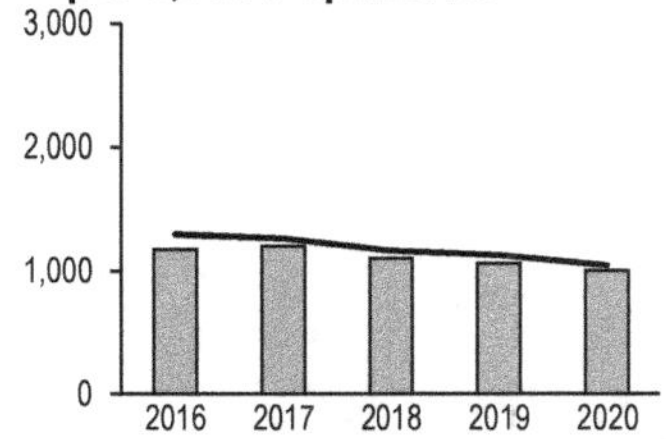

	2016	2017	2018	2019	2020
Concord	1,177	1,204	1,104	1,059	1,004
Average	1,296	1,264	1,166	1,130	1,042

Calls Dispatched per 1,000 Population

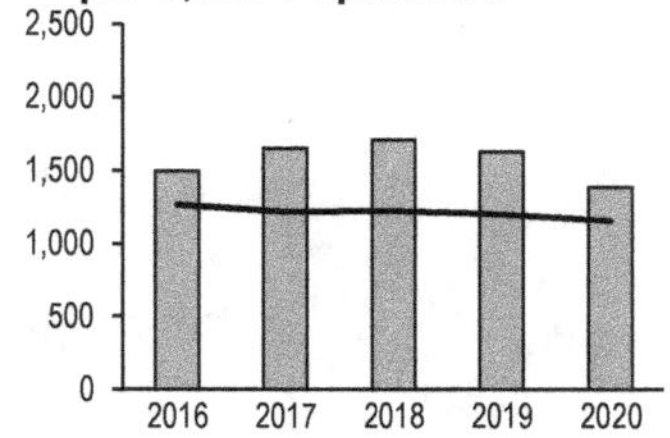

	2016	2017	2018	2019	2020
Concord	1,495	1,650	1,708	1,629	1,389
Average	1,267	1,222	1,225	1,204	1,159

E-911 Calls as a Percentage of All Incoming Calls

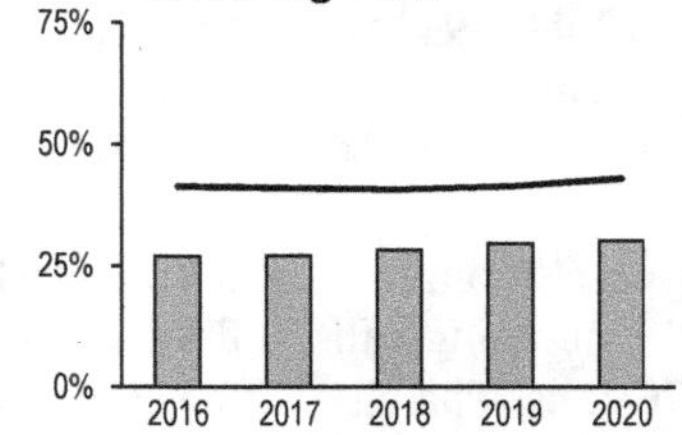

	2016	2017	2018	2019	2020
Concord	27.0%	27.1%	28.3%	29.7%	30.3%
Average	41.3%	41.0%	40.8%	41.4%	43.1%

Efficiency Measures

Calls Answered per Telecommunicator

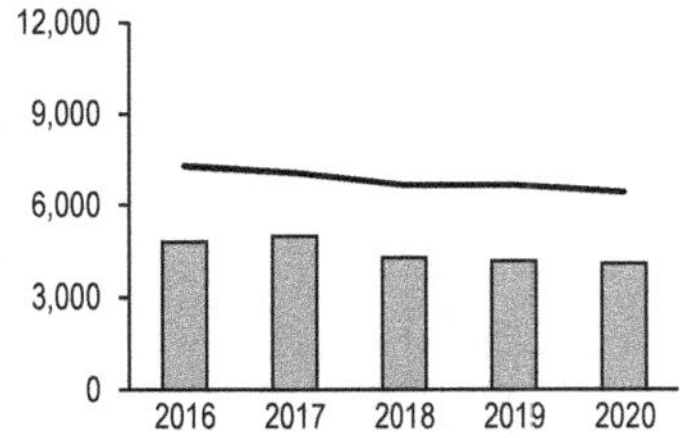

	2016	2017	2018	2019	2020
Concord	4,769	4,974	4,267	4,171	4,078
Average	7,274	7,068	6,655	6,675	6,425

Calls Dispatched per Telecommunicator

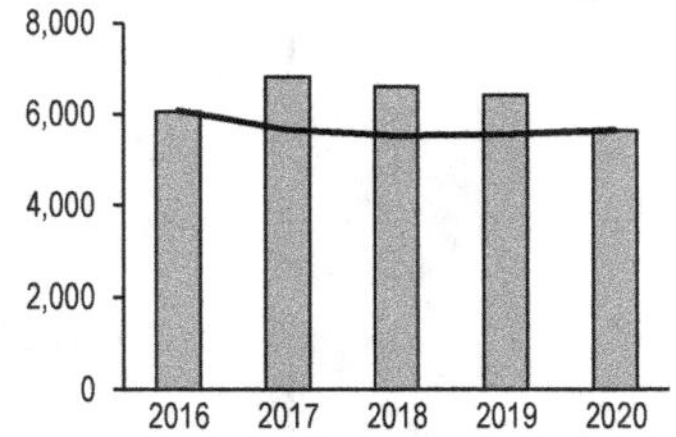

	2016	2017	2018	2019	2020
Concord	6,057	6,817	6,603	6,417	5,642
Average	6,069	5,660	5,529	5,556	5,650

Emergency Communications Cost per Call Dispatched

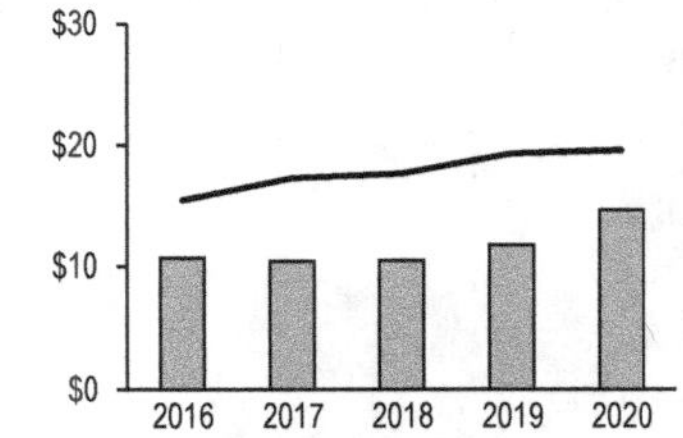

	2016	2017	2018	2019	2020
Concord	$10.64	$10.40	$10.48	$11.71	$14.63
Average	$15.44	$17.28	$17.65	$19.34	$19.57

Effectiveness Measures

Number of Seconds from Initial Ring to Answer

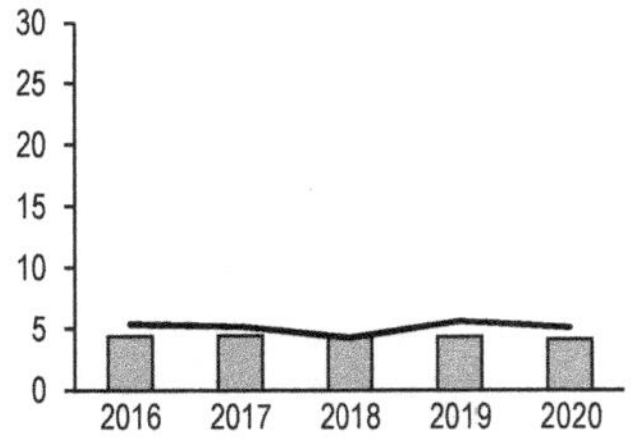

	2016	2017	2018	2019	2020
Concord	4	4	4	4	4
Average	5	5	4	6	5

Percent of E-911 Calls Answered within Twenty Seconds

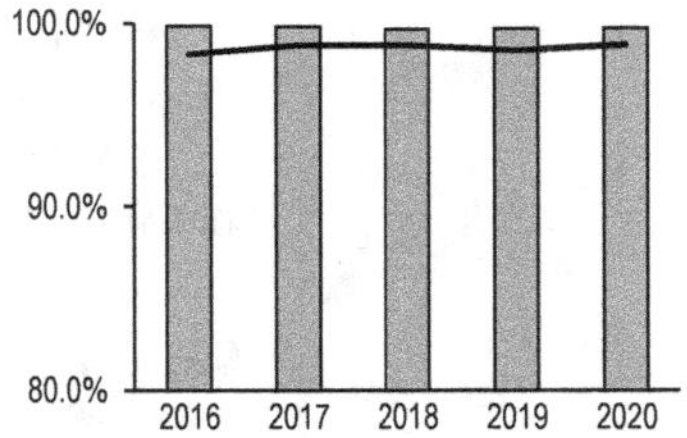

	2016	2017	2018	2019	2020
Concord	99.8%	99.8%	99.7%	99.7%	99.7%
Average	98.3%	98.8%	98.8%	98.5%	98.8%

Average Time in Seconds from CAD Entry to Dispatch for Priority One Calls

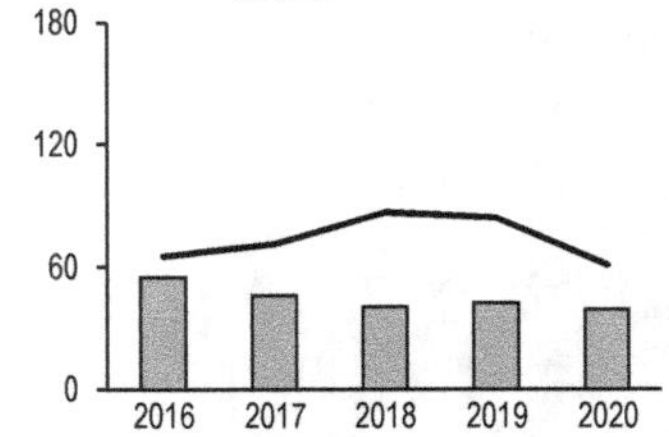

	2016	2017	2018	2019	2020
Concord	55	46	40	42	39
Average	65	71	86	84	61

Fiscal Year 2019-20

Explanatory Information

Service Level and Delivery

Guilford Metro 911 operates under an interlocal agreement between the City of Greensboro and Guilford County. The public safety answering point serves as a separate department providing emergency communications for the City of Greensboro, Guilford County, and Gibsonville (except for the City of High Point Police and Fire departments). The services include dispatch and call intake for all law agencies, fire agencies, and EMS. The consolidation process enabled the first update of all 911 equipment in ten years and the creation of a back-up E-911 center to improve disaster preparedness. These changes contributed to slightly higher operational costs.

Guilford Metro 911 uses Motorola Trunked P25 Regional radio system. The system has nine tower sites and is jointly owned with Guilford County.

Greensboro's communications center handled a total of 524,888 incoming calls in the fiscal year, dispatching 421,076 calls. The city defines highest-priority emergency calls as call types that require the fastest response, such as shootings, robberies, and domestic violence.

Greensboro received $2,594,180 in E-911 revenues to support system operations.

Conditions Affecting Service, Performance, and Costs

Municipal Profile

Population (OSBM 2019)–Guilford County	536,096
Land Area (Square Miles)	649.42
Persons per Square Mile	825
Median Household Income U.S. Census 2016	$40,760
County	Guilford

Service Profile

Primary or Secondary Answering Point	Primary
Calls Dispatched	
Police	Yes
Fire	Yes
Other	Yes
FTE Positions	
Telecommunicators/Call-Takers	92.0
Other	6.0
Total Positions	98.0
Average Length of Service for Call-Takers	10.5 years
Total Incoming Calls	524,888
Total 911 Calls	323,899
Total Calls Dispatched	421,076
Outgoing Calls Other than Dispatch	194,238
Revenue from E-911 Fees	$2,594,180

Full Cost Profile

Cost Breakdown by Percentage	
Personal Services	81.4%
Operating Costs	18.6%
Capital Costs	0.0%
TOTAL	100.0%
Cost Breakdown in Dollars	
Personal Services	$7,238,005
Operating Costs	$1,657,215
Capital Costs	$0
TOTAL	$8,895,220

Greensboro — Emergency Communications

Key: Greensboro ▇ Benchmarking Average — Fiscal Years 2016 through 2020

Resource Measures

Emergency Communications Services Costs per Capita

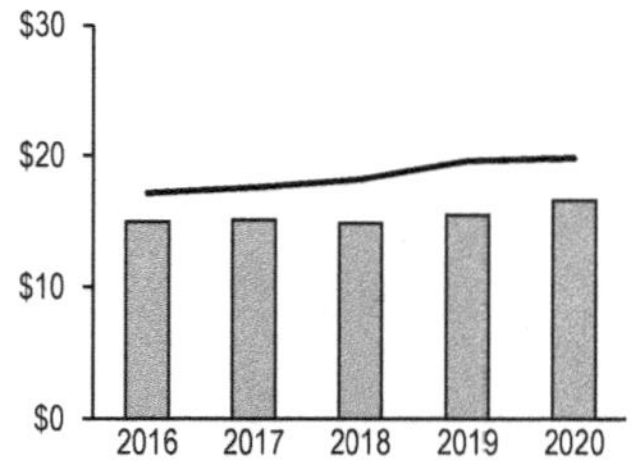

	2016	2017	2018	2019	2020
Greensboro	$14.91	$15.07	$14.82	$15.47	$16.59
Average	$17.16	$17.58	$18.22	$19.62	$19.83

Emergency Communications FTEs per 10,000 Population

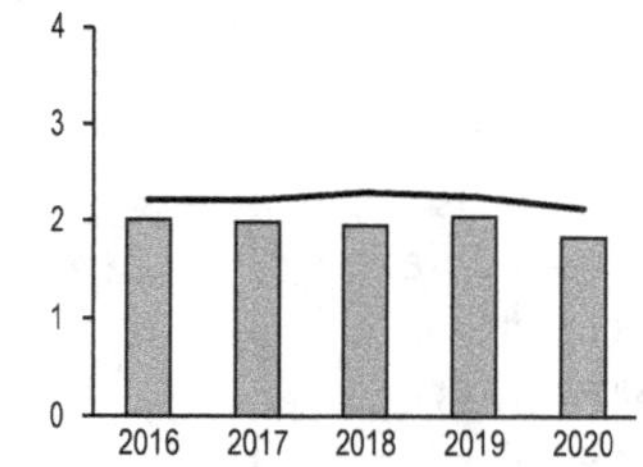

	2016	2017	2018	2019	2020
Greensboro	2.01	1.98	1.95	2.04	1.83
Average	2.22	2.21	2.30	2.26	2.13

Workload Measures

Total Calls Answered per 1,000 Population

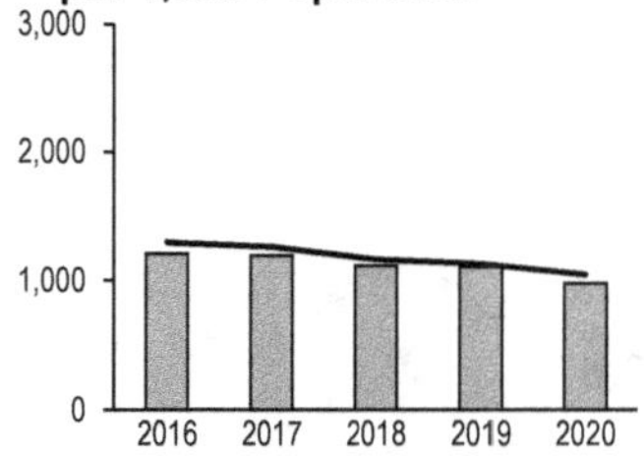

	2016	2017	2018	2019	2020
Greensboro	1,207	1,196	1,115	1,105	979
Average	1,296	1,264	1,166	1,130	1,042

Calls Dispatched per 1,000 Population

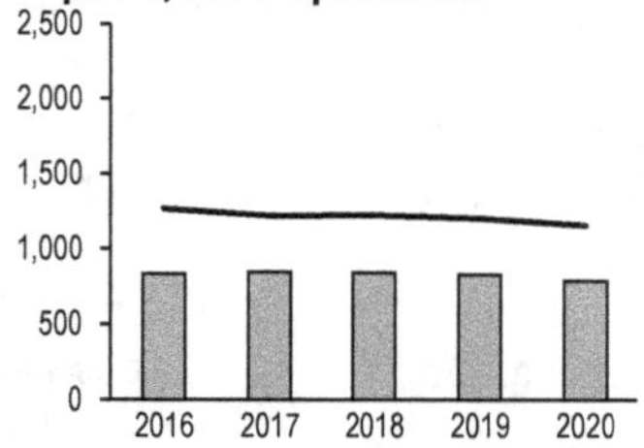

	2016	2017	2018	2019	2020
Greensboro	831	843	838	829	785
Average	1,267	1,222	1,225	1,204	1,159

E-911 Calls as a Percentage of All Incoming Calls

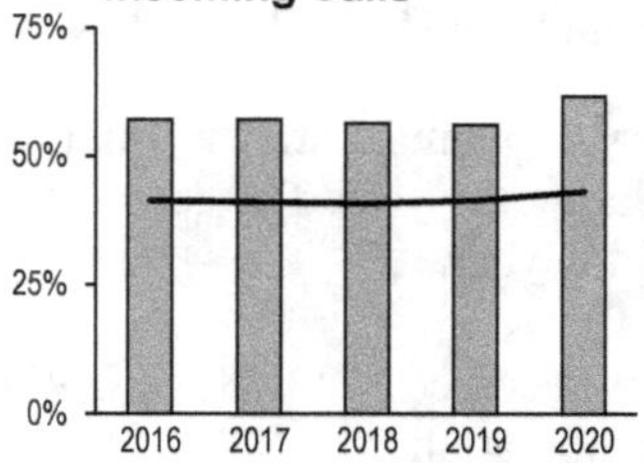

	2016	2017	2018	2019	2020
Greensboro	57.1%	57.0%	56.4%	56.1%	61.7%
Average	41.3%	41.0%	40.8%	41.4%	43.1%

Efficiency Measures

Calls Answered per Telecommunicator

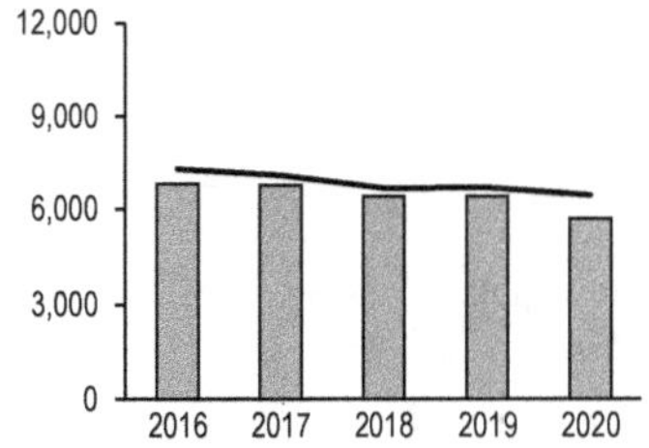

	2016	2017	2018	2019	2020
Greensboro	6,786	6,764	6,396	6,406	5,705
Average	7,274	7,068	6,655	6,675	6,425

Calls Dispatched per Telecommunicator

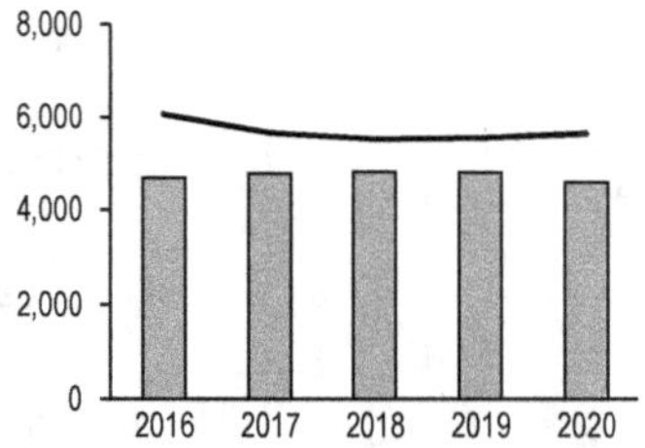

	2016	2017	2018	2019	2020
Greensboro	4,673	4,765	4,811	4,803	4,577
Average	6,069	5,660	5,529	5,556	5,650

Emergency Communications Cost per Call Dispatched

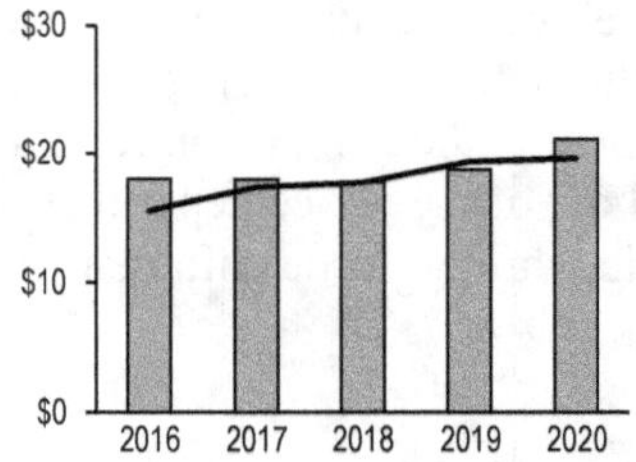

	2016	2017	2018	2019	2020
Greensboro	$17.94	$17.88	$17.67	$18.66	$21.12
Average	$15.44	$17.28	$17.65	$19.34	$19.57

Effectiveness Measures

Number of Seconds from Initial Ring to Answer

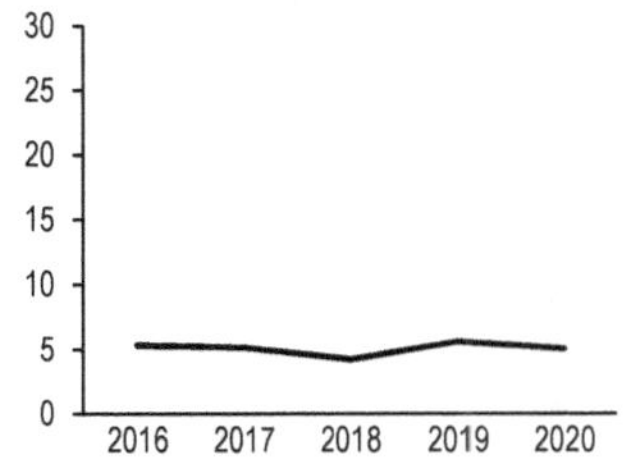

	2016	2017	2018	2019	2020
Greensboro					
Average	5	5	4	6	5

Percent of E-911 Calls Answered within Twenty Seconds

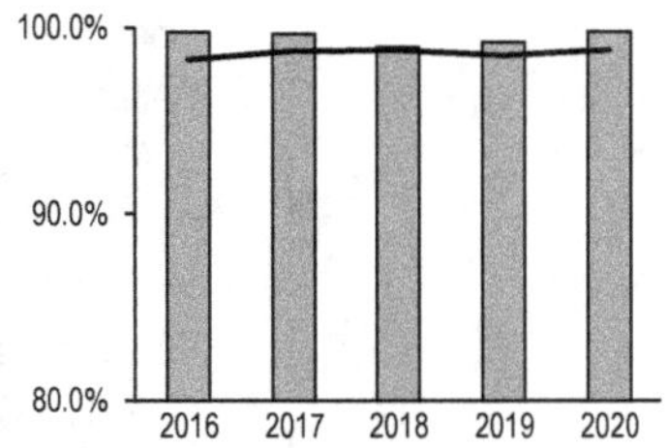

	2016	2017	2018	2019	2020
Greensboro	99.7%	99.6%	99.0%	99.2%	99.8%
Average	98.3%	98.8%	98.8%	98.5%	98.8%

Average Time in Seconds from CAD Entry to Dispatch for Priority One Calls

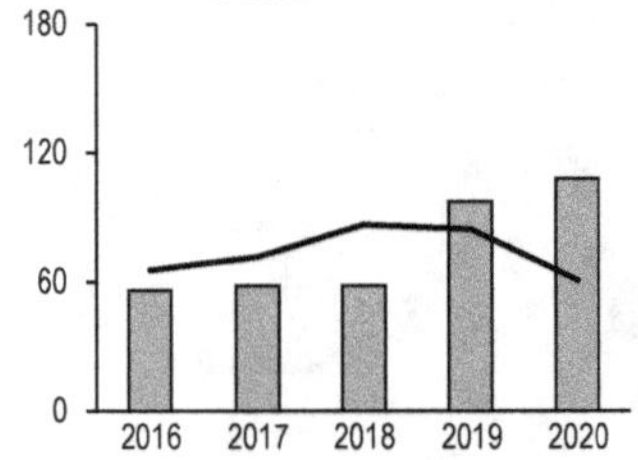

	2016	2017	2018	2019	2020
Greensboro	56	58	58	97	108
Average	65	71	86	84	61

Hickory — Emergency Communications

Fiscal Year 2019-20

Explanatory Information

Service Level and Delivery

Hickory's emergency communications center is a secondary public safety answering point, with Catawba County being the primary answering point. Catawaba County initially receives all 911 calls and dispatches fire and EMS calls inside the city limits. All 911 calls for police services are transferred to the emergency communications center for dispatch. Any emergency calls for other city services are transferred to the emergency communications center between 3:30 p.m. and 7:00 a.m.

The city owns its communications system and infrastructure. It uses an Ericsson 800 MHz radio system. There is one 1,350-foot tower and antennas at two other sites. The system serves approximately 200 users in five city departments.

Hickory's communications center took in 114,966 incoming calls during the year. The center dispatched 98,159 calls during the year.

Hickory received $213,786 in E-911 revenues to support system operations.

Conditions Affecting Service, Performance, and Costs

Incoming calls in Hickory are down over time because of changes in how calls are routed. Several special units now have their own administrative phones, so calls no longer come through the emergency communications center. Additionally, the animal control unit's operations were moved out of the police department, so their calls are now being fed through code enforcement.

Municipal Profile

Population (OSBM 2019)	41,409
Land Area (Square Miles)	29.92
Persons per Square Mile	1,384
Median Household Income U.S. Census 2016	$35,353
County	Catawba

Service Profile

Primary or Secondary Answering Point	Secondary
Calls Dispatched	
Police	Yes
Fire	No
Other	No
FTE Positions	
Telecommunicators/Call-Takers	14.0
Other	0.0
Total Positions	14.0
Average Length of Service for Call-Takers	4.5 years
Total Incoming Calls	114,966
Total 911 Calls	15,042
Total Calls Dispatched	98,159
Outgoing Calls Other than Dispatch	27,561
Revenue from E-911 Fees	$213,786

Full Cost Profile

Cost Breakdown by Percentage	
Personal Services	66.5%
Operating Costs	24.5%
Capital Costs	8.9%
TOTAL	100.0%
Cost Breakdown in Dollars	
Personal Services	$720,649
Operating Costs	$265,930
Capital Costs	$96,807
TOTAL	$1,083,386

Hickory — Emergency Communications

Key: Hickory ▒ Benchmarking Average — Fiscal Years 2016 through 2020

Resource Measures

Emergency Communications Services Costs per Capita

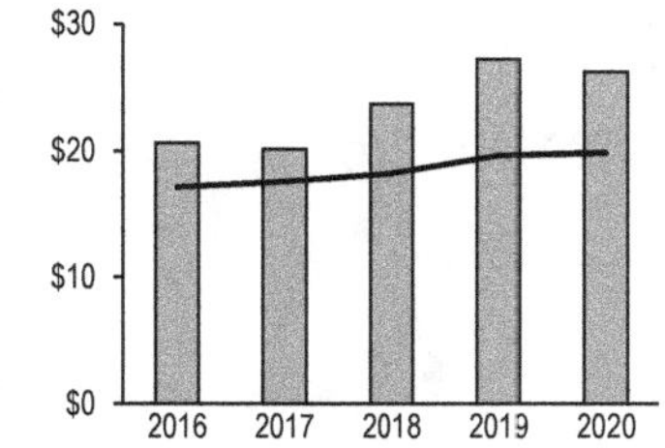

	2016	2017	2018	2019	2020
Hickory	$20.62	$20.12	$23.68	$27.18	$26.16
Average	$17.16	$17.58	$18.22	$19.62	$19.83

Emergency Communications FTEs per 10,000 Population

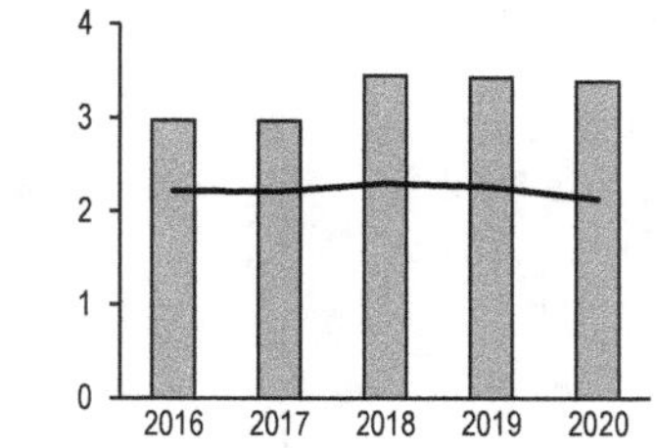

	2016	2017	2018	2019	2020
Hickory	2.97	2.97	3.44	3.42	3.38
Average	2.22	2.21	2.30	2.26	2.13

Workload Measures

Total Calls Answered per 1,000 Population

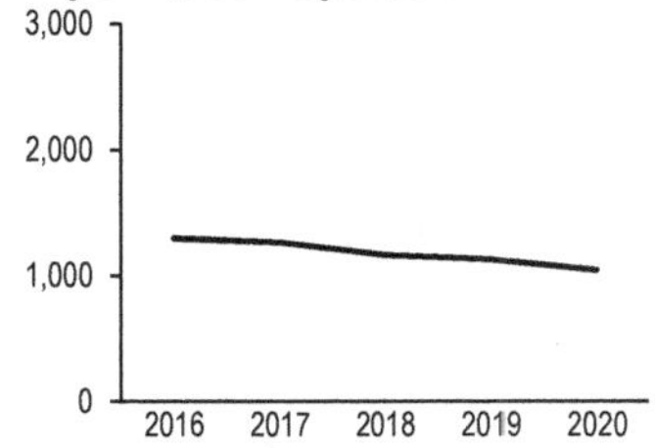

	2016	2017	2018	2019	2020
Hickory					
Average	1,296	1,264	1,166	1,130	1,042

Calls Dispatched per 1,000 Population

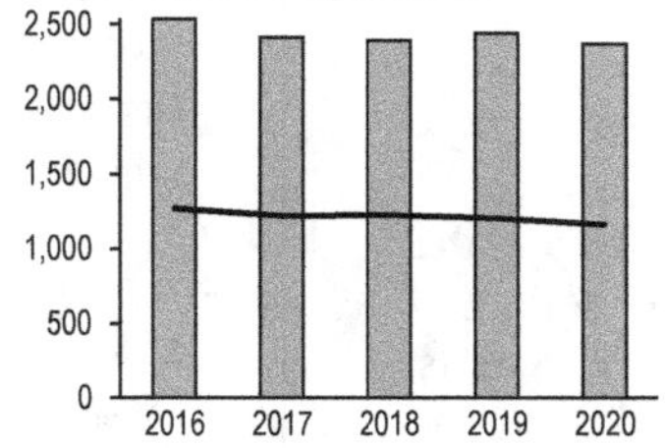

	2016	2017	2018	2019	2020
Hickory	2,535	2,413	2,394	2,444	2,370
Average	1,267	1,222	1,225	1,204	1,159

E-911 Calls as a Percentage of All Incoming Calls

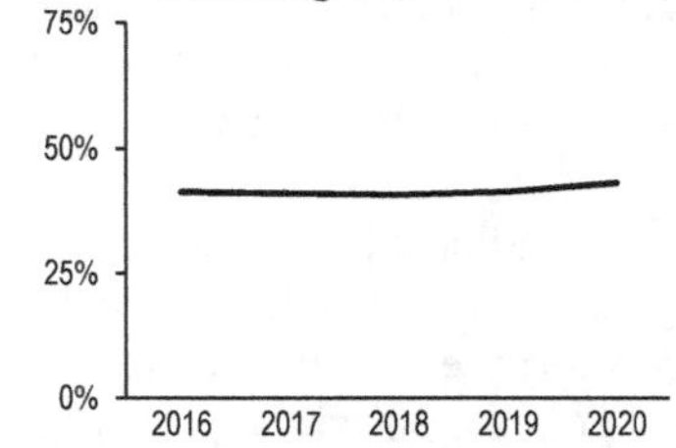

	2016	2017	2018	2019	2020
Hickory					
Average	41.3%	41.0%	40.8%	41.4%	43.1%

Efficiency Measures

Calls Answered per Telecommunicator

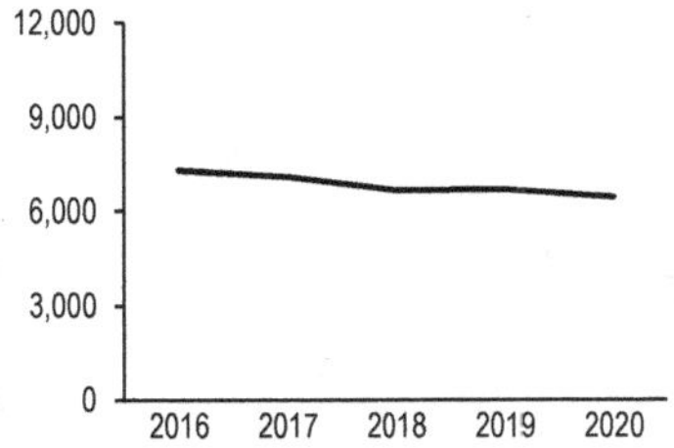

	2016	2017	2018	2019	2020
Hickory					
Average	7,274	7,068	6,655	6,675	6,425

Calls Dispatched per Telecommunicator

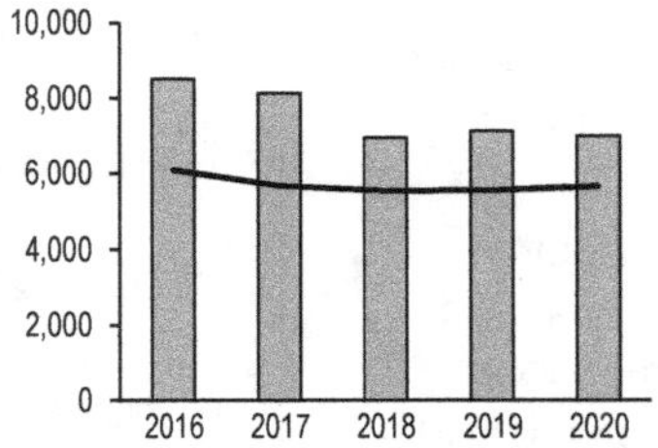

	2016	2017	2018	2019	2020
Hickory	8,525	8,133	6,951	7,146	7,011
Average	6,069	5,660	5,529	5,556	5,650

Emergency Communications Cost per Call Dispatched

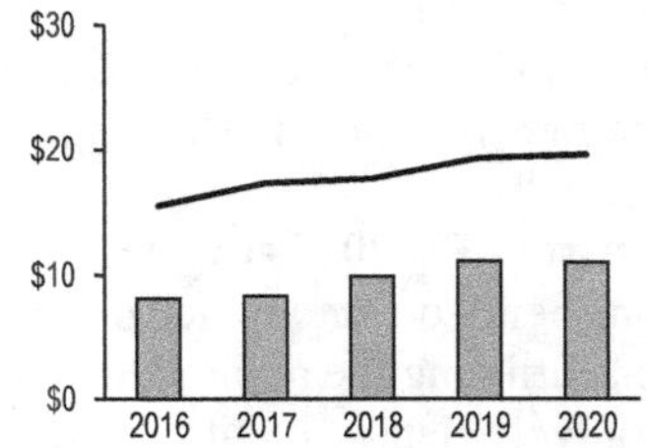

	2016	2017	2018	2019	2020
Hickory	$8.13	$8.34	$9.89	$11.12	$11.04
Average	$15.44	$17.28	$17.65	$19.34	$19.57

Effectiveness Measures

Number of Seconds from Initial Ring to Answer

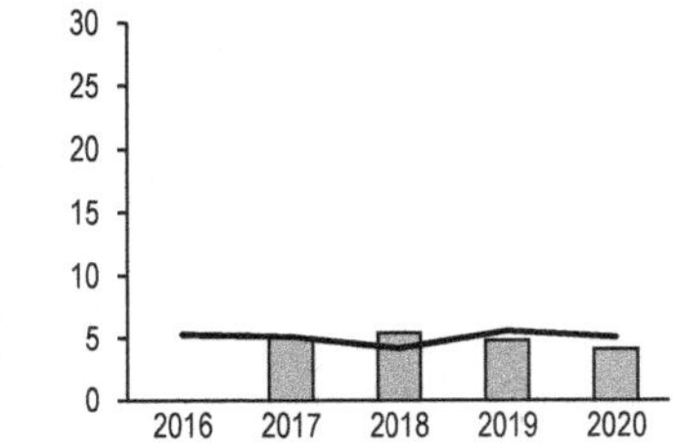

	2016	2017	2018	2019	2020
Hickory		5	5	5	4
Average	5	5	4	6	5

Percent of E-911 Calls Answered within Twenty Seconds

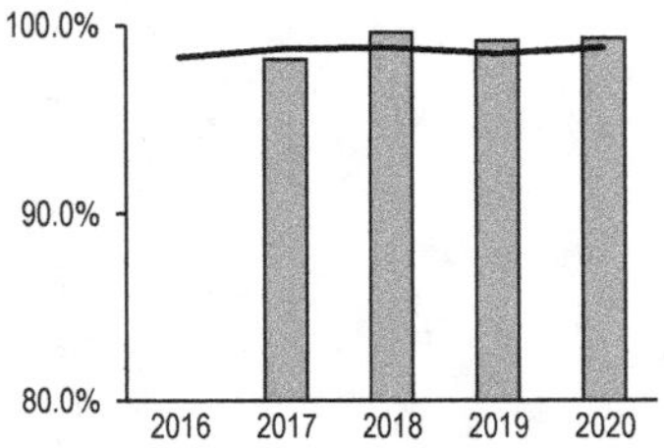

	2016	2017	2018	2019	2020
Hickory		98.2%	99.6%	99.2%	99.3%
Average	98.3%	98.8%	98.8%	98.5%	98.8%

Average Time in Seconds from CAD Entry to Dispatch for Priority One Calls

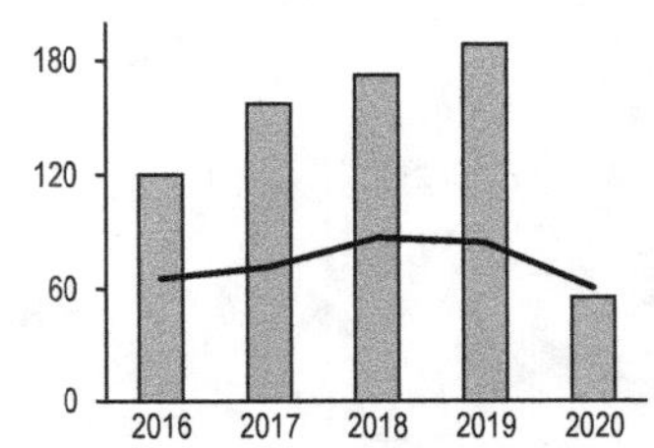

	2016	2017	2018	2019	2020
Hickory	120	157	172	188	55
Average	65	71	86	84	61

Fiscal Year 2019-20

Explanatory Information

Service Level and Delivery

The Emergency Communications Center (ECC) is the answering and dispatch agency for all of Wake County. It provides dispatch services for forty-four law enforcement, fire, EMS, rescue, and public service agencies. The ECC takes 911 calls for the Wake County Sheriff's Department, but these calls are transferred to the sheriff's telecommunicators.

The Town of Cary provides its own services for fire and police, but the ECC provides EMS call service for Cary.

The ECC uses a combination of city-owned and leased tower and transmitter sites. The system uses an 800 MHz system. Over 7,000 mobile and portable radios have been issued to public safety and non-public safety users within Wake County for use of the system.

The ECC handled a total of 835,150 incoming calls in the fiscal year, dispatching 487,264 calls. The ECC defines highest-priority emergency calls as all fire and EMS calls and also police calls with a priority of "0" or "1" as defined by the police agency being dispatched.

Raleigh received $2,587,879 in E-911 revenues to support system operations.

Conditions Affecting Service, Performance, and Costs

Raleigh rejoined the Benchmarking Project in July 2016, with the first year of data showing for FY 2015–16.

At the start of FY 2015–16, the ECC switched from all positions being on automatic call distribution to specific positions utilizing the automatic system. This decreased answering efficiency, but it helped increase responder safety issues that were identified when all positions used the automatic system. Additionally during this year, the ECC had a one-fourth attrition rate, which impacted answering efficiencies as well.

Municipal Profile

Population (OSBM 2017)-Wake County	1,085,297
Land Area (Square Miles)	831.92
Persons per Square Mile	1,305
Median Household Income U.S. Census 2016	$46,612
County	Wake

Service Profile

Primary or Secondary Answering Point	Primary
Calls Dispatched	
Police	Yes
Fire	Yes
Other	Yes
FTE Positions	
Telecommunicators/Call-Takers	102.0
Other	27.0
Total Positions	129.0
Average Length of Service for Call-Takers	5.5 years
Total Incoming Calls	835,150
Total 911 Calls	553,997
Total Calls Dispatched	487,264
Outgoing Calls Other than Dispatch	288,455
Revenue from E-911 Fees	$2,587,879

Full Cost Profile

Cost Breakdown by Percentage	
Personal Services	66.6%
Operating Costs	31.7%
Capital Costs	1.7%
TOTAL	100.0%
Cost Breakdown in Dollars	
Personal Services	$8,180,013
Operating Costs	$3,895,638
Capital Costs	$214,830
TOTAL	$12,290,481

Raleigh Emergency Communications

Key: Raleigh ■ Benchmarking Average — Fiscal Years 2016 through 2020

Resource Measures

Emergency Communications Services Costs per Capita

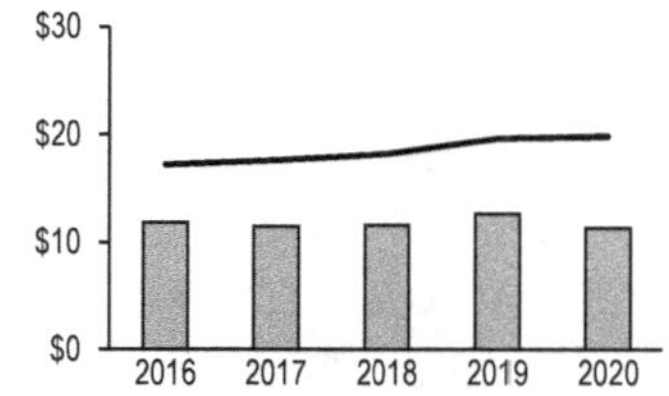

	2016	2017	2018	2019	2020
Raleigh	$11.80	$11.47	$11.58	$12.64	$11.32
Average	$17.16	$17.58	$18.22	$19.62	$19.83

Emergency Communications FTEs per 10,000 Population

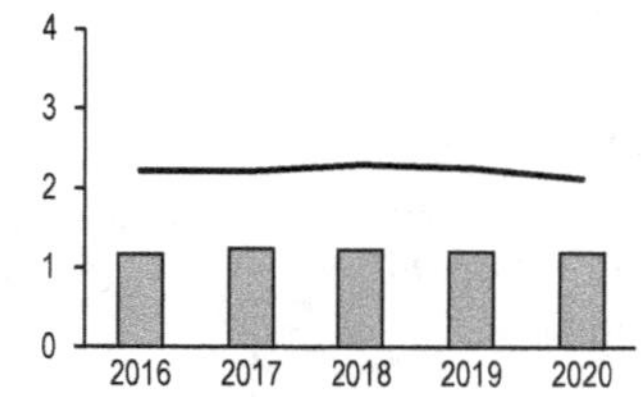

	2016	2017	2018	2019	2020
Raleigh	1.17	1.24	1.23	1.20	1.19
Average	2.22	2.21	2.30	2.26	2.13

Workload Measures

Total Calls Answered per 1,000 Population

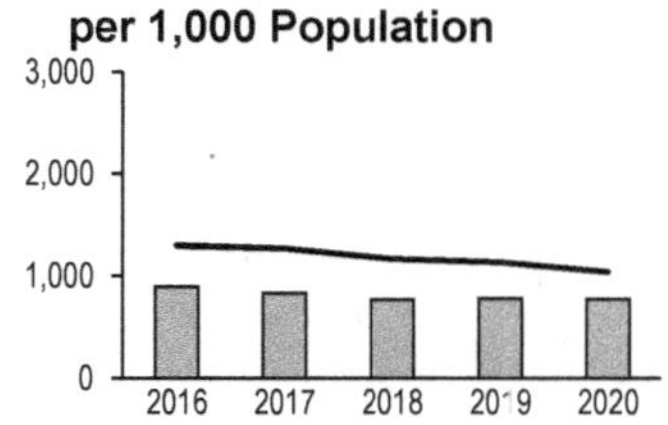

	2016	2017	2018	2019	2020
Raleigh	893	828	767	778	770
Average	1,296	1,264	1,166	1,130	1,042

Calls Dispatched per 1,000 Population

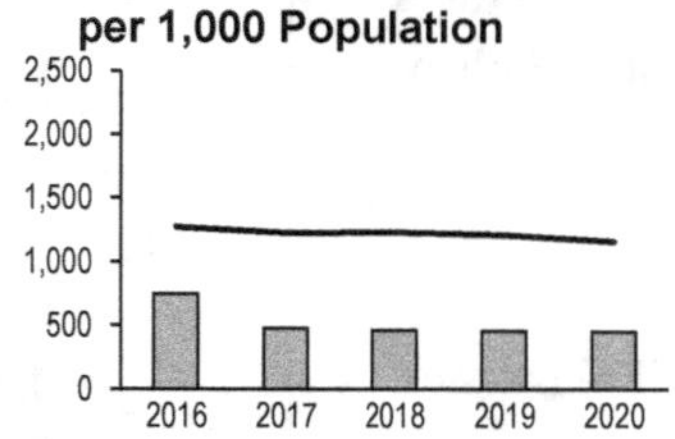

	2016	2017	2018	2019	2020
Raleigh	743	475	458	454	449
Average	1,267	1,222	1,225	1,204	1,159

E-911 Calls as a Percentage of All Incoming Calls

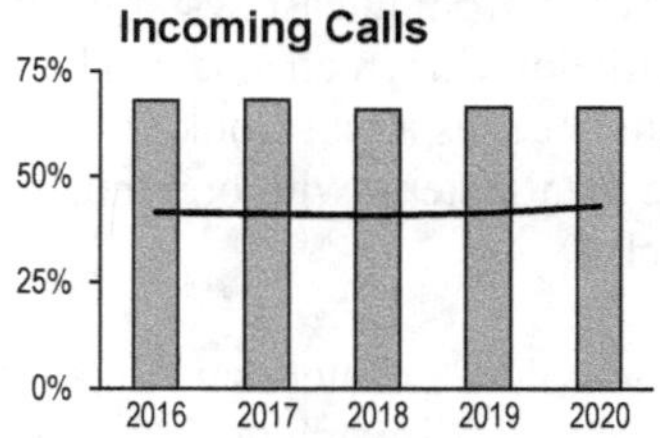

	2016	2017	2018	2019	2020
Raleigh	67.9%	68.0%	65.7%	66.3%	66.3%
Average	41.3%	41.0%	40.8%	41.4%	43.1%

Efficiency Measures

Calls Answered per Telecommunicator

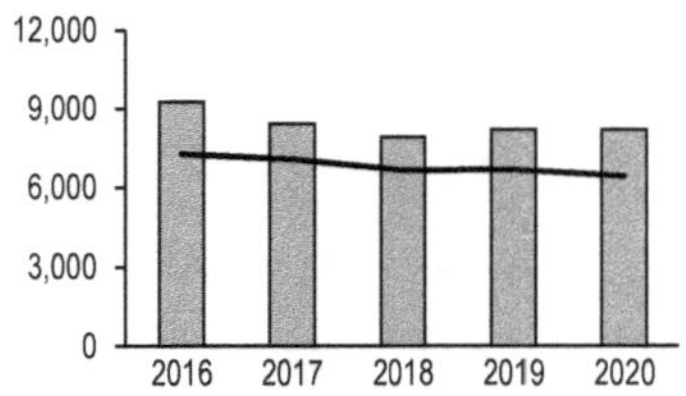

	2016	2017	2018	2019	2020
Raleigh	9,273	8,419	7,915	8,188	8,188
Average	7,274	7,068	6,655	6,675	6,425

Calls Dispatched per Telecommunicator

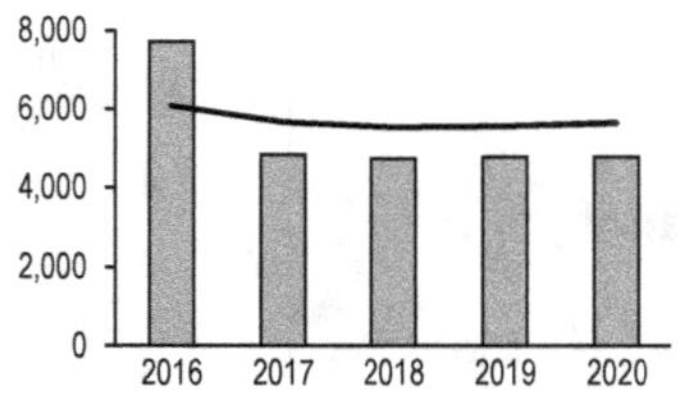

	2016	2017	2018	2019	2020
Raleigh	7,722	4,829	4,728	4,777	4,777
Average	6,069	5,660	5,529	5,556	5,650

Emergency Communications Cost per Call Dispatched

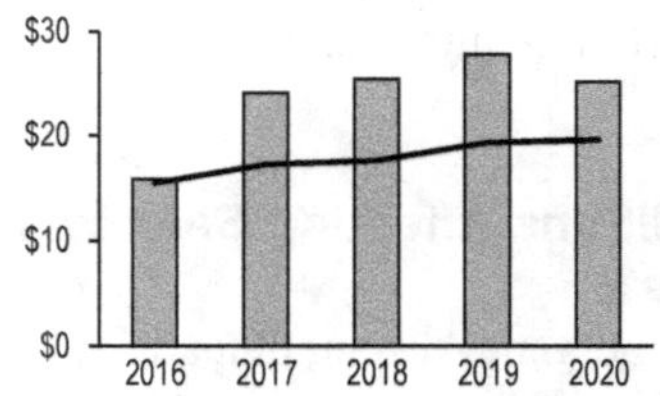

	2016	2017	2018	2019	2020
Raleigh	$15.88	$24.15	$25.49	$27.87	$25.22
Average	$15.44	$17.28	$17.65	$19.34	$19.57

Effectiveness Measures

Number of Seconds from Initial Ring to Answer

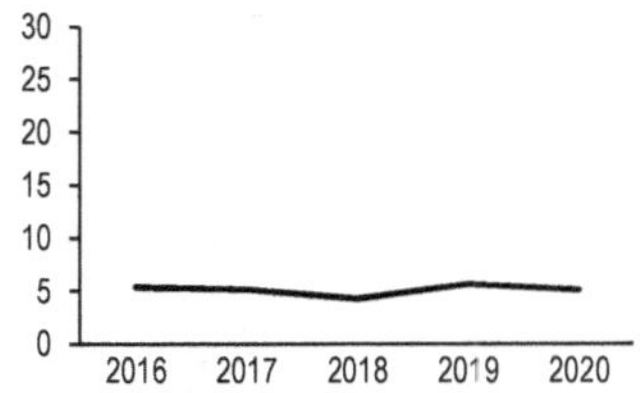

	2016	2017	2018	2019	2020
Raleigh					0
Average	5	5	4	6	5

Percent of E-911 Calls Answered within Twenty Seconds

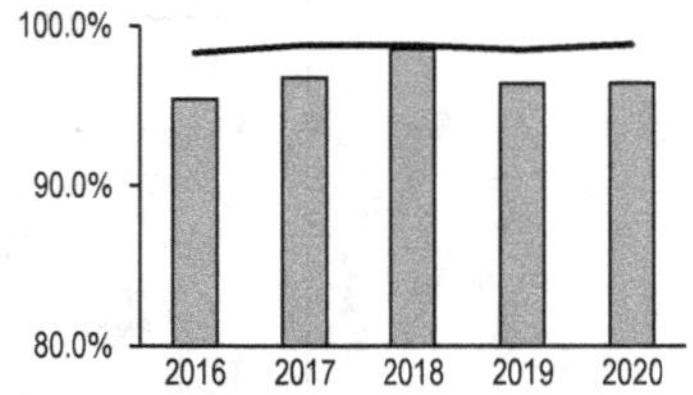

	2016	2017	2018	2019	2020
Raleigh	95.4%	96.7%	98.5%	96.4%	96.4%
Average	98.3%	98.8%	98.8%	98.5%	98.8%

Average Time in Seconds from CAD Entry to Dispatch for Priority One Calls

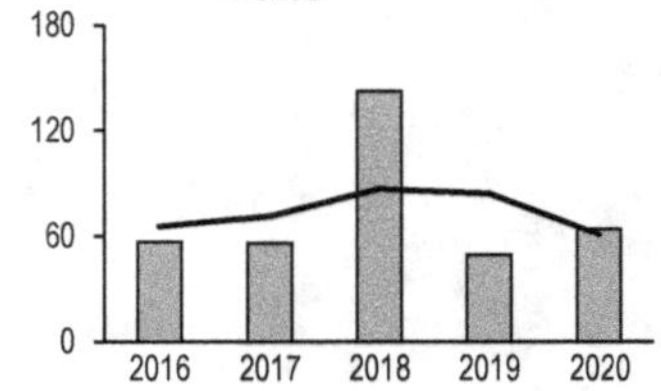

	2016	2017	2018	2019	2020
Raleigh	56	56	142	49	64
Average	65	71	86	84	61

Winston-Salem — Emergency Communications

Fiscal Year 2019-20

Explanatory Information

Service Level and Delivery

Winston-Salem's Emergency Communications Division is part of the police department and handles 911 and non-emergency calls for police and fire. Calls received for EMS, the sheriff's office, county fire, and the highway patrol are transferred to the appropriate agency. All telecommunicators are hired and trained as call-takers and dispatchers.

The city owns the infrastructure but contracts with local vendors to provide telecommunications services. The City of Winston-Salem and Forsyth County implemented a voice radio system in October 2004. The Motorola ASTRO 800 MHz Trunked Simulcast system is made up of eight tower sites utilizing fifteen channels. The Winston-Salem Police Department uses a non-trunked 800 MHz system for the mobile data system, with one transmitter site using three channels.

Winston-Salem's center handled a total of 446,177 calls in the fiscal year, dispatching 237,578 calls. The city defines highest-priority emergency calls as calls with a significant threat of imminent injury to persons or calls for crimes against persons that are in progress or have just occurred and the suspect is still there.

Winston-Salem received $528,588 in E-911 revenues to support system operations.

Conditions Affecting Service, Performance, and Costs

The Emergency Communications Division has been short operators from its authorized total during some of the years.

The system has not been able to provide data on calls answered in the 20-second interval in the past, but improvements now show this data.

Municipal Profile

Population (OSBM 2019)	244,739
Land Area (Square Miles)	132.55
Persons per Square Mile	1,846
Median Household Income U.S. Census 2016	$40,584
County	Forsyth

Service Profile

Primary or Secondary Answering Point	Primary
Calls Dispatched	
Police	Yes
Fire	Yes
Other	No
FTE Positions	
Telecommunicators/Call-Takers	45.0
Other	2.0
Total Positions	47.0
Average Length of Service for Call-Takers	9.5 years
Total Incoming Calls	446,177
Total 911 Calls	209,526
Total Calls Dispatched	237,578
Outgoing Calls Other than Dispatch	70,822
Revenue from E-911 Fees	$528,588

Full Cost Profile

Cost Breakdown by Percentage	
Personal Services	69.3%
Operating Costs	26.2%
Capital Costs	4.5%
TOTAL	100.0%
Cost Breakdown in Dollars	
Personal Services	$3,693,329
Operating Costs	$1,395,281
Capital Costs	$241,988
TOTAL	$5,330,598

Winston-Salem — Emergency Communications

Key: Winston-Salem ■ Benchmarking Average — Fiscal Years 2016 through 2020

Resource Measures

Emergency Communications Services Costs per Capita

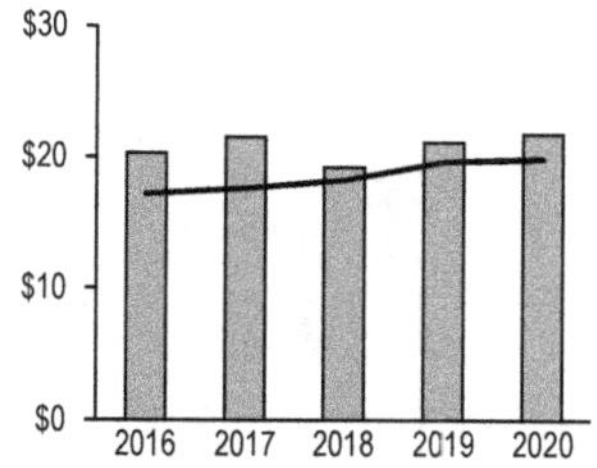

	2016	2017	2018	2019	2020
Winston-Salem	$20.29	$21.49	$19.18	$21.11	$21.78
Average	$17.16	$17.58	$18.22	$19.62	$19.83

Emergency Communications FTEs per 10,000 Population

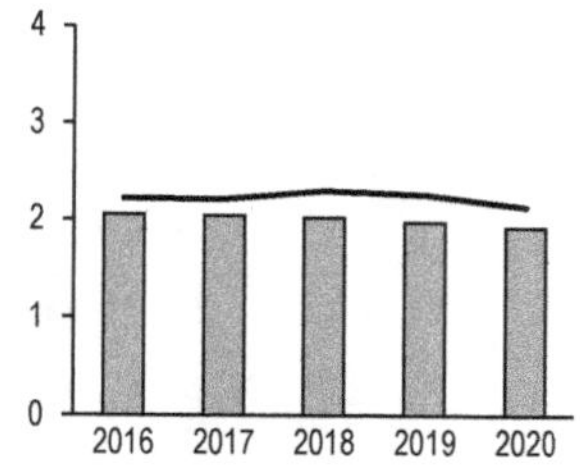

	2016	2017	2018	2019	2020
Winston-Salem	2.05	2.04	2.02	1.97	1.92
Average	2.22	2.21	2.30	2.26	2.13

Workload Measures

Total Calls Answered per 1,000 Population

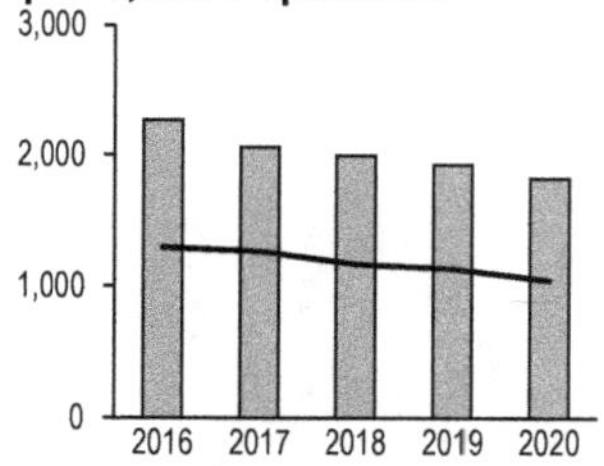

	2016	2017	2018	2019	2020
Winston-Salem	2,268	2,060	1,997	1,929	1,823
Average	1,296	1,264	1,166	1,130	1,042

Calls Dispatched per 1,000 Population

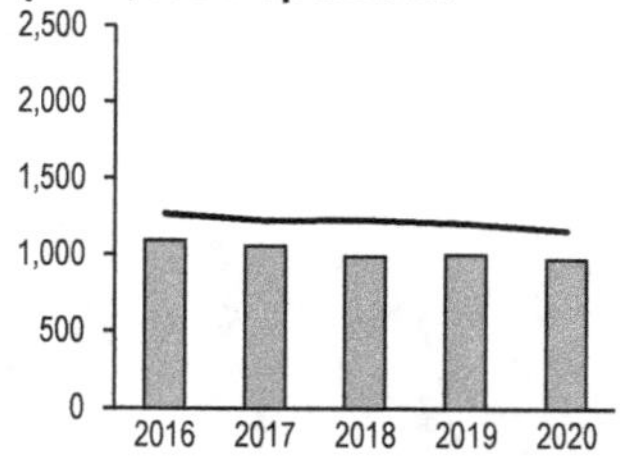

	2016	2017	2018	2019	2020
Winston-Salem	1,091	1,052	986	998	971
Average	1,267	1,222	1,225	1,204	1,159

E-911 Calls as a Percentage of All Incoming Calls

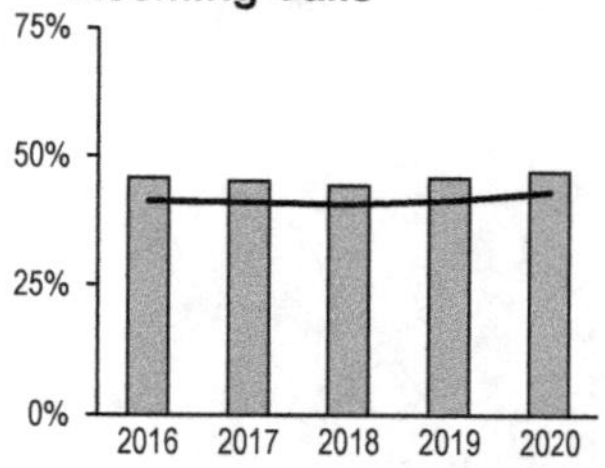

	2016	2017	2018	2019	2020
Winston-Salem	45.8%	45.2%	44.2%	45.8%	47.0%
Average	41.3%	41.0%	40.8%	41.4%	43.1%

Efficiency Measures

Calls Answered per Telecommunicator

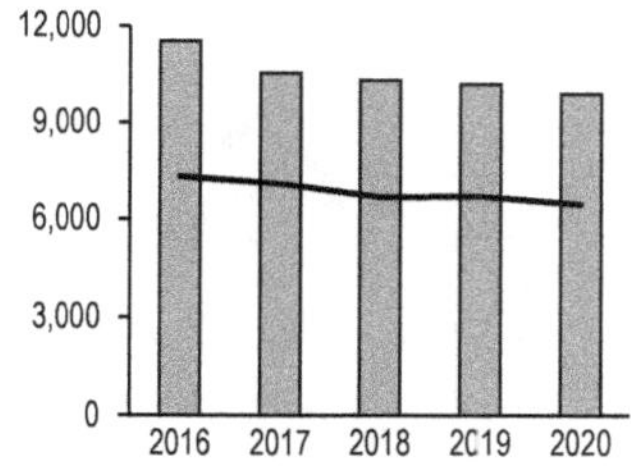

	2016	2017	2018	2019	2020
Winston-Salem	11,528	10,545	10,327	10,209	9,915
Average	7,274	7,068	6,655	6,675	6,425

Calls Dispatched per Telecommunicator

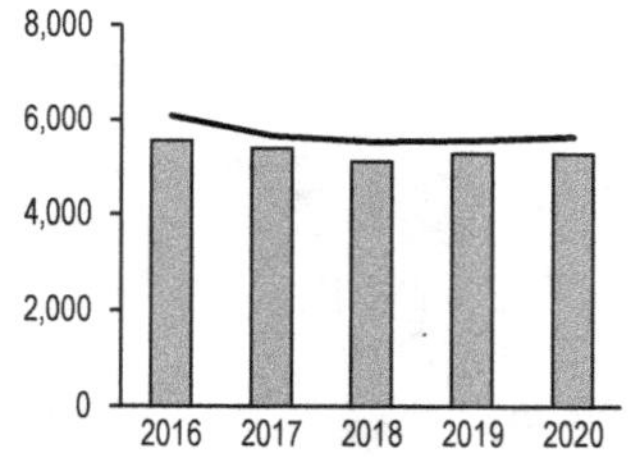

	2016	2017	2018	2019	2020
Winston-Salem	5,544	5,383	5,101	5,281	5,280
Average	6,069	5,660	5,529	5,556	5,650

Emergency Communications Cost per Call Dispatched

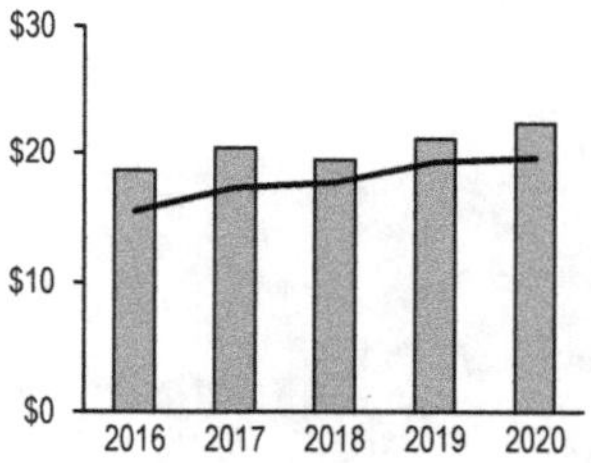

	2016	2017	2018	2019	2020
Winston-Salem	$18.60	$20.43	$19.44	$21.15	$22.44
Average	$15.44	$17.28	$17.65	$19.34	$19.57

Effectiveness Measures

Number of Seconds from Initial Ring to Answer

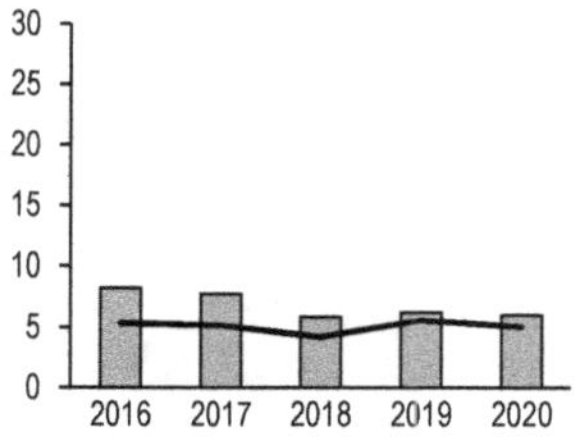

	2016	2017	2018	2019	2020
Winston-Salem	8	8	6	6	6
Average	5	5	4	6	5

Percent of E-911 Calls Answered within Twenty Seconds

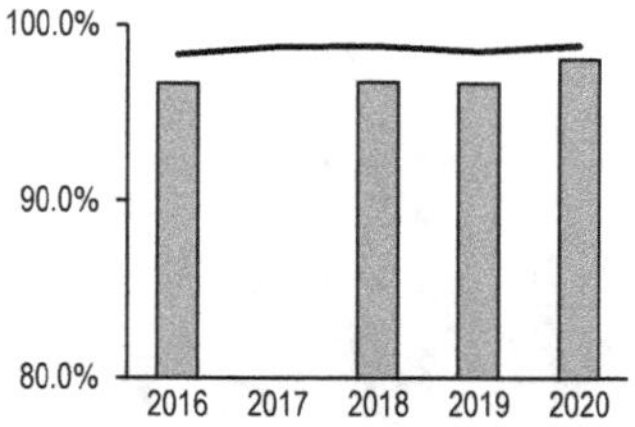

	2016	2017	2018	2019	2020
Winston-Salem	96.6%		96.7%	96.7%	98.1%
Average	98.3%	98.8%	98.8%	98.5%	98.8%

Average Time in Seconds from CAD Entry to Dispatch for Priority One Calls

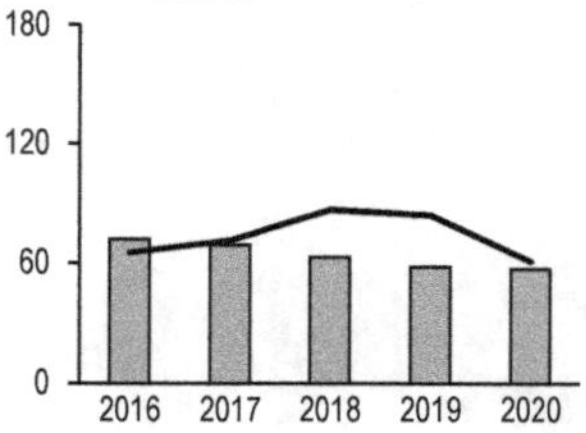

	2016	2017	2018	2019	2020
Winston-Salem	72	69	63	58	57
Average	65	71	86	84	61

UNC | SCHOOL OF GOVERNMENT
North Carolina Benchmarking Project

Performance and Cost Data

ASPHALT MAINTENANCE AND REPAIR

PERFORMANCE MEASURES FOR ASPHALT MAINTENANCE AND REPAIR

SERVICE DEFINITION

Asphalt Maintenance and Repair includes the activities of pothole repair, repaving, surface treatment, structure adjustments, milling, and utility cuts. It does not include work on reconstruction, handicap ramps, storm drainage, sidewalks, curb and gutter, right-of-way maintenance, street cleaning and sweeping, pavement marking, lane widening, unpaved street maintenance, or snow and ice removal.

NOTES ON PERFORMANCE MEASURES

1. Lane Miles Maintained

This measure refers to total lane miles that a municipality maintains, including state streets and municipal streets. The standard lane mile is 12 feet in width and 5,280 feet in length. Some jurisdictions do not track lane miles. Therefore, a methodology must be employed to calculate lane miles for participation.

2. Potholes and Utility Cuts per Lane Mile

Breaks in pavement due to potholes or to intentional utility cuts affect asphalt maintenance workload in the short term and long term because of breaks in the pavement integrity.

3. Cost of Road Treatment per Lane Mile

This is the cost of different types of asphalt treatment that a municipality may use to maintain or repair roads. Treatments include preservation work, such as crack or slurry sealing; resurfacing, which is typically one to two inches of new asphalt; and rehabilitation, which combines resurfacing with milling work to repair more damaged roads.

4. Cost of Asphalt Maintenance and Repair

Total cost of asphalt maintenance and repair represents the total direct, indirect, and capital costs taken from the accounting form. "Cost of maintenance" represents total cost from the accounting form minus cost of any treatment efforts by contract and municipal crews.

5. Percentage of Street Segments Rated 85 or Better and Below 45

Many municipalities use standard rating systems for assessing street pavement condition. These systems apply professionally determined criteria and embody scales that provide relatively objective ratings. These measures indicate the proportion of street segments that are rated 85 or better, which is good condition, and those rated below 45, which is poor condition, on the most recent street pavement assessment.

6. Percentage of Potholes Repaired within Twenty-Four Hours

Repair of potholes in a timely manner is important for maintaining pavement integrity and minimizing further damage to the street and vehicle traffic.

Asphalt Maintenance and Repair

Summary of Key Dimensions of Service

City or Town	Lane Miles Maintained	Total Lane Miles Treated by Type			Percent Treated			FTE Positions for City Staff
		Preservation	Resurfacing	Rehabilitation	Preservation	Resurfacing	Rehabilitation	
Apex	431.49	26.1	0.0	6.0	6.0%	0.0%	1.4%	14.0
Chapel Hill	333.40	0.0	0.0	5.3	0.0%	0.0%	1.6%	4.6
Charlotte	5,445.03	0.6	2.6	138.8	0.0%	0.0%	2.5%	120.0
Concord	712.92	0.0	0.0	0.0	0.0%	0.0%	0.0%	12.3
Goldsboro	324.68	0.0	0.0	21.4	0.0%	0.0%	6.6%	6.0
Greensboro	2,431.00	23.7	68.7	0.0	1.0%	2.8%	0.0%	51.0
Hickory	719.79	0.0	7.0	1.7	0.0%	1.0%	0.2%	7.0
Raleigh	2,356.00	16.0	27.0	0.0	0.7%	1.1%	0.0%	41.0
Wilson	697.17	2.2	20.9	0.0	0.3%	3.0%	0.0%	5.5
Winston-Salem	2,805.50	7.2	22.3	0.0	0.3%	0.8%	0.0%	43.3

EXPLANATORY FACTORS

These are factors that the project found affected asphalt maintenance and repair performance and cost in one or more of the municipalities:

Costs of materials in different cities
Weather conditions and terrain
Vehicle burden placed on streets
Age of street infrastructure
Depth of materials applied in repaving
Extent of contracting

Asphalt Maintenance and Repair

Fiscal Year 2019-20

Explanatory Information

Service Level and Delivery

The Town of Apex's Streets Department was responsible for maintaining approximately 431.5 lane miles during the fiscal year. The Streets Department is part of the Public Works and Utilities Division for the town.

The town rehabilitated 6.0 lane miles during the year, which involves milling and resurfacing. The Town also did preservation work on 26.1 lane miles. This represented treatment of about 7.4 percent of total lane miles maintained.

The city reported that 42 percent of its lane miles were rated 85 or better on the pavement condition rating. The rating was performed by US Infrastructure of Carolina, Inc. using surveying in 2020.

The number of potholes reported for the fiscal year was sixty-four. The town only repairs within one day those potholes that are considered large and dangerous. Smaller potholes are repaired when the streets crews can get to them.

The Streets Department also repaired fifty-five utility cuts and twenty-seven maintenance patches.

Conditions Affecting Service, Performance, and Costs

Hurricane Matthew in September 2016 had impacts on Apex, which raised the event to a Federal Emergency Management Agency (FEMA) event and response.

Municipal Profile

Population (OSBM 2019)	61,319
Land Area (Square Miles)	23.61
Persons per Square Mile	2,597
Topography	Flat; gently rolling
Climate	Temperate; little ice and snow

Service Profile

FTE Positions—Crews	12.00
FTE Positions—Other	2.00
Lane Miles Maintained	431.5
Lane Miles Treated	
Preservation	26.1
Resurfacing	0.0
Rehabilitation	6.0
TOTAL	32.1
Total Costs for All Treatment Types	$628,252
Potholes Repaired	64
Number of Utility Cuts	55
Number of Maintenance Patches (exclusive of potholes and utility cuts)	27
Average Cost per Ton of Hot Asphalt during Year	$82.28

Full Cost Profile

Cost Breakdown by Percentage	
Personal Services	17.9%
Operating Costs	78.1%
Capital Costs	3.9%
TOTAL	100.0%
Cost Breakdown in Dollars	
Personal Services	$341,097
Operating Costs	$1,484,664
Capital Costs	$74,725
TOTAL	$1,900,486

Key: Apex ■ Benchmarking Average — Fiscal Years 2016 through 2020

Resource Measures

Asphalt Maintenance and Repair Services Costs per Capita

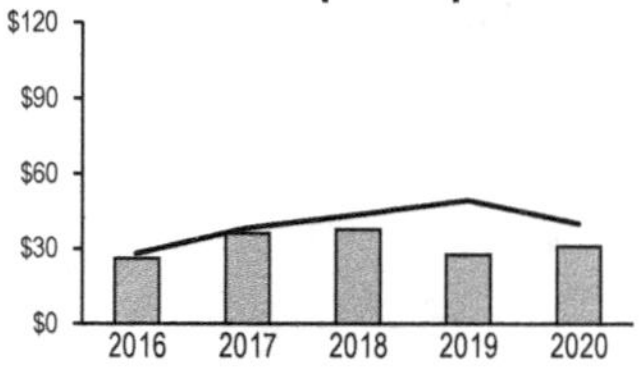

	2016	2017	2018	2019	2020
Apex	$26.08	$36.24	$37.60	$27.68	$30.99
Average	$27.80	$38.27	$43.58	$49.28	$39.86

Asphalt Maintenance and Repair FTEs per 10,000 Population

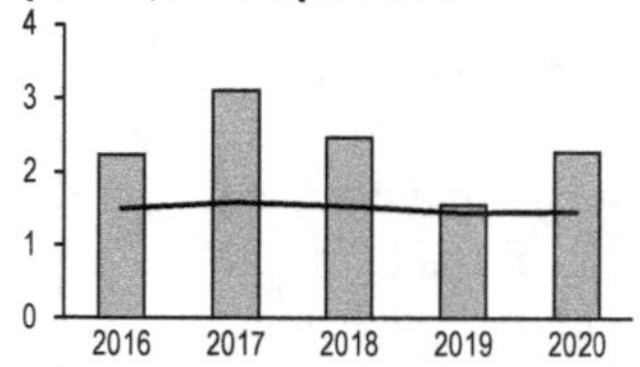

	2016	2017	2018	2019	2020
Apex	2.23	3.11	2.48	1.56	2.28
Average	1.49	1.58	1.53	1.44	1.46

Service Costs per Lane Mile of Road Maintained

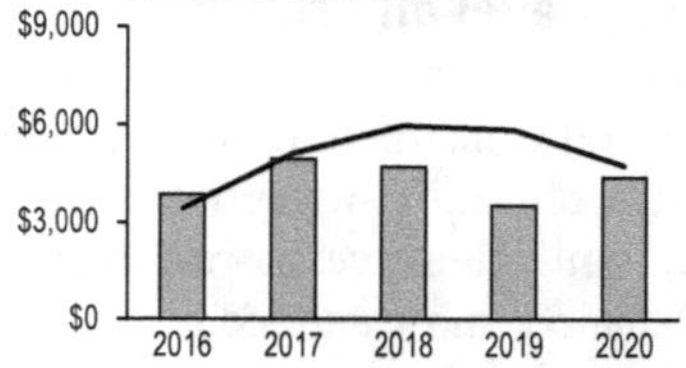

	2016	2017	2018	2019	2020
Apex	$3,863	$4,949	$4,714	$3,530	$4,404
Average	$3,426	$5,133	$5,961	$5,839	$4,759

Workload Measures

Number of Lane Miles Maintained per 1,000 Population

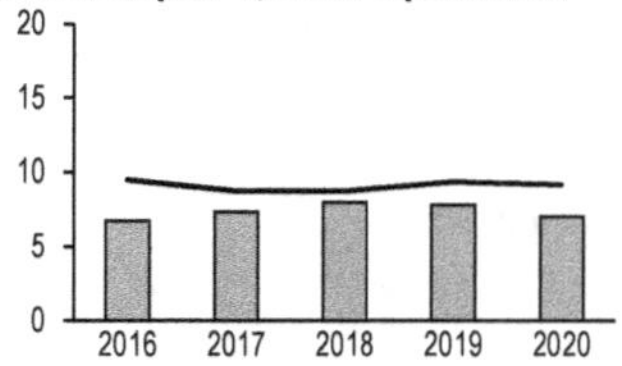

	2016	2017	2018	2019	2020
Apex	6.8	7.3	8.0	7.8	7.0
Average	9.5	8.7	8.8	9.3	9.2

Reported Potholes per Lane Mile Maintained

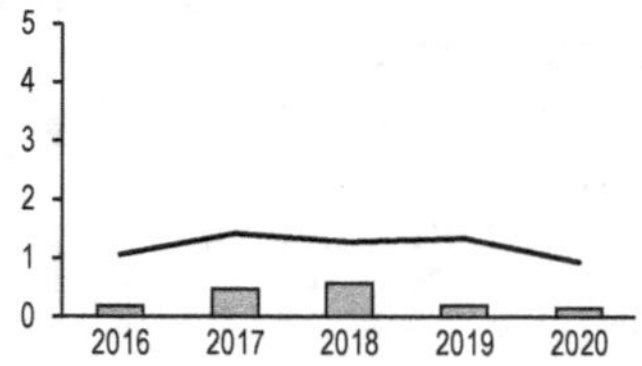

	2016	2017	2018	2019	2020
Apex	0.18	0.47	0.57	0.20	0.15
Average	1.06	1.42	1.27	1.34	0.92

Repaired Utility Cuts per Lane Mile Maintained

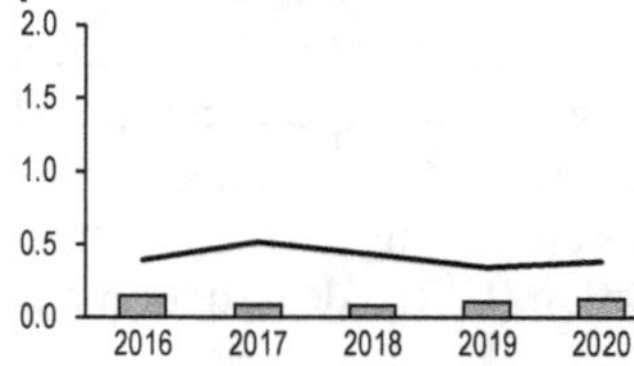

	2016	2017	2018	2019	2020
Apex	0.15	0.09	0.08	0.11	0.13
Average	0.39	0.51	0.43	0.34	0.38

Efficiency Measures

Cost of Maintenance per Lane Mile Maintained

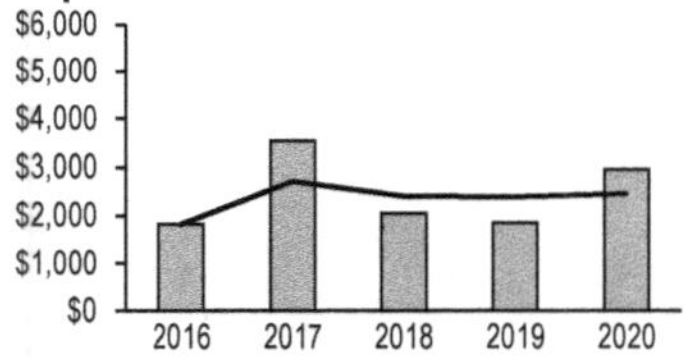

	2016	2017	2018	2019	2020
Apex	$1,827	$3,545	$2,050	$1,852	$2,948
Average	$1,806	$2,696	$2,403	$2,379	$2,446

Cost per Lane Mile for Preservation Treatment

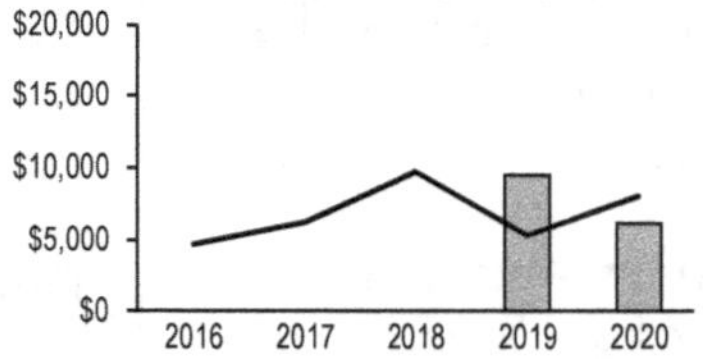

	2016	2017	2018	2019	2020
Apex				$9,508	$6,165
Average	$4,648	$6,231	$9,697	$5,320	$8,025

Cost per Lane Mile for Resurfacing Treatment

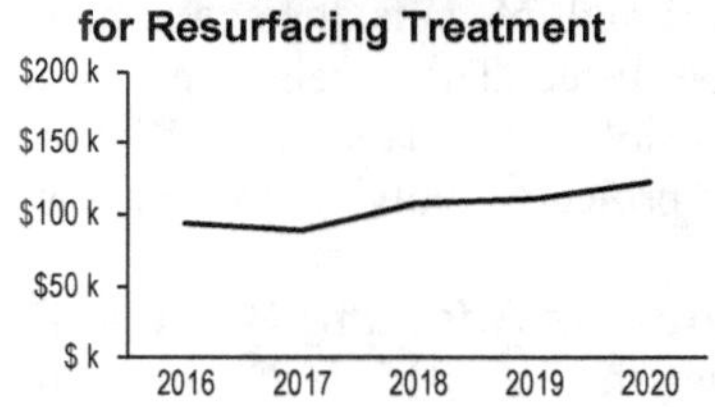

	2016	2017	2018	2019	2020
Apex					
Average	$93 k	$89 k	$107 k	$110 k	$122 k

Cost per Lane Mile for Rehabilitation Treatment

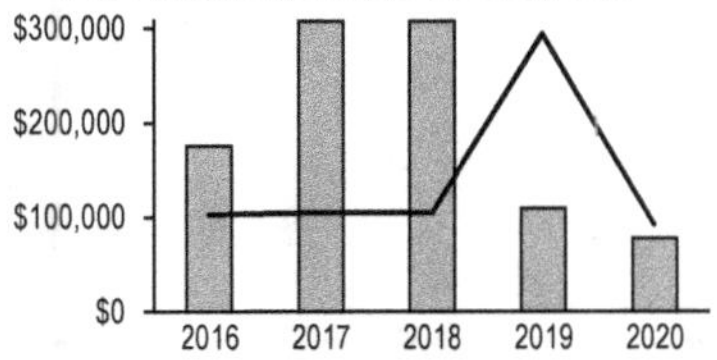

	2016	2017	2018	2019	2020
Apex	$176 k	$308 k	$308 k	$110 k	$78 k
Average	$103 k	$105 k	$105 k	$294 k	$92 k

Cost per Ton for Contract Resurfacing

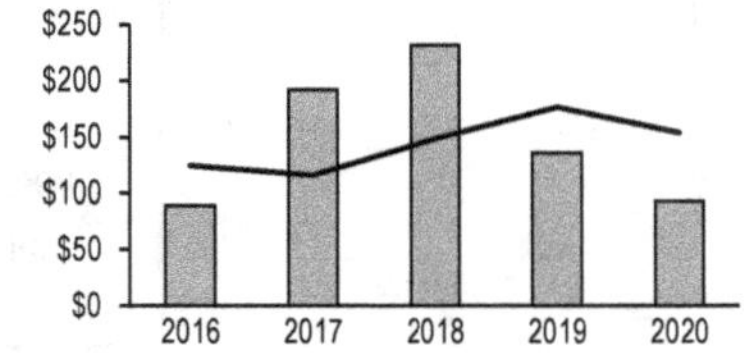

	2016	2017	2018	2019	2020
Apex	$89	$192	$231	$136	$93
Average	$124	$115	$148	$176	$154

Effectiveness Measures

Percent of Lane Miles Rated 85 or Better

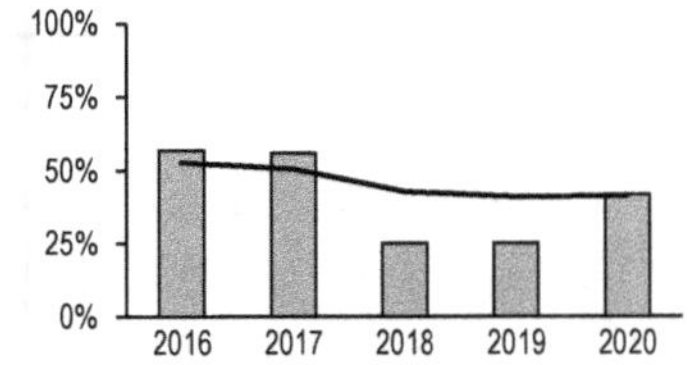

	2016	2017	2018	2019	2020
Apex	57%	56%	25%	25%	42%
Average	53%	50%	43%	41%	41%

Percent of Lane Miles Rated Below 45

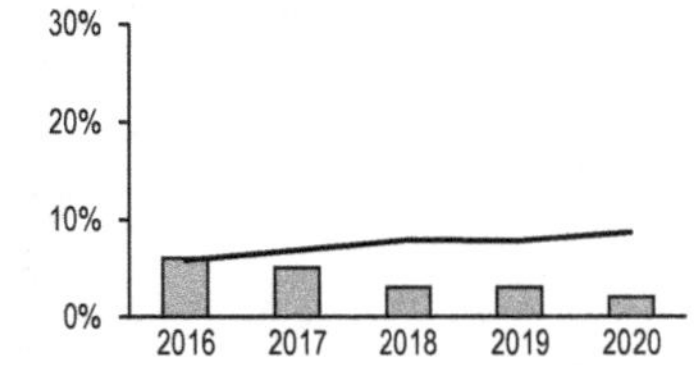

	2016	2017	2018	2019	2020
Apex	6.0%	5.0%	3.0%	3.0%	2.0%
Average	5.7%	6.8%	7.9%	7.8%	8.7%

Percentage of Potholes Repaired within 24 hours

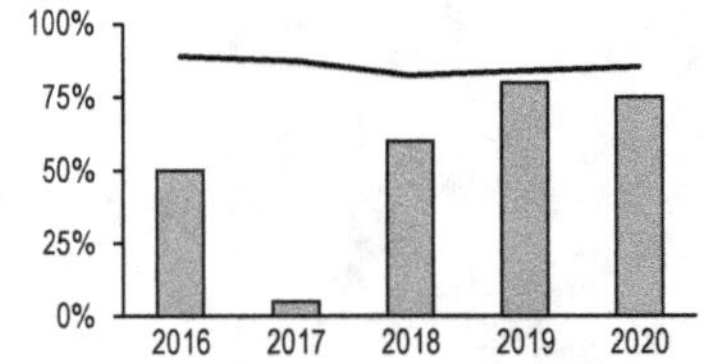

	2016	2017	2018	2019	2020
Apex	50%	5%	60%	80%	75%
Average	89%	87%	83%	84%	85%

Chapel Hill — Asphalt Maintenance and Repair

Fiscal Year 2019-20

Explanatory Information

Service Level and Delivery

Asphalt maintenance is performed by the Town of Chapel Hill Streets and Construction Services Division of the Public Works Department. The Town provides services in asphalt maintenance, sidewalk maintenance, storm debris cleanup, gravel road maintenance, snow and ice removal, and cleanup following special events. During the fiscal year the town was responsible for maintaining approximately 333 lane miles. During the year 5.3 lane miles were treatedby contract crews doing rehabilitation work or about 1.6 percent of total lane miles.

The town reported that 43.6 percent of its lane miles rated 85 or above on its most recent pavement condition rating conducted in 2018. The roads were rated by US Infrastructure of Carolina using the system relying on the Institute for Transportation Research and Education (ITRE) degradation curves.

The number of potholes reported for the year was sixty. Permit holders repaired thirty-four utility cuts during the year. A permit is required for any non-town entity cutting inside the right-of-way. The permit holder is responsible for all repairs. Because one permit can involve multiple cuts, the actual number of cuts is higher than the number listed. The streets inspector monitors the work and bills the responsible party. The Public Works Engineering Division inspects larger projects involving a water or sewer line replacement.

Conditions Affecting Service, Performance, and Costs

Though the FY 2015–16 Chapel Hill budget included $585,222 for annual resurfacing work, this funding was encumbered and carried forward into FY 2016–17 and was not reflected in the costs for this service area for that report year. A total of 5.5 lane miles were resurfaced using FY 2015–16 funds but at the beginning of FY 2016–17. These costs were reported in that year.

The town experienced two significant snow storms in the FY 2017–18 fiscal year which impacted operations and funding.

Municipal Profile

Population (OSBM 2019)	63,639
Land Area (Square Miles)	21.31
Persons per Square Mile	2,987
Topography	Flat; gently rolling
Climate	Temperate; little ice and snow

Service Profile

FTE Positions—Crews	3.10
FTE Positions—Other	1.50
Lane Miles Maintained	333.4
Lane Miles Treated	
Preservation	0.0
Resurfacing	0.0
Rehabilitation	5.3
TOTAL	5.3
Total Costs for All Treatment Types	$538,249
Potholes Repaired	60
Number of Utility Cuts	66
Number of Maintenance Patches (exclusive of potholes and utility cuts)	na
Average Cost per Ton of Hot Asphalt during Year	$68.00

Full Cost Profile

Cost Breakdown by Percentage	
Personal Services	28.6%
Operating Costs	54.8%
Capital Costs	16.7%
TOTAL	100.0%
Cost Breakdown in Dollars	
Personal Services	$464,139
Operating Costs	$890,224
Capital Costs	$270,934
TOTAL	$1,625,297

Chapel Hill — Asphalt Maintenance and Repair

Key: Chapel Hill ■ Benchmarking Average — Fiscal Years 2016 through 2020

Resource Measures

Asphalt Maintenance and Repair Services Costs per Capita

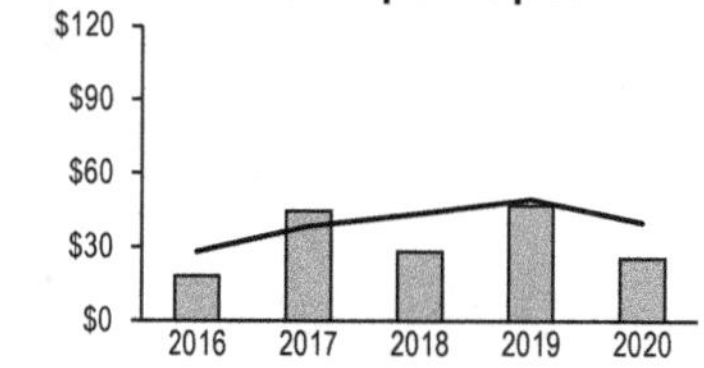

	2016	2017	2018	2019	2020
Chapel Hill	$18.14	$44.52	$28.07	$46.91	$25.54
Average	$27.80	$38.27	$43.58	$49.28	$39.86

Asphalt Maintenance and Repair FTEs per 10,000 Population

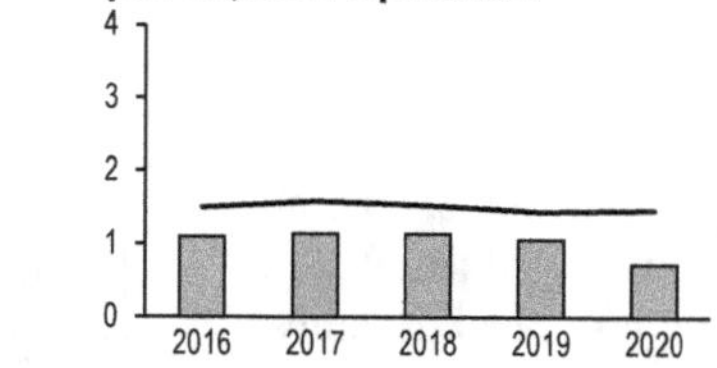

	2016	2017	2018	2019	2020
Chapel Hill	1.09	1.14	1.14	1.06	0.72
Average	1.49	1.58	1.53	1.44	1.46

Service Costs per Lane Mile of Road Maintained

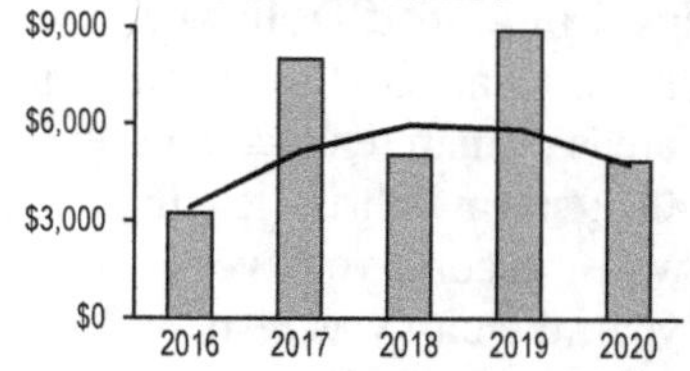

	2016	2017	2018	2019	2020
Chapel Hill	$3,242	$7,992	$5,044	$8,890	$4,875
Average	$3,426	$5,133	$5,961	$5,839	$4,759

Workload Measures

Number of Lane Miles Maintained per 1,000 Population

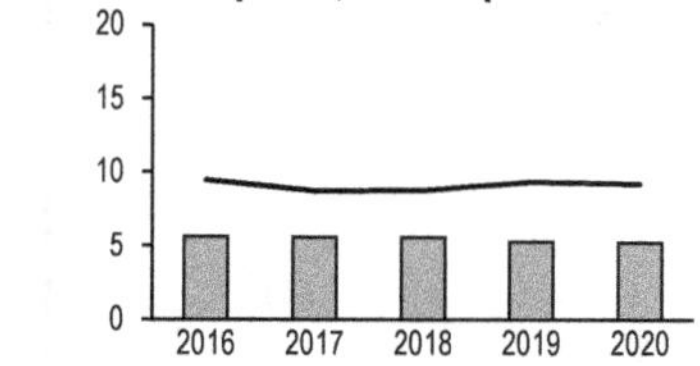

	2016	2017	2018	2019	2020
Chapel Hill	5.6	5.6	5.6	5.3	5.2
Average	9.5	8.7	8.8	9.3	9.2

Reported Potholes per Lane Mile Maintained

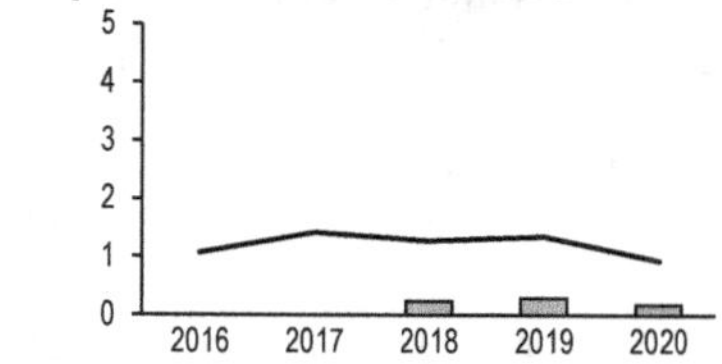

	2016	2017	2018	2019	2020
Chapel Hill			0.23	0.29	0.18
Average	1.06	1.42	1.27	1.34	0.92

Repaired Utility Cuts per Lane Mile Maintained

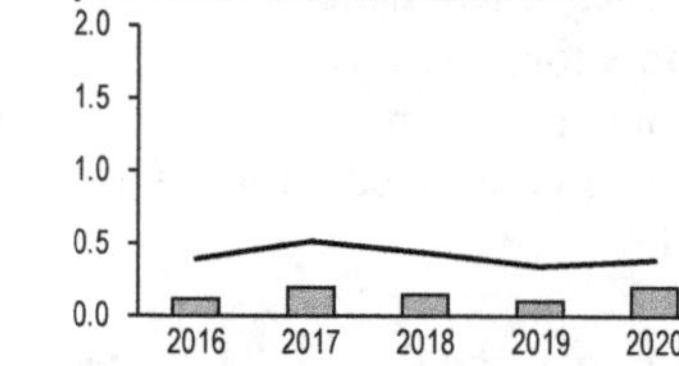

	2016	2017	2018	2019	2020
Chapel Hill	0.12	0.19	0.14	0.10	0.20
Average	0.39	0.51	0.43	0.34	0.38

Efficiency Measures

Cost of Maintenance per Lane Mile Maintained

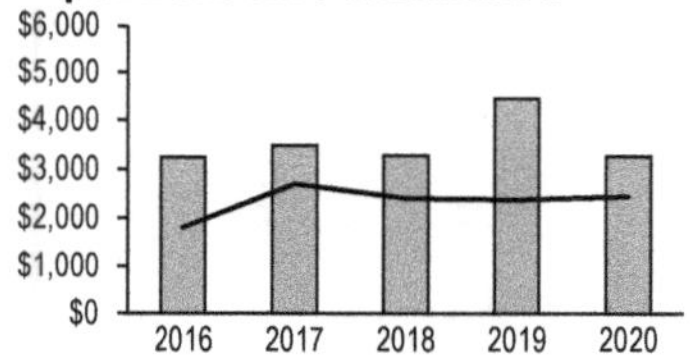

	2016	2017	2018	2019	2020
Chapel Hill	$3,242	$3,479	$3,282	$4,452	$3,260
Average	$1,806	$2,696	$2,403	$2,379	$2,446

Cost per Lane Mile for Preservation Treatment

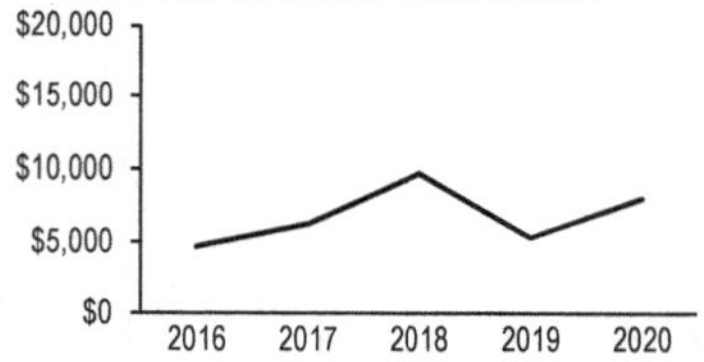

	2016	2017	2018	2019	2020
Chapel Hill					
Average	$4,648	$6,231	$9,697	$5,320	$8,025

Cost per Lane Mile for Resurfacing Treatment

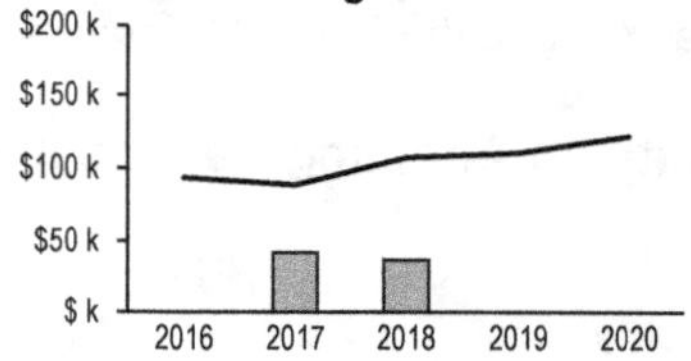

	2016	2017	2018	2019	2020
Chapel Hill		$42 k	$37 k		
Average	$93 k	$89 k	$107 k	$110 k	$122 k

Cost per Lane Mile for Rehabilitation Treatment

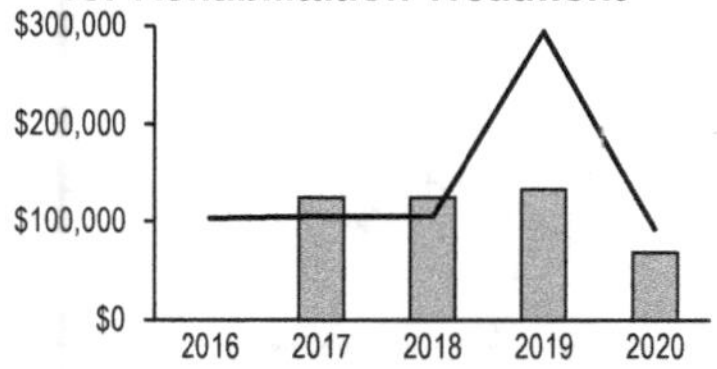

	2016	2017	2018	2019	2020
Chapel Hill		$125 k	$125 k	$133 k	$68 k
Average	$103 k	$105 k	$105 k	$294 k	$92 k

Cost per Ton for Contract Resurfacing

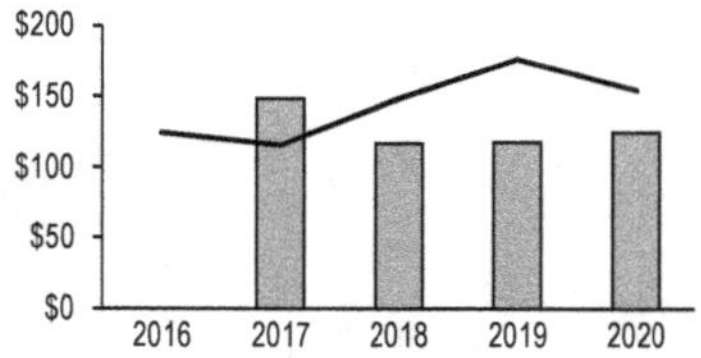

	2016	2017	2018	2019	2020
Chapel Hill		$148	$117	$118	$125
Average	$124	$115	$148	$176	$154

Effectiveness Measures

Percent of Lane Miles Rated 85 or Better

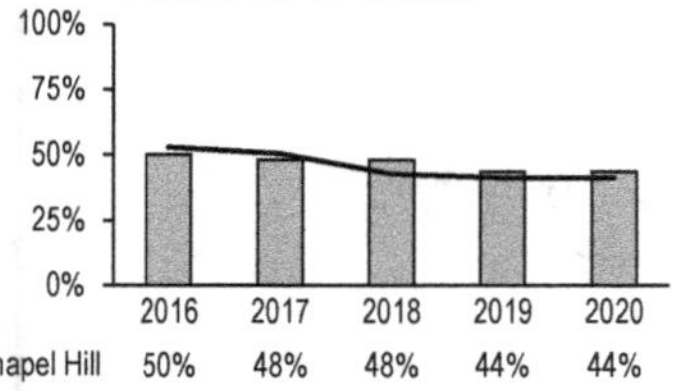

	2016	2017	2018	2019	2020
Chapel Hill	50%	48%	48%	44%	44%
Average	53%	50%	43%	41%	41%

Percent of Lane Miles Rated Below 45

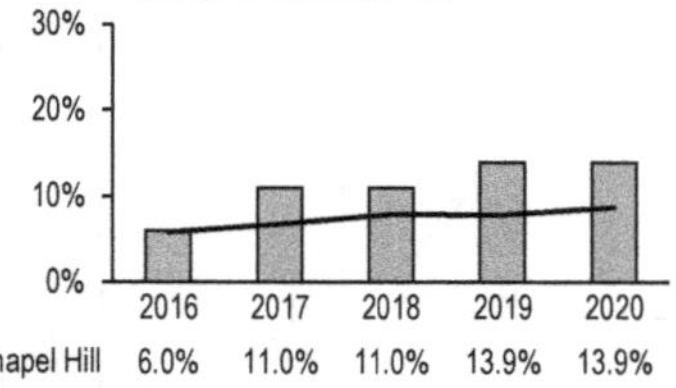

	2016	2017	2018	2019	2020
Chapel Hill	6.0%	11.0%	11.0%	13.9%	13.9%
Average	5.7%	6.8%	7.9%	7.8%	8.7%

Percentage of Potholes Repaired within 24 hours

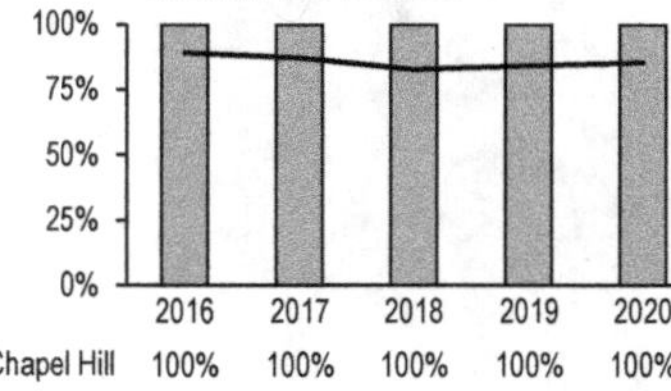

	2016	2017	2018	2019	2020
Chapel Hill	100%	100%	100%	100%	100%
Average	89%	87%	83%	84%	85%

Charlotte — Asphalt Maintenance and Repair

Fiscal Year 2019-20

Explanatory Information

Service Level and Delivery

The City of Charlotte Street Maintenance Division provides service in the areas of maintenance and repair of street drainage structures; sidewalks; storm debris cleanup; and specialty repair items, such as brick walls, decorative pavers, fences, and guardrails. During the fiscal year, the city was responsible for maintaining approximately 5,445 lane miles and treated 142 lane miles, equating to approximately 2.6 percent of total lane miles.

Of the treatment work done during the year, 0.62 lane miles received preservation work, completed by city crews, such as crack sealing or thin overlays. Resurfacing work covered 2.6 lane miles and was done by contractors and city crews. Additionally, 120.8 lane miles were rehabilitated by contractors with milling followed by resurfacing. City crews completed a further 18 lane miles of rehabilitation work as well.

The city reported that 40.81 percent of its lane miles rated 85 or above on its most recent pavement condition rating conducted in 2019.

The number of potholes reported for the fiscal year was 2,244. . A total of 1,188 utility cuts was also repaired during the year by contractors and the Street Maintenance Division.

Conditions Affecting Service, Performance, and Costs

Municipal Profile

Population (OSBM 2019)	863,985
Land Area (Square Miles)	307.41
Persons per Square Mile	2,811
Topography	Flat; gently rolling
Climate	Temperate; little ice and snow

Service Profile

FTE Positions—Crews	101.00
FTE Positions—Other	19.00
Lane Miles Maintained	5,445.0
Lane Miles Treated	
Preservation	0.6
Resurfacing	2.6
Rehabilitation	138.8
TOTAL	142.0
Total Costs for All Treatment Types	$12,510,646
Potholes Repaired	2,244
Number of Utility Cuts	1,188
Number of Maintenance Patches (exclusive of potholes and utility cuts)	na
Average Cost per Ton of Hot Asphalt during Year	$43.82

Full Cost Profile

Cost Breakdown by Percentage	
Personal Services	28.1%
Operating Costs	60.3%
Capital Costs	11.6%
TOTAL	100.0%
Cost Breakdown in Dollars	
Personal Services	$8,291,898
Operating Costs	$17,794,870
Capital Costs	$3,416,455
TOTAL	$29,503,223

Charlotte — Asphalt Maintenance and Repair

Key: Charlotte ▒ Benchmarking Average — Fiscal Years 2016 through 2020

Resource Measures

Asphalt Maintenance and Repair Services Costs per Capita

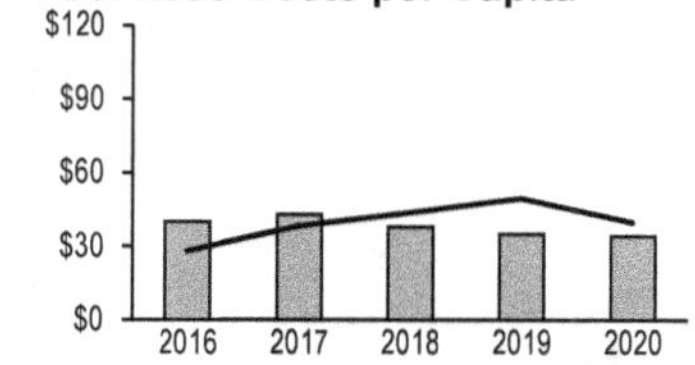

	2016	2017	2018	2019	2020
Charlotte	$40.02	$43.01	$38.01	$35.05	$34.15
Average	$27.80	$38.27	$43.58	$49.28	$39.86

Asphalt Maintenance and Repair FTEs per 10,000 Population

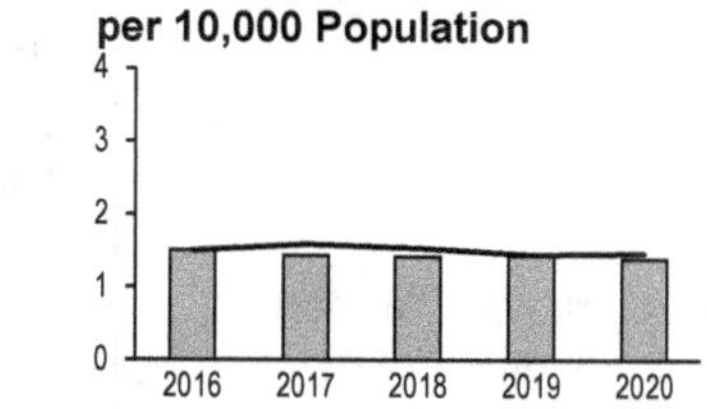

	2016	2017	2018	2019	2020
Charlotte	1.50	1.43	1.42	1.43	1.39
Average	1.49	1.58	1.53	1.44	1.46

Service Costs per Lane Mile of Road Maintained

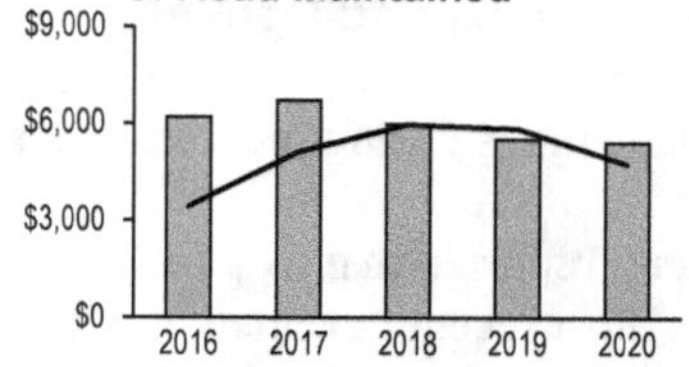

	2016	2017	2018	2019	2020
Charlotte	$6,199	$6,709	$5,982	$5,522	$5,418
Average	$3,426	$5,133	$5,961	$5,839	$4,759

Workload Measures

Number of Lane Miles Maintained per 1,000 Population

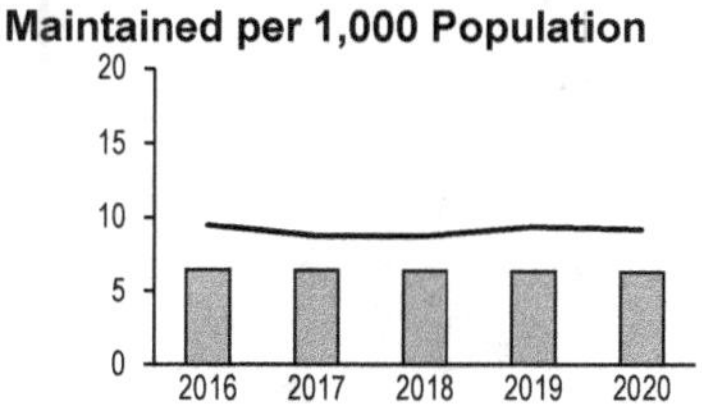

	2016	2017	2018	2019	2020
Charlotte	6.5	6.4	6.4	6.3	6.3
Average	9.5	8.7	8.8	9.3	9.2

Reported Potholes per Lane Mile Maintained

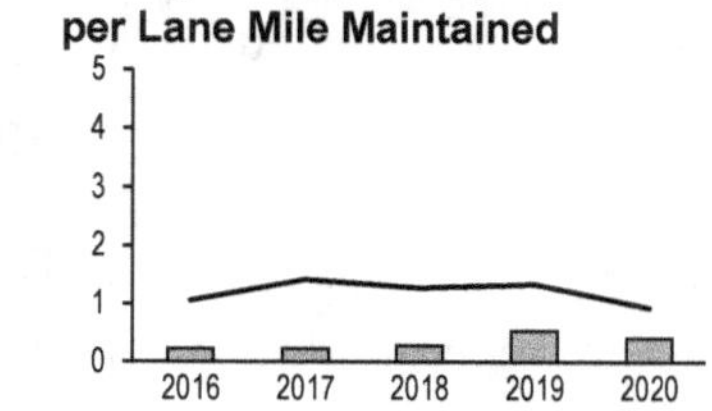

	2016	2017	2018	2019	2020
Charlotte	0.22	0.22	0.28	0.53	0.41
Average	1.06	1.42	1.27	1.34	0.92

Repaired Utility Cuts per Lane Mile Maintained

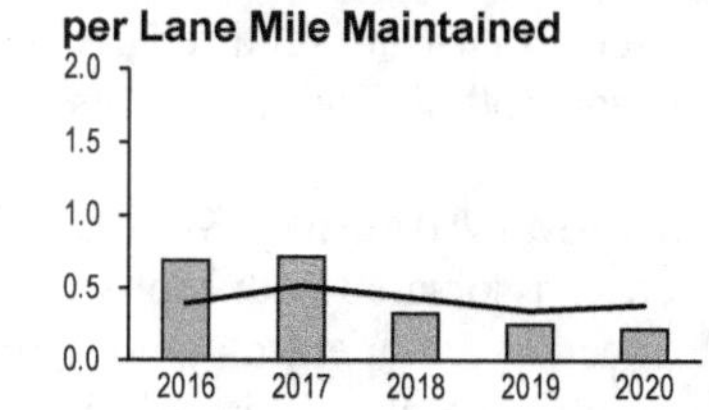

	2016	2017	2018	2019	2020
Charlotte	0.69	0.72	0.33	0.25	0.22
Average	0.39	0.51	0.43	0.34	0.38

Efficiency Measures

Cost of Maintenance per Lane Mile Maintained

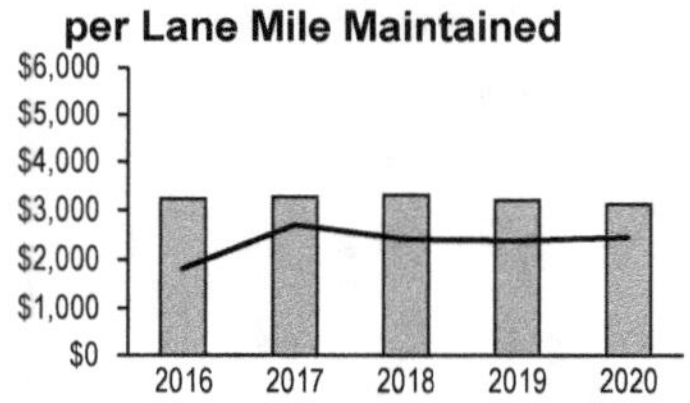

	2016	2017	2018	2019	2020
Charlotte	$3,237	$3,273	$3,317	$3,208	$3,121
Average	$1,806	$2,696	$2,403	$2,379	$2,446

Cost per Lane Mile for Preservation Treatment

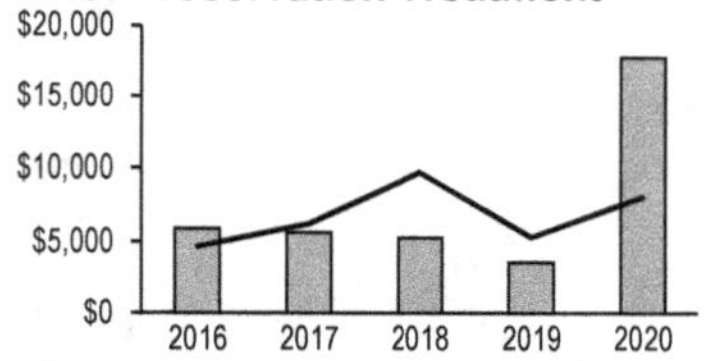

	2016	2017	2018	2019	2020
Charlotte	$5,915	$5,624	$5,293	$3,599	$17,789
Average	$4,648	$6,231	$9,697	$5,320	$8,025

Cost per Lane Mile for Resurfacing Treatment

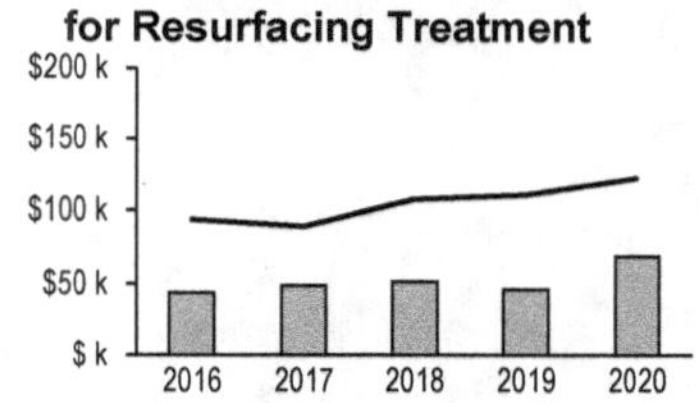

	2016	2017	2018	2019	2020
Charlotte	$44 k	$49 k	$52 k	$46 k	$69 k
Average	$93 k	$89 k	$107 k	$110 k	$122 k

Cost per Lane Mile for Rehabilitation Treatment

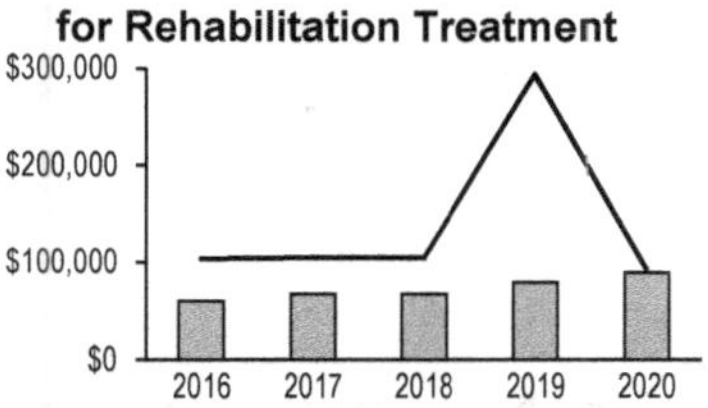

	2016	2017	2018	2019	2020
Charlotte	$60 k	$67 k	$67 k	$79 k	$89 k
Average	$103 k	$105 k	$105 k	$294 k	$92 k

Cost per Ton for Contract Resurfacing

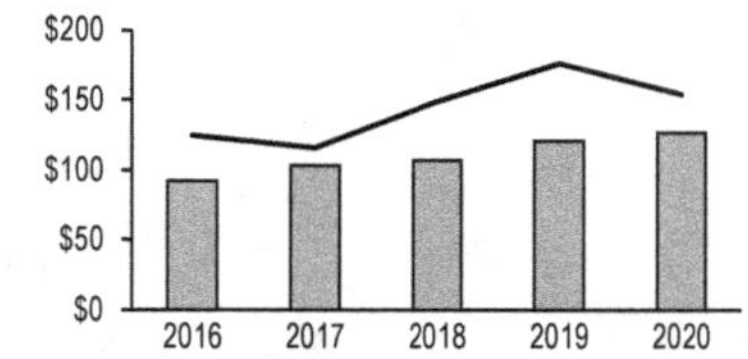

	2016	2017	2018	2019	2020
Charlotte	$92	$103	$107	$121	$127
Average	$124	$115	$148	$176	$154

Effectiveness Measures

Percent of Lane Miles Rated 85 or Better

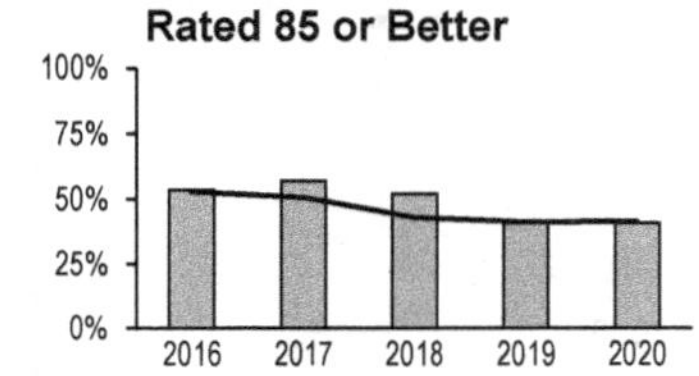

	2016	2017	2018	2019	2020
Charlotte	54%	57%	52%	41%	41%
Average	53%	50%	43%	41%	41%

Percent of Lane Miles Rated Below 45

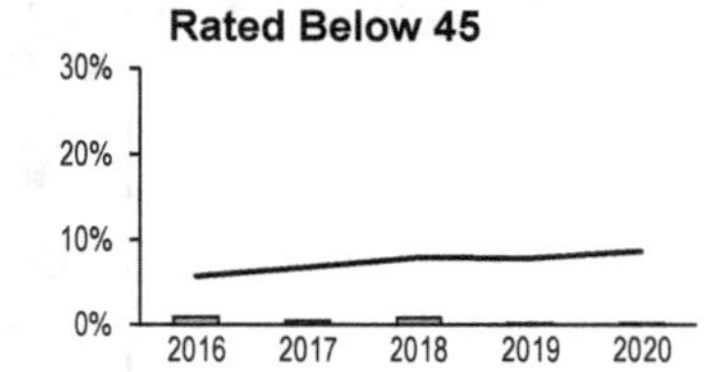

	2016	2017	2018	2019	2020
Charlotte	0.9%	0.5%	0.8%	0.2%	0.2%
Average	5.7%	6.8%	7.9%	7.8%	8.7%

Percentage of Potholes Repaired within 24 hours

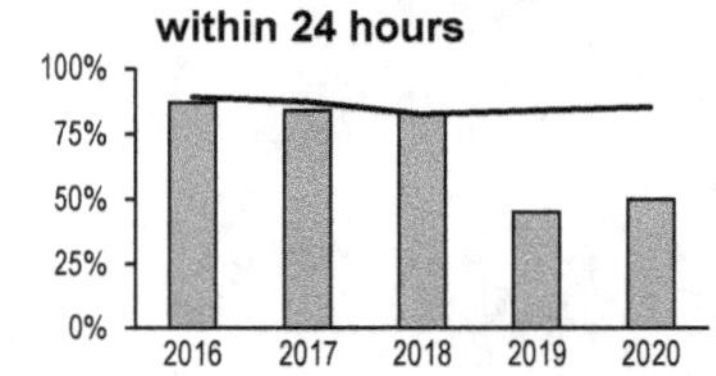

	2016	2017	2018	2019	2020
Charlotte	87%	84%	83%	45%	50%
Average	89%	87%	83%	84%	85%

Concord

Asphalt Maintenance and Repair

Fiscal Year 2019-20

Explanatory Information

Service Level and Delivery

The City of Concord was responsible for maintaining approximately 713 lane miles during the fiscal year.

The city reported that 31 percent of its lane miles rated 85 or above on its most recent pavement condition rating, conducted in 2019 using a city system based on North Carolina Department of Transportation ratings.

The number of potholes reported for the year was 176, including those reported by citizens and the city. Concord also reported 360 utility cuts that were repaired and 163 maintenance patches for work other than potholes or utility cuts.

Conditions Affecting Service, Performance, and Costs

The costs associated with asphalt maintenance and resurfacing are influenced by competition among providers due to the location of three asphalt plants within the city limits.

Municipal Profile

Population (OSBM 2019)	95,453
Land Area (Square Miles)	63.65
Persons per Square Mile	1,500
Topography	Flat; gently rolling
Climate	Temperate; little ice and snow

Service Profile

FTE Positions—Crews	10.75
FTE Positions—Other	1.55
Lane Miles Maintained	712.9
Lane Miles Treated	
Preservation	0.0
Resurfacing	0.0
Rehabilitation	0.0
TOTAL	0.0
Total Costs for All Treatment Types	$0
Potholes Repaired	176
Number of Utility Cuts	360
Number of Maintenance Patches (exclusive of potholes and utility cuts)	163
Average Cost per Ton of Hot Asphalt during Year	$65.00

Full Cost Profile

Cost Breakdown by Percentage	
Personal Services	54.0%
Operating Costs	32.0%
Capital Costs	13.9%
TOTAL	100.0%
Cost Breakdown in Dollars	
Personal Services	$765,499
Operating Costs	$454,091
Capital Costs	$197,386
TOTAL	$1,416,976

Concord — Asphalt Maintenance and Repair

Key: Concord ▒ Benchmarking Average — Fiscal Years 2016 through 2020

Resource Measures

Asphalt Maintenance and Repair Services Costs per Capita

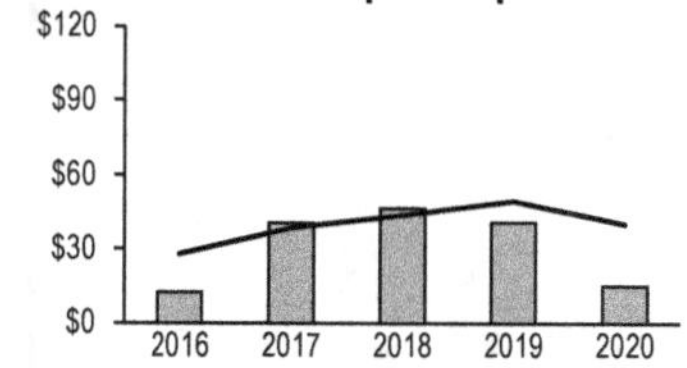

	2016	2017	2018	2019	2020
Concord	$12.21	$40.44	$46.37	$40.73	$14.84
Average	$27.80	$38.27	$43.58	$49.28	$39.86

Asphalt Maintenance and Repair FTEs per 10,000 Population

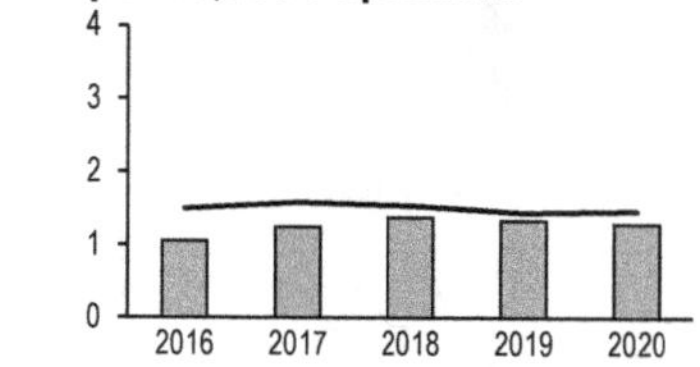

	2016	2017	2018	2019	2020
Concord	1.05	1.24	1.38	1.33	1.29
Average	1.49	1.58	1.53	1.44	1.46

Service Costs per Lane Mile of Road Maintained

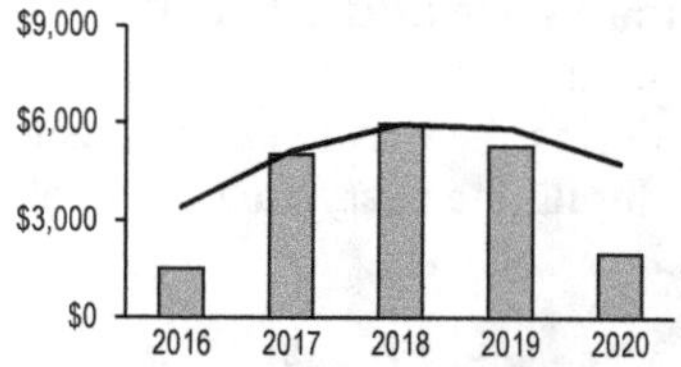

	2016	2017	2018	2019	2020
Concord	$1,515	$5,046	$5,973	$5,299	$1,988
Average	$3,426	$5,133	$5,961	$5,839	$4,759

Workload Measures

Number of Lane Miles Maintained per 1,000 Population

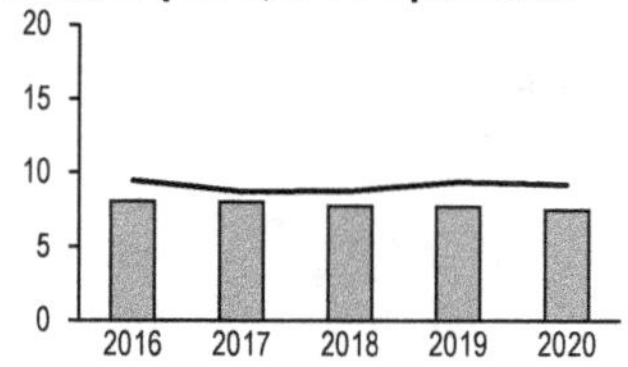

	2016	2017	2018	2019	2020
Concord	8.1	8.0	7.8	7.7	7.5
Average	9.5	8.7	8.8	9.3	9.2

Reported Potholes per Lane Mile Maintained

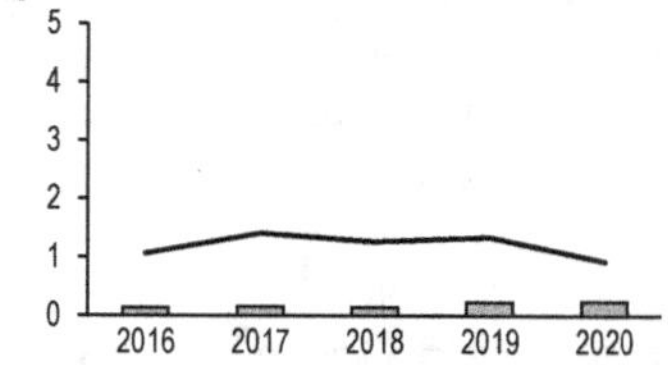

	2016	2017	2018	2019	2020
Concord	0.13	0.16	0.14	0.23	0.25
Average	1.06	1.42	1.27	1.34	0.92

Repaired Utility Cuts per Lane Mile Maintained

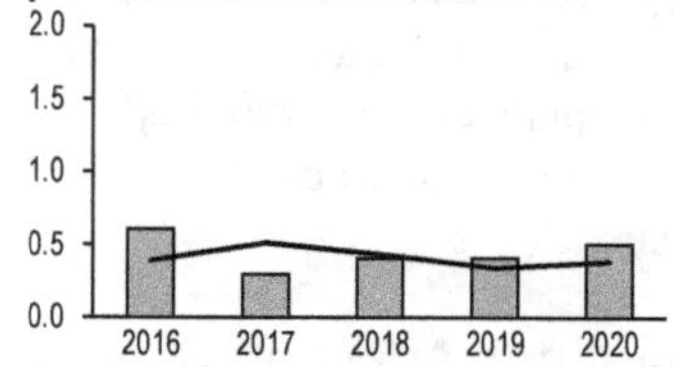

	2016	2017	2018	2019	2020
Concord	0.61	0.29	0.40	0.41	0.50
Average	0.39	0.51	0.43	0.34	0.38

Efficiency Measures

Cost of Maintenance per Lane Mile Maintained

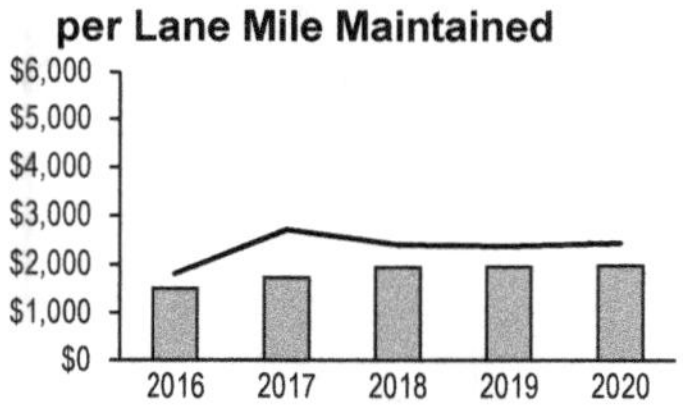

	2016	2017	2018	2019	2020
Concord	$1,515	$1,740	$1,949	$1,961	$1,988
Average	$1,806	$2,696	$2,403	$2,379	$2,446

Cost per Lane Mile for Preservation Treatment

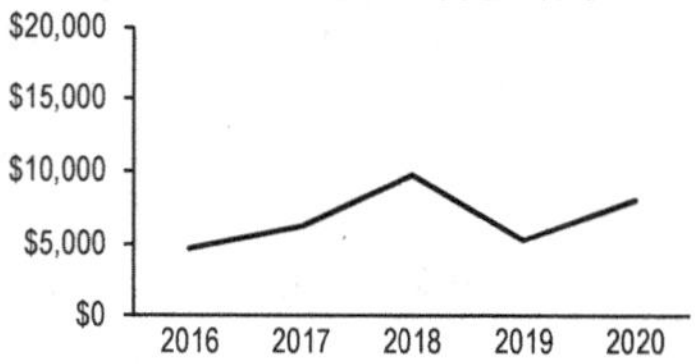

	2016	2017	2018	2019	2020
Concord					
Average	$4,648	$6,231	$9,697	$5,320	$8,025

Cost per Lane Mile for Resurfacing Treatment

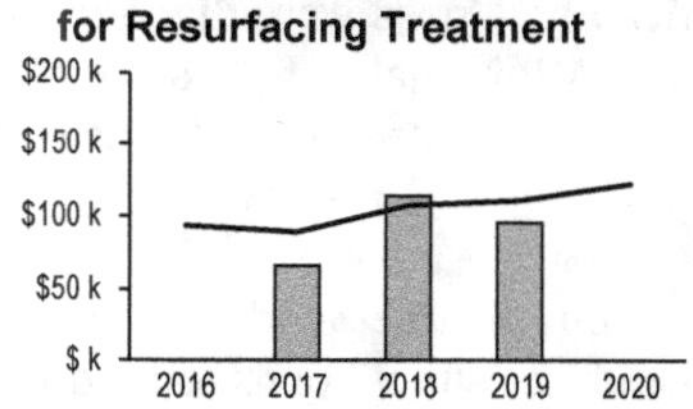

	2016	2017	2018	2019	2020
Concord		$66 k	$113 k	$95 k	
Average	$93 k	$89 k	$107 k	$110 k	$122 k

Cost per Lane Mile for Rehabilitation Treatment

	2016	2017	2018	2019	2020
Concord		$10 k	$10 k		
Average	$103 k	$105 k	$105 k	$294 k	$92 k

Cost per Ton for Contract Resurfacing

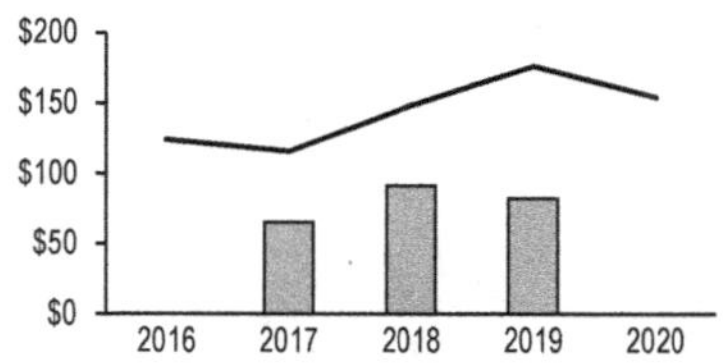

	2016	2017	2018	2019	2020
Concord		$65	$91	$82	
Average	$124	$115	$148	$176	$154

Effectiveness Measures

Percent of Lane Miles Rated 85 or Better

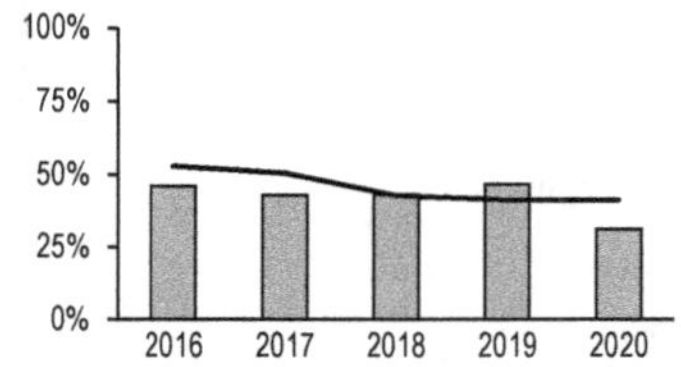

	2016	2017	2018	2019	2020
Concord	46%	43%	43%	47%	31%
Average	53%	50%	43%	41%	41%

Percent of Lane Miles Rated Below 45

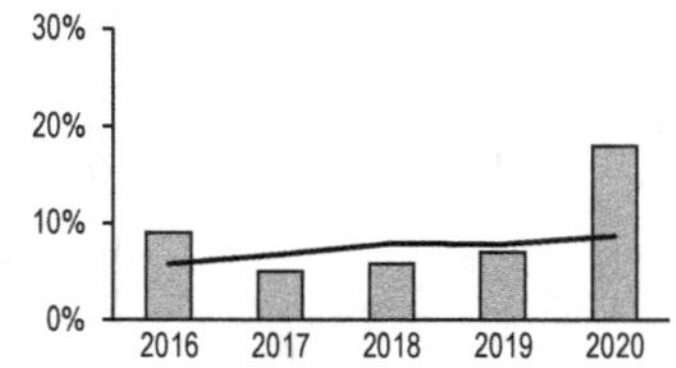

	2016	2017	2018	2019	2020
Concord	9.0%	5.0%	5.8%	7.0%	18.0%
Average	5.7%	6.8%	7.9%	7.8%	8.7%

Percentage of Potholes Repaired within 24 hours

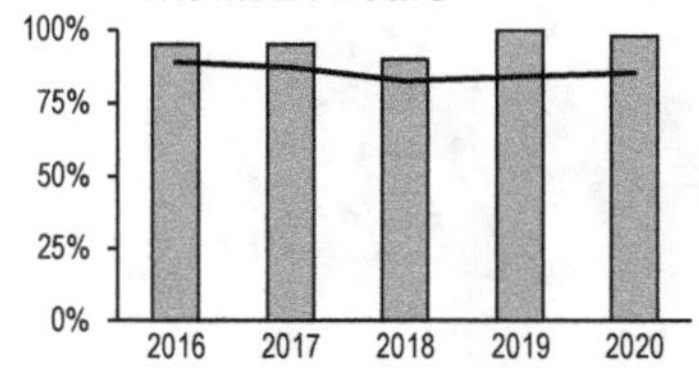

	2016	2017	2018	2019	2020
Concord	95%	95%	90%	100%	98%
Average	89%	87%	83%	84%	85%

Goldsboro — Asphalt Maintenance and Repair

Fiscal Year 2019-20

Explanatory Information

Service Level and Delivery

The City of Goldsboro was responsible for maintaining 325 lane miles during the fiscal year. Goldsboro treated a total of 21.4 lane miles during the year, equating to about 6.6 percent of total lane miles.

Of the treatment work done on Goldsboro's streets, all 21.36 lane miles received rehabilitation work done by contractors. Rehabiltation work requires milling work and is then followed by resurfacing.

The number of potholes reported for the year was 315. The city has one person driving around the city every day looking for potholes that need to be repaired and fixing them on the spot. A total of 135 utility cuts were also repaired, with city crews repairing water and sewer cuts reported by the city's Distribution and Collections Division.

Conditions Affecting Service, Performance, and Costs

The City of Goldsboro joined the Benchmarking Project in July 2017, with the first year of data showing for FY 2016–17.

Hurricane Matthew in October 2016 impacted asphalt work significantly. Crews were diverted to recovery efforts such as tree removal. Additionally, fifty-one sink holes developed over the year in roads due to storm water infrastructure failures under the asphalt surfaces.

The amount of street work done in FY 2017–18 was up significantly due the use of street bonds to fund the work.

Municipal Profile

Population (OSBM 2019)	33,969
Land Area (Square Miles)	29.45
Persons per Square Mile	1,154
Topography	Flat
Climate	Temperate; little ice and snow

Service Profile

FTE Positions—Crews	4.00
FTE Positions—Other	2.00
Lane Miles Maintained	324.7
Lane Miles Treated	
Preservation	0.0
Resurfacing	0.0
Rehabilitation	21.4
TOTAL	21.4
Total Costs for All Treatment Types	$2,627,358
Potholes Repaired	315
Number of Utility Cuts	135
Number of Maintenance Patches (exclusive of potholes and utility cuts)	na
Average Cost per Ton of Hot Asphalt during Year	$72.50

Full Cost Profile

Cost Breakdown by Percentage	
Personal Services	9.1%
Operating Costs	86.0%
Capital Costs	4.9%
TOTAL	100.0%
Cost Breakdown in Dollars	
Personal Services	$284,895
Operating Costs	$2,693,210
Capital Costs	$152,744
TOTAL	$3,130,849

Goldsboro Asphalt Maintenance and Repair

Key: Goldsboro ■ Benchmarking Average — Fiscal Years 2016 through 2020

Resource Measures

Asphalt Maintenance and Repair Services Costs per Capita

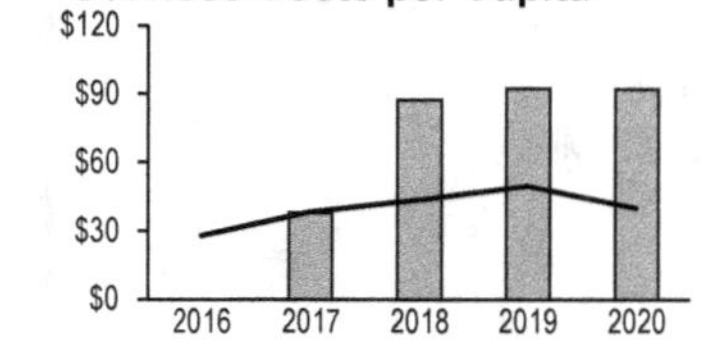

	2016	2017	2018	2019	2020
Goldsboro		$37.86	$87.22	$92.43	$92.17
Average	$27.80	$38.27	$43.58	$49.28	$39.86

Asphalt Maintenance and Repair FTEs per 10,000 Population

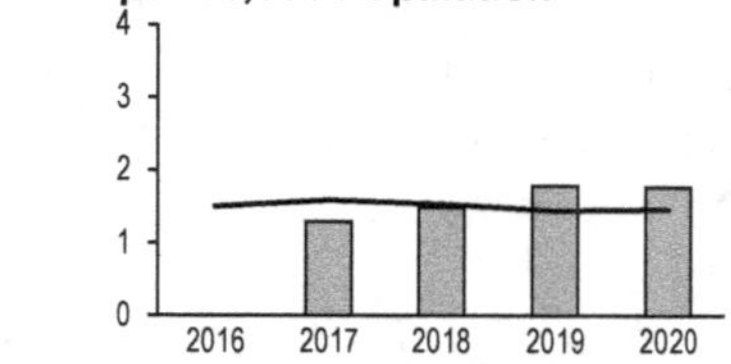

	2016	2017	2018	2019	2020
Goldsboro		1.29	1.48	1.78	1.77
Average	1.49	1.58	1.53	1.44	1.46

Service Costs per Lane Mile of Road Maintained

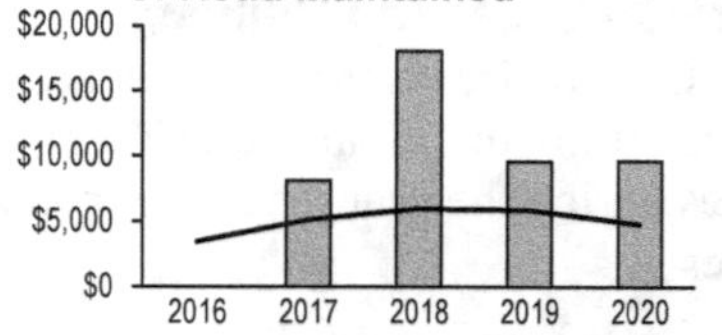

	2016	2017	2018	2019	2020
Goldsboro		$8,094	$18,072	$9,576	$9,643
Average	$3,426	$5,133	$5,961	$5,839	$4,759

Workload Measures

Number of Lane Miles Maintained per 1,000 Population

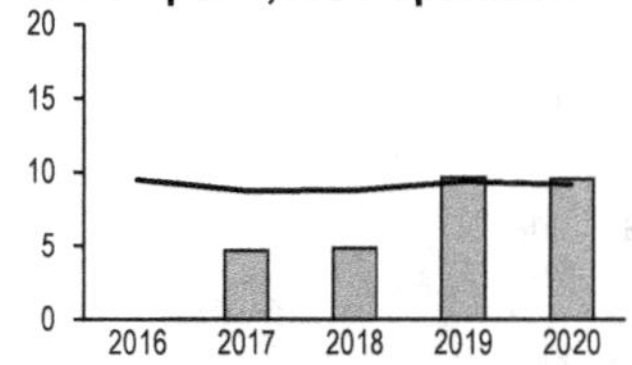

	2016	2017	2018	2019	2020
Goldsboro		4.7	4.8	9.7	9.6
Average	9.5	8.7	8.8	9.3	9.2

Reported Potholes per Lane Mile Maintained

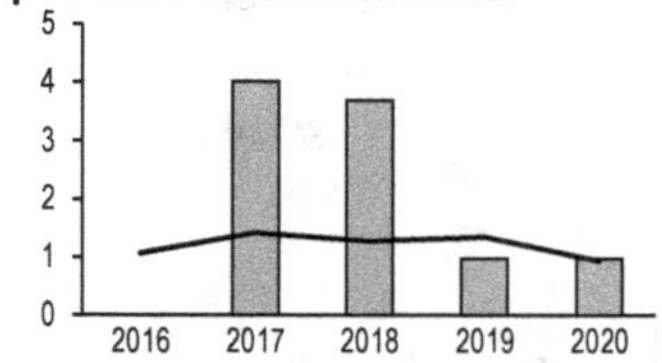

	2016	2017	2018	2019	2020
Goldsboro		4.02	3.70	0.97	0.97
Average	1.06	1.42	1.27	1.34	0.92

Repaired Utility Cuts per Lane Mile Maintained

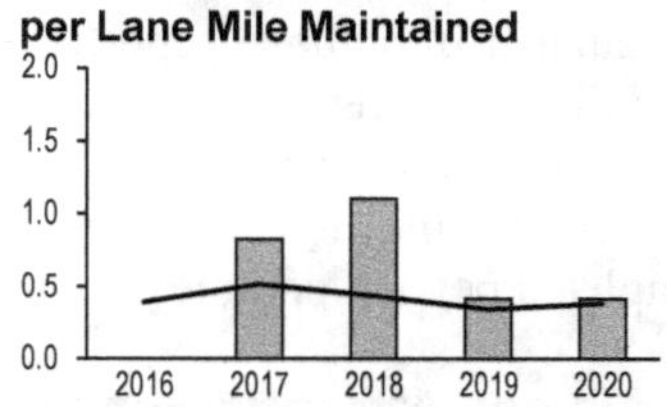

	2016	2017	2018	2019	2020
Goldsboro		0.82	1.10	0.42	0.42
Average	0.39	0.51	0.43	0.34	0.38

Efficiency Measures

Cost of Maintenance per Lane Mile Maintained

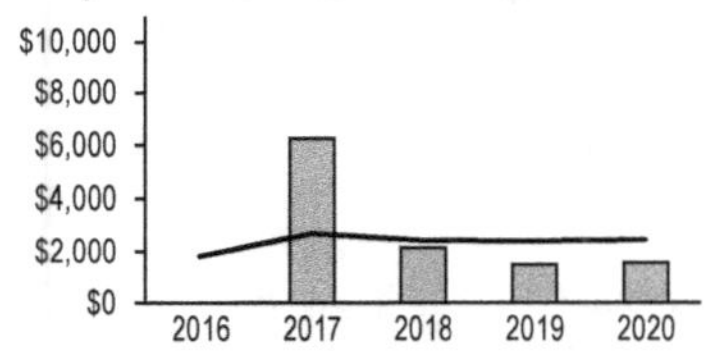

	2016	2017	2018	2019	2020
Goldsboro		$6,237	$2,143	$1,484	$1,551
Average	$1,806	$2,696	$2,403	$2,379	$2,446

Cost per Lane Mile for Preservation Treatment

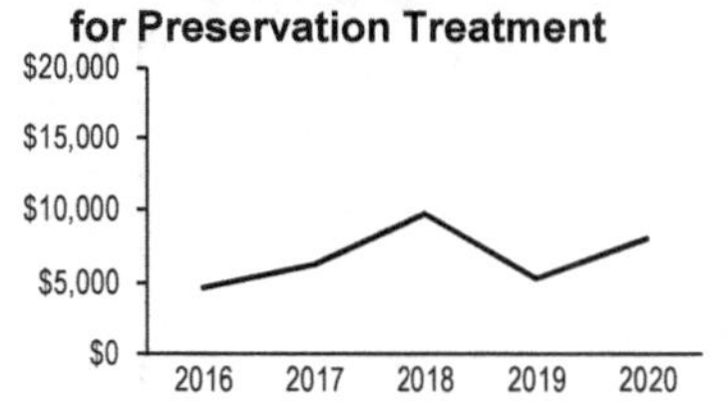

	2016	2017	2018	2019	2020
Goldsboro					
Average	$4,648	$6,231	$9,697	$5,320	$8,025

Cost per Lane Mile for Resurfacing Treatment

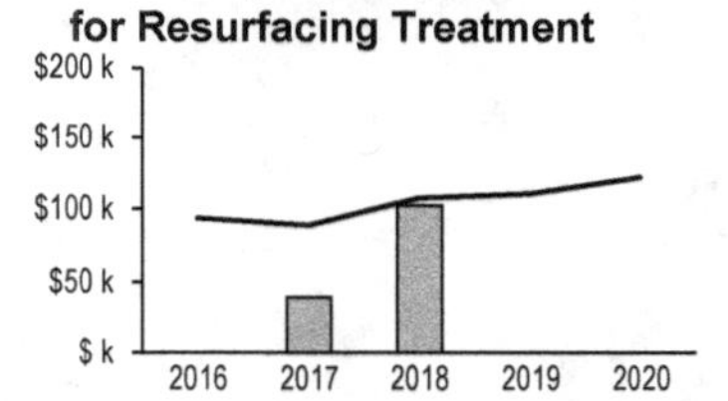

	2016	2017	2018	2019	2020
Goldsboro		$39 k	$103 k		
Average	$93 k	$89 k	$107 k	$110 k	$122 k

Cost per Lane Mile for Rehabilitation Treatment

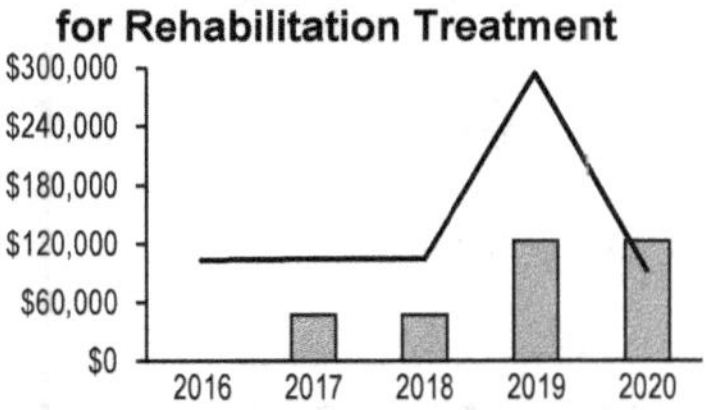

	2016	2017	2018	2019	2020
Goldsboro		$47 k	$47 k	$123 k	$123 k
Average	$103 k	$105 k	$105 k	$294 k	$92 k

Cost per Ton for Contract Resurfacing

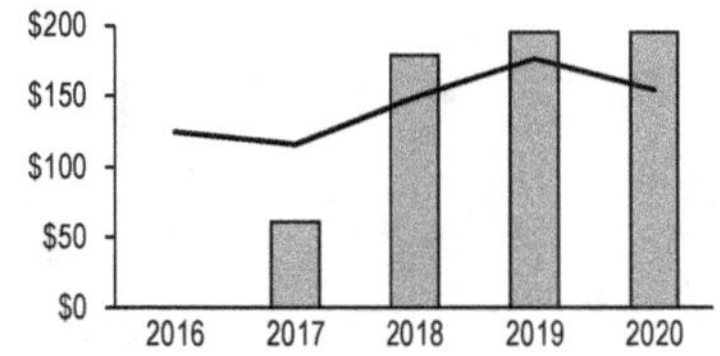

	2016	2017	2018	2019	2020
Goldsboro		$61	$179	$195	$195
Average	$124	$115	$148	$176	$154

Effectiveness Measures

Percent of Lane Miles Rated 85 or Better

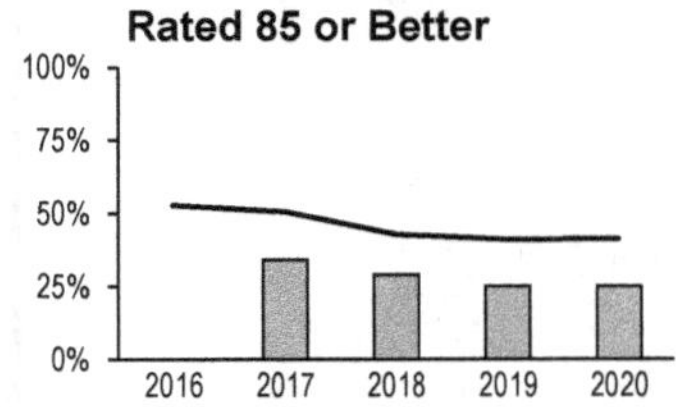

	2016	2017	2018	2019	2020
Goldsboro		34%	29%	25%	25%
Average	53%	50%	43%	41%	41%

Percent of Lane Miles Rated Below 45

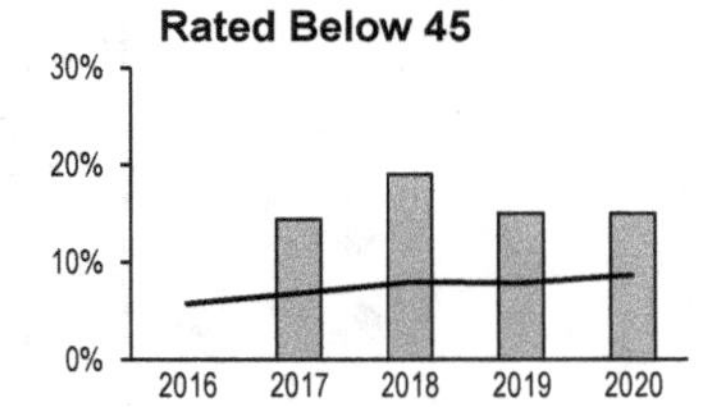

	2016	2017	2018	2019	2020
Goldsboro		14.4%	19.0%	15.0%	15.0%
Average	5.7%	6.8%	7.9%	7.8%	8.7%

Percentage of Potholes Repaired within 24 hours

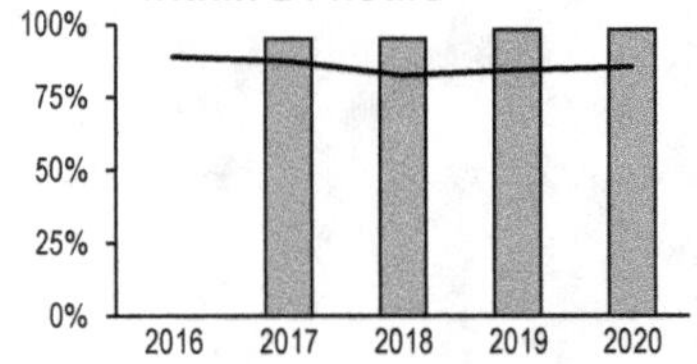

	2016	2017	2018	2019	2020
Goldsboro		95%	95%	98%	98%
Average	89%	87%	83%	84%	85%

Greensboro — Asphalt Maintenance and Repair

Fiscal Year 2019-20

Explanatory Information

Service Level and Delivery

The City of Greensboro was responsible for maintaining 2,431 lane miles during the fiscal year. Greensboro treated a total of 92.4 lane miles during the year, equating to about 3.8 percent of total lane miles.

Of the treatment work done on Greensboro's streets, 23.7 of the lane miles had preservation work performed, such as crack sealing or thin overlays. All of this preservation work was done by city crews. Resurfacing work was done on 68.7 lane miles by contract crews.

The number of potholes reported for the year was 4,895. A total of 256 utility cuts were also repaired, with city crews repairing water and sewer cuts but private contractors repairing others after getting permits from the city. A further 118 maintenance patches were completed beyond potholes and utility cuts.

Conditions Affecting Service, Performance, and Costs

Changes in tracking software have improved the accuracy of potholes reported and asphalt used over time.

Municipal Profile

Population (OSBM 2019)	293,730
Land Area (Square Miles)	129.62
Persons per Square Mile	2,266
Topography	Flat; gently rolling
Climate	Temperate; little ice and snow

Service Profile

FTE Positions—Crews	45.00
FTE Positions—Other	6.00
Lane Miles Maintained	2,431.0
Lane Miles Treated	
Preservation	23.7
Resurfacing	68.7
Rehabilitation	0.0
TOTAL	92.4
Total Costs for All Treatment Types	$7,176,130
Potholes Repaired	4,895
Number of Utility Cuts	256
Number of Maintenance Patches (exclusive of potholes and utility cuts)	118
Average Cost per Ton of Hot Asphalt during Year	$68.41

Full Cost Profile

Cost Breakdown by Percentage	
Personal Services	20.0%
Operating Costs	80.0%
Capital Costs	0.0%
TOTAL	100.0%
Cost Breakdown in Dollars	
Personal Services	$2,515,991
Operating Costs	$10,032,966
Capital Costs	$0
TOTAL	$12,548,957

Greensboro

Asphalt Maintenance and Repair

Key: Greensboro ▒ Benchmarking Average — Fiscal Years 2016 through 2020

Resource Measures

Asphalt Maintenance and Repair Services Costs per Capita

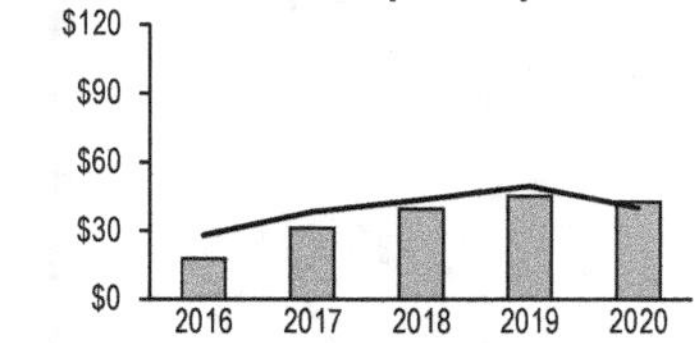

	2016	2017	2018	2019	2020
Greensboro	$17.78	$31.23	$39.80	$45.17	$42.72
Average	$27.80	$38.27	$43.58	$49.28	$39.86

Asphalt Maintenance and Repair FTEs per 10,000 Population

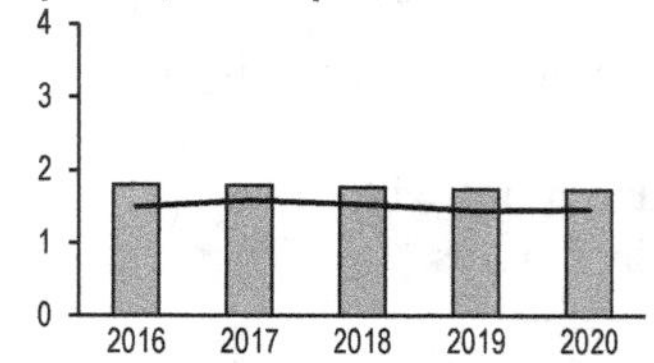

	2016	2017	2018	2019	2020
Greensboro	1.80	1.79	1.77	1.74	1.74
Average	1.49	1.58	1.53	1.44	1.46

Service Costs per Lane Mile of Road Maintained

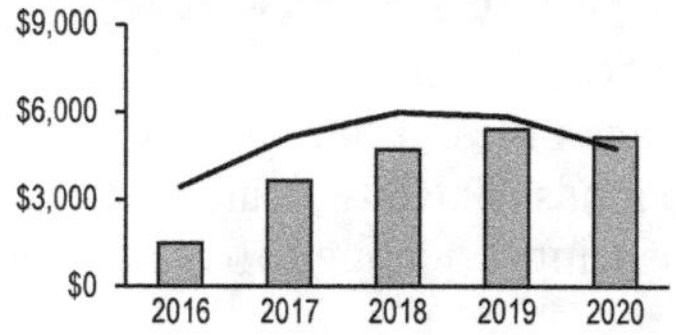

	2016	2017	2018	2019	2020
Greensboro	$1,498	$3,652	$4,716	$5,432	$5,162
Average	$3,426	$5,133	$5,961	$5,839	$4,759

Workload Measures

Number of Lane Miles Maintained per 1,000 Population

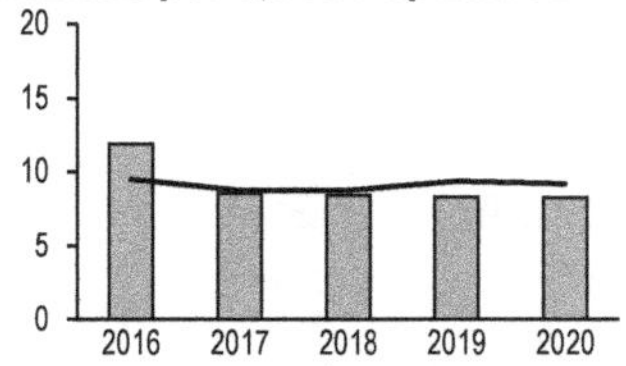

	2016	2017	2018	2019	2020
Greensboro	11.9	8.5	8.4	8.3	8.3
Average	9.5	8.7	8.8	9.3	9.2

Reported Potholes per Lane Mile Maintained

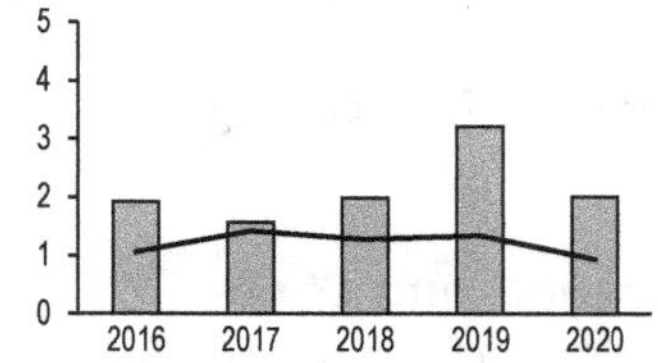

	2016	2017	2018	2019	2020
Greensboro	1.93	1.57	1.99	3.21	2.01
Average	1.06	1.42	1.27	1.34	0.92

Repaired Utility Cuts per Lane Mile Maintained

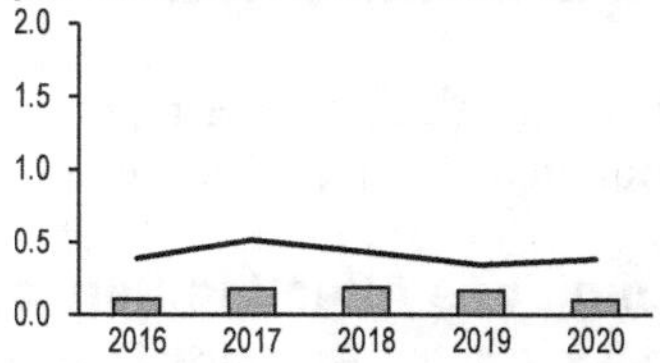

	2016	2017	2018	2019	2020
Greensboro	0.11	0.18	0.19	0.16	0.11
Average	0.39	0.51	0.43	0.34	0.38

Efficiency Measures

Cost of Maintenance per Lane Mile Maintained

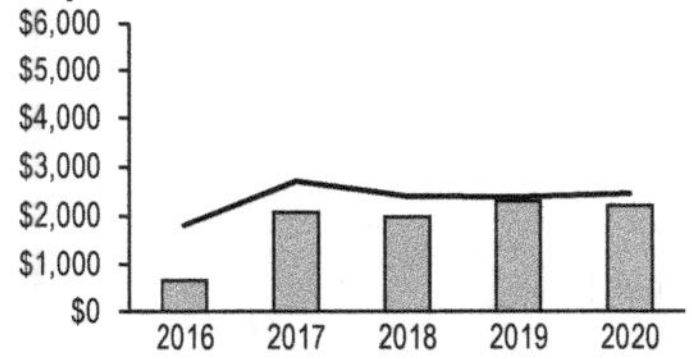

	2016	2017	2018	2019	2020
Greensboro	$657	$2,080	$1,992	$2,301	$2,210
Average	$1,806	$2,696	$2,403	$2,379	$2,446

Cost per Lane Mile for Preservation Treatment

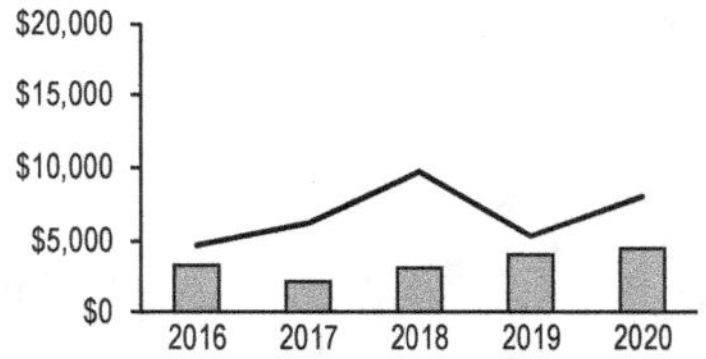

	2016	2017	2018	2019	2020
Greensboro	$3,282	$2,148	$3,128	$4,044	$4,507
Average	$4,648	$6,231	$9,697	$5,320	$8,025

Cost per Lane Mile for Resurfacing Treatment

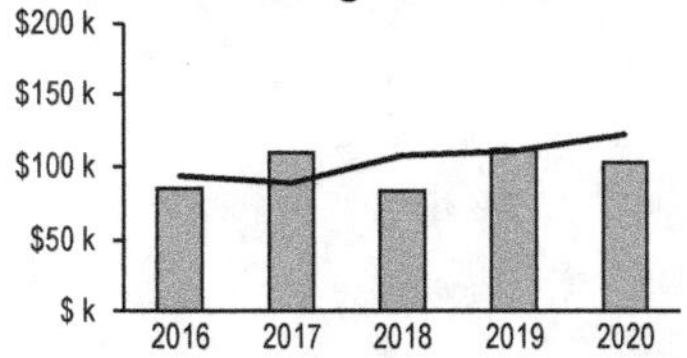

	2016	2017	2018	2019	2020
Greensboro	$85 k	$109 k	$84 k	$112 k	$103 k
Average	$93 k	$89 k	$107 k	$110 k	$122 k

Cost per Lane Mile for Rehabilitation Treatment

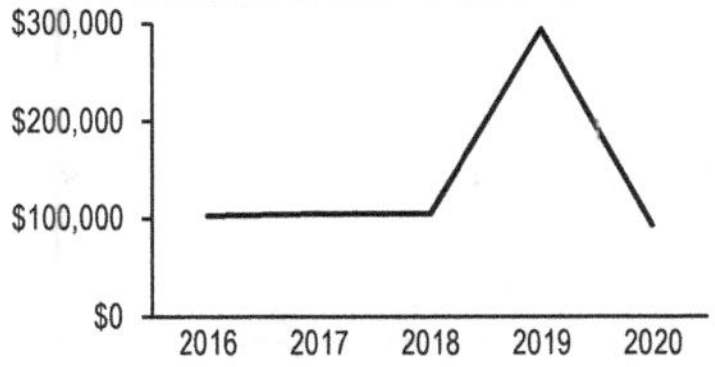

	2016	2017	2018	2019	2020
Greensboro					
Average	$103 k	$105 k	$105 k	$294 k	$92 k

Cost per Ton for Contract Resurfacing

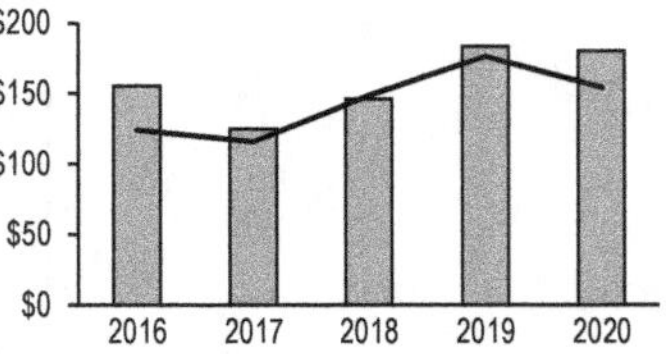

	2016	2017	2018	2019	2020
Greensboro	$155	$125	$146	$183	$180
Average	$124	$115	$148	$176	$154

Effectiveness Measures

Percent of Lane Miles Rated 85 or Better

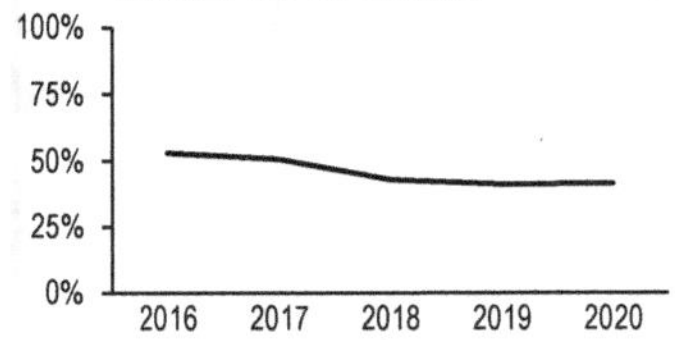

	2016	2017	2018	2019	2020
Greensboro					
Average	53%	50%	43%	41%	41%

Percent of Lane Miles Rated Below 45

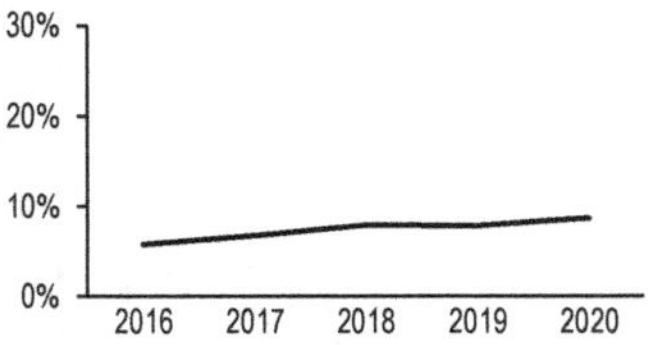

	2016	2017	2018	2019	2020
Greensboro					
Average	5.7%	6.8%	7.9%	7.8%	8.7%

Percentage of Potholes Repaired within 24 hours

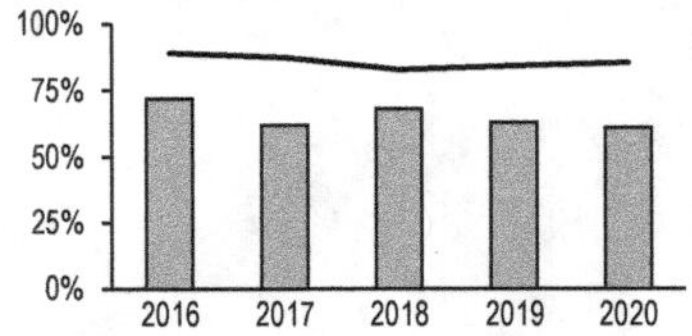

	2016	2017	2018	2019	2020
Greensboro	72%	62%	68%	63%	61%
Average	89%	87%	83%	84%	85%

Asphalt Maintenance and Repair

Fiscal Year 2019-20

Explanatory Information

Service Level and Delivery

The City of Hickory was responsible for maintaining approximately 720 lane miles during the fiscal year, including 238.8 lane miles of state roads. The city treated a total of nine lane miles with resurfacing, equating to 1.2 percent of total lane miles.

The city resurfaced seven lane miles and did rehabilitation work on an additional 1.7 lane miles using contractors. The city reported that 37 percent of its lane miles rated 85 or above on its most recent pavement condition rating, conducted in 2017. The city used the Institute for Transportation Research and Education (ITRE) to conduct its rating system.

The number of potholes reported for the year was 372, including self-reported and citizen-reported potholes.

Conditions Affecting Service, Performance, and Costs

Winter weather has caused maintenance problems in a number of the fiscal years reported here.

Municipal Profile

Population (OSBM 2019)	41,409
Land Area (Square Miles)	30.50
Persons per Square Mile	1,358
Topography	Gently rolling
Climate	Temperate; some ice and snow

Service Profile

FTE Positions—Crews	6.00
FTE Positions—Other	1.00
Lane Miles Maintained	719.8
Lane Miles Treated	
Preservation	0.0
Resurfacing	7.0
Rehabilitation	1.7
TOTAL	8.7
Total Costs for All Treatment Types	$900,775
Potholes Repaired	372
Number of Utility Cuts	na
Number of Maintenance Patches (exclusive of potholes and utility cuts)	na
Average Cost per Ton of Hot Asphalt during Year	$67.00

Full Cost Profile

Cost Breakdown by Percentage	
Personal Services	15.5%
Operating Costs	78.9%
Capital Costs	5.6%
TOTAL	100.0%
Cost Breakdown in Dollars	
Personal Services	$238,948
Operating Costs	$1,213,199
Capital Costs	$85,828
TOTAL	$1,537,975

Key: Hickory ■ Benchmarking Average — Fiscal Years 2016 through 2020

Resource Measures

Asphalt Maintenance and Repair Services Costs per Capita

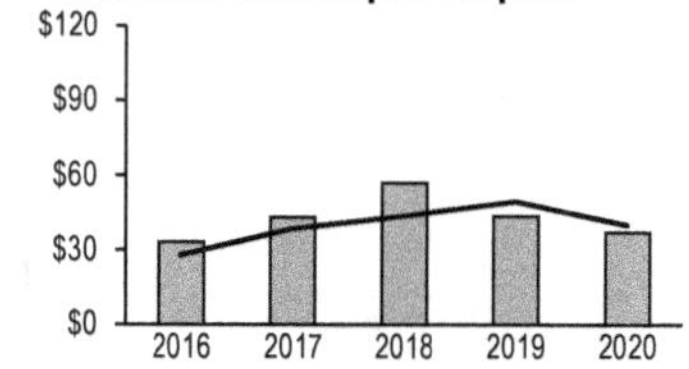

	2016	2017	2018	2019	2020
Hickory	$33.22	$43.10	$56.92	$43.63	$37.14
Average	$27.80	$38.27	$43.58	$49.28	$39.86

Asphalt Maintenance and Repair FTEs per 10,000 Population

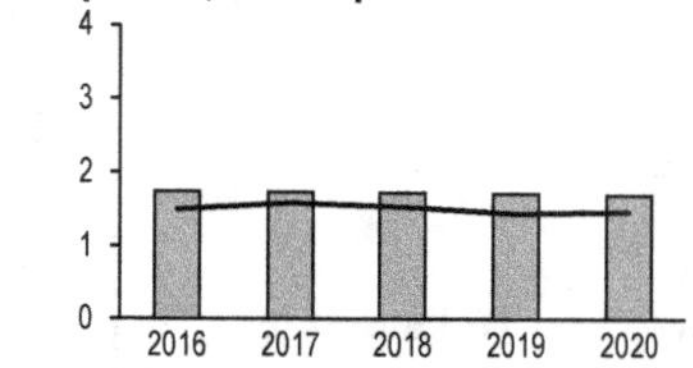

	2016	2017	2018	2019	2020
Hickory	1.73	1.73	1.72	1.71	1.69
Average	1.49	1.58	1.53	1.44	1.46

Service Costs per Lane Mile of Road Maintained

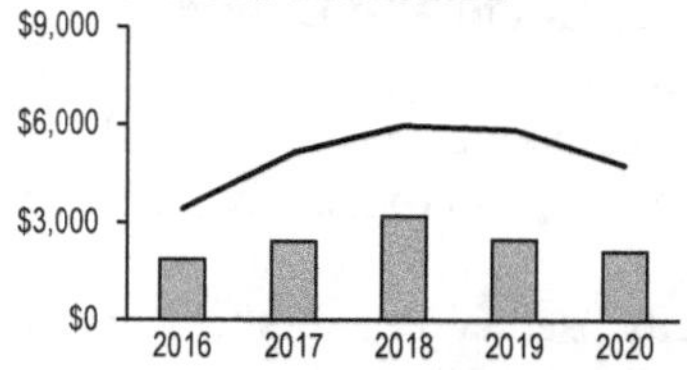

	2016	2017	2018	2019	2020
Hickory	$1,862	$2,423	$3,208	$2,476	$2,137
Average	$3,426	$5,133	$5,961	$5,839	$4,759

Workload Measures

Number of Lane Miles Maintained per 1,000 Population

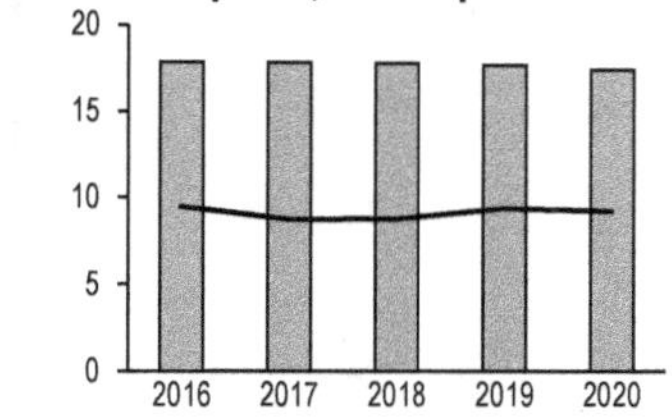

	2016	2017	2018	2019	2020
Hickory	17.8	17.8	17.7	17.6	17.4
Average	9.5	8.7	8.8	9.3	9.2

Reported Potholes per Lane Mile Maintained

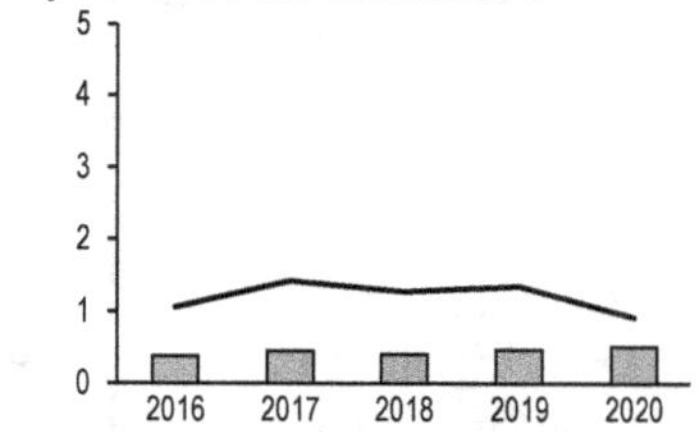

	2016	2017	2018	2019	2020
Hickory	0.38	0.45	0.41	0.47	0.52
Average	1.06	1.42	1.27	1.34	0.92

Repaired Utility Cuts per Lane Mile Maintained

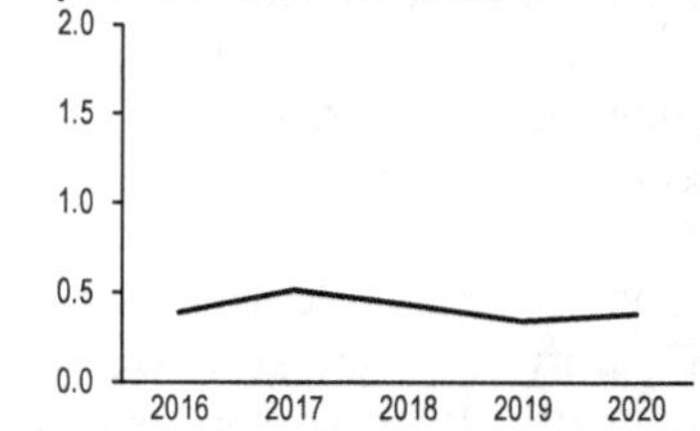

	2016	2017	2018	2019	2020
Hickory					0.00
Average	0.39	0.51	0.43	0.34	0.38

Efficiency Measures

Cost of Maintenance per Lane Mile Maintained

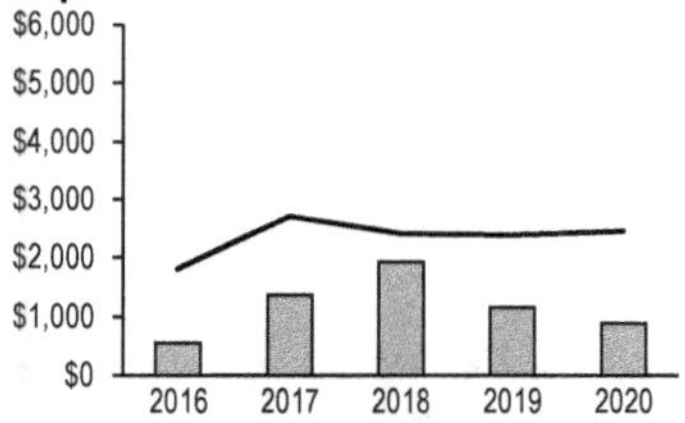

	2016	2017	2018	2019	2020
Hickory	$545	$1,366	$1,928	$1,160	$885
Average	$1,806	$2,696	$2,403	$2,379	$2,446

Cost per Lane Mile for Preservation Treatment

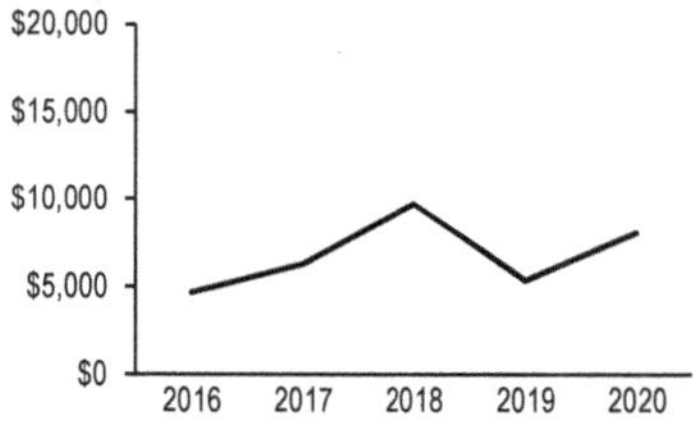

	2016	2017	2018	2019	2020
Hickory					
Average	$4,648	$6,231	$9,697	$5,320	$8,025

Cost per Lane Mile for Resurfacing Treatment

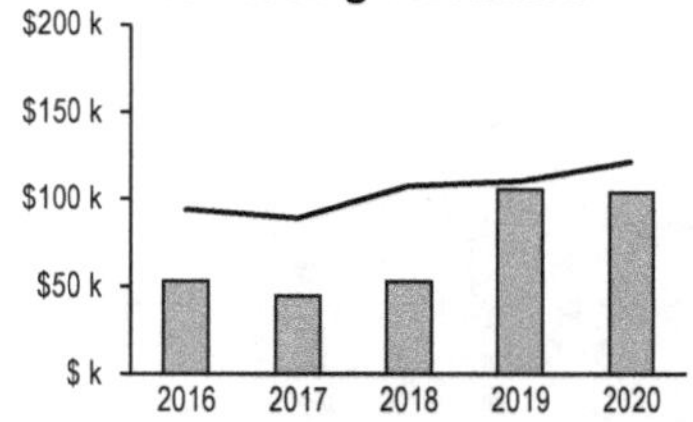

	2016	2017	2018	2019	2020
Hickory	$53 k	$44 k	$52 k	$105 k	$104 k
Average	$93 k	$89 k	$107 k	$110 k	$122 k

Cost per Lane Mile for Rehabilitation Treatment

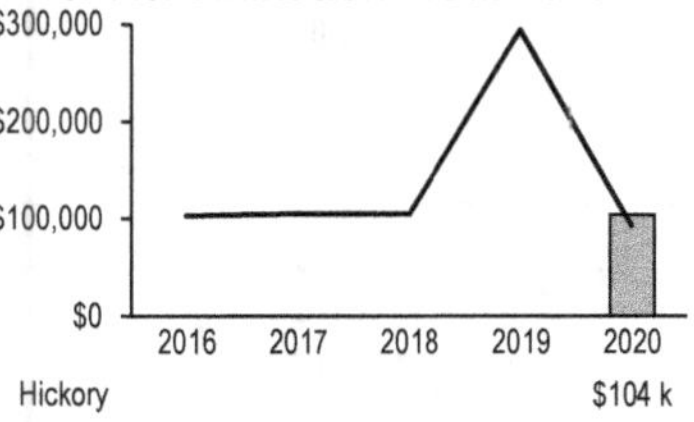

	2016	2017	2018	2019	2020
Hickory					$104 k
Average	$103 k	$105 k	$105 k	$294 k	$92 k

Cost per Ton for Contract Resurfacing

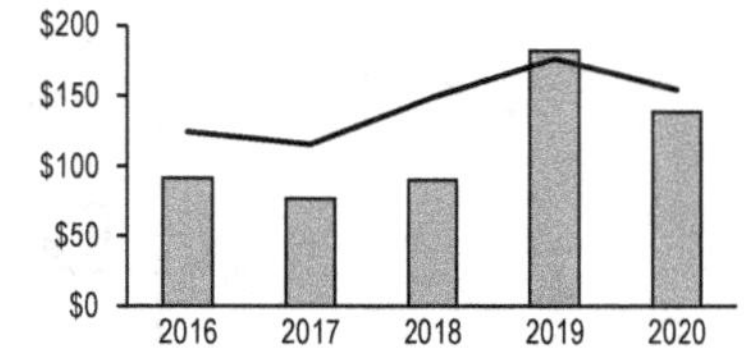

	2016	2017	2018	2019	2020
Hickory	$92	$77	$90	$182	$138
Average	$124	$115	$148	$176	$154

Effectiveness Measures

Percent of Lane Miles Rated 85 or Better

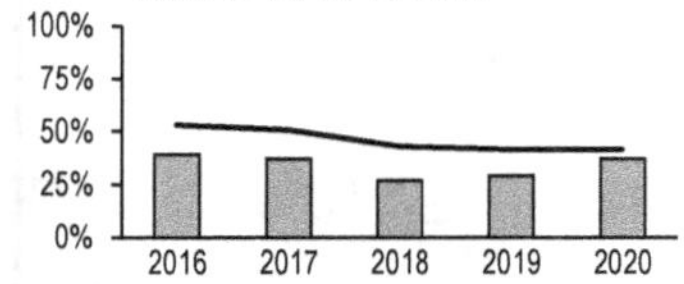

	2016	2017	2018	2019	2020
Hickory	39%	37%	27%	29%	37%
Average	53%	50%	43%	41%	41%

Percent of Lane Miles Rated Below 45

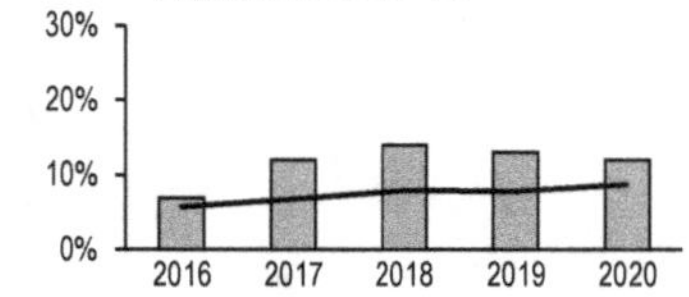

	2016	2017	2018	2019	2020
Hickory	7.0%	12.0%	14.0%	13.0%	12.0%
Average	5.7%	6.8%	7.9%	7.8%	8.7%

Percentage of Potholes Repaired within 24 hours

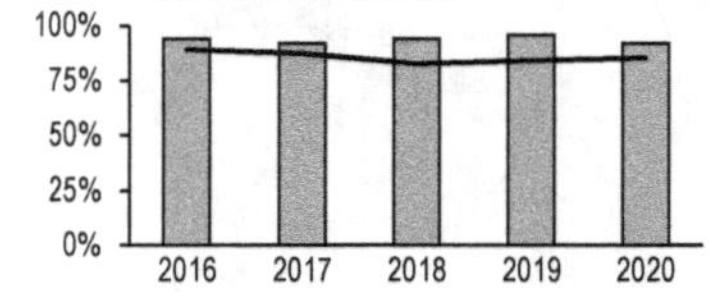

	2016	2017	2018	2019	2020
Hickory	94%	92%	94%	96%	92%
Average	89%	87%	83%	84%	85%

Raleigh

Asphalt Maintenance and Repair

Fiscal Year 2019-20

Explanatory Information

Service Level and Delivery

The City of Raleigh's Department of Transportation is responsible for for street maintenance. During the year the city was responsible for maintaining approximately 2,356 lane miles.

The city used contractors to do preservation work on 16 lane miles. An additional 27 lane miles were resrucefaced by contractors during the year. This treatment work represented about 1.8 percent of total lane miles.

The city reported that 54 percent of its lane miles rated 85 or above on its most recent pavement condition rating, conducted in 2019. The city used city staff conducting a windshield survey following the Institute for Transportation Research and Education (ITRE) rating system.

The number of potholes reported for the year was 3,838. A total of 1,168 utility cuts were also made, with the city repairing all of these. Additionally, 258 maintenance patches were completed, which are exclusive of potholes and utility cut repairs.

Conditions Affecting Service, Performance, and Costs

Raleigh rejoined the Benchmarking Project in July 2016, with the first year of data showing for FY 2015–16.

Municipal Profile

Population (OSBM 2019)	475,580
Land Area (Square Miles)	146.47
Persons per Square Mile	3,247
Topography	Flat; gently rolling
Climate	Temperate; little ice and snow

Service Profile

FTE Positions—Crews	33.00
FTE Positions—Other	8.00
Lane Miles Maintained	2,356.0
Lane Miles Treated	
Preservation	16.0
Resurfacing	27.0
Rehabilitation	0.0
TOTAL	43.0
Total Costs for All Treatment Types	$4,233,879
Potholes Repaired	3,838
Number of Utility Cuts	1,168
Number of Maintenance Patches (exclusive of potholes and utility cuts)	258
Average Cost per Ton of Hot Asphalt during Year	$58.25

Full Cost Profile

Cost Breakdown by Percentage	
Personal Services	19.3%
Operating Costs	67.8%
Capital Costs	12.9%
TOTAL	100.0%
Cost Breakdown in Dollars	
Personal Services	$3,355,081
Operating Costs	$11,781,041
Capital Costs	$2,247,505
TOTAL	$17,383,627

Raleigh

Asphalt Maintenance and Repair

Key: Raleigh ▒ Benchmarking Average — Fiscal Years 2016 through 2020

Resource Measures

Asphalt Maintenance and Repair Services Costs per Capita

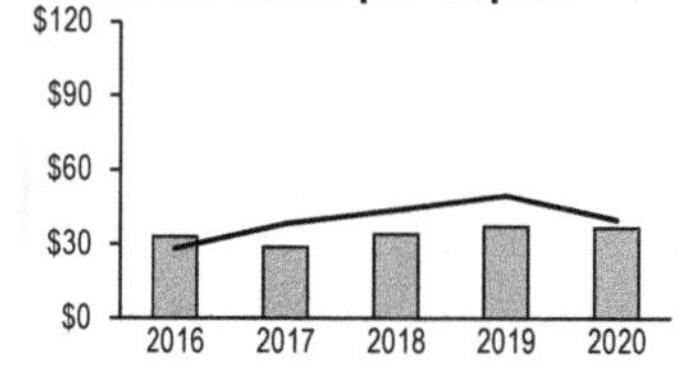

	2016	2017	2018	2019	2020
Raleigh	$32.95	$28.73	$33.98	$37.08	$36.55
Average	$27.80	$38.27	$43.58	$49.28	$39.86

Asphalt Maintenance and Repair FTEs per 10,000 Population

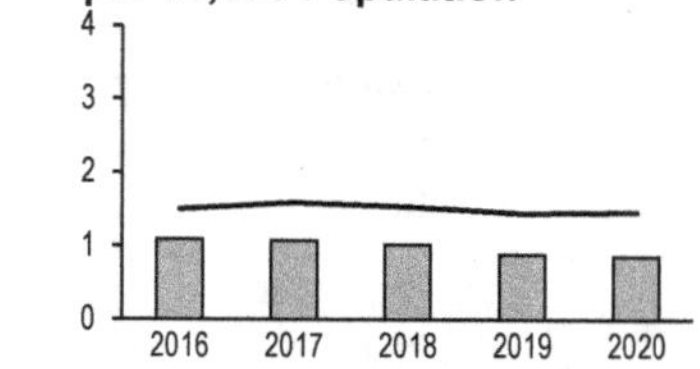

	2016	2017	2018	2019	2020
Raleigh	1.09	1.07	1.02	0.88	0.86
Average	1.49	1.58	1.53	1.44	1.46

Service Costs per Lane Mile of Road Maintained

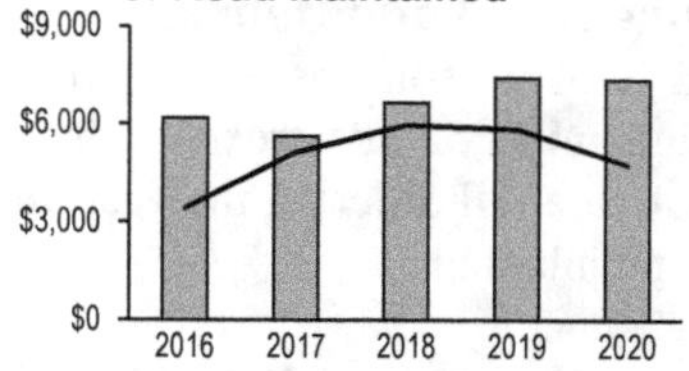

	2016	2017	2018	2019	2020
Raleigh	$6,180	$5,621	$6,656	$7,432	$7,378
Average	$3,426	$5,133	$5,961	$5,839	$4,759

Workload Measures

Number of Lane Miles Maintained per 1,000 Population

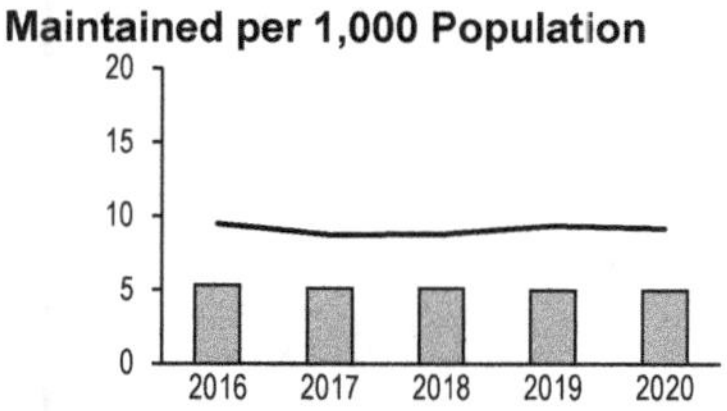

	2016	2017	2018	2019	2020
Raleigh	5.3	5.1	5.1	5.0	5.0
Average	9.5	8.7	8.8	9.3	9.2

Reported Potholes per Lane Mile Maintained

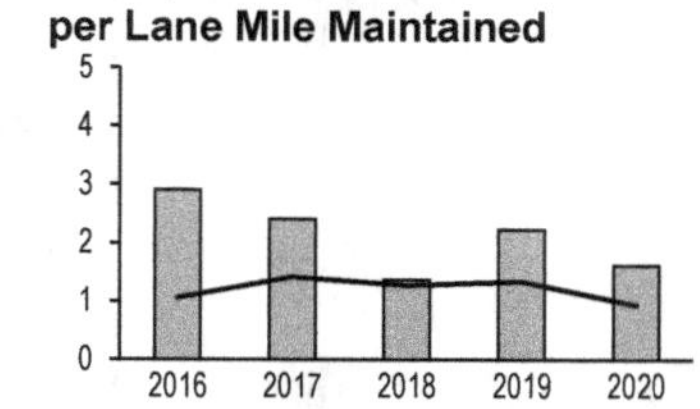

	2016	2017	2018	2019	2020
Raleigh	2.91	2.40	1.37	2.23	1.63
Average	1.06	1.42	1.27	1.34	0.92

Repaired Utility Cuts per Lane Mile Maintained

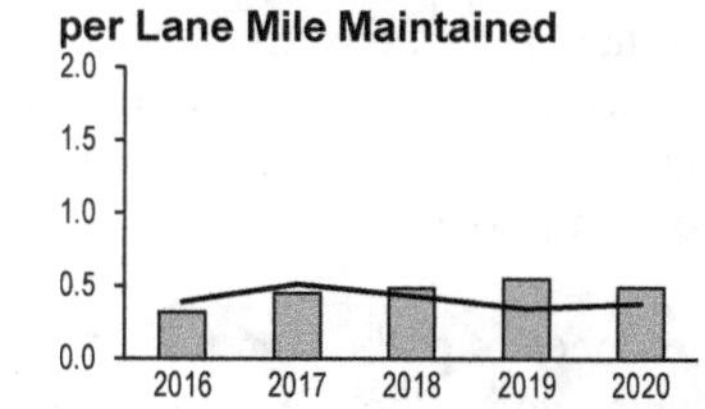

	2016	2017	2018	2019	2020
Raleigh	0.32	0.45	0.49	0.55	0.50
Average	0.39	0.51	0.43	0.34	0.38

Efficiency Measures

Cost of Maintenance per Lane Mile Maintained

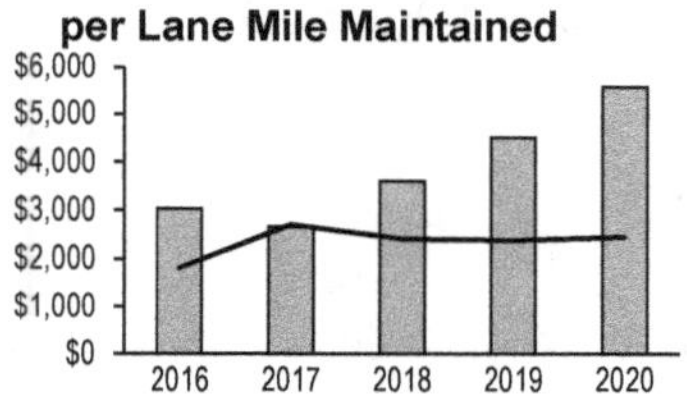

	2016	2017	2018	2019	2020
Raleigh	$3,030	$2,662	$3,603	$4,511	$5,581
Average	$1,806	$2,696	$2,403	$2,379	$2,446

Cost per Lane Mile for Preservation Treatment

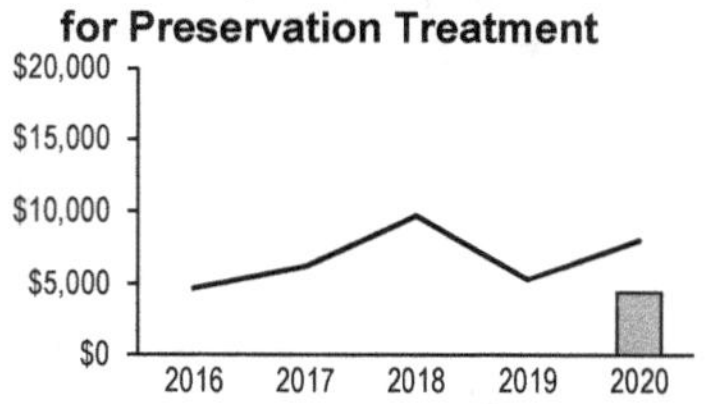

	2016	2017	2018	2019	2020
Raleigh					$4,451
Average	$4,648	$6,231	$9,697	$5,320	$8,025

Cost per Lane Mile for Resurfacing Treatment

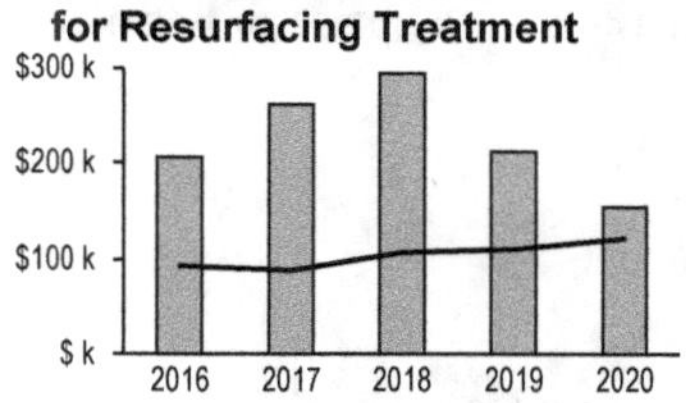

	2016	2017	2018	2019	2020
Raleigh	$206 k	$261 k	$295 k	$212 k	$154 k
Average	$93 k	$89 k	$107 k	$110 k	$122 k

Cost per Lane Mile for Rehabilitation Treatment

	2016	2017	2018	2019	2020
Raleigh					
Average	$103 k	$105 k	$105 k	$294 k	$92 k

Cost per Ton for Contract Resurfacing

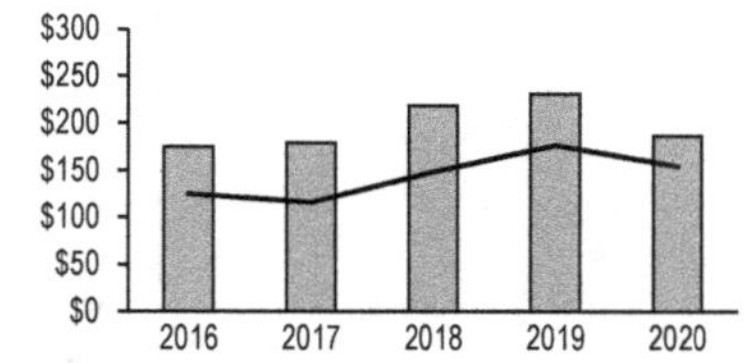

	2016	2017	2018	2019	2020
Raleigh	$175	$179	$219	$230	$187
Average	$124	$115	$148	$176	$154

Effectiveness Measures

Percent of Lane Miles Rated 85 or Better

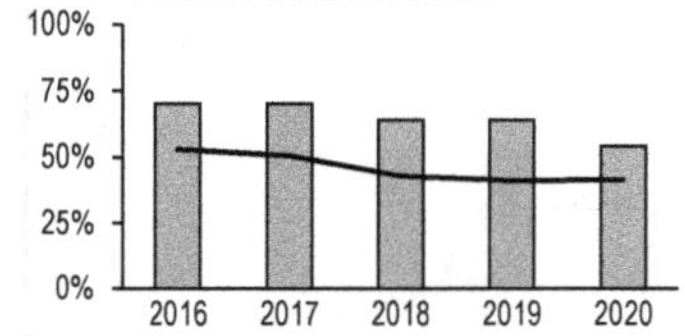

	2016	2017	2018	2019	2020
Raleigh	70%	70%	64%	64%	54%
Average	53%	50%	43%	41%	41%

Percent of Lane Miles Rated Below 45

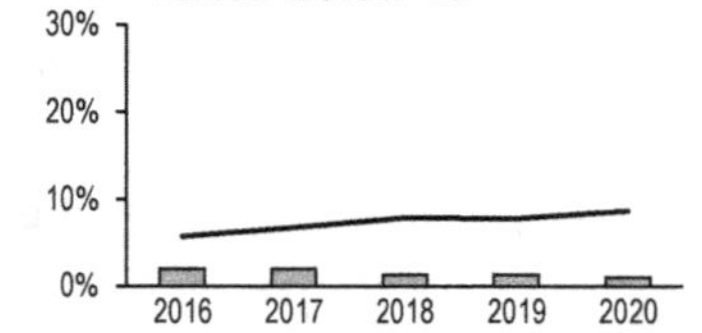

	2016	2017	2018	2019	2020
Raleigh	2.0%	2.0%	1.3%	1.3%	1.0%
Average	5.7%	6.8%	7.9%	7.8%	8.7%

Percentage of Potholes Repaired within 24 hours

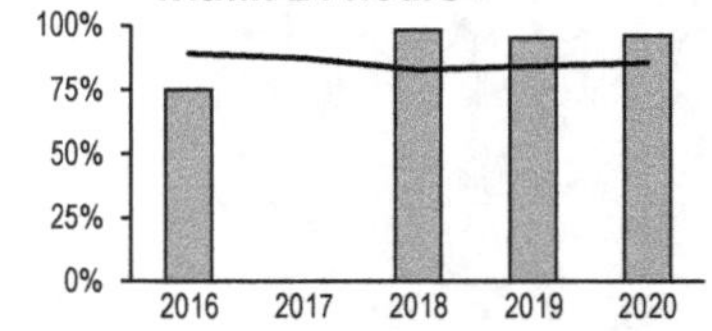

	2016	2017	2018	2019	2020
Raleigh	75%		98%	95%	96%
Average	89%	87%	83%	84%	85%

Wilson

Asphalt Maintenance and Repair

Fiscal Year 2019-20

Explanatory Information

Service Level and Delivery

The City of Wilson was responsible for maintaining approximately 697 lane miles of city streets during the year. The city treated a total of 23.1 lane miles during the year, or 3.3 percent of the total lane miles maintained.

Contract crews treated 20.94 lane miles with resurfacing. City crews performed preservation work on 2.18 lane miles. Preservation techniques include methods such as crack sealing or thin overlays.

The city reported that 47 percent of its lane miles rated 85 or above on its most recent pavement condition rating, conducted in 2018. The city relied on a consultant for the rating, who used a customized rating based on the Institute for Transportation Research and Education (ITRE) system.

The number of potholes reported for the year was 1,484. The percentage of potholes repaired within twenty-four hours was 90 percent. Repairs to 894 utility cuts were also made during the year.

Conditions Affecting Service, Performance, and Costs

The cost of asphalt and maintenance materials is directly related to fluctuations in the price of petroleum.

Municipal Profile

Population (OSBM 2019)	49,384
Land Area (Square Miles)	31.02
Persons per Square Mile	1,592
Topography	Flat
Climate	Temperate; little ice and snow

Service Profile

FTE Positions—Crews	5.00
FTE Positions—Other	0.50
Lane Miles Maintained	697.2
Lane Miles Treated	
Preservation	2.2
Resurfacing	20.9
Rehabilitation	0.0
TOTAL	23.1
Total Costs for All Treatment Types	$1,182,046
Potholes Repaired	1,484
Number of Utility Cuts	894
Number of Maintenance Patches (exclusive of potholes and utility cuts)	609
Average Cost per Ton of Hot Asphalt during Year	$74.55

Full Cost Profile

Cost Breakdown by Percentage	
Personal Services	18.7%
Operating Costs	76.7%
Capital Costs	4.6%
TOTAL	100.0%
Cost Breakdown in Dollars	
Personal Services	$443,159
Operating Costs	$1,820,091
Capital Costs	$109,737
TOTAL	$2,372,987

Wilson — Asphalt Maintenance and Repair

Key: Wilson ▒ Benchmarking Average — Fiscal Years 2016 through 2020

Resource Measures

Asphalt Maintenance and Repair Services Costs per Capita

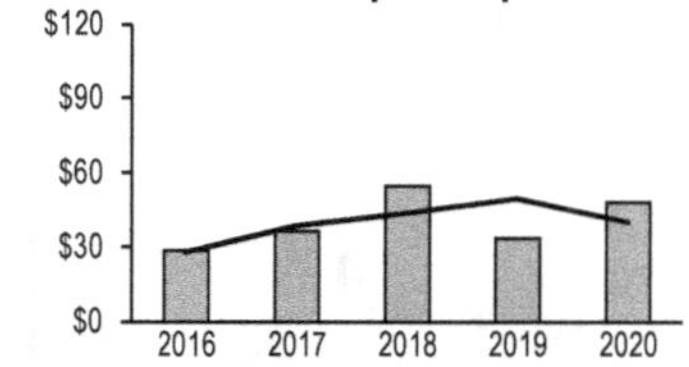

	2016	2017	2018	2019	2020
Wilson	$28.44	$36.32	$54.57	$33.28	$48.05
Average	$27.80	$38.27	$43.58	$49.28	$39.86

Asphalt Maintenance and Repair FTEs per 10,000 Population

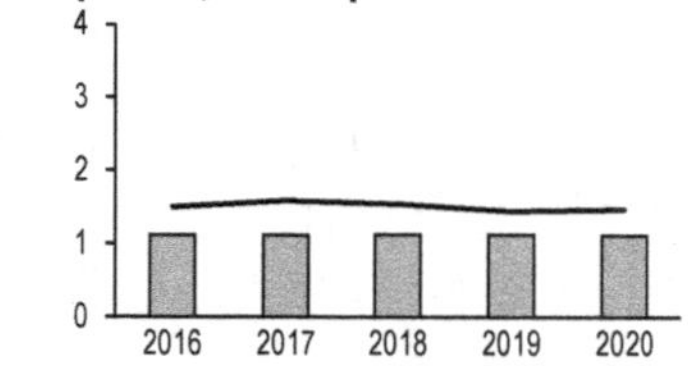

	2016	2017	2018	2019	2020
Wilson	1.11	1.11	1.12	1.12	1.11
Average	1.49	1.58	1.53	1.44	1.46

Service Costs per Lane Mile of Road Maintained

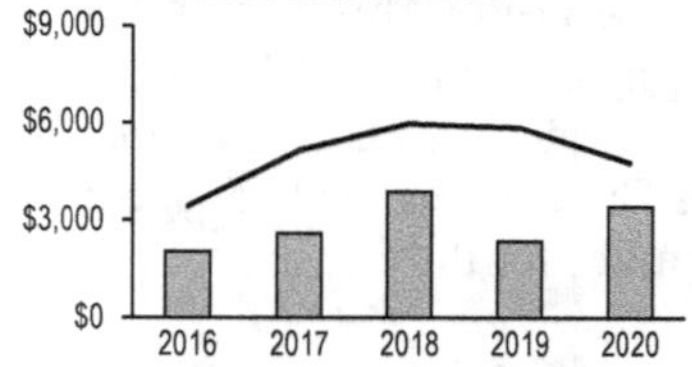

	2016	2017	2018	2019	2020
Wilson	$2,019	$2,580	$3,859	$2,347	$3,404
Average	$3,426	$5,133	$5,961	$5,839	$4,759

Workload Measures

Number of Lane Miles Maintained per 1,000 Population

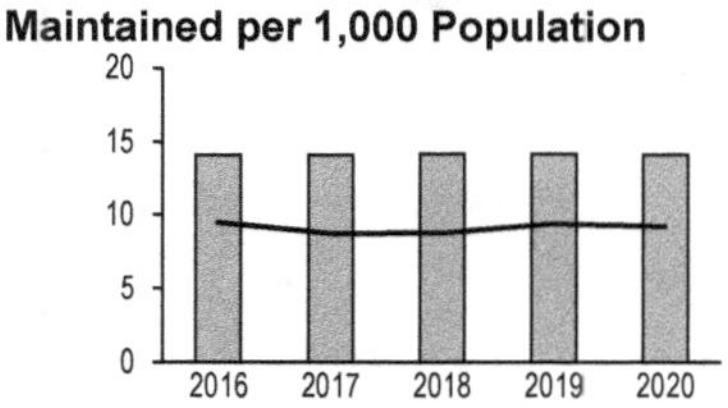

	2016	2017	2018	2019	2020
Wilson	14.1	14.1	14.1	14.2	14.1
Average	9.5	8.7	8.8	9.3	9.2

Reported Potholes per Lane Mile Maintained

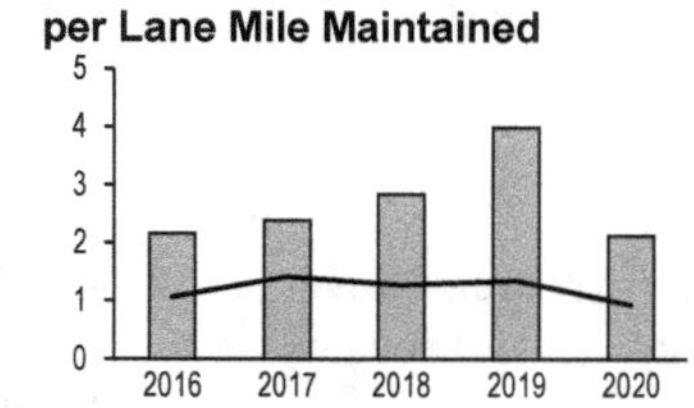

	2016	2017	2018	2019	2020
Wilson	2.15	2.38	2.83	3.99	2.13
Average	1.06	1.42	1.27	1.34	0.92

Repaired Utility Cuts per Lane Mile Maintained

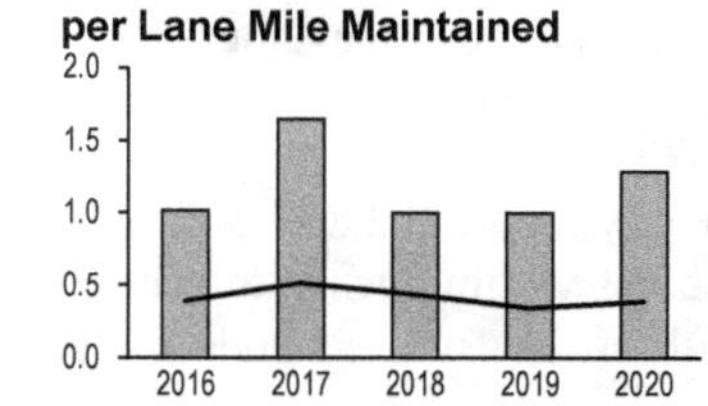

	2016	2017	2018	2019	2020
Wilson	1.01	1.64	0.99	0.99	1.28
Average	0.39	0.51	0.43	0.34	0.38

Efficiency Measures

Cost of Maintenance per Lane Mile Maintained

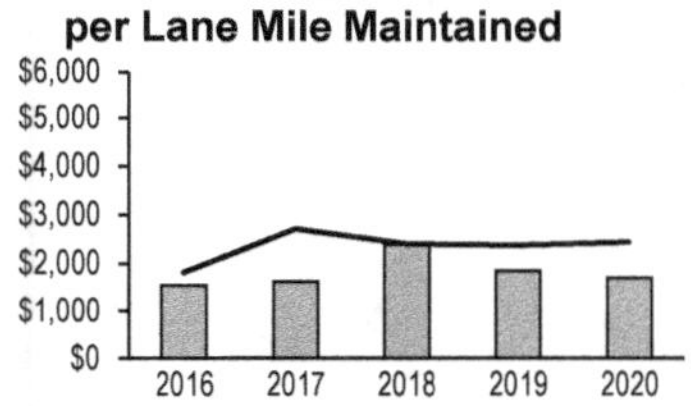

	2016	2017	2018	2019	2020
Wilson	$1,548	$1,626	$2,404	$1,862	$1,708
Average	$1,806	$2,696	$2,403	$2,379	$2,446

Cost per Lane Mile for Preservation Treatment

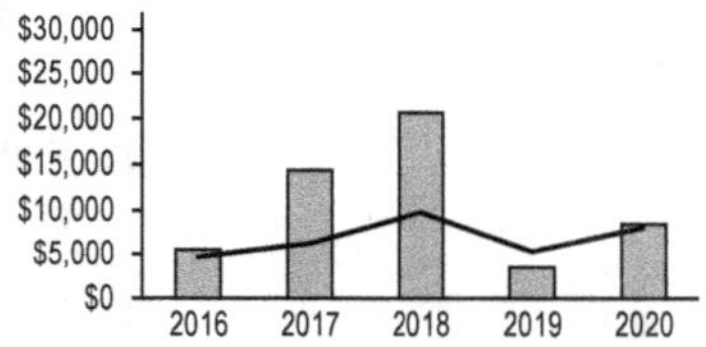

	2016	2017	2018	2019	2020
Wilson	$5,500	$14,360	$20,671	$3,536	$8,498
Average	$4,648	$6,231	$9,697	$5,320	$8,025

Cost per Lane Mile for Resurfacing Treatment

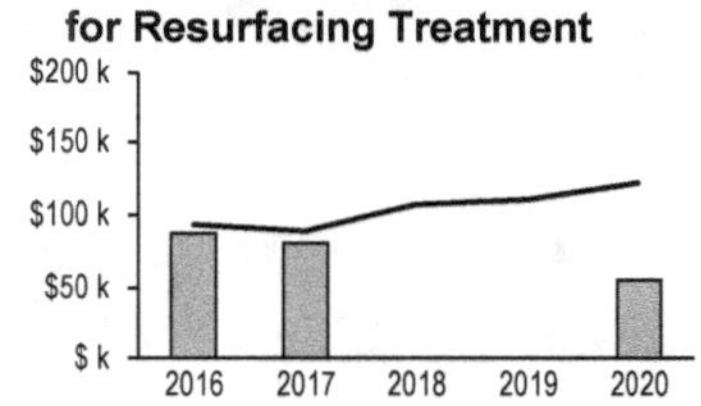

	2016	2017	2018	2019	2020
Wilson	$88 k	$81 k			$56 k
Average	$93 k	$89 k	$107 k	$110 k	$122 k

Cost per Lane Mile for Rehabilitation Treatment

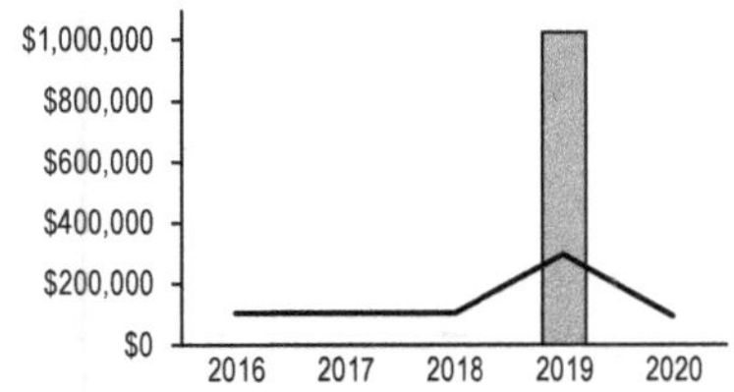

	2016	2017	2018	2019	2020
Wilson				$1024 k	
Average	$103 k	$105 k	$105 k	$294 k	$92 k

Cost per Ton for Contract Resurfacing

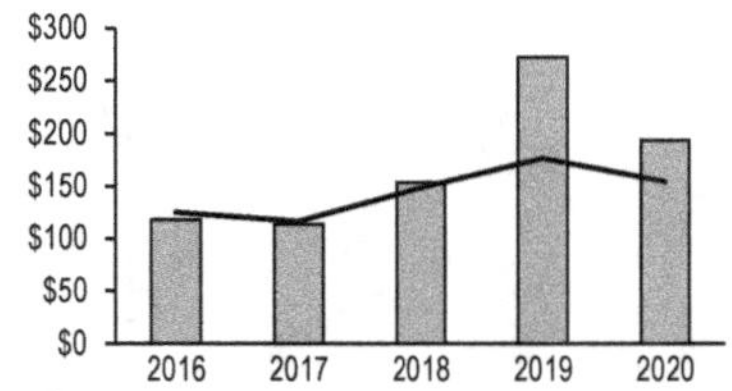

	2016	2017	2018	2019	2020
Wilson	$118	$113	$154	$272	$193
Average	$124	$115	$148	$176	$154

Effectiveness Measures

Percent of Lane Miles Rated 85 or Better

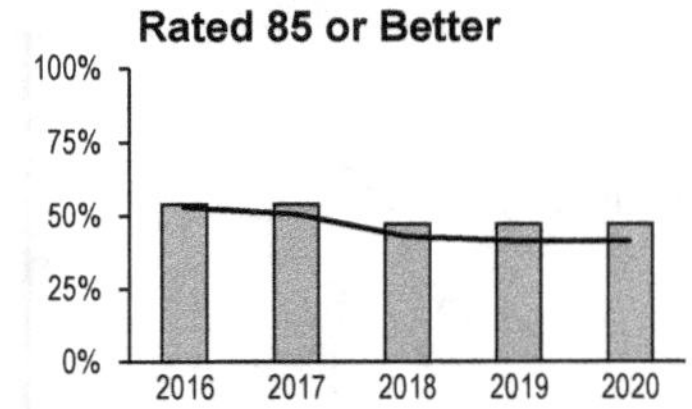

	2016	2017	2018	2019	2020
Wilson	54%	54%	47%	47%	47%
Average	53%	50%	43%	41%	41%

Percent of Lane Miles Rated Below 45

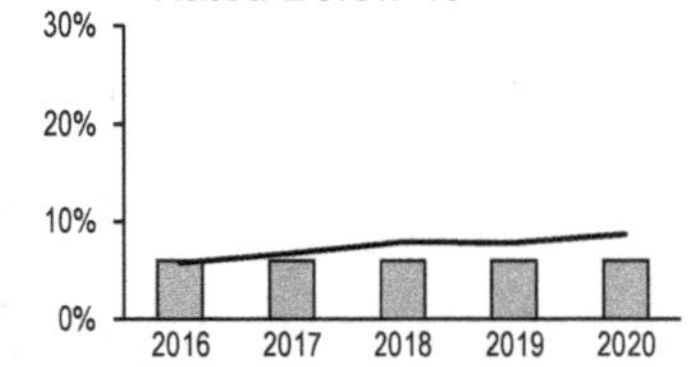

	2016	2017	2018	2019	2020
Wilson	6.0%	6.0%	6.0%	6.0%	6.0%
Average	5.7%	6.8%	7.9%	7.8%	8.7%

Percentage of Potholes Repaired within 24 hours

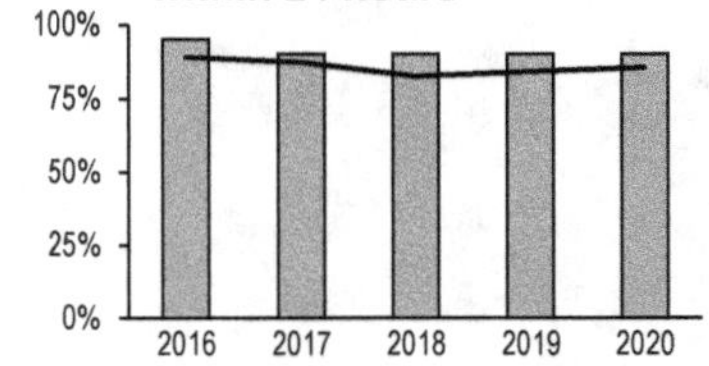

	2016	2017	2018	2019	2020
Wilson	95%	90%	90%	90%	90%
Average	89%	87%	83%	84%	85%

Winston-Salem — Asphalt Maintenance and Repair

Fiscal Year 2019-20

Explanatory Information

Service Level and Delivery

The City of Winston-Salem was responsible for maintaining approximately 2,805.5 lane miles of city streets during the fiscal year. The city treated 29.5 lane miles or approximately 1.1% of total lane miles for the city.

Contractors did 7.2 lane miles of preservation work and 22.3 lane miles of resurfacing, City crews did an additional 0.04 lane miles of resurfacing work as well.

The city reported that 50 percent of its lane miles rated 85 or above on its most recent pavement condition rating, conducted in 2019. The city used the Pavement Tracking System (PTS).

The city reported 2,802 potholes for the year. City policy is to repair potholes within twenty-four hours, but the lower response level is a result of calls on weekends and sick or vacation time of repair crews.

Conditions Affecting Service, Performance, and Costs

Winston-Salem's Department of Transportation has had several major snow storm events and higher than normal rainfall for past years, which lowered road repair work and maintenance activities and expenses.

Municipal Profile

Population (OSBM 2019)	244,739
Land Area (Square Miles)	132.59
Persons per Square Mile	1,846
Topography	Gently rolling
Climate	Temperate; some ice and snow

Service Profile

FTE Positions—Crews	40.00
FTE Positions—Other	3.25
Lane Miles Maintained	2,805.5
Lane Miles Treated	
Preservation	7.2
Resurfacing	22.3
Rehabilitation	0.0
TOTAL	29.5
Total Costs for All Treatment Types	$5,530,027
Potholes Repaired	2,802
Number of Utility Cuts	259
Number of Maintenance Patches (exclusive of potholes and utility cuts)	48
Average Cost per Ton of Hot Asphalt during Year	$65.13

Full Cost Profile

Cost Breakdown by Percentage	
Personal Services	16.1%
Operating Costs	76.8%
Capital Costs	7.1%
TOTAL	100.0%
Cost Breakdown in Dollars	
Personal Services	$1,437,098
Operating Costs	$6,857,642
Capital Costs	$629,560
TOTAL	$8,924,300

Winston-Salem — Asphalt Maintenance and Repair

Key: Winston-Salem ■ Benchmarking Average — Fiscal Years 2016 through 2020

Resource Measures

Asphalt Maintenance and Repair Services Costs per Capita

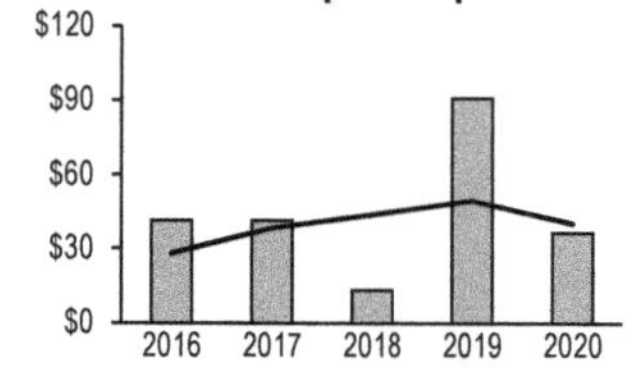

	2016	2017	2018	2019	2020
Winston-Salem	$41.38	$41.24	$13.26	$90.83	$36.46
Average	$27.80	$38.27	$43.58	$49.28	$39.86

Asphalt Maintenance and Repair FTEs per 10,000 Population

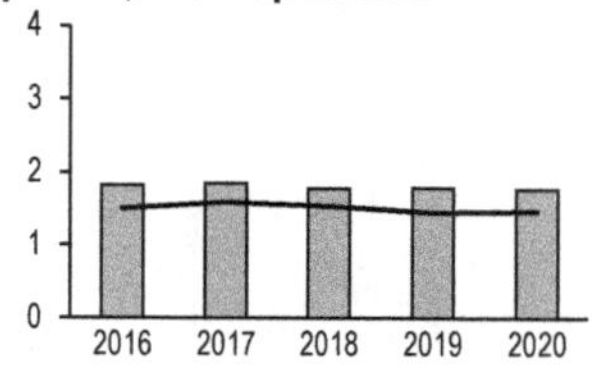

	2016	2017	2018	2019	2020
Winston-Salem	1.82	1.85	1.78	1.78	1.77
Average	1.49	1.58	1.53	1.44	1.46

Service Costs per Lane Mile of Road Maintained

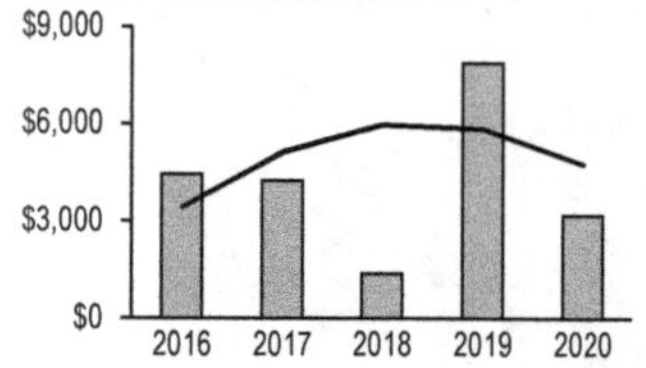

	2016	2017	2018	2019	2020
Winston-Salem	$4,455	$4,259	$1,382	$7,882	$3,181
Average	$3,426	$5,133	$5,961	$5,839	$4,759

Workload Measures

Number of Lane Miles Maintained per 1,000 Population

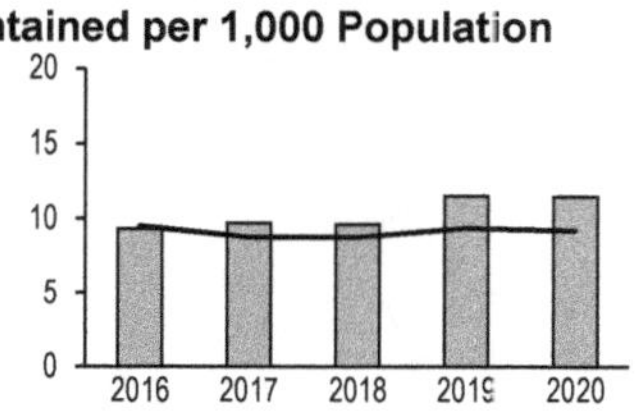

	2016	2017	2018	2019	2020
Winston-Salem	9.3	9.7	9.6	11.5	11.5
Average	9.5	8.7	8.8	9.3	9.2

Reported Potholes per Lane Mile Maintained

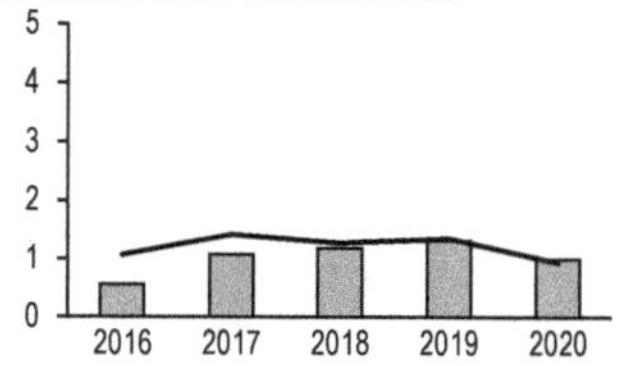

	2016	2017	2018	2019	2020
Winston-Salem	0.55	1.07	1.19	1.32	1.00
Average	1.06	1.42	1.27	1.34	0.92

Repaired Utility Cuts per Lane Mile Maintained

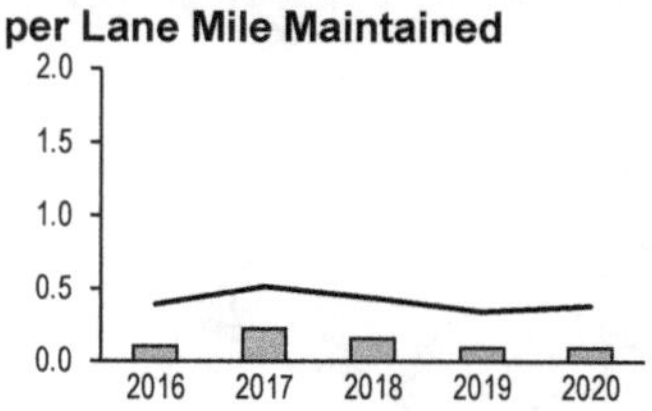

	2016	2017	2018	2019	2020
Winston-Salem	0.10	0.22	0.16	0.09	0.09
Average	0.39	0.51	0.43	0.34	0.38

Efficiency Measures

Cost of Maintenance per Lane Mile Maintained

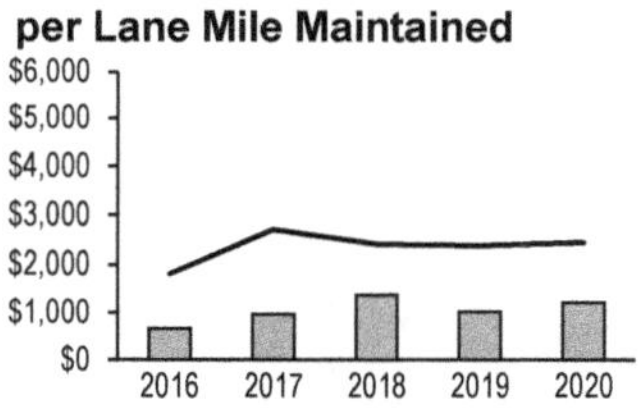

	2016	2017	2018	2019	2020
Winston-Salem	$652	$955	$1,363	$1,004	$1,210
Average	$1,806	$2,696	$2,403	$2,379	$2,446

Cost per Lane Mile for Preservation Treatment

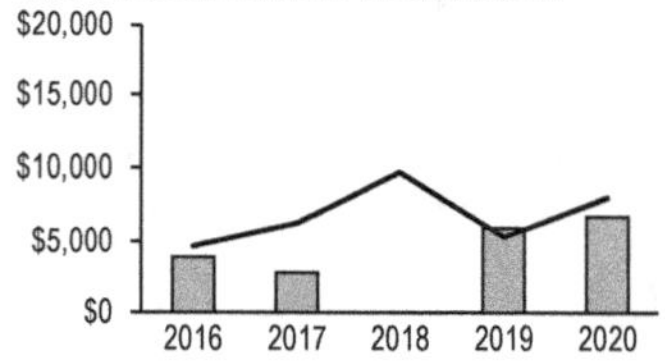

	2016	2017	2018	2019	2020
Winston-Salem	$3,895	$2,791		$5,914	$6,737
Average	$4,648	$6,231	$9,697	$5,320	$8,025

Cost per Lane Mile for Resurfacing Treatment

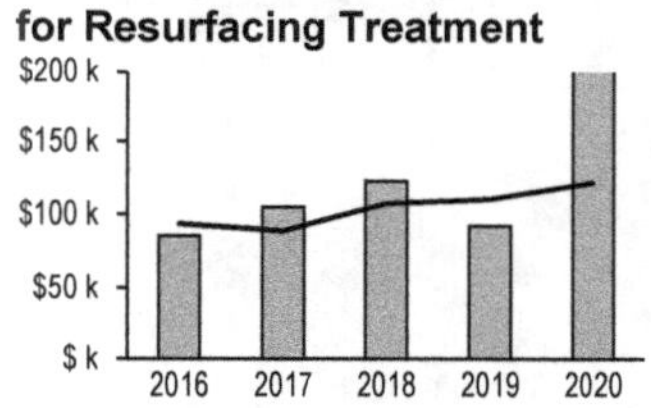

	2016	2017	2018	2019	2020
Winston-Salem	$85 k	$105 k	$123 k	$92 k	$246 k
Average	$93 k	$89 k	$107 k	$110 k	$122 k

Cost per Lane Mile for Rehabilitation Treatment

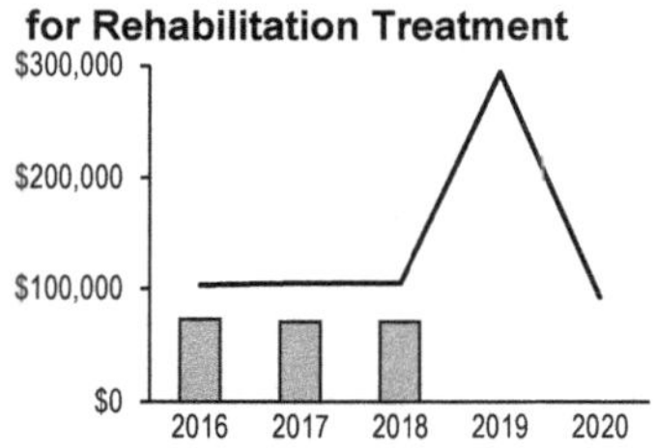

	2016	2017	2018	2019	2020
Winston-Salem	$73 k	$71 k	$71 k		
Average	$103 k	$105 k	$105 k	$294 k	$92 k

Cost per Ton for Contract Resurfacing

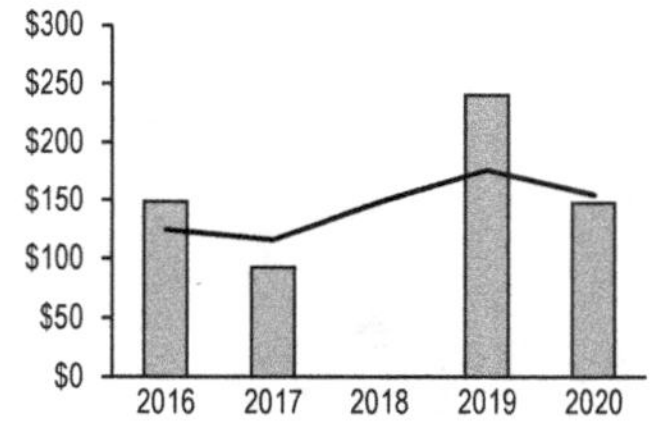

	2016	2017	2018	2019	2020
Winston-Salem	$148	$92		$240	$147
Average	$124	$115	$148	$176	$154

Effectiveness Measures

Percent of Lane Miles Rated 85 or Better

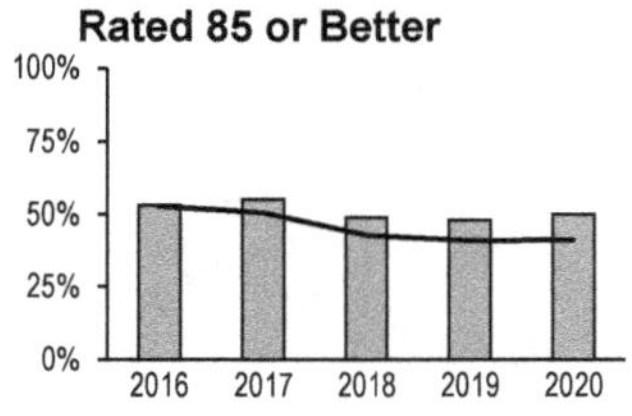

	2016	2017	2018	2019	2020
Winston-Salem	53%	55%	49%	48%	50%
Average	53%	50%	43%	41%	41%

Percent of Lane Miles Rated Below 45

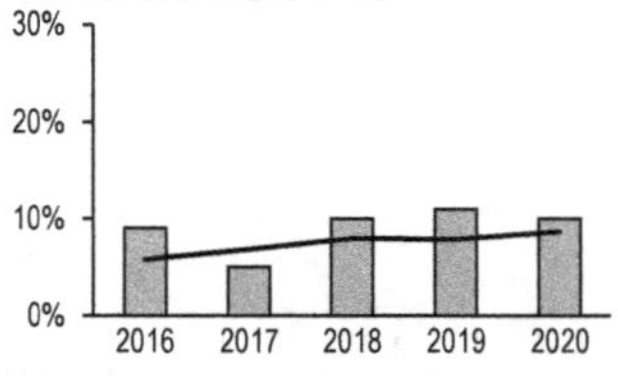

	2016	2017	2018	2019	2020
Winston-Salem	9.0%	5.0%	10.0%	11.0%	10.0%
Average	5.7%	6.8%	7.9%	7.8%	8.7%

Percentage of Potholes Repaired within 24 hours

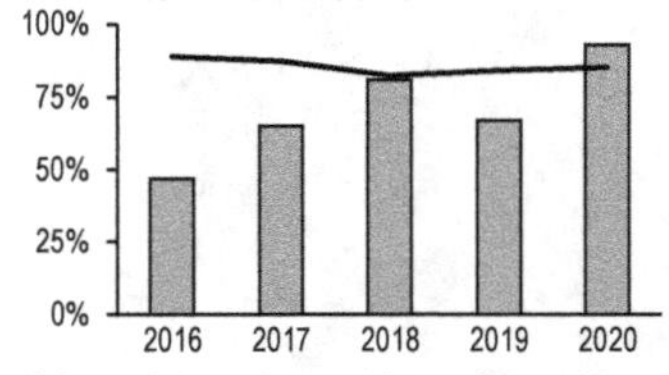

	2016	2017	2018	2019	2020
Winston-Salem	47%	65%	81%	67%	93%
Average	89%	87%	83%	84%	85%

SCHOOL OF GOVERNMENT
North Carolina Benchmarking Project

Performance and Cost Data

FIRE SERVICES

SCHOOL OF GOVERNMENT
North Carolina Benchmarking Project

PERFORMANCE MEASURES FOR FIRE SERVICES

SERVICE DEFINITION

Fire Services refers to activities and programs relating to the prevention and suppression of fires, responses to calls for service, rescue service (if provided), fire inspections (if provided), responses to hazardous materials calls (if provided), and fire education services. The services provided by fire departments vary from city to city, but the common goal remains the same: to protect the lives and property of the community served.

NOTES ON PERFORMANCE MEASURES

1. Number of Actual Fires per 1,000 Population

The total number of actual fires includes all types of fires, including structural fires.

2. Fire Inspections Completed per 1,000 Population

Fire inspections include Level I, II, and III inspections.

3. Number of Fire Department Responses per 1,000 Population

Responses include those to fires, medical emergencies, false alarms, and other types of situations that result in mobilization of fire equipment and personnel.

4. Cost per Fire Department Response

The cost represents the total cost of fire services and is calculated using a full cost accounting model that captures direct, indirect, and capital costs. Response is as defined above.

5. Number of Inspections Completed per Fire Inspector FTE

One full-time equivalent (FTE) position equals 2,080 hours of work per year. Any combination of employees providing 2,080 hours of work per year is counted as one FTE.

6. Average Turnout and Travel Time for First Unit Dispatched under "Priority One" Situations

Fast response is a critical determinant in how successful fire responders will be. Response time is calculated by adding both the turnout time (the time the dispatch is received until the first unit is out the door) and the travel time (the time the first unit is out the door until the unit arrives on the scene).

7. Percentage of Full Responses within Eight Minutes

The speed of fire department responses can be judged both by the time for the first unit arriving and also by how long it takes a full complement of trucks and personnel to respond to an emergency. The percentage within eight minutes takes into account travel time.

8. Percentage of Fires Confined to Object or Room of Origin

Containment of fires to as small an area as possible limits total damages. The degree of containment depends on how quickly the fire department is called and is also an effectiveness measure that is reported to the state.

9. Percentage of Fires for Which Cause Is Determined

Investigation of the causes of fires can be an important part of prevention and suppression efforts. While the cause of all fires cannot always be determined, being able to identify causes is important if lessons are to be learned from the investigations.

10. Percentage of Fire Code Violations "Cleared" by Correction or Imposition of Penalty within Ninety Days

Fire code violations are violations of state and local laws and regulations as found through fire inspections. The violators are given time to correct the violation before a penalty is imposed. This is an effectiveness measure that provides an indication of timeliness of follow-up.

11. Percentage of Cases with Lost Pulse Where Pulse Is Recovered at Time of Transfer for Transport

Fire departments frequently are the first responders to medical calls, including cases where an individual has no pulse either at the time of arrival or during the response. This effectiveness measure reports the percentage of these cases in which the patient has recovered a pulse by the time responsibility for care has been transferred to emergency responders who will transport the patient to a hospital. Many patients cannot be saved, and recovery of pulse does not guarantee survival at the hospital.

Fire Services

Summary of Key Dimensions of Service

City or Town	Population Served	Land Area Served (in Square Miles)	Value of Property in Service Area (in Billions)	Total Number of Fire Department Responses	Fire Code Violations Found	Number of Community Fire Stations	Number of Fire Services FTEs	ISO* Rating
Apex	68,488	67.4	$8.8	3,503	1,357	5	98	3—town 6—outlying
Chapel Hill	64,225	22.9	$8.4	4,385	na	5	96	2
Charlotte	880,649	315.3	$147.1	119,581	35,696	41 + 1 airport	1,237	1
Concord	99,228	70.1	$12.2	12,154	2,708	10 + 1 airport	229	1
Goldsboro	33,969	29.4	$2.6	2,296	2,013	5	84	2
Greensboro	302,728	140.5	$29.2	38,952	9,840	26	584	1
Hickory	46,565	43.4	$5.7	5,677	3,073	6 + 1 airport	139	3
Raleigh	475,580	146.5	$61.6	43,779	26,545	28	621	1
Wilson	49,384	31.0	$4.2	4,272	2,945	5	100	1
Winston-Salem	244,739	132.6	$23.0	23,483	6,644	19	368	2

NOTES

*ISO—Insurance Service Office

EXPLANATORY FACTORS

These are factors that the project found affected fire services performance and cost in one or more of the municipalities:

Population and area served
Value of property area protected in service area
Number of engine companies
Number of fire department responses
Fire code violations
ISO rating
Age of housing stock

Fiscal Year 2019-20

Explanatory Information

Service Level and Delivery

The mission of the Apex Fire Department is to protect life, property, and the environment from fire, medical emergencies, natural disasters, and other emergencies for those who live, work, and travel in and through the town and surrounding area. In addition to the town, the fire department serves an additional forty-nine square miles in surrounding fire districts.

The fire department uses a shift schedule with one twenty-four-hour shift on schedule and one off every three days, followed by a four-day break. On average, shift personnel work ten to eleven days per twenty-eight-day cycle.

The area within the Town of Apex has an ISO rating of 3, while the surrounding fire districts served have an ISO rating of 6. The rating was done during 2013 and was an upgrade from the prior rating for both areas.

The Apex Fire Department conducted 1,407 fire maintenance, construction, and reinspections during the fiscal year. The fire department handles all inspections within town limits and coordinates with the Wake County Fire Marshal for joint inspections in the extra-territorial jurisdiction for new construction, fire alarms, and sprinkler reviews and inspections. Apex has a fire marshal and one inspector.

All fire investigations in Apex are handled by the Wake County Fire Marshal. Apex assists in investigations but does not provide the investigative reports.

Conditions Affecting Service, Performance, and Costs

Municipal Profile

Service Population	68,488
Land Area (Square Miles)	67.35
Persons per Square Mile	1,017
Median Household Income	$84,000
U.S. Census 2016	

Service Profile

FTE Positions—Firefighters	88.0
FTE Positions—Other	10.0
Fire Stations	5
First-Line Fire Apparatus	
Pumpers	4
Aerial Trucks	2
Quints	1
Squads	0
Rescue	1
Other	6
Fire Department Responses	3,503
Responses for Fires	127
Structural Fires Reported	30
Inspections Completed for Maintenance, Construction, and Reinspections	1,407
Fire Code Violations Reported	1,357
Estimated Fire Loss (millions)	$0.66
Amount of Property Protected in Service Area (millions)	$8,802
Number of Fire Education Programs or Events	13

Full Cost Profile

Cost Breakdown by Percentage	
Personal Services	68.5%
Operating Costs	20.2%
Capital Costs	11.3%
TOTAL	100.0%
Cost Breakdown in Dollars	
Personal Services	$8,086,246
Operating Costs	$2,378,725
Capital Costs	$1,337,100
TOTAL	$11,802,071

Apex

Fire Services

Key: Apex ■ Benchmarking Average — Fiscal Years 2016 through 2020

Resource Measures

Fire Services Costs per Capita

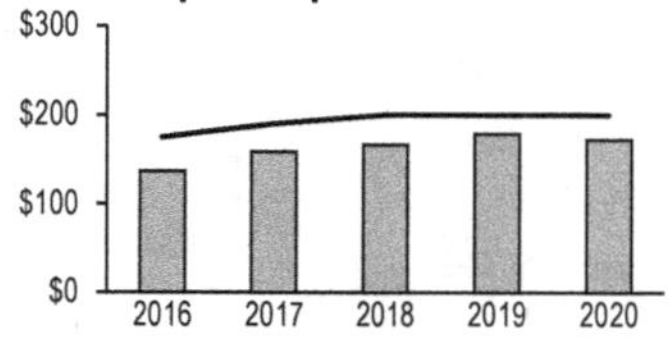

	2016	2017	2018	2019	2020
Apex	$137	$159	$166	$178	$172
Average	$174	$190	$199	$200	$200

Fire Services Total FTEs per 10,000 Population

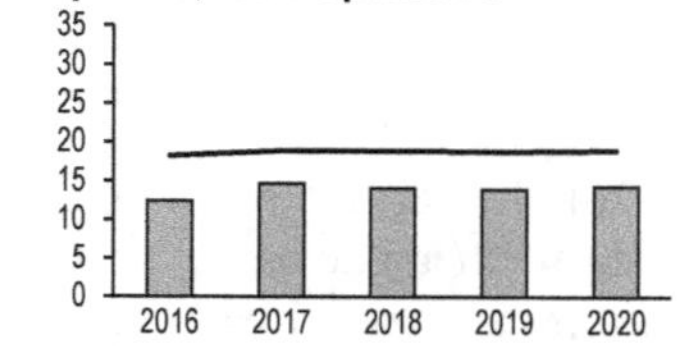

	2016	2017	2018	2019	2020
Apex	12.4	14.7	14.0	13.9	14.3
Average	18.1	18.8	18.8	18.7	18.8

Fire Services Cost per Thousand Dollars of Property Protected

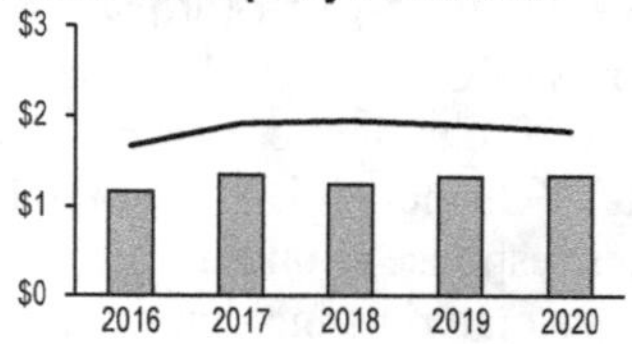

	2016	2017	2018	2019	2020
Apex	$1.16	$1.35	$1.24	$1.33	$1.34
Average	$1.66	$1.91	$1.94	$1.90	$1.83

Workload Measures

Actual Fires per 1,000 Population

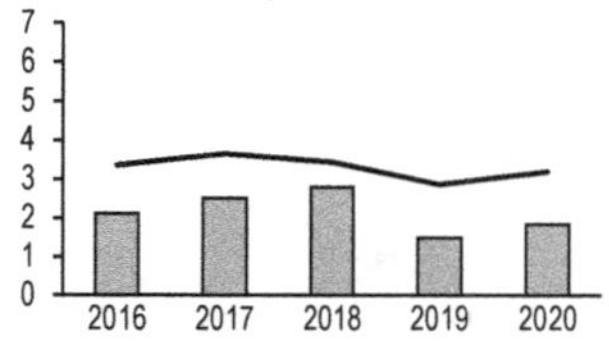

	2016	2017	2018	2019	2020
Apex	2.12	2.52	2.81	1.51	1.85
Average	3.34	3.65	3.44	2.87	3.19

Fire Department Responses per 1,000 Population

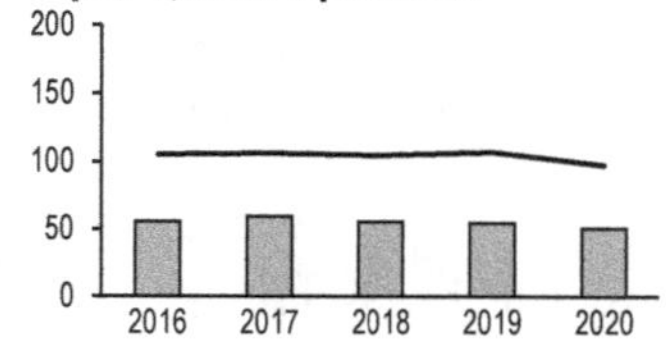

	2016	2017	2018	2019	2020
Apex	56	60	56	55	51
Average	105	106	105	107	97

Fire Inspections Completed per 1,000 Population

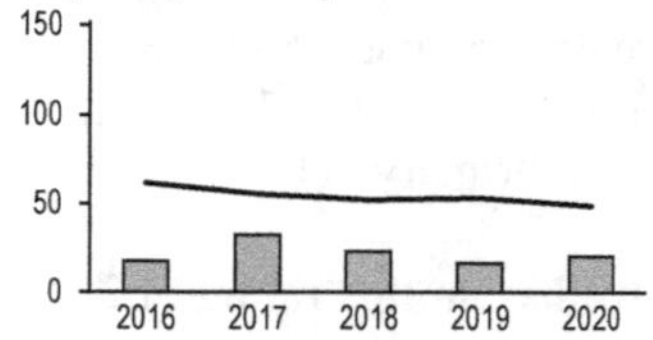

	2016	2017	2018	2019	2020
Apex	18	33	23	17	21
Average	62	55	52	53	49

Efficiency Measures

Fire Services Cost per Fire Department Response

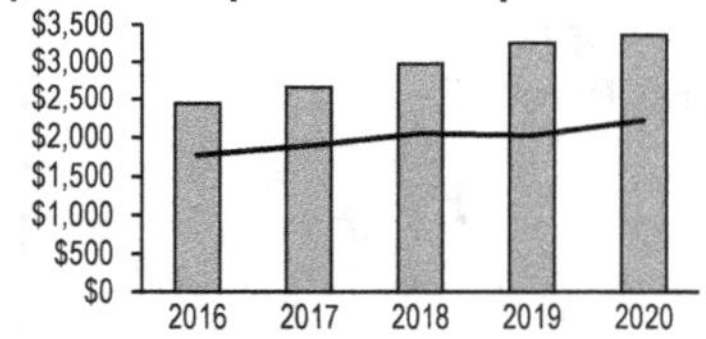

	2016	2017	2018	2019	2020
Apex	$2,443	$2,659	$2,972	$3,257	$3,369
Average	$1,765	$1,892	$2,051	$2,021	$2,219

Inspections Completed per Inspector FTE

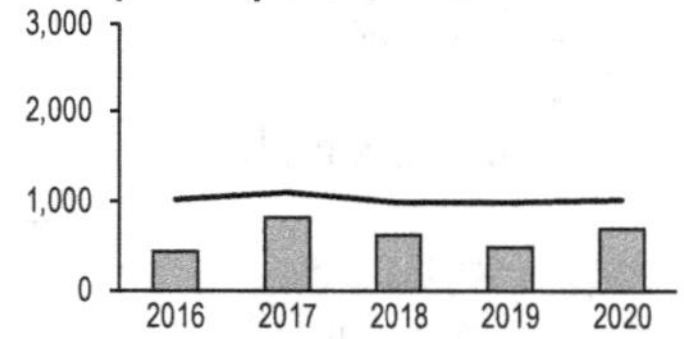

	2016	2017	2018	2019	2020
Apex	445	822	630	492	704
Average	1,014	1,095	985	989	1,017

Effectiveness Measures

Average Response Time to Priority One Calls in Minutes

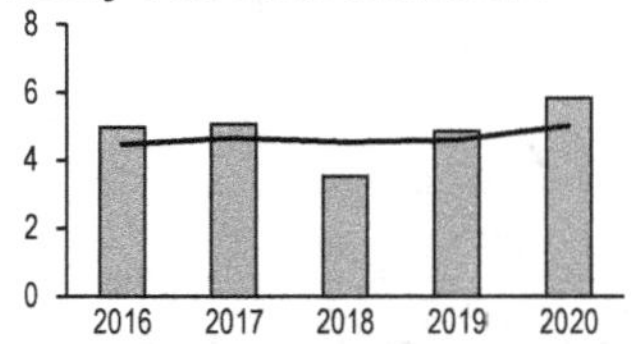

	2016	2017	2018	2019	2020
Apex	5.0	5.1	3.5	4.9	5.8
Average	4.4	4.6	4.5	4.6	5.0

Percentage of Fire Code Violations Cleared within 90 Days

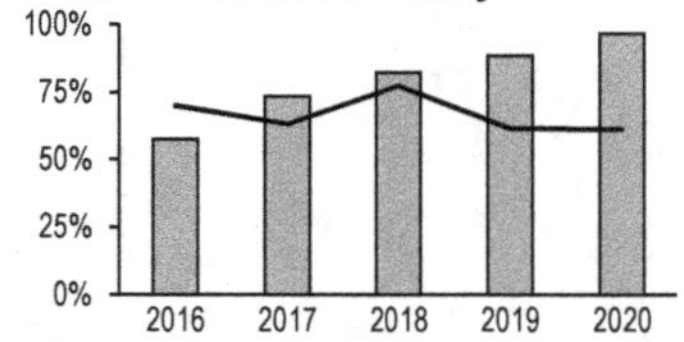

	2016	2017	2018	2019	2020
Apex	57%	73%	82%	89%	97%
Average	70%	63%	77%	61%	61%

Percentage of Fires Confined to Rooms or Objects Involved on Arrival

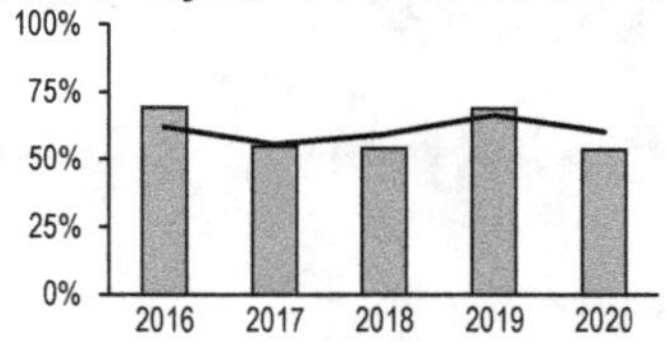

	2016	2017	2018	2019	2020
Apex	69%	55%	54%	69%	53%
Average	62%	55%	59%	66%	60%

Percentage of Fires for Which Cause Was Determined

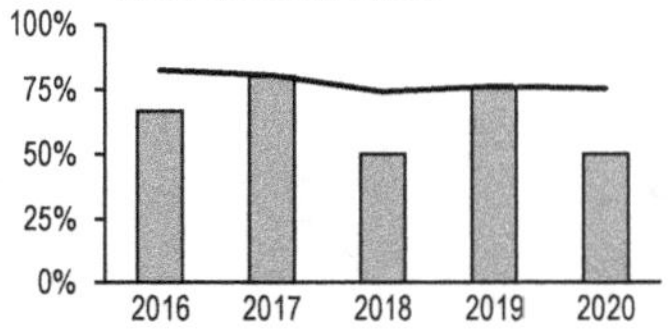

	2016	2017	2018	2019	2020
Apex	67%	80%	50%	76%	50%
Average	82%	80%	74%	76%	75%

Percentage of Full Response within 8 Minutes Travel Time

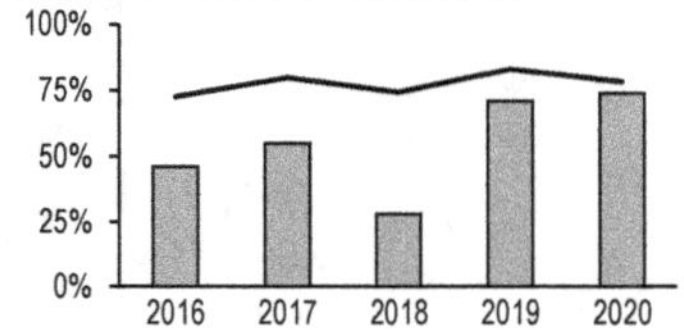

	2016	2017	2018	2019	2020
Apex	46%	55%	28%	71%	74%
Average	72%	80%	74%	83%	78%

Percentage of Lost Pulse Cases Recovered Pulse at Transfer of Care

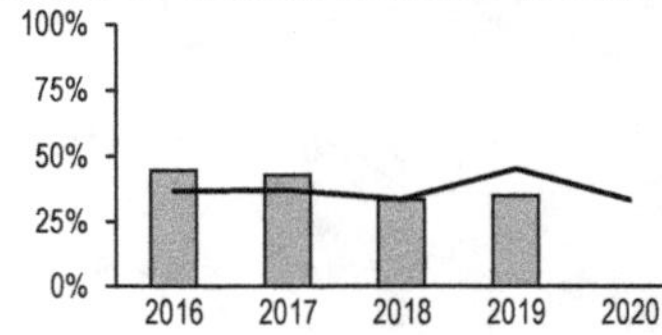

	2016	2017	2018	2019	2020
Apex	44.4%	42.9%	33.3%	35.0%	
Average	36.6%	36.9%	33.5%	45.1%	33.3%

Fiscal Year 2019-20

Explanatory Information

Service Level and Delivery

The Town of Chapel Hill Fire Department's mission is to minimize the risk of fire and other hazards to the life and property of the citizens of Chapel Hill. To accomplish this mission, the department provides response to and mitigation of fires, medical emergencies, hazardous materials incidents, and other emergencies as they arise.

The fire department is organized into three divisions: operations, administration, and life safety. Operations and life safety are administered by a deputy chief with support staff. Administration consists of the fire chief and support staff.

The fire department works a 3/4 system, where personnel are on duty for 24 hours starting at 7 a.m. The town has five community stations with seven primary vehicles for response.

The town has an ISO rating of 2 received in 2016, which was an upgrade from the year before.

Fire inspections are performed by fire inspectors and are designed to be completed in accordance with the State of North Carolina's inspection schedule. Initial inspections may generate findings for reinspection. The department counts malls as one inspection per occupancy and one per building structure. High rises have one inspection per building plus one per commercial occupancy. Multi-structure apartment complexes have just one inspection per complex.

Conditions Affecting Service, Performance, and Costs

Complete data on fire code violations and fire safety complaints was not available for the last few years.

Municipal Profile

Service Population	64,225
Land Area (Square Miles)	22.91
Persons per Square Mile	2,804
Median Household Income U.S. Census 2016	$60,802

Service Profile

FTE Positions—Firefighters	78.0
FTE Positions—Other	18.0
Fire Stations	5
First-Line Fire Apparatus	
Pumpers	5
Aerial Trucks	2
Quints	0
Squads	0
Rescue	2
Other	32
Fire Department Responses	4,385
Responses for Fires	99
Structural Fires Reported	46
Inspections Completed for Maintenance, Construction, and Reinspections	0
Fire Code Violations Reported	NA
Estimated Fire Loss (millions)	$0.31
Amount of Property Protected in Service Area (millions)	$8,384
Number of Fire Education Programs or Events	NA

Full Cost Profile

Cost Breakdown by Percentage	
Personal Services	63.0%
Operating Costs	28.1%
Capital Costs	8.9%
TOTAL	100.0%
Cost Breakdown in Dollars	
Personal Services	$8,171,061
Operating Costs	$3,645,217
Capital Costs	$1,152,707
TOTAL	$12,968,985

Key: Chapel Hill ■ Benchmarking Average — Fiscal Years 2016 through 2020

Resource Measures

Fire Services Costs per Capita

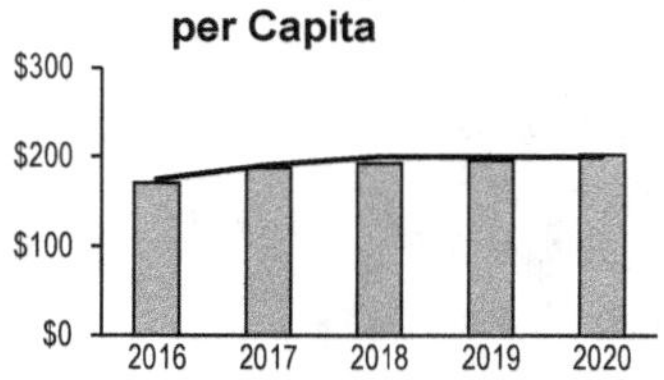

	2016	2017	2018	2019	2020
Chapel Hill	$170	$187	$192	$196	$202
Average	$174	$190	$199	$200	$200

Fire Services Total FTEs per 10,000 Population

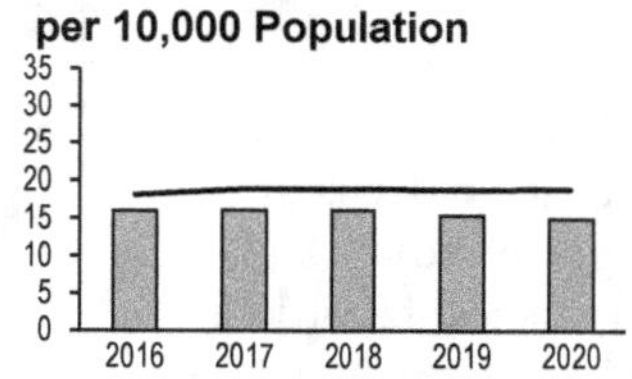

	2016	2017	2018	2019	2020
Chapel Hill	16.0	16.1	16.0	15.4	14.9
Average	18.1	18.8	18.8	18.7	18.8

Fire Services Cost per Thousand Dollars of Property Protected

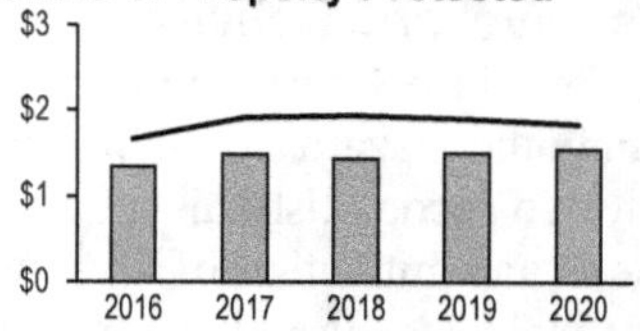

	2016	2017	2018	2019	2020
Chapel Hill	$1.35	$1.49	$1.44	$1.50	$1.55
Average	$1.66	$1.91	$1.94	$1.90	$1.83

Workload Measures

Actual Fires per 1,000 Population

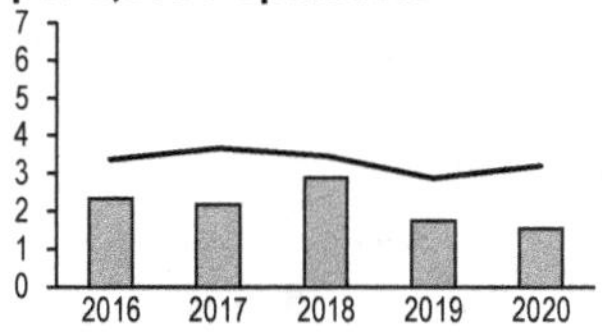

	2016	2017	2018	2019	2020
Chapel Hill	2.33	2.17	2.88	1.76	1.54
Average	3.34	3.65	3.44	2.87	3.19

Fire Department Responses per 1,000 Population

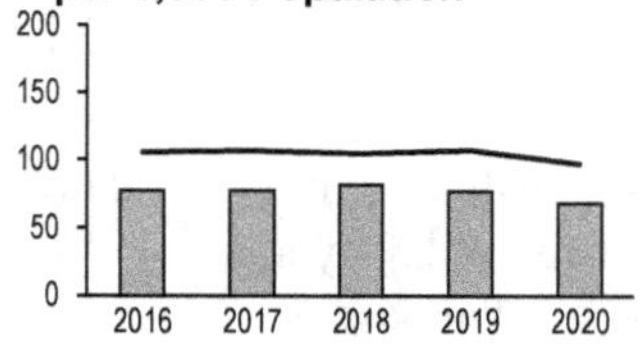

	2016	2017	2018	2019	2020
Chapel Hill	77	77	81	77	68
Average	105	106	105	107	97

Fire Inspections Completed per 1,000 Population

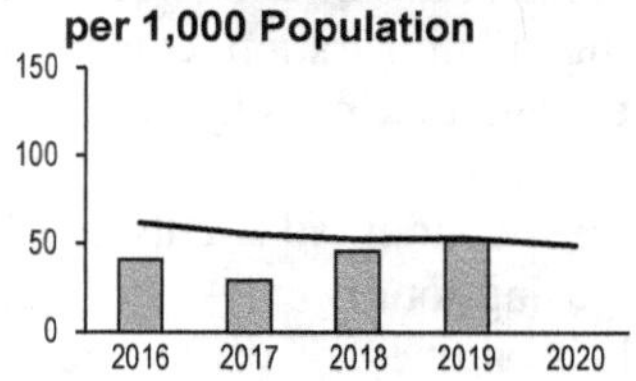

	2016	2017	2018	2019	2020
Chapel Hill	41	29	46	52	
Average	62	55	52	53	49

Efficiency Measures

Fire Services Cost per Fire Department Response

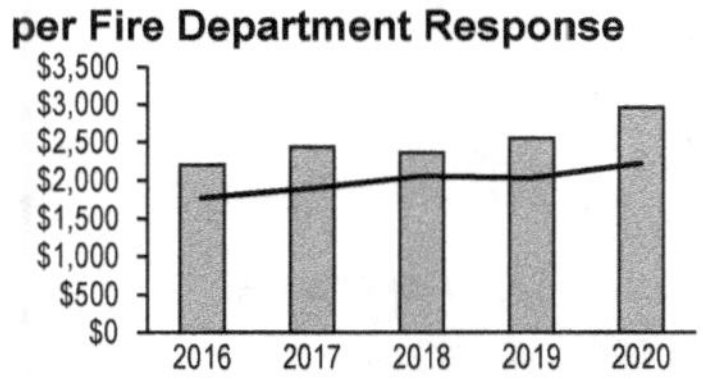

	2016	2017	2018	2019	2020
Chapel Hill	$2,203	$2,432	$2,360	$2,553	$2,958
Average	$1,765	$1,892	$2,051	$2,021	$2,219

Inspections Completed per Inspector FTE

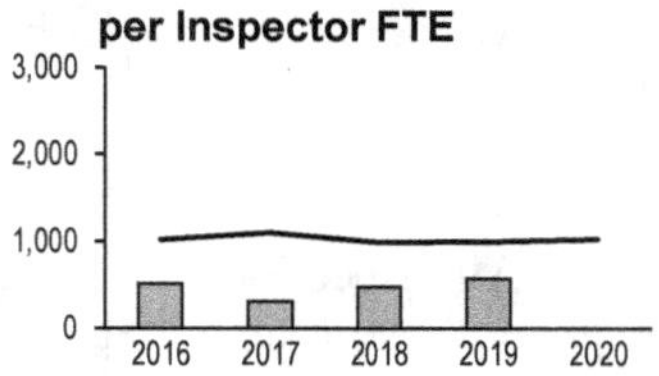

	2016	2017	2018	2019	2020
Chapel Hill	517	310	479	575	
Average	1,014	1,095	985	989	1,017

Effectiveness Measures

Average Response Time to Priority One Calls in Minutes

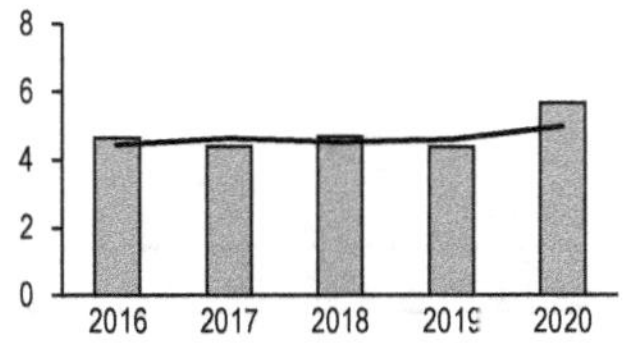

	2016	2017	2018	2019	2020
Chapel Hill	4.7	4.4	4.7	4.4	5.7
Average	4.4	4.6	4.5	4.6	5.0

Percentage of Fire Code Violations Cleared within 90 Days

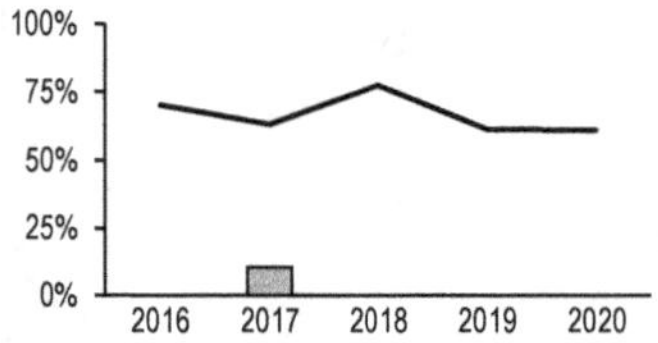

	2016	2017	2018	2019	2020
Chapel Hill		11%			
Average	70%	63%	77%	61%	61%

Percentage of Fires Confined to Rooms or Objects Involved on Arrival

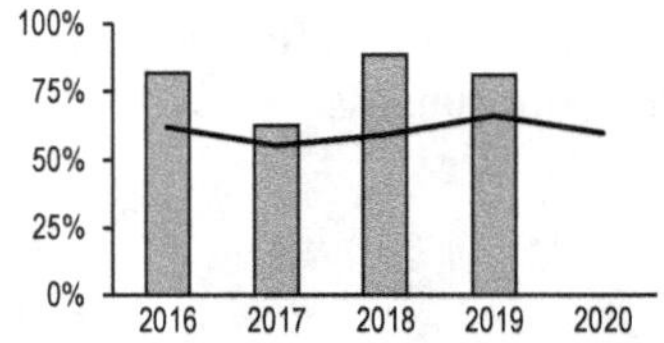

	2016	2017	2018	2019	2020
Chapel Hill	82%	63%	88%	81%	
Average	62%	55%	59%	66%	60%

Percentage of Fires for Which Cause Was Determined

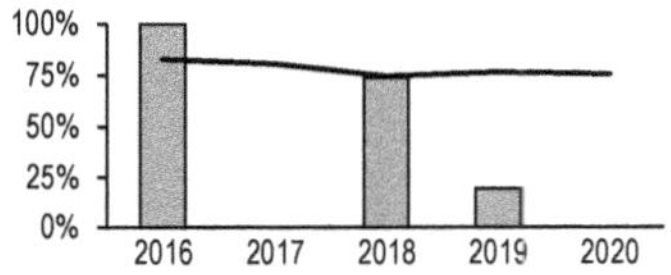

	2016	2017	2018	2019	2020
Chapel Hill	100%		74%	19%	
Average	82%	80%	74%	76%	75%

Percentage of Full Response within 8 Minutes Travel Time

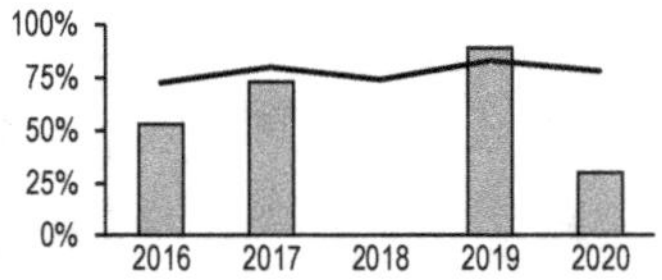

	2016	2017	2018	2019	2020
Chapel Hill	53%	73%		89%	30%
Average	72%	80%	74%	83%	78%

Percentage of Lost Pulse Cases Recovered Pulse at Transfer of Care

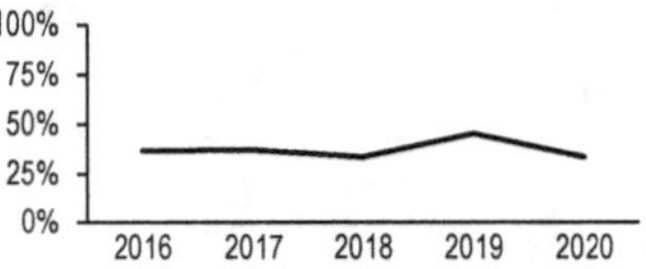

	2016	2017	2018	2019	2020
Chapel Hill					
Average	36.6%	36.9%	33.5%	45.1%	33.3%

Fiscal Year 2019-20

Explanatory Information

Service Level and Delivery
The mission of the Charlotte Fire Department is to minimize the risk of fire and other hazards to the life and property of the citizens of Charlotte. To accomplish this mission, the department provides response to and mitigation of fires, medical emergencies, hazardous materials incidents, aircraft emergencies, technical rescues, and other emergencies as they arise. These services are provided immediately to any person who has a need anywhere within the corporate limits of Charlotte.

The divisions of the Charlotte Fire Department are operations (A, B, C), training, administration, communications, logistics, fire prevention, and fire investigation.

The city uses a modified twenty-four-hour/forty-eight-hour shift schedule, using four twenty-four-hour shifts in a twelve-day cycle. The cycle is on one day, off one day, on one day, off two days, on one day, off one day, on one day, off four days. In addition, firefighters receive a Kelley day (ten hours) off and a Kelley night (fourteen hours) off every seven weeks to maintain the number of hours worked per week at fifty-two.

The city has an ISO rating of 1, which is the highest level possible. The Charlotte Fire Department has been accredited since 2000.

The fire department conducted 37,869 fire maintenance, construction, and reinspections during the fiscal year. All inspections are performed by certified fire inspectors who are employees of the Fire Prevention Bureau. The inspectors handle certificate of occupancy inspections, permit inspections and issuances, regular code enforcement inspections, and reinspections. The Bureau currently uses separate inspections on each building of an apartment complex.

Conditions Affecting Service, Performance, and Costs
Charlotte staffs a fire station at the airport in addition to forty-one community fire stations.

Municipal Profile

Service Population	880,649
Land Area (Square Miles)	315.34
Persons per Square Mile	2,793
Median Household Income U.S. Census 2016	$46,975

Service Profile

FTE Positions—Firefighters	1,101.0
FTE Positions—Other	136.0
Fire Stations	42
First-Line Fire Apparatus	
Pumpers	42
Aerial Trucks	0
Quints	16
Squads	0
Rescue	2
Other	37
Fire Department Responses	119,581
Responses for Fires	2,260
Structural Fires Reported	448
Inspections Completed for Maintenance, Construction, and Reinspections	37,869
Fire Code Violations Reported	35,696
Estimated Fire Loss (millions)	$66.97
Amount of Property Protected in Service Area (millions)	$147,146
Number of Fire Education Programs or Events	900

Full Cost Profile

Cost Breakdown by Percentage	
Personal Services	66.5%
Operating Costs	21.7%
Capital Costs	11.8%
TOTAL	100.0%
Cost Breakdown in Dollars	
Personal Services	$115,180,502
Operating Costs	$20,635,528
Capital Costs	$9,544,408
TOTAL	$145,360,438

Key: Charlotte ▪ Benchmarking Average — Fiscal Years 2016 through 2020

Resource Measures

Fire Services Costs per Capita

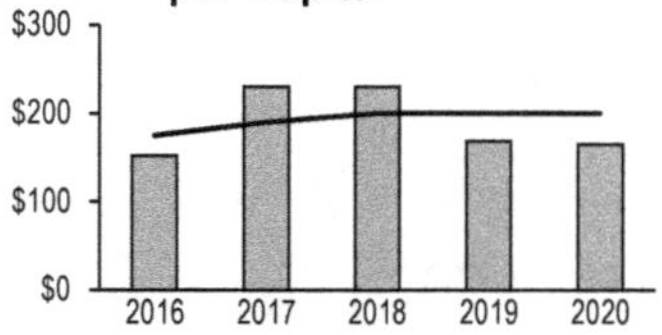

	2016	2017	2018	2019	2020
Charlotte	$152	$230	$230	$168	$165
Average	$174	$190	$199	$200	$200

Fire Services Total FTEs per 10,000 Population

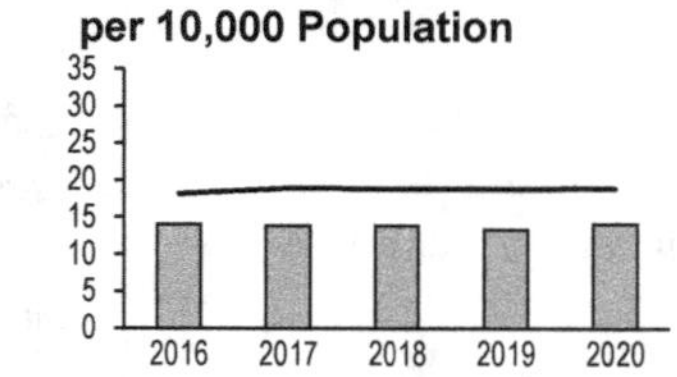

	2016	2017	2018	2019	2020
Charlotte	14.0	13.8	13.9	13.3	14.0
Average	18.1	18.8	18.8	18.7	18.8

Fire Services Cost per Thousand Dollars of Property Protected

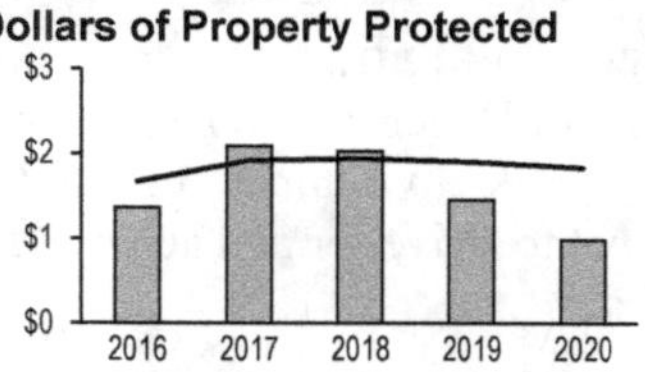

	2016	2017	2018	2019	2020
Charlotte	$1.36	$2.09	$2.03	$1.46	$0.99
Average	$1.66	$1.91	$1.94	$1.90	$1.83

Workload Measures

Actual Fires per 1,000 Population

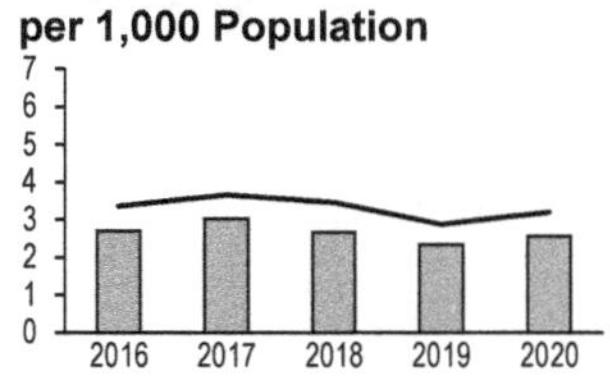

	2016	2017	2018	2019	2020
Charlotte	2.70	3.01	2.66	2.34	2.57
Average	3.34	3.65	3.44	2.87	3.19

Fire Department Responses per 1,000 Population

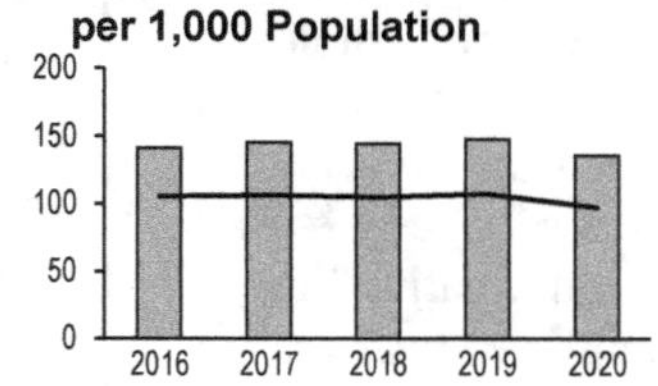

	2016	2017	2018	2019	2020
Charlotte	141	146	145	148	136
Average	105	106	105	107	97

Fire Inspections Completed per 1,000 Population

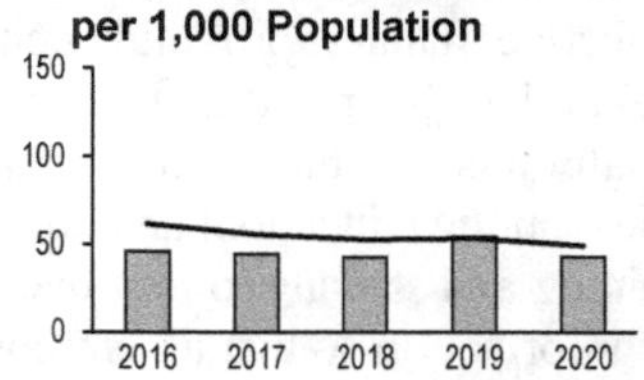

	2016	2017	2018	2019	2020
Charlotte	46	44	43	54	43
Average	62	55	52	53	49

Efficiency Measures

Fire Services Cost per Fire Department Response

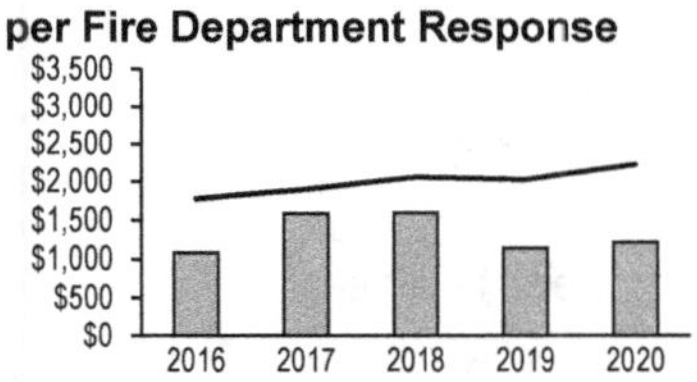

	2016	2017	2018	2019	2020
Charlotte	$1,078	$1,582	$1,594	$1,141	$1,216
Average	$1,765	$1,892	$2,051	$2,021	$2,219

Inspections Completed per Inspector FTE

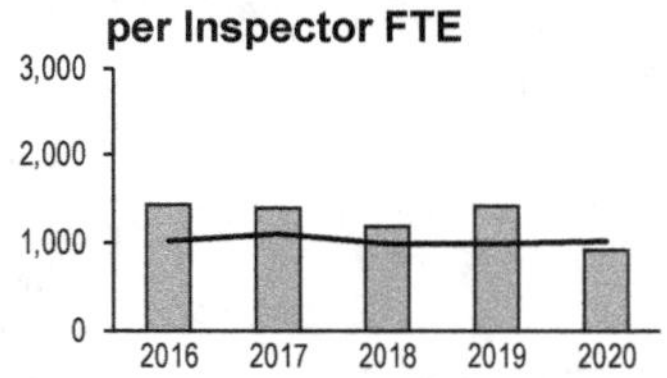

	2016	2017	2018	2019	2020
Charlotte	1,421	1,387	1,184	1,409	924
Average	1,014	1,095	985	989	1,017

Effectiveness Measures

Average Response Time to Priority One Calls in Minutes

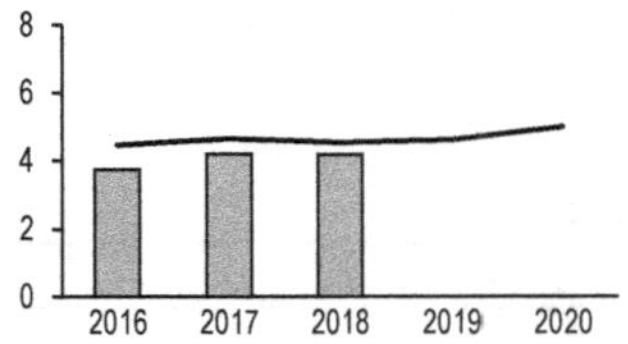

	2016	2017	2018	2019	2020
Charlotte	3.7	4.2	4.2		
Average	4.4	4.6	4.5	4.6	5.0

Percentage of Fire Code Violations Cleared within 90 Days

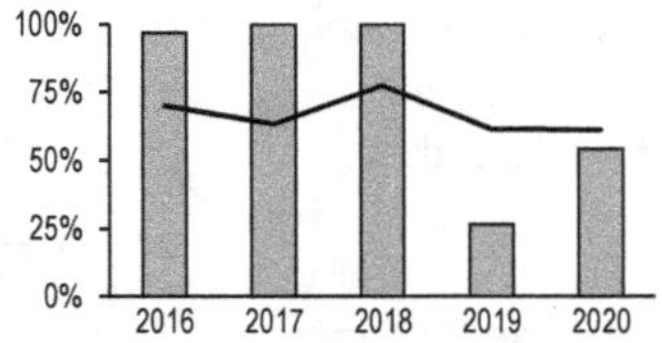

	2016	2017	2018	2019	2020
Charlotte	97%	100%	100%	27%	54%
Average	70%	63%	77%	61%	61%

Percentage of Fires Confined to Rooms or Objects Involved on Arrival

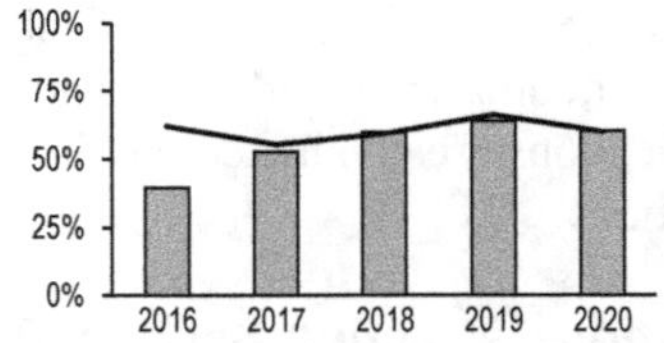

	2016	2017	2018	2019	2020
Charlotte	39%	53%	60%	64%	60%
Average	62%	55%	59%	66%	60%

Percentage of Fires for Which Cause Was Determined

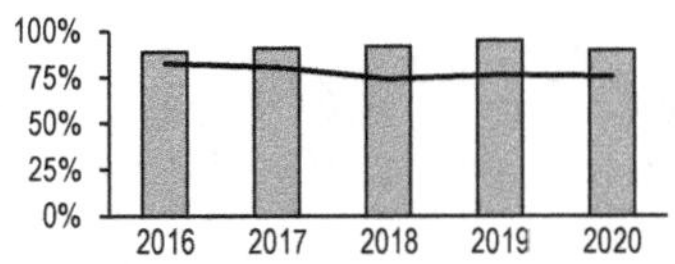

	2016	2017	2018	2019	2020
Charlotte	89%	91%	92%	95%	90%
Average	82%	80%	74%	76%	75%

Percentage of Full Response within 8 Minutes Travel Time

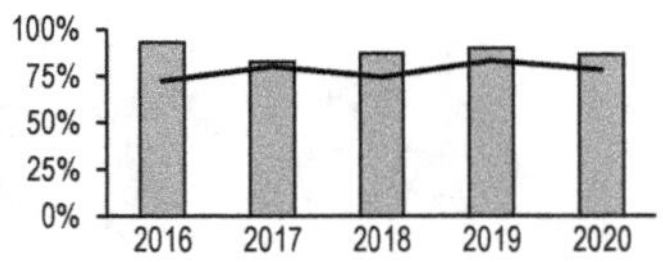

	2016	2017	2018	2019	2020
Charlotte	93%	82%	87%	90%	86%
Average	72%	80%	74%	83%	78%

Percentage of Lost Pulse Cases Recovered Pulse at Transfer of Care

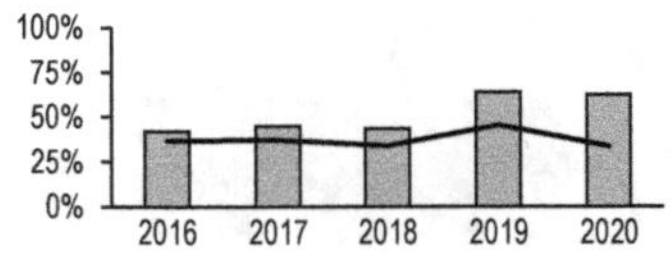

	2016	2017	2018	2019	2020
Charlotte	41.7%	44.7%	43.4%	63.7%	62.5%
Average	36.6%	36.9%	33.5%	45.1%	33.3%

Fiscal Year 2019-20

Explanatory Information

Service Level and Delivery

The City of Concord Fire Department is committed to providing a positive work environment to enable the department and its personnel to strive for and achieve excellence in fire protection services.

The department is committed to the following: providing leadership through a management/employee team organizational concept that is dedicated to modern-day management principles and practices; providing the citizens with the best possible modern-day fire protection and life safety services in a courteous, professional, and cost-effective manner; providing equal opportunity for all employees to excel in their job performance and career development; striving to continually increase the public's awareness through fire prevention activities, public education, and community-based services; maintaining and striving to improve on an open, informative flow of correct information so that all employees and employee teams reach their goals and objectives; subscribing to departmental values of honesty, professionalism, teamwork, loyalty, dedication, and commitment to serving the public; and planning for change to develop and prepare the department to always strive for excellence.

The fire department in Concord contains the following divisions: administration, operations, training, and fire prevention..

The fire department utilizes a shift schedule that includes twenty-four hours on and forty-eight hours off.

The city has an ISO rating of 1, as rated in 2018. This is the highest level rating possible and was an upgrade from the last rating.

The fire department conducted 4,771 fire maintenance, construction, and reinspections during the fiscal year. Inspections are conducted by the Fire-Risk Management Division. Each inspector has an assigned area of the city and a specific number of inspections to complete. Each occupancy is counted separately in the inspections number. An apartment complex would be considered as one occupancy. Reinspections are conducted within forty-five days to confirm corrections.

Conditions Affecting Service, Performance, and Costs

Concord staffs a fire station at the airport in addition to ten community fire stations.

Municipal Profile

Service Population	99,228
Land Area (Square Miles)	70.10
Persons per Square Mile	1,416
Median Household Income U.S. Census 2016	$50,863

Service Profile

FTE Positions—Firefighters	209.0
FTE Positions—Other	19.5
Fire Stations	11
First-Line Fire Apparatus	
Pumpers	10
Aerial Trucks	3
Quints	0
Squads	0
Rescue	1
Other	12
Fire Department Responses	12,154
Responses for Fires	264
Structural Fires Reported	44
Inspections Completed for Maintenance, Construction, and Reinspections	4,771
Fire Code Violations Reported	2,708
Estimated Fire Loss (millions)	$3.08
Amount of Property Protected in Service Area (millions)	$12,152
Number of Fire Education Programs or Events	158

Full Cost Profile

Cost Breakdown by Percentage	
Personal Services	67.7%
Operating Costs	21.2%
Capital Costs	11.1%
TOTAL	100.0%

Cost Breakdown in Dollars	
Personal Services	$17,246,933
Operating Costs	$5,392,269
Capital Costs	$2,819,527
TOTAL	$25,458,729

Concord

Fire Services

Key: Concord ▪ Benchmarking Average —

Fiscal Years 2016 through 2020

Resource Measures

Fire Services Costs per Capita

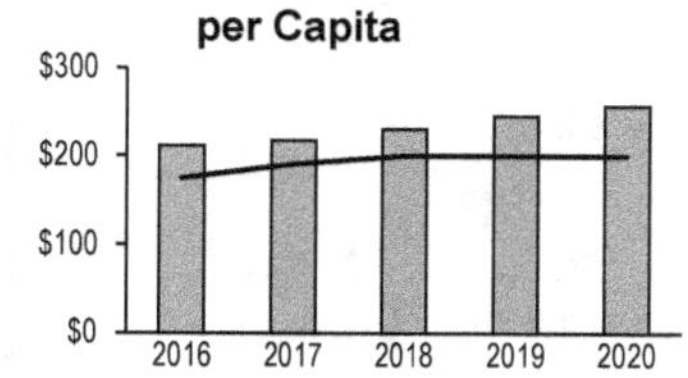

	2016	2017	2018	2019	2020
Concord	$211	$217	$230	$245	$257
Average	$174	$190	$199	$200	$200

Fire Services Total FTEs per 10,000 Population

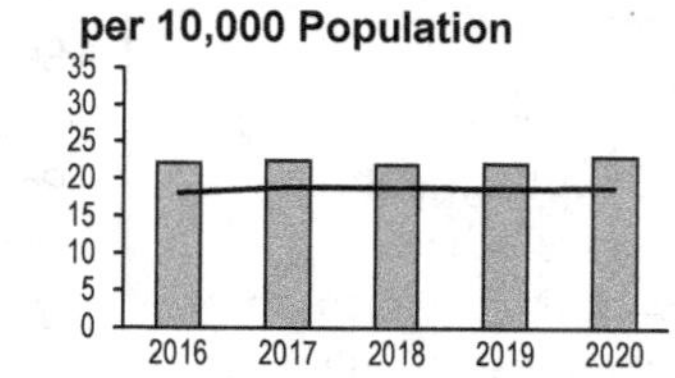

	2016	2017	2018	2019	2020
Concord	22.1	22.4	21.9	22.1	23.0
Average	18.1	18.8	18.8	18.7	18.8

Fire Services Cost per Thousand Dollars of Property Protected

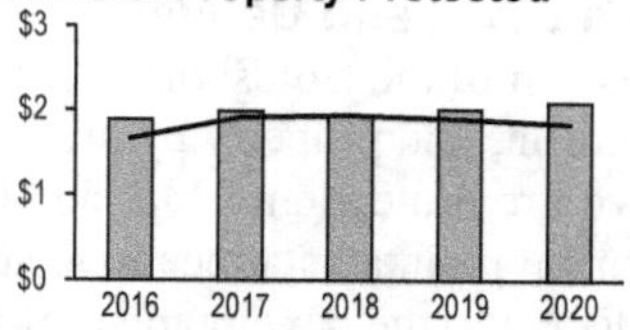

	2016	2017	2018	2019	2020
Concord	$1.89	$1.98	$1.92	$2.01	$2.10
Average	$1.66	$1.91	$1.94	$1.90	$1.83

Workload Measures

Actual Fires per 1,000 Population

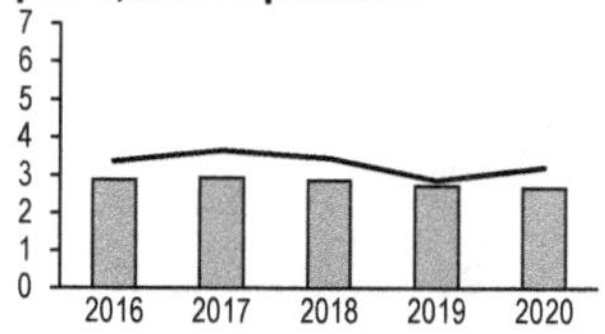

	2016	2017	2018	2019	2020
Concord	2.88	2.92	2.85	2.71	2.66
Average	3.34	3.65	3.44	2.87	3.19

Fire Department Responses per 1,000 Population

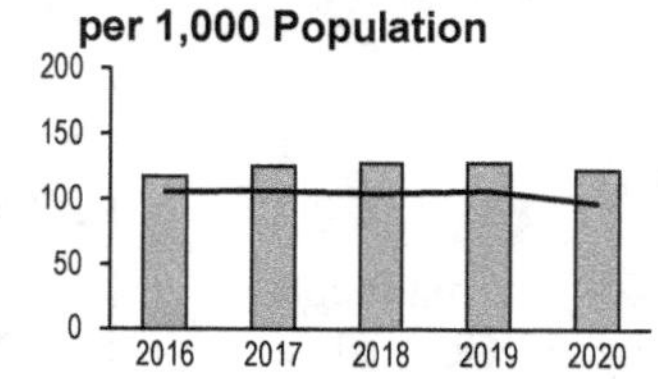

	2016	2017	2018	2019	2020
Concord	117	125	128	128	122
Average	105	106	105	107	97

Fire Inspections Completed per 1,000 Population

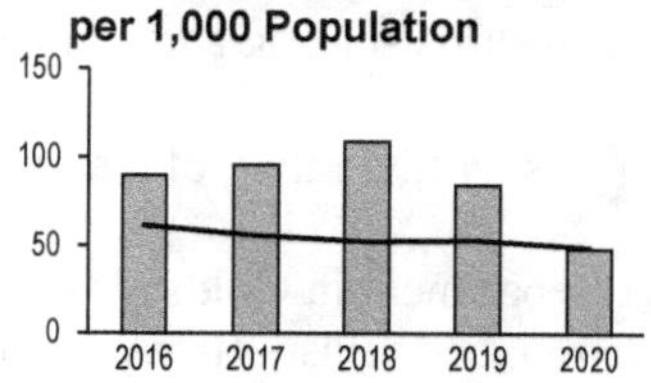

	2016	2017	2018	2019	2020
Concord	90	96	109	84	48
Average	62	55	52	53	49

Efficiency Measures

Fire Services Cost per Fire Department Response

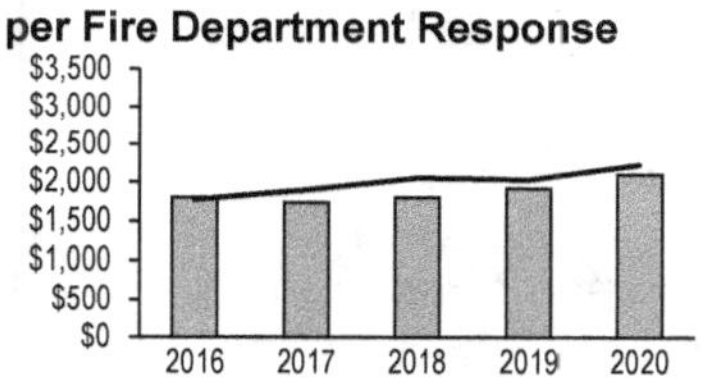

	2016	2017	2018	2019	2020
Concord	$1,797	$1,733	$1,799	$1,916	$2,095
Average	$1,765	$1,892	$2,051	$2,021	$2,219

Inspections Completed per Inspector FTE

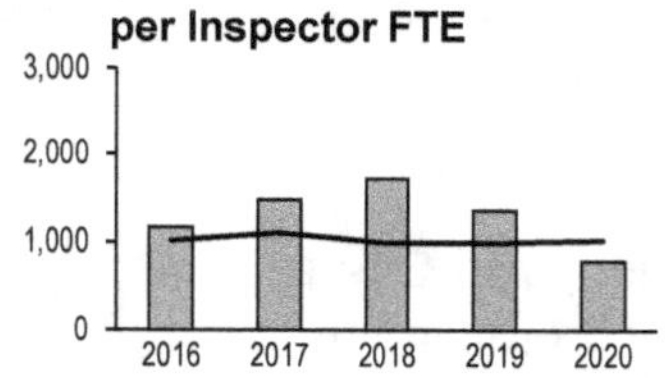

	2016	2017	2018	2019	2020
Concord	1,163	1,472	1,712	1,353	795
Average	1,014	1,095	985	989	1,017

Effectiveness Measures

Average Response Time to Priority One Calls in Minutes

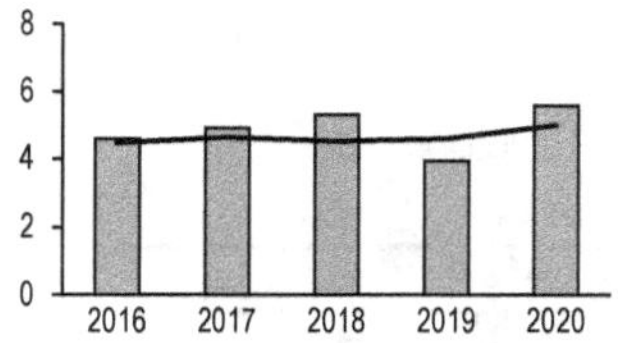

	2016	2017	2018	2019	2020
Concord	4.6	4.9	5.3	3.9	5.6
Average	4.4	4.6	4.5	4.6	5.0

Percentage of Fire Code Violations Cleared within 90 Days

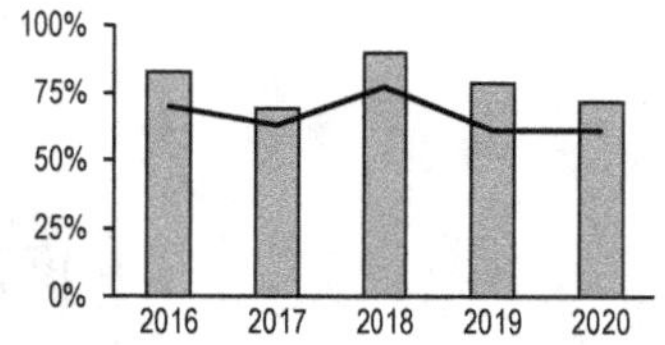

	2016	2017	2018	2019	2020
Concord	83%	69%	90%	79%	72%
Average	70%	63%	77%	61%	61%

Percentage of Fires Confined to Rooms or Objects Involved on Arrival

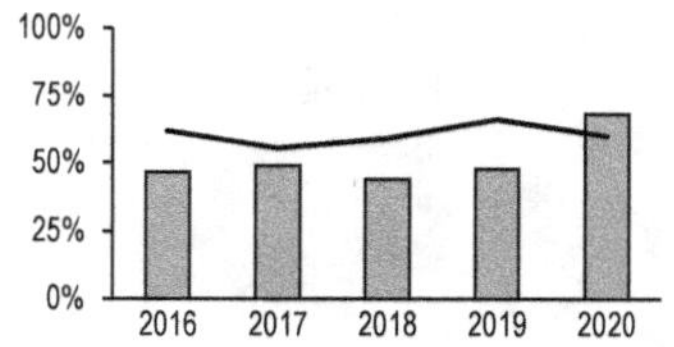

	2016	2017	2018	2019	2020
Concord	47%	49%	44%	48%	68%
Average	62%	55%	59%	66%	60%

Percentage of Fires for Which Cause Was Determined

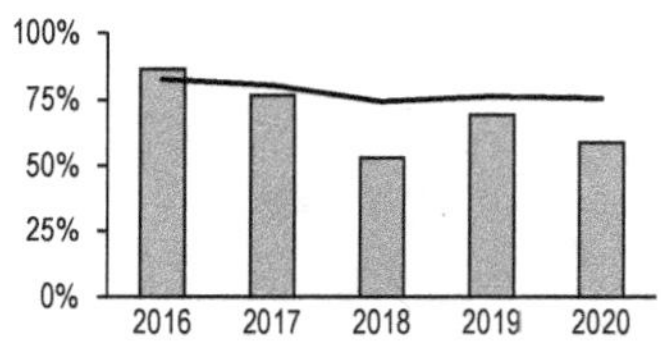

	2016	2017	2018	2019	2020
Concord	86%	77%	53%	69%	59%
Average	82%	80%	74%	76%	75%

Percentage of Full Response within 8 Minutes Travel Time

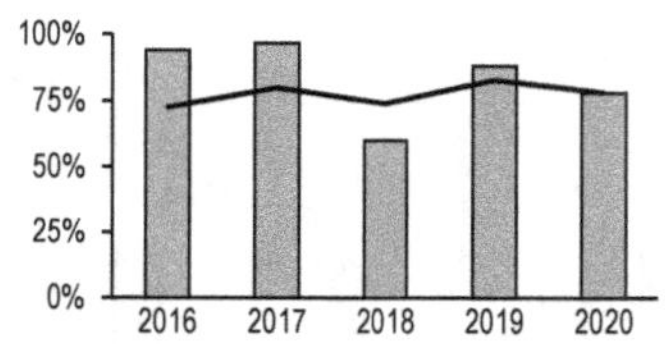

	2016	2017	2018	2019	2020
Concord	94%	97%	60%	88%	78%
Average	72%	80%	74%	83%	78%

Percentage of Lost Pulse Cases Recovered Pulse at Transfer of Care

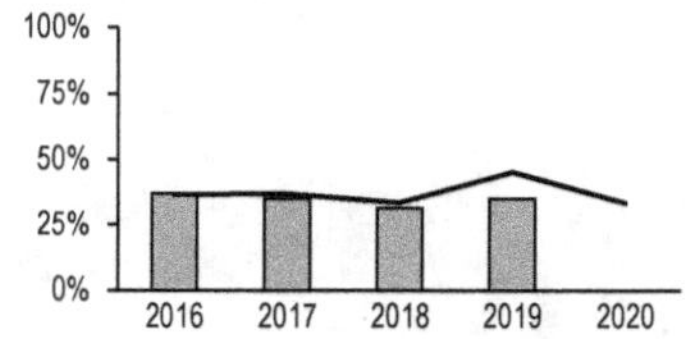

	2016	2017	2018	2019	2020
Concord	37.0%	35.2%	31.5%	35.0%	0.0%
Average	36.6%	36.9%	33.5%	45.1%	33.3%

Goldsboro — Fire Services

Fiscal Year 2019-20

Explanatory Information

Service Level and Delivery

The mission of the Goldsboro Fire Department is to protect lives, the environment, and property by providing prompt, skillful, and cost-effective fire protection, EMS, and life safety service. The Department maintains a receptive and ethical work environment that is conducive to the development of innovative and creative solutions by employees to meet the ever-changing needs of the community.

The fire department utilizes a shift schedule that includes alternates twenty-four hours on and twenty-four hours off for five days followed by four days off. This works out to fifty-six hour work weeks with shifts starting and ending at 8 a.m.

The city has an ISO rating of 2 as rated in 2020.

The fire department in Goldsboro conducted 1,400 fire maintenance, construction, and reinspections during the fiscal year. General inspections are performed according to the mandated inspection schedule, which is based on occupancy type established in the International Fire Code. Maintenance fire inspections are assigned by the fire marshal to the fire inspectors, fire company inspectors, and the fire marshal's office as well. The fire inspector or fire marshal perform all site plan reviews, fumigation, tent inspections, and construction inspections for fire suppression and sprinklers, tanks, and fire alarm systems.

Conditions Affecting Service, Performance, and Costs

The City of Goldsboro joined the Benchmarking Project in July 2017, with the first year of data showing for FY 2016–17.

Municipal Profile

Service Population	34,793
Land Area (Square Miles)	29.35
Persons per Square Mile	1,186
Median Household Income U.S. Census 2016	$32,148

Service Profile

FTE Positions—Firefighters	75.0
FTE Positions—Other	9.0
Fire Stations	5
First-Line Fire Apparatus	
Pumpers	4
Aerial Trucks	1
Quints	1
Squads	0
Rescue	0
Other	0
Fire Department Responses	2,296
Responses for Fires	156
Structural Fires Reported	47
Inspections Completed for Maintenance, Construction, and Reinspections	1,400
Fire Code Violations Reported	2,013
Estimated Fire Loss (millions)	$0.90
Amount of Property Protected in Service Area (millions)	$2,551
Number of Fire Education Programs or Events	154

Full Cost Profile

Cost Breakdown by Percentage	
Personal Services	89.2%
Operating Costs	8.6%
Capital Costs	2.2%
TOTAL	100.0%
Cost Breakdown in Dollars	
Personal Services	$5,659,202
Operating Costs	$547,526
Capital Costs	$139,659
TOTAL	$6,346,387

Goldsboro

Fire Services

Key: Goldsboro ■ Benchmarking Average — Fiscal Years 2016 through 2020

Resource Measures

Fire Services Costs per Capita

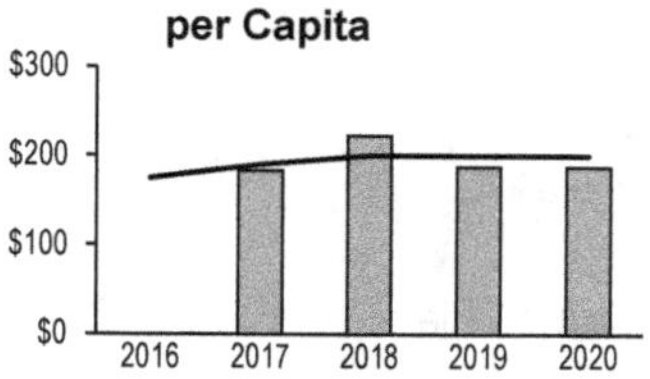

	2016	2017	2018	2019	2020
Goldsboro		$182	$222	$187	$187
Average	$174	$190	$199	$200	$200

Fire Services Total FTEs per 10,000 Population

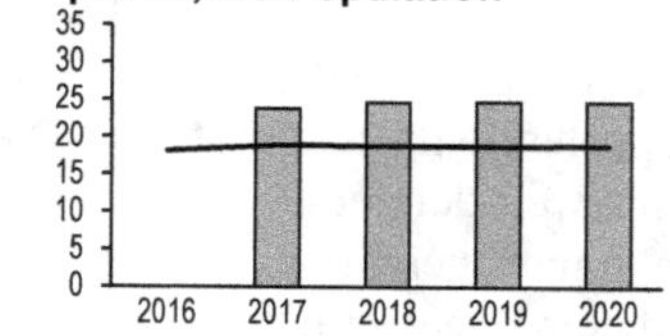

	2016	2017	2018	2019	2020
Goldsboro		23.7	24.6	24.7	24.7
Average	18.1	18.8	18.8	18.7	18.8

Fire Services Cost per Thousand Dollars of Property Protected

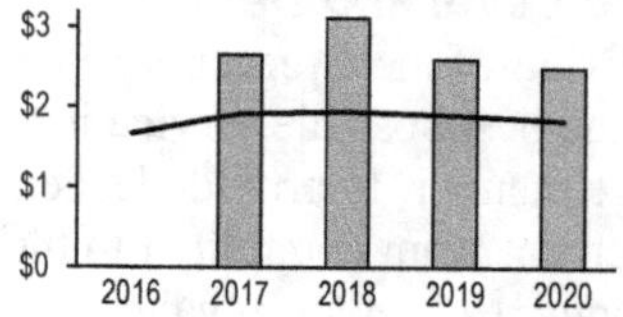

	2016	2017	2018	2019	2020
Goldsboro		$2.65	$3.11	$2.60	$2.49
Average	$1.66	$1.91	$1.94	$1.90	$1.83

Workload Measures

Actual Fires per 1,000 Population

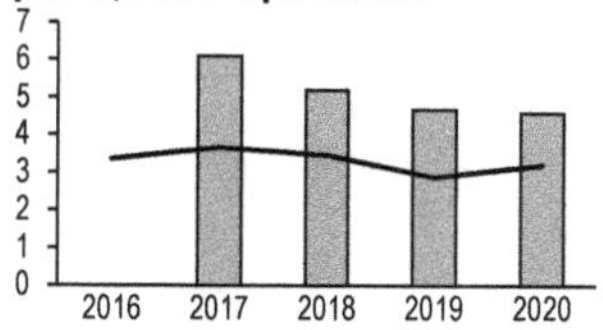

	2016	2017	2018	2019	2020
Goldsboro		6.09	5.20	4.67	4.59
Average	3.34	3.65	3.44	2.87	3.19

Fire Department Responses per 1,000 Population

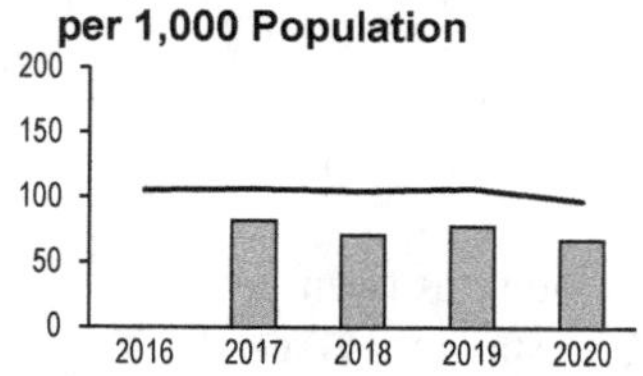

	2016	2017	2018	2019	2020
Goldsboro		82	71	78	68
Average	105	106	105	107	97

Fire Inspections Completed per 1,000 Population

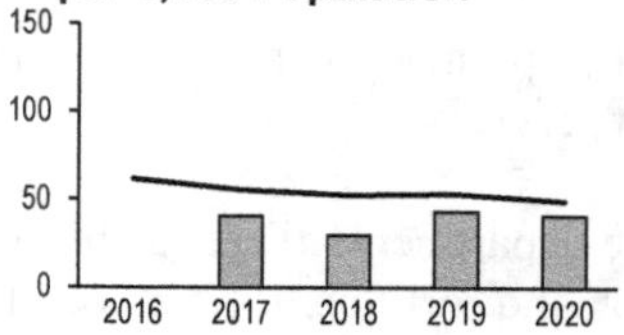

	2016	2017	2018	2019	2020
Goldsboro		41	30	43	41
Average	62	55	52	53	49

Efficiency Measures

Fire Services Cost per Fire Department Response

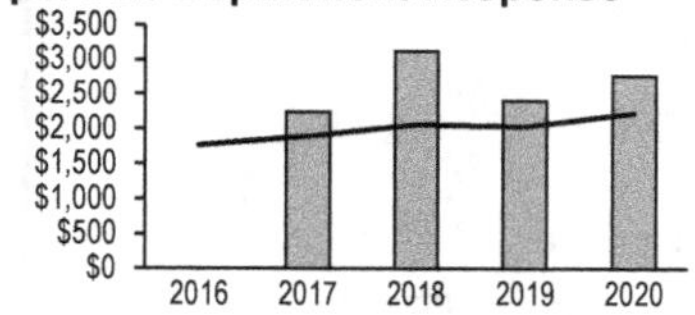

	2016	2017	2018	2019	2020
Goldsboro		$2,236	$3,125	$2,397	$2,764
Average	$1,765	$1,892	$2,051	$2,021	$2,219

Inspections Completed per Inspector FTE

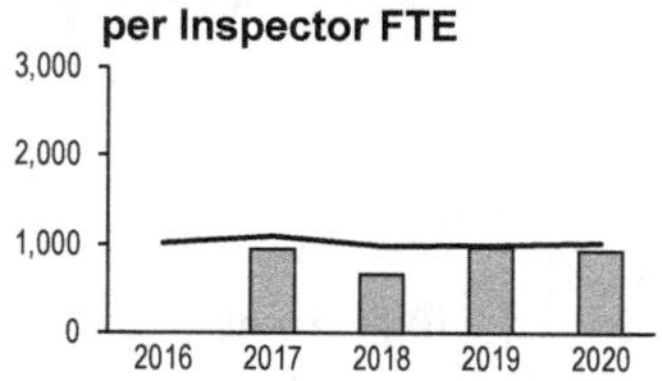

	2016	2017	2018	2019	2020
Goldsboro		947	669	966	933
Average	1,014	1,095	985	989	1,017

Effectiveness Measures

Average Response Time to Priority One Calls in Minutes

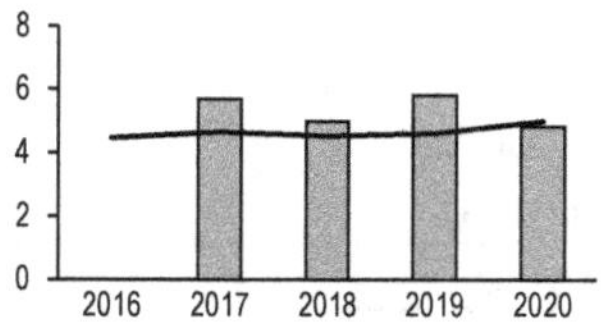

	2016	2017	2018	2019	2020
Goldsboro		5.7	5.0	5.8	4.8
Average	4.4	4.6	4.5	4.6	5.0

Percentage of Fire Code Violations Cleared within 90 Days

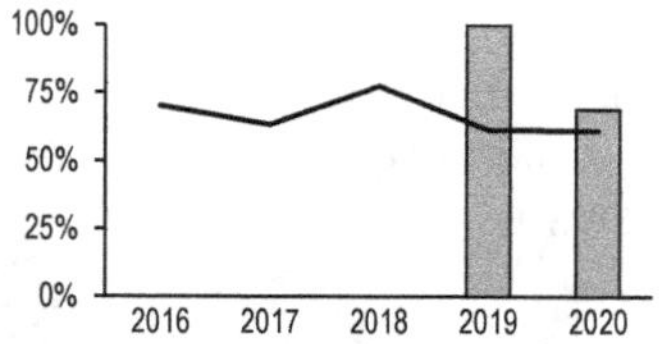

	2016	2017	2018	2019	2020
Goldsboro				100%	69%
Average	70%	63%	77%	61%	61%

Percentage of Fires Confined to Rooms or Objects Involved on Arrival

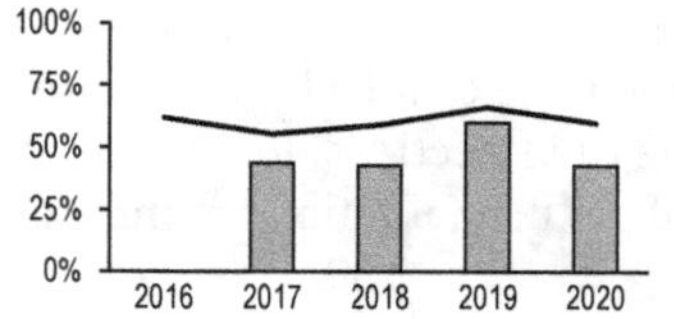

	2016	2017	2018	2019	2020
Goldsboro		44%	43%	60%	43%
Average	62%	55%	59%	66%	60%

Percentage of Fires for Which Cause Was Determined

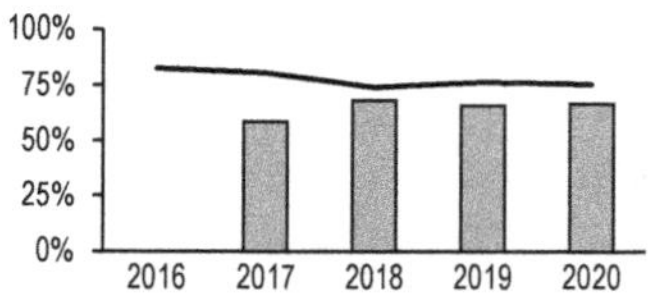

	2016	2017	2018	2019	2020
Goldsboro		58%	68%	66%	67%
Average	82%	80%	74%	76%	75%

Percentage of Full Response within 8 Minutes Travel Time

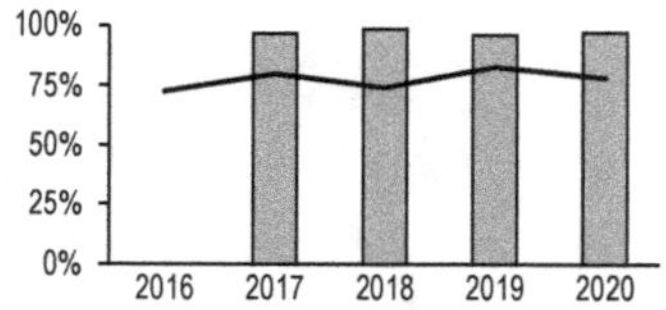

	2016	2017	2018	2019	2020
Goldsboro		97%	98%	96%	97%
Average	72%	80%	74%	83%	78%

Percentage of Lost Pulse Cases Recovered Pulse at Transfer of Care

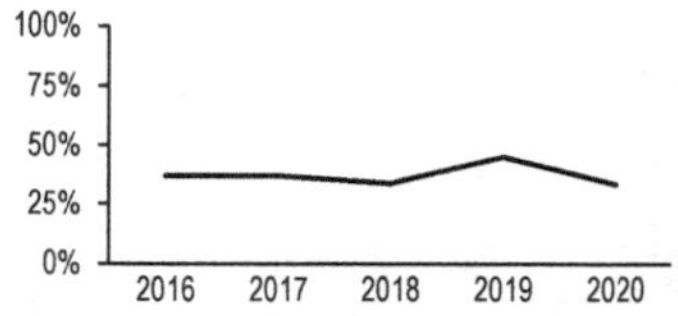

	2016	2017	2018	2019	2020
Goldsboro					
Average	36.6%	36.9%	33.5%	45.1%	33.3%

Greensboro

Fire Services

Fiscal Year 2019-20

Explanatory Information

Service Level and Delivery

The mission of the Greensboro Fire Department is to provide the public the best possible service in a courteous, professional, and cost-effective manner; to provide leadership through a well-defined management team committed to the departmental management philosophy; to provide equal opportunity for all employees in job performance and career development; to enhance public awareness through education, activities, and services; to maintain an open, informative flow of information so that all municipal departments may reach their goals and objectives; and to subscribe to honesty, integrity, and fairness.

The fire department contains two branches: emergency services and support services.

The fire department utilizes a shift schedule that includes twenty-four hours on and forty-eight hours off. For Fair Labor Standards Act (FLSA) purposes, the department utilizes a twenty-seven-day cycle.

The city has an ISO rating of 1, the highest rating possible, as rated in 2019. The Greensboro Fire Department has been accredited since 1997.

The fire department in Greensboro conducted 7,650 fire maintenance, construction, and reinspections during the fiscal year. General inspections are performed according to the mandated inspection schedule, which is based on occupancy type established in the International Fire Code. Complaints are addressed within twenty-four hours and are handled twenty-four hours a day as shift personnel are available. Inspectors generally work in districts and work in specialized areas, including educational, institutional, high rise, privilege licenses, and certificates of compliance. Apartment complexes are assigned one file number for the entire complex.

Conditions Affecting Service, Performance, and Costs

For clearance of fire code violations, Greensboro requires the violation to be cleared by witness of an inspector in person. With a backlog of inspections, this has meant some violations have not been cleared per the definition but may have been addressed.

Municipal Profile

Service Population	302,728
Land Area (Square Miles)	140.52
Persons per Square Mile	2,154
Median Household Income U.S. Census 2016	$40,760

Service Profile

FTE Positions—Firefighters	527.0
FTE Positions—Other	57.0
Fire Stations	26
First-Line Fire Apparatus	
Pumpers	24
Aerial Trucks	0
Quints	11
Squads	0
Rescue	1
Other	0
Fire Department Responses	38,952
Responses for Fires	1,101
Structural Fires Reported	250
Inspections Completed for Maintenance, Construction, and Reinspections	7,650
Fire Code Violations Reported	9,840
Estimated Fire Loss (millions)	$6.80
Amount of Property Protected in Service Area (millions)	$29,154
Number of Fire Education Programs or Events	1,120

Full Cost Profile

Cost Breakdown by Percentage	
Personal Services	80.2%
Operating Costs	19.8%
Capital Costs	0.0%
TOTAL	100.0%
Cost Breakdown in Dollars	
Personal Services	$47,934,959
Operating Costs	$11,870,813
Capital Costs	$0
TOTAL	$59,805,772

Key: Greensboro ■ Benchmarking Average — Fiscal Years 2016 through 2020

Resource Measures

Fire Services Costs per Capita

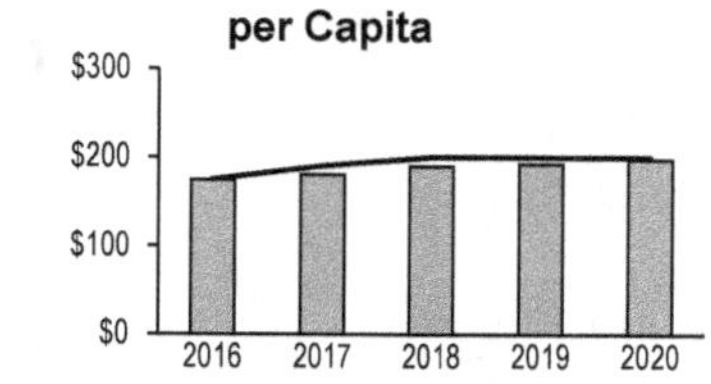

	2016	2017	2018	2019	2020
Greensboro	$175	$180	$189	$193	$198
Average	$174	$190	$199	$200	$200

Fire Services Total FTEs per 10,000 Population

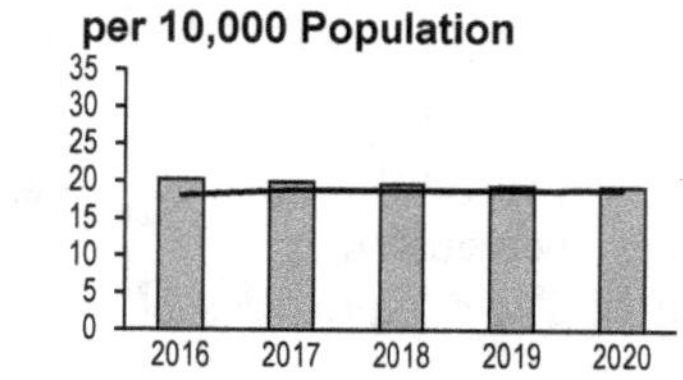

	2016	2017	2018	2019	2020
Greensboro	20.2	19.9	19.6	19.4	19.3
Average	18.1	18.8	18.8	18.7	18.8

Fire Services Cost per Thousand Dollars of Property Protected

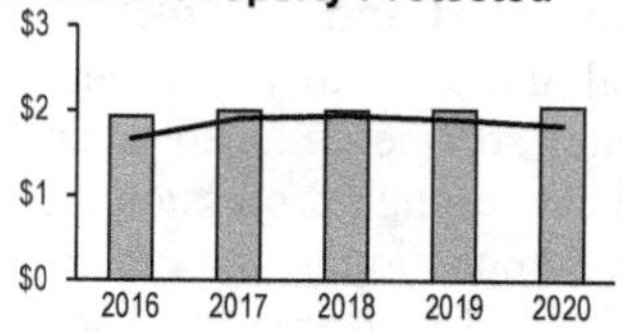

	2016	2017	2018	2019	2020
Greensboro	$1.93	$2.00	$2.00	$2.02	$2.05
Average	$1.66	$1.91	$1.94	$1.90	$1.83

Workload Measures

Actual Fires per 1,000 Population

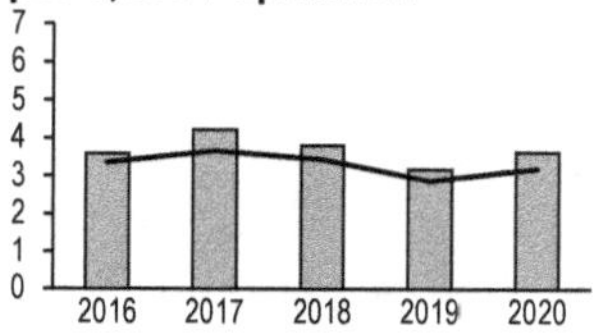

	2016	2017	2018	2019	2020
Greensboro	3.58	4.22	3.81	3.17	3.64
Average	3.34	3.65	3.44	2.87	3.19

Fire Department Responses per 1,000 Population

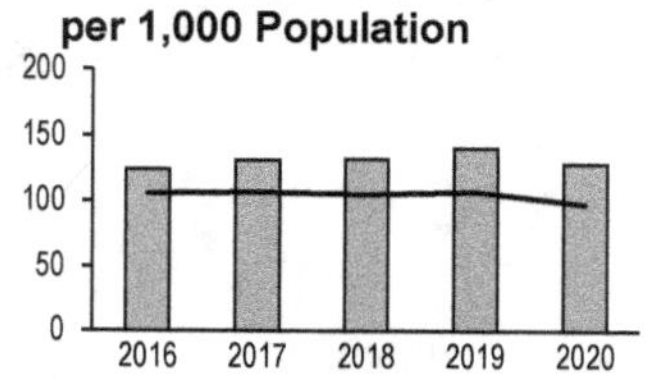

	2016	2017	2018	2019	2020
Greensboro	124	131	132	140	129
Average	105	106	105	107	97

Fire Inspections Completed per 1,000 Population

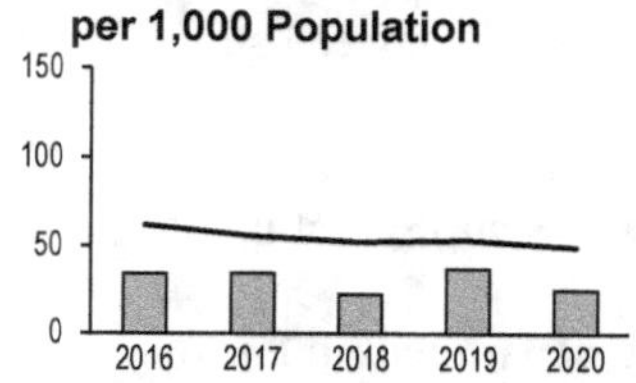

	2016	2017	2018	2019	2020
Greensboro	34	35	22	37	25
Average	62	55	52	53	49

Efficiency Measures

Fire Services Cost per Fire Department Response

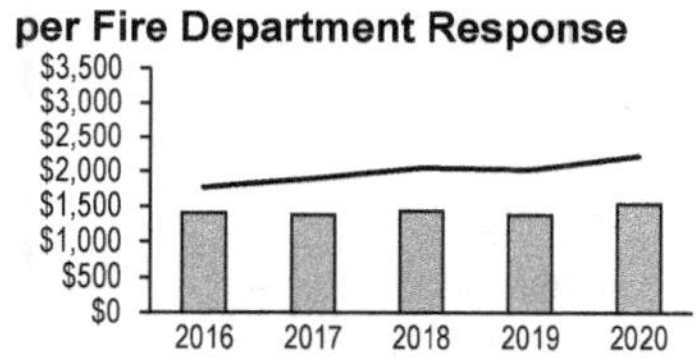

	2016	2017	2018	2019	2020
Greensboro	$1,406	$1,376	$1,438	$1,375	$1,535
Average	$1,765	$1,892	$2,051	$2,021	$2,219

Inspections Completed per Inspector FTE

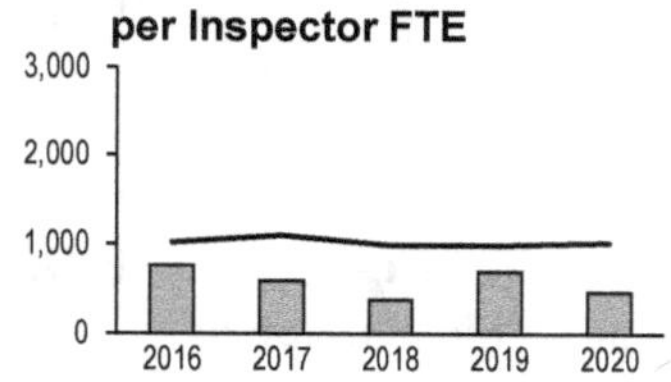

	2016	2017	2018	2019	2020
Greensboro	768	599	393	701	478
Average	1,014	1,095	985	989	1,017

Effectiveness Measures

Average Response Time to Priority One Calls in Minutes

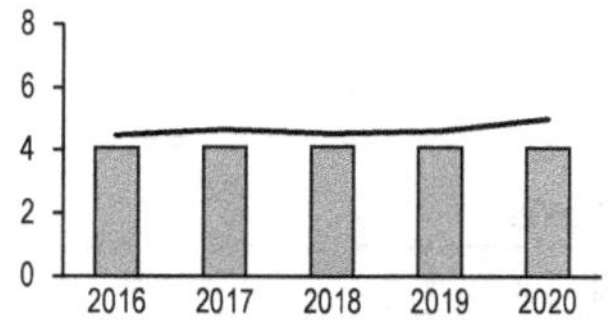

	2016	2017	2018	2019	2020
Greensboro	4.1	4.1	4.1	4.1	4.1
Average	4.4	4.6	4.5	4.6	5.0

Percentage of Fire Code Violations Cleared within 90 Days

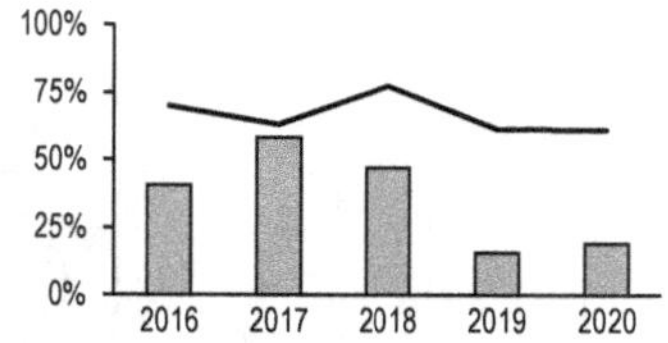

	2016	2017	2018	2019	2020
Greensboro	40%	58%	47%	16%	19%
Average	70%	63%	77%	61%	61%

Percentage of Fires Confined to Rooms or Objects Involved on Arrival

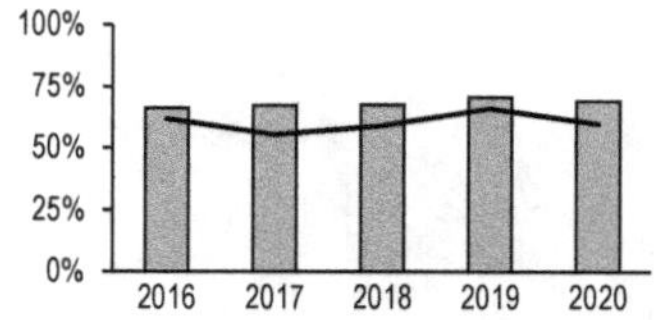

	2016	2017	2018	2019	2020
Greensboro	66%	67%	68%	71%	69%
Average	62%	55%	59%	66%	60%

Percentage of Fires for Which Cause Was Determined

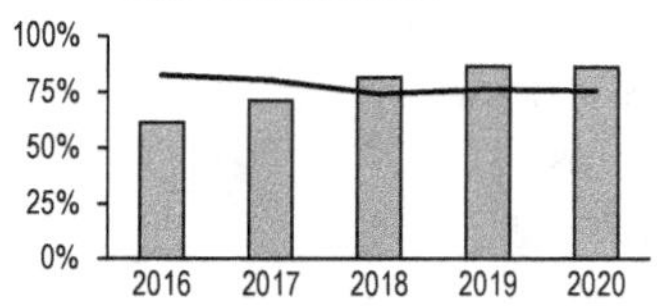

	2016	2017	2018	2019	2020
Greensboro	61%	71%	82%	86%	86%
Average	82%	80%	74%	76%	75%

Percentage of Full Response within 8 Minutes Travel Time

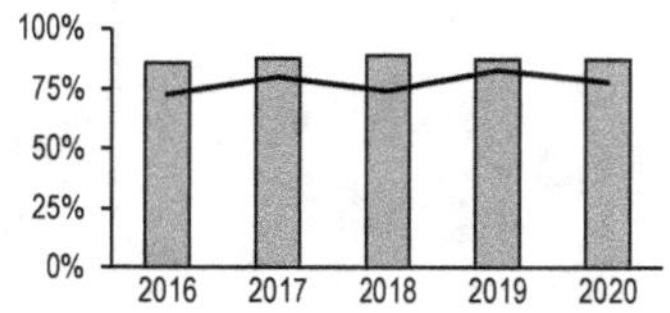

	2016	2017	2018	2019	2020
Greensboro	86%	88%	89%	88%	88%
Average	72%	80%	74%	83%	78%

Percentage of Lost Pulse Cases Recovered Pulse at Transfer of Care

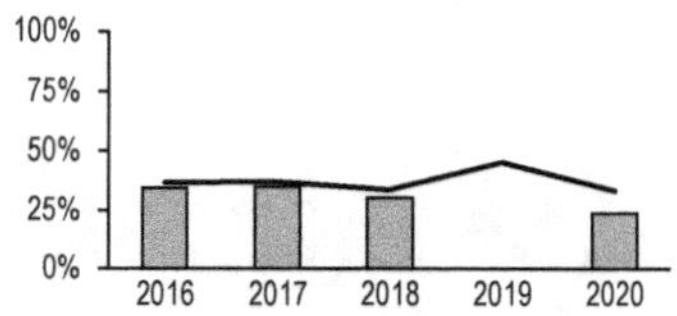

	2016	2017	2018	2019	2020
Greensboro	34.5%	34.8%	30.4%		23.7%
Average	36.6%	36.9%	33.5%	45.1%	33.3%

Fiscal Year 2019-20

Explanatory Information

Service Level and Delivery

The goal of the Hickory Fire Department is to provide high quality emergency services, education, and prevention that protect the community through professional coworkers focused on customer service, compassion, commitment, and innovation. The city provides fire coverage for an area of 13 square miles beyond city boundaries.

The fire department contains the following divisions: administration, fire and life safety, training, maintenance, and fire suppression.

Fire suppression personnel work a twenty-four-hour shift with forty-eight hours off between shifts. The twenty-four-hour shift begins at 8 a.m.

The city has an ISO rating of 3, as rated in 2005.

The fire department in Hickory conducted 5,124 fire maintenance, construction, and reinspections during the fiscal year. Fire prevention inspectors are assigned Level I, Level II, and Level III inspections. They also review construction and fire protection plans and inspect the installation of fire protection systems. The inspectors also accompany building inspectors during certificate of occupancy inspections and are responsible for conducting fire investigations, fire hydrant flow tests, occupancy and site visits, and other activities as assigned.

Conditions Affecting Service, Performance, and Costs

Hickory has a fire station staffed at the regional airport in addition to the six community fire stations.

Municipal Profile

Service Population	46,565
Land Area (Square Miles)	43.42
Persons per Square Mile	1,072
Median Household Income U.S. Census 2016	$35,353

Service Profile

FTE Positions—Firefighters	118.0
FTE Positions—Other	20.5
Fire Stations	7
First-Line Fire Apparatus	
Pumpers	6
Aerial Trucks	2
Quints	0
Squads	0
Rescue	0
Other	1
Fire Department Responses	5,677
Responses for Fires	217
Structural Fires Reported	42
Inspections Completed for Maintenance, Construction, and Reinspections	5,124
Fire Code Violations Reported	3,073
Estimated Fire Loss (millions)	$1.78
Amount of Property Protected in Service Area (millions)	$5,686
Number of Fire Education Programs or Events	412

Full Cost Profile

Cost Breakdown by Percentage	
Personal Services	76.0%
Operating Costs	17.4%
Capital Costs	6.6%
TOTAL	100.0%
Cost Breakdown in Dollars	
Personal Services	$9,203,623
Operating Costs	$2,101,987
Capital Costs	$804,919
TOTAL	$12,110,529

Key: Hickory ▒ Benchmarking Average — Fiscal Years 2016 through 2020

Resource Measures

Fire Services Costs per Capita

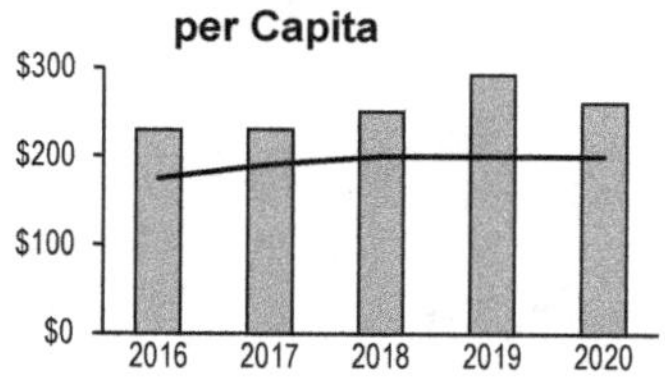

	2016	2017	2018	2019	2020
Hickory	$229	$230	$250	$292	$260
Average	$174	$190	$199	$200	$200

Fire Services Total FTEs per 10,000 Population

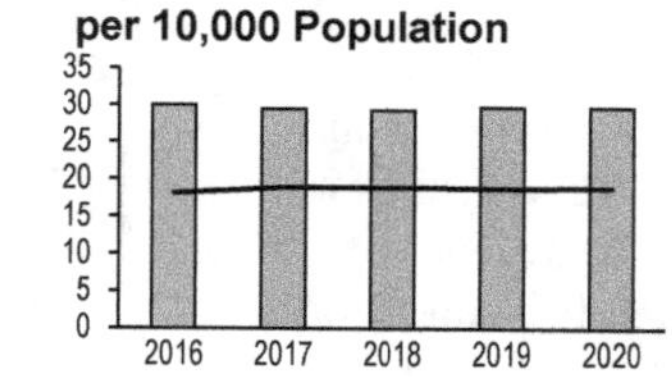

	2016	2017	2018	2019	2020
Hickory	30.0	29.4	29.3	29.7	29.7
Average	18.1	18.8	18.8	18.7	18.8

Fire Services Cost per Thousand Dollars of Property Protected

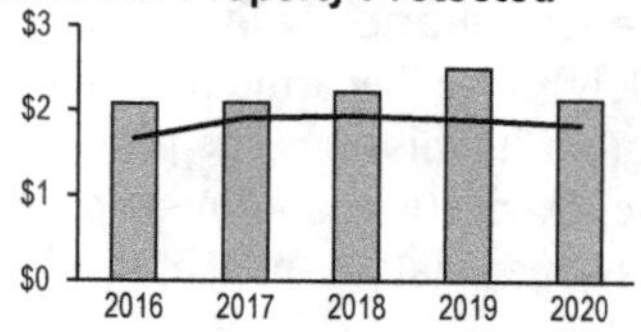

	2016	2017	2018	2019	2020
Hickory	$2.08	$2.09	$2.22	$2.50	$2.13
Average	$1.66	$1.91	$1.94	$1.90	$1.83

Workload Measures

Actual Fires per 1,000 Population

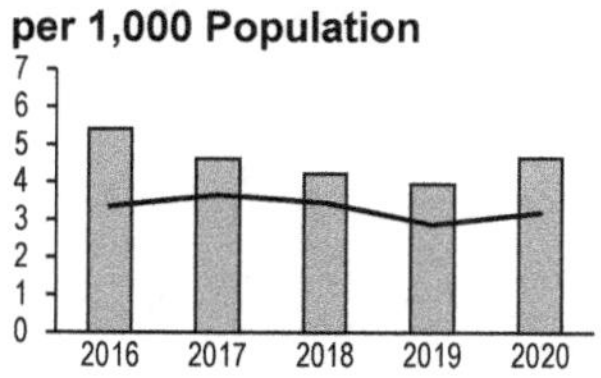

	2016	2017	2018	2019	2020
Hickory	5.40	4.61	4.22	3.95	4.66
Average	3.34	3.65	3.44	2.87	3.19

Fire Department Responses per 1,000 Population

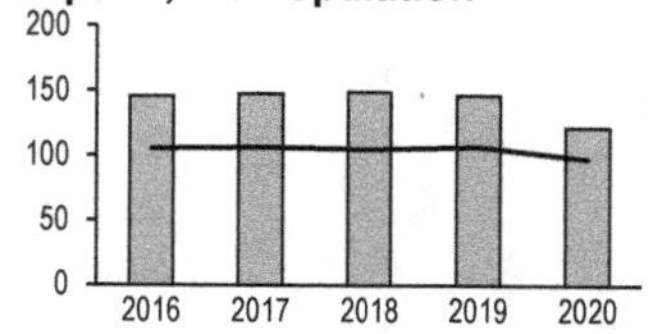

	2016	2017	2018	2019	2020
Hickory	146	148	149	146	122
Average	105	106	105	107	97

Fire Inspections Completed per 1,000 Population

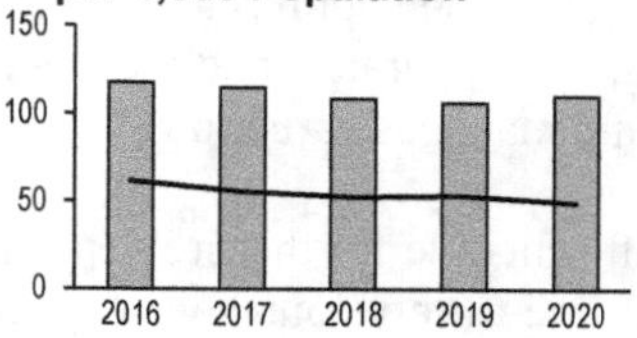

	2016	2017	2018	2019	2020
Hickory	118	114	109	106	110
Average	62	55	52	53	49

Efficiency Measures

Fire Services Cost per Fire Department Response

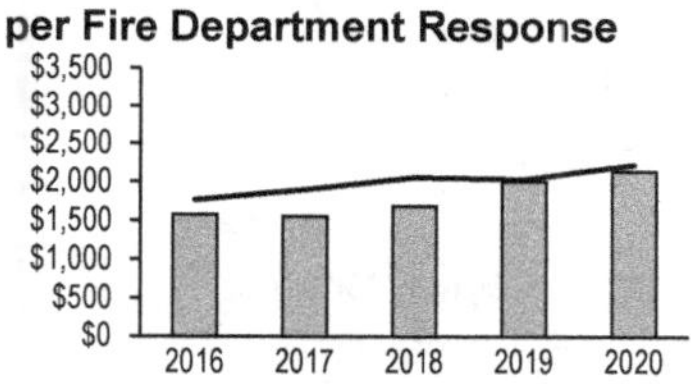

	2016	2017	2018	2019	2020
Hickory	$1,575	$1,555	$1,680	$1,996	$2,133
Average	$1,765	$1,892	$2,051	$2,021	$2,219

Inspections Completed per Inspector FTE

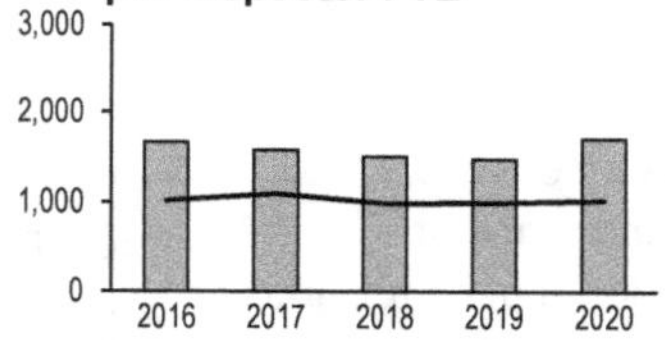

	2016	2017	2018	2019	2020
Hickory	1,667	1,579	1,504	1,481	1,708
Average	1,014	1,095	985	989	1,017

Effectiveness Measures

Average Response Time to Priority One Calls in Minutes

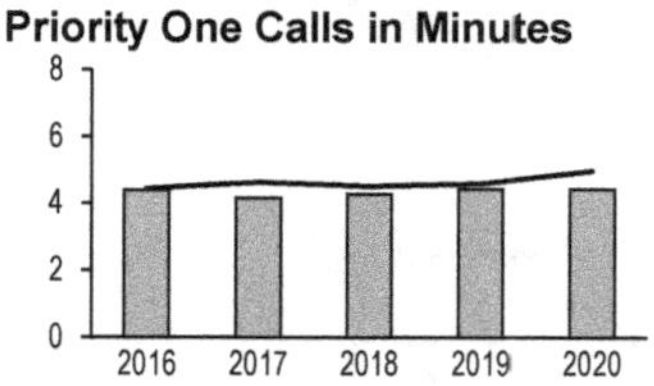

	2016	2017	2018	2019	2020
Hickory	4.4	4.2	4.3	4.4	4.4
Average	4.4	4.6	4.5	4.6	5.0

Percentage of Fire Code Violations Cleared within 90 Days

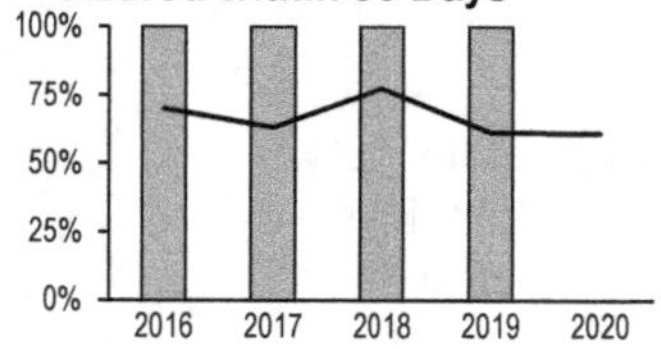

	2016	2017	2018	2019	2020
Hickory	100%	100%	100%	100%	
Average	70%	63%	77%	61%	61%

Percentage of Fires Confined to Rooms or Objects Involved on Arrival

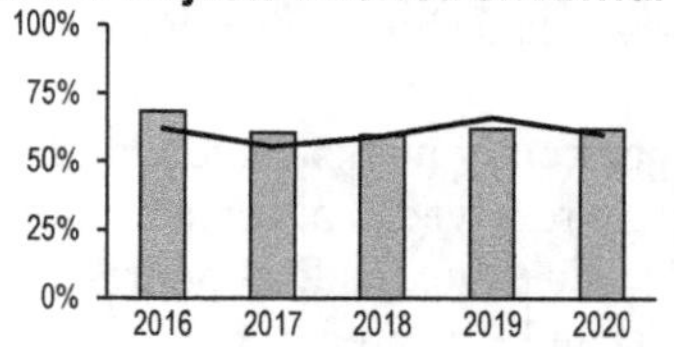

	2016	2017	2018	2019	2020
Hickory	68%	61%	60%	62%	62%
Average	62%	55%	59%	66%	60%

Percentage of Fires for Which Cause Was Determined

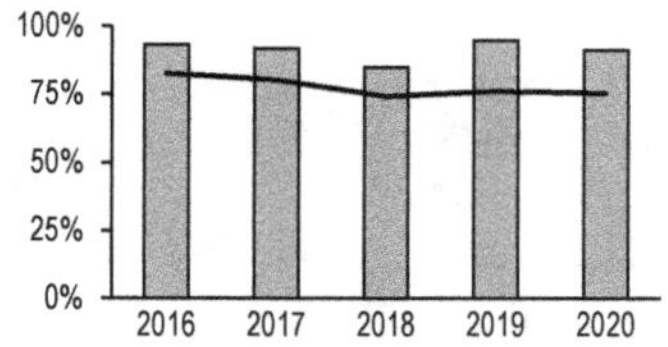

	2016	2017	2018	2019	2020
Hickory	93%	92%	85%	95%	91%
Average	82%	80%	74%	76%	75%

Percentage of Full Response within 8 Minutes Travel Time

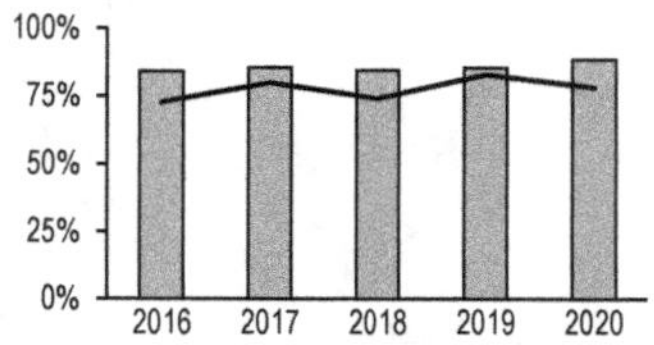

	2016	2017	2018	2019	2020
Hickory	84%	85%	84%	86%	89%
Average	72%	80%	74%	83%	78%

Percentage of Lost Pulse Cases Recovered Pulse at Transfer of Care

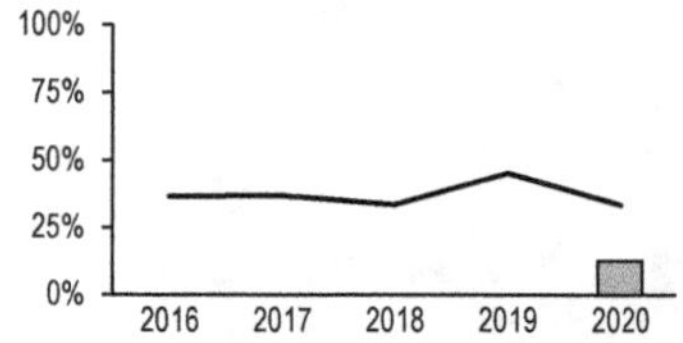

	2016	2017	2018	2019	2020
Hickory					12.8%
Average	36.6%	36.9%	33.5%	45.1%	33.3%

Raleigh

Fire Services

Fiscal Year 2019-20

Explanatory Information

Service Level and Delivery

The Raleigh Fire Department provides the following services in carrying out its mission: fire protection, emergency medical first response, extrication, confined space and high-angle rescue, hazardous materials response, fire inspections, and fire education.

The fire department is broken into five primary function areas. The Office of the Fire Chief provides administrative services and oversight; the Office of the Fire Marshal is the enforcement, educational, and informational arm; the Operations Division responds to and manages incidents and special events; the Support Services Division supplies and maintains infrastructure, equipment, clothing, and apparatus; and the Training Division recruits, hires, trains, and manages career development.

The shift schedule for the fire department is a nine-day cycle as follows: five twenty-four-hour days alternating on and off followed by four days off.

The city received an ISO rating of 1 in 2016. This is the highest rating possible.

The fire department in Raleigh conducted 23,245 fire maintenance, construction, and reinspections during the fiscal year. Fire inspections are scheduled by the Office of the Fire Marshal through an automated process based on a priority basis and consistent with section 106 of the NC State Fire Code. Other inspections are scheduled as requested for special events, operational permits, and special requests. Apartment complexes are counted as one inspection per building, and high rises are considered as one inspection with one file.

Conditions Affecting Service, Performance, and Costs

Raleigh rejoined the Benchmarking Project in July 2016, with the first year of data showing for FY 2015–16.

Raleigh currently marks some violations as repaired but not yet completely resolved. This creates more open violations in the system while decisions are made about referrals or penalties before the violation can be cleared.

Municipal Profile

Service Population	475,580
Land Area (Square Miles)	146.47
Persons per Square Mile	3,247
Median Household Income U.S. Census 2016	$46,612

Service Profile

FTE Positions—Firefighters	552.0
FTE Positions—Other	69.0
Fire Stations	28
First-Line Fire Apparatus	
Pumpers	27
Aerial Trucks	9
Quints	0
Squads	2
Rescue	1
Other	12
Fire Department Responses	43,779
Responses for Fires	1,048
Structural Fires Reported	263
Inspections Completed for Maintenance, Construction, and Reinspections	23,245
Fire Code Violations Reported	26,545
Estimated Fire Loss (millions)	$18.94
Amount of Property Protected in Service Area (millions)	$61,648
Number of Fire Education Programs or Events	197

Full Cost Profile

Cost Breakdown by Percentage	
Personal Services	74.4%
Operating Costs	16.9%
Capital Costs	8.7%
TOTAL	100.0%
Cost Breakdown in Dollars	
Personal Services	$56,630,547
Operating Costs	$12,819,925
Capital Costs	$6,631,835
TOTAL	$76,082,307

Key: Raleigh ▒ Benchmarking Average — Fiscal Years 2016 through 2020

Resource Measures

Fire Services Costs per Capita

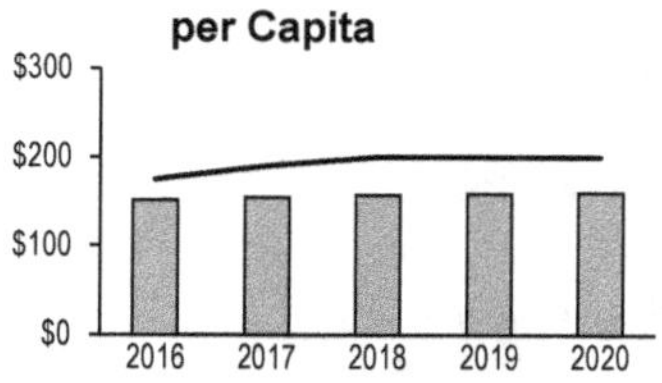

	2016	2017	2018	2019	2020
Raleigh	$151	$154	$157	$159	$160
Average	$174	$190	$199	$200	$200

Fire Services Total FTEs per 10,000 Population

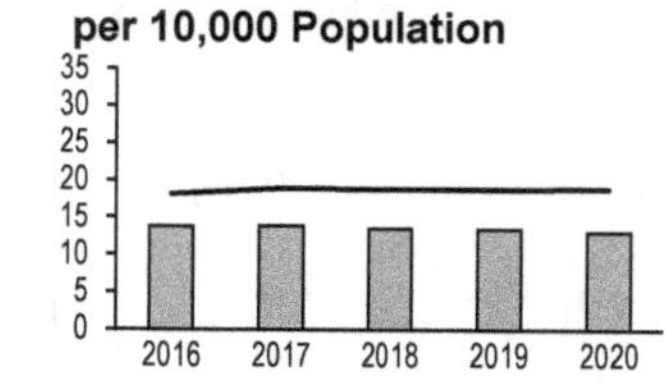

	2016	2017	2018	2019	2020
Raleigh	13.8	13.8	13.5	13.4	13.1
Average	18.1	18.8	18.8	18.7	18.8

Fire Services Cost per Thousand Dollars of Property Protected

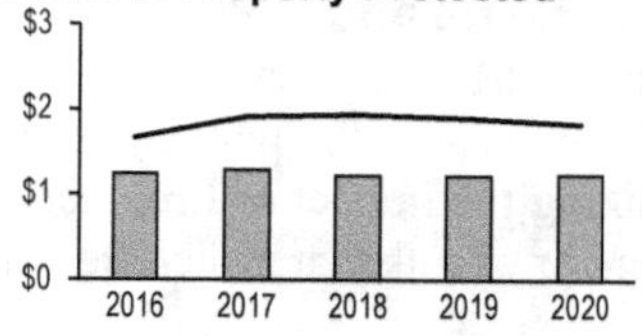

	2016	2017	2018	2019	2020
Raleigh	$1.24	$1.29	$1.22	$1.22	$1.23
Average	$1.66	$1.91	$1.94	$1.90	$1.83

Workload Measures

Actual Fires per 1,000 Population

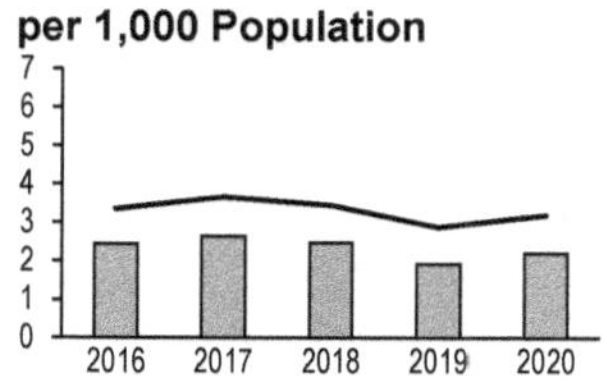

	2016	2017	2018	2019	2020
Raleigh	2.45	2.65	2.47	1.93	2.20
Average	3.34	3.65	3.44	2.87	3.19

Fire Department Responses per 1,000 Population

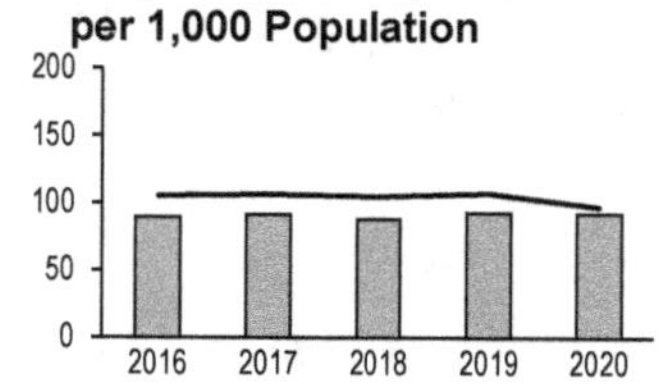

	2016	2017	2018	2019	2020
Raleigh	89	91	88	93	92
Average	105	106	105	107	97

Fire Inspections Completed per 1,000 Population

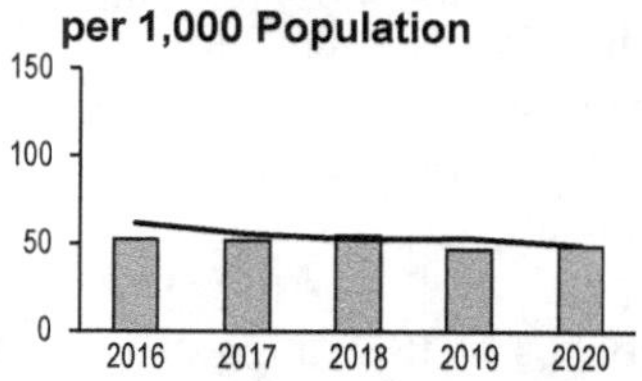

	2016	2017	2018	2019	2020
Raleigh	53	52	55	47	49
Average	62	55	52	53	49

Efficiency Measures

Fire Services Cost per Fire Department Response

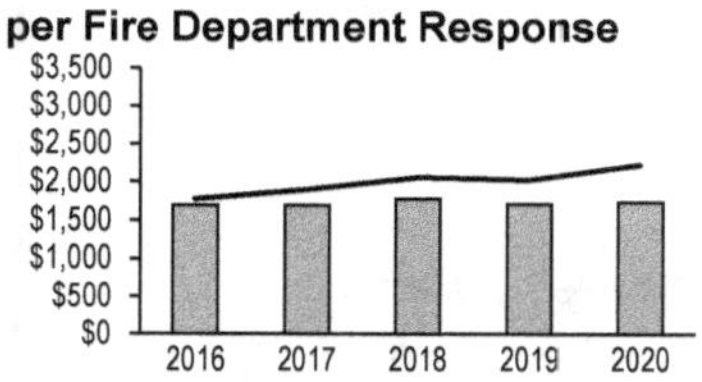

	2016	2017	2018	2019	2020
Raleigh	$1,690	$1,689	$1,779	$1,711	$1,738
Average	$1,765	$1,892	$2,051	$2,021	$2,219

Inspections Completed per Inspector FTE

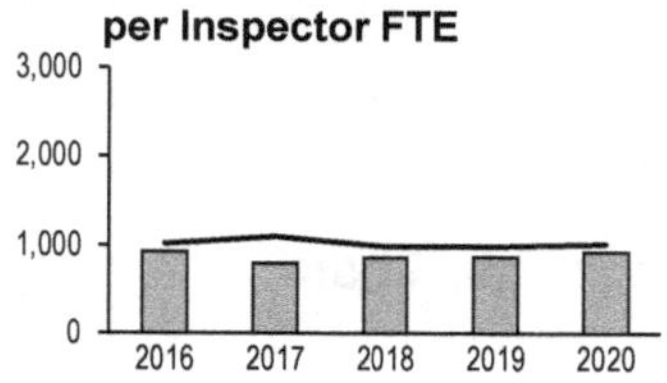

	2016	2017	2018	2019	2020
Raleigh	926	801	867	871	930
Average	1,014	1,095	985	989	1,017

Effectiveness Measures

Average Response Time to Priority One Calls in Minutes

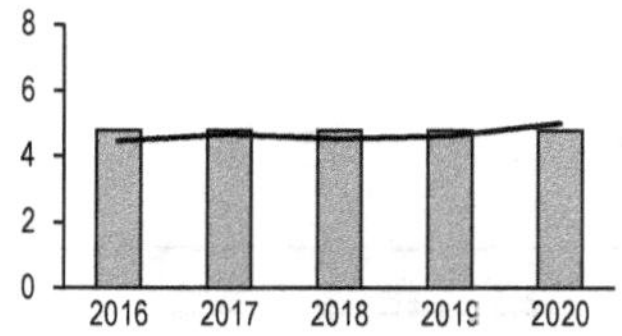

	2016	2017	2018	2019	2020
Raleigh	4.8	4.8	4.8	4.8	4.8
Average	4.4	4.6	4.5	4.6	5.0

Percentage of Fire Code Violations Cleared within 90 Days

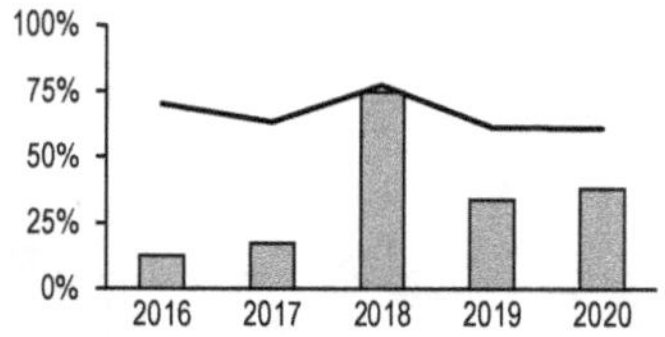

	2016	2017	2018	2019	2020
Raleigh	13%	17%	75%	34%	38%
Average	70%	63%	77%	61%	61%

Percentage of Fires Confined to Rooms or Objects Involved on Arrival

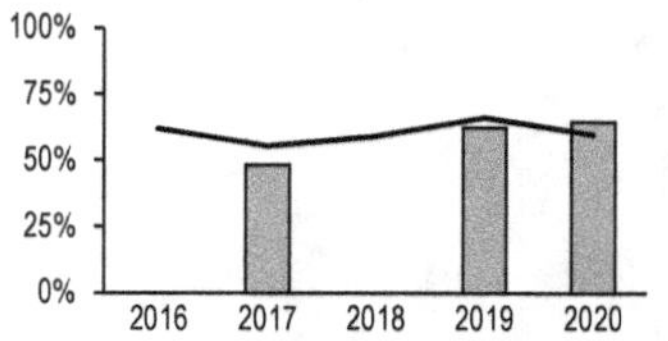

	2016	2017	2018	2019	2020
Raleigh		48%		62%	65%
Average	62%	55%	59%	66%	60%

Percentage of Fires for Which Cause Was Determined

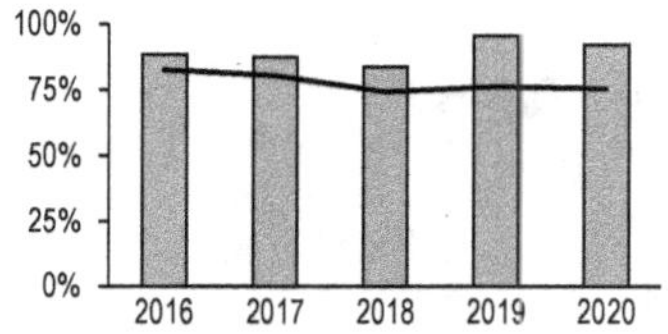

	2016	2017	2018	2019	2020
Raleigh	88%	87%	84%	96%	92%
Average	82%	80%	74%	76%	75%

Percentage of Full Response within 8 Minutes Travel Time

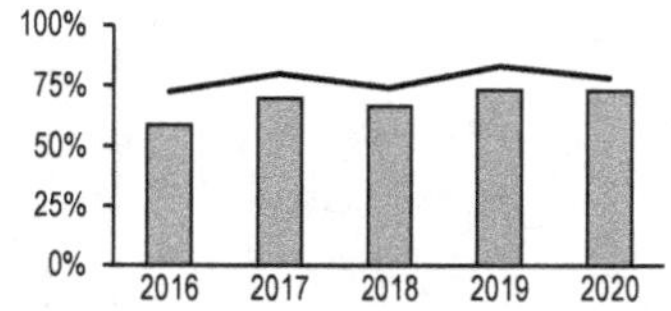

	2016	2017	2018	2019	2020
Raleigh	59%	70%	66%	73%	73%
Average	72%	80%	74%	83%	78%

Percentage of Lost Pulse Cases Recovered Pulse at Transfer of Care

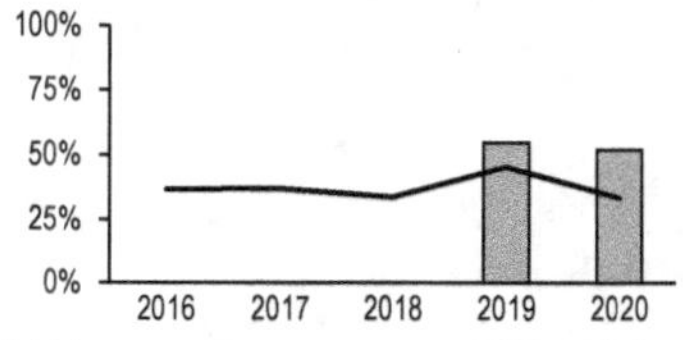

	2016	2017	2018	2019	2020
Raleigh				54.8%	51.9%
Average	36.6%	36.9%	33.5%	45.1%	33.3%

Fiscal Year 2019-20

Explanatory Information

Service Level and Delivery

Wilson Fire/Rescue Services is a public safety organization whose mission is to assist the public in the protection of life and property by minimizing the impact of fire, medical emergencies, and potential disasters or events that affect the community and the environment.

Wilson Fire/Rescue Services has two major divisions. Operations handles emergency responses and equipment maintenance. Support Services handles fire prevention and education, facility maintenance, IM/GIS, and budget.

Firefighters work twenty-four hours on and twenty-four hours off. Each work cycle consists of three twenty-four-hour shifts with a day off between shifts. A four-day break is then provided before the cycle repeats itself.

The city has an ISO rating of 1, as rated in 2018. This is the highest rating that can be achieved. The Wilson Fire Department has been accredited since 2002.

The fire department in Wilson conducted 3,545 fire maintenance, construction, and reinspections during the fiscal year. Fire inspections are conducted by the Fire Prevention Bureau on a daily basis. Each inspector is assigned a district in which he or she handles all inspections. A charge is made on the third reinspection.

Conditions Affecting Service, Performance, and Costs

Municipal Profile

Service Population	49,384
Land Area (Square Miles)	31.02
Persons per Square Mile	1,592
Median Household Income U.S. Census 2016	$35,409

Service Profile

FTE Positions—Firefighters	85.0
FTE Positions—Other	15.0
Fire Stations	5
First-Line Fire Apparatus	
Pumpers	4
Aerial Trucks	1
Quints	1
Squads	0
Rescue	0
Other	1
Fire Department Responses	4,272
Responses for Fires	248
Structural Fires Reported	59
Inspections Completed for Maintenance, Construction, and Reinspections	3,545
Fire Code Violations Reported	2,945
Estimated Fire Loss (millions)	$0.89
Amount of Property Protected in Service Area (millions)	$4,212
Number of Fire Education Programs or Events	51

Full Cost Profile

Cost Breakdown by Percentage	
Personal Services	73.3%
Operating Costs	17.8%
Capital Costs	8.9%
TOTAL	100.0%

Cost Breakdown in Dollars	
Personal Services	$8,377,282
Operating Costs	$2,032,630
Capital Costs	$1,023,134
TOTAL	$11,433,046

Key: Wilson ▒ Benchmarking Average — Fiscal Years 2016 through 2020

Resource Measures

Fire Services Costs per Capita

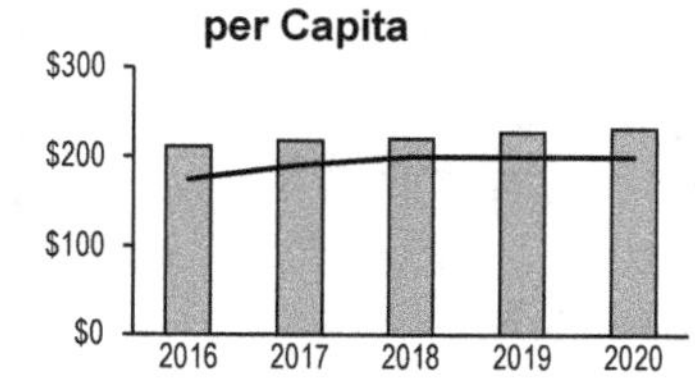

	2016	2017	2018	2019	2020
Wilson	$211	$217	$219	$227	$232
Average	$174	$190	$199	$200	$200

Fire Services Total FTEs per 10,000 Population

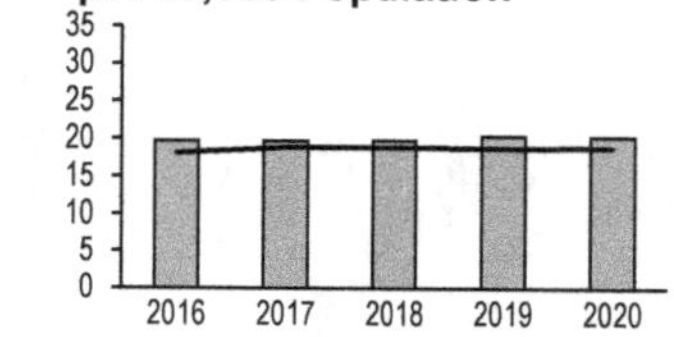

	2016	2017	2018	2019	2020
Wilson	19.7	19.6	19.7	20.4	20.2
Average	18.1	18.8	18.8	18.7	18.8

Fire Services Cost per Thousand Dollars of Property Protected

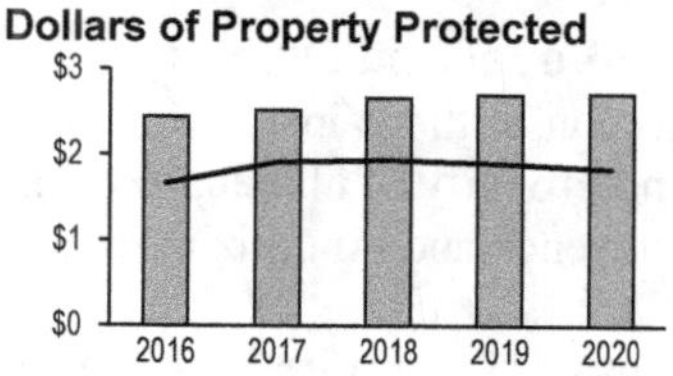

	2016	2017	2018	2019	2020
Wilson	$2.44	$2.51	$2.66	$2.70	$2.71
Average	$1.66	$1.91	$1.94	$1.90	$1.83

Workload Measures

Actual Fires per 1,000 Population

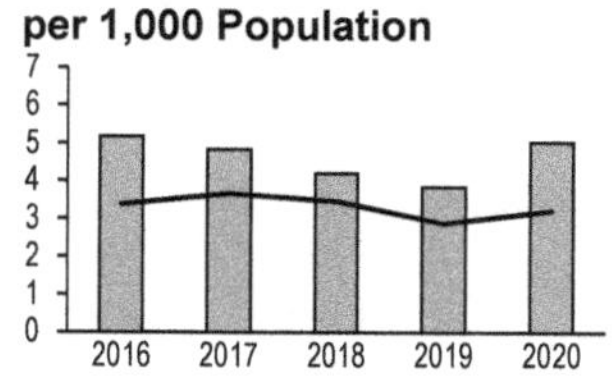

	2016	2017	2018	2019	2020
Wilson	5.17	4.82	4.19	3.83	5.02
Average	3.34	3.65	3.44	2.87	3.19

Fire Department Responses per 1,000 Population

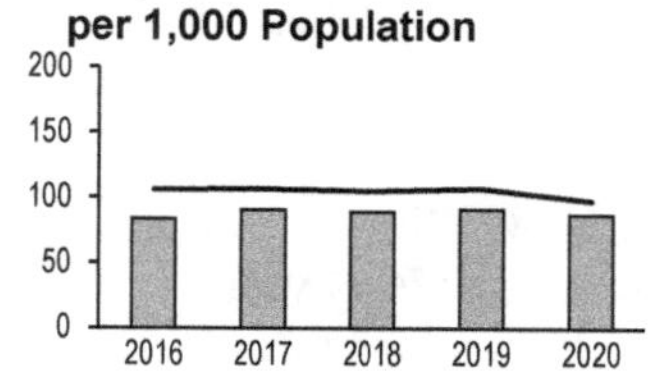

	2016	2017	2018	2019	2020
Wilson	83	90	89	90	87
Average	105	106	105	107	97

Fire Inspections Completed per 1,000 Population

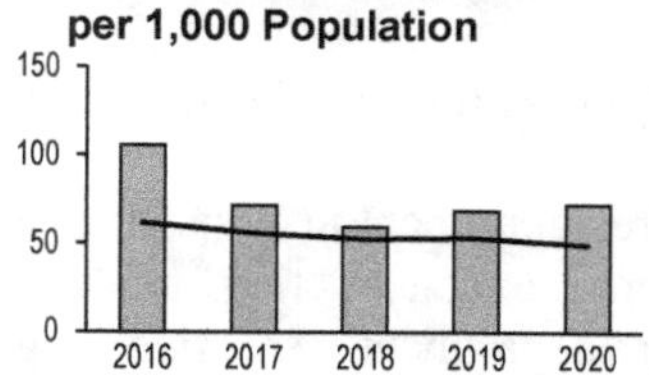

	2016	2017	2018	2019	2020
Wilson	105	71	59	68	72
Average	62	55	52	53	49

Efficiency Measures

Fire Services Cost per Fire Department Response

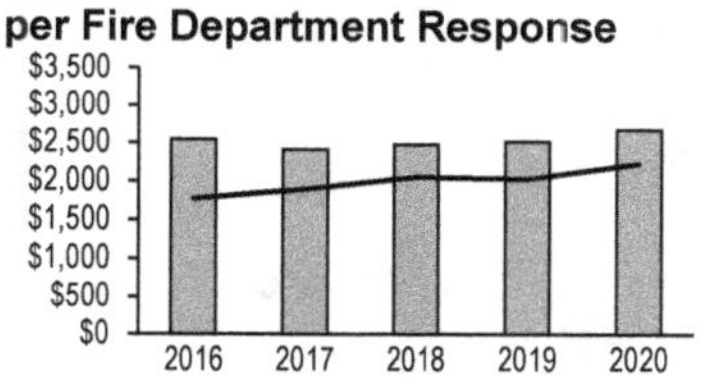

	2016	2017	2018	2019	2020
Wilson	$2,543	$2,410	$2,472	$2,511	$2,676
Average	$1,765	$1,892	$2,051	$2,021	$2,219

Inspections Completed per Inspector FTE

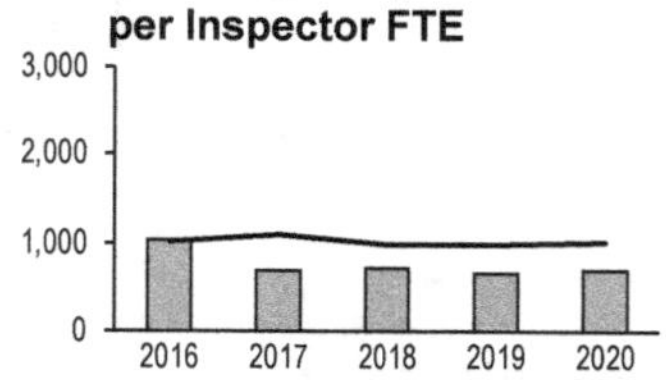

	2016	2017	2018	2019	2020
Wilson	1,041	704	728	670	709
Average	1,014	1,095	985	989	1,017

Effectiveness Measures

Average Response Time to Priority One Calls in Minutes

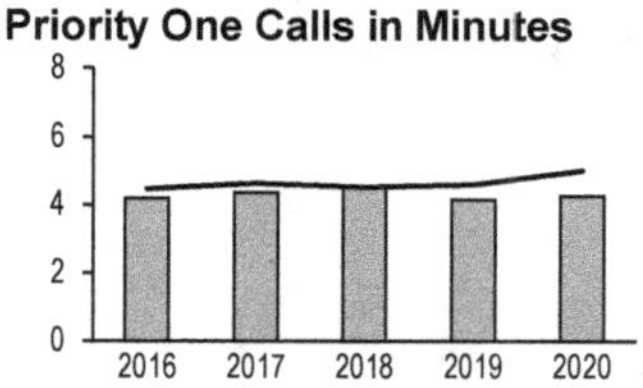

	2016	2017	2018	2019	2020
Wilson	4.2	4.4	4.5	4.1	4.3
Average	4.4	4.6	4.5	4.6	5.0

Percentage of Fire Code Violations Cleared within 90 Days

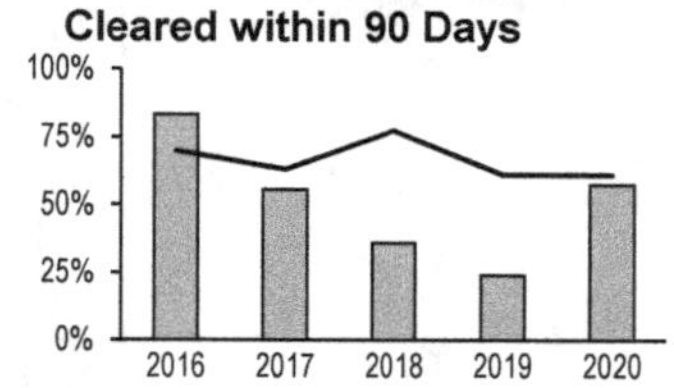

	2016	2017	2018	2019	2020
Wilson	83%	56%	36%	24%	58%
Average	70%	63%	77%	61%	61%

Percentage of Fires Confined to Rooms or Objects Involved on Arrival

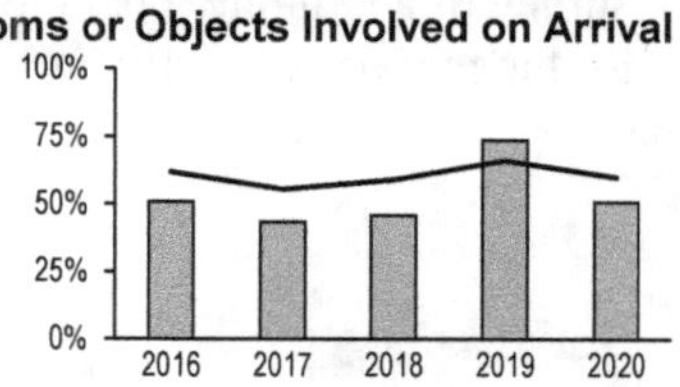

	2016	2017	2018	2019	2020
Wilson	51%	43%	46%	74%	51%
Average	62%	55%	59%	66%	60%

Percentage of Fires for Which Cause Was Determined

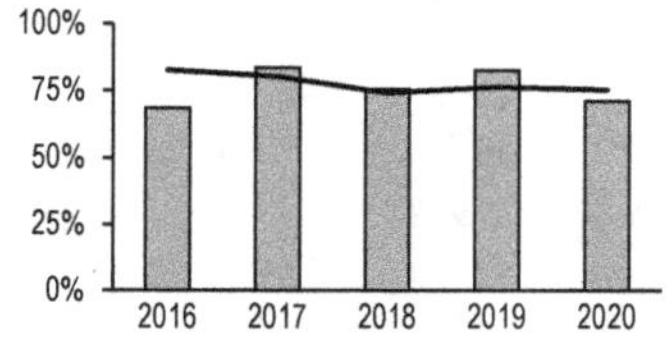

	2016	2017	2018	2019	2020
Wilson	68%	84%	76%	82%	71%
Average	82%	80%	74%	76%	75%

Percentage of Full Response within 8 Minutes Travel Time

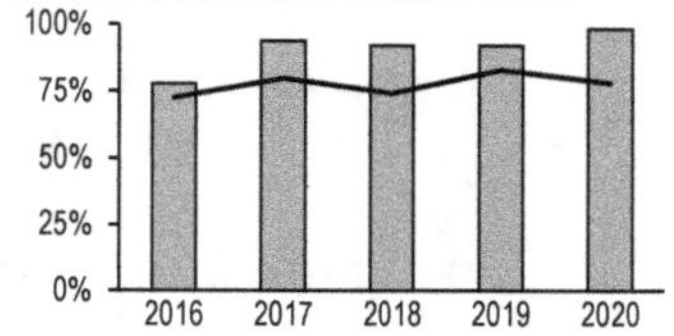

	2016	2017	2018	2019	2020
Wilson	78%	94%	92%	92%	98%
Average	72%	80%	74%	83%	78%

Percentage of Lost Pulse Cases Recovered Pulse at Transfer of Care

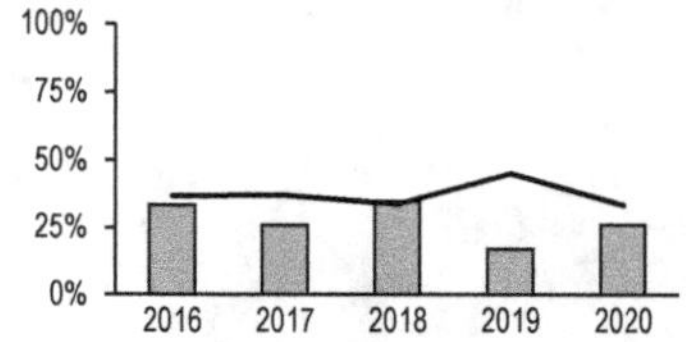

	2016	2017	2018	2019	2020
Wilson	33.3%	25.8%	34.7%	17.1%	26.2%
Average	36.6%	36.9%	33.5%	45.1%	33.3%

Fiscal Year 2019-20

Explanatory Information

Service Level and Delivery
The mission of the Winston-Salem Fire Department is to protect the lives and property of all people within Winston-Salem by reducing the occurrence and minimizing the effects of fires.

The Winston-Salem Fire Department contains the following six divisions: fire suppression, vehicle maintenance, planning, community education, fire prevention, and administration.

Fire suppression personnel work a twenty-one-day cycle with an average of fifty-six hours per week.

The city has an ISO rating of 2, as rated in 2015.

The fire department in Winston-Salem conducted 7,892 fire maintenance, construction, and reinspections during the fiscal year. The fire department inspection program includes inspections that (1) ensure reasonable life safety conditions within a structure; (2) identify fire hazards; and (3) determine the proper installation, operation, and maintenance of fire protection features, systems, and appliances within buildings. The fire department inspection program involves both the Fire Prevention Bureau and the fire engine companies. Similar to the Fire Prevention Bureau, all fire stations have inspection responsibilities and conduct building inspections within their assigned territories. Each business within the city limits is inspected annually and receives as many return visits as necessary for fire code compliance.

Conditions Affecting Service, Performance, and Costs
Winston-Salem has a high number of inspections per inspector full-time equivalent (FTE) when compared to the other jurisdictions due to the fact that many inspections are performed by fire company personnel. The city defines an inspection as a site interior and/or exterior survey of a building, operation, event, condition, and/or activity for the purpose of verifying fire and building code compliance.

Municipal Profile

Service Population	244,739
Land Area (Square Miles)	132.59
Persons per Square Mile	1,846
Median Household Income U.S. Census 2016	$40,584

Service Profile

FTE Positions—Firefighters	339.0
FTE Positions—Other	29.0
Fire Stations	19
First-Line Fire Apparatus	
Pumpers	18
Aerial Trucks	5
Quints	0
Squads	0
Rescue	2
Other	13
Fire Department Responses	23,483
Responses for Fires	780
Structural Fires Reported	231
Inspections Completed for Maintenance, Construction, and Reinspections	7,892
Fire Code Violations Reported	6,644
Estimated Fire Loss (millions)	$7.31
Amount of Property Protected in Service Area (millions)	$22,956
Number of Fire Education Programs or Events	205

Full Cost Profile

Cost Breakdown by Percentage	
Personal Services	79.6%
Operating Costs	13.5%
Capital Costs	7.0%
TOTAL	100.0%

Cost Breakdown in Dollars	
Personal Services	$31,883,389
Operating Costs	$5,391,829
Capital Costs	$2,788,743
TOTAL	$40,063,961

Winston-Salem

Fire Services

Key: Winston-Salem ▒ Benchmarking Average — Fiscal Years 2016 through 2020

Resource Measures

Fire Services Costs per Capita

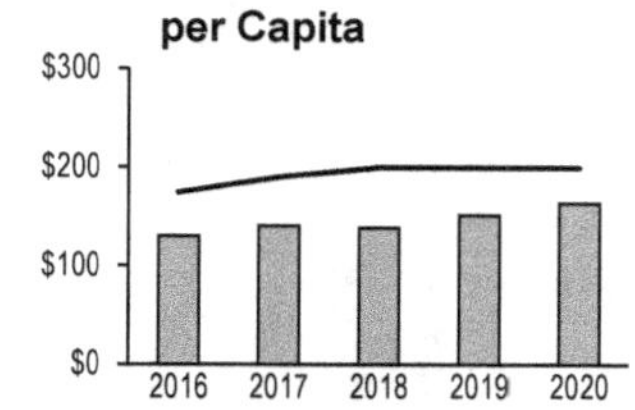

	2016	2017	2018	2019	2020
Winston-Salem	$130	$140	$138	$152	$164
Average	$174	$190	$199	$200	$200

Fire Services Total FTEs per 10,000 Population

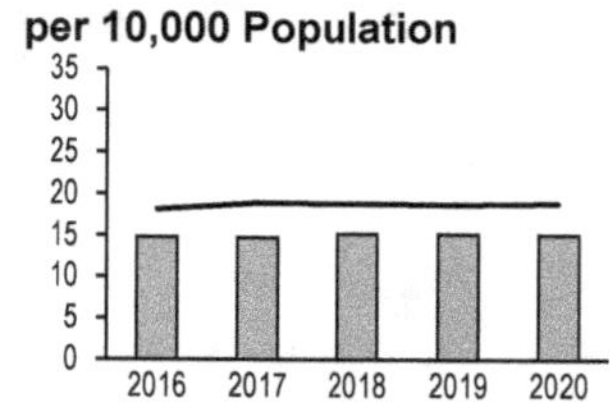

	2016	2017	2018	2019	2020
Winston-Salem	14.8	14.7	15.1	15.1	15.0
Average	18.1	18.8	18.8	18.7	18.8

Fire Services Cost per Thousand Dollars of Property Protected

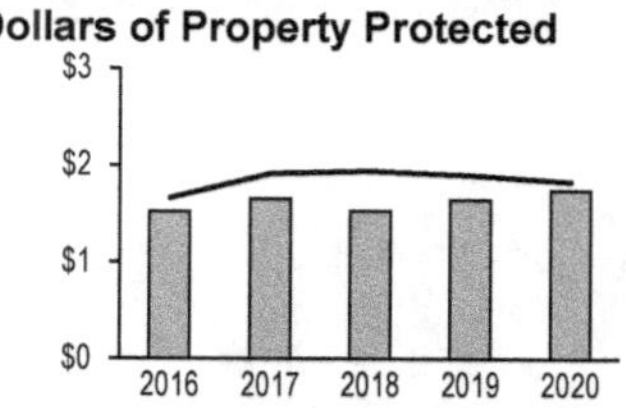

	2016	2017	2018	2019	2020
Winston-Salem	$1.52	$1.65	$1.53	$1.65	$1.75
Average	$1.66	$1.91	$1.94	$1.90	$1.83

Workload Measures

Actual Fires per 1,000 Population

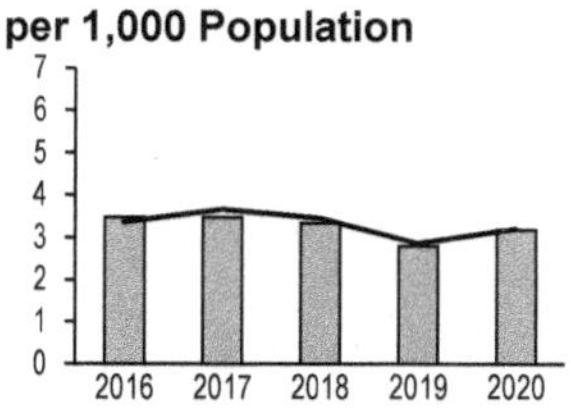

	2016	2017	2018	2019	2020
Winston-Salem	3.47	3.47	3.34	2.80	3.19
Average	3.34	3.65	3.44	2.87	3.19

Fire Department Responses per 1,000 Population

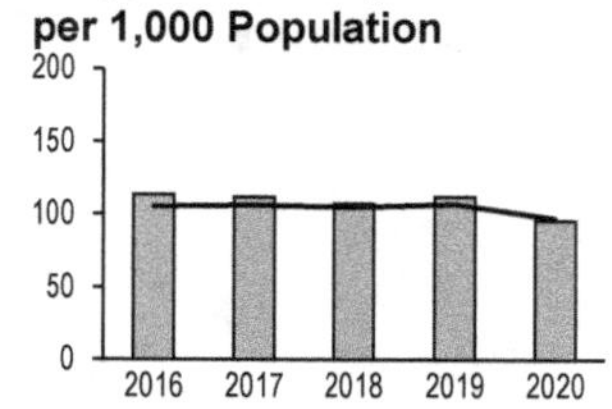

	2016	2017	2018	2019	2020
Winston-Salem	113	112	107	112	96
Average	105	106	105	107	97

Fire Inspections Completed per 1,000 Population

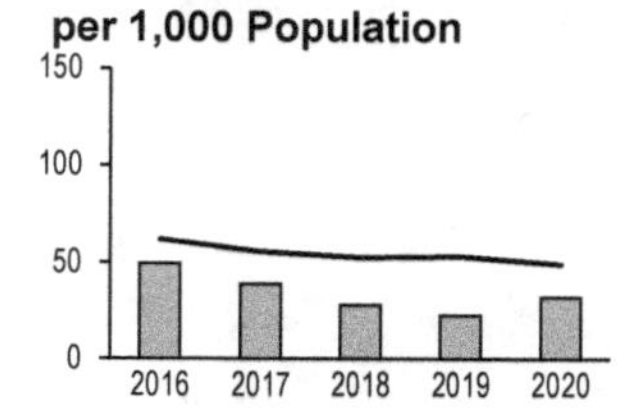

	2016	2017	2018	2019	2020
Winston-Salem	49	39	28	23	32
Average	62	55	52	53	49

Efficiency Measures

Fire Services Cost per Fire Department Response

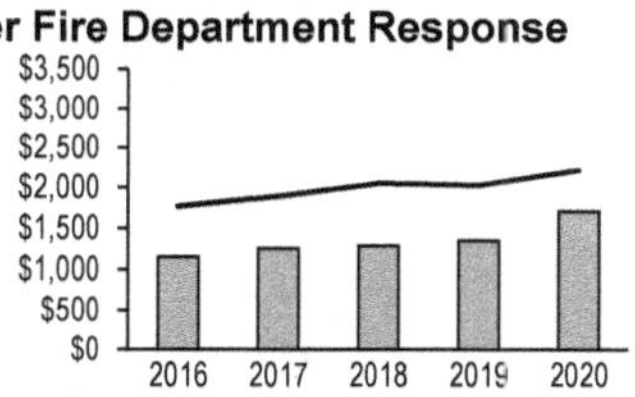

	2016	2017	2018	2019	2020
Winston-Salem	$1,148	$1,253	$1,290	$1,352	$1,706
Average	$1,765	$1,892	$2,051	$2,021	$2,219

Inspections Completed per Inspector FTE

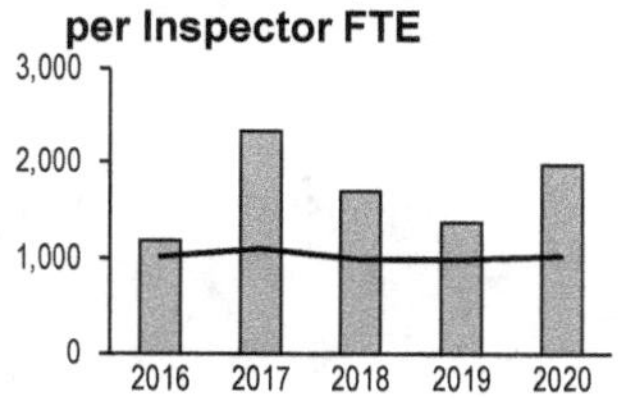

	2016	2017	2018	2019	2020
Winston-Salem	1,182	2,331	1,688	1,370	1,973
Average	1,014	1,095	985	989	1,017

Effectiveness Measures

Average Response Time to Priority One Calls in Minutes

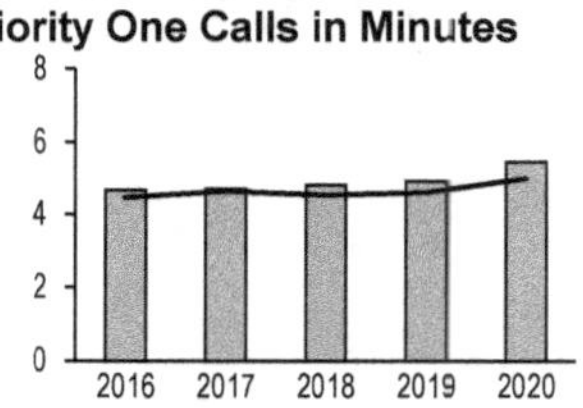

	2016	2017	2018	2019	2020
Winston-Salem	4.7	4.7	4.8	4.9	5.5
Average	4.4	4.6	4.5	4.6	5.0

Percentage of Fire Code Violations Cleared within 90 Days

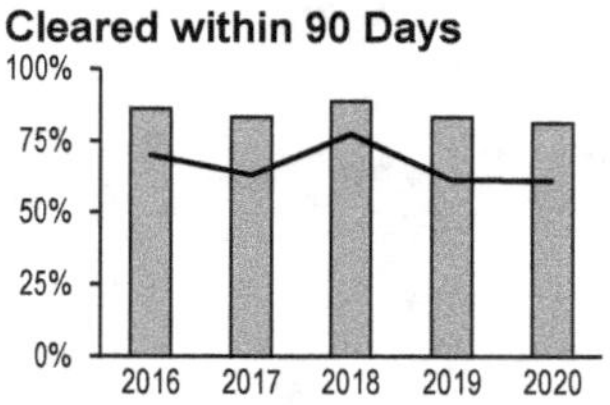

	2016	2017	2018	2019	2020
Winston-Salem	86%	83%	89%	83%	81%
Average	70%	63%	77%	61%	61%

Percentage of Fires Confined to Rooms or Objects Involved on Arrival

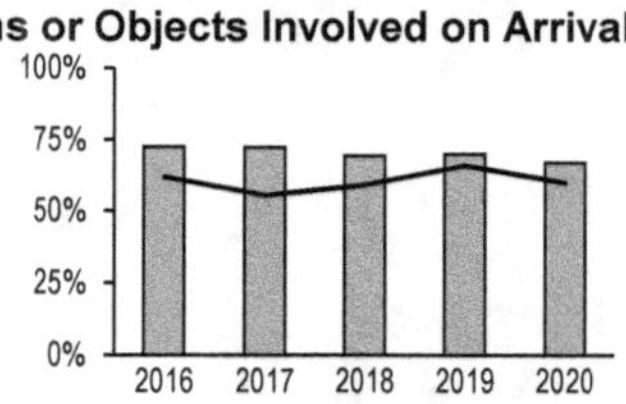

	2016	2017	2018	2019	2020
Winston-Salem	73%	72%	69%	70%	67%
Average	62%	55%	59%	66%	60%

Percentage of Fires for Which Cause Was Determined

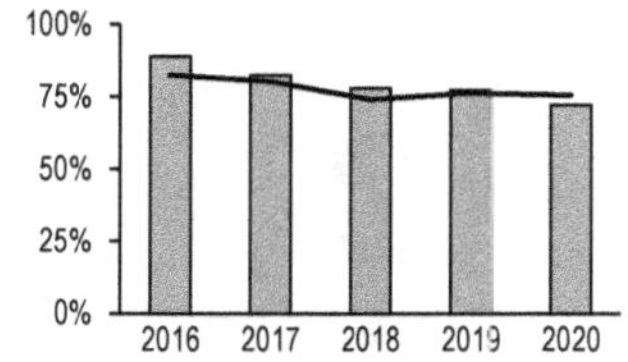

	2016	2017	2018	2019	2020
Winston-Salem	89%	82%	78%	77%	72%
Average	82%	80%	74%	76%	75%

Percentage of Full Response within 8 Minutes Travel Time

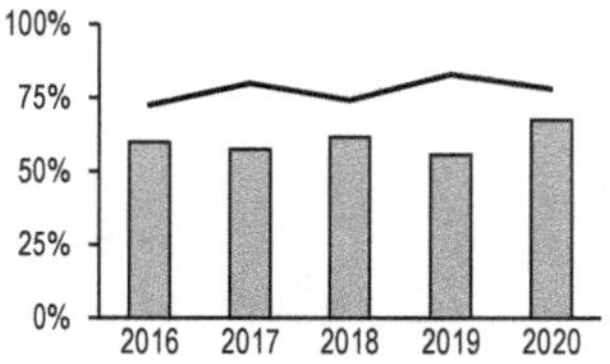

	2016	2017	2018	2019	2020
Winston-Salem	60%	57%	62%	56%	68%
Average	72%	80%	74%	83%	78%

Percentage of Lost Pulse Cases Recovered Pulse at Transfer of Care

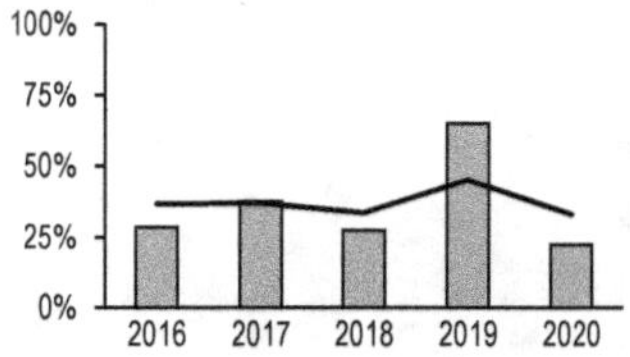

	2016	2017	2018	2019	2020
Winston-Salem	28.6%	37.7%	27.5%	65.1%	22.5%
Average	36.6%	36.9%	33.5%	45.1%	33.3%

UNC | SCHOOL OF GOVERNMENT
North Carolina Benchmarking Project

Performance and Cost Data

BUILDING INSPECTIONS

SCHOOL OF GOVERNMENT
North Carolina Benchmarking Project

PERFORMANCE MEASURES FOR BUILDING INSPECTIONS

SERVICE DEFINITION

Building Inspection Services refers to permit issuance and inspections for building, electrical, mechanical (including heating and cooling), and plumbing work on new residential and commercial construction or additions and alterations to enforce the North Carolina State Building Code and related local building regulations. The inspection process includes the receipt of permit applications, review of plans and specifications, issuance of permits, and follow-up field inspections to ensure compliance. Excluded are the enforcement of zoning and subdivision regulations, fire codes, minimum housing codes, erosion and sedimentation control regulations, watershed regulations, historic preservation ordinances, and other development regulations or plans.

NOTES ON PERFORMANCE MEASURES

1. Building Inspections per 1,000 Population

Building inspections are those required by the North Carolina State Building Code for general building, electrical, mechanical (including heating and cooling), and plumbing work associated with construction projects. Inspections include re-inspections. They do not include non–building code inspections or consultation visits.

2. Value of Total Building Permits as Percentage of Tax Base of Area Served

When a building permit is issued, the dollar amount of the work specified in the contract(s) authorizing the work is recorded as the value of the building permit. Tax base refers to the taxable valuation used for levying the fiscal year property tax for the area served.

3. Value of Commercial Permits as Percentage of Tax Base of Area Served

Commercial building permits are issued for construction of business, manufacturing, institutional, and other nonresidential buildings or improvements. Tax base is defined above.

4. Cost per Building Inspection and Inspections per Day per Inspector

Building inspections are defined above. Cost is determined using the project's full cost accounting model, including direct, indirect, and capital costs. An inspector full-time equivalent (FTE) is calculated using a work year of 235 days. Inspector FTEs include permanent, temporary, part-time, and full-time inspectors.

5. Value of Building Permits per FTE

Value of building permits is defined above. Inspectors must be certified by the state to enforce the state building code and be able to review plans and conduct inspections to enforce that code. Inspector FTEs exclude supervisors, who may be certified but who spend less than 50 percent of their time performing inspections. Inspector FTEs also exclude support personnel who are not certified.

6. Number of Plan Reviews per Reviewer FTE

The state building code requires that plans and specifications for most commercial and residential construction be reviewed before permits are issued for such construction. Reviewer FTEs are calculated using a 2,080-hour work year, the actual number of plan reviews conducted during the fiscal year, and the number of plan reviewers.

7. Percentage of Inspection Responses within One Working Day of Request

A request for inspection may be made by phone, in person, or in writing. A response refers to at least beginning an inspection, regardless of whether approval of the work occurs. The majority of inspections are completed the same day as initiated. A response to a request within one working day means that the inspection is initiated before the end of the workday following the day on which the request is made.

8. Percentage of Inspections That Are Re-inspections

A re-inspection occurs when a building inspector must inspect work that has previously been inspected. A re-inspection can occur due to problems found in the original inspection or for other reasons.

Building Inspections

Summary of Key Dimensions of Service

City or Town	Area Served (in Square Miles)	Population Growth from 2010 to 2017	Building Inspections by Trade					Number of Plan Reviewers	Building Inspector FTEs	Total Staff FTEs
			Building	Electrical	Mechanical	Plumbing	Total			
Apex	37.3	29.3%	24,118	11,871	8,849	12,380	57,218	4.0	12.0	22.0
Chapel Hill	27.5	4.7%	3,223	2,596	2,712	1,771	10,302	2.0	7.0	15.0
Goldsboro	57.6	-7.6%	1,440	2,139	1,317	787	5,683	1.0	4.0	8.0
Greensboro	134.6	6.9%	18,482	17,346	14,327	10,694	60,849	4.5	16.0	30.5
Raleigh	181.5	14.0%	24,073	33,669	23,479	15,791	97,012	14.0	42.0	80.0
Wilson	31.9	0.0%	2,384	2,408	2,168	1,393	8,353	1.0	4.0	7.0
Winston-Salem	396.0	5.8%	16,832	23,209	17,092	12,910	70,043	3.0	18.0	38.4

** Total Inspections for Chapel Hill includes 347 that did not fit into the four major categories.*

EXPLANATORY FACTORS

These are factors that the project found affected building inspection performance and cost in one or more of the municipalities:

Rate of growth and development in city
Size and complexity of construction projects
Geographic area served by county building inspections
Inspectors' enforcement of local development regulations
Emphasis given to plan review in each jurisdiction
Inspector specialization
Organization of the building inspection function

Fiscal Year 2019-20

Explanatory Information

Service Level and Delivery

The Town of Apex provides building inspection services though the Building Inspections and Permits Department. The department is organized into two major divisions: building inspections and engineering. The department provides inspections for all of Apex and just over twenty-one square miles of area in its extraterritorial jurisdiction (ETJ).

All building inspectors in Apex serve each of the major trades. The department enforces the North Carolina State Building Code.

The department has a goal of having all inspectors fully qualified for the technical, administrative, and customer service aspects of their job. Training is accomplished primarily by off-site seminars and conferences offered by state-approved sponsors.

Apex has a standard that all inspection requests recorded by a permit technician or the permit office voicemail by 3 a.m. are to be performed on the next business day. Due to high workload during the latter part of the fiscal year, the city was not able to always meet this standard of service.

Total revenue received from inspection fees amounted to $3,184,148 for the fiscal year.

Conditions Affecting Service, Performance, and Costs

The population served is calculated by adding the population of Apex with the population of the ETJ. The tax base served is calculated by adding the tax base of Apex with the tax base of the ETJ. The population and the tax base of the ETJ are calculated by taking the population and tax base per square mile of Wake County and multiplying them by the square miles of the ETJ.

Apex does not track multifamily as a category of reporting for inspections or plan reviews. Instead, townhomes are included with residential, and condos and apartments are included with commercial.

While Apex has the goal of providing next-day service for building inspections, the large volume of work in the strong growth community has made this goal difficult to achieve at all times.

Municipal Profile

Population Served	78,670
Land Area Inspected (Square Miles)	37.29
Persons per Square Mile	2,110
Estimated Tax Base in Service Area (billions)	$10.34
Median Household Income U.S. Census 2016	$84,000

Service Profile

FTE Inspectors	
Building	0.0
Electrical	0.0
Mechanical	0.0
Plumbing	0.0
All Trades	12.0
Total Inspectors	12.0
FTE Plan Reviewers	4.0
Other FTE Positions	6.0
Total of All Positions	22.0
Number of Inspections by Type	
Building	24,118
Electrical	11,871
Mechanical	8,849
Plumbing	12,380
TOTAL	57,218
Building Permit Values	
Residential	$355,298,464
Multifamily	included with residential
Commercial	$92,248,929
TOTAL	$447,547,393
Inspection Fee Revenue	$3,184,148

Full Cost Profile

Cost Breakdown by Percentage	
Personal Services	73.2%
Operating Costs	19.7%
Capital Costs	7.1%
TOTAL	100.0%
Cost Breakdown in Dollars	
Personal Services	$1,978,011
Operating Costs	$532,465
Capital Costs	$192,805
TOTAL	$2,703,281

Key: Apex ▒ Benchmarking Average — Fiscal Years 2016 through 2020

Resource Measures

Building Inspections Services Costs per Capita

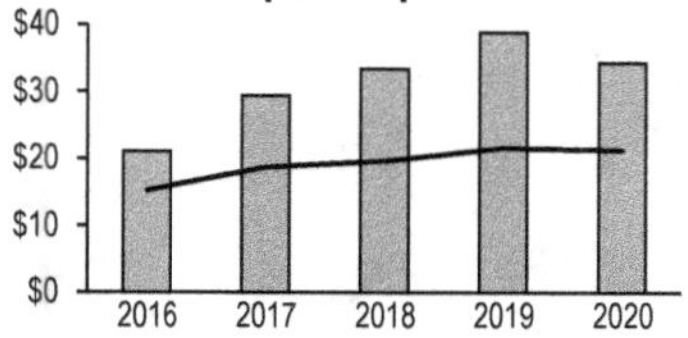

	2016	2017	2018	2019	2020
Apex	$21.07	$29.34	$33.41	$38.87	$34.36
Average	$15.18	$18.61	$19.55	$21.51	$21.21

Building Inspections Services FTEs per 10,000 Population

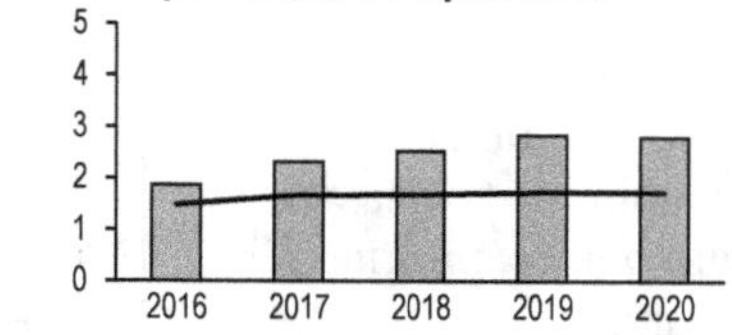

	2016	2017	2018	2019	2020
Apex	1.87	2.32	2.53	2.84	2.80
Average	1.48	1.66	1.68	1.73	1.73

Building Inspections Services Cost per Million Dollars of Tax Base

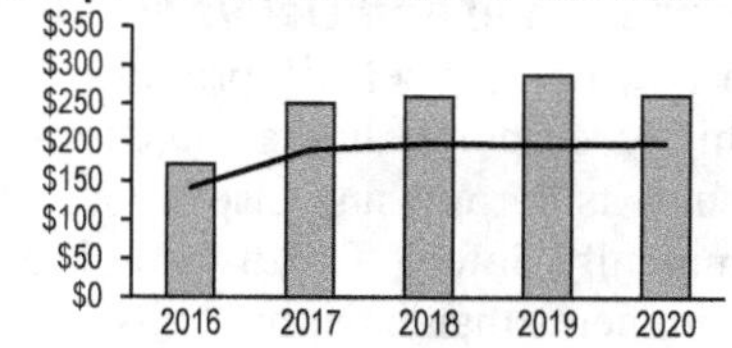

	2016	2017	2018	2019	2020
Apex	$172	$250	$259	$287	$262
Average	$141	$190	$197	$197	$199

Workload Measures

Inspections per 1,000 Population in Service Area

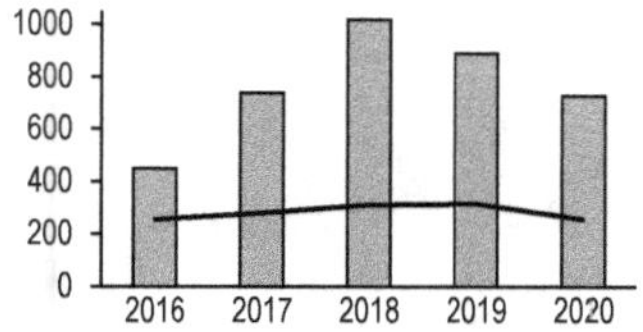

	2016	2017	2018	2019	2020
Apex	450	739	1016	890	727
Average	253	277	309	314	255

Inspections per Square Mile in Service Area

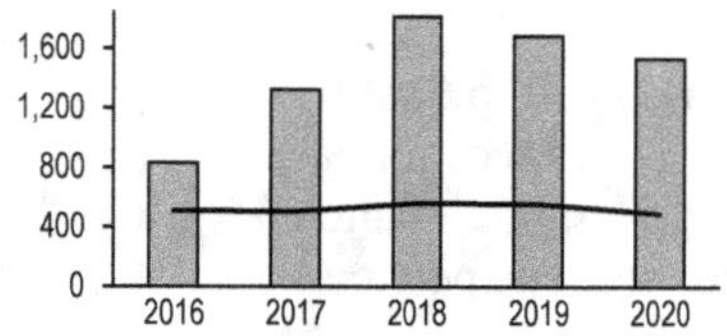

	2016	2017	2018	2019	2020
Apex	828	1,323	1,814	1,683	1,534
Average	505	504	560	555	490

Value of Building Permits as Percentage of Tax Base of Area Served

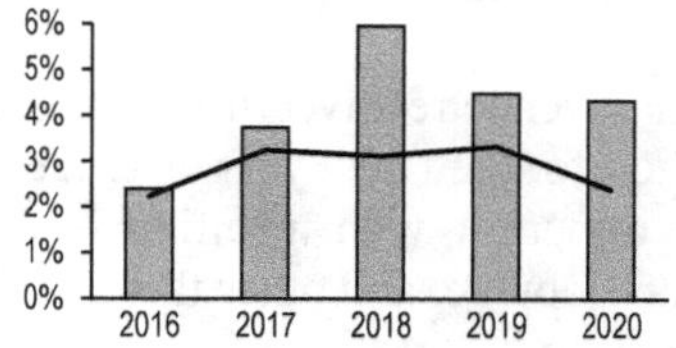

	2016	2017	2018	2019	2020
Apex	2.39%	3.73%	5.94%	4.49%	4.33%
Average	2.23%	3.23%	3.10%	3.32%	2.38%

Value of Commercial Permits as Percentage of Tax Base of Area Served

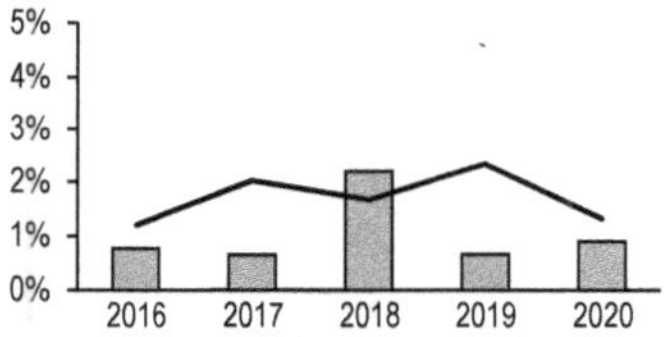

	2016	2017	2018	2019	2020
Apex	0.77%	0.65%	2.19%	0.66%	0.89%
Average	1.20%	2.02%	1.67%	2.33%	1.32%

Value of Building Permits per Inspector FTE in Millions of Dollars

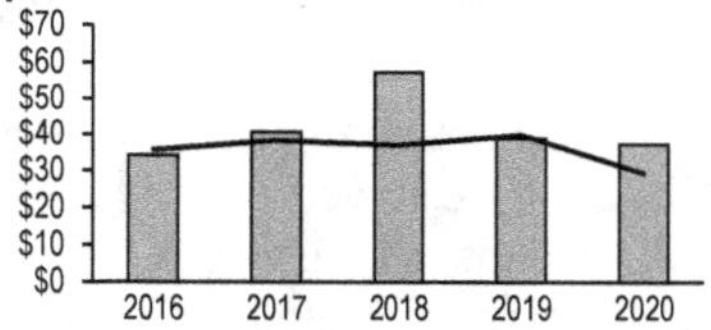

	2016	2017	2018	2019	2020
Apex	$34.1	$40.6	$57.4	$38.9	$37.3
Average	$35.6	$38.1	$36.9	$39.8	$29.3

Efficiency Measures

Building Services Cost per Inspection—All Types

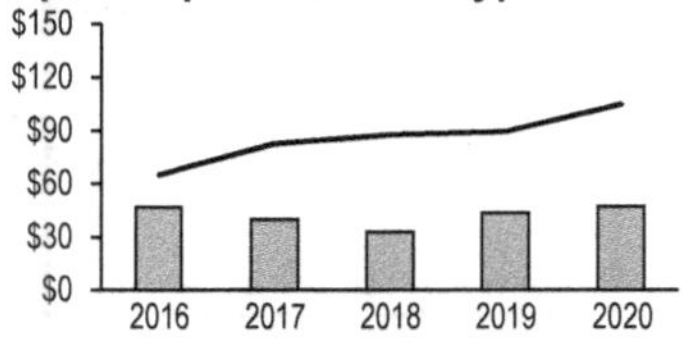

	2016	2017	2018	2019	2020
Apex	$46.84	$39.71	$32.89	$43.69	$47.25
Average	$64.77	$82.44	$87.41	$89.47	$104.76

Inspections per Day per Inspector FTE

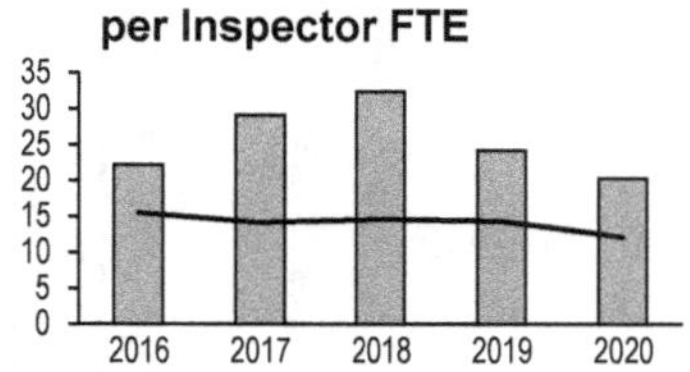

	2016	2017	2018	2019	2020
Apex	22.2	29.1	32.3	24.2	20.3
Average	15.4	14.1	14.5	14.3	12.0

Plan Reviews per Year per Reviewer FTE

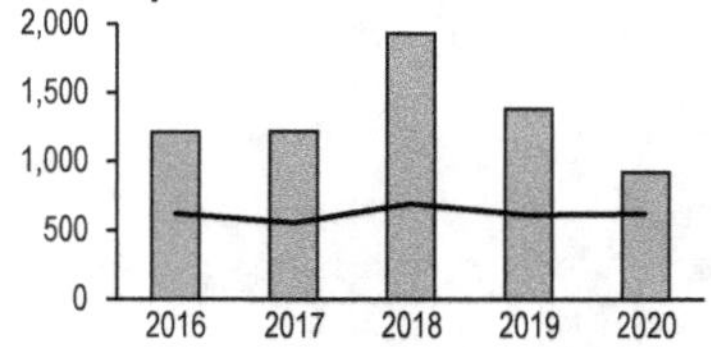

	2016	2017	2018	2019	2020
Apex	1,213	1,217	1,931	1,383	923
Average	620	552	690	608	617

Effectiveness Measures

Percentage of Inspection Responses within One Working Day of Request

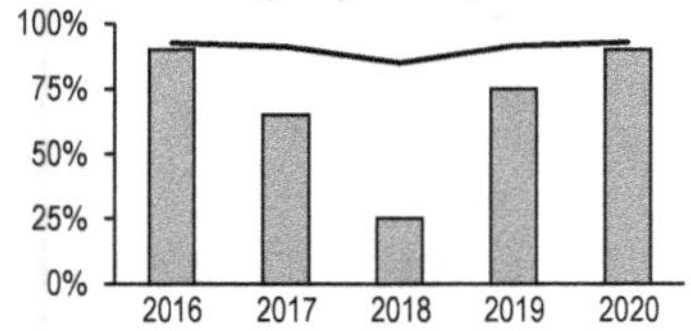

	2016	2017	2018	2019	2020
Apex	90.0%	65.0%	25.0%	75.0%	90.0%
Average	92.7%	91.1%	84.8%	91.4%	92.7%

Percentage of Inspections That Are Reinspections

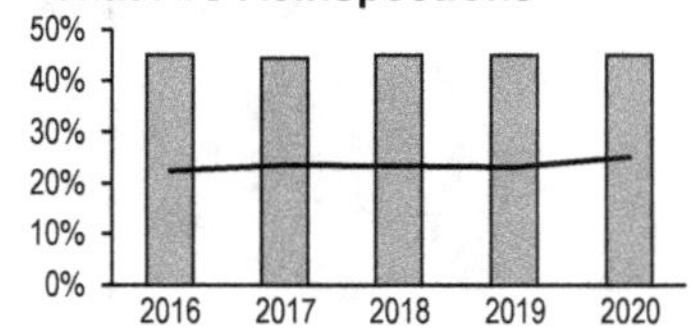

	2016	2017	2018	2019	2020
Apex	45.0%	44.4%	45.0%	45.0%	45.0%
Average	22.4%	23.4%	23.4%	23.1%	25.1%

Fiscal Year 2019-20

Explanatory Information

Service Level and Delivery

The Town of Chapel Hill provides building inspection services within its corporate limits and extra-territorial jurisdiction (ETJ) through its Permits and Inspections Division within the Office of Community Safety. The division is a full-service entity, meeting all requirements mandated by the N.C. General Statutes.

Inspectors have a main discipline in one of the building trades and usually perform Level 3 inspections, plus they perform inspections in other disciplines when needed. On occasion retired part-time inspectors are brought in to help with overloads and the need for plan review in field inspections.

Total revenue received from inspection fees amounted to $1.89 million for the fiscal year. The fee schedule separates fees for each type of permit, with specific fees depending on a minimum amount, square footage, and other factors. There is a fee for reinspections.

Conditions Affecting Service, Performance, and Costs

Although data for the earlier years are not shown here, Chapel Hill has noted an uptick in permits and construction over prior years. There has particularly been an increase in larger and more complex projects requiring staff attention.

The population served is calculated by adding the population of Chapel Hill with the population of the ETJ. The tax base served is calculated by adding the tax base of Chapel Hill with the tax base of the ETJ. The population and the tax base of the ETJ are calculated by taking the population and tax base per square mile of Orange County and multiplying them by the square miles of the ETJ.

Municipal Profile

Population Served	65,911
Land Area Inspected (Square Miles)	27.50
Persons per Square Mile	2,397
Estimated Tax Base in Service Area (billions)	$8.60
Median Household Income U.S. Census 2016	$60,802

Service Profile

FTE Inspectors	
Building	0.0
Electrical	0.0
Mechanical	0.0
Plumbing	0.0
All Trades	7.0
Total Inspectors	7.0
FTE Plan Reviewers	2.0
Other FTE Positions	6.0
Total of All Positions	15.0
Number of Inspections by Type	
Building	2,876
Electrical	2,596
Mechanical	2,712
Plumbing	1,771
TOTAL	10,302
Building Permit Values	
Residential	$59,596,590
Multifamily	included with commercial
Commercial	$137,875,121
TOTAL	$197,471,711
Inspection Fee Revenue	$1,893,585

Full Cost Profile

Cost Breakdown by Percentage	
Personal Services	52.2%
Operating Costs	23.0%
Capital Costs	24.7%
TOTAL	100.0%
Cost Breakdown in Dollars	
Personal Services	$1,270,789
Operating Costs	$560,277
Capital Costs	$601,086
TOTAL	$2,432,152

Chapel Hill — Building Inspections

Key: Chapel Hill ■ Benchmarking Average — Fiscal Years 2016 through 2020

Resource Measures

Building Inspections Services Costs per Capita

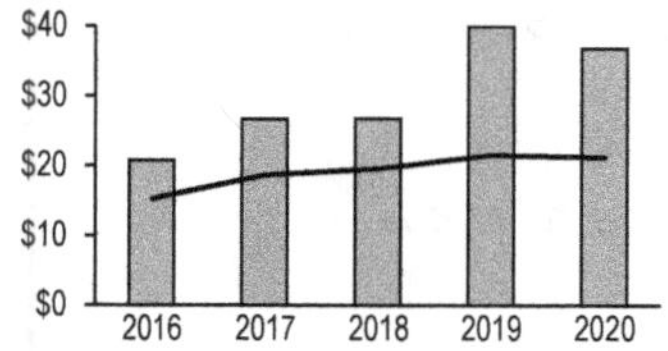

	2016	2017	2018	2019	2020
Chapel Hill	$20.78	$26.64	$26.81	$40.00	$36.90
Average	$15.18	$18.61	$19.55	$21.51	$21.21

Building Inspections Services FTEs per 10,000 Population

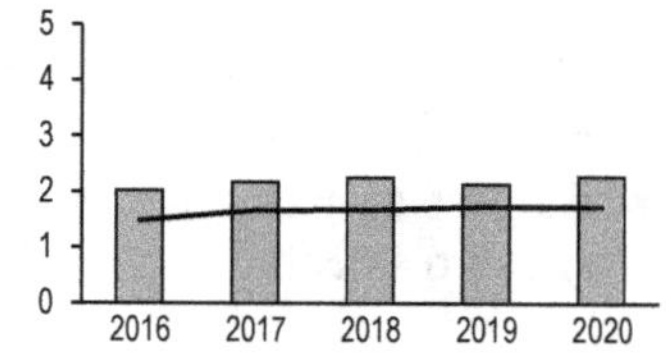

	2016	2017	2018	2019	2020
Chapel Hill	2.02	2.18	2.25	2.14	2.28
Average	1.48	1.66	1.68	1.73	1.73

Building Inspections Services Cost per Million Dollars of Tax Base

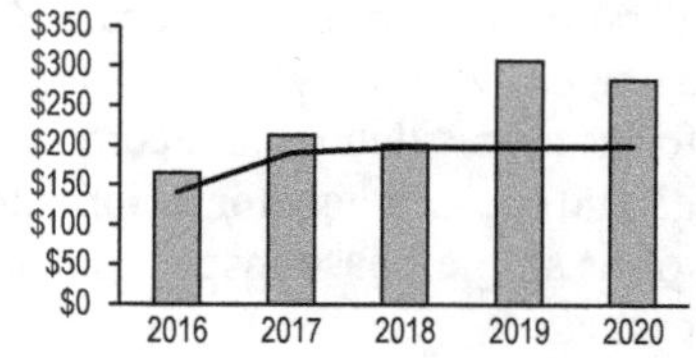

	2016	2017	2018	2019	2020
Chapel Hill	$165	$212	$201	$307	$283
Average	$141	$190	$197	$197	$199

Workload Measures

Inspections per 1,000 Population in Service Area

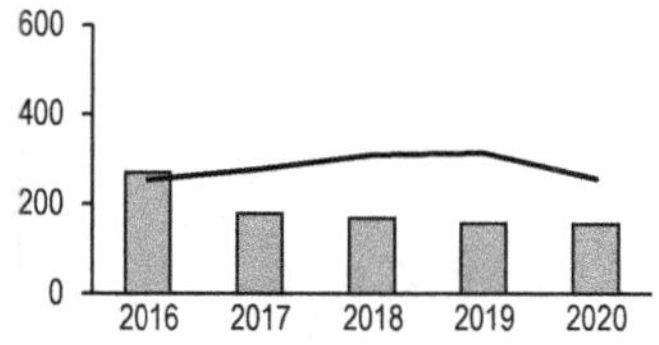

	2016	2017	2018	2019	2020
Chapel Hill	270	178	169	157	156
Average	253	277	309	314	255

Inspections per Square Mile in Service Area

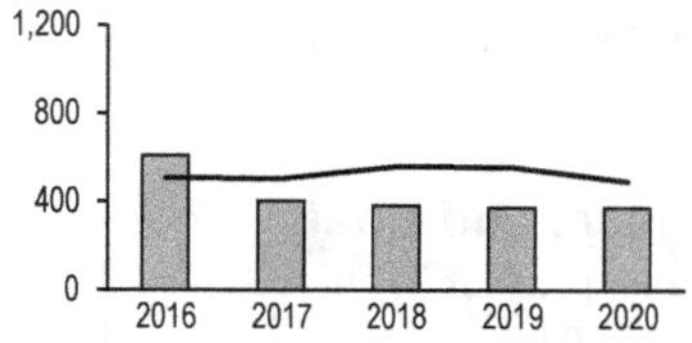

	2016	2017	2018	2019	2020
Chapel Hill	609	402	381	373	375
Average	505	504	560	555	490

Value of Building Permits as Percentage of Tax Base of Area Served

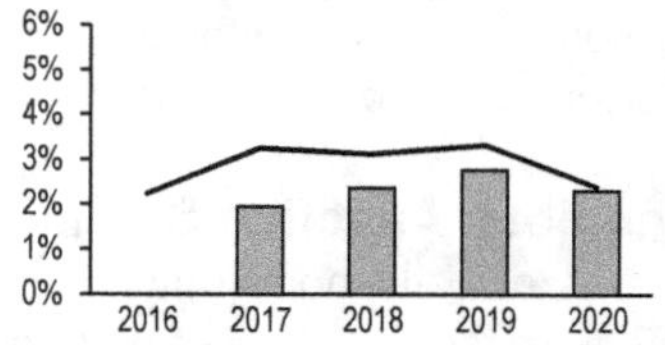

	2016	2017	2018	2019	2020
Chapel Hill		1.95%	2.35%	2.77%	2.30%
Average	2.23%	3.23%	3.10%	3.32%	2.38%

Value of Commercial Permits as Percentage of Tax Base of Area Served

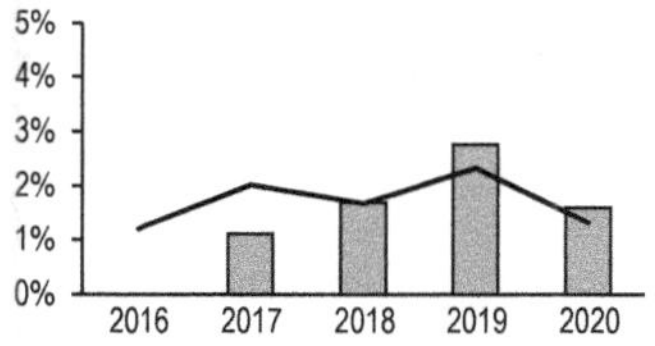

	2016	2017	2018	2019	2020
Chapel Hill		1.10%	1.69%	2.77%	1.60%
Average	1.20%	2.02%	1.67%	2.33%	1.32%

Value of Building Permits per Inspector FTE in Millions of Dollars

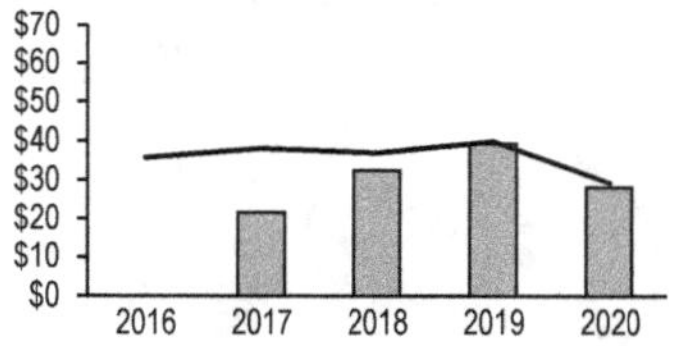

	2016	2017	2018	2019	2020
Chapel Hill		$21.6	$32.5	$39.3	$28.2
Average	$35.6	$38.1	$36.9	$39.8	$29.3

Efficiency Measures

Building Services Cost per Inspection—All Types

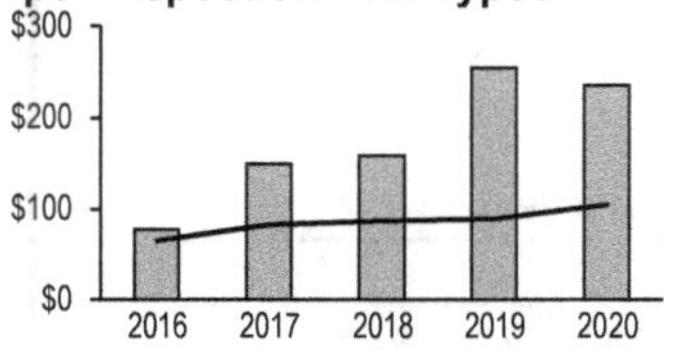

	2016	2017	2018	2019	2020
Chapel Hill	$76.95	$149.46	$158.76	$255.09	$236.09
Average	$64.77	$82.44	$87.41	$89.47	$104.76

Inspections per Day per Inspector FTE

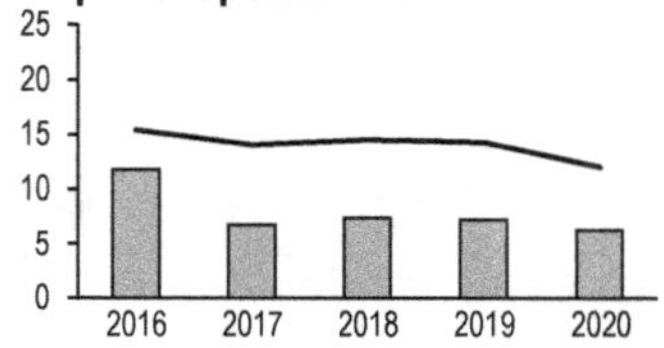

	2016	2017	2018	2019	2020
Chapel Hill	11.8	6.7	7.4	7.3	6.3
Average	15.4	14.1	14.5	14.3	12.0

Plan Reviews per Year per Reviewer FTE

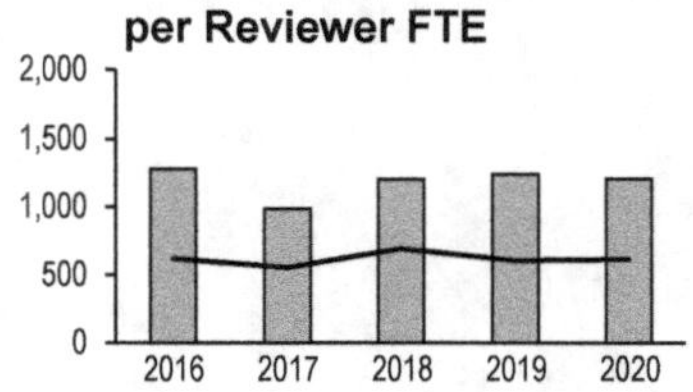

	2016	2017	2018	2019	2020
Chapel Hill	1,281	985	1,203	1,242	1,209
Average	620	552	690	608	617

Effectiveness Measures

Percentage of Inspection Responses within One Working Day of Request

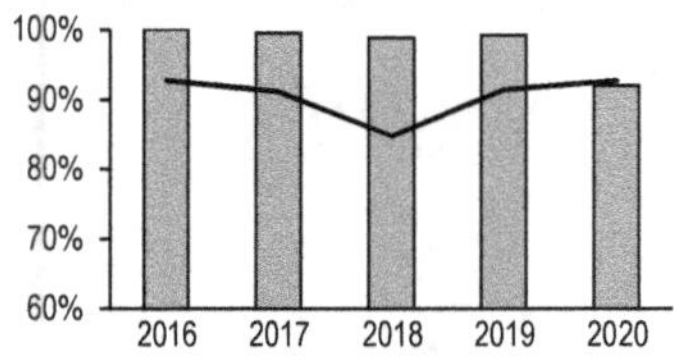

	2016	2017	2018	2019	2020
Chapel Hill	100.0%	99.4%	98.8%	99.2%	92.0%
Average	92.7%	91.1%	84.8%	91.4%	92.7%

Percentage of Inspections That Are Reinspections

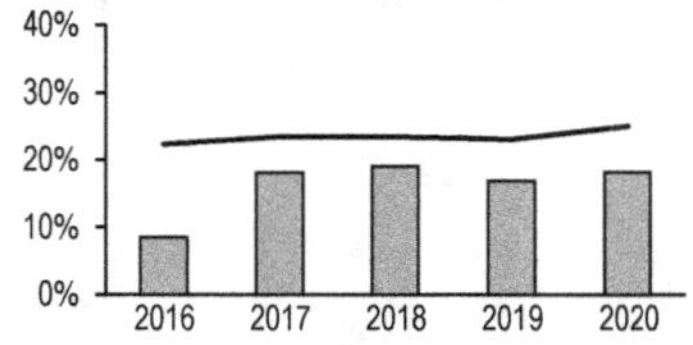

	2016	2017	2018	2019	2020
Chapel Hill	8.5%	18.1%	19.0%	16.9%	18.2%
Average	22.4%	23.4%	23.4%	23.1%	25.1%

Fiscal Year 2019-20

Explanatory Information

Service Level and Delivery

Goldsboro Inspections is a separate department that operates independently of the Wayne County inspections function. Goldsboro performs all residential and commercial inspections within the city limits and the extraterritorial jurisdiction areas. The Department performs single-phase inspections for commercial and residential properties.

Inspectors for the city are trade-specific. Inspectors are required to take at least six hours of trade specific training each year in addition to thirty hours of state mandated training.

All requests for inspections have a goal of a response within twenty-four hours. Re-inspections are charged $75 for the first time and $125 for each subsequent time.

Conditions Affecting Service, Performance, and Costs

The City of Goldsboro joined the Benchmarking Project in July 2017, with the first year of data showing for FY 2016–17.

Goldsboro combines residential and multifamily when reporting the dollar value of permits.

The City of Goldsboro had a noticeably higher level of residential and building permits for FY 2016–17 due to recovery work following Hurricane Matthew in October 2016.

Municipal Profile

Population Served	40,543
Land Area Inspected (Square Miles)	57.55
Persons per Square Mile	704
Estimated Tax Base in Service Area (billions)	$3.01
Median Household Income U.S. Census 2016	$32,148

Service Profile

FTE Inspectors	
Building	1.0
Electrical	1.0
Mechanical	1.0
Plumbing	1.0
All Trades	0.0
Total Inspectors	4.0
FTE Plan Reviewers	1.0
Other FTE Positions	3.0
Total of All Positions	8.0
Number of Inspections by Type	
Building	1,440
Electrical	2,139
Mechanical	1,317
Plumbing	787
TOTAL	5,683
Building Permit Values	
Residential	$15,200,000
Multifamily	included with residential
Commercial	$45,700,000
TOTAL	$60,900,000
Inspection Fee Revenue	$457,836

Full Cost Profile

Cost Breakdown by Percentage	
Personal Services	72.0%
Operating Costs	25.5%
Capital Costs	2.5%
TOTAL	100.0%
Cost Breakdown in Dollars	
Personal Services	$587,361
Operating Costs	$207,745
Capital Costs	$20,403
TOTAL	$815,509

Goldsboro

Building Inspections

Key: Goldsboro ■ Benchmarking Average — Fiscal Years 2016 through 2020

Resource Measures

Building Inspections Services Costs per Capita

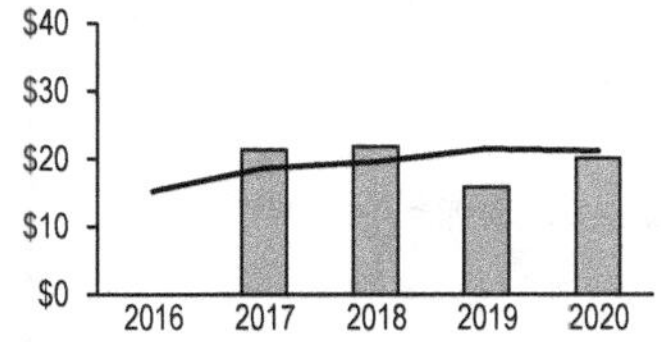

	2016	2017	2018	2019	2020
Goldsboro		$21.41	$21.85	$15.85	$20.11
Average	$15.18	$18.61	$19.55	$21.51	$21.21

Building Inspections Services FTEs per 10,000 Population

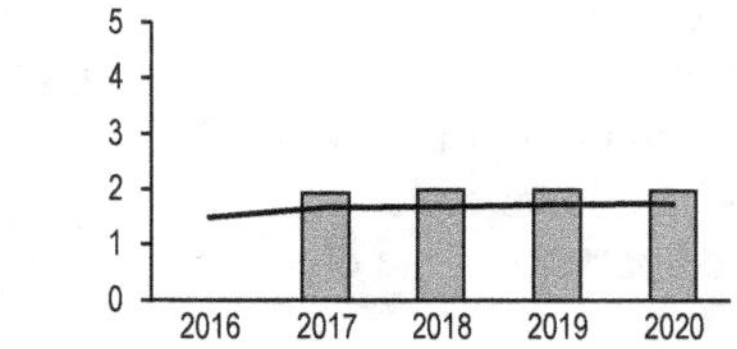

	2016	2017	2018	2019	2020
Goldsboro		1.94	1.99	1.99	1.97
Average	1.48	1.66	1.68	1.73	1.73

Building Inspections Services Cost per Million Dollars of Tax Base

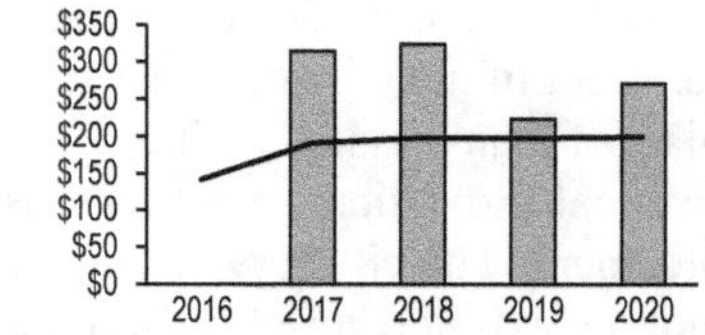

	2016	2017	2018	2019	2020
Goldsboro		$314	$324	$223	$271
Average	$141	$190	$197	$197	$199

Workload Measures

Inspections per 1,000 Population in Service Area

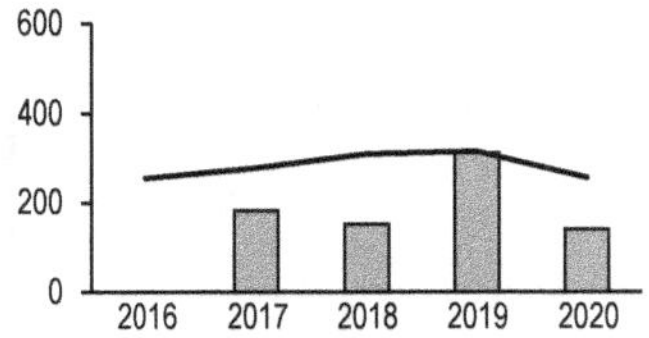

	2016	2017	2018	2019	2020
Goldsboro		182	152	311	140
Average	253	277	309	314	255

Inspections per Square Mile in Service Area

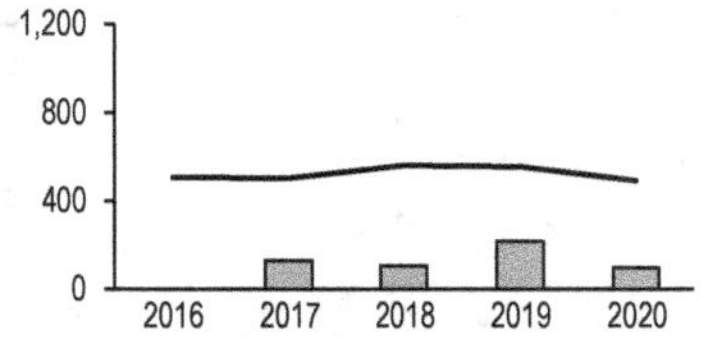

	2016	2017	2018	2019	2020
Goldsboro		130	106	217	99
Average	505	504	560	555	490

Value of Building Permits as Percentage of Tax Base of Area Served

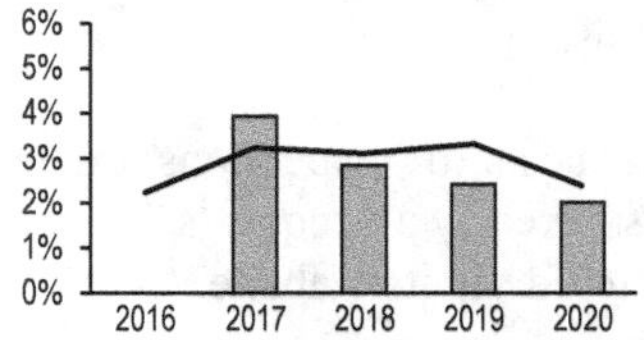

	2016	2017	2018	2019	2020
Goldsboro		3.94%	2.84%	2.42%	2.02%
Average	2.23%	3.23%	3.10%	3.32%	2.38%

Value of Commercial Permits as Percentage of Tax Base of Area Served

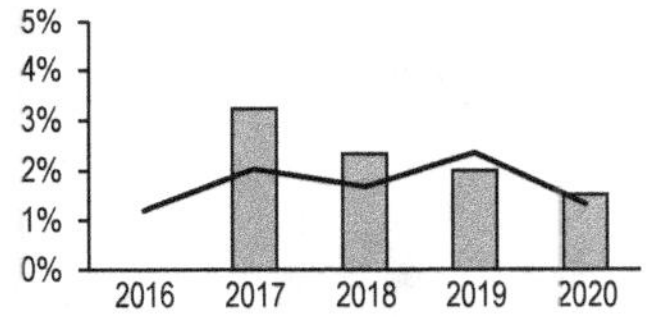

	2016	2017	2018	2019	2020
Goldsboro		3.23%	2.32%	2.00%	1.52%
Average	1.20%	2.02%	1.67%	2.33%	1.32%

Value of Building Permits per Inspector FTE in Millions of Dollars

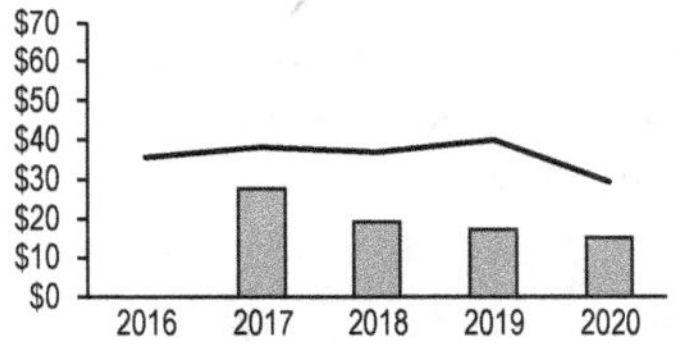

	2016	2017	2018	2019	2020
Goldsboro		$27.8	$19.3	$17.3	$15.2
Average	$35.6	$38.1	$36.9	$39.8	$29.3

Efficiency Measures

Building Services Cost per Inspection—All Types

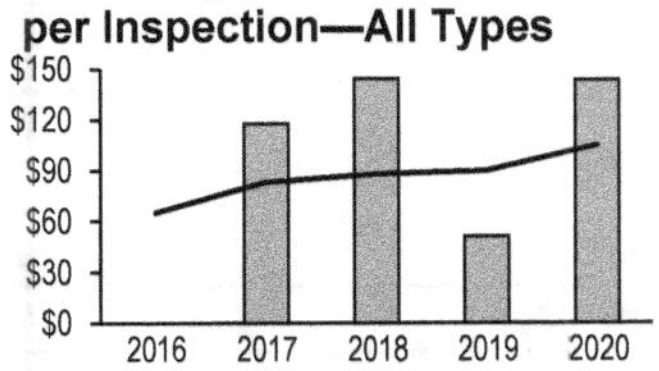

	2016	2017	2018	2019	2020
Goldsboro		$117.66	$144.20	$50.92	$143.50
Average	$64.77	$82.44	$87.41	$89.47	$104.76

Inspections per Day per Inspector FTE

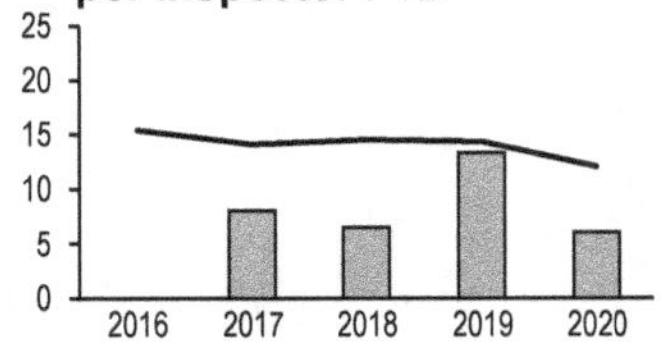

	2016	2017	2018	2019	2020
Goldsboro		8.0	6.5	13.3	6.0
Average	15.4	14.1	14.5	14.3	12.0

Plan Reviews per Year per Reviewer FTE

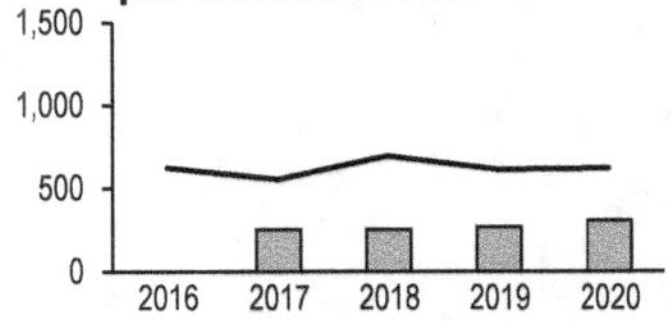

	2016	2017	2018	2019	2020
Goldsboro		249	249	266	306
Average	620	552	690	608	617

Effectiveness Measures

Percentage of Inspection Responses within One Working Day of Request

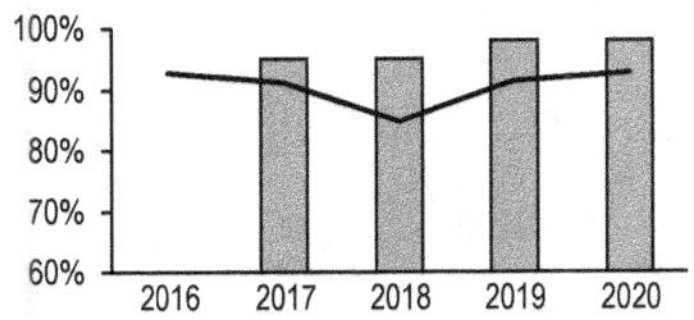

	2016	2017	2018	2019	2020
Goldsboro		95.0%	95.0%	98.0%	98.0%
Average	92.7%	91.1%	84.8%	91.4%	92.7%

Percentage of Inspections That Are Reinspections

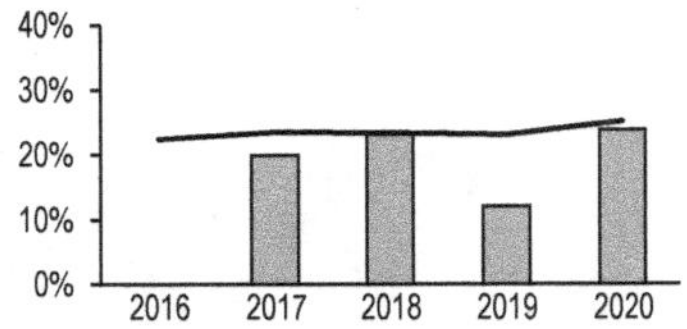

	2016	2017	2018	2019	2020
Goldsboro		19.9%	23.2%	12.0%	23.9%
Average	22.4%	23.4%	23.4%	23.1%	25.1%

Fiscal Year 2019-20

Explanatory Information

Service Level and Delivery

Inspections is a division of the Engineering and Inspections Department of the City of Greensboro. The inspections division consists of plans review, building inspections, plumbing inspections, mechanical inspections, electrical inspections, and local code enforcement. The city services the incorporated portion of the city but not the extraterritorial jurisdiction areas.

Trade inspectors are required to attain a Level III certification of their primary building trade within two years. Mechanical and plumbing inspectors are required to attain a secondary certification. Local ordinance inspectors are required to attain a Level I certification. All certified inspectors are required to take and pass a law and administrative course.

All requests for inspections are responded to within forty-eight hours or less. Nearly all requests are called into the city's automated system or entered via its website.

Total revenue received from inspection fees amounted to $2.7 million for the fiscal year. If a request for inspection is made and the job is not ready or corrections have not been made, a $45 fee for each reinspection is assessed.

Conditions Affecting Service, Performance, and Costs

The broad downturn in the economy reduced building activity and the number of requests for inspections in the earlier years.

Municipal Profile

Population Served	293,730
Land Area Inspected (Square Miles)	134.62
Persons per Square Mile	2,182
Estimated Tax Base in Service Area (billions)	$28.27
Median Household Income U.S. Census 2016	$40,760

Service Profile

FTE Inspectors	
Building	5.0
Electrical	5.0
Mechanical	3.0
Plumbing	3.0
All Trades	0.0
Total Inspectors	16.0
FTE Plan Reviewers	4.5
Other FTE Positions	10.0
Total of All Positions	30.5
Number of Inspections by Type	
Building	18,482
Electrical	17,346
Mechanical	14,327
Plumbing	10,694
TOTAL	60,849
Building Permit Values	
Residential	$132,151,383
Multifamily	$101,256,027
Commercial	$317,576,277
TOTAL	$550,983,687
Inspection Fee Revenue	$2,675,987

Full Cost Profile

Cost Breakdown by Percentage	
Personal Services	83.0%
Operating Costs	17.0%
Capital Costs	0.0%
TOTAL	100.0%
Cost Breakdown in Dollars	
Personal Services	$2,830,829
Operating Costs	$581,281
Capital Costs	$0
TOTAL	$3,412,110

Greensboro

Building Inspections

Key: Greensboro ▒ Benchmarking Average — Fiscal Years 2016 through 2020

Resource Measures

Building Inspections Services Costs per Capita

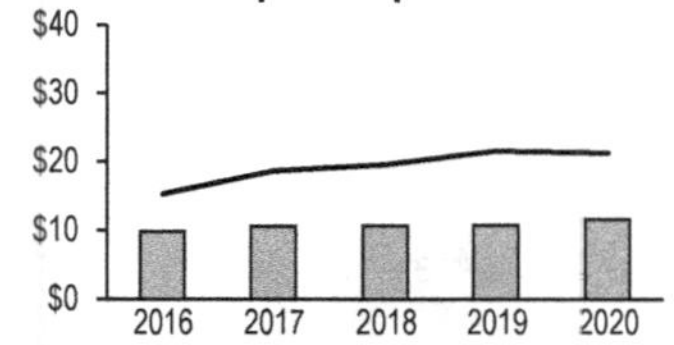

	2016	2017	2018	2019	2020
Greensboro	$9.80	$10.60	$10.68	$10.70	$11.62
Average	$15.18	$18.61	$19.55	$21.51	$21.21

Building Inspections Services FTEs per 10,000 Population

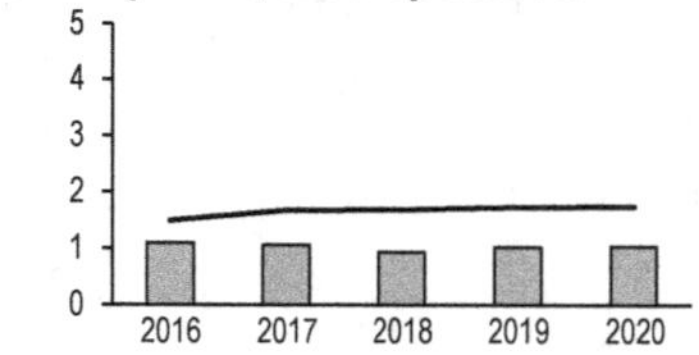

	2016	2017	2018	2019	2020
Greensboro	1.10	1.06	0.94	1.03	1.04
Average	1.48	1.66	1.68	1.73	1.73

Building Inspections Services Cost per Million Dollars of Tax Base

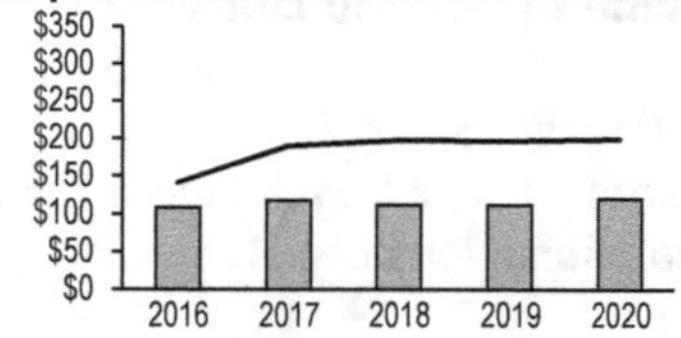

	2016	2017	2018	2019	2020
Greensboro	$108	$118	$112	$112	$121
Average	$141	$190	$197	$197	$199

Workload Measures

Inspections per 1,000 Population in Service Area

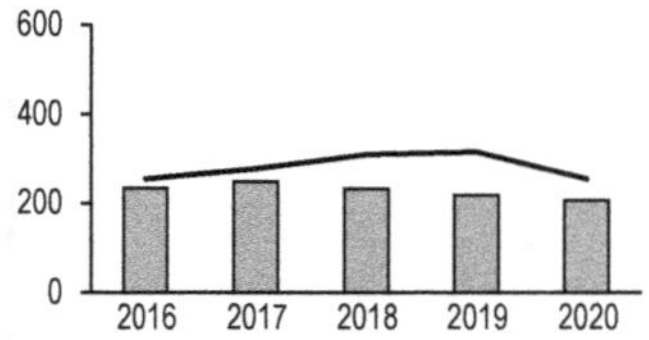

	2016	2017	2018	2019	2020
Greensboro	234	249	233	218	207
Average	253	277	309	314	255

Inspections per Square Mile in Service Area

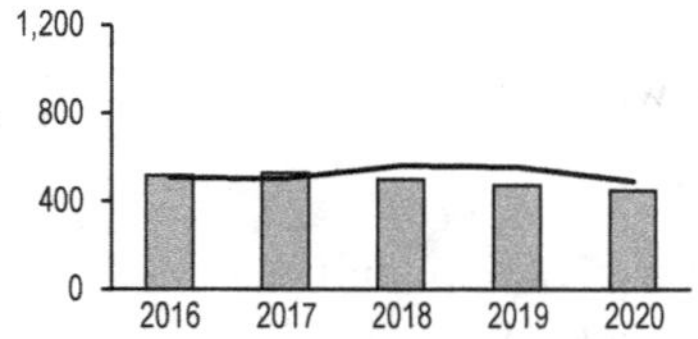

	2016	2017	2018	2019	2020
Greensboro	516	529	501	474	452
Average	505	504	560	555	490

Value of Building Permits as Percentage of Tax Base of Area Served

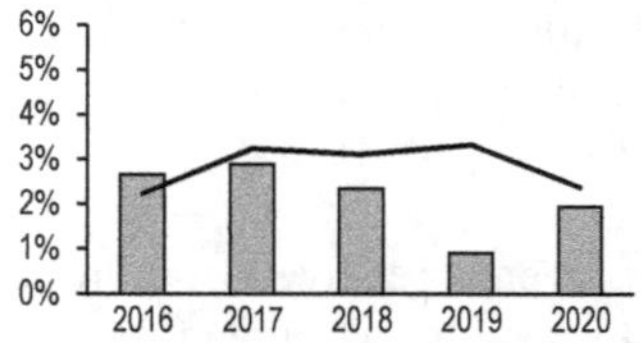

	2016	2017	2018	2019	2020
Greensboro	2.66%	2.89%	2.35%	0.90%	1.95%
Average	2.23%	3.23%	3.10%	3.32%	2.38%

Value of Commercial Permits as Percentage of Tax Base of Area Served

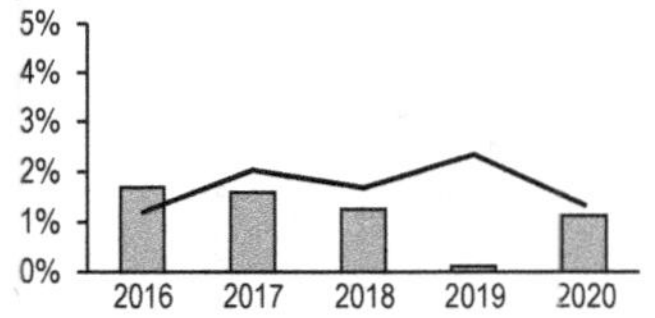

	2016	2017	2018	2019	2020
Greensboro	1.69%	1.59%	1.25%	0.11%	1.12%
Average	1.20%	2.02%	1.67%	2.33%	1.32%

Value of Building Permits per Inspector FTE in Millions of Dollars

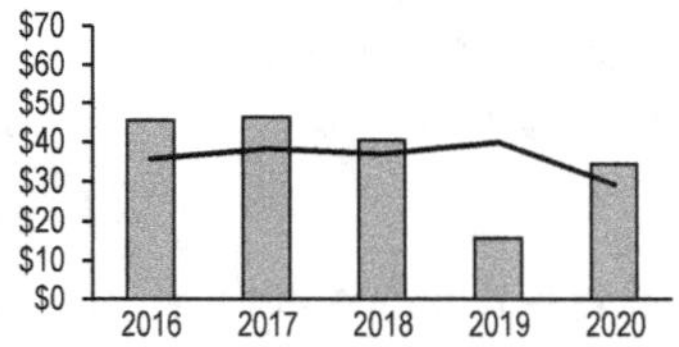

	2016	2017	2018	2019	2020
Greensboro	$45.4	$46.3	$40.5	$15.8	$34.4
Average	$35.6	$38.1	$36.9	$39.8	$29.3

Efficiency Measures

Building Services Cost per Inspection—All Types

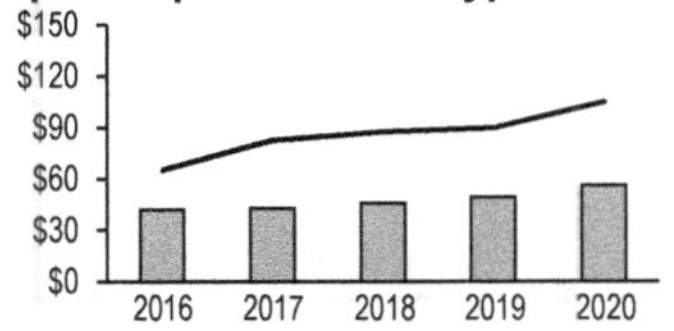

	2016	2017	2018	2019	2020
Greensboro	$41.90	$42.56	$45.90	$49.04	$56.08
Average	$64.77	$82.44	$87.41	$89.47	$104.76

Inspections per Day per Inspector FTE

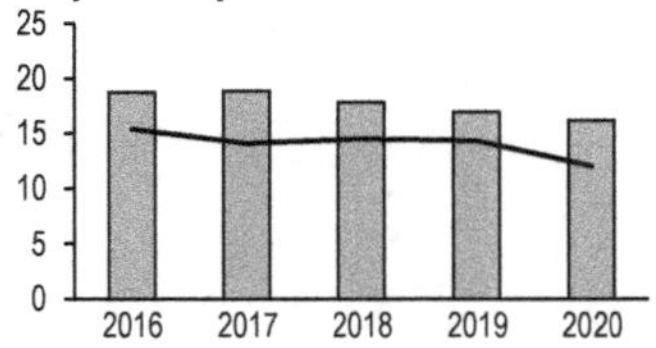

	2016	2017	2018	2019	2020
Greensboro	18.8	18.8	17.8	17.0	16.2
Average	15.4	14.1	14.5	14.3	12.0

Plan Reviews per Year per Reviewer FTE

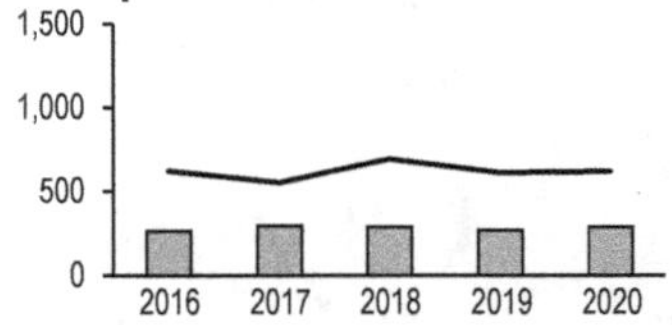

	2016	2017	2018	2019	2020
Greensboro	265	293	286	267	287
Average	620	552	690	608	617

Effectiveness Measures

Percentage of Inspection Responses within One Working Day of Request

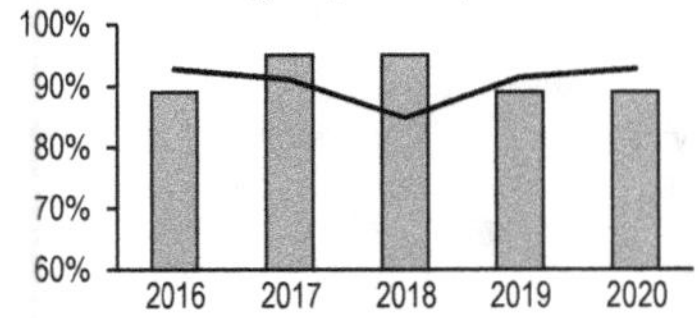

	2016	2017	2018	2019	2020
Greensboro	89.0%	95.0%	95.0%	89.0%	89.0%
Average	92.7%	91.1%	84.8%	91.4%	92.7%

Percentage of Inspections That Are Reinspections

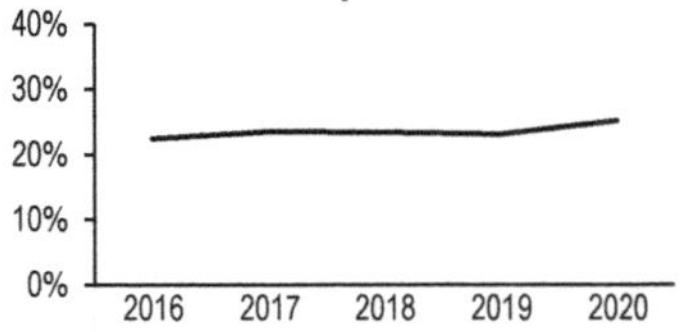

	2016	2017	2018	2019	2020
Greensboro					
Average	22.4%	23.4%	23.4%	23.1%	25.1%

Fiscal Year 2019-20

Explanatory Information

Service Level and Delivery

The City of Raleigh conducts building inspections through its Building and Safety Division of the Development Services Department. The Development Services Department serves the entire jurisdictional territory of the City of Raleigh.

Inspection services are currently provided by inspectors specializing in each of the major service trades as well as inspectors who cover all trades. A staff of plan reviewers and support specialists further the work in the division.

It is the policy of the inspection work team to respond to an inspection request within twenty-four hours for each type of construction. Most inspections are completed within one day of a request.

Total revenue received from inspection fees was $9.8 million for the fiscal year. Inspection and permit fees depend on the type of construction or work, the value of construction, and other factors. Reinspections are not charged for the first time. Reinspections of the same inspection item that has failed for a second time are subject to a reinspection fee.

Conditions Affecting Service, Performance, and Costs

Raleigh rejoined the Benchmarking Project in July 2016, with the first year of data showing for FY 2015–16.

The permit value of multifamily building projects is included in the totals for commercial projects.

Municipal Profile

Population Served	519,152
Land Area Inspected (Square Miles)	181.50
Persons per Square Mile	2,860
Estimated Tax Base in Service Area (billions)	$67.81
Median Household Income U.S. Census 2016	$46,612

Service Profile

FTE Inspectors	
Building	8.0
Electrical	10.0
Mechanical	7.0
Plumbing	5.0
All Trades	12.0
Total Inspectors	42.0
FTE Plan Reviewers	14.0
Other FTE Positions	24.0
Total of All Positions	80.0
Number of Inspections by Type	
Building	24,073
Electrical	33,669
Mechanical	23,479
Plumbing	15,791
TOTAL	97,012
Building Permit Values	
Residential	$332,617,463
Multifamily	with commercial
Commercial	$1,145,981,538
TOTAL	$1,478,599,001
Inspection Fee Revenue	$9,796,737

Full Cost Profile

Cost Breakdown by Percentage	
Personal Services	71.9%
Operating Costs	20.5%
Capital Costs	7.7%
TOTAL	100.0%
Cost Breakdown in Dollars	
Personal Services	$5,251,120
Operating Costs	$1,496,345
Capital Costs	$559,202
TOTAL	$7,306,667

Raleigh

Building Inspections

Key: Raleigh ▒ Benchmarking Average — Fiscal Years 2016 through 2020

Resource Measures

Building Inspections Services Costs per Capita

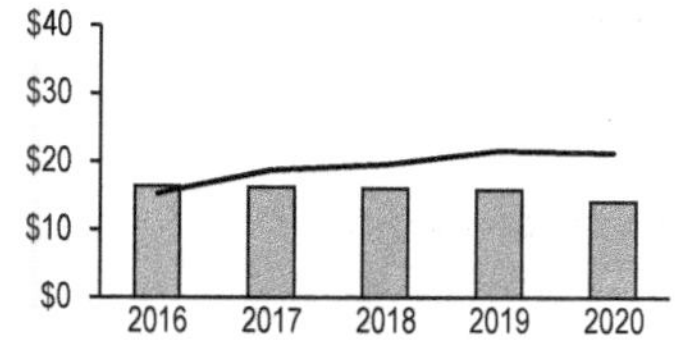

	2016	2017	2018	2019	2020
Raleigh	$16.32	$16.19	$15.95	$15.80	$14.07
Average	$15.18	$18.61	$19.55	$21.51	$21.21

Building Inspections Services FTEs per 10,000 Population

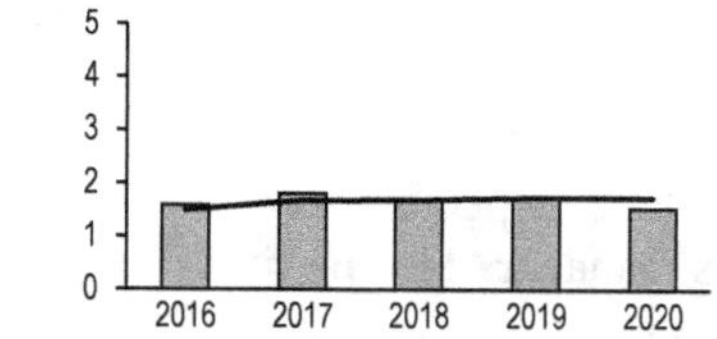

	2016	2017	2018	2019	2020
Raleigh	1.59	1.81	1.69	1.72	1.54
Average	1.48	1.66	1.68	1.73	1.73

Building Inspections Services Cost per Million Dollars of Tax Base

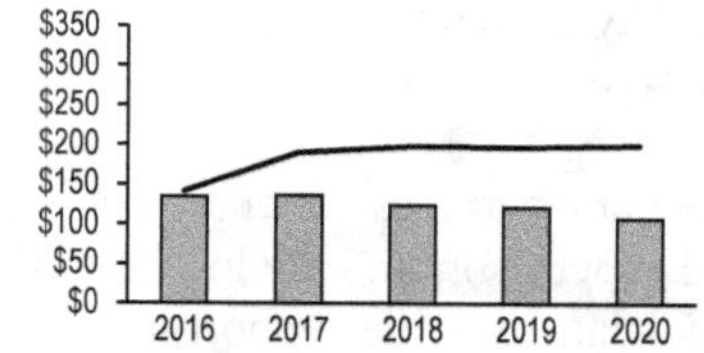

	2016	2017	2018	2019	2020
Raleigh	$134	$136	$124	$122	$108
Average	$141	$190	$197	$197	$199

Workload Measures

Inspections per 1,000 Population in Service Area

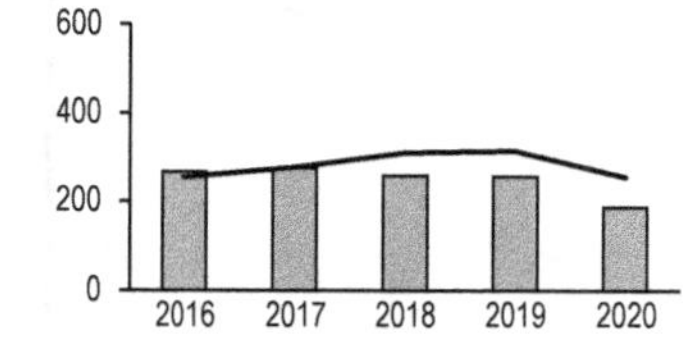

	2016	2017	2018	2019	2020
Raleigh	266	274	257	257	187
Average	253	277	309	314	255

Inspections per Square Mile in Service Area

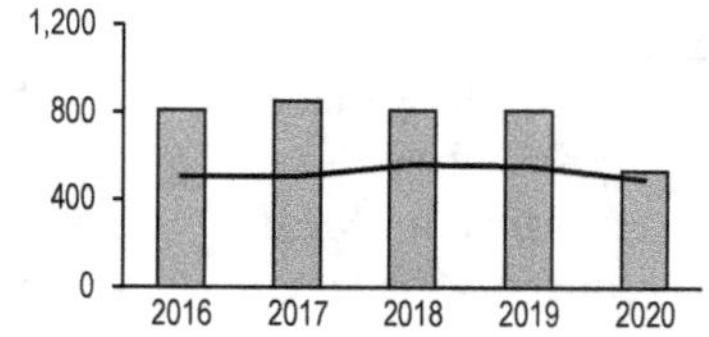

	2016	2017	2018	2019	2020
Raleigh	808	850	808	811	535
Average	505	504	560	555	490

Value of Building Permits as Percentage of Tax Base of Area Served

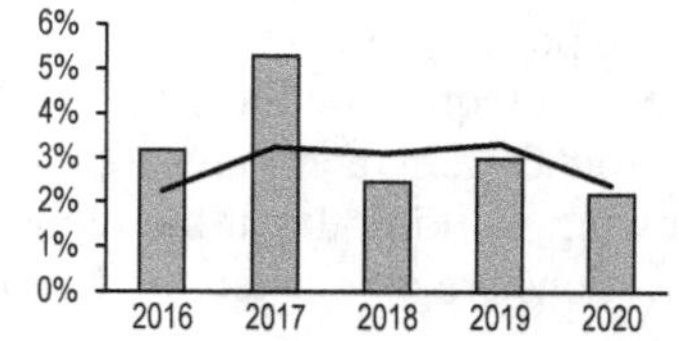

	2016	2017	2018	2019	2020
Raleigh	3.18%	5.29%	2.46%	2.98%	2.18%
Average	2.23%	3.23%	3.10%	3.32%	2.38%

Value of Commercial Permits as Percentage of Tax Base of Area Served

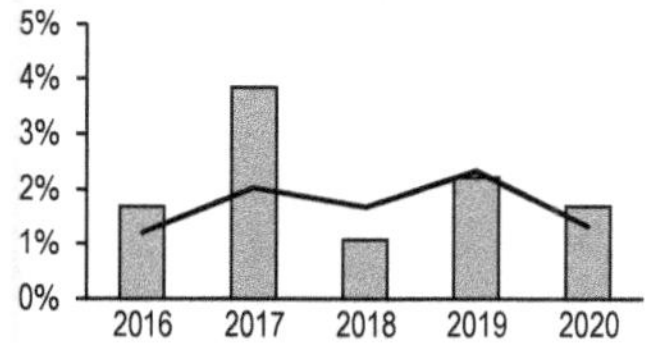

	2016	2017	2018	2019	2020
Raleigh	1.68%	3.83%	1.08%	2.22%	1.69%
Average	1.20%	2.02%	1.67%	2.33%	1.32%

Value of Building Permits per Inspector FTE in Millions of Dollars

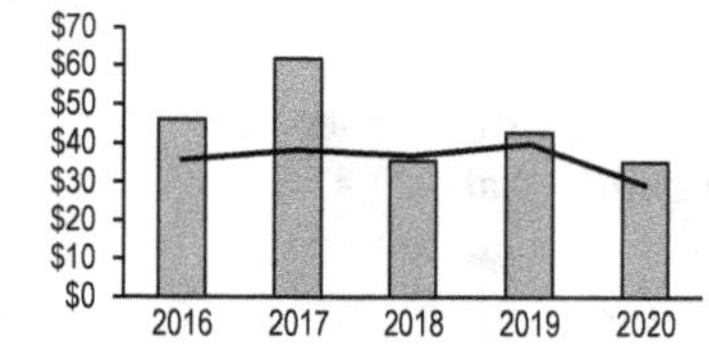

	2016	2017	2018	2019	2020
Raleigh	$46.0	$61.6	$35.5	$42.8	$35.2
Average	$35.6	$38.1	$36.9	$39.8	$29.3

Efficiency Measures

Building Services Cost per Inspection—All Types

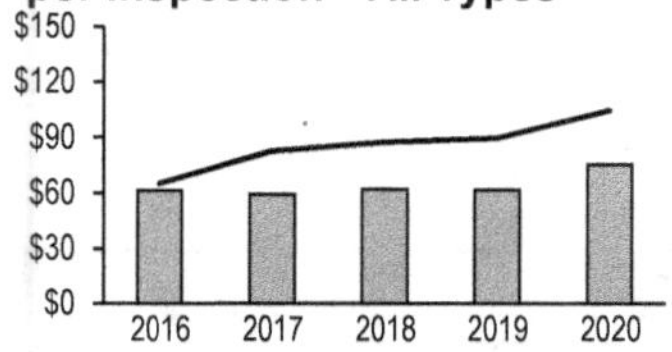

	2016	2017	2018	2019	2020
Raleigh	$61.30	$58.98	$62.01	$61.60	$75.32
Average	$64.77	$82.44	$87.41	$89.47	$104.76

Inspections per Day per Inspector FTE

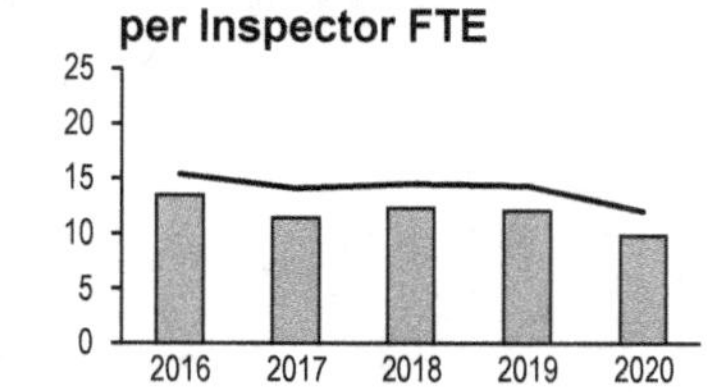

	2016	2017	2018	2019	2020
Raleigh	13.5	11.4	12.3	12.1	9.8
Average	15.4	14.1	14.5	14.3	12.0

Plan Reviews per Year per Reviewer FTE

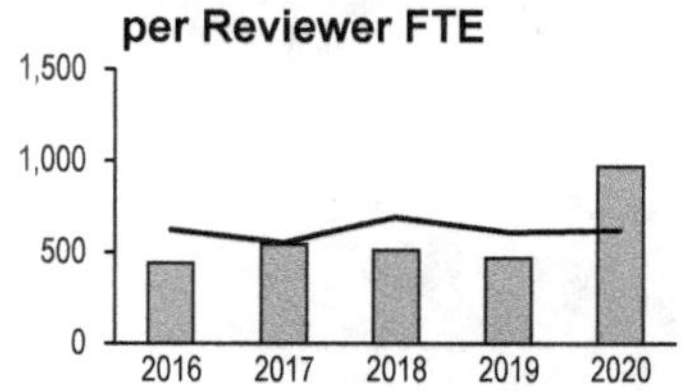

	2016	2017	2018	2019	2020
Raleigh	439	542	511	469	970
Average	620	552	690	608	617

Effectiveness Measures

Percentage of Inspection Responses within One Working Day of Request

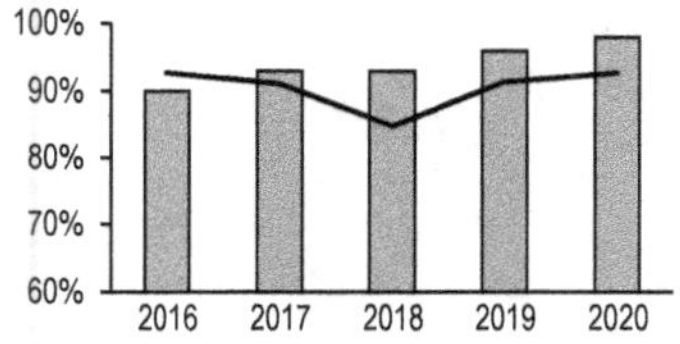

	2016	2017	2018	2019	2020
Raleigh	90.0%	93.0%	93.0%	96.0%	98.0%
Average	92.7%	91.1%	84.8%	91.4%	92.7%

Percentage of Inspections That Are Reinspections

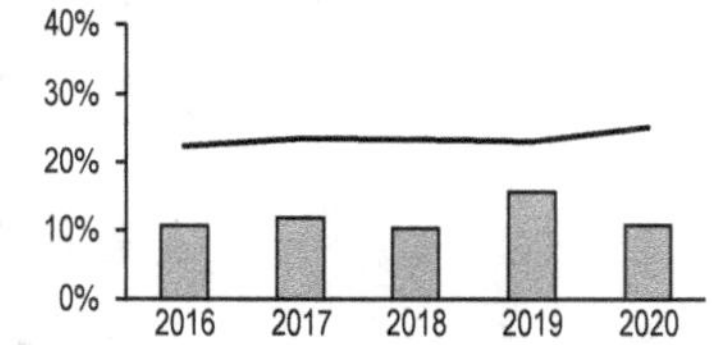

	2016	2017	2018	2019	2020
Raleigh	10.7%	11.8%	10.3%	15.6%	10.8%
Average	22.4%	23.4%	23.4%	23.1%	25.1%

Fiscal Year 2019-20

Explanatory Information

Service Level and Delivery
The City of Wilson's inspection team serves the area within the city's corporate.

Inspection services are currently provided by three inspectors, one field supervisor, and the inspections divisions manager. Two permit technicians provide support to this function. For commercial jobs, each inspector is assigned a primary inspection field. For residential jobs, inspectors hold certificates in all trade areas. Fire inspections are typically handled by certified inspectors in the fire department but are occasionally conducted by building inspectors who have fire inspection certification.

It is the policy of the inspection work team to respond to an inspection request on the same working day if the request is made prior to 8:30 a.m. and to respond to an inspection request by the following working day if the request is made after 8:30 a.m. Most inspections are completed on the same day the request is made.

Total revenue received from inspection fees was $315,291 for the fiscal year. Inspection and permit fees depend on the type of construction or work, the value of construction, and other factors. A reinspection fee is assessed when making an inspection for the same trade that had been previously rejected.

Conditions Affecting Service, Performance, and Costs
The broad downturn in the economy reduced building activity and the number of requests for inspections in the earlier years, but in FY 2018–19 activity in commercial buildings has picked up.

Municipal Profile

Population Served	49,384
Land Area Inspected (Square Miles)	31.92
Persons per Square Mile	1,547
Estimated Tax Base in Service Area (billions)	$4.21
Median Household Income U.S. Census 2016	$35,409

Service Profile

FTE Inspectors	
Building	0.0
Electrical	0.0
Mechanical	0.0
Plumbing	0.0
All Trades	4.0
Total Inspectors	4.0
FTE Plan Reviewers	1.0
Other FTE Positions	2.0
Total of All Positions	7.0
Number of Inspections by Type	
Building	2,384
Electrical	2,408
Mechanical	2,168
Plumbing	1,393
TOTAL	8,353
Building Permit Values	
Residential	$21,528,272
Multifamily	$9,694,000
Commercial	$67,409,536
TOTAL	$98,631,808
Inspection Fee Revenue	$315,291

Full Cost Profile

Cost Breakdown by Percentage	
Personal Services	76.7%
Operating Costs	17.0%
Capital Costs	6.4%
TOTAL	100.0%
Cost Breakdown in Dollars	
Personal Services	$731,404
Operating Costs	$161,776
Capital Costs	$60,819
TOTAL	$953,999

Key: Wilson ▒ Benchmarking Average — Fiscal Years 2016 through 2020

Resource Measures

Building Inspections Services Costs per Capita

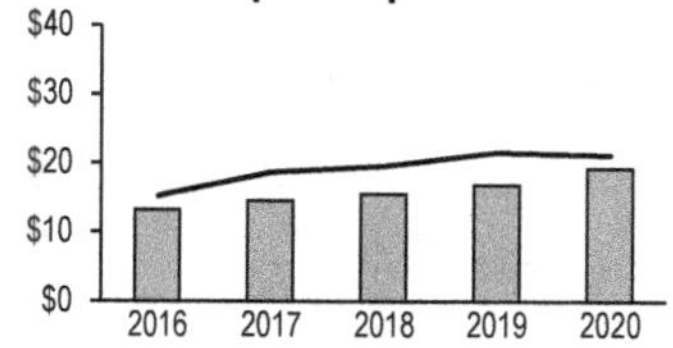

	2016	2017	2018	2019	2020
Wilson	$13.19	$14.56	$15.53	$16.82	$19.32
Average	$15.18	$18.61	$19.55	$21.51	$21.21

Building Inspections Services FTEs per 10,000 Population

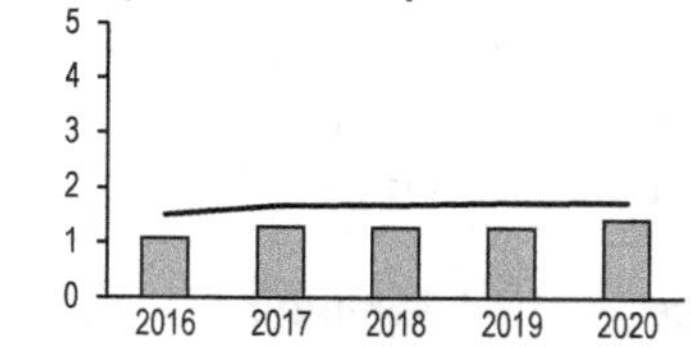

	2016	2017	2018	2019	2020
Wilson	1.07	1.28	1.27	1.27	1.42
Average	1.48	1.66	1.68	1.73	1.73

Building Inspections Services Cost per Million Dollars of Tax Base

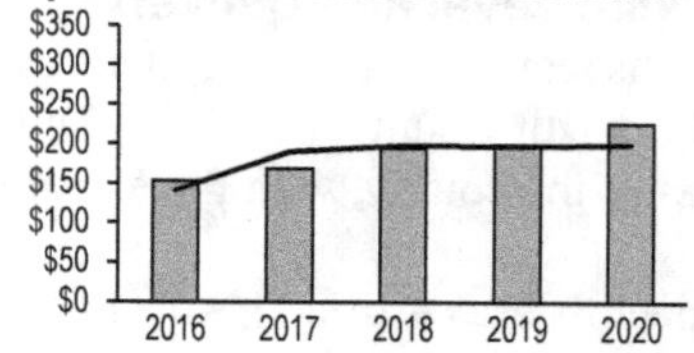

	2016	2017	2018	2019	2020
Wilson	$153	$169	$194	$200	$226
Average	$141	$190	$197	$197	$199

Workload Measures

Inspections per 1,000 Population in Service Area

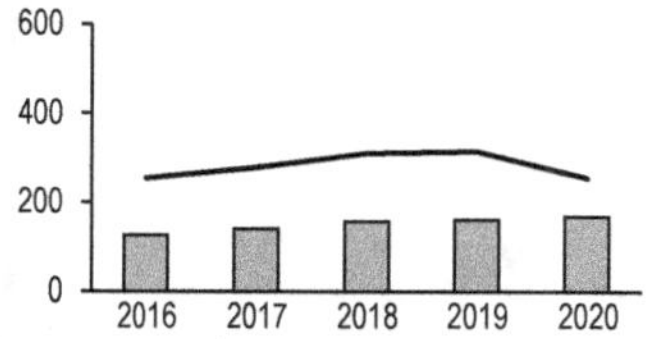

	2016	2017	2018	2019	2020
Wilson	126	139	157	162	169
Average	253	277	309	314	255

Inspections per Square Mile in Service Area

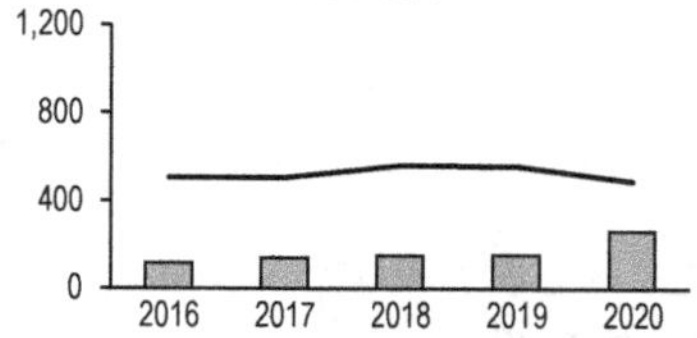

	2016	2017	2018	2019	2020
Wilson	114	138	148	152	262
Average	505	504	560	555	490

Value of Building Permits as Percentage of Tax Base of Area Served

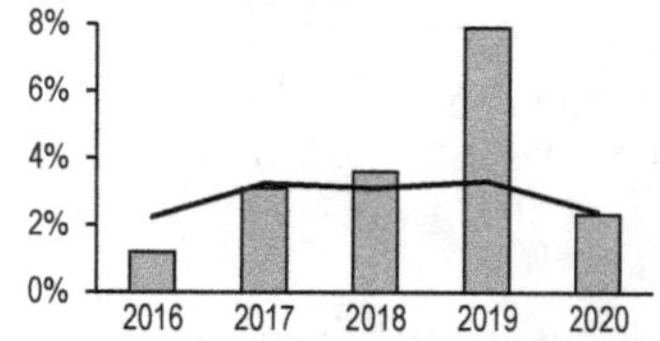

	2016	2017	2018	2019	2020
Wilson	1.17%	3.10%	3.60%	7.89%	2.34%
Average	2.23%	3.23%	3.10%	3.32%	2.38%

Value of Commercial Permits as Percentage of Tax Base of Area Served

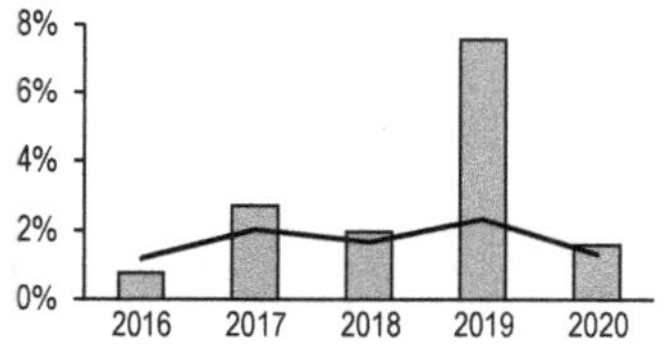

	2016	2017	2018	2019	2020
Wilson	0.78%	2.70%	1.96%	7.56%	1.60%
Average	1.20%	2.02%	1.67%	2.33%	1.32%

Value of Building Permits per Inspector FTE in Millions of Dollars

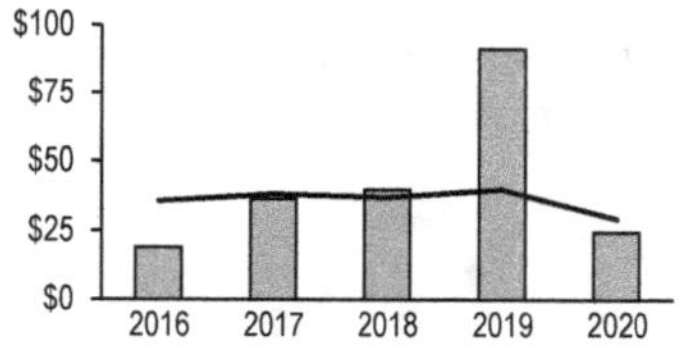

	2016	2017	2018	2019	2020
Wilson	$18.9	$36.5	$39.6	$91.2	$24.7
Average	$35.6	$38.1	$36.9	$39.8	$29.3

Efficiency Measures

Building Services Cost per Inspection—All Types

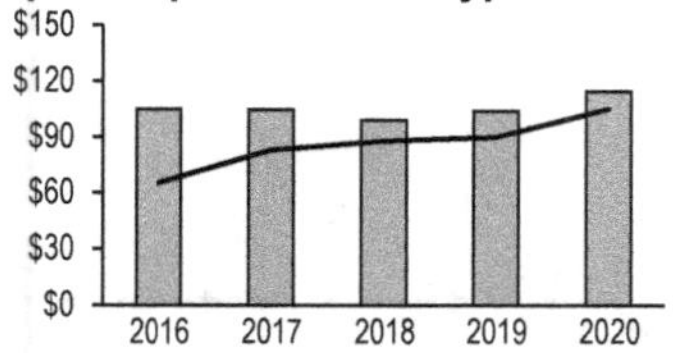

	2016	2017	2018	2019	2020
Wilson	$104.80	$104.40	$98.95	$103.92	$114.21
Average	$64.77	$82.44	$87.41	$89.47	$104.76

Inspections per Day per Inspector FTE

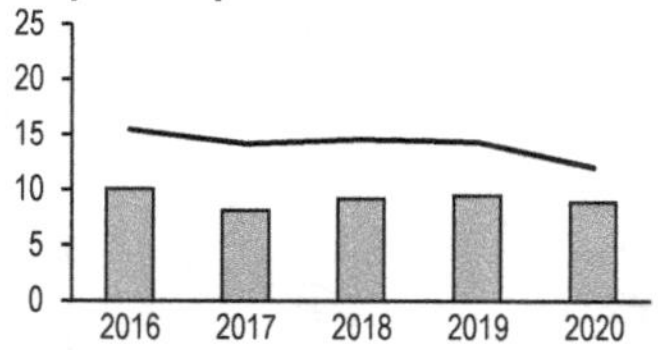

	2016	2017	2018	2019	2020
Wilson	10.0	8.1	9.2	9.5	8.9
Average	15.4	14.1	14.5	14.3	12.0

Plan Reviews per Year per Reviewer FTE

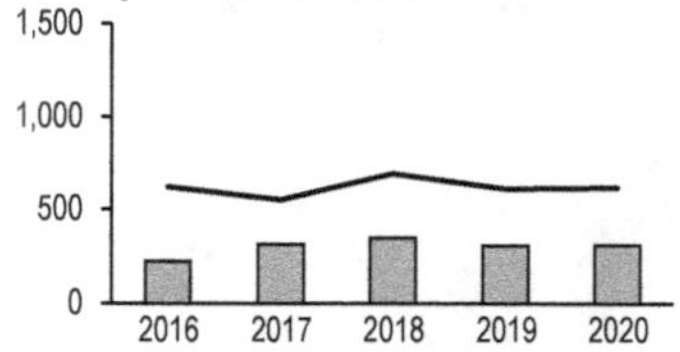

	2016	2017	2018	2019	2020
Wilson	222	313	350	306	311
Average	620	552	690	608	617

Effectiveness Measures

Percentage of Inspection Responses within One Working Day of Request

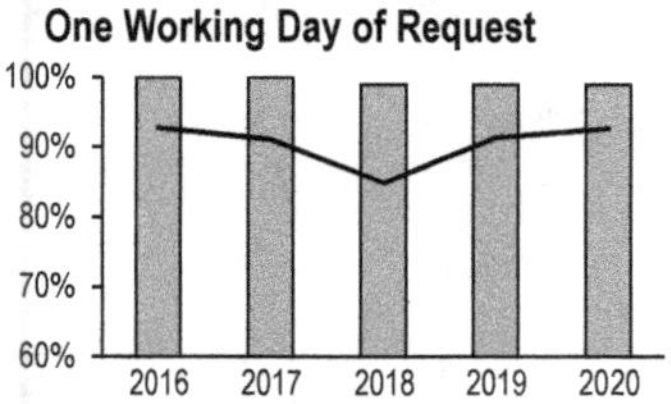

	2016	2017	2018	2019	2020
Wilson	100.0%	100.0%	99.0%	99.0%	99.0%
Average	92.7%	91.1%	84.8%	91.4%	92.7%

Percentage of Inspections That Are Reinspections

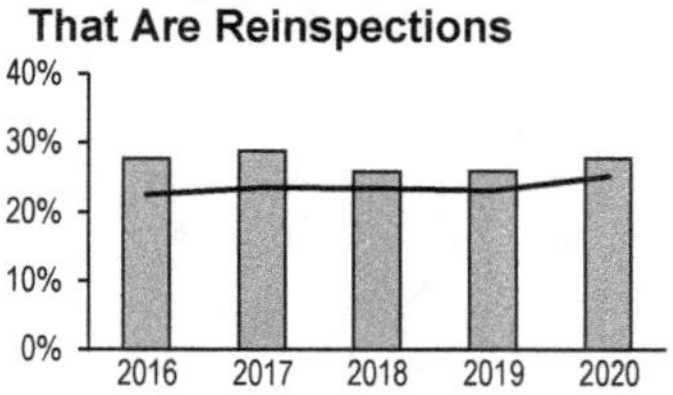

	2016	2017	2018	2019	2020
Wilson	27.7%	28.8%	25.8%	25.9%	27.8%
Average	22.4%	23.4%	23.4%	23.1%	25.1%

Fiscal Year 2019-20

Explanatory Information

Service Level and Delivery

The Inspections Division is a combined program for Winston-Salem and Forsyth County, providing building inspections services for all areas of the county, with the exception of the Town of Kernersville.

Inspectors are certified in one of the following four trades: building, electrical, mechanical, or plumbing. Inspectors drive to and from inspection sites in city-owned vehicles. Besides the North Carolina State Building Code, the Inspections Division enforces zoning codes and soil and sedimentation control regulations. Full-time equivalent positions and costs for these responsibilities are excluded from the project's figures for building inspections.

It is the policy of the Inspections Division to respond to inspection requests within one working day; 90 percent of the time it achieves this goal.

Total revenue received from inspection fees amounted to $4.2 million for the fiscal year. Inspection and permit fees depend on the type of construction or work, value of the construction, and other factors. An extra trip charge of $40 is assessed for each reinspection due to a second and subsequent failed inspection on each permit.

Conditions Affecting Service, Performance, and Costs

Municipal Profile

Population Served	352,157
Land Area Inspected (Square Miles)	396.00
Persons per Square Mile	889
Estimated Tax Base in Service Area (billions)	$34.47
Median Household Income U.S. Census 2016	$40,584

Service Profile

FTE Inspectors	
Building	4.0
Electrical	5.0
Mechanical	6.0
Plumbing	3.0
All Trades	0.0
Total Inspectors	18.0
FTE Plan Reviewers	3.0
Other FTE Positions	17.4
Total of All Positions	38.4
Number of Inspections by Type	
Building	16,832
Electrical	23,209
Mechanical	17,092
Plumbing	12,910
TOTAL	70,043
Building Permit Values	
Residential	$252,943,207
Multifamily	with residential
Commercial	$287,419,415
TOTAL	$540,362,622
Inspection Fee Revenue	$4,248,799

Full Cost Profile

Cost Breakdown by Percentage	
Personal Services	64.3%
Operating Costs	28.1%
Capital Costs	7.6%
TOTAL	100.0%
Cost Breakdown in Dollars	
Personal Services	$2,742,324
Operating Costs	$1,199,281
Capital Costs	$324,785
TOTAL	$4,266,390

Winston-Salem — Building Inspections

Key: Winston-Salem ■ Benchmarking Average — Fiscal Years 2016 through 2020

Resource Measures

Building Inspections Services Costs per Capita

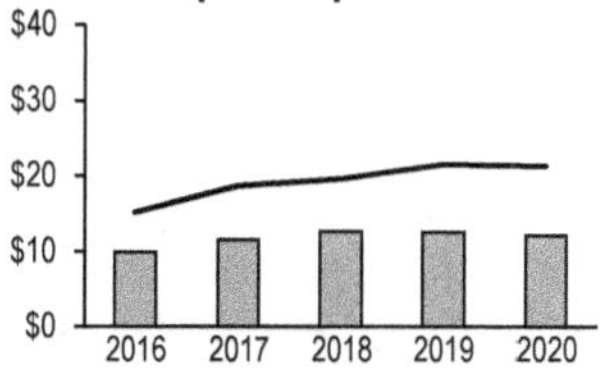

	2016	2017	2018	2019	2020
Winston-Salem	$9.93	$11.53	$12.62	$12.51	$12.12
Average	$15.18	$18.61	$19.55	$21.51	$21.21

Building Inspections Services FTEs per 10,000 Population

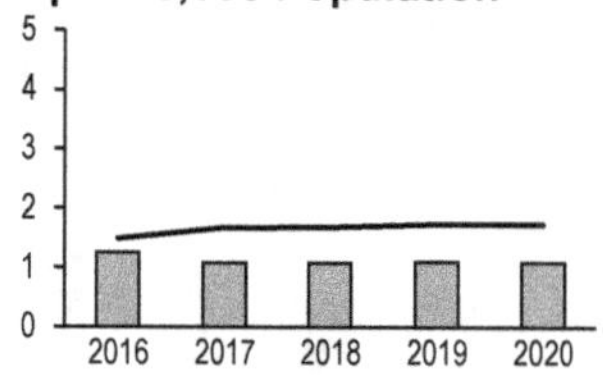

	2016	2017	2018	2019	2020
Winston-Salem	1.26	1.08	1.08	1.10	1.09
Average	1.48	1.66	1.68	1.73	1.73

Building Inspections Services Cost per Million Dollars of Tax Base

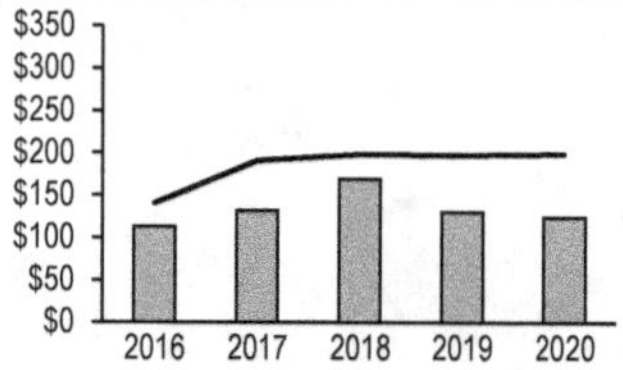

	2016	2017	2018	2019	2020
Winston-Salem	$112	$131	$169	$130	$124
Average	$141	$190	$197	$197	$199

Workload Measures

Inspections per 1,000 Population in Service Area

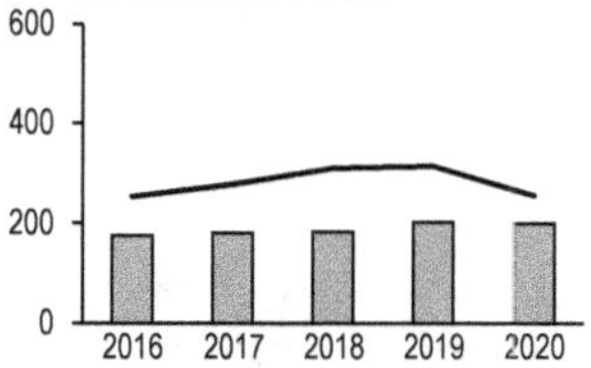

	2016	2017	2018	2019	2020
Winston-Salem	175	179	182	202	199
Average	253	277	309	314	255

Inspections per Square Mile in Service Area

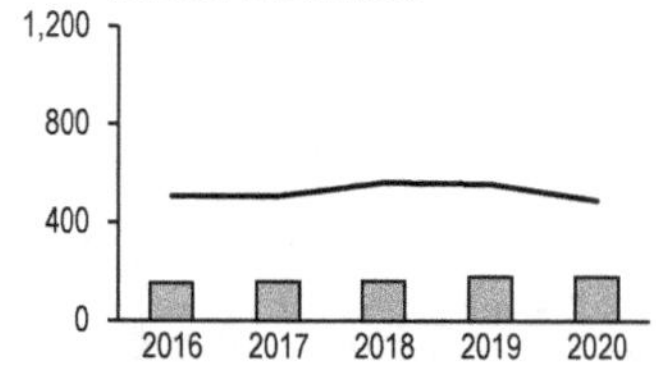

	2016	2017	2018	2019	2020
Winston-Salem	152	156	161	178	177
Average	505	504	560	555	490

Value of Building Permits as Percentage of Tax Base of Area Served

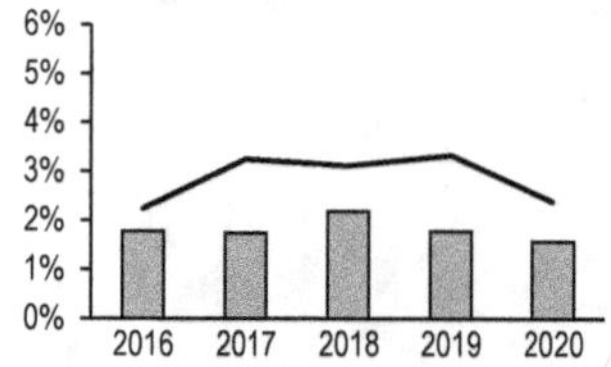

	2016	2017	2018	2019	2020
Winston-Salem	1.77%	1.73%	2.18%	1.77%	1.57%
Average	2.23%	3.23%	3.10%	3.32%	2.38%

Value of Commercial Permits as Percentage of Tax Base of Area Served

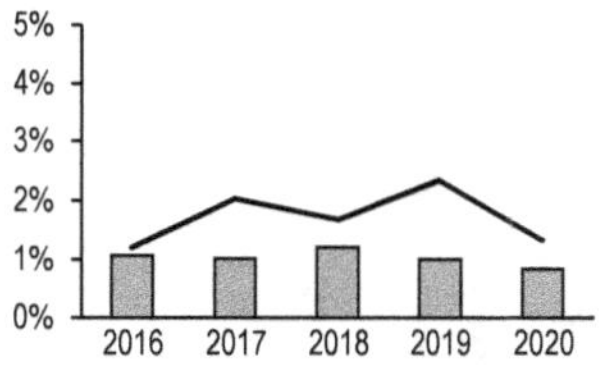

	2016	2017	2018	2019	2020
Winston-Salem	1.06%	1.00%	1.20%	1.00%	0.83%
Average	1.20%	2.02%	1.67%	2.33%	1.32%

Value of Building Permits per Inspector FTE in Millions of Dollars

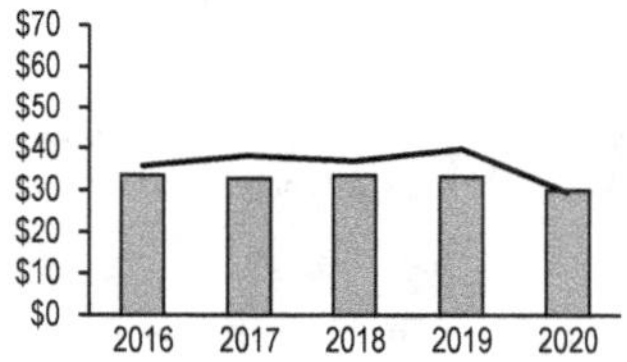

	2016	2017	2018	2019	2020
Winston-Salem	$33.4	$32.7	$33.4	$33.2	$30.0
Average	$35.6	$38.1	$36.9	$39.8	$29.3

Efficiency Measures

Building Services Cost per Inspection—All Types

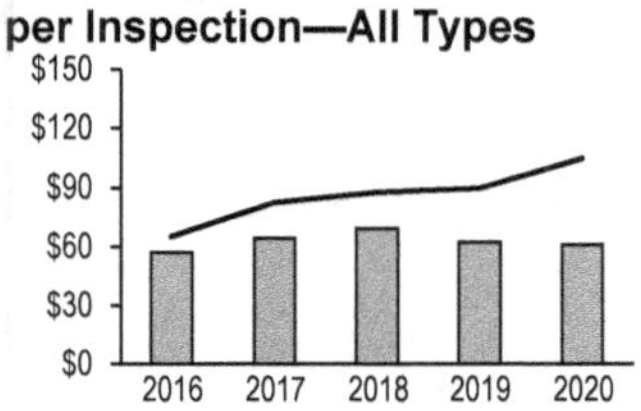

	2016	2017	2018	2019	2020
Winston-Salem	$56.83	$64.31	$69.18	$62.07	$60.91
Average	$64.77	$82.44	$87.41	$89.47	$104.76

Inspections per Day per Inspector FTE

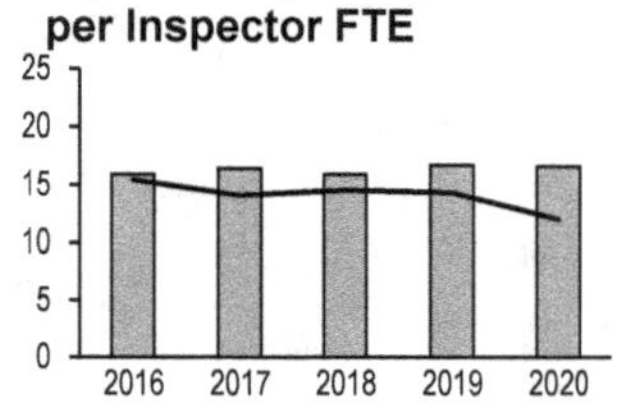

	2016	2017	2018	2019	2020
Winston-Salem	15.9	16.4	15.9	16.7	16.6
Average	15.4	14.1	14.5	14.3	12.0

Plan Reviews per Year per Reviewer FTE

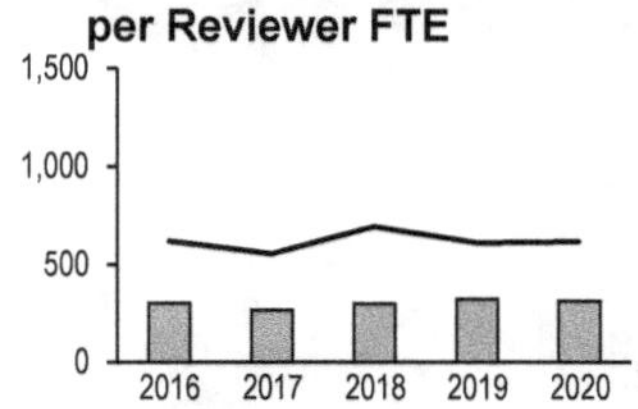

	2016	2017	2018	2019	2020
Winston-Salem	304	266	298	324	312
Average	620	552	690	608	617

Effectiveness Measures

Percentage of Inspection Responses within One Working Day of Request

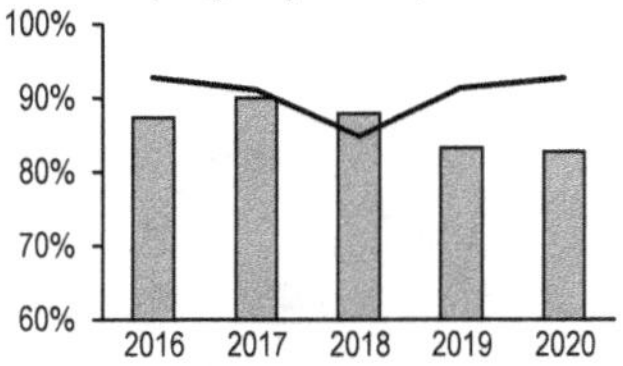

	2016	2017	2018	2019	2020
Winston-Salem	87.4%	90.1%	87.9%	83.3%	82.8%
Average	92.7%	91.1%	84.8%	91.4%	92.7%

Percentage of Inspections That Are Reinspections

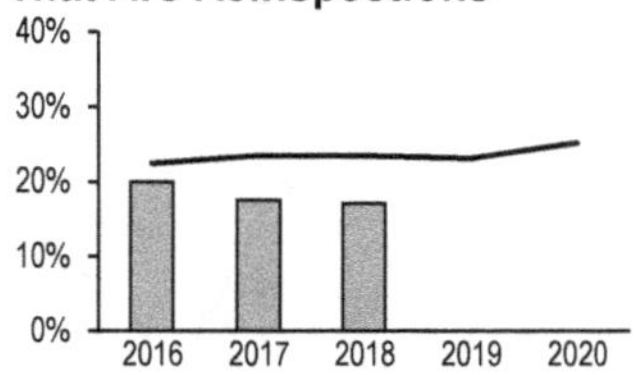

	2016	2017	2018	2019	2020
Winston-Salem	20.0%	17.6%	17.1%		
Average	22.4%	23.4%	23.4%	23.1%	25.1%

SCHOOL OF GOVERNMENT
North Carolina Benchmarking Project

Performance and Cost Data

FLEET MAINTENANCE

SCHOOL OF GOVERNMENT

North Carolina Benchmarking Project

PERFORMANCE MEASURES FOR FLEET MAINTENANCE

SERVICE DEFINITION

Fleet Maintenance represents the scheduled and unscheduled maintenance of rolling stock performed by the central garage and contractual work assigned by the central garage. This includes preventive, predictive, corrective, and breakdown maintenance. Excluded from this definition are rolling stock not maintained by the central garage and the broader activities of fleet services, such as rolling stock replacement and disposal, fuel station operation, and pool vehicle management.

NOTES ON PERFORMANCE MEASURES

1. Number of Vehicle Equivalent Units (VEUs) per Technician FTE

Vehicle Equivalent Units (VEUs) are a weighted measure of the maintenance effort associated with different classes of vehicles. A normal-use car is considered equal to one VEU. Vehicles such as fire trucks or police cars have higher VEUs, reflecting greater expected levels of maintenance effort. The number of VEUs in a municipality is determined by taking the number of rolling stock units in different classes of vehicles and multiplying them by a class weight for that category of vehicle. Vehicle categories include cars; light, medium, and heavy vehicles; trailed equipment; off-road/construction/tractor units; and buses. The number of full-time equivalent (FTE) positions for technicians is the number of employees directly involved in providing the maintenance services for the municipality's rolling stock as approved in the annual operating budget for the fiscal year.

2. Number of Preventive Maintenances Completed In-House per Technician FTE

The number of preventive maintenance jobs (PMs) completed in-house is the total number completed for the fiscal year ending June 30 that are done by the municipality's staff. The number of FTE positions for technicians is the same as defined above.

3. Cost per Work Order

This measure represents the total cost of fleet maintenance and is calculated using the full cost accounting model that captures direct, indirect, and capital costs. Work orders include the total number of work orders produced, including those related to contractual work, for the fiscal year ending June 30.

4. Cost per Vehicle Equivalent Unit (VEU)

This measure represents the total cost of fleet maintenance and is calculated using the full cost accounting model that captures direct, indirect, and capital costs. VEUs are calculated as defined above for the fiscal year ending June 30.

5. Hours Billed as a Percentage of Total Hours
The total number of billable hours includes all hours for technicians available for work during the fiscal year. Billable hours are calculated by multiplying 2,080 (hours in a normal working year) by the number of FTE positions for technicians as defined above. However, this number of FTEs is adjusted for vacancies. Hours billed represents actual hours billed during the fiscal year by the central garage to departments, divisions, and programs.

5. Preventive Maintenances (PMs) as a Percentage of All Work Orders
This measure is based on the total number of PMs (done in-house or by outside contractors) completed during the fiscal year divided by the total number of work orders (including contractual work) completed during the fiscal year for that jurisdiction.

7. Percentage of PMs Completed on Schedule
Based on the total number of PMs as defined above, this measure represents the percentage of PMs completed as scheduled as defined by the respective jurisdiction's standards.

8. Percentage of Work Orders Completed within Twenty-Four Hours
Based on the total number of work orders as defined above, this measure represents the percentage of work orders completed during the fiscal year within twenty-four hours of being received.

9. Percentage of Rolling Stock Available per Day
Based on the total number of rolling stock units as defined above, this measure represents the average percentage of rolling stock available for use per working day of the jurisdiction.

10. Percentage of Work Orders Requiring Repeat Repair within Thirty Days
Based on the total number of work orders as defined above, this measure represents the percentage of work orders (completed work on a unit of rolling stock) requiring repeat repair for the same problem within thirty days.

Fleet Maintenance

Summary of Key Dimensions of Service

City or Town	Number of Rolling Stock Maintained	Average Age of Rolling Stock (in Years)	Number of Work Orders	Number of Preventive Maintenances	Number of Work Bays	Authorized Technician FTEs	Labor Rate (per Hour)	Fund Type
Apex	500	4.4	1,874	1,266	6	4.0	NA	General Fund
Chapel Hill	354	9.2	1,482	503	10	5.5	$100.00	Internal Service
Charlotte	4,191	6.6	39,787	14,427	90	78.0	$80.75	General Fund
Concord	995	7.6	3,889	1,842	8	8.0	$60.00	General Fund
Goldsboro	549	9.2	3,389	818	11	7.0	$13.50	General Fund
Greensboro	1,697	6.6	11,265	5,061	34	32.0	$65.00	Internal Service
Hickory	556	9.4	5,354	1,252	14	6.0	$60.00	Internal Service
Raleigh	2,713	6.4	23,453	8,038	51	46.0	Heavy&Lead Mech - $72, Motor Mech - $72, Welder - $44, Auto Specialist - $44, Auto Tire-$44, PM Tech - $44	Internal Service
Wilson	884	11.0	6,639	1,646	15	11.0	$44.00	General Fund
Winston-Salem	1,889	7.5	10,401	2,379	30	19.0	$50.00	Internal Service

EXPLANATORY FACTORS

These are factors that the project found affected fleet maintenance performance and cost in one or more of the municipalities:

Number of vehicles maintained
Types of vehicles maintained
Fleet replacement plan
Average age of vehicles by type
Average miles driven for each type of vehicle
Preventive maintenance classification system
Preventive maintenance schedule

Fiscal Year 2019-20

Explanatory Information

Service Level and Delivery

Fleet Services is a division of the Facility and Fleet Services Department in the Town of Apex. The activities for this operation are accounted for in the general fund.

The town does not charge departments for labor but does track time technicians spend on work orders. There is no charge to departments for parts or sublet work. Parts inventory turned over approximately nine times during the fiscal year.

The following services were contracted out:

- transmission repairs
- extended repair order work
- major engine repairs
- body work
- EMS ambulance body service work
- electric line truck repairs
- major hydraulic cylinder repairs
- fire truck pump repairs.

Conditions Affecting Service, Performance, and Costs

Vehicle Equivalent Units (VEUs) are a weighted measure of the maintenance effort associated with different classes of vehicles. A normal-use car is considered equal to one VEU. Vehicles such as fire trucks or police cars have higher VEUs, reflecting greater expected levels of maintenance.

The measure "hours billed as a percentage of total hours" is based on a work year of 2,080 hours and only counts those positions that were filled. It should be noted that technicians have responsibilities that do not result in billable hours, and they take normal vacation and sick leave. Therefore, this percentage should not be expected to be near 100 percent.

In Apex the preventive maintenance (PM) completion standard for "percentage of PMs completed as scheduled" is within thirty days of the scheduled date or within mileage parameters.

In addition to rolling stock, Apex's fleet services has maintenance responsibilities for other pieces of equipment, including asphalt rollers, whacker and roller tamps, portable generators, ballfield conditioners, various types of ATVs, weedeaters, lawnmowers, chainsaws, sump pumps, water pumps, snow plows, flail mowers, boat motors, light towers, and stump grinders.

The Apex Fleet Services supervisor provides technician support on an as needed basis.

Municipal Profile

Population (OSBM 2019)	61,319
Land Area (Square Miles)	23.61
Persons per Square Mile	2,597

Service Profile

FTE Positions—Technician	4.0
FTE Positions—Other	1.5
Work Bays	6

Rolling Stock Maintained	No.	Average Age
Cars—Normal Usage	28	8.1 Years
Cars—Severe Usage	102	3.6 Years
Motorcycles	3	7.0 Years
Light Utility Vehicles	13	10.0 Years
Light Vehicles	138	6.4 Years
Medium Vehicles	20	9.5 Years
Heavy—Sanitation	3	8.6 Years
Heavy—Sewer	3	5.7 Years
Heavy—Fire Apparatus	12	10.7 Years
Heavy—Other	27	8.9 Years
Trailed Equipment	83	NA
Off-Road/Construction/Tractors	68	NA
Buses	0	NA
TOTAL	500	

Vehicle Equivalent Units (VEUs)	1,415
Average Rolling Stock Units Available per Day	492
Hours Billed	5,378
Work Orders	1,874
Repeat Repairs within 30 Days	6
Work Orders Completed within 24 hours	1,592
Preventive Maintenance Jobs (PMs)	1,266
PMs Completed as Scheduled	1,135

Full Cost Profile

Cost Breakdown by Percentage	
Personal Services	31.0%
Operating Costs	58.1%
Capital Costs	10.9%
TOTAL	100.0%

Cost Breakdown in Dollars	
Personal Services	$385,704
Operating Costs	$723,761
Capital Costs	$135,245
TOTAL	$1,244,710

Key: Apex ■ Benchmarking Average — Fiscal Years 2016 through 2020

Resource Measures

Fleet Maintenance Services Cost per Capita

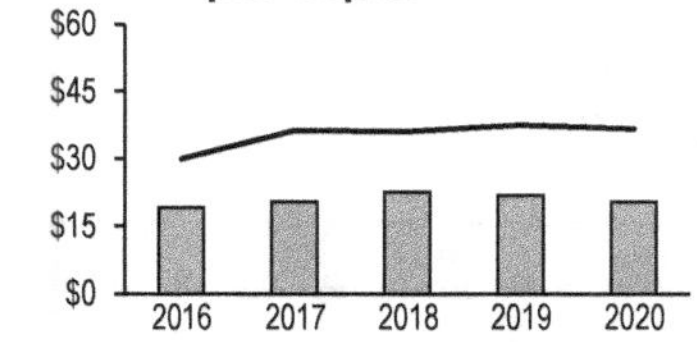

	2016	2017	2018	2019	2020
Apex	$18.99	$20.38	$22.49	$21.77	$20.30
Average	$29.83	$36.10	$36.06	$37.55	$36.51

Fleet Maintenance FTEs per 10,000 Population

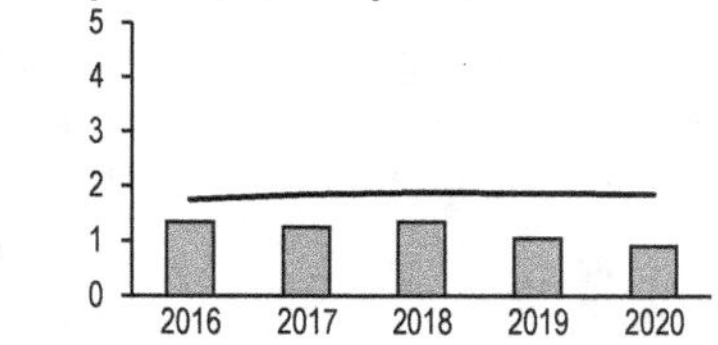

	2016	2017	2018	2019	2020
Apex	1.34	1.24	1.34	1.04	0.90
Average	1.74	1.83	1.88	1.85	1.85

Fleet Maintenance FTEs per 100 Municipal Employees

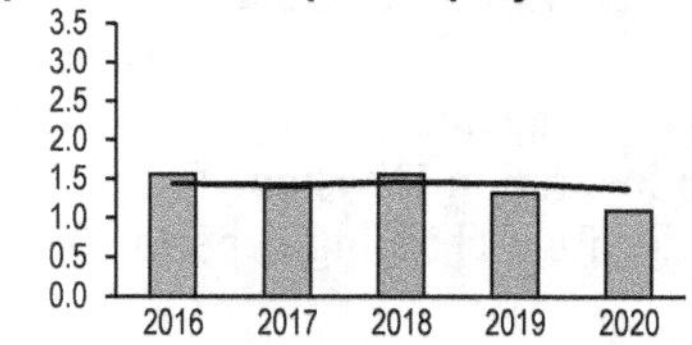

	2016	2017	2018	2019	2020
Apex	1.55	1.39	1.56	1.32	1.09
Average	1.43	1.42	1.45	1.44	1.37

Workload Measures

Number of Vehicle Equivalent Units (VEUs) per Technician FTE

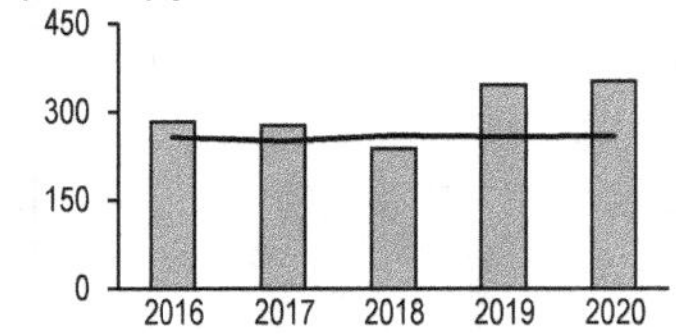

	2016	2017	2018	2019	2020
Apex	284	277	238	347	354
Average	256	249	259	257	258

Preventive Maintenances (PMs) Completed In-House per Tech FTE

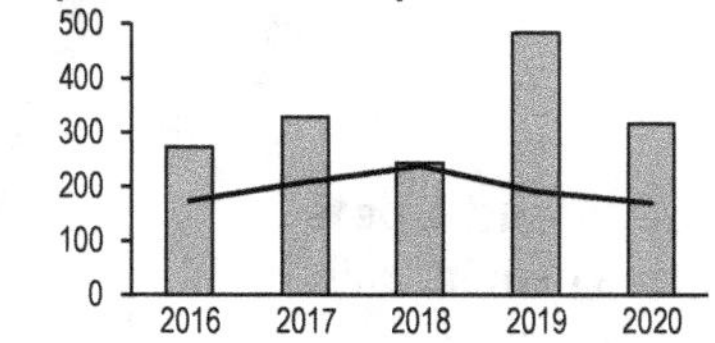

	2016	2017	2018	2019	2020
Apex	273	328	243	484	316
Average	173	207	237	191	170

Efficiency Measures

Fleet Maintenance Cost per Work Order

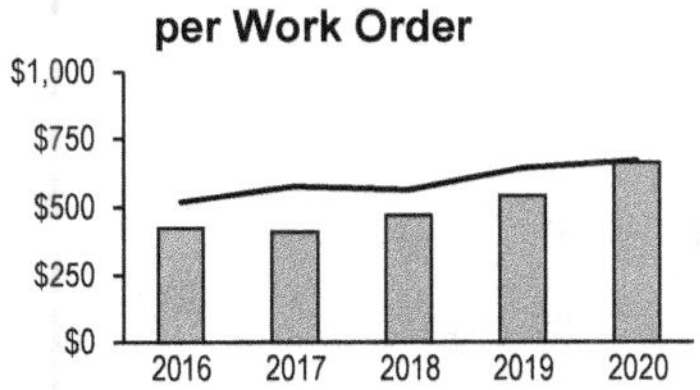

	2016	2017	2018	2019	2020
Apex	$425	$411	$471	$544	$664
Average	$520	$577	$564	$642	$670

Fleet Maintenance Cost per Vehicle Equivalent Unit (VEU)

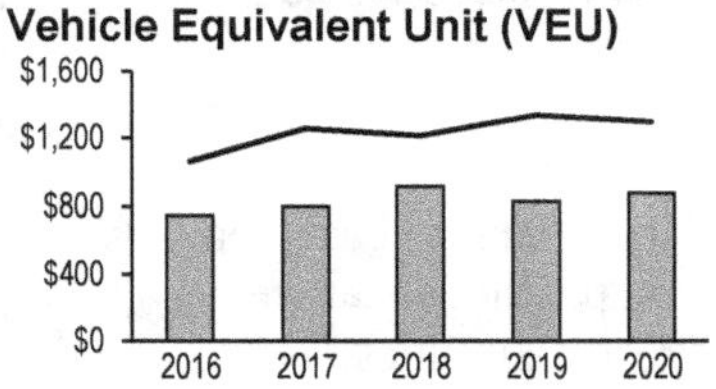

	2016	2017	2018	2019	2020
Apex	$749	$800	$917	$830	$880
Average	$1,060	$1,254	$1,212	$1,334	$1,297

Hours Billed as a Percentage of Total Hours

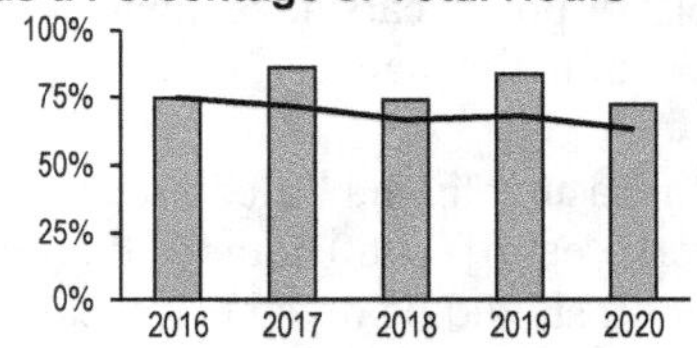

	2016	2017	2018	2019	2020
Apex	74%	86%	74%	84%	72%
Average	74%	72%	67%	68%	63%

Effectiveness Measures

Preventive Maintenances (PMs) as a Percentage of All Work Orders

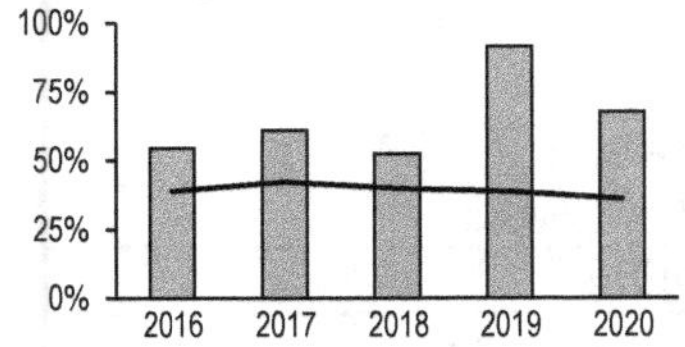

	2016	2017	2018	2019	2020
Apex	54%	61%	52%	91%	68%
Average	39%	42%	40%	39%	36%

Percentage of Preventive Maintenances (PMs) Completed as Scheduled

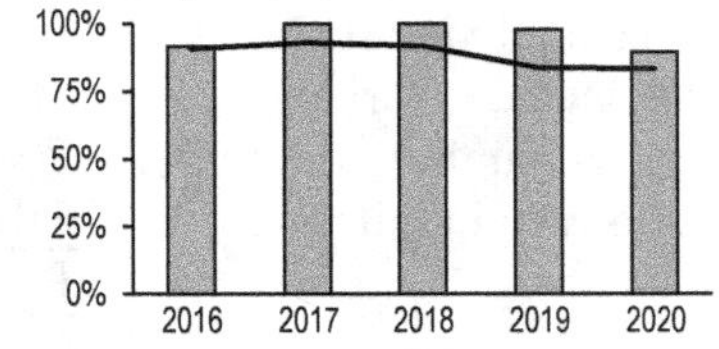

	2016	2017	2018	2019	2020
Apex	92%	100%	100%	98%	90%
Average	91%	93%	92%	84%	83%

Percentage of Work Orders Completed within 24 Hours

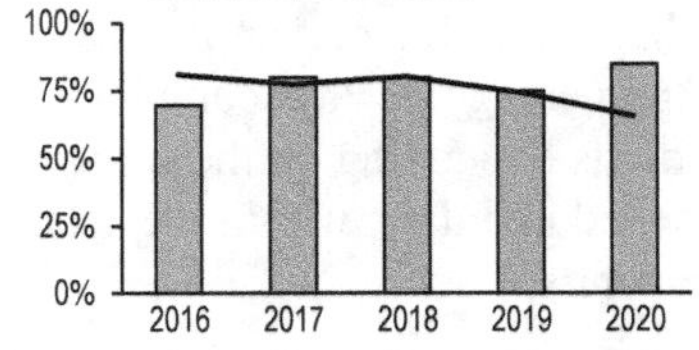

	2016	2017	2018	2019	2020
Apex	70%	80%	80%	75%	85%
Average	81%	77%	80%	74%	65%

Percentage of Rolling Stock Available per Day

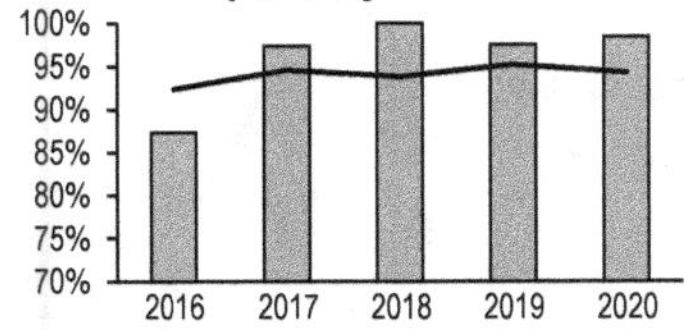

	2016	2017	2018	2019	2020
Apex	87%	97%	100%	97%	98%
Average	92%	95%	94%	95%	94%

Percentage of Work Orders Requiring Repeat Repair within 30 Days

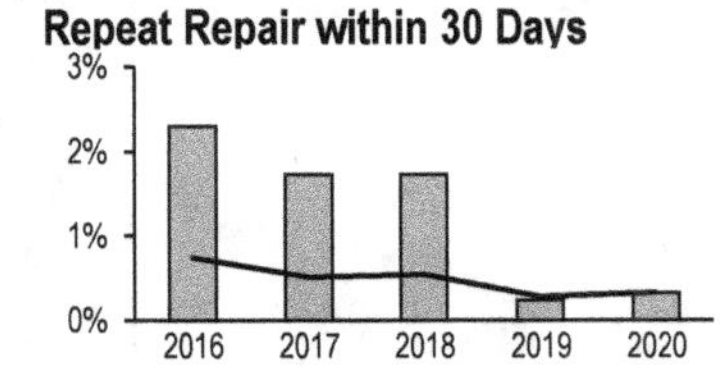

	2016	2017	2018	2019	2020
Apex	2.30%	1.73%	1.73%	0.24%	0.32%
Average	0.74%	0.50%	0.53%	0.28%	0.32%

Fiscal Year 2019-20

Explanatory Information

Service Level and Delivery

The Town of Chapel Hill provides fleet maintenance through the Fleet Management Program in the Public Works Department Administration Division. The program is operated as an internal service fund charging departments for services.

A labor rate of $100 per hour is charged for maintenance work. Additionally, a parts markup of 15 percent is applied to the cost of parts, and a 10 percent markup is charged for overseeing sublet work.

The town contracted out some maintenance services during the fiscal year, including towing, body work, lift truck inspections, and parts inventory. The overall turnover in parts was estimated at three times per year.

Conditions Affecting Service, Performance, and Costs

Chapel Hill improved its tracking of repeat repairs to more closely follow the benchmarking directions of repairs to the same component, as opposed to repairs to address the same complaint.

Vehicle Equivalent Units (VEUs) are a weighted measure of the maintenance effort associated with different classes of vehicles. A normal-use car is considered equal to one VEU. Vehicles such as fire trucks or police cars have higher VEUs, reflecting greater expected levels of maintenance.

The measure "hours billed as a percentage of total hours" is based on a work year of 2,080 hours and only counts those positions that were filled. It should be noted that technicians have responsibilities that do not result in billable hours, and they take normal vacation and sick leave. Therefore, this percentage should not be expected to be near 100 percent. There was a large degree of turnover in the shop during the prior year, with a full complement only reached at the start of FY 2015–16.

In Chapel Hill the preventive maintenance (PM) completion standard for "percentage of PMs completed as scheduled" includes varying standards depending on the work but must occur within thirty days of the scheduled date, within the scheduled month, or within mileage parameters.

In addition to rolling stock, Chapel Hill's fleet services has maintenance responsibilities for generators, light towers, mowers, weed wackers, leaf blowers, leaf vacuum machines, and sign towers.

Municipal Profile

Population (OSBM 2019)	63,639
Land Area (Square Miles)	21.31
Persons per Square Mile	2,987

Service Profile

FTE Positions—Technician		5.50
FTE Positions—Other		2.25
Work Bays		10
Rolling Stock Maintained	No.	Average Age
Cars—Normal Usage	41	9.2 Years
Cars—Severe Usage	52	6.8 Years
Motorcycles	0	NA
Light Utility Vehicles	10	12.9 Years
Light Vehicles	128	9.4 Years
Medium Vehicles	18	9.6 Years
Heavy—Sanitation	17	6.2 Years
Heavy—Sewer	2	16.9 Years
Heavy—Fire Apparatus	9	9.4 Years
Heavy—Other	10	6.8 Years
Trailed Equipment	50	11.3 Years
Off-Road/Construction/Tractors	17	9.9 Years
Buses	0	NA
TOTAL	354	
Vehicle Equivalent Units (VEUs)		1,100
Average Rolling Stock Units Available per Day		336
Hours Billed		6,015
Work Orders		1,482
Repeat Repairs within 30 Days		4
Work Orders Completed within 24 hours		733
Preventive Maintenance Jobs (PMs)		503
PMs Completed as Scheduled		447

Full Cost Profile

Cost Breakdown by Percentage	
Personal Services	23.3%
Operating Costs	44.7%
Capital Costs	32.0%
TOTAL	100.0%

Cost Breakdown in Dollars	
Personal Services	$539,105
Operating Costs	$1,032,991
Capital Costs	$739,345
TOTAL	$2,311,441

Key: Chapel Hill ▒ Benchmarking Average — Fiscal Years 2016 through 2020

Resource Measures

Fleet Maintenance Services Cost per Capita

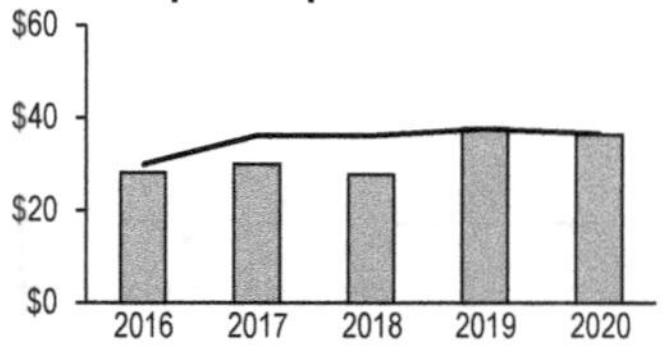

	2016	2017	2018	2019	2020
Chapel Hill	$28.25	$30.04	$27.79	$37.75	$36.32
Average	$29.83	$36.10	$36.06	$37.55	$36.51

Fleet Maintenance FTEs per 10,000 Population

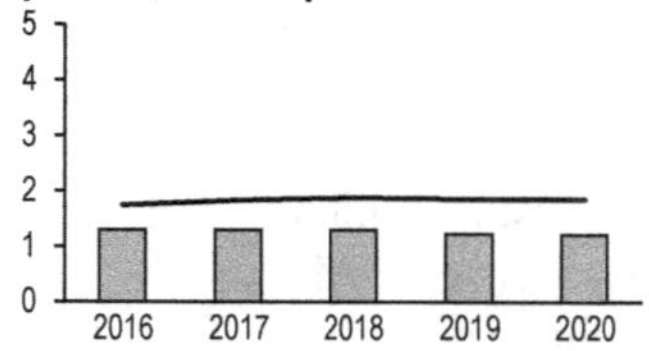

	2016	2017	2018	2019	2020
Chapel Hill	1.30	1.29	1.29	1.23	1.22
Average	1.74	1.83	1.88	1.85	1.85

Fleet Maintenance FTEs per 100 Municipal Employees

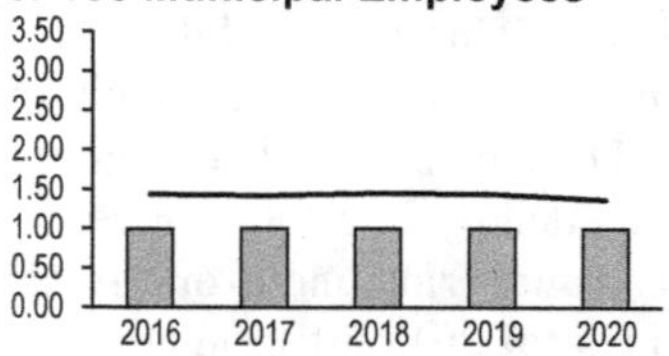

	2016	2017	2018	2019	2020
Chapel Hill	0.99	1.00	1.00	1.00	1.00
Average	1.43	1.42	1.45	1.44	1.37

Workload Measures

Number of Vehicle Equivalent Units (VEUs) per Technician FTE

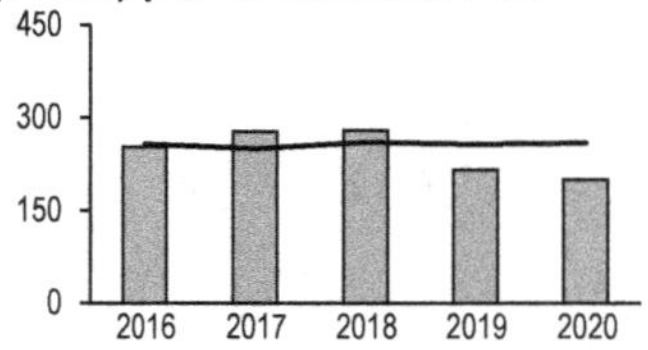

	2016	2017	2018	2019	2020
Chapel Hill	252	277	279	216	200
Average	256	249	259	257	258

Preventive Maintenances (PMs) Completed In-House per Tech FTE

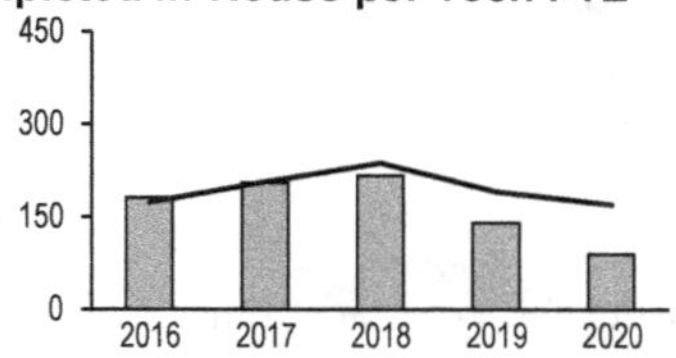

	2016	2017	2018	2019	2020
Chapel Hill	182	205	217	141	90
Average	173	207	237	191	170

Efficiency Measures

Fleet Maintenance Cost per Work Order

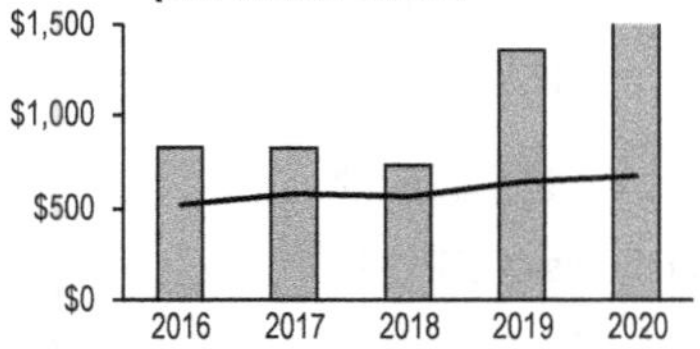

	2016	2017	2018	2019	2020
Chapel Hill	$824	$822	$732	$1,356	$1,560
Average	$520	$577	$564	$642	$670

Fleet Maintenance Cost per Vehicle Equivalent Unit (VEU)

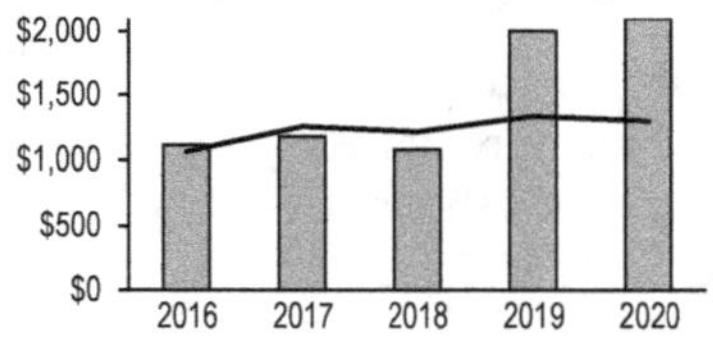

	2016	2017	2018	2019	2020
Chapel Hill	$1,114	$1,179	$1,083	$2,008	$2,102
Average	$1,060	$1,254	$1,212	$1,334	$1,297

Hours Billed as a Percentage of Total Hours

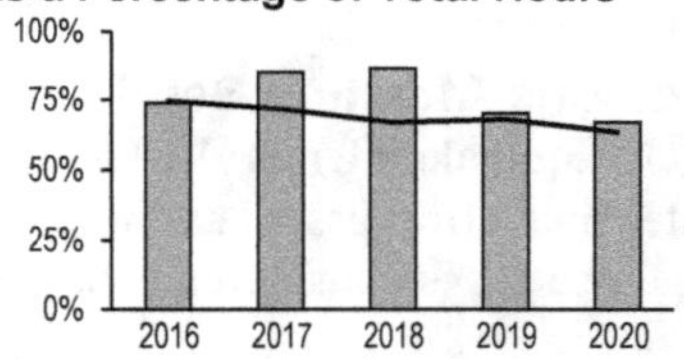

	2016	2017	2018	2019	2020
Chapel Hill	74%	85%	86%	70%	67%
Average	74%	72%	67%	68%	63%

Effectiveness Measures

Preventive Maintenances (PMs) as a Percentage of All Work Orders

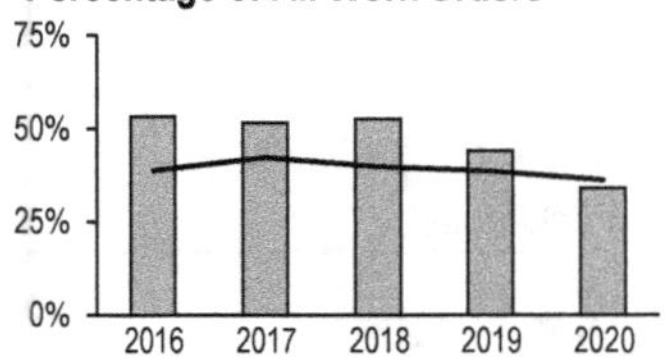

	2016	2017	2018	2019	2020
Chapel Hill	53%	52%	53%	44%	34%
Average	39%	42%	40%	39%	36%

Percentage of Preventive Maintenances (PMs) Completed as Scheduled

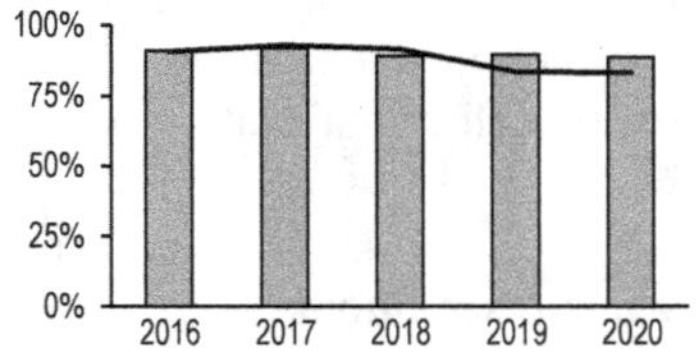

	2016	2017	2018	2019	2020
Chapel Hill	91%	92%	89%	90%	89%
Average	91%	93%	92%	84%	83%

Percentage of Work Orders Completed within 24 Hours

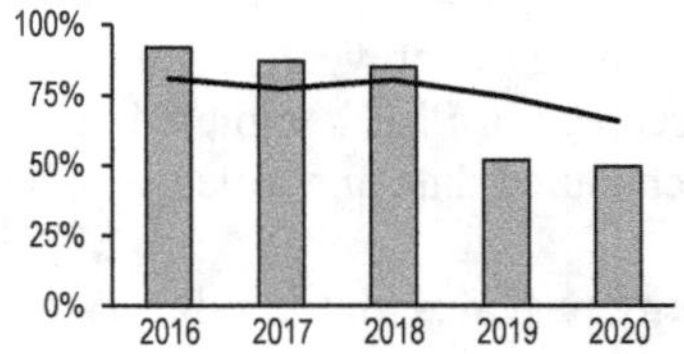

	2016	2017	2018	2019	2020
Chapel Hill	92%	87%	85%	52%	49%
Average	81%	77%	80%	74%	65%

Percentage of Rolling Stock Available per Day

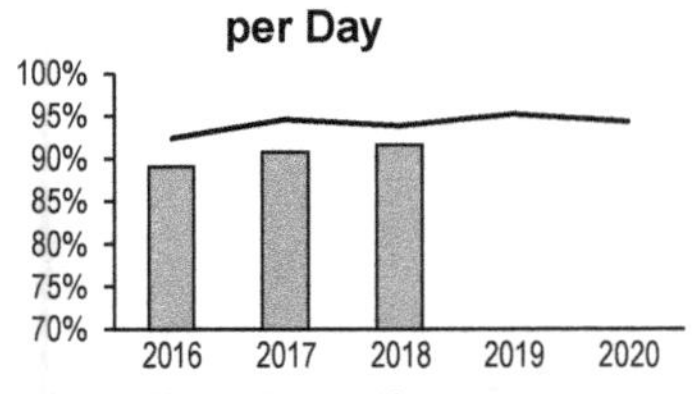

	2016	2017	2018	2019	2020
Chapel Hill	89%	91%	92%		
Average	92%	95%	94%	95%	94%

Percentage of Work Orders Requiring Repeat Repair within 30 Days

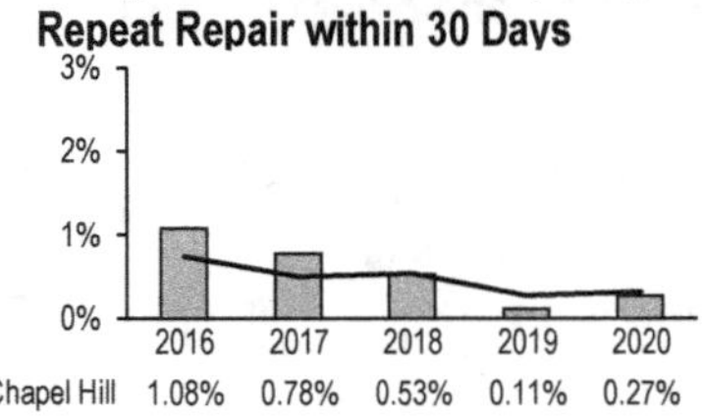

	2016	2017	2018	2019	2020
Chapel Hill	1.08%	0.78%	0.53%	0.11%	0.27%
Average	0.74%	0.50%	0.53%	0.28%	0.32%

Charlotte — Fleet Maintenance

Fiscal Year 2019-20

Explanatory Information

Service Level and Delivery

The City of Charlotte and the County of Mecklenburg merged fleet maintenance services under a city-operated program beginning July 1, 2009. The data reported here are inclusive of both fleets. The services are provided by Charlotte's Fleet Management Division, which is part of the Engineering and Property Management Department. All activities for this operation are accounted for in the general fund. The Fleet Management Division currently charges an administrative fee per unit to compensate for the overhead of administrative staff, including tags and title work, specification writing, and fleet analysis.

Charges for maintenance services included a $80.75-per-hour labor rate, a 13.4 percent markup charge on parts sold, and a 20.8 percent markup charge on sublet work. Part caps are negotiated individually, based on very special and specific needs. All sublet transactions are subject to a $500 cap.

The following services were contracted out during the year: accident repair, body work, spring repairs, front-end alignment, glass replacement, fuel system repair, engine overhauls, transmission overhauls, towing, some tire service, police car preparation, heavy tire replacement and repair, some light-vehicle preventive maintenance, painting/graphic installation, and radio/computer installation or removal.

Conditions Affecting Service, Performance, and Costs

Vehicle Equivalent Units (VEUs) are a weighted measure of the maintenance effort associated with different classes of vehicles. A normal-use car is considered equal to one VEU.

The measure "hours billed as a percentage of total hours" is based on a work year of 2,080 hours and only counts those positions that were filled. Technicians have responsibilities that do not result in billable hours, and they take normal vacation and sick leave. Therefore, this percentage should not be expected to be near 100 percent.

In Charlotte the preventive maintenance (PM) completion standard for "percentage of PMs completed as scheduled" is within thirty days of the scheduled date and mileage parameters.

The city provides motorpool services. These include reservations, tracking, cleaning, parking, and check-in. In addition to rolling stock, Charlotte's fleet services had maintenance responsibilities for generators, mowers, weed whackers, compressors, saws, blowers, fans, asphalt-tar/kettles, edgers, snow plows, spreaders, tamps, mixers, chippers, posthole diggers, grinders, pressure washers, and other city equipment.

The measure Fleet personnel per 100 municipal employees includes county employees in the denominator due to the Fleet Division effectively serving both city and county employees.

Municipal Profile

Population (OSBM 2019)	863,985
Land Area (Square Miles)	307.41
Persons per Square Mile	2,811

Service Profile

FTE Positions—Technician	78.00
FTE Positions—Other	46.0
Work Bays	90

Rolling Stock Maintained	No.	Average Age
Cars—Normal Usage	336	6.4 Years
Cars—Severe Usage	839	3.5 Years
Motorcycles	84	5.7 Years
Light Utility Vehicles	87	5.9 Years
Light Vehicles	1,541	5.4 Years
Medium Vehicles	136	10.5 Years
Heavy—Sanitation	174	6.2 Years
Heavy—Sewer	33	6.6 Years
Heavy—Fire Apparatus	109	8.6 Years
Heavy—Other	146	7.8 Years
Trailed Equipment	353	12.1 Years
Off-Road/Construction/Tractors	351	11.5 Years
Buses	2	11.4 Years
TOTAL	4,191	

Vehicle Equivalent Units (VEUs)	13,513
Average Rolling Stock Units Available per Day	3,451
Hours Billed	NA
Work Orders	39,787
Repeat Repairs within 30 Days	0
Work Orders Completed within 24 hours	9,940
Preventive Maintenance Jobs (PMs)	14,427
PMs Completed as Scheduled	NA

Full Cost Profile

Cost Breakdown by Percentage	
Personal Services	40.6%
Operating Costs	58.9%
Capital Costs	0.5%
TOTAL	100.0%

Cost Breakdown in Dollars	
Personal Services	$9,686,879
Operating Costs	$14,071,025
Capital Costs	$123,117
TOTAL	$23,881,021

Key: Charlotte ▒ Benchmarking Average — Fiscal Years 2016 through 2020

Resource Measures

Fleet Maintenance Services Cost per Capita

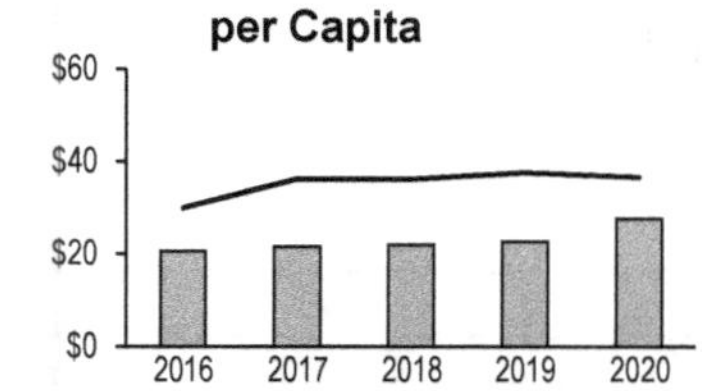

	2016	2017	2018	2019	2020
Charlotte	$20.51	$21.47	$21.96	$22.67	$27.64
Average	$29.83	$36.10	$36.06	$37.55	$36.51

Fleet Maintenance FTEs per 10,000 Population

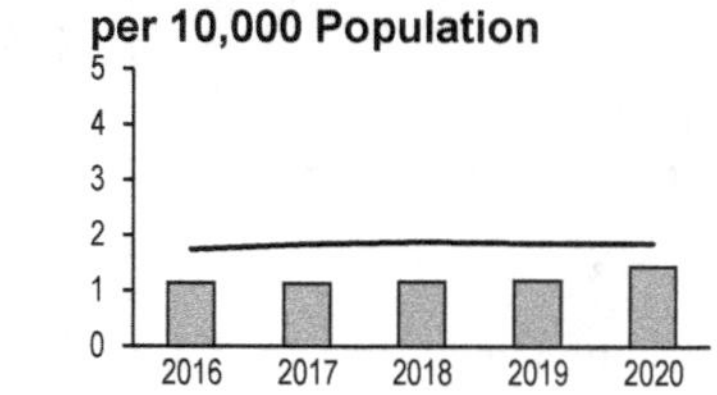

	2016	2017	2018	2019	2020
Charlotte	1.14	1.13	1.15	1.18	1.44
Average	1.74	1.83	1.88	1.85	1.85

Fleet Maintenance FTEs per 100 Municipal Employees

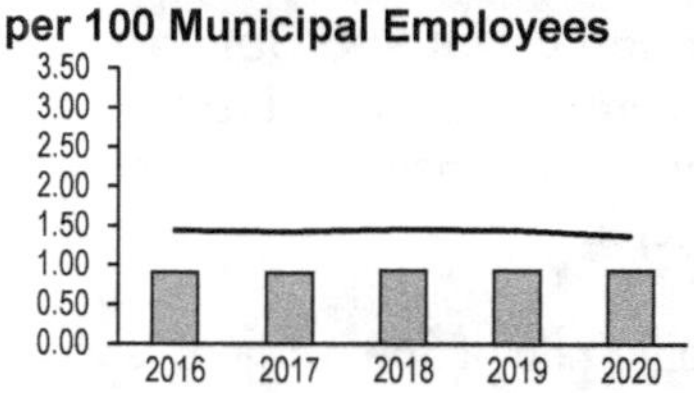

	2016	2017	2018	2019	2020
Charlotte	0.90	0.90	0.93	0.93	0.93
Average	1.43	1.42	1.45	1.44	1.37

Charlotte includes county employees too.

Workload Measures

Number of Vehicle Equivalent Units (VEUs) per Technician FTE

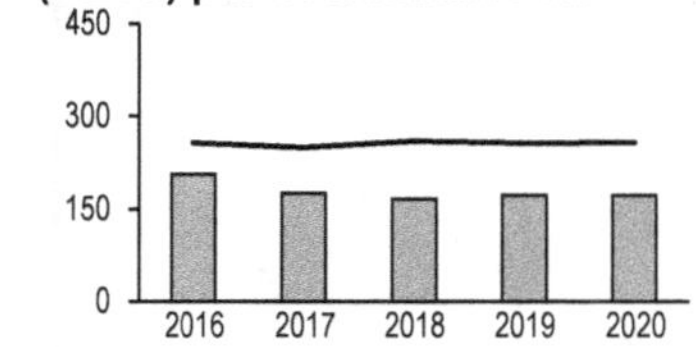

	2016	2017	2018	2019	2020
Charlotte	206	176	166	173	173
Average	256	249	259	257	258

Preventive Maintenances (PMs) Completed In-House per Tech FTE

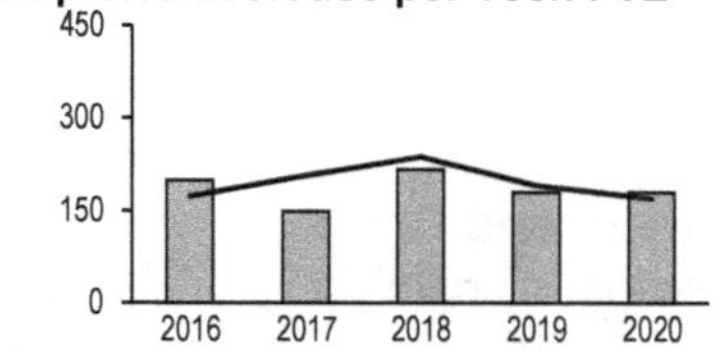

	2016	2017	2018	2019	2020
Charlotte	200	150	218	181	181
Average	173	207	237	191	170

Efficiency Measures

Fleet Maintenance Cost per Work Order

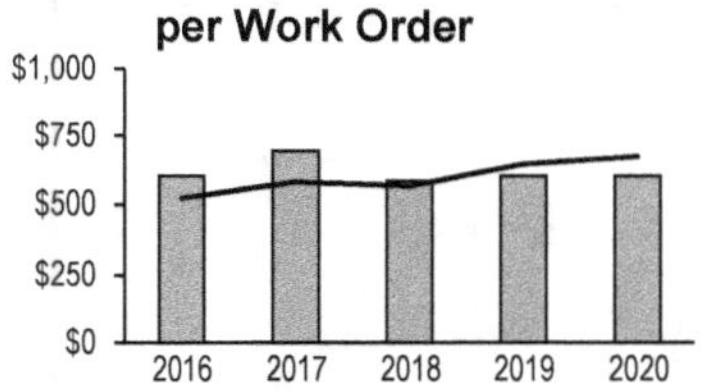

	2016	2017	2018	2019	2020
Charlotte	$601	$692	$582	$600	$600
Average	$520	$577	$564	$642	$670

Fleet Maintenance Cost per Vehicle Equivalent Unit (VEU)

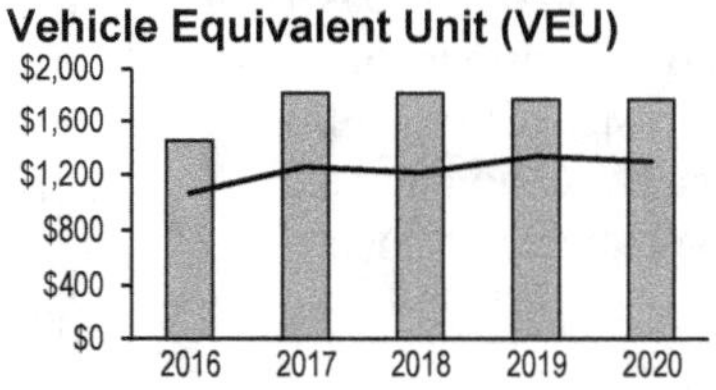

	2016	2017	2018	2019	2020
Charlotte	$1,456	$1,816	$1,818	$1,767	$1,767
Average	$1,060	$1,254	$1,212	$1,334	$1,297

Hours Billed as a Percentage of Total Hours

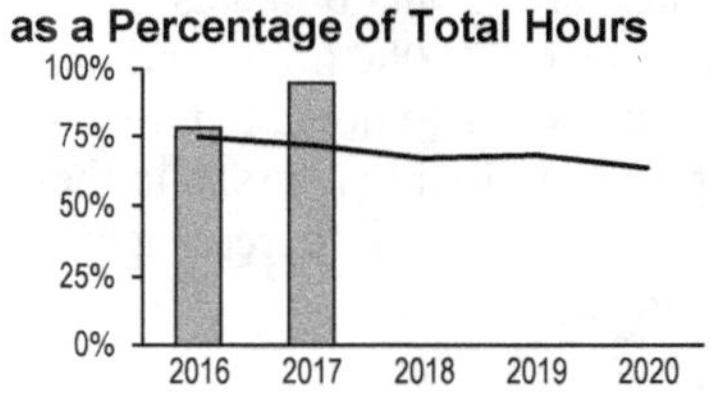

	2016	2017	2018	2019	2020
Charlotte	78%	95%			
Average	74%	72%	67%	68%	63%

Effectiveness Measures

Preventive Maintenances (PMs) as a Percentage of All Work Orders

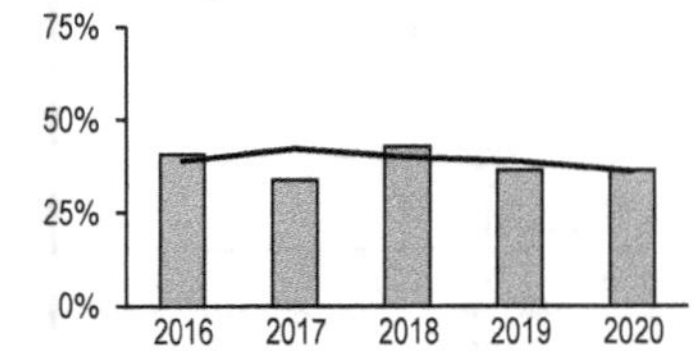

	2016	2017	2018	2019	2020
Charlotte	41%	34%	43%	36%	36%
Average	39%	42%	40%	39%	36%

Percentage of Preventive Maintenances (PMs) Completed as Scheduled

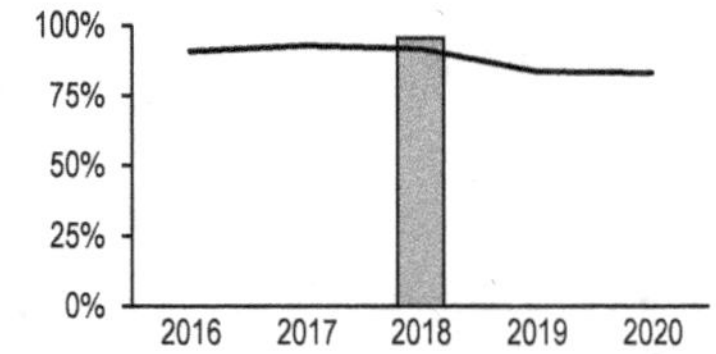

	2016	2017	2018	2019	2020
Charlotte			96%		
Average	91%	93%	92%	84%	83%

Percentage of Work Orders Completed within 24 Hours

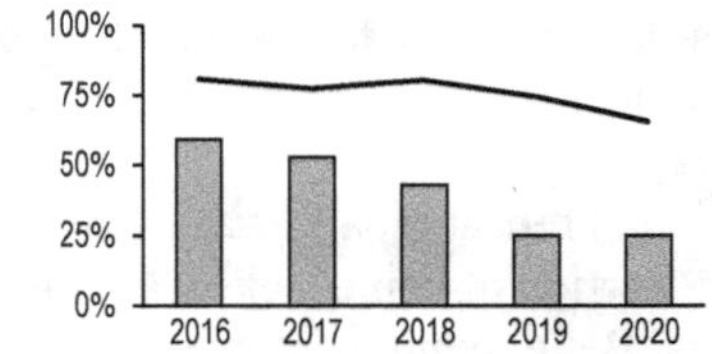

	2016	2017	2018	2019	2020
Charlotte	59%	53%	43%	25%	25%
Average	81%	77%	80%	74%	65%

Percentage of Rolling Stock Available per Day

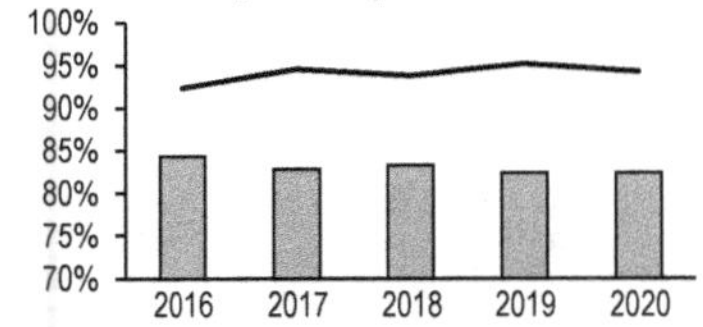

	2016	2017	2018	2019	2020
Charlotte	84%	83%	83%	82%	82%
Average	92%	95%	94%	95%	94%

Percentage of Work Orders Requiring Repeat Repair within 30 Days

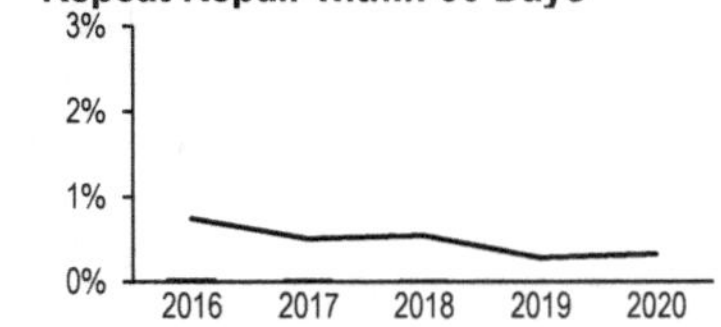

	2016	2017	2018	2019	2020
Charlotte	0.02%	0.02%	0.00%	0.00%	0.00%
Average	0.74%	0.50%	0.53%	0.28%	0.32%

Fiscal Year 2019-20

Explanatory Information

Service Level and Delivery

Concord's Fleet Department operates as a separate city department through the general fund, charging other departments for services rendered.

A labor rate of $60 per hour is charged for all maintenance services. There is a 25 percent markup charge for parts and a 10 percent markup on sublet work.

The following services were contracted out:

- body repairs
- aerial device repairs
- front-end alignments.

Conditions Affecting Service, Performance, and Costs

Vehicle Equivalent Units (VEUs) are a weighted measure of the maintenance effort associated with different classes of vehicles. A normal-use car is considered equal to one VEU. Vehicles such as fire trucks or police cars have higher VEUs, reflecting greater expected levels of maintenance.

The measure "hours billed as a percentage of total hours" is based on a work year of 2,080 hours and only counts those positions that were filled. It should be noted that technicians have responsibilities that do not result in billable hours, and they take normal vacation and sick leave. Therefore, this percentage should not be expected to be near 100 percent.

In Concord, the preventive maintenance (PM) completion standard for "percentage of PMs completed as scheduled" is within thirty days of the scheduled date.

In addition to rolling stock, Concord's fleet services has maintenance responsibilities for generators, mowers, weedeaters, chainsaws, chop saws, leaf blowers, tamps, pumps, power washers, and other city equipment.

A drop in repeat repairs was driven by an analysis that showed that a large portion of comebacks were due to A/C and charging system issues. Better equipment was purchased for these repairs, and a master mechanic was hired to do most of the A/C repair work, leading to lower repeat repairs.

Municipal Profile

Population (OSBM 2019)	95,453
Land Area (Square Miles)	63.65
Persons per Square Mile	1,500

Service Profile

FTE Positions—Technician	8.00
FTE Positions—Other	6.0
Work Bays	8

Rolling Stock Maintained	No.	Average Age
Cars—Normal Usage	4	5.0 Years
Cars—Severe Usage	191	4.7 Years
Motorcycles	6	2.5 Years
Light Utility Vehicles	62	7.9 Years
Light Vehicles	262	6.3 Years
Medium Vehicles	56	6.4 Years
Heavy—Sanitation	15	6.1 Years
Heavy—Sewer	3	4.2 Years
Heavy—Fire Apparatus	25	9.3 Years
Heavy—Other	67	8.5 Years
Trailed Equipment	178	12.0 Years
Off-Road/Construction/Tractors	115	8.6 Years
Buses	11	6.3 Years
TOTAL	995	

Vehicle Equivalent Units (VEUs)	3,050
Average Rolling Stock Units Available per Day	984
Hours Billed	10,374
Work Orders	3,889
Repeat Repairs within 30 Days	15
Work Orders Completed within 24 hours	3,845
Preventive Maintenance Jobs (PMs)	1,842
PMs Completed as Scheduled	1,801

Full Cost Profile

Cost Breakdown by Percentage	
Personal Services	46.9%
Operating Costs	48.7%
Capital Costs	4.4%
TOTAL	100.0%

Cost Breakdown in Dollars	
Personal Services	$1,084,614
Operating Costs	$1,125,920
Capital Costs	$100,854
TOTAL	$2,311,388

Concord

Fleet Maintenance

Key: Concord ▒ Benchmarking Average — Fiscal Years 2016 through 2020

Resource Measures

Fleet Maintenance Services Cost per Capita

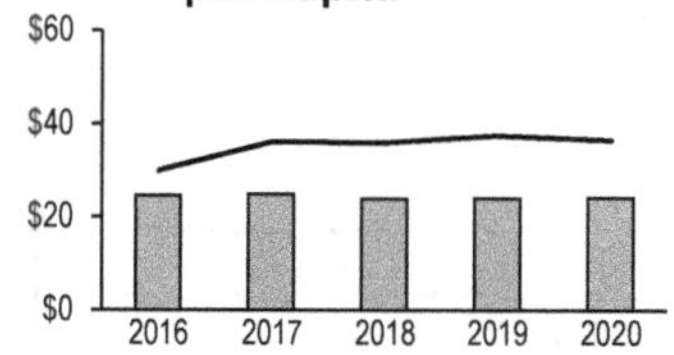

	2016	2017	2018	2019	2020
Concord	$24.55	$24.90	$23.88	$24.01	$24.21
Average	$29.83	$36.10	$36.06	$37.55	$36.51

Fleet Maintenance FTEs per 10,000 Population

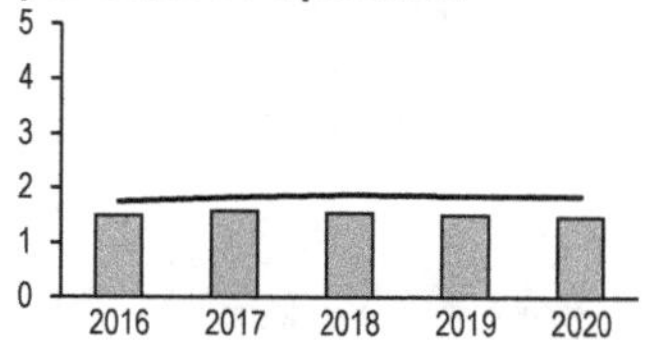

	2016	2017	2018	2019	2020
Concord	1.49	1.58	1.54	1.51	1.47
Average	1.74	1.83	1.88	1.85	1.85

Fleet Maintenance FTEs per 100 Municipal Employees

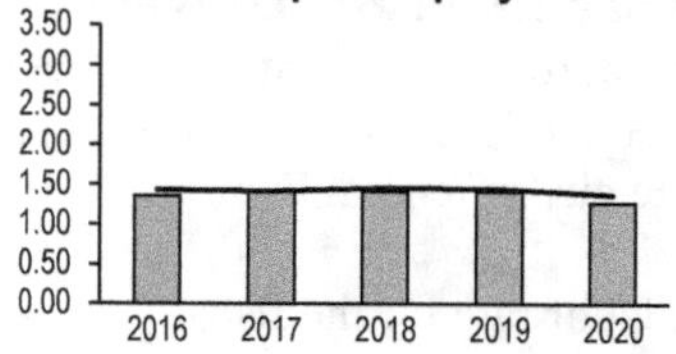

	2016	2017	2018	2019	2020
Concord	1.35	1.41	1.41	1.41	1.28
Average	1.43	1.42	1.45	1.44	1.37

Workload Measures

Number of Vehicle Equivalent Units (VEUs) per Technician FTE

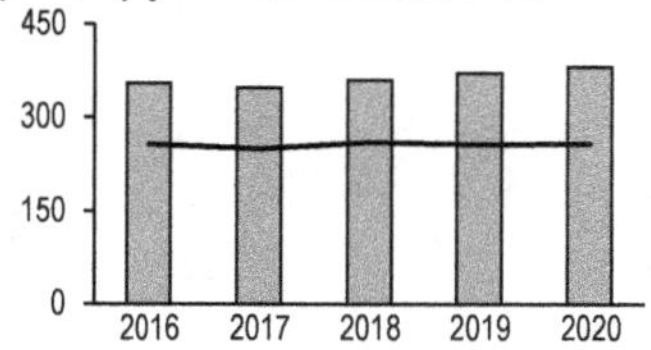

	2016	2017	2018	2019	2020
Concord	354	348	360	372	381
Average	256	249	259	257	258

Preventive Maintenances (PMs) Completed In-House per Tech FTE

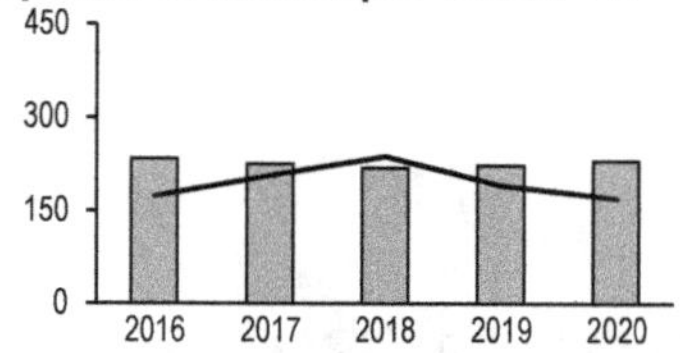

	2016	2017	2018	2019	2020
Concord	234	226	220	223	230
Average	173	207	237	191	170

Efficiency Measures

Fleet Maintenance Cost per Work Order

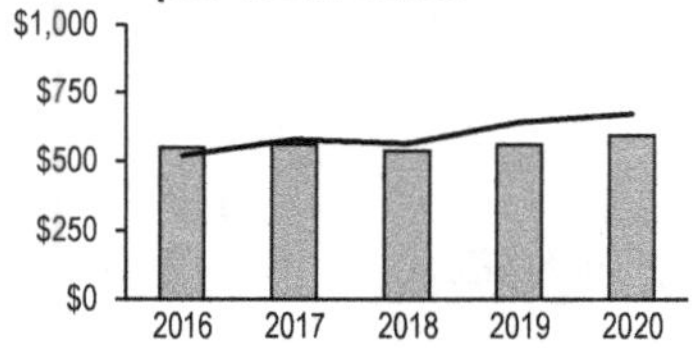

	2016	2017	2018	2019	2020
Concord	$552	$561	$537	$562	$594
Average	$520	$577	$564	$642	$670

Fleet Maintenance Cost per Vehicle Equivalent Unit (VEU)

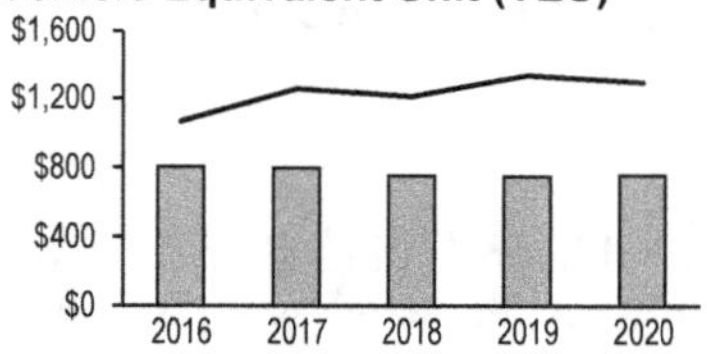

	2016	2017	2018	2019	2020
Concord	$805	$795	$753	$747	$758
Average	$1,060	$1,254	$1,212	$1,334	$1,297

Hours Billed as a Percentage of Total Hours

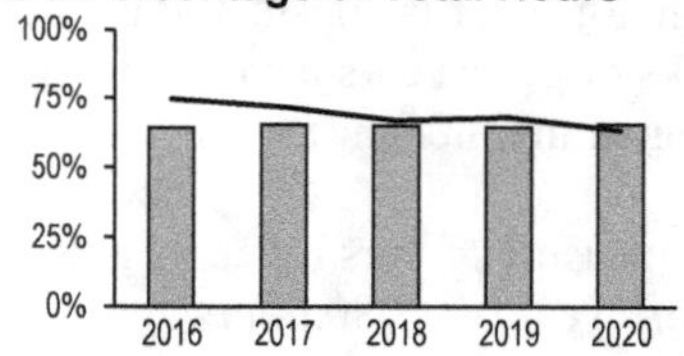

	2016	2017	2018	2019	2020
Concord	64%	65%	65%	65%	66%
Average	74%	72%	67%	68%	63%

Effectiveness Measures

Preventive Maintenances (PMs) as a Percentage of All Work Orders

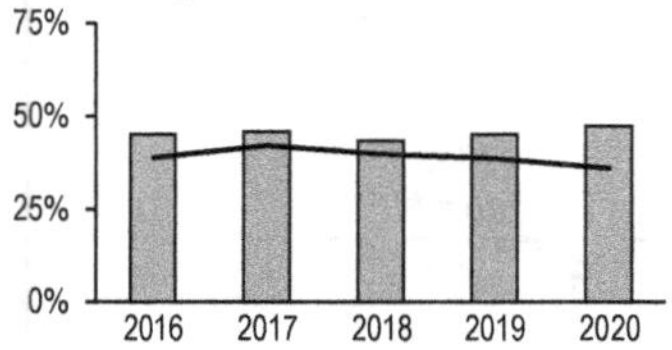

	2016	2017	2018	2019	2020
Concord	45%	46%	43%	45%	47%
Average	39%	42%	40%	39%	36%

Percentage of Preventive Maintenances (PMs) Completed as Scheduled

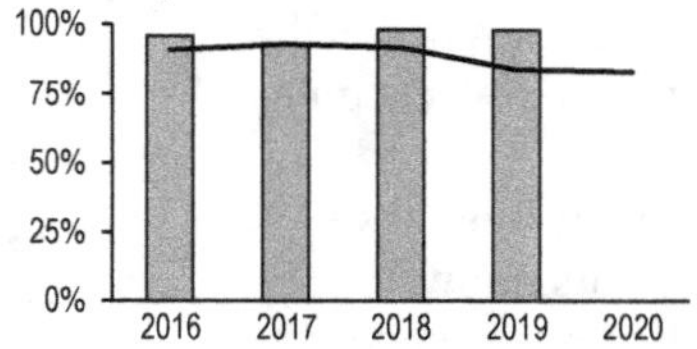

	2016	2017	2018	2019	2020
Concord	96%	93%	98%	98%	
Average	91%	93%	92%	84%	83%

Percentage of Work Orders Completed within 24 Hours

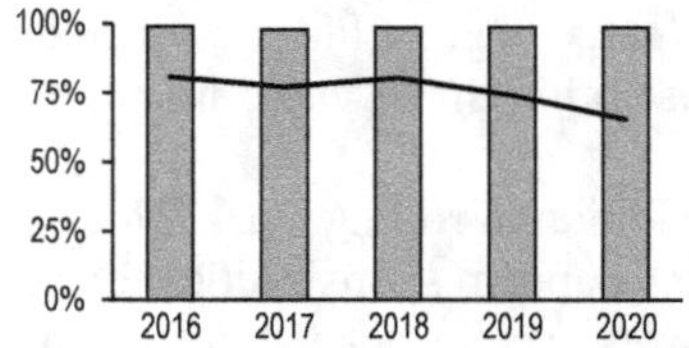

	2016	2017	2018	2019	2020
Concord	99%	98%	99%	99%	99%
Average	81%	77%	80%	74%	65%

Percentage of Rolling Stock Available per Day

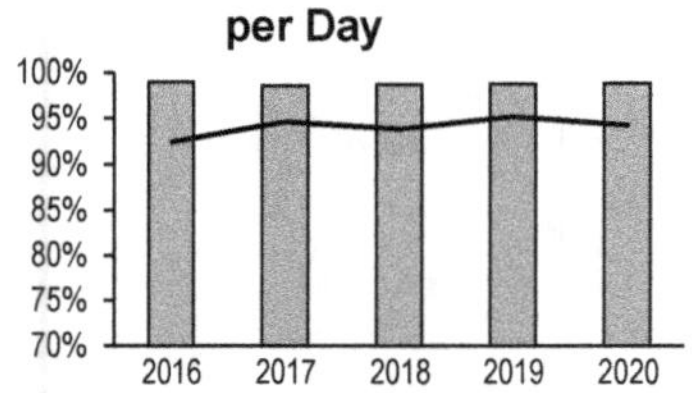

	2016	2017	2018	2019	2020
Concord	99%	99%	99%	99%	99%
Average	92%	95%	94%	95%	94%

Percentage of Work Orders Requiring Repeat Repair within 30 Days

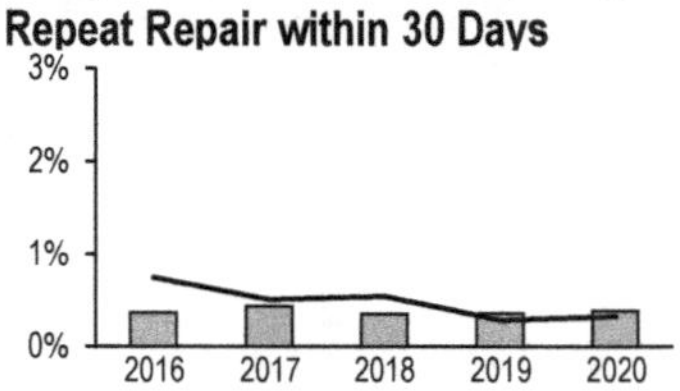

	2016	2017	2018	2019	2020
Concord	0.36%	0.43%	0.35%	0.35%	0.39%
Average	0.74%	0.50%	0.53%	0.28%	0.32%

Fiscal Year 2019-20

Explanatory Information

Service Level and Delivery

Goldsboro's fleet maintenance operation is housed within the Garage Division of the Public Works Department. The division is funded out of the city's General Fund.

The labor rate for the fiscal year was $13.50 an hour. No markup charges are placed on parts or sublet work performed by the Garage Division.

The following services were contracted out:

- body work
- engine repairs requiring specialized tools
- engine diagnostics
- wheel alignments
- hydraulics.

Conditions Affecting Service, Performance, and Costs

The City of Goldsboro joined the Benchmarking Project in July 2017, with the first year of data showing for FY 2016–17.

Vehicle Equivalent Units (VEUs) are a weighted measure of the maintenance effort associated with different classes of vehicles. A normal-use car is considered equal to one VEU. Vehicles such as fire trucks or police cars have higher VEUs, reflecting greater expected levels of maintenance.

The measure "hours billed as a percentage of total hours" is based on a work year of 2,080 hours and only counts those positions that were filled. It should be noted that technicians have responsibilities that do not result in billable hours, and they take normal vacation and sick leave. Therefore, this percentage should not be expected to be near 100 percent.

In Goldsboro, the preventive maintenance (PM) completion standard for "percentage of PMs completed as scheduled" uses scheduled dates within the calendar month or within thirty days of schedule.

In addition to rolling stock, Goldsboro's Garage Division has maintenance responsibilities for portable generators, mowers, blowers, weed wackers, pressure washers, and other equipment.

Municipal Profile

Population (OSBM 2019)	33,969
Land Area (Square Miles)	29.45
Persons per Square Mile	1,154

Service Profile

FTE Positions—Technician		7.0
FTE Positions—Other		4.0
Work Bays		11
Rolling Stock Maintained	No.	Average Age
Cars—Normal Usage	10	13.1 Years
Cars—Severe Usage	114	5.8 Years
Motorcycles	0	NA
Light Utility Vehicles	154	7.4 Years
Light Vehicles	87	7.3 Years
Medium Vehicles	3	8.3 Years
Heavy—Sanitation	40	12.7 Years
Heavy—Sewer	3	5.0 Years
Heavy—Fire Apparatus	12	24.5 Years
Heavy—Other	20	11.2 Years
Trailed Equipment	65	14.5 Years
Off-Road/Construction/Tractors	39	11.6 Years
Buses	2	1.5 Years
TOTAL	549	
Vehicle Equivalent Units (VEUs)		1,809
Average Rolling Stock Units Available per Day		547
Hours Billed		4,297
Work Orders		3,389
Repeat Repairs within 30 Days		0
Work Orders Completed within 24 hours		0
Preventive Maintenance Jobs (PMs)		818
PMs Completed as Scheduled		818

Full Cost Profile

Cost Breakdown by Percentage	
Personal Services	49.0%
Operating Costs	51.0%
Capital Costs	0.0%
TOTAL	100.0%

Cost Breakdown in Dollars	
Personal Services	$687,396
Operating Costs	$716,260
Capital Costs	$0
TOTAL	$1,403,656

Goldsboro

Fleet Maintenance

Key: Goldsboro ▒ Benchmarking Average — Fiscal Years 2016 through 2020

Resource Measures

Fleet Maintenance Services Cost per Capita

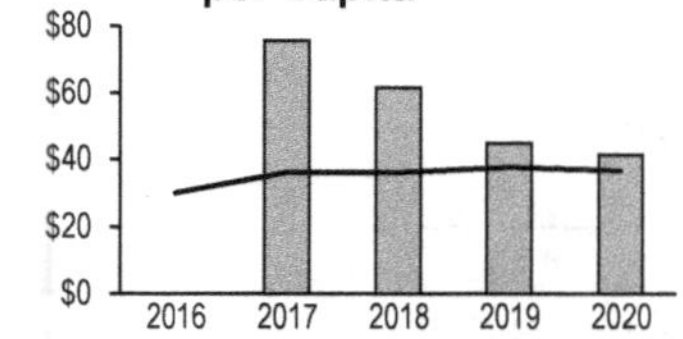

	2016	2017	2018	2019	2020
Goldsboro		$75.58	$61.49	$44.77	$41.32
Average	$29.83	$36.10	$36.06	$37.55	$36.51

Fleet Maintenance FTEs per 10,000 Population

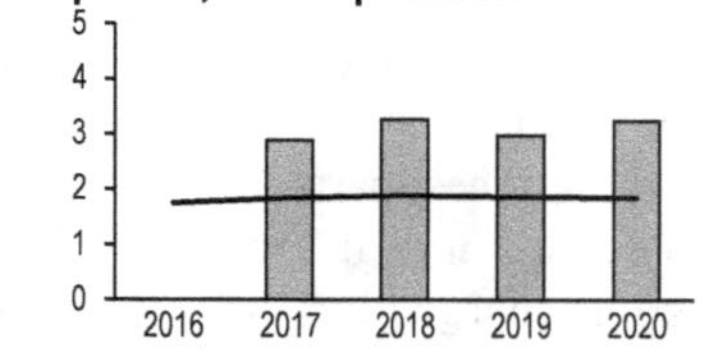

	2016	2017	2018	2019	2020
Goldsboro		2.87	3.27	2.97	3.24
Average	1.74	1.83	1.88	1.85	1.85

Fleet Maintenance FTEs per 100 Municipal Employees

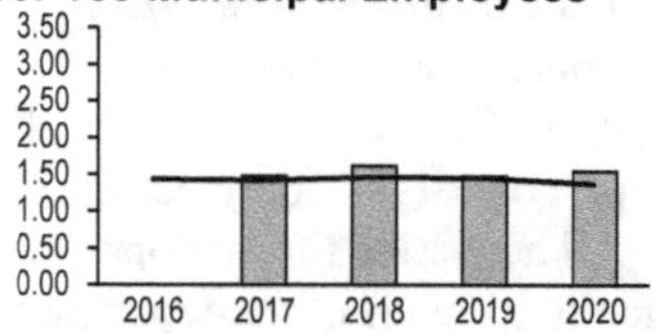

	2016	2017	2018	2019	2020
Goldsboro		1.47	1.62	1.47	1.54
Average	1.43	1.42	1.45	1.44	1.37

Workload Measures

Number of Vehicle Equivalent Units (VEUs) per Technician FTE

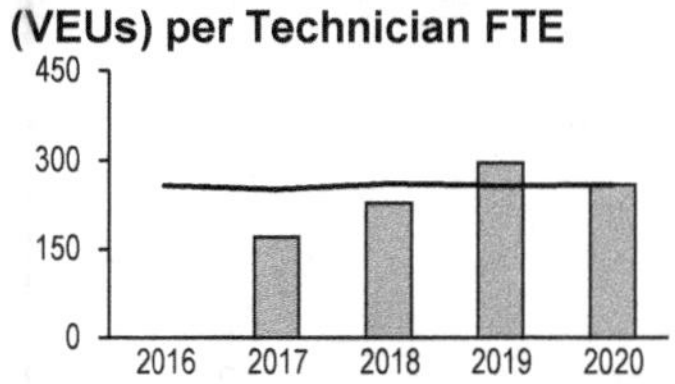

	2016	2017	2018	2019	2020
Goldsboro		170	227	295	258
Average	256	249	259	257	258

Preventive Maintenances (PMs) Completed In-House per Tech FTE

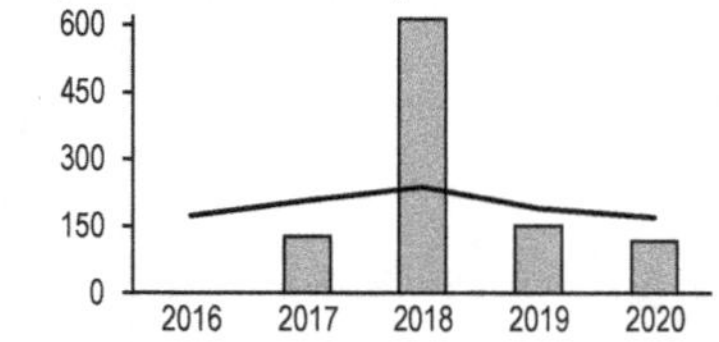

	2016	2017	2018	2019	2020
Goldsboro		128	613	152	117
Average	173	207	237	191	170

Efficiency Measures

Fleet Maintenance Cost per Work Order

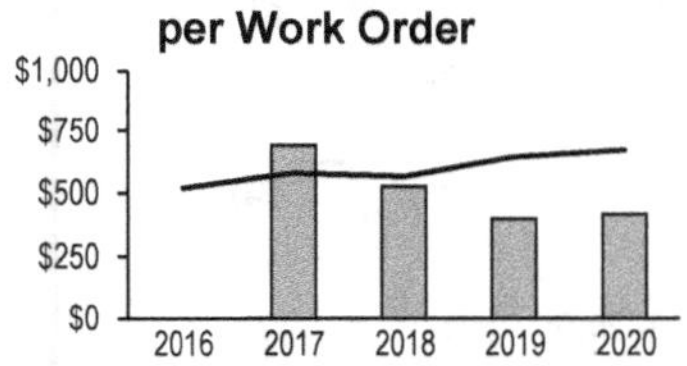

	2016	2017	2018	2019	2020
Goldsboro		$689	$526	$396	$414
Average	$520	$577	$564	$642	$670

Fleet Maintenance Cost per Vehicle Equivalent Unit (VEU)

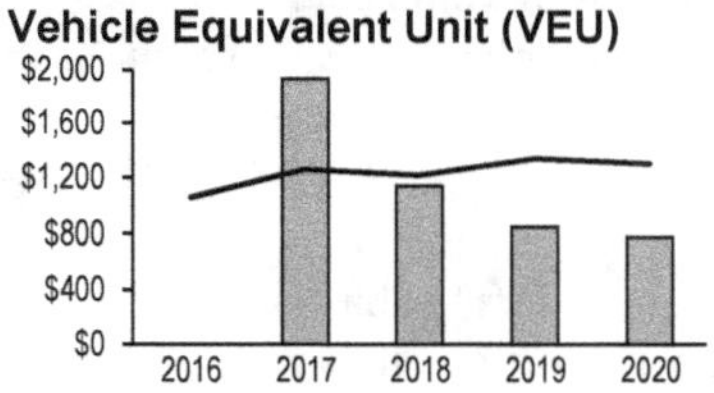

	2016	2017	2018	2019	2020
Goldsboro		$1,931	$1,138	$851	$776
Average	$1,060	$1,254	$1,212	$1,334	$1,297

Hours Billed as a Percentage of Total Hours

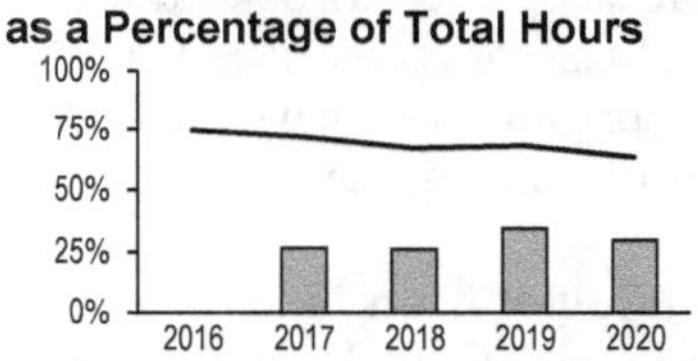

	2016	2017	2018	2019	2020
Goldsboro		27%	26%	34%	30%
Average	74%	72%	67%	68%	63%

Effectiveness Measures

Preventive Maintenances (PMs) as a Percentage of All Work Orders

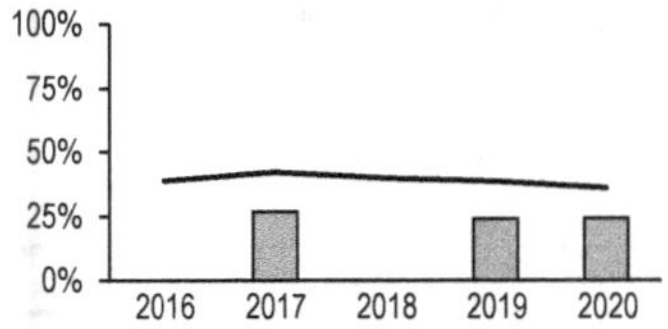

	2016	2017	2018	2019	2020
Goldsboro		27%		24%	24%
Average	39%	42%	40%	39%	36%

Percentage of Preventive Maintenances (PMs) Completed as Scheduled

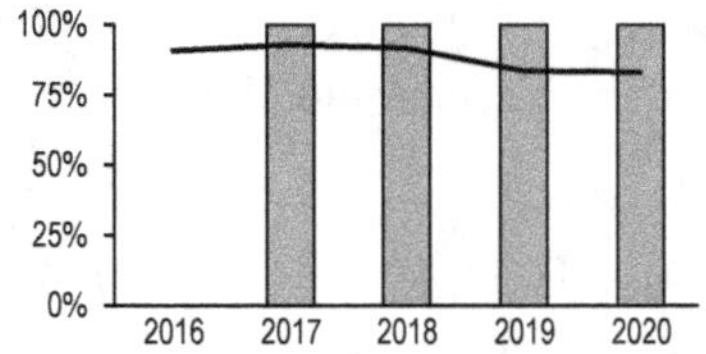

	2016	2017	2018	2019	2020
Goldsboro		100%	100%	100%	100%
Average	91%	93%	92%	84%	83%

Percentage of Work Orders Completed within 24 Hours

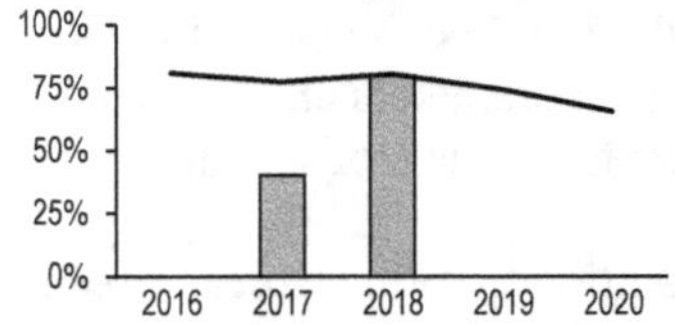

	2016	2017	2018	2019	2020
Goldsboro		40%	80%		
Average	81%	77%	80%	74%	65%

Percentage of Rolling Stock Available per Day

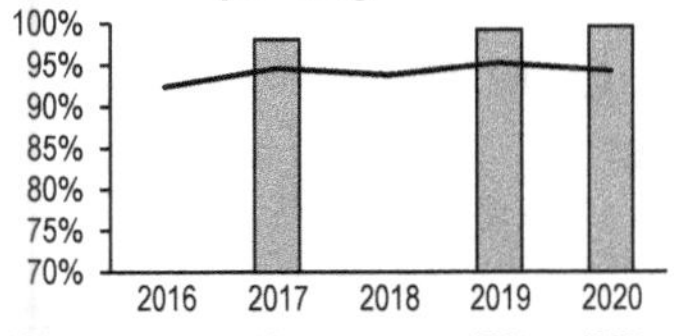

	2016	2017	2018	2019	2020
Goldsboro		98%		99%	100%
Average	92%	95%	94%	95%	94%

Percentage of Work Orders Requiring Repeat Repair within 30 Days

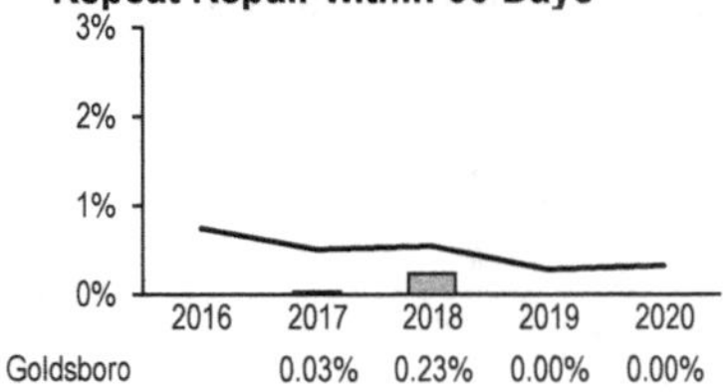

	2016	2017	2018	2019	2020
Goldsboro		0.03%	0.23%	0.00%	0.00%
Average	0.74%	0.50%	0.53%	0.28%	0.32%

Fiscal Year 2019-20

Explanatory Information

Service Level and Delivery
Greensboro's fleet maintenance operation is housed within the Equipment Services Division of the Finance Department. The division consists of four sections: administration, services, parts, and tires. All activities for this operation are accounted for in an internal service fund, with other departments and programs charged for its maintenance services on a cost recovery basis.

The labor rate for the fiscal year was $65 an hour. Charges included a 25 percent markup for parts sold and a 5 percent markup for sublet work.

The following services were contracted out:

- body work
- glass repair
- upholstery repair
- most automotive and light-duty oil changes
- other repairs when workload exceeded in-house capacity.

Conditions Affecting Service, Performance, and Costs
Vehicle Equivalent Units (VEUs) are a weighted measure of the maintenance effort associated with different classes of vehicles. A normal-use car is considered equal to one VEU. Vehicles such as fire trucks or police cars have higher VEUs, reflecting greater expected levels of maintenance.

The measure "hours billed as a percentage of total hours" is based on a work year of 2,080 hours and only counts those positions that were filled. It should be noted that technicians have responsibilities that do not result in billable hours, and they take normal vacation and sick leave. Therefore, this percentage should not be expected to be near 100 percent.

In Greensboro, the preventive maintenance (PM) completion standard for "percentage of PMs completed as scheduled" uses mileage parameters and scheduled dates within the calendar month or within thirty days of schedule.

In addition to rolling stock, Greensboro's fleet services has maintenance responsibilities for generators, saws, blowers, various police equipment, asphalt pavers, sprayers, hydraulic hammers, a motor mixer, pumps, snow plows, spreaders, and other equipment.

In Greensboro, maintenance on fire vehicles is performed by mechanics in the fire department. The work performed is not counted here.

Municipal Profile

Population (OSBM 2019)	293,730
Land Area (Square Miles)	129.62
Persons per Square Mile	2,266

Service Profile

FTE Positions—Technician	32.0
FTE Positions—Other	17.0
Work Bays	34

Rolling Stock Maintained	No.	Average Age
Cars—Normal Usage	161	6.0 Years
Cars—Severe Usage	380	3.0 Years
Motorcycles	7	4.0 Years
Light Utility Vehicles	35	14.0 Years
Light Vehicles	430	6.0 Years
Medium Vehicles	120	8.0 Years
Heavy—Sanitation	98	5.0 Years
Heavy—Sewer	9	6.0 Years
Heavy—Fire Apparatus	0	NA
Heavy—Other	112	9.0 Years
Trailed Equipment	210	12.0 Years
Off-Road/Construction/Tractors	132	7.0 Years
Buses	3	16.0 Years
TOTAL	1,697	

Vehicle Equivalent Units (VEUs)	5,530
Average Rolling Stock Units Available per Day	1,568
Hours Billed	39,106
Work Orders	11,265
Repeat Repairs within 30 Days	50
Work Orders Completed within 24 hours	10,409
Preventive Maintenance Jobs (PMs)	5,061
PMs Completed as Scheduled	5,061

Full Cost Profile

Cost Breakdown by Percentage	
Personal Services	41.6%
Operating Costs	58.4%
Capital Costs	0.0%
TOTAL	100.0%

Cost Breakdown in Dollars	
Personal Services	$3,438,237
Operating Costs	$4,817,269
Capital Costs	$0
TOTAL	$8,255,506

Key: Greensboro ■ Benchmarking Average — Fiscal Years 2016 through 2020

Resource Measures

Fleet Maintenance Services Cost per Capita

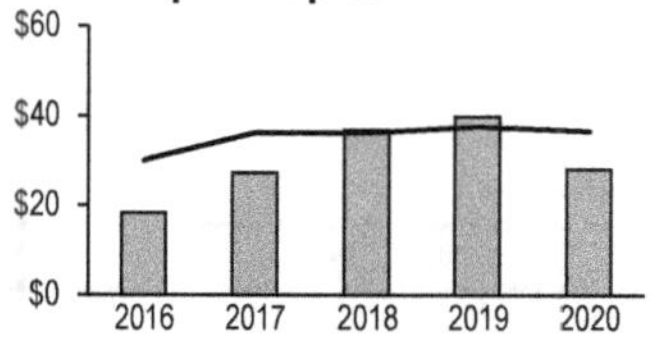

	2016	2017	2018	2019	2020
Greensboro	$18.22	$27.22	$36.76	$39.88	$28.11
Average	$29.83	$36.10	$36.06	$37.55	$36.51

Fleet Maintenance FTEs per 10,000 Population

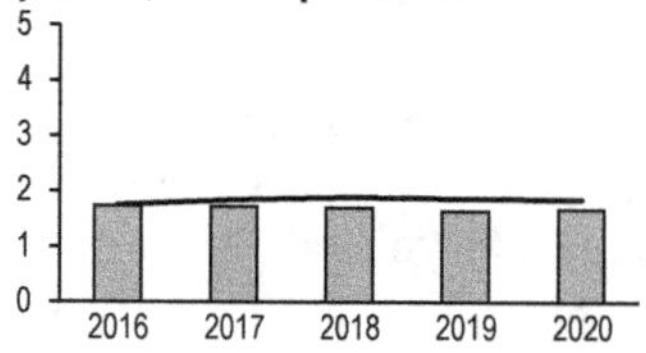

	2016	2017	2018	2019	2020
Greensboro	1.73	1.72	1.70	1.64	1.67
Average	1.74	1.83	1.88	1.85	1.85

Fleet Maintenance FTEs per 100 Municipal Employees

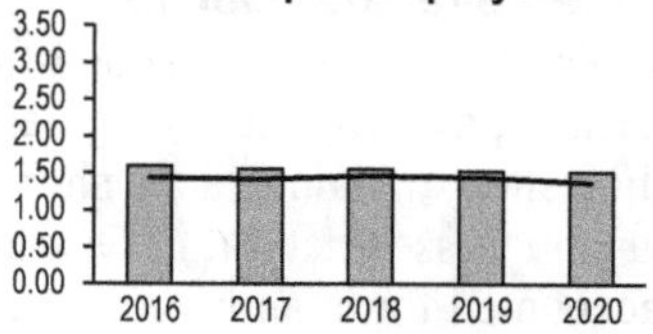

	2016	2017	2018	2019	2020
Greensboro	1.60	1.56	1.56	1.52	1.52
Average	1.43	1.42	1.45	1.44	1.37

Workload Measures

Number of Vehicle Equivalent Units (VEUs) per Technician FTE

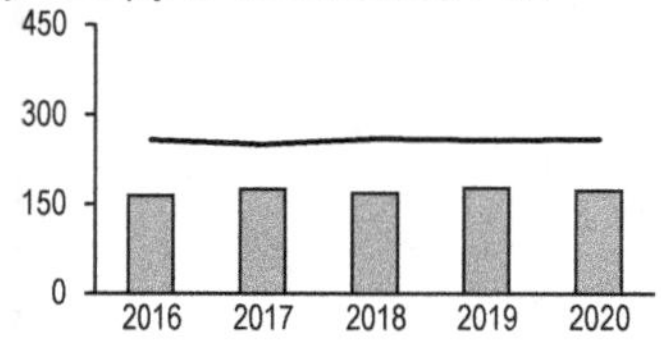

	2016	2017	2018	2019	2020
Greensboro	165	175	168	177	173
Average	256	249	259	257	258

Preventive Maintenances (PMs) Completed In-House per Tech FTE

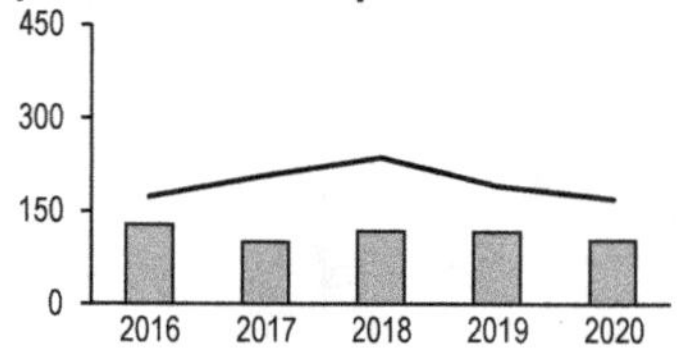

	2016	2017	2018	2019	2020
Greensboro	128	100	118	117	103
Average	173	207	237	191	170

Efficiency Measures

Fleet Maintenance Cost per Work Order

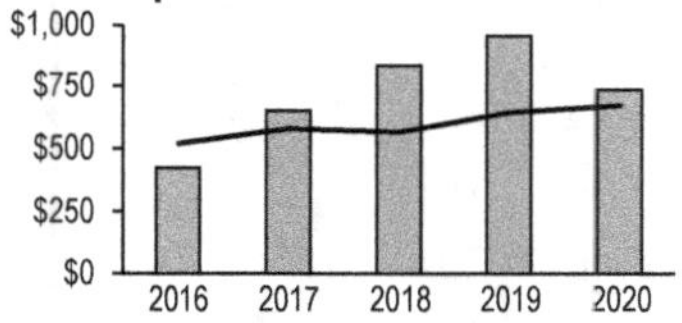

	2016	2017	2018	2019	2020
Greensboro	$422	$648	$832	$955	$733
Average	$520	$577	$564	$642	$670

Fleet Maintenance Cost per Vehicle Equivalent Unit (VEU)

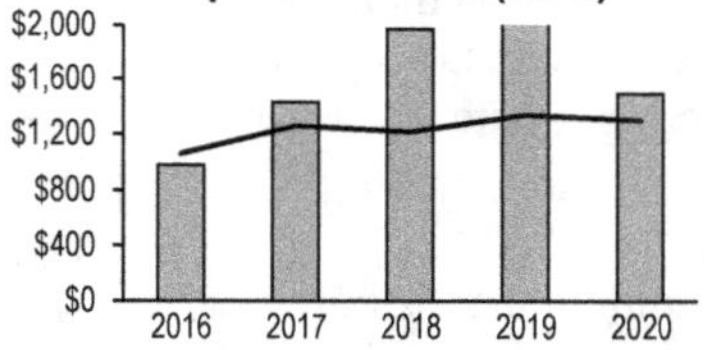

	2016	2017	2018	2019	2020
Greensboro	$979	$1,429	$1,970	$2,125	$1,493
Average	$1,060	$1,254	$1,212	$1,334	$1,297

Hours Billed as a Percentage of Total Hours

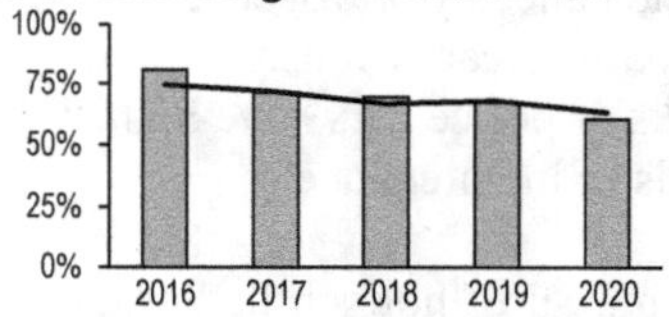

	2016	2017	2018	2019	2020
Greensboro	81%	71%	69%	67%	61%
Average	74%	72%	67%	68%	63%

Effectiveness Measures

Preventive Maintenances (PMs) as a Percentage of All Work Orders

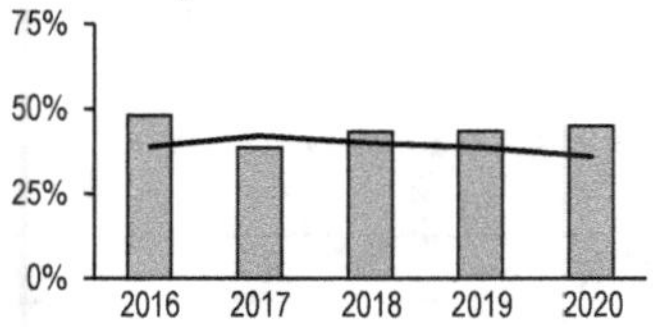

	2016	2017	2018	2019	2020
Greensboro	48%	39%	43%	43%	45%
Average	39%	42%	40%	39%	36%

Percentage of Preventive Maintenances (PMs) Completed as Scheduled

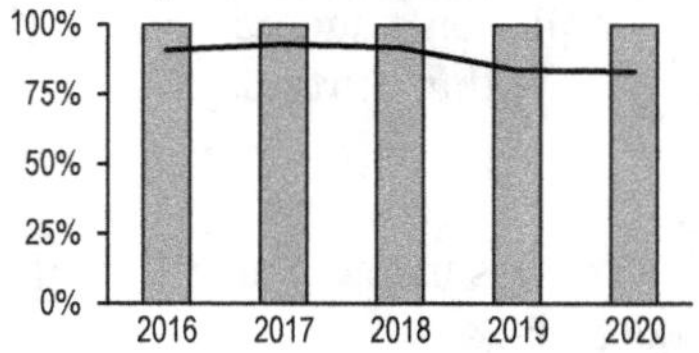

	2016	2017	2018	2019	2020
Greensboro	100%	100%	100%	100%	100%
Average	91%	93%	92%	84%	83%

Percentage of Work Orders Completed within 24 Hours

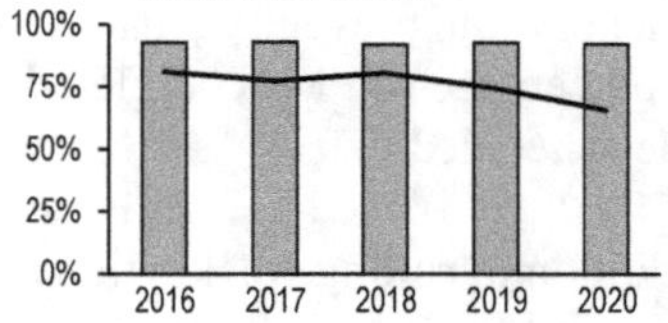

	2016	2017	2018	2019	2020
Greensboro	93%	93%	92%	93%	92%
Average	81%	77%	80%	74%	65%

Percentage of Rolling Stock Available per Day

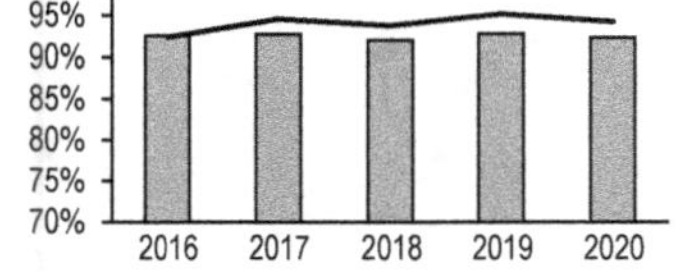

	2016	2017	2018	2019	2020
Greensboro	93%	93%	92%	93%	92%
Average	92%	95%	94%	95%	94%

Percentage of Work Orders Requiring Repeat Repair within 30 Days

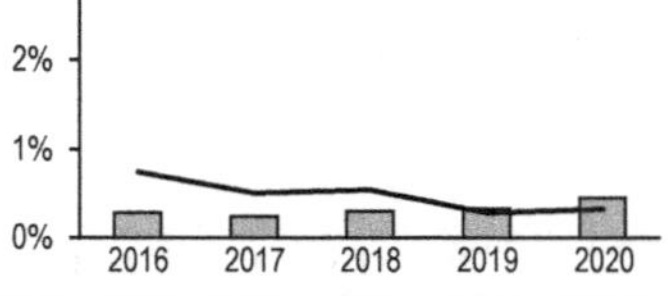

	2016	2017	2018	2019	2020
Greensboro	0.28%	0.23%	0.30%	0.33%	0.44%
Average	0.74%	0.50%	0.53%	0.28%	0.32%

Hickory — Fleet Maintenance

Fiscal Year 2019-20

Explanatory Information

Service Level and Delivery

Fleet Maintenance is a division of Hickory's Public Services Department and consists of a garage office, a parts warehouse, a welding shop, a maintenance shop, a fleet wash station, a fuel station, and a compressed natural gas station. All activities for this operation are accounted for in an internal service fund.

The division charges a $60-per-hour labor rate for maintenance services and a 25 percent markup charge on parts sold. There is no markup charge for sublet work.

The following services were contracted out:

- alignments
- body work
- large wrecker service
- special machine work
- starter/alternator repair
- glass repair or replacement
- transmission repairs.

Conditions Affecting Service, Performance, and Costs

Vehicle Equivalent Units (VEUs) are a weighted measure of the maintenance effort associated with different classes of vehicles. A normal-use car is considered equal to one VEU. Vehicles such as fire trucks or police cars have higher VEUs, reflecting greater expected levels of maintenance.

The measure "hours billed as a percentage of total hours" is based on a work year of 2,080 hours and only counts those positions that were filled. It should be noted that technicians have responsibilities that do not result in billable hours, and they take normal vacation and sick leave. Therefore, this percentage should not be expected to be near 100 percent.

In Hickory, the preventive maintenance (PM) completion standard for "percentage of PMs completed as scheduled" is within thirty days of the scheduled date.

In addition to rolling stock, Hickory's fleet services has maintenance responsibilities for electronic signs, saws, weedeaters, sewer machines, hole piercing tools, boring machines, pumps, mowers, edgers, a sand blaster, pressure washers, blowers, mules, spreaders, generators, tamps, vacuums, airport equipment, grinders, a fleet wash station, a compressed natural gas fuel station, a gasoline and diesel fuel station, and other equipment.

In Hickory, maintenance on fire vehicles is performed by mechanics in the fire department. The work performed is not counted here.

Municipal Profile

Population (OSBM 2019)	41,409
Land Area (Square Miles)	30.50
Persons per Square Mile	1,358

Service Profile

FTE Positions—Technician	6.0
FTE Positions—Other	4.0
Work Bays	14

Rolling Stock Maintained	No.	Average Age
Cars—Normal Usage	24	9.5 Years
Cars—Severe Usage	141	6.9 Years
Motorcycles	0	NA
Light Utility Vehicles	6	NA
Light Vehicles	110	7.7 Years
Medium Vehicles	38	12.4 Years
Heavy—Sanitation	31	10.2 Years
Heavy—Sewer	5	10.4 Years
Heavy—Fire Apparatus	0	NA
Heavy—Other	21	17.6 Years
Trailed Equipment	62	5.5 Years
Off-Road/Construction/Tractors	118	13.7 Years
Buses	0	NA
TOTAL	556	

Vehicle Equivalent Units (VEUs)	1,916
Average Rolling Stock Units Available per Day	515
Hours Billed	11,094
Work Orders	5,354
Repeat Repairs within 30 Days	0
Work Orders Completed within 24 hours	45
Preventive Maintenance Jobs (PMs)	1,252
PMs Completed as Scheduled	862

Full Cost Profile

Cost Breakdown by Percentage	
Personal Services	28.6%
Operating Costs	70.3%
Capital Costs	1.1%
TOTAL	100.0%

Cost Breakdown in Dollars	
Personal Services	$652,639
Operating Costs	$1,603,050
Capital Costs	$24,123
TOTAL	$2,279,812

Key: Hickory ▒ Benchmarking Average — Fiscal Years 2016 through 2020

Resource Measures

Fleet Maintenance Services Cost per Capita

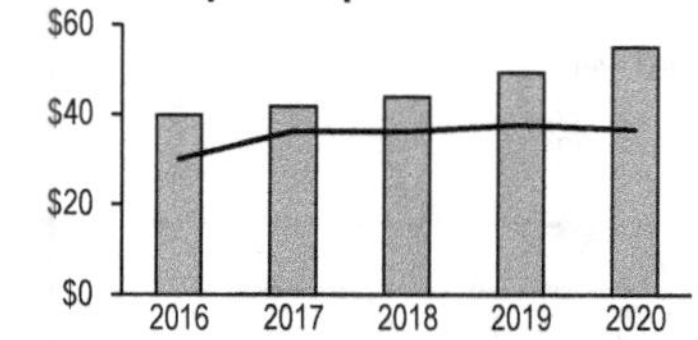

	2016	2017	2018	2019	2020
Hickory	$39.78	$41.75	$43.90	$49.34	$55.06
Average	$29.83	$36.10	$36.06	$37.55	$36.51

Fleet Maintenance FTEs per 10,000 Population

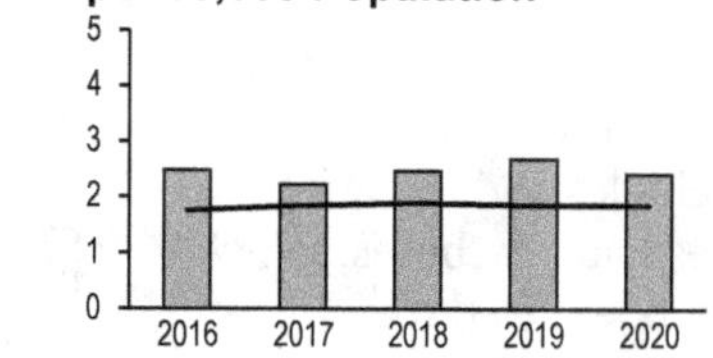

	2016	2017	2018	2019	2020
Hickory	2.48	2.22	2.46	2.69	2.41
Average	1.74	1.83	1.88	1.85	1.85

Fleet Maintenance FTEs per 100 Municipal Employees

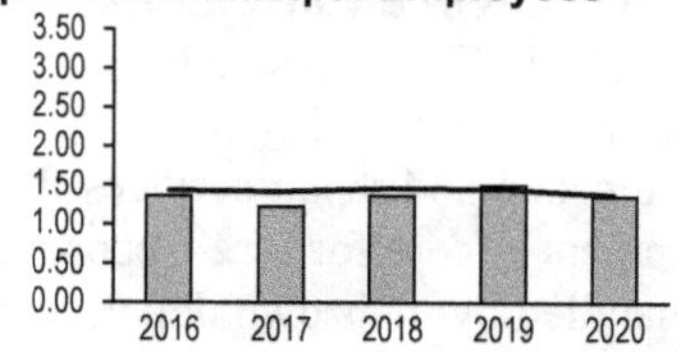

	2016	2017	2018	2019	2020
Hickory	1.36	1.22	1.36	1.49	1.35
Average	1.43	1.42	1.45	1.44	1.37

Workload Measures

Number of Vehicle Equivalent Units (VEUs) per Technician FTE

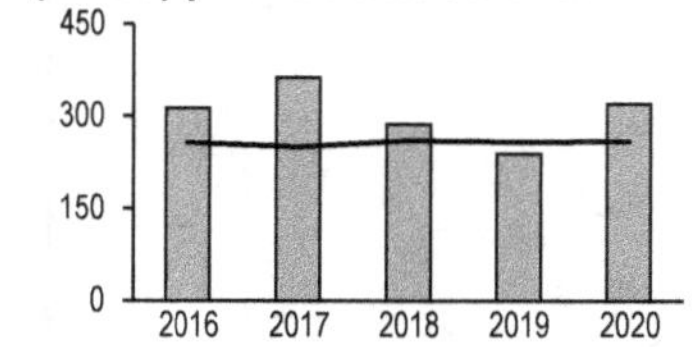

	2016	2017	2018	2019	2020
Hickory	312	362	286	238	319
Average	256	249	259	257	258

Preventive Maintenances (PMs) Completed In-House per Tech FTE

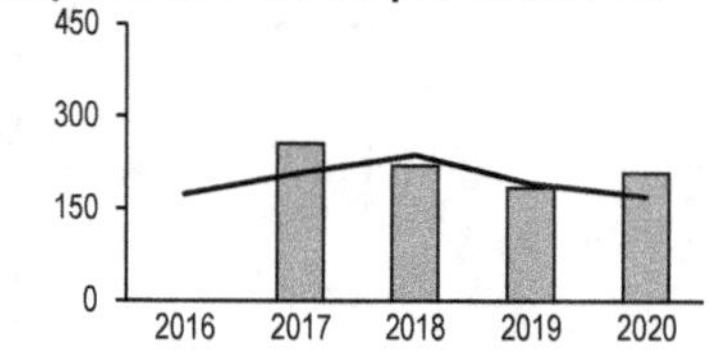

	2016	2017	2018	2019	2020
Hickory		256	220	184	209
Average	173	207	237	191	170

Efficiency Measures

Fleet Maintenance Cost per Work Order

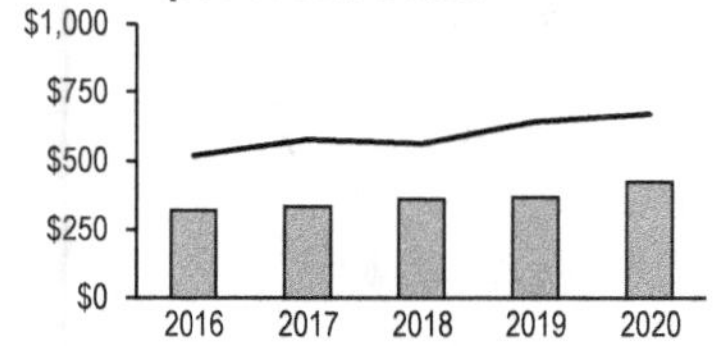

	2016	2017	2018	2019	2020
Hickory	$322	$336	$364	$370	$426
Average	$520	$577	$564	$642	$670

Fleet Maintenance Cost per Vehicle Equivalent Unit (VEU)

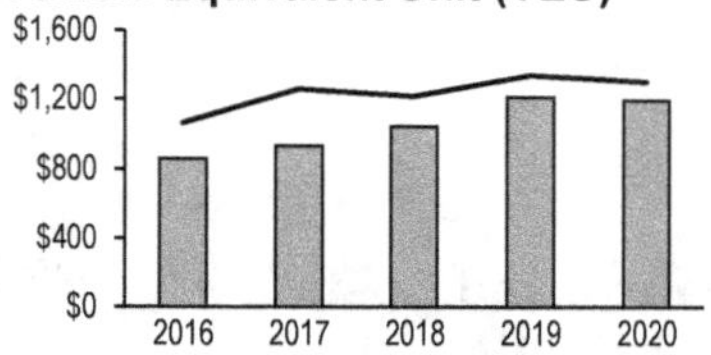

	2016	2017	2018	2019	2020
Hickory	$857	$932	$1,040	$1,211	$1,190
Average	$1,060	$1,254	$1,212	$1,334	$1,297

Hours Billed as a Percentage of Total Hours

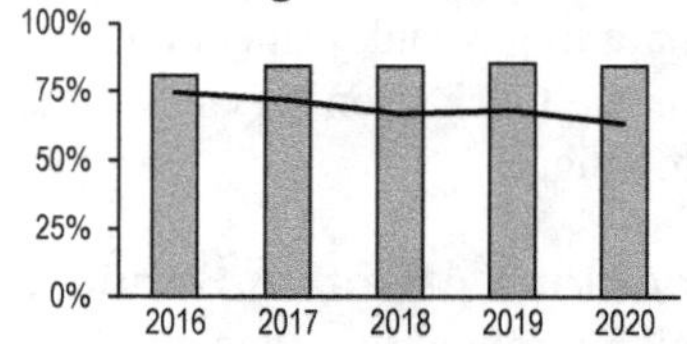

	2016	2017	2018	2019	2020
Hickory	81%	84%	84%	85%	84%
Average	74%	72%	67%	68%	63%

Effectiveness Measures

Preventive Maintenances (PMs) as a Percentage of All Work Orders

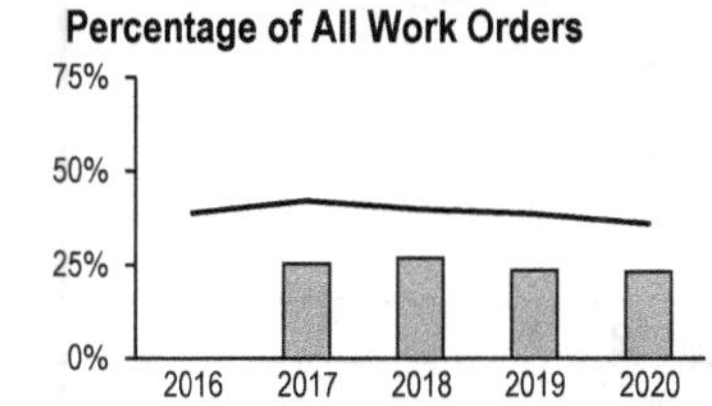

	2016	2017	2018	2019	2020
Hickory		25%	27%	24%	23%
Average	39%	42%	40%	39%	36%

Percentage of Preventive Maintenances (PMs) Completed as Scheduled

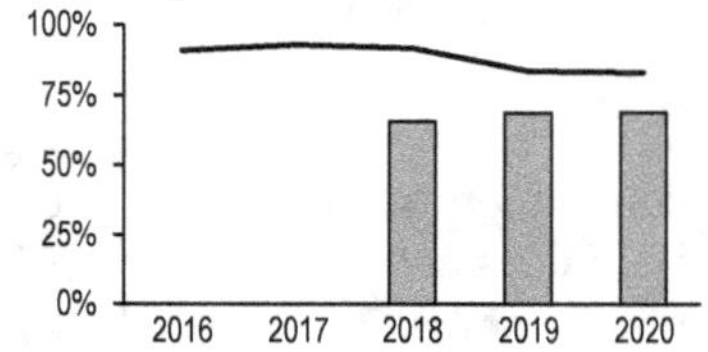

	2016	2017	2018	2019	2020
Hickory			66%	69%	69%
Average	91%	93%	92%	84%	83%

Percentage of Work Orders Completed within 24 Hours

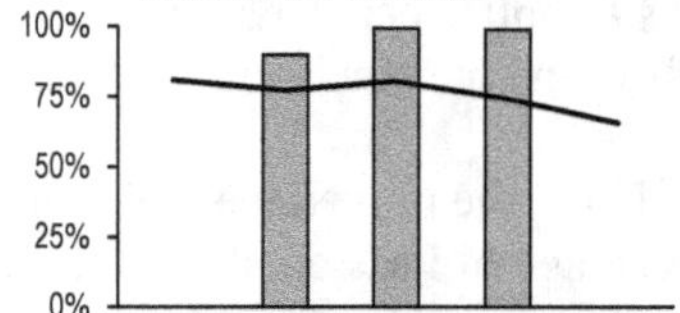

	2016	2017	2018	2019	2020
Hickory		90%	99%	99%	
Average	81%	77%	80%	74%	65%

Percentage of Rolling Stock Available per Day

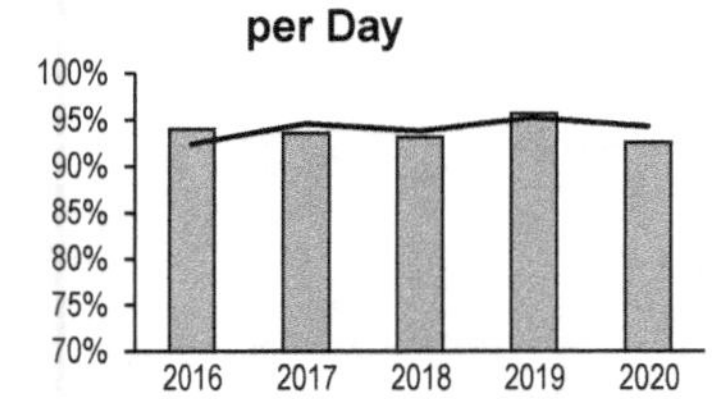

	2016	2017	2018	2019	2020
Hickory	94%	94%	93%	96%	93%
Average	92%	95%	94%	95%	94%

Percentage of Work Orders Requiring Repeat Repair within 30 Days

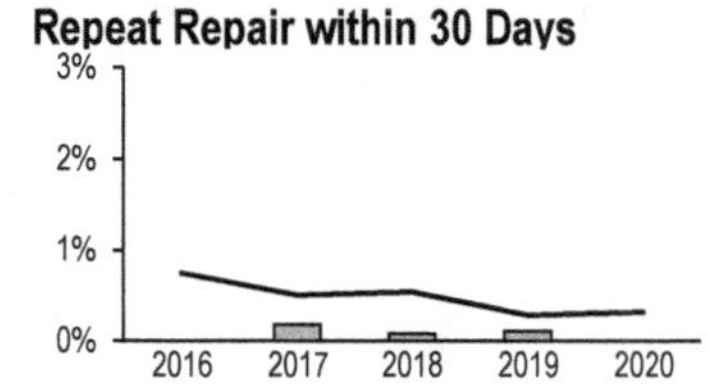

	2016	2017	2018	2019	2020
Hickory		0.18%	0.08%	0.11%	0.00%
Average	0.74%	0.50%	0.53%	0.28%	0.32%

Fiscal Year 2019-20

Explanatory Information

Service Level and Delivery

The Vehicle Fleet Service Division is under the Engineering Services Department for the City of Raleigh. The division provides maintenance and repair services for all city vehicles and motorized equipment except for Fire Department vehicles and city buses, which are handled by their own department. The city operates three separate locations to service vehicles. The division also handles replacement of new vehicles and equipment, managing fuel operations, and the city motor pool. The division is run as an internal service fund for the city.

Varying labor rates are used for different types of workers ranging from $44 per hour for preventative maintenance technicians up to $72 for heavy equipment mechanics. A markup of 30 percent is added for parts, and a 20 percent markup is added for sublet work.

The following services were contracted out:

- body work
- painting of new vehicles
- transmission work and overhauls
- some engine replacements
- spring work
- natural gas tank inspections
- onsite lubrication services for refuse vehicles
- towing.

Conditions Affecting Service, Performance, and Costs

Raleigh rejoined the Benchmarking Project in July 2016, with the first year of data showing for FY 2015–16.

Vehicle Equivalent Units (VEUs) are a weighted measure of the maintenance effort associated with different classes of vehicles. A normal-use car is considered equal to one VEU. Vehicles such as fire trucks or police cars have higher VEUs, reflecting greater expected levels of maintenance.

In Raleigh, the preventive maintenance (PM) completion standard for "percentage of PMs completed as scheduled" is 45 days and a 30 percent variance for meters, which could be miles or hours.

In addition to maintenance responsibilities for the city's rolling stock, the division also has responsibility for equipment, including pumps, weed eaters, concrete saws, mowers, blowers, compressors, light towers, scissor lifts, vacuums, pipe saws, flashing light arrows, chippers, spray washes, line markers, leaf vacuums, outboard motors, spreaders, generators, paint sprayers, grass trimmers, yard waste handlers, power rodders, golf carts, forklifts, and other city equipment.

Municipal Profile

Population (OSBM 2019)	475,580
Land Area (Square Miles)	146.47
Persons per Square Mile	3,247

Service Profile

FTE Positions—Technician	46.0
FTE Positions—Other	31.0
Work Bays	51

Rolling Stock Maintained	No.	Average Age
Cars—Normal Usage	238	5.4 Years
Cars—Severe Usage	454	4.5 Years
Motorcycles	8	3.3 Years
Light Utility Vehicles	91	6.6 Years
Light Vehicles	889	5.7 Years
Medium Vehicles	150	6.4 Years
Heavy—Sanitation	107	5.2 Years
Heavy—Sewer	25	5.7 Years
Heavy—Fire Apparatus	0	NA
Heavy—Other	156	6.8 Years
Trailed Equipment	360	10.2 Years
Off-Road/Construction/Tractors	216	8.9 Years
Buses	19	10.4 Years
TOTAL	2,713	

Vehicle Equivalent Units (VEUs)	7,993
Average Rolling Stock Units Available per Day	2,588
Hours Billed	53,545
Work Orders	23,453
Repeat Repairs within 30 Days	153
Work Orders Completed within 24 hours	5,304
Preventive Maintenance Jobs (PMs)	8,038
PMs Completed as Scheduled	6,409

Full Cost Profile

Cost Breakdown by Percentage	
Personal Services	48.0%
Operating Costs	46.3%
Capital Costs	5.8%
TOTAL	100.0%

Cost Breakdown in Dollars	
Personal Services	$5,522,911
Operating Costs	$5,327,734
Capital Costs	$666,423
TOTAL	$11,517,068

Key: Raleigh ■ Benchmarking Average — Fiscal Years 2016 through 2020

Resource Measures

Fleet Maintenance Services Cost per Capita

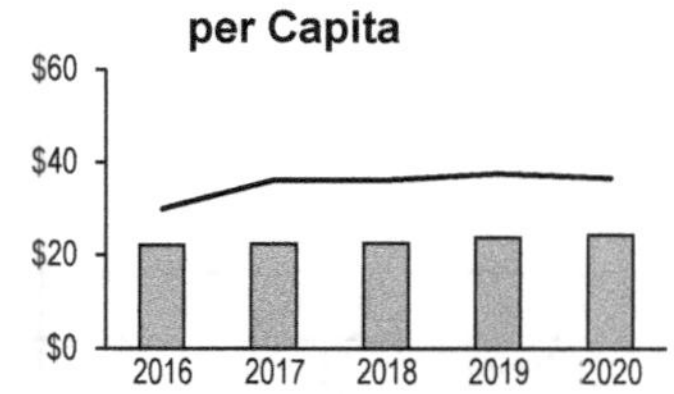

	2016	2017	2018	2019	2020
Raleigh	$21.97	$22.36	$22.51	$23.74	$24.22
Average	$29.83	$36.10	$36.06	$37.55	$36.51

Fleet Maintenance FTEs per 10,000 Population

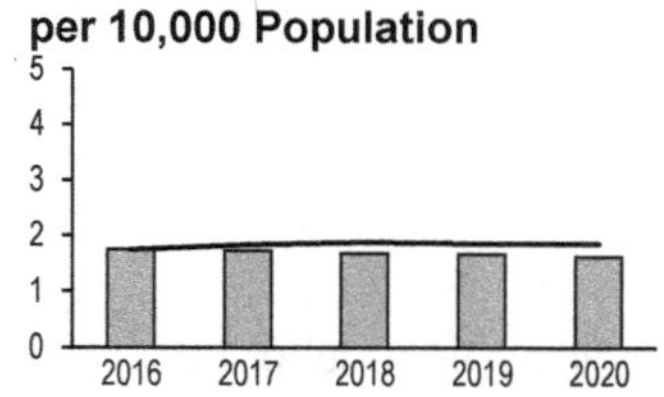

	2016	2017	2018	2019	2020
Raleigh	1.75	1.72	1.67	1.66	1.62
Average	1.74	1.83	1.88	1.85	1.85

Fleet Maintenance FTEs per 100 Municipal Employees

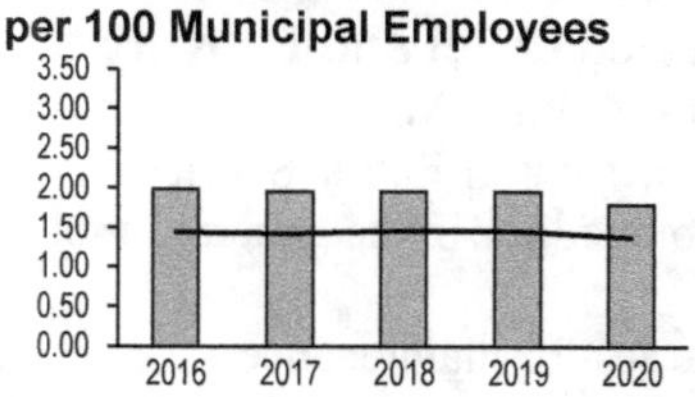

	2016	2017	2018	2019	2020
Raleigh	1.98	1.95	1.95	1.95	1.79
Average	1.43	1.42	1.45	1.44	1.37

Workload Measures

Number of Vehicle Equivalent Units (VEUs) per Technician FTE

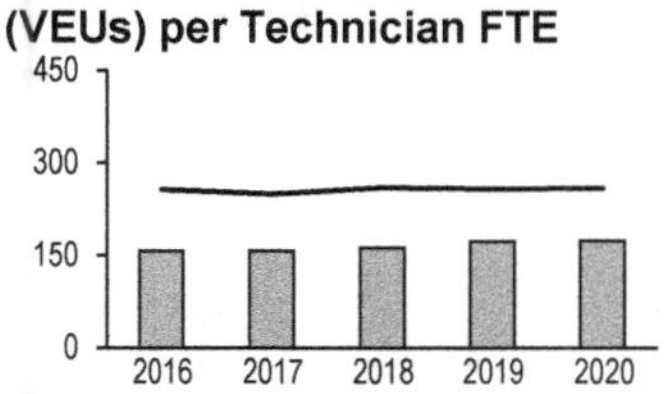

	2016	2017	2018	2019	2020
Raleigh	157	157	162	172	174
Average	256	249	259	257	258

Preventive Maintenances (PMs) Completed In-House per Tech FTE

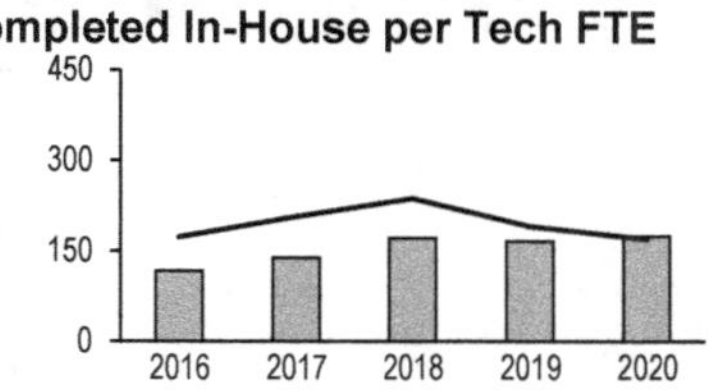

	2016	2017	2018	2019	2020
Raleigh	116	139	171	166	175
Average	173	207	237	191	170

Efficiency Measures

Fleet Maintenance Cost per Work Order

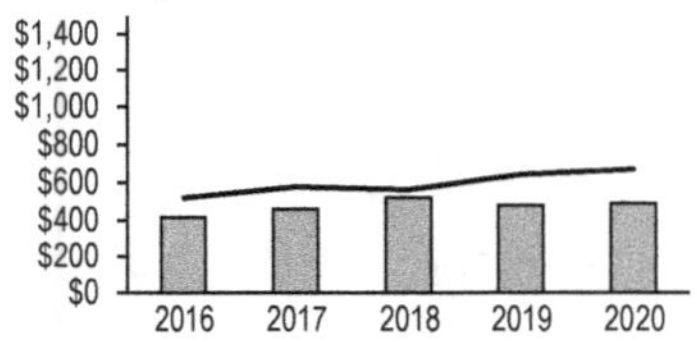

	2016	2017	2018	2019	2020
Raleigh	$416	$459	$522	$481	$491
Average	$520	$577	$564	$642	$670

Fleet Maintenance Cost per Vehicle Equivalent Unit (VEU)

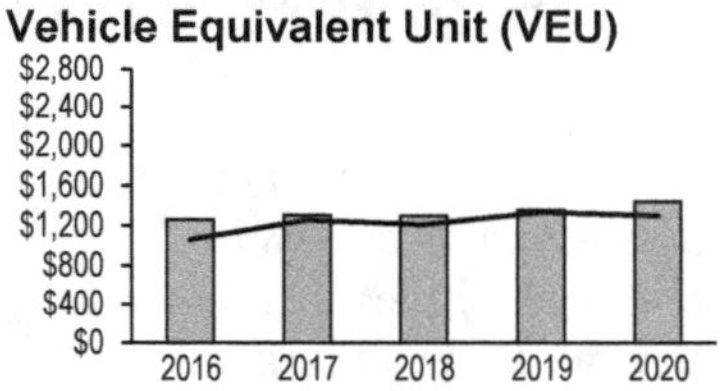

	2016	2017	2018	2019	2020
Raleigh	$1,260	$1,306	$1,302	$1,362	$1,441
Average	$1,060	$1,254	$1,212	$1,334	$1,297

Hours Billed as a Percentage of Total Hours

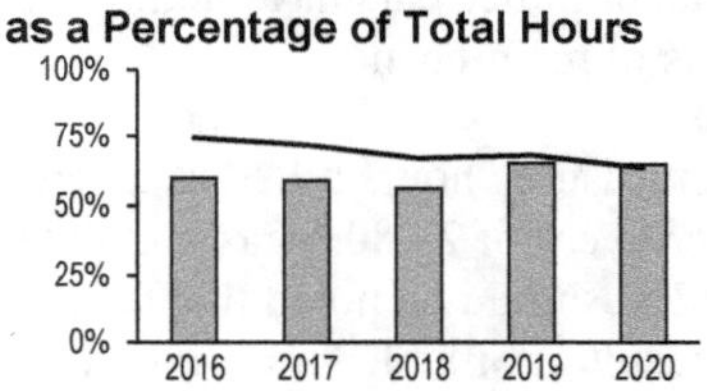

	2016	2017	2018	2019	2020
Raleigh	60%	59%	56%	65%	65%
Average	74%	72%	67%	68%	63%

Effectiveness Measures

Preventive Maintenances (PMs) as a Percentage of All Work Orders

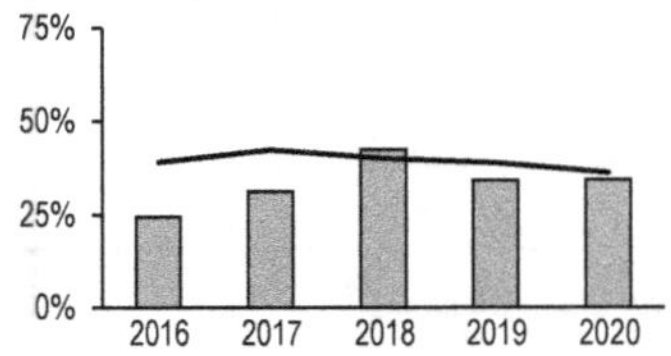

	2016	2017	2018	2019	2020
Raleigh	24%	31%	42%	34%	34%
Average	39%	42%	40%	39%	36%

Percentage of Preventive Maintenances (PMs) Completed as Scheduled

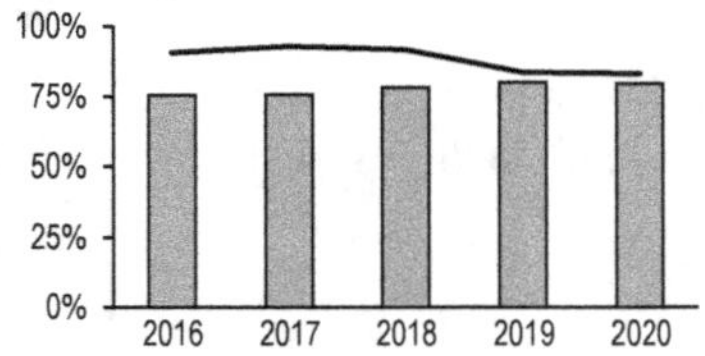

	2016	2017	2018	2019	2020
Raleigh	76%	76%	78%	80%	80%
Average	91%	93%	92%	84%	83%

Percentage of Work Orders Completed within 24 Hours

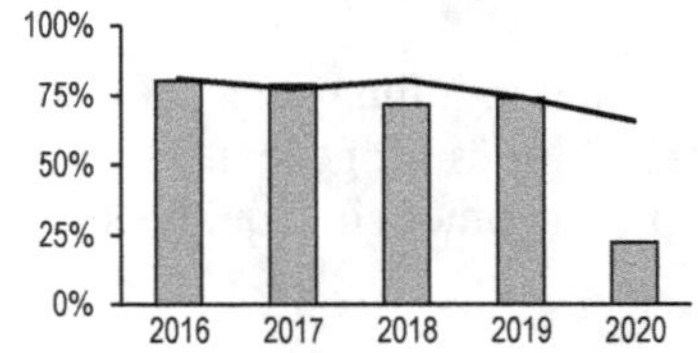

	2016	2017	2018	2019	2020
Raleigh	80%	79%	72%	74%	23%
Average	81%	77%	80%	74%	65%

Percentage of Rolling Stock Available per Day

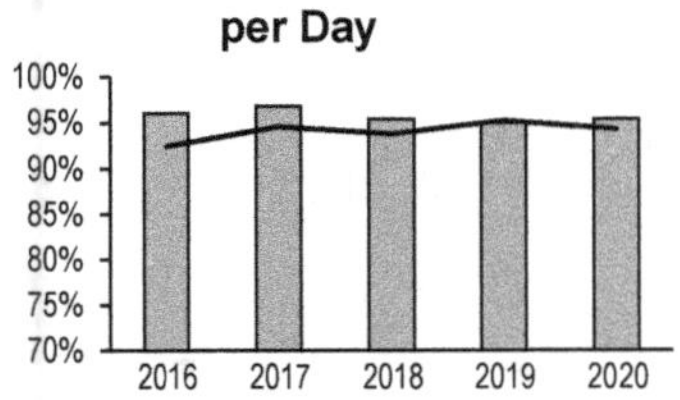

	2016	2017	2018	2019	2020
Raleigh	96%	97%	95%	95%	95%
Average	92%	95%	94%	95%	94%

Percentage of Work Orders Requiring Repeat Repair within 30 Days

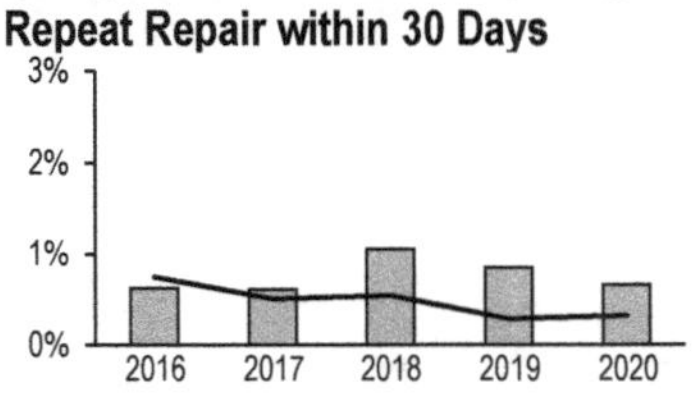

	2016	2017	2018	2019	2020
Raleigh	0.62%	0.61%	1.06%	0.85%	0.65%
Average	0.74%	0.50%	0.53%	0.28%	0.32%

Fiscal Year 2019-20

Explanatory Information

Service Level and Delivery

Wilson's Fleet Maintenance Division is housed within the Department of Public Services. All activities in this operation are accounted for in the general fund.

Charges for maintenance services included a $44-per-hour labor rate, a 25 percent markup charge on parts sold, and a 5 percent markup charge on sublet work.

The following services were contracted out:

- body repairs
- paint work
- wrecker service
- radiator repairs
- alignment
- muffler repairs.

Conditions Affecting Service, Performance, and Costs

Vehicle Equivalent Units (VEUs) are a weighted measure of the maintenance effort associated with different classes of vehicles. A normal-use car is considered equal to one VEU. Vehicles such as fire trucks or police cars have higher VEUs, reflecting greater expected levels of maintenance.

The measure "hours billed as a percentage of total hours" is based on a work year of 2,080 hours and only counts those positions that were filled. It should be noted that technicians have responsibilities that do not result in billable hours, and they take normal vacation and sick leave. Therefore, this percentage should not be expected to be near 100 percent.

In Wilson, the preventive maintenance (PM) completion standard for "percentage of PMs completed as scheduled" varies, including both calendar and mileage standards.

In addition to rolling stock, Wilson's fleet services has maintenance responsibilities for generators, mowers, tamps, leaf machines, water pumps, and other city equipment.

Municipal Profile

Population (OSBM 2019)	49,384
Land Area (Square Miles)	31.02
Persons per Square Mile	1,592

Service Profile

FTE Positions—Technician	11.0
FTE Positions—Other	5.0
Work Bays	15

Rolling Stock Maintained	No.	Average Age
Cars—Normal Usage	29	8.1 Years
Cars—Severe Usage	118	6.7 Years
Motorcycles	3	4.0 Years
Light Utility Vehicles	19	10.1 Years
Light Vehicles	214	8.6 Years
Medium Vehicles	59	13.0 Years
Heavy—Sanitation	33	8.8 Years
Heavy—Sewer	4	6.5 Years
Heavy—Fire Apparatus	10	13.6 Years
Heavy—Other	62	9.5 Years
Trailed Equipment	167	15.0 Years
Off-Road/Construction/Tractors	162	14.0 Years
Buses	4	15.0 Years
TOTAL	884	

Vehicle Equivalent Units (VEUs)	2,891
Average Rolling Stock Units Available per Day	849
Hours Billed	18,563
Work Orders	6,639
Repeat Repairs within 30 Days	21
Work Orders Completed within 24 hours	5,643
Preventive Maintenance Jobs (PMs)	1,646
PMs Completed as Scheduled	1,481

Full Cost Profile

Cost Breakdown by Percentage	
Personal Services	30.2%
Operating Costs	65.7%
Capital Costs	4.0%
TOTAL	100.0%

Cost Breakdown in Dollars	
Personal Services	$1,229,061
Operating Costs	$2,670,683
Capital Costs	$163,957
TOTAL	$4,063,701

Wilson — Fleet Maintenance

Key: Wilson ■ Benchmarking Average — Fiscal Years 2016 through 2020

Resource Measures

Fleet Maintenance Services Cost per Capita

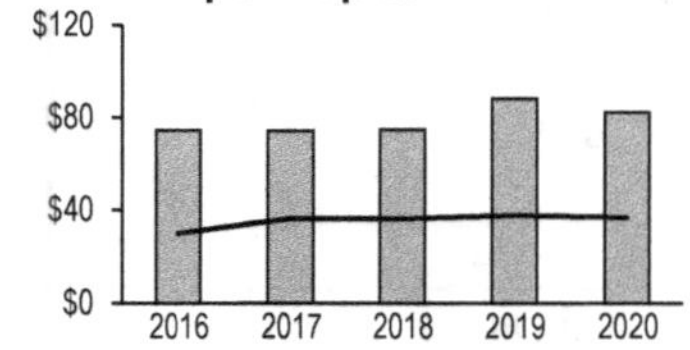

	2016	2017	2018	2019	2020
Wilson	$74.36	$74.24	$74.80	$88.02	$82.29
Average	$29.83	$36.10	$36.06	$37.55	$36.51

Fleet Maintenance FTEs per 10,000 Population

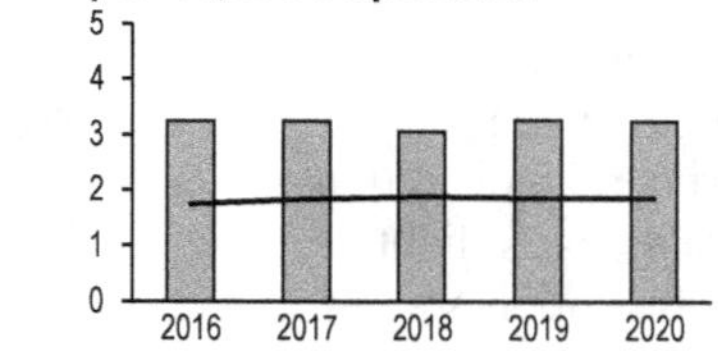

	2016	2017	2018	2019	2020
Wilson	3.24	3.24	3.05	3.26	3.24
Average	1.74	1.83	1.88	1.85	1.85

Fleet Maintenance FTEs per 100 Municipal Employees

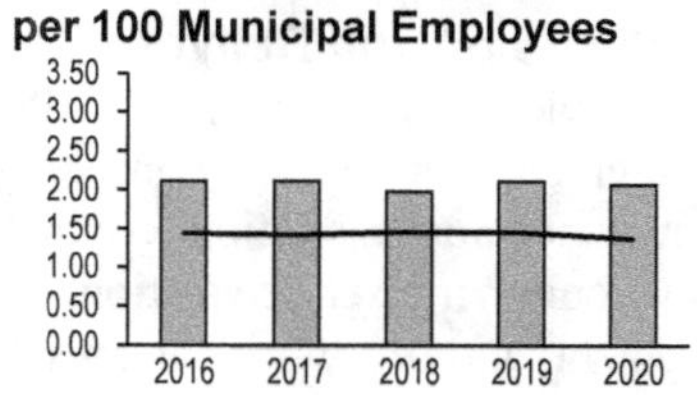

	2016	2017	2018	2019	2020
Wilson	2.11	2.11	1.97	2.11	2.07
Average	1.43	1.42	1.45	1.44	1.37

Workload Measures

Number of Vehicle Equivalent Units (VEUs) per Technician FTE

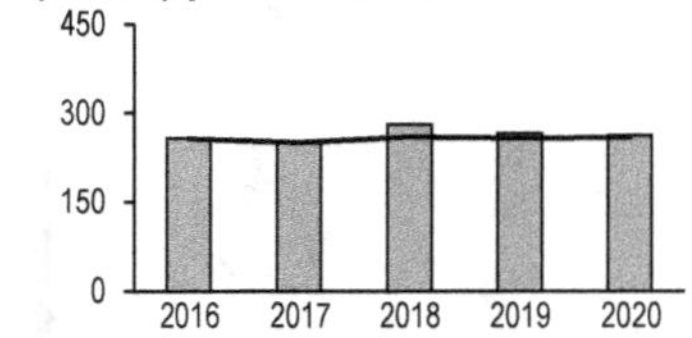

	2016	2017	2018	2019	2020
Wilson	257	250	281	266	263
Average	256	249	259	257	258

Preventive Maintenances (PMs) Completed In-House per Tech FTE

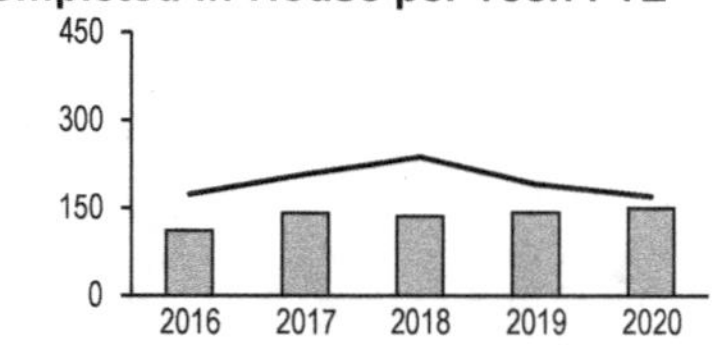

	2016	2017	2018	2019	2020
Wilson	110	141	135	143	150
Average	173	207	237	191	170

Efficiency Measures

Fleet Maintenance Cost per Work Order

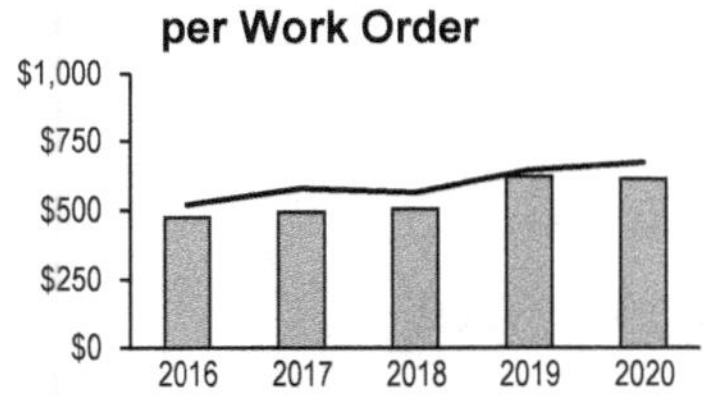

	2016	2017	2018	2019	2020
Wilson	$475	$495	$505	$621	$612
Average	$520	$577	$564	$642	$670

Fleet Maintenance Cost per Vehicle Equivalent Unit (VEU)

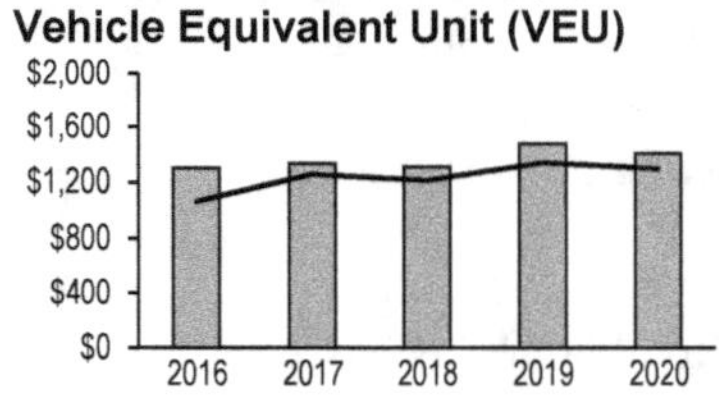

	2016	2017	2018	2019	2020
Wilson	$1,298	$1,333	$1,308	$1,474	$1,406
Average	$1,060	$1,254	$1,212	$1,334	$1,297

Hours Billed as a Percentage of Total Hours

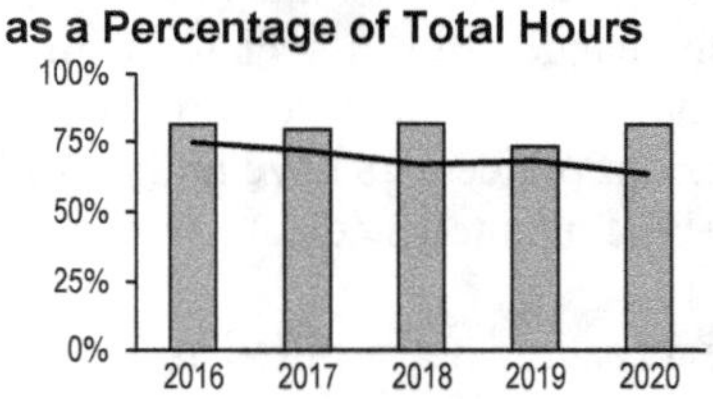

	2016	2017	2018	2019	2020
Wilson	81%	79%	81%	73%	81%
Average	74%	72%	67%	68%	63%

Effectiveness Measures

Preventive Maintenances (PMs) as a Percentage of All Work Orders

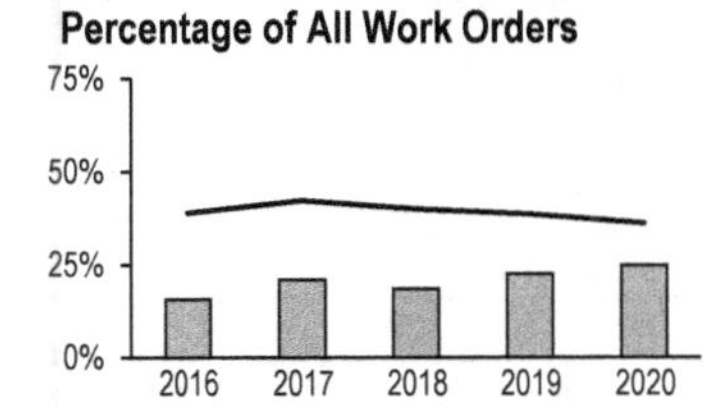

	2016	2017	2018	2019	2020
Wilson	16%	21%	19%	23%	25%
Average	39%	42%	40%	39%	36%

Percentage of Preventive Maintenances (PMs) Completed as Scheduled

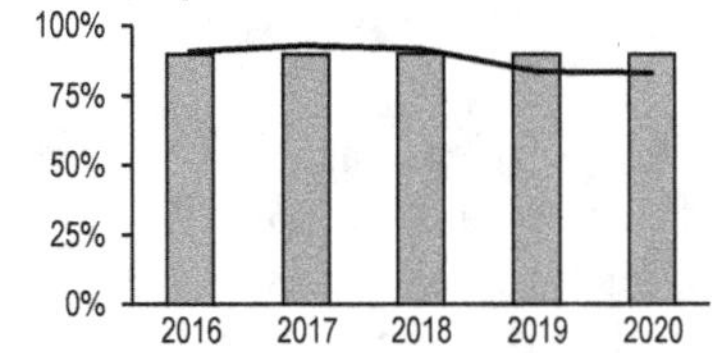

	2016	2017	2018	2019	2020
Wilson	90%	90%	90%	90%	90%
Average	91%	93%	92%	84%	83%

Percentage of Work Orders Completed within 24 Hours

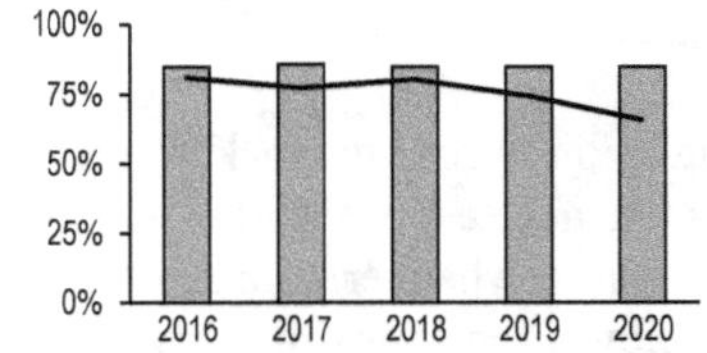

	2016	2017	2018	2019	2020
Wilson	85%	86%	85%	85%	85%
Average	81%	77%	80%	74%	65%

Percentage of Rolling Stock Available per Day

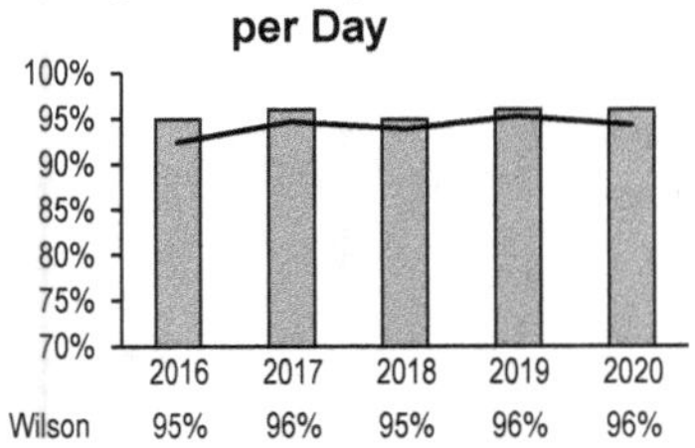

	2016	2017	2018	2019	2020
Wilson	95%	96%	95%	96%	96%
Average	92%	95%	94%	95%	94%

Percentage of Work Orders Requiring Repeat Repair within 30 Days

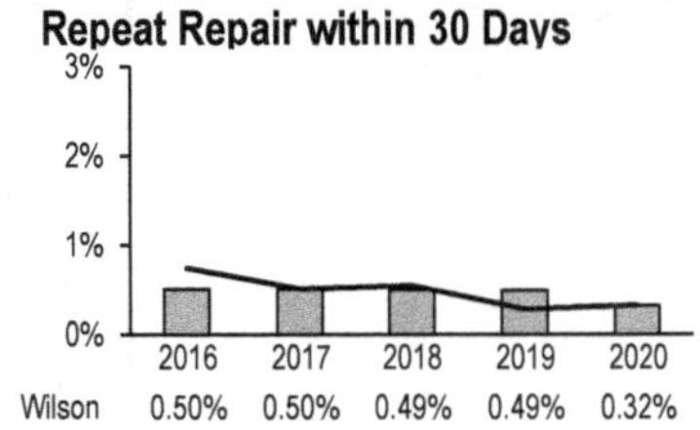

	2016	2017	2018	2019	2020
Wilson	0.50%	0.50%	0.49%	0.49%	0.32%
Average	0.74%	0.50%	0.53%	0.28%	0.32%

Winston-Salem — Fleet Maintenance

Fiscal Year 2019-20

Explanatory Information

Service Level and Delivery

Fleet Services is a division of the Property and Facilities Management Department, consisting of eight units: vehicle maintenance administration, contract monitoring administration, heavy equipment, service station, vehicle leasing, parts, light equipment, and tire shop. All activities in this operation are accounted for in an internal service fund.

Charges for maintenance services included a $50-per-hour labor rate, a 26 percent markup charge for parts sold, and a 13 percent markup charge for sublet work.

The following services were contracted out:

- body work
- welding
- hydraulic cylinder and pump repair
- glass repair
- towing
- transmission repair.

Conditions Affecting Service, Performance, and Costs

Vehicle Equivalent Units (VEUs) are a weighted measure of the maintenance effort associated with different classes of vehicles. A normal-use car is considered equal to one VEU. Vehicles such as fire trucks or police cars have higher VEUs, reflecting greater expected levels of maintenance.

The measure "hours billed as a percentage of total hours" is based on a work year of 2,080 hours and only counts those positions that were filled. It should be noted that technicians have responsibilities that do not result in billable hours, and they take normal vacation and sick leave. Therefore, this percentage should not be expected to be near 100 percent. Winston-Salem indicated that seventeen technician FTEs were actually working during the fiscal year for this calculation.

In addition to rolling stock, Winston-Salem's Fleet Services has maintenance responsibilities for mowers, weedeaters, water pumps, chain saws, whacker tamps, pavement stripers, tractor implements, leaf blowers, power trimmers, salt spreaders, snow plows, and other city equipment.

In Winston-Salem, maintenance on fire vehicles is performed by mechanics in the fire department. Those mechanics and that work performed are not counted here.

Municipal Profile

Population (OSBM 2019)	244,739
Land Area (Square Miles)	132.59
Persons per Square Mile	1,846

Service Profile

FTE Positions—Technician	19.0
FTE Positions—Other	13.0
Work Bays	30

Rolling Stock Maintained	No.	Average Age
Cars—Normal Usage	265	8.0 Years
Cars—Severe Usage	444	7.0 Years
Motorcycles	15	NA
Light Utility Vehicles	11	NA
Light Vehicles	442	9.0 Years
Medium Vehicles	144	10.0 Years
Heavy—Sanitation	55	7.0 Years
Heavy—Sewer	11	4.0 Years
Heavy—Fire Apparatus	0	NA
Heavy—Other	66	7.0 Years
Trailed Equipment	172	NA
Off-Road/Construction/Tractors	264	10.0 Years
Buses	0	NA
TOTAL	1,889	

Vehicle Equivalent Units (VEUs)	5,419
Average Rolling Stock Units Available per Day	1,749
Hours Billed	20,627
Work Orders	10,401
Repeat Repairs within 30 Days	81
Work Orders Completed within 24 hours	6,814
Preventive Maintenance Jobs (PMs)	2,379
PMs Completed as Scheduled	1,146

Full Cost Profile

Cost Breakdown by Percentage	
Personal Services	28.6%
Operating Costs	69.6%
Capital Costs	1.8%
TOTAL	100.0%

Cost Breakdown in Dollars	
Personal Services	$1,796,700
Operating Costs	$4,375,447
Capital Costs	$110,470
TOTAL	$6,282,617

Winston-Salem

Fleet Maintenance

Key: Winston-Salem ▒ Benchmarking Average — Fiscal Years 2016 through 2020

Resource Measures

Fleet Maintenance Services Cost per Capita

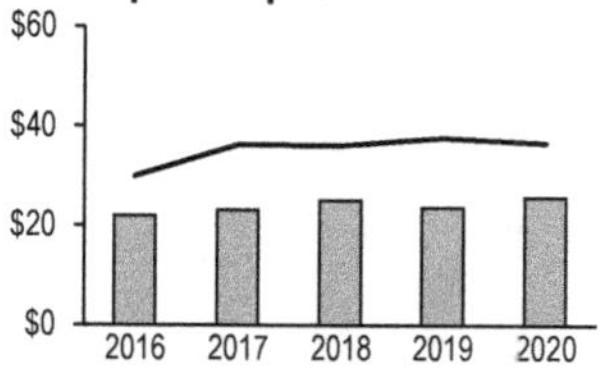

	2016	2017	2018	2019	2020
Winston-Salem	$21.87	$23.08	$24.98	$23.53	$25.67
Average	$29.83	$36.10	$36.06	$37.55	$36.51

Fleet Maintenance FTEs per 10,000 Population

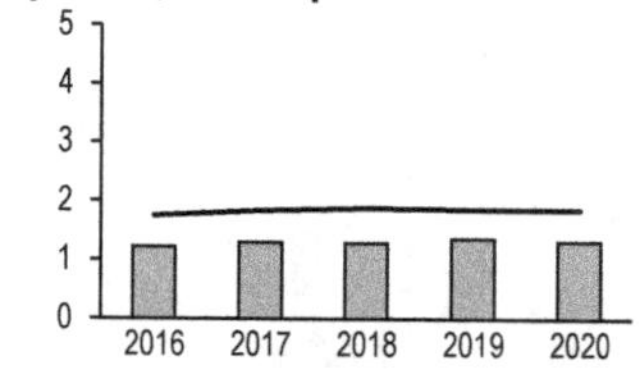

	2016	2017	2018	2019	2020
Winston-Salem	1.21	1.29	1.28	1.36	1.31
Average	1.74	1.83	1.88	1.85	1.85

Fleet Maintenance FTEs per 100 Municipal Employees

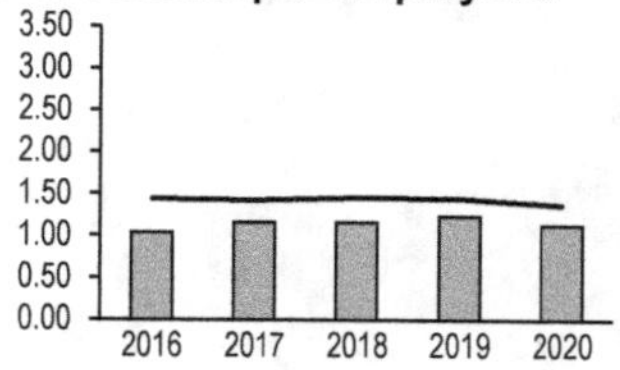

	2016	2017	2018	2019	2020
Winston-Salem	1.04	1.16	1.16	1.23	1.13
Average	1.43	1.42	1.45	1.44	1.37

Workload Measures

Number of Vehicle Equivalent Units (VEUs) per Technician FTE

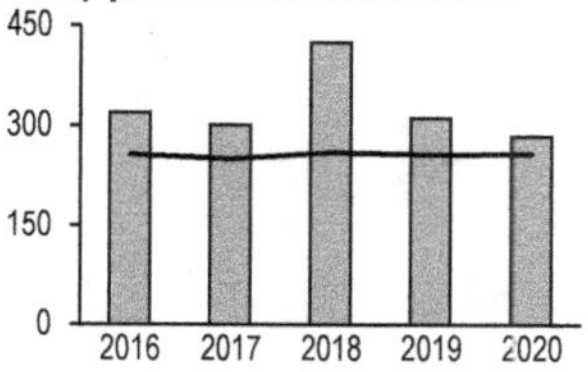

	2016	2017	2018	2019	2020
Winston-Salem	320	302	425	312	285
Average	256	249	259	257	258

Preventive Maintenances (PMs) Completed In-House per Tech FTE

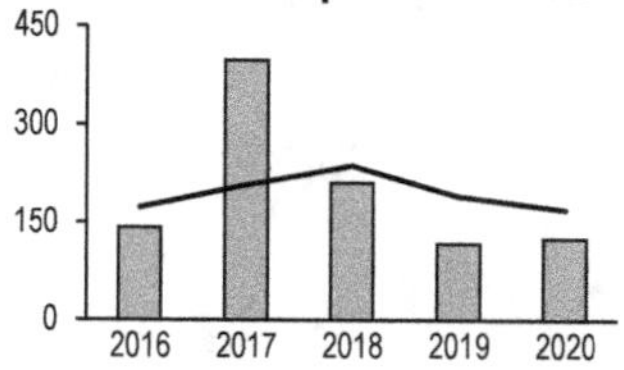

	2016	2017	2018	2019	2020
Winston-Salem	142	398	211	118	125
Average	173	207	237	191	170

Efficiency Measures

Fleet Maintenance Cost per Work Order

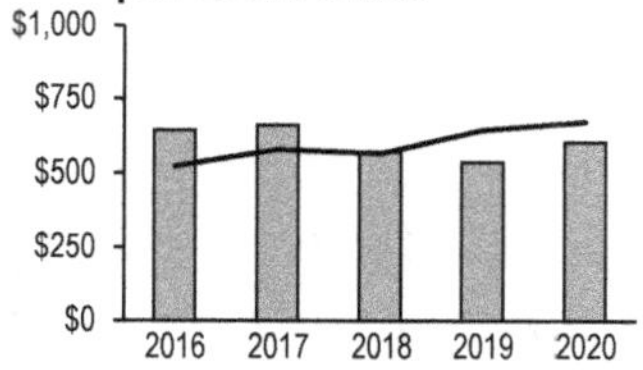

	2016	2017	2018	2019	2020
Winston-Salem	$642	$661	$572	$535	$604
Average	$520	$577	$564	$642	$670

Fleet Maintenance Cost per Vehicle Equivalent Unit (VEU)

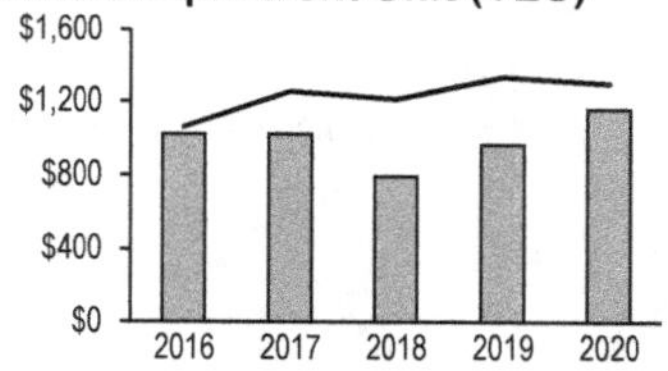

	2016	2017	2018	2019	2020
Winston-Salem	$1,021	$1,022	$793	$966	$1,159
Average	$1,060	$1,254	$1,212	$1,334	$1,297

Hours Billed as a Percentage of Total Hours

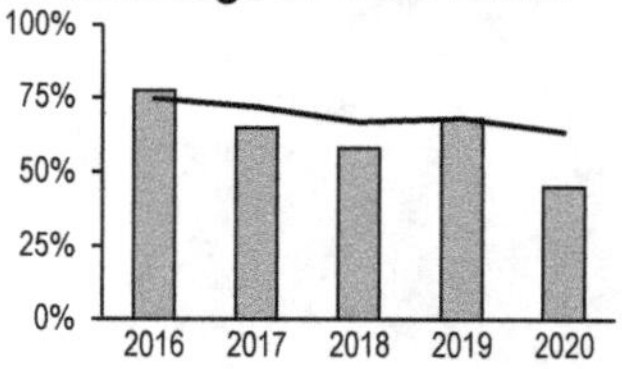

	2016	2017	2018	2019	2020
Winston-Salem	77%	65%	58%	68%	45%
Average	74%	72%	67%	68%	63%

Effectiveness Measures

Preventive Maintenances (PMs) as a Percentage of All Work Orders

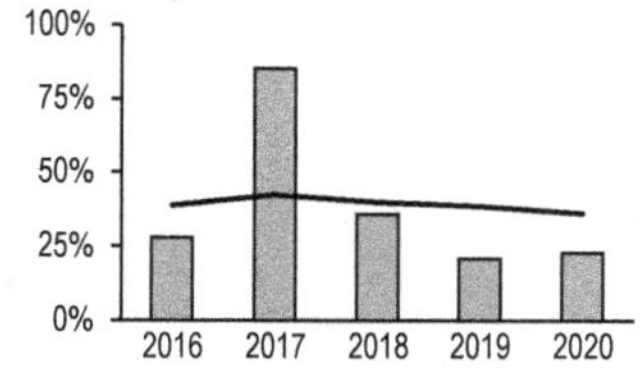

	2016	2017	2018	2019	2020
Winston-Salem	28%	85%	36%	21%	23%
Average	39%	42%	40%	39%	36%

Percentage of Preventive Maintenances (PMs) Completed as Scheduled

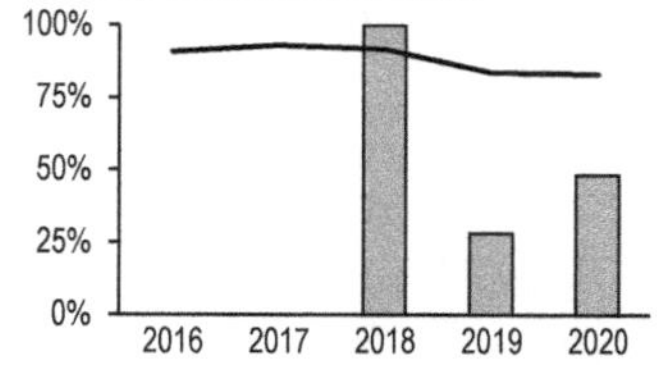

	2016	2017	2018	2019	2020
Winston-Salem			100%	28%	48%
Average	91%	93%	92%	84%	83%

Percentage of Work Orders Completed within 24 Hours

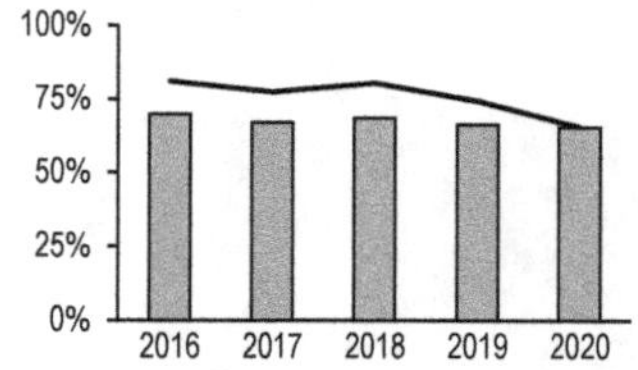

	2016	2017	2018	2019	2020
Winston-Salem	70%	67%	68%	66%	66%
Average	81%	77%	80%	74%	65%

Percentage of Rolling Stock Available per Day

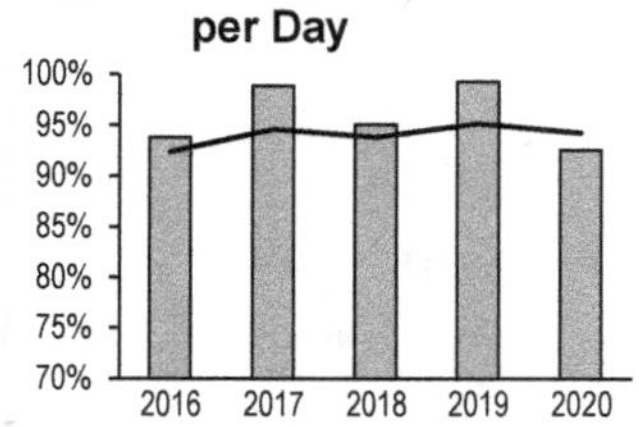

	2016	2017	2018	2019	2020
Winston-Salem	94%	99%	95%	99%	93%
Average	92%	95%	94%	95%	94%

Percentage of Work Orders Requiring Repeat Repair within 30 Days

	2016	2017	2018	2019	2020
Winston-Salem			0.57%		0.78%
Average	0.74%	0.50%	0.53%	0.28%	0.32%

UNC | SCHOOL OF GOVERNMENT
North Carolina Benchmarking Project

Performance and Cost Data

CENTRAL HUMAN RESOURCES

SCHOOL OF GOVERNMENT
North Carolina Benchmarking Project

PERFORMANCE MEASURES FOR CENTRAL HUMAN RESOURCES

SERVICE DEFINITION

Central Human Resources represents an internal support service. It is characterized by various functions related to the daily management of human capital or personnel, including compensation analysis; position classification; benefits administration; management of employee training and development; employee relations; position control; employee performance evaluations; recruitment and selection; occupational health, wellness, and safety programs; administration of the Human Resources Information System (HRIS); and general administration of the central human resources office. Excluded from the counts here are staff who may be assisting with certain human resource functions but who are not in the central human resources department, such as employees who might be assigned to individual departments. Also excluded from this service area is risk financing, including general liability insurance and workers' compensation.

NOTES ON PERFORMANCE MEASURES

1. Total Workforce FTEs per 10,000 Population

The number of full-time equivalent (FTE) positions includes all permanent full-time and permanent part-time employees budgeted for the municipality. One FTE equates to 2,080 hours of work per year. Any combination of employees providing 2,080 hours of annual work equals one FTE.

2. Number of Applications Received per 100 Employees

Human resources is responsible for the recruitment and selection of applicants to fill new or vacant positions.

3. Number of Position Requisitions per 100 Employees

Position requisitions are submitted to the human resources office by departments seeking to fill vacant positions.

4. Cost per Employee

This measure represents the total cost of human resources for the fiscal year ending June 30 and is calculated using the project's full cost accounting model, which captures direct, indirect, and capital costs. Cost per employee is the primary measure of cost efficiency for this service area.

5. Ratio of Human Resources Staff to Total Workforce

This is a calculation of human resource FTEs divided by the total number of employees in the permanent municipal workforce, including full- and part-time staff.

6. Probationary Period Completion Rate (New Hires)

Most organizations require that new employees complete a probationary employment period, typically lasting three to eighteen months from the hire date, depending on the job classification. This effectiveness measure is calculated by dividing the total number of employees that completed the probationary period by the number of employees eligible to complete the probationary period during the fiscal year.

7. Employee Total Turnover Rate

The employee turnover rate is calculated by dividing the total number of separated staff during the fiscal year by the total number of authorized positions.

8. Employee Voluntary Turnover Rate

The employee voluntary turnover rate is calculated by dividing the number of voluntarily separated staff during the fiscal year by the total number of authorized positions. Voluntary separations include retirements and resignations.

9. Percentage of Grievances Resolved at Department Level

Most jurisdictions have a process in place for handling formal grievances filed by employees. This effectiveness measure is calculated by dividing the number of formal grievances that were resolved within the respective department (prior to going to a higher level or third party for resolution) by the total number of grievances filed during the fiscal year.

10. Average Number of Days from Position Post Date to Hire Date

This includes the number of working days from the date a job is posted to the hire date (first day of employment). It includes only recruitments for permanent full-time and part-time positions that were completed during the fiscal year. This measure excludes recruitment of temporary workers.

Central Human Resources

Summary of Key Dimensions of Service

City or Town	Total Number of Authorized Municipal Positions	Average Length of Service (in Years)	Number of Position Requisitions	Number of Employment Applications Processed	Number of Retirees Serviced	Probationary Period	Turnover Rate	Number of HR FTEs
Apex	504	7.0	56	3,552	54	6 & 12 months	7.1%	5.0
Chapel Hill	775	9.8	144	4,931	50	6 & 12 months	12.1%	8.0
Charlotte	7,620	10.5	579	56,611	na	6 & 12 months	9.4%	47.0
Concord	1,097	9.6	175	5,101	398	6 & 12 months	10.5%	13.0
Goldsboro	714	10.4	123	3,311	5	6 & 12 months	8.8%	5.0
Greensboro	3,229	11.1	590	22,720	600	6 & 12 months	8.8%	35.0
Hickory	740	9.9	70	2,398	92	12 months	11.9%	8.0
Raleigh	4,299	10.3	827	46,275	107	6 & 12 months	8.3%	32.0
Wilson	773	10.1	73	3,883	61	12 months	8.8%	8.0
Winston-Salem	2,835	10.6	487	21,291	1,017	6 & 12 months	9.0%	15.0

NOTES

For municipalities with varying probationary periods, typically fire and/or police personnel have longer probationary periods.

EXPLANATORY FACTORS

These are factors that the project found affected human resources performance and cost in one or more of the municipalities:

Decentralization of HR functions
Personnel policies
External economic climate
Unemployment rate
Extent of contracting out for services
Departmental discretion regarding vacancies
Hiring freezes
State and/or federal mandates

Apex

Central Human Resources

Fiscal Year 2019-20

Explanatory Information

Service Level and Delivery

The Human Resources Department for Apex provides a comprehensive assortment of services, including occupational health and wellness, benefits, recruitment and selection, compensation, employee relations, and training and development programs.

One employee compensation study was completed during the fiscal year covering ninety-six positions. The Town of Apex tries to study one-third of the job classifications every three years and uses a consultant to assist in this process.

The town's probationary period for new employees is six months for general employees and twelve months for sworn police, fire, and EMS personnel.

Conditions Affecting Service, Performance, and Costs

Municipal Profile

Population (OSBM 2019)	61,319
Land Area (Square Miles)	23.61
Persons per Square Mile	2,597
Median Household Income U.S. Census 2016	$84,000

Service Profile

Central HR FTE Positions	
Administration	2.0
Generalist/Specialist	2.0
Staff Support/Clerical	1.00
Total Authorized Workforce	504.0
Authorized FTEs	501.5
Average Length of Service (Months)	84
Number of Position Requisitions	56
Employment Applications Processed	3,552
Length of Probationary Employment Period	6 & 12 months
Compensation Studies Completed	1
Positions Studied	96
Employee Turnover	
Voluntary Separations	30
Involuntary Separations	6
TOTAL SEPARATIONS	36
Formal Grievances Filed by Employees	0
Equal Employment Opportunity Commission (EEOC) Complaints Filed	0

Full Cost Profile

Cost Breakdown by Percentage	
Personal Services	63.6%
Operating Costs	35.0%
Capital Costs	1.4%
TOTAL	100.0%
Cost Breakdown in Dollars	
Personal Services	$446,693
Operating Costs	$245,522
Capital Costs	$9,620
TOTAL	$701,835

Key: Apex ▪ Benchmarking Average — Fiscal Years 2016 through 2020

Resource Measures

Human Resources Services Cost per Capita

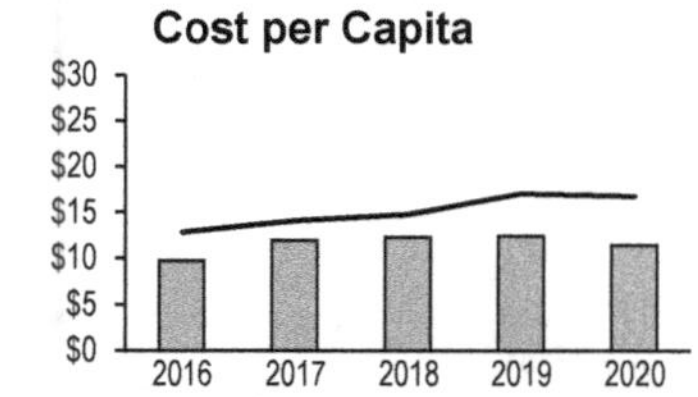

	2016	2017	2018	2019	2020
Apex	$9.73	$11.95	$12.27	$12.43	$11.45
Average	$12.81	$14.05	$14.72	$17.01	$16.75

Human Resources FTEs per 10,000 Population

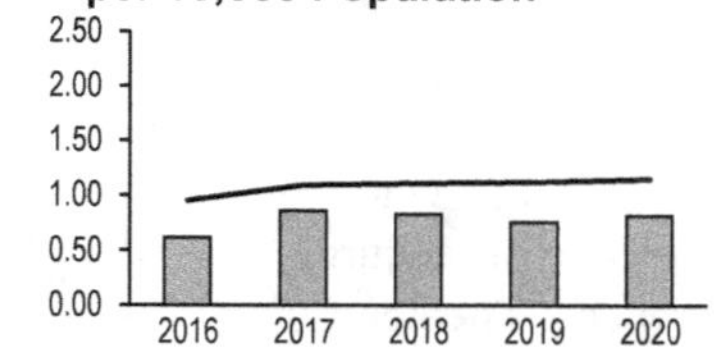

	2016	2017	2018	2019	2020
Apex	0.61	0.86	0.83	0.76	0.82
Average	0.95	1.09	1.10	1.12	1.15

Workload Measures

Total Municipal FTEs per 10,000 Population

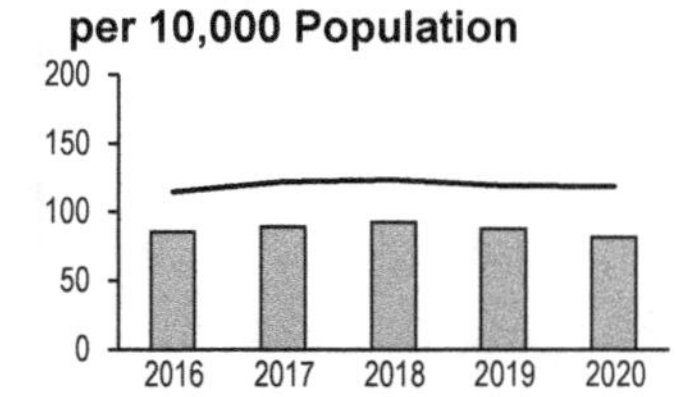

	2016	2017	2018	2019	2020
Apex	86	89	92	88	82
Average	114	122	123	119	118

Applications Processed per 100 Municipal Employees

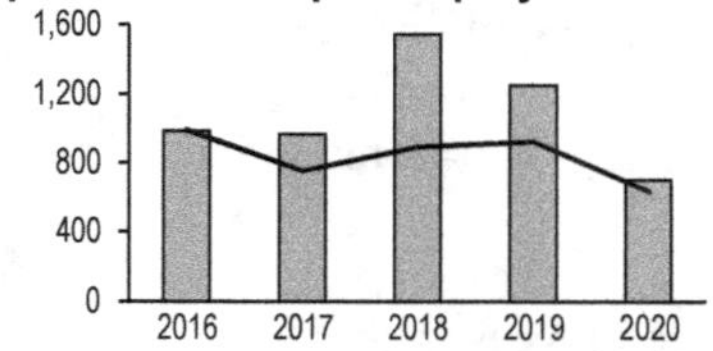

	2016	2017	2018	2019	2020
Apex	982	962	1,545	1,249	705
Average	988	752	888	921	637

Position Requisitions per 100 Municipal Employees

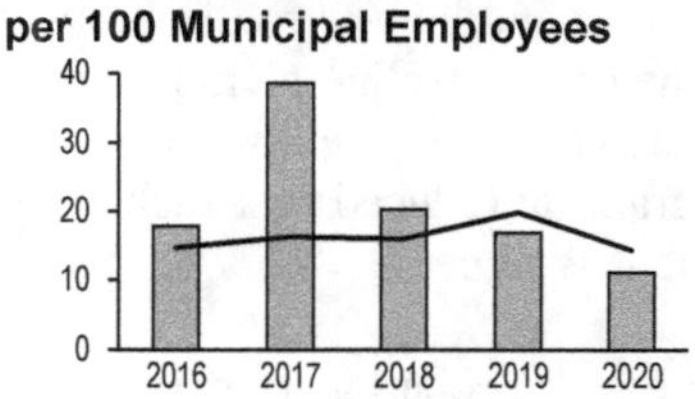

	2016	2017	2018	2019	2020
Apex	17.9	38.6	20.3	17.0	11.1
Average	14.7	16.2	16.0	19.8	14.4

Efficiency Measures

Human Resources Cost per Municipal Employee

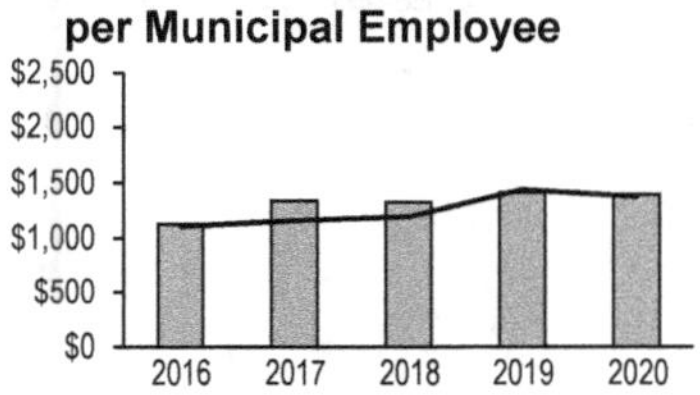

	2016	2017	2018	2019	2020
Apex	$1,128	$1,338	$1,324	$1,411	$1,393
Average	$1,105	$1,154	$1,188	$1,434	$1,372

Ratio of Human Resources Staff to 100 Municipal Employees

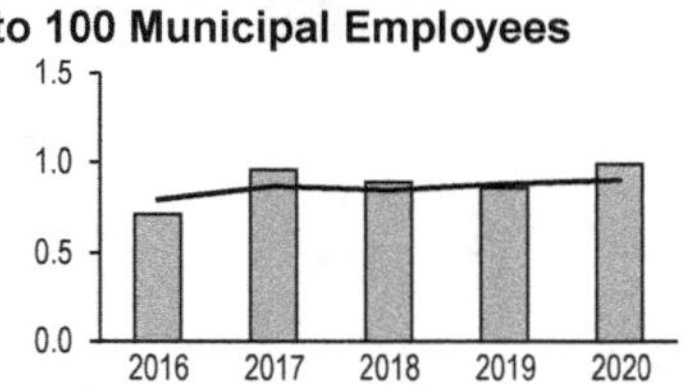

	2016	2017	2018	2019	2020
Apex	0.71	0.96	0.89	0.86	0.99
Average	0.79	0.87	0.84	0.88	0.90

Effectiveness Measures

Probationary Period Completion Rate (New Hires)

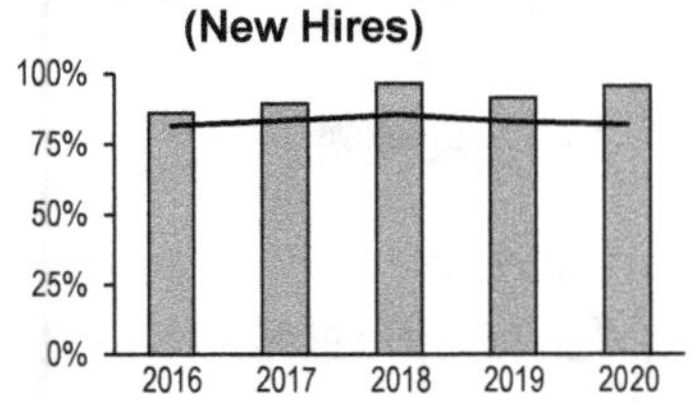

	2016	2017	2018	2019	2020
Apex	86%	89%	97%	92%	96%
Average	81%	84%	86%	83%	82%

Employee Turnover Rate (All Separations)

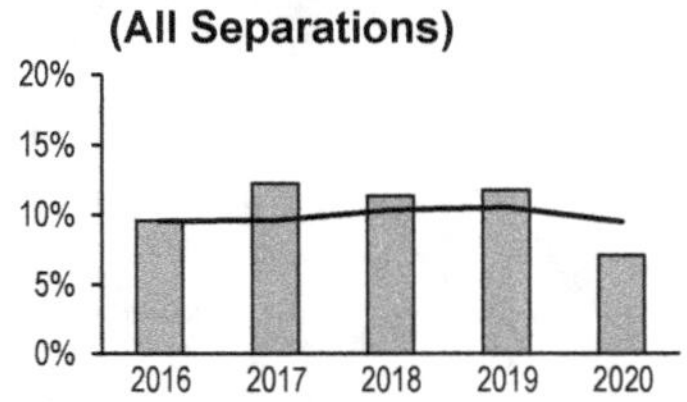

	2016	2017	2018	2019	2020
Apex	9.6%	12.2%	11.4%	11.8%	7.1%
Average	9.6%	9.6%	10.3%	10.5%	9.5%

Employee Turnover Rate (Voluntary Separations)

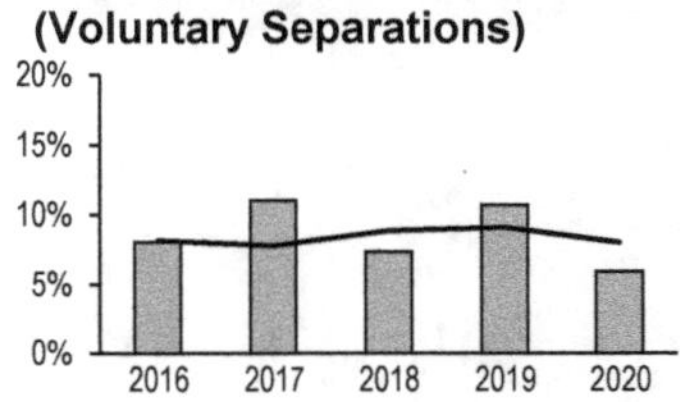

	2016	2017	2018	2019	2020
Apex	8.0%	11.0%	7.3%	10.7%	6.0%
Average	8.1%	7.7%	8.8%	9.1%	8.0%

Percentage of Grievances Resolved at Department Level

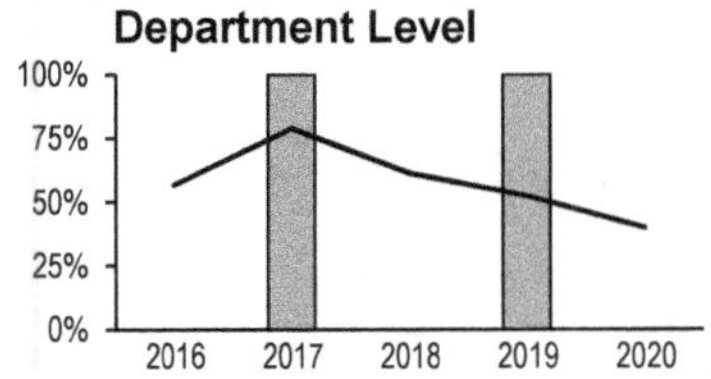

	2016	2017	2018	2019	2020
Apex		100%		100%	
Average	57%	79%	61%	52%	40%

Average Days from Post Date to Hire Date (First Day of Employment)

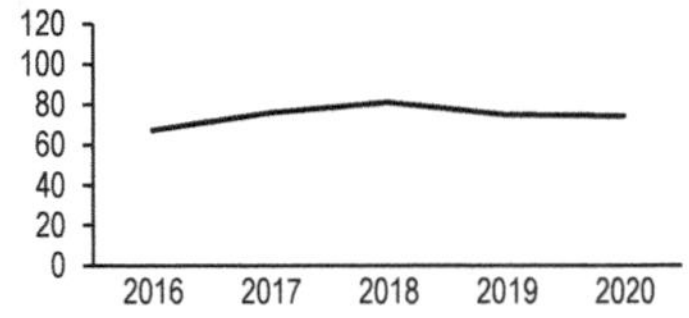

	2016	2017	2018	2019	2020
Apex					
Average	67	76	81	75	74

Fiscal Year 2019-20

Explanatory Information

Service Level and Delivery

The Town of Chapel Hill's Human Resource Development Department is organized into one centralized HR department using a specialist structure with several departmental HR liasons who facilitate communication of the town'sprocesses and procedures, benefits paperwork, and predisciplinary conferences. The department ensures standard operating procedures are followed and coordinates departmental interviews for job openings.

The town provides an employee assistance program at no cost to town staff. Chapel Hill also provides some life insurance coverage and short and long-term disability at no cost to employees. The town has an on-site wellness clinic staffed with a nurse practitioner and registered nurse. The town also offers a variety of other wellness programs at reduced cost such, as gym membership, nutritionists, and Weight Watchers.

The town's probationary period for most new employees is six months. Department heads and police personnel serve a twelve-month period.

Conditions Affecting Service, Performance, and Costs

Municipal Profile

Population (OSBM 2019)	63,639
Land Area (Square Miles)	21.31
Persons per Square Mile	2,987
Median Household Income U.S. Census 2016	$60,802

Service Profile

Central HR FTE Positions	
Administration	3.0
Generalist/Specialist	4.0
Staff Support/Clerical	1.0
Total Authorized Workforce	775.0
Authorized FTEs	771.93
Average Length of Service (Months)	117.91
Number of Position Requisitions	144
Employment Applications Processed	4,931
Length of Probationary Employment Period	6 & 12 months
Compensation Studies Completed	1
Positions Studied	312
Employee Turnover	
Voluntary Separations	82
Involuntary Separations	12
TOTAL SEPARATIONS	94
Formal Grievances Filed by Employees	0
Equal Employment Opportunity Commission (EEOC) Complaints Filed	0

Full Cost Profile

Cost Breakdown by Percentage	
Personal Services	16.0%
Operating Costs	58.9%
Capital Costs	25.1%
TOTAL	100.0%
Cost Breakdown in Dollars	
Personal Services	$355,769
Operating Costs	$1,310,187
Capital Costs	$557,081
TOTAL	$2,223,037

Chapel Hill

Central Human Resources

Key: Chapel Hill ■ Benchmarking Average — Fiscal Years 2016 through 2020

Resource Measures

Human Resources Services Cost per Capita

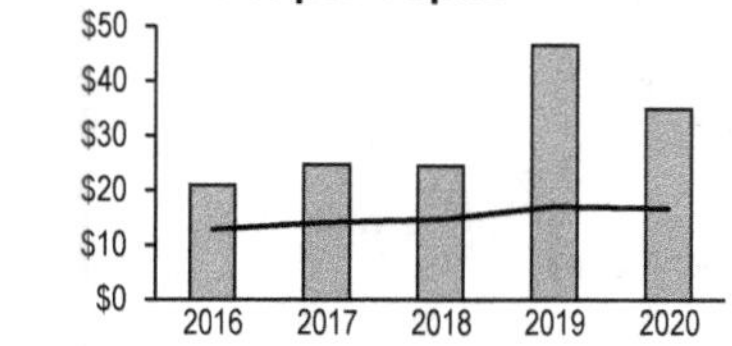

	2016	2017	2018	2019	2020
Chapel Hill	$20.98	$24.65	$24.43	$46.55	$34.93
Average	$12.81	$14.05	$14.72	$17.01	$16.75

Human Resources FTEs per 10,000 Population

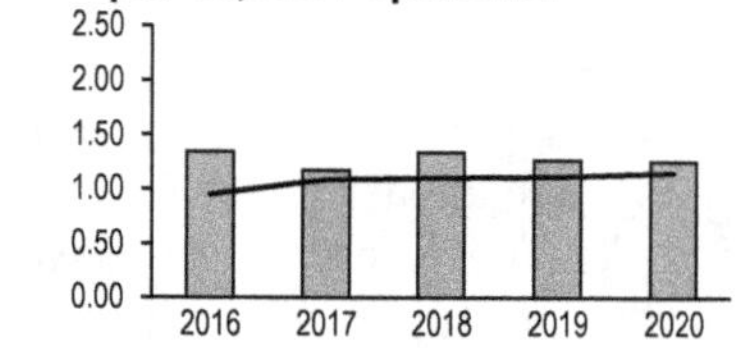

	2016	2017	2018	2019	2020
Chapel Hill	1.34	1.17	1.34	1.27	1.26
Average	0.95	1.09	1.10	1.12	1.15

Workload Measures

Total Municipal FTEs per 10,000 Population

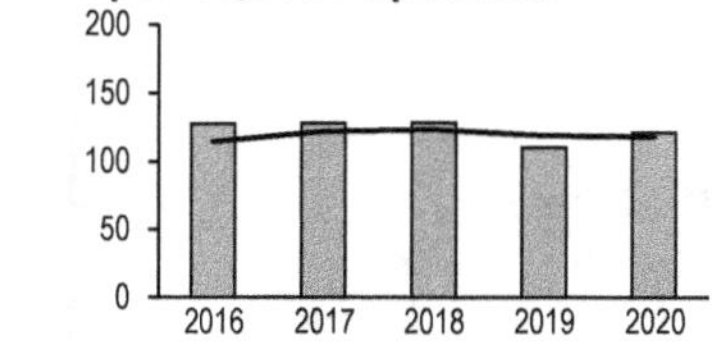

	2016	2017	2018	2019	2020
Chapel Hill	128	128	128	110	121
Average	114	122	123	119	118

Applications Processed per 100 Municipal Employees

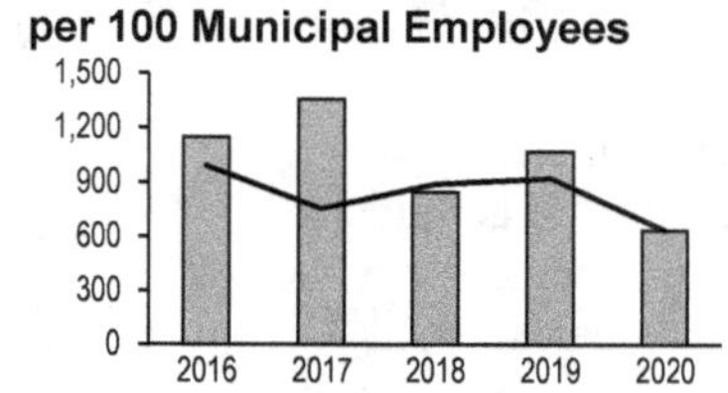

	2016	2017	2018	2019	2020
Chapel Hill	1,148	1,357	845	1,070	636
Average	988	752	888	921	637

Position Requisitions per 100 Municipal Employees

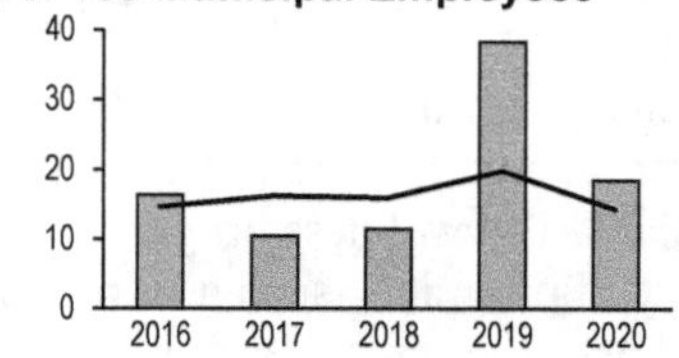

	2016	2017	2018	2019	2020
Chapel Hill	16.4	10.5	11.5	38.4	18.6
Average	14.7	16.2	16.0	19.8	14.4

Efficiency Measures

Human Resources Cost per Municipal Employee

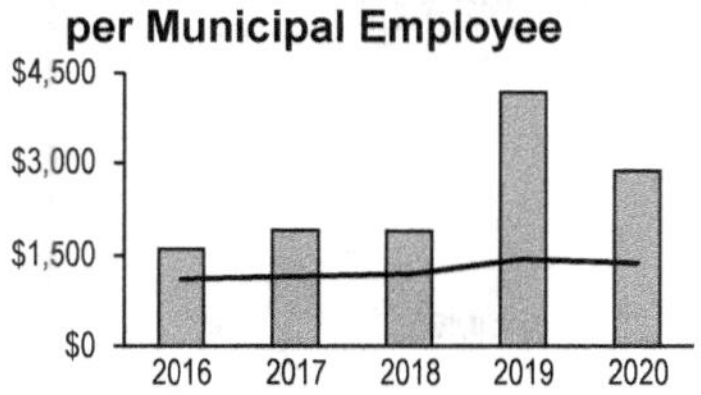

	2016	2017	2018	2019	2020
Chapel Hill	$1,599	$1,904	$1,894	$4,183	$2,868
Average	$1,105	$1,154	$1,188	$1,434	$1,372

Ratio of Human Resources Staff to 100 Municipal Employees

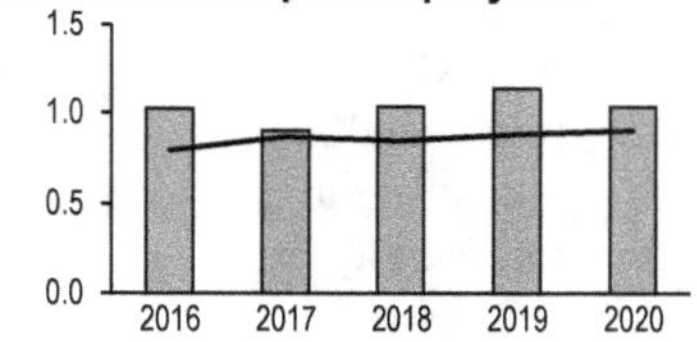

	2016	2017	2018	2019	2020
Chapel Hill	1.02	0.90	1.03	1.14	1.03
Average	0.79	0.87	0.84	0.88	0.90

Effectiveness Measures

Probationary Period Completion Rate (New Hires)

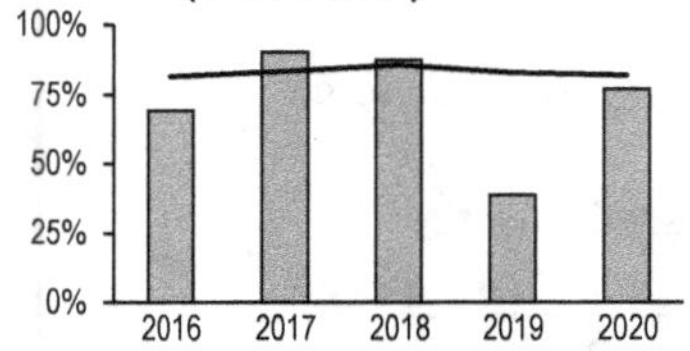

	2016	2017	2018	2019	2020
Chapel Hill	69%	90%	88%	39%	77%
Average	81%	84%	86%	83%	82%

Employee Turnover Rate (All Separations)

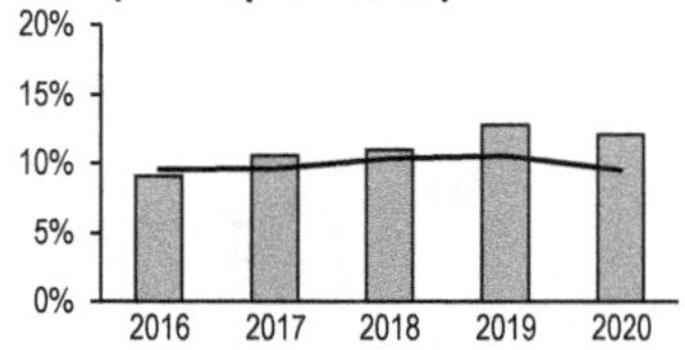

	2016	2017	2018	2019	2020
Chapel Hill	9.1%	10.6%	11.0%	12.8%	12.1%
Average	9.6%	9.6%	10.3%	10.5%	9.5%

Employee Turnover Rate (Voluntary Separations)

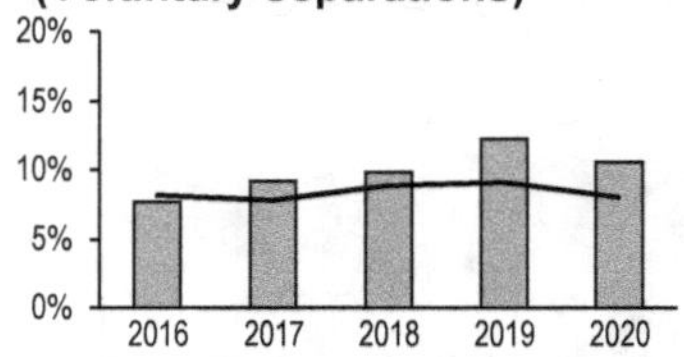

	2016	2017	2018	2019	2020
Chapel Hill	7.7%	9.2%	9.8%	12.2%	10.6%
Average	8.1%	7.7%	8.8%	9.1%	8.0%

Percentage of Grievances Resolved at Department Level

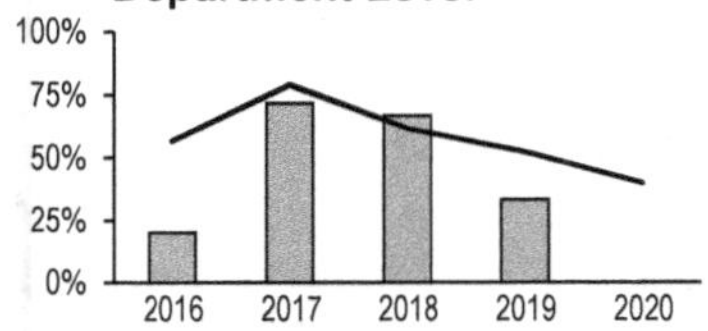

	2016	2017	2018	2019	2020
Chapel Hill	20%	71%	67%	33%	
Average	57%	79%	61%	52%	40%

Average Days from Post Date to Hire Date (First Day of Employment)

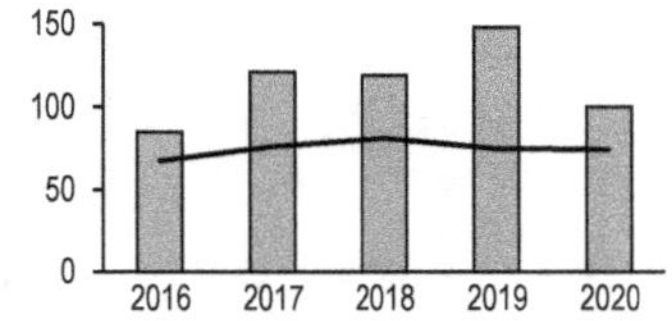

	2016	2017	2018	2019	2020
Chapel Hill	85	121	119	148	100
Average	67	76	81	75	74

Fiscal Year 2019-20

Explanatory Information

Service Level and Delivery

Charlotte's Human Resources Department is organized into six core services: benefits, organization development and learning, human resources management systems and payroll, employee relations and compliance, talent acquisition, and compensation planning. These functional areas perform a variety of strategic, tactical, and transactional services. Some of the transactional services are outsourced.

There were 56,611 employment applications processed for open positions. All applicants must use the PeopleSoft online job application software for each position for which they wish to apply.

The city is self-insured for medical, prescription drug, and dental insurance, and third-party administrators are retained to administer the plans. The wellness program, Wellness Works, includes a wide variety of programs, such as tobacco cessation, annual flu shots, blood pressure screenings, on-site fitness education programs, and weight loss programs. The city partners with OurHealth for health clinic operations for employees, retirees, and dependents, which in addition to health coaching and health risk assessments, provides many health care services. In 2011, the city began offering a premium differential to employees who take a health screening.

Conditions Affecting Service, Performance, and Costs

Charlotte has a very robust wellness program, including a health clinic. Many resources are devoted to the success of this program. There are wellness ambassadors in every department in the city.

The payroll function in many cities is located in finance; it resides in Human Resources in Charlotte.

Municipal Profile

Population (OSBM 2019)	863,985
Land Area (Square Miles)	307.41
Persons per Square Mile	2,811
Median Household Income U.S. Census 2016	$46,975

Service Profile

Central HR FTE Positions	
Administration	2.0
Generalist/Specialist	43.0
Staff Support/Clerical	2.0
Total Authorized Workforce	7,620.0
Authorized FTEs	7,613.6
Average Length of Service (Months)	125.4
Number of Position Requisitions	579
Employment Applications Processed	56,611
Length of Probationary Employment Period	6 & 12 months
Compensation Studies Completed	8
Positions Studied	6
Employee Turnover	
Voluntary Separations	613
Involuntary Separations	101
TOTAL SEPARATIONS	714
Formal Grievances Filed by Employees	18
Equal Employment Opportunity Commission (EEOC) Complaints Filed	16

Full Cost Profile

Cost Breakdown by Percentage	
Personal Services	64.3%
Operating Costs	33.7%
Capital Costs	2.0%
TOTAL	100.0%
Cost Breakdown in Dollars	
Personal Services	$4,908,726
Operating Costs	$2,577,333
Capital Costs	$152,164
TOTAL	$7,638,223

Key: Charlotte ▒ Benchmarking Average — Fiscal Years 2016 through 2020

Resource Measures

Human Resources Services Cost per Capita

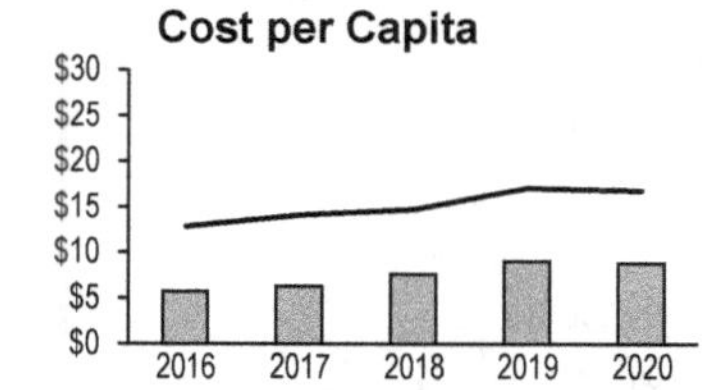

	2016	2017	2018	2019	2020
Charlotte	$5.68	$6.29	$7.63	$9.02	$8.84
Average	$12.81	$14.05	$14.72	$17.01	$16.75

Human Resources FTEs per 10,000 Population

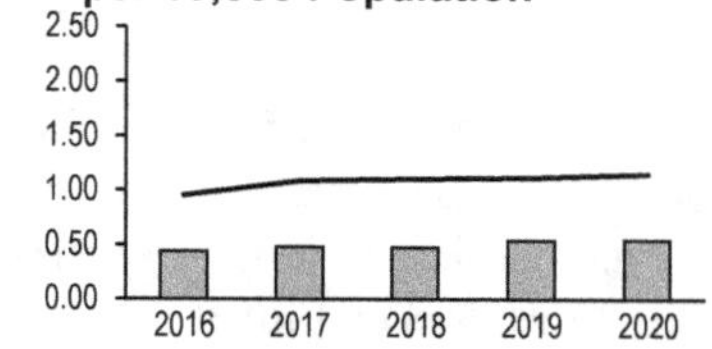

	2016	2017	2018	2019	2020
Charlotte	0.44	0.48	0.47	0.54	0.54
Average	0.95	1.09	1.10	1.12	1.15

Workload Measures

Total Municipal FTEs per 10,000 Population

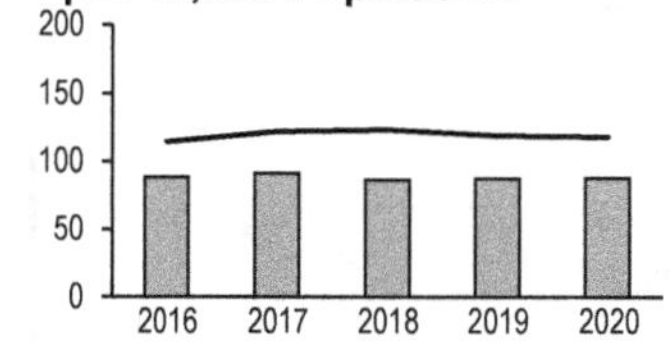

	2016	2017	2018	2019	2020
Charlotte	88	91	87	88	88
Average	114	122	123	119	118

Applications Processed per 100 Municipal Employees

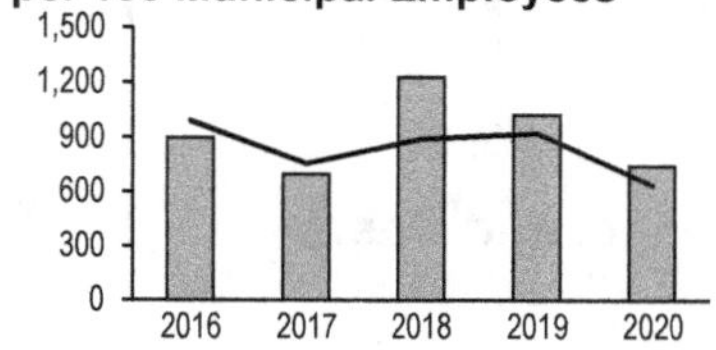

	2016	2017	2018	2019	2020
Charlotte	895	698	1,227	1,023	743
Average	988	752	888	921	637

Position Requisitions per 100 Municipal Employees

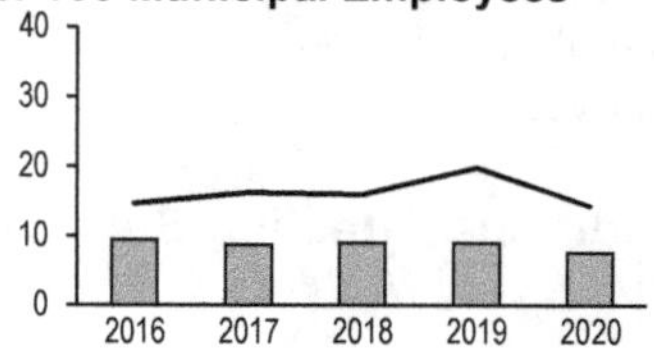

	2016	2017	2018	2019	2020
Charlotte	9.4	8.7	9.0	9.0	7.6
Average	14.7	16.2	16.0	19.8	14.4

Efficiency Measures

Human Resources Cost per Municipal Employee

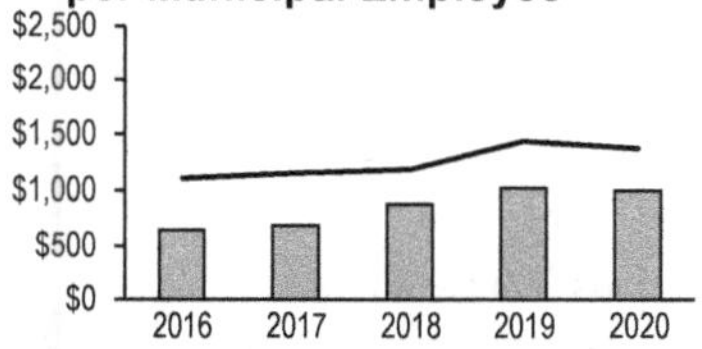

	2016	2017	2018	2019	2020
Charlotte	$643	$688	$880	$1,024	$1,002
Average	$1,105	$1,154	$1,188	$1,434	$1,372

Ratio of Human Resources Staff to 100 Municipal Employees

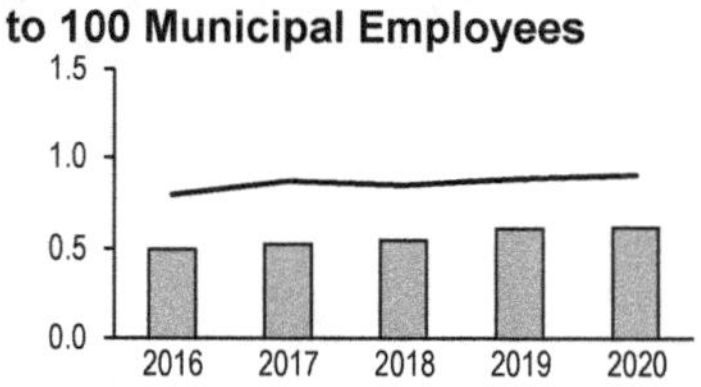

	2016	2017	2018	2019	2020
Charlotte	0.50	0.53	0.55	0.61	0.62
Average	0.79	0.87	0.84	0.88	0.90

Effectiveness Measures

Probationary Period Completion Rate (New Hires)

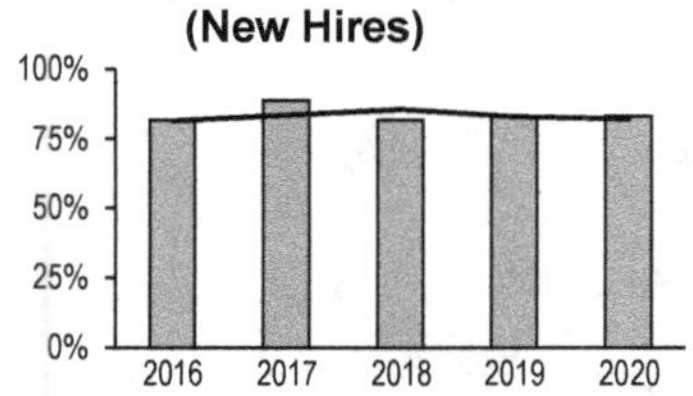

	2016	2017	2018	2019	2020
Charlotte	82%	89%	82%	83%	83%
Average	81%	84%	86%	83%	82%

Employee Turnover Rate (All Separations)

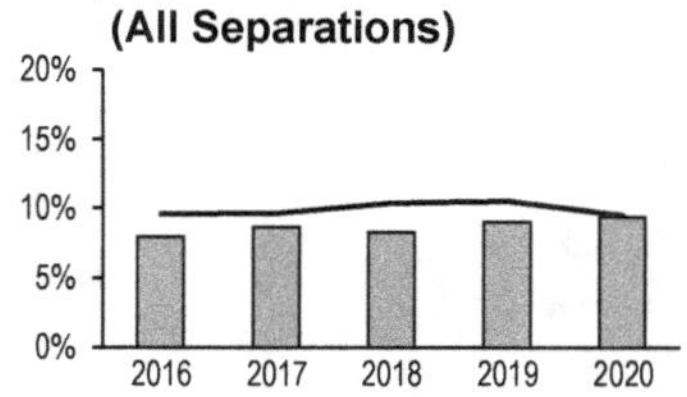

	2016	2017	2018	2019	2020
Charlotte	7.9%	8.6%	8.3%	9.0%	9.4%
Average	9.6%	9.6%	10.3%	10.5%	9.5%

Employee Turnover Rate (Voluntary Separations)

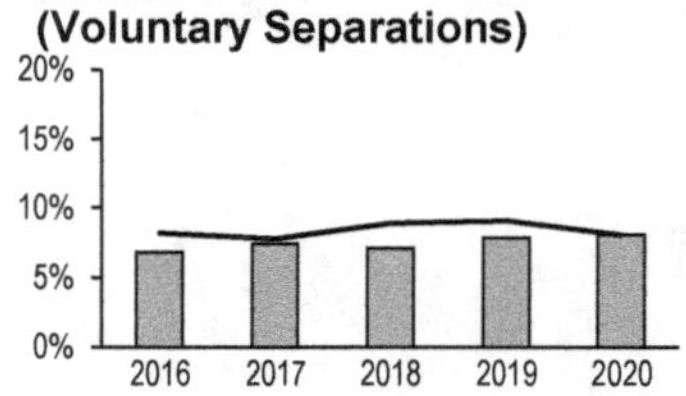

	2016	2017	2018	2019	2020
Charlotte	6.8%	7.4%	7.1%	7.8%	8.0%
Average	8.1%	7.7%	8.8%	9.1%	8.0%

Percentage of Grievances Resolved at Department Level

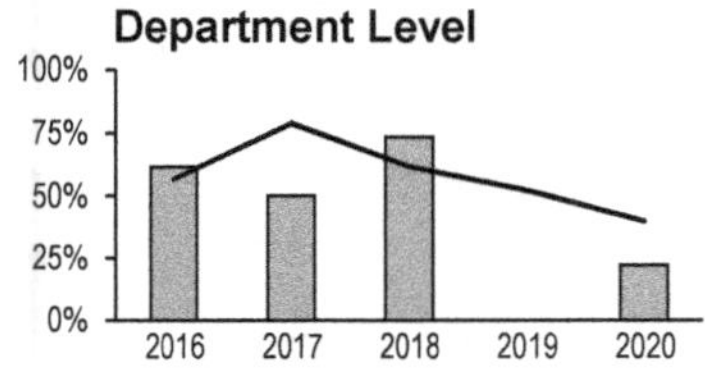

	2016	2017	2018	2019	2020
Charlotte	62%	50%	73%		22%
Average	57%	79%	61%	52%	40%

Average Days from Post Date to Hire Date (First Day of Employment)

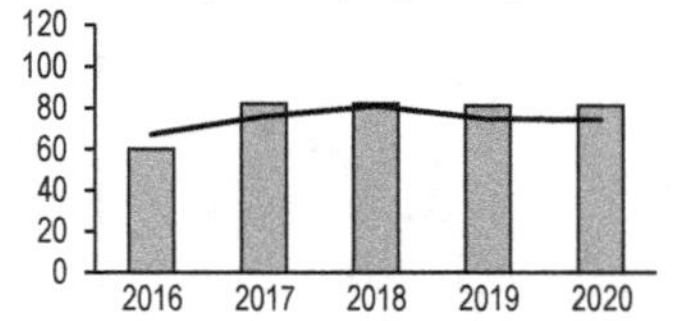

	2016	2017	2018	2019	2020
Charlotte	60	82	82	81	81
Average	67	76	81	75	74

Explanatory Information

Service Level and Delivery

The Human Resources Department for the City of Concord is responsible for the following functions: departmental management, policy design and administration, classification and compensation design and administration, benefits plan design and administration, employee relations, grievance and disciplinary actions, and employee rewards.

The department conducted one compensation study during the most recent year covering fourteen positions.

The city's probationary period for new employees is six months for non–public safety employees and twelve months for public safety employees.

Conditions Affecting Service, Performance, and Costs

Municipal Profile

Population (OSBM 2019)	95,453
Land Area (Square Miles)	63.65
Persons per Square Mile	1,500
Median Household Income U.S. Census 2016	$50,863

Service Profile

Central HR FTE Positions	
Administration	4.0
Generalist/Specialist	8.0
Staff Support/Clerical	1.0
Total Authorized Workforce	1,097.0
Authorized FTEs	1,078.5
Average Length of Service (Months)	114.96
Number of Position Requisitions	175
Employment Applications Processed	5,101
Length of Probationary Employment Period	6 & 12 months
Compensation Studies Completed	1
Positions Studied	14
Employee Turnover	
Voluntary Separations	100
Involuntary Separations	15
TOTAL SEPARATIONS	115
Formal Grievances Filed by Employees	5
Equal Employment Opportunity Commission (EEOC) Complaints Filed	4

Full Cost Profile

Cost Breakdown by Percentage	
Personal Services	67.4%
Operating Costs	31.0%
Capital Costs	1.6%
TOTAL	100.0%
Cost Breakdown in Dollars	
Personal Services	$1,102,917
Operating Costs	$506,366
Capital Costs	$26,381
TOTAL	$1,635,664

Concord — Central Human Resources

Key: Concord ▪ Benchmarking Average — Fiscal Years 2016 through 2020

Resource Measures

Human Resources Services Cost per Capita

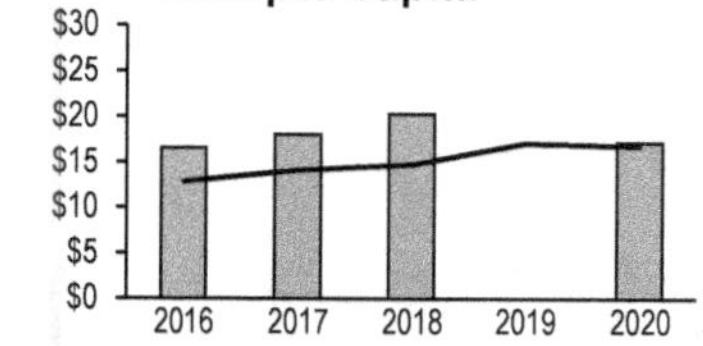

	2016	2017	2018	2019	2020
Concord	$16.51	$17.98	$20.30		$17.14
Average	$12.81	$14.05	$14.72	$17.01	$16.75

Human Resources FTEs per 10,000 Population

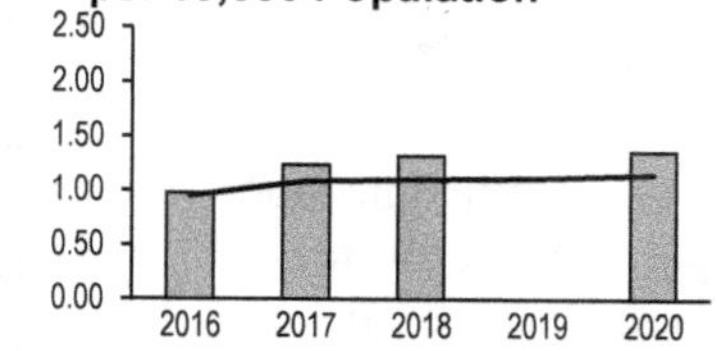

	2016	2017	2018	2019	2020
Concord	0.98	1.24	1.32		1.36
Average	0.95	1.09	1.10	1.12	1.15

Workload Measures

Total Municipal FTEs per 10,000 Population

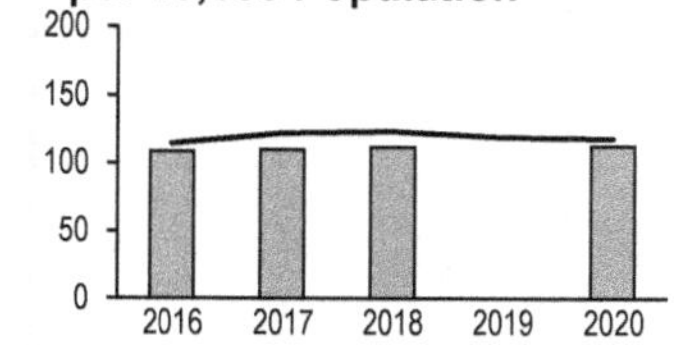

	2016	2017	2018	2019	2020
Concord	108	110	112		113
Average	114	122	123	119	118

Applications Processed per 100 Municipal Employees

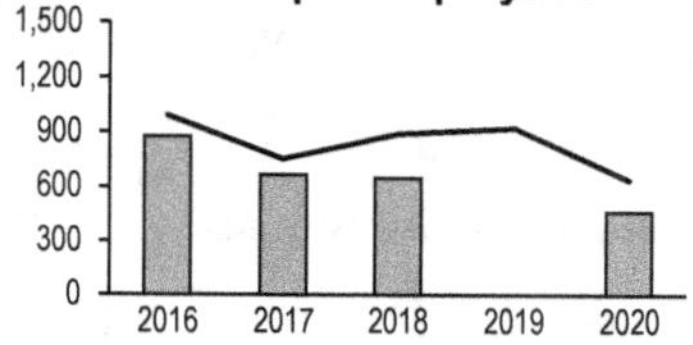

	2016	2017	2018	2019	2020
Concord	876	665	647		465
Average	988	752	888	921	637

Position Requisitions per 100 Municipal Employees

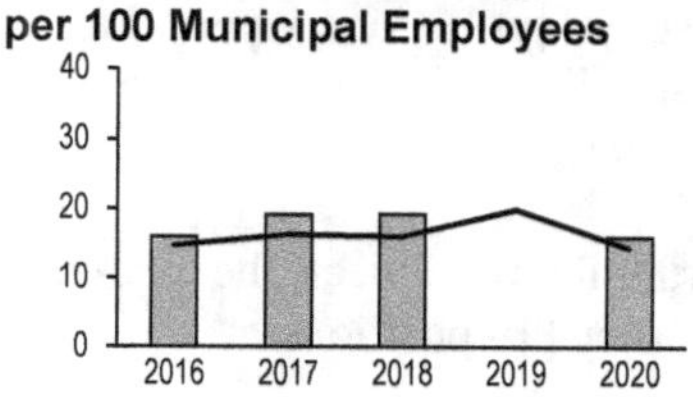

	2016	2017	2018	2019	2020
Concord	15.9	19.1	19.2		16.0
Average	14.7	16.2	16.0	19.8	14.4

Efficiency Measures

Human Resources Cost per Municipal Employee

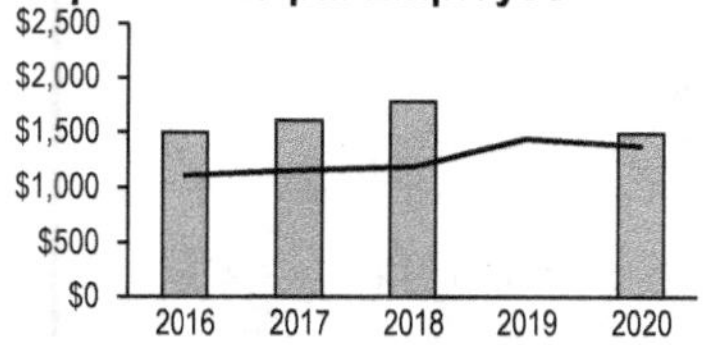

	2016	2017	2018	2019	2020
Concord	$1,498	$1,609	$1,785		$1,491
Average	$1,105	$1,154	$1,188	$1,434	$1,372

Ratio of Human Resources Staff to 100 Municipal Employees

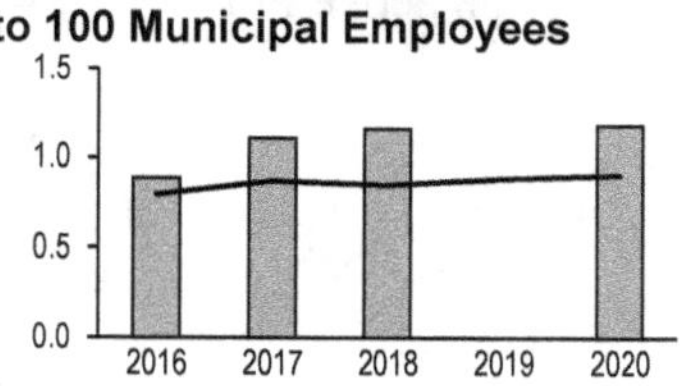

	2016	2017	2018	2019	2020
Concord	0.89	1.11	1.16		1.19
Average	0.79	0.87	0.84	0.88	0.90

Effectiveness Measures

Probationary Period Completion Rate (New Hires)

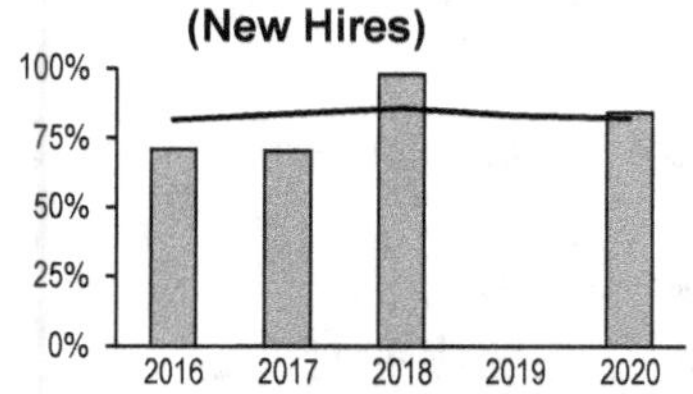

	2016	2017	2018	2019	2020
Concord	71%	70%	98%		84%
Average	81%	84%	86%	83%	82%

Employee Turnover Rate (All Separations)

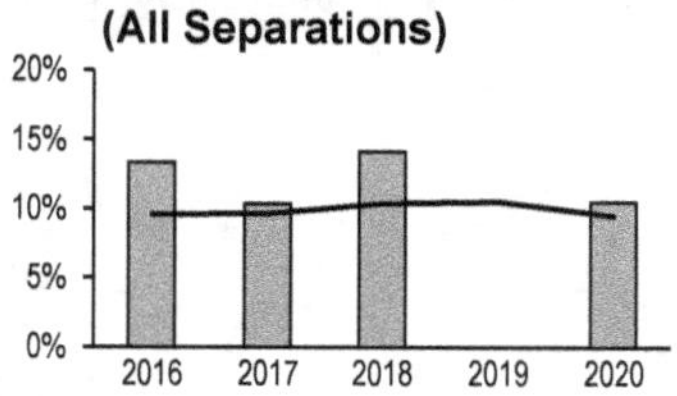

	2016	2017	2018	2019	2020
Concord	13.3%	10.4%	14.1%		10.5%
Average	9.6%	9.6%	10.3%	10.5%	9.5%

Employee Turnover Rate (Voluntary Separations)

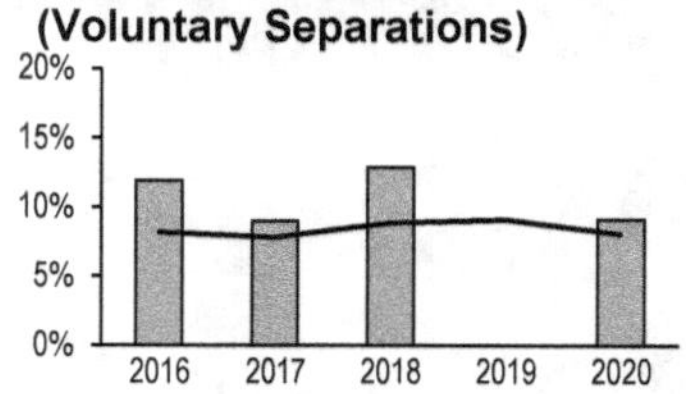

	2016	2017	2018	2019	2020
Concord	11.9%	9.0%	12.9%		9.1%
Average	8.1%	7.7%	8.8%	9.1%	8.0%

Percentage of Grievances Resolved at Department Level

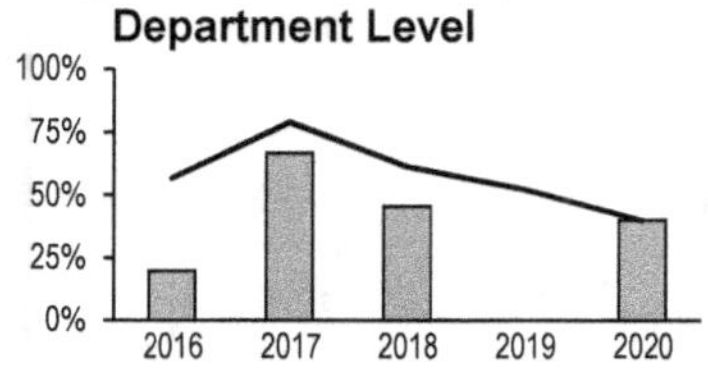

	2016	2017	2018	2019	2020
Concord	20%	67%	45%		40%
Average	57%	79%	61%	52%	40%

Average Days from Post Date to Hire Date (First Day of Employment)

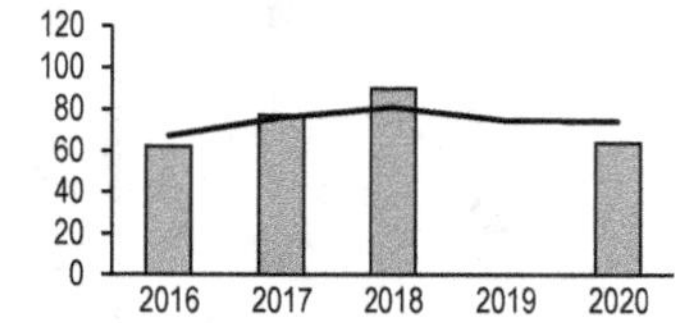

	2016	2017	2018	2019	2020
Concord	62	77	90		64
Average	67	76	81	75	74

Fiscal Year 2019-20

Explanatory Information

Service Level and Delivery

The mission of the Human Resources Department for the City of Goldsboro is to provide services that promote a work environment that is characterized by fair treatment of staff, open communications, personal accountability, trust, and mutual respect. The department provides a comprehensive array of services that includes employee selection and recruitment, salary and compensation, benefits, professional development, employee relations, employee health/wellness, and compliance with federal and state safety regulations.

The city's probationary period for new employees is six months for non-public safety employees and twelve months for public safety employees.

During the fiscal year, the city conducted five compensation studies covering 114 positions.

Conditions Affecting Service, Performance, and Costs

The City of Goldsboro joined the Benchmarking Project in July 2017, with the first year of data showing for FY 2016–17.

The city provides a $20,000 life insurance policy for all active full-time employees.

Municipal Profile

Population (OSBM 2019)	33,969
Land Area (Square Miles)	29.45
Persons per Square Mile	1,154
Median Household Income U.S. Census 2016	$32,148

Service Profile

Central HR FTE Positions	
Administration	1.0
Generalist/Specialist	3.0
Staff Support/Clerical	1.0
Total Authorized Workforce	714.0
Authorized FTEs	564.0
Average Length of Service (Months)	125
Number of Position Requisitions	123
Employment Applications Processed	3,311
Length of Probationary Employment Period	6 & 12 months
Compensation Studies Completed	5
Positions Studied	114
Employee Turnover	
Voluntary Separations	57
Involuntary Separations	6
TOTAL SEPARATIONS	63
Formal Grievances Filed by Employees	3
Equal Employment Opportunity Commission (EEOC) Complaints Filed	1

Full Cost Profile

Cost Breakdown by Percentage	
Personal Services	70.0%
Operating Costs	30.0%
Capital Costs	0.0%
TOTAL	100.0%
Cost Breakdown in Dollars	
Personal Services	$445,299
Operating Costs	$190,818
Capital Costs	$0
TOTAL	$636,117

Key: Goldsboro ▒ Benchmarking Average — Fiscal Years 2016 through 2020

Resource Measures

Human Resources Services Cost per Capita

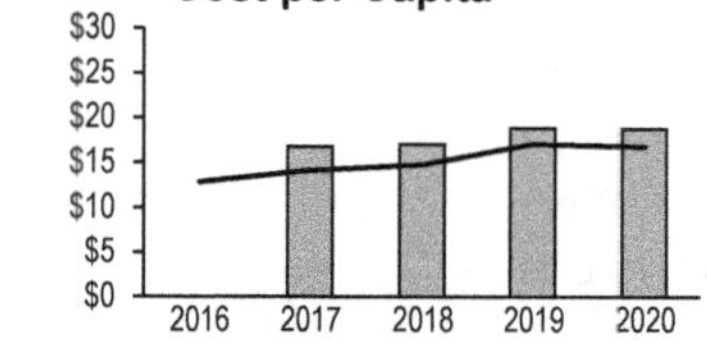

	2016	2017	2018	2019	2020
Goldsboro		$16.74	$17.03	$18.80	$18.73
Average	$12.81	$14.05	$14.72	$17.01	$16.75

Human Resources FTEs per 10,000 Population

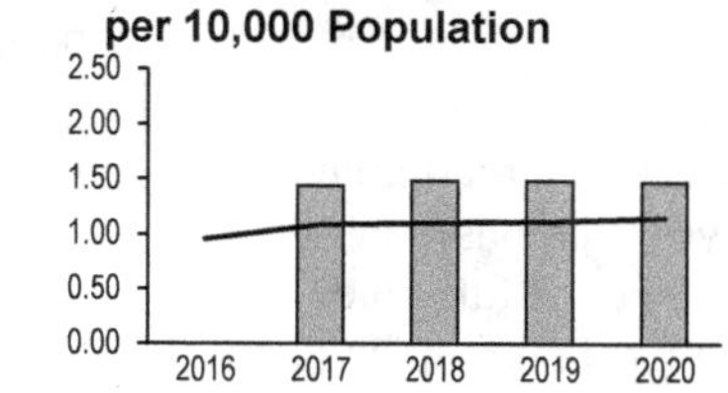

	2016	2017	2018	2019	2020
Goldsboro		1.44	1.48	1.49	1.47
Average	0.95	1.09	1.10	1.12	1.15

Workload Measures

Total Municipal FTEs per 10,000 Population

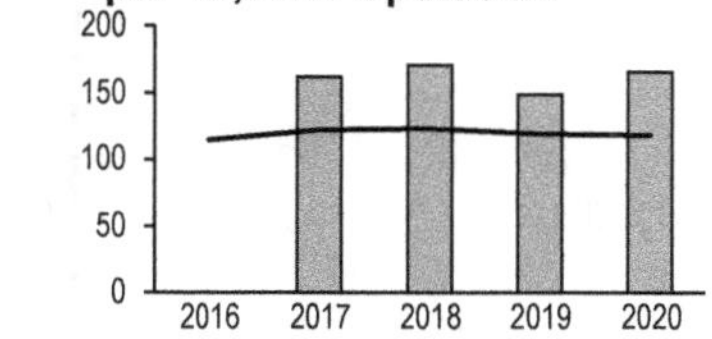

	2016	2017	2018	2019	2020
Goldsboro		162	171	149	166
Average	114	122	123	119	118

Applications Processed per 100 Municipal Employees

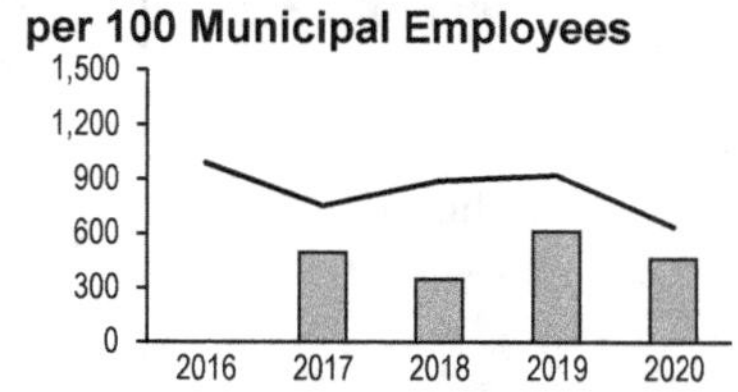

	2016	2017	2018	2019	2020
Goldsboro		497	352	613	464
Average	988	752	888	921	637

Position Requisitions per 100 Municipal Employees

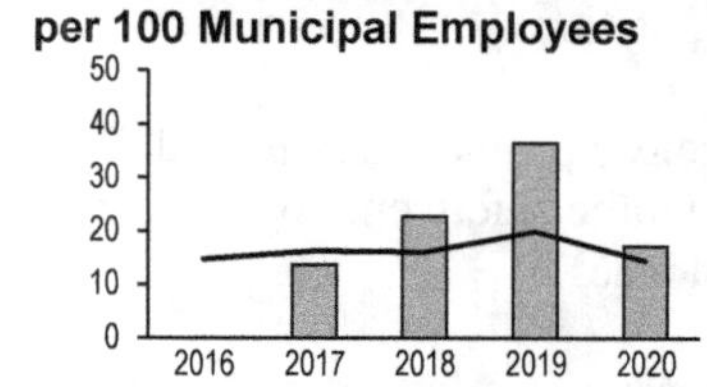

	2016	2017	2018	2019	2020
Goldsboro		13.7	22.8	36.5	17.2
Average	14.7	16.2	16.0	19.8	14.4

Efficiency Measures

Human Resources Cost per Municipal Employee

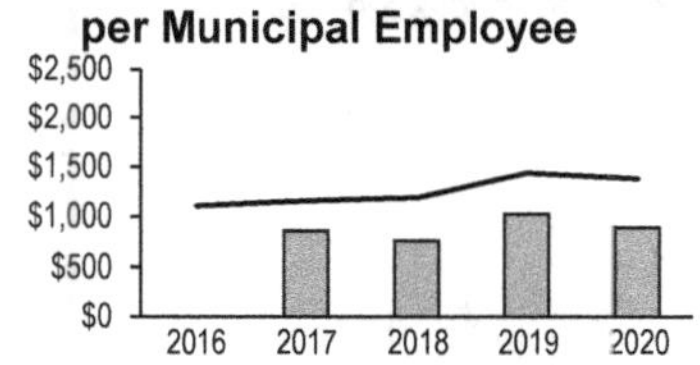

	2016	2017	2018	2019	2020
Goldsboro		$857	$759	$1,025	$891
Average	$1,105	$1,154	$1,188	$1,434	$1,372

Ratio of Human Resources Staff to 100 Municipal Employees

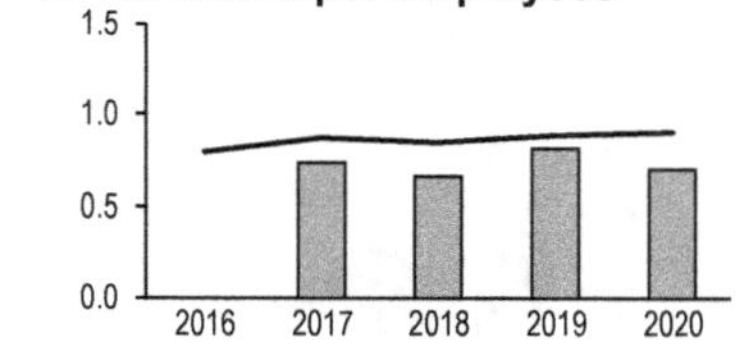

	2016	2017	2018	2019	2020
Goldsboro		0.74	0.66	0.81	0.70
Average	0.79	0.87	0.84	0.88	0.90

Effectiveness Measures

Probationary Period Completion Rate (New Hires)

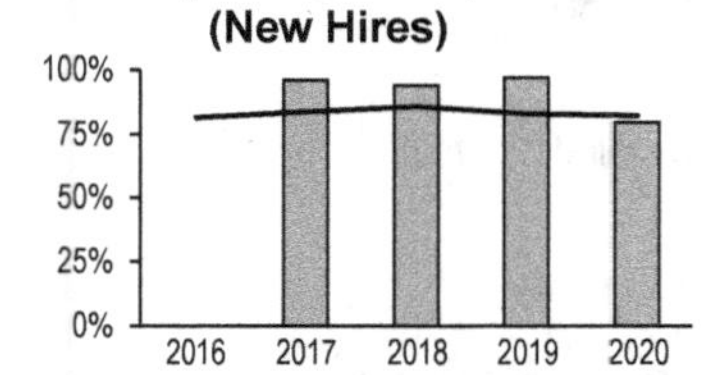

	2016	2017	2018	2019	2020
Goldsboro		96%	94%	97%	79%
Average	81%	84%	86%	83%	82%

Employee Turnover Rate (All Separations)

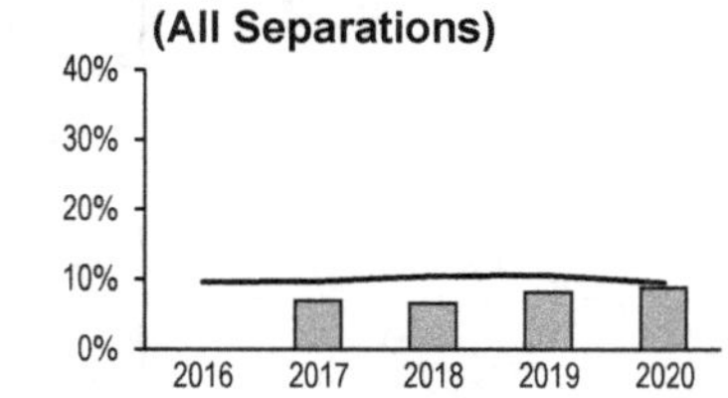

	2016	2017	2018	2019	2020
Goldsboro		6.9%	6.6%	8.1%	8.8%
Average	9.6%	9.6%	10.3%	10.5%	9.5%

Employee Turnover Rate (Voluntary Separations)

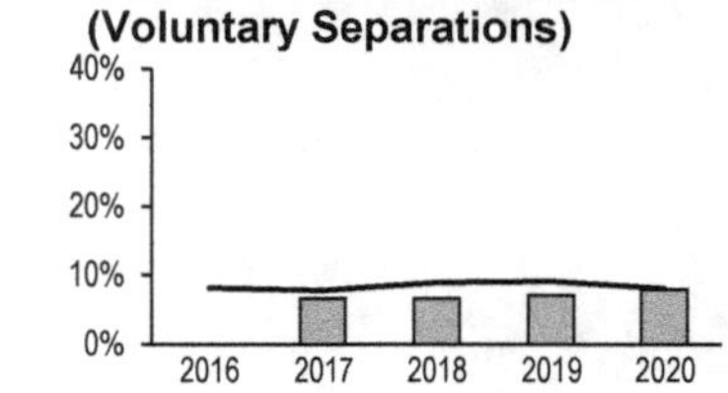

	2016	2017	2018	2019	2020
Goldsboro		6.6%	6.6%	7.1%	8.0%
Average	8.1%	7.7%	8.8%	9.1%	8.0%

Percentage of Grievances Resolved at Department Level

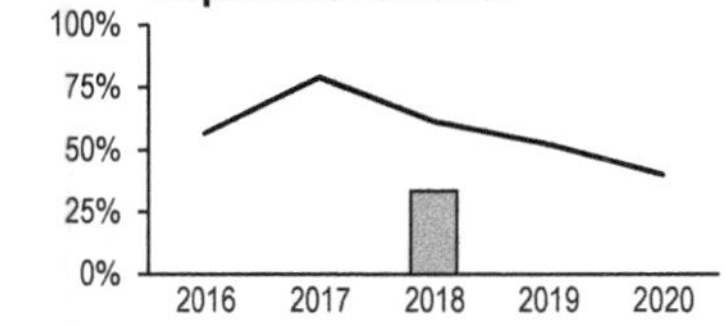

	2016	2017	2018	2019	2020
Goldsboro			33%	0%	0%
Average	57%	79%	61%	52%	40%

Average Days from Post Date to Hire Date (First Day of Employment)

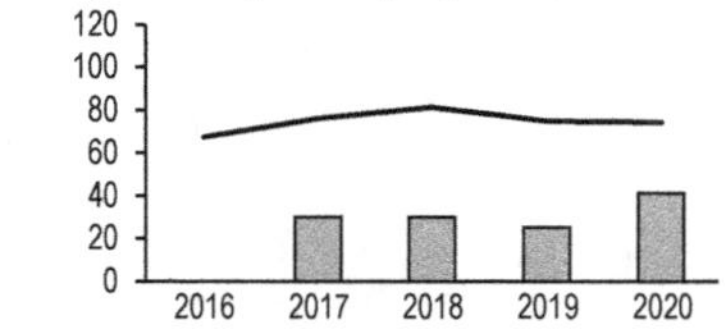

	2016	2017	2018	2019	2020
Goldsboro		30	30	25	41
Average	67	76	81	75	74

Fiscal Year 2019-20

Explanatory Information

Service Level and Delivery

The Human Resources Department for the City of Greensboro provides comprehensive personnel services, including recruitment and selection, compensation, benefits, employee relations, safety, and occupational health and wellness. The total number of full-time equivalent (FTE) positions includes staff from the Training Division, which is housed in a separate department from Human Resources. The HR department has a staff attorney who is able to provide legal consultation on a variety of issues confronting the HR department.

The city conducted one compensation study for the year covering 123 positions.

The city's probationary period for new employees is six months for non-public safety employees and twelve months for public safety employees.

Conditions Affecting Service, Performance, and Costs

Municipal Profile

Population (OSBM 2019)	293,730
Land Area (Square Miles)	129.62
Persons per Square Mile	2,266
Median Household Income U.S. Census 2016	$40,760

Service Profile

Central HR FTE Positions	
Administration	3.0
Generalist/Specialist	3.0
Staff Support/Clerical	29.0
Total Authorized Workforce	3,229.0
Authorized FTEs	3,031.0
Average Length of Service (Months)	133.68
Number of Position Requisitions	590
Employment Applications Processed	22,720
Length of Probationary Employment Period	6 & 12 months
Compensation Studies Completed	1
Positions Studied	123
Employee Turnover	
Voluntary Separations	233
Involuntary Separations	50
TOTAL SEPARATIONS	283
Formal Grievances Filed by Employees	38
Equal Employment Opportunity Commission (EEOC) Complaints Filed	8

Full Cost Profile

Cost Breakdown by Percentage	
Personal Services	78.8%
Operating Costs	21.2%
Capital Costs	0.0%
TOTAL	100.0%
Cost Breakdown in Dollars	
Personal Services	$2,837,391
Operating Costs	$761,178
Capital Costs	$0
TOTAL	$3,598,569

Key: Greensboro ▪ Benchmarking Average — Fiscal Years 2016 through 2020

Resource Measures

Human Resources Services Cost per Capita

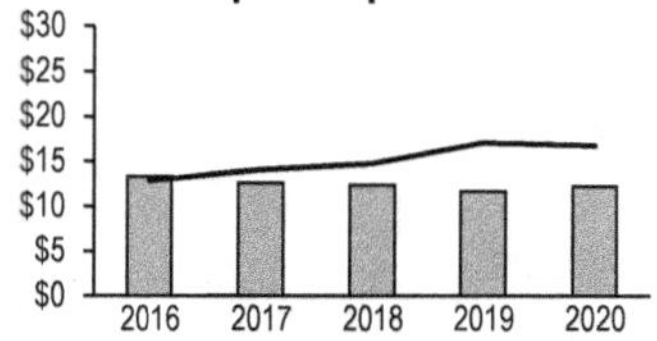

	2016	2017	2018	2019	2020
Greensboro	$13.28	$12.58	$12.38	$11.68	$12.25
Average	$12.81	$14.05	$14.72	$17.01	$16.75

Human Resources FTEs per 10,000 Population

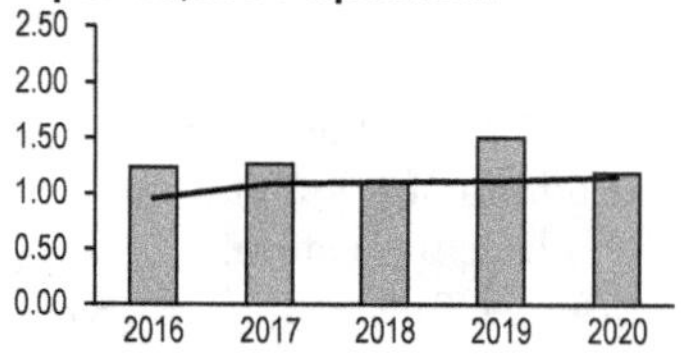

	2016	2017	2018	2019	2020
Greensboro	1.24	1.27	1.11	1.51	1.19
Average	0.95	1.09	1.10	1.12	1.15

Workload Measures

Total Municipal FTEs per 10,000 Population

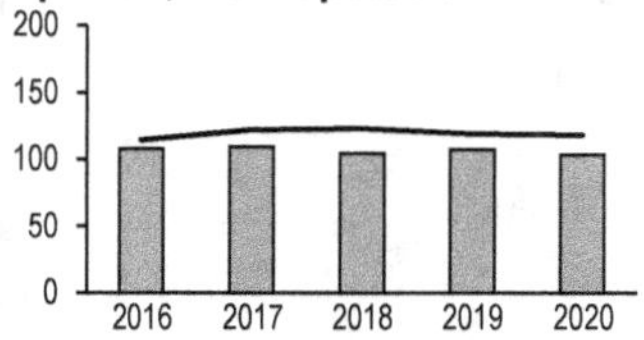

	2016	2017	2018	2019	2020
Greensboro	108	110	104	108	103
Average	114	122	123	119	118

Applications Processed per 100 Municipal Employees

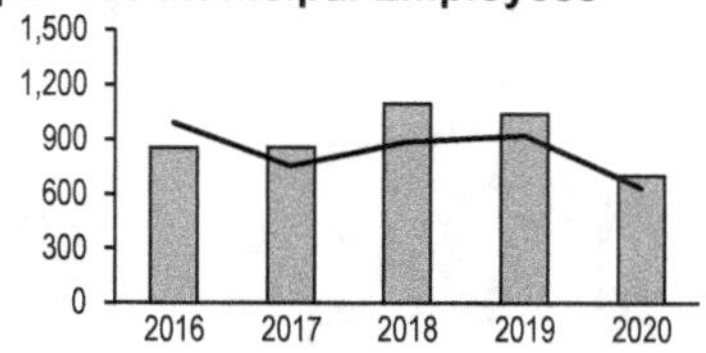

	2016	2017	2018	2019	2020
Greensboro	855	857	1,098	1,044	704
Average	988	752	888	921	637

Position Requisitions per 100 Municipal Employees

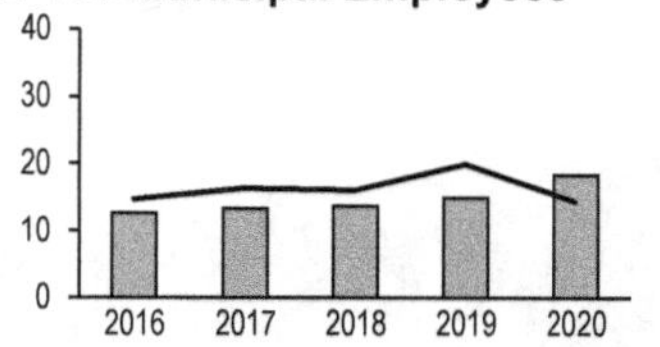

	2016	2017	2018	2019	2020
Greensboro	12.6	13.2	13.6	14.9	18.3
Average	14.7	16.2	16.0	19.8	14.4

Efficiency Measures

Human Resources Cost per Municipal Employee

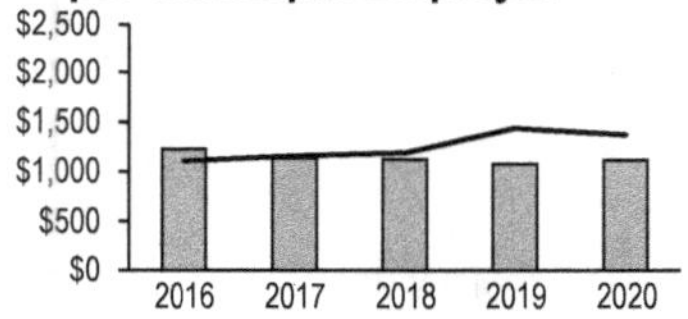

	2016	2017	2018	2019	2020
Greensboro	$1,226	$1,137	$1,126	$1,078	$1,114
Average	$1,105	$1,154	$1,188	$1,434	$1,372

Ratio of Human Resources Staff to 100 Municipal Employees

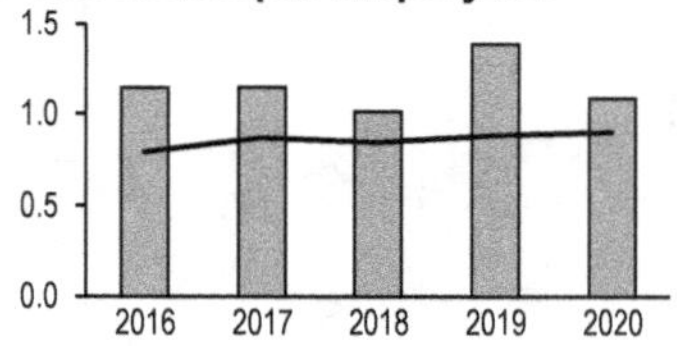

	2016	2017	2018	2019	2020
Greensboro	1.14	1.14	1.01	1.39	1.08
Average	0.79	0.87	0.84	0.88	0.90

Effectiveness Measures

Probationary Period Completion Rate (New Hires)

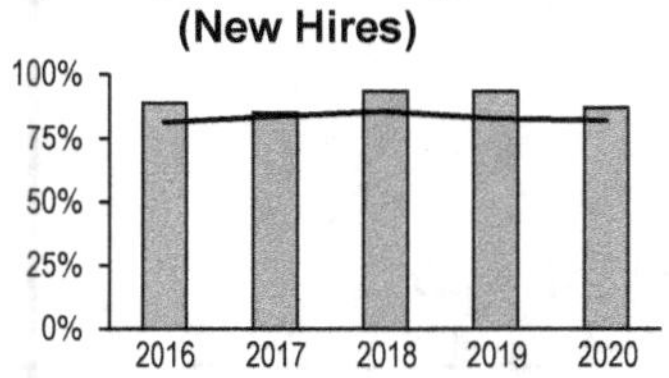

	2016	2017	2018	2019	2020
Greensboro	89%	85%	94%	93%	87%
Average	81%	84%	86%	83%	82%

Employee Turnover Rate (All Separations)

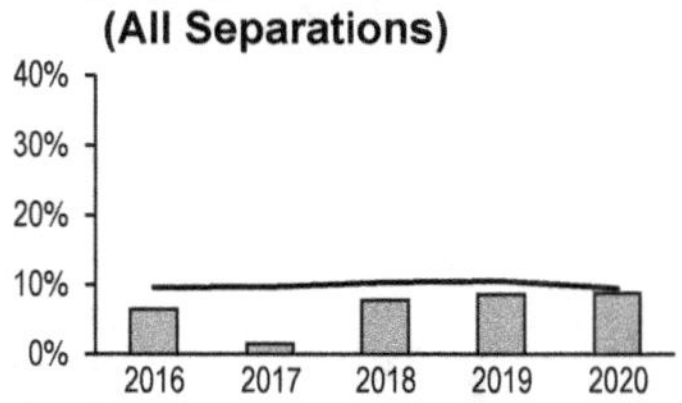

	2016	2017	2018	2019	2020
Greensboro	6.5%	1.5%	7.8%	8.6%	8.8%
Average	9.6%	9.6%	10.3%	10.5%	9.5%

Employee Turnover Rate (Voluntary Separations)

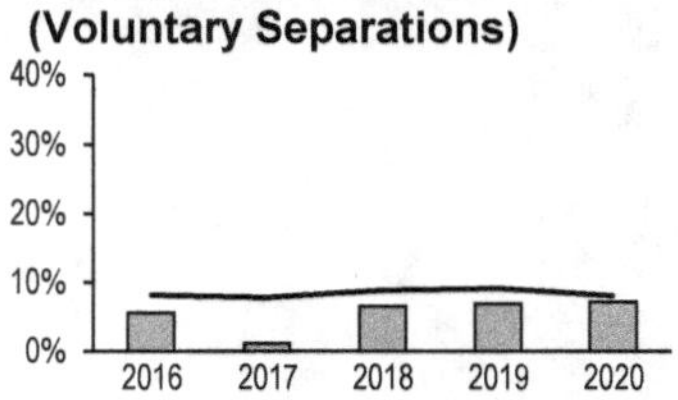

	2016	2017	2018	2019	2020
Greensboro	5.6%	1.2%	6.6%	6.9%	7.2%
Average	8.1%	7.7%	8.8%	9.1%	8.0%

Percentage of Grievances Resolved at Department Level

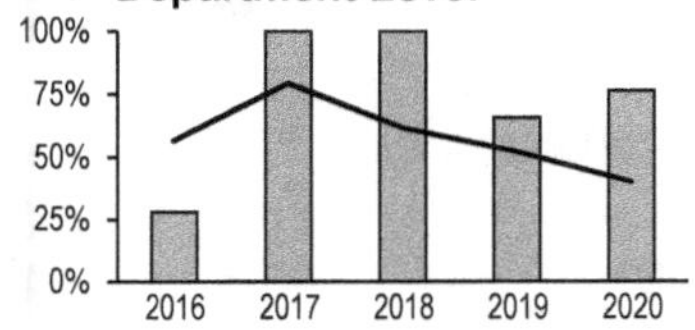

	2016	2017	2018	2019	2020
Greensboro	28%	100%	100%	66%	76%
Average	57%	79%	61%	52%	40%

Average Days from Post Date to Hire Date (First Day of Employment)

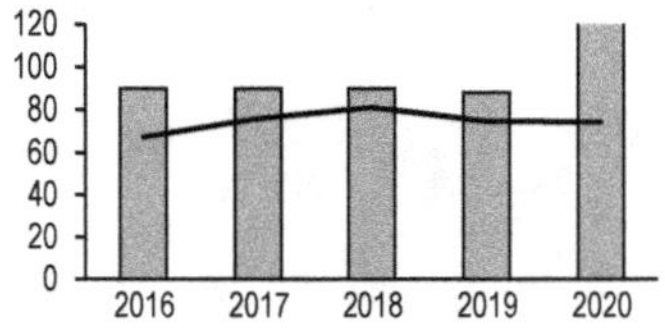

	2016	2017	2018	2019	2020
Greensboro	90	90	90	88	133
Average	67	76	81	75	74

Hickory

Central Human Resources

Fiscal Year 2019-20

Explanatory Information

Service Level and Delivery

The human resources function for the City of Hickory contains a director, an organizational development coordinator, a city nurse, two human resources analysts (one oversees benefits administration and the other oversees general employment), and one clerical position. Risk management is a division of the human resources function, which includes a risk manager and a clerical support position.

The city's probationary period is twelve months for all new city employees.

Conditions Affecting Service, Performance, and Costs

Municipal Profile

Population (OSBM 2019)	41,409
Land Area (Square Miles)	30.50
Persons per Square Mile	1,358
Median Household Income U.S. Census 2016	$35,353

Service Profile

Central HR FTE Positions	
Administration	1.00
Generalist/Specialist	5.0
Staff Support/Clerical	2.00
Total Authorized Workforce	740.0
Authorized FTEs	700.5
Average Length of Service (Months)	118.73
Number of Position Requisitions	70
Employment Applications Processed	2,398
Length of Probationary Employment Period	12 months
Compensation Studies Completed	0
Positions Studied	0
Employee Turnover	
Voluntary Separations	71
Involuntary Separations	17
TOTAL SEPARATIONS	88
Formal Grievances Filed by Employees	1
Equal Employment Opportunity Commission (EEOC) Complaints Filed	1

Full Cost Profile

Cost Breakdown by Percentage	
Personal Services	68.6%
Operating Costs	30.3%
Capital Costs	1.1%
TOTAL	100.0%
Cost Breakdown in Dollars	
Personal Services	$469,309
Operating Costs	$207,467
Capital Costs	$7,324
TOTAL	$684,100

Key: Hickory ▒ Benchmarking Average — Fiscal Years 2016 through 2020

Resource Measures

Human Resources Services Cost per Capita

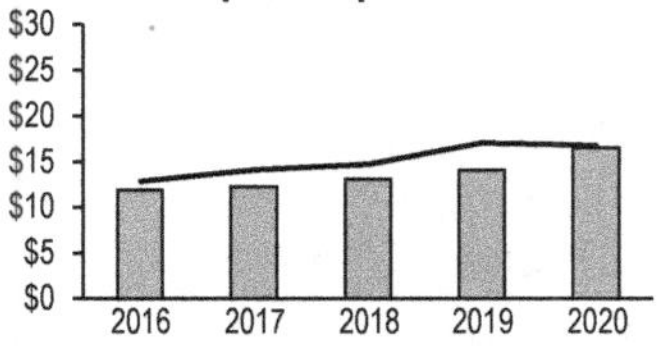

	2016	2017	2018	2019	2020
Hickory	$11.92	$12.25	$13.08	$14.08	$16.52
Average	$12.81	$14.05	$14.72	$17.01	$16.75

Human Resources FTEs per 10,000 Population

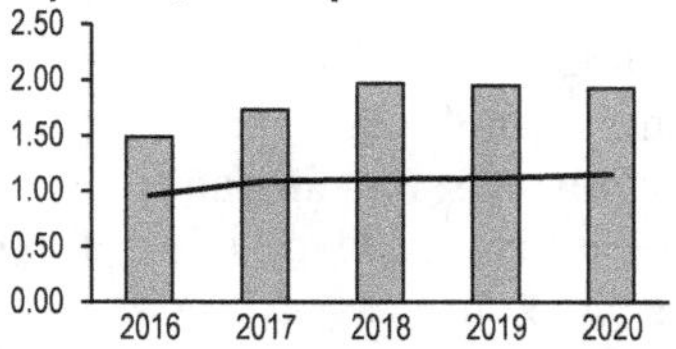

	2016	2017	2018	2019	2020
Hickory	1.49	1.73	1.97	1.95	1.93
Average	0.95	1.09	1.10	1.12	1.15

Workload Measures

Total Municipal FTEs per 10,000 Population

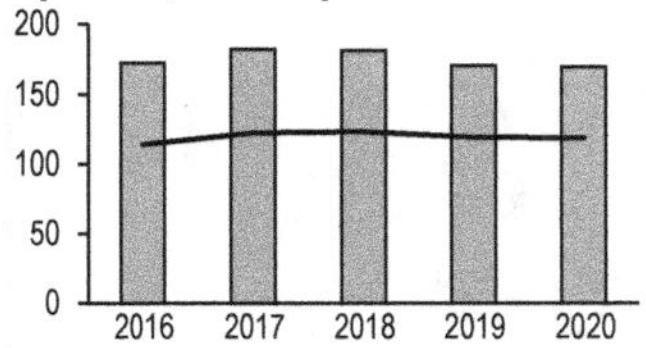

	2016	2017	2018	2019	2020
Hickory	172	182	181	170	169
Average	114	122	123	119	118

Applications Processed per 100 Municipal Employees

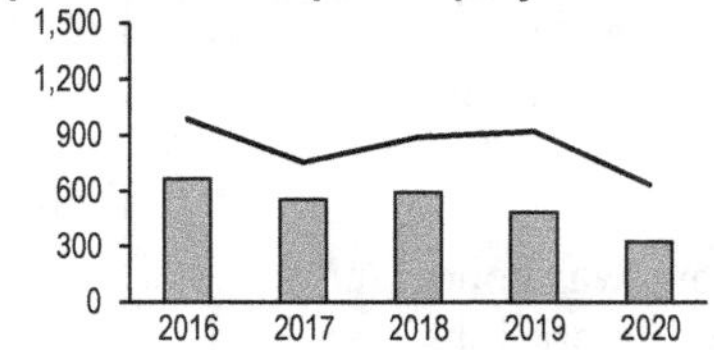

	2016	2017	2018	2019	2020
Hickory	667	555	593	484	324
Average	988	752	888	921	637

Position Requisitions per 100 Municipal Employees

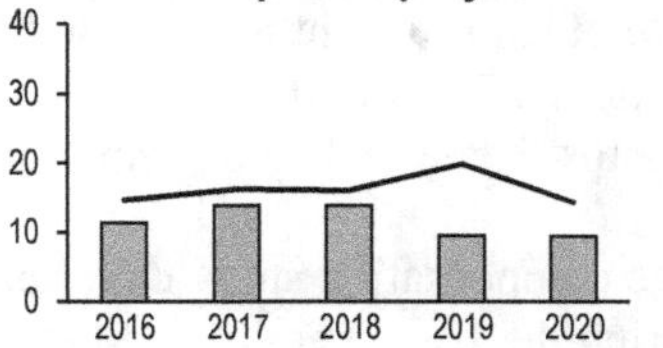

	2016	2017	2018	2019	2020
Hickory	11.4	13.9	13.9	9.5	9.5
Average	14.7	16.2	16.0	19.8	14.4

Efficiency Measures

Human Resources Cost per Municipal Employee

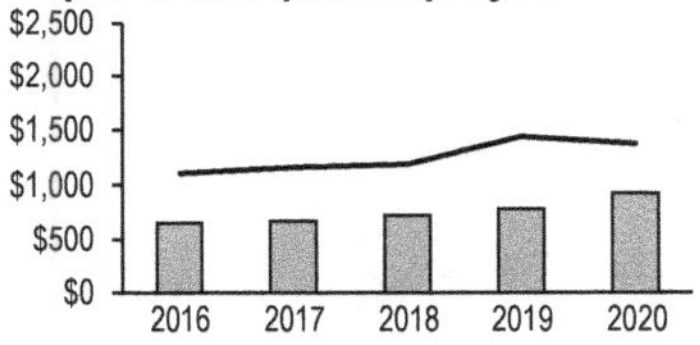

	2016	2017	2018	2019	2020
Hickory	$654	$673	$723	$782	$924
Average	$1,105	$1,154	$1,188	$1,434	$1,372

Ratio of Human Resources Staff to 100 Municipal Employees

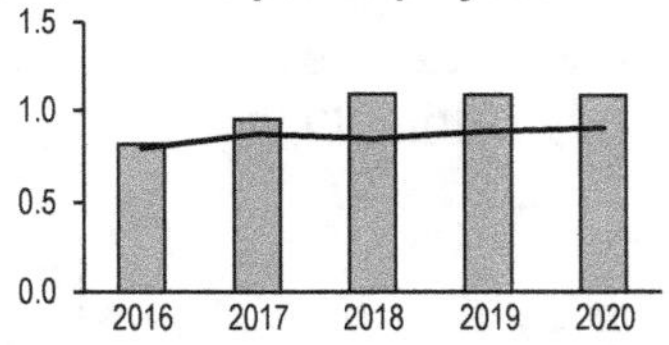

	2016	2017	2018	2019	2020
Hickory	0.82	0.95	1.09	1.09	1.08
Average	0.79	0.87	0.84	0.88	0.90

Effectiveness Measures

Probationary Period Completion Rate (New Hires)

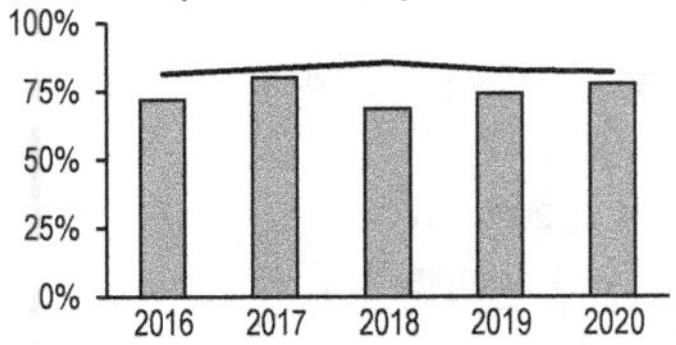

	2016	2017	2018	2019	2020
Hickory	72%	80%	69%	74%	78%
Average	81%	84%	86%	83%	82%

Employee Turnover Rate (All Separations)

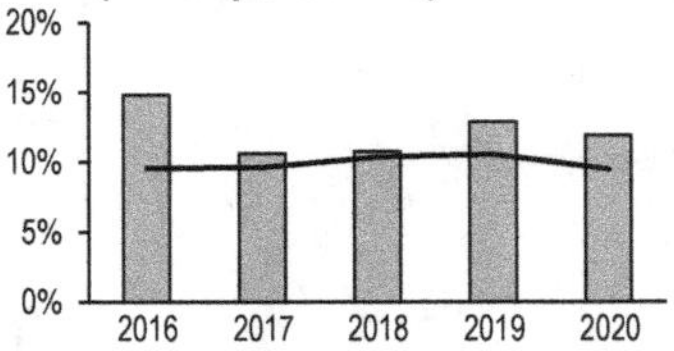

	2016	2017	2018	2019	2020
Hickory	14.8%	10.6%	10.7%	12.9%	11.9%
Average	9.6%	9.6%	10.3%	10.5%	9.5%

Employee Turnover Rate (Voluntary Separations)

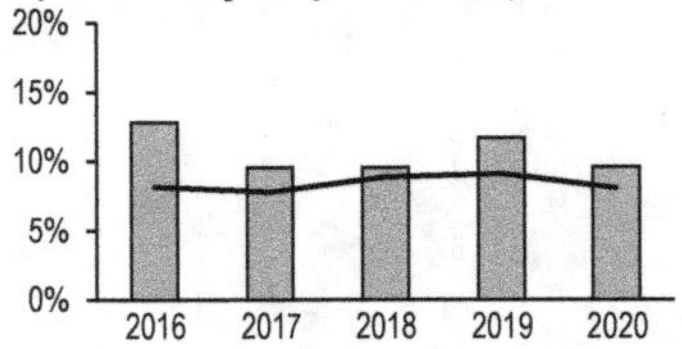

	2016	2017	2018	2019	2020
Hickory	12.8%	9.5%	9.5%	11.7%	9.6%
Average	8.1%	7.7%	8.8%	9.1%	8.0%

Percentage of Grievances Resolved at Department Level

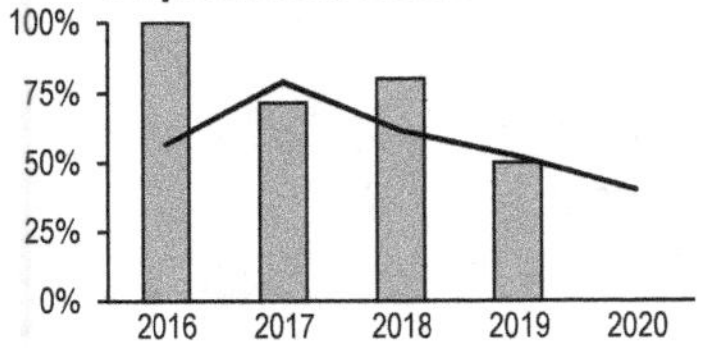

	2016	2017	2018	2019	2020
Hickory	100%	71%	80%	50%	0%
Average	57%	79%	61%	52%	40%

Average Days from Post Date to Hire Date (First Day of Employment)

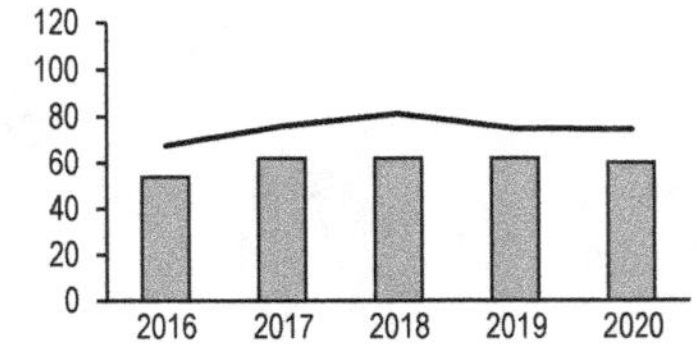

	2016	2017	2018	2019	2020
Hickory	54	62	62	62	60
Average	67	76	81	75	74

Fiscal Year 2019-20

Explanatory Information

Service Level and Delivery

The City of Raleigh's Human Resource Department is organized around work units covering benefits and wellness, employee training and organizational development, talent acquisition, classification and compensation, HRIS administration, and health, safety, and worker's compensation. In addition, the department has three business partners who align with the city's assistant city managers and their respective departments.

The city's probationary period for law enforcement officers is twelve months from the date of employment or successful completion of field training. For firefighters, the probationary period is from the date of employment to six months after graduation from the academy. For all other employees, the probation period lasts six months from the date of employment.

One compensation study covering 840 positions was conducted during the fiscal year. A market review of benchmark jobs was conducted for comparison.

All applications for employment must be completed electronically. HR conducts an initial scan based on minimum qualifications and secondarily by screening questions developed by the hiring manager.

Conditions Affecting Service, Performance, and Costs

Raleigh rejoined the Benchmarking Project in July 2016, with the first year of data showing for FY 2015–16.

Municipal Profile

Population (OSBM 2019)	475,580
Land Area (Square Miles)	146.47
Persons per Square Mile	3,247
Median Household Income U.S. Census 2016	$46,612

Service Profile

Central HR FTE Positions	
Administration	7.0
Generalist/Specialist	21.0
Staff Support/Clerical	4.0
Total Authorized Workforce	4,299.0
Authorized FTEs	4,299.0
Average Length of Service (Months)	124
Number of Position Requisitions	827
Employment Applications Processed	46,275
Length of Probationary Employment Period	6 & 12 months
Compensation Studies Completed	1
Positions Studied	840
Employee Turnover	
Voluntary Separations	305
Involuntary Separations	51
TOTAL SEPARATIONS	356
Formal Grievances Filed by Employees	41
Equal Employment Opportunity Commission (EEOC) Complaints Filed	2

Full Cost Profile

Cost Breakdown by Percentage	
Personal Services	72.4%
Operating Costs	26.9%
Capital Costs	0.7%
TOTAL	100.0%
Cost Breakdown in Dollars	
Personal Services	$3,177,209
Operating Costs	$1,178,652
Capital Costs	$30,398
TOTAL	$4,386,259

Key: Raleigh ▒ Benchmarking Average — Fiscal Years 2016 through 2020

Resource Measures

Human Resources Services Cost per Capita

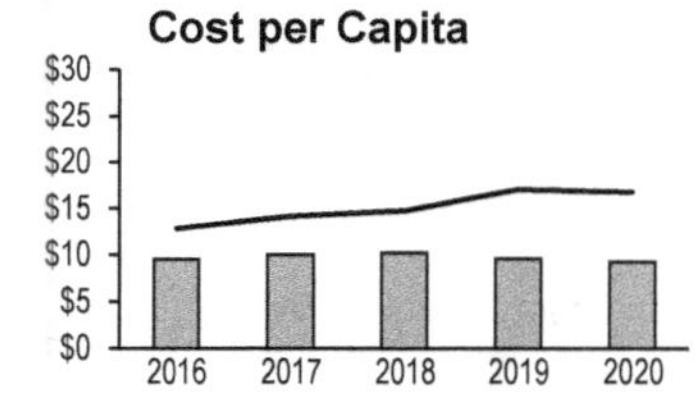

	2016	2017	2018	2019	2020
Raleigh	$9.52	$9.97	$10.15	$9.55	$9.22
Average	$12.81	$14.05	$14.72	$17.01	$16.75

Human Resources FTEs per 10,000 Population

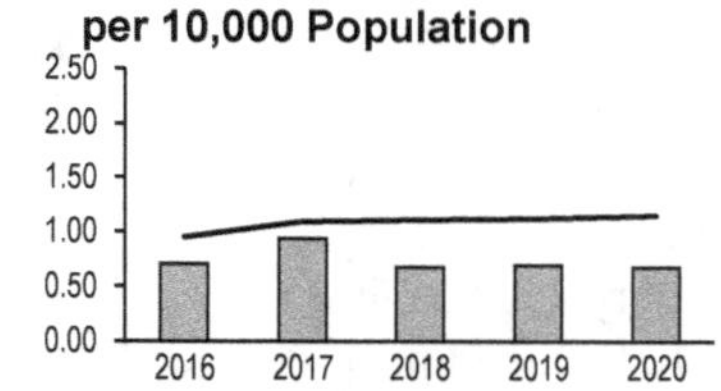

	2016	2017	2018	2019	2020
Raleigh	0.70	0.94	0.67	0.69	0.67
Average	0.95	1.09	1.10	1.12	1.15

Workload Measures

Total Municipal FTEs per 10,000 Population

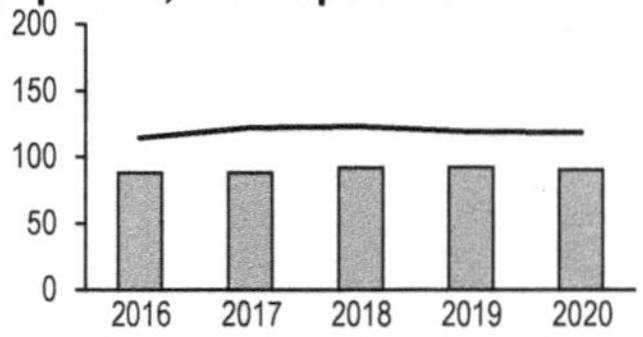

	2016	2017	2018	2019	2020
Raleigh	88	88	92	92	90
Average	114	122	123	119	118

Applications Processed per 100 Municipal Employees

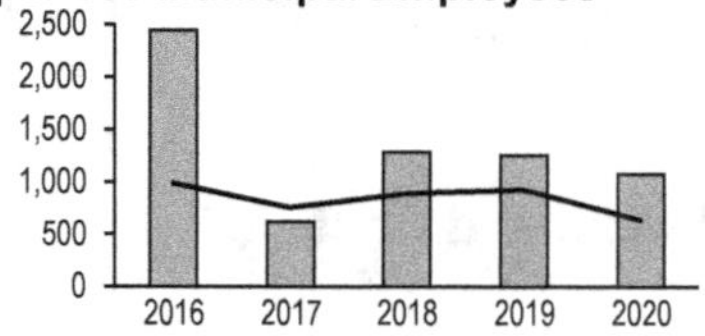

	2016	2017	2018	2019	2020
Raleigh	2,447	621	1,282	1,257	1,076
Average	988	752	888	921	637

Position Requisitions per 100 Municipal Employees

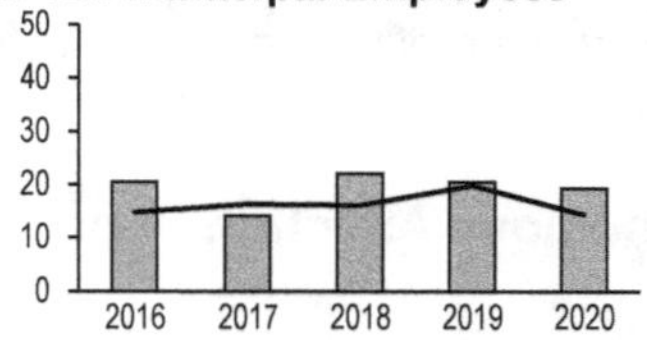

	2016	2017	2018	2019	2020
Raleigh	20.5	14.1	22.0	20.4	19.2
Average	14.7	16.2	16.0	19.8	14.4

Efficiency Measures

Human Resources Cost per Municipal Employee

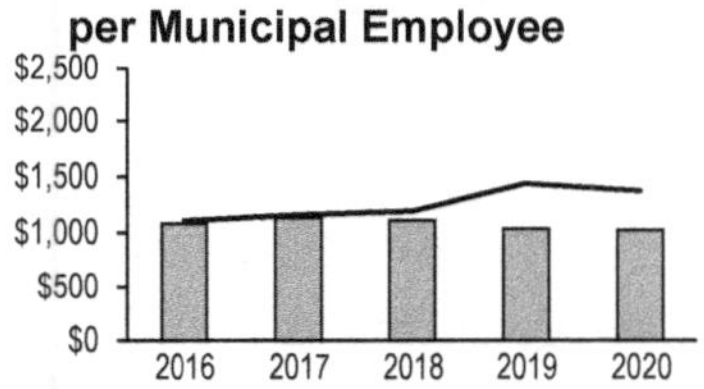

	2016	2017	2018	2019	2020
Raleigh	$1,080	$1,133	$1,108	$1,035	$1,020
Average	$1,105	$1,154	$1,188	$1,434	$1,372

Ratio of Human Resources Staff to 100 Municipal Employees

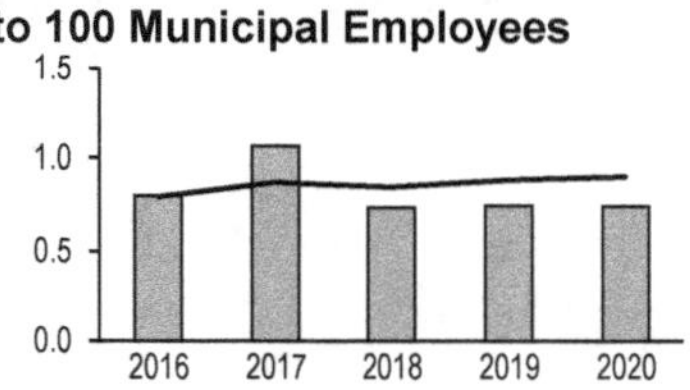

	2016	2017	2018	2019	2020
Raleigh	0.80	1.06	0.73	0.75	0.74
Average	0.79	0.87	0.84	0.88	0.90

Effectiveness Measures

Probationary Period Completion Rate (New Hires)

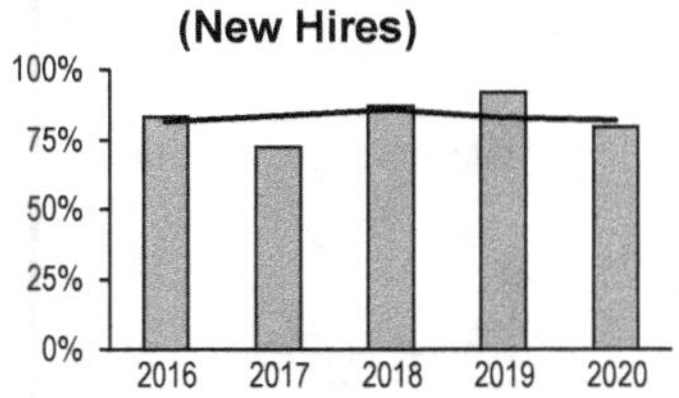

	2016	2017	2018	2019	2020
Raleigh	83%	72%	87%	92%	80%
Average	81%	84%	86%	83%	82%

Employee Turnover Rate (All Separations)

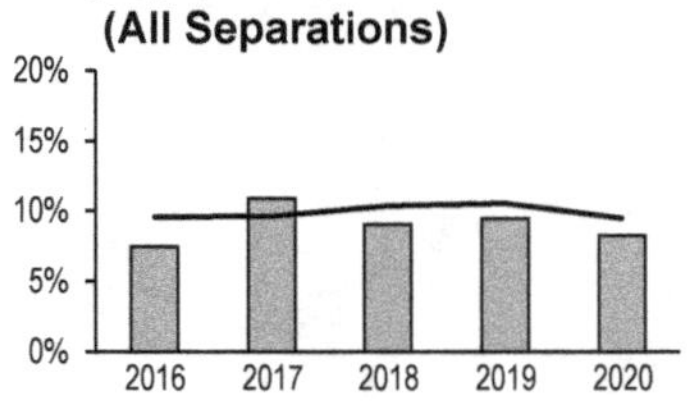

	2016	2017	2018	2019	2020
Raleigh	7.5%	10.9%	9.0%	9.5%	8.3%
Average	9.6%	9.6%	10.3%	10.5%	9.5%

Employee Turnover Rate (Voluntary Separations)

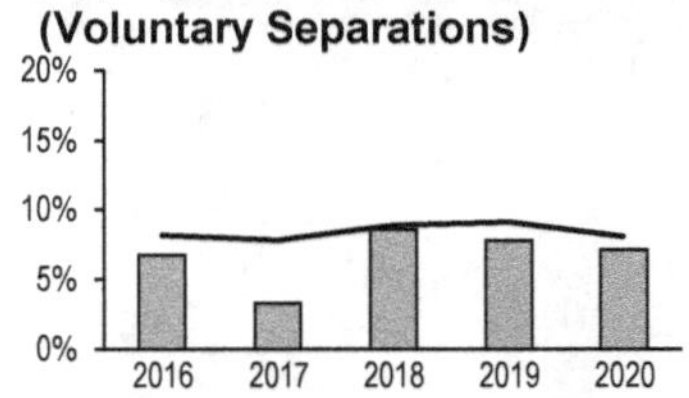

	2016	2017	2018	2019	2020
Raleigh	6.7%	3.3%	8.5%	7.8%	7.1%
Average	8.1%	7.7%	8.8%	9.1%	8.0%

Percentage of Grievances Resolved at Department Level

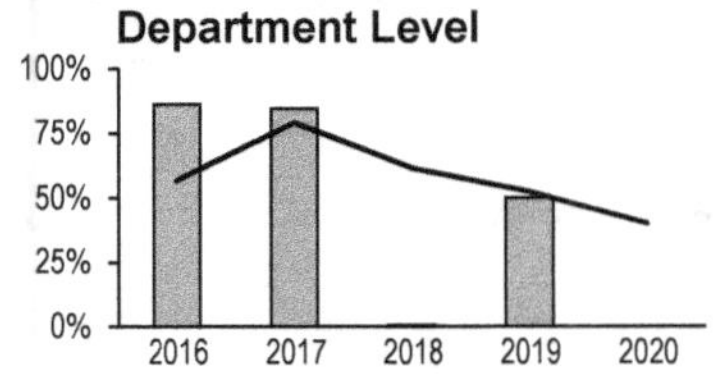

	2016	2017	2018	2019	2020
Raleigh	86%	85%	1%	50%	
Average	57%	79%	61%	52%	40%

Average Days from Post Date to Hire Date (First Day of Employment)

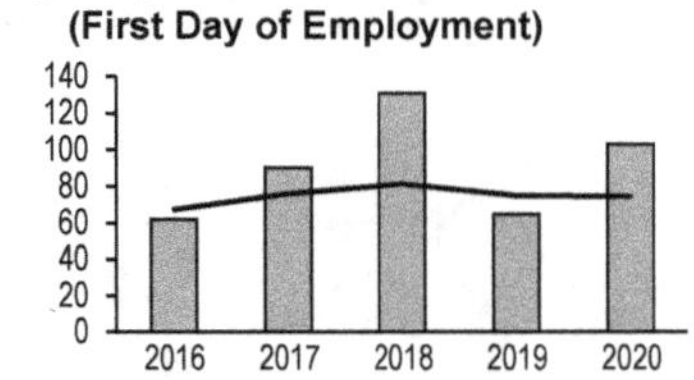

	2016	2017	2018	2019	2020
Raleigh	62	90	131	65	103
Average	67	76	81	75	74

Fiscal Year 2019-20

Explanatory Information

Service Level and Delivery

The City of Wilson has a centralized Human Resources Department that includes policy development and implementation, classification and pay administration, recruitment and selection, benefits administration, and employee relations. The safety and health program is a function of the Risk Management Division under another department. Occupational health needs are met through a contract with the Wilson Medical Center.

The city conducted two compensation studies during the fiscal year, covering 77 positions.

The city's probationary period is twelve months for new city employees.

Conditions Affecting Service, Performance, and Costs

Municipal Profile

Population (OSBM 2019)	49,384
Land Area (Square Miles)	31.02
Persons per Square Mile	1,592
Median Household Income U.S. Census 2016	$35,409

Service Profile

Central HR FTE Positions	
Administration	1.0
Generalist/Specialist	3.0
Staff Support/Clerical	4.0
Total Authorized Workforce	773.0
Authorized FTEs	726.0
Average Length of Service (Months)	121
Number of Position Requisitions	73
Employment Applications Processed	3,883
Length of Probationary Employment Period	12 months
Compensation Studies Completed	2
Positions Studied	77
Employee Turnover	
Voluntary Separations	54
Involuntary Separations	14
TOTAL SEPARATIONS	68
Formal Grievances Filed by Employees	5
Equal Employment Opportunity Commission (EEOC) Complaints Filed	1

Full Cost Profile

Cost Breakdown by Percentage	
Personal Services	77.8%
Operating Costs	19.9%
Capital Costs	2.3%
TOTAL	100.0%
Cost Breakdown in Dollars	
Personal Services	$516,637
Operating Costs	$132,275
Capital Costs	$15,021
TOTAL	$663,933

Key: Wilson ▪ Benchmarking Average — Fiscal Years 2016 through 2020

Resource Measures

Human Resources Services Cost per Capita

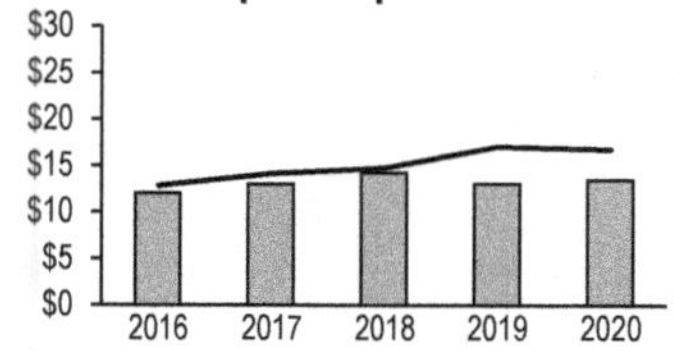

	2016	2017	2018	2019	2020
Wilson	$12.02	$12.94	$14.20	$13.07	$13.44
Average	$12.81	$14.05	$14.72	$17.01	$16.75

Human Resources FTEs per 10,000 Population

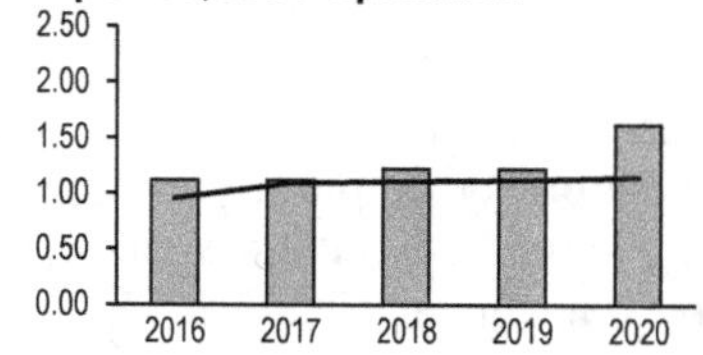

	2016	2017	2018	2019	2020
Wilson	1.11	1.11	1.22	1.22	1.62
Average	0.95	1.09	1.10	1.12	1.15

Workload Measures

Total Municipal FTEs per 10,000 Population

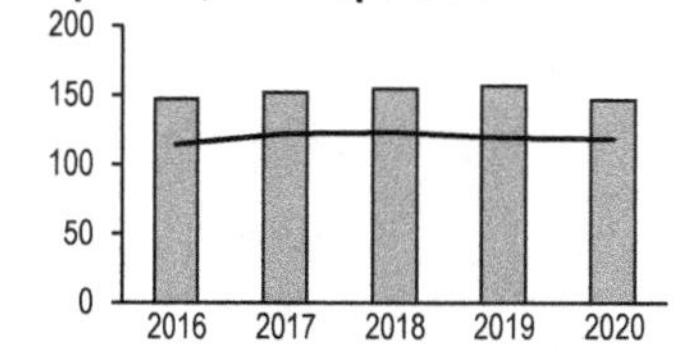

	2016	2017	2018	2019	2020
Wilson	147	152	155	157	147
Average	114	122	123	119	118

Applications Processed per 100 Municipal Employees

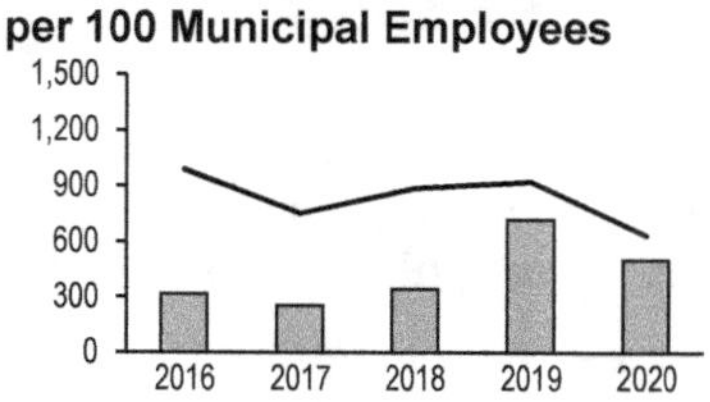

	2016	2017	2018	2019	2020
Wilson	315	251	343	719	502
Average	988	752	888	921	637

Position Requisitions per 100 Municipal Employees

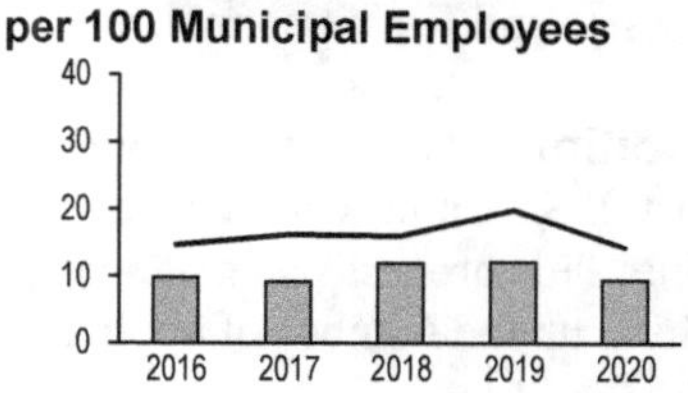

	2016	2017	2018	2019	2020
Wilson	9.9	9.2	11.9	12.2	9.4
Average	14.7	16.2	16.0	19.8	14.4

Efficiency Measures

Human Resources Cost per Municipal Employee

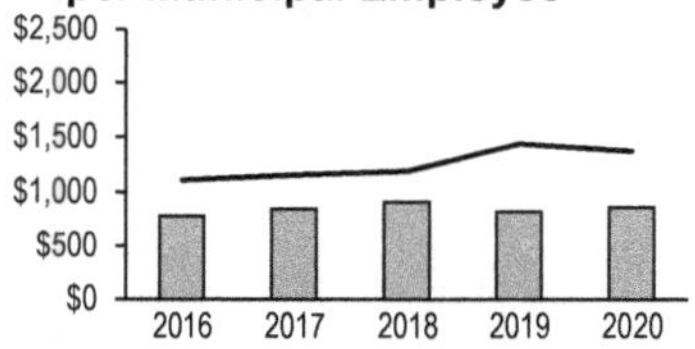

	2016	2017	2018	2019	2020
Wilson	$781	$841	$907	$823	$859
Average	$1,105	$1,154	$1,188	$1,434	$1,372

Ratio of Human Resources Staff to 100 Municipal Employees

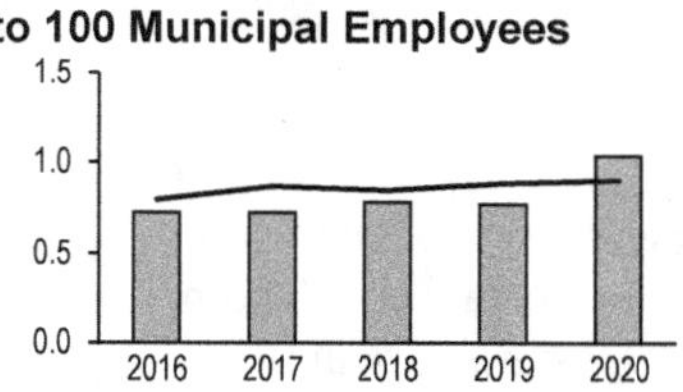

	2016	2017	2018	2019	2020
Wilson	0.72	0.72	0.78	0.77	1.03
Average	0.79	0.87	0.84	0.88	0.90

Effectiveness Measures

Probationary Period Completion Rate (New Hires)

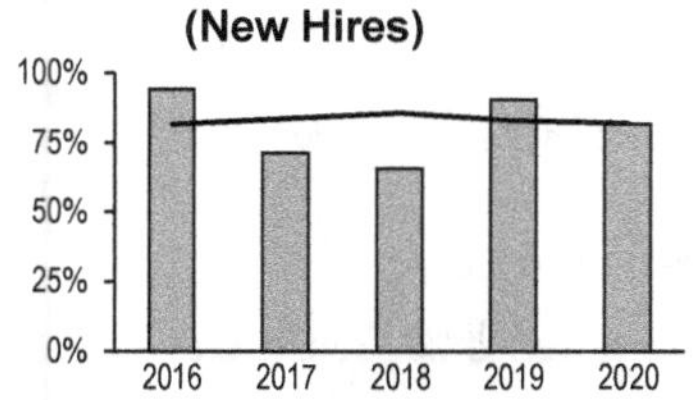

	2016	2017	2018	2019	2020
Wilson	94%	71%	66%	91%	82%
Average	81%	84%	86%	83%	82%

Employee Turnover Rate (All Separations)

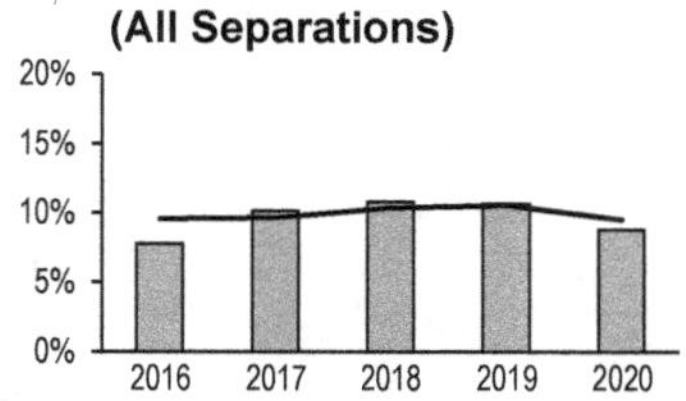

	2016	2017	2018	2019	2020
Wilson	7.8%	10.1%	10.8%	10.7%	8.8%
Average	9.6%	9.6%	10.3%	10.5%	9.5%

Employee Turnover Rate (Voluntary Separations)

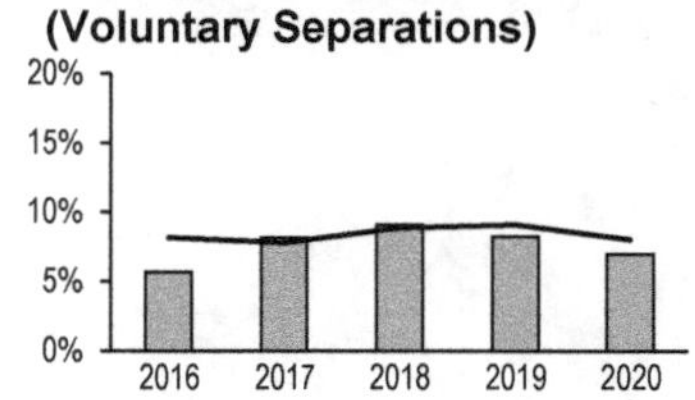

	2016	2017	2018	2019	2020
Wilson	5.7%	8.2%	9.1%	8.2%	7.0%
Average	8.1%	7.7%	8.8%	9.1%	8.0%

Percentage of Grievances Resolved at Department Level

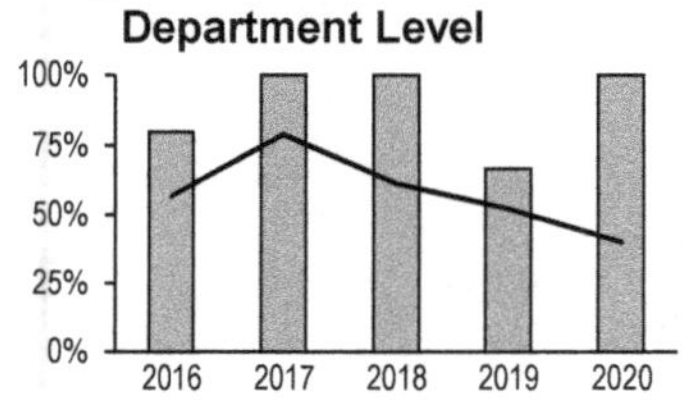

	2016	2017	2018	2019	2020
Wilson	80%	100%	100%	67%	100%
Average	57%	79%	61%	52%	40%

Average Days from Post Date to Hire Date (First Day of Employment)

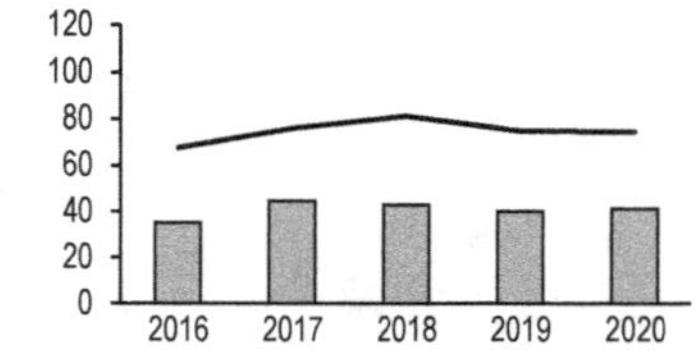

	2016	2017	2018	2019	2020
Wilson	35	44	43	40	41
Average	67	76	81	75	74

Fiscal Year 2019-20

Explanatory Information

Service Level and Delivery

The human resources function is housed under two separate departments: Human Resources (HR) and Finance. The finance department is responsible for benefits administration and employee safety. The human resources department has three separate sections: general human resources management, employee health, and employee training.

Winston-Salem began having employees go through a probationary period in FY 2015–16 for the first time. The city's probationary period for new general employees is six months and twelve months for police and fire personnel.

Conditions Affecting Service, Performance, and Costs

Winston-Salem now requires all job applications to be submitted online. This process has made it substantially easier to apply for jobs, pushing up the number of applications.

The city has two health insurance plans: a basic plan and the Basic Plus Plan, which has richer benefits and more expensive premiums for employees. The city offers a dental reimbursement plan instead of a dental insurance plan.

The City Attorney's Office handles all Equal Employment Opportunity Commission (EEOC) charges.

Winston-Salem's HR department manually calculates the time from post date to hire by subtracting the "approved for posting date" from the actual hire date as noted in the department's system. Certain current policies can effectively stretch this time period, which accounts for the long time reported in the length of time to hire new employees. For example, graduates from the fire academy may sometimes require five months before all evaluations are completed.

Municipal Profile

Population (OSBM 2019)	244,739
Land Area (Square Miles)	132.59
Persons per Square Mile	1,846
Median Household Income U.S. Census 2016	$40,584

Service Profile

Central HR FTE Positions	
Administration	3.0
Generalist/Specialist	10.0
Staff Support/Clerical	2.0
Total Authorized Workforce	2,835.0
Authorized FTEs	2,497.0
Average Length of Service (Months)	127.44
Number of Position Requisitions	487
Employment Applications Processed	21,291
Length of Probationary Employment Period	6 & 12 months
Compensation Studies Completed	0
Positions Studied	0
Employee Turnover	
Voluntary Separations	217
Involuntary Separations	39
TOTAL SEPARATIONS	256
Formal Grievances Filed by Employees	39
Equal Employment Opportunity Commission (EEOC) Complaints Filed	2

Full Cost Profile

Cost Breakdown by Percentage	
Personal Services	29.3%
Operating Costs	68.7%
Capital Costs	2.1%
TOTAL	100.0%
Cost Breakdown in Dollars	
Personal Services	$1,785,652
Operating Costs	$4,189,204
Capital Costs	$126,870
TOTAL	$6,101,726

Winston-Salem — Central Human Resources

Key: Winston-Salem ■ Benchmarking Average — Fiscal Years 2016 through 2020

Resource Measures

Human Resources Services Cost per Capita

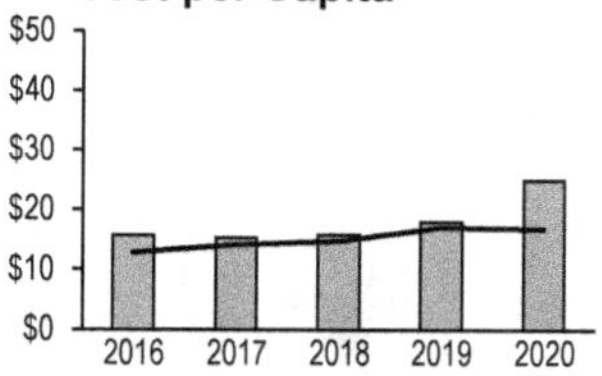

	2016	2017	2018	2019	2020
Winston-Salem	$15.65	$15.17	$15.71	$17.96	$24.93
Average	$12.81	$14.05	$14.72	$17.01	$16.75

Human Resources FTEs per 10,000 Population

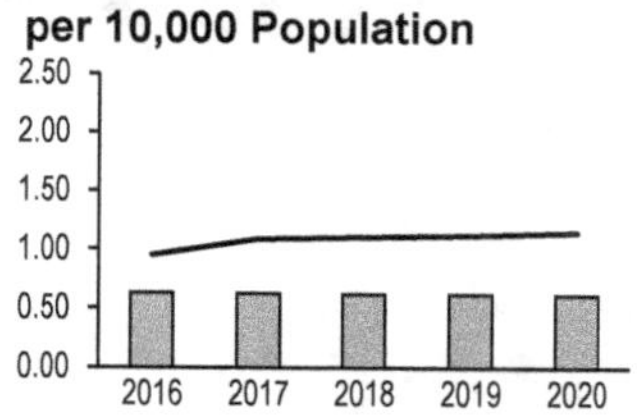

	2016	2017	2018	2019	2020
Winston-Salem	0.63	0.62	0.62	0.62	0.61
Average	0.95	1.09	1.10	1.12	1.15

Workload Measures

Total Municipal FTEs per 10,000 Population

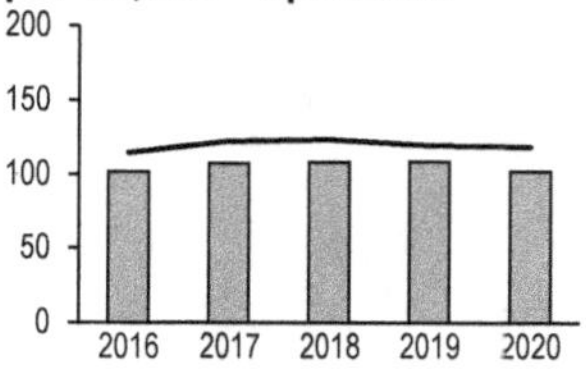

	2016	2017	2018	2019	2020
Winston-Salem	101	107	108	109	102
Average	114	122	123	119	118

Applications Processed per 100 Municipal Employees

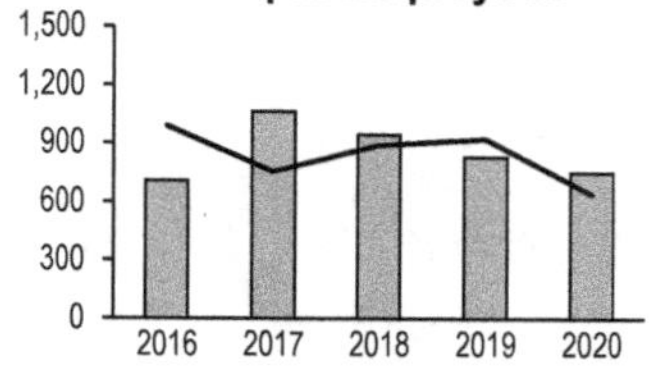

	2016	2017	2018	2019	2020
Winston-Salem	709	1,063	946	828	751
Average	988	752	888	921	637

Position Requisitions per 100 Municipal Employees

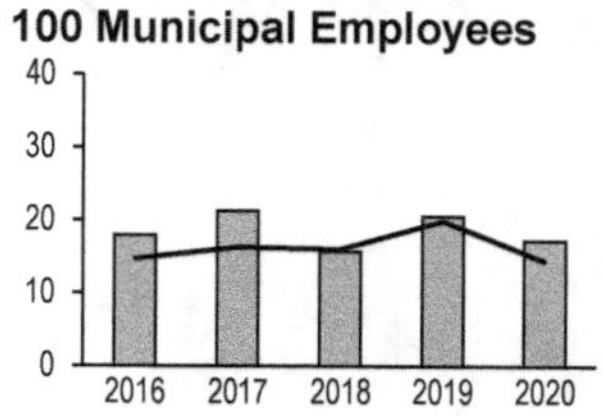

	2016	2017	2018	2019	2020
Winston-Salem	17.9	21.3	15.7	20.5	17.2
Average	14.7	16.2	16.0	19.8	14.4

Efficiency Measures

Human Resources Cost per Municipal Employee

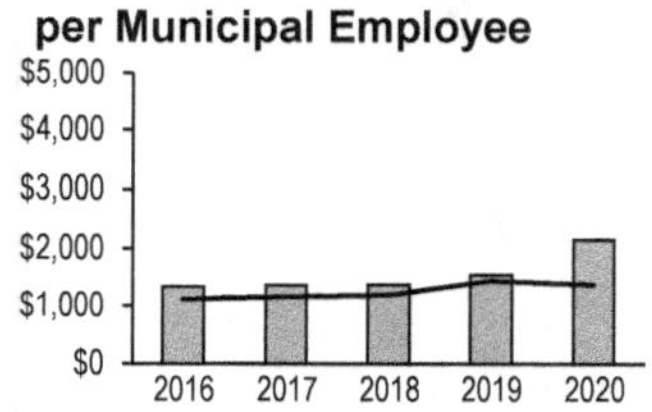

	2016	2017	2018	2019	2020
Winston-Salem	$1,338	$1,364	$1,373	$1,543	$2,152
Average	$1,105	$1,154	$1,188	$1,434	$1,372

Ratio of Human Resources Staff to 100 Municipal Employees

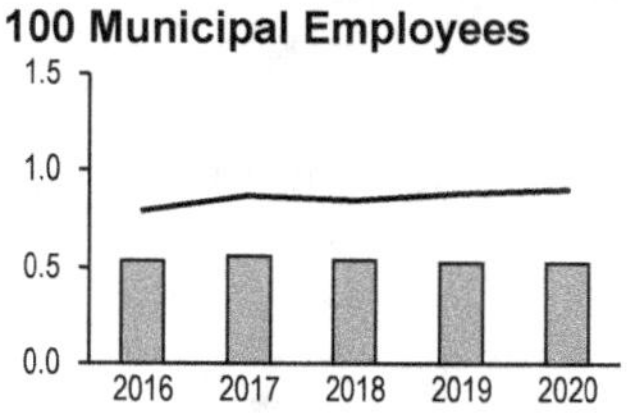

	2016	2017	2018	2019	2020
Winston-Salem	0.54	0.56	0.54	0.53	0.53
Average	0.79	0.87	0.84	0.88	0.90

Effectiveness Measures

Probationary Period Completion Rate (New Hires)

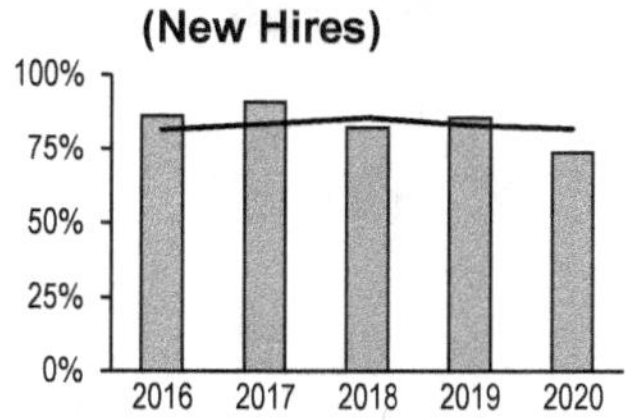

	2016	2017	2018	2019	2020
Winston-Salem	86%	91%	82%	86%	74%
Average	81%	84%	86%	83%	82%

Employee Turnover Rate (All Separations)

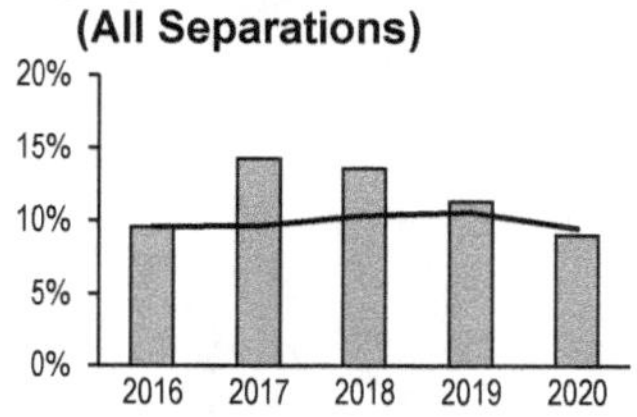

	2016	2017	2018	2019	2020
Winston-Salem	9.6%	14.3%	13.6%	11.3%	9.0%
Average	9.6%	9.6%	10.3%	10.5%	9.5%

Employee Turnover Rate (Voluntary Separations)

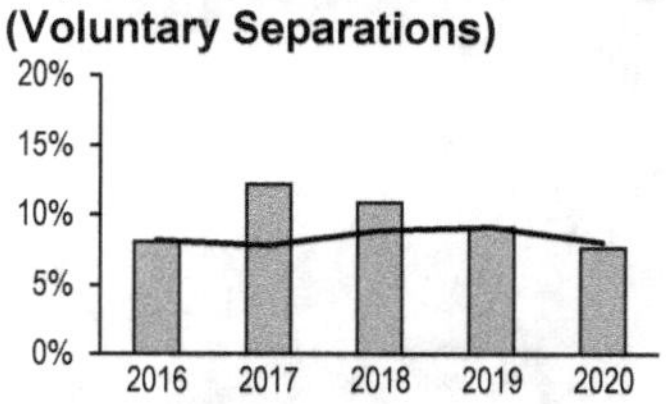

	2016	2017	2018	2019	2020
Winston-Salem	8.1%	12.1%	10.9%	9.1%	7.7%
Average	8.1%	7.7%	8.8%	9.1%	8.0%

Percentage of Grievances Resolved at Department Level

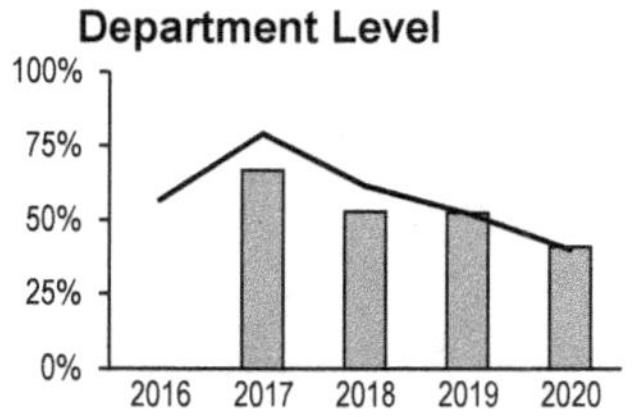

	2016	2017	2018	2019	2020
Winston-Salem		67%	53%	52%	41%
Average	57%	79%	61%	52%	40%

Average Days from Post Date to Hire Date (First Day of Employment)

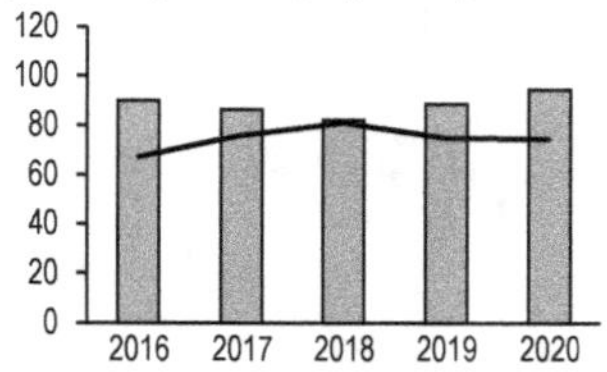

	2016	2017	2018	2019	2020
Winston-Salem	90	86	82	89	94
Average	67	76	81	75	74

UNC | SCHOOL OF GOVERNMENT
North Carolina Benchmarking Project

Performance and Cost Data

WATER SERVICES

SCHOOL OF GOVERNMENT
North Carolina Benchmarking Project

PERFORMANCE MEASURES FOR WATER SERVICES

SERVICE DEFINITION

This service area includes the collection, treatment, distribution, and billing related to drinking water services. It includes reservoirs where appropriate, pumping stations, pipes to and from treatment plants, storage tanks, and treatment plants. Activities and costs include the operation, maintenance, and installation of infrastructure. Also included are costs and activities associated with the installation, upkeep, and reading of meters; billing and collection costs for drinking water services; and administrative activities, such as planning, engineering, and testing. Excluded are reclaimed water, sewer collection, and wastewater treatment services.

NOTES ON PERFORMANCE MEASURES

1. Thousands of Gallons Billed Water per Meter

This workload measure captures the amount of water provided per meter in the system. Water that does not make it to customer taps is not included.

2. Miles of Main Line Pipe per Square Mile of Service Area

The amount of pipe per square mile shows the density of the pipe infrastructure to be maintained relative to the geographic size of the area served.

3. Total Cost per Thousand Gallons of Billed Water

This efficiency measure shows the total system costs per 1,000 gallons of water that is actually billed to customers.

4. Million Gallons of Billed Water per All Staff FTEs

Large numbers of staff including treatment staff, line maintenance staff, meter readers, billing staff, and others are required to bring drinking water to customer taps. Based on all staff who help support the delivery of drinking water to customers, this efficiency measure shows how much billable water is produced per full-time equivalent (FTE) staff member.

5. Billed Water as a Percentage of Finished Water

Not all water produced at treatment plants makes it to customer meters. Some water is lost through leaks or breaks in the system. Other water is unbilled but authorized for uses such as fighting fires or flushing lines. This efficiency measure shows the percentage of water produced that makes it to customer taps.

6. Percentage of Existing Pipeline Renewed

Replacement or rehabilitation of existing pipeline is needed to ensure that the distribution infrastructure can continue to function. This effectiveness measure shows the percentage of existing water lines that are renewed each year.

7. Percentage of Bills Not Collected

Collection of water bills sent to customers is necessary to ensure revenues for system operation. Adjustments to bills reflecting water loss adjustments are not included in the amount of billings.

8. Peak Daily Demand as a Percentage of Treatment Capacity

A water system needs sufficient capacity to meet not only average demands, but also peak demands. This measure looks at peak historical demand relative to the water system treatment capacity in a day.

9. Breaks and Leaks per Mile of Main Line Pipe

Breaks or leaks in water distribution lines mean the loss of treated water.

10. Customer Complaints about Water Quality per Thousand Meters

Concerns for the adequacy of water are matched with the quality of the water delivered to customers. This effectiveness measure assesses customers' perceptions about their water quality.

Water Services

Summary of Key Dimensions of Service

City or Town	Estimated Residential Population in Service Area	Service Area (in Square Miles)	Average Daily Demand for Water (in MGD)	Operating Treatment Plants	Total Treatment Capacity for Finished Water (in MGD)	Miles of Water Main Lines	Number of Water Meters	Water System FTE Positions
Apex	65,682	24.0	4.2	Shared with Cary	Shared with Cary	318.2	22,988	30.0
Charlotte	1,110,356	546.0	108.9	3	242.0	4,431.0	306,397	467.0
Concord	98,064	142.8	13.1	2	24.0	752.3	43,138	67.0
Goldsboro	34,959	25.0	6.5	1	12.0	270.0	14,744	26.0
Greensboro	315,328	148.0	32.2	2	63.7	1,514.0	107,267	164.0
Hickory	99,530	326.0	11.3	1	32.0	947.7	27,903	55.0
Raleigh	591,943	299.0	51.4	2	106.0	2,351.0	207,954	297.0
Wilson	54,500	40.0	9.1	2	22.0	433.0	22,267	48.0
Winston-Salem	351,733	227.0	36.1	3	91.0	2,341.0	131,935	172.2

NOTES

MGD stands for millions of gallons per day.

EXPLANATORY FACTORS

These are factors that the project found affected water services performance and cost in one or more of the municipalities:

Topography
Water quality of source water
Size of service area
Population density
Age of infrastructure
Growth of population and businesses

Fiscal Year 2019-20

Explanatory Information

Service Level and Delivery

The Town of Apex Water Distribution Division is housed within the Department of Public Works. It consists of repairs, preventive maintenance, meter installation and replacement, and testing. The town is co-owner of the Cary/Apex water treatment facility, which draws raw water from Jordan Lake. The Town of Cary provides the operational staff for the treatment plant, but Apex shares in the costs of operation and capital.

Apex bases replacement of water lines on customer complaints, frequency of repairs, street rehabilitation needs, age and material of pipes, and flow concerns.

Currently, nearly all water meters are read by automatic means. Replacement of meters is based on a combination of factors, as is water line replacement.

Conditions Affecting Service, Performance, and Costs

The costs of water services as captured here do not include debt service but do capture depreciation.

Municipal Profile

Estimated Service Population	65,682
Service Land Area (Square Miles)	24.0
Persons per Square Mile	2,737
Topography	Flat; gently rolling
Climate	Temperate; little ice and snow
Median Household Income U.S. Census 2016	$84,000

Service Profile

FTE Staff Positions	
Treatment Plant	0.0
Line Crews	18.0
Meter Readers	5.0
Billing/Collection	4.0
Other	3.0
Total	30.0
Number of Treatment Plants	NA
Total Treatment Capacity	NA
Average Daily Demand	4.2 MGD
Miles of Main Line Pipe	318
Average Age of Main Line Pipe	17 years
Number of Breaks/Leaks	92
Number of Water Meters	22,988
Percent of Meters Read Automatically	99.4%
Total Revenues Collected	$11,809,743

Full Cost Profile

Cost Breakdown by Percentage	
Personal Services	29.1%
Operating Costs	28.8%
Capital Costs	42.1%
TOTAL	100.0%
Cost Breakdown in Dollars	
Personal Services	$1,889,697
Operating Costs	$1,869,349
Capital Costs	$2,729,274
TOTAL	$6,488,320

Key: Apex ▪ Benchmarking Average — Fiscal Years 2016 through 2020

Resource Measures

Water Services Cost per Capita

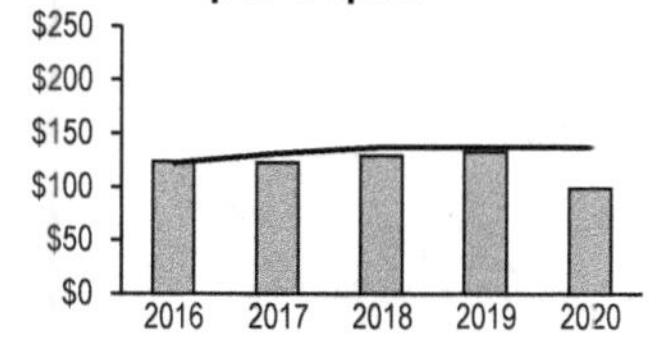

	2016	2017	2018	2019	2020
Apex	$124	$122	$129	$133	$99
Average	$122	$131	$137	$137	$137

Water Services FTEs per 10,000 Population

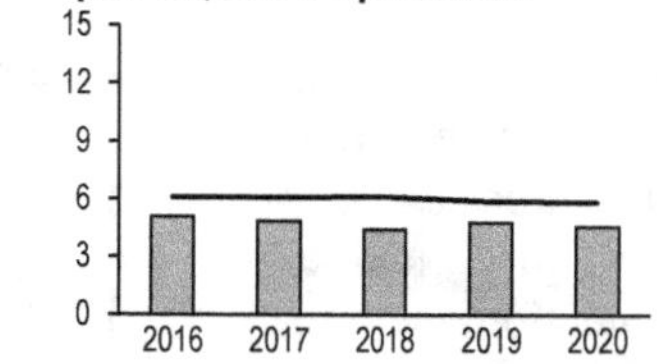

	2016	2017	2018	2019	2020
Apex	5.0	4.8	4.4	4.8	4.6
Average	6.1	6.1	6.1	5.9	5.8

Water Services Cost per Meter

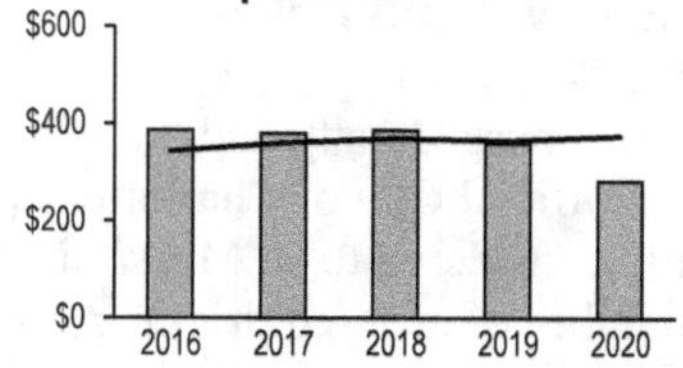

	2016	2017	2018	2019	2020
Apex	$387	$380	$387	$360	$282
Average	$343	$360	$369	$365	$375

Workload Measures

Thousands of Gallons of Billed Water per Meter

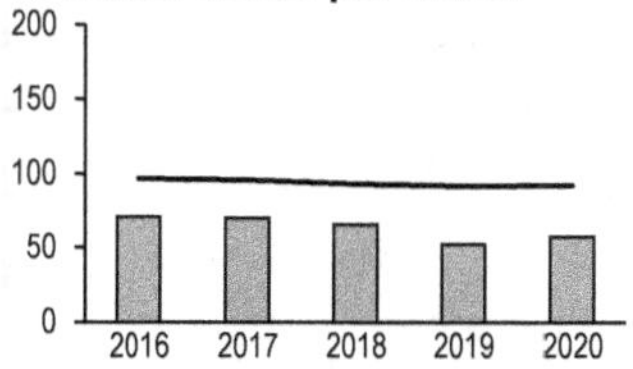

	2016	2017	2018	2019	2020
Apex	70.8	70.0	65.8	52.4	57.5
Average	96.4	95.5	92.8	91.6	92.2

Miles of Main Line Pipe per Square Mile of Service Area

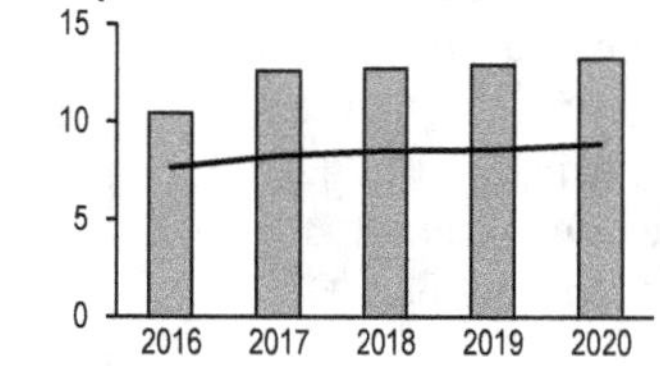

	2016	2017	2018	2019	2020
Apex	10.4	12.6	12.7	12.9	13.3
Average	7.6	8.2	8.5	8.6	8.8

Efficiency Measures

Total Cost per Thousand Gallons of Billed Water

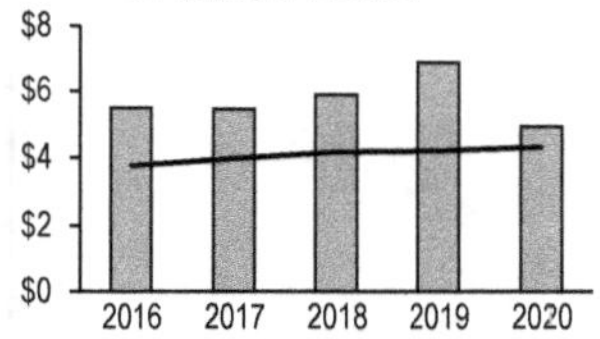

	2016	2017	2018	2019	2020
Apex	$5.47	$5.43	$5.88	$6.87	$4.91
Average	$3.75	$3.95	$4.15	$4.18	$4.30

Million Gallons of Billed Water per Water Services FTEs

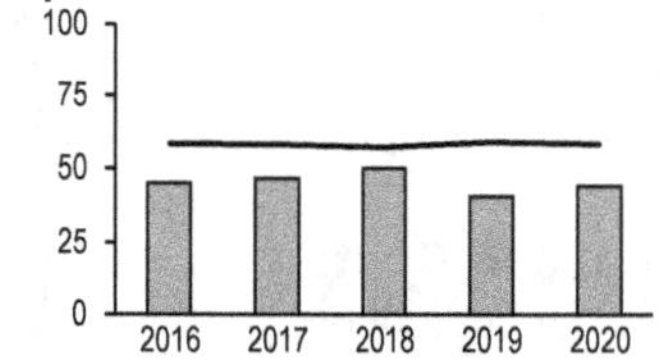

	2016	2017	2018	2019	2020
Apex	44.9	46.6	50.0	40.6	44.1
Average	58.1	57.9	57.0	58.7	58.2

Billed Water as a Percentage of Finished Water

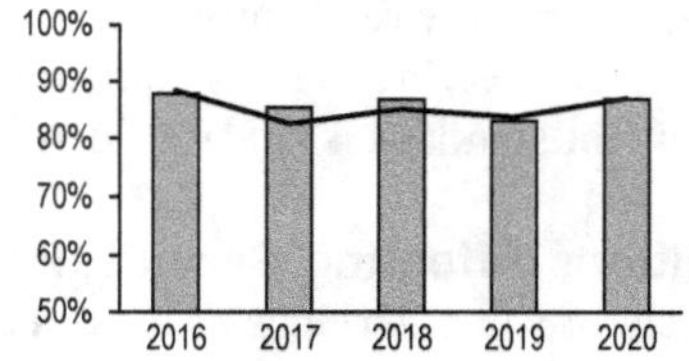

	2016	2017	2018	2019	2020
Apex	88%	85%	87%	83%	87%
Average	88%	82%	85%	84%	87%

Effectiveness Measures

Percentage of Existing Pipeline Replaced or Rehabbed

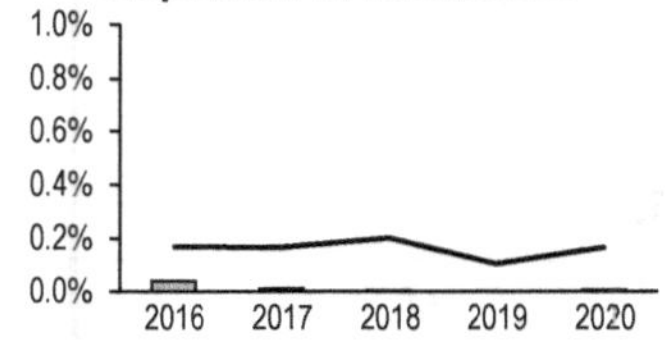

	2016	2017	2018	2019	2020
Apex	0.0%	0.0%	0.0%	0.0%	0.0%
Average	0.2%	0.2%	0.2%	0.1%	0.2%

Percentage of Water Bills Not Collected

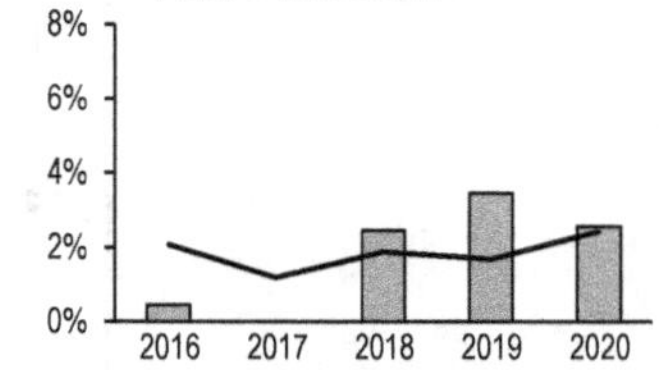

	2016	2017	2018	2019	2020
Apex	0.46%	0.00%	2.46%	3.47%	2.57%
Average	2.08%	1.19%	1.88%	1.68%	2.42%

Peak Daily Demand as a Percentage of Treatment Capacity

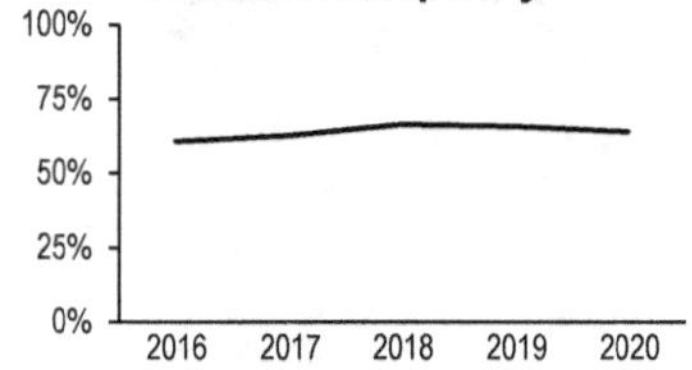

	2016	2017	2018	2019	2020
Apex					
Average	61%	63%	66%	66%	64%

Breaks and Leaks per Mile of Main Line Pipe

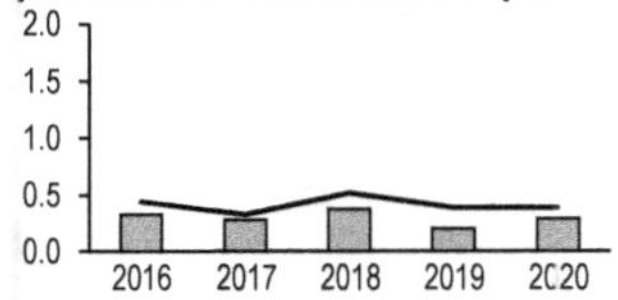

	2016	2017	2018	2019	2020
Apex	0.33	0.28	0.37	0.20	0.29
Average	0.44	0.32	0.52	0.38	0.38

Customer Complaints about Water Quality per 1,000 Meters

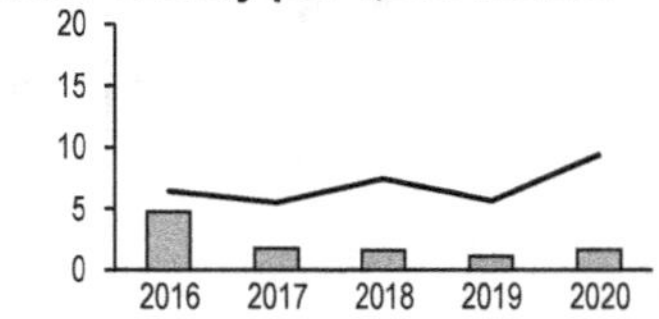

	2016	2017	2018	2019	2020
Apex	4.73	1.69	1.54	1.06	1.61
Average	6.43	5.48	7.42	5.61	9.38

Fiscal Year 2019-20

Explanatory Information

Service Level and Delivery
Charlotte Water (CLTWater) is a combined water and sewer utility for Mecklenburg County and the City of Charlotte. The department is run as an official City of Charlotte department. The area served is generally considered to be Mecklenburg County but also includes a small number of metered drinking water interconnections with the City of Concord and the counties of Union in North Carolina and Lancaster and York in South Carolina. The service area covers approximately 546 square miles and serves over one million people.

Source water for the system is drawn from two impounded lakes on the Catawba River, Lake Norman and Mountain Island Lake, which are operated by Duke Energy. The combined estimated safe yield is between 376 and 503 million gallons per day. The system operates three treatment plants with a combined treatment capacity of 242 million gallons per day. The treatment plants are conventional facilities using rapid mix, flocculation, settling, filtration, and chemical application.

The estimated average age of main line pipes in the system is twenty-nine years. CMU's replacement policy for pipe is based on flow and quality standards.

All meters are now read automatically. CMU uses a system that allows vans traveling the city to read meters as they drive by. The replacement standard is every fifteen years for water meters.

Conditions Affecting Service, Performance, and Costs
The costs of water services as captured here do not include debt service but do capture depreciation.

The reduction in reported leaks and breaks over time is in large part due to improvements in tracking and data reporting. CMU staff worked on improving how the work order system is used to determine the number of leaks or breaks in the water system.

Municipal Profile

Estimated Service Population	1,110,356
Service Land Area (Square Miles)	546.0
Persons per Square Mile	2,034
Topography	Flat; gently rolling
Climate	Temperate; little ice and snow
Median Household Income U.S. Census 2016	$46,975

Service Profile

FTE Staff Positions	
Treatment Plant	53.0
Line Crews	177.0
Meter Readers	4.0
Billing/Collection	12.0
Other	221.0
Total	467.0
Number of Treatment Plants	3
Total Treatment Capacity	242.0 MGD
Average Daily Demand	108.9 MGD
Miles of Main Line Pipe	4,431
Average Age of Main Line Pipe	33 years
Number of Breaks/Leaks	4,171
Number of Water Meters	306,397
Percent of Meters Read Automatically	100.0%
Total Revenues Collected	$174,761,331

Full Cost Profile

Cost Breakdown by Percentage	
Personal Services	26.0%
Operating Costs	34.4%
Capital Costs	39.6%
TOTAL	100.0%
Cost Breakdown in Dollars	
Personal Services	$30,982,400
Operating Costs	$40,879,850
Capital Costs	$47,127,673
TOTAL	$118,989,923

Charlotte

Water Services

Key: Charlotte ▒ Benchmarking Average — Fiscal Years 2016 through 2020

Resource Measures

Water Services Cost per Capita

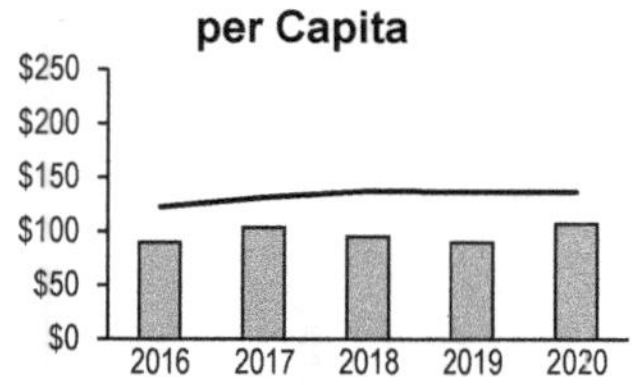

	2016	2017	2018	2019	2020
Charlotte	$90	$103	$95	$89	$107
Average	$122	$131	$137	$137	$137

Water Services FTEs per 10,000 Population

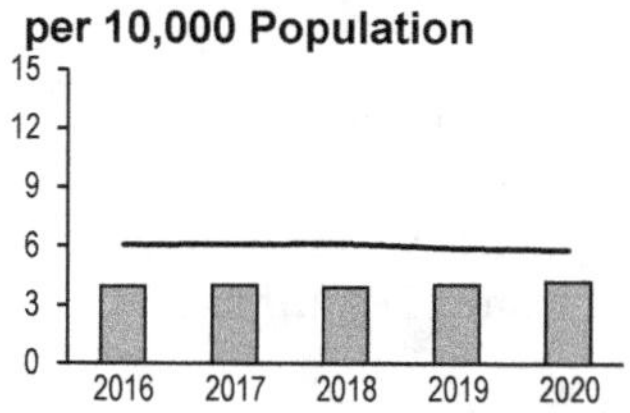

	2016	2017	2018	2019	2020
Charlotte	3.9	4.0	3.9	4.0	4.2
Average	6.1	6.1	6.1	5.9	5.8

Water Services Cost per Meter

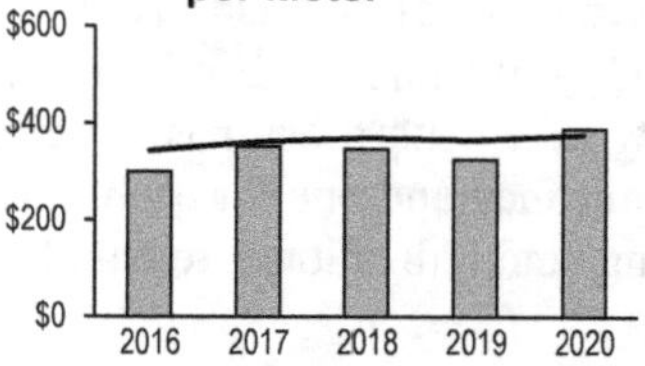

	2016	2017	2018	2019	2020
Charlotte	$300	$351	$346	$326	$388
Average	$343	$360	$369	$365	$375

Workload Measures

Thousands of Gallons of Billed Water per Meter

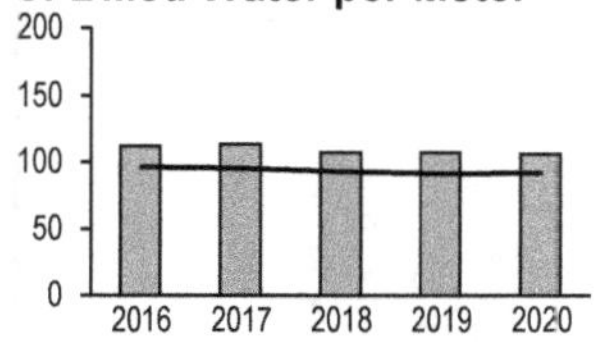

	2016	2017	2018	2019	2020
Charlotte	112.3	113.7	107.6	107.3	106.3
Average	96.4	95.5	92.8	91.6	92.2

Miles of Main Line Pipe per Square Mile of Service Area

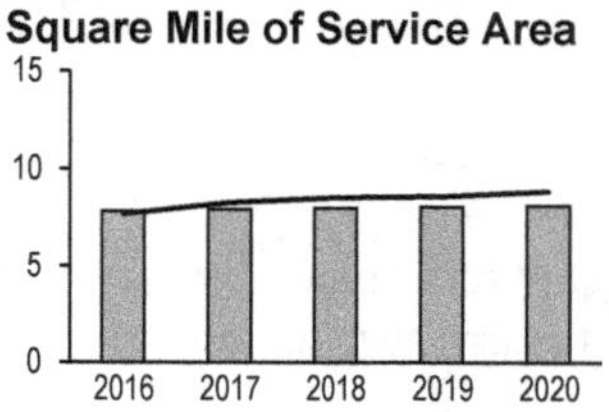

	2016	2017	2018	2019	2020
Charlotte	7.8	7.9	8.0	8.0	8.1
Average	7.6	8.2	8.5	8.6	8.8

Efficiency Measures

Total Cost per Thousand Gallons of Billed Water

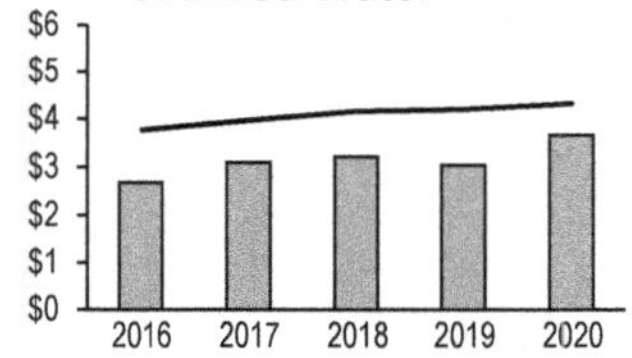

	2016	2017	2018	2019	2020
Charlotte	$2.67	$3.09	$3.22	$3.03	$3.65
Average	$3.75	$3.95	$4.15	$4.18	$4.30

Million Gallons of Billed Water per Water Services FTEs

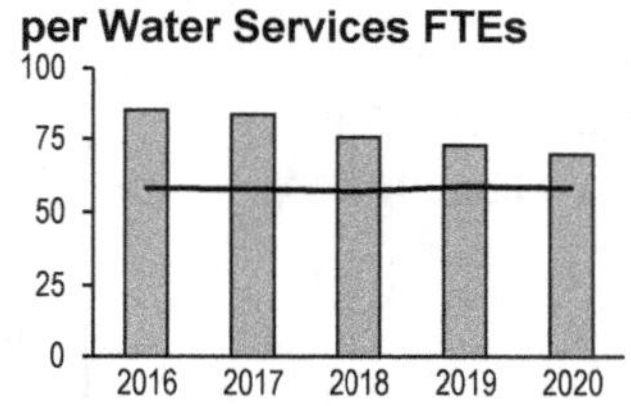

	2016	2017	2018	2019	2020
Charlotte	85.2	83.6	75.8	72.9	69.7
Average	58.1	57.9	57.0	58.7	58.2

Billed Water as a Percentage of Finished Water

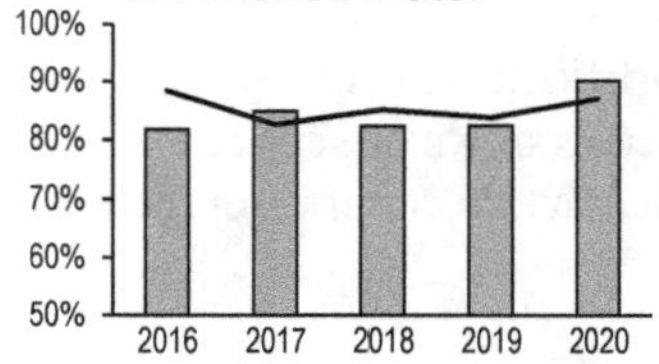

	2016	2017	2018	2019	2020
Charlotte	82%	85%	82%	82%	90%
Average	88%	82%	85%	84%	87%

Effectiveness Measures

Percentage of Existing Pipeline Replaced or Rehabbed

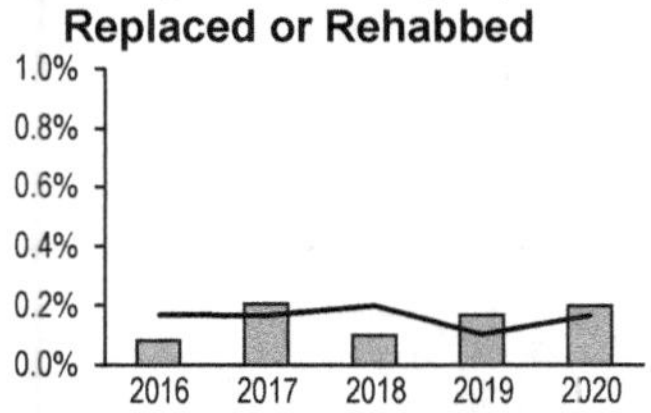

	2016	2017	2018	2019	2020
Charlotte	0.1%	0.2%	0.1%	0.2%	0.2%
Average	0.2%	0.2%	0.2%	0.1%	0.2%

Percentage of Water Bills Not Collected

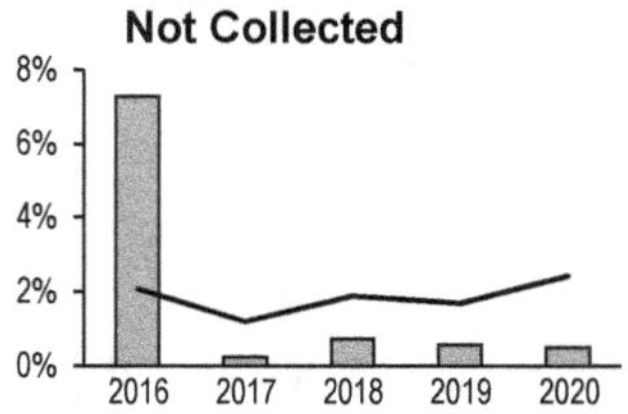

	2016	2017	2018	2019	2020
Charlotte	7.29%	0.24%	0.73%	0.58%	0.49%
Average	2.08%	1.19%	1.88%	1.68%	2.42%

Peak Daily Demand as a Percentage of Treatment Capacity

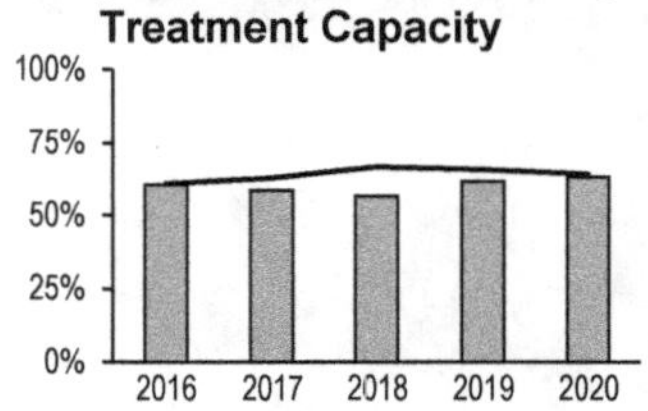

	2016	2017	2018	2019	2020
Charlotte	60%	58%	57%	62%	63%
Average	61%	63%	66%	66%	64%

Breaks and Leaks per Mile of Main Line Pipe

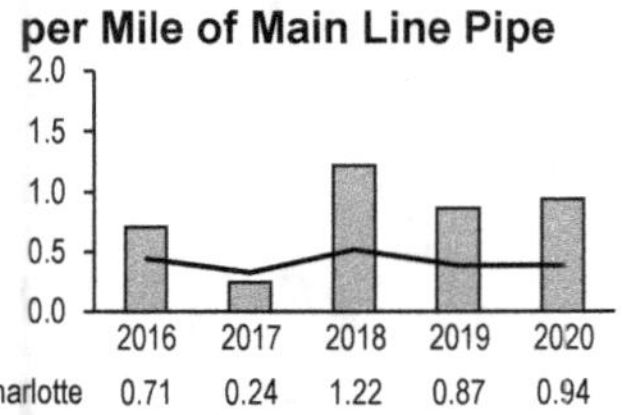

	2016	2017	2018	2019	2020
Charlotte	0.71	0.24	1.22	0.87	0.94
Average	0.44	0.32	0.52	0.38	0.38

Customer Complaints about Water Quality per 1,000 Meters

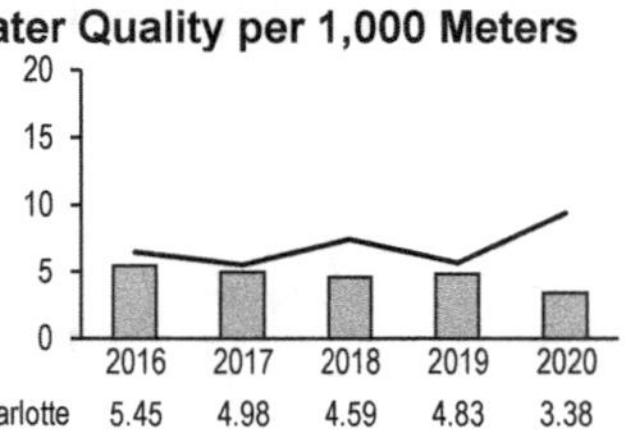

	2016	2017	2018	2019	2020
Charlotte	5.45	4.98	4.59	4.83	3.38
Average	6.43	5.48	7.42	5.61	9.38

Fiscal Year 2019-20

Explanatory Information

Service Level and Delivery

The City of Concord Water Resources Department is a water-only utility. The department has three divisions: one for operations and maintenance and one for each of two treatment plants. Meter reading, billing, and collections are handled by the city Finance Department.

Concord's system serves approximately 98,000 people and covers the City of Concord, the Town of Midland, and approximately one-fourth of Cabarrus County. Water sources for the system are Lake Fisher, owned by the city, and Lakes Howell and Concord, reservoirs owned by the Water and Sewer Authority of Cabarrus County. The combined estimated safe yield is 24 million gallons per day.

The city operates two treatment plants with a combined treatment capacity of 24 million gallons per day. Concord has emergency connections with the City of Charlotte and the City of Kannapolis and sells small amounts of water to the Town of Harrisburg and the Town of Midland.

The estimated average age of main line pipes in the system is thirty-six years. Water meters are read monthly, with all being read using automatic means. The replacement standard for water meters is fifteen years.

Conditions Affecting Service, Performance, and Costs

The costs of water services as captured here do not include debt service but do capture depreciation.

Municipal Profile

Estimated Service Population	98,064
Service Land Area (Square Miles)	142.8
Persons per Square Mile	687
Topography	Flat; gently rolling
Climate	Temperate; little ice and snow
Median Household Income U.S. Census 2016	$50,863

Service Profile

FTE Staff Positions	
Treatment Plant	18.0
Line Crews	25.0
Meter Readers	0.0
Billing/Collection	0.0
Other	24.0
Total	67.0
Number of Treatment Plants	2
Total Treatment Capacity	24.0 MGD
Average Daily Demand	13.1 MGD
Miles of Main Line Pipe	752
Average Age of Main Line Pipe	36 years
Number of Breaks/Leaks	57
Number of Water Meters	43,138
Percent of Meters Read Automatically	100.0%
Total Revenues Collected	$26,524,010

Full Cost Profile

Cost Breakdown by Percentage	
Personal Services	36.4%
Operating Costs	45.3%
Capital Costs	18.4%
TOTAL	100.0%
Cost Breakdown in Dollars	
Personal Services	$8,447,248
Operating Costs	$10,514,231
Capital Costs	$4,268,280
TOTAL	$23,229,759

Concord

Water Services

Key: Concord ■ Benchmarking Average — Fiscal Years 2016 through 2020

Resource Measures

Water Services Cost per Capita

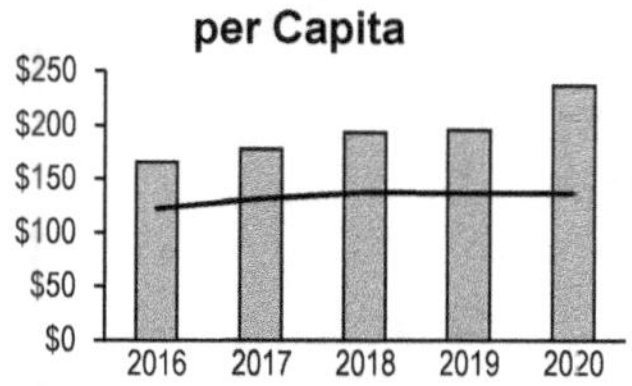

	2016	2017	2018	2019	2020
Concord	$166	$177	$193	$196	$237
Average	$122	$131	$137	$137	$137

Water Services FTEs per 10,000 Population

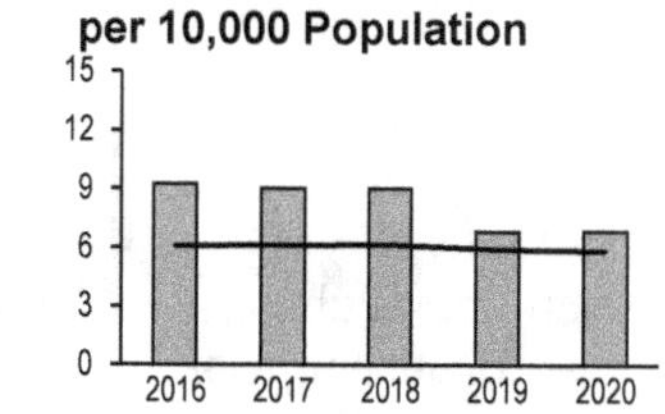

	2016	2017	2018	2019	2020
Concord	9.2	9.0	9.0	6.8	6.8
Average	6.1	6.1	6.1	5.9	5.8

Water Services Cost per Meter

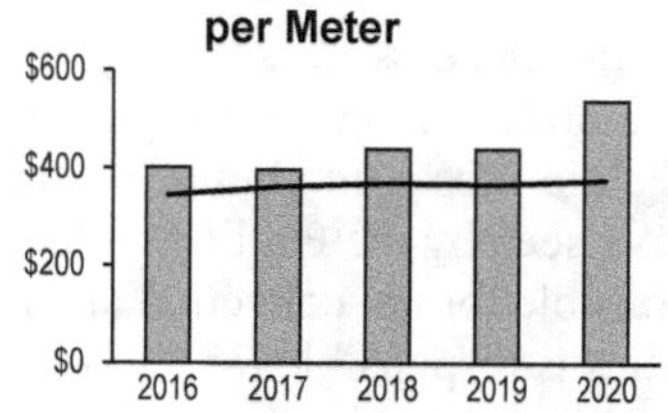

	2016	2017	2018	2019	2020
Concord	$401	$395	$440	$440	$538
Average	$343	$360	$369	$365	$375

Workload Measures

Thousands of Gallons of Billed Water per Meter

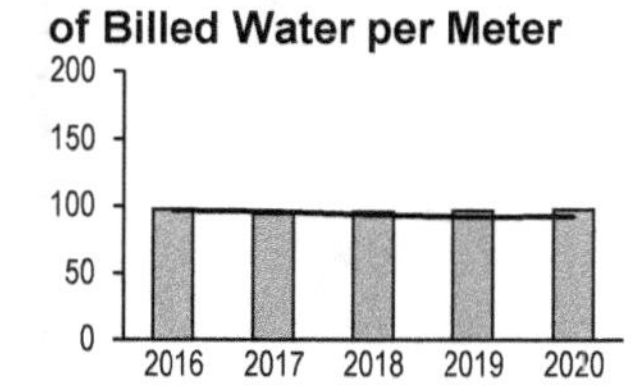

	2016	2017	2018	2019	2020
Concord	97.4	94.0	95.6	96.5	97.4
Average	96.4	95.5	92.8	91.6	92.2

Miles of Main Line Pipe per Square Mile of Service Area

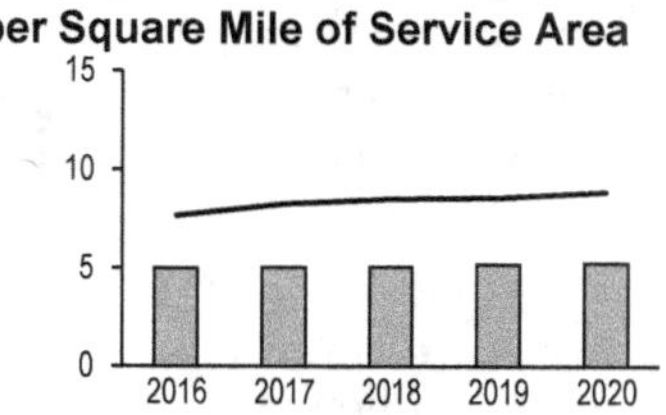

	2016	2017	2018	2019	2020
Concord	5.0	5.0	5.1	5.2	5.3
Average	7.6	8.2	8.5	8.6	8.8

Efficiency Measures

Total Cost per Thousand Gallons of Billed Water

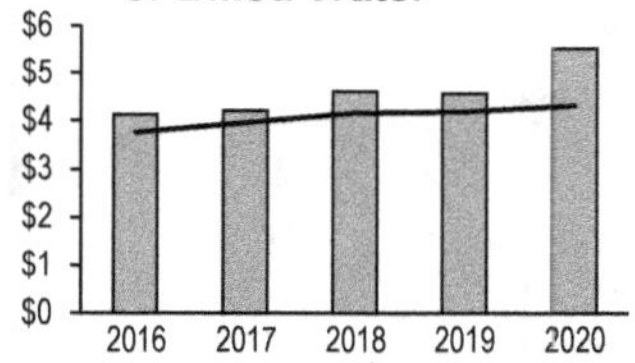

	2016	2017	2018	2019	2020
Concord	$4.12	$4.21	$4.60	$4.56	$5.53
Average	$3.75	$3.95	$4.15	$4.18	$4.30

Million Gallons of Billed Water per Water Services FTEs

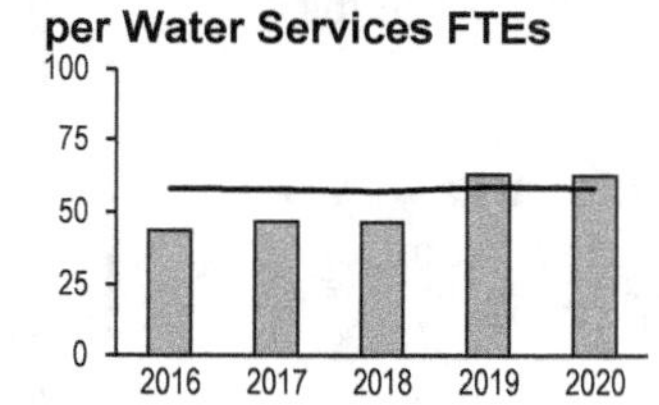

	2016	2017	2018	2019	2020
Concord	43.6	46.8	46.5	63.1	62.7
Average	58.1	57.9	57.0	58.7	58.2

Billed Water as a Percentage of Finished Water

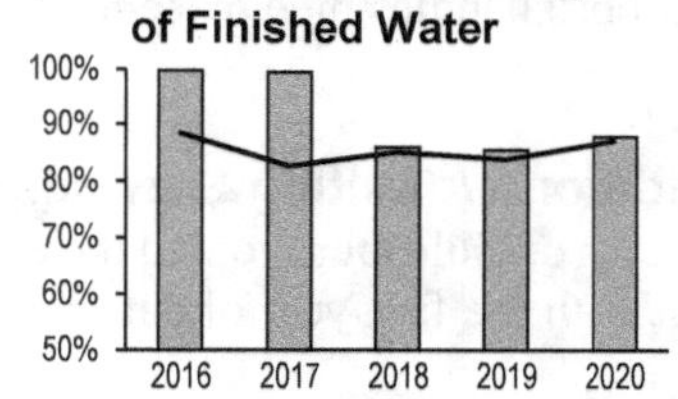

	2016	2017	2018	2019	2020
Concord	100%	100%	86%	85%	88%
Average	88%	82%	85%	84%	87%

Effectiveness Measures

Percentage of Existing Pipeline Replaced or Rehabbed

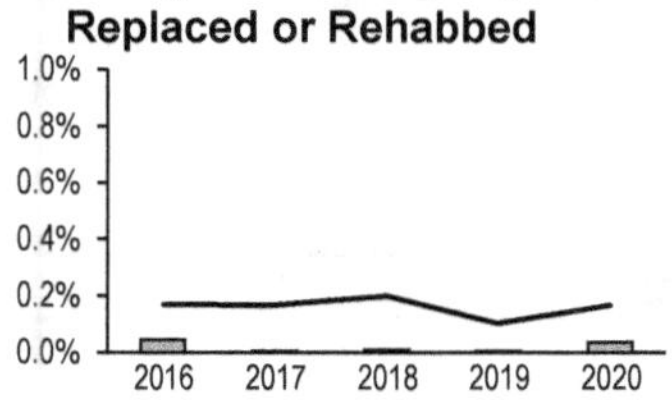

	2016	2017	2018	2019	2020
Concord	0.0%	0.0%	0.0%	0.0%	0.0%
Average	0.2%	0.2%	0.2%	0.1%	0.2%

Percentage of Water Bills Not Collected

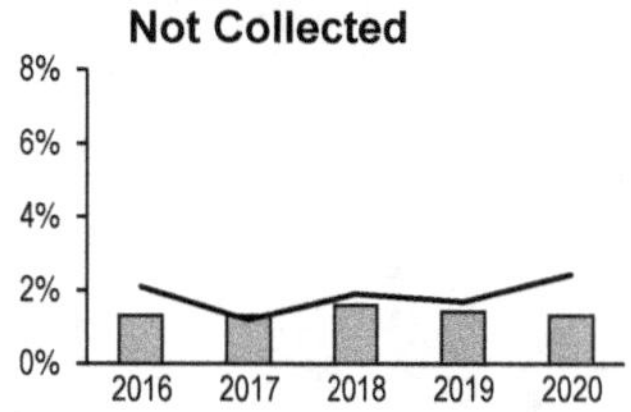

	2016	2017	2018	2019	2020
Concord	1.31%	1.31%	1.58%	1.42%	1.31%
Average	2.08%	1.19%	1.88%	1.68%	2.42%

Peak Daily Demand as a Percentage of Treatment Capacity

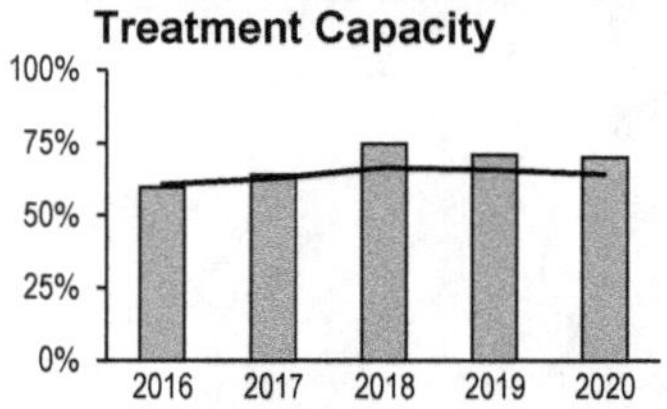

	2016	2017	2018	2019	2020
Concord	60%	64%	75%	71%	70%
Average	61%	63%	66%	66%	64%

Breaks and Leaks per Mile of Main Line Pipe

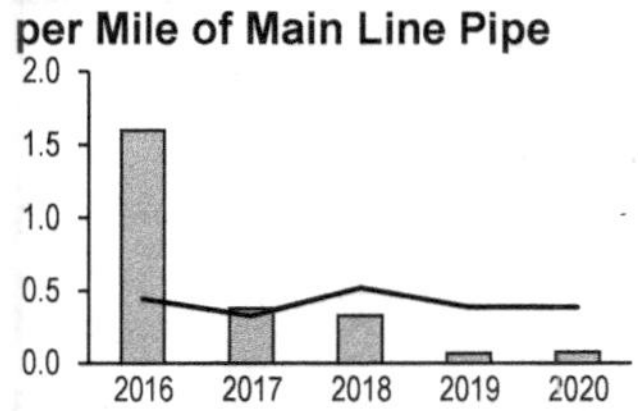

	2016	2017	2018	2019	2020
Concord	1.60	0.38	0.33	0.07	0.08
Average	0.44	0.32	0.52	0.38	0.38

Customer Complaints about Water Quality per 1,000 Meters

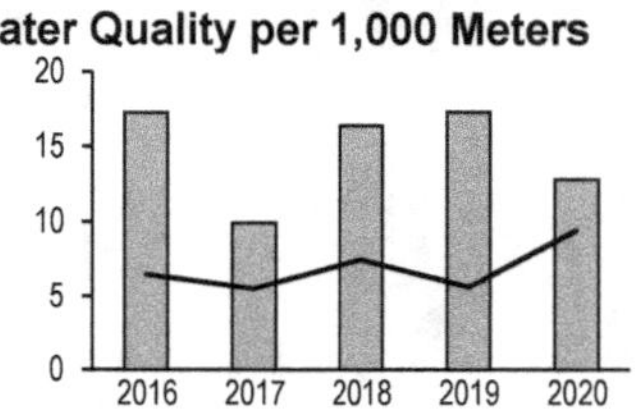

	2016	2017	2018	2019	2020
Concord	17.26	9.89	16.39	17.32	12.82
Average	6.43	5.48	7.42	5.61	9.38

Fiscal Year 2019-20

Explanatory Information

Service Level and Delivery

Goldsboro's drinking water services are a joint responsibility between the Public Works and Public Utilities Departments. Both departments are overseen by the Public Works Director. Public Works is responsible for the collection and distribution system lines. Public Utilities is responsible for the operations of the water treatment plant, the water reclamation facility, and pump stations.

The Goldsboro system serves approximately 35,000 people in an area covering twenty-five square miles. Water is collected from the Neuse River. The system also has an emergency option to collect from the Littler River, but this option has not been needed for several years. The estimated safe yield of the system is 6 million gallons per day based on an analysis performed by consultants. The system has emergency connections with Eastern Wayne, Belfast-Patetown, Fork Town, and Southern Wayne Sanitary districts.

The city runs one treatment plant with a capacity of 12 million gallons per day. The plant uses traditional surface water treatment consisting of coagulation, flocculation, sedimentation, filtration, and disinfection.

Goldsboro handles pipe placement by focusing on breaks in the system.

Conditions Affecting Service, Performance, and Costs

The City of Goldsboro joined the Benchmarking Project in July 2017, with the first year of data showing for FY 2016–17.

The costs of water services as captured here do not include debt service but do capture depreciation.

Hurricane Matthew in October 2016 put stress on the water system due to the extensive flooding.

Municipal Profile

Estimated Service Population	34,959
Service Land Area (Square Miles)	25.0
Persons per Square Mile	1,398
Topography	Flat
Climate	Temperate; little ice and snow
Median Household Income U.S. Census 2016	$32,148

Service Profile

FTE Staff Positions	
Treatment Plant	9.0
Line Crews	5.0
Meter Readers	4.0
Billing/Collection	6.0
Other	2.0
Total	26.0
Number of Treatment Plants	1
Total Treatment Capacity	12.0 MGD
Average Daily Demand	6.5 MGD
Miles of Main Line Pipe	270
Average Age of Main Line Pipe	70 years
Number of Breaks/Leaks	41
Number of Water Meters	14,744
Percent of Meters Read Automatically	100.0%
Total Revenues Collected	$6,894,973

Full Cost Profile

Cost Breakdown by Percentage	
Personal Services	17.7%
Operating Costs	80.5%
Capital Costs	1.8%
TOTAL	100.0%
Cost Breakdown in Dollars	
Personal Services	$684,023
Operating Costs	$3,110,005
Capital Costs	$69,862
TOTAL	$3,863,890

Goldsboro

Water Services

Key: Goldsboro ▪ Benchmarking Average — Fiscal Years 2016 through 2020

Resource Measures

Water Services Cost per Capita

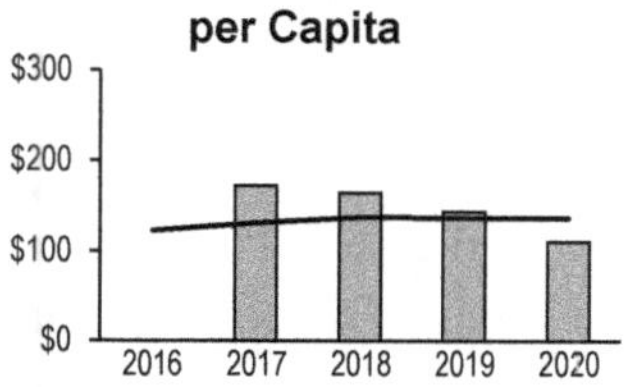

	2016	2017	2018	2019	2020
Goldsboro		$172	$164	$143	$111
Average	$122	$131	$137	$137	$137

Water Services FTEs per 10,000 Population

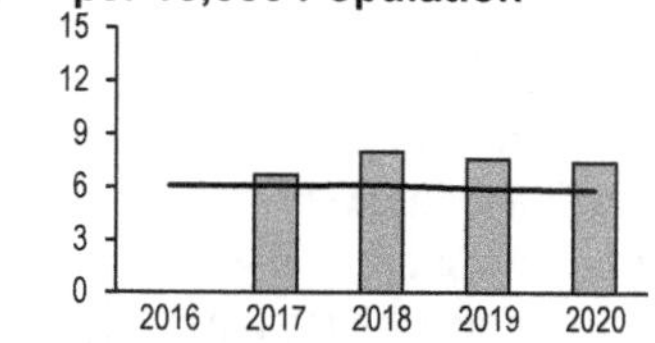

	2016	2017	2018	2019	2020
Goldsboro		6.7	8.0	7.6	7.4
Average	6.1	6.1	6.1	5.9	5.8

Water Services Cost per Meter

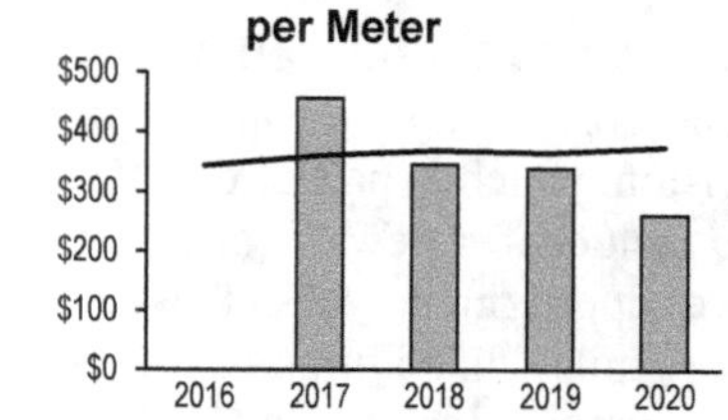

	2016	2017	2018	2019	2020
Goldsboro		$457	$346	$340	$262
Average	$343	$360	$369	$365	$375

Workload Measures

Thousands of Gallons of Billed Water per Meter

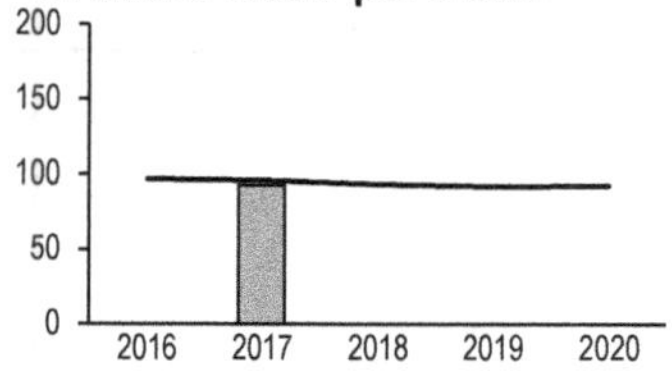

	2016	2017	2018	2019	2020
Goldsboro		92.6			
Average	96.4	95.5	92.8	91.6	92.2

Miles of Main Line Pipe per Square Mile of Service Area

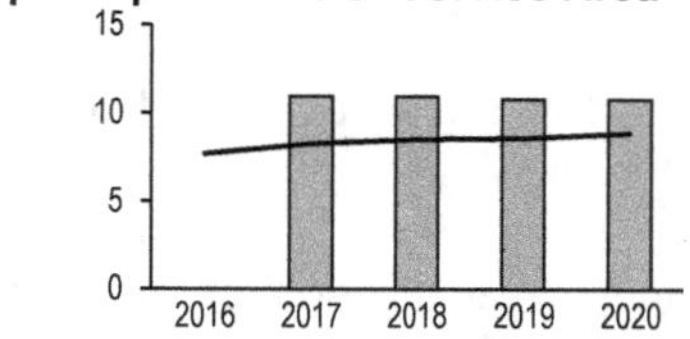

	2016	2017	2018	2019	2020
Goldsboro		11.0	11.0	10.8	10.8
Average	7.6	8.2	8.5	8.6	8.8

Efficiency Measures

Total Cost per Thousand Gallons of Billed Water

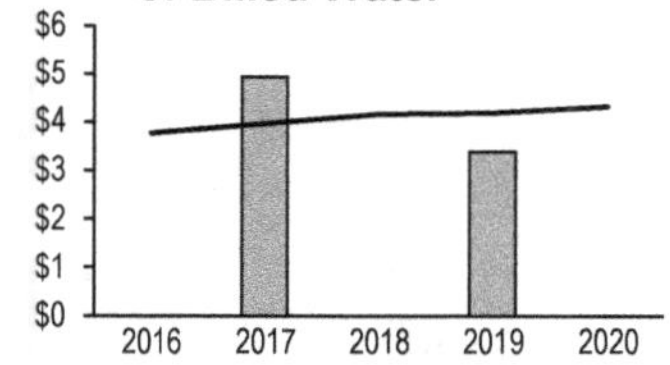

	2016	2017	2018	2019	2020
Goldsboro		$4.93		$3.38	
Average	$3.75	$3.95	$4.15	$4.18	$4.30

Million Gallons of Billed Water per Water Services FTEs

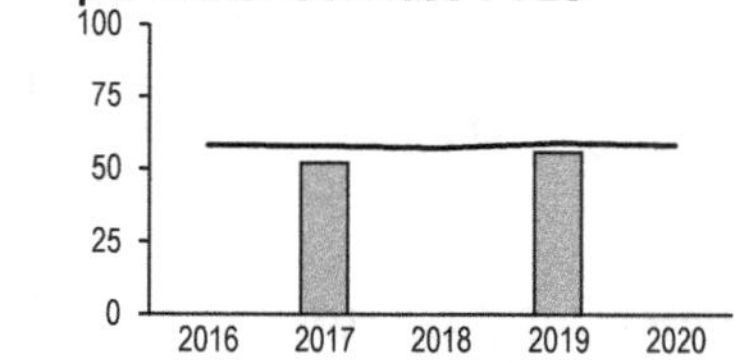

	2016	2017	2018	2019	2020
Goldsboro		52.1		55.8	
Average	58.1	57.9	57.0	58.7	58.2

Billed Water as a Percentage of Finished Water

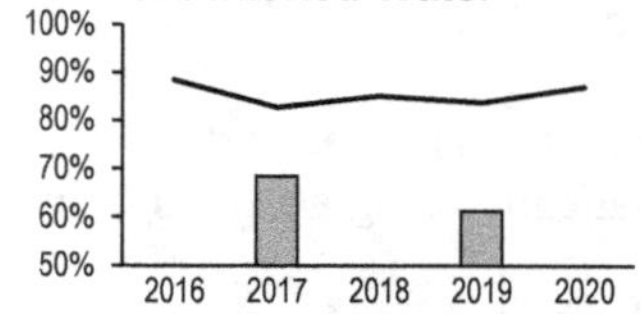

	2016	2017	2018	2019	2020
Goldsboro		68%		61%	
Average	88%	82%	85%	84%	87%

Effectiveness Measures

Percentage of Existing Pipeline Replaced or Rehabbed

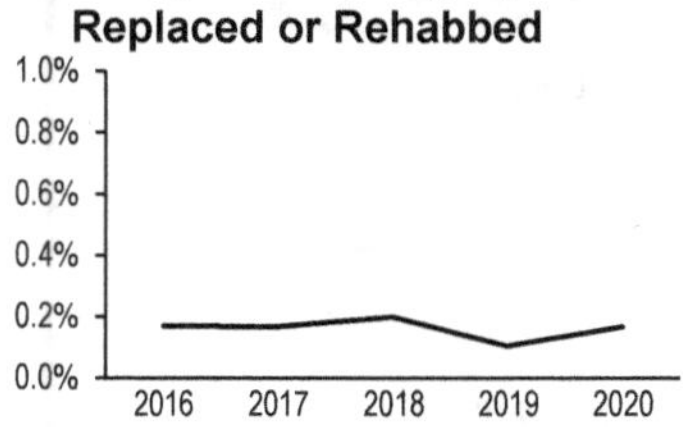

	2016	2017	2018	2019	2020
Goldsboro		0.0%	0.0%	0.0%	0.0%
Average	0.2%	0.2%	0.2%	0.1%	0.2%

Percentage of Water Bills Not Collected

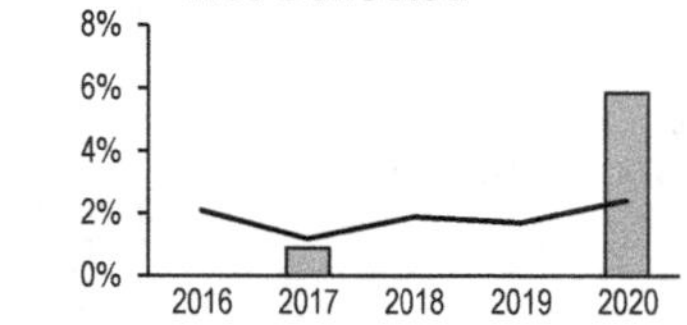

	2016	2017	2018	2019	2020
Goldsboro		0.88%			5.84%
Average	2.08%	1.19%	1.88%	1.68%	2.42%

Peak Daily Demand as a Percentage of Treatment Capacity

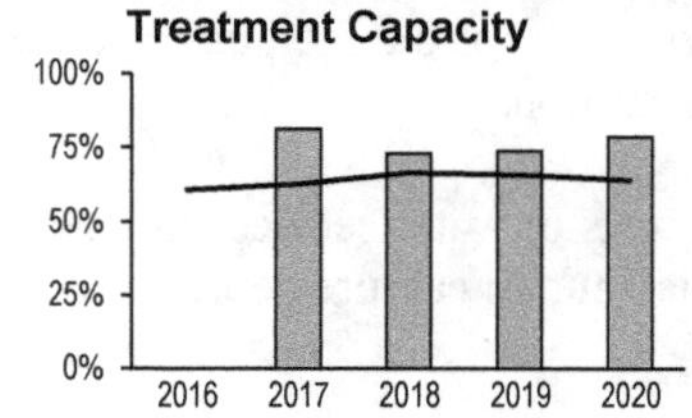

	2016	2017	2018	2019	2020
Goldsboro		81%	73%	74%	79%
Average	61%	63%	66%	66%	64%

Breaks and Leaks per Mile of Main Line Pipe

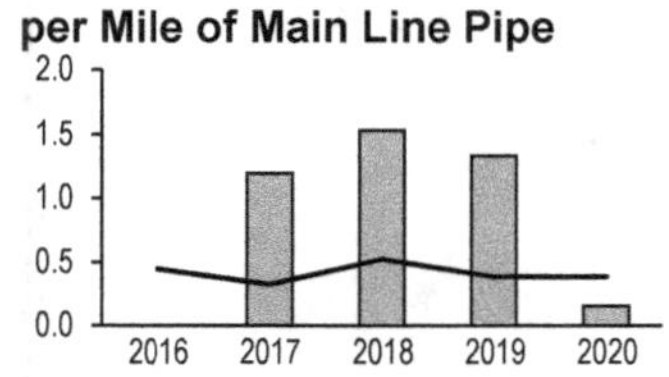

	2016	2017	2018	2019	2020
Goldsboro		1.19	1.53	1.33	0.15
Average	0.44	0.32	0.52	0.38	0.38

Customer Complaints about Water Quality per 1,000 Meters

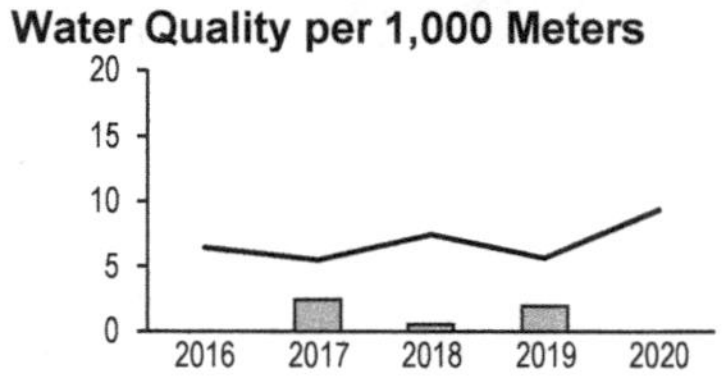

	2016	2017	2018	2019	2020
Goldsboro		2.45	0.56	1.94	
Average	6.43	5.48	7.42	5.61	9.38

Fiscal Year 2019-20

Explanatory Information

Service Level and Delivery

Greensboro's drinking water is provided by the Water Supply Division, which is part of the Water Resources Department, which also includes wastewater and stormwater services. The water system serves approximately 315,000 people in an area covering about 148 square miles. In addition to City of Greensboro residents, the system serves many addresses in Guilford County in areas adjacent to the city limits.

Water sources for the system are three city-owned reservoirs in the Haw River basin, which is part of the Upper Cape Fear River basin. The estimated safe yield of the system is 36.7 million gallons per day, based on a fifty-year estimate as certified by engineers. The system has emergency interconnections with High Point, Burlington, Reidsville, Winston-Salem, and Piedmont Triad Water Authority.

The city runs two treatment plants with a combined capacity of 63.7 million gallons. Both plants use conventional surface water treatment.

The estimated average age of main line pipes in the system is forty-one years. Greensboro has begun a spending program on water line rehabilitation and plans to increase funding for this activity for the next several years.

Water meters are read and billed monthly. All meters are read automatically using a radio system.

Conditions Affecting Service, Performance, and Costs

Greensboro has a very high collection rate for water bills. The city has a lien law, so only a small portion of billed amounts goes unpaid. The lien law was changed during FY 2010–11 so that it now only includes owners and not tenants.

Greensboro has a large public education program to encourage water conservation.

The costs of water services as captured here do not include debt service but do capture depreciation.

Municipal Profile

Estimated Service Population	315,328
Service Land Area (Square Miles)	148.0
Persons per Square Mile	2,131
Topography	Flat; gently rolling
Climate	Temperate; little ice and snow
Median Household Income U.S. Census 2016	$40,760

Service Profile

FTE Staff Positions	
Treatment Plant	54.0
Line Crews	54.5
Meter Readers	25.0
Billing/Collection	7.5
Other	23.0
Total	164.0
Number of Treatment Plants	2
Total Treatment Capacity	63.7 MGD
Average Daily Demand	32.2 MGD
Miles of Main Line Pipe	1,514
Average Age of Main Line Pipe	41 years
Number of Breaks/Leaks	259
Number of Water Meters	107,267
Percent of Meters Read Automatically	100.0%
Total Revenues Collected	$58,748,798

Full Cost Profile

Cost Breakdown by Percentage	
Personal Services	17.2%
Operating Costs	65.8%
Capital Costs	17.0%
TOTAL	100.0%
Cost Breakdown in Dollars	
Personal Services	$7,188,943
Operating Costs	$27,563,408
Capital Costs	$7,123,223
TOTAL	$41,875,574

Greensboro

Water Services

Key: Greensboro ■ Benchmarking Average — Fiscal Years 2016 through 2020

Resource Measures

Water Services Cost per Capita

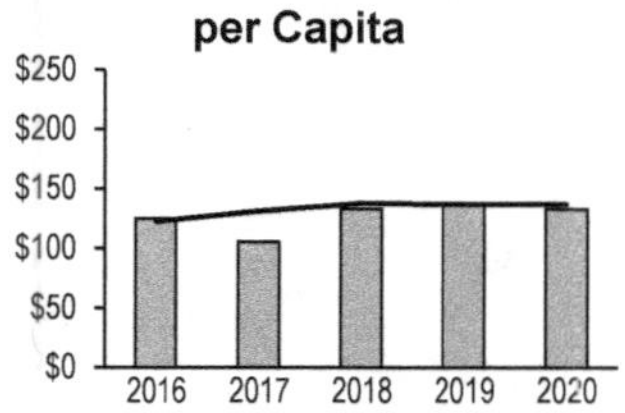

	2016	2017	2018	2019	2020
Greensboro	$125	$106	$133	$138	$133
Average	$122	$131	$137	$137	$137

Water Services FTEs per 10,000 Population

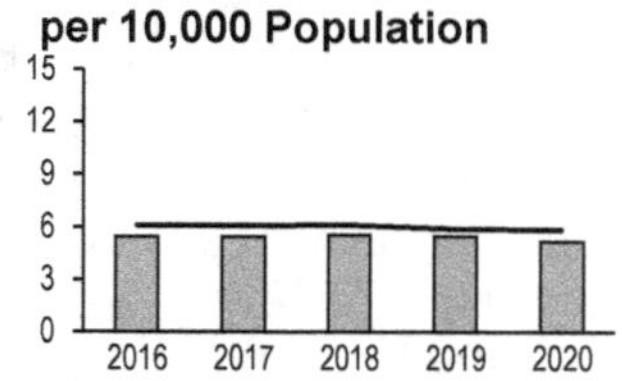

	2016	2017	2018	2019	2020
Greensboro	5.4	5.4	5.6	5.5	5.2
Average	6.1	6.1	6.1	5.9	5.8

Water Services Cost per Meter

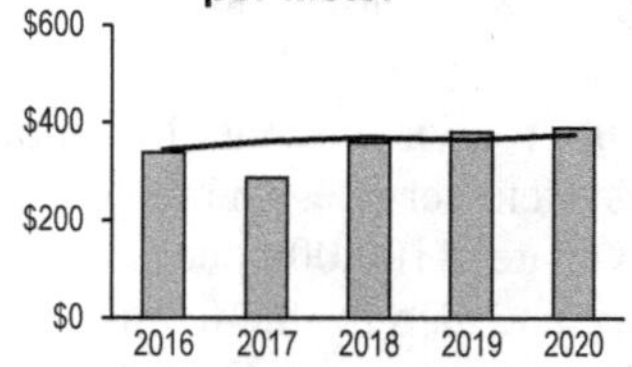

	2016	2017	2018	2019	2020
Greensboro	$338	$287	$360	$381	$390
Average	$343	$360	$369	$365	$375

Workload Measures

Thousands of Gallons of Billed Water per Meter

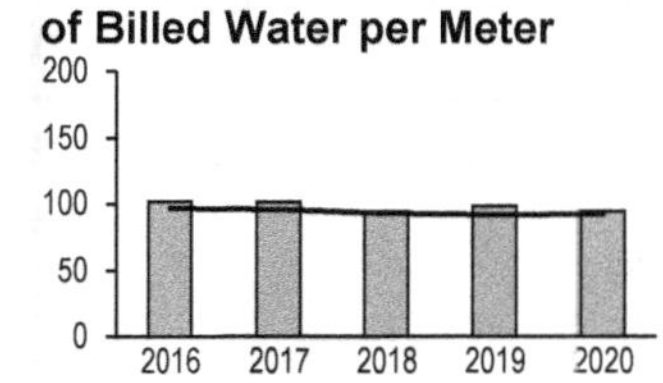

	2016	2017	2018	2019	2020
Greensboro	101.6	101.5	94.2	98.2	94.4
Average	96.4	95.5	92.8	91.6	92.2

Miles of Main Line Pipe per Square Mile of Service Area

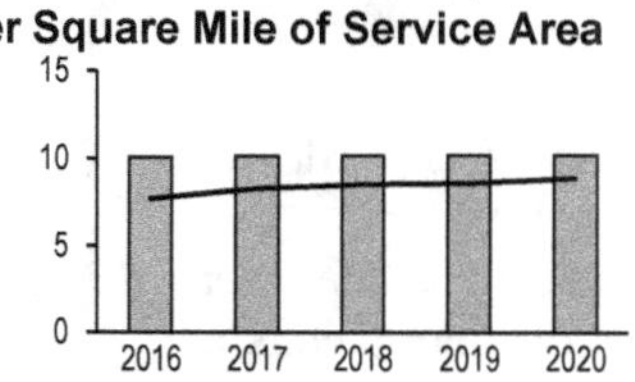

	2016	2017	2018	2019	2020
Greensboro	10.1	10.2	10.2	10.2	10.2
Average	7.6	8.2	8.5	8.6	8.8

Efficiency Measures

Total Cost per Thousand Gallons of Billed Water

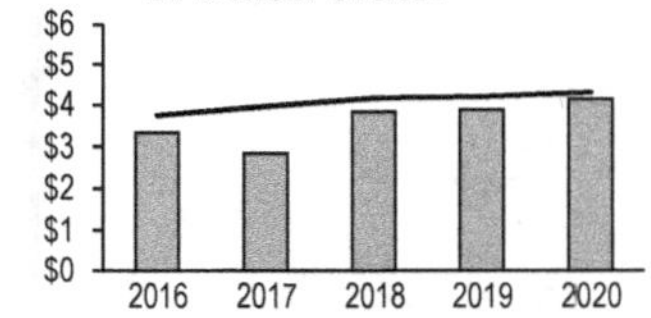

	2016	2017	2018	2019	2020
Greensboro	$3.33	$2.83	$3.82	$3.88	$4.13
Average	$3.75	$3.95	$4.15	$4.18	$4.30

Million Gallons of Billed Water per Water Services FTEs

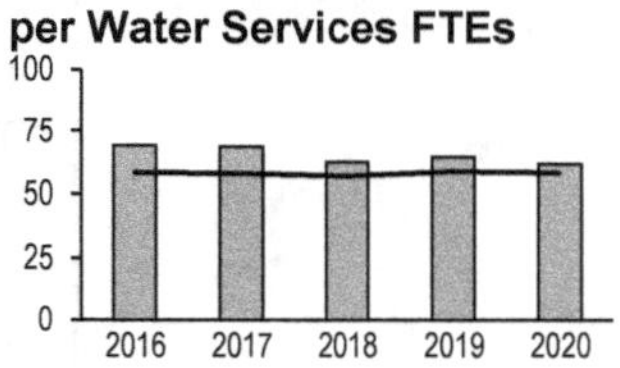

	2016	2017	2018	2019	2020
Greensboro	68.9	68.5	62.4	64.6	61.8
Average	58.1	57.9	57.0	58.7	58.2

Billed Water as a Percentage of Finished Water

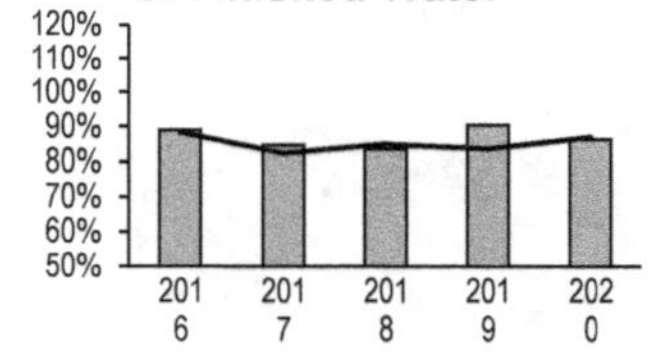

	2016	2017	2018	2019	2020
Greensboro	89%	85%	84%	90%	86%
Average	88%	82%	85%	84%	87%

Effectiveness Measures

Percentage of Existing Pipeline Replaced or Rehabbed

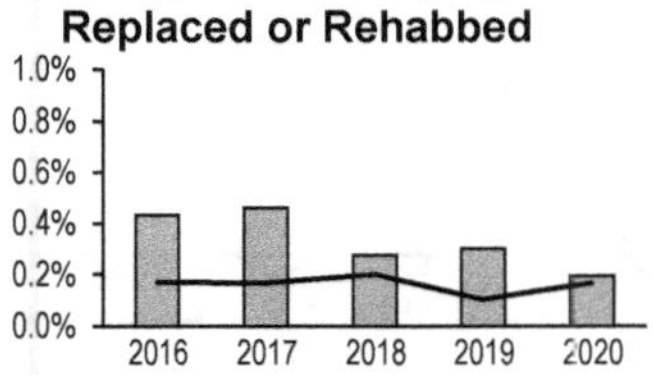

	2016	2017	2018	2019	2020
Greensboro	0.4%	0.5%	0.3%	0.3%	0.2%
Average	0.2%	0.2%	0.2%	0.1%	0.2%

Percentage of Water Bills Not Collected

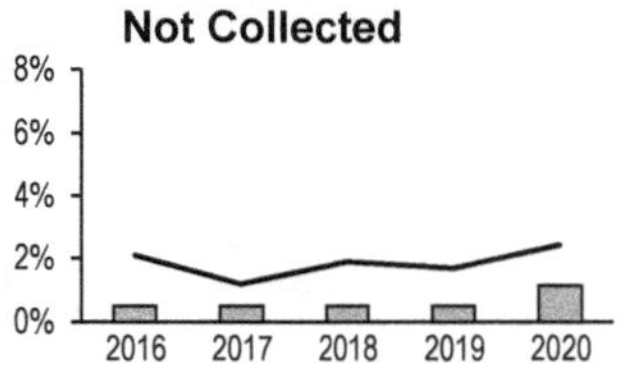

	2016	2017	2018	2019	2020
Greensboro	0.50%	0.50%	0.50%	0.50%	1.14%
Average	2.08%	1.19%	1.88%	1.68%	2.42%

Peak Daily Demand as a Percentage of Treatment Capacity

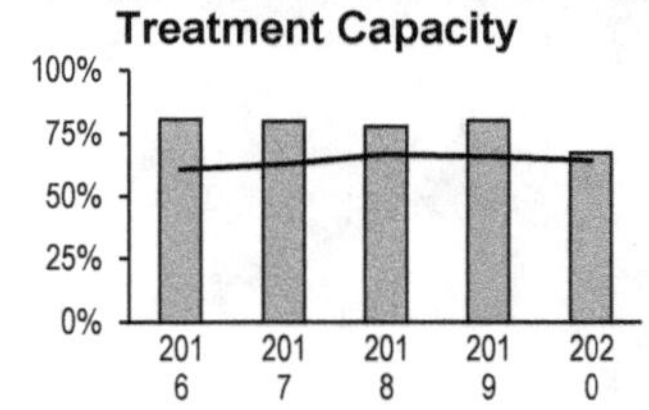

	2016	2017	2018	2019	2020
Greensboro	81%	80%	78%	80%	67%
Average	61%	63%	66%	66%	64%

Breaks and Leaks per Mile of Main Line Pipe

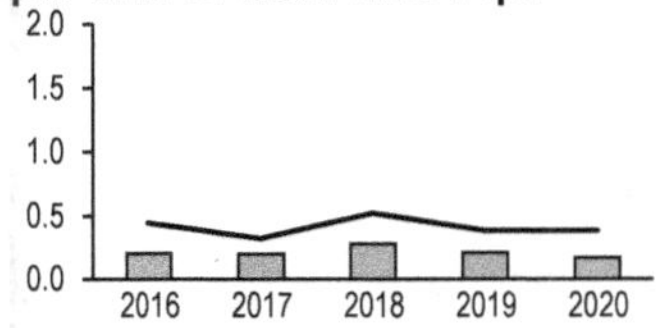

	2016	2017	2018	2019	2020
Greensboro	0.20	0.20	0.28	0.21	0.17
Average	0.44	0.32	0.52	0.38	0.38

Customer Complaints about Water Quality per 1,000 Meters

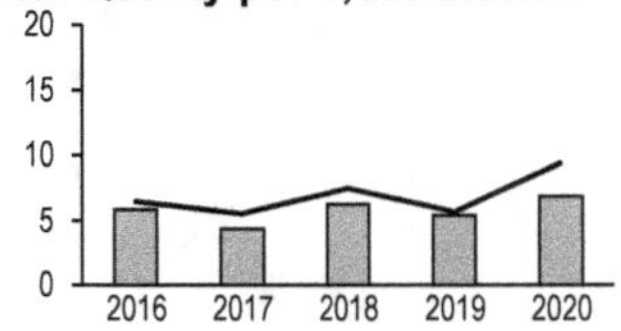

	2016	2017	2018	2019	2020
Greensboro	5.80	4.32	6.20	5.39	6.81
Average	6.43	5.48	7.42	5.61	9.38

Fiscal Year 2019-20

Explanatory Information

Service Level and Delivery

Water services in Hickory are provided by a combined water distribution division under the Public Services Department. The water system services an area covering roughly 326 square miles and approximately 100,000 people. Water is provided for the City of Hickory and also for the towns of Hildenbran, Brookford, and Catawba; the Sherrill's Ford, Mountain View, and Cooksville communities of Catawba County; and the Bethlehem, Sugarloaf, and Highway 16 communities of Alexander County.

Source water is from the Catawba River basin, with an estimated safe yield of 54 million gallons per day. Hickory sells water to the systems in Conover, Claremont, and Icard Township. The system has one treatment plant with a capacity of 32 million gallons per day.

Water meters are read monthly. Hickory's replacement standard for water meters is twenty years. About 19.7 percent of water meters in the system are read by automatic means.

Conditions Affecting Service, Performance, and Costs

The costs of water services as captured here do not include debt service but do capture depreciation.

Municipal Profile

Estimated Service Population	99,530
Service Land Area (Square Miles)	326.0
Persons per Square Mile	305
Topography	Flat; gently rolling
Climate	Temperate; some ice and snow
Median Household Income U.S. Census 2016	$35,353

Service Profile

FTE Staff Positions	
Treatment Plant	13.0
Line Crews	25.0
Meter Readers	6.0
Billing/Collection	5.0
Other	6.0
Total	55.0
Number of Treatment Plants	1
Total Treatment Capacity	32.0 MGD
Average Daily Demand	11.3 MGD
Miles of Main Line Pipe	948
Average Age of Main Line Pipe	40 years
Number of Breaks/Leaks	147
Number of Water Meters	27,903
Percent of Meters Read Automatically	19.7%
Total Revenues Collected	$17,094,746

Full Cost Profile

Cost Breakdown by Percentage	
Personal Services	27.1%
Operating Costs	49.5%
Capital Costs	23.4%
TOTAL	100.0%
Cost Breakdown in Dollars	
Personal Services	$2,863,250
Operating Costs	$5,225,962
Capital Costs	$2,473,741
TOTAL	$10,562,953

Key: Hickory ▩ Benchmarking Average — Fiscal Years 2016 through 2020

Resource Measures

Water Services Cost per Capita

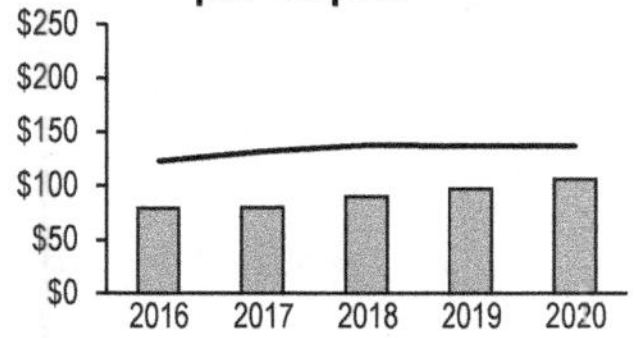

	2016	2017	2018	2019	2020
Hickory	$79	$80	$90	$97	$106
Average	$122	$131	$137	$137	$137

Water Services FTEs per 10,000 Population

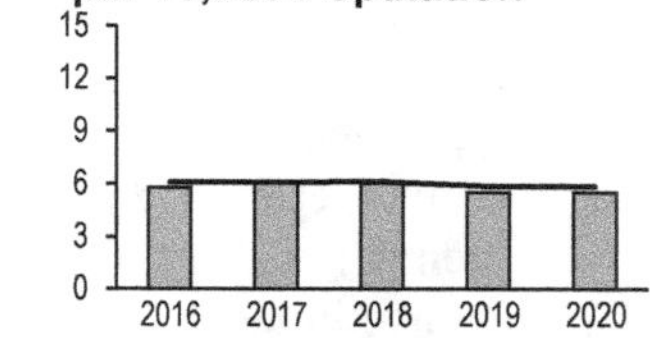

	2016	2017	2018	2019	2020
Hickory	5.8	6.0	6.0	5.5	5.5
Average	6.1	6.1	6.1	5.9	5.8

Water Services Cost per Meter

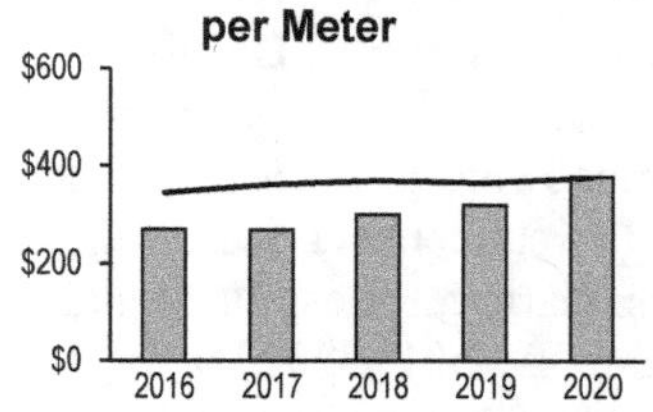

	2016	2017	2018	2019	2020
Hickory	$270	$269	$300	$320	$379
Average	$343	$360	$369	$365	$375

Workload Measures

Thousands of Gallons of Billed Water per Meter

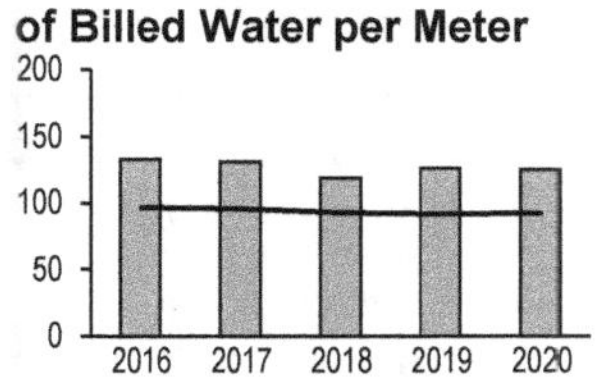

	2016	2017	2018	2019	2020
Hickory	133.0	131.5	119.4	126.4	125.3
Average	96.4	95.5	92.8	91.6	92.2

Miles of Main Line Pipe per Square Mile of Service Area

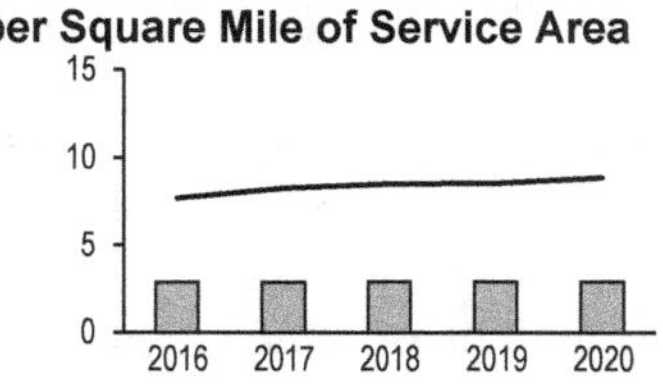

	2016	2017	2018	2019	2020
Hickory	2.9	2.9	2.9	2.9	2.9
Average	7.6	8.2	8.5	8.6	8.8

Efficiency Measures

Total Cost per Thousand Gallons of Billed Water

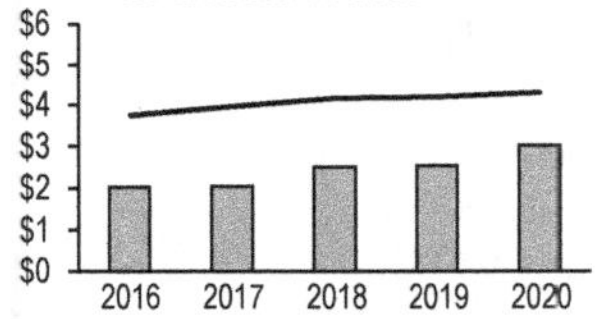

	2016	2017	2018	2019	2020
Hickory	$2.03	$2.05	$2.52	$2.53	$3.02
Average	$3.75	$3.95	$4.15	$4.18	$4.30

Million Gallons of Billed Water per Water Services FTEs

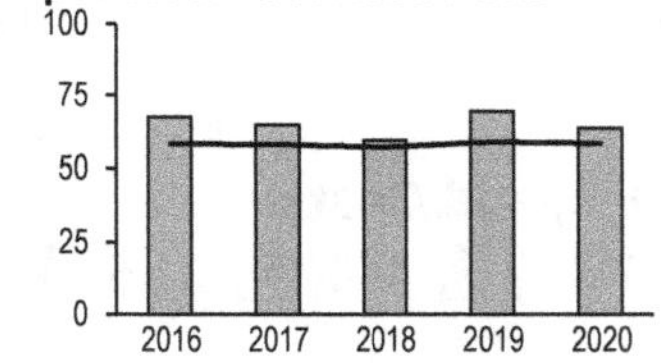

	2016	2017	2018	2019	2020
Hickory	67.3	64.6	59.3	69.3	63.6
Average	58.1	57.9	57.0	58.7	58.2

Billed Water as a Percentage of Finished Water

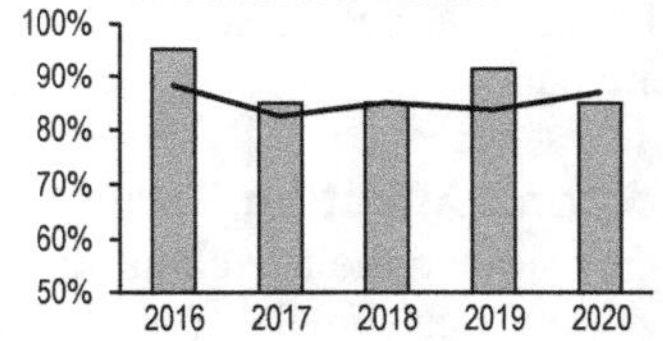

	2016	2017	2018	2019	2020
Hickory	95%	85%	85%	92%	85%
Average	88%	82%	85%	84%	87%

Effectiveness Measures

Percentage of Existing Pipeline Replaced or Rehabbed

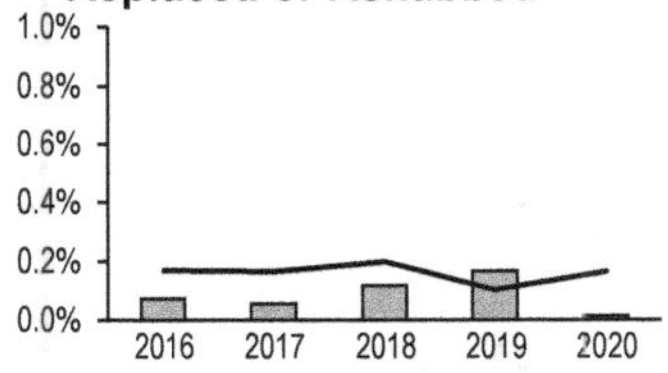

	2016	2017	2018	2019	2020
Hickory	0.1%	0.1%	0.1%	0.2%	0.0%
Average	0.2%	0.2%	0.2%	0.1%	0.2%

Percentage of Water Bills Not Collected

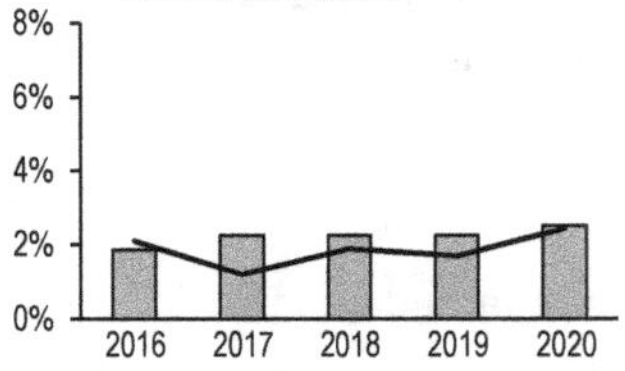

	2016	2017	2018	2019	2020
Hickory	1.86%	2.24%	2.24%	2.25%	2.50%
Average	2.08%	1.19%	1.88%	1.68%	2.42%

Peak Daily Demand as a Percentage of Treatment Capacity

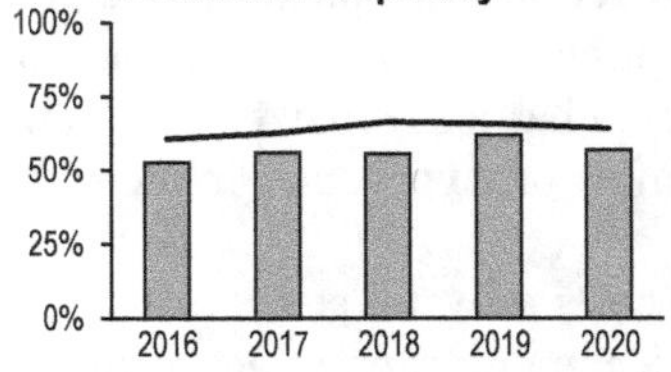

	2016	2017	2018	2019	2020
Hickory	53%	56%	55%	62%	57%
Average	61%	63%	66%	66%	64%

Breaks and Leaks per Mile of Main Line Pipe

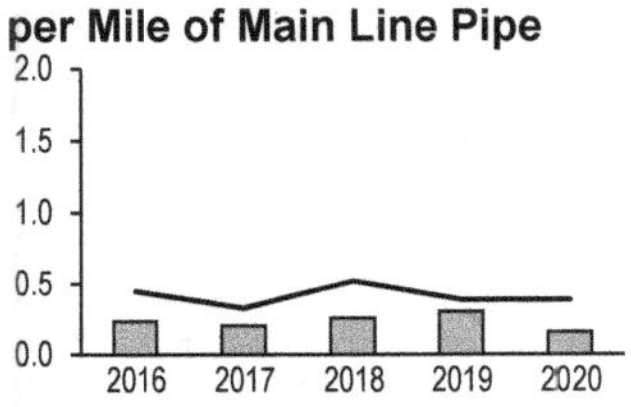

	2016	2017	2018	2019	2020
Hickory	0.23	0.20	0.25	0.30	0.16
Average	0.44	0.32	0.52	0.38	0.38

Customer Complaints about Water Quality per 1,000 Meters

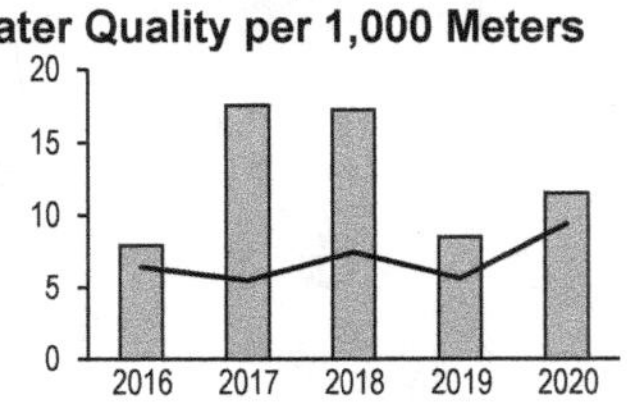

	2016	2017	2018	2019	2020
Hickory	7.94	17.57	17.27	8.53	11.54
Average	6.43	5.48	7.42	5.61	9.38

Fiscal Year 2019-20

Explanatory Information

Service Level and Delivery

Public Utilities is a department within the City of Raleigh. It is a combined enterprise system which provides drinking water and sewage treatment services to the City of Raleigh and six merger towns: Garner, Rolesville, Knightdale, Wake Forest, Wendell, and Zebulon. As of FY 2020, approximately 592,000 people live in the contractual service area of 299 square miles. Source water supply is from Falls Lake located in the Neuse River watershed and from Lake Wheeler and Lake Benson, which are in the Swift Creek watershed. During FY 2019, the Utility received a reallocation of its water supply that increased the system's 50-year reliable yield to 98 million gallons per day.

The Utility operates two surface water treatment plants with a total permitted treatment capacity of 106 million gallons per day. The E.M. Johnson plant provides 86 percent of the potable water using an enhanced coagulation treatment process with the addition of settled water ozone. The Dempsey E. Benton plant also utilizes an enhanced coagulation treatment process using raw water ozone, solids contact sedimentation, a two-stage filter process, and ultraviolet disinfection prior to clearwell storage.

Water meters are read once per month. Currently, most meters are read by automatic means. The standard for meter replacement is fifteen years.

Conditions Affecting Service, Performance, and Costs

Raleigh rejoined the Benchmarking Project in July 2016, with the first year of data showing for FY 2015–16.

The approved reallocation of supply water resources in FY 2019 comes with increased costs to maintain and finance the improvement. Due to source water organics both treatment plants utilize enhanced coagulation with ferric sulfate and chloramine disinfection to control disinfection byproducts. These processes have higher chemical and operating costs than traditional treatment processes. Additionally, Raleigh has a specialized program to manage water age and disinfection byproducts in the distribution system.

The costs of water services as captured here do not include debt service but do capture depreciation.

Municipal Profile

Estimated Service Population	591,943
Service Land Area (Square Miles)	299.0
Persons per Square Mile	1,980
Topography	Flat; gently rolling
Climate	Temperate; little ice and snow
Median Household Income U.S. Census 2016	$46,612

Service Profile

FTE Staff Positions	
Treatment Plant	61.0
Line Crews	79.0
Meter Readers	2.0
Billing/Collection	29.0
Other	126.0
Total	297.0
Number of Treatment Plants	2
Total Treatment Capacity	106.0 MGD
Average Daily Demand	51.4 MGD
Miles of Main Line Pipe	2,351
Average Age of Main Line Pipe	30 years
Number of Breaks/Leaks	407
Number of Water Meters	207,954
Percent of Meters Read Automatically	92.5%
Total Revenues Collected	$118,919,370

Full Cost Profile

Cost Breakdown by Percentage	
Personal Services	35.9%
Operating Costs	45.3%
Capital Costs	18.8%
TOTAL	100.0%
Cost Breakdown in Dollars	
Personal Services	$25,087,694
Operating Costs	$31,706,359
Capital Costs	$13,121,252
TOTAL	$69,915,305

Key: Raleigh ▒ Benchmarking Average — Fiscal Years 2016 through 2020

Resource Measures

Water Services Cost per Capita

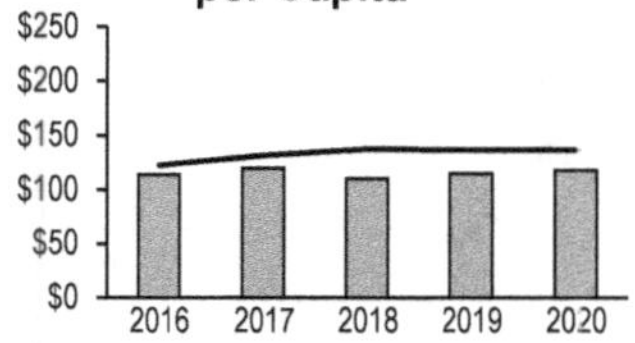

	2016	2017	2018	2019	2020
Raleigh	$114	$120	$110	$115	$118
Average	$122	$131	$137	$137	$137

Water Services FTEs per 10,000 Population

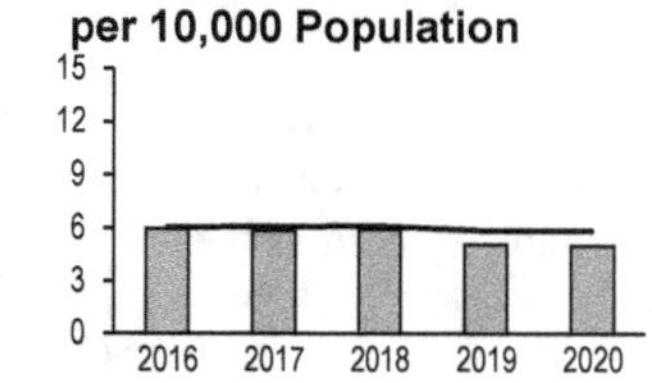

	2016	2017	2018	2019	2020
Raleigh	6.0	5.8	5.9	5.1	5.0
Average	6.1	6.1	6.1	5.9	5.8

Water Services Cost per Meter

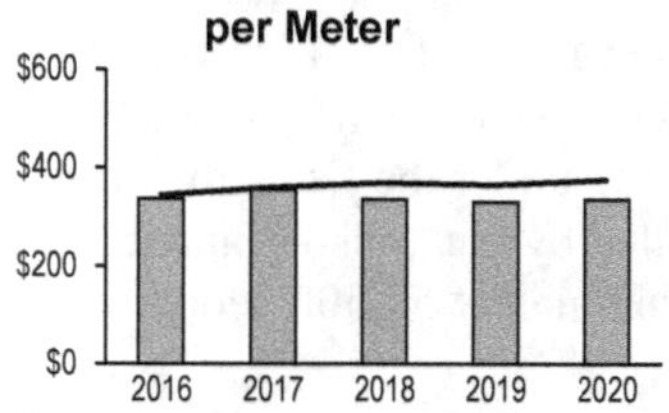

	2016	2017	2018	2019	2020
Raleigh	$337	$356	$336	$331	$336
Average	$343	$360	$369	$365	$375

Workload Measures

Thousands of Gallons of Billed Water per Meter

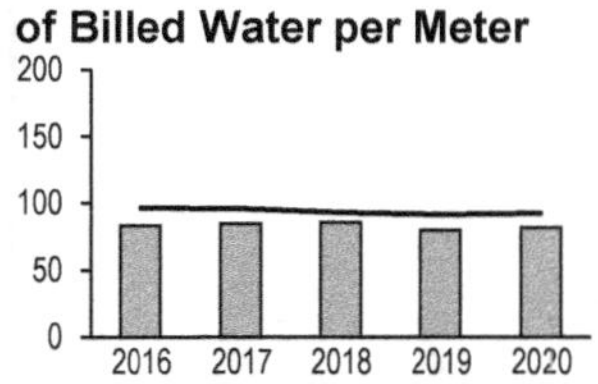

	2016	2017	2018	2019	2020
Raleigh	83.2	84.5	85.7	79.7	81.7
Average	96.4	95.5	92.8	91.6	92.2

Miles of Main Line Pipe per Square Mile of Service Area

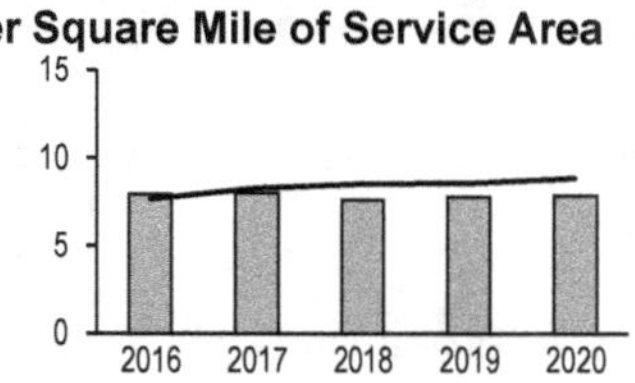

	2016	2017	2018	2019	2020
Raleigh	7.9	8.0	7.6	7.8	7.9
Average	7.6	8.2	8.5	8.6	8.8

Efficiency Measures

Total Cost per Thousand Gallons of Billed Water

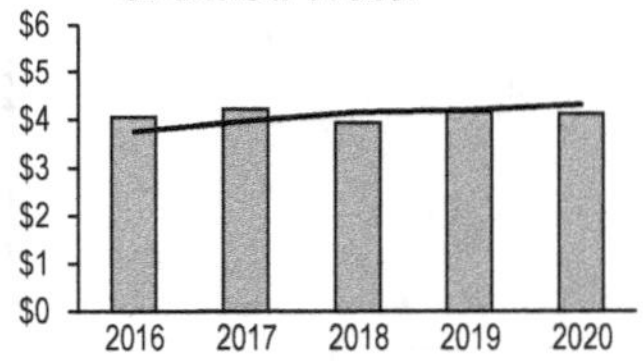

	2016	2017	2018	2019	2020
Raleigh	$4.06	$4.21	$3.92	$4.15	$4.11
Average	$3.75	$3.95	$4.15	$4.18	$4.30

Million Gallons of Billed Water per Water Services FTEs

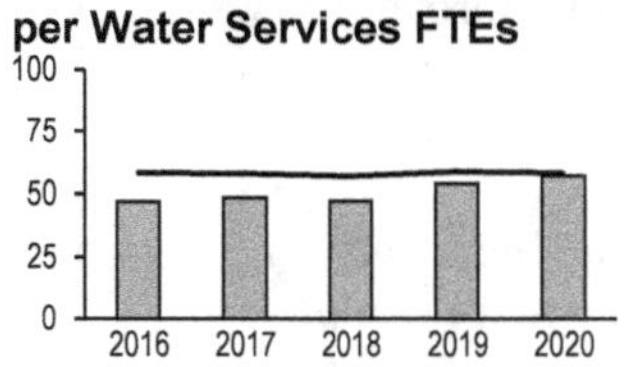

	2016	2017	2018	2019	2020
Raleigh	47.0	48.6	47.4	54.2	57.2
Average	58.1	57.9	57.0	58.7	58.2

Billed Water as a Percentage of Finished Water

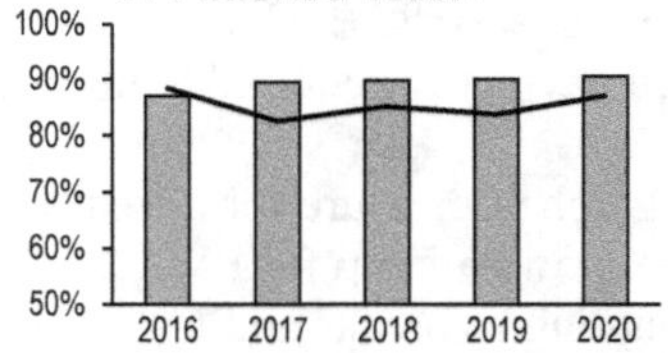

	2016	2017	2018	2019	2020
Raleigh	87%	89%	90%	90%	91%
Average	88%	82%	85%	84%	87%

Effectiveness Measures

Percentage of Existing Pipeline Replaced or Rehabbed

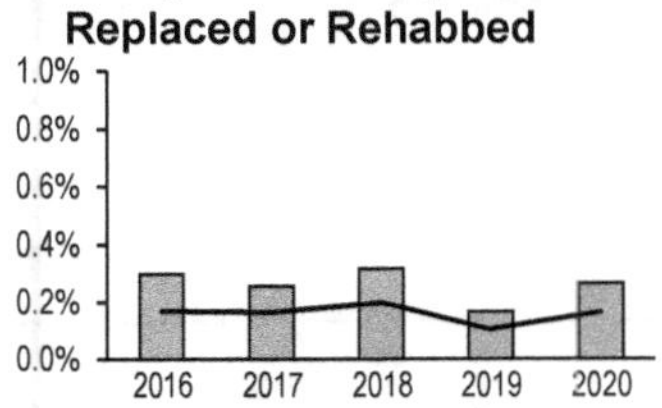

	2016	2017	2018	2019	2020
Raleigh	0.3%	0.3%	0.3%	0.2%	0.3%
Average	0.2%	0.2%	0.2%	0.1%	0.2%

Percentage of Water Bills Not Collected

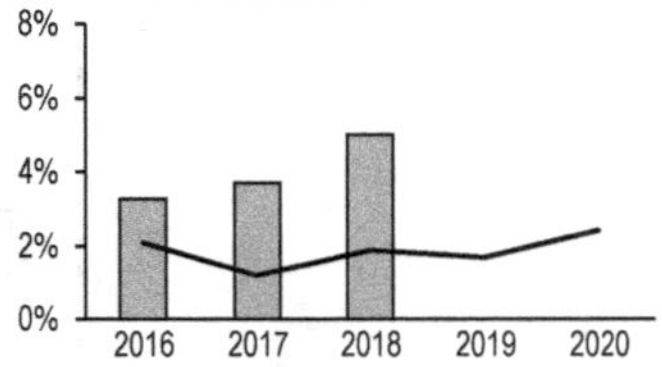

	2016	2017	2018	2019	2020
Raleigh	3.28%	3.70%	5.00%		
Average	2.08%	1.19%	1.88%	1.68%	2.42%

Peak Daily Demand as a Percentage of Treatment Capacity

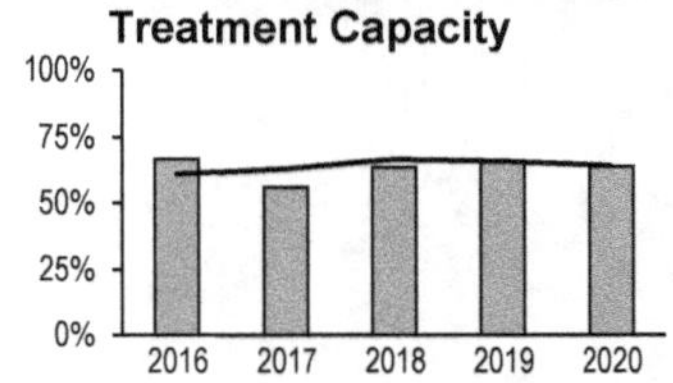

	2016	2017	2018	2019	2020
Raleigh	67%	56%	63%	65%	64%
Average	61%	63%	66%	66%	64%

Breaks and Leaks per Mile of Main Line Pipe

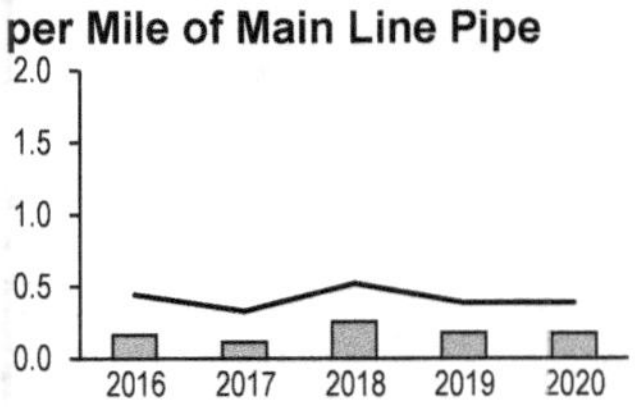

	2016	2017	2018	2019	2020
Raleigh	0.16	0.11	0.25	0.18	0.17
Average	0.44	0.32	0.52	0.38	0.38

Customer Complaints about Water Quality per 1,000 Meters

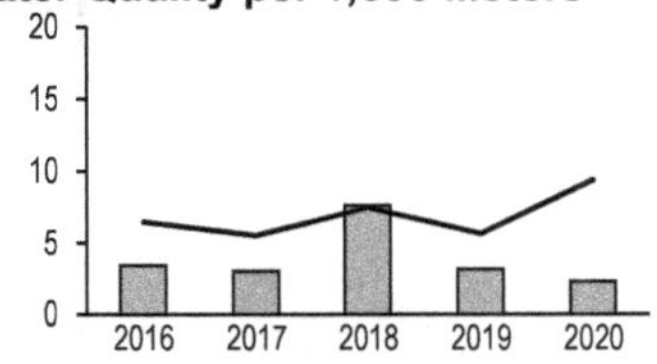

	2016	2017	2018	2019	2020
Raleigh	3.40	3.00	7.59	3.16	2.28
Average	6.43	5.48	7.42	5.61	9.38

Fiscal Year 2019-20

Explanatory Information

Service Level and Delivery

Water services in Wilson are handled by a combined water/sewer division under the Department of Public Works. Billing services are handled by the Wilson Finance Department. The water system serves approximately 54,500 people over forty square miles.

Source water for the system comes from four city-owned reservoirs. Water is also pumped from two different reservoirs in the Neuse River basin. The estimated safe yield for the system is 29 million gallons per day.

The system has two treatment plants with a combined treatment capacity of 22 million gallons per day. The plants use conventional surface water treatment with flocculation, sedimentation, and filtration.

Water meters are read once per month in Wilson. Approximately 80 percent of the water meters in the system are read by automatic remote means using a radio system by Itron.

Conditions Affecting Service, Performance, and Costs

The costs of water services as captured here do not include debt service but do capture depreciation. Large capital improvements are being made to the Buckhorn Lake Dam and Wastewater Projects, which have been required to meet advanced nutrient removal.

The graphed measure for "Breaks and Leaks per Mile of Main Line Pipe" shows a jump for FY2020. This is due to a more complete accounting of breaks and leaks rather than a change in performance. In earlier years, Wilson had only reported the smaller number of breaks in the main lines themselves. This new reporting is more inclusive as it includes all breaks and leaks for which crews were dispatched.

Municipal Profile

Estimated Service Population	54,500
Service Land Area (Square Miles)	40.0
Persons per Square Mile	1,363
Topography	Flat; gently rolling
Climate	Temperate; little ice and snow
Median Household Income U.S. Census 2016	$35,409

Service Profile

FTE Staff Positions	
Treatment Plant	19.0
Line Crews	20.0
Meter Readers	3.0
Billing/Collection	3.0
Other	3.0
Total	48.0
Number of Treatment Plants	2
Total Treatment Capacity	22.0 MGD
Average Daily Demand	9.1 MGD
Miles of Main Line Pipe	433
Average Age of Main Line Pipe	41 years
Number of Breaks/Leaks	534
Number of Water Meters	22,267
Percent of Meters Read Automatically	80.8%
Total Revenues Collected	$13,476,000

Full Cost Profile

Cost Breakdown by Percentage	
Personal Services	27.0%
Operating Costs	45.4%
Capital Costs	27.6%
TOTAL	100.0%
Cost Breakdown in Dollars	
Personal Services	$3,219,559
Operating Costs	$5,406,079
Capital Costs	$3,284,864
TOTAL	$11,910,502

Wilson

Water Services

Key: Wilson ■ Benchmarking Average — Fiscal Years 2016 through 2020

Resource Measures

Water Services Cost per Capita

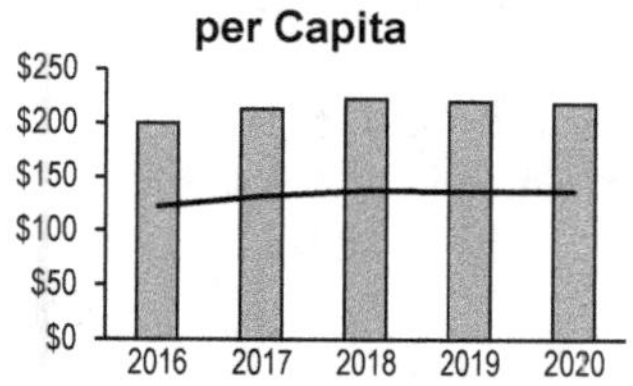

	2016	2017	2018	2019	2020
Wilson	$200	$213	$223	$220	$219
Average	$122	$131	$137	$137	$137

Water Services FTEs per 10,000 Population

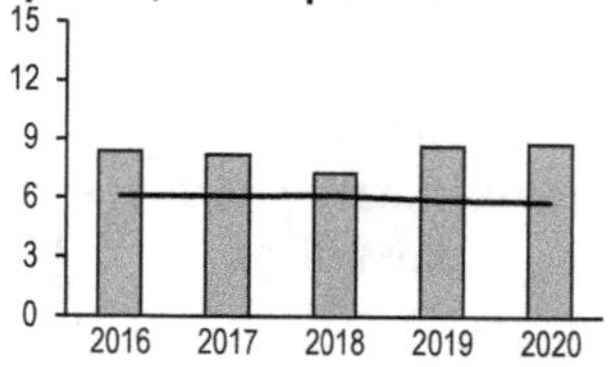

	2016	2017	2018	2019	2020
Wilson	8.3	8.2	7.2	8.6	8.8
Average	6.1	6.1	6.1	5.9	5.8

Water Services Cost per Meter

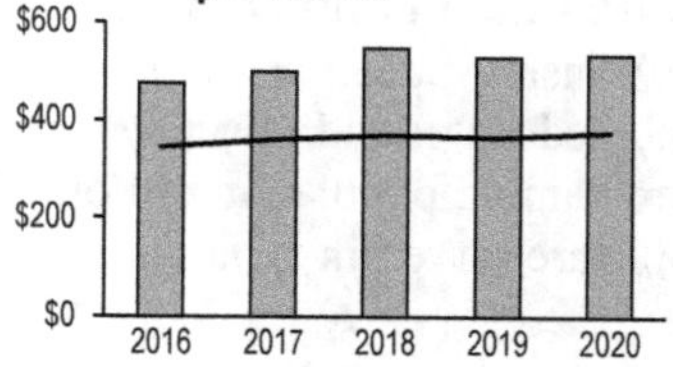

	2016	2017	2018	2019	2020
Wilson	$475	$500	$548	$530	$535
Average	$343	$360	$369	$365	$375

Workload Measures

Thousands of Gallons of Billed Water per Meter

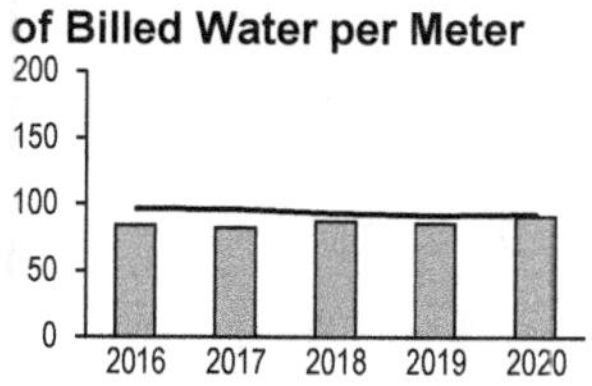

	2016	2017	2018	2019	2020
Wilson	84.1	82.2	87.1	85.6	90.3
Average	96.4	95.5	92.8	91.6	92.2

Miles of Main Line Pipe per Square Mile of Service Area

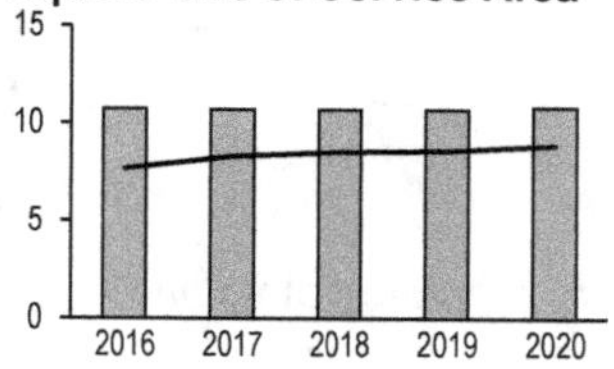

	2016	2017	2018	2019	2020
Wilson	10.7	10.7	10.7	10.7	10.8
Average	7.6	8.2	8.5	8.6	8.8

Efficiency Measures

Total Cost per Thousand Gallons of Billed Water

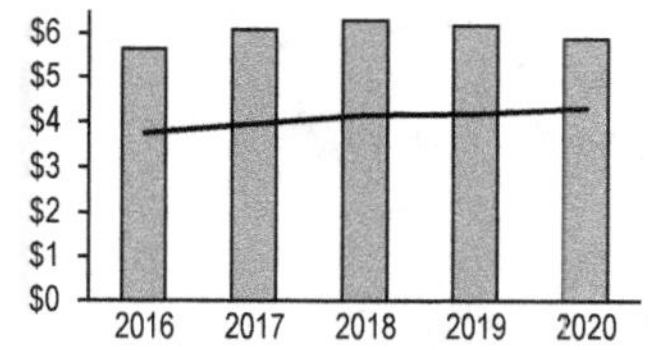

	2016	2017	2018	2019	2020
Wilson	$5.65	$6.08	$6.30	$6.19	$5.89
Average	$3.75	$3.95	$4.15	$4.18	$4.30

Million Gallons of Billed Water per Water Services FTEs

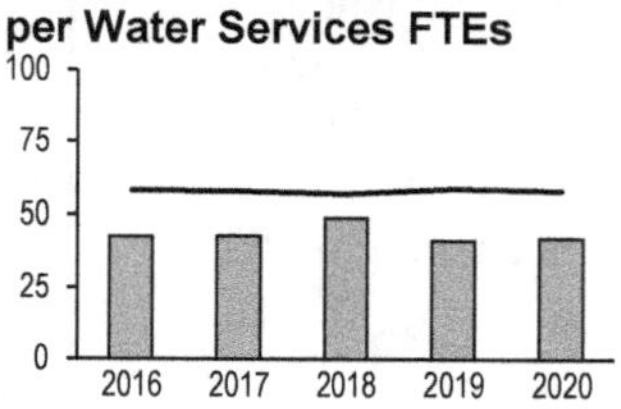

	2016	2017	2018	2019	2020
Wilson	42.4	42.8	48.9	41.3	42.1
Average	58.1	57.9	57.0	58.7	58.2

Billed Water as a Percentage of Finished Water

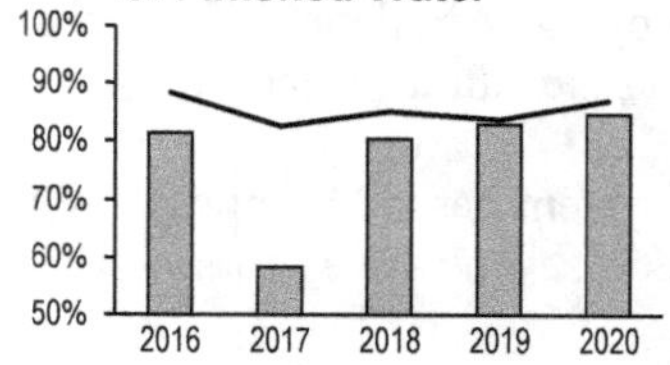

	2016	2017	2018	2019	2020
Wilson	81%	58%	80%	83%	85%
Average	88%	82%	85%	84%	87%

Effectiveness Measures

Percentage of Existing Pipeline Replaced or Rehabbed

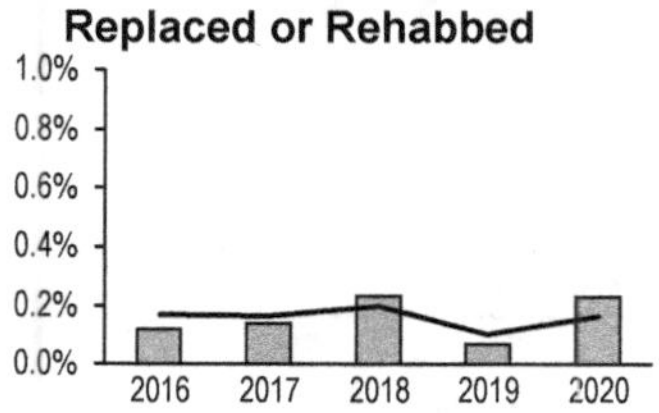

	2016	2017	2018	2019	2020
Wilson	0.1%	0.1%	0.2%	0.1%	0.2%
Average	0.2%	0.2%	0.2%	0.1%	0.2%

Percentage of Water Bills Not Collected

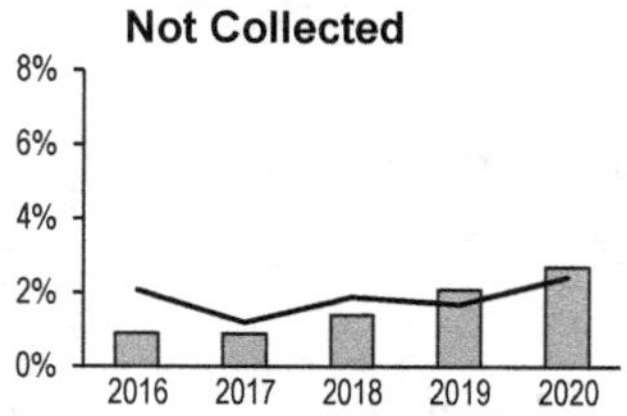

	2016	2017	2018	2019	2020
Wilson	0.92%	0.89%	1.40%	2.09%	2.71%
Average	2.08%	1.19%	1.88%	1.68%	2.42%

Peak Daily Demand as a Percentage of Treatment Capacity

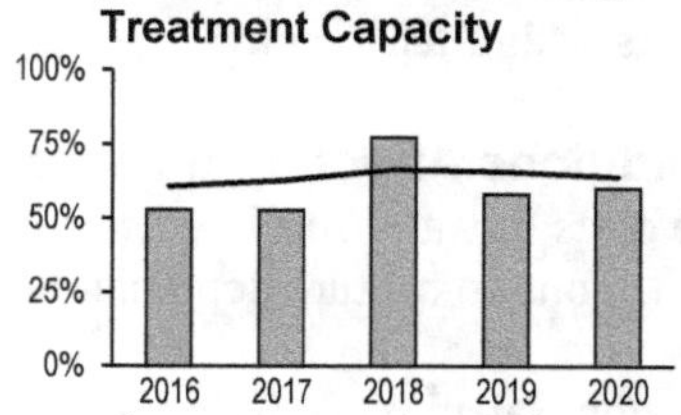

	2016	2017	2018	2019	2020
Wilson	53%	53%	77%	58%	60%
Average	61%	63%	66%	66%	64%

Breaks and Leaks per Mile of Main Line Pipe

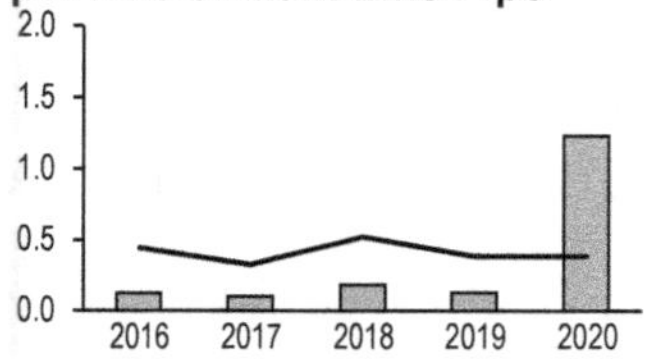

	2016	2017	2018	2019	2020
Wilson	0.12	0.10	0.18	0.13	1.23
Average	0.44	0.32	0.52	0.38	0.38

Customer Complaints about Water Quality per 1,000 Meters

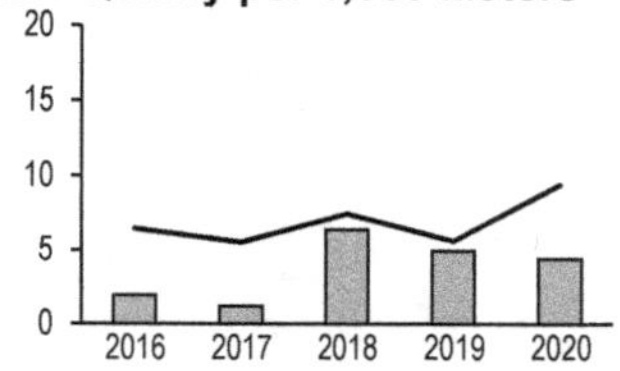

	2016	2017	2018	2019	2020
Wilson	1.94	1.21	6.38	4.94	4.40
Average	6.43	5.48	7.42	5.61	9.38

Winston-Salem — Water Services

Fiscal Year 2019-20

Explanatory Information

Service Level and Delivery

The Winston-Salem and Forsyth County Utilities Division operates a combined water and sewer system that covers the city and most of the remaining population of Forsyth County. Approximately 352,000 people are served in an area covering roughly 227 square miles.

The system has an eleven-member utility commission that was created by an interlocal agreement between the City of Winston-Salem and Forsyth County. The commission sets policy for publicly owned water, wastewater, and solid waste disposal facilities. The commission is also charged with the responsibility for long-range planning, authorizing funding for projects, operation and maintenance of facilities, and setting policies and rate structures. The commission is not authorized to issue bonds to finance capital improvements.

Water sources for the system are drawn from two separate points on the Yadkin River. The city also uses Salem Lake as a water source. The estimated safe yield for the system is 100 million gallons per day.

The city uses three treatment plants with a daily treatment capacity of 91 million gallons. The plants all use conventional treatment, employing coagulation, flocculation, and sedimentation followed by rapid sand filtration and then chlorine treatment for disinfection.

The system has 2,341 miles of pipeline. The replacement goal for pipes is seventy-five years.

Water meters are read both monthly and bi-monthly depending on the account type. Currently the system has a small number of meters read by automatic means, totaling approximately 13 percent. The replacement standard for water meters is approximately every ten years. The goal is to have completely switched to automatically read meters within ten years.

Conditions Affecting Service, Performance, and Costs

The costs of water services as captured here do not include debt service but do capture depreciation.

Winston-Salem made improvements in their calculation of population served and area covered to improve the accuracy of their data. This had the effect of decreasing the reported population and size of area served from earlier years. The changes seen in FY 2017–18 are due to this improved estimation and not a change in services.

Municipal Profile

Estimated Service Population	351,733
Service Land Area (Square Miles)	227.0
Persons per Square Mile	1,549
Topography	Gently rolling
Climate	Temperate; some ice and snow
Median Household Income U.S. Census 2016	$40,584

Service Profile

FTE Staff Positions	
Treatment Plant	54.0
Line Crews	77.0
Meter Readers	13.0
Billing/Collection	8.2
Other	20.0
Total	172.2
Number of Treatment Plants	3
Total Treatment Capacity	91.0 MGD
Average Daily Demand	36.1 MGD
Miles of Main Line Pipe	2,341
Average Age of Main Line Pipe	75 years
Number of Breaks/Leaks	596
Number of Water Meters	131,935
Percent of Meters Read Automatically	13.4%
Total Revenues Collected	$60,821,971

Full Cost Profile

Cost Breakdown by Percentage	
Personal Services	28.0%
Operating Costs	37.3%
Capital Costs	34.7%
TOTAL	100.0%
Cost Breakdown in Dollars	
Personal Services	$9,868,188
Operating Costs	$13,126,186
Capital Costs	$12,234,886
TOTAL	$35,229,260

Winston-Salem — Water Services

Key: Winston-Salem ■ Benchmarking Average — Fiscal Years 2016 through 2020

Resource Measures

Water Services Cost per Capita

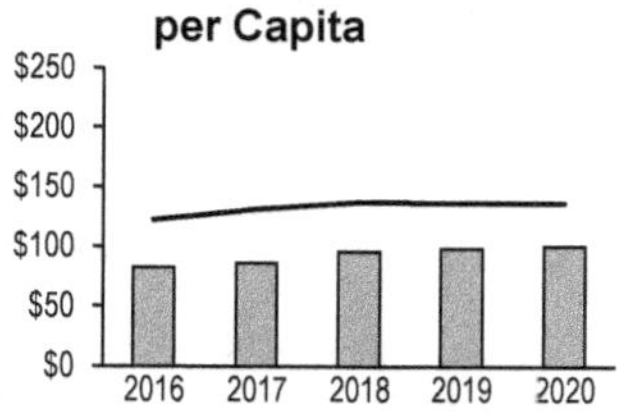

	2016	2017	2018	2019	2020
Winston-Salem	$82	$86	$95	$98	$100
Average	$122	$131	$137	$137	$137

Water Services FTEs per 10,000 Population

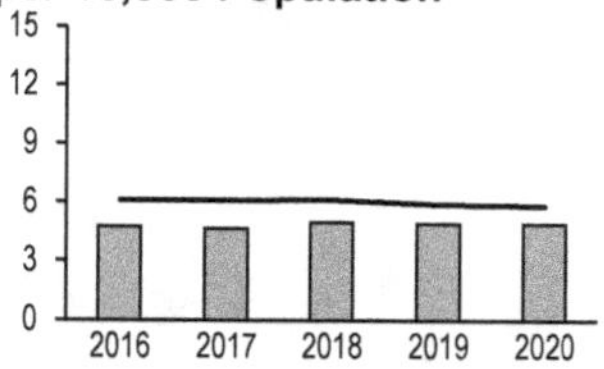

	2016	2017	2018	2019	2020
Winston-Salem	4.7	4.6	4.9	4.9	4.9
Average	6.1	6.1	6.1	5.9	5.8

Water Services Cost per Meter

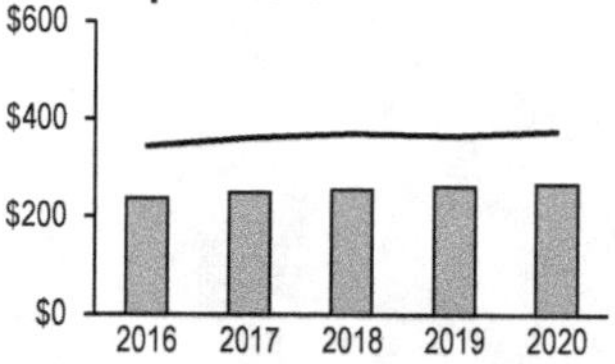

	2016	2017	2018	2019	2020
Winston-Salem	$237	$248	$255	$261	$267
Average	$343	$360	$369	$365	$375

Workload Measures

Thousands of Gallons of Billed Water per Meter

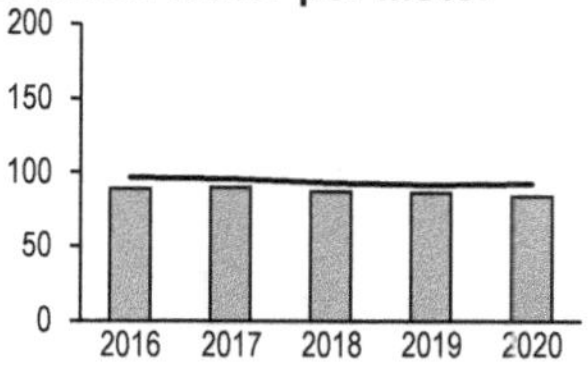

	2016	2017	2018	2019	2020
Winston-Salem	88.9	89.7	87.2	86.5	84.2
Average	96.4	95.5	92.8	91.6	92.2

Miles of Main Line Pipe per Square Mile of Service Area

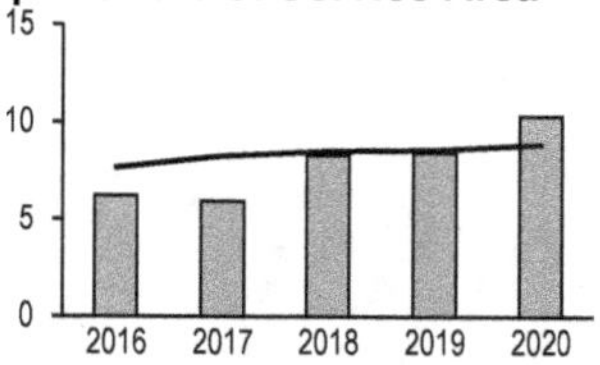

	2016	2017	2018	2019	2020
Winston-Salem	6.2	5.9	8.3	8.4	10.3
Average	7.6	8.2	8.5	8.6	8.8

Efficiency Measures

Total Cost per Thousand Gallons of Billed Water

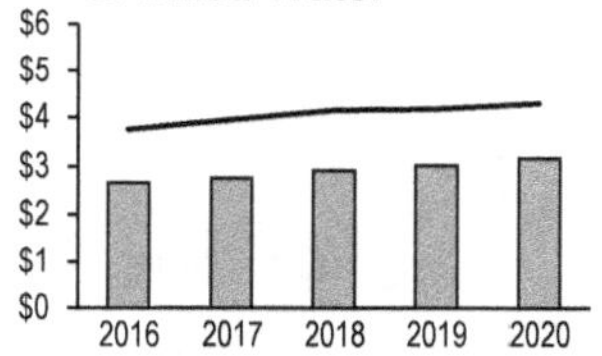

	2016	2017	2018	2019	2020
Winston-Salem	$2.66	$2.76	$2.92	$3.02	$3.17
Average	$3.75	$3.95	$4.15	$4.18	$4.30

Million Gallons of Billed Water per Water Services FTEs

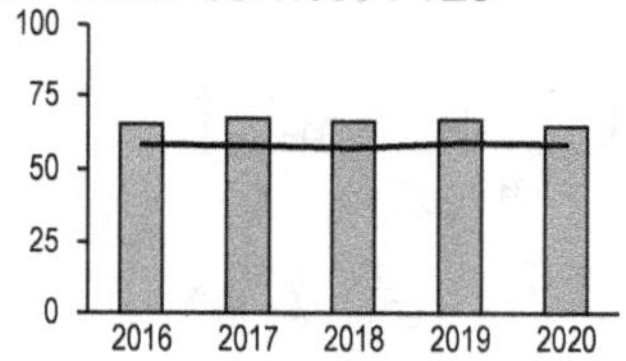

	2016	2017	2018	2019	2020
Winston-Salem	65.1	67.1	66.1	66.7	64.5
Average	58.1	57.9	57.0	58.7	58.2

Billed Water as a Percentage of Finished Water

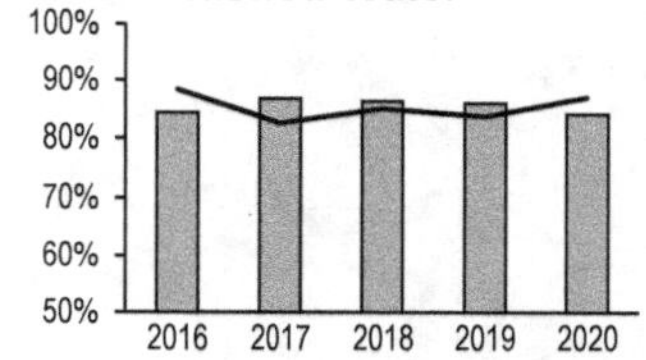

	2016	2017	2018	2019	2020
Winston-Salem	84%	87%	86%	86%	84%
Average	88%	82%	85%	84%	87%

Effectiveness Measures

Percentage of Existing Pipeline Replaced or Rehabbed

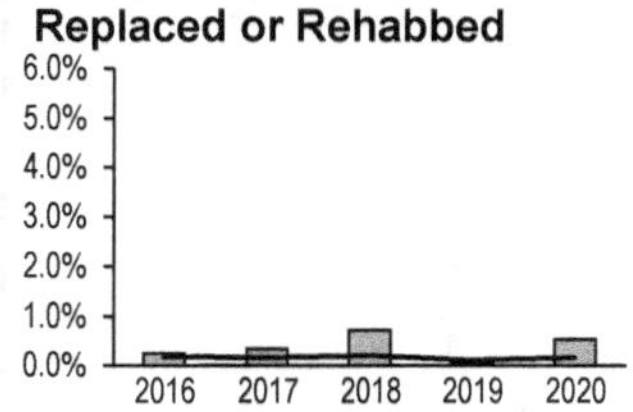

	2016	2017	2018	2019	2020
Winston-Salem	0.3%	0.3%	0.7%	0.1%	0.5%
Average	0.2%	0.2%	0.2%	0.1%	0.2%

Percentage of Water Bills Not Collected

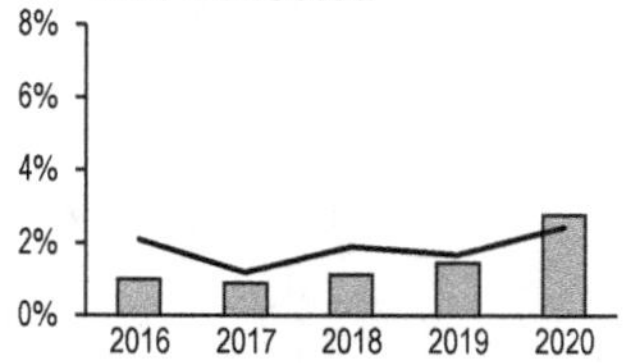

	2016	2017	2018	2019	2020
Winston-Salem	1.02%	0.91%	1.14%	1.47%	2.76%
Average	2.08%	1.19%	1.88%	1.68%	2.42%

Peak Daily Demand as a Percentage of Treatment Capacity

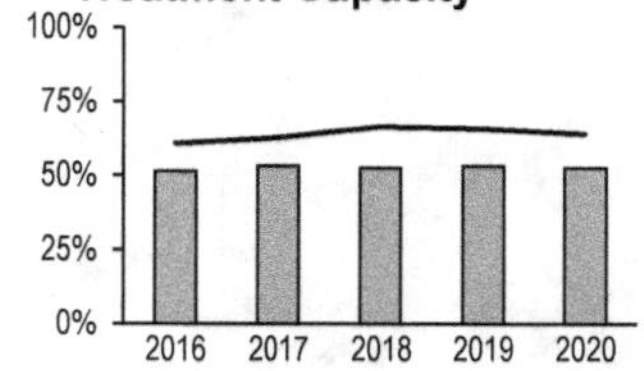

	2016	2017	2018	2019	2020
Winston-Salem	51%	53%	52%	53%	52%
Average	61%	63%	66%	66%	64%

Breaks and Leaks per Mile of Main Line Pipe

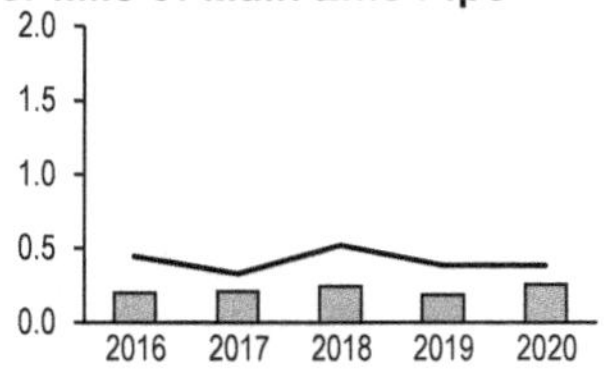

	2016	2017	2018	2019	2020
Winston-Salem	0.19	0.20	0.24	0.18	0.25
Average	0.44	0.32	0.52	0.38	0.38

Customer Complaints about Water Quality per 1,000 Meters

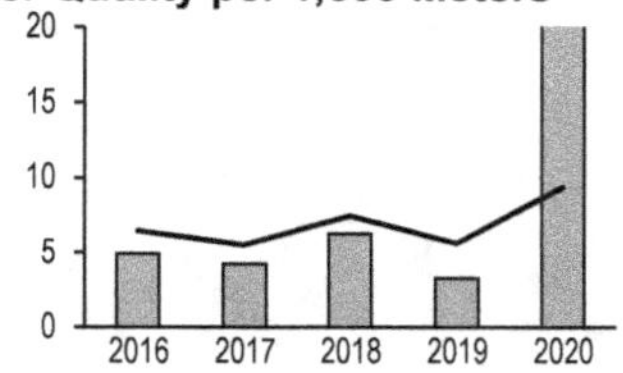

	2016	2017	2018	2019	2020
Winston-Salem	4.93	4.21	6.26	3.29	32.20
Average	6.43	5.48	7.42	5.61	9.38

SCHOOL OF GOVERNMENT
North Carolina Benchmarking Project

Performance and Cost Data

WASTEWATER SERVICES

UNC | SCHOOL OF GOVERNMENT
North Carolina Benchmarking Project

PERFORMANCE MEASURES FOR WASTEWATER SERVICES

SERVICE DEFINITION

Wastewater Services includes the collection, treatment, wastewater discharge, solids disposal, and billing related to sewer services. This service area includes the collection system after leaving the customer's outlet, lift stations, pretreatment, and treatment plants. Activities and costs include the operation, maintenance, and installation of infrastructure. Also included are costs and activities associated with billing and collection for sewer services and administrative activities, such as planning, engineering, and testing. This includes wastewater treated for reuse at the plant site and for other purposes. Excluded are potable water systems and stormwater systems.

NOTES ON PERFORMANCE MEASURES

1. Volume of Sewage per Account

This workload measure captures the amount of wastewater generated and received at the treatment plant relative to the number of customers.

2. Miles of Sewer Main Line Pipe per Square Mile of Service Area

The amount of sewer main line pipe per square mile shows the density of the pipe infrastructure to be maintained relative to the geographic size of the area served.

3. Number of Lift Stations per Thousand Accounts

This workload measure provides some idea of the amount of reliance on pumping in a system to supplement gravity-fed delivery. Lift stations also generate additional maintenance workload.

4. Cost per Thousand Gallons of Collected and Treated Wastewater

This efficiency measure shows total system costs relative to the volume of wastewater reaching treatment plants. Some wastewater does not make it to treatment plants.

5. Wastewater Volume in Millions of Gallons per FTE

This efficiency measure captures the number of workers the system is using relative to the volume of wastewater treated.

6. Customer Accounts per FTE

The number of customer accounts relative to the number of workers is another efficiency measure showing how many customers are being served per worker.

7. Percentage of Bills Collected
Collection of wastewater bills sent to customers is necessary to ensure revenues for system operation. Bills not collected reflect potential lost revenue to the system, but some loss is unavoidable.

8. Average Daily Treatment as a Percent of Permitted Capacity
A wastewater system needs sufficient capacity to meet not only average demands, but also peak demands. This measure looks at average daily demand relative to the wastewater system treatment capacity in a day. Some excess capacity is needed to allow for daily service variations and to plan for future expansion needs.

9. Percent of Existing Main Line Pipe Rehabilitated or Replaced
As the wastewater systems age, pipe needs to be replaced to ensure that service will not be interrupted. This effectiveness measure captures the amount of current stock being replaced or rehabilitated during a given year.

10. Overflows Per 100 Miles of Main Line Pipe
Sanitary system overflows may be due to blockages or breaks in pipe. Keeping these breaks to a low level is an important measure of the effectiveness of preventive maintenance and system upkeep. Overflows, if large enough, may also represent a public health concern.

11. Sewer Backups per 100 Miles of Main Line Pipe
Backups in sewer pipes are another measure of potential maintenance concerns and potential public health concerns. Backups may also be a sign of insufficient maintenance.

12. Billed Sewer Effluents as a Percent of Treated Effluent
The volume of wastewater that is billed relative to the volume received at the treatment plant is an effectiveness measure that points to potential losses in the collection system. Some loss is inevitable in sewer systems, and not all drinking water billed for is used in such a way that it should make it back to the wastewater treatment plant. But comparisons may reveal excessive infiltration or leakage.

Wastewater Services

Summary of Key Dimensions of Service

City or Town	Estimated Residential Population in Service Area	Service Area (in Square Miles)	Operating Treatment Plants	Average Daily Flow of Wastewater at Plants (in MGD)	Total Treatment Capacity for Wastewater (in MGD)	Miles of Gravity and Forced Main Lines	Number of Wastewater Accounts	Sewer System FTE Positions
Apex	65,682	24.0	1 + 1 jointly operated with Cary	3.7	9.7	303.2	21,701	24.0
Charlotte	1,110,356	546.0	7	88.7	123.2	4,420.0	270,641	530.0
Concord	91,938	105.7	0	na	na	604.7	38,330	33.0
Goldsboro	34,234	25.0	1	9.0	14.2	244.0	11,392	30.0
Greensboro	315,328	148.0	1	35.5	56.0	1,519.1	106,024	153.0
Hickory	37,478	65.0	3	5.9	16.5	544.0	16,153	44.0
Raleigh	591,943	299.0	3	50.2	80.2	2,504.0	179,463	347.0
Wilson	54,600	42.0	1	8.9	14.0	363.0	20,294	65.0
Winston-Salem	299,808	148.0	2	36.7	51.0	1,805.0	101,900	175.2

NOTES

MGD stands for millions of gallons per day.

EXPLANATORY FACTORS

These are factors that the project found affected wastewater services performance and cost in one or more of the municipalities:

Topography
Size of service area
Population density
Age of infrastructure
Growth of population and businesses

Fiscal Year 2019-20

Explanatory Information

Service Level and Delivery

Wastewater services for the Town of Apex are managed by the Water Reclamation and Wastewater Collections Division under the Department of Water Resources. The system covers the area within the municipal limits.

Apex has one treatment plant, which uses bar screens, grit removal, biological nutrient removal (BNR), oxidation ditches, secondary clarifiers, sand filters, ultraviolet disinfection, aerobic sludge digestion, and rotary drum sludge dewatering as part of its treatment process. The Apex wastewater system has nutrient limits in place that restrict what can be discharged from the plant to protect water quality. Apex uses land application for biosolids resulting from treatment and also dries some biosolids as fertilizer pellets. Apex also pays for one-third of the operation of a separate treatment plant, which is jointly owned with the Town of Cary.

The town's system had one regulatory violation for the treatment portion of the system and two violations connected to the collection system during the fiscal year.

Conditions Affecting Service, Performance, and Costs

The costs of wastewater or sewer services as captured here do not include debt service but do capture depreciation of capital.

Municipal Profile

Estimated Service Population	65,682
Service Land Area (Square Miles)	24.0
Persons per Square Mile	2,737
Topography	Flat; gently rolling
Climate	Temperate; little ice and snow
Median Household Income U.S. Census 2016	$84,000

Service Profile

Total FTE Staff Positions	24.0
Treatment Plant	8.0
Line Crews	12.0
Billing/Collection	2.0
Other	2.0
Number of Treatment Plants	2
Total Treatment Capacity	9.7 MGD
Average Daily Flow	3.7 MGD
River Basin into Which System Discharges	Neuse
Miles of Gravity Main Line Pipe	265
Miles of Forced Main Line Pipe	38
Average Age of Main Line Pipe	16 years
Blocks in Sewer Mains	28
Number of System Breaks	18
Sanitary System Overflows	2
Number of Customer Accounts	21,701
Total Revenues Collected	$16,323,164

Full Cost Profile

Cost Breakdown by Percentage	
Personal Services	16.0%
Operating Costs	45.9%
Capital Costs	38.1%
TOTAL	100.0%
Cost Breakdown in Dollars	
Personal Services	$1,631,043
Operating Costs	$4,691,464
Capital Costs	$3,894,460
TOTAL	$10,216,967

Key: Apex ▒ Benchmarking Average — Fiscal Years 2016 through 2020

Resource Measures

Wastewater Services Cost per Capita

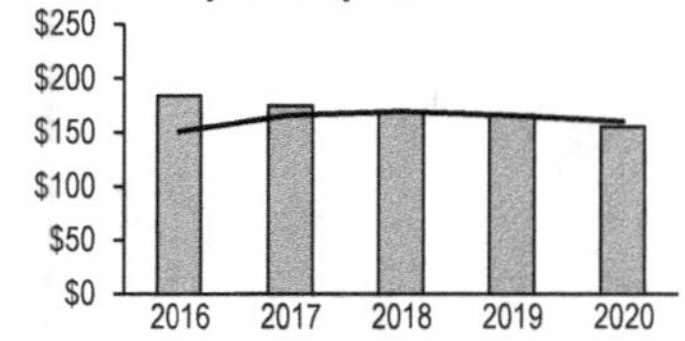

	2016	2017	2018	2019	2020
Apex	$184	$175	$169	$166	$156
Average	$151	$166	$169	$165	$160

Wastewater Services FTEs per 10,000 Population

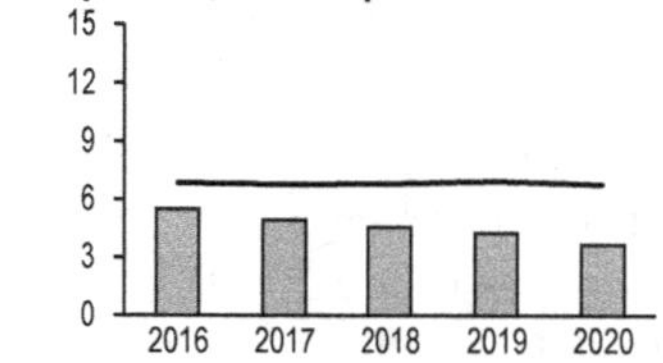

	2016	2017	2018	2019	2020
Apex	5.5	4.9	4.6	4.3	3.7
Average	6.8	6.8	6.8	6.9	6.8

Wastewater Services Cost per Customer Account

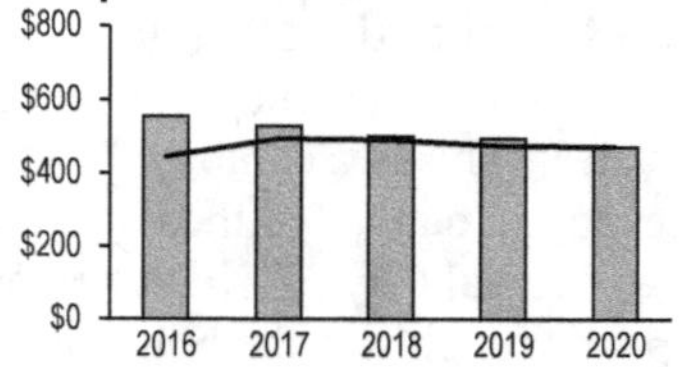

	2016	2017	2018	2019	2020
Apex	$554	$527	$499	$494	$471
Average	$445	$494	$490	$473	$471

Workload Measures

Thousands of Gallons of Wastewater per Account

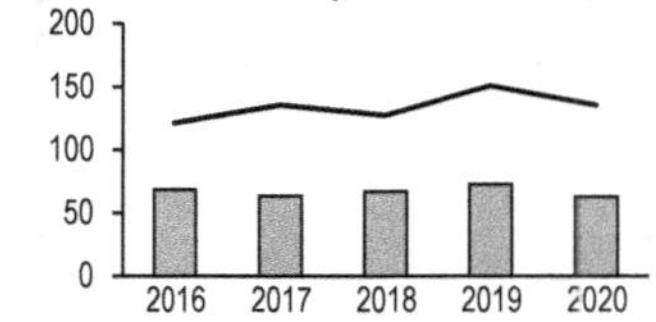

	2016	2017	2018	2019	2020
Apex	68.6	63.6	67.2	72.5	63.1
Average	121.0	135.0	126.9	150.7	135.2

Miles of Sewer Main Line Pipe per Square Mile of Service Area

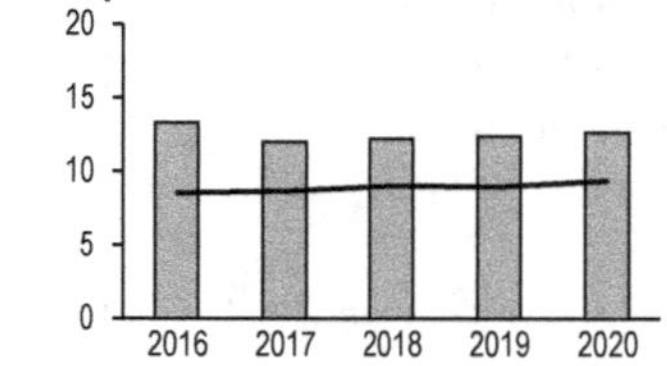

	2016	2017	2018	2019	2020
Apex	13.3	12.0	12.2	12.4	12.6
Average	8.5	8.6	9.0	8.9	9.3

Number of Lift Stations per 1,000 Accounts

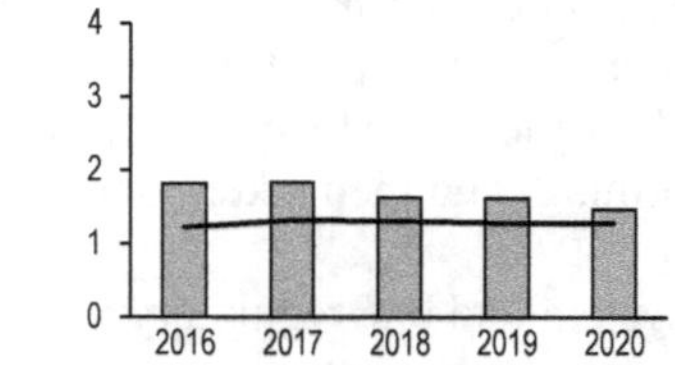

	2016	2017	2018	2019	2020
Apex	1.82	1.83	1.63	1.62	1.47
Average	1.22	1.31	1.30	1.28	1.28

Efficiency Measures

Total Cost per 1,000 Gallons of Treated Wastewater

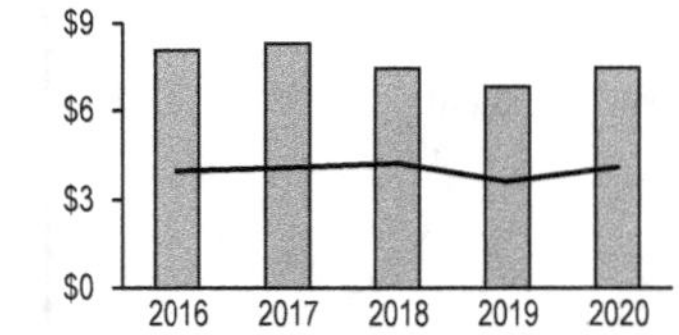

	2016	2017	2018	2019	2020
Apex	$8.07	$8.29	$7.43	$6.81	$7.46
Average	$3.96	$4.07	$4.21	$3.59	$4.08

Million Gallons of Wastewater per Wastewater Services FTE

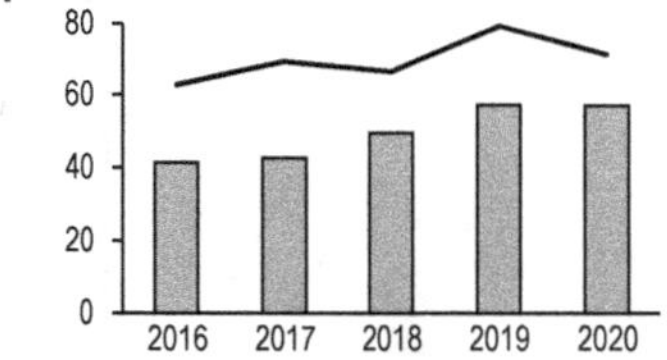

	2016	2017	2018	2019	2020
Apex	41.5	42.6	49.6	57.2	57.0
Average	62.7	69.2	66.3	79.4	71.2

Customer Accounts per Wastewater Services FTE

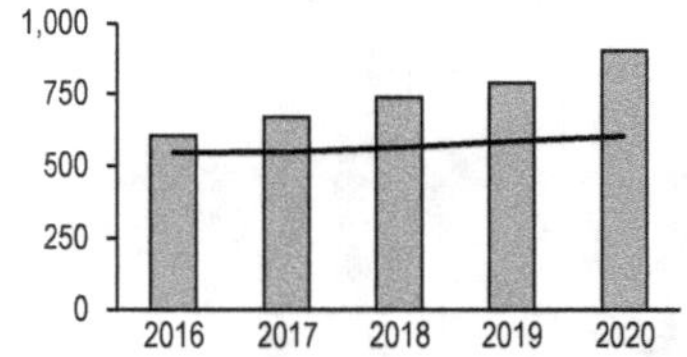

	2016	2017	2018	2019	2020
Apex	605	669	737	789	904
Average	545	547	563	584	603

Effectiveness Measures

Percentage of Wastewater Bills Not Collected

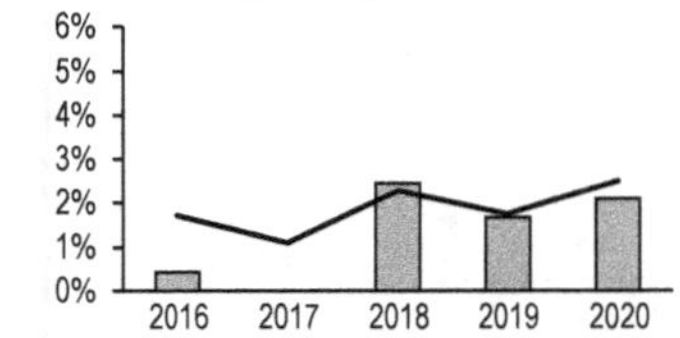

	2016	2017	2018	2019	2020
Apex	0.44%	0.00%	2.45%	1.66%	2.10%
Average	1.72%	1.09%	2.27%	1.74%	2.49%

Average Daily Treatment as a Percentage of Capacity

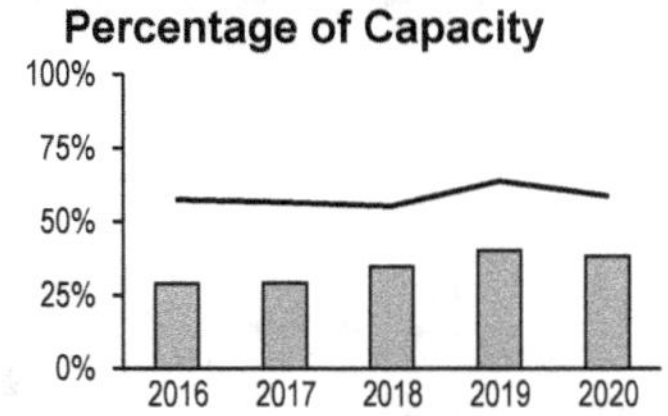

	2016	2017	2018	2019	2020
Apex	29.1%	29.3%	34.8%	40.1%	38.3%
Average	57.6%	56.7%	55.3%	63.8%	58.8%

Percent of Main Line Rehabbed or Replaced

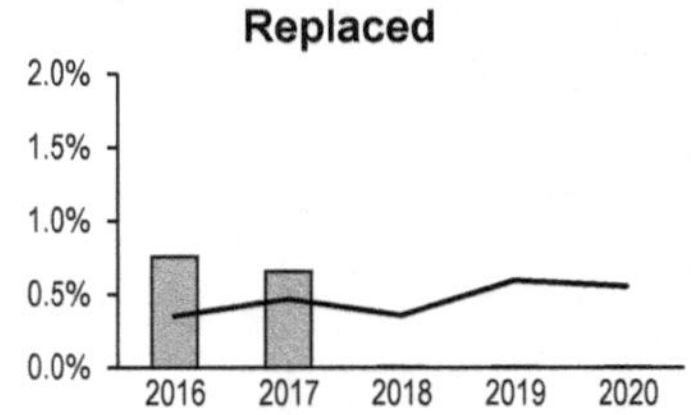

	2016	2017	2018	2019	2020
Apex	0.76%	0.65%	0.01%	0.00%	0.00%
Average	0.35%	0.47%	0.36%	0.59%	0.56%

Overflows per 100 Miles of Main Line Pipe

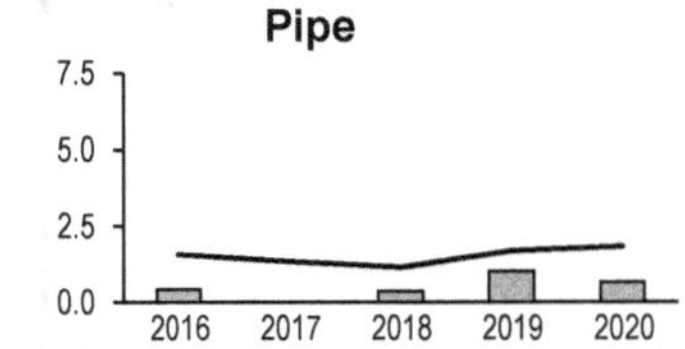

	2016	2017	2018	2019	2020
Apex	0.42	0.00	0.36	1.01	0.66
Average	1.57	1.34	1.17	1.68	1.85

Backups per 100 Miles of Main Line Pipe

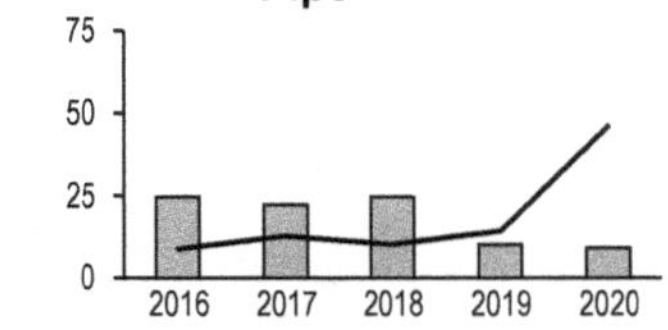

	2016	2017	2018	2019	2020
Apex	24.64	22.36	24.64	10.12	9.24
Average	8.83	12.62	10.08	14.21	45.98

Billed Wastewater as a Percent of Treated Effluent

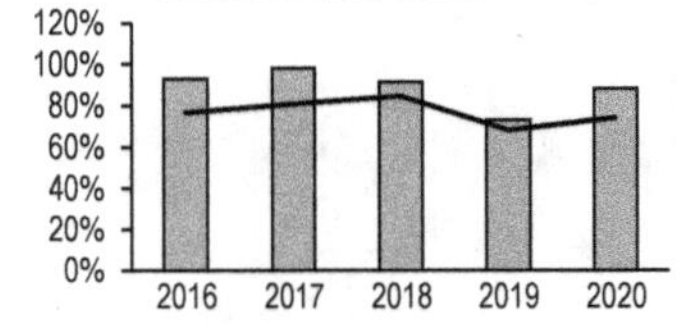

	2016	2017	2018	2019	2020
Apex	93%	98%	91%	73%	88%
Average	76%	81%	84%	68%	74%

Charlotte — Wastewater Services

Fiscal Year 2019-20

Explanatory Information

Service Level and Delivery

Wastewater collection and treatment are handled by Charlotte Water (CLTWater). This is a combined water and sewer utility for Mecklenburg County and the City of Charlotte. The department is run as an official City of Charlotte department. The service area corresponds roughly to the boundaries of Mecklenburg County.

There are seven wastewater treatment plants owned and operated by Charlotte Water. Each of CLTWater's treatment plants applies primary, secondary, and advanced treatment to the waste stream. The system does have regulatory limits in place on nutrient loads, which can be discharged in order to protect water quality. In addition to the treatment of wastewater, the system handles biosolids, most of which are applied to land (unless non-conforming) and then taken to the landfill.

The system had one regulatory violations connected to treatment issues and three regulatory violation connected to the collection portion of the system during the year.

Conditions Affecting Service, Performance, and Costs

The costs of wastewater or sewer services as captured here do not include debt service but do capture depreciation of capital.

Municipal Profile

Estimated Service Population	1,110,356
Service Land Area (Square Miles)	546
Persons per Square Mile	2,034
Topography	Flat; gently rolling
Climate	Temperate; little ice and snow
Median Household Income U.S. Census 2016	$46,975

Service Profile

Total FTE Staff Positions	530.0
Treatment Plant	120.0
Line Crews	177.0
Billing/Collection	12.0
Other	221.0
Number of Treatment Plants	7
Total Treatment Capacity	123.2 MGD
Average Daily Flow	88.7 MGD
River Basin into Which System Discharges	Catawba and Yadkin
Miles of Gravity Main Line Pipe	4,284
Miles of Forced Main Line Pipe	136
Average Age of Main Line Pipe	34 years
Blocks in Sewer Mains	114
Number of System Breaks	122
Sanitary System Overflows	151
Number of Customer Accounts	270,641
Total Revenues Collected	$272,695,202

Full Cost Profile

Cost Breakdown by Percentage	
Personal Services	18.1%
Operating Costs	38.4%
Capital Costs	43.5%
TOTAL	100.0%
Cost Breakdown in Dollars	
Personal Services	$36,056,447
Operating Costs	$76,305,233
Capital Costs	$86,474,586
TOTAL	$198,836,266

Charlotte

Wastewater Services

Key: Charlotte ■ Benchmarking Average — Fiscal Years 2016 through 2020

Resource Measures

Wastewater Services Cost per Capita

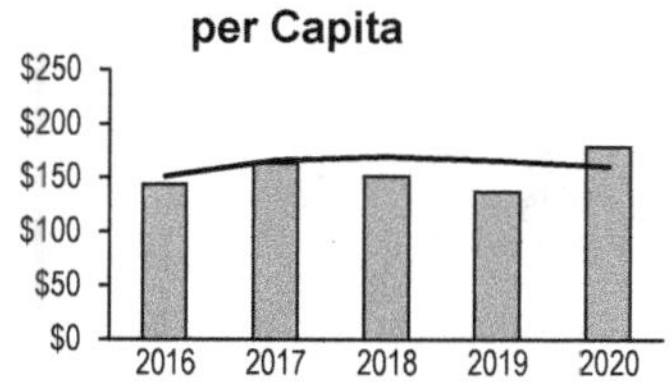

	2016	2017	2018	2019	2020
Charlotte	$144	$163	$151	$137	$179
Average	$151	$166	$169	$165	$160

Wastewater Services FTEs per 10,000 Population

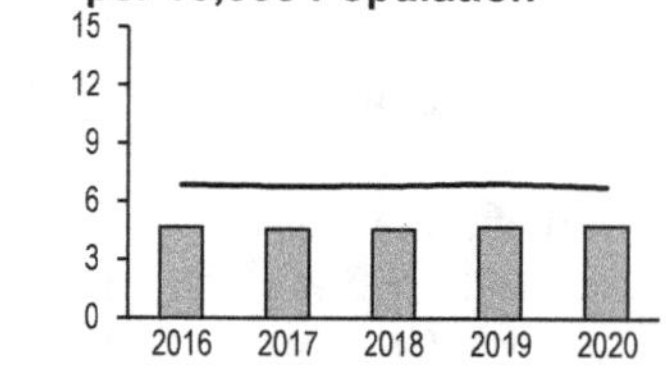

	2016	2017	2018	2019	2020
Charlotte	4.7	4.6	4.6	4.7	4.8
Average	6.8	6.8	6.8	6.9	6.8

Wastewater Services Cost per Customer Account

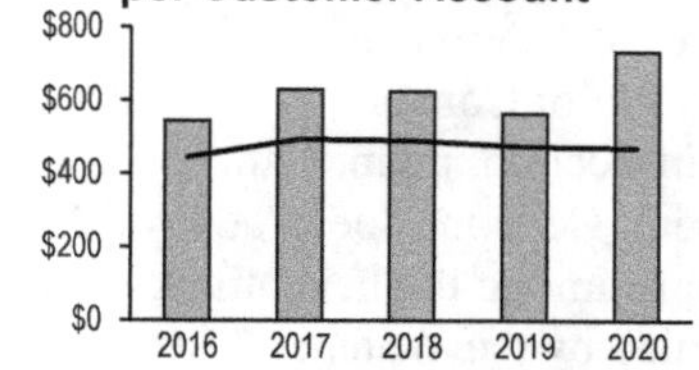

	2016	2017	2018	2019	2020
Charlotte	$544	$630	$624	$565	$735
Average	$445	$494	$490	$473	$471

Workload Measures

Thousands of Gallons of Wastewater per Account

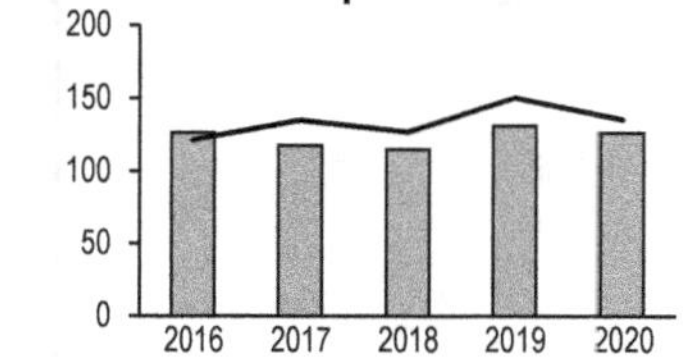

	2016	2017	2018	2019	2020
Charlotte	126.6	117.5	114.9	131.6	126.4
Average	121.0	135.0	126.9	150.7	135.2

Miles of Sewer Main Line Pipe per Square Mile of Service Area

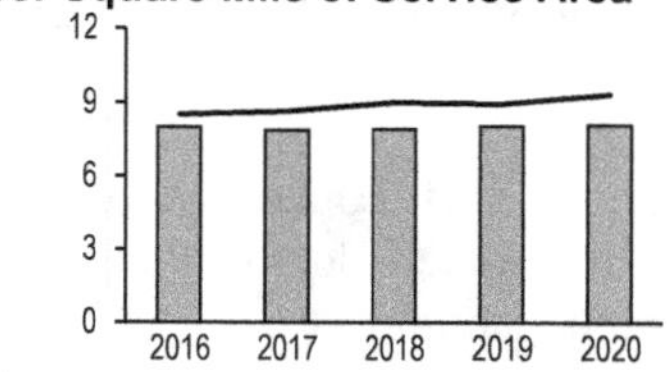

	2016	2017	2018	2019	2020
Charlotte	8.0	7.9	7.9	8.0	8.1
Average	8.5	8.6	9.0	8.9	9.3

Number of Lift Stations per 1,000 Accounts

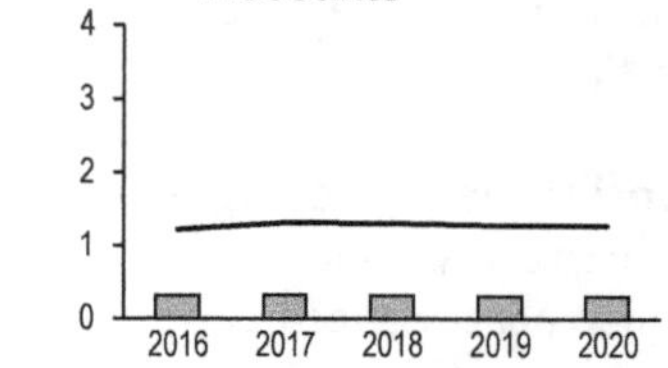

	2016	2017	2018	2019	2020
Charlotte	0.32	0.32	0.31	0.31	0.31
Average	1.22	1.31	1.30	1.28	1.28

Efficiency Measures

Total Cost per 1,000 Gallons of Treated Wastewater

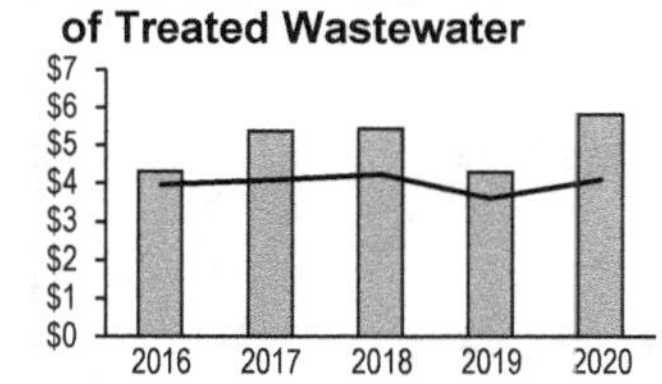

	2016	2017	2018	2019	2020
Charlotte	$4.30	$5.36	$5.43	$4.29	$5.81
Average	$3.96	$4.07	$4.21	$3.59	$4.08

Million Gallons of Wastewater per Wastewater Services FTE

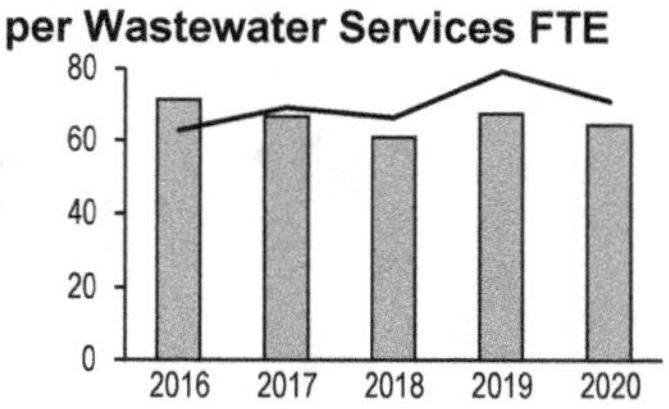

	2016	2017	2018	2019	2020
Charlotte	71.5	66.8	60.9	67.6	64.5
Average	62.7	69.2	66.3	79.4	71.2

Customer Accounts per Wastewater Services FTE

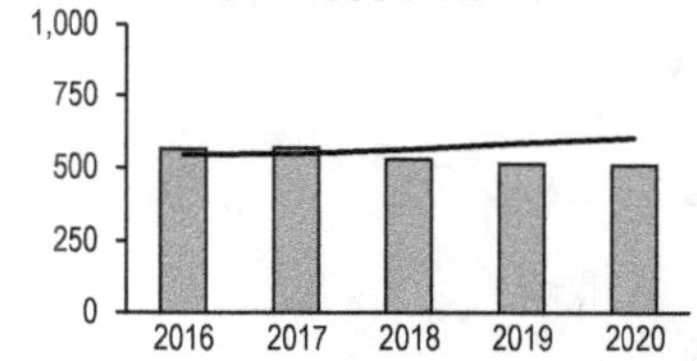

	2016	2017	2018	2019	2020
Charlotte	565	568	530	514	511
Average	545	547	563	584	603

Effectiveness Measures

Percentage of Wastewater Bills Not Collected

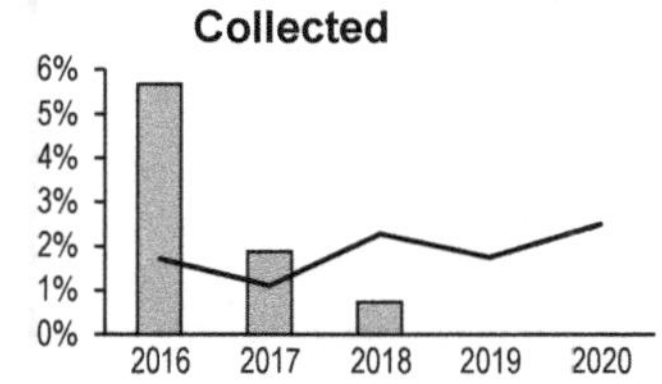

	2016	2017	2018	2019	2020
Charlotte	5.67%	1.88%	0.72%		
Average	1.72%	1.09%	2.27%	1.74%	2.49%

Average Daily Treatment as a Percentage of Capacity

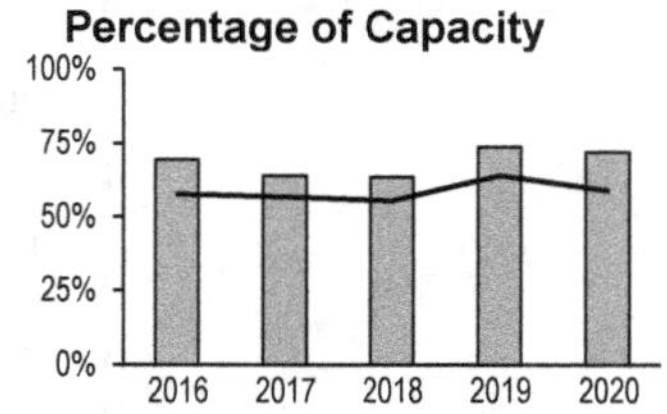

	2016	2017	2018	2019	2020
Charlotte	69.4%	64.0%	63.4%	73.9%	72.0%
Average	57.6%	56.7%	55.3%	63.8%	58.8%

Percent of Main Line Rehabbed or Replaced

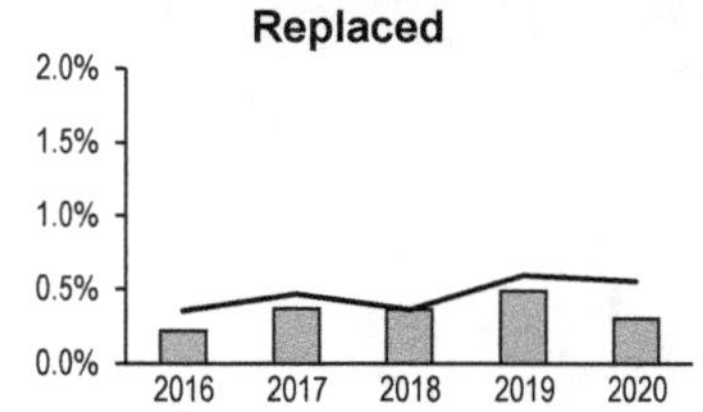

	2016	2017	2018	2019	2020
Charlotte	0.22%	0.37%	0.36%	0.49%	0.30%
Average	0.35%	0.47%	0.36%	0.59%	0.56%

Overflows per 100 Miles of Main Line Pipe

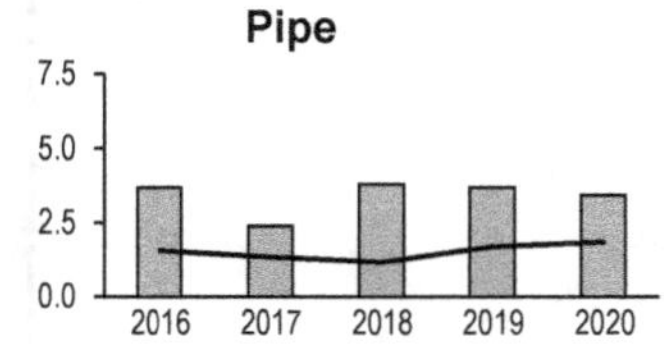

	2016	2017	2018	2019	2020
Charlotte	3.67	2.39	3.79	3.69	3.42
Average	1.57	1.34	1.17	1.68	1.85

Backups per 100 Miles of Main Line Pipe

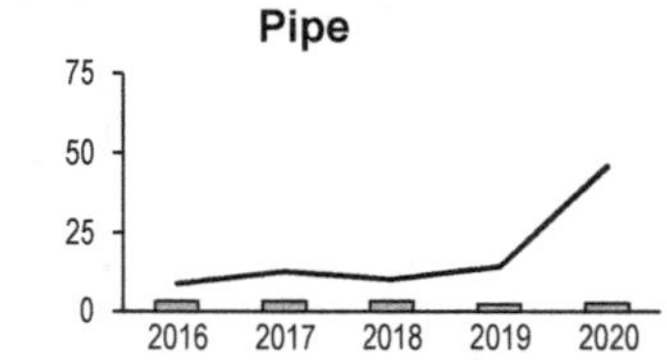

	2016	2017	2018	2019	2020
Charlotte	3.25	3.18	3.19	2.30	2.58
Average	8.83	12.62	10.08	14.21	45.98

Billed Wastewater as a Percent of Treated Effluent

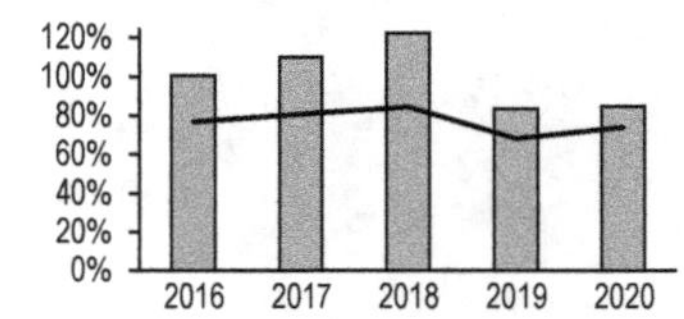

	2016	2017	2018	2019	2020
Charlotte	100%	110%	122%	83%	85%
Average	76%	81%	84%	68%	74%

Fiscal Year 2019-20

Explanatory Information

Service Level and Delivery

The City of Concord has a wastewater department that focuses on the inspection, maintenance, and repair of the wastewater collection system. Concord does not have its own treatment plant, making it unique among the benchmarking partner cities. Instead, treatment is handled by the Water and Sewer Authority of Cabarrus County, a regional system. All treatment and disposal of wastewater and biosolids are handled by the regional authority using two treatment plants.

The Concord wastewater collection system had one violation on the collection portion of the system involving sanitary system overflows.

Conditions Affecting Service, Performance, and Costs

The costs of wastewater or sewer services as captured here do not include debt service but do capture depreciation of capital.

Municipal Profile

Estimated Service Population	91,938
Service Land Area (Square Miles)	105.7
Persons per Square Mile	870
Topography	Flat; gently rolling
Climate	Temperate; little ice and snow
Median Household Income U.S. Census 2016	$50,863

Service Profile

Total FTE Staff Positions	33.0
Treatment Plant	NA
Line Crews	27.0
Billing/Collection	0.0
Other	6.0
Number of Treatment Plants	0
Total Treatment Capacity	NA
Average Daily Flow	NA
River Basin into Which System Discharges	Yadkin and Pee-Dee
Miles of Gravity Main Line Pipe	592
Miles of Forced Main Line Pipe	13
Average Age of Main Line Pipe	41 years
Blocks in Sewer Mains	3
Number of System Breaks	0
Sanitary System Overflows	3
Number of Customer Accounts	38,330
Total Revenues Collected	$18,337,136

Full Cost Profile

Cost Breakdown by Percentage	
Personal Services	19.6%
Operating Costs	57.2%
Capital Costs	23.2%
TOTAL	100.0%

Cost Breakdown in Dollars	
Personal Services	$2,915,791
Operating Costs	$8,534,710
Capital Costs	$3,463,283
TOTAL	$14,913,784

Concord

Wastewater Services

Key: Concord ▒ Benchmarking Average — Fiscal Years 2016 through 2020

Resource Measures

Wastewater Services Cost per Capita

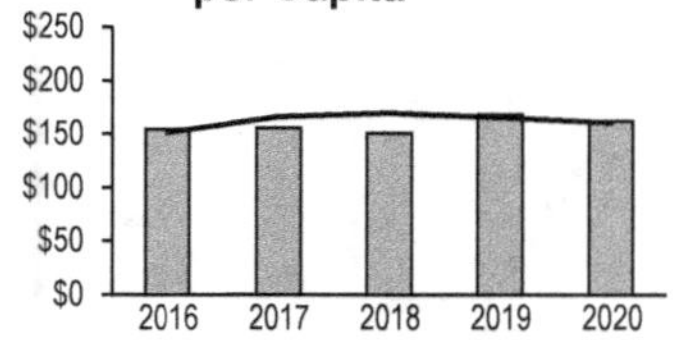

	2016	2017	2018	2019	2020
Concord	$155	$155	$151	$168	$162
Average	$151	$166	$169	$165	$160

Wastewater Services FTEs per 10,000 Population

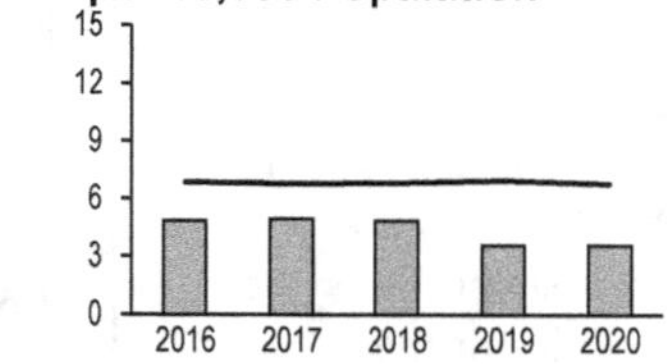

	2016	2017	2018	2019	2020
Concord	4.8	5.0	4.8	3.6	3.6
Average	6.8	6.8	6.8	6.9	6.8

Wastewater Services Cost per Customer Account

	2016	2017	2018	2019	2020
Concord	$398	$395	$381	$420	$389
Average	$445	$494	$490	$473	$471

Workload Measures

Thousands of Gallons of Wastewater per Account

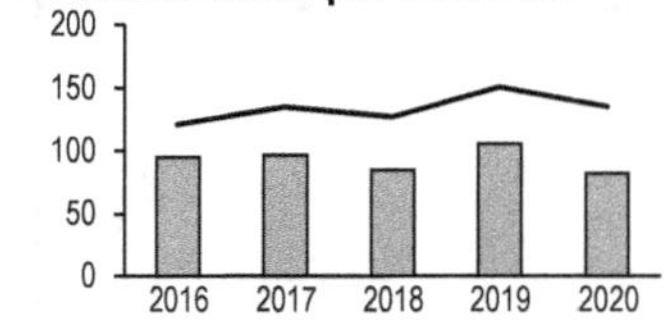

	2016	2017	2018	2019	2020
Concord	95.0	96.3	84.7	105.6	82.0
Average	121.0	135.0	126.9	150.7	135.2

Miles of Sewer Main Line Pipe per Square Mile of Service Area

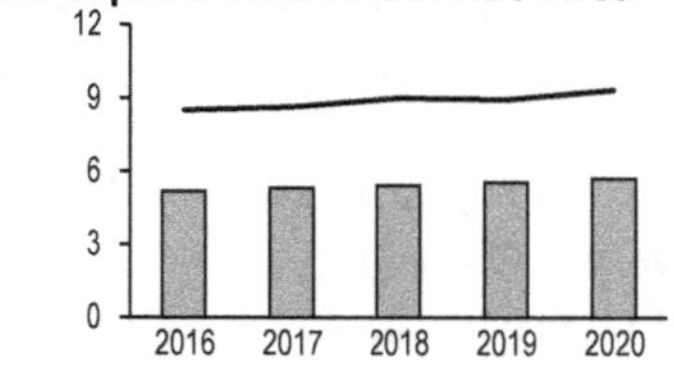

	2016	2017	2018	2019	2020
Concord	5.2	5.3	5.4	5.5	5.7
Average	8.5	8.6	9.0	8.9	9.3

Number of Lift Stations per 1,000 Accounts

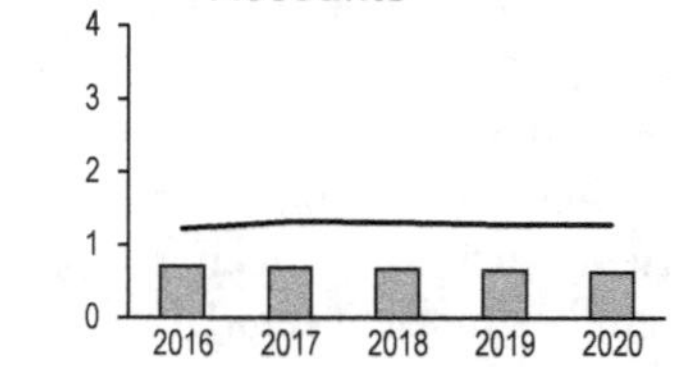

	2016	2017	2018	2019	2020
Concord	0.70	0.69	0.67	0.65	0.63
Average	1.22	1.31	1.30	1.28	1.28

Efficiency Measures

Total Cost per 1,000 Gallons of Treated Wastewater

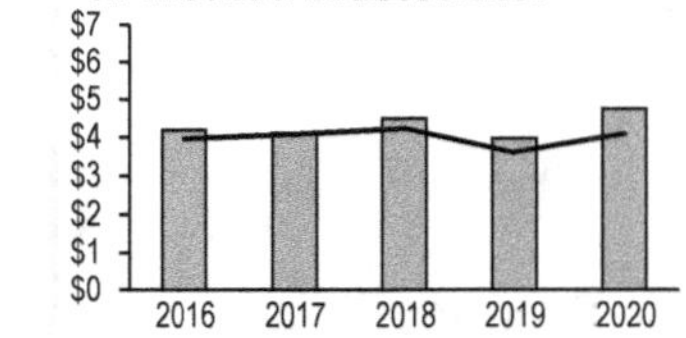

	2016	2017	2018	2019	2020
Concord	$4.19	$4.10	$4.50	$3.98	$4.75
Average	$3.96	$4.07	$4.21	$3.59	$4.08

Million Gallons of Wastewater per Wastewater Services FTE

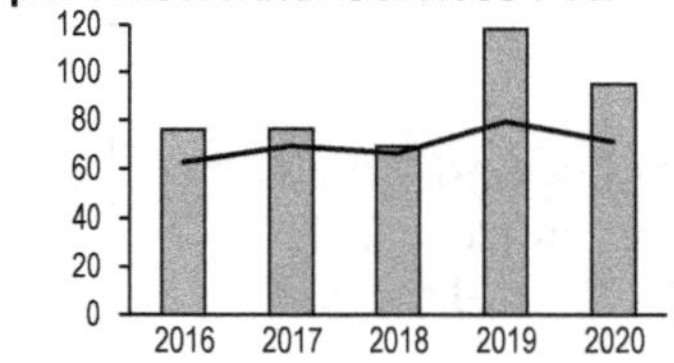

	2016	2017	2018	2019	2020
Concord	76.2	76.4	69.3	118.6	95.2
Average	62.7	69.2	66.3	79.4	71.2

Customer Accounts per Wastewater Services FTE

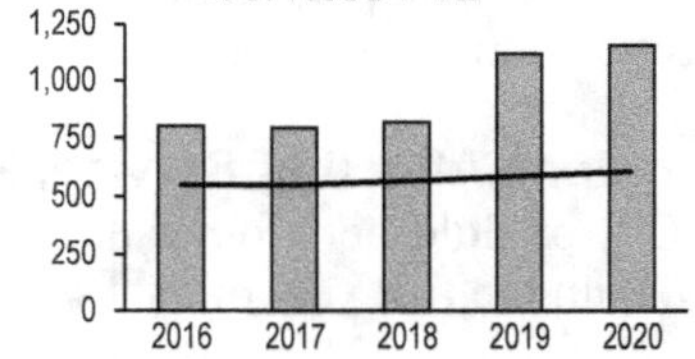

	2016	2017	2018	2019	2020
Concord	802	793	818	1,123	1,162
Average	545	547	563	584	603

Effectiveness Measures

Percentage of Wastewater Bills Not Collected

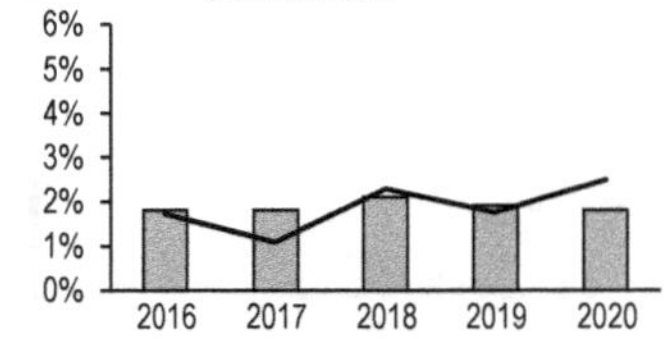

	2016	2017	2018	2019	2020
Concord	1.81%	1.81%	2.10%	1.91%	1.81%
Average	1.72%	1.09%	2.27%	1.74%	2.49%

Average Daily Treatment as a Percentage of Capacity

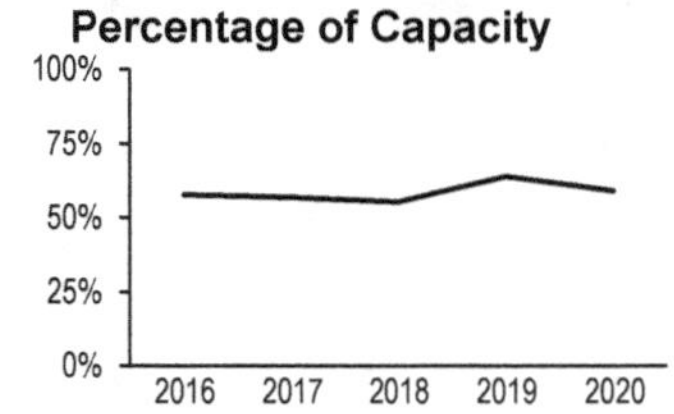

	2016	2017	2018	2019	2020
Concord					
Average	57.6%	56.7%	55.3%	63.8%	58.8%

Percent of Main Line Rehabbed or Replaced

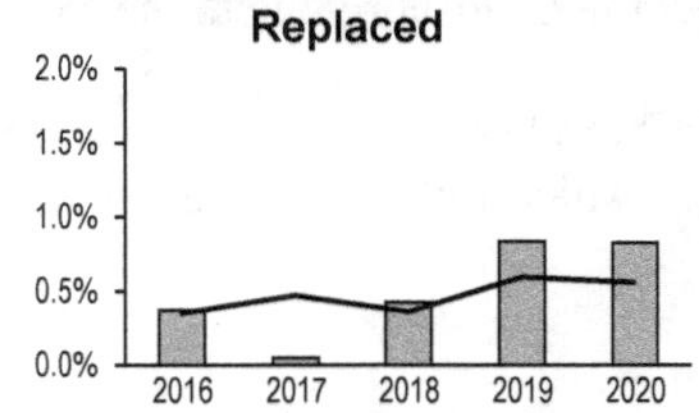

	2016	2017	2018	2019	2020
Concord	0.37%	0.05%	0.43%	0.83%	0.82%
Average	0.35%	0.47%	0.36%	0.59%	0.56%

Overflows per 100 Miles of Main Line Pipe

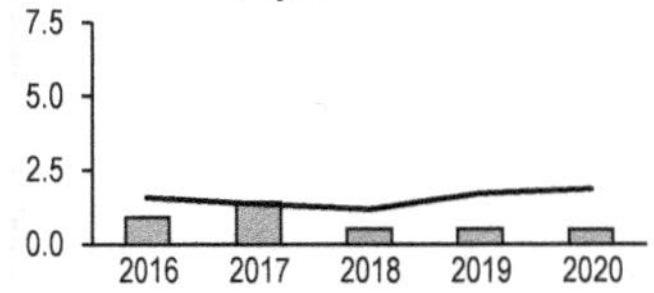

	2016	2017	2018	2019	2020
Concord	0.92	1.42	0.52	0.51	0.50
Average	1.57	1.34	1.17	1.68	1.85

Backups per 100 Miles of Main Line Pipe

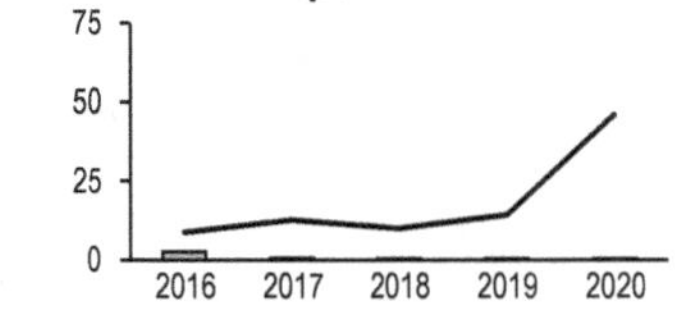

	2016	2017	2018	2019	2020
Concord	2.75	0.53	0.52	0.51	0.50
Average	8.83	12.62	10.08	14.21	45.98

Billed Wastewater as a Percent of Treated Effluent

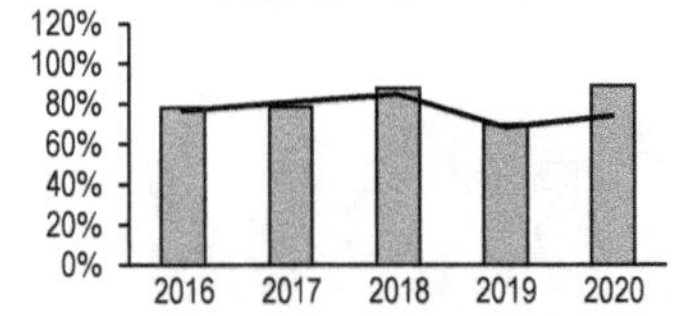

	2016	2017	2018	2019	2020
Concord	78%	78%	88%	70%	89%
Average	76%	81%	84%	68%	74%

Fiscal Year 2019-20

Explanatory Information

Service Level and Delivery

Wastewater treatment in Goldsboro is a joint responsibility between the Public Works and Public Utilities Departments. The Public Works Director oversees both departments. The Public Works Department is responsible for the collection and distribution system lines. The Public Utilities Department is responsible for the operation of the water treatment plant, the water reclamation facility, and pump stations.

The sewer system covers the city of Goldsboro and receives wastewater from neighboring systems in Wayne County. Wastewater treatment is done by one plant with a total treatment capacity of 14.2 million gallons per day. The plant uses advanced biological processes to remove pollutants from the water. Besides removing oxygen consuming wastes, the facility is able to remove nutrients such as nitrogen and phosphorus to very low levels. The system has nutrient regulatory limits in place that restrict what can be discharged in order to protect water quality. All biosolids produced by the Goldsboro treatment plant are dewatered and then composted.

During the fiscal year, the system had two regulatory violations with the treatment portion of the system and one violation for the collection portion of the system.

Conditions Affecting Service, Performance, and Costs

The City of Goldsboro joined the Benchmarking Project in July 2017, with the first year of data showing for FY 2016–17.

The costs of wastewater or sewer services as captured here do not include debt service but do capture depreciation of capital.

Hurricane Matthew in October 2016 put stress on the wastewater system in Goldsboro due to the extensive flooding.

Goldsboro has improved its tracking system for a number of data items, which reflects greater accuracy in the most recent year.

Municipal Profile

Estimated Service Population	34,234
Service Land Area (Square Miles)	25
Persons per Square Mile	1,369
Topography	Flat; gently rolling
Climate	Temperate; little ice and snow
Median Household Income U.S. Census 2016	$32,148

Service Profile

Total FTE Staff Positions	30.0
Treatment Plant	10.0
Line Crews	5.0
Billing/Collection	6.0
Other	9.0
Number of Treatment Plants	1
Total Treatment Capacity	14.2 MGD
Average Daily Flow	9.0 MGD
River Basin into Which System Discharges	Neuse
Miles of Gravity Main Line Pipe	227
Miles of Forced Main Line Pipe	17
Average Age of Main Line Pipe	70 years
Blocks in Sewer Mains	40
Number of System Breaks	27
Sanitary System Overflows	5
Number of Customer Accounts	11,392
Total Revenues Collected	$8,360,137

Full Cost Profile

Cost Breakdown by Percentage	
Personal Services	33.6%
Operating Costs	62.8%
Capital Costs	3.6%
TOTAL	100.0%

Cost Breakdown in Dollars	
Personal Services	$1,317,265
Operating Costs	$2,459,698
Capital Costs	$140,897
TOTAL	$3,917,860

Key: Goldsboro ▪ Benchmarking Average — Fiscal Years 2016 through 2020

Resource Measures

Wastewater Services Cost per Capita

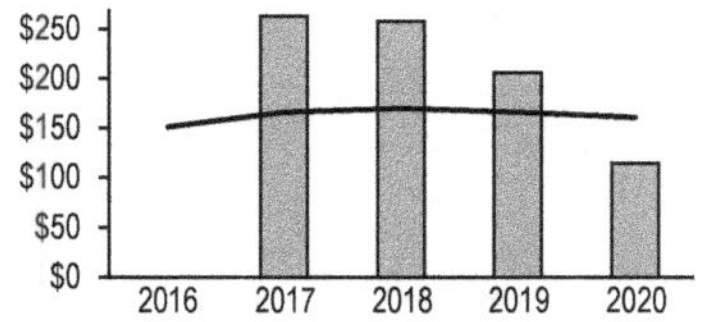

	2016	2017	2018	2019	2020
Goldsboro		$263	$258	$206	$114
Average	$151	$166	$169	$165	$160

Wastewater Services FTEs per 10,000 Population

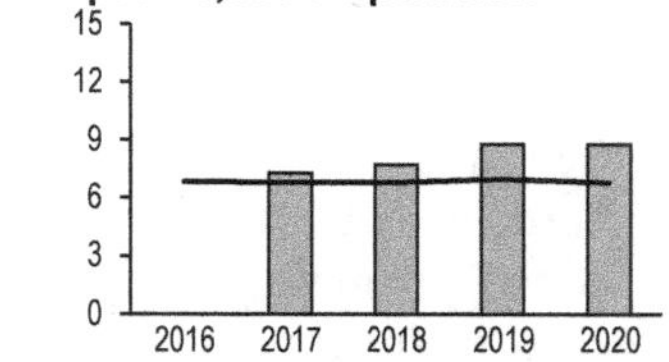

	2016	2017	2018	2019	2020
Goldsboro		7.3	7.7	8.8	8.8
Average	6.8	6.8	6.8	6.9	6.8

Wastewater Services Cost per Customer Account

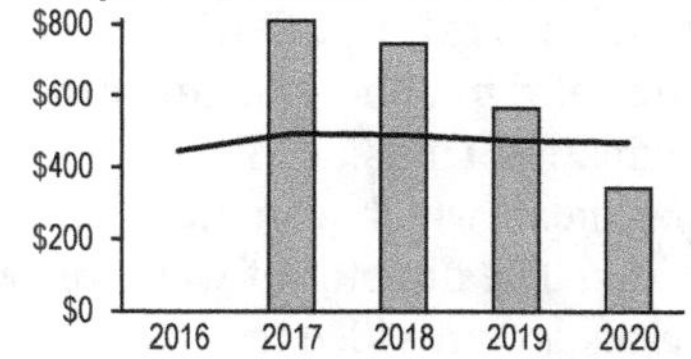

	2016	2017	2018	2019	2020
Goldsboro		$810	$746	$565	$344
Average	$445	$494	$490	$473	$471

Workload Measures

Thousands of Gallons of Wastewater per Account

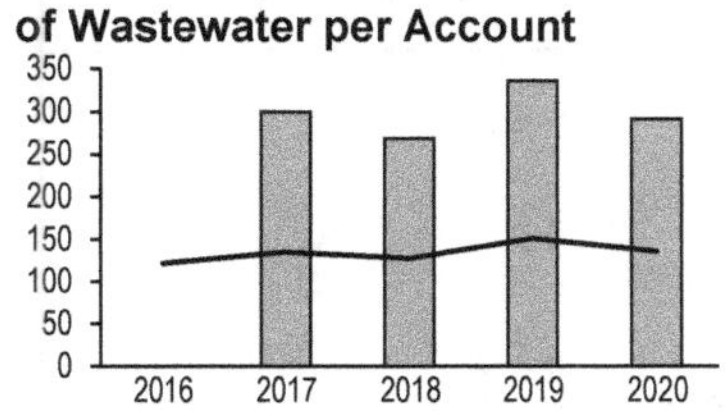

	2016	2017	2018	2019	2020
Goldsboro		299.3	268.3	335.7	291.6
Average	121.0	135.0	126.9	150.7	135.2

Miles of Sewer Main Line Pipe per Square Mile of Service Area

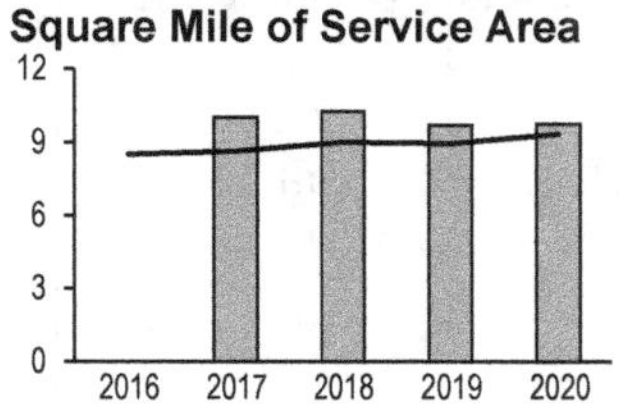

	2016	2017	2018	2019	2020
Goldsboro		10.0	10.3	9.7	9.8
Average	8.5	8.6	9.0	8.9	9.3

Number of Lift Stations per 1,000 Accounts

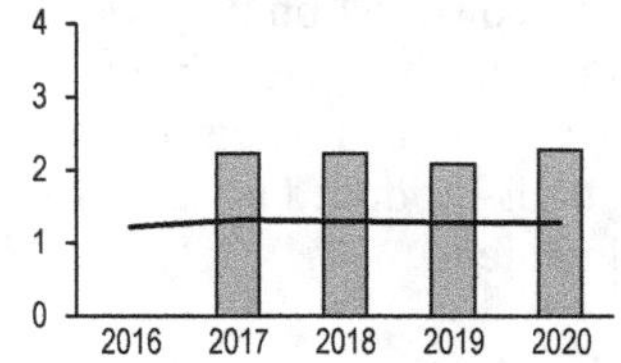

	2016	2017	2018	2019	2020
Goldsboro		2.23	2.23	2.09	2.28
Average	1.22	1.31	1.30	1.28	1.28

Efficiency Measures

Total Cost per 1,000 Gallons of Treated Wastewater

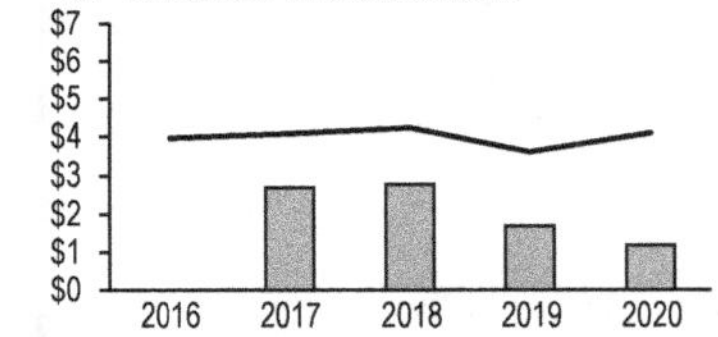

	2016	2017	2018	2019	2020
Goldsboro		$2.70	$2.78	$1.68	$1.18
Average	$3.96	$4.07	$4.21	$3.59	$4.08

Million Gallons of Wastewater per Wastewater Services FTE

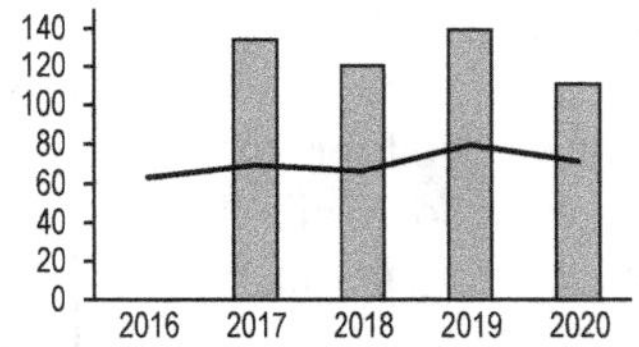

	2016	2017	2018	2019	2020
Goldsboro		134.0	120.1	139.4	110.7
Average	62.7	69.2	66.3	79.4	71.2

Customer Accounts per Wastewater Services FTE

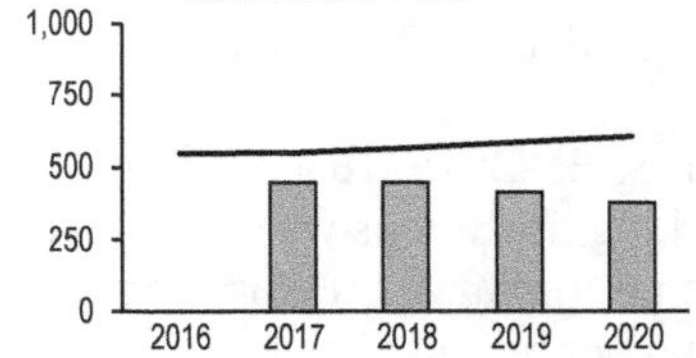

	2016	2017	2018	2019	2020
Goldsboro		448	448	415	380
Average	545	547	563	584	603

Effectiveness Measures

Percentage of Wastewater Bills Not Collected

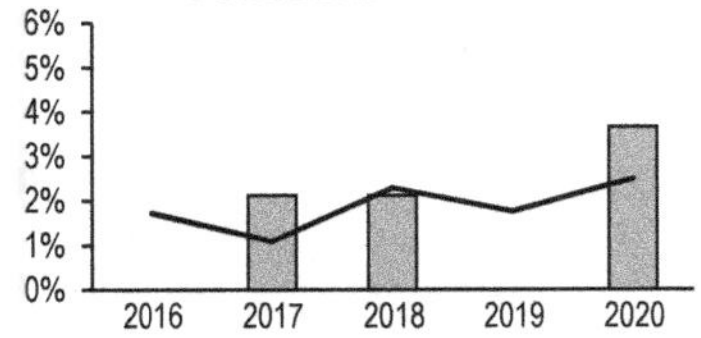

	2016	2017	2018	2019	2020
Goldsboro		2.11%	2.11%		3.66%
Average	1.72%	1.09%	2.27%	1.74%	2.49%

Average Daily Treatment as a Percentage of Capacity

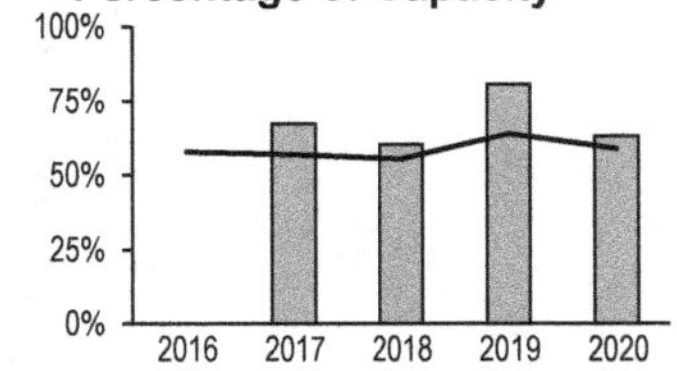

	2016	2017	2018	2019	2020
Goldsboro		67.3%	60.3%	80.7%	63.2%
Average	57.6%	56.7%	55.3%	63.8%	58.8%

Percent of Main Line Rehabbed or Replaced

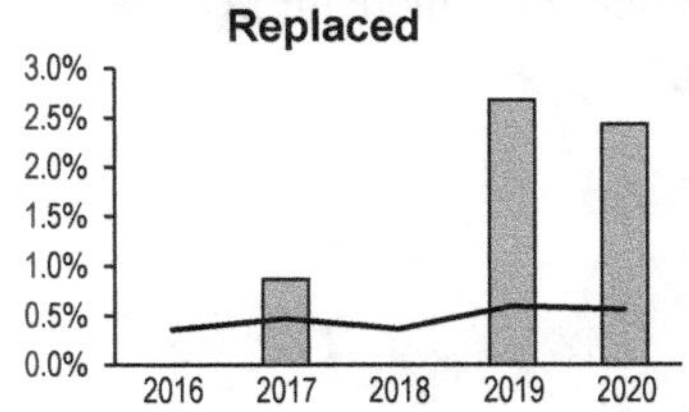

	2016	2017	2018	2019	2020
Goldsboro		0.87%	0.00%	2.68%	2.43%
Average	0.35%	0.47%	0.36%	0.59%	0.56%

Overflows per 100 Miles of Main Line Pipe

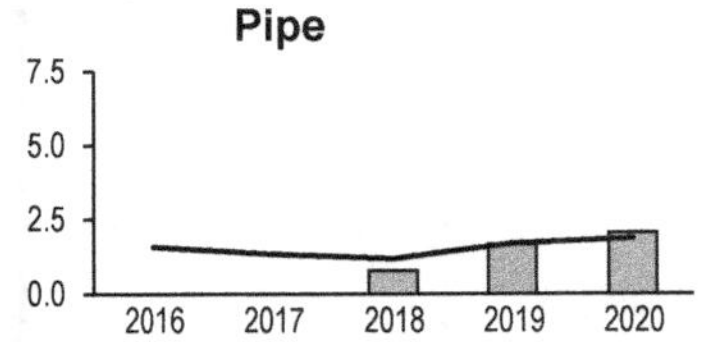

	2016	2017	2018	2019	2020
Goldsboro		0.00	0.78	1.65	2.05
Average	1.57	1.34	1.17	1.68	1.85

Backups per 100 Miles of Main Line Pipe

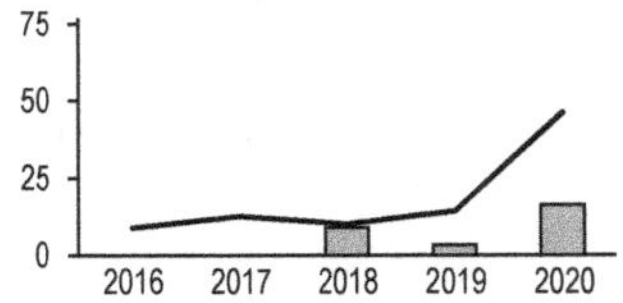

	2016	2017	2018	2019	2020
Goldsboro		0.00	8.95	3.29	16.39
Average	8.83	12.62	10.08	14.21	45.98

Billed Wastewater as a Percent of Treated Effluent

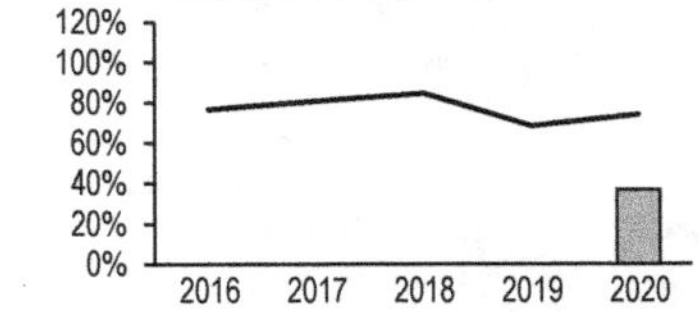

	2016	2017	2018	2019	2020
Goldsboro					37%
Average	76%	81%	84%	68%	74%

Fiscal Year 2019-20

Explanatory Information

Service Level and Delivery

Wastewater treatment in Greensboro is handled by the Water Reclamation Division. This is part of the Water Resources Department, which also includes stormwater and drinking water services. The director of water resources reports to the city manager. Services are provided to most of the City of Greensboro and to some addresses outside city limits within Guilford County.

Wastewater treatment in Greensboro is now handled by one treatment plant. In October 2017 one plant was decommissioned, with the effective capacity transferred to the remaining plant through a large construction upgrade. This plant uses advanced tertiary treatment. The system has nutrient regulatory limits in place that restrict what can be discharged in order to protect water quality. All biosolids produced by the Greensboro treatment plant are incinerated.

During the fiscal year, the system had three regulatory violations connected to the treatment portion of the system. No violations connected to the collection portion of the system were reported.

Conditions Affecting Service, Performance, and Costs

The costs of wastewater or sewer services as captured here do not include debt service but do capture depreciation of capital.

During FY 2015–16 a conversion to a new database used for tracking operations was undertaken. Some data were not available. The performance measure "backups per 100 miles of main line pipe" could not be calculated.

The full implementation of a new asset management system designed for utilities took place in FY 2016–17. Work orders are now assigned and tracked by more specific types of duties, which resulted in an increase in certain metrics over prior years.

Municipal Profile

Estimated Service Population	315,328
Service Land Area (Square Miles)	148
Persons per Square Mile	2,131
Topography	Flat; gently rolling
Climate	Temperate; little ice and snow
Median Household Income U.S. Census 2016	$40,760

Service Profile

Total FTE Staff Positions	153.0
Treatment Plant	50.0
Line Crews	72.5
Billing/Collection	7.5
Other	23.0
Number of Treatment Plants	1
Total Treatment Capacity	56.0 MGD
Average Daily Flow	35.5 MGD
River Basin into Which System Discharges	Cape Fear
Miles of Gravity Main Line Pipe	1,444
Miles of Forced Main Line Pipe	75
Average Age of Main Line Pipe	40 years
Blocks in Sewer Mains	2,886
Number of System Breaks	909
Sanitary System Overflows	47
Number of Customer Accounts	106,024
Total Revenues Collected	$62,177,944

Full Cost Profile

Cost Breakdown by Percentage	
Personal Services	18.5%
Operating Costs	55.7%
Capital Costs	25.7%
TOTAL	100.0%

Cost Breakdown in Dollars	
Personal Services	$7,854,398
Operating Costs	$23,597,678
Capital Costs	$10,892,688
TOTAL	$42,344,764

Greensboro — Wastewater Services

Key: Greensboro ▒ Benchmarking Average — Fiscal Years 2016 through 2020

Resource Measures

Wastewater Services Cost per Capita

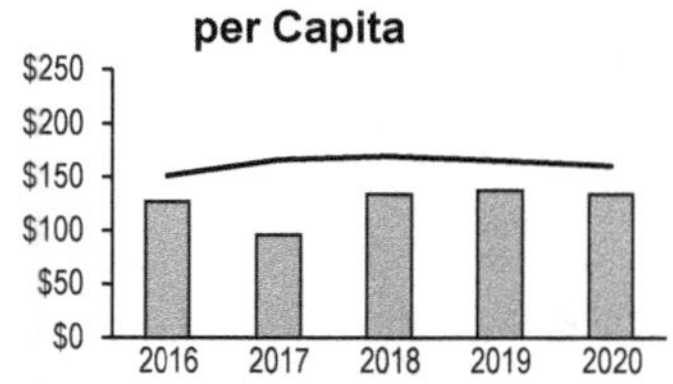

	2016	2017	2018	2019	2020
Greensboro	$127	$96	$134	$138	$134
Average	$151	$166	$169	$165	$160

Wastewater Services FTEs per 10,000 Population

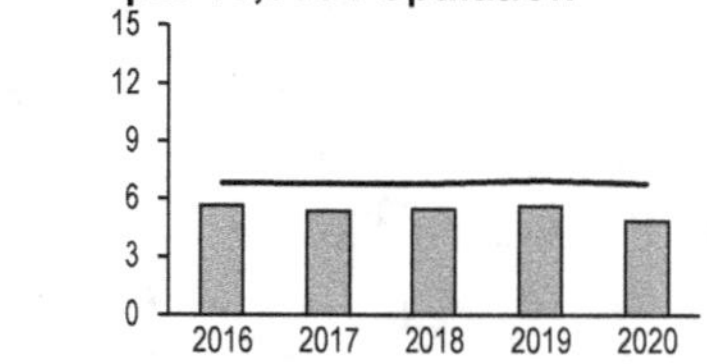

	2016	2017	2018	2019	2020
Greensboro	5.7	5.3	5.4	5.6	4.9
Average	6.8	6.8	6.8	6.9	6.8

Wastewater Services Cost per Customer Account

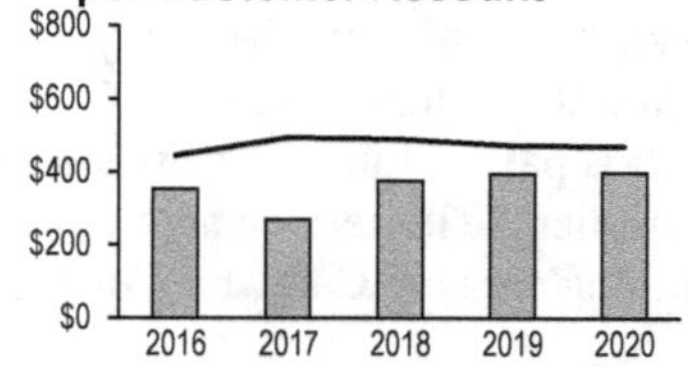

	2016	2017	2018	2019	2020
Greensboro	$353	$268	$375	$395	$399
Average	$445	$494	$490	$473	$471

Workload Measures

Thousands of Gallons of Wastewater per Account

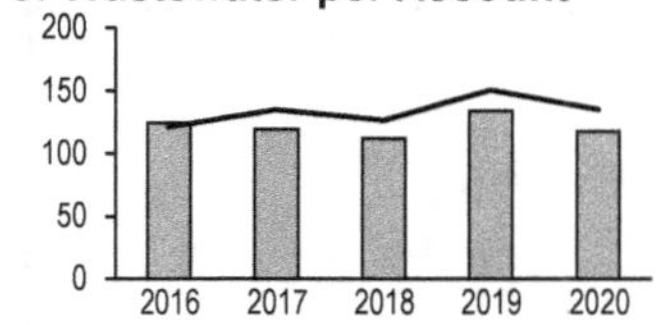

	2016	2017	2018	2019	2020
Greensboro	124.9	119.3	112.2	134.3	118.1
Average	121.0	135.0	126.9	150.7	135.2

Miles of Sewer Main Line Pipe per Square Mile of Service Area

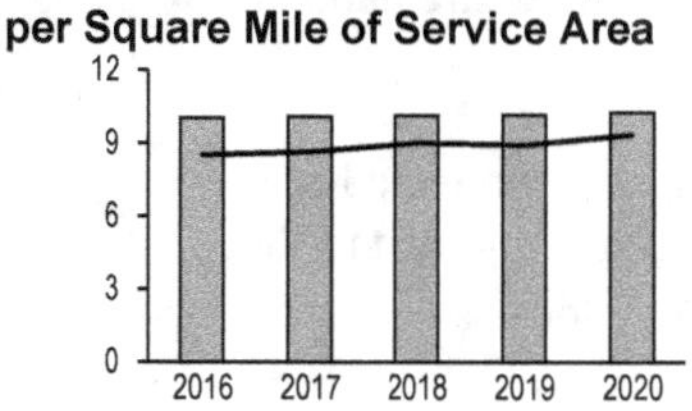

	2016	2017	2018	2019	2020
Greensboro	10.0	10.1	10.2	10.2	10.3
Average	8.5	8.6	9.0	8.9	9.3

Number of Lift Stations per 1,000 Accounts

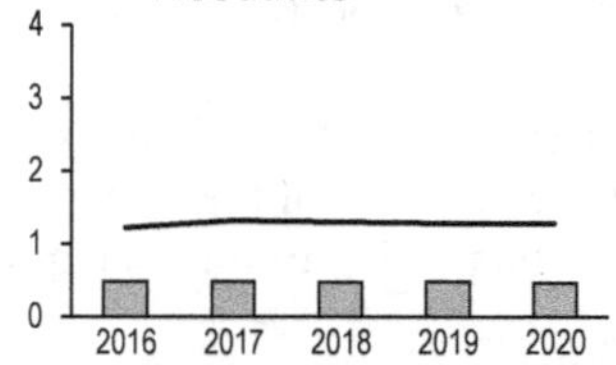

	2016	2017	2018	2019	2020
Greensboro	0.48	0.48	0.48	0.49	0.47
Average	1.22	1.31	1.30	1.28	1.28

Efficiency Measures

Total Cost per 1,000 Gallons of Treated Wastewater

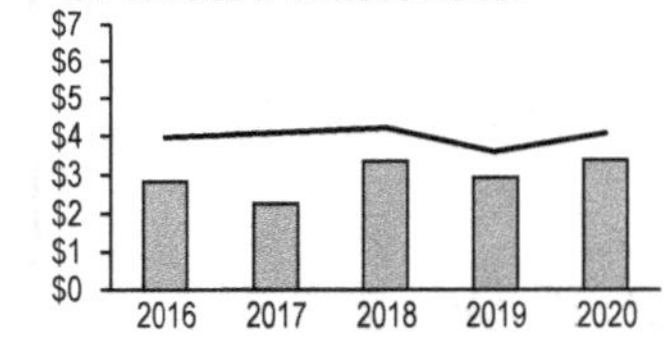

	2016	2017	2018	2019	2020
Greensboro	$2.82	$2.25	$3.34	$2.94	$3.38
Average	$3.96	$4.07	$4.21	$3.59	$4.08

Million Gallons of Wastewater per Wastewater Services FTE

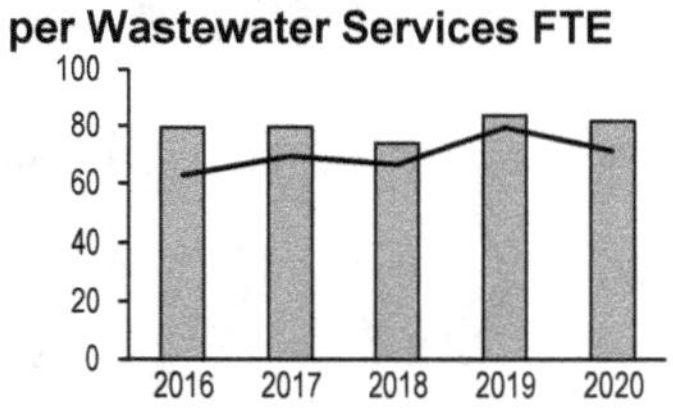

	2016	2017	2018	2019	2020
Greensboro	79.4	79.6	73.8	83.7	81.8
Average	62.7	69.2	66.3	79.4	71.2

Customer Accounts per Wastewater Services FTE

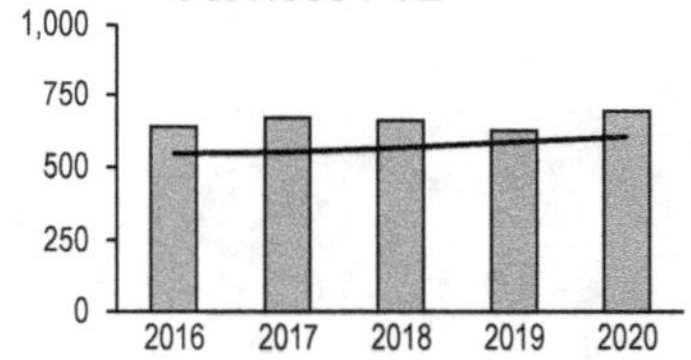

	2016	2017	2018	2019	2020
Greensboro	636	668	658	623	693
Average	545	547	563	584	603

Effectiveness Measures

Percentage of Wastewater Bills Not Collected

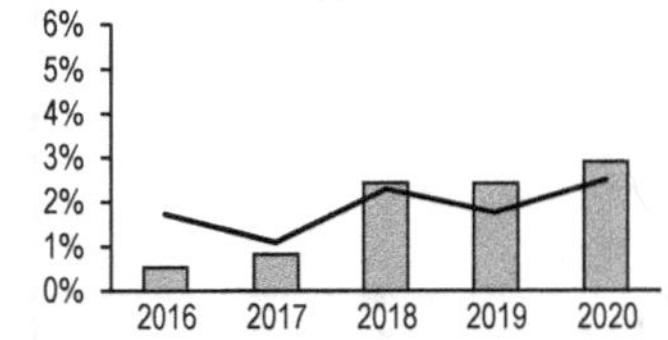

	2016	2017	2018	2019	2020
Greensboro	0.53%	0.82%	2.42%	2.40%	2.90%
Average	1.72%	1.09%	2.27%	1.74%	2.49%

Average Daily Treatment as a Percentage of Capacity

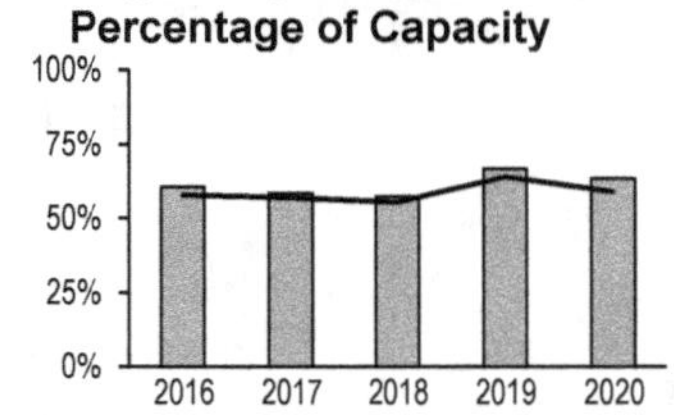

	2016	2017	2018	2019	2020
Greensboro	60.5%	58.3%	57.3%	66.7%	63.4%
Average	57.6%	56.7%	55.3%	63.8%	58.8%

Percent of Main Line Rehabbed or Replaced

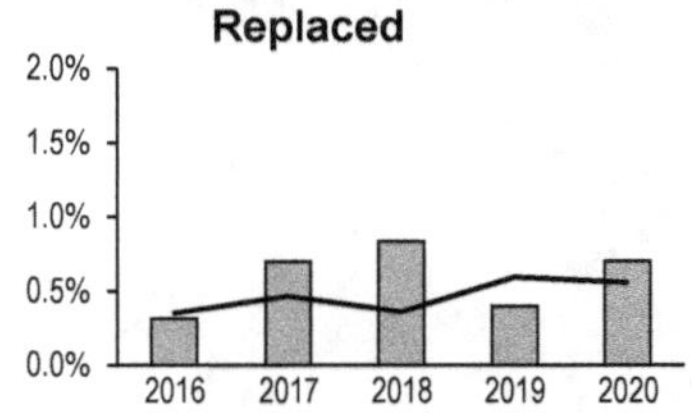

	2016	2017	2018	2019	2020
Greensboro	0.32%	0.70%	0.83%	0.40%	0.70%
Average	0.35%	0.47%	0.36%	0.59%	0.56%

Overflows per 100 Miles of Main Line Pipe

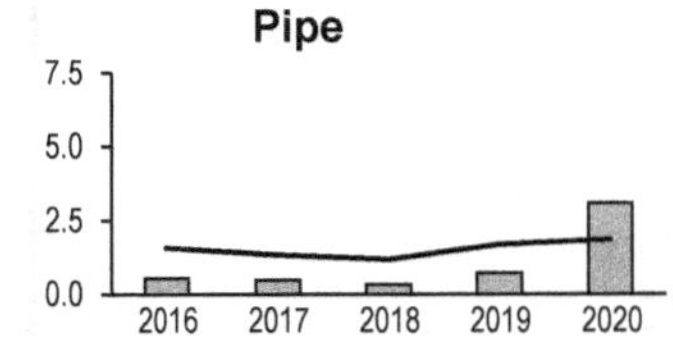

	2016	2017	2018	2019	2020
Greensboro	0.54	0.47	0.33	0.73	3.09
Average	1.57	1.34	1.17	1.68	1.85

Backups per 100 Miles of Main Line Pipe

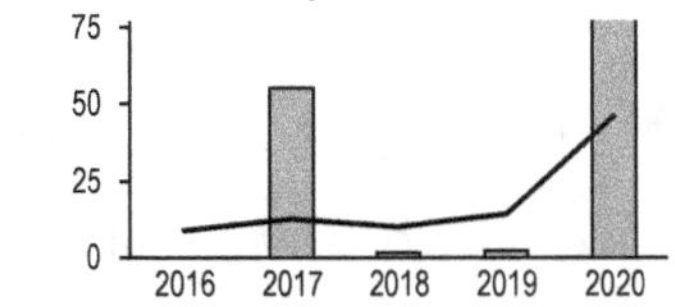

	2016	2017	2018	2019	2020
Greensboro		55.13	1.66	2.46	189.98
Average	8.83	12.62	10.08	14.21	45.98

Billed Wastewater as a Percent of Treated Effluent

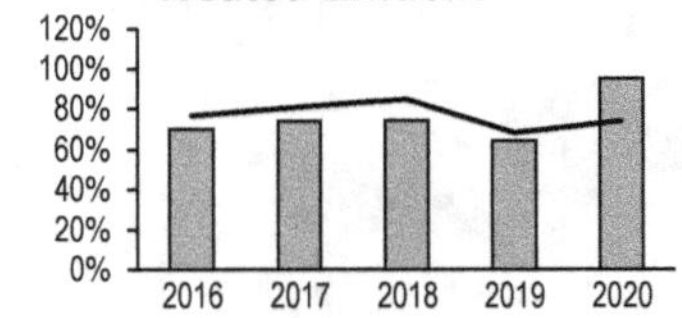

	2016	2017	2018	2019	2020
Greensboro	70%	74%	74%	64%	95%
Average	76%	81%	84%	68%	74%

Fiscal Year 2019-20

Explanatory Information

Service Level and Delivery

Wastewater is handled by the City of Hickory's Collection Division, which is part of Public Utilities under the Public Services Department. The service area covers the City of Hickory and several adjoining areas in Catawba County.

The system relies on three treatment plants to handle wastewater. One plant uses activated-sludge biological nutrient removal (BNR), the second uses oxidation-ditch-activated-sludge BNR, and the third uses conventional activated sludge. The entire system does not have nutrient limits in place at this time. Biosolids generated are handled as Class A compost.

The system in Hickory had six regulatory violations connected to the treatment portion of the system and five violations connected to the collection portion of the system during the fiscal year.

Conditions Affecting Service, Performance, and Costs

The costs of wastewater or sewer services as captured here do not include debt service but do capture depreciation of capital.

Municipal Profile

Estimated Service Population	37,478
Service Land Area (Square Miles)	65.0
Persons per Square Mile	577
Topography	Gently rolling
Climate	Temperate; some ice and snow
Median Household Income U.S. Census 2016	$35,353

Service Profile

Total FTE Staff Positions	44.0
Treatment Plant	29.0
Line Crews	10.0
Billing/Collection	2.5
Other	2.5
Number of Treatment Plants	3
Total Treatment Capacity	16.5 MGD
Average Daily Flow	5.9 MGD
River Basin into Which System Discharges	Catawba
Miles of Gravity Main Line Pipe	501
Miles of Forced Main Line Pipe	43
Average Age of Main Line Pipe	48 years
Blocks in Sewer Mains	188
Number of System Breaks	12
Sanitary System Overflows	5
Number of Customer Accounts	16,153
Total Revenues Collected	$11,619,690

Full Cost Profile

Cost Breakdown by Percentage	
Personal Services	38.7%
Operating Costs	44.8%
Capital Costs	16.6%
TOTAL	100.0%

Cost Breakdown in Dollars	
Personal Services	$3,125,920
Operating Costs	$3,622,469
Capital Costs	$1,338,507
TOTAL	$8,086,896

Hickory — Wastewater Services

Key: Hickory ■ Benchmarking Average — Fiscal Years 2016 through 2020

Resource Measures

Wastewater Services Cost per Capita

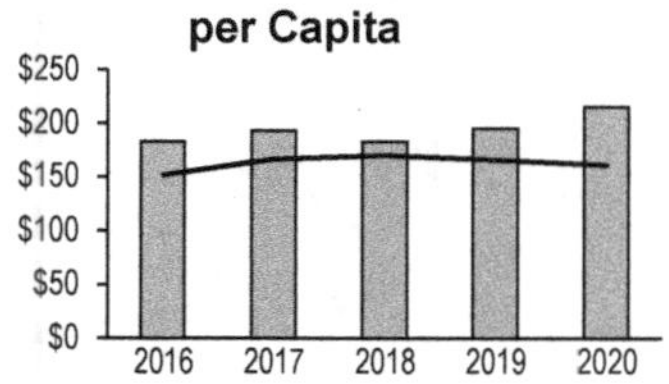

	2016	2017	2018	2019	2020
Hickory	$183	$193	$182	$195	$216
Average	$151	$166	$169	$165	$160

Wastewater Services FTEs per 10,000 Population

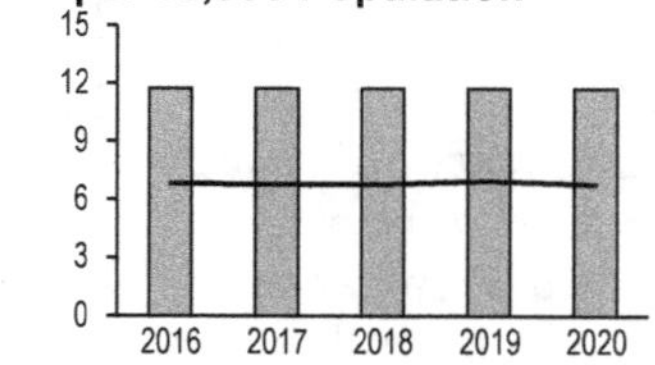

	2016	2017	2018	2019	2020
Hickory	11.7	11.7	11.7	11.7	11.7
Average	6.8	6.8	6.8	6.9	6.8

Wastewater Services Cost per Customer Account

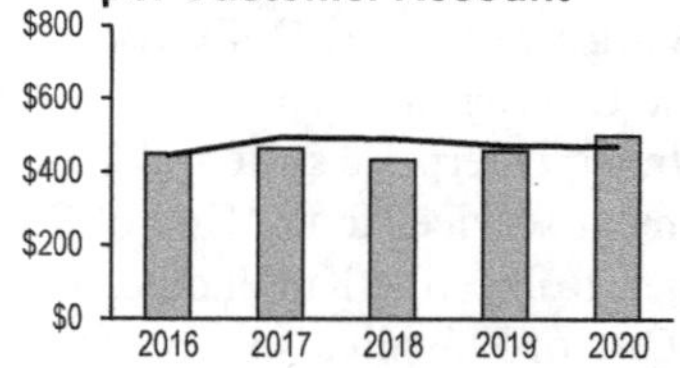

	2016	2017	2018	2019	2020
Hickory	$450	$465	$435	$459	$501
Average	$445	$494	$490	$473	$471

Workload Measures

Thousands of Gallons of Wastewater per Account

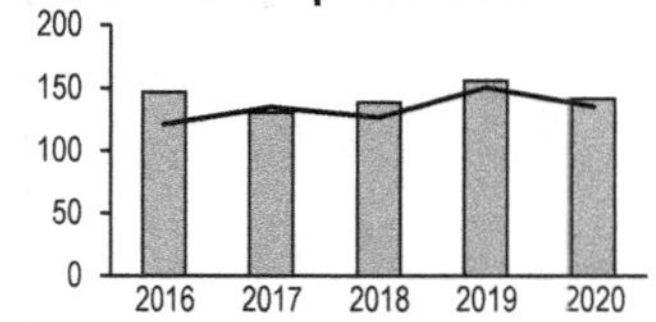

	2016	2017	2018	2019	2020
Hickory	147.3	131.0	138.7	156.6	142.3
Average	121.0	135.0	126.9	150.7	135.2

Miles of Sewer Main Line Pipe per Square Mile of Service Area

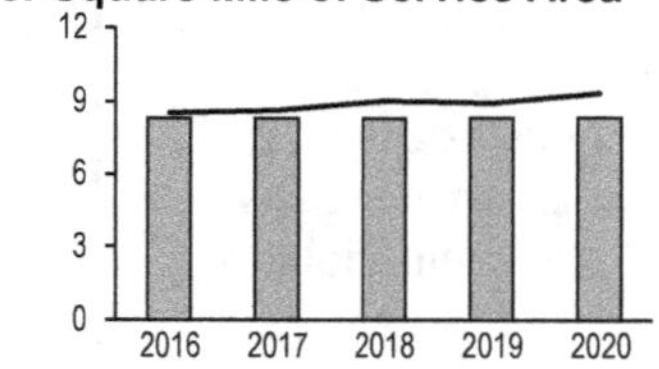

	2016	2017	2018	2019	2020
Hickory	8.3	8.3	8.3	8.3	8.4
Average	8.5	8.6	9.0	8.9	9.3

Number of Lift Stations per 1,000 Accounts

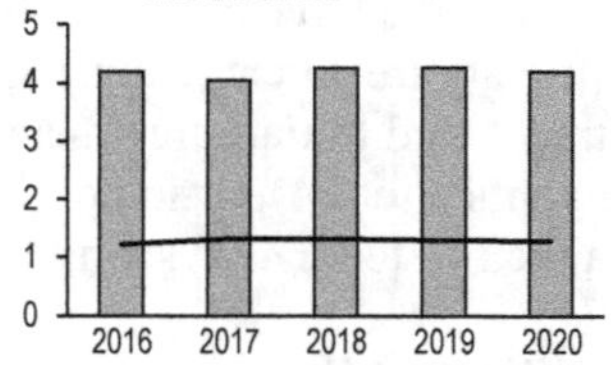

	2016	2017	2018	2019	2020
Hickory	4.20	4.05	4.26	4.27	4.21
Average	1.22	1.31	1.30	1.28	1.28

Efficiency Measures

Total Cost per 1,000 Gallons of Treated Wastewater

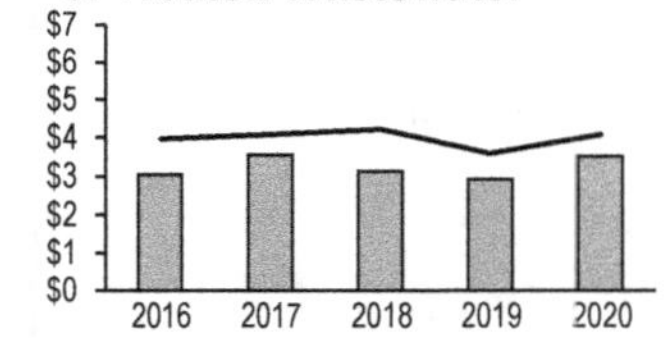

	2016	2017	2018	2019	2020
Hickory	$3.05	$3.55	$3.13	$2.93	$3.52
Average	$3.96	$4.07	$4.21	$3.59	$4.08

Million Gallons of Wastewater per Wastewater Services FTE

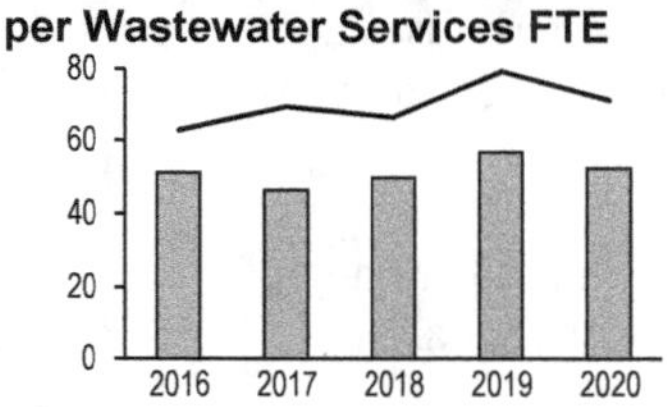

	2016	2017	2018	2019	2020
Hickory	51.0	46.3	49.6	56.7	52.2
Average	62.7	69.2	66.3	79.4	71.2

Customer Accounts per Wastewater Services FTE

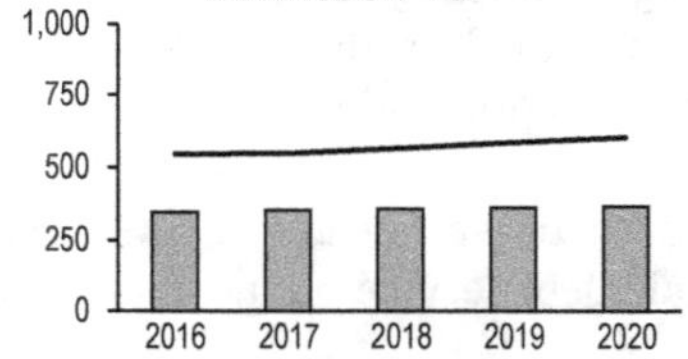

	2016	2017	2018	2019	2020
Hickory	346	353	358	362	367
Average	545	547	563	584	603

Effectiveness Measures

Percentage of Wastewater Bills Not Collected

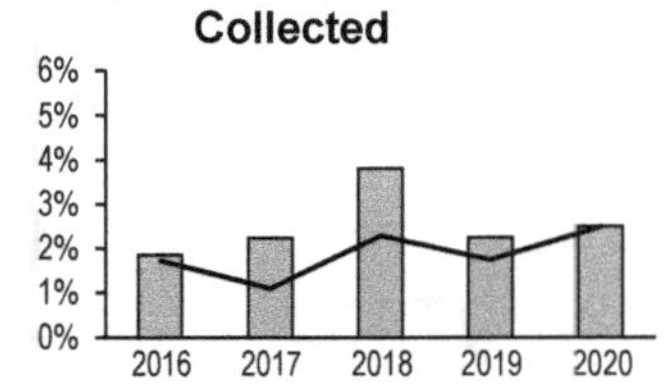

	2016	2017	2018	2019	2020
Hickory	1.86%	2.24%	3.81%	2.25%	2.50%
Average	1.72%	1.09%	2.27%	1.74%	2.49%

Average Daily Treatment as a Percentage of Capacity

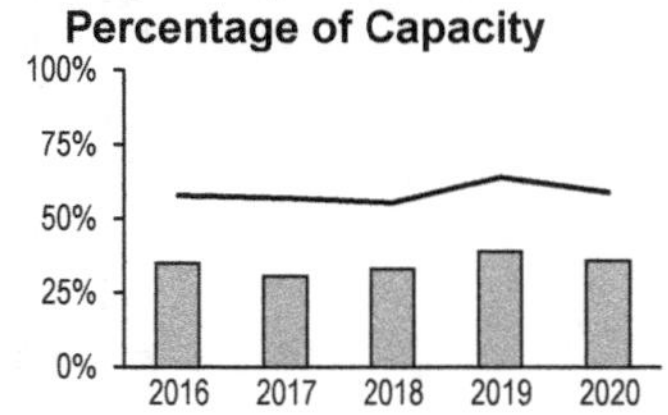

	2016	2017	2018	2019	2020
Hickory	34.8%	30.6%	32.9%	38.8%	35.7%
Average	57.6%	56.7%	55.3%	63.8%	58.8%

Percent of Main Line Rehabbed or Replaced

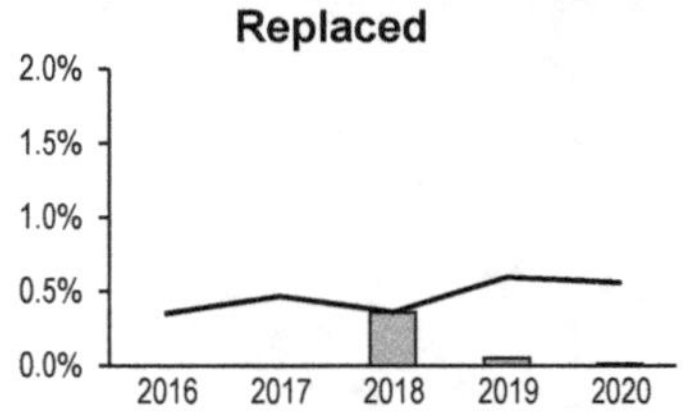

	2016	2017	2018	2019	2020
Hickory	0.00%	0.00%	0.36%	0.05%	0.01%
Average	0.35%	0.47%	0.36%	0.59%	0.56%

Overflows per 100 Miles of Main Line Pipe

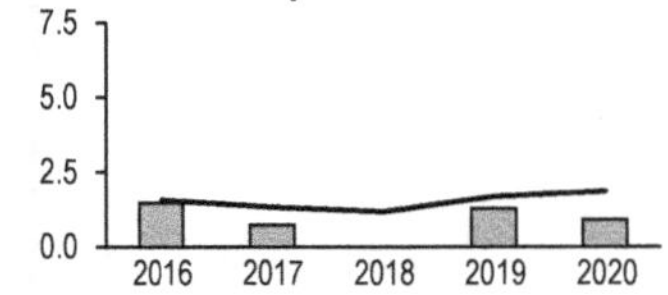

	2016	2017	2018	2019	2020
Hickory	1.48	0.74	0.00	1.29	0.92
Average	1.57	1.34	1.17	1.68	1.85

Backups per 100 Miles of Main Line Pipe

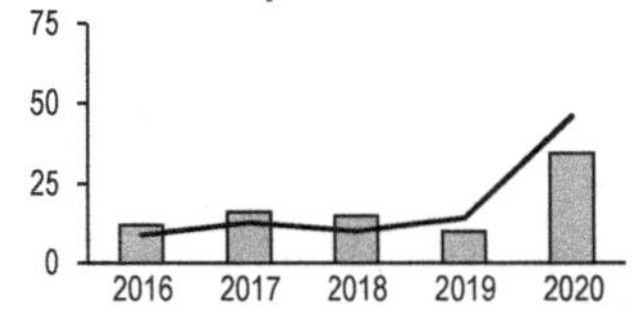

	2016	2017	2018	2019	2020
Hickory	12.04	16.11	15.00	10.16	34.56
Average	8.83	12.62	10.08	14.21	45.98

Billed Wastewater as a Percent of Treated Effluent

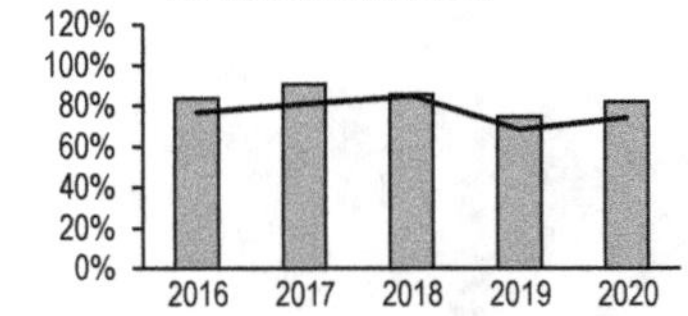

	2016	2017	2018	2019	2020
Hickory	83%	91%	86%	75%	82%
Average	76%	81%	84%	68%	74%

Fiscal Year 2019-20

Explanatory Information

Service Level and Delivery

Public Utilities is a department within the City of Raleigh. It is a combined enterprise system that provides drinking water and sewage treatment services to the City of Raleigh and six merger towns: Garner, Rolesville, Knightdale, Wake Forest, Wendell, and Zebulon. The City of Raleigh also provides wastewater treatment for the Towns of Middlesex and Clayton. As of FY 2020, approximately 592,000 people live in the contractual service area of 299 square miles.

Wastewater is treated at three plants. The total combined treatment capacity at the three plants is 80.2 million gallons per day. The plants use primary treatment, a nutrient removal process for secondary treatment, and tertiary treatment along with biosolids treatment and land application. A portion of the treated effluent is distributed as reclaimed water. The system had no wastewater treatment violations.

Conditions Affecting Service, Performance, and Costs

Raleigh rejoined the Benchmarking Project in July 2016, with the first year of data showing for FY 2015–16.

The Utility has a full-functioning farm with a dedicated Land Management program consisting of 15 FTEs. The farm uses a portion of the biosolids produced at the plant as fertilizer to grow soybeans, corn, and hay.

The costs of wastewater or sewer services as captured here do not include debt service but do capture depreciation of capital.

Municipal Profile

Estimated Service Population	591,943
Service Land Area (Square Miles)	299.0
Persons per Square Mile	1,980
Topography	Flat; gently rolling
Climate	Temperate; little ice and snow
Median Household Income U.S. Census 2016	$46,612

Service Profile

Total FTE Staff Positions	347.0
Treatment Plant	46.0
Line Crews	140.0
Billing/Collection	35.0
Other	126.0
Number of Treatment Plants	3
Total Treatment Capacity	80.2 MGD
Average Daily Flow	50.2 MGD
River Basin into Which System Discharges	Neuse
Miles of Gravity Main Line Pipe	2,374
Miles of Forced Main Line Pipe	130
Average Age of Main Line Pipe	34 years
Blocks in Sewer Mains	na
Number of System Breaks	238
Sanitary System Overflows	36
Number of Customer Accounts	179,463
Total Revenues Collected	$146,295,529

Full Cost Profile

Cost Breakdown by Percentage	
Personal Services	38.5%
Operating Costs	42.7%
Capital Costs	18.7%
TOTAL	100.0%
Cost Breakdown in Dollars	
Personal Services	$27,029,979
Operating Costs	$29,976,417
Capital Costs	$13,143,676
TOTAL	$70,150,072

Raleigh — Wastewater Services

Key: Raleigh ▒ Benchmarking Average — Fiscal Years 2016 through 2020

Resource Measures

Wastewater Services Cost per Capita

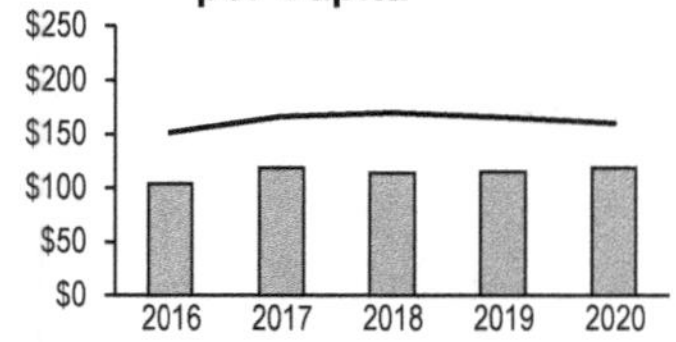

	2016	2017	2018	2019	2020
Raleigh	$104	$119	$114	$115	$119
Average	$151	$166	$169	$165	$160

Wastewater Services FTEs per 10,000 Population

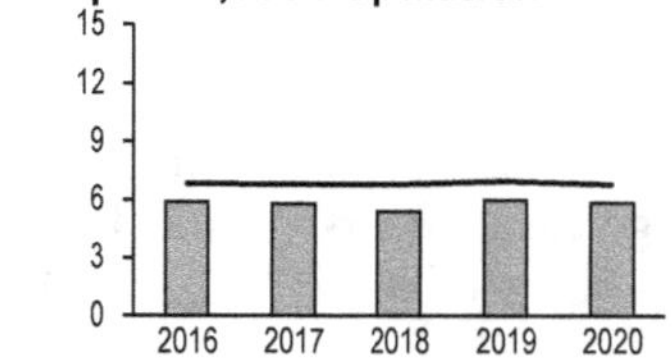

	2016	2017	2018	2019	2020
Raleigh	5.9	5.8	5.4	6.0	5.9
Average	6.8	6.8	6.8	6.9	6.8

Wastewater Services Cost per Customer Account

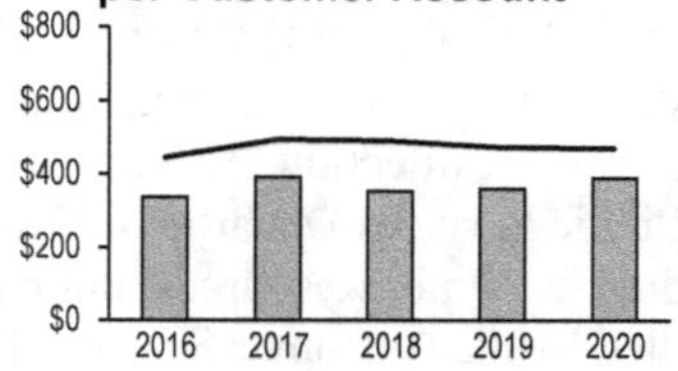

	2016	2017	2018	2019	2020
Raleigh	$337	$391	$353	$360	$391
Average	$445	$494	$490	$473	$471

Workload Measures

Thousands of Gallons of Wastewater per Account

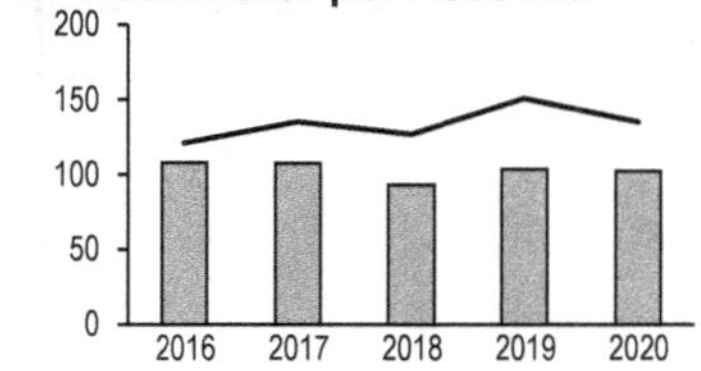

	2016	2017	2018	2019	2020
Raleigh	107.9	107.3	93.2	103.4	102.4
Average	121.0	135.0	126.9	150.7	135.2

Miles of Sewer Main Line Pipe per Square Mile of Service Area

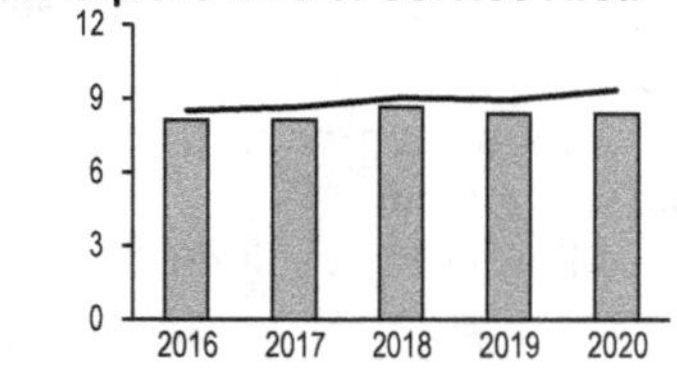

	2016	2017	2018	2019	2020
Raleigh	8.1	8.1	8.6	8.4	8.4
Average	8.5	8.6	9.0	8.9	9.3

Number of Lift Stations per 1,000 Accounts

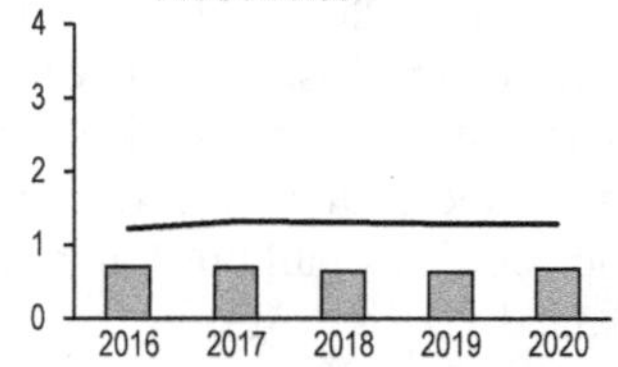

	2016	2017	2018	2019	2020
Raleigh	0.70	0.69	0.64	0.63	0.67
Average	1.22	1.31	1.30	1.28	1.28

Efficiency Measures

Total Cost per 1,000 Gallons of Treated Wastewater

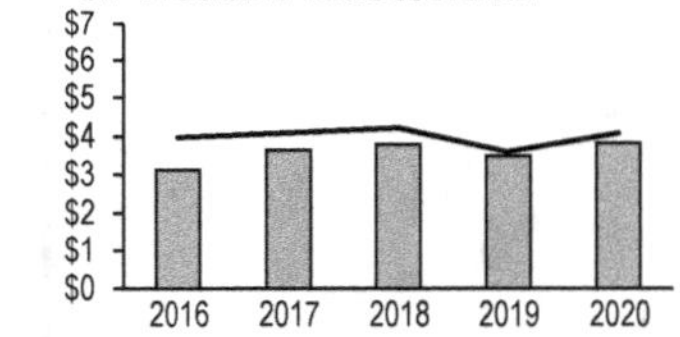

	2016	2017	2018	2019	2020
Raleigh	$3.12	$3.65	$3.78	$3.49	$3.82
Average	$3.96	$4.07	$4.21	$3.59	$4.08

Million Gallons of Wastewater per Wastewater Services FTE

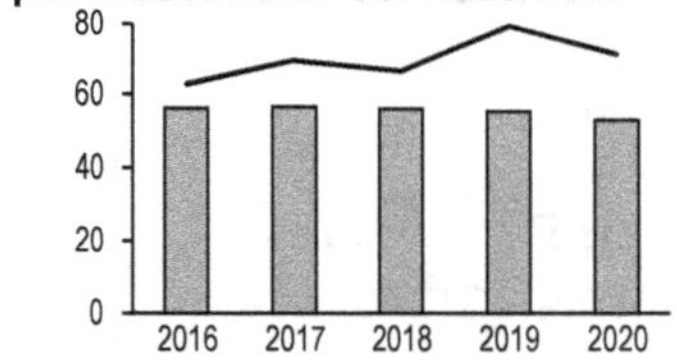

	2016	2017	2018	2019	2020
Raleigh	56.2	56.4	56.0	55.2	53.0
Average	62.7	69.2	66.3	79.4	71.2

Customer Accounts per Wastewater Services FTE

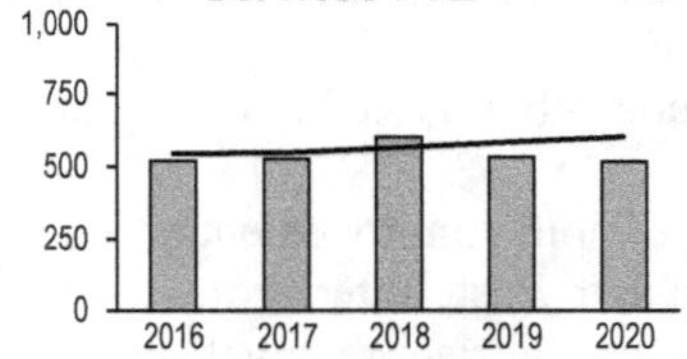

	2016	2017	2018	2019	2020
Raleigh	520	526	601	534	517
Average	545	547	563	584	603

Effectiveness Measures

Percentage of Wastewater Bills Not Collected

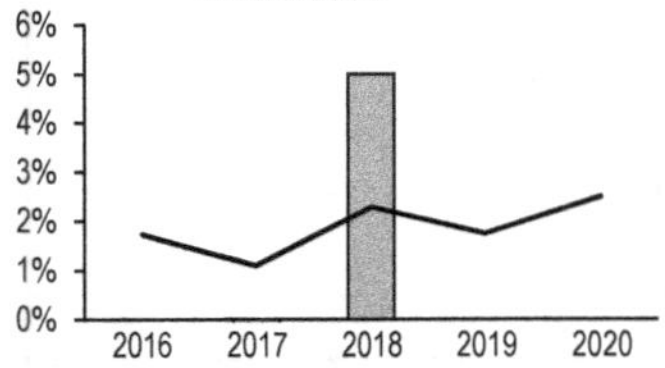

	2016	2017	2018	2019	2020
Raleigh		-0.98%	5.00%		
Average	1.72%	1.09%	2.27%	1.74%	2.49%

Average Daily Treatment as a Percentage of Capacity

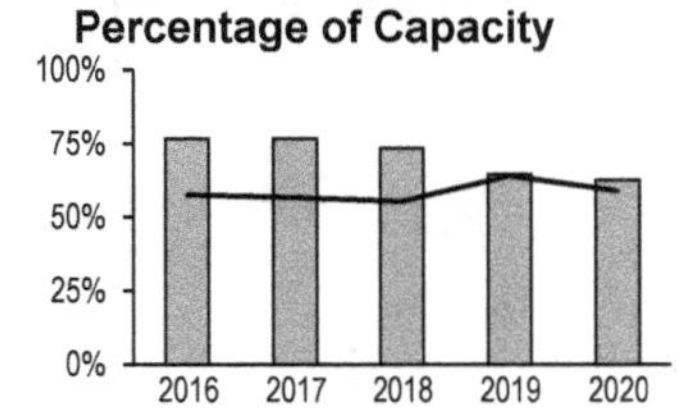

	2016	2017	2018	2019	2020
Raleigh	76.8%	76.9%	73.4%	64.6%	62.6%
Average	57.6%	56.7%	55.3%	63.8%	58.8%

Percent of Main Line Rehabbed or Replaced

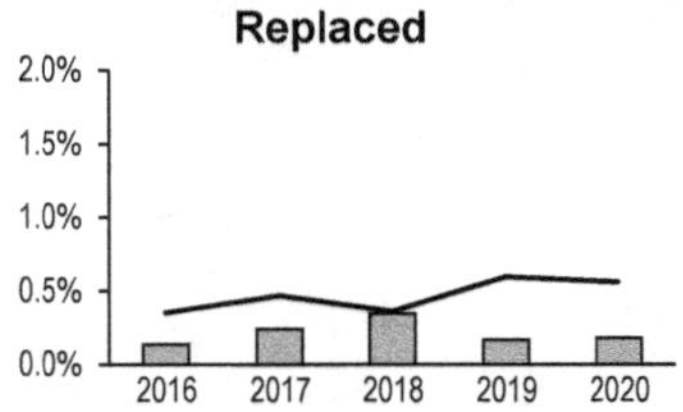

	2016	2017	2018	2019	2020
Raleigh	0.13%	0.24%	0.35%	0.17%	0.18%
Average	0.35%	0.47%	0.36%	0.59%	0.56%

Overflows per 100 Miles of Main Line Pipe

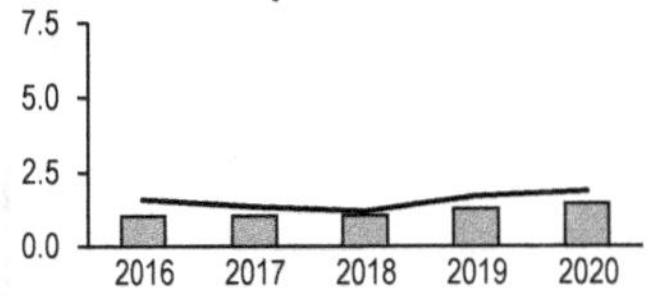

	2016	2017	2018	2019	2020
Raleigh	1.03	1.03	1.04	1.27	1.44
Average	1.57	1.34	1.17	1.68	1.85

Backups per 100 Miles of Main Line Pipe

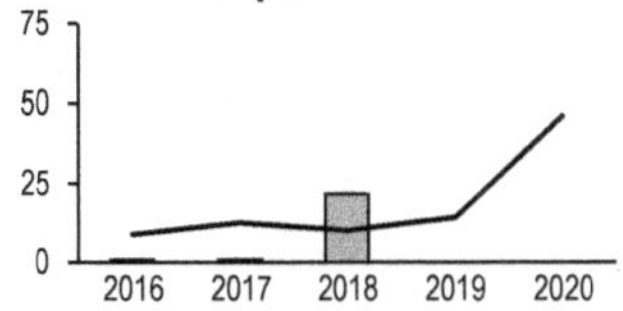

	2016	2017	2018	2019	2020
Raleigh	1.03	1.03	21.77		
Average	8.83	12.62	10.08	14.21	45.98

Billed Wastewater as a Percent of Treated Effluent

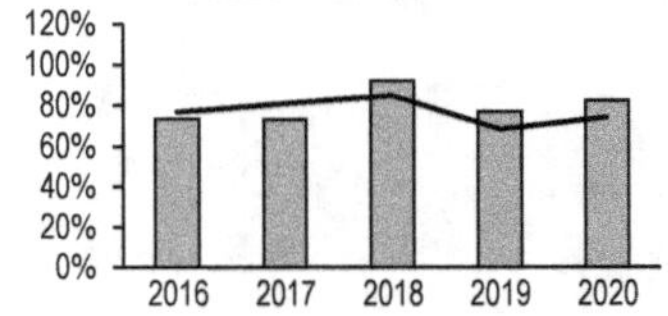

	2016	2017	2018	2019	2020
Raleigh	74%	73%	92%	77%	82%
Average	76%	81%	84%	68%	74%

Fiscal Year 2019-20

Explanatory Information

Service Level and Delivery

Wastewater in Wilson is handled by the Water Reclamation and Wastewater Collection Division, which is part of Water Resources in the Public Services Department. Billing for large customers is handled by Water Resources, but residential customer billing is handled by the Customer Services Division in the Finance Department. The system covers the City of Wilson and several small adjoining areas outside the city in Wilson County.

Wastewater treatment is handled by one plant. The treatment plant uses advanced five-stage biological nutrient removal with deep-bed filters with methanol and biological and chemical phosphorous reduction. The system had very stringent nutrient limits in place to protect water quality in the Neuse River basin. The system produced Class A and B biosolids, with most of this solid waste being composted. A small portion is applied on city land or other permitted farmland.

The system had no reported regulatory violations for the treatment system, but one violation for the collection portion of the system during the fiscal year.

Conditions Affecting Service, Performance, and Costs

The costs of wastewater or sewer services as captured here do not include debt service but do capture depreciation of capital.

Large capital improvements are being made to the Buckhorn Lake Dam and Wastewater Projects, which have been required to meet advanced nutrient removal standards.

Municipal Profile

Estimated Service Population	54,600
Service Land Area (Square Miles)	42
Persons per Square Mile	1,300
Topography	Flat
Climate	Temperate; little ice and snow
Median Household Income U.S. Census 2016	$35,409

Service Profile

Total FTE Staff Positions	65.0
Treatment Plant	31.0
Line Crews	28.0
Billing/Collection	3.0
Other	3.0
Number of Treatment Plants	1
Total Treatment Capacity	14.0 MGD
Average Daily Flow	8.9 MGD
River Basin into Which System Discharges	Neuse
Miles of Gravity Main Line Pipe	351
Miles of Forced Main Line Pipe	12
Average Age of Main Line Pipe	44 years
Blocks in Sewer Mains	394
Number of System Breaks	1
Sanitary System Overflows	1
Number of Customer Accounts	20,294
Total Revenues Collected	$14,275,000

Full Cost Profile

Cost Breakdown by Percentage	
Personal Services	36.4%
Operating Costs	39.2%
Capital Costs	24.4%
TOTAL	100.0%
Cost Breakdown in Dollars	
Personal Services	$4,666,762
Operating Costs	$5,030,197
Capital Costs	$3,121,700
TOTAL	$12,818,659

Key: Wilson ▒ Benchmarking Average — Fiscal Years 2016 through 2020

Resource Measures

Wastewater Services Cost per Capita

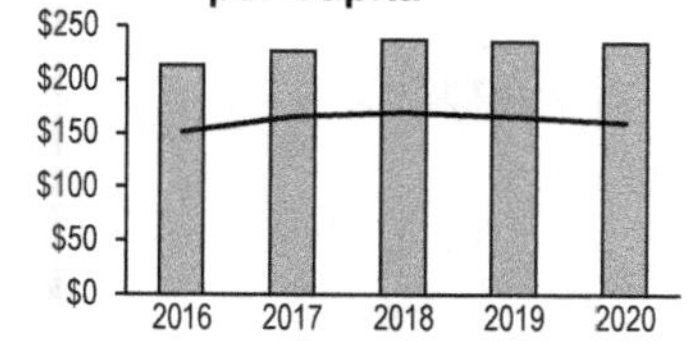

	2016	2017	2018	2019	2020
Wilson	$214	$227	$238	$236	$235
Average	$151	$166	$169	$165	$160

Wastewater Services FTEs per 10,000 Population

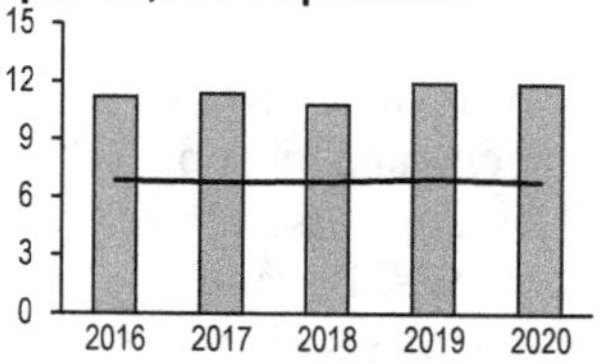

	2016	2017	2018	2019	2020
Wilson	11.2	11.4	10.8	11.9	11.9
Average	6.8	6.8	6.8	6.9	6.8

Wastewater Services Cost per Customer Account

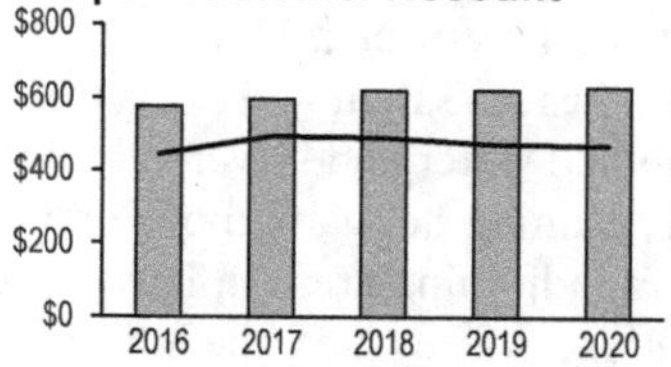

	2016	2017	2018	2019	2020
Wilson	$577	$596	$620	$622	$632
Average	$445	$494	$490	$473	$471

Workload Measures

Thousands of Gallons of Wastewater per Account

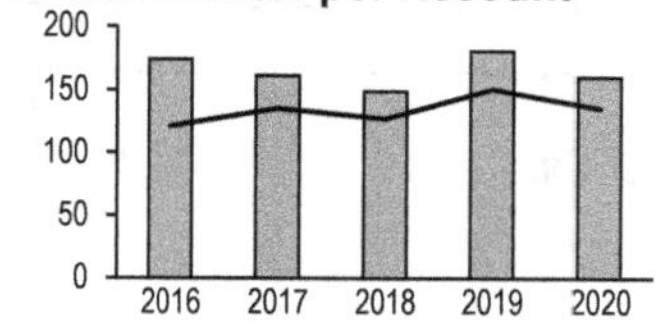

	2016	2017	2018	2019	2020
Wilson	173.7	161.2	148.6	180.6	159.9
Average	121.0	135.0	126.9	150.7	135.2

Miles of Sewer Main Line Pipe per Square Mile of Service Area

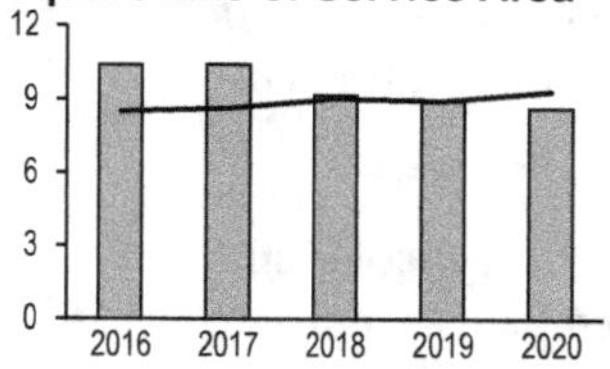

	2016	2017	2018	2019	2020
Wilson	10.4	10.4	9.2	9.0	8.6
Average	8.5	8.6	9.0	8.9	9.3

Number of Lift Stations per 1,000 Accounts

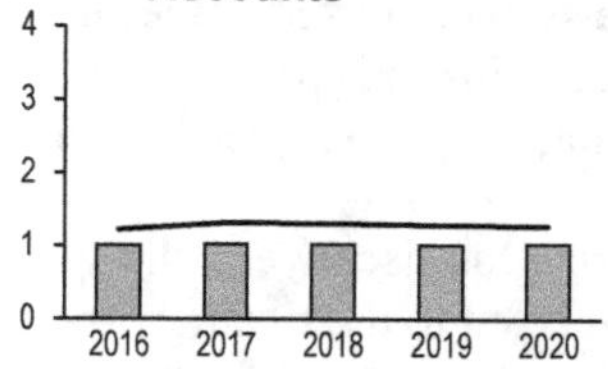

	2016	2017	2018	2019	2020
Wilson	1.01	1.03	1.02	1.02	1.03
Average	1.22	1.31	1.30	1.28	1.28

Efficiency Measures

Total Cost per 1,000 Gallons of Treated Wastewater

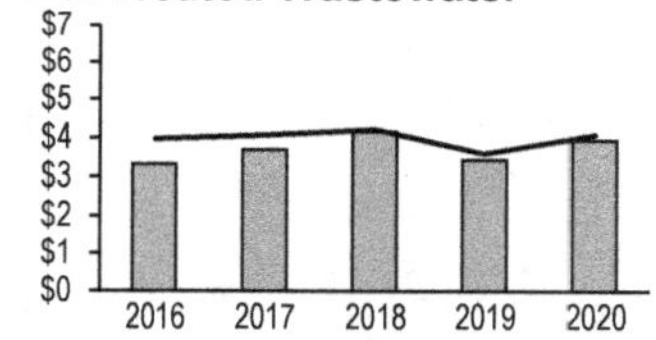

	2016	2017	2018	2019	2020
Wilson	$3.32	$3.70	$4.17	$3.44	$3.95
Average	$3.96	$4.07	$4.21	$3.59	$4.08

Million Gallons of Wastewater per Wastewater Services FTE

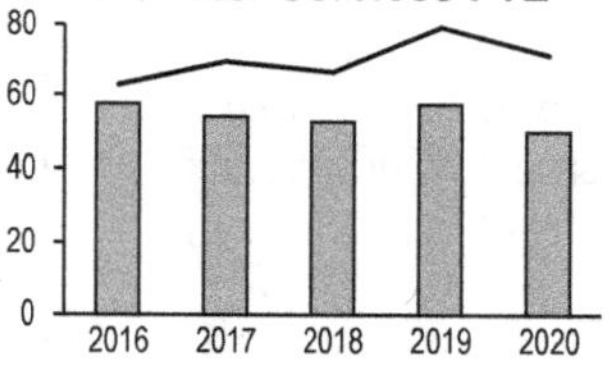

	2016	2017	2018	2019	2020
Wilson	57.6	54.0	52.7	57.3	49.9
Average	62.7	69.2	66.3	79.4	71.2

Customer Accounts per Wastewater Services FTE

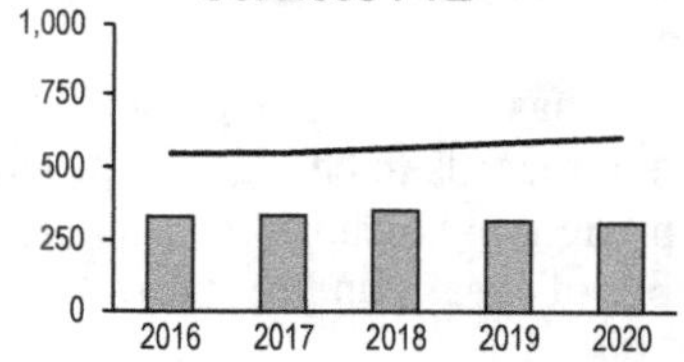

	2016	2017	2018	2019	2020
Wilson	331	335	355	318	312
Average	545	547	563	584	603

Effectiveness Measures

Percentage of Wastewater Bills Not Collected

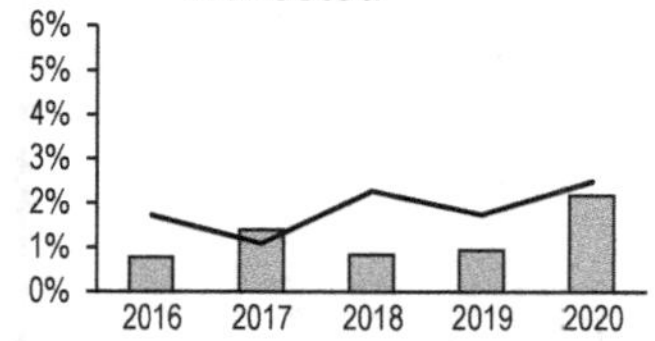

	2016	2017	2018	2019	2020
Wilson	0.78%	1.41%	0.85%	0.95%	2.18%
Average	1.72%	1.09%	2.27%	1.74%	2.49%

Average Daily Treatment as a Percentage of Capacity

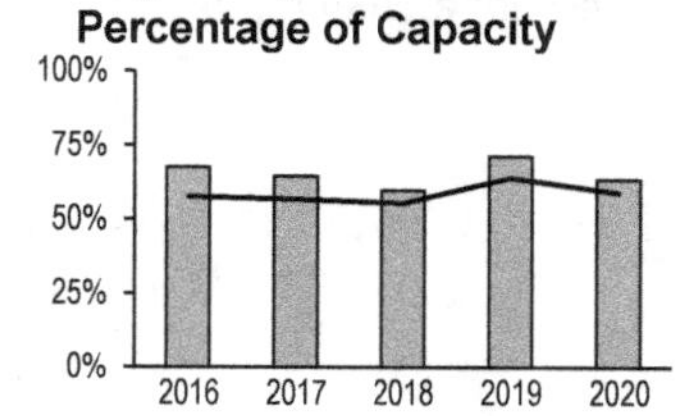

	2016	2017	2018	2019	2020
Wilson	67.6%	64.5%	59.8%	71.3%	63.5%
Average	57.6%	56.7%	55.3%	63.8%	58.8%

Percent of Main Line Rehabbed or Replaced

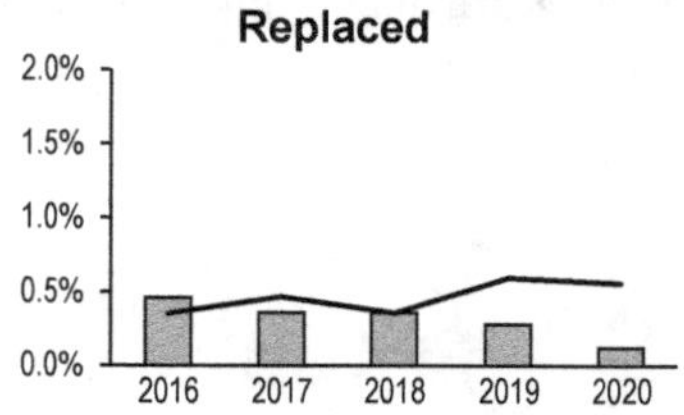

	2016	2017	2018	2019	2020
Wilson	0.46%	0.36%	0.36%	0.28%	0.12%
Average	0.35%	0.47%	0.36%	0.59%	0.56%

Overflows per 100 Miles of Main Line Pipe

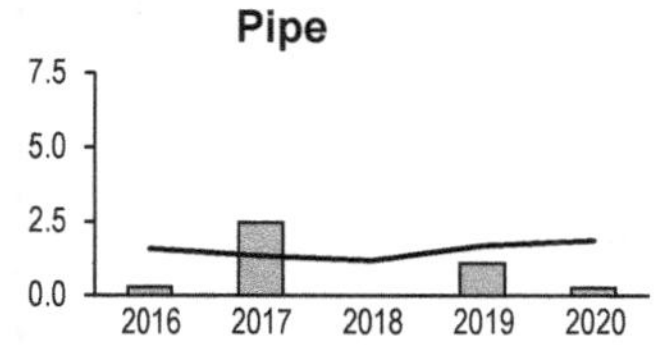

	2016	2017	2018	2019	2020
Wilson	0.28	2.47	0.00	1.09	0.28
Average	1.57	1.34	1.17	1.68	1.85

Backups per 100 Miles of Main Line Pipe

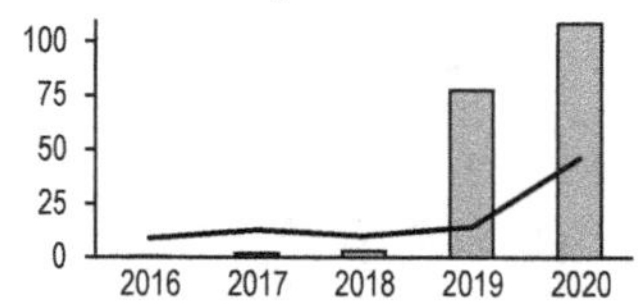

	2016	2017	2018	2019	2020
Wilson	0.57	1.92	3.27	77.66	108.54
Average	8.83	12.62	10.08	14.21	45.98

Billed Wastewater as a Percent of Treated Effluent

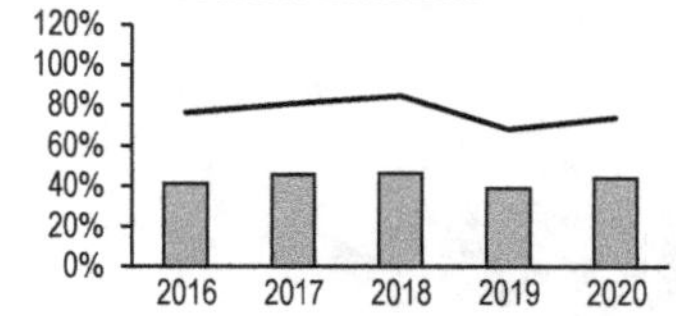

	2016	2017	2018	2019	2020
Wilson	42%	46%	46%	39%	44%
Average	76%	81%	84%	68%	74%

Fiscal Year 2019-20

Explanatory Information

Service Level and Delivery

The Winston-Salem and Forsyth County Utilities Division operates a combined water and sewer system that covers the city and most of the remaining population of Forsyth County. The system also serves several adjoining areas in Davie and Davidson counties. Beyond water and wastewater, the Utilities Division also handles solid waste disposal. Operations are divided among several divisions by function.

The system has two separate treatment plants. The plants use conventional activated sludge with anaerobic digestion for treatment. The system currently does not have regulatory nutrient limits in place. Biosolids produced are disposed after first using thermal drying with subsequent reuse as a soil amendment.

During the fiscal year, the system had one regulatory violation connected to the treatment portion of the system and seventy-seven reported violations for the collection portion of the system connected to sanitary system overflows.

Conditions Affecting Service, Performance, and Costs

The costs of wastewater or sewer services as captured here do not include debt service but do capture depreciation of capital.

The city has used improvements in its GIS mapping systems and incident records to change the process by which the division ranks and proactively cleans pipes. This process is expected to lower the number of breaks and overflows.

Winston-Salem made improvements in their calculation of population served and area covered to improve the accuracy of their data. This had the effect of decreasing the reported population and size of the area served from earlier years. The changes seen in FY 2017–2018 are due to this improved estimation and not a change in services.

Municipal Profile

Estimated Service Population	299,808
Service Land Area (Square Miles)	148
Persons per Square Mile	2,026
Topography	Gently rolling
Climate	Temperate; some ice and snow
Median Household Income U.S. Census 2016	$40,584

Service Profile

Total FTE Staff Positions	175.2
Treatment Plant	88.0
Line Crews	59.0
Billing/Collection	8.2
Other	20.0
Number of Treatment Plants	2
Total Treatment Capacity	51.0 MGD
Average Daily Flow	36.7 MGD
River Basin into Which System Discharges	Yadkin
Miles of Gravity Main Line Pipe	1,802
Miles of Forced Main Line Pipe	4
Average Age of Main Line Pipe	39 years
Blocks in Sewer Mains	110
Number of System Breaks	202
Sanitary System Overflows	77
Number of Customer Accounts	101,900
Total Revenues Collected	$61,501,544

Full Cost Profile

Cost Breakdown by Percentage	
Personal Services	27.7%
Operating Costs	32.6%
Capital Costs	39.8%
TOTAL	100.0%

Cost Breakdown in Dollars	
Personal Services	$10,600,283
Operating Costs	$12,473,360
Capital Costs	$15,224,940
TOTAL	$38,298,583

Winston-Salem

Wastewater Services

Key: Winston-Salem ▪ Benchmarking Average — Fiscal Years 2016 through 2020

Resource Measures

Wastewater Services Cost per Capita

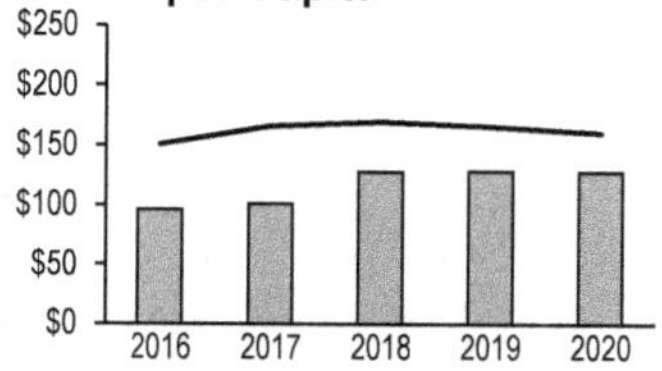

	2016	2017	2018	2019	2020
Winston-Salem	$96	$101	$128	$129	$128
Average	$151	$166	$169	$165	$160

Wastewater Services FTEs per 10,000 Population

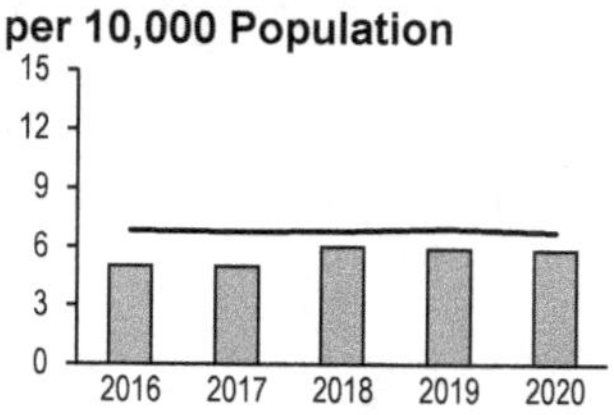

	2016	2017	2018	2019	2020
Winston-Salem	5.0	5.0	6.0	5.9	5.8
Average	6.8	6.8	6.8	6.9	6.8

Wastewater Services Cost per Customer Account

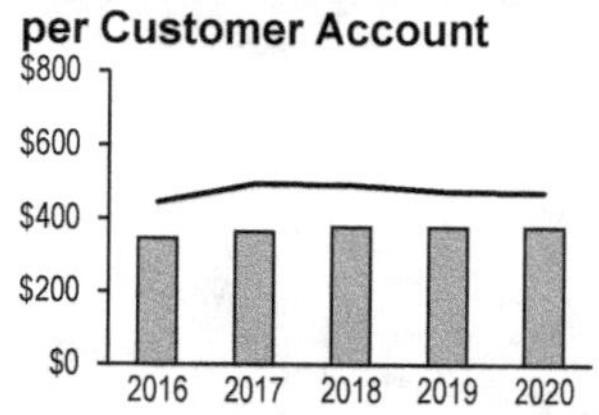

	2016	2017	2018	2019	2020
Winston-Salem	$346	$362	$376	$377	$376
Average	$445	$494	$490	$473	$471

Workload Measures

Thousands of Gallons of Wastewater per Account

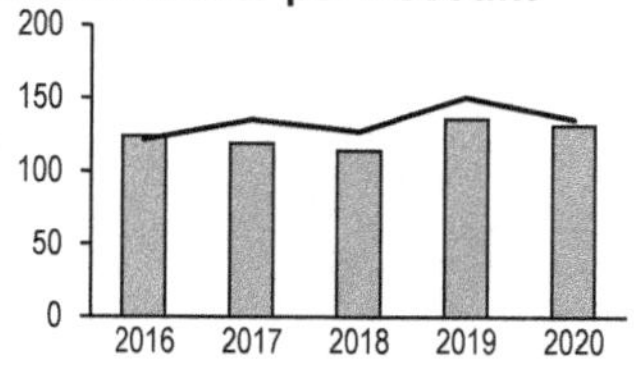

	2016	2017	2018	2019	2020
Winston-Salem	124.0	119.1	114.0	135.8	131.4
Average	121.0	135.0	126.9	150.7	135.2

Miles of Sewer Main Line Pipe per Square Mile of Service Area

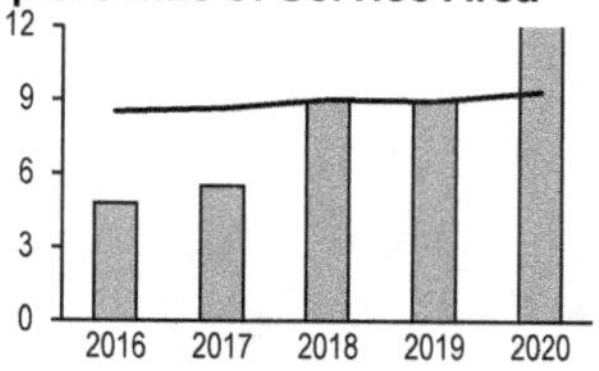

	2016	2017	2018	2019	2020
Winston-Salem	4.8	5.5	9.0	9.0	12.2
Average	8.5	8.6	9.0	8.9	9.3

Number of Lift Stations per 1,000 Accounts

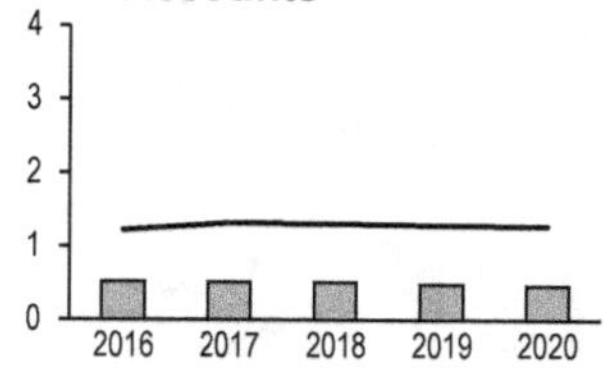

	2016	2017	2018	2019	2020
Winston-Salem	0.51	0.51	0.50	0.48	0.46
Average	1.22	1.31	1.30	1.28	1.28

Efficiency Measures

Total Cost per 1,000 Gallons of Treated Wastewater

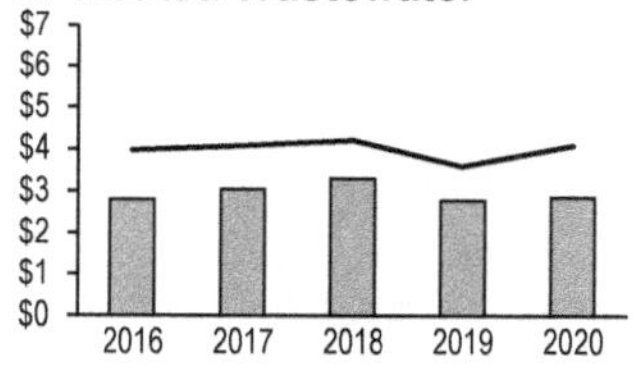

	2016	2017	2018	2019	2020
Winston-Salem	$2.79	$3.04	$3.30	$2.78	$2.86
Average	$3.96	$4.07	$4.21	$3.59	$4.08

Million Gallons of Wastewater per Wastewater Services FTE

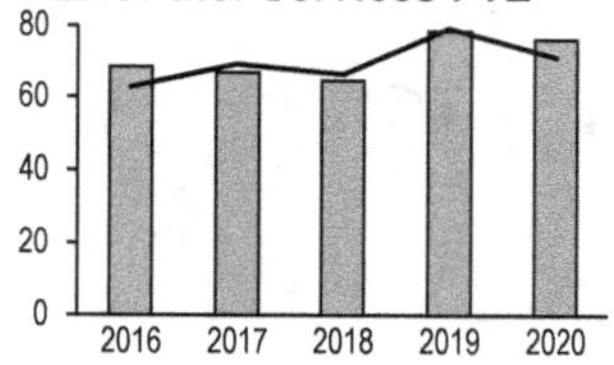

	2016	2017	2018	2019	2020
Winston-Salem	68.5	66.9	64.6	78.6	76.4
Average	62.7	69.2	66.3	79.4	71.2

Customer Accounts per Wastewater Services FTE

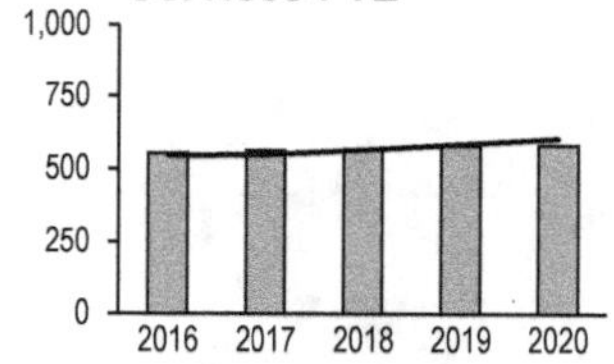

	2016	2017	2018	2019	2020
Winston-Salem	553	562	567	578	582
Average	545	547	563	584	603

Effectiveness Measures

Percentage of Wastewater Bills Not Collected

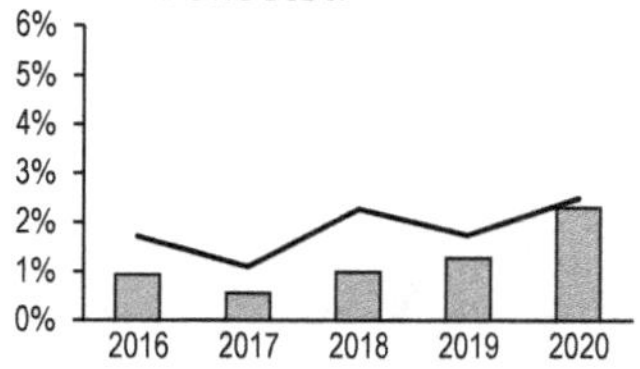

	2016	2017	2018	2019	2020
Winston-Salem	0.94%	0.56%	0.99%	1.28%	2.30%
Average	1.72%	1.09%	2.27%	1.74%	2.49%

Average Daily Treatment as a Percentage of Capacity

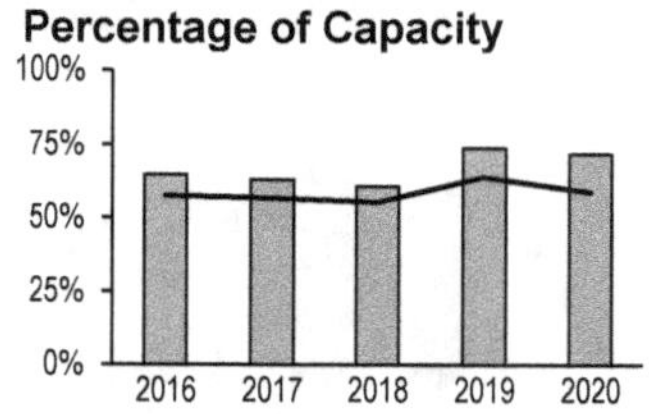

	2016	2017	2018	2019	2020
Winston-Salem	64.8%	62.9%	60.8%	73.9%	71.9%
Average	57.6%	56.7%	55.3%	63.8%	58.8%

Percent of Main Line Rehabbed or Replaced

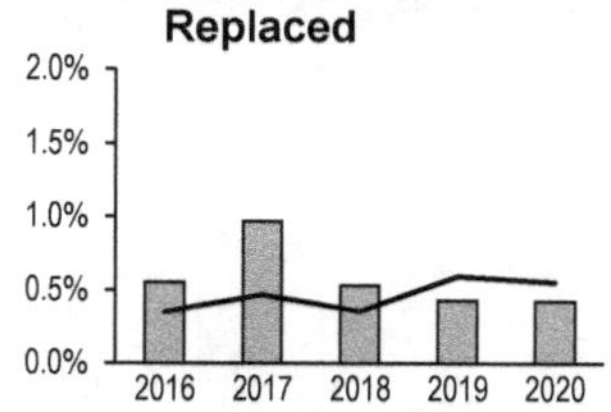

	2016	2017	2018	2019	2020
Winston-Salem	0.55%	0.97%	0.53%	0.43%	0.43%
Average	0.35%	0.47%	0.36%	0.59%	0.56%

Overflows per 100 Miles of Main Line Pipe

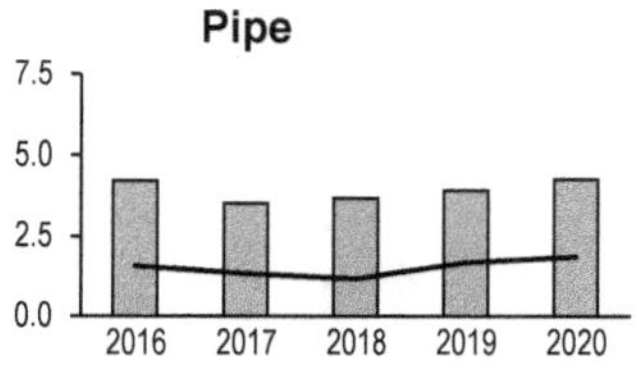

	2016	2017	2018	2019	2020
Winston-Salem	4.23	3.52	3.67	3.92	4.27
Average	1.57	1.34	1.17	1.68	1.85

Backups per 100 Miles of Main Line Pipe

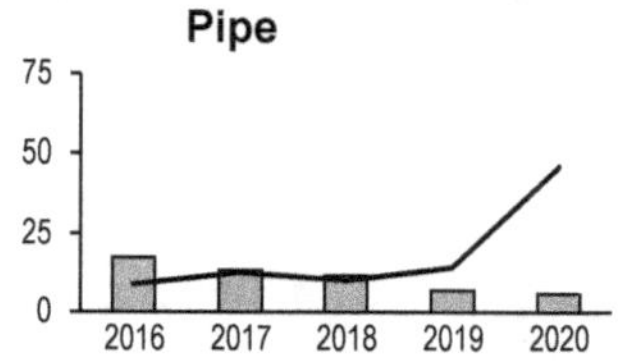

	2016	2017	2018	2019	2020
Winston-Salem	17.54	13.34	11.75	7.16	6.09
Average	8.83	12.62	10.08	14.21	45.98

Billed Wastewater as a Percent of Treated Effluent

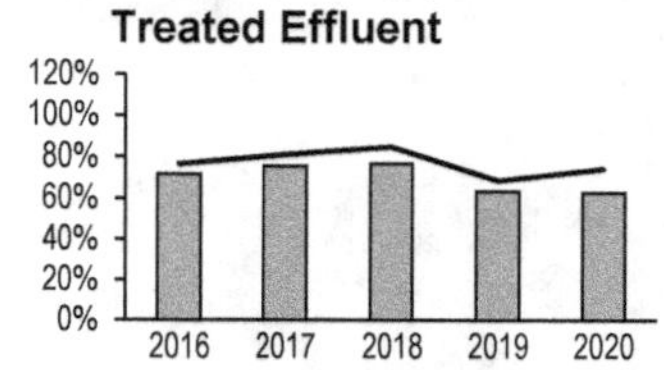

	2016	2017	2018	2019	2020
Winston-Salem	71%	75%	77%	63%	63%
Average	76%	81%	84%	68%	74%

SCHOOL OF GOVERNMENT
North Carolina Benchmarking Project

Performance and Cost Data

CORE PARKS AND RECREATION

SCHOOL OF GOVERNMENT
North Carolina Benchmarking Project

PERFORMANCE MEASURES FOR CORE PARKS AND RECREATION SERVICES

SERVICE DEFINITION

Parks and Recreation includes both passive and active recreation opportunities maintained and operated by a local government. For the purposes of this benchmarking effort, this includes core operational functions, such as parks, multipurpose recreation facilities, athletic facilities, greenways, and trails. This also includes programs and events.

However, Parks and Recreation departments frequently may include a variety of other activities and facilities. To support reasonable comparisons, this service benchmarking excludes these secondary recreational activities, including performance venues, museums, historic sites, golf courses, marinas/boat ramps, and professional stadiums. Also excluded are other non-recreational activities sometimes performed by parks and recreation departments, such as care of cemeteries; maintenance of rights-of-way along city streets; maintenance of facilities owned by a municipality but not parks-related; and maintenance of city lots. The dollars and people associated with these secondary and non-park activities are excluded.

Parks and Recreation does offer an important difference from many of the other services provided by local governments. Much of the objective of this service area is to provide facilities for use by citizens. Use of many of these facilities is not easily tracked. Many of the measures shown for this service area are accordingly measures of facility availability rather than the traditional workload type of measures seen in other service areas.

NOTES ON PERFORMANCE MEASURES

1. Land Acres of All Municipal Parks per 10,000 Population

This resource measure captures the amount of park land that is available relative to the population in the communities.

2. Recreation Centers per 10,000 Population

Recreation centers provide space for a variety of indoor recreational activities. This measure shows the number of centers relative to the population.

3. Swimming Pools per 10,000 Population

Indoor and outdoor pools are a desirable recreational facility. This resource measure captures the number of pools relative to the population.

4. Athletic Fields per 10,000 Population

Outdoor athletic fields are used for organized and informal recreation. This measure counts the number of formal athletic fields, including rectangular fields such as those for football and soccer, diamond fields as for baseball, and nondesignated fields that can be used for multiple activities. The count includes both natural grass and artificial-surface fields, where available.

5. Playgrounds per 10,000 Population
Formal playgrounds include a variety of fixed equipment, such as swings, jungle gyms, slides, and other apparatus. This measure captures these playgrounds relative to the population.

6. Miles of Trails per 10,000 Population
Outdoor trails of all types represent an important type of active recreation. This measure captures the total miles of trails in a community relative to the population. The miles total includes paved and unpaved trails and covers various types of trail, such as those for walking, bike riding, and equestrian riding.

7. Total Core Parks and Recreation Costs
This efficiency measure represents the level of spending relative to the park acreage in a community. Although funds may be spent on facilities and activities, this measure provides some comparison of the intensity of spending.

8. Acres of Park Maintained per Maintenance Full-Time Equivalent (FTE)
This efficiency measure compares the amount of acres in the park system relative to the number of FTEs used by a jurisdiction to provide maintenance.

9. Volunteer Hours in FTEs as a Percent of Paid Staff FTEs
Volunteers represent an important resource to help support Parks and Recreation activities. This efficiency measure compares the estimated amount of volunteer labor relative to the paid staff in order to provide a measure of the benefit these volunteers bring to a community.

10. Revenue Gained as a Percent of Total Core Parks and Recreation Costs
Parks and Recreation is a service that is primarily supported by general funding from a local government budget. But gaining additional revenues in the form of user fees, grants, donations, and sponsorships helps to leverage spending and provide services. This effectiveness measure shows how much revenue has been raised from these other sources relative to the total costs reported.

11. Acts of Vandalism per 10,000 Population
Vandalism damages parks and recreation facilities, making them unavailable or less useful to citizens. This effectiveness measure compares the number of acts of vandalism relative to the population to indicate the extent of this problem.

Core Parks and Recreation

Summary of Key Dimensions of Service

City or Town	Municipal Population as of July 2019	Core Parks and Recreation FTEs	Number of Parks	Park Land Acreage	Number of Recreation and Senior Centers	Number of Playgrounds	Number of Athletic Fields	Miles of Trails
Apex	61,319	41.5	13	618.3	1	12	27	21.9
Chapel Hill	63,639	71.0	31	1,114.0	2	11	16	15.5
Concord	95,453	36.0	13	383.6	4	13	27	15.8
Goldsboro	33,969	48.3	14	233.0	4	10	25	4.5
Greensboro	293,730	162.0	486	7,432.7	12	105	75	100.2
Hickory	41,409	23.0	24	447.6	7	40	23	16.0
Raleigh	475,580	753.4	175	6,224.0	41	106	99	156.0
Wilson	49,384	44.5	28	400.0	4	26	26	7.5
Winston-Salem	244,739	212.0	84	4,279.2	17	46	97	23.3

EXPLANATORY FACTORS

These are some factors that the project found affected core parks and recreation services performance and cost in one or more of the municipalities:

Youth Population
Total Acreage
Miles of Trails
Number of Facilities

Fiscal Year 2019-20

Explanatory Information

Service Level and Delivery

The Town of Apex provides recreation services through the separate Parks, Recreation, and Cultural Resources Department. The city has priority use agreements with the Wake County School System in exchange for maintenance of areas used by the town.

The town has thirteen separate parks and sites. These parks cover 618 land acres; most of this area is currently developed. The city has nearly twenty-two miles of trails.

In addition to the core parks and recreational facilities, Apex has a performing arts center. The operation of this other facility is not included in the Core Parks and Recreation comparisons reported here. This facility is not included here in dollars or staff as part of core parks and recreation facilities and activities.

Conditions Affecting Service, Performance, and Costs

Municipal Profile

Population (OSBM 2019)	61,319
Land Area (Square Miles)	23.61
Persons per Square Mile	2,597
Topography	Flat; gently rolling
Climate	Temperate; little ice and snow

Service Profile

Parks and Recreation Staff	
Administrative Position FTEs	5.0
Maintenance Staff FTEs	25.5
Program and Facility FTEs	11.0
Other Staff FTEs	0.0
TOTAL	41.5
Number of Parks and Sites	13
Total Land Acreage in Parks	618.3
Miles of Trails in Parks	21.9
Recreational Facilities	
Indoor and Outdoor Pools	0
Recreation Centers	1
Outdoor Basketball Courts	15
Outdoor Tennis Courts	15
Playgrounds	12
Diamond Fields	13
Rectangular Fields	12
Other Athletic Fields	2
Picnic Shelters	11
Parks and Recreation Revenues	
User Fees	$561,311
Grants	$167,770
Sponsorships	$0
Donations	$0

Full Cost Profile

Cost Breakdown by Percentage	
Personal Services	48.2%
Operating Costs	43.0%
Capital Costs	8.8%
TOTAL	100.0%
Cost Breakdown in Dollars	
Personal Services	$2,665,525
Operating Costs	$2,377,264
Capital Costs	$488,053
TOTAL	$5,530,842

Key: Apex ▒ Benchmarking Average — Fiscal Years 2016 through 2020

Resource Measures

Core Parks and Recreation Services per Capita

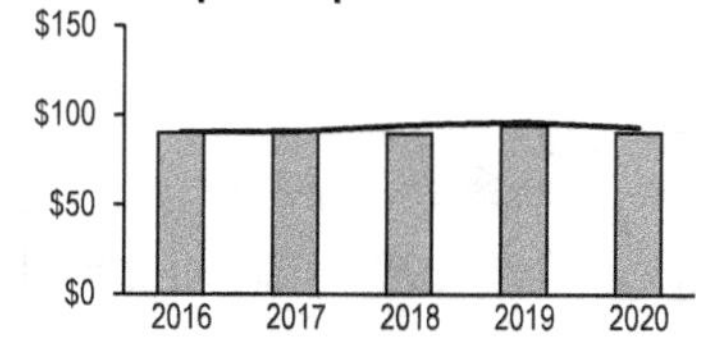

	2016	2017	2018	2019	2020
Apex	$90	$91	$90	$94	$90
Average	$91	$90	$94	$96	$93

Core Parks and Recreation Staff per 10,000 Population

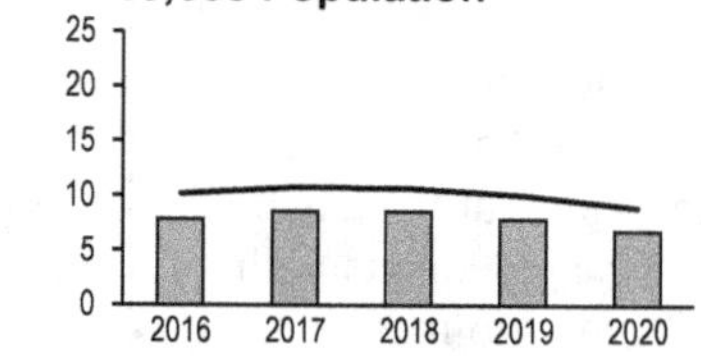

	2016	2017	2018	2019	2020
Apex	7.8	8.6	8.6	7.8	6.8
Average	10.2	10.8	10.7	10.0	8.9

Facilities Measures

Land Acres of Parks per 10,000 Population

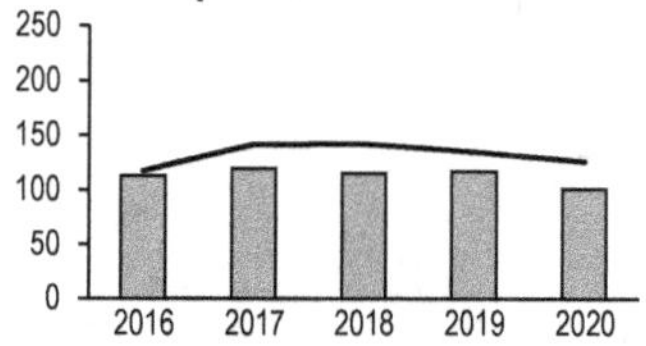

	2016	2017	2018	2019	2020
Apex	113.09	119.52	115.12	116.86	100.83
Average	117.20	140.99	141.65	134.43	125.84

Recreation Centers per 10,000 Population

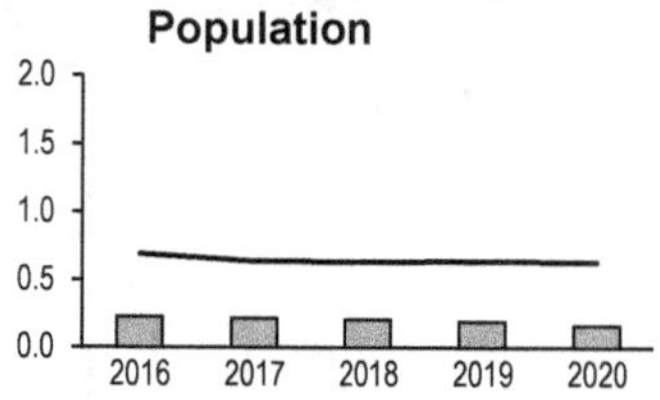

	2016	2017	2018	2019	2020
Apex	0.22	0.21	0.21	0.19	0.16
Average	0.69	0.64	0.63	0.64	0.63

Swimming Pools per 10,000 Population

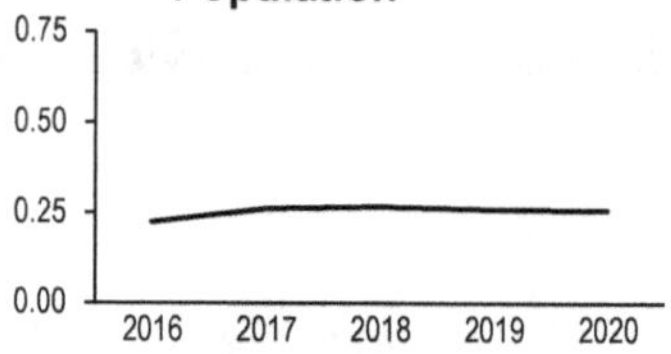

	2016	2017	2018	2019	2020
Apex	0.00	0.00	0.00	0.00	0.00
Average	0.22	0.26	0.27	0.26	0.26

Athletic Fields per 10,000 Population

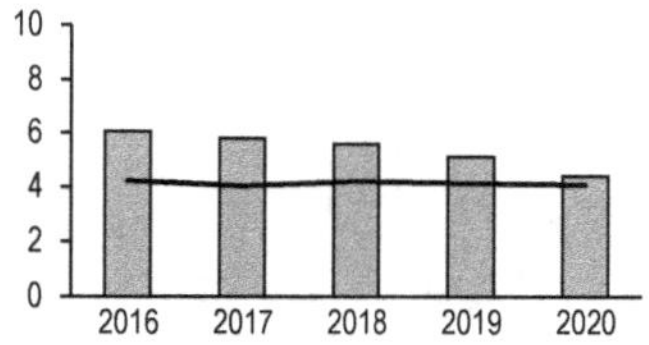

	2016	2017	2018	2019	2020
Apex	6.03	5.78	5.57	5.10	4.40
Average	4.19	4.00	4.19	4.12	4.06

Playgrounds per 10,000 Population

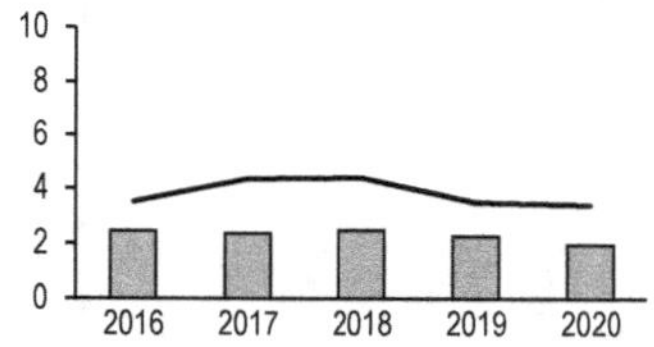

	2016	2017	2018	2019	2020
Apex	2.46	2.36	2.48	2.27	1.96
Average	3.51	4.35	4.39	3.48	3.40

Miles of Land Trails per 10,000 Population

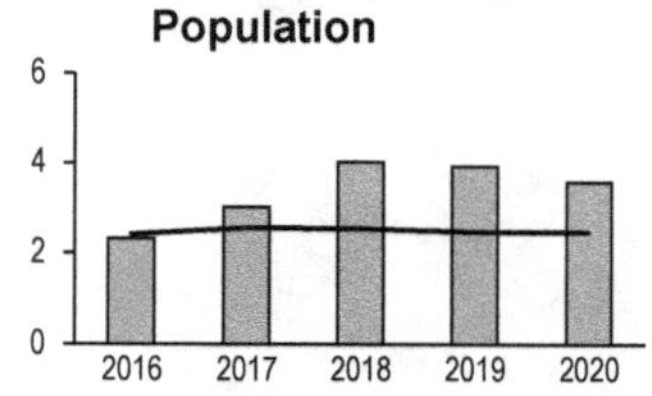

	2016	2017	2018	2019	2020
Apex	2.30	3.00	4.02	3.92	3.56
Average	2.38	2.54	2.52	2.44	2.45

Efficiency Measures

Total Core Parks and Recreation Costs per Acre

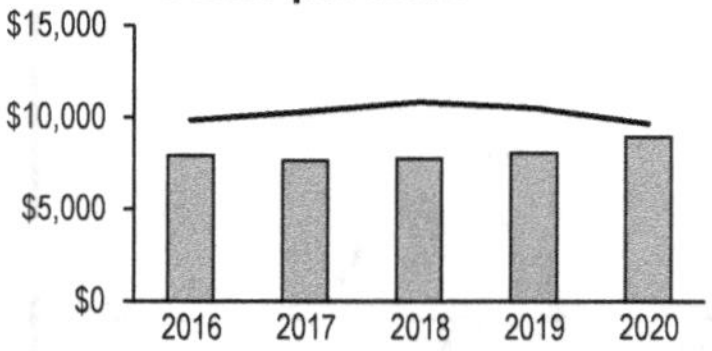

	2016	2017	2018	2019	2020
Apex	$7,949	$7,652	$7,777	$8,075	$8,946
Average	$9,857	$10,296	$10,807	$10,512	$9,650

Acres of Park Maintained per Maintenance FTE

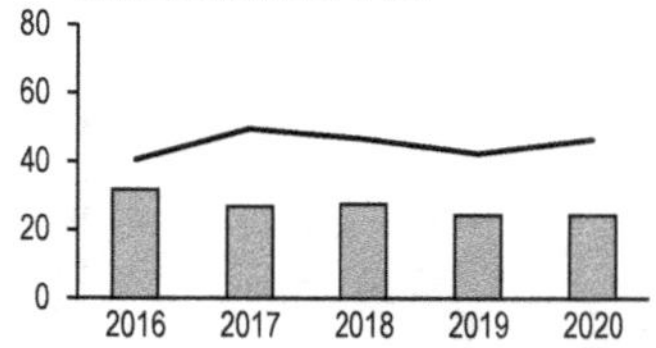

	2016	2017	2018	2019	2020
Apex	31.6	26.8	27.5	24.2	24.2
Average	40.3	49.4	46.7	42.3	46.4

Volunteer Hours in FTEs as a Percent of Paid Staff FTEs

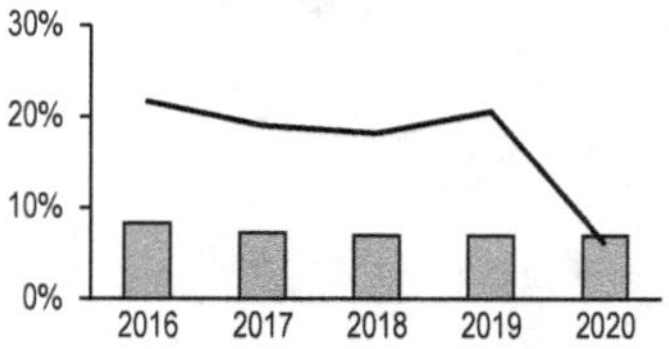

	2016	2017	2018	2019	2020
Apex	8.2%	7.2%	7.0%	7.0%	7.0%
Average	21.6%	19.0%	18.1%	20.5%	6.1%

Effectiveness Measures

Revenue Gained as a Percent of Total Core Costs

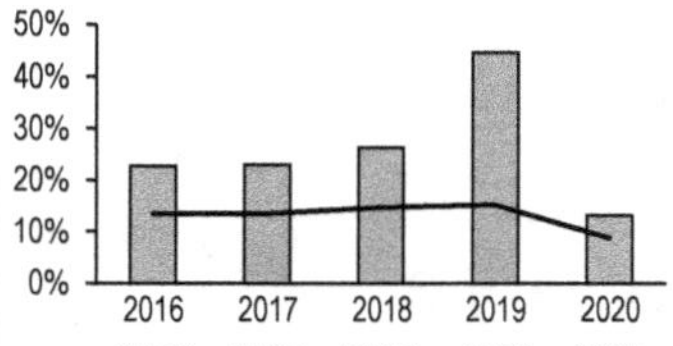

	2016	2017	2018	2019	2020
Apex	22.7%	22.9%	26.3%	44.6%	13.2%
Average	13.4%	13.4%	14.7%	15.2%	8.7%

Acts of Vandalism at Parks Facilities per 10,000 Population

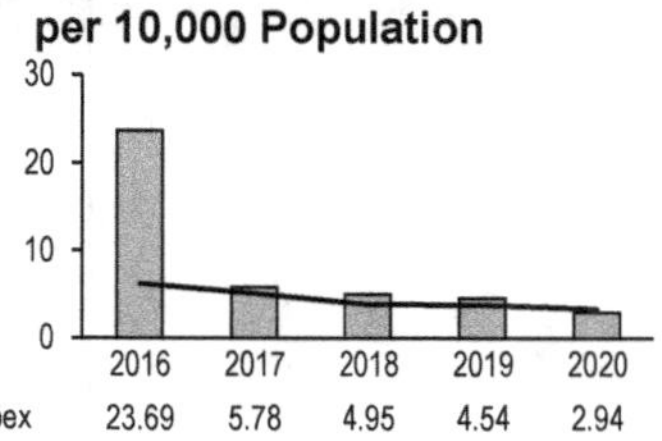

	2016	2017	2018	2019	2020
Apex	23.69	5.78	4.95	4.54	2.94
Average	6.18	5.02	3.76	3.75	3.32

Fiscal Year 2019-20

Explanatory Information

Service Level and Delivery

The Town of Chapel Hill provides recreation services through the separate Parks and Recreation Department. The town has agreements with Orange County for use of the senior center and county resident participation in other programs. The town also has agreements with the Town of Carrboro, the Street Scene Teen Center, Holmes Childcare Center, and Chapel Hill-Carrboro City Schools.

The town has thirty-one separate parks and sites. These parks cover 1,114 land acres, much of which is currently undeveloped. The town has about sixteen miles of trails.

Conditions Affecting Service, Performance, and Costs

Municipal Profile

Population (OSBM 2019)	63,639
Land Area (Square Miles)	21.31
Persons per Square Mile	2,987
Topography	Flat; gently rolling
Climate	Temperate; little ice and snow

Service Profile

Parks and Recreation Staff	
Administrative Position FTEs	7.0
Maintenance Staff FTEs	15.5
Program and Facility FTEs	48.5
Other Staff FTEs	0.0
TOTAL	71.0
Number of Parks and Sites	31
Total Land Acreage in Parks	1,114.0
Miles of Trails in Parks	15.5
Recreational Facilities	
Indoor and Outdoor Pools	3
Recreation Centers	2
Outdoor Basketball Courts	7
Outdoor Tennis Courts	18
Playgrounds	11
Diamond Fields	7
Rectangular Fields	9
Other Athletic Fields	0
Picnic Shelters	8
Parks and Recreation Revenues	
User Fees	$958,796
Grants	$0
Sponsorships	$9,396
Donations	$339

Full Cost Profile

Cost Breakdown by Percentage	
Personal Services	50.2%
Operating Costs	38.5%
Capital Costs	11.3%
TOTAL	100.0%
Cost Breakdown in Dollars	
Personal Services	$3,632,362
Operating Costs	$2,788,989
Capital Costs	$817,443
TOTAL	$7,238,794

Chapel Hill — Core Parks and Recreation

Key: Chapel Hill ▒ Benchmarking Average — Fiscal Years 2016 through 2020

Resource Measures

Core Parks and Recreation Services per Capita

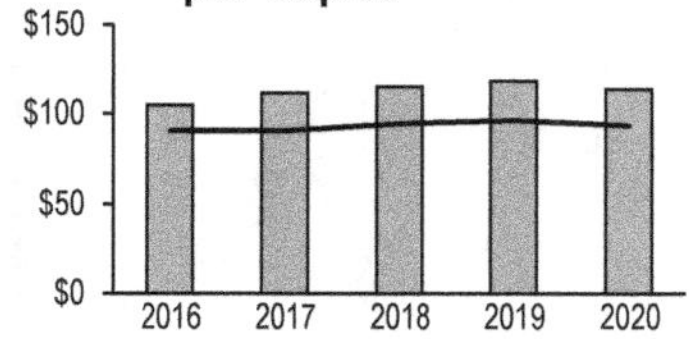

	2016	2017	2018	2019	2020
Chapel Hill	$105	$112	$115	$118	$114
Average	$91	$90	$94	$96	$93

Core Parks and Recreation Staff per 10,000 Population

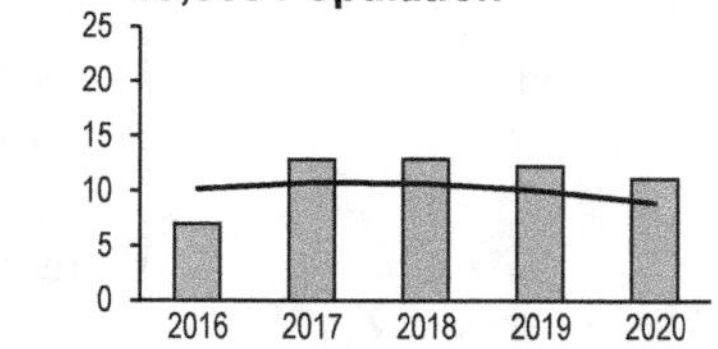

	2016	2017	2018	2019	2020
Chapel Hill	7.0	12.8	12.9	12.3	11.2
Average	10.2	10.8	10.7	10.0	8.9

Facilities Measures

Land Acres of Parks per 10,000 Population

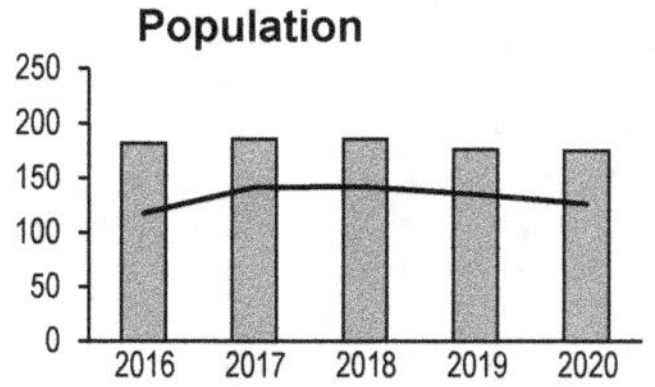

	2016	2017	2018	2019	2020
Chapel Hill	181.53	186.13	185.97	176.33	175.05
Average	117.20	140.99	141.65	134.43	125.84

Recreation Centers per 10,000 Population

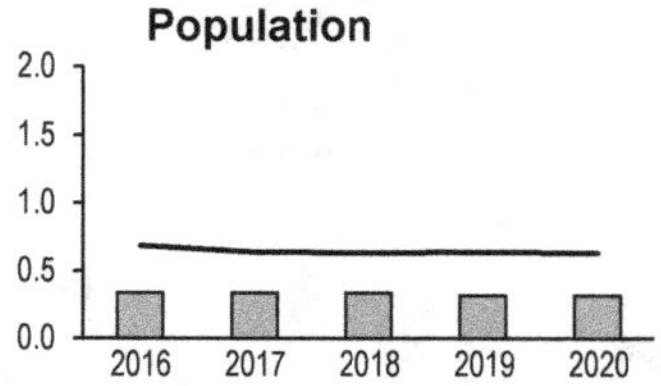

	2016	2017	2018	2019	2020
Chapel Hill	0.34	0.33	0.33	0.32	0.31
Average	0.69	0.64	0.63	0.64	0.63

Swimming Pools per 10,000 Population

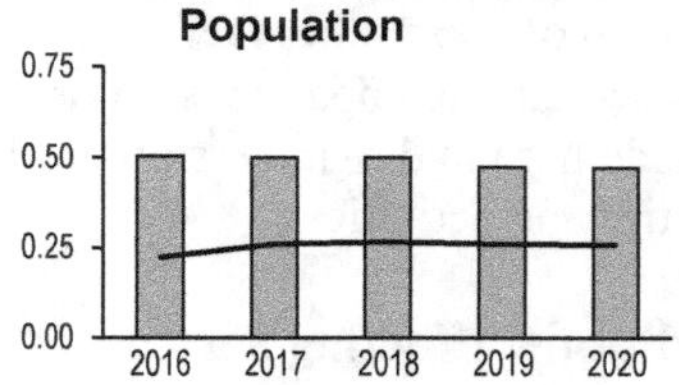

	2016	2017	2018	2019	2020
Chapel Hill	0.50	0.50	0.50	0.47	0.47
Average	0.22	0.26	0.27	0.26	0.26

Athletic Fields per 10,000 Population

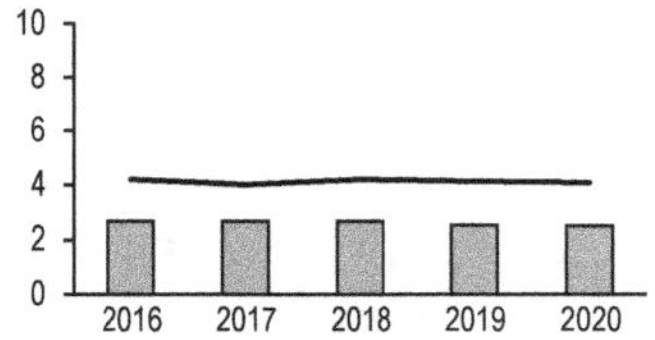

	2016	2017	2018	2019	2020
Chapel Hill	2.68	2.67	2.67	2.53	2.51
Average	4.19	4.00	4.19	4.12	4.06

Playgrounds per 10,000 Population

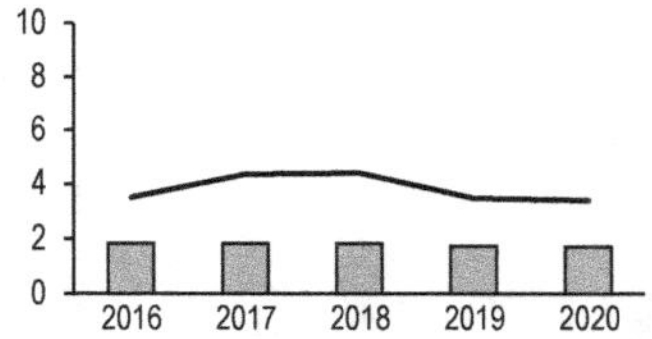

	2016	2017	2018	2019	2020
Chapel Hill	1.85	1.84	1.84	1.74	1.73
Average	3.51	4.35	4.39	3.48	3.40

Miles of Land Trails per 10,000 Population

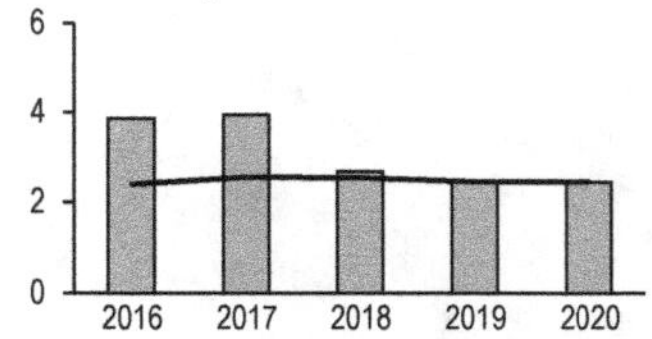

	2016	2017	2018	2019	2020
Chapel Hill	3.85	3.94	2.67	2.45	2.44
Average	2.38	2.54	2.52	2.44	2.45

Efficiency Measures

Total Core Parks and Recreation Costs per Acre

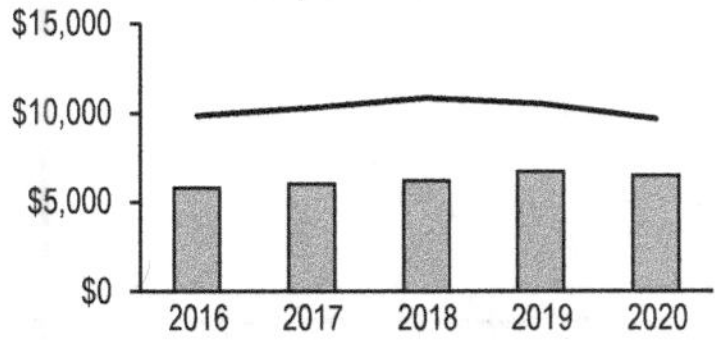

	2016	2017	2018	2019	2020
Chapel Hill	$5,780	$6,000	$6,201	$6,706	$6,498
Average	$9,857	$10,296	$10,807	$10,512	$9,650

Acres of Park Maintained per Maintenance FTE

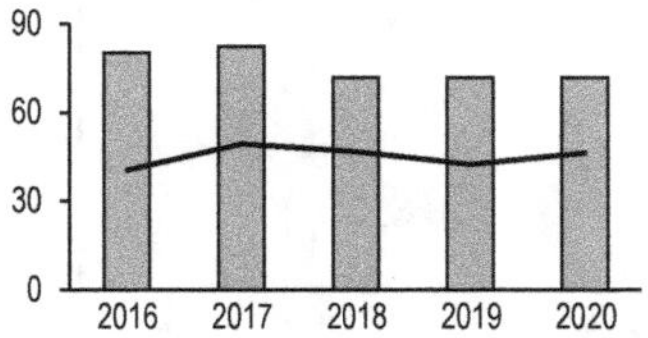

	2016	2017	2018	2019	2020
Chapel Hill	80.1	82.5	71.9	71.9	71.9
Average	40.3	49.4	46.7	42.3	46.4

Volunteer Hours in FTEs as a Percent of Paid Staff FTEs

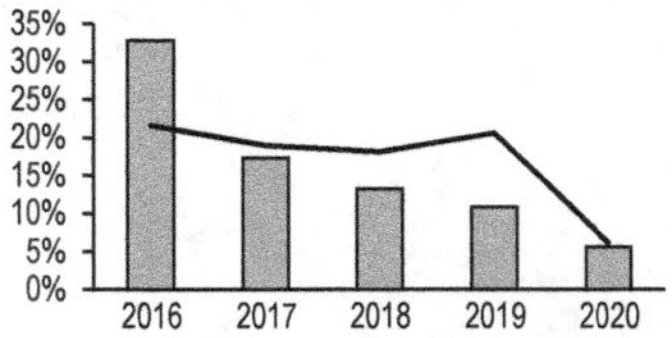

	2016	2017	2018	2019	2020
Chapel Hill	32.8%	17.4%	13.2%	10.8%	5.6%
Average	21.6%	19.0%	18.1%	20.5%	6.1%

Effectiveness Measures

Revenue Gained as a Percent of Total Core Costs

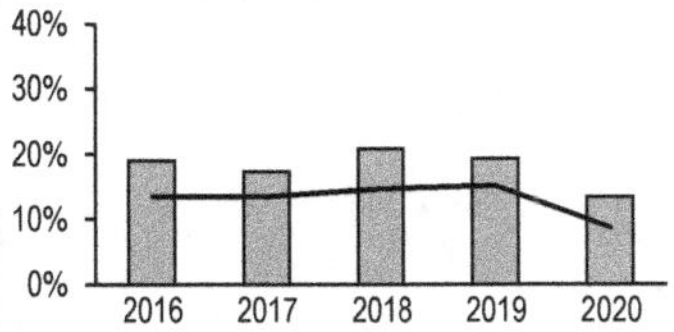

	2016	2017	2018	2019	2020
Chapel Hill	19.1%	17.3%	20.8%	19.3%	13.4%
Average	13.4%	13.4%	14.7%	15.2%	8.7%

Acts of Vandalism at Parks Facilities per 10,000 Population

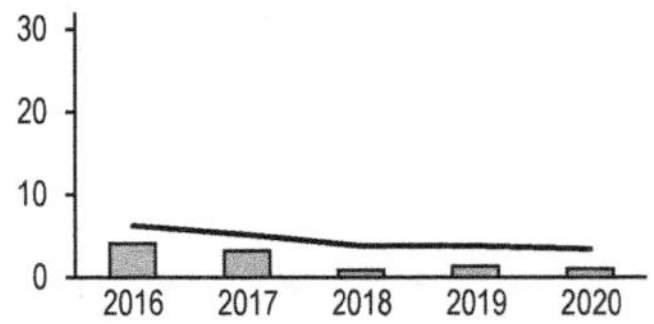

	2016	2017	2018	2019	2020
Chapel Hill	4.03	3.17	0.83	1.27	0.94
Average	6.18	5.02	3.76	3.75	3.32

Fiscal Year 2019-20

Explanatory Information

Service Level and Delivery

The City of Concord provides recreation services through the separate Parks and Recreation Department. The city provides an array of facilities and activities for recreation.

The city has thirteen separate parks and sites. These parks cover 384 land acres. The city has nearly sixteen miles of recreational trails, most of them paved.

In addition to the core parks and recreational facilities, Concord has one large outdoor performance event site and one boat ramp. The operation of these other facilities is not included in the Core Parks and Recreation comparisons reported here. These facilities are not included here in dollars or staff as part of core parks and recreation facilities and activities.

Conditions Affecting Service, Performance, and Costs

Municipal Profile

Population (OSBM 2019)	95,453
Land Area (Square Miles)	63.65
Persons per Square Mile	1,500
Topography	Flat; gently rolling
Climate	Temperate; little ice and snow

Service Profile

Parks and Recreation Staff	
Administrative Position FTEs	7.0
Maintenance Staff FTEs	0.0
Program and Facility FTEs	27.0
Other Staff FTEs	2.0
TOTAL	36.0
Number of Parks and Sites	13
Total Land Acreage in Parks	383.6
Miles of Trails in Parks	15.8
Recreational Facilities	
Indoor and Outdoor Pools	1
Recreation Centers	4
Outdoor Basketball Courts	5
Outdoor Tennis Courts	14
Playgrounds	13
Diamond Fields	17
Rectangular Fields	7
Other Athletic Fields	3
Picnic Shelters	15
Parks and Recreation Revenues	
User Fees	$191,815
Grants	$0
Sponsorships	$6,125
Donations	$0

Full Cost Profile

Cost Breakdown by Percentage	
Personal Services	26.7%
Operating Costs	66.6%
Capital Costs	6.7%
TOTAL	100.0%
Cost Breakdown in Dollars	
Personal Services	$1,808,931
Operating Costs	$4,518,858
Capital Costs	$455,611
TOTAL	$6,783,400

Key: Concord ▒ Benchmarking Average — Fiscal Years 2016 through 2020

Resource Measures

Core Parks and Recreation Services per Capita

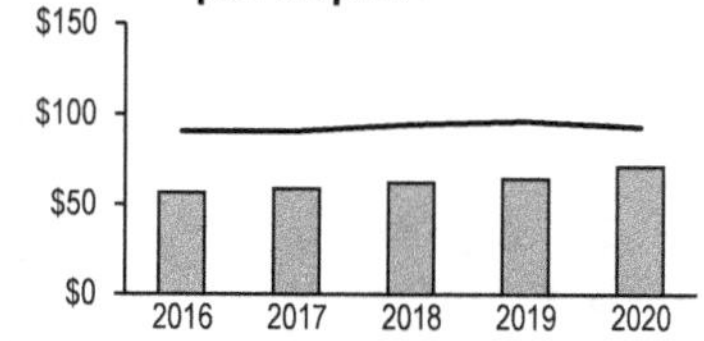

	2016	2017	2018	2019	2020
Concord	$56	$59	$62	$64	$71
Average	$91	$90	$94	$96	$93

Core Parks and Recreation Staff per 10,000 Population

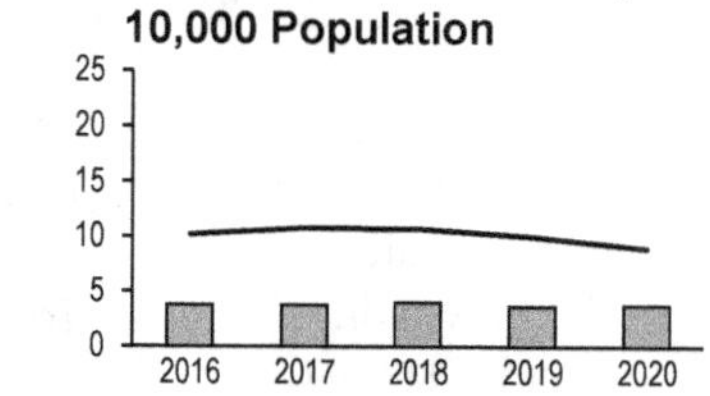

	2016	2017	2018	2019	2020
Concord	3.8	3.8	4.0	3.6	3.8
Average	10.2	10.8	10.7	10.0	8.9

Facilities Measures

Land Acres of Parks per 10,000 Population

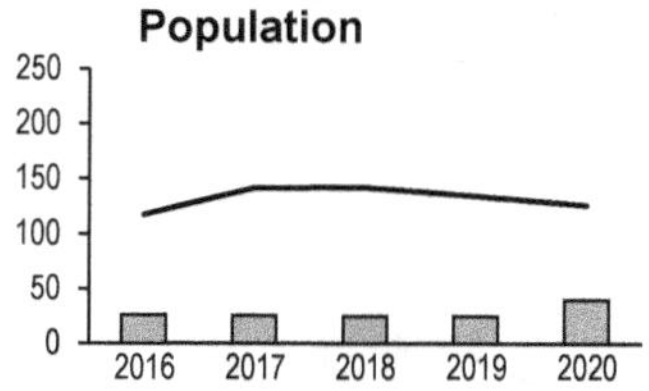

	2016	2017	2018	2019	2020
Concord	25.94	25.45	24.88	24.41	40.19
Average	117.20	140.99	141.65	134.43	125.84

Recreation Centers per 10,000 Population

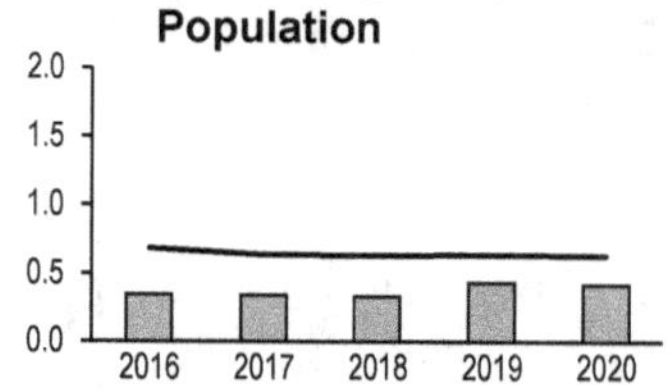

	2016	2017	2018	2019	2020
Concord	0.34	0.34	0.33	0.43	0.42
Average	0.69	0.64	0.63	0.64	0.63

Swimming Pools per 10,000 Population

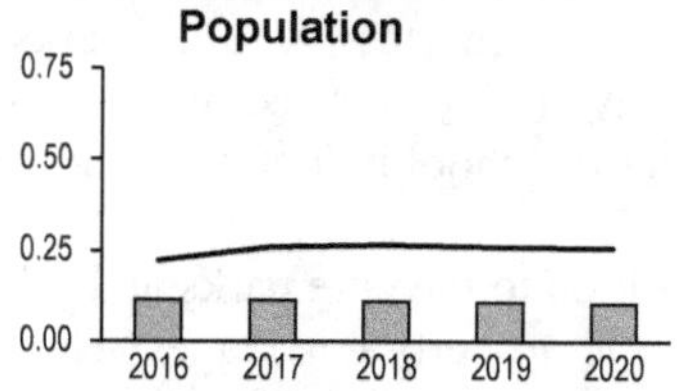

	2016	2017	2018	2019	2020
Concord	0.11	0.11	0.11	0.11	0.10
Average	0.22	0.26	0.27	0.26	0.26

Athletic Fields per 10,000 Population

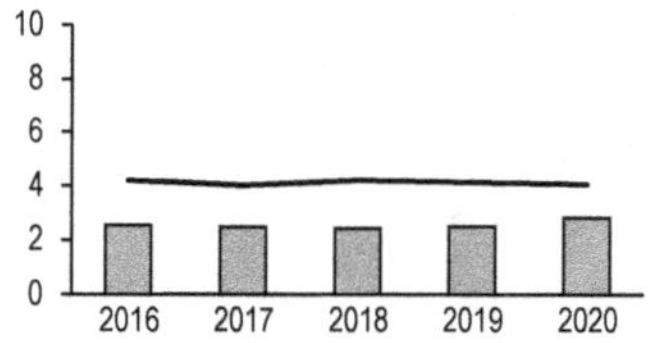

	2016	2017	2018	2019	2020
Concord	2.52	2.48	2.42	2.48	2.83
Average	4.19	4.00	4.19	4.12	4.06

Playgrounds per 10,000 Population

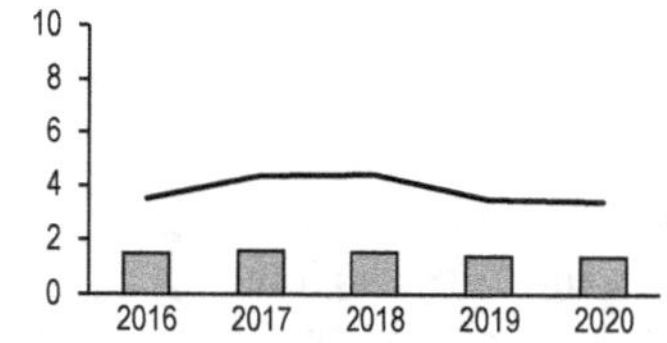

	2016	2017	2018	2019	2020
Concord	1.49	1.58	1.54	1.40	1.36
Average	3.51	4.35	4.39	3.48	3.40

Miles of Land Trails per 10,000 Population

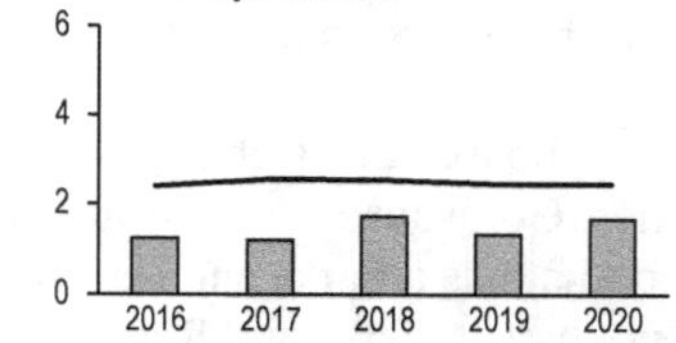

	2016	2017	2018	2019	2020
Concord	1.24	1.20	1.71	1.32	1.66
Average	2.38	2.54	2.52	2.44	2.45

Efficiency Measures

Total Core Parks and Recreation Costs per Acre

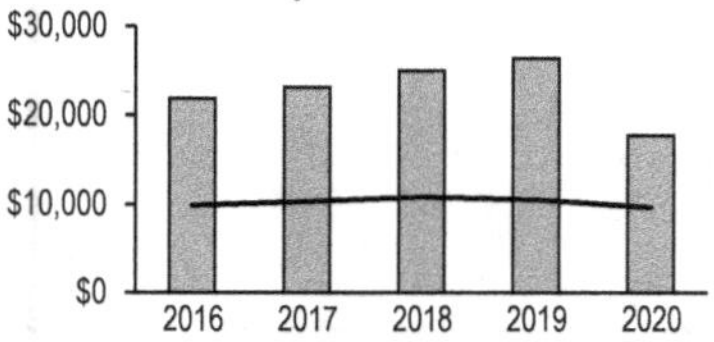

	2016	2017	2018	2019	2020
Concord	$21,782	$23,056	$24,913	$26,303	$17,683
Average	$9,857	$10,296	$10,807	$10,512	$9,650

Acres of Park Maintained per Maintenance FTE

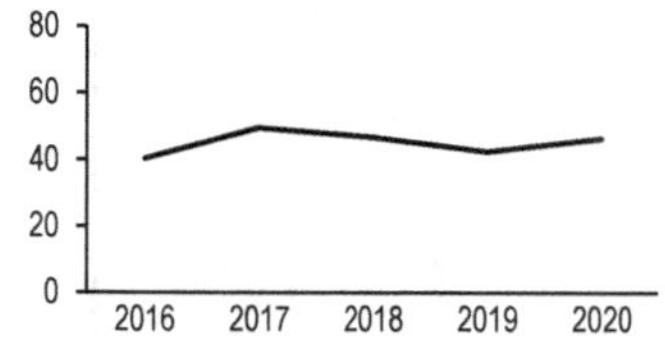

	2016	2017	2018	2019	2020
Concord					0.0
Average	40.3	49.4	46.7	42.3	46.4

Volunteer Hours in FTEs as a Percent of Paid Staff FTEs

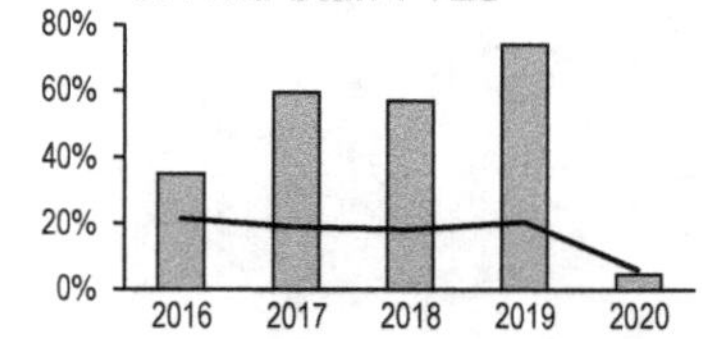

	2016	2017	2018	2019	2020
Concord	35.0%	59.5%	56.9%	74.2%	4.6%
Average	21.6%	19.0%	18.1%	20.5%	6.1%

Effectiveness Measures

Revenue Gained as a Percent of Total Core Costs

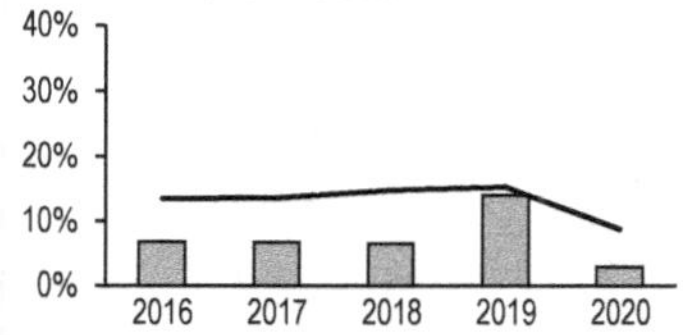

	2016	2017	2018	2019	2020
Concord	6.8%	6.7%	6.5%	14.0%	2.9%
Average	13.4%	13.4%	14.7%	15.2%	8.7%

Acts of Vandalism at Parks Facilities per 10,000 Population

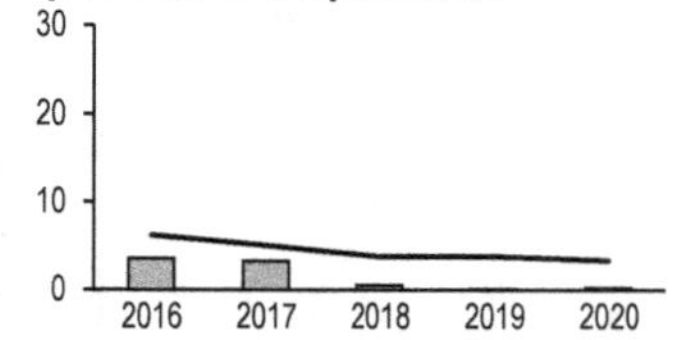

	2016	2017	2018	2019	2020
Concord	3.56	3.27	0.55	0.11	0.21
Average	6.18	5.02	3.76	3.75	3.32

Fiscal Year 2019-20

Explanatory Information

Service Level and Delivery

The City of Goldsboro provides recreation services through the separate Parks and Recreation Department. The department aims to serve the community through programs in youth athletics, adult athletics, seniors, and special populations both adult and youth. The city has a cooperative agreement with the public school system. The city has also formalized an agreement with the U.S. Air Force Base Seymour Johnson for the use of certain base facilities. County residents from outside the city are also users of the Goldsboro city system facilities and programmed activities.

The city has fourteen separate parks covering 233 acres. There are about five miles of trails, two outdoor pools, greenways, and a number of school indoor and outdoor facilities.

In addition to the core parks and recreational facilities, Goldsboro has a historic property it manages. The city also runs a municipal golf course. The operation of this course is not included here in dollars or staff as part of core parks and recreation facilities and activities.

Conditions Affecting Service, Performance, and Costs

The City of Goldsboro joined the Benchmarking Project in July 2017, with the first year of data showing for FY 2016–17.

There are no extra fees charged for non-resident users of Goldsboro's facilities. Goldsboro is one of just two municipalities in Wayne County that has a Parks and Recreation Department. Wayne County does not have a Parks and Recreation Department as one of its services offered. Goldsboro Parks and Recreation has team up with the Travel and Tourism Department to bring sports tournaments to Goldsboro. This helps expose more people to the city's offering of services and facilities.

Municipal Profile

Population (OSBM 2019)	33,969
Land Area (Square Miles)	29.45
Persons per Square Mile	1,154
Topography	Flat
Climate	Temperate; little ice and snow

Service Profile

Parks and Recreation Staff	
Administrative Position FTEs	5.0
Maintenance Staff FTEs	21.3
Program and Facility FTEs	18.3
Other Staff FTEs	3.8
TOTAL	48.3
Number of Parks and Sites	14
Total Land Acreage in Parks	233.0
Miles of Trails in Parks	4.5
Recreational Facilities	
Indoor and Outdoor Pools	2
Recreation Centers	4
Outdoor Basketball Courts	11
Outdoor Tennis Courts	18
Playgrounds	10
Diamond Fields	4
Rectangular Fields	15
Other Athletic Fields	6
Picnic Shelters	13
Parks and Recreation Revenues	
User Fees	$185,075
Grants	$2,500
Sponsorships	$52,500
Donations	$0

Full Cost Profile

Cost Breakdown by Percentage	
Personal Services	69.6%
Operating Costs	22.7%
Capital Costs	7.7%
TOTAL	100.0%
Cost Breakdown in Dollars	
Personal Services	$2,268,956
Operating Costs	$741,914
Capital Costs	$250,763
TOTAL	$3,261,633

Goldsboro — Core Parks and Recreation

Key: Goldsboro ▩ Benchmarking Average — Fiscal Years 2016 through 2020

Resource Measures

Core Parks and Recreation Services per Capita

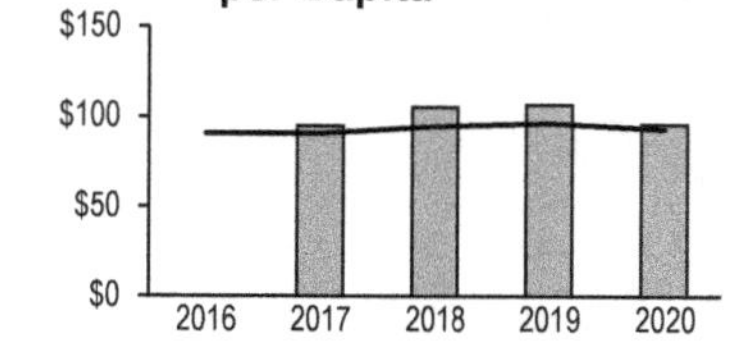

	2016	2017	2018	2019	2020
Goldsboro		$95	$105	$107	$96
Average	$91	$90	$94	$96	$93

Core Parks and Recreation Staff per 10,000 Population

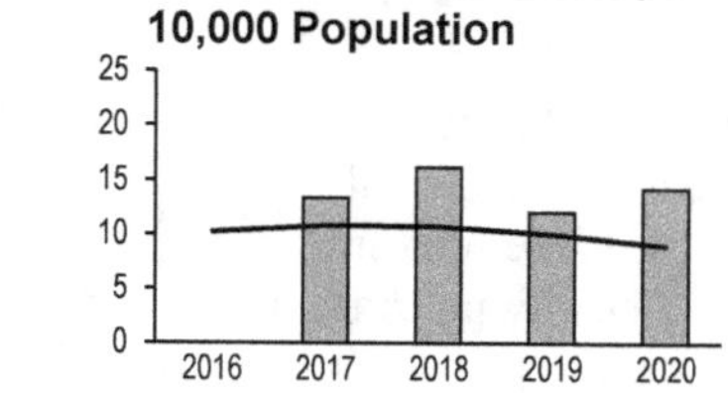

	2016	2017	2018	2019	2020
Goldsboro		13.3	16.1	12.0	14.2
Average	10.2	10.8	10.7	10.0	8.9

Facilities Measures

Land Acres of Parks per 10,000 Population

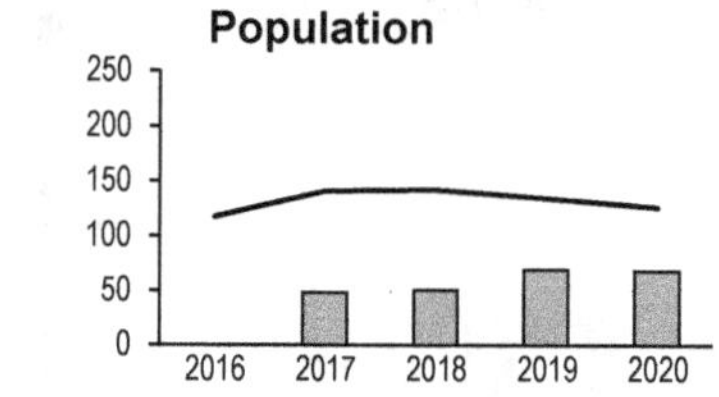

	2016	2017	2018	2019	2020
Goldsboro		48.51	50.47	69.27	68.59
Average	117.20	140.99	141.65	134.43	125.84

Recreation Centers per 10,000 Population

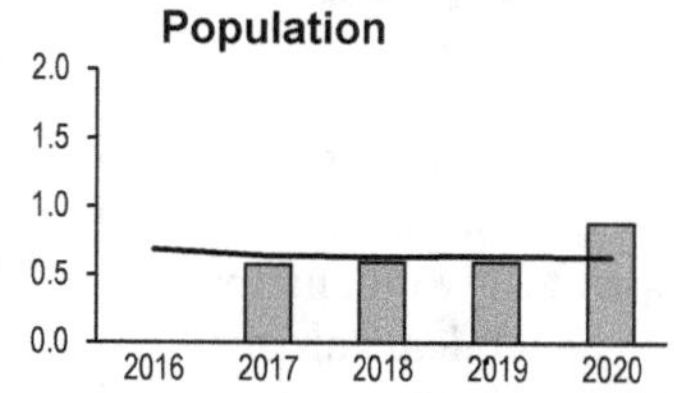

	2016	2017	2018	2019	2020
Goldsboro		0.57	0.59	0.59	0.88
Average	0.69	0.64	0.63	0.64	0.63

Swimming Pools per 10,000 Population

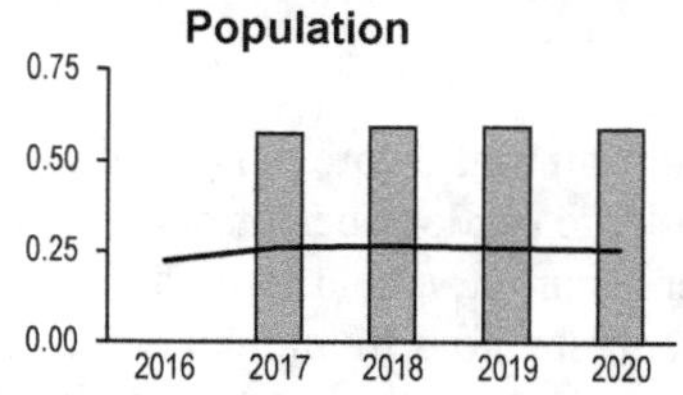

	2016	2017	2018	2019	2020
Goldsboro		0.57	0.59	0.59	0.59
Average	0.22	0.26	0.27	0.26	0.26

Athletic Fields per 10,000 Population

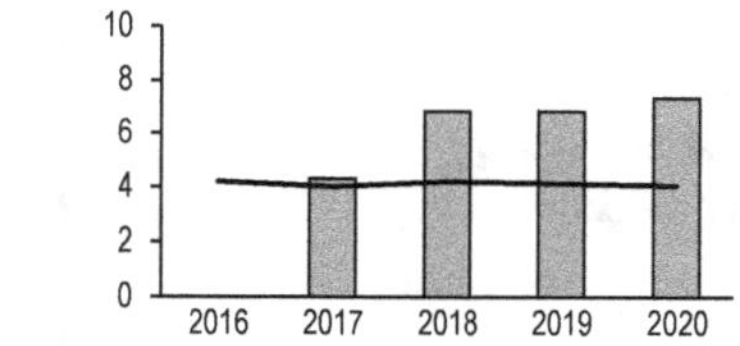

	2016	2017	2018	2019	2020
Goldsboro		4.31	6.83	6.84	7.36
Average	4.19	4.00	4.19	4.12	4.06

Playgrounds per 10,000 Population

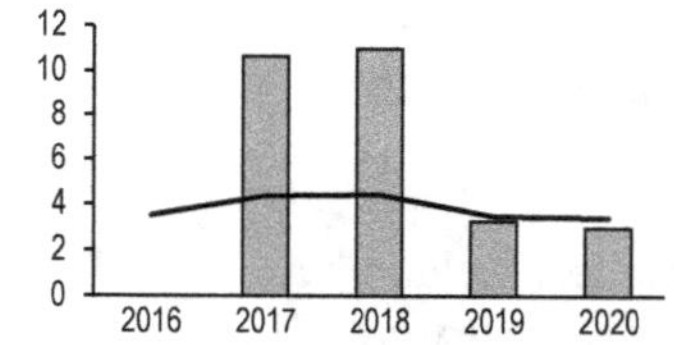

	2016	2017	2018	2019	2020
Goldsboro		10.63	10.98	3.27	2.94
Average	3.51	4.35	4.39	3.48	3.40

Miles of Land Trails per 10,000 Population

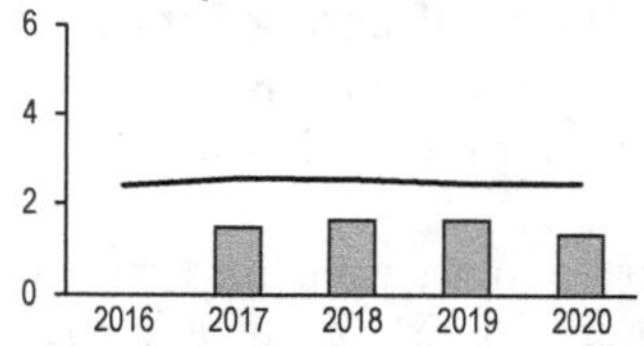

	2016	2017	2018	2019	2020
Goldsboro		1.47	1.63	1.64	1.32
Average	2.38	2.54	2.52	2.44	2.45

Efficiency Measures

Total Core Parks and Recreation Costs per Acre

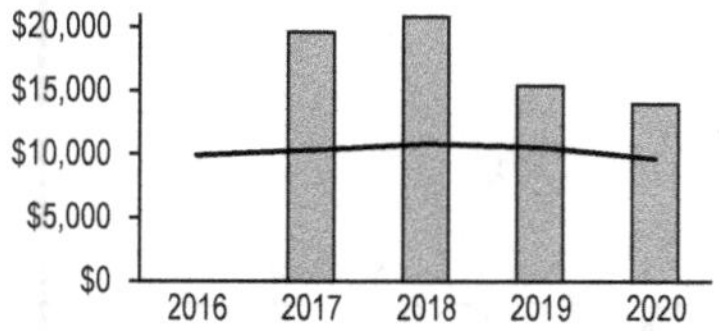

	2016	2017	2018	2019	2020
Goldsboro		$19,567	$20,815	$15,420	$13,998
Average	$9,857	$10,296	$10,807	$10,512	$9,650

Acres of Park Maintained per Maintenance FTE

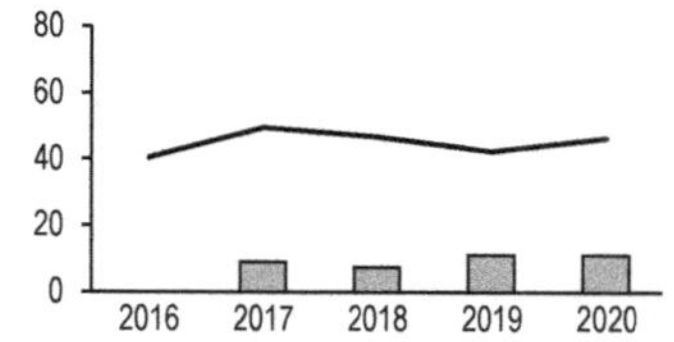

	2016	2017	2018	2019	2020
Goldsboro		8.9	7.4	11.0	11.0
Average	40.3	49.4	46.7	42.3	46.4

Volunteer Hours in FTEs as a Percent of Paid Staff FTEs

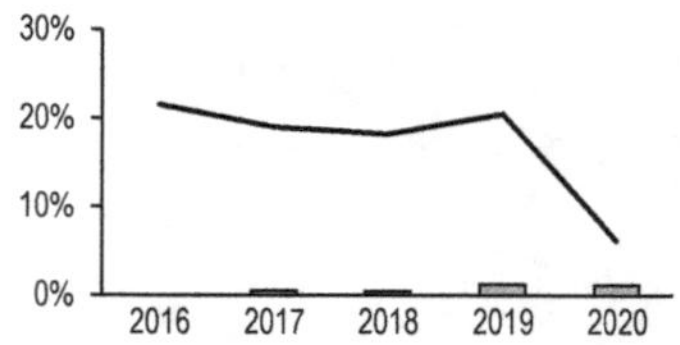

	2016	2017	2018	2019	2020
Goldsboro		0.5%	0.4%	1.2%	1.1%
Average	21.6%	19.0%	18.1%	20.5%	6.1%

Effectiveness Measures

Revenue Gained as a Percent of Total Core Costs

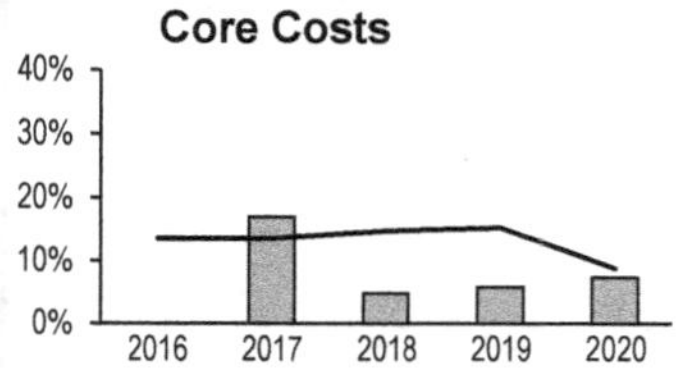

	2016	2017	2018	2019	2020
Goldsboro		16.9%	4.7%	5.8%	7.4%
Average	13.4%	13.4%	14.7%	15.2%	8.7%

Acts of Vandalism at Parks Facilities per 10,000 Population

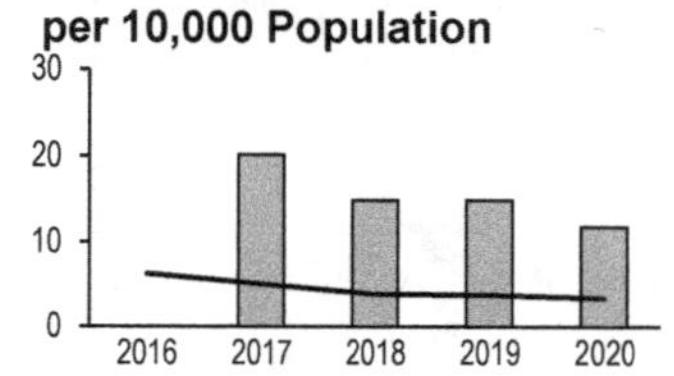

	2016	2017	2018	2019	2020
Goldsboro		20.12	14.84	14.87	11.78
Average	6.18	5.02	3.76	3.75	3.32

Fiscal Year 2019-20

Explanatory Information

Service Level and Delivery

The City of Greensboro provides recreation services through the separate Parks and Recreation Department. The city has several cooperative agreements with the local schools and some non-profits for the provision of services or use of facilities. The city provides a full array of recreational facilities and activities.

The city has 486 separate parks and sites. These parks cover 7,433 land acres; most of them are developed and include dedicated drainageway and open spaces. In addition, the city has a number of acres in water space as part of the parks system. The city has 100 miles of trails.

In addition to the core parks and recreational facilities, Greensboro has a large outdoor performance event site, a historic property, a famers' market, a boat ramp and marina, and operates two municipal golf courses, four municipal cemetaries, and four botanical gardens. The operation of these other facilities is not included in the Core Parks and Recreation comparisons reported here. These facilities are not included here in dollars or staff as part of core parks and recreation facilities and activities.

Conditions Affecting Service, Performance, and Costs

Greensboro did not report data for Core Parks and Recreation services for FY 2015–16.

Greensboro has been updating its lists of properties, including a number of drainage way and open space properties that were dedicated to the city but never accepted. These parcels have been added to the inventory of parks, which has increased the number of parks reported.

Municipal Profile

Population (OSBM 2019)	293,730
Land Area (Square Miles)	129.62
Persons per Square Mile	2,266
Topography	Flat
Climate	Temperate; little ice and snow

Service Profile

Parks and Recreation Staff	
Administrative Position FTEs	16.5
Maintenance Staff FTEs	78.5
Program and Facility FTEs	61.0
Other Staff FTEs	6.0
TOTAL	162.0
Number of Parks and Sites	486
Total Land Acreage in Parks	7,432.7
Miles of Trails in Parks	100.2
Recreational Facilities	
Indoor and Outdoor Pools	5
Recreation Centers	12
Outdoor Basketball Courts	46
Outdoor Tennis Courts	75
Playgrounds	105
Diamond Fields	39
Rectangular Fields	36
Other Athletic Fields	0
Picnic Shelters	40
Parks and Recreation Revenues	
User Fees	$1,177,202
Grants	$613,074
Sponsorships	$17,383
Donations	$83,572

Full Cost Profile

Cost Breakdown by Percentage	
Personal Services	60.9%
Operating Costs	39.1%
Capital Costs	0.0%
TOTAL	100.0%
Cost Breakdown in Dollars	
Personal Services	$10,680,734
Operating Costs	$6,843,432
Capital Costs	$0
TOTAL	$17,524,166

Greensboro — Core Parks and Recreation

Key: Greensboro ▪ Benchmarking Average — Fiscal Years 2016 through 2020

Resource Measures

Core Parks and Recreation Services per Capita

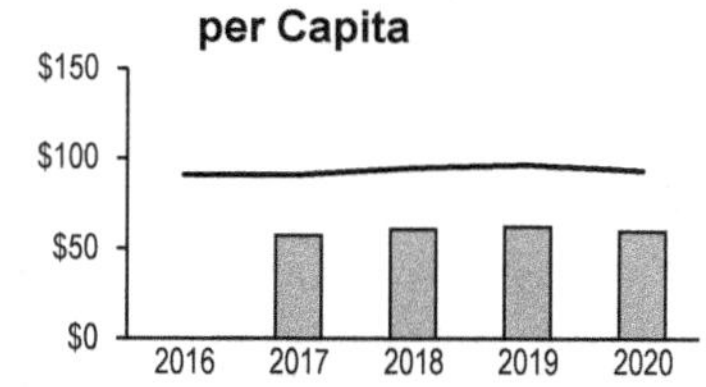

	2016	2017	2018	2019	2020
Greensboro		$57	$61	$62	$60
Average	$91	$90	$94	$96	$93

Core Parks and Recreation Staff per 10,000 Population

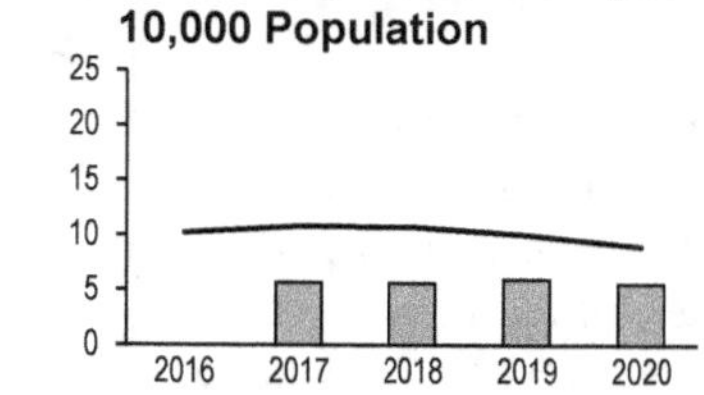

	2016	2017	2018	2019	2020
Greensboro		5.7	5.6	5.9	5.5
Average	10.2	10.8	10.7	10.0	8.9

Facilities Measures

Land Acres of Parks per 10,000 Population

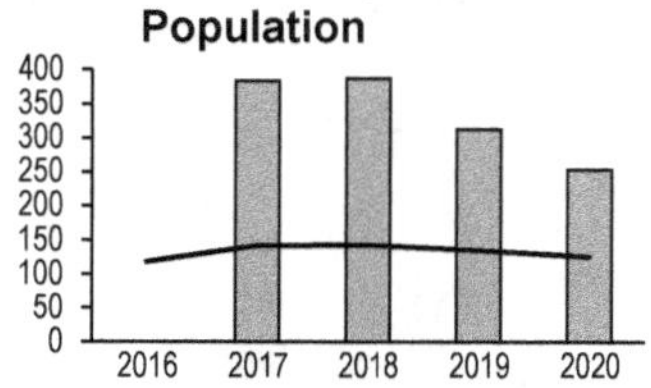

	2016	2017	2018	2019	2020
Greensboro		383.59	387.24	313.21	253.04
Average	117.20	140.99	141.65	134.43	125.84

Recreation Centers per 10,000 Population

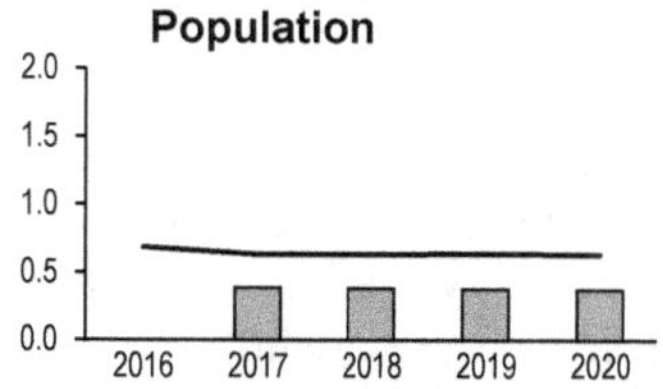

	2016	2017	2018	2019	2020
Greensboro		0.39	0.38	0.38	0.37
Average	0.69	0.64	0.63	0.64	0.63

Swimming Pools per 10,000 Population

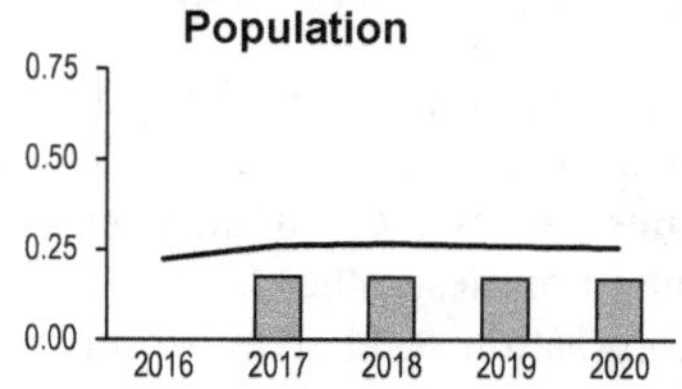

	2016	2017	2018	2019	2020
Greensboro		0.18	0.17	0.17	0.17
Average	0.22	0.26	0.27	0.26	0.26

Athletic Fields per 10,000 Population

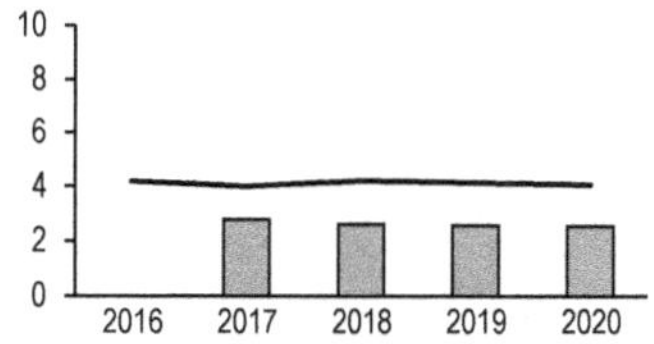

	2016	2017	2018	2019	2020
Greensboro		2.78	2.60	2.57	2.55
Average	4.19	4.00	4.19	4.12	4.06

Playgrounds per 10,000 Population

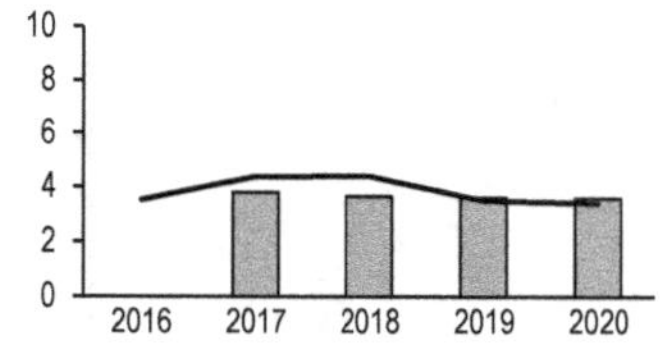

	2016	2017	2018	2019	2020
Greensboro		3.80	3.64	3.59	3.57
Average	3.51	4.35	4.39	3.48	3.40

Miles of Land Trails per 10,000 Population

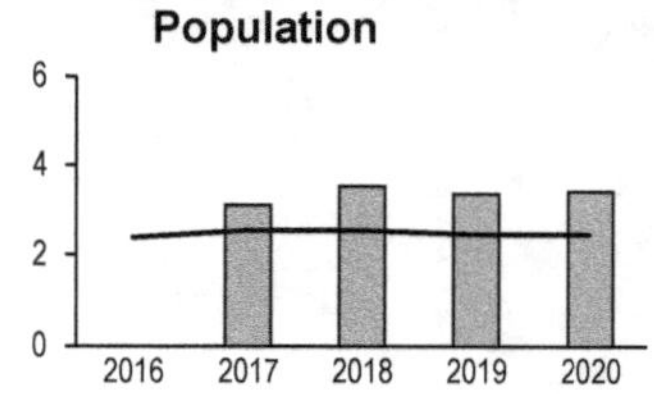

	2016	2017	2018	2019	2020
Greensboro		3.10	3.53	3.35	3.41
Average	2.38	2.54	2.52	2.44	2.45

Efficiency Measures

Total Core Parks and Recreation Costs per Acre

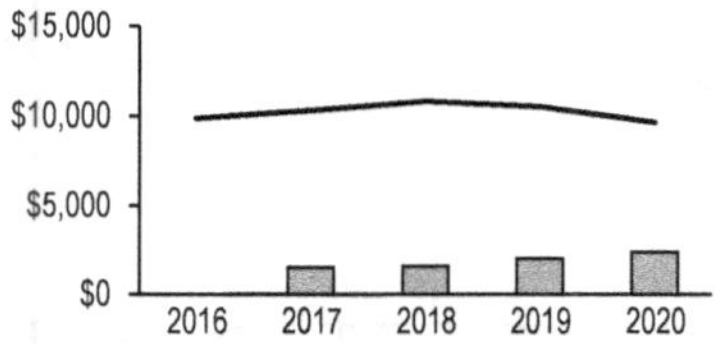

	2016	2017	2018	2019	2020
Greensboro		$1,493	$1,570	$1,991	$2,358
Average	$9,857	$10,296	$10,807	$10,512	$9,650

Acres of Park Maintained per Maintenance FTE

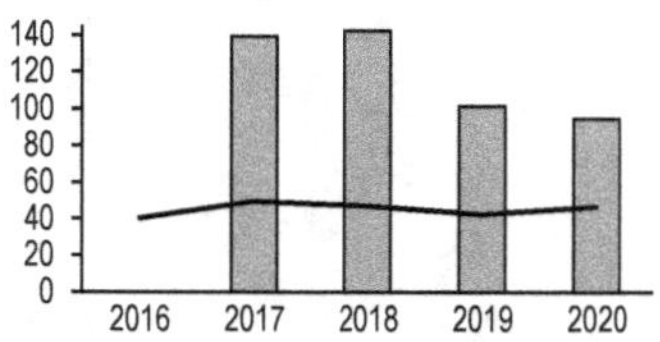

	2016	2017	2018	2019	2020
Greensboro		138.9	142.2	101.1	94.7
Average	40.3	49.4	46.7	42.3	46.4

Volunteer Hours in FTEs as a Percent of Paid Staff FTEs

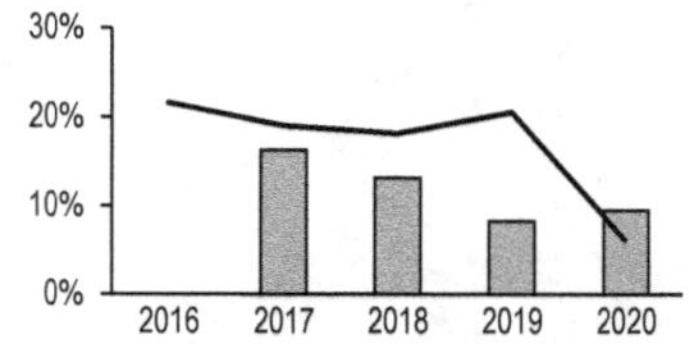

	2016	2017	2018	2019	2020
Greensboro		16.3%	13.1%	8.2%	9.5%
Average	21.6%	19.0%	18.1%	20.5%	6.1%

Effectiveness Measures

Revenue Gained as a Percent of Total Core Costs

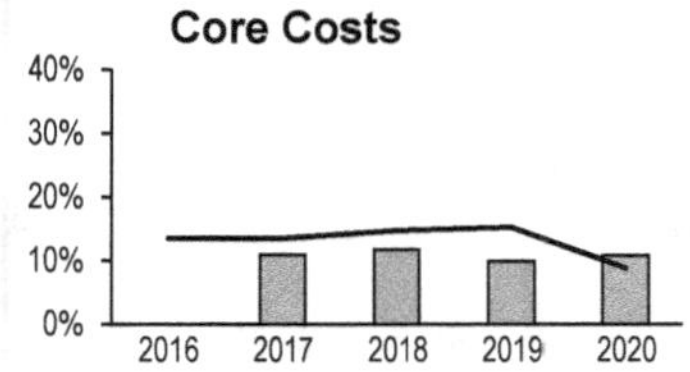

	2016	2017	2018	2019	2020
Greensboro		10.9%	11.7%	9.9%	10.8%
Average	13.4%	13.4%	14.7%	15.2%	8.7%

Acts of Vandalism at Parks Facilities per 10,000 Population

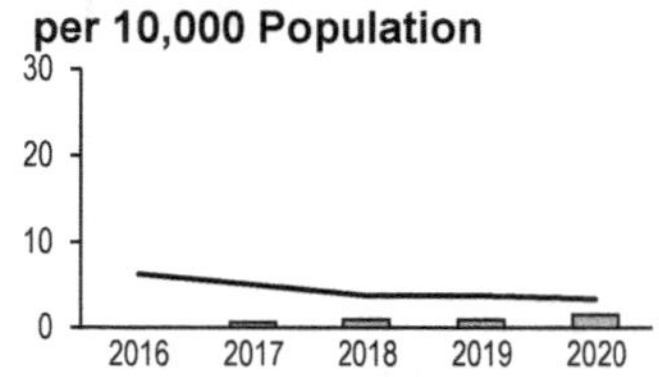

	2016	2017	2018	2019	2020
Greensboro		0.67	0.94	0.92	1.57
Average	6.18	5.02	3.76	3.75	3.32

Fiscal Year 2019-20

Explanatory Information

Service Level and Delivery

The City of Hickory Parks and Recreation Department is a separate department under the city organization. The city has partnerships with other organizations to provide recreational services, including a priority-use agreement with local schools for use of facilities over other non-school users and a priority-use agreement with Catawba Valley Youth Soccer for use of city soccer fields.

The city has twenty-four separate parks and sites. This includes 448 acres of park acreage, mostly developed. The city has sixteen miles of trails.

In addition to the core parks and recreational facilities, Hickory has one historic property, one professional sports facility, one boat ramp, one museum, two community gardens, and a tower ropes course. The operation of these other facilities is not included in the Core Parks and Recreation comparisons reported here. These facilities are not included here in dollars or staff as part of core parks and recreation facilities and activities.

Conditions Affecting Service, Performance, and Costs

Municipal Profile

Population (OSBM 2019)	41,409
Land Area (Square Miles)	30.50
Persons per Square Mile	1,358
Topography	Gently rolling
Climate	Temperate; some ice and snow

Service Profile

Parks and Recreation Staff	
Administrative Position FTEs	3.0
Maintenance Staff FTEs	0.0
Program and Facility FTEs	20.0
Other Staff FTEs	0.0
TOTAL	23.0
Number of Parks and Sites	24
Total Land Acreage in Parks	447.6
Miles of Trails in Parks	16.0
Recreational Facilities	
Indoor and Outdoor Pools	0
Recreation Centers	7
Outdoor Basketball Courts	17
Outdoor Tennis Courts	16
Playgrounds	40
Diamond Fields	11
Rectangular Fields	12
Other Athletic Fields	0
Picnic Shelters	13
Parks and Recreation Revenues	
User Fees	$136,562
Grants	$0
Sponsorships	$0
Donations	$60,000

Full Cost Profile

Cost Breakdown by Percentage	
Personal Services	43.8%
Operating Costs	40.9%
Capital Costs	15.3%
TOTAL	100.0%
Cost Breakdown in Dollars	
Personal Services	$2,161,664
Operating Costs	$2,018,488
Capital Costs	$752,723
TOTAL	$4,932,875

Hickory — Core Parks and Recreation

Key: Hickory ■ Benchmarking Average — Fiscal Years 2016 through 2020

Resource Measures

Core Parks and Recreation Services per Capita

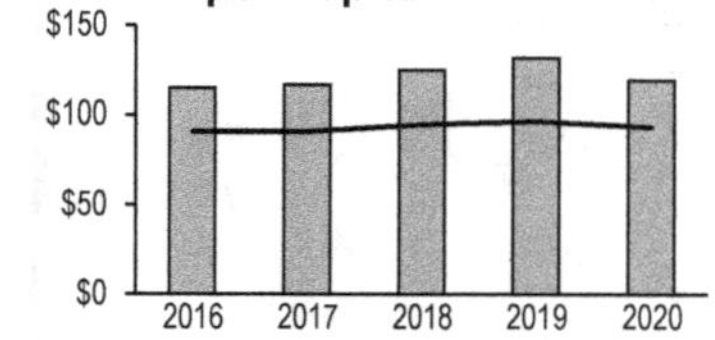

	2016	2017	2018	2019	2020
Hickory	$115	$117	$125	$132	$119
Average	$91	$90	$94	$96	$93

Core Parks and Recreation Staff per 10,000 Population

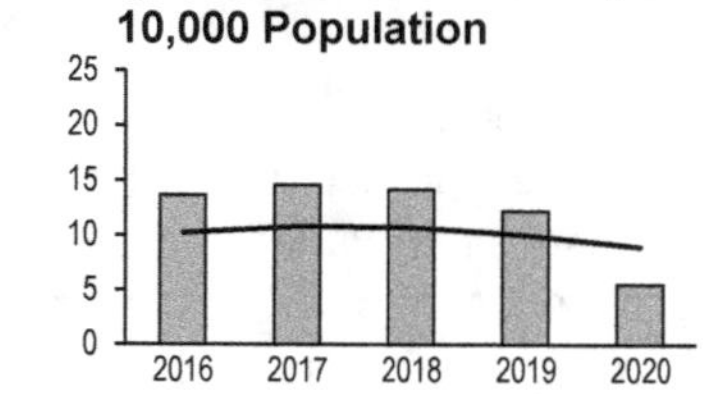

	2016	2017	2018	2019	2020
Hickory	13.6	14.6	14.1	12.2	5.6
Average	10.2	10.8	10.7	10.0	8.9

Facilities Measures

Land Acres of Parks per 10,000 Population

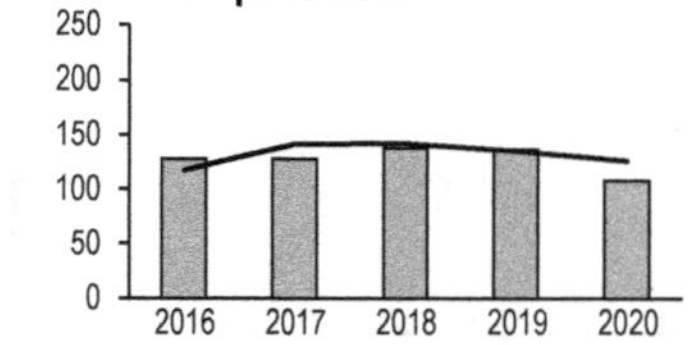

	2016	2017	2018	2019	2020
Hickory	127.38	127.31	137.27	136.32	108.10
Average	117.20	140.99	141.65	134.43	125.84

Recreation Centers per 10,000 Population

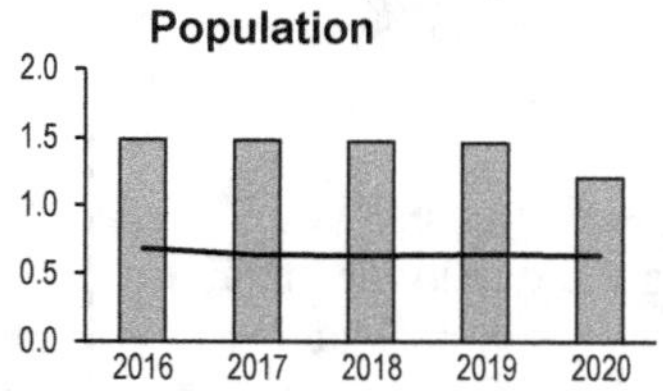

	2016	2017	2018	2019	2020
Hickory	1.49	1.48	1.48	1.47	1.21
Average	0.69	0.64	0.63	0.64	0.63

Swimming Pools per 10,000 Population

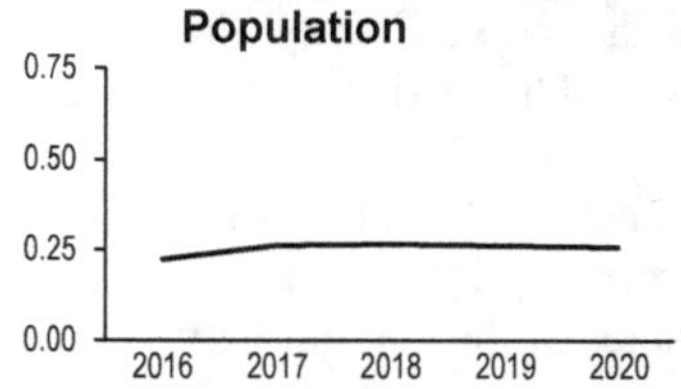

	2016	2017	2018	2019	2020
Hickory	0.00	0.00	0.00	0.00	0.00
Average	0.22	0.26	0.27	0.26	0.26

Athletic Fields per 10,000 Population

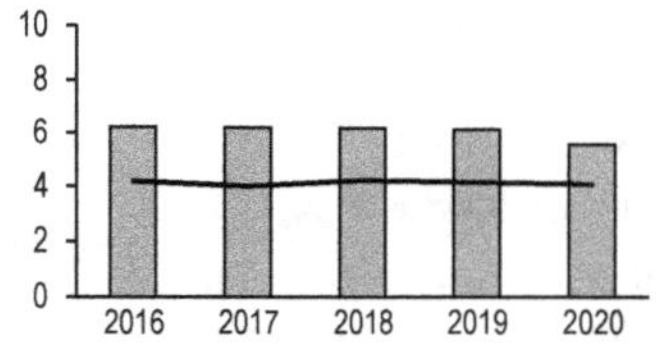

	2016	2017	2018	2019	2020
Hickory	6.20	6.18	6.15	6.11	5.55
Average	4.19	4.00	4.19	4.12	4.06

Playgrounds per 10,000 Population

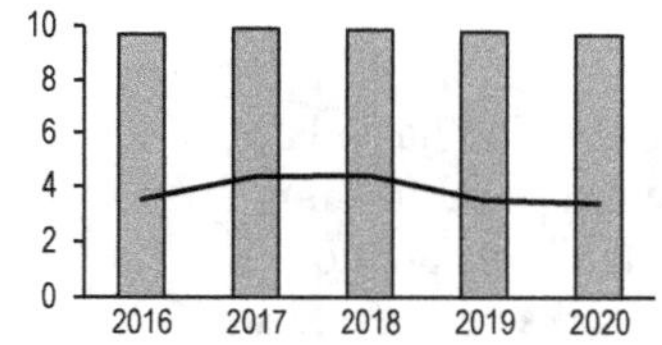

	2016	2017	2018	2019	2020
Hickory	9.67	9.89	9.84	9.77	9.66
Average	3.51	4.35	4.39	3.48	3.40

Miles of Land Trails per 10,000 Population

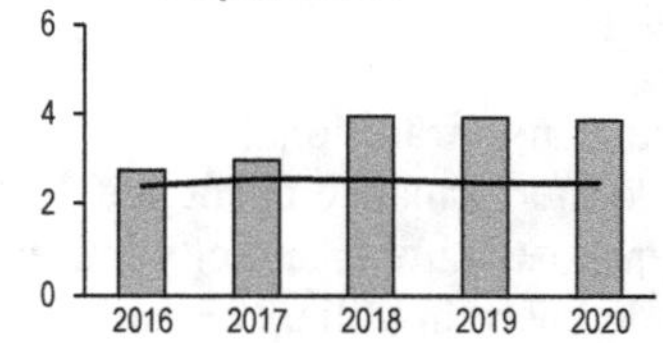

	2016	2017	2018	2019	2020
Hickory	2.73	2.96	3.95	3.92	3.86
Average	2.38	2.54	2.52	2.44	2.45

Efficiency Measures

Total Core Parks and Recreation Costs per Acre

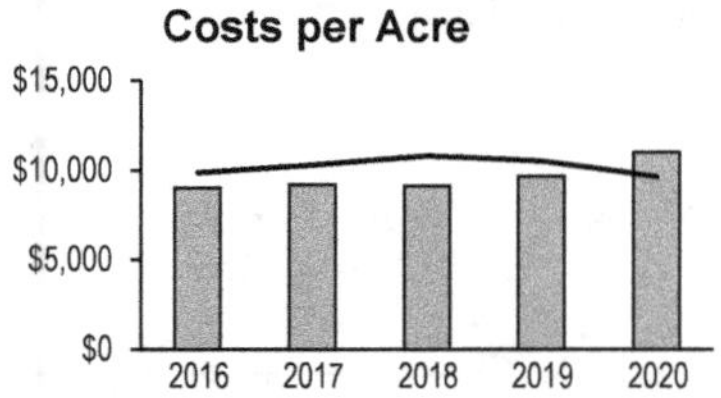

	2016	2017	2018	2019	2020
Hickory	$9,020	$9,184	$9,119	$9,684	$11,020
Average	$9,857	$10,296	$10,807	$10,512	$9,650

Acres of Park Maintained per Maintenance FTE

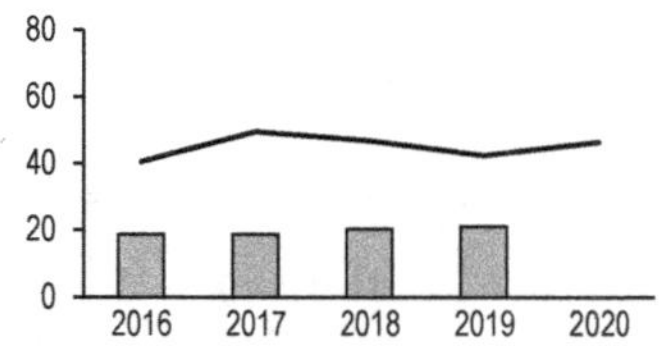

	2016	2017	2018	2019	2020
Hickory	18.7	18.7	20.3	21.1	0.0
Average	40.3	49.4	46.7	42.3	46.4

Volunteer Hours in FTEs as a Percent of Paid Staff FTEs

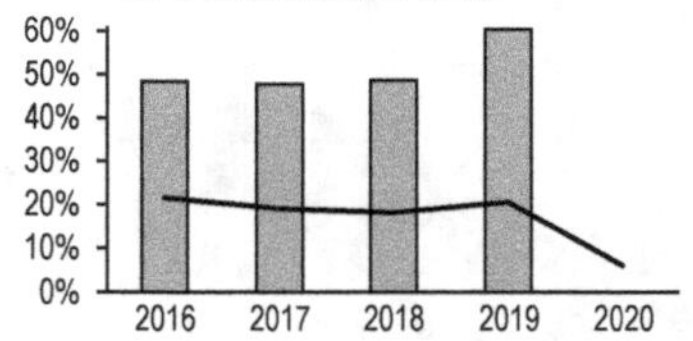

	2016	2017	2018	2019	2020
Hickory	48.3%	47.7%	48.6%	60.4%	
Average	21.6%	19.0%	18.1%	20.5%	6.1%

Effectiveness Measures

Revenue Gained as a Percent of Total Core Costs

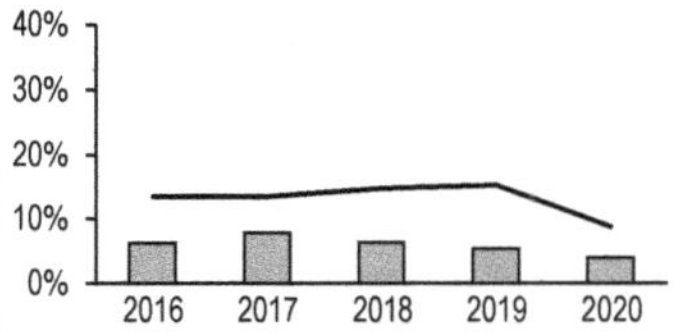

	2016	2017	2018	2019	2020
Hickory	6.2%	7.8%	6.4%	5.3%	4.0%
Average	13.4%	13.4%	14.7%	15.2%	8.7%

Acts of Vandalism at Parks Facilities per 10,000 Population

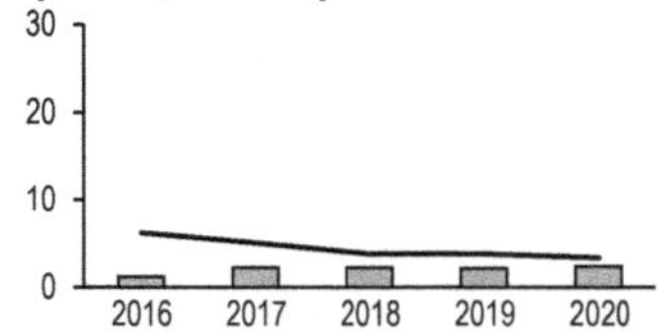

	2016	2017	2018	2019	2020
Hickory	1.24	2.22	2.21	2.20	2.41
Average	6.18	5.02	3.76	3.75	3.32

Fiscal Year 2019-20

Explanatory Information

Service Level and Delivery

The City of Raleigh Parks, Recreation, and Cultural Resources Department is a stand-alone unit within the city. The department is comprised of five divisions: Business Process Management, Park Development and Communications, Parks, Recreation, and Resources.

The department has a public/private partnership with the Dix Park Conservancy to provide funding for master planning and programming at Dorothea Dix Park. The city also has joint-use agreements and memorandums of understanding with other entities, including Wake County, the Wake County Public School System, NC State University, and local non-profit organizations.

Raleigh has a full array of recreational facilities available. The department plays a leading role in determining the quality of life and character of the Capital City. With over 6,200 acres of parkland, 156 miles of greenway trails, and over 1.3 million square feet of facilities, the department provides a wide range of creative programming opportunities that promote the social, cultural, mental, and physical well-being of citizens. The city's vision for its parks, recreation, and cultural resources system is "bringing people to parks and parks to people."

In addition to traditional recreational facilities, Raleigh has a large outdoor performance event site, historic properties, a performing arts center, boats ramps, and city museums. These facilities are not included here in dollars or staff as part of core parks and recreation facilities and activities.

Conditions Affecting Service, Performance, and Costs

Raleigh rejoined the Benchmarking Project in July 2016, with the first year of data showing for FY 2015–16.

Municipal Profile

Population (OSBM 2019)	475,580
Land Area (Square Miles)	146.47
Persons per Square Mile	3,247
Topography	Flat; gently rolling
Climate	Temperate; little ice and snow

Service Profile

Parks and Recreation Staff	
Administrative Position FTEs	20.9
Maintenance Staff FTEs	179.0
Program and Facility FTEs	520.5
Other Staff FTEs	33.0
TOTAL	753.4
Number of Parks and Sites	175
Total Land Acreage in Parks	6,224.0
Miles of Trails in Parks	156.0
Recreational Facilities	
Indoor and Outdoor Pools	8
Recreation Centers	41
Outdoor Basketball Courts	64
Outdoor Tennis Courts	114
Playgrounds	106
Diamond Fields	58
Rectangular Fields	0
Other Athletic Fields	41
Picnic Shelters	90
Parks and Recreation Revenues	
User Fees	$5,855,201
Grants	$200,998
Sponsorships	$0
Donations	$959,487

Full Cost Profile

Cost Breakdown by Percentage	
Personal Services	61.0%
Operating Costs	34.0%
Capital Costs	5.0%
TOTAL	100.0%
Cost Breakdown in Dollars	
Personal Services	$34,708,940
Operating Costs	$19,355,097
Capital Costs	$2,843,290
TOTAL	$56,907,327

Raleigh

Core Parks and Recreation

Key: Raleigh ▒ Benchmarking Average — Fiscal Years 2016 through 2020

Resource Measures

Core Parks and Recreation Services per Capita

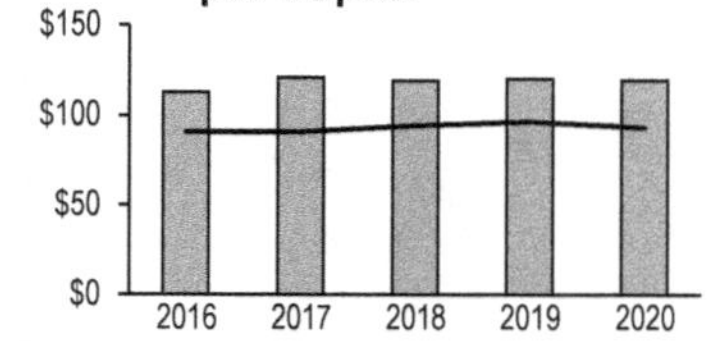

	2016	2017	2018	2019	2020
Raleigh	$113	$121	$119	$120	$120
Average	$91	$90	$94	$96	$93

Core Parks and Recreation Staff per 10,000 Population

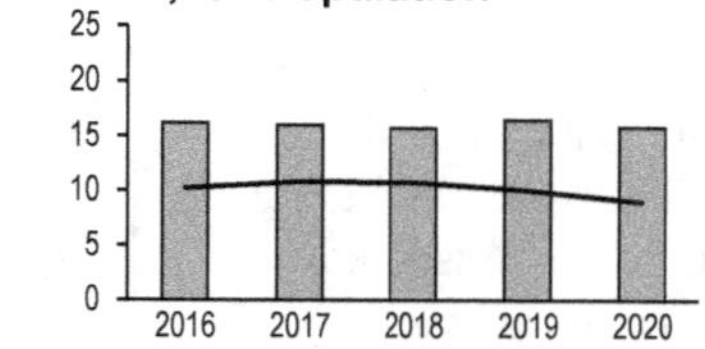

	2016	2017	2018	2019	2020
Raleigh	16.2	16.0	15.7	16.5	15.8
Average	10.2	10.8	10.7	10.0	8.9

Facilities Measures

Land Acres of Parks per 10,000 Population

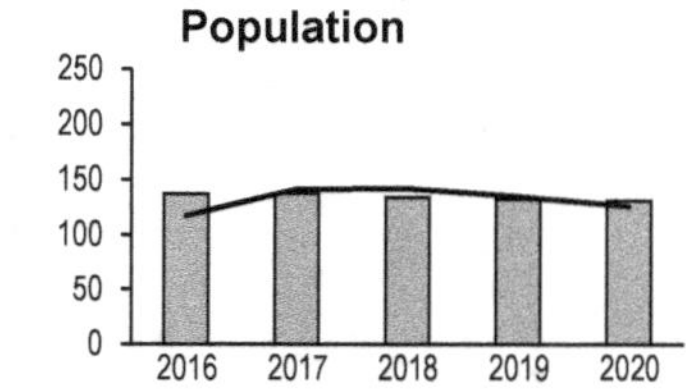

	2016	2017	2018	2019	2020
Raleigh	137.03	137.38	133.92	131.92	130.87
Average	117.20	140.99	141.65	134.43	125.84

Recreation Centers per 10,000 Population

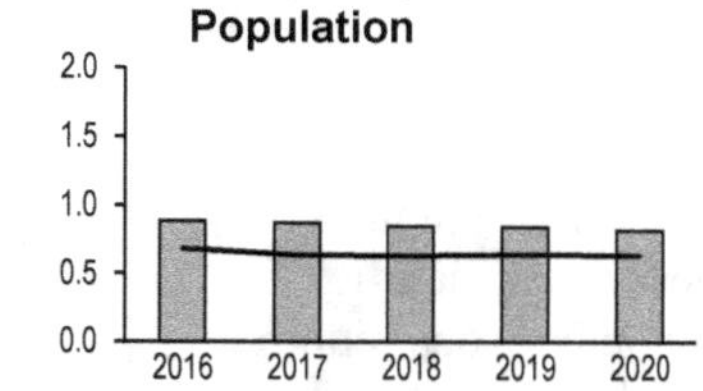

	2016	2017	2018	2019	2020
Raleigh	0.88	0.87	0.85	0.84	0.82
Average	0.69	0.64	0.63	0.64	0.63

Swimming Pools per 10,000 Population

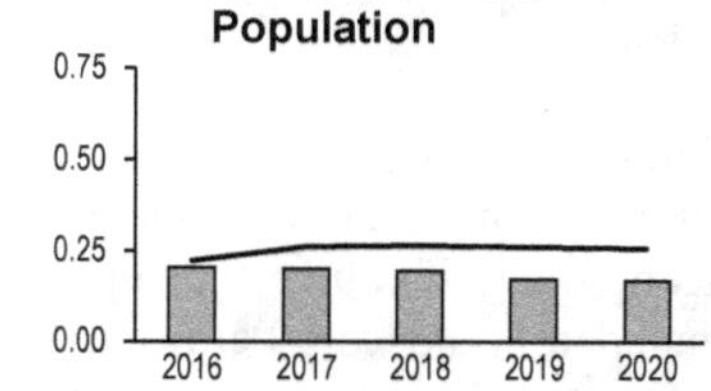

	2016	2017	2018	2019	2020
Raleigh	0.20	0.20	0.20	0.17	0.17
Average	0.22	0.26	0.27	0.26	0.26

Athletic Fields per 10,000 Population

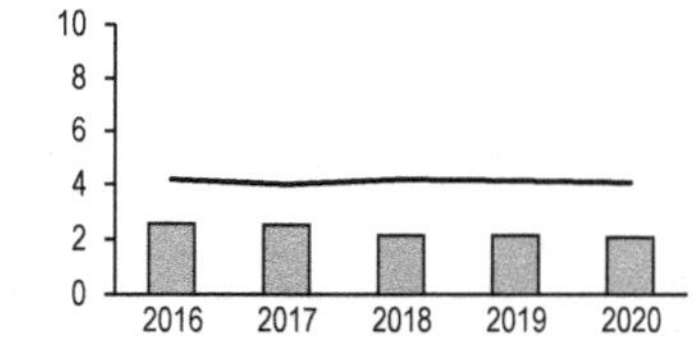

	2016	2017	2018	2019	2020
Raleigh	2.56	2.52	2.15	2.15	2.08
Average	4.19	4.00	4.19	4.12	4.06

Playgrounds per 10,000 Population

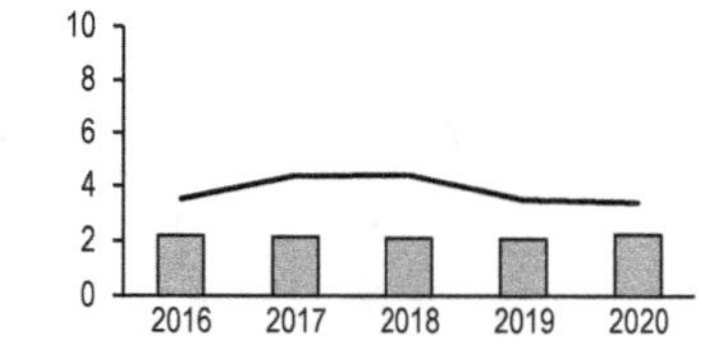

	2016	2017	2018	2019	2020
Raleigh	2.18	2.14	2.09	2.07	2.23
Average	3.51	4.35	4.39	3.48	3.40

Miles of Land Trails per 10,000 Population

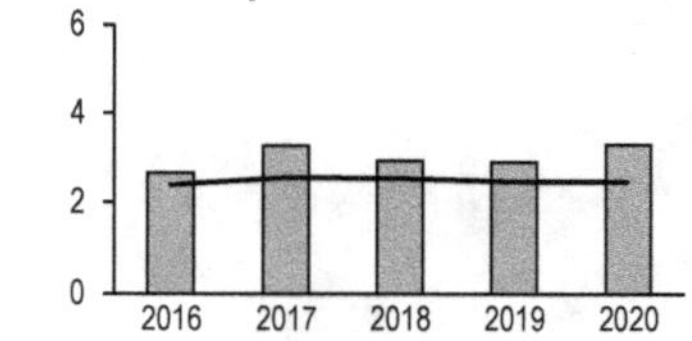

	2016	2017	2018	2019	2020
Raleigh	2.65	3.26	2.91	2.89	3.28
Average	2.38	2.54	2.52	2.44	2.45

Efficiency Measures

Total Core Parks and Recreation Costs per Acre

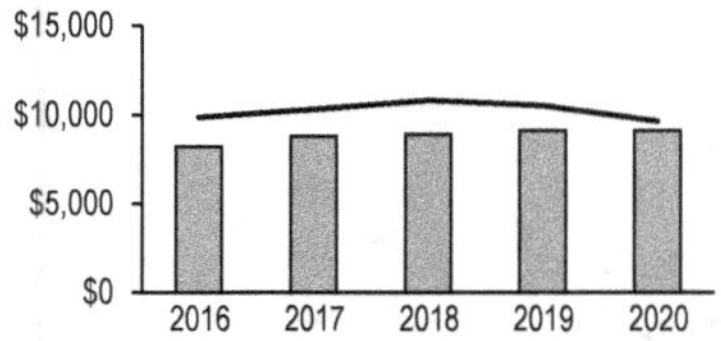

	2016	2017	2018	2019	2020
Raleigh	$8,240	$8,806	$8,909	$9,131	$9,143
Average	$9,857	$10,296	$10,807	$10,512	$9,650

Acres of Park Maintained per Maintenance FTE

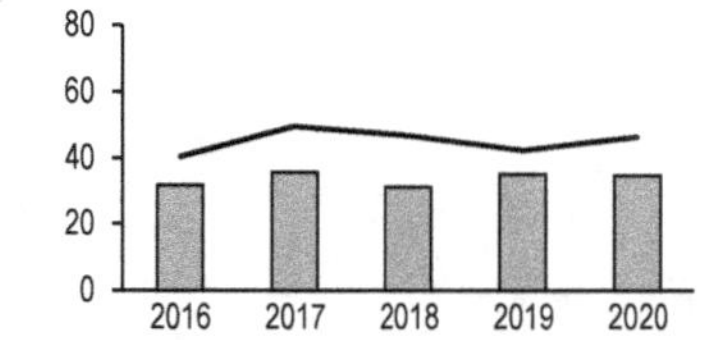

	2016	2017	2018	2019	2020
Raleigh	31.8	35.7	31.3	35.1	34.8
Average	40.3	49.4	46.7	42.3	46.4

Volunteer Hours in FTEs as a Percent of Paid Staff FTEs

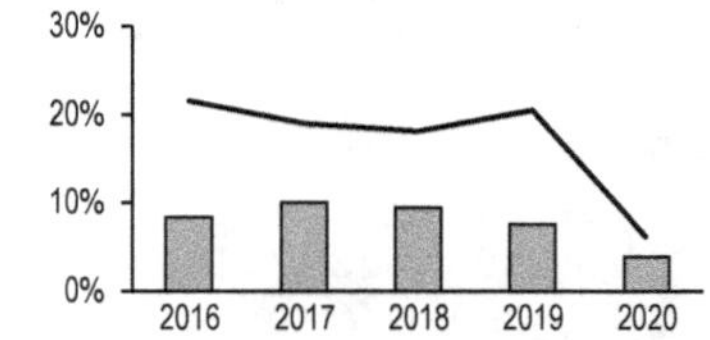

	2016	2017	2018	2019	2020
Raleigh	8.3%	10.0%	9.4%	7.5%	3.9%
Average	21.6%	19.0%	18.1%	20.5%	6.1%

Effectiveness Measures

Revenue Gained as a Percent of Total Core Costs

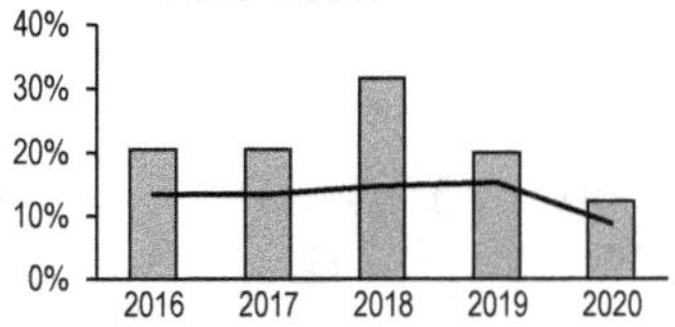

	2016	2017	2018	2019	2020
Raleigh	20.5%	20.5%	31.7%	20.1%	12.3%
Average	13.4%	13.4%	14.7%	15.2%	8.7%

Acts of Vandalism at Parks Facilities per 10,000 Population

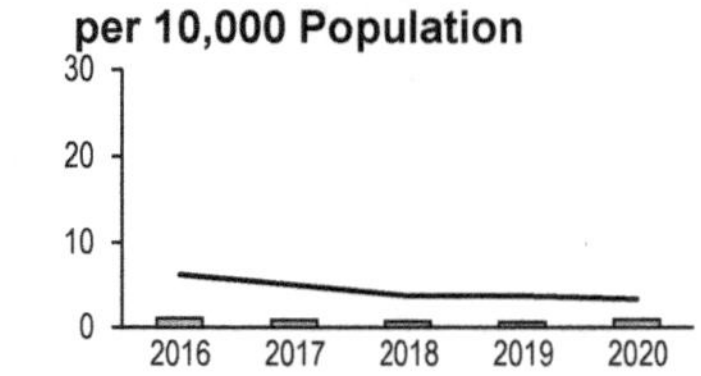

	2016	2017	2018	2019	2020
Raleigh	1.09	0.85	0.76	0.65	0.99
Average	6.18	5.02	3.76	3.75	3.32

Fiscal Year 2019-20

Explanatory Information

Service Level and Delivery

The City of Wilson Parks and Recreation Department is a separate department under the city organization. The city has partnerships with other organizations to provide recreational services, including the Wilson County Schools, the Wilson Youth Soccer Association, Wilson City Little League, Special Olympics, Youth Soccer Association, the Senior Games of North Carolina, and the Wilson Arts Council.

The city has twenty-eight separate parks and sites. This includes 400 acres, most currently undeveloped. The city has seven and half miles of trails.

In addition to the core parks and recreational facilities, Wilson has three boat ramps and one museum. The city also runs a municipal eighteen-hole golf course. The operation of these other facilities is not included in the Core Parks and Recreation comparisons reported here. These facilities are not included here in dollars or staff as part of core parks and recreation facilities and activities.

Conditions Affecting Service, Performance, and Costs

Municipal Profile

Population (OSBM 2019)	49,384
Land Area (Square Miles)	31.02
Persons per Square Mile	1,592
Topography	Flat
Climate	Temperate; little ice and snow

Service Profile

Parks and Recreation Staff	
Administrative Position FTEs	6.5
Maintenance Staff FTEs	16.0
Program and Facility FTEs	18.0
Other Staff FTEs	4.0
TOTAL	44.5
Number of Parks and Sites	28
Total Land Acreage in Parks	400.0
Miles of Trails in Parks	7.5
Recreational Facilities	
Indoor and Outdoor Pools	2
Recreation Centers	4
Outdoor Basketball Courts	7
Outdoor Tennis Courts	16
Playgrounds	26
Diamond Fields	11
Rectangular Fields	14
Other Athletic Fields	1
Picnic Shelters	19
Parks and Recreation Revenues	
User Fees	$485,000
Grants	$0
Sponsorships	$65,000
Donations	$0

Full Cost Profile

Cost Breakdown by Percentage	
Personal Services	59.4%
Operating Costs	32.4%
Capital Costs	8.2%
TOTAL	100.0%
Cost Breakdown in Dollars	
Personal Services	$3,350,082
Operating Costs	$1,826,752
Capital Costs	$461,967
TOTAL	$5,638,801

Wilson

Core Parks and Recreation

Key: Wilson ▒ Benchmarking Average — Fiscal Years 2016 through 2020

Resource Measures

Core Parks and Recreation Services per Capita

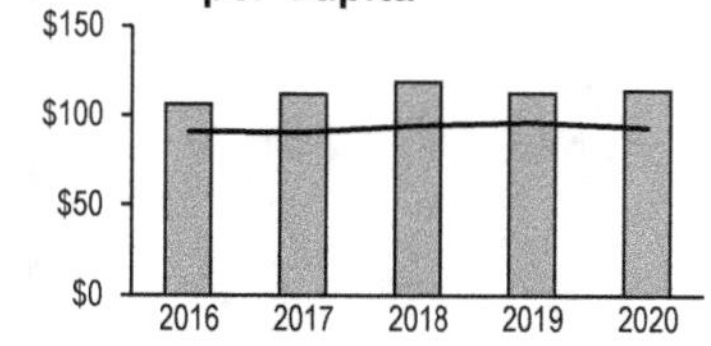

	2016	2017	2018	2019	2020
Wilson	$106	$112	$119	$113	$114
Average	$91	$90	$94	$96	$93

Core Parks and Recreation Staff per 10,000 Population

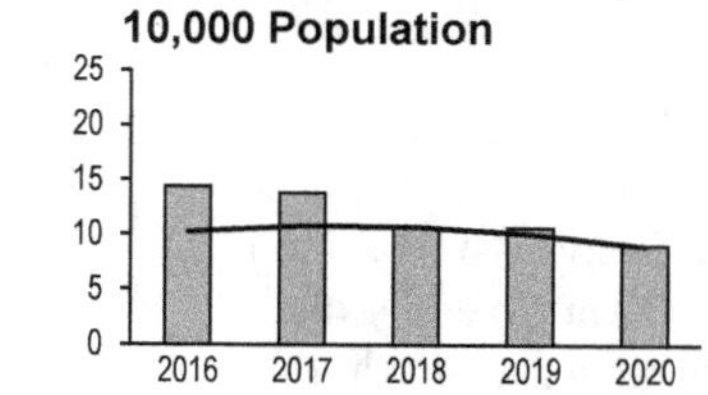

	2016	2017	2018	2019	2020
Wilson	14.4	13.8	10.6	10.6	9.0
Average	10.2	10.8	10.7	10.0	8.9

Facilities Measures

Land Acres of Parks per 10,000 Population

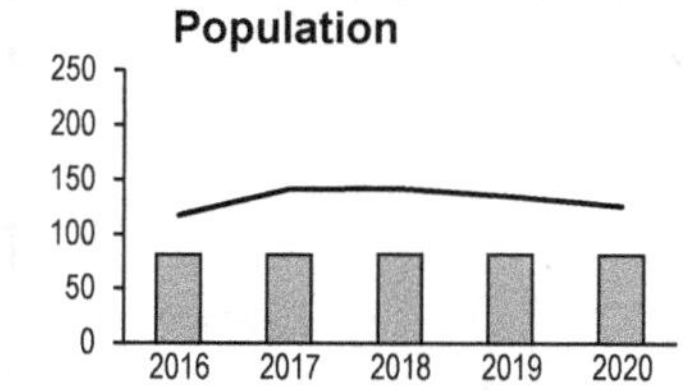

	2016	2017	2018	2019	2020
Wilson	81.04	80.96	81.35	81.54	81.00
Average	117.20	140.99	141.65	134.43	125.84

Recreation Centers per 10,000 Population

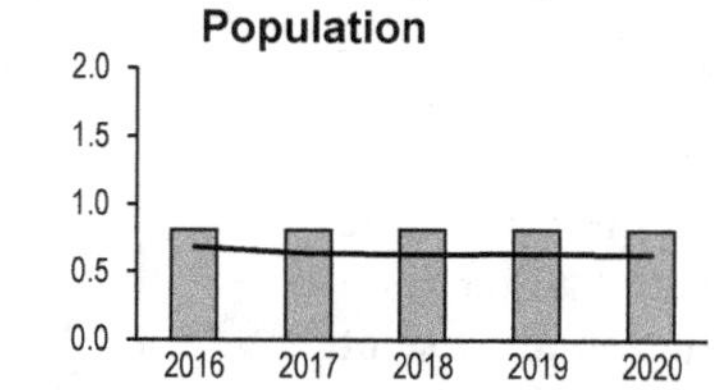

	2016	2017	2018	2019	2020
Wilson	0.81	0.81	0.81	0.82	0.81
Average	0.69	0.64	0.63	0.64	0.63

Swimming Pools per 10,000 Population

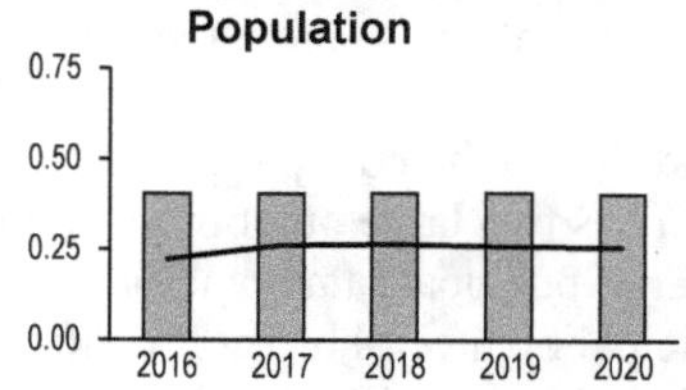

	2016	2017	2018	2019	2020
Wilson	0.41	0.40	0.41	0.41	0.40
Average	0.22	0.26	0.27	0.26	0.26

Athletic Fields per 10,000 Population

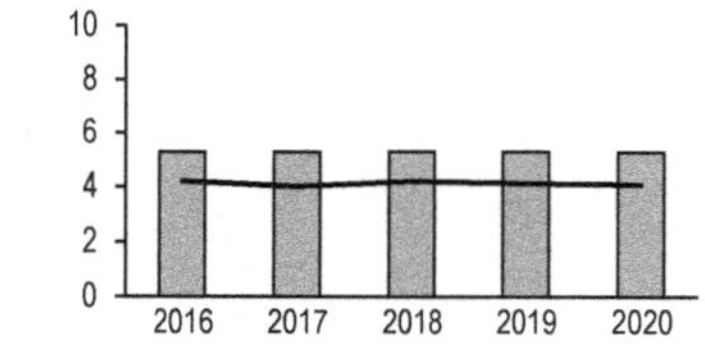

	2016	2017	2018	2019	2020
Wilson	5.27	5.26	5.29	5.30	5.26
Average	4.19	4.00	4.19	4.12	4.06

Playgrounds per 10,000 Population

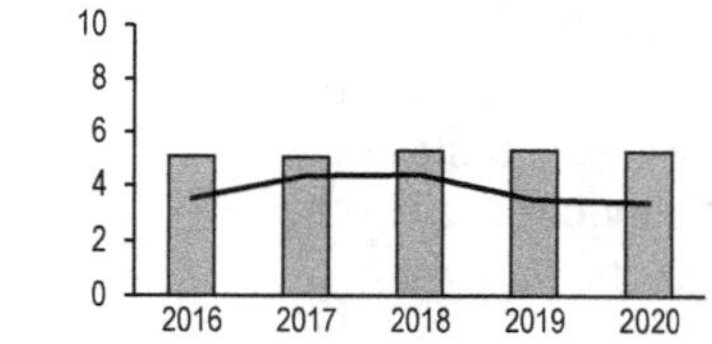

	2016	2017	2018	2019	2020
Wilson	5.06	5.06	5.29	5.30	5.26
Average	3.51	4.35	4.39	3.48	3.40

Miles of Land Trails per 10,000 Population

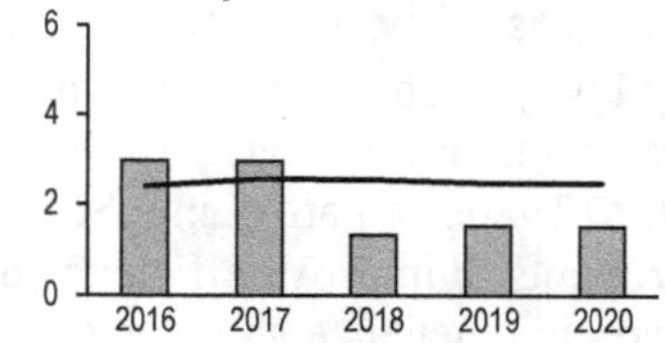

	2016	2017	2018	2019	2020
Wilson	2.94	2.93	1.32	1.53	1.52
Average	2.38	2.54	2.52	2.44	2.45

Efficiency Measures

Total Core Parks and Recreation Costs per Acre

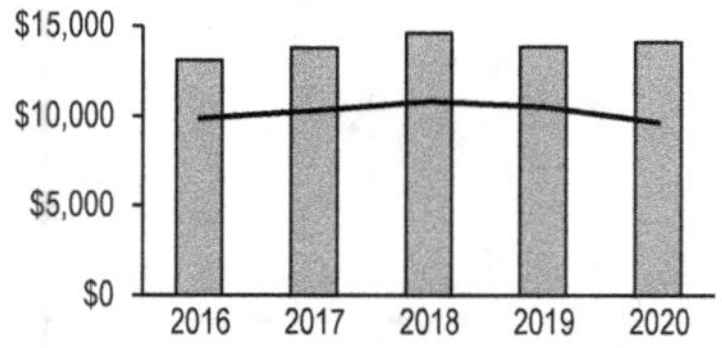

	2016	2017	2018	2019	2020
Wilson	$13,079	$13,802	$14,616	$13,852	$14,097
Average	$9,857	$10,296	$10,807	$10,512	$9,650

Acres of Park Maintained per Maintenance FTE

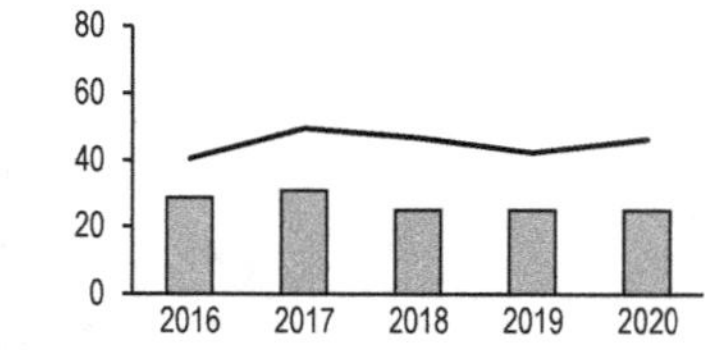

	2016	2017	2018	2019	2020
Wilson	28.6	30.8	25.0	25.0	25.0
Average	40.3	49.4	46.7	42.3	46.4

Volunteer Hours in FTEs as a Percent of Paid Staff FTEs

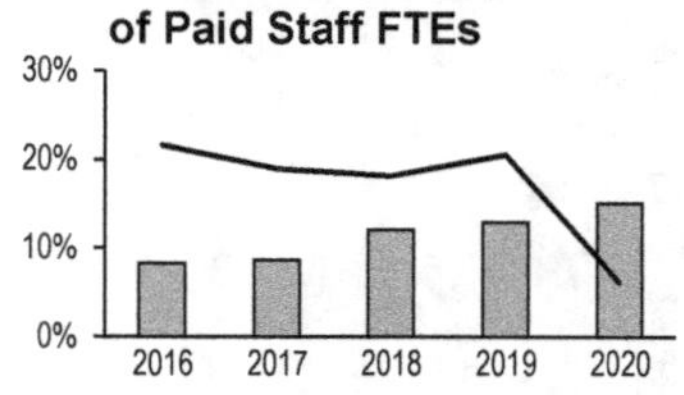

	2016	2017	2018	2019	2020
Wilson	8.3%	8.6%	12.0%	12.9%	15.1%
Average	21.6%	19.0%	18.1%	20.5%	6.1%

Effectiveness Measures

Revenue Gained as a Percent of Total Core Costs

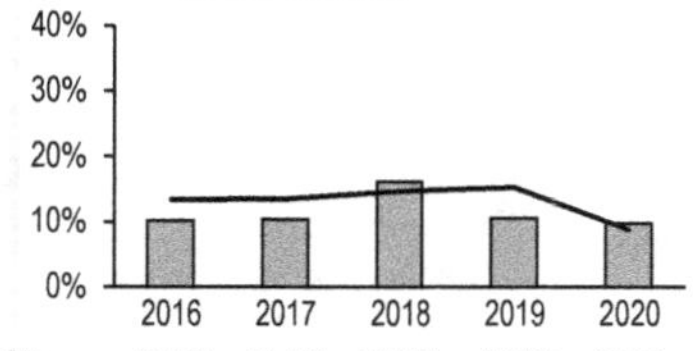

	2016	2017	2018	2019	2020
Wilson	10.2%	10.4%	16.1%	10.6%	9.8%
Average	13.4%	13.4%	14.7%	15.2%	8.7%

Acts of Vandalism at Parks Facilities per 10,000 Population

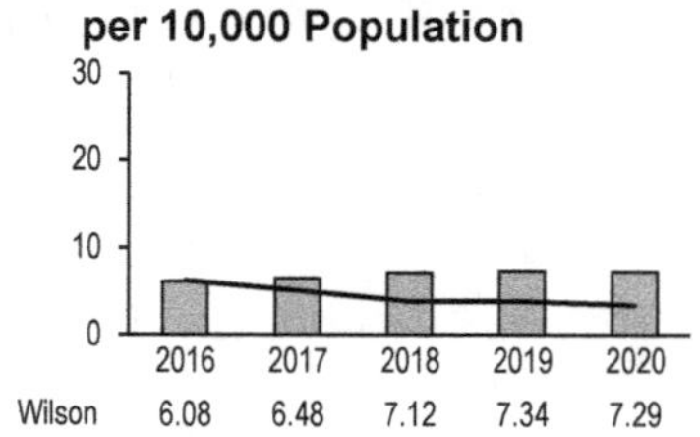

	2016	2017	2018	2019	2020
Wilson	6.08	6.48	7.12	7.34	7.29
Average	6.18	5.02	3.76	3.75	3.32

Fiscal Year 2019-20

Explanatory Information

Service Level and Delivery

The City of Winston-Salem Recreation and Parks Department is a separate department under the city organization. The department is overseen by the advisory Parks and Recreation Commission, which has eleven members appointed by the mayor and approved by the city council. The city has formal cooperative arrangements with Forsyth County and various public-private partnerships with other organizations to provide recreational services.

The city has eighty-four separate parks and sites. This includes 4,279 acres of parkland, most of which is developed. The city has twenty-three miles of trails, about two-thirds of which are paved.

In addition to the core parks and recreational facilities, Winston-Salem has two large outdoor performance event sites, a historic property, one boat ramp, and one museum. The city also runs two municipal eighteen-hole golf courses. The operation of these other facilities is not included in the Core Parks and Recreation comparisons reported here. These facilities are not included here in dollars or staff as part of core parks and recreation facilities and activities.

Conditions Affecting Service, Performance, and Costs

Many Forsyth County residents make use of the city's parks and recreational facilities. Most of the city's facilities were built in the 1960s to 1980s and are aging. Several support services are in other departments to improve efficiency and reduce costs, including property maintenance and vegetation management.

Municipal Profile

Population (OSBM 2019)	244,739
Land Area (Square Miles)	132.59
Persons per Square Mile	1,846
Topography	Gently rolling
Climate	Temperate; some ice and snow

Service Profile

Parks and Recreation Staff	
Administrative Position FTEs	30.3
Maintenance Staff FTEs	67.8
Program and Facility FTEs	111.9
Other Staff FTEs	2.0
TOTAL	212.0
Number of Parks and Sites	84
Total Land Acreage in Parks	4,279.2
Miles of Trails in Parks	23.3
Recreational Facilities	
Indoor and Outdoor Pools	10
Recreation Centers	17
Outdoor Basketball Courts	23
Outdoor Tennis Courts	106
Playgrounds	46
Diamond Fields	47
Rectangular Fields	50
Other Athletic Fields	0
Picnic Shelters	51
Parks and Recreation Revenues	
User Fees	$415,412
Grants	$125,698
Sponsorships	$5,226
Donations	$78,616

Full Cost Profile

Cost Breakdown by Percentage	
Personal Services	53.7%
Operating Costs	33.5%
Capital Costs	12.8%
TOTAL	100.0%
Cost Breakdown in Dollars	
Personal Services	$7,145,622
Operating Costs	$4,454,415
Capital Costs	$1,695,685
TOTAL	$13,295,722

Winston-Salem — Core Parks and Recreation

Key: Winston-Salem ▒ Benchmarking Average — Fiscal Years 2016 through 2020

Resource Measures

Core Parks and Recreation Services per Capita

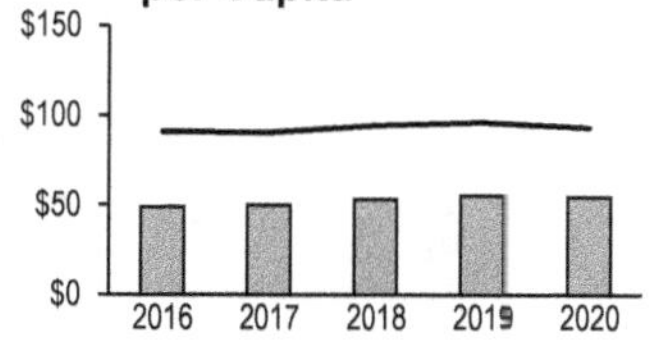

	2016	2017	2018	2019	2020
Winston-Salem	$49	$50	$53	$55	$54
Average	$91	$90	$94	$96	$93

Core Parks and Recreation Staff per 10,000 Population

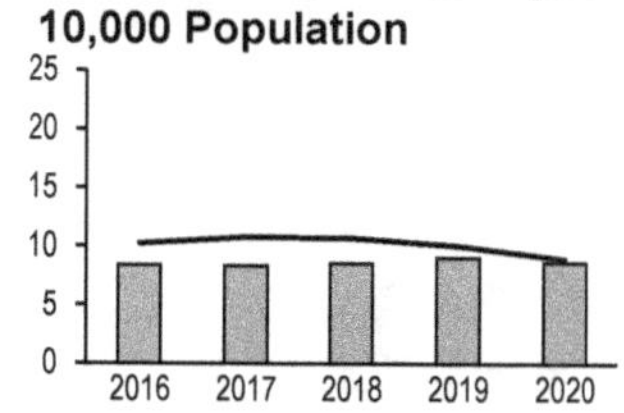

	2016	2017	2018	2019	2020
Winston-Salem	8.4	8.3	8.5	9.0	8.7
Average	10.2	10.8	10.7	10.0	8.9

Facilities Measures

Land Acres of Parks per 10,000 Population

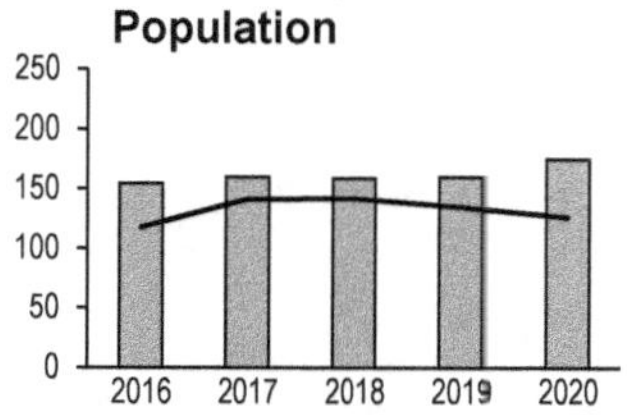

	2016	2017	2018	2019	2020
Winston-Salem	154.37	160.10	158.66	159.99	174.85
Average	117.20	140.99	141.65	134.43	125.84

Recreation Centers per 10,000 Population

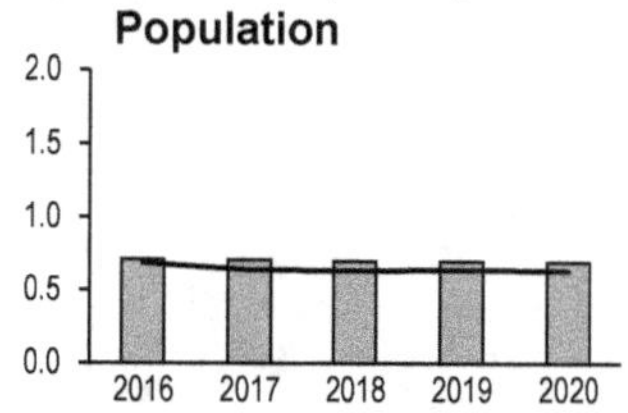

	2016	2017	2018	2019	2020
Winston-Salem	0.71	0.71	0.70	0.70	0.69
Average	0.69	0.64	0.63	0.64	0.63

Swimming Pools per 10,000 Population

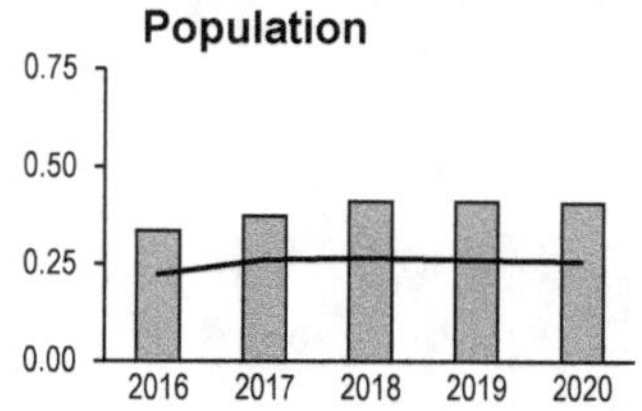

	2016	2017	2018	2019	2020
Winston-Salem	0.33	0.37	0.41	0.41	0.41
Average	0.22	0.26	0.27	0.26	0.26

Athletic Fields per 10,000 Population

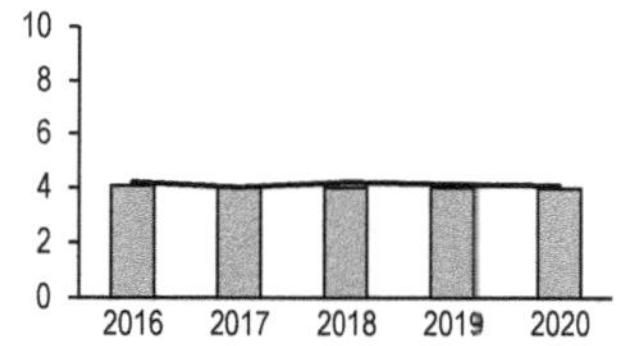

	2016	2017	2018	2019	2020
Winston-Salem	4.06	4.03	3.99	3.96	3.96
Average	4.19	4.00	4.19	4.12	4.06

Playgrounds per 10,000 Population

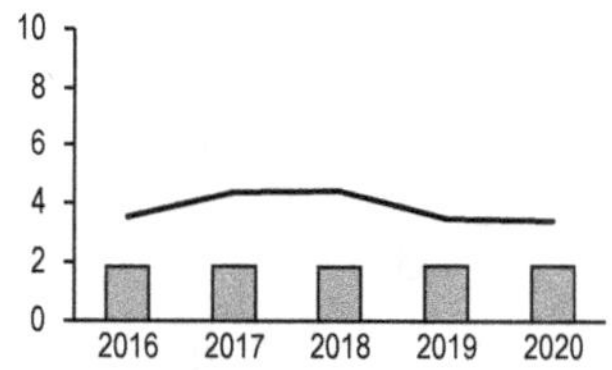

	2016	2017	2018	2019	2020
Winston-Salem	1.84	1.87	1.85	1.89	1.88
Average	3.51	4.35	4.39	3.48	3.40

Miles of Land Trails per 10,000 Population

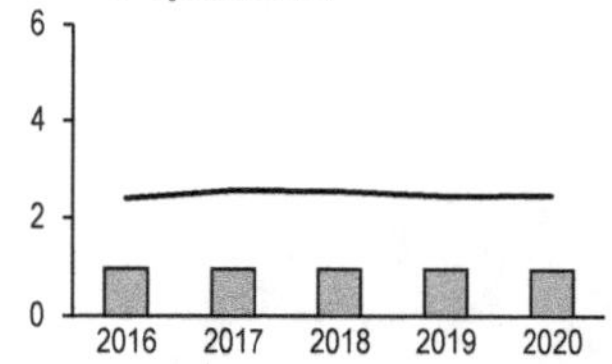

	2016	2017	2018	2019	2020
Winston-Salem	0.97	0.97	0.96	0.96	0.95
Average	2.38	2.54	2.52	2.44	2.45

Efficiency Measures

Total Core Parks and Recreation Costs per Acre

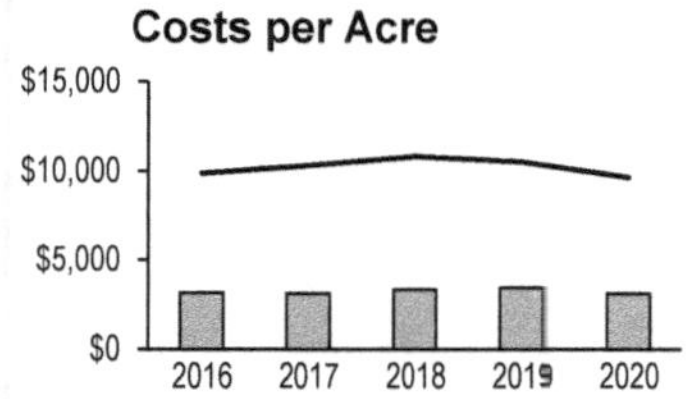

	2016	2017	2018	2019	2020
Winston-Salem	$3,147	$3,104	$3,344	$3,444	$3,107
Average	$9,857	$10,296	$10,807	$10,512	$9,650

Acres of Park Maintained per Maintenance FTE

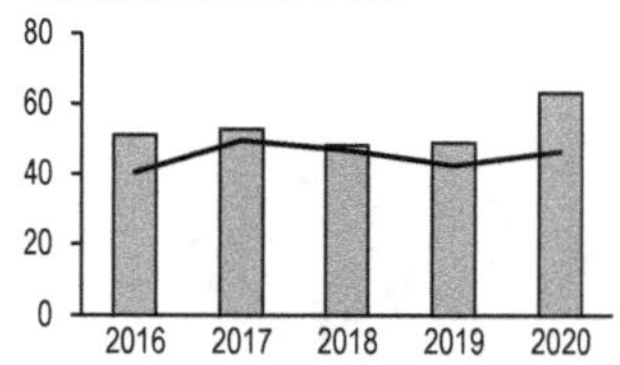

	2016	2017	2018	2019	2020
Winston-Salem	51.2	52.9	48.3	49.0	63.1
Average	40.3	49.4	46.7	42.3	46.4

Volunteer Hours in FTEs as a Percent of Paid Staff FTEs

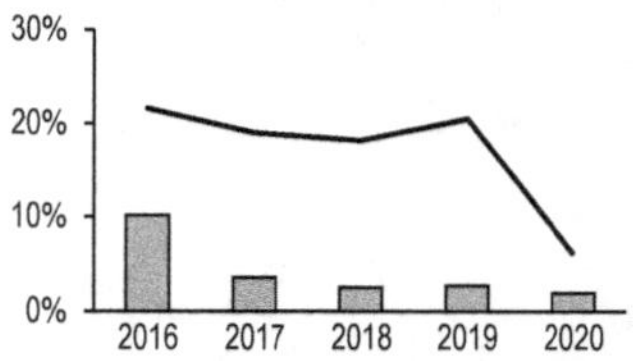

	2016	2017	2018	2019	2020
Winston-Salem	10.1%	3.5%	2.5%	2.7%	2.0%
Average	21.6%	19.0%	18.1%	20.5%	6.1%

Effectiveness Measures

Revenue Gained as a Percent of Total Core Costs

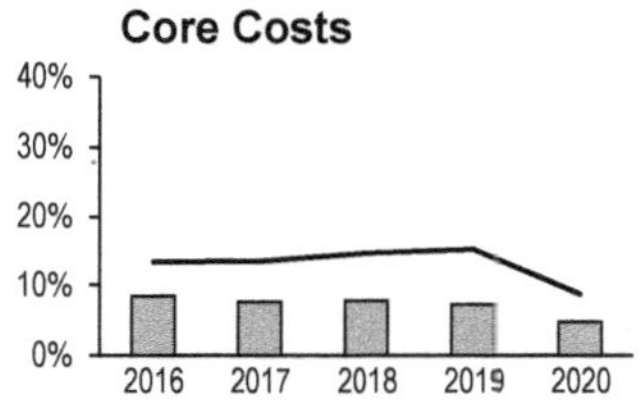

	2016	2017	2018	2019	2020
Winston-Salem	8.4%	7.5%	7.8%	7.2%	4.7%
Average	13.4%	13.4%	14.7%	15.2%	8.7%

Acts of Vandalism at Parks Facilities per 10,000 Population

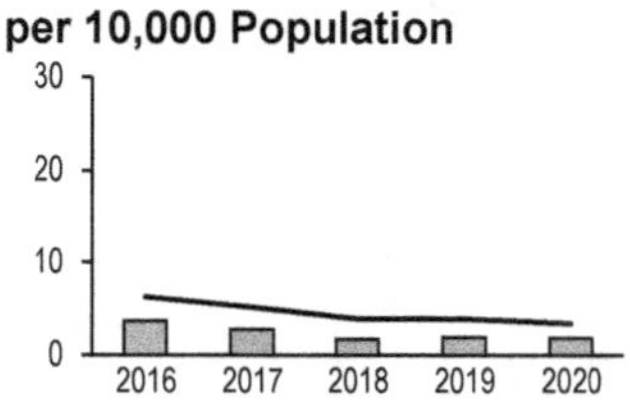

	2016	2017	2018	2019	2020
Winston-Salem	3.56	2.66	1.65	1.85	1.76
Average	6.18	5.02	3.76	3.75	3.32

www.ingramcontent.com/pod-product-compliance
Lightning Source LLC
LaVergne TN
LVHW080028210926
848481LV00011B/3128
* 9 7 8 1 6 4 2 3 8 0 3 6 1 *